WEBSTER'S II
New Riverside
Desk Reference

HOME AND OFFICE
EDITION

HOUGHTON MIFFLIN COMPANY
Boston   New York   London

Library of Congress Cataloging-in-Publication Data

Webster's II new Riverside desk reference.—Home and office ed.

     p.   cm.

  Includes index.

    ISBN 0-395-59520-7. — ISBN 0-395-62026-0 (deluxe)

    1. Encyclopedias and dictionaries. I. Title: Webster's two new Riverside desk reference. II. Title: Webster's 2 new Riverside desk reference.

AG6.W33 1992

031—dc20   91-41366

                                        CIP

TABLE OF CONTENTS

Calendar and Holidays 1
   Perpetual Calendar 8
U.S. Statistics 10
U.S. Geography 30
U.S. States and Cities 35
   U.S. States 35
   U.S. Territories 62
   U.S. Cities 66
U.S. History and Government 79
   Declaration of Independence 79
   U.S. Constitution 81
   Other Historical Documents 91
   Firsts in America 97
   Presidents of the U.S. 98
   Presidential Elections 100
   Cabinet Members 106
   Executive Departments and Agencies 111
   Congress of the U.S. 114
   U.S. Supreme Court 119
   U.S. Government 121
   Military 123
   Law Enforcement and Crime 130
   Taxes 137
   Postal Regulations 145
World Statistics 149
World Geography 159
The United Nations 178
Countries of the World 182
Business and the Economy 325

Resource Guide 352
  Social Security 352
  Copyrights 359
  Unemployment Insurance 361
  Trademarks 363
  Patents 363
  State Consumer Protection Offices 364
  How to Write a Complaint Letter 365
  Toll-Free Numbers 366
  U.S. Societies and Associations 369
Education 381
  Senior Colleges and Universities 385
  Degree Abbreviations 411
Writer's Guide 412
  A Concise Guide to Style 412
  Reference Books and Other Sources 417
Weather and Climate 419
Weights and Measures 429
Travel 438
  U.S. Passport and Customs Information 438
  Foreign Embassies 439
  Health Hints for the Traveler 444
  State and City Tourism Offices 447
  Distances 450
  World's Busiest Airports 456
Index 457

CALENDAR AND HOLIDAYS

The Calendar

History of the Calendar

The purpose of a calendar is to reckon time in advance, to show how many days have to elapse until a certain event takes place—the harvest, a religious festival, or whatever. The earliest calendars, naturally, were crude, and they must have been strongly influenced by the geographical location of the people who made them. In the Scandinavian countries, for example, where the seasons are pronounced, the concept of the year was determined by the seasons, specifically by the end of winter. The Norsemen, before becoming Christians, are said to have had a calendar consisting of ten months of 30 days each.

But in warmer countries, where the seasons are less pronounced, the Moon became the basic unit for time reckoning; an old Jewish book actually makes the statement that "the Moon was created for the counting of the days." All the oldest calendars of which we have reliable information were lunar calendars, based on the time interval from one new moon to the next—a so-called "lunation." But even in a warm climate there are annual events that pay no attention to the phases of the Moon. In some areas it was a rainy season; in Egypt it was the annual flooding of the Nile. It was, therefore, necessary to regulate daily life and religious festivals by lunations, but to take care of the annual event in some other manner.

The calendar of the Assyrians was based on the phases of the Moon. The month began with the first appearance of the lunar crescent, and since this can best be observed in the evening, the day began with sunset. They knew that a lunation was 29 1/2 days long, so their lunar year had a duration of 354 days, falling eleven days short of the solar year.[1] After three years such a lunar calendar would be off by 33 days, or more than one lunation. We know that the Assyrians added an extra month from time to time, but we do not know whether they had developed a special rule for doing so or whether the priests proclaimed the necessity for an extra month from observation. If they made every third year a year of 13 lunations, their three-year period would cover 1,091 1/2 days (using their value of 29 1/2 days for one lunation), or just about four days too short. In one century this mistake would add up to 133 days by their reckoning (in reality closer to 134 days), requiring four extra lunations per century.

We now know that an eight-year period, consisting of five years with 12 months and three years with 13 months would lead to a difference of only 20 days per century, but we do not know whether such a calendar was actually used.

The best approximation that was possible in antiquity was a 19-year period, with seven of these 19 years having 13 months. This means that the period contained 235 months. This, still using the old value for a lunation, made a total of 6,932 1/2 days, while 19 solar years added up to 6,939.7 days, a difference of just one week per period and about five weeks per

1. The correct figures are: lunation: 29 d, 12 h, 44 min, 2.8 sec (29.530585 d); solar year: 365 d, 5 h, 48 min, 46 sec (365.242216 d); 12 lunations: 354 d, 8 h, 48 min, 34 sec (354.3671 d).

century. Even the 19-year period required constant adjustment, but it was the period that became the basis of the religious calendar of the Jews. The Arabs used the same calendar at first, but Mohammed forbade shifting from 12 months to 13 months, so that the Islamic religious calendar, even today, has a lunar year of 354 days. As a result the Islamic religious festivals run through all the seasons of the year three times per century.

The Egyptians had a traditional calendar with 12 months of 30 days each. At one time they added five extra days at the end of every year. These turned into a five-day festival because it was thought to be unlucky to work during that time.

When Rome emerged as a world power, the difficulties of making a calendar were well known, but the Romans complicated their lives because of their superstition that even numbers were unlucky. Hence their months were 29 or 31 days, with the exception of February, which had 28 days. However, four months of 31 days, seven months of 29 days, and one month of 28 days added up to only 355 days. Therefore, the Romans invented an extra month called Mercedonius of 22 or 23 days. It was added every second year.

Even with Mercedonius, the Roman calendar was so far off that Caesar, advised by the astronomer Sosigenes, ordered a sweeping reform in 45 B.C. One year, made 445 days long by imperial decree, brought the calendar back in step with the seasons. Then the solar year (with the value of 365 days and 6 hours) was made the basis of the calendar. The months were 30 or 31 days in length, and to take care of the six hours, every fourth year was made a 366-day year. Moreover, Caesar decreed, the year began with the first of January, not with the vernal equinox in late March.

This was the Julian calendar, named after Julius Caesar. It is still the calendar of the Eastern Orthodox churches.

However, the year is 11 1/2 minutes shorter than the figure written into Caesar's calendar by Sosigenes, and after a number of centuries, even 11 1/2 minutes add up. See table.

While Caesar could decree that the vernal equinox should not be used as the first day of the new year, the vernal equinox is still a fact of Nature that could not be disregarded. One of the first (as far as we know) to become alarmed about this was Roger Bacon. He sent a memorandum to Pope Clement IV, who apparently was not impressed. But Pope Sixtus IV (reigned 1471 to 1484) decided that another reform was needed and called the German astronomer Regiomontanus to Rome to advise him. Regiomontanus arrived in 1475, but one year later he died in an epidemic, one of the recurrent outbreaks of the plague. The Pope himself survived, but his reform plans died with Regiomontanus.

Less than a hundred years later, in 1545, the Council of Trent authorized the then Pope, Paul III, to reform the calendar once more. Most of the mathematical and astronomical work was done by Father Christopher Clavius, S.J. The immediate correction, advised by Father Clavius and ordered by Pope Gregory XIII, was that Thursday, Oct. 4, 1582, was to be the last day of the Julian calendar. The next day was

Drift of the Vernal Equinox in the Julian Calendar

Date	Julian year	Date	Julian year	Date	Julian Year
March 21	325 A.D.	March 17	837 A.D.	March 13	1349 A.D.
March 20	453 A.D.	March 16	965 A.D.	March 12	1477 A.D.
March 19	581 A.D.	March 15	1093 A.D.	March 11	1605 A.D.
March 18	709 A.D.	March 14	1221 A.D.		

Friday, with the date of October 15. For long-range accuracy, a formula suggested by the Vatican librarian Aloysius Giglio (latinized into Lilius) was adopted: every fourth year is a leap year *unless* it is a century year like 1700 or 1800. Century years can be leap years *only* when they are divisible by 400 (e.g., 1600). This rule eliminates three leap years in four centuries, making the calendar sufficiently correct for all ordinary purposes.

Unfortunately, all the Protestant princes in 1582 chose to ignore the papal bull; they continued with the Julian calendar. It was not until 1698 that the German professor Erhard Weigel persuaded the Protestant rulers of Germany and of the Netherlands to change to the new calendar. In England the shift took place in 1752, and in Russia it needed the revolution to introduce the Gregorian calendar in 1918.

The average year of the Gregorian calendar, in spite of the leap year rule, is about 26 seconds longer than the earth's orbital period. But this discrepancy will need 3,323 years to build up to a single day.

Modern proposals for calendar reform do not aim at a "better" calendar, but at one that is more convenient to use, especially for commercial purposes. A 365-day year cannot be divided into equal halves or quarters; the number of days per month is haphazard; the months begin or end in the middle of a week; a holiday fixed by date (e.g., the Fourth of July) will wander through a week; a holiday fixed in another manner (e.g., Easter) can fall on thirty-five possible dates. The Gregorian calendar, admittedly, keeps the calendar dates in reasonable unison with astronomical events, but it still is full of minor annoyances. Moreover, you need a calendar every year to look up dates; an ideal calendar should be one that you can memorize for one year and that is valid for all other years, too.

In 1834 an Italian priest, Marco Mastrofini, suggested taking one day out of every year. It would be made a holiday and *not* be given the name of a weekday. That would make every year begin with January 1 as a Sunday. The leap-year day would be treated the same way, so that in leap years there would be two unnamed holidays at the end of the year.

About a decade later the philosopher Auguste Comte also suggested a 364-day calendar with an extra day, which he called Year Day.

Since then there have been other unsuccessful attempts at calendar reform.

Time and Calendar

The two natural cycles on which time measurements are based are the year and the day. The year is defined as the time required for the Earth to complete one revolution around the Sun, while the day is the time required for the Earth to complete one turn upon its axis. Unfortunately the Earth needs 365 days plus about six hours to go around the Sun once, so that the year does not consist of so and so many days; the fractional day has to be taken care of by an extra day every fourth year.

But because the Earth, while turning upon its axis, also moves around the Sun there are two kinds of days. A day may be defined as the interval between the highest point of the Sun in the sky on two successive days. This, averaged out over the year, produces the customary 24-hour day. But one might also define a day as the time interval between the moments when a certain point in the sky, say a conveniently located star, is directly overhead. This is called:

Sidereal time. Astronomers use a point which they call the "vernal equinox" for the actual determination. Such a sidereal day is somewhat shorter than the "solar day," namely by about 3 minutes and 56 seconds of so-called "mean solar time."

Apparent solar time is the time based directly on the Sun's position in the sky. In ordinary life the day runs from midnight to midnight. It begins when the Sun is invisible by being 12 hours from its zenith. Astronomers use the so-called "Julian Day," which runs from noon to noon; the concept was invented by the astronomer Joseph Scaliger, who named it after his father Julius. To avoid the problems caused by leap-year days and so forth, Scaliger picked a conveniently remote date in the past and suggested just counting days without regard to weeks, months, and years. The Julian Day for 0ʰ Jan. 31, 1992 is 244 8621.5. The reason for having the Julian Day run from noon to noon is the practical one that astronomical observations usually extend across the midnight hour, which would require a change in date (or in the Julian Day number) if the astronomical day, like the civil day, ran from midnight to midnight.

Mean solar time, rather than apparent solar time, is what is actually used most of the time. The mean solar time is based on the position of a fictitious "mean sun." The reason why this fictitious sun has to be introduced is the following: the Earth turns on its axis regularly; it needs the same number of seconds regardless of the season. But the movement of the Earth around the Sun is not regular because the Earth's orbit is an ellipse. This has the result (as explained in the section The Seasons) that the Earth moves faster in January and slower in July. Though it is the Earth that changes velocity, it looks to us as if the Sun did. In January, when the Earth moves faster, the *apparent* movement of the Sun looks faster. The "mean sun" of time measurements, then, is a sun that moves regularly all year round; the real Sun will be either ahead of or behind the "mean sun." The difference between the real Sun and the fictitious mean sun is called the *equation of time*.

When the real Sun is west of the mean sun we have the "sun fast" condition, with the real Sun crossing the meridian ahead of the mean sun. The opposite is the "sun slow" situation when the real Sun crosses the meridian after the mean sun. Of course, what is observed is the real Sun. The equation of time is needed to establish mean solar time, kept by the reference clocks.

But if all clocks were actually set by mean solar time we would be plagued by a welter of time differences that would be "correct" but a major nuisance.

The Names of Days

Latin	Saxon	English	French	Italian	Spanish	German
Dies Solis	Sun's Day	Sunday	dimanche	domenica	domingo	Sonntag
Dies Lunae	Moon's Day	Monday	lundi	lunedi	lunes	Montag
Dies Martis	Tiw's Day	Tuesday	mardi	martedi	martes	Dienstag
Dies Mercurii	Woden's Day	Wednesday	mercredi	mercoledi	miércoles	Mittwoch
Dies Jovis	Thor's Day	Thursday	jeudi	giovedi	jueves	Donnerstag
Dies Veneris	Frigg's Day	Friday	vendredi	venedri	viernes	Freitag
Dies Saturni	Seterne's Day	Saturday	samedi	sabato	sábado	Sonnabend

NOTE: The Romans gave one day of the week to each planet known, the Sun and Moon being considered planets in this connection. The Saxon names are a kind of translation of the Roman names: Tiw was substituted for Mars, Woden (Wotan) for Mercury, Thor for Jupiter (Jove), Frigg for Venus, and Seterne for Saturn. The English names are adapted Saxon. The Spanish, Italian, and French names, which are normally not capitalized, are derived from the Latin. The German names follow the Saxon pattern with two exceptions: Wednesday is Mittwoch (Middle of the Week), and Saturday is Sonnabend (Sunday's Eve).

A clock on Long Island, correctly showing mean solar time for its location (this would be *local civil time*), would be slightly ahead of a clock in Newark, N.J. The Newark clock would be slightly ahead of a clock in Trenton, N.J., which, in turn, would be ahead of a clock in Philadelphia. This condition actually prevailed in the past until 1883, when *standard time* was introduced. Standard time is the correct mean solar time for a designated meridian, and this time is used for a certain area to the east and west of this meridian. In the U.S. four meridians have been designated to supply standard times; they are 75°, 90°, 105°, and 120° west of Greenwich. The 75° meridian determines Eastern Standard Time. It happens to run through Camden, N.J., where standard time, therefore, is also mean solar time and local civil time. The 90° meridian (which happens to pass through the western part of Memphis, Tenn.) determines Central Standard Time, the 105° meridian (passing through Denver) determines Mountain Standard Time, and the 120° meridian (which runs through Lake Tahoe) determines Pacific Standard Time.

Canada, extending over more territory from west to east, adds one time zone on either side: Atlantic Standard Time (based on 60° west of Greenwich) for New Brunswick, Nova Scotia, and Quebec, and Yukon Standard Time (determined by the 135° meridian) for its extreme West. Alaska, extending still farther to the west, adds two more time zones, Alaska Standard Time (determined by the 150° meridian that passes through Anchorage) and Nome Standard Time, based on the 165° meridian just east of Nome.

In general the Earth is divided into 24 such time zones, which run one hour apart. For practical purposes the time zones sometimes show indentations, and there are a few "subzones" that differ from the neighboring zone by only half an hour, e.g., Newfoundland.

The date line. While the time zones are based on the natural event of the Sun crossing the meridian, the date must be an arbitrary decision. The meridians are traditionally counted from the meridian of the observatory of Greenwich in England, which is called the zero meridian. The logical place for changing the date is 12 hours, or 180° from Greenwich. Fortunately, the 180th meridian runs mostly through the open Pacific. The date line makes a zigzag in the north to incorporate the eastern tip of Siberia into the Siberian time system and then another one to incorporate a number of islands into the Alaska time system. In the south there is a similar zigzag for the purpose of tying a number of British-owned islands to the New Zealand time system. Otherwise the date line is the same as 180° from Greenwich. At points to the east of the date line the calendar is one day earlier than at points to the west of it. A traveller going eastward across the date line from one island to another would not have to re-set his watch because he would stay inside the time zone (provided he does so where the date line does *not* coincide with the 180° meridian), but it would be the same time of the previous day.

The Seasons

The seasons are caused by the tilt of the Earth's axis (23.4°) and not by the fact that the Earth's orbit around the Sun is an ellipse. The average distance of the Earth from the Sun is 93 million miles; the difference between aphelion (farthest away) and perihelion (closest to the Sun) is 3 million miles, so that perihelion is about 91.4 million miles from the Sun. The Earth goes through the perihelion point a few days after New Year, just when the northern hemisphere has winter. Aphelion is passed during the first days in July. This by itself shows that the distance from the

The Names of the Months

January: named after Janus, protector of the gateway to heaven

February: named after Februalia, a time period when sacrifices were made to atone for sins

March: named after Mars, the god of war, presumably signifying that the campaigns interrupted by the winter could be resumed

April: from *aperire*, Latin for "to open" (buds)

May: named after Maia, the goddess of growth of plants

June: from *juvenis*, Latin for "youth"

July: named after Julius Caesar

August: named after Augustus, the first Roman Emperor

September: from *septem*, Latin for "seven"

October: from *octo*, Latin for "eight"

November: from *novem*, Latin for "nine"

December: from *decem*, Latin for "ten"

NOTE: The earliest Latin calendar was a 10-month one; thus September was the seventh month, October, the eighth, etc. July was originally called Quintilis, as the fifth month; August was originally called Sextilis, as the sixth month.

Sun is not important within these limits. What is important is that when the Earth passes through perihelion, the northern end of the Earth's axis happens to tilt away from the Sun, so that the areas beyond the Tropic of Cancer receive only slanting rays from a Sun low in the sky.

The tilt of the Earth's axis is responsible for four lines you find on every globe. When, say, the North Pole is tilted away from the Sun as much as possible, the farthest points in the North which can still be reached by the Sun's rays are 23 1/2° from the pole. This is the Arctic Circle. The Antarctic Circle is the corresponding limit 23.4° from the South Pole; the Sun's rays cannot reach beyond this point when we have mid-summer in the North.

When the Sun is vertically above the equator, the day is of equal length all over the Earth. This happens twice a year, and these are the "equinoxes" in March and in September. After having been over the equator in March, the Sun will seem to move northward. The northernmost point where the Sun can be straight overhead is 23.4° north of the equator. This is the Tropic of Cancer; the Sun can never be vertically overhead to the north of this line. Similarly the Sun cannot be vertically overhead to the south of a line 23.4° south of the equator—the Tropic of Capricorn.

This explains the climatic zones. In the belt (the Greek word *zone* means "belt") between the Tropic of Cancer and the Tropic of Capricorn, the Sun can be straight overhead; this is the tropical zone. The two zones where the Sun cannot be overhead but will be above the horizon every day of the year are the two temperate zones; the two areas where the Sun will not rise at all for varying lengths of time are the two polar areas, Arctic and Antarctic.

Holidays

Religious and Secular

Since 1971, by federal law, Washington's Birthday, Memorial Day, Columbus Day, and Veterans' Day have been celebrated on Mondays to create three-day weekends for federal employees. Many states now observe these holidays on the same Mondays. The dates given for the holidays listed below are the traditional ones.

New Year's Day, Jan. 1. A legal holiday in all states and the District of Columbia, New Year's Day has its origin in Roman Times, when sacrifices were offered to Janus, the two-faced Roman deity who looked back on the past and forward to the future.

Epiphany, Jan. 6. Falls the twelfth day after Christmas and commemorates the manifestation of Jesus as the Son of God, as represented by the adoration of the Magi, the baptism of Jesus, and the miracle of the wine at the marriage feast at Cana. Epiphany originally marked the beginning of the carnival season preceding Lent, and the evening (sometimes the eve) is known as Twelfth Night.

Martin Luther King, Jr.'s Birthday, Jan. 15. Observed on the third Monday in January. Honors the late civil rights leader. Became a legal public holiday in 1986.

Ground-hog Day, Feb. 2. Legend has it that if the ground-hog sees his shadow, he'll return to his hole, and winter will last another six weeks.

Lincoln's Birthday, Feb. 12. A legal holiday in many states, this day was first formally observed in Washington, D.C., in 1866, when both houses of Congress gathered for a memorial address in tribute to the assassinated President.

St. Valentine's Day, Feb. 14. This day is the festival of two third-century martyrs, both named St. Valentine. It is not known why this day is associated with lovers. It may derive from an old pagan festival about this time of year, or it may have been inspired by the belief that birds mate on this day.

Washington's Birthday, Feb. 22. Observed on the third Monday in February. The birthday of George Washington is celebrated as a legal holiday in every state of the Union, the District of Columbia, and all territories. The observance began in 1796.

Shrove Tuesday. Falls the day before Ash Wednesday and marks the end of the carnival season, which once began on Epiphany but is now usually celebrated the last three days before Lent. In France, the day is known as Mardi Gras (Fat Tuesday), and Mardi Gras celebrations are also held in several American cities, particularly in New Orleans. The day is sometimes called Pancake Tuesday by the English because fats, which were prohibited during Lent, had to be used up.

Ash Wednesday. The first day of the Lenten season, which lasts 40 days. Having its origin sometime before A.D. 1000, it is a day of public penance and is marked in the Roman Catholic Church by the burning of the palms blessed on the previous year's Palm Sunday. With his thumb, the priest then marks a cross upon the forehead of each worshipper. The Anglican Church and a few Protestant groups in the United States also observe the day, but generally without the use of ashes.

St. Patrick's Day, March 17. St. Patrick, patron saint of Ireland, has been honored in America since the first days of the nation. There are many dinners and meetings but perhaps the most notable part of the observance is the annual St. Patrick's Day parade on Fifth Avenue in New York City.

Purim (Feast of Lots). Usually observed in February or March. A day of joy and feasting celebrating deliverance of the Jews from a massacre planned by the Persian Minister Haman. The Jewish Queen Esther interceded with her husband, King Ahasuerus, to spare the life of her uncle, Mordecai, and Haman was hanged on the same gallows he had built for Mordecai. The holiday is marked by the reading of the Book of Esther (megillah), and by the exchange of gifts, donations to the poor, and the presentation of Purim plays.

Palm Sunday. Is observed the Sunday before Easter

to commemorate the entry of Jesus into Jerusalem. The procession and the ceremonies introducing the benediction of palms probably had their origin in Jerusalem.

Good Friday. Is observed the Friday before Easter. This day commemorates the Crucifixion, which is retold during services from the Gospel according to St. John. A feature in Roman Catholic churches is the Liturgy of the Passion; there is no Consecration, the Host having been consecrated the previous day. The eating of hot cross buns on this day is said to have started in England.

First Day of Passover (Pesach). Usually observed in March or April. The Feast of the Passover, also called the Feast of Unleavened Bread, commemorates the escape of the Jews from Egypt. As the Jews fled they ate unleavened bread, and from that time the Jews have allowed no leavening in the houses during Passover, bread being replaced by matzoh.

Easter Sunday. Observed in all Christian churches, Easter commemorates the Resurrection of Jesus. It is celebrated on the first Sunday after the full moon which occurs on or next after March 21 and is therefore celebrated between March 22 and April 25 inclusive. This date was fixed by the Council of Nicaea in A.D. 325.

Mother's Day. Observed the second Sunday in May, as proposed by Anna Jarvis of Philadelphia in 1907.

Ascension Day. Took place in the presence of His apostles 40 days after the Resurrection of Jesus. It is traditionally held to have occurred on Mount Olivet in Bethany.

Memorial Day. Observed on the last Monday in May. Also known as Decoration Day, Memorial Day is a legal holiday in most of the states and the territories, and is also observed by the armed forces. In 1868, Gen. John A. Logan, Commander in Chief of the Grand Army of the Republic, issued an order designating the day as one in which the graves of soldiers would be decorated. The holiday was originally devoted to honoring the memory of those who fell in the Civil War, but is now also dedicated to the memory of all war dead.

First Day of Shavuot (Hebrew Pentecost). Usually observed in May or June. This festival, sometimes called the Feast of Weeks, or of Harvest, or of the First Fruits, falls 50 days after Passover and originally celebrated the end of the seven-week grain harvesting season. In later tradition, it also celebrated the giving of the Law to Moses on Mount Sinai.

Pentecost (Whitsunday). This day commemorates the descent of the Holy Ghost upon the apostles 50 days after the Resurrection. The sermon by the Apostle Peter, which led to the baptism of 3,000 who professed belief, originated the ceremonies that have since been followed. "Whitsunday" is believed to have come from "white Sunday" when, among the English, white robes were worn by those baptized on the day.

Flag Day, June 14. This day commemorates the adoption by the Continental Congress on June 14, 1777, of the Stars and Stripes as the U.S. flag. Although it is a legal holiday only in Pennsylvania, President Truman, on Aug. 3, 1949, signed a bill re-

questing the President to call for its observance each year by proclamation.

Father's Day. Observed the third Sunday in June. First celebrated June 19, 1910.

Independence Day, July 4. The day of the adoption of the Declaration of Independence in 1776, celebrated in all states and territories. The observance began the next year in Philadelphia.

Labor Day. Observed the first Monday in September in all states and territories. Labor Day was first celebrated in New York in 1882 under the sponsorship of the Central Labor Union, following the suggestion of Peter J. McGuire, of the Knights of Labor, that the day be set aside in honor of labor.

First Day of Rosh Hashana (Jewish New Year). Usually observed in September. This day marks the beginning of the Jewish year 5753 and opens the Ten Days of Penitence closing with Yom Kippur.

Yom Kippur (Day of Atonement). Usually observed in September or October. This day marks the end of the Ten Days of Penitence that began with Rosh Hashana. It is described in *Leviticus* as a "Sabbath of rest," and synagogue services begin the preceding sundown, resume the following morning, and continue to sundown.

First Day of Sukkot (Feast of Tabernacles). Usually observed in September or October. This festival, also known as the Feast of the Ingathering, originally celebrated the fruit harvest, and the name comes from the booths or tabernacles in which the Jews lived during the harvest, although one tradition traces it to the shelters used by the Jews in their wandering through the wilderness. During the festival many Jews build small huts in their back yards or on the roofs of their houses.

Columbus Day. Is observed the second Monday in October. A legal holiday in many states, commemorating the discovery of America by Columbus in 1492. Quite likely the first celebration of Columbus Day was that organized in 1792 by the Society of St. Tammany, or Columbian Order, widely known as Tammany Hall.

Simhat Torah (Rejoicing of the Law). Usually observed in September or October. This joyous holiday falls on the eighth day of Sukkot. It marks the end of the year's reading of the Torah (Five Books of Moses) in the synagogue every Saturday and the beginning of the new cycle of reading.

United Nations Day, Oct. 24. Marking the founding of the United Nations.

Halloween, Oct. 31. Eve of All Saints' Day, formerly called All Hallows and Hallowmass. Halloween is traditionally associated in some countries with old customs such as bonfires, masquerading, and the telling of ghost stories. These are old Celtic practices marking the beginning of winter.

All Saints' Day, Nov. 1. A Roman Catholic and Anglican holiday celebrating all saints, known and unknown.

Election Day, (legal holiday in certain states). Since 1845, by Act of Congress, the first Tuesday after the first Monday in November is the date for choosing Presidential electors. State elections are also generally held on this day.

Veterans Day, Nov. 11. Armistice Day was established in 1926 to commemorate the signing in 1918 of the Armistice ending World War I. On June 1, 1954, the name was changed to Veterans Day to honor all men and women who have served America in its armed forces.

Thanksgiving. Observed nationally on the fourth Thursday in November by Act of Congress (1941), the first such national proclamation having been issued by President Lincoln in 1863, on the urging of Mrs. Sarah J. Hale, editor of *Godey's Lady's Book.* Most Americans believe that the holiday dates back to the day of thanks ordered by Governor Bradford of Plymouth Colony in New England in 1621, but scholars point out that days of thanks stem from ancient times.

First Sunday of Advent. Advent is the season in which the faithful must prepare themselves for the advent of the Saviour on Christmas. The four Sundays before Christmas are marked by special church services.

First Day of Hanukkah (Festival of Lights). Usually observed in November or December. This festival was instituted by Judas Maccabaeus in 165 B.C. to celebrate the purification of the Temple of Jerusalem, which had been desecrated three years earlier by Antiochus Epiphanes, who set up a pagan altar and offered sacrifices to Zeus Olympius. In Jewish homes, a light is lighted on each night of the eight-day festival.

Christmas (Feast of the Nativity), Dec. 25. The most widely celebrated holiday of the Christian year, Christmas is observed as the anniversary of the birth of Jesus. Christmas customs are centuries old. The mistletoe, for example, comes from the Druids, who, in hanging the mistletoe, hoped for peace and good fortune. Use of such plants as holly comes from the ancient belief that such plants blossomed at Christmas. Comparatively recent is the Christmas tree, first set up in Germany in the 17th century, and the use of candles on trees developed from the belief that candles appeared by miracle on the trees at Christmas. Colonial Manhattan Islanders introduced the name Santa Claus, a corruption of the Dutch name for the 4th-century Asia Minor St. Nicholas.

State Observances

January 6, Three Kings' Day: Puerto Rico.
January 8, Battle of New Orleans Day: Louisiana.
January 11, De Hostos' Birthday: Puerto Rico.
January 19, Robert E. Lee's Birthday: Arkansas, Florida, Kentucky, Louisiana, South Carolina, **(third Monday)** Alabama, Mississippi.
January 19, Confederate Heroes Day: Texas.
January (third Monday): Lee-Jackson-King Day: Virginia.
January 30, F.D. Roosevelt's Birthday: Kentucky.
February 15, Susan B. Anthony's Birthday: Florida, Minnesota.
March (first Tuesday), Town Meeting Day: Vermont.
March 2, Texas Independence Day: Texas.
March (first Monday), Casimir Pulaski's Birthday: Illinois.
March 17, Evacuation Day: Massachusetts (in Suffolk County).
March 20 (First Day of Spring), Youth Day: Oklahoma.
March 22, Abolition Day: Puerto Rico.
March 25, Maryland Day: Maryland.
March 26, Prince Jonah Kuhio Kalanianaole Day: Hawaii.
March (last Monday), Seward's Day: Alaska.
April 2, Pascua Florida Day: Florida
April 13, Thomas Jefferson's Birthday: Alabama, Oklahoma.
April 16, De Diego's Birthday: Puerto Rico.
April (third Monday), Patriots' Day: Maine, Massachusetts.
April 21, San Jacinto Day: Texas.
April 22, Arbor Day: Nebraska.
April 22, Oklahoma Day: Oklahoma.
April 26, Confederate Memorial Day: Florida, Georgia.
April (fourth Monday), Fast Day: New Hampshire.
April (last Monday), Confederate Memorial Day: Alabama, Mississippi.
May 1, Bird Day: Oklahoma.
May 8, Truman Day: Missouri.
May 11, Minnesota Day: Minnesota.

May 20, Mecklenburg Independence Day: North Carolina.
June (first Monday), Jefferson Davis's Birthday: Alabama, Mississippi.
June 3, Jefferson Davis's Birthday: Florida, South Carolina.
June 3, Confederate Memorial Day: Kentucky, Louisiana.
June 9, Senior Citizens Day: Oklahoma.
June 11, King Kamehameha I Day: Hawaii.
June 15, Separation Day: Delaware.
June 17, Bunker Hill Day: Massachusetts (in Suffolk County).
June 19, Emancipation Day: Texas.
June 20, West Virginia Day: West Virginia.
July 17, Muñoz Rivera's Birthday: Puerto Rico.
July 24, Pioneer Day: Utah.
July 25, Constitution Day: Puerto Rico.
July 27, Barbosa's Birthday: Puerto Rico.
August (first Sunday), American Family Day: Arizona.
August (first Monday), Colorado Day: Colorado.
August (second Monday), Victory Day: Rhode Island.
August 16, Bennington Battle Day: Vermont.
August (third Friday), Admission Day: Hawaii.
August 27, Lyndon B. Johnson's Birthday: Texas.
August 30, Huey P. Long Day: Louisiana.
September 9, Admission Day: California.
September 12, Defenders' Day: Maryland.
September 16, Cherokee Strip Day: Oklahoma.
September (first Saturday after full moon), Indian Day: Oklahoma.
October 10, Leif Erickson Day: Minnesota.
October 10, Oklahoma Historical Day: Oklahoma.
October 18, Alaska Day: Alaska.
October 31, Nevada Day: Nevada.
November 4, Will Rogers Day: Oklahoma.
November (week of the 16th), Oklahoma Heritage Week: Oklahoma.
November 19, Discovery Day: Puerto Rico.
December 7, Delaware Day: Delaware.

National Holidays Around the World

Country	Date	Country	Date	Country	Date
Afghanistan	April 27	Gabon	Aug. 17	Pakistan	March 23
Albania	Nov. 29	Gambia	Feb. 18	Panama	Nov. 3
Algeria	Nov. 1	Ghana	March 6	Papua New Guinea	Sept. 16
Angola	Nov. 11	Greece	March 25	Paraguay	May 14
Antigua and Barbuda	Nov. 1	Grenada	Feb. 7	Peru	July 28
Argentina	May 25	Guatemala	Sept. 15	Philippines	June 12
Australia	Jan. 26	Guinea	Oct. 2	Poland	July 22
Austria	Oct. 26	Guinea-Bissau	Sept. 24	Portugal	June 10
Bahamas	July 10	Guyana	Feb. 23	Qatar	Sept. 3
Bahrain	Dec. 16	Haiti	Jan. 1	Romania	Dec. 1
Bangladesh	March 26	Honduras	Sept. 15	Rwanda	July 1
Barbados	Nov. 30	Hungary	March 15	St. Kitts and Nevis	Sept. 19
Belgium	July 21	Iceland	June 17	St. Lucia	Feb. 22
Belize	Sept. 21	India	Jan. 26	St. Vincent and	
Benin	Nov. 30	Indonesia	Aug. 17	the Grenadines	Oct. 27
Bhutan	Dec. 17	Iran	Feb. 11	São Tomé and Príncipe	July 12
Bolivia	Aug. 6	Iraq	July 17	Saudi Arabia	Sept. 23
Botswana	Sept. 30	Ireland	March 17	Senegal	April 4
Brazil	Sept. 7	Israel	(1)	Seychelles	June 5
Brunei	Feb. 23	Italy	June 2	Sierra Leone	April 27
Bulgaria	March 3	Jamaica	(2)	Singapore	Aug. 9
Burkina Faso	Aug. 4	Japan	April 29	Solomon Islands	July 7
Burundi	July 1	Jordan	May 25	Somalia	Oct. 21
Cambodia	April 17	Kenya	Dec. 12	South Africa	May 31
Cameroon	May 20	Kuwait	Feb. 25	Spain	Oct. 12
Canada	July 1	Laos	Dec. 2	Sri Lanka	Feb. 4
Cape Verde	Sept. 12	Lebanon	Nov. 22	Sudan	Jan. 1
Central African Republic	Dec. 1	Lesotho	Oct. 4	Suriname	Nov. 25
Chad	June 7	Liberia	July 26	Swaziland	Sept. 6
Chile	Sept. 18	Libya	Sept. 1	Sweden	June 6
China	Oct. 1	Luxembourg	June 23	Switzerland	Aug. 1
Colombia	July 20	Madagascar	June 26	Syria	April 17
Comoros	July 6	Malawi	July 6	Tanzania	April 26
Congo	Aug. 15	Malaysia	Aug. 31	Thailand	Dec. 5
Costa Rica	Sept. 15	Maldives	July 26	Togo	April 27
Côte d'Ivoire	Dec. 7	Mali	Sept. 22	Trinidad and Tobago	Aug. 31
Cuba	Jan. 1	Malta	March 31	Tunisia	June 1
Cyprus	Oct. 1	Mauritania	Nov. 28	Turkey	Oct. 29
Czechoslovakia	May 9,	Mauritius	March 12	Uganda	Oct. 9
	Oct. 28	Mexico	Sept. 16	U.S.S.R.	Nov. 7
		Mongolia	July 11	United Arab Emirates	Dec. 2
Denmark	April 16	Morocco	March 3	United Kingdom	(3)
Djibouti	June 27	Mozambique	June 25	United States	July 4
Dominica	Nov. 3	Myanmar	Jan. 4	Uruguay	Aug. 25
Dominican Republic	Feb. 27	Nepal	Dec. 28	Vanuatu	July 30
Ecuador	Aug. 10	Netherlands	April 30	Venezuela	July 5
Egypt	July 23	New Zealand	Feb. 6	Viet Nam	Sept. 2
El Salvador	Sept. 15	Nicaragua	Sept. 15	Western Samoa	June 1
Equatorial Guinea	Oct. 12	Niger	Dec. 18	Yemen, Republic of	Sept. 26
Ethiopia	Sept. 12	Nigeria	Oct. 1	Yugoslavia	Nov. 29
Fiji	Oct. 10	Norway	May 17	Zaire	June 30
Finland	Dec. 6	Oman	Nov. 18	Zambia	Oct. 24
France	July 14			Zimbabwe	April 18

1. Changes yearly according to Hebrew calendar. 2. Celebrated on first Monday in August. 3. Celebrated the second Saturday in June.

Modern Wedding Anniversary Gift List

Anniversay	Gift	Anniversay	Gift	Anniversay	Gift
1st	Gold jewelry	7th	Onyx	30th	Pearl jubilee
2nd	Garnet	8th	Tourmaline	35th	Emerald
3rd	Pearls	9th	Lapis	40th	Ruby
4th	Blue topaz	10th	Diamond jewelry	45th	Sapphire
5th	Sapphire	20th	Emerald	50th	Golden jubilee
6th	Amethyst	25th	Silver jubilee	60th	Diamond jubilee

Source: Jewelry Industry Council

PERPETUAL CALENDAR

```
1800 .. 4    1844 .. 9    1888 .. 8    1932 . 13    1976 . 12    2020 . 11
1801 .. 5    1845 .. 4    1889 .. 3    1933 .. 1    1977 .. 7    2021 .. 6
1802 .. 6    1846 .. 5    1890 .. 4    1934 .. 2    1978 .. 1    2022 .. 7
1803 .. 7    1847 .. 6    1891 .. 5    1935 .. 3    1979 .. 2    2023 .. 1
1804 .. 8    1848 . 14    1892 . 13    1936 . 11    1980 . 10    2024 .. 9
1805 .. 3    1849 .. 2    1893 .. 1    1937 .. 6    1981 .. 5    2025 .. 4
1806 .. 4    1850 .. 3    1894 .. 2    1938 .. 7    1982 .. 6    2026 .. 5
1807 .. 5    1851 .. 4    1895 .. 3    1939 .. 1    1983 .. 7    2027 .. 6
1808 . 13    1852 . 12    1896 . 11    1940 .. 9    1984 .. 8    2028 . 14
1809 .. 1    1853 .. 7    1897 .. 6    1941 .. 4    1985 .. 3    2029 .. 2
1810 .. 2    1854 .. 1    1898 .. 7    1942 .. 5    1986 .. 4    2030 .. 3
1811 .. 3    1855 .. 2    1899 .. 1    1943 .. 6    1987 .. 5    2031 .. 4
1812 . 11    1856 . 10    1900 .. 2    1944 . 14    1988 . 13    2032 . 12
1813 .. 6    1857 .. 5    1901 .. 3    1945 .. 2    1989 .. 1    2033 .. 7
1814 .. 7    1858 .. 6    1902 .. 4    1946 .. 3    1990 .. 2    2034 .. 1
1815 .. 1    1859 .. 7    1903 .. 5    1947 .. 4    1991 .. 3    2035 .. 2
1816 .. 9    1860 .. 8    1904 . 13    1948 . 12    1992 . 11    2036 . 10
1817 .. 4    1861 .. 3    1905 .. 1    1949 .. 7    1993 .. 6    2037 .. 5
1818 .. 5    1862 .. 4    1906 .. 2    1950 .. 1    1994 .. 7    2038 .. 6
1819 .. 6    1863 .. 5    1907 .. 3    1951 .. 2    1995 .. 1    2039 .. 7
1820 . 14    1864 . 13    1908 . 11    1952 . 10    1996 .. 9    2040 .. 8
1821 .. 2    1865 .. 1    1909 .. 6    1953 .. 5    1997 .. 4    2041 .. 3
1822 .. 3    1866 .. 2    1910 .. 7    1954 .. 6    1998 .. 5    2042 .. 4
1823 .. 4    1867 .. 3    1911 .. 1    1955 .. 7    1999 .. 6    2043 .. 5
1824 . 12    1868 . 11    1912 .. 9    1956 .. 8    2000 . 14    2044 . 13
1825 .. 7    1869 .. 6    1913 .. 4    1957 .. 3    2001 .. 2    2045 .. 1
1826 .. 1    1870 .. 7    1914 .. 5    1958 .. 4    2002 .. 3    2046 .. 2
1827 .. 2    1871 .. 1    1915 .. 6    1959 .. 5    2003 .. 4    2047 .. 3
1828 . 10    1872 .. 9    1916 . 14    1960 . 13    2004 . 12    2048 . 11
1829 .. 5    1873 .. 4    1917 .. 2    1961 .. 1    2005 .. 7    2049 .. 6
1830 .. 6    1874 .. 5    1918 .. 3    1962 .. 2    2006 .. 1    2050 .. 7
1831 .. 7    1875 .. 6    1919 .. 4    1963 .. 3    2007 .. 2    2051 .. 1
1832 .. 8    1876 . 14    1920 . 12    1964 . 11    2008 . 10    2052 .. 9
1833 .. 3    1877 .. 2    1921 .. 7    1965 .. 6    2009 .. 5    2053 .. 4
1834 .. 4    1878 .. 3    1922 .. 1    1966 .. 7    2010 .. 6    2054 .. 5
1835 .. 5    1879 .. 4    1923 .. 2    1967 .. 1    2011 .. 7    2055 .. 6
1836 . 13    1880 . 12    1924 . 10    1968 .. 9    2012 .. 8    2056 . 14
1837 .. 1    1881 .. 7    1925 .. 5    1969 .. 4    2013 .. 3    2057 .. 2
1838 .. 2    1882 .. 1    1926 .. 6    1970 .. 5    2014 .. 4    2058 .. 3
1839 .. 3    1883 .. 2    1927 .. 7    1971 .. 6    2015 .. 5    2059 .. 4
1840 . 11    1884 . 10    1928 .. 8    1972 . 14    2016 . 13    2060 . 12
1841 .. 6    1885 .. 5    1929 .. 3    1973 .. 2    2017 .. 1    2061 .. 7
1842 .. 7    1886 .. 6    1930 .. 4    1974 .. 3    2018 .. 2    2062 .. 1
1843 .. 1    1887 .. 7    1931 .. 5    1975 .. 4    2019 .. 3    2063 .. 5
```

DIRECTIONS: The number given with each year in the key above is number of calendar to use for that year

Calendar 1

```
JANUARY                 FEBRUARY                MARCH                   APRIL
S  M  T  W  T  F  S      S  M  T  W  T  F  S      S  M  T  W  T  F  S      S  M  T  W  T  F  S
 1  2  3  4  5  6  7                  1  2  3  4                  1  2  3  4                        1
 8  9 10 11 12 13 14      5  6  7  8  9 10 11      5  6  7  8  9 10 11      2  3  4  5  6  7  8
15 16 17 18 19 20 21     12 13 14 15 16 17 18     12 13 14 15 16 17 18      9 10 11 12 13 14 15
22 23 24 25 26 27 28     19 20 21 22 23 24 25     19 20 21 22 23 24 25     16 17 18 19 20 21 22
29 30 31                 26 27 28                 26 27 28 29 30 31        23 24 25 26 27 28 29
                                                                          30

MAY                     JUNE                    JULY                    AUGUST
S  M  T  W  T  F  S      S  M  T  W  T  F  S      S  M  T  W  T  F  S      S  M  T  W  T  F  S
    1  2  3  4  5  6                  1  2  3                        1            1  2  3  4  5
 7  8  9 10 11 12 13      4  5  6  7  8  9 10      2  3  4  5  6  7  8      6  7  8  9 10 11 12
14 15 16 17 18 19 20     11 12 13 14 15 16 17      9 10 11 12 13 14 15     13 14 15 16 17 18 19
21 22 23 24 25 26 27     18 19 20 21 22 23 24     16 17 18 19 20 21 22     20 21 22 23 24 25 26
28 29 30 31              25 26 27 28 29 30        23 24 25 26 27 28 29     27 28 29 30 31
                                                  30 31

SEPTEMBER               OCTOBER                 NOVEMBER                DECEMBER
S  M  T  W  T  F  S      S  M  T  W  T  F  S      S  M  T  W  T  F  S      S  M  T  W  T  F  S
             1  2        1  2  3  4  5  6  7                  1  2  3  4                  1  2
 3  4  5  6  7  8  9      8  9 10 11 12 13 14      5  6  7  8  9 10 11      3  4  5  6  7  8  9
10 11 12 13 14 15 16     15 16 17 18 19 20 21     12 13 14 15 16 17 18     10 11 12 13 14 15 16
17 18 19 20 21 22 23     22 23 24 25 26 27 28     19 20 21 22 23 24 25     17 18 19 20 21 22 23
24 25 26 27 28 29 30     29 30 31                 26 27 28 29 30           24 25 26 27 28 29 30
                                                                          31
```

Calendar 2

```
JANUARY                 FEBRUARY                MARCH                   APRIL
S  M  T  W  T  F  S      S  M  T  W  T  F  S      S  M  T  W  T  F  S      S  M  T  W  T  F  S
    1  2  3  4  5  6                  1  2  3                  1  2  3      1  2  3  4  5  6  7
 7  8  9 10 11 12 13      4  5  6  7  8  9 10      4  5  6  7  8  9 10      8  9 10 11 12 13 14
14 15 16 17 18 19 20     11 12 13 14 15 16 17     11 12 13 14 15 16 17     15 16 17 18 19 20 21
21 22 23 24 25 26 27     18 19 20 21 22 23 24     18 19 20 21 22 23 24     22 23 24 25 26 27 28
28 29 30 31              25 26 27 28              25 26 27 28 29 30 31     29 30

MAY                     JUNE                    JULY                    AUGUST
S  M  T  W  T  F  S      S  M  T  W  T  F  S      S  M  T  W  T  F  S      S  M  T  W  T  F  S
       1  2  3  4  5                  1  2        1  2  3  4  5  6  7                  1  2  3  4
 6  7  8  9 10 11 12      3  4  5  6  7  8  9      8  9 10 11 12 13 14      5  6  7  8  9 10 11
13 14 15 16 17 18 19     10 11 12 13 14 15 16     15 16 17 18 19 20 21     12 13 14 15 16 17 18
20 21 22 23 24 25 26     17 18 19 20 21 22 23     22 23 24 25 26 27 28     19 20 21 22 23 24 25
27 28 29 30 31           24 25 26 27 28 29 30     29 30 31                 26 27 28 29 30 31

SEPTEMBER               OCTOBER                 NOVEMBER                DECEMBER
S  M  T  W  T  F  S      S  M  T  W  T  F  S      S  M  T  W  T  F  S      S  M  T  W  T  F  S
                   1        1  2  3  4  5  6                  1  2  3                        1
 2  3  4  5  6  7  8      7  8  9 10 11 12 13      4  5  6  7  8  9 10      2  3  4  5  6  7  8
 9 10 11 12 13 14 15     14 15 16 17 18 19 20     11 12 13 14 15 16 17      9 10 11 12 13 14 15
16 17 18 19 20 21 22     21 22 23 24 25 26 27     18 19 20 21 22 23 24     16 17 18 19 20 21 22
23 24 25 26 27 28 29     28 29 30 31              25 26 27 28 29 30        23 24 25 26 27 28 29
30                                                                        30 31
```

Calendar 3

```
JANUARY                 FEBRUARY                MARCH                   APRIL
S  M  T  W  T  F  S      S  M  T  W  T  F  S      S  M  T  W  T  F  S      S  M  T  W  T  F  S
       1  2  3  4  5                  1  2                  1  2            1  2  3  4  5  6
 6  7  8  9 10 11 12      3  4  5  6  7  8  9      3  4  5  6  7  8  9      7  8  9 10 11 12 13
13 14 15 16 17 18 19     10 11 12 13 14 15 16     10 11 12 13 14 15 16     14 15 16 17 18 19 20
20 21 22 23 24 25 26     17 18 19 20 21 22 23     17 18 19 20 21 22 23     21 22 23 24 25 26 27
27 28 29 30 31           24 25 26 27 28           24 25 26 27 28 29 30     28 29 30
                                                  31

MAY                     JUNE                    JULY                    AUGUST
S  M  T  W  T  F  S      S  M  T  W  T  F  S      S  M  T  W  T  F  S      S  M  T  W  T  F  S
          1  2  3  4                        1         1  2  3  4  5  6                  1  2  3
 5  6  7  8  9 10 11      2  3  4  5  6  7  8      7  8  9 10 11 12 13      4  5  6  7  8  9 10
12 13 14 15 16 17 18      9 10 11 12 13 14 15     14 15 16 17 18 19 20     11 12 13 14 15 16 17
19 20 21 22 23 24 25     16 17 18 19 20 21 22     21 22 23 24 25 26 27     18 19 20 21 22 23 24
26 27 28 29 30 31        23 24 25 26 27 28 29     28 29 30 31              25 26 27 28 29 30 31
                         30

SEPTEMBER               OCTOBER                 NOVEMBER                DECEMBER
S  M  T  W  T  F  S      S  M  T  W  T  F  S      S  M  T  W  T  F  S      S  M  T  W  T  F  S
 1  2  3  4  5  6  7           1  2  3  4  5                     1  2      1  2  3  4  5  6  7
 8  9 10 11 12 13 14      6  7  8  9 10 11 12      3  4  5  6  7  8  9      8  9 10 11 12 13 14
15 16 17 18 19 20 21     13 14 15 16 17 18 19     10 11 12 13 14 15 16     15 16 17 18 19 20 21
22 23 24 25 26 27 28     20 21 22 23 24 25 26     17 18 19 20 21 22 23     22 23 24 25 26 27 28
29 30                    27 28 29 30 31           24 25 26 27 28 29 30     29 30 31
```

Calendar 4

```
JANUARY                 FEBRUARY                MARCH                   APRIL
S  M  T  W  T  F  S      S  M  T  W  T  F  S      S  M  T  W  T  F  S      S  M  T  W  T  F  S
          1  2  3  4                        1                        1         1  2  3  4  5
 5  6  7  8  9 10 11      2  3  4  5  6  7  8      2  3  4  5  6  7  8      6  7  8  9 10 11 12
12 13 14 15 16 17 18      9 10 11 12 13 14 15      9 10 11 12 13 14 15     13 14 15 16 17 18 19
19 20 21 22 23 24 25     16 17 18 19 20 21 22     16 17 18 19 20 21 22     20 21 22 23 24 25 26
26 27 28 29 30 31        23 24 25 26 27 28        23 24 25 26 27 28 29     27 28 29 30
                                                  30 31

MAY                     JUNE                    JULY                    AUGUST
S  M  T  W  T  F  S      S  M  T  W  T  F  S      S  M  T  W  T  F  S      S  M  T  W  T  F  S
             1  2  3      1  2  3  4  5  6  7            1  2  3  4  5                     1  2
 4  5  6  7  8  9 10      8  9 10 11 12 13 14      6  7  8  9 10 11 12      3  4  5  6  7  8  9
11 12 13 14 15 16 17     15 16 17 18 19 20 21     13 14 15 16 17 18 19     10 11 12 13 14 15 16
18 19 20 21 22 23 24     22 23 24 25 26 27 28     20 21 22 23 24 25 26     17 18 19 20 21 22 23
25 26 27 28 29 30 31     29 30                    27 28 29 30 31           24 25 26 27 28 29 30
                                                                          31

SEPTEMBER               OCTOBER                 NOVEMBER                DECEMBER
S  M  T  W  T  F  S      S  M  T  W  T  F  S      S  M  T  W  T  F  S      S  M  T  W  T  F  S
    1  2  3  4  5  6                  1  2  3  4                        1         1  2  3  4  5  6
 7  8  9 10 11 12 13      5  6  7  8  9 10 11      2  3  4  5  6  7  8      7  8  9 10 11 12 13
14 15 16 17 18 19 20     12 13 14 15 16 17 18      9 10 11 12 13 14 15     14 15 16 17 18 19 20
21 22 23 24 25 26 27     19 20 21 22 23 24 25     16 17 18 19 20 21 22     21 22 23 24 25 26 27
28 29 30                 26 27 28 29 30 31        23 24 25 26 27 28 29     28 29 30 31
                                                  30
```

Calendar 5

```
JANUARY                 FEBRUARY                MARCH                   APRIL
S  M  T  W  T  F  S      S  M  T  W  T  F  S      S  M  T  W  T  F  S      S  M  T  W  T  F  S
             1  2  3      1  2  3  4  5  6  7      1  2  3  4  5  6  7                  1  2  3  4
 4  5  6  7  8  9 10      8  9 10 11 12 13 14      8  9 10 11 12 13 14      5  6  7  8  9 10 11
11 12 13 14 15 16 17     15 16 17 18 19 20 21     15 16 17 18 19 20 21     12 13 14 15 16 17 18
18 19 20 21 22 23 24     22 23 24 25 26 27 28     22 23 24 25 26 27 28     19 20 21 22 23 24 25
25 26 27 28 29 30 31                             29 30 31                 26 27 28 29 30

MAY                     JUNE                    JULY                    AUGUST
S  M  T  W  T  F  S      S  M  T  W  T  F  S      S  M  T  W  T  F  S      S  M  T  W  T  F  S
                1  2        1  2  3  4  5  6            1  2  3  4                        1
 3  4  5  6  7  8  9      7  8  9 10 11 12 13      5  6  7  8  9 10 11      2  3  4  5  6  7  8
10 11 12 13 14 15 16     14 15 16 17 18 19 20     12 13 14 15 16 17 18      9 10 11 12 13 14 15
17 18 19 20 21 22 23     21 22 23 24 25 26 27     19 20 21 22 23 24 25     16 17 18 19 20 21 22
24 25 26 27 28 29 30     28 29 30                 26 27 28 29 30 31        23 24 25 26 27 28 29
31                                                                        30 31

SEPTEMBER               OCTOBER                 NOVEMBER                DECEMBER
S  M  T  W  T  F  S      S  M  T  W  T  F  S      S  M  T  W  T  F  S      S  M  T  W  T  F  S
       1  2  3  4  5                  1  2  3      1  2  3  4  5  6  7            1  2  3  4  5
 6  7  8  9 10 11 12      4  5  6  7  8  9 10      8  9 10 11 12 13 14      6  7  8  9 10 11 12
13 14 15 16 17 18 19     11 12 13 14 15 16 17     15 16 17 18 19 20 21     13 14 15 16 17 18 19
20 21 22 23 24 25 26     18 19 20 21 22 23 24     22 23 24 25 26 27 28     20 21 22 23 24 25 26
27 28 29 30              25 26 27 28 29 30 31     29 30                    27 28 29 30 31
```

Calendar 6

```
JANUARY                 FEBRUARY                MARCH                   APRIL
S  M  T  W  T  F  S      S  M  T  W  T  F  S      S  M  T  W  T  F  S      S  M  T  W  T  F  S
                1  2         1  2  3  4  5  6         1  2  3  4  5  6                  1  2  3
 3  4  5  6  7  8  9      7  8  9 10 11 12 13      7  8  9 10 11 12 13      4  5  6  7  8  9 10
10 11 12 13 14 15 16     14 15 16 17 18 19 20     14 15 16 17 18 19 20     11 12 13 14 15 16 17
17 18 19 20 21 22 23     21 22 23 24 25 26 27     21 22 23 24 25 26 27     18 19 20 21 22 23 24
24 25 26 27 28 29 30     28                       28 29 30 31             25 26 27 28 29 30
31

MAY                     JUNE                    JULY                    AUGUST
S  M  T  W  T  F  S      S  M  T  W  T  F  S      S  M  T  W  T  F  S      S  M  T  W  T  F  S
                   1            1  2  3  4  5                  1  2  3      1  2  3  4  5  6  7
 2  3  4  5  6  7  8      6  7  8  9 10 11 12      4  5  6  7  8  9 10      8  9 10 11 12 13 14
 9 10 11 12 13 14 15     13 14 15 16 17 18 19     11 12 13 14 15 16 17     15 16 17 18 19 20 21
16 17 18 19 20 21 22     20 21 22 23 24 25 26     18 19 20 21 22 23 24     22 23 24 25 26 27 28
23 24 25 26 27 28 29     27 28 29 30              25 26 27 28 29 30 31     29 30 31
30 31

SEPTEMBER               OCTOBER                 NOVEMBER                DECEMBER
S  M  T  W  T  F  S      S  M  T  W  T  F  S      S  M  T  W  T  F  S      S  M  T  W  T  F  S
          1  2  3  4                  1  2        1  2  3  4  5  6                  1  2  3  4
 5  6  7  8  9 10 11      3  4  5  6  7  8  9      7  8  9 10 11 12 13      5  6  7  8  9 10 11
12 13 14 15 16 17 18     10 11 12 13 14 15 16     14 15 16 17 18 19 20     12 13 14 15 16 17 18
19 20 21 22 23 24 25     17 18 19 20 21 22 23     21 22 23 24 25 26 27     19 20 21 22 23 24 25
26 27 28 29 30           24 25 26 27 28 29 30     28 29 30                 26 27 28 29 30 31
                         31
```

7

JANUARY

S	M	T	W	T	F	S
						1
2	3	4	5	6	7	8
9	10	11	12	13	14	15
16	17	18	19	20	21	22
23	24	25	26	27	28	29
30	31					

FEBRUARY

S	M	T	W	T	F	S
		1	2	3	4	5
6	7	8	9	10	11	12
13	14	15	16	17	18	19
20	21	22	23	24	25	26
27	28					

MARCH

S	M	T	W	T	F	S
		1	2	3	4	5
6	7	8	9	10	11	12
13	14	15	16	17	18	19
20	21	22	23	24	25	26
27	28	29	30	31		

APRIL

S	M	T	W	T	F	S
					1	2
3	4	5	6	7	8	9
10	11	12	13	14	15	16
17	18	19	20	21	22	23
24	25	26	27	28	29	30

MAY

S	M	T	W	T	F	S
1	2	3	4	5	6	7
8	9	10	11	12	13	14
15	16	17	18	19	20	21
22	23	24	25	26	27	28
29	30	31				

JUNE

S	M	T	W	T	F	S
			1	2	3	4
5	6	7	8	9	10	11
12	13	14	15	16	17	18
19	20	21	22	23	24	25
26	27	28	29	30		

JULY

S	M	T	W	T	F	S
					1	2
3	4	5	6	7	8	9
10	11	12	13	14	15	16
17	18	19	20	21	22	23
24	25	26	27	28	29	30
31						

AUGUST

S	M	T	W	T	F	S
	1	2	3	4	5	6
7	8	9	10	11	12	13
14	15	16	17	18	19	20
21	22	23	24	25	26	27
28	29	30	31			

SEPTEMBER

S	M	T	W	T	F	S
				1	2	3
4	5	6	7	8	9	10
11	12	13	14	15	16	17
18	19	20	21	22	23	24
25	26	27	28	29	30	

OCTOBER

S	M	T	W	T	F	S
						1
2	3	4	5	6	7	8
9	10	11	12	13	14	15
16	17	18	19	20	21	22
23	24	25	26	27	28	29
30	31					

NOVEMBER

S	M	T	W	T	F	S
		1	2	3	4	5
6	7	8	9	10	11	12
13	14	15	16	17	18	19
20	21	22	23	24	25	26
27	28	29	30			

DECEMBER

S	M	T	W	T	F	S
				1	2	3
4	5	6	7	8	9	10
11	12	13	14	15	16	17
18	19	20	21	22	23	24
25	26	27	28	29	30	31

8

JANUARY

S	M	T	W	T	F	S
1	2	3	4	5	6	7
89	10	11	12	13	14	
15	16	17	18	19	20	21
22	23	24	25	26	27	28
29	30	31				

FEBRUARY

S	M	T	W	T	F	S
			1	2	3	4
5	6	7	8	9	10	11
12	13	14	15	16	17	18
19	20	21	22	23	24	25
26	27	28	29			

MARCH

S	M	T	W	T	F	S
				1	2	3
4	5	6	7	8	9	10
11	12	13	14	15	16	17
18	19	20	21	22	23	24
25	26	27	28	29	30	31

APRIL

S	M	T	W	T	F	S
1	2	3	4	5	6	7
8	9	10	11	12	13	14
15	16	17	18	19	20	21
22	23	24	25	26	27	28
29	30					

MAY

S	M	T	W	T	F	S
		1	2	3	4	5
6	7	8	9	10	11	12
13	14	15	16	17	18	19
20	21	22	23	24	25	26
27	28	29	30	31		

JUNE

S	M	T	W	T	F	S
					1	2
3	4	5	6	7	8	9
10	11	12	13	14	15	16
17	18	19	20	21	22	23
24	25	26	27	28	29	30

JULY

S	M	T	W	T	F	S
1	2	3	4	5	6	7
8	9	10	11	12	13	14
15	16	17	18	19	20	21
22	23	24	25	26	27	28
29	30	31				

AUGUST

S	M	T	W	T	F	S
			1	2	3	4
5	6	7	8	9	10	11
12	13	14	15	16	17	18
19	20	21	22	23	24	25
26	27	28	29	30	31	

SEPTEMBER

S	M	T	W	T	F	S
						1
2	3	4	5	6	7	8
9	10	11	12	13	14	15
16	17	18	19	20	21	22
23	24	25	26	27	28	29
30						

OCTOBER

S	M	T	W	T	F	S
	1	2	3	4	5	6
7	8	9	10	11	12	13
14	15	16	17	18	19	20
21	22	23	24	25	26	27
28	29	30	31			

NOVEMBER

S	M	T	W	T	F	S
				1	2	3
4	5	6	7	8	9	10
11	12	13	14	15	16	17
18	19	20	21	22	23	24
25	26	27	28	29	30	

DECEMBER

S	M	T	W	T	F	S
						1
2	3	4	5	6	7	8
9	10	11	12	13	14	15
16	17	18	19	20	21	22
23	24	25	26	27	28	29
30	31					

9

JANUARY

S	M	T	W	T	F	S
	1	2	3	4	5	6
7	8	9	10	11	12	13
14	15	16	17	18	19	20
21	22	23	24	25	26	27
28	29	30	31			

FEBRUARY

S	M	T	W	T	F	S
				1	2	3
4	5	6	7	8	9	10
11	12	13	14	15	16	17
18	19	20	21	22	23	24
25	26	27	28	29		

MARCH

S	M	T	W	T	F	S
					1	2
3	4	5	6	7	8	9
10	11	12	13	14	15	16
17	18	19	20	21	22	23
24	25	26	27	28	29	30
31						

APRIL

S	M	T	W	T	F	S
	1	2	3	4	5	6
7	8	9	10	11	12	13
14	15	16	17	18	19	20
21	22	23	24	25	26	27
28	29	30				

MAY

S	M	T	W	T	F	S
			1	2	3	4
5	6	7	8	9	10	11
12	13	14	15	16	17	18
19	20	21	22	23	24	25
26	27	28	29	30	31	

JUNE

S	M	T	W	T	F	S
						1
2	3	4	5	6	7	8
9	10	11	12	13	14	15
16	17	18	19	20	21	22
23	24	25	26	27	28	29
30						

JULY

S	M	T	W	T	F	S
	1	2	3	4	5	6
7	8	9	10	11	12	13
14	15	16	17	18	19	20
21	22	23	24	25	26	27
28	29	30	31			

AUGUST

S	M	T	W	T	F	S
				1	2	3
4	5	6	7	8	9	10
11	12	13	14	15	16	17
18	19	20	21	22	23	24
25	26	27	28	29	30	31

SEPTEMBER

S	M	T	W	T	F	S
1	2	3	4	5	6	7
8	9	10	11	12	13	14
15	16	17	18	19	20	21
22	23	24	25	26	27	28
29	30					

OCTOBER

S	M	T	W	T	F	S
		1	2	3	4	5
6	7	8	9	10	11	12
13	14	15	16	17	18	19
20	21	22	23	24	25	26
27	28	29	30	31		

NOVEMBER

S	M	T	W	T	F	S
					1	2
3	4	5	6	7	8	9
10	11	12	13	14	15	16
17	18	19	20	21	22	23
24	25	26	27	28	29	30

DECEMBER

S	M	T	W	T	F	S
1	2	3	4	5	6	7
8	9	10	11	12	13	14
15	16	17	18	19	20	21
22	23	24	25	26	27	28
29	30	31				

10

JANUARY

S	M	T	W	T	F	S
		1	2	3	4	5
6	7	8	9	10	11	12
13	14	15	16	17	18	19
20	21	22	23	24	25	26
27	28	29	30	31		

FEBRUARY

S	M	T	W	T	F	S
					1	2
3	4	5	6	7	8	9
10	11	12	13	14	15	16
17	18	19	20	21	22	23
24	25	26	27	28	29	

MARCH

S	M	T	W	T	F	S
						1
2	3	4	5	6	7	8
9	10	11	12	13	14	15
16	17	18	19	20	21	22
23	24	25	26	27	28	29
30	31					

APRIL

S	M	T	W	T	F	S
		1	2	3	4	5
6	7	8	9	10	11	12
13	14	15	16	17	18	19
20	21	22	23	24	25	26
27	28	29	30			

MAY

S	M	T	W	T	F	S
				1	2	3
4	5	6	7	8	9	10
11	12	13	14	15	16	17
18	19	20	21	22	23	24
25	26	27	28	29	30	31

JUNE

S	M	T	W	T	F	S
1	2	3	4	5	6	7
8	9	10	11	12	13	14
15	16	17	18	19	20	21
22	23	24	25	26	27	28
29	30					

JULY

S	M	T	W	T	F	S
		1	2	3	4	5
6	7	8	9	10	11	12
13	14	15	16	17	18	19
20	21	22	23	24	25	26
27	28	29	30	31		

AUGUST

S	M	T	W	T	F	S
					1	2
3	4	5	6	7	8	9
10	11	12	13	14	15	16
17	18	19	20	21	22	23
24	25	26	27	28	29	30
31						

SEPTEMBER

S	M	T	W	T	F	S
	1	2	3	4	5	6
7	8	9	10	11	12	13
14	15	16	17	18	19	20
21	22	23	24	25	26	27
28	29	30				

OCTOBER

S	M	T	W	T	F	S
			1	2	3	4
5	6	7	8	9	10	11
12	13	14	15	16	17	18
19	20	21	22	23	24	25
26	27	28	29	30	31	

NOVEMBER

S	M	T	W	T	F	S
						1
2	3	4	5	6	7	8
9	10	11	12	13	14	15
16	17	18	19	20	21	22
23	24	25	26	27	28	29
30						

DECEMBER

S	M	T	W	T	F	S
	1	2	3	4	5	6
7	8	9	10	11	12	13
14	15	16	17	18	19	20
21	22	23	24	25	26	27
28	29	30	31			

11

JANUARY

S	M	T	W	T	F	S
			1	2	3	4
5	6	7	8	9	10	11
12	13	14	15	16	17	18
19	20	21	22	23	24	25
26	27	28	29	30	31	

FEBRUARY

S	M	T	W	T	F	S
						1
2	3	4	5	6	7	8
9	10	11	12	13	14	15
16	17	18	19	20	21	22
23	24	25	26	27	28	29

MARCH

S	M	T	W	T	F	S
1	2	3	4	5	6	7
8	9	10	11	12	13	14
15	16	17	18	19	20	21
22	23	24	25	26	27	28
29	30	31				

APRIL

S	M	T	W	T	F	S
			1	2	3	4
5	6	7	8	9	10	11
12	13	14	15	16	17	18
19	20	21	22	23	24	25
26	27	28	29	30		

MAY

S	M	T	W	T	F	S
					1	2
3	4	5	6	7	8	9
10	11	12	13	14	15	16
17	18	19	20	21	22	23
24	25	26	27	28	29	30
31						

JUNE

S	M	T	W	T	F	S
	1	2	3	4	5	6
7	8	9	10	11	12	13
14	15	16	17	18	19	20
21	22	23	24	25	26	27
28	29	30				

JULY

S	M	T	W	T	F	S
			1	2	3	4
5	6	7	8	9	10	11
12	13	14	15	16	17	18
19	20	21	22	23	24	25
26	27	28	29	30	31	

AUGUST

S	M	T	W	T	F	S
						1
2	3	4	5	6	7	8
9	10	11	12	13	14	15
16	17	18	19	20	21	22
23	24	25	26	27	28	29
30	31					

SEPTEMBER

S	M	T	W	T	F	S
		1	2	3	4	5
6	7	8	9	10	11	12
13	14	15	16	17	18	19
20	21	22	23	24	25	26
27	28	29	30			

OCTOBER

S	M	T	W	T	F	S
				1	2	3
4	5	6	7	8	9	10
11	12	13	14	15	16	17
18	19	20	21	22	23	24
25	26	27	28	29	30	31

NOVEMBER

S	M	T	W	T	F	S
1	2	3	4	5	6	7
8	9	10	11	12	13	14
15	16	17	18	19	20	21
22	23	24	25	26	27	28
29	30					

DECEMBER

S	M	T	W	T	F	S
		1	2	3	4	5
6	7	8	9	10	11	12
13	14	15	16	17	18	19
20	21	22	23	24	25	26
27	28	29	30	31		

12

JANUARY

S	M	T	W	T	F	S
				1	2	3
4	5	6	7	8	9	10
11	12	13	14	15	16	17
18	19	20	21	22	23	24
25	26	27	28	29	30	31

FEBRUARY

S	M	T	W	T	F	S
1	2	3	4	5	6	7
8	9	10	11	12	13	14
15	16	17	18	19	20	21
22	23	24	25	26	27	28
29						

MARCH

S	M	T	W	T	F	S
	1	2	3	4	5	6
7	8	9	10	11	12	13
14	15	16	17	18	19	20
21	22	23	24	25	26	27
28	29	30	31			

APRIL

S	M	T	W	T	F	S
				1	2	3
4	5	6	7	8	9	10
11	12	13	14	15	16	17
18	19	20	21	22	23	24
25	26	27	28	29	30	

MAY

S	M	T	W	T	F	S
						1
2	3	4	5	6	7	8
9	10	11	12	13	14	15
16	17	18	19	20	21	22
23	24	25	26	27	28	29
30	31					

JUNE

S	M	T	W	T	F	S
		1	2	3	4	5
6	7	8	9	10	11	12
13	14	15	16	17	18	19
20	21	22	23	24	25	26
27	28	29	30			

JULY

S	M	T	W	T	F	S
				1	2	3
4	5	6	7	8	9	10
11	12	13	14	15	16	17
18	19	20	21	22	23	24
25	26	27	28	29	30	31

AUGUST

S	M	T	W	T	F	S
1	2	3	4	5	6	7
8	9	10	11	12	13	14
15	16	17	18	19	20	21
22	23	24	25	26	27	28
29	30	31				

SEPTEMBER

S	M	T	W	T	F	S
			1	2	3	4
5	6	7	8	9	10	11
12	13	14	15	16	17	18
19	20	21	22	23	24	25
26	27	28	29	30		

OCTOBER

S	M	T	W	T	F	S
					1	2
3	4	5	6	7	8	9
10	11	12	13	14	15	16
17	18	19	20	21	22	23
24	25	26	27	28	29	30
31						

NOVEMBER

S	M	T	W	T	F	S
	1	2	3	4	5	6
7	8	9	10	11	12	13
14	15	16	17	18	19	20
21	22	23	24	25	26	27
28	29	30				

DECEMBER

S	M	T	W	T	F	S
			1	2	3	4
5	6	7	8	9	10	11
12	13	14	15	16	17	18
19	20	21	22	23	24	25
26	27	28	29	30	31	

13

JANUARY

S	M	T	W	T	F	S
					1	2
3	4	5	6	7	8	9
10	11	12	13	14	15	16
17	18	19	20	21	22	23
24	25	26	27	28	29	30
31						

FEBRUARY

S	M	T	W	T	F	S
	1	2	3	4	5	6
7	8	9	10	11	12	13
14	15	16	17	18	19	20
21	22	23	24	25	26	27
28	29					

MARCH

S	M	T	W	T	F	S
		1	2	3	4	5
6	7	8	9	10	11	12
13	14	15	16	17	18	19
20	21	22	23	24	25	26
27	28	29	30	31		

APRIL

S	M	T	W	T	F	S
					1	2
3	4	5	6	7	8	9
10	11	12	13	14	15	16
17	18	19	20	21	22	23
24	25	26	27	28	29	30

MAY

S	M	T	W	T	F	S
1	2	3	4	5	6	7
8	9	10	11	12	13	14
15	16	17	18	19	20	21
22	23	24	25	26	27	28
29	30	31				

JUNE

S	M	T	W	T	F	S
			1	2	3	4
5	6	7	8	9	10	11
12	13	14	15	16	17	18
19	20	21	22	23	24	25
26	27	28	29	30		

JULY

S	M	T	W	T	F	S
					1	2
3	4	5	6	7	8	9
10	11	12	13	14	15	16
17	18	19	20	21	22	23
24	25	26	27	28	29	30
31						

AUGUST

S	M	T	W	T	F	S
	1	2	3	4	5	6
7	8	9	10	11	12	13
14	15	16	17	18	19	20
21	22	23	24	25	26	27
28	29	30	31			

SEPTEMBER

S	M	T	W	T	F	S
				1	2	3
4	5	6	7	8	9	10
11	12	13	14	15	16	17
18	19	20	21	22	23	24
25	26	27	28	29	30	

OCTOBER

S	M	T	W	T	F	S
						1
2	3	4	5	6	7	8
9	10	11	12	13	14	15
16	17	18	19	20	21	22
23	24	25	26	27	28	29
30	31					

NOVEMBER

S	M	T	W	T	F	S
		1	2	3	4	5
6	7	8	9	10	11	12
13	14	15	16	17	18	19
20	21	22	23	24	25	26
27	28	29	30			

DECEMBER

S	M	T	W	T	F	S
				1	2	3
4	5	6	7	8	9	10
11	12	13	14	15	16	17
18	19	20	21	22	23	24
25	26	27	28	29	30	31

14

JANUARY

S	M	T	W	T	F	S
						1
2	3	4	5	6	7	8
9	10	11	12	13	14	15
16	17	18	19	20	21	22
23	24	25	26	27	28	29
30	31					

FEBRUARY

S	M	T	W	T	F	S
		1	2	3	4	5
6	7	8	9	10	11	12
13	14	15	16	17	18	19
20	21	22	23	24	25	26
27	28	29				

MARCH

S	M	T	W	T	F	S
			1	2	3	4
5	6	7	8	9	10	11
12	13	14	15	16	17	18
19	20	21	22	23	24	25
26	27	28	29	30	31	

APRIL

S	M	T	W	T	F	S
						1
2	3	4	5	6	7	8
9	10	11	12	13	14	15
16	17	18	19	20	21	22
23	24	25	26	27	28	29
30						

MAY

S	M	T	W	T	F	S
	1	2	3	4	5	6
7	8	9	10	11	12	13
14	15	16	17	18	19	20
21	22	23	24	25	26	27
28	29	30	31			

JUNE

S	M	T	W	T	F	S
				1	2	3
4	5	6	7	8	9	10
11	12	13	14	15	16	17
18	19	20	21	22	23	24
25	26	27	28	29	30	

JULY

S	M	T	W	T	F	S
						1
2	3	4	5	6	7	8
9	10	11	12	13	14	15
16	17	18	19	20	21	22
23	24	25	26	27	28	29
30	31					

AUGUST

S	M	T	W	T	F	S
		1	2	3	4	5
6	7	8	9	10	11	12
13	14	15	16	17	18	19
20	21	22	23	24	25	26
27	28	29	30	31		

SEPTEMBER

S	M	T	W	T	F	S
					1	2
3	4	5	6	7	8	9
10	11	12	13	14	15	16
17	18	19	20	21	22	23
24	25	26	27	28	29	30

OCTOBER

S	M	T	W	T	F	S
1	2	3	4	5	6	7
8	9	10	11	12	13	14
15	16	17	18	19	20	21
22	23	24	25	26	27	28
29	30	31				

NOVEMBER

S	M	T	W	T	F	S
			1	2	3	4
5	6	7	8	9	10	11
12	13	14	15	16	17	18
19	20	21	22	23	24	25
26	27	28	29	30		

DECEMBER

S	M	T	W	T	F	S
					1	2
3	4	5	6	7	8	9
10	11	12	13	14	15	16
17	18	19	20	21	22	23
24	25	26	27	28	29	30
31						

U.S. STATISTICS

This profile was created from many data sources. Most figures are approximate. The figures given are latest available.

GEOGRAPHY

Number of states: 50
Land area (1990): 3,615,100 sq. mi. Share of world land area (1990): 6.2%
Northernmost point: Point Barrow, Alaska
Easternmost point: West Quoddy Head, Maine
Southernmost point: Ka Lae (South Cape), Hawaii
Westernmost point: Pochnoi Point, Alaska
Geographic center: in Butte County, S.D. (44" 58' N. lat., 103" 46' W. long.)

POPULATION

Total (1990): 248,709,873
Center of population (1990): 9.7 miles northwest of Steelville in Crawford County, Missouri
Males (1990): 121,239,418
Females (1990): 127,470,418
White (1990): 199,686,070
Black (1990): 29,986,070
Hispanic origin (can be of any race) (1990): 22,354,059
American Indian, Eskimo, Aleut (1990): 1,959,234
Asian or Pacific Islander (1990): 7,273,662
Other race (1990): 9,804,847
Breakdown by age groups (1990):
Under 5 years: 18,354,443
5–17 years: 45,249,989
18–20 years: 11,726,868
21–24 years: 15,010,835
25–44 years: 80,754,835
45–54 years: 25,223,086
55–59 years: 10,531,756
60–64 years: 10,616,167
65–74 years: 18,106,558
75–84 years: 10,055,108
85 and over: 3,080,165
Median age (1990): 32.9
Rural population (1990): 66,964,000
Metropolitan population (1990): 192,725,741
Total households (1990): 91,947,410
Family households (1990): 64,517,947
Non-family households (1990): 27,429,463
Average no. of persons per household (1990): 2.63
Average family size (1990): 3.17
No. of owner households (1990): 59,846,000
Married couples (1990): 52,317,000
Unmarried households (1990): 2,856,000
Single parent (1990): female, 6,599,000; male, 1,153,000
Widows (1990): 11,477,000
Widowers (1990): 2,333,000

VITAL STATISTICS

Births (est. 1990): 4,179,000
Deaths (est. 1990): 2,152,000
Marriages (est. 1990): 2,448,000
Divorces (est. 1990): 1,175,000
Infant mortality rate (est. 1990): 9.1/1,000
Legal abortions (est. 1987): 1,600,000
Life expectancy (1988): white male, 72.3; white female, 78.9; black male, 64.9; black female, 73.4

CIVILIAN LABOR FORCE

Males (1991): 63,405,000 (92.6% employed)
Females (1991): 53,479,000 (93.5% employed)
Teenagers, 16–19 (1991): 5,537,000 (80.8% employed)

Work at home (est. 1991): 38,400,000

INCOME AND CREDIT

Gross National Product (1990): $5,465,100,000,000
Personal income per capita (1990): $21,974
Average family income (1989): $41,506
Individual shareholders (1990): 51,400,000
Number below poverty level (1989): 31,534,000
Tax returns with reported adjusted gross income of $1 million or more (1989): 61,987
Credit market debt outstanding (1988): $11,415,000,000,000
Mortgage debt outstanding (1988): $3,254,000,000,000
Consumer credit outstanding (1988): $728,900,000,000

EDUCATION

Public elementary and secondary pupils (est. 1989–1991): 41,047,643
Public elementary and secondary classroom teachers (est. 1990–1991): 2,408,836; women, 1,745,041; men, 663,795
Average annual salaries of public elementary and secondary teachers (est. 1990–1991): $33,015
Public high-school graduates (est. 1990–1991): 2,285,030
Persons completing 4 years of college or more (1989): 34,457,000
Current expenditures for public elementary and secondary day schools (est. 1990–1991): 198,435,420,000

CONVENIENCES

Radio sets (1988): households with, 99%; average no. of radio sets per household, 5.6
Radio stations (1991): 8,051
Television stations (1991): 1,367
Automobiles (1990): 143,864,000
Households with telephones (1988): 85,300,000; (93%)
Newspaper circulation (morning and evening, Sept. 30, 1990): 62,327,962
Cable television subscribers (1989): 47,800,000
Television sets in homes (1989): 176,000,000
Households with television sets (1989): 90,000,000
Households with VCRs (1989): 58,000,000
Personal computers used at home (1988): 22,380,000

CRIME

Total arrests (1989): 11,261,295; males, 9,224,132; under 18 male, 1,362,814; female, 2,037,163; under 18 female, 382,004
Child neglect and abuse (1987): 2,178,384 children reported; 1,404,242 families reported
Prisoners under sentence of death (Dec. 31, 1989): 2,250
Law enforcement officers killed (1990): 132
Murder victims (1989): 21,500
Households touched by crime (1989): 22,800,000 (25%)

1990 Census Profile

Source: U.S. Department of Commerce, Economics and Statistics Administration, Bureau of the Census.

Population Trends

The resident population of the United States as of April 1, 1990, was 248.7 million persons. This is 9.8% above the 1980 census count of 226.5 million.

The growth rate for the 1980–90 decade is the second lowest in census history. The rate exceeded only the 7.3% increase of the Depression decade of the 1930s, when the rate of childbearing dropped close to two births per woman and net immigration from abroad was negligible. In contrast, the growth rate reached 18.5% in the 1950s, which included the peak of the post-World War II baby boom (1946–64) and a rate of childbearing averaging over three births per woman.

Despite an increase in net immigration since the 1950s, the growth rate has been lower subsequently. The decline is due primarily to the drop in the rate of childbearing, which averaged about two births per woman during the past two decades.

The numerical growth in the 1980–90 decade was 22.2 million. The numerical growth also exceeded 20 million in the three preceding decades, with a peak figure of 28.0 million in the 1950s.

The population growth rate exceeded 30% in each decade from 1790 to 1860 and remained above 20% in each decade from 1860 to 1910, before dropping to 7.3% in the 1930s. The decrease is due primarily to the long-term decline in the average rate of childbearing from about seven births per woman at the beginning of the 19th century. The effect of declining fertility on the growth rate was offset in part by declining mortality, and by large-scale immigration during most of the period from the 1840s to the 1920s.

Fastest Growing Regions

The West had the highest growth rate (22.3%) among the four census regions of the United States during the 1980s. This was down slightly from the 1970s (23.9%), but still more than twice the national rate. The South's growth rate fell more sharply (20.0% to 13.4%), but remained above the national rate. The growth rate rose in the Northeast (0.2% to 3.4%) and fell in the Midwest (4.0% to 1.4%). These two regions had growth rates far below the national rate in both the 1970s and 1980s.

The difference in growth rates among the regions in the 1980s reflect differences in migration among States and immigration, and in rates of natural increase (birth rates minus death rates). There was net migration into the South and West, negligible net migration in the Northeast, and net migration out of the Midwest. The rate of natural increase was highest in the West and lowest in the Northeast.

The South and West together accounted for 89% of national population growth in the 1980s and 90% in the 1970s. Their combined share of the national population increased from 48.0% in 1970 to 52.3% in 1980 and to 55.6% in 1990.

Fastest Growing States

The five States with the highest percent increases in population during the 1980–90 decade were Nevada (50.1), Alaska (36.9), Arizona (34.8), Florida (32.7), and California (25.7).

During the past five decades (the 1940s through the 1980s), five states have dominated the list of most rapidly growing states. Arizona, Florida, and Nevada were included in each decade, while Alaska and California missed only in the 1970s. Nevada had the highest growth rate in each of the last three decades.

The only Northeastern or Midwestern States with growth rates above the national figure during the 1980s were New Hampshire (20.5%) and Vermont (10.0%), while Maine's growth rate was slightly lower (9.2%). These three were the only Northeastern or Midwestern States with growth rates above the national rate in the 1970s.

Four states lost population during the 1980s after increases in the 1970s: Iowa, North Dakota, West Virginia, and Wyoming. New York and Rhode Island gained population in the 1980s after losses in the 1970s. The District of Columbia lost population in both decades.

California, Florida, and Texas

The combined population growth in California (6.1 million), Florida (3.2 million), and Texas (2.8 million) in the 1980–90 decade totaled 12.0 million, or 54% of the 22.2-million national population increase. This is the first time in the nation's 200-year census history that as few as three states accounted for over half of the national population growth.

California's numerical growth of 6.1 million and its 27% share of U.S. population growth during the 1980s are record highs for a single State. Its population of 29.8 million in 1990 was larger than that of the 21 least populous States combined, and its 12.0% share of U.S. population was the highest in one State since 1860 when New York had 12.3%.

Congressional Apportionment

As a result of population changes from 1980 to 1990, eight states will have more representatives in the 103rd Congress, which will convene in January 1993.[1] The largest gains will be in California (+7), Florida (+4), and Texas (+3), while five other states will each gain one seat: Arizona, Georgia, North Carolina, Virginia, and Washington. Thirteen states will have fewer representatives. The largest losses will be in New York (–3), and in Illinois, Michigan, Ohio, and Pennsylvania (–2 each). Eight other states will each lose one seat: Iowa, Kansas, Kentucky, Louisiana, Massachusetts, Montana, New Jersey, and West Virginia.

In the upcoming reapportionment, the new increase of 7 seats in the South reflects a gain of 10 seats and a loss of 1 seat each in Kentucky, Louisiana, and West Virginia. The net increase of 8 seats in the West reflects a gain of 9 seats and a loss of 1 seat in Montana. □

---

1. The 1990 census apportionment population was 249.0 million. This number includes 0.9 million overseas military and Federal civilian employees and their dependents and excludes the District of Columbia.

Population

Colonial Population Estimates (in round numbers)

Year	Population	Year	Population	Year	Population	Year	Population
1610	350	1660	75,100	1710	331,700	1760	1,593,600
1620	2,300	1670	111,900	1720	466,200	1770	2,148,100
1630	4,600	1680	151,500	1730	629,400	1780	2,780,400
1640	26,600	1690	210,400	1740	905,600		
1650	50,400	1700	250,900	1750	1,170,800		

National Censuses[1]

Year	Resident population[2]	Land area, sq mi.	Pop. per sq mi.	Year	Resident population[2]	Land area, sq mi.	Pop. per sq mi.
1790	3,929,214	864,746	4.5	1900	75,994,575	2,969,834	25.6
1800	5,308,483	864,746	6.1	1910	91,972,266	2,969,565	31.0
1810	7,239,881	1,681,828	4.3	1920	105,710,620	2,969,451	35.6
1820	9,638,453	1,749,462	5.5	1930	122,775,046	2,977,128	41.2
1830	12,866,020	1,749,462	7.4	1940	131,669,275	2,977,128	44.2
1840	17,069,453	1,749,462	9.8	1950	150,697,361	2,974,726	50.7
1850	23,191,876	2,940,042	7.9	1960	179,323,175	3,540,911	50.6
1860	31,443,321	2,969,640	10.6	1970	203,302,031	3,540,023	57.4
1870	39,818,449	2,969,640	13.4	1980	226,545,805	3,539,289	64.0
1880	50,155,783	2,969,640	16.9	1990	248,709,873	3,618,770	68.7
1890	62,947,714	2,969,640	21.2				

1. Beginning with 1960, figures include Alaska and Hawaii. 2. Excludes armed forces overseas. *Source:* Department of Commerce, Bureau of the Census.

Population Distribution by Age, Race, Nativity, and Sex

Year	Total	Age Under 5	Age 5–19	Age 20–44	Age 45–64	Age 65 and over	White[1] Total	White[1] Native born	White[1] Foreign born	Black	Other races[1]
PERCENT DISTRIBUTION											
1860[2]	100.0	15.4	35.8	35.7	10.4	2.7	85.6	72.6	13.0	14.1	0.3
1870[2]	100.0	14.3	35.4	35.4	11.9	3.0	87.1	72.9	14.2	12.7	0.2
1880[2]	100.0	13.8	34.3	35.9	12.6	3.4	86.5	73.4	13.1	13.1	0.3
1890[3]	100.0	12.2	33.9	36.9	13.1	3.9	87.5	73.0	14.5	11.9	0.3
1900	100.0	12.1	32.3	37.7	13.7	4.1	87.9	74.5	13.4	11.6	0.5
1910	100.0	11.6	30.4	39.0	14.6	4.3	88.9	74.4	14.5	10.7	0.4
1920	100.0	10.9	29.8	38.4	16.1	4.7	89.7	76.7	13.0	9.9	0.4
1930	100.0	9.3	29.5	38.3	17.4	5.4	89.8	78.4	11.4	9.7	0.5
1940	100.0	8.0	26.4	38.9	19.8	6.8	89.8	81.1	8.7	9.8	0.4
1950	100.0	10.7	23.2	37.6	20.3	8.1	89.5	82.8	6.7	10.0	0.5
1960	100.0	11.3	27.1	32.2	20.1	9.2	88.6	83.4	5.2	10.5	0.9
1970[2]	100.0	8.4	29.5	31.7	20.6	9.8	87.6	83.4	4.3	11.1	1.4
1980	100.0	7.2	24.8	37.1	19.6	11.3	83.1	n.a.	n.a.	11.7	5.2
MALES PER 100 FEMALES											
1860[2]	104.7	102.4	101.2	107.9	111.5	98.3	105.3	103.7	115.1	99.6	260.8
1870[2]	102.2	102.9	101.2	99.2	114.5	100.5	102.8	100.6	115.3	96.2	400.7
1880[2]	103.6	103.0	101.3	104.0	110.2	101.4	104.0	102.1	115.9	97.8	362.2
1890[3]	105.0	103.6	101.4	107.3	108.3	104.2	105.4	102.9	118.7	99.5	165.2
1900	104.4	102.1	100.9	105.8	110.7	102.0	104.9	102.8	117.4	98.6	185.2
1910	106.0	102.5	101.3	108.1	114.4	101.1	106.6	102.7	129.2	98.9	185.6
1920	104.0	102.5	100.8	102.8	115.2	101.3	104.4	101.7	121.7	99.2	156.6
1930	102.5	103.0	101.4	100.5	109.1	100.5	102.9	101.1	115.8	97.0	150.6
1940	100.7	103.2	102.0	98.1	105.2	95.5	101.2	100.1	111.1	95.0	140.5

| | | | | Age | | | | Race and Nativity | | | | |
| | | | | | | | | White[1] | | | | |
Year	Total	Under 5	5–19	20–44	45–64	65 and over	Total	Native born	Foreign born	Black	Other races[1]
1950	98.6	103.9	102.5	96.2	100.1	89.6	99.0	98.8	102.0	93.7	129.7
1960	97.1	103.4	102.7	95.6	95.7	82.8	97.4	97.6	94.2	93.3	109.7
1970[2]	94.8	104.0	103.3	95.1	91.6	72.1	95.3	95.9	83.8	90.8	100.2
1980	94.5	104.7	104.0	98.1	90.7	67.6	94.8	n.a.	n.a.	89.6	100.3

1. The 1980 census data for white and other races categories are not directly comparable to those shown for the preceding years because of the changes in the way some persons reported their race, as well as changes in 1980 procedures relating to racial classification. 2. Excludes persons for whom age is not available. 3. Excludes persons enumerated in the Indian Territory and on Indian reservations. NOTES: Data exclude Armed Forces overseas. Beginning in 1960, includes Alaska and Hawaii. n.a. = not available. 1990 Census data not available at press time. *Source:* Department of Commerce, Bureau of the Census.

Population and Rank of Large Metropolitan Areas, 1990

(over 100,000)

Rank	Standard metropolitan statistical area	Population
1	New York–Northern New Jersey–Long Island–NY–NJ–CT	18,087,251
	New York, NY	8,546,846
	Nassau–Suffolk, NY	2,609,212
	Newark, NJ	1,824,321
	Bergen–Passaic, NJ	1,278,440
	Middlesex–Somerset–Hunterdon, NJ	1,019,835
	Monmouth–Ocean, NJ	986,327
	Jersey City, NJ	553,099
	Bridgeport–Milford, CT	443,772
	Orange County, NY	307,647
	Stamford, CT	202,557
	Danbury, CT	187,867
	Norwalk, CT	127,378
2	Los Angeles–Anaheim–Riverside, CA	14,531,529
	Los Angeles–Long Beach, CA	8,863,164
	Riverside–San Bernardino, CA	2,588,793
	Anaheim–Santa Ana, CA	2,410,556
	Oxnard–Ventura, CA	669,016
3	Chicago–Gary–Lake County, IL–IN–WI	8,065,633
	Chicago, IL	6,069,974
	Gary–Hammond, IN	604,526
	Lake County, IL	516,418
	Joliet, IL	389,650
	Aurora–Elgin, IL	356,884
	Kenosha, WI	128,181
4	San Francisco–Oakland–San Jose, CA	6,253,311
	Oakland, CA	2,082,914
	San Francisco, CA	1,603,678
	San Jose, CA	1,497,577
	Vallejo–Fairfield–Napa, CA	451,186
	Santa Rosa–Petaluma, CA	388,222
	Santa Cruz, CA	229,734
5	Philadelphia–Wilmington–Trenton, PA–NJ–DE–MD	5,899,345
	Philadelphia, PA–NJ	4,856,881
	Wilmington, DE–NJ–MD	578,587
	Trenton, NJ	325,824
	Vineland–Millville–Bridgeton, NJ	138,053
6	Detroit–Ann Arbor, MI	4,665,236
	Detroit, MI	4,382,299
	Ann Arbor, MI	282,937
7	Boston–Lawrence–Salem, MA–NH	4,171,643
	Boston, MA	2,870,669
	Lawrence–Haverhill, MA–NH	393,516
	Lowell, MA–NH	273,067
	Salem–Gloucester, MA	264,356

Rank	Standard metropolitan statistical area	Population
	Brockton, MA	189,478
	Nashua, NH	180,557
8	Washington, DC–MD–VA	3,923,574
9	Dallas–Fort Worth, TX	3,885,415
	Dallas, TX	2,553,362
	Fort Worth–Arlington, TX	1,332,053
10	Houston–Galveston–Brazoria, TX	3,711,043
	Houston, TX	3,301,937
	Galveston–Texas City, TX	217,399
	Brazoria, TX	191,707
11	Miami–Fort Lauderdale, FL	3,192,582
	Miami–Hialeah, FL	1,937,094
	Fort Lauderdale–Hollywood–Pompano Beach, FL	1,255,488
12	Atlanta, GA	2,833,511
13	Cleveland–Akron–Lorain, OH	2,759,823
	Cleveland, OH	1,831,122
	Akron, OH	657,575
	Lorain–Elyria, OH	271,126
14	Seattle–Tacoma, WA	2,559,164
	Seattle, WA	1,972,961
	Tacoma, WA	586,203
15	San Diego, CA	2,498,016
16	Minneapolis–St. Paul, MN–WI	2,464,124
17	St. Louis, MO–WI	2,444,099
18	Baltimore, MD	2,382,172
19	Pittsburgh–Beaver Valley, PA	2,242,798
	Pittsburgh, PA	2,056,705
	Beaver County, PA	186,093
20	Phoenix, AZ	2,122,101
21	Tampa–St. Petersburg–Clearwater, FL	2,067,959
22	Denver–Boulder, CO	1,848,319
	Denver, CO	1,622,980
	Boulder–Longmont, CO	225,339
23	Cincinnati–Hamilton, OH–KY–IN	1,744,124
	Cincinnati, OH–KY–IN	1,452,645
	Hamilton–Middletown, OH	291,479
24	Milwaukee–Racine, WI	1,607,183
	Milwaukee, WI	1,432,149
	Racine, WI	175,034
25	Kansas City, MO–KS	1,566,280
26	Sacramento, CA	1,481,102
27	Portland–Vancouver, OR–WA	1,477,895
	Portland, OR	1,239,842
	Vancouver, WA	238,053
28	Norfolk–Virginia Beach–Newport News, VA	1,396,107
29	Columbus, OH	1,377,419

Rank	Standard metropolitan statistical area	Population
30	San Antonio, TX	1,302,099
31	Indianapolis, IN	1,249,822
32	New Orleans, LA	1,238,816
33	Buffalo–Niagara Falls, NY	1,189,288
	Buffalo, NY	968,532
	Niagara Falls, NY	220,756
34	Charlotte–Gastonia–Rock Hill, NC–SC	1,162,093
35	Providence–Pawtucket–Fall River, RI–MA	1,141,510
	Providence, RI	654,854
	Pawtucket–Woonsocket–Attleboro, RI–MA	329,384
	Fall River, MA–RI	157,272
36	Hartford–New Britain–Middletown, CT	1,085,837
	Hartford, CT	767,841
	New Britain, CT	148,188
	Middletown, CT	90,320
	Bristol, CT	79,488
37	Orlando, FL	1,072,748
38	Salt Lake City–Ogden, UT	1,072,227
39	Rochester, NY	1,002,410
40	Nashville, TN	985,026
41	Memphis, TN–AR–MS	981,747
42	Oklahoma City, OK	958,839
43	Louisville, KY–IN	952,662
44	Dayton–Springfield, OH	951,270
45	Greensboro–Winston-Salem–High Point, NC	942,091
46	Birmingham, AL	907,810
47	Jacksonville, FL	906,727
48	Albany–Schenectady–Troy, NY	874,304
49	Richmond–Petersburg, VA	865,640
50	West Palm Beach–Boca Raton–Delray Beach, FL	863,518
51	Honolulu, HI	836,231
52	Austin, TX	781,572
53	Las Vegas, NV	741,459
54	Raleigh–Durham, NC	735,480
55	Scranton–Wilkes-Barre, PA	734,175
56	Tulsa, OK	708,954
57	Grand Rapids, MI	688,399
58	Allentown–Bethlehem–Easton, PA–NJ	686,688
59	Fresno, CA	667,490
60	Tucson, AZ	666,880
61	Syracuse, NY	659,864
62	Greenville–Spartanburg, SC	640,861
63	Omaha, NE–IA	618,262
64	Toledo, OH	614,128
65	Knoxville, TN	604,816
66	El Paso, TX	591,610
67	Harrisburg–Lebanon–Carlisle, PA	587,986
68	Bakersfield, CA	543,477
69	New Haven–Meriden, CT	530,180
70	Springfield, MA	529,519
71	Baton Rouge, LA	528,264
72	Little Rock–North Little Rock, AR	513,117
73	Charleston, SC	506,875
74	Youngstown–Warren, OH	492,619
75	Wichita, KS	485,270
76	Stockton, CA	480,628
77	Albuquerque, NM	480,577
78	Mobile, AL	476,923
79	Columbia, SC	453,331
80	Worcester, MA	436,905
81	Johnson City–Kingsport–Bristol, TN–VA	436,047
82	Chattanooga, TN–GA	433,210
83	Lansing–East Lansing, MI	432,674
84	Flint, MI	430,459
85	Lancaster, PA	422,822

Rank	Standard metropolitan statistical area	Population
86	York, PA	417,848
87	Lakeland–Winter Haven, FL	405,382
88	Saginaw–Bay City–Midland, MI	399,320
89	Melbourne–Titusville–Palm Bay, FL	398,978
90	Colorado Springs, CO	397,014
91	Augusta, GA–SC	396,809
92	Jackson, MS	395,396
93	Canton, OH	394,106
94	Des Moines, IA	392,928
95	McAllen–Edinburg–Mission, TX	383,543
96	Daytona Beach, FL	370,712
97	Modesto, CA	370,522
98	Santa Barbara–Santa Maria–Lompoc, CA	369,608
99	Madison, WI	367,085
100	Fort Wayne, IN	363,811
101	Spokane, WA	361,364
102	Beaumont–Port Arthur, TX	361,226
103	Salinas–Seaside–Monterey, CA	355,660
104	Davenport–Rock Island–Moline, IA–IL	350,861
105	Corpus Christi, TX	349,894
106	Lexington–Fayette, KY	348,428
107	Pensacola, FL	344,406
108	Peoria, IL	339,172
109	Reading, PA	336,523
110	Fort Myers–Cape Coral, FL	335,113
111	Shreveport, LA	334,341
112	Atlantic City, NJ	319,416
113	Utica–Rome, NY	316,633
114	Appleton–Oshkosh–Neenah, WI	315,121
115	Huntington–Ashland, WV–KY–OH	312,529
116	Visalia–Tulare–Porterville, CA	311,921
117	Montgomery, AL	292,517
118	Rockford, IL	283,719
119	Eugene–Springfield, OR	282,912
120	Macon–Warner Robins, GA	281,103
121	Evansville, IN–KY	278,990
122	Salem, OR	278,024
123	Sarasota, FL	277,776
124	Erie, PA	275,572
125	Fayetteville, NC	274,566
126	New London–Norwich, CT–RI	266,819
127	Binghamton, NY	264,497
128	Provo–Orem, UT	263,590
129	Brownsville–Harlingen, TX	260,120
130	Poughkeepsie, NY	259,462
131	Killeen–Temple, TX	255,301
132	Reno, NV	254,667
133	Fort Pierce, FL	251,071
134	Charleston, WV	250,454
135	South Bend–Mishawaka, IN	247,052
136	Columbus, GA–AL	243,072
137	Savannah, GA	242,622
138	Johnstown, PA	241,247
139	Springfield, MO	240,593
140	Duluth, MN–WI	239,971
141	Huntsville, AL	238,912
142	Tallahassee, FL	233,598
143	Anchorage, AK	226,338
144	Roanoke, VA	224,477
145	Portsmouth–Dover–Rochester, NH–ME	223,578
146	Kalamazoo, MI	223,411
147	Lubbock, TX	222,636
148	Hickory–Morganton, NC	221,700
149	Waterbury, CT	221,629
150	Portland, ME	215,281
151	Lincoln, NE	213,641
152	Bradenton, FL	211,707
153	Lafayette, LA	208,740

Rank	Standard metropolitan statistical area	Population	Rank	Standard metropolitan statistical area	Population
154	Boise City, ID	205,775	207	Joplin, MO	134,910
155	Gainesville, FL	204,111	208	Laredo, TX	133,239
156	Biloxi–Gulfport, MS	197,125	209	Greeley, CO	131,821
157	Ocala, FL	194,833	210	Decatur, AL	131,556
158	Green Bay, WI	194,594	211	Alexandria, LA	131,556
159	St. Cloud, MN	190,921	212	Burlington, VT	131,439
160	Bremerton, WA	189,731	213	Florence, AL	131,327
161	Springfield, IL	189,550	214	Charlottesville, VA	131,107
162	Waco, TX	189,123	215	Dothan, AL	130,964
163	Yakima, WA	188,823	216	Terre Haute, IN	130,812
164	Amarillo, TX	187,547	217	Anderson, IN	130,669
165	Fort Collins–Loveland, CO	186,136	218	Lafayette–West Lafayette, IN	130,598
166	Houma–Thibodaux, LA	182,842	219	Altoona, PA	130,542
167	Chico, CA	182,120	220	Bloomington–Normal, IL	129,180
168	Merced, CA	178,403	221	Bellingham, WA	127,780
169	Fort Smith, AR–OK	175,911	222	Panama City, FL	126,994
170	New Bedrofd, MA	175,641	223	Mansfield, OH	126,137
171	Asheville, NC	174,821	224	Sioux Falls, SD	123,809
172	Champaign–Urbana–Rantoul, IL	173,025	225	State College, PA	123,786
173	Clarksville–Hopkinsville, TN–KY	169,439	226	Pueblo, CO	123,051
174	Cedar Rapids, IA	168,767	227	Yuba City, CA	122,643
175	Lake Charles, LA	168,134	228	Wichita Falls, TX	122,378
176	Longview–Marshall, TX	162,431	229	Bryan–College Station, TX	121,862
177	Benton Harbor, MI	161,378	230	Hagerstown, MD	121,393
178	Olympia, WA	161,238	231	Sharon, PA	121,003
179	Topeka, KS	160,976	232	Wilmington, NC	120,284
180	Wheeling, WV–OH	159,301	233	Texarkana, TX–Texarkana, AR	120,132
181	Muskegon, MI	158,983	234	Muncie, IN	119,659
182	Athens, GA	156,267	235	Abilene, TX	119,655
183	Elkhart–Goshen, IN	156,198	236	Odessa, TX	118,934
184	Lima, OH	154,340	237	Williamsport, PA	118,710
185	Fargo–Moorhead, ND–MN	153,296	238	Glens Falls, NY	118,539
186	Naples, FL	152,099	239	Decatur, IL	117,206
187	Tyler, TX	151,309	240	Santa Fe, NM	117,043
188	Tuscaloosa, AL	150,522	241	Anniston, AL	116,034
189	Richland–Kennewick–Pasco, WA	150,033	242	Wausau, WI	115,400
190	Jacksonville, NC	149,838	243	Pascagoula, MS	115,243
191	Jackson, MI	149,756	244	Sioux City, IA–NE	115,018
192	Parkersburg–Marietta, WV–OH	149,169	245	Florence, SC	114,344
193	Manchester, NH	147,809	246	Billings, MT	113,419
194	Redding, CA	147,036	247	Fayetteville–Springdale, AR	113,409
195	Waterlook–Cedar Falls, IA	146,611	248	Albany, GA	112,561
196	Medford, OR	146,389	249	Columbia, MO	112,379
197	Anderson, SC	145,196	250	Lawton, OK	111,486
198	Fort Walton Beach, FL	143,776	251	Bloomington, IN	108,978
199	Stebuenville–Weirton, OH–WV	142,523	252	Danville, VA	108,711
200	Lynchburg, VA	142,199	253	Burlington, NC	108,213
201	Monroe, LA	142,191	254	Yuma, AZ	106,895
202	Jamestown–Dunkirk, NY	141,895	255	Midland, TX	106,611
203	Janesville–Beloit, WI	139,510	256	Rochester, MN	106,470
204	Eau Claire, WI	137,543	257	Sheboygan, WI	103,877
205	Battle Creek, MI	135,982	258	Fitchburg–Leominster, MA	102,797
206	Las Cruces, NM	135,510	259	Cumberland, MD–WV	101,643

NOTE: A standard metropolitan statistical area (SMSA) is one of a large population nucleus together with adjacent communities that have a high degree of economic and social integration with that nucleus.—Source does not list rank separately. It is given for the Consolidated Metropolitan Statistical Area of which this area is a part. *Source:* Bureau of the Census.

Half of the U.S. Population Lives in the Largest Metro Areas

Final 1990 census figures show that the Nation has 39 metropolitan areas of at least one million people. These 39 areas have 124.8 million inhabitants or 50.2% of the United States total population.

The census figures show that the U.S. population living in all of the metro areas has reached 192,725,741, an increase of 20 million (11.6%) since 1980.

The metropolitan population now constitutes 77.5% of the U.S. total, compared with 76.2% in 1980. Ninety percent of the Nation's growth in the 1980s took place in metropolitan areas.

Only five metropolitan areas as large as one million lost population in the 1980s, compared with eight in the 1970s. However, many middle-sized and smaller metro areas grew more slowly in the 1980s than in the 1970s.

The Los Angeles–Anaheim–Riverside metropolitan area gained three million inhabitants for a total of over 14.5 million. The increase brings that area to within 3.5 million of the New York metropolitan area, the Nation's largest, which gained about 550,000 people for a total of 18.1 million.

Territorial Expansion

Accession	Date	Area[1]
United States	—	3,618,770
Territory in 1790	—	891,364
Louisiana Purchase	1803	831,321
Florida	1819	69,866
Texas	1845	384,958
Oregon	1846	283,439
Mexican Cession	1848	530,706
Gadsden Purchase	1853	29,640
Alaska	1867	591,004
Hawaii	1898	6,471
Other territory	—	4,664
Philippines	1898	115,600 [2]
Puerto Rico	1899	3,515
Guam	1899	209
American Samoa	1900	77
Canal Zone[3]	1904	553
Virgin Islands of U.S.	1917	132
Trust Territory of Pacific Islands	1947	717 [4]
All other	—	14
Total, 1980	**—**	**3,623,434**

1. Total land and water area in square miles. 2. Became independent in 1946. 3. Reverted to Panama. 4. Land area only; includes Northern Mariana Islands. NOTE: 1990 Census data not available at press time. *Source:* Department of Commerce, Bureau of the Census.

Total Population

Area	1980	1970	1960
50 states of U.S.	226,545,805	203,302,031	179,323,175
48 conter-			
minous	225,179,263	202,229,535	178,464,236
Alaska	401,851	302,583	226,167
Hawaii	964,691	769,913	632,772
American Samoa	32,297	27,159	20,051
Canal Zone	(1)	44,198	42,122
Canton Island	—	n.a.	320
Corn Islands	—	(2)	1,872
Guam	105,979	84,996	67,044
Johnston Atoll	327	1,007	156
Midway	453	2,220	2,356
Puerto Rico	3,196,520	2,712,033	2,349,544
Swan Islands	n.a.	22	28
Trust Ter. of Pac. Is.	132,929 [3]	90,940	70,724
Virgin Is. of U.S.	96,569	62,468	32,099
Wake Island	302	1,647	1,097
Population abroad	995,546	1,737,836	1,374,421
Armed forces	515,408	1,057,776	609,720
Other[4]	n.a.	n.a.	n.a.
Total	**231,106,727**	**208,066,557**	**183,285,009**

1. Granted independence on Oct. 1, 1979. 2. Returned to Nicaragua April 25, 1971. 3. Includes Northern Mariana Islands. 4. Includes Baker Island, Enderbury Island, Howland Island, and Jarvis Island, all uninhabited. NOTE: n.a.= unavailable. 1990 Census data not available at press time. *Source:* Department of Commerce, Bureau of the Census.

Resident Population by Age, Sex, Race, and Hispanic Origin, 1989[1]

(in thousands)

Age	White Male	White Female	Black Male	Black Female	Other races Male	Other races Female	Hispanic origin[2] Male	Hispanic origin[2] Female	All persons Male	All persons Female
Under 5	7,716	7,335	1,469	1,421	414	399	1,131	1,091	9,598	9,155
5–9	7,504	7,124	1,423	1,378	394	389	1,019	977	9,321	8,891
10–14	6,973	6,601	1,362	1,318	355	342	957	920	8,689	8,260
15–19	7,327	7,015	1,394	1,365	371	341	905	868	9,091	8,721
20–24	7,731	7,628	1,279	1,372	357	335	996	928	9,368	9,334
25–29	9,142	8,960	1,342	1,485	381	389	1,159	1,029	10,865	10,834
30–34	9,385	9,182	1,289	1,455	404	420	1,026	933	11,078	11,058
35–39	8,342	8,283	1,035	1,225	354	382	779	757	9,731	9,890
40–44	7,229	7,321	782	945	283	322	582	603	8,294	8,588
45–49	5,758	5,915	626	769	217	237	427	457	6,601	6,920
50–54	4,791	4,998	544	679	174	189	346	380	5,509	5,866
55–59	4,480	4,830	508	608	133	167	293	329	5,121	5,605
60–64	4,498	5,071	467	567	113	150	249	291	5,079	5,788
65–69	4,130	4,899	402	515	100	125	181	220	4,631	5,538
70–74	3,120	4,074	274	386	69	89	110	153	3,464	4,549
75–79	2,147	3,282	187	299	51	66	77	120	2,385	3,648
80–84	1,189	2,220	91	165	26	37	46	74	1,306	2,422
85 and over	761	2,000	72	165	17	27	32	59	850	2,192
All ages	102,223	106,738	14,545	16,115	4,213	4,404	10,317	10,188	120,982	127,258
16 and over	78,686	84,404	10,027	11,743	2,979	3,208	7,027	7,024	91,693	99,354
18 and over	75,862	81,725	9,466	11,200	2,832	3,072	6,666	6,678	88,160	95,997
65 and over	11,347	16,475	1,025	1,529	264	344	447	626	12,636	18,348
Median age	32.5	34.7	26.3	29.1	27.9	30.1	25.7	26.5	31.6	33.8
Mean age	34.6	37.4	29.3	32.0	29.7	31.7	27.4	29.0	33.8	36.5

1. July 1, 1989. 2. Persons of Hispanic origin may be of any race. NOTE: 1990 Census data not available at press time. *Source:* U.S. Bureau of the Census.

Population by State

State	1990	Percent change, 1980–90	Pop. per sq mi., 1990	Pop. rank, 1990	1980	1950	1900	1790
Alabama	4,040,587	+3.8	79.6	22	3,893,888	3,061,743	1,828,697	—
Alaska	550,403	+36.9	1.0	49	401,851	128,643	63,592	—
Arizona	3,665,228	+34.8	32.3	24	2,718,215	749,587	122,931	—
Arkansas	2,350,725	+2.8	45.1	33	2,286,435	1,909,511	1,311,564	—
California	29,760,021	+25.7	190.4	1	23,667,902	10,586,223	1,485,053	—
Colorado	3,294,394	+14.0	31.8	26	2,889,964	1,325,089	539,700	—
Connecticut	3,287,116	+5.8	674.7	27	3,107,576	2,007,280	908,420	237,946
Delaware	666,168	+12.1	344.8	46	594,338	318,085	184,735	59,096
D.C.	606,900	−4.9	—	—	638,333	802,178	278,718	—
Florida	12,937,926	+32.7	238.9	4	9,746,324	2,771,305	528,542	—
Georgia	6,478,216	+18.6	109.9	11	5,463,105	3,444,578	2,216,331	82,548
Hawaii	1,108,229	+14.9	172.5	41	964,691	499,794	154,001	—
Idaho	1,006,749	+6.7	12.2	42	943,935	588,637	161,772	—
Illinois	11,430,602	0.0	205.4	6	11,426,518	8,712,176	4,821,550	—
Indiana	5,544,159	+1.0	154.2	14	5,490,224	3,934,224	2,516,462	—
Iowa	2,776,755	−4.7	49.6	30	2,913,808	2,621,073	2,231,853	—
Kansas	2,477,574	+4.8	30.3	32	2,363,679	1,905,299	1,470,495	—
Kentucky	3,685,296	+0.7	92.9	23	3,660,777	2,944,806	2,147,174	73,677
Louisiana	4,219,973	+0.3	94.8	21	4,205,900	2,683,516	1,381,625	—
Maine	1,227,928	+9.2	39.6	38	1,124,660	913,774	694,466	96,540
Maryland	4,781,468	+13.4	486.0	19	4,216,975	2,343,001	1,188,044	319,728
Massachusetts	6,016,425	+4.9	768.9	13	5,737,037	4,690,514	2,805,346	378,787
Michigan	9,295,297	+0.4	163.2	8	9,262,078	6,371,766	2,420,982	—
Minnesota	4,375,099	+7.3	55.0	20	4,075,970	2,982,483	1,751,394	—
Mississippi	2,573,216	+2.1	54.5	31	2,520,638	2,178,914	1,551,270	—
Missouri	5,117,073	+4.1	74.2	15	4,916,686	3,954,653	3,106,665	—
Montana	799,065	+1.6	5.5	44	786,690	591,024	243,329	—
Nebraska	1,578,385	+0.5	20.6	36	1,569,825	1,325,510	1,066,300	—
Nevada	1,201,833	+50.1	10.9	39	800,493	160,083	42,335	—
New Hampshire	1,109,252	+20.5	123.3	40	920,610	533,242	411,588	141,885
New Jersey	7,730,188	+5.0	1,035.1	9	7,364,823	4,835,329	1,883,669	184,139
New Mexico	1,515,069	+16.3	12.5	37	1,302,894	681,187	195,310	—
New York	17,990,455	+2.5	379.7	2	17,558,072	14,830,192	7,268,894	340,120
North Carolina	6,628,637	+12.7	135.7	10	5,881,766	4,061,929	1,893,810	393,751
North Dakota	638,800	−2.1	9.0	47	652,717	619,636	319,146	—
Ohio	10,847,115	+0.5	264.5	7	10,797,630	7,946,627	4,157,545	—
Oklahoma	3,145,585	+4.0	45.8	28	3,025,290	2,233,351	790,391[1]	—
Oregon	2,842,321	+7.9	29.5	29	2,633,105	1,521,341	413,536	—
Pennsylvania	11,881,643	+0.1	264.7	5	11,863,895	10,498,012	6,302,115	434,373
Rhode Island	1,003,464	+5.9	951.1	43	947,154	791,896	428,556	68,825
South Carolina	3,486,703	+11.7	115.4	25	3,121,820	2,117,027	1,340,316	249,073
South Dakota	696,004	+0.8	9.1	45	690,768	652,740	401,570	—
Tennessee	4,877,185	+6.2	118.5	17	4,591,120	3,291,718	2,020,616	35,691
Texas	16,986,510	+19.4	64.8	3	14,229,191	7,711,194	3,048,710	—
Utah	1,722,850	+17.9	20.9	35	1,461,037	688,862	276,749	—
Vermont	562,758	+10.0	60.7	48	511,456	377,747	343,641	85,425
Virginia	6,187,358	+15.7	155.8	12	5,346,818	3,318,680	1,854,184	747,610 [2]
Washington	4,866,692	+17.8	73.1	18	4,132,156	2,378,963	518,103	—
West Virginia	1,793,477	−8.0	73.8	34	1,949,644	2,005,552	958,800	—
Wisconsin	4,891,769	+4.0	89.9	16	4,705,767	3,434,575	2,069,042	—
Wyoming	453,588	−3.4	4.7	50	469,557	290,529	92,531	—
Total U.S.	**248,709,873**	**+9.8**	**—**	**—**	**226,545,805**	**151,325,798**	**76,212,168**	**3,929,214**

1. Includes population of Indian Territory: 1900, 392,960. 2. Until 1863, Virginia included what is now West Virginia. *Source:* Department of Commerce, Bureau of the Census.

The U.S. Population Grows Older

According to the 1990 census, the nation's median age is 32.9 years, up 2.9 years from 1980. Regionally the Northeast has the oldest median, 34.2 years, followed by the Midwest with 33.0 years, and the South with a median of 32.8 years. The West has a median age of 31.8 years, the nation's lowest and below the national median.

In addition the percent of people over the age of 65 has increased from 11 percent in 1980 to 13 percent in 1990. Again the Northeast leads the other regions, with 14 percent of its population aged 65 and over. The Midwest and South have 13 percent of their population in the older group and the West again has the smallest proportion of the elderly, 11 percent.

Immigration to U.S. by Country of Origin

(Figures are totals, not annual averages, and were tabulated as follows: 1820–67, alien passengers arrived; 1868–91 and 1895–97, immigrant aliens arrived; 1892–94 and 1898 to present, immigrant aliens admitted. 1989 and 1990 totals include legalized immigrants. (Data before 1906 relate to country whence alien came; 1906–80, to country of last permanent residence; 1981 to present data based on country of birth.)

Countries	1990	1820–1990	1981–90	1971–80	1961–70	1951–60	1941–50	1820–1940
Europe: Albania[1]	78	3,090	479	329	98	59	85	2,040
Austria[2]	675	2,661,318	4,636	9,478	20,621	67,106	24,860	2,534,617
Belgium	682	209,196	5,706	5,329	9,192	18,575	12,189	158,205
Bulgaria[3]	428	70,484	2,342	1,188	619	104	375	65,856
Czechoslovakia[1]	1,412	150,074	11,500	6,023	3,273	918	8,347	120,013
Denmark	666	370,422	5,380	4,439	9,201	10,984	5,393	335,025
Estonia[1]	20	1,294	137	91	163	185	212	506
Finland[1]	369	37,346	3,265	2,868	4,192	4,925	2,503	19,593
France	2,849	778,358	23,124	25,069	45,237	51,121	38,809	594,998
Germany[2]	7,493	7,061,615	70,111	74,414	190,796	477,765	226,578	6,021,951
Great Britain	15,928	5,102,100	142,123	137,374	213,822	202,824	139,306	4,266,561
Greece	2,742	694,657	29,130	92,369	85,969	47,608	8,973	430,608
Hungary[2]	1,655	1,670,979	9,764	6,550	5,401	36,637	3,469	1,609,158
Ireland	10,333	4,725,987	32,823	11,490	32,966	48,362	14,789	4,580,557
Italy	3,287	5,338,748	32,894	129,368	214,111	185,491	57,661	4,719,223
Latvia[1]	45	2,981	359	207	510	352	361	1,192
Lithuania[1]	67	4,418	482	248	562	242	683	2,201
Luxembourg[1]	31	3,166	234	307	556	684	820	565
Netherlands	1,424	373,952	11,958	10,492	30,606	52,277	14,860	253,759
Norway[4]	524	753,456	3,901	3,941	15,484	22,935	10,100	697,095
Poland[5]	20,537	620,474	97,390	37,234	53,539	9,985	7,571	414,755
Portugal	4,035	500,850	40,020	101,710	76,065	19,588	7,423	256,044
Romania[6]	4,647	212,947	39,963	12,393	2,531	1,039	1,076	156,945
Spain	1,886	280,413	15,698	39,141	44,659	7,894	2,898	170,123
Sweden[4]	1,196	1,391,428	10,211	6,531	17,116	21,697	10,665	1,325,208
Switzerland	845	357,666	7,076	8,235	18,453	17,675	10,547	295,680
U.S.S.R.[7]	25,524	3,470,110	84,081	38,961	2,465	671	571	3,343,361
Yugoslavia[3]	2,828	136,691	19,182	30,540	20,381	8,225	1,576	56,787
Other Europe	195	60,920	2,661	4,049	4,904	9,799	3,447	36,060
Total Europe	112,401	37,045,140	705,630	800,368	1,123,492	1,325,727	621,147	32,468,776
Asia: China[8]	46,966	956,315	388,686	124,326	34,764	9,657	16,709	382,173
India	30,667	466,771	261,841	164,134	27,189	1,973	1,761	9,873
Israel[9]	4,664	129,620	36,353	37,713	29,602	25,476	476	—
Japan[9]	5,734	458,407	43,248	49,775	39,988	46,250	1,555	277,591
Turkey	2,468	409,937	20,843	13,399	10,142	3,519	798	361,236
Other Asia	248,082	3,677,389	2,042,025	1,198,831	285,957	66,374	15,729	44,053
Total Asia[10]	338,581	6,098,449	2,066,455	1,588,178	427,642	153,249	37,028	1,074,926
America: Canada and Newfoundland[11]	16,812	4,257,851	119,204	169,939	413,310	377,952	171,718	3,005,728
Central America	146,202	810,293	458,753	134,640	101,330	44,751	21,665	49,154
Mexico[12]	679,068	3,886,136	1,653,250	640,294	453,937	299,811	60,589	778,255
South America	85,819	1,244,433	455,977	295,741	257,954	91,628	21,831	121,302
West Indies	115,065	2,723,518	892,392	741,126	470,213	123,091	49,725	446,971
Other America[12]	411	111,020	1,352	995	19,630	59,711	29,276	56
Total America	1,043,377	13,033,251	3,580,928	1,982,735	1,716,374	996,944	354,804	4,401,466
Africa	35,893	349,464	192,212	80,779	28,954	14,092	7,367	26,060
Australia and New Zealand	2,583	143,627	20,169	23,788	19,562	11,506	13,805	54,437
Pacific Islands[13]	3,599	57,460	21,041	17,454	5,560	1,470	746	11,089
Countries not specified[14]	49	266,623	196	12	93	12,491	142	253,689
Total all countries	1,536,483	56,994,014	7,338,062	4,493,314	3,321,677	2,515,479	1,035,039	38,290,443

1. Countries established since beginning of World War I are included with countries to which they belonged. 2. Data for Austria–Hungary not reported until 1861. Austria and Hungary recorded separately after 1905, Austria included with Germany 1938–45. 3. Bulgaria, Serbia, Montenegro first reported in 1899. Bulgaria reported separately since 1920. In 1920, separate enumeration for Kingdom of Serbs, Croats, Slovenes; since 1922, recorded as Yugoslavia. 4. Norway included with Sweden 1820–68. 5. Included with Austria–Hungary, Germany, and Russia 1899–1919. 6. No record of immigration until 1880. 7. From 1931–63, the U.S.S.R. was broken down into European U.S.S.R. and Asian U.S.S.R. Since 1964, total U.S.S.R. has been reported in Europe. 8. Beginning in 1957, China includes Taiwan. 9. No record of immigration until 1861. 10. From 1934, Asia included Philippines; before 1934, recorded in separate tables as insular travel. 11. Includes all British North American possessions, 1820–98. 12. No record of immigration, 1886–93. 13. Included with "Countries not specified" prior to 1925. 14. Includes 32,897 persons returning in 1906 to their homes in U.S. *Source:* Department of Justice, Immigration and Naturalization Service. NOTE: Data are latest available.

Immigrant and Nonimmigrant Aliens Admitted to U.S.

Period[1]	Immigrants	Non–immigrants	Total	Period[1]	Immigrants	Non–immigrants	Total
1901–10	8,795,386	1,007,909	9,803,295	1983[2]	559,763	9,849,458	10,409,221
1911–20	5,735,811	1,376,271	7,112,082	1984	543,903	9,426,759	9,970,662
1921–30	4,107,209	1,774,896	5,882,090	1985	570,009	9,675,650	10,245,659
1931–40	528,431	1,574,071	2,102,502	1986	601,708	10,471,024	11,072,732
1941–50	1,035,039	2,461,359	3,496,398	1987	601,516	12,272,866	12,874,382
1951–60	2,515,479	7,113,023	9,628,502	1988	643,025	14,591,735	15,234,760
1961–70	3,321,677	24,107,224	27,428,901	1989	1,090,924[3]	16,144,576	17,235,500
1971–77	2,797,209	45,236,597	48,033,806	1990	1,536,483[3]	17,145,680	18,682,163

1. Fiscal year ending June 30 prior to 1977. After 1977 for fiscal year ending Sept. 30. 2. Nonimmigrant figures for calendar year 1983. Nonimmigrant aliens include visitors for business or pleasure, students, foreign government officials, and others temporarily in the U.S. 3. Includes immigrants and legalized immigrants. *Source:* Department of Justice, Immigration and Naturalization Service.

Persons Naturalized Since 1907

Period[1]	Civilian	Military	Total	Period[1]	Civilian	Military	Total
1907–30	2,713,389	300,506	3,013,895	1985	238,394	3,266	244,717[2]
1930–40	1,498,573	19,891	1,518,464	1986	275,352	2,901	280,623[3]
1941–50	1,837,229	149,799	1,987,028	1987	224,100	2,402	227,008[4]
1951–60	1,148,241	41,705	1,189,946	1988	239,541	2,296	242,063[5]
1961–70	1,084,195	36,068	1,120,263	1989	231,198	1,954	233,777[6]
1971–80	1,397,846	66,926	1,464,772	1907–89	11,588,147	641,582	12,238,532[7]

1. Fiscal year ending June 30. Starting 1977, fiscal year ending Sept. 30. 2. Including 3,057 unidentified. 3. Including 2,370 unidentified. 4. Including 506 unidentified. 5. Including 226 unidentified. 6. Including 625 unidentified. 7. Including 8,803 unidentified. *Source:* Department of Justice, Immigration and Naturalization Service. NOTE: Data are latest available.

Population of Largest Indian Reservations, Jan. 1989

Navajo (Ariz., N.M., Utah)	185,661	Rosebud (S.D.)	17,128	Zuni (N.M.)	8,244
Cherokee (Okla.)	87,059	Gila River (Ariz.)	11,700	Pawnee (Okla.)	2,229
Creek (Okla.)	56,244	Tohono O'odham (Ariz.)	16,531	Northern Pueblos (N.M.)	6,866
Choctaw (Okla.)	26,884	Turtle Mountain (N.D.)	12,312	Shawnee (Okla., Texas)	1,034
Pine Ridge (S.D.)	20,206	Hopi (Ariz.)	9,617	Blackfeet (Mont.)	7,179
Southern Pueblos (N.M.)	18,837	Standing Rock (N.D., S.D.)	10,306	Yakima (Wash.)	6,706
Chicksaw (Okla.)	12,369	Fort Apache (Ariz.)	8,726	Wind River (Wyo.)	4,935

NOTE: The Bureau of Indian Affairs lists 861,500 Indians residing on or near Federal reservations as of January 1987. The total Indian population of the United States, according to the 1980 updated census, is 1,534,000, including Aleuts and Eskimos. *Source:* Department of the Interior, Bureau of Indian Affairs. NOTE: Figures are most recent available.

Persons Below Poverty Level
by Age, Region, Race, and Hispanic Origin, 1989

Age and region	Number below poverty level				Percent below poverty level			
	All races[2]	White	Black	Hispanic origin[1]	All races[2]	White	Black	Hispanic origin[1]
Under 18 years	12,590	7,599	4,375	2,603	19.6	14.8	43.7	36.2
18 to 21	2,201	1,456	611	425	15.3	12.4	29.8	27.0
22 to 44	9,447	6,471	2,505	1,684	10.3	8.4	22.7	20.9
45 to 54	1,883	1,323	462	289	7.4	6.1	17.4	17.0
55 to 59	1,027	693	309	111	9.7	7.6	28.6	17.4
60 to 64	1,017	705	277	107	9.5	7.5	27.0	18.8
65 and over	3,369	2,542	766	211	11.4	9.6	30.8	20.6
Northeast	5,061	3,502	1,303	958	10.0	8.0	24.7	29.6
Midwest	7,043	4,718	2,181	352	11.9	9.0	36.4	24.7
South	12,943	7,498	5,220	1,855	15.4	11.4	31.6	28.7
West	6,487	5,070	601	2,266	12.5	11.3	23.5	23.6
Total	**31,534**	**20,788**	**9,305**	**5,430**	**12.8**	**10.0**	**30.7**	**26.2**

1. Persons of Hispanic origin may be of any race. 2. Includes race not shown separately. *Source:* U.S. Bureau of the Census.

Revised Population Projections to 2080[1,2]
(in millions)

Sex, race, age group	2000	2050	2070	2080	Sex, race, age group	2000	2050	2070	2080
MALE, WHITE	108.8	110.3	105.6	103.6	**FEMALE, BLACK**	18.3	24.7	25.0	25.0
Up to 19 years	29.7	37.3	23.9	23.4	Up to 19 years	5.8	5.6	5.3	5.2
20 to 39 years	31.4	27.4	25.9	25.3	20 to 39 years	5.6	6.2	5.9	5.7
40 to 59 years	30.7	27.6	26.7	25.7	40 to 59 years	4.4	6.0	6.1	6.0
60 to 79 years	14.2	22.8	21.7	21.6	60 to 79 years	2.0	5.0	5.4	5.6
80 and over	2.8	7.4	7.5	7.6	80 and over	0.4	1.8	2.2	2.4
FEMALE, WHITE	112.7	116.2	110.9	108.7	**TOTALS**[3]	268.3	299.8	294.6	292.2
Up to 19 years	28.2	24.0	22.7	22.2	Up to 19 years	73.3	66.7	64.0	63.0
20 to 39 years	30.6	26.7	25.2	24.6	20 to 39 years	76.6	73.1	70.4	69.2
40 to 59 years	31.0	27.6	26.6	25.6	40 to 59 years	72.8	73.0	72.5	70.9
60 to 79 years	17.2	25.1	23.8	23.5	60 to 79 years	36.2	62.0	61.7	62.2
80 and over	5.7	12.9	12.5	12.7	80 and over	9.3	24.9	25.9	26.9
MALE, BLACK	16.7	22.4	22.7	22.6	Males	131.2	145.3	142.9	141.7
Up to 19 years	6.1	5.9	5.6	5.4	Females	137.1	154.5	151.7	150.5
20 to 39 years	5.2	5.8	5.5	5.4	White	221.5	226.6	216.5	212.3
40 to 59 years	3.7	5.3	5.4	5.3	Black	35.1	47.1	47.7	47.6
60 to 79 years	1.6	4.3	4.8	5.0	Median age	36.4	42.7	43.6	43.9
80 and over	0.2	1.1	1.4	1.5					

1. Based on Population Report issued January 1989 revising prior Report issued May 1984. 2. Based on average of 1.8 lifetime births per woman. 3. Includes all races. NOTE: Zero population growth is expected to be reached by 2050. Details may not add because of rounding. *Source:* Department of Commerce, Bureau of the Census.

Marriage and Divorce

Marriages and Divorces

Year	Marriage Number	Marriage Rate[2]	Divorce[1] Number	Divorce[1] Rate[2]	Year	Marriage Number	Marriage Rate[2]	Divorce[1] Number	Divorce[1] Rate[2]
1900	709,000	9.3	55,751	.7	1967	1,927,000	9.7	523,000	2.6
1905	842,000	10.0	67,976	.8	1968	2,069,258	10.4	584,000	2.9
1910	948,166	10.3	83,045	.9	1969	2,145,438	10.6	639,000	3.2
1915	1,007,595	10.0	104,298	1.0	1970	2,158,802	10.6	708,000	3.5
1920	1,274,476	12.0	170,505	1.6	1971	2,190,481	10.6	773,000	3.7
1925	1,188,334	10.3	175,449	1.5	1972	2,282,154	11.0	845,000	4.1
1930	1,126,856	9.2	195,961	1.6	1973	2,284,108	10.9	915,000	4.4
1935	1,327,000	10.4	218,000	1.7	1974	2,229,667	10.5	977,000	4.6
1940	1,595,879	12.1	264,000	2.0	1975	2,152,662	10.1	1,036,000	4.9
1945	1,612,992	12.2	485,000	3.5	1976	2,154,807	10.0	1,083,000	5.0
1950	1,667,231	11.1	385,144	2.6	1977	2,178,367	10.1	1,091,000	5.0
1954	1,490,000	9.2	379,000	2.4	1978	2,282,272	10.5	1,130,000	5.2
1955	1,531,000	9.3	377,000	2.3	1979	2,341,799	10.6	1,181,000	5.4
1956	1,585,000	9.5	382,000	2.3	1980	2,406,708	10.6	1,182,000	5.2
1957	1,518,000	8.9	381,000	2.2	1981	2,438,000	10.6	1,219,000	5.3
1958	1,451,000	8.4	368,000	2.1	1982	2,495,000	10.8	1,180,000	5.1
1959	1,494,000	8.5	395,000	2.2	1983	2,444,000	10.5	1,179,000	5.0
1960	1,523,000	8.5	393,000	2.2	1984	2,487,000	10.5	1,155,000	4.9
1961	1,548,000	8.5	414,000	2.3	1985	2,425,000	10.2	1,187,000	5.0
1962	1,577,000	8.5	413,000	2.2	1986	2,400,000	10.0	1,159,000	4.8
1963	1,654,000	8.8	428,000	2.3	1987	2,421,000	9.9	1,157,000	4.8
1964	1,725,000	9.0	450,000	2.4	1988	2,389,000	9.7	1,183,000	4.8
1965	1,800,000	9.3	479,000	2.5	1989	2,404,000	9.7	1,163,000	4.7
1966	1,857,000	9.5	499,000	2.5	1990[3]	2,448,000	9.8	1,175,000	4.7

1. Includes annulments. 2. Per 1,000 population. Divorce rates for 1941–46 are based on population including armed forces overseas. Marriage rates are based on population excluding armed forces overseas. 3. Provisional. NOTE: Marriage and divorce figures for most years include some estimated data. Alaska is included beginning 1959, Hawaii beginning 1960. *Source:* Department of Health and Human Services, National Center for Health Statistics.

Percent of Population Ever Married

Age group, years[1]	1990	1980	1970	1960	1950	1940	1930	1920	1910	1900
Males: 15 to 19	1.5	2.7	2.6	3.3	2.9	1.5	1.5	1.8	1.0	0.9
20 to 24	20.7	31.2	45.3	46.9	41.0	27.8	29.0	29.1	24.7	22.2
25 to 29	54.8	67.0	80.9	79.2	76.2	64.0	63.2	60.5	57.1	54.1
30 to 34	73.0	84.1	90.6	88.1	86.8	79.3	78.8	75.8	73.9	72.3
35 to 44	87.2	92.5	93.3	91.9	90.4	86.0	85.7	83.8	83.3	83.0
45 to 54	93.7	93.9	92.5	92.6	91.5	88.9	88.6	88.0	88.8	89.7
Females: 15 to 19	5.0	8.8	9.7	13.5	14.4	10.0	10.9	10.8	9.8	9.4
20 to 24	37.2	49.8	64.2	71.6	67.7	52.8	53.9	54.4	51.5	48.4
25 to 29	68.9	79.1	89.5	89.5	86.7	77.2	78.3	76.9	75.0	72.4
30 to 34	83.6	90.5	93.8	93.1	90.7	85.3	86.8	85.1	83.8	83.4
35 to 44	90.7	94.5	94.8	93.9	91.7	89.6	90.0	88.6	88.6	88.9
45 to 54	95.0	95.3	95.1	93.0	92.2	91.3	90.9	90.4	91.4	92.2

1. Prior to 1980 data are for persons 14 years and older. *Source:* Department of Commerce, Bureau of the Census.

Persons Living Alone, by Sex and Age
(numbers in thousands)

Sex and Age[1]	1990 Number	1990 Percent	1980 Number	1980 Percent	1975 Number	1975 Percent	1970 Number	1970 Percent	1960 Number	1960 Percent
BOTH SEXES										
15 to 24 years	1,210	5.3	1,726	9.4	1,111	8.0	556	5.1	234	3.3
25 to 44 years	7,110	30.9	4,729	25.8	2,744	19.7	1,604	14.8	1,212	17.2
45 to 64 years	5,502	23.9	4,514	24.7	4,076	29.2	3,622	33.4	2,720	38.5
65 years and over	9,176	39.9	7,328	40.1	6,008	43.1	5,071	46.7	2,898	41.0
Total, 15 years and over	**22,999**	**100.0**	**18,296**	**100.0**	**13,939**	**100.0**	**10,851**	**100.0**	**7,063**	**100.0**
MALE										
15 to 24 years	674	7.4	947	13.6	610	4.4	274	2.5	124	1.8
25 to 44 years	4,231	46.8	2,920	41.9	1,689	12.1	933	8.6	686	9.7
45 to 64 years	2,203	24.3	1,613	23.2	1,329	9.5	1,152	10.6	965	13.7
65 years and over	1,942	21.5	1,486	21.3	1,290	9.3	1,174	10.8	853	12.1
Total, 15 years and over	**9,049**	**100.0**	**6,966**	**100.0**	**4,918**	**35.3**	**3,532**	**32.5**	**2,628**	**37.2**
FEMALE										
15 to 24 years	536	3.8	779	6.9	501	3.6	282	2.6	110	1.6
25 to 44 years	2,881	20.7	1,809	16.0	1,055	7.6	671	6.2	526	7.4
45 to 64 years	3,300	23.7	2,901	25.6	2,747	19.7	2,470	22.8	1,755	24.8
65 years and over	7,233	51.8	5,842	51.6	4,718	33.8	3,897	35.9	2,045	29.0
Total, 15 years and over	**13,950**	**100.0**	**11,330**	**100.0**	**9,021**	**64.7**	**7,319**	**67.5**	**4,436**	**62.8**

1. Prior to 1980, data are for persons 14 years and older. NOTE: Details may not add because of rounding. *Source:* Department of Commerce, Bureau of the Census.

Characteristics of Unmarried–Couple Households, 1990
(number in thousands)

Characteristics	Number	Percent	Characteristics	Number	Percent
Unmarried–couple households	2,856	100.0	Presence of children:		
			No children under 15 years	1,966	68.8
Age of householders:			Some children under 15 years	891	31.2
Under 25 years	596	20.0			
25–44 years	1,775	62.1	Sex of householders:		
45–64 years	358	12.5	Male	1,651	57.8
65 years and over	127	4.4	Female	1,205	42.2

Source: U.S. Bureau of the Census.

Households, Families, and Married Couples

	Households		Families		Maried couples
Date	Number	Average population per household	Number	Average population per family	Number
June 1890	12,690,000	4.93	—	—	—
April 1930	29,905,000	4.11	—	—	25,174,000
April 1940	34,949,000	3.67	32,166,000	3.76	28,517,000
March 1950	43,554,000	3.37	39,303,000	3.54	36,091,000
April 1955	47,874,000	3.33	41,951,000	3.59	37,556,000
March 1960[1]	52,799,000	3.33	45,111,000	3.67	40,200,000
March 1965	57,436,000	3.29	47,956,000	3.70	42,478,000
March 1970	63,401,000	3.14	51,586,000	3.58	45,373,000
March 1975	71,120,000	2.94	55,712,000	3.42	47,547,000
March 1980	80,776,000	2.76	59,550,000	3.29	49,714,000
March 1985	86,789,000	2.69	62,706,000	3.23	51,114,000
March 1988	91,066,000	2.64	65,133,000	3.17	52,613,000
March 1989	92,830,000	2.62	65,837,000	3.16	52,517,000
March 1990	93,347,000	2.63	66,090,000	3.17	53,256,000

1. First year in which figures for Alaska and Hawaii are included. *Source:* Department of Commerce, Bureau of the Census.

Families Maintained by Women, With No Husband Present
(numbers in thousands)

	1990		1980		1975		1970		1960	
	Number	Percent	Number	Percent	Number	Percent	Number	Percent	Number	Percent
Age of women:										
Under 35 years	3,699	34.0	3,015	34.6	2,356	32.5	1,364	24.4	796	17.7
35 to 44 years	2,929	26.9	1,916	22.0	1,510	20.9	1,074	19.2	940	20.9
45 to 64 years	2,790	25.6	2,514	28.9	2,266	31.3	2,021	36.1	1,731	38.5
65 years and over	1,471	13.5	1,260	14.5	1,108	15.3	1,131	20.2	1,027	22.9
Median age	40.7	—	41.7	—	43.4	—	48.5	—	50.1	—
Presence of children:										
No own children under 18 years	4,290	39.4	3,260	37.4	2,838	39.2	2,665	47.7	2,397	53.3
With own children under 18 years	6,599	60.6	5,445	62.6	4,404	60.8	2,926	52.3	2,097	46.7
Total own children under 18 years	11,378	—	10,204	—	9,227	—	6,694	—	4,674	—
Average per family	1.04	—	1.17	—	1.27	—	1.20	—	1.04	—
Average per family with children	1.72	—	1.87	—	2.10	—	2.29	—	2.24	—
Race:										
White	7,306	67.1	6,052	69.5	5,212	72.0	4,165	74.5	3,547	78.9
Black[1]	3,275	30.1	2,495	28.7	1,940	26.8	1,382	24.7	947	21.1
Other	309	2.8	158	1.8	90	1.2	44	0.8	n.a.	n.a.
Marital status:										
Married, husband absent	1,947	17.9	1,769	20.3	1,647	22.7	1,326	23.7	1,099	24.5
Widowed	2,536	23.3	2,570	29.5	2,559	35.3	2,396	42.9	2,325	51.7
Divorced	3,949	36.3	3,008	34.6	2,110	29.1	1,259	22.5	694	15.4
Never married	2,457	22.6	1,359	15.6	926	12.8	610	10.9	376	8.4
Total families maintained by women	10,890	100.0	8,705	100.0	7,242	100.0	5,591	100.0	4,494	100.0

1. Includes other races in 1960. NOTE: n.a. = not available. (—) as shown in this table, means "not applicable." *Source:* Department of Commerce, Bureau of the Census.

Median Age at First Marriage

Year	Males	Females	Year	Males	Females	Year	Males	Females	Year	Males	Females
1900	25.9	21.9	1930	24.3	21.3	1960	22.8	20.3	1988	25.9	23.6
1910	25.1	21.6	1940	24.3	21.5	1970	23.2	20.8	1989	26.2	23.8
1920	24.6	21.2	1950	22.8	20.3	1980	24.7	22.0	1990	26.1	23.9

Source: Department of Commerce, Bureau of the Census.

Selected Family Characteristics

Characteristics[1]	1989 Number (thous.)	1989 Median income
ALL RACES		
All families	66,090	34,213
Type of residence		
Nonfarm	64,701	34,300
Farm	1,390	30,809
Location of residence		
Inside metropolitan areas	50,619	36,896
1,000,000 or more	31,836	39,265
Inside central cities	11,535	30,578
Outside central cities	20,301	43,801
Under 1,000,000	18,783	33,280
Inside central cities	7,499	30,832
Outside central cities	11,284	35,118
Outside metropolitan areas	15,471	26,979
Region		
Northeast	13,494	39,484
Midwest	16,059	34,613
South	23,244	30,499
West	13,293	35,698
Type of family		
Married–couple family	52,317	38,547
Wife in paid labor force	30,188	45,266
Wife not in paid labor force	22,129	28,747
Male householder, no wife present	2,884	27,847
Female householder, no husband present	10,890	16,442
Number of earners		
No earners	9,439	14,285
1 earner	18,146	25,226
2 earners	29,235	40,658
3 earners	6,724	51,758
4 earners or more	2,546	65,722
Size of family		
2 persons	27,606	28,834
3 persons	15,353	35,963
4 persons	14,026	40,763
5 persons	5,938	39,077
6 persons	1,997	35,801
7 persons or more	1,170	32,259
Occupation group of longest job of householder (No longer available)		
Tenure status		
Owner occupied	n.a.	n.a.
Renter occupied	n.a.	n.a.
Occupier paid no cash rent	n.a.	n.a.
Educational attainment of householder		
Elementary	n.a.	n.a.
High school	n.a.	n.a.
College	n.a.	n.a.
1 to 3 years	n.a.	n.a.
4 years or more	n.a.	n.a.
4 years	n.a.	n.a.
5 years or more	n.a.	n.a.
Total, 25 years and over	n.a.	n.a.
WHITE		
All families	56,590	35,975

Characteristics[1]	1989 Number (thous.)	1989 Median income
Type of residence		
Nonfarm	55,225	36,104
Farm	1,365	31,020
Location of residence		
Inside metropolitan areas	42,592	39,103
1,000,000 or more	26,080	41,719
Inside central cities	7,946	34,758
Outside central cities	18,134	44,686
Under 1,000,000	16,512	35,182
Inside central cities	6,018	33,684
Outside central cities	10,493	35,848
Outside metropolitan areas	13,999	28,154
Region		
Northeast	11,837	40,990
Midwest	14,370	35,789
South	18,746	32,939
West	11,638	36,144
Type of family		
Married–couple family	46,918	39,208
Wife in paid labor force	26,829	45,803
Wife not in paid labor force	20,153	29,689
Male householder, no wife present	2,303	30,487
Female householder, no husband present	7,306	18,946
Number of earners		
No earners	7,816	16,360
1 earner	14,970	27,145
2 earners	25,737	41,429
3 earners	5,832	52,582
4 earners or more	2,236	66,890
BLACK		
All families	7,470	20,209
Type of residence		
Nonfarm	7,453	20,248
Farm	17	(B)
Location of residence		
Inside metropolitan areas	6,256	21,593
1,000,000 or more	4,416	22,986
Inside central cities	2,949	19,472
Outside central cities	1,467	32,270
Under 1,000,000	1,839	19,037
Inside central cities	1,248	18,531
Outside central cities	591	20,001
Outside metropolitan areas	1,215	14,370
Region		
Northeast	1,279	25,391
Midwest	1,446	18,301
South	4,147	19,029
West	598	25,670
Type of family		
Married–couple family	3,750	30,650
Wife in paid labor force	2,400	37,787
Wife not in paid labor force	13,450	18,727
Male householder, no wife present	446	18,395
Female householder, no husband present	3,275	11,630

Characteristics[1]	1989		Characteristics[1]	1989	
	Number (thous.)	Median income		Number (thous.)	Median income
Number of earners			Region		
No earners	1,396	6,166	Northeast	815	22,627
1 earner	2,601	15,440	Midwest	330	26,359
2 earners	2,609	32,171	South	1,596	20,520
3 earners	659	43,693	West	2,101	25,511
4 earners or more	205	53,258			
			Type of family		
HISPANIC ORIGIN OF HOUSEHOLDER[2]			Married–couple family	3,395	27,382
All families	4,840	23,446	Wife in paid labor force	1,763	34,821
Type of residence			Wife not in paid labor force	1,633	20,717
Nonfarm	4,813	23,456	Male householder, no		
Farm	28	(B)	wife present	329	25,176
Location of residence			Female householder, no		
Inside metropolitan areas	4,463	24,050	husband present	1,116	11,745
1,000,000 or more	3,353	25,304			
Inside central cities	1,898	21,662	Number of earners		
Outside central cities	1,456	31,213	No earners	615	7,486
Under 1,000,000	1,110	20,373	1 earner	1,554	17,250
Inside central cities	625	19,347	2 earners	1,860	29,420
Outside central cities	485	21,996	3 earners	541	40,480
Outside metropolitan areas	377	18,343	4 earners or more	271	46,858

1. Family data as of March 1990. 2. Persons of Hispanic origin may be of any race. n.a. = not available. (B) Base less than 75,000. *Source:* Department of Commerce, Bureau of the Census. NOTE: Data are the latest available.

Births

Live Births and Birth Rates

Year	Births[1]	Rate[2]	Year	Births[1]	Rate[2]	Year	Births[1]	Rate[2]
1910	2,777,000	30.1	1956[3]	4,218,000	25.2	1973	3,136,965	14.9
1915	2,965,000	29.5	1957[3]	4,308,000	25.3	1974	3,159,958	14.9
1920	2,950,000	27.7	1958[3]	4,255,000	24.5	1975	3,144,198	14.8
1925	2,909,000	25.1	1959[3]	4,295,000	24.3	1976	3,167,788	14.8
1930	2,618,000	21.3	1960[3]	4,257,850	23.7	1977	3,326,632	15.4
1935	2,377,000	18.7	1961[3]	4,268,326	23.3	1978	3,333,279	15.3
1940	2,559,000	19.4	1962[3]	4,167,362	22.4	1979	3,494,398	15.9
1945	2,858,000	20.4	1963[3]	4,098,020	21.7	1980	3,612,258	15.9
1947	3,817,000	26.6	1964[3]	4,027,490	21.0	1982	3,680,537	15.9
1948	3,637,000	24.9	1965[3]	3,760,358	19.4	1983	3,638,933	15.5
1949	3,649,000	24.5	1966[3]	3,606,274	18.4	1984	3,669,141	15.5
1950	3,632,000	24.1	1967[4]	3,520,959	17.8	1985	3,760,561	15.8
1951[3]	3,823,000	24.9	1968[3]	3,501,564	17.5	1986	3,731,000	15.5
1952[3]	3,913,000	25.1	1969[3]	3,600,206	17.8	1987	3,829,000	15.7
1953[3]	3,965,000	25.1	1970[3]	3,731,386	18.4	1988	3,913,000	15.9
1954[3]	4,078,000	25.3	1971[3]	3,555,970	17.2	1989	4,021,000	16.2
1955	4,104,000	25.0	1972	3,258,411	15.6	1990[5]	4,179,000	16.7

1. Figures through 1959 include adjustment for underregistration; beginning 1960, figures represent number registered. For comparison, the 1959 registered count was 4,245,000. 2. Rates are per 1,000 population estimated as of July 1 for each year except 1940, 1950, 1960, 1970, and 1980, which are as of April 1, the census date; for 1942–46 based on population including armed forces overseas. 3. Based on 50% sample of births. 4. Based on a 20 to 50% sample of births. 5. Provisional. NOTE: Alaska is included beginning 1959; Hawaii beginning 1960. Since 1972, based on 100% of births in selected states and on 50% sample in all other states. *Sources:* Department of Health and Human Services, National Center for Health Statistics.

Live Births by Age of Mother

Year[1] and race	Total	Age of Mother							
		Under 15 yr	15–19 yr	20–24 yr	25–29 yr	30–34 yr	35–39 yr	40–44 yr	45 yr and over
1940	2,558,647	3,865	332,667	799,537	693,268	431,468	222,015	68,269	7,558
1945	2,858,449	4,028	298,868	832,746	785,299	554,906	296,852	78,853	6,897
1950	3,631,512	5,413	432,911	1,155,167	1,041,360	610,816	302,780	77,743	5,322
1955	4,014,112	6,181	493,770	1,290,939	1,133,155	732,540	352,320	89,777	5,430
1960	4,257,850	6,780	586,966	1,426,912	1,092,816	687,722	359,908	91,564	5,182
1965	3,760,358	7,768	590,894	1,337,350	925,732	529,376	282,908	81,716	4,614
1970	3,731,386	11,752	644,708	1,418,874	994,904	427,806	180,244	49,952	3,146
1975	3,144,198	12,642	582,238	1,093,676	936,786	375,500	115,409	26,319	1,628
1980	3,612,258	10,169	552,161	1,226,200	1,108,291	550,354	140,793	23,090	1,200
1985	3,760,561	10,220	467,485	1,141,320	1,201,350	696,354	214,336	28,334	1,162
1986	3,756,547	10,176	461,905	1,102,119	1,199,519	721,395	230,335	29,847	1,251
1987	3,809,394	10,311	462,312	1,075,856	1,216,080	760,695	247,984	34,781	1,375
1988	3,909,510	10,588	478,353	1,067,472	1,239,256	803,547	269,518	39,349	1,427
White	3,046,162	4,073	315,471	804,622	1,010,748	661,414	217,754	31,068	1,012
Black	671,976	6,182	146,326	220,301	167,684	93,765	32,534	4,981	203
Other	191,372	333	16,556	42,549	60,824	48,368	19,230	3,300	212

1. Data for 1940–55 are adjusted for underregistration. Beginning 1960, registered births only are shown. Data for 1960–70 based on a 50% sample of births. For 1972–84, based on 100% of births in selected states and on 50% sample in all other states. Beginning 1960, including Alaska and Hawaii. NOTE: Data refer only to births occurring within the U.S. Figures are shown to the last digit as computed for convenience in summation. They are not assumed to be accurate to the last digit. Figures for age of mother not stated are distributed. *Source:* Department of Health and Human Services, National Center for Health Statistics.

Births to Unmarried Women

(in thousands, except as indicated)

Age and race	1988	1985	1980	1975	1970	1965	1960	1955	1950
By age of mother:									
Under 15 years	9.9	9.4	9.0	11.0	9.5	6.1	4.6	3.9	3.2
15–19 years	312.5	270.9	262.8	222.5	190.4	123.1	87.1	68.9	56.0
20–24 years	350.9	300.4	237.3	134.0	126.7	90.7	68.0	55.7	43.1
25–29 years	196.4	152.0	99.6	50.2	40.6	36.8	32.1	28.0	20.9
30–34 years	94.9	67.3	41.0	19.8	19.1	19.6	18.9	16.1	10.8
35–39 years	34.4	24.0	13.2	8.1	9.4	11.4	10.6	8.3	6.0
40 years and over	6.3	4.1	2.9	2.3	3.0	3.7	3.0	2.4	1.7
By race:									
White	539.7	433.0	320.1	186.4	175.1	123.7	82.5	64.2	53.5
Black and other	465.6	395.2	345.7	261.6	223.6	167.5	141.8	119.2	88.1
Total of above births	**1,005.3**	**828.2**	**665.8**	**447.9**	**398.7**	**291.2**	**224.3**	**183.4**	**141.6**
Percent of all births[1]	25.7	22.0	18.4	14.2	10.7	7.7	5.3	4.5	3.9
Rate[2]	38.6	32.8	29.4	24.8	26.4	23.4	21.8	19.3	14.1

1. Through 1955, based on data adjusted for underregistration; thereafter, registered births. 2. Rate per 1,000 unmarried (never married, widowed, and divorced) women, 15–44 years old. *Source:* Department of Health and Human Services, National Center for Health Statistics. NOTE: Data are latest available.

Live Births and Birth Rates

State	1989[1] number	1989[1] rate	1988 number	1988 rate	State	1989[1] number	1989[1] rate	1988 number	1988 rate
Alabama	58,360	14.2	60,745	14.8	Montana	11,394	14.1	11,692	14.5
Alaska	11,545	21.9	11,232	21.4	Nebraska	24,317	15.1	23,907	14.9
Arizona	67,609	19.0	65,623	18.8	Nevada	18,297	16.5	18,008	17.1
Arkansas	34,997	14.5	35,035	14.6	New Hampshire	17,946	16.2	17,364	16.0
California	557,003	19.2	533,148	18.8	New Jersey	116,554	15.1	117,764	15.3
Colorado	52,863	15.9	53,367	16.2	New Mexico	27,324	17.9	27,015	17.9
Connecticut	47,560	14.7	48,077	14.9	New York	291,145	16.2	280,650	15.7
Delaware	11,492	17.1	10,406	15.8	North Carolina	102,817	15.6	97,579	15.0
D.C.[2]	22,549	37.3	10,540	17.1	North Dakota	10,862	16.5	10,103	15.1
Florida	192,813	15.2	184,119	14.9	Ohio	162,793	14.9	160,529	14.8
Georgia	109,905	17.1	105,923	16.7	Oklahoma	46,455	14.4	47,408	14.6
Hawaii	19,545	17.6	19,045	17.3	Oregon	43,835	15.5	40,052	14.5
Idaho	15,459	15.2	15,741	15.7	Pennsylvania	170,261	14.1	165,639	13.8
Illinois	186,500	16.0	184,841	15.9	Rhode Island	15,302	15.3	14,224	14.3
Indiana	82,764	14.8	81,643	14.7	South Carolina	55,214	15.7	55,114	15.9
Iowa	37,241	13.1	38,119	13.5	South Dakota	10,991	15.4	11,194	15.7
Kansas	35,632	14.2	38,792	15.5	Tennessee	76,780	15.5	70,711	14.4
Kentucky	52,591	14.1	51,058	13.7	Texas	301,360	17.7	303,418	18.0
Louisiana	68,813	15.7	73,902	16.8	Utah	36,208	21.2	36,055	21.3
Maine	16,842	13.8	17,172	14.3	Vermont	7,920	14.0	8,111	14.6
Maryland	67,550	14.4	75,768	16.4	Virginia	93,453	15.3	93,127	15.5
Massachusetts	96,457	16.3	88,194	15.0	Washington	73,261	15.4	72,503	15.6
Michigan	142,673	15.4	139,714	15.1	West Virginia	23,079	12.4	21,846	11.6
Minnesota	66,593	15.3	66,748	15.5	Wisconsin	72,100	14.8	70,817	14.6
Mississippi	42,263	16.1	42,074	16.1	Wyoming	6,491	13.7	7,162	15.0
Missouri	80,126	15.5	76,492	14.9	**Total**	**4,021,000**	**16.2**	**3,909,510**	**15.9**

1. Provisional. 2. The anomaly in the 1988 and 1989 figures is due to the District's unique situation. The 1988 figures refer to place of residence whereas the 1989 figure (as noted) refers to place of occurrence which for D.C. residents can be Maryland or Virginia. NOTE: Provisional data by place of occurrence. Rates are per 1,000 population. *Source:* Department of Health and Human Services, National Center for Health Statistics.

Live Births by Race or National Origin

Race	1988	1987	Race	1988	1987
White	3,046,162	2,992,488	Chinese	22,904	19,293
Black	671,976	641,567	Filipino	24,612	23,636
American Indian[1]	45,871	43,707	Other[2]	84,259	75,880
Japanese	10,483	9,822	**Total[3]**	**3,909,510**	**3,809,394**

1. Includes Eskimos and Aleuts. 2. Hawaiian and other Asian or Pacific Islander. 3. Includes births of other races not shown separately. Data are latest available. *Source:* Department of Health and Human Services, National Center for Health Statistics.

Live Births by Sex and Sex Ratio[1]

Year	Total[2] Male	Total[2] Female	Total[2] Males per 1,000 females	White Male	White Female	White Males per 1,000 females	Black Male	Black Female	Black Males per 1,000 females
1979[3]	1,791,267	1,703,131	1,052	1,442,981	1,365,439	1,057	293,013	284,842	1,029
1980[3]	1,852,616	1,759,642	1,053	1,490,140	1,408,592	1,058	299,033	290,583	1,029
1981[3]	1,860,272	1,768,966	1,052	1,494,437	1,414,232	1,057	297,864	289,933	1,027
1982[3]	1,885,676	1,794,861	1,051	1,509,704	1,432,350	1,054	301,121	291,520	1,033
1983[3]	1,865,553	1,773,380	1,052	1,492,385	1,411,865	1,057	297,011	289,016	1,028
1984[3]	1,879,490	1,789,651	1,050	1,500,326	1,423,176	1,054	300,951	291,794	1,031
1985	1,927,983	1,832,578	1,052	1,536,646	1,454,727	1,056	308,575	299,618	1,030
1986	1,924,868	1,831,679	1,051	1,523,914	1,446,525	1,053	315,788	305,433	1,034
1987	1,951,153	1,858,241	1,050	1,535,517	1,456,971	1,054	325,259	316,308	1,028
1988	2,002,424	1,907,086	1,050	1,562,675	1,483,487	1,053	341,441	330,535	1,033

1. Excludes births to nonresidents of U.S. 2. Includes races other than white and black. 3. Based on 100% of births for selected states and 50% sample in all others. *Source:* Department of Health and Human Services, National Center for Health Statistics. NOTE: Data are latest available.

Mortality
Death Rates for Selected Causes

Cause of death	Death rates per 100,000							
	1990[1]	1989[1]	1985	1980	1950	1945–49	1920–24[4]	1900–04[4]
Typhoid fever	n.a.	n.a.	—	0.0	0.1	0.2	7.3	26.7
Communicable diseases of childhood	n.a.	n.a.	n.a.	0.0	1.3	2.3	33.8	65.2
Measles	0.0	0.0	—	0.0	0.3	0.6	7.3	10.0
Scarlet fever	n.a.	n.a.	1.0	0.0	0.2	0.1	4.0	11.8
Whooping cough	0.0	0.0	—	0.0	0.7	1.0	8.9	10.7
Diphtheria	n.a.	n.a.	—	0.0	0.3	0.7	13.7	32.7
Pneumonia and influenza	31.4	30.3	27.9	23.3	31.3	41.3	140.3	184.3
Influenza	0.8	0.5	0.8	1.1	4.4	5.0	34.8	22.8
Pneumonia	30.6	29.7	27.1	22.0	26.9	37.2	105.5	161.5
Tuberculosis	0.7	0.7	0.7	0.8	22.5	33.3	96.7	184.7
Cancer	202.1	199.9	191.7	182.5	139.8	134.0	86.9	67.7
Diabetes mellitus	19.0	18.7	16.2	15.0	16.2	24.1	17.1	12.2
Major cardiovascular diseases	366.2	375.3	410.7	434.5	510.8	493.1	369.9	359.5
Diseases of the heart	288.5	295.9	325.0	335.2	356.8	325.1	169.8	153.0
Cerebrovascular diseases	57.5	58.9	64.0	74.6	104.0	93.8	93.5	106.3
Nephritis and nephrosis	8.5	8.9	9.4	7.6	16.4	48.4	81.5	84.3
Syphilis	0.0	0.0	0.0	0.1	5.0	8.4	17.6	12.9
Appendicitis	0.2	0.2	0.2	0.3	2.0	3.5	14.0	9.4
Accidents, all forms	36.5	37.2	38.6	46.0	60.6	67.6	70.8	79.2
Motor vehicle accidents	18.6	18.9	18.8	23.0	23.1	22.3	12.9	n.a.
Infant mortality[2]	n.a.	n.a.	10.6	12.5	29.2	33.3	76.7	n.a.
Neonatal mortality[2]	n.a.	n.a.	7.0	8.4	20.5	22.9	39.7	n.a.
Fetal mortality[3]	n.a.	n.a.	7.9	9.2	19.2	21.6	n.a	n.a.
Maternal mortality[2]	n.a.	n.a.	0.1	0.1	0.8	1.4	6.9	n.a.
All causes	861.9	868.1	890.8	883.4	960.1	1,000.6	1,157.4	1,621.6

1. Provisional, based on a 10% sample of deaths. 2. Rates per 1,000 live births. 3. Ratio per 1,000 births. 4. Includes only deaths occurring within the registration areas. Beginning with 1933, area includes the entire United States; Alaska included beginning in 1959 and Hawaii in 1960. Rates per 100,000 population residing in areas, enumerated as of April 1 for 1940, 1950, and 1980 and estimated as of July 1 for all other years. Due to changes in statistical methods, death rates are not strictly comparable. n.a. = not available. *Source:* Department of Health and Human Services, National Center for Health Statistics.

Accident Rates, 1989

Class of accident		One every	Class of accident		One every
All accidents	Deaths	6 minutes	Workers off-job	Deaths	14 minutes
	Injuries	4 seconds		Injuries	11 seconds
Motor-vehicle	Deaths	11 minutes	Home	Deaths	23 minutes
	Injuries	19 seconds		Injuries	9 seconds
Work	Deaths	51 minutes	Public non-motor-	Deaths	28 minutes
	Injuries	19 seconds	vehicle	Injuries	13 seconds

NOTE: Data are latest available. *Source:* National Safety Council.

Improper Driving as Factor in Accidents, 1989

Kind of improper driving	Fatal accidents			Injury accidents			All accidents		
	Total	Urban	Rural	Total	Urban	Rural	Total	Urban	Rural
Improper driving	61.9	61.3	62.3	73.7	75.3	70.5	72.7	74.2	68.9
Speed too fast[1]	26.7	27.5	26.3	23.1	21.3	26.8	18.9	17.4	22.5
Right of way	12.2	15.4	10.5	25.4	29.8	16.3	23.4	26.5	15.7
Failed to yield	8.4	10.1	7.5	18.2	20.6	13.2	17.8	19.8	13.1
Passed stop sign	2.1	1.7	2.3	2.0	2.2	1.7	1.6	1.6	1.4
Disregarded signal	1.7	3.6	0.7	5.2	7.0	1.4	4.0	5.1	1.2
Drove left of center	4.5	2.4	5.6	1.5	0.9	2.7	1.7	1.2	2.8
Improper overtaking	6.2	3.9	7.3	2.0	1.5	3.2	2.4	2.1	3.3
Made improper turn	0.4	0.6	0.4	1.5	1.6	1.2	2.6	2.9	1.8
Followed too closely	0.7	0.7	0.7	6.1	6.9	4.5	6.4	7.0	5.0
Other improper driving	11.2	10.8	11.5	14.1	13.3	15.8	17.3	17.1	17.8
No improper driving stated	38.1	38.7	37.7	26.3	24.7	29.5	27.3	25.8	31.1
Total	100.0%	100.0%	100.0%	100.0%	100.0%	100.0%	100.0%	100.0%	100.0%

1. Includes "speed too fast for conditions." *Source:* Motor-vehicle reports from six state traffic authorities to National Safety Council. NOTE: Figures are latest available.

Annual Death Rates

Year	Rate	Year	Rate	Year	Deaths	Rate
1900	17.2	1943	10.9	1967	1,851,323	9.4
1905	15.9	1944	10.6	1968	1,930,082	9.7
1910	14.7	1945	10.6	1969	1,921,990	9.5
1915	13.2	1946	10.0	1970[1]	1,921,031	9.5
1920	13.0	1947	10.1	1971	1,927,542	9.3
1925	11.7	1948	9.9	1972	1,963,944	9.4
1926	12.1	1949	9.7	1973	1,973,003	9.3
1927	11.3	1950	9.6	1974	1,934,388	9.1
1928	12.0	1951	9.7	1975	1,892,879	8.8
1929	11.9	1952	9.6	1976	1,909,440	8.8
1930	11.3	1953	9.6	1977	1,899,597	8.6
1931	11.1	1954	9.2	1978	1,927,788	8.7
1932	10.9	1955	9.3	1979	1,913,841	8.5
1933	10.7	1956	9.4	1980	1,989,841	8.7
1934	11.1	1957	9.6	1982	1,974,797	8.5
1935	10.9	1958	9.5	1983	2,019,201	8.6
1936	11.6	1959	9.4	1984	2,039,369	8.6
1937	11.3	1960	9.5	1985	2,086,440	8.7
1938	10.6	1962	9.5	1986	2,099,000	8.7
1939	10.6	1963	9.6	1987	2,127,000	8.7
1940	10.8	1964	9.4	1988	2,171,000	8.8
1941	10.5	1965	9.4	1989	2,155,000	8.7
1942	10.3	1966	9.5	1990[2]	2,162,000	8.6

1. First year for which deaths of nonresidents are excluded. 2. Provisional. NOTE: Includes only deaths occurring within the registration states. Beginning with 1933, area includes entire U.S.; with 1959 includes Alaska, and with 1960 includes Hawaii. Excludes fetal deaths. Rates per 1,000 population residing in area, as of April 1 for 1940, 1950, 1960, 1970, and 1980, and estimated as of July 1 for all other years. *Sources:* Department of Health and Human Services, National Center for Health Statistics.

Death Rates by Age, Race, and Sex

Age	1989[1]	1988	1987	1980	1970[2]	1960	1989[1]	1988	1987	1980	1970[2]	1960
	White males						White females					
Under 1 year	9.1	9.3	9.4	12.3	21.1	26.9	7.1	7.2	7.4	9.6	16.1	20.1
1–4	0.4	0.5	0.5	0.7	0.8	1.0	0.3	0.4	0.4	0.5	0.8	0.9
5–14	0.3	0.2	0.3	0.4	0.5	0.5	0.1	0.1	0.2	0.2	0.3	0.3
15–24	1.3	1.3	1.4	1.7	1.7	1.4	0.5	0.4	0.5	0.5	0.6	0.5
25–34	1.7	1.6	1.7	1.7	1.8	1.6	0.6	0.6	0.6	0.7	0.8	0.9
35–44	2.6	2.5	2.5	2.6	3.4	3.3	1.2	1.1	1.2	1.2	1.9	1.9
45–54	5.6	5.6	5.8	7.0	8.8	9.3	3.0	3.1	3.3	3.7	4.6	4.6
55–64	14.9	15.3	15.5	17.3	22.0	22.3	8.4	8.5	8.5	8.8	10.1	10.8
65–74	33.4	35.0	35.5	40.4	48.1	48.5	19.4	19.9	20.0	20.7	24.7	27.8
75–84	79.3	82.0	82.1	88.3	101.0	103.0	50.7	51.2	50.8	54.0	67.0	77.0
85 and over	181.1	188.1	184.3	191.0	185.5	217.5	140.3	147.5	144.9	149.8	159.8	194.8
	All other males						All other females					
Under 1 year	17.5	18.9	19.4	23.5	40.2	51.9	15.6	16.0	15.7	19.4	31.7	40.7
1–4	0.6	0.7	0.8	1.0	1.4	2.1	0.6	0.6	0.7	0.8	1.2	1.7
5–14	0.4	0.3	0.4	0.4	0.6	0.8	0.2	0.2	0.2	0.3	0.4	0.5
15–24	2.0	2.0	1.9	2.0	3.0	2.1	0.6	0.6	0.6	0.7	1.1	1.1
25–34	3.6	3.4	3.3	3.6	5.0	3.9	1.3	1.3	1.3	1.4	2.2	2.6
35–44	5.6	5.8	5.7	5.9	8.7	7.3	2.5	2.5	2.5	2.9	4.9	5.5
45–54	10.6	10.6	10.6	13.1	16.5	15.5	5.0	5.4	5.6	6.9	9.8	11.4
55–64	21.0	21.8	21.8	26.1	30.5	31.5	11.9	12.7	12.7	14.2	18.9	24.1
65–74	39.8	41.7	42.3	47.5	54.7	56.6	24.0	25.5	25.7	28.6	36.8	39.8
75–84	80.1	84.0	83.4	86.9	89.8	86.6	52.0	56.2	55.4	58.6	63.9	67.1
85 and over	141.0	145.5	145.1	157.7	114.1	152.4	115.0	119.6	118.1	119.2	102.9	128.7

1. Provisional. Based on a 10% sample of deaths. 2. Beginning 1970 excludes deaths of nonresidents of U.S. NOTE: Excludes fetal deaths. Rates are per 1,000 population in each group, enumerated as of April 1 for 1960, 1970, and 1980, and estimated as of July 1 for all other years. *Sources:* Department of Health and Human Services, National Center for Health Statistics.

Expectation of Life

Expectation of Life in the United States

Calendar period	Age								
	0	10	20	30	40	50	60	70	80
WHITE MALES									
1850[1]	38.3	48.0	40.1	34.0	27.9	21.6	15.6	10.2	5.9
1890[1]	42.50	48.45	40.66	34.05	27.37	20.72	14.73	9.35	5.40
1900–1902[2]	48.23	50.59	42.19	34.88	27.74	20.76	14.35	9.03	5.10
1909–1911[2]	50.23	51.32	42.71	34.87	27.43	20.39	13.98	8.83	5.09
1919–1921[3]	56.34	54.15	45.60	37.65	29.86	22.22	15.25	9.51	5.47
1929–1931	59.12	54.96	46.02	37.54	29.22	21.51	14.72	9.20	5.26
1939–1941	62.81	57.03	47.76	38.80	30.03	21.96	15.05	9.42	5.38
1949–1951	66.31	58.98	49.52	40.29	31.17	22.83	15.76	10.07	5.88
1959–1961[5]	67.55	59.78	50.25	40.98	31.73	23.22	16.01	10.29	5.89
1969–1971[6]	67.94	59.69	50.22	41.07	31.87	23.34	16.07	10.38	6.18
1979–1981	70.82	61.98	52.45	43.31	34.04	25.26	17.56	11.35	6.76
1986	72.0	62.9	53.4	44.2	34.9	26.1	18.2	11.7	6.9
1987	72.2	63.1	53.6	44.3	35.1	26.2	18.3	11.8	6.9
1988	72.3	63.2	53.6	44.4	35.2	26.3	18.4	11.8	6.8
WHITE FEMALES									
1850[1]	40.5	47.2	40.2	35.4	29.8	23.5	17.0	11.3	6.4
1890[1]	44.46	49.62	42.03	35.36	28.76	22.09	15.70	10.15	5.75
1900–1902[2]	51.08	52.15	43.77	36.42	29.17	21.89	15.23	9.59	5.50
1909–1911[2]	53.62	53.57	44.88	36.96	29.26	21.74	14.92	9.38	5.35
1919–1921[3]	58.53	55.17	46.46	38.72	30.94	23.12	15.93	9.94	5.70
1929–1931	62.67	57.65	48.52	39.99	31.52	23.41	16.05	9.98	5.63
1939–1941	67.29	60.85	51.38	42.21	33.25	24.72	17.00	10.50	5.88
1949–1951	72.03	64.26	54.56	45.00	35.64	26.76	18.64	11.68	6.59
1959–1961[5]	74.19	66.05	56.29	46.63	37.13	28.08	19.69	12.38	6.67
1969–1971[6]	75.49	66.97	57.24	47.60	38.12	29.11	20.79	13.37	7.59
1979–1981	78.22	69.21	59.44	49.76	40.16	30.96	22.45	14.89	8.65
1986	78.8	69.6	59.9	50.1	40.5	31.2	22.6	15.1	8.8
1987	78.9	69.7	59.9	50.2	40.6	31.3	22.7	15.1	8.8
1988	78.9	69.7	59.9	50.2	40.6	31.2	22.6	15.0	8.7
ALL OTHER MALES[4]									
1900–1902[2]	32.54	41.90	35.11	29.25	23.12	17.34	12.62	8.33	5.12
1909–1911[2]	34.05	40.65	33.46	27.33	21.57	16.21	11.67	8.00	5.53
1919–1921[3]	47.14	45.99	38.36	32.51	26.53	20.47	14.74	9.58	5.83
1929–1931	47.55	44.27	35.95	29.45	23.36	17.92	13.15	8.78	5.42
1939–1941	52.33	48.54	39.74	32.25	25.23	19.18	14.38	10.06	6.46
1949–1951	58.91	52.96	43.73	35.31	27.29	20.25	14.91	10.74	7.07
1959–1961[5]	61.48	55.19	45.78	37.05	28.72	21.28	15.29	10.81	6.87
1969–1971[6]	60.98	53.67	44.37	36.20	28.29	21.24	15.35	10.68	7.57
1979–1981	65.63	57.40	47.87	39.13	30.64	22.92	16.54	11.36	7.22
1986	67.2	58.7	49.1	40.3	31.8	.23.9	17.0	11.5	7.1
1987	67.3	58.8	49.2	40.4	32.0	24.1	17.2	11.6	7.2
1988	67.1	58.6	49.1	40.3	32.0	24.1	17.2	11.6	7.2
ALL OTHER FEMALES[4]									
1900–1902[2]	35.04	43.02	36.89	30.70	24.37	18.67	13.60	9.62	6.48
1909–1911[2]	37.67	42.84	36.14	29.61	23.34	17.65	12.78	9.22	6.05
1919–1921[3]	46.92	44.54	37.15	31.48	25.60	19.76	14.69	10.25	6.58
1929–1931	49.51	45.33	37.22	30.67	24.30	18.60	14.22	10.38	6.90
1939–1941	55.51	50.83	42.14	34.52	27.31	21.04	16.14	11.81	8.00
1949–1951	62.70	56.17	46.77	38.02	29.82	22.67	16.95	12.29	8.15
1959–1961[5]	66.47	59.72	50.07	40.83	32.16	24.31	17.83	12.46	7.66
1969–1971[6]	69.05	61.49	51.85	42.61	33.87	25.97	19.02	13.30	9.01
1979–1981	74.00	65.64	55.88	46.39	37.16	28.59	20.49	14.44	9.17
1986	75.1	66.4	56.6	47.1	37.8	29.1	21.2	14.5	8.9
1987	75.2	66.5	56.7	47.2	38.0	29.2	21.3	14.6	8.9
1988	75.1	66.4	56.7	47.1	37.9	29.2	21.3	14.5	8.8

1. Massachusetts only; white and nonwhite combined, the latter being about 1% of the total. 2. Original Death Registration States. 3. Death Registration States of 1920. 4. Data for periods 1900–1902 to 1929–1931 relate to blacks only. 5. Alaska and Hawaii included beginning in 1959. 6. Deaths of nonresidents of the United States excluded starting in 1970. *Sources:* Department of Health and Human Services, National Center for Health Statistics.

U.S. GEOGRAPHY

Miscellaneous Data for the United States

Source: Department of the Interior, U.S. Geological Survey.

Highest point: Mount McKinley, Alaska	20,320 ft (6,198 m)
Lowest point: Death Valley, Calif.	282 ft (86 m) below sea level
Approximate mean altitude	2,500 ft (763 m)
Points farthest apart (50 states):	5,859 mi. (9,429 km)
Log Point, Elliot Key, Fla., and Kure Island, Hawaii	
Geographic center (50 states):	44° 58' N. lat.103° 46' W. long.
In Butte County, S.D. (west of Castle Rock)	
Geographic center (48 conterminous states):	39° 50' N. lat.98° 35' W. long.
In Smith County, Kan. (near Lebanon)	
Boundaries:	
Between Alaska and Canada	1,538 mi. (2,475 km)
Between the 48 conterminous states and Canada (incl. Great Lakes)	3,987 mi. (6,416 km)
Between the United States and Mexico	1,933 mi. (3,111 km)

Extreme Points of the United States (50 States)

			Distance[1]	
Extreme point	Latitude	Longitude	mi.	km
Northernmost point: Point Barrow, Alaska	71°23' N	156°29' W	2,507	4,034
Easternmost point: West Quoddy Head, Me.	44°49' N	66°57' W	1,788	2,997
Southernmost point: Ka Lae (South Cape), Hawaii	18°55' N	155°41' W	3,463	5,573
Westernmost point: Pochnoi Point, Alaska (Semisopochnoi Island)	51°17' N	172°09' E	3,372	5,426

1. From geographic center of United States (incl. Alaska and Hawaii), west of Castle Rock, S.D., 44°58' N. lat., 103°46' W long.

Coastline of the United States

	Lengths, statute miles			Lengths, statute miles	
State	General coastline[1]	Tidal shoreline[2]	State	General coastline[1]	Tidal shoreline[2]
Atlantic Coast:			Gulf Coast:		
Maine	228	3,478	Florida (Gulf)	770	5,095
New Hampshire	13	131	Alabama	53	607
Massachusetts	192	1,519	Mississippi	44	359
Rhode Island	40	384	Louisiana	397	7,721
Connecticut	—	618	Texas	367	3,359
New York	127	1,850	Total Gulf coast	1,631	17,141
New Jersey	130	1,792	Pacific Coast:		
Pennsylvania	—	89	California	840	3,427
Delaware	28	381	Oregon	296	1,410
Maryland	31	3,190	Washington	157	3,026
Virginia	112	3,315	Hawaii	750	1,052
North Carolina	301	3,375	Alaska (Pacific)	5,580	31,383
South Carolina	187	2,876	Total Pacific coast	7,623	40,298
Georgia	100	2,344	Arctic Coast:		
Florida (Atlantic)	580	3,331	Alaska (Arctic)	1,060	2,521
Total Atlantic coast	2,069	28,673	Total Arctic coast	1,060	2,521
			States Total	**12,383**	**88,633**

1. Figures are lengths of general outline of seacoast. Measurements made with unit measure of 30 minutes of latitude on charts as near scale of 1:1,200,000 as possible. Coastline of bays and sounds is included to point where they narrow to width of unit measure, and distance across at such point is included. 2. Figures obtained in 1939–40 with recording instrument on largest–scale maps and charts then available. Shoreline of outer coast, offshore islands, sounds, bays, rivers, and creeks is included to head of tidewater, or to point where tidal waters narrow to width of 100 feet. *Source:* Department of Commerce, National Oceanic and Atmospheric Administration, National Ocean Service.

Highest, Lowest, and Mean Altitudes in the United States

State	Altitude ft[1]	Highest point	Altitude ft[1]	Lowest point	Altitude ft[1]
Alabama	500	Cheaha Mountain	2,405	Gulf of Mexico	Sea level
Alaska	1,900	Mount McKinley	20,320	Pacific Ocean	Sea level
Arizona	4,100	Humphreys Peak	12,633	Colorado River	70
Arkansas	650	Magazine Mountain	2,753	Ouachita River	55
California	2,900	Mount Whitney	14,491[2]	Death Valley	282[3]
Colorado	6,800	Mount Elbert	14,433	Arkansas River	3,350
Connecticut	500	Mount Frissell, on south slope	2,380	Long Island Sound	Sea level
Delaware	60	On Ebright Road	442	Atlantic Ocean	Sea level
D.C.	150	Tenleytown, at Reno Reservoir	410	Potomac River	1
Florida	100	Sec. 30, T6N, R20W[4]	345	Atlantic Ocean	Sea level
Georgia	600	Brasstown Bald	4,784	Atlantic Ocean	Sea level
Hawaii	3,030	Puu Wekiu, Mauna Kea	13,796	Pacific Ocean	Sea level
Idaho	5,000	Borah Peak	12,662	Snake River	710
Illinois	600	Charles Mound	1,235	Mississippi River	279[5]
Indiana	700	Franklin Township, Wayne County	1,257	Ohio River	320[5]
Iowa	1,100	Sec. 29, T100N, R41W[6]	1,670	Mississippi River	480
Kansas	2,000	Mount Sunflower	4,039[7]	Verdigris River	679
Kentucky	750	Black Mountain	4,139	Mississippi River	257[5]
Louisiana	100	Driskill Mountain	535	New Orleans	8[3]
Maine	600	Mount Katahdin	5,267	Atlantic Ocean	Sea level
Maryland	350	Backbone Mountain	3,360	Atlantic Ocean	Sea level
Massachusetts	500	Mount Greylock	3,487	Atlantic Ocean	Sea level
Michigan	900	Mount Arvon	1,979	Lake Erie	572[5]
Minnesota	1,200	Eagle Mountain	2,301	Lake Superior	600
Mississippi	300	Woodall Mountain	806	Gulf of Mexico	Sea level
Missouri	800	Taum Sauk Mountain	1,772	St. Francis River	230[5]
Montana	3,400	Granite Peak	12,799	Kootenai River	1,800
Nebraska	2,600	Johnson Township, Kimball County	5,424	Missouri River	840
Nevada	5,500	Boundary Peak	13,140	Colorado River	479
New Hampshire	1,000	Mount Washington	6,288	Atlantic Ocean	Sea level
New Jersey	250	High Point	1,803[7]	Atlantic Ocean	Sea level
New Mexico	5,700	Wheeler Peak	13,161	Red Bluff Reservoir	2,842
New York	1,000	Mount Marcy	5,344	Atlantic Ocean	Sea level
North Carolina	700	Mount Mitchell	6,684	Atlantic Ocean	Sea level
North Dakota	1,900	White Butte	3,506	Red River	750
Ohio	850	Campbell Hill	1,549	Ohio River	455[5]
Oklahoma	1,300	Black Mesa	4,973	Little River	289
Oregon	3,300	Mount Hood	11,239	Pacific Ocean	Sea level
Pennsylvania	1,100	Mount Davis	3,213	Delaware River	Sea level
Rhode Island	200	Jerimoth Hill	812	Atlantic Ocean	Sea level
South Carolina	350	Sassafras Mountain	3,560	Atlantic Ocean	Sea level
South Dakota	2,200	Harney Peak	7,242	Big Stone Lake	966
Tennessee	900	Clingmans Dome	6,643	Mississippi River	178[5]
Texas	1,700	Guadalupe Peak	8,749	Gulf of Mexico	Sea level
Utah	6,100	Kings Peak	13,528	Beaverdam Wash	2,000
Vermont	1,000	Mount Mansfield	4,393	Lake Champlain	95
Virginia	950	Mount Rogers	5,729	Atlantic Ocean	Sea level
Washington	1,700	Mount Rainier	14,411	Pacific Ocean	Sea level
West Virginia	1,500	Spruce Knob	4,861	Potomac River	240
Wisconsin	1,050	Timms Hill	1,951	Lake Michigan	579[5]
Wyoming	6,700	Gannett Peak	13,804	Belle Fourche River	3,099
United States	2,500	Mount McKinley (Alaska)	20,320	Death Valley (California)	282[3]

1. Approximate mean altitude. 2. National Geodetic Survey. 3. Below sea level. 4. Walton County. 5. Corps of Engineers 6. Osceola County. 7. State Surveys *Source:* Department of the Interior, U.S. Geological Survey.

The Continental Divide

The Continental Divide is a ridge of high ground which runs irregularly north and south through the Rocky Mountains and separates eastward-flowing from westward-flowing streams. The waters which flow eastward empty into the Atlantic Ocean, chiefly by way of the Gulf of Mexico; those which flow westward empty into the Pacific.

Mason and Dixon's Line

Mason and Dixon's Line (often called the Mason-Dixon Line) is the boundary between Pennsylvania and Maryland, running at a north latitude of 39°43'19.11". The greater part of it was surveyed from 1763–67 by Charles Mason and Jeremiah Dixon, English astronomers who had been appointed to settle a dispute between the colonies. As the line was partly the boundary between the free and the slave states, it has come to signify the division between the North and the South.

Latitude and Longitude of U.S. and Canadian Cities

(and time corresponding to 12:00 noon, eastern standard time)

City	Lat. °	Lat. ′	Long. °	Long. ′	Time	City	Lat. °	Lat. ′	Long. °	Long. ′	Time
Albany, N.Y.	42	40	73	45	12:00 noon	Memphis, Tenn	35	9	90	3	11:00 a.m.
Albuquerque, N.M.	35	05	106	39	10:00 a.m.	Miami, Fla.	25	46	80	12	12:00 noon
Amarillo, Tex.	35	11	101	50	11:00 a.m.	Milwaukee	43	2	87	55	11:00 a.m.
Anchorage, Alaska	61	13	149	54	7:00 a.m.	Minneapolis	44	59	93	14	11:00 a.m.
Atlanta	33	45	84	23	12:00 noon	Mobile, Ala.	30	42	88	3	11:00 a.m.
Austin, Tex.	30	16	97	44	11:00 a.m.	Montgomery, Ala.	32	21	86	18	11:00 a.m.
Baker, Ore.	44	47	117	50	9:00 a.m.	Montpelier, Vt.	44	15	72	32	12:00 noon
Baltimore	39	18	76	38	12:00 noon	Montreal, Que.	45	30	73	35	12:00 noon
Bangor, Me.	44	48	68	47	12:00 noon	Moose Jaw, Sask.	50	37	105	31	10:00 a.m.
Birmingham, Ala.	33	30	86	50	11:00 a.m.	Nashville, Tenn.	36	10	86	47	11:00 a.m.
Bismarck, N.D.	46	48	100	47	11:00 a.m.	Nelson, B.C.	49	30	117	17	9:00 a.m.
Boise, Idaho	43	36	116	13	10:00 a.m.	Newark, N.J.	40	44	74	10	12:00 noon
Boston	42	21	71	5	12:00 noon	New Haven, Conn.	41	19	72	55	12:00 noon
Buffalo, N.Y.	42	55	78	50	12:00 noon	New Orleans	29	57	90	4	11:00 a.m.
Calgary, Alberta	51	1	114	1	10:00 a.m.	New York	40	47	73	58	12:00 noon
Carlsbad, N.M.	32	26	104	15	10:00 a.m.	Nome, Alaska	64	25	165	30	6:00 a.m.
Charleston, S.C.	32	47	79	56	12:00 noon	Oakland, Calif.	37	48	122	16	9:00 a.m.
Charleston, W. Va.	38	21	81	38	12:00 noon	Oklahoma City	35	26	97	28	11:00 a.m.
Charlotte, N.C.	35	14	80	50	12:00 noon	Omaha, Neb.	41	15	95	56	11:00 a.m.
Cheyenne, Wyo.	41	9	104	52	10:00 a.m.	Ottawa, Ont.	45	24	75	43	12:00 noon
Chicago	41	50	87	37	11:00 a.m.	Philadelphia	39	57	75	10	12:00 noon
Cincinnati	39	8	84	30	12:00 noon	Phoenix, Ariz.	33	29	112	4	10:00 a.m.
Cleveland	41	28	81	37	12:00 noon	Pierre, S.D.	44	22	100	21	11:00 a.m.
Columbia, S.C.	34	0	81	2	12:00 noon	Pittsburgh	40	27	79	57	12:00 noon
Columbus, Ohio	40	0	83	1	12:00 noon	Port Arthur, Ont.	48	30	89	17	12:00 noon
Dallas	32	46	96	46	11:00 a.m.	Portland, Me.	43	40	70	15	12:00 noon
Denver	39	45	105	0	10:00 a.m.	Portland, Ore.	45	31	122	41	9:00 a.m.
Des Moines, Iowa	41	35	93	37	11:00 a.m.	Providence, R.I.	41	50	71	24	12:00 noon
Detroit	42	20	83	3	12:00 noon	Quebec, Que.	46	49	71	11	12:00 noon
Dubuque, Iowa	42	31	90	40	11:00 a.m.	Raleigh, N.C.	35	46	78	39	12:00 noon
Duluth, Minn.	46	49	92	5	11:00 a.m.	Reno, Nev.	39	30	119	49	9:00 a.m.
Eastport, Me.	44	54	67	0	12:00 noon	Richfield, Utah	38	46	112	5	10:00 a.m.
El Centro, Calif.	32	38	115	33	9:00 a.m.	Richmond, Va.	37	33	77	29	12:00 noon
El Paso	31	46	106	29	10:00 a.m.	Roanoke, Va.	37	17	79	57	12:00 noon
Eugene, Ore.	44	3	123	5	9:00 a.m.	Sacramento, Calif.	38	35	121	30	9:00 a.m.
Fargo, N.D.	46	52	96	48	11:00 a.m.	St. John, N.B.	45	18	66	10	1:00 p.m.
Flagstaff, Ariz.	35	13	111	41	10:00 a.m.	St. Louis	38	35	90	12	11:00 a.m.
Fort Worth, Tex.	32	43	97	19	11:00 a.m.	Salt Lake City, Utah	40	46	111	54	10:00 a.m.
Fresno, Calif.	36	44	119	48	9:00 a.m.	San Antonio	29	23	98	33	11:00 a.m.
Grand Junction, Colo.	39	5	108	33	10:00 a.m.	San Diego, Calif.	32	42	117	10	9:00 a.m.
Grand Rapids, Mich.	42	58	85	40	12:00 noon	San Francisco	37	47	122	26	9:00 a.m.
Havre, Mont.	48	33	109	43	10:00 a.m.	San Jose, Calif.	37	20	121	53	9:00 a.m.
Helena, Mont.	46	35	112	2	10:00 a.m.	San Juan, P.R.	18	30	66	10	1:00 p.m.
Honolulu	21	18	157	50	7:00 a.m.	Santa Fe, N.M.	35	41	105	57	10:00 a.m.
Hot Springs, Ark.	34	31	93	3	11:00 a.m.	Savannah, Ga.	32	5	81	5	12:00 noon
Houston, Tex.	29	45	95	21	11:00 a.m.	Seattle	47	37	122	20	9:00 a.m.
Idaho Falls, Idaho	43	30	112	1	10:00 a.m.	Shreveport, La.	32	28	93	42	11:00 a.m.
Indianapolis	39	46	86	10	12:00 noon	Sioux Falls, S.D.	43	33	96	44	11:00 a.m.
Jackson, Miss.	32	20	90	12	11:00 a.m.	Sitka, Alaska	57	10	135	15	9:00 a.m.
Jacksonville, Fla.	30	22	81	40	12:00 noon	Spokane, Wash.	47	40	117	26	9:00 a.m.
Juneau, Alaska	58	18	134	24	9:00 a.m.	Springfield, Ill.	39	48	89	38	11:00 a.m.
Kansas City, Mo.	39	6	94	35	11:00 a.m.	Springfield, Mass.	42	6	72	34	12:00 noon
Key West, Fla.	24	33	81	48	12:00 noon	Springfield, Mo.	37	13	93	17	11:00 a.m.
Kingston, Ont.	44	15	76	30	12:00 noon	Syracuse, N.Y.	43	2	76	8	12:00 noon
Klamath Falls, Ore.	42	10	121	44	9:00 a.m.	Tampa, Fla.	27	57	82	27	12:00 noon
Knoxville, Tenn.	35	57	83	56	12:00 noon	Toledo, Ohio	41	39	83	33	12:00 noon
Las Vegas, Nev.	36	10	115	12	9:00 a.m.	Toronto, Ont.	43	40	79	24	12:00 noon
Lewiston, Idaho	46	24	117	2	9:00 a.m.	Tulsa, Okla.	36	09	95	59	11:00 a.m.
Lincoln, Neb.	40	50	96	40	11:00 a.m.	Victoria, B.C.	48	25	123	21	9:00 a.m.
London, Ont.	43	2	81	34	12:00 noon	Virginia Beach, Va.	36	51	75	58	12:00 noon
Long Beach, Calif.	33	46	118	11	9:00 a.m.	Washington, D.C.	38	53	77	02	12:00 noon
Los Angeles	34	3	118	15	9:00 a.m.	Wichita, Kan.	37	43	97	17	11:00 a.m.
Louisville, Ky.	38	15	85	46	12:00 noon	Wilmington, N.C.	34	14	77	57	12:00 noon
Manchester, N.H.	43	0	71	30	12:00 noon	Winnipeg, Man.	49	54	97	7	11:00 a.m.

Named Summits in the U.S. Over 14,000 Feet Above Sea Level

Name	State	Height	Name	State	Height	Name	State	Height
Mt. McKinley	Alaska	20,320	Castle Peak	Colo.	14,265	Mt. Eolus	Colo.	14,083
Mt. St. Elias	Alaska	18,008	Quandary Peak	Colo.	14,265	Windom Peak	Colo.	14,082
Mt. Foraker	Alaska	17,400	Mt. Evans	Colo.	14,264	Mt. Columbia	Colo.	14,073
Mt. Bona	Alaska	16,500	Longs Peak	Colo.	14,255	Mt. Augusta	Alaska	14,070
Mt. Blackburn	Alaska	16,390	Mt. Wilson	Colo.	14,246	Missouri Mtn.	Colo.	14,067
Mt. Sanford	Alaska	16,237	White Mtn.	Calif.	14,246	Humboldt Peak	Colo.	14,064
Mt. Vancouver	Alaska	15,979	North Palisade	Calif.	14,242	Mt. Bierstadt	Colo.	14,060
South Buttress	Alaska	15,885	Mt. Cameron	Colo.	14,238	Sunlight Peak	Colo.	14,059
Mt. Churchill	Alaska	15,638	Shavano Peak	Colo.	14,229	Split Mtn.	Calif.	14,058
Mt. Fairweather	Alaska	15,300	Crestone Needle	Colo.	14,197	Handies Peak	Colo.	14,048
Mt. Hubbard	Alaska	14,950	Mt. Belford	Colo.	14,197	Culebra Peak	Colo.	14,047
Mt. Bear	Alaska	14,831	Mt. Princeton	Colo.	14,197	Mt. Lindsey	Colo.	14,042
East Buttress	Alaska	14,730	Mt. Yale	Colo.	14,196	Ellingwood Point	Colo.	14,042
Mt. Hunter	Alaska	14,573	Mt. Bross	Colo.	14,172	Little Bear Peak	Colo.	14,037
Browne Tower	Alaska	14,530	Kit Carson Mtn.	Colo.	14,165	Mt. Sherman	Colo.	14,036
Mt. Alverstone	Alaska	14,500	Mt. Wrangell	Alaska	14,163	Redcloud Peak	Colo.	14,034
Mt. Whitney	Calif.	14,494 [1]	Mt. Shasta	Calif.	14,162	Mt. Langley	Calif.	14,026
University Peak	Alaska	14,470	El Diente Peak	Colo.	14,159	Conundrum Peak	Colo.	14,022
Mt. Elbert	Colo.	14,433	Point Success	Wash.	14,158	Mt. Tyndall	Calif.	14,019
Mt. Massive	Colo.	14,421	Maroon Peak	Colo.	14,156	Pyramid Peak	Colo.	14,018
Mt. Harvard	Colo.	14,420	Tabeguache Mtn.	Colo.	14,155	Wilson Peak	Colo.	14,017
Mt. Rainier	Wash.	14,411	Mt. Oxford	Colo.	14,153	Wetterhorn Peak	Colo.	14,015
Mt. Williamson	Calif.	14,370	Mt. Sill	Calif.	14,153	North Maroon Peak	Colo.	14,014
La Plata Peak	Colo.	14,361	Mt. Sneffels	Colo.	14,150	San Luis Peak	Colo.	14,014
Blanca Peak	Colo.	14,345	Mt. Democrat	Colo.	14,148	Middle Palisade	Calif.	14,012
Uncompahgre Peak	Colo.	14,309	Capitol Peak	Colo.	14,130	Mt. Muir	Calif.	14,012
Crestone Peak	Colo.	14,294	Liberty Cap	Wash.	14,112	Mt. of the Holy Cross	Colo.	14,005
Mt. Lincoln	Colo.	14,286	Pikes Peak	Colo.	14,110	Huron Peak	Colo.	14,003
Grays Peak	Colo.	14,270	Snowmass Mtn.	Colo.	14,092	Thunderbolt Peak	Calif.	14,003
Mt. Antero	Colo.	14,269	Mt. Russell	Calif.	14,088	Sunshine Peak	Colo.	14,001
Torreys Peak	Colo.	14,267						

1. National Geodetic Survey. *Source:* Department of the Interior, U.S. Geological Survey.

Rivers of the United States

(350 or more miles long)

Alabama-Coosa (600 mi.; 966 km): From junction of Oostanula and Etowah R. in Georgia to Mobile R.

Altamaha-Ocmulgee (392 mi.; 631 km): From junction of Yellow R. and South R., Newton Co. in Georgia to Atlantic Ocean.

Apalachicola-Chattahoochee (524 mi.; 843 km): From Towns Co. in Georgia to Gulf of Mexico in Florida.

Arkansas (1,459 mi.; 2,348 km): From Lake Co. in Colorado to Mississippi R. in Arkansas.

Brazos (923 mi.; 1,490 km): From junction of Salt Fork and Double Mountain Fork in Texas to Gulf of Mexico.

Canadian (906 mi.; 1,458 km): From Las Animas Co. in Colorado to Arkansas R. in Oklahoma.

Cimarron (600 mi.; 966 km): From Colfax Co. in New Mexico to Arkansas R. in Oklahoma.

Colorado (1,450 mi.; 2,333 km): From Rocky Mountain National Park in Colorado to Gulf of California in Mexico.

Colorado (862 mi.; 1,387 km): From Dawson Co. in Texas to Matagorda Bay.

Columbia (1,243 mi.; 2,000 km): From Columbia Lake in British Columbia to Pacific Ocean (entering between Oregon and Washington).

Colville (350 mi.; 563 km): From Brooks Range in Alaska to Beaufort Sea.

Connecticut (407 mi.; 655 km): From Third Connecticut Lake in New Hampshire to Long Island Sound in Connecticut.

Cumberland (720 mi.; 1,159 km): From junction of Poor and Clover Forks in Harlan Co. in Kentucky to Ohio R.

Delaware (390 mi.; 628 km): From Schoharie Co. in New York to Liston Point, Delaware Bay.

Gila (649 mi.; 1,044 km): From Catron Co. in New Mexico to Colorado R. in Arizona.

Green (360 mi.; 579 km): From Lincoln Co. in Kentucky to Ohio R. in Kentucky.

Green (730 mi.; 1,175 km): From Sublette Co. in Wyoming to Colorado R. in Utah.

Illinois (420 mi.; 676 km): From St. Joseph Co. in Indiana to Mississippi R. at Grafton in Illinois.

James (sometimes called *Dakota*) (710 mi.; 1,143 km): From Wells Co. in North Dakota to Missouri R. in South Dakota.

Kanawha-New (352 mi.; 566 km): From junction of North and South Forks of New R. in North Carolina, through Virginia and West Virginia (New River becoming Kanawha River), to Ohio River.

Koyukuk (470 mi.; 756 km): From Brooks Range in Alaska to Yukon R.

Kuskokwim (724 mi.; 1,165 km): From Alaska Range in Alaska to Kuskokwim Bay.

Licking (350 mi.; 563 km): From Magoffin Co. in Kentucky to Ohio R. at Cincinnati in Ohio.

Little Missouri (560 mi.; 901 km): From Crook Co. in Wyoming to Missouri R. in North Dakota.

Milk (625 mi.; 1,006 km): From junction of forks in Alberta Province to Missouri R.

Mississippi (2,340 mi.; 3,766 km): From Lake Itasca in Minnesota to mouth of Southwest Pass in La.

Mississippi-Missouri-Red Rock (3,710 mi.; 5,970 km): From source of Red Rock R. in Montana to mouth of Southwest Pass in Louisiana.

Missouri (2,315 mi.; 3,726 km): From junction of Jefferson R., Gallatin R., and Madison R. in Montana to Mississippi R. near St. Louis.

Missouri-Red Rock (2,540 mi.; 4,090 km): From source of Red Rock R. in Montana to Mississippi R. near St. Louis.

Mobile-Alabama-Coosa (645 mi.; 1,040 km): From junction of Etowah R. and Oostanula R. in Georgia to Mobile Bay.

Neosho (460 mi.; 740 km): From Morris Co. in Kansas to Arkansas R. in Oklahoma.

Niobrara (431 mi.; 694 km): From Niobrara Co. in Wyoming to Missouri R. in Nebraska.

Noatak (350 mi.; 563 km): From Brooks Range in Alaska to Kotzebue Sound.

North Canadian (800 mi.; 1,290 km): From Union Co. in New Mexico to Canadian R. in Oklahoma.

North Platte (618 mi.; 995 km): From Jackson Co. in Colorado to junction with So. Platte R. in Nebraska to form Platte R.

Ohio (981 mi.; 1,579 km): From junction of Allegheny R. and Monongahela R. at Pittsburgh to Mississippi R. between Illinois and Kentucky.

Ohio-Allegheny (1,306 mi.; 2,102 km): From Potter Co. in Pennsylvania to Mississippi R. at Cairo in Illinois.

Osage (500 mi.; 805 km): From east-central Kansas to Missouri R. near Jefferson City in Missouri.

Ouachita (605 mi.; 974 km): From Polk Co. in Arkansas to Red R. in Louisiana.

Pearl (411 mi.; 661 km): From Neshoba County in Mississippi to Gulf of Mexico (Mississippi-Louisiana).

Pecos (926 mi.; 1,490 km): From Mora Co. in New Mexico to Rio Grande in Texas.

Pee Dee-Yadkin (435 mi.; 700 km): From Watauga Co. in North Carolina to Winyah Bay in South Carolina.

Pend Oreille-Clark Fork (531 mi.; 855 km): Near Butte in Montana to Columbia R. on Washington-Canada border.

Porcupine (569 mi.; 916 km): From Yukon Territory, Canada, to Yukon R. in Alaska.

Potomac (383 mi.; 616 km): From Garrett Co. in Md. to Chesapeake Bay at Point Lookout in Md.

Powder (375 mi.; 603 km): From junction of forks in Johnson Co. in Wyoming to Yellowstone R. in Montana.

Red (1,290 mi.; 2,080 km): From source of Tierra Blanca Creek in Curry County, New Mexico to Mississippi R. in Louisiana.

Red (also called *Red River of the North*) (545 mi.; 877 km): From junction of Otter Tail R. and Bois de Sioux R. in Minnesota to Lake Winnipeg in Manitoba.

Republican (445 mi.; 716 km): From junction of North Fork and Arikaree R. in Nebraska to junction with Smoky Hill R. in Kansas to form the Kansas R.

Rio Grande (1,900 mi.; 3,060 km): From San Juan Co. in Colorado to Gulf of Mexico.

Roanoke (380 mi.; 612 km): From junction of forks in Montgomery Co. in Virginia to Albemarle Sound in North Carolina.

Sabine (380 mi.; 612 km): From junction of forks in Hunt Co. in Texas to Sabine Lake between Texas and Louisiana.

Sacramento (377 mi.; 607 km): From Siskiyou Co. in California to Suisun Bay.

Saint Francis (425 mi.; 684 km): From Iron Co. in Missouri to Mississippi R. in Arkansas.

Salmon (420 mi.; 676 km): From Custer Co. in Idaho to Snake R.

San Joaquin (350 mi.; 563 km): From junction of forks in Madera Co. in California to Suisun Bay.

San Juan (360 mi.; 579 km): From Archuleta Co. in Colorado to Colorado R. in Utah.

Santee-Wateree-Catawba (538 mi.; 866 km): From McDowell Co. in North Carolina to Atlantic Ocean in South Carolina.

Smoky Hill (540 mi.; 869 km): From Cheyenne Co. in Colorado to junction with Republican R. in Kansas to form Kansas R.

Snake (1,038 mi.; 1,670 km): From Ocean Plateau in Wyoming to Columbia R. in Washington.

South Platte (424 mi.; 682 km): From Park Co. in Colorado to junction with North Platte R. in Nebraska to form Platte R.

Susquehanna (444 mi.; 715 km): From Otsego Lake in New York to Chesapeake Bay in Maryland.

Tanana (659 mi.; 1,060 km): From Wrangell Mts. in Yukon Territory, Canada, to Yukon R. in Alaska.

Tennessee (652 mi.; 1,049 km): From junction of Holston R. and French Broad R. in Tennessee to Ohio R. in Kentucky.

Tennessee-French Broad (870 mi.; 1,400 km): From Bland Co. in Virginia to Ohio R. at Paducah in Kentucky.

Tombigbee (525 mil; 845 km): From junction of forks in Itawamba Co. in Mississippi to Mobile R. in Alabama.

Trinity (360 mi.; 579 km): From junction of forks in Dallas Co. in Texas to Galveston Bay.

Wabash (512 mi.; 824 km): From Darke Co. in Ohio to Ohio R. between Illinois and Indiana.

Washita (500 mi.; 805 km): From Hemphill Co. in Texas to Red R. in Oklahoma.

White (722 mi.; 1,160 km): From Madison Co. in Arkansas to Mississippi R.

Wisconsin (430 mi.; 692 km): From Vilas Co. in Wisconsin to Mississippi R.

Yellowstone (692 mi.; 1,110 km): From Park Co. in Wyoming to Missouri R. in North Dakota.

Yukon (1,979 mi.; 3,185 km): From junction of Lewes R. and Pelly R. in Yukon Territory, Canada, to Bering Sea in Alaska.

U.S. STATES & CITIES

States and Territories

Sources for state populations, populations under 18, over 65, median age, largest cities and counties, and population by race are latest data provided by the U.S. Census Bureau. NOTE: Persons of Hispanic origin can be of any race. The population counts set forth herein by the Census Bureau are subject to possible correction for undercount or overcount. They include Armed Forces residing in each state. Largest cities include incorporated places only, as defined by the U.S. Census Bureau. They do not include adjacent or suburban areas as do the Metropolitan Statistical Areas found in the "U.S. Statistics" section. For secession and readmission dates of the former Confederate states, *see* Index.

ALABAMA

Capital: Montgomery
Governor: Billy Joe Camp, D
Organized as territory: March 3, 1817
Entered Union & (rank): Dec. 14, 1819 (22)
Present constitution adopted: 1901
Motto: *Audemus jura nostra defendere* (We dare defend our rights)
STATE SYMBOLS: flower, Camellia (1959); **bird,** Yellowhammer (1927); **song,** "Alabama" (1931); **tree,** Southern pine (longleaf) (1949); **salt water fish,** Tarpon (1955); **fresh water fish,** Largemouth bass (1975); **horse,** Racking horse; **mineral,** Hematite (1967); **rock,** Marble (1969); **game bird,** Wild turkey (1980); **dance,** Square dance (1981); **nut,** Pecan (1982); **fossil,** species *Basilosaurus Cetoides* (1984).
Nickname: Yellowhammer State
Origin of name: May come from Choctaw meaning "thicket-clearers" or "vegetation-gatherers"
10 largest cities (1990 census): Birmingham, 265,968; Mobile, 196,278; Montgomery, 187,106; Huntsville, 159,789; Tuscaloosa, 77,759; Dothan, 53,589; Decatur, 48,761; Gadsden, 42,523; Hoover, 39,788; Florence, 36,426
Land area & (rank): 50,767 sq mi. (131,487 sq km) (28)
Geographic center: In Chilton Co., 12 mi. SW of Clanton
Number of counties: 67
Largest county (1990 census): Jefferson, 651,525
State forests: 21 (48,000 ac.)
State parks: 22 (45,614 ac.)
1980 resident census population & (rank): 3,893,888 (22)
1990 census population, sex, & (rank): 4,040,587 (22).
Male: 1,936,162; **Female:** 2,104,425. **White:** 2,975,797 (73.6%); **Black:** 1,020,705 (25.3%); **American Indian, Eskimo, or Aleut:** 16,506 (0.4%); **Asian or Pacific Islander:** 21,797 (0.5%); **Other race:** 5,782 (0.1%); **Hispanic:** 24,629 (0.6%). **1990 percent population under 18:** 26.2; **65 and over:** 12.9; **median age:** 33.0.

Spanish explorers are believed to have arrived at Mobile Bay in 1519, and the territory was visited in 1540 by the explorer Hernando de Soto. The first permanent European settlement in Alabama was founded by the French at Fort Louis in 1702. The British gained control of the area in 1763 by the Treaty of Paris, but had to cede almost all the Alabama region to the U.S. after the American Revolution. The Confederacy was founded at Montgomery in February 1861 and, for a time, the city was the Confederate capital.

During the last part of the 19th century, the economy of the state slowly improved. At Tuskegee Institute, founded in 1881 by Booker T. Washington, Dr. George Washington Carver carried out his famous agricultural research.

In the 1950s and '60s, Alabama was the site of such landmark civil-rights actions as the bus boycott in Montgomery (1955–56) and the "Freedom March" from Selma to Montgomery (1965).

Today paper, chemicals, rubber and plastics, apparel and textiles, and primary metals comprise the leading industries of Alabama. Continuing as a major manufacturer of coal, iron, and steel, Birmingham is also noted for its world-renowned medical center, especially for heart surgery. The state ranks high in the production of poultry, soybeans, milk, vegetables, livestock, wheat, cattle, cotton, peanuts, fruits, hogs, and corn.

Points of interest include the Space and Rocket Center at Huntsville, the White House of the Confederacy, and Shakespeare Festival Theater Complex in Montgomery, and Russell Cave near Bridgeport, and the Gulf Coast area.

ALASKA

Capital: Juneau
Governor: Walter J. Hickel, Ind-R[1]
Organized as territory: 1912
Entered Union & (rank): Jan. 3, 1959 (49)
Constitution ratified: April 24, 1956
Motto: North to the Future
STATE SYMBOLS: flower, Forget-me-not (1949); **tree,** Sitka spruce (1962); **bird,** Willow ptarmigan (1955); **fish,** King salmon (1962); **song,** "Alaska's Flag" (1955); **gem,** Jade (1968); **marine mammal,** Bowhead Whale (1983); **fossil,** Woolly Mammoth (1986); **mineral,** Gold (1968); **sport,** Dog Mushing (1972)
Nickname: The state is commonly called "The Last Frontier" or "Land of the Midnight Sun"
Origin of name: Corruption of Aleut word meaning "great land" or "that which the sea breaks against"
10 largest cities (1990 census): Anchorage, 226,338; Fairbanks, 30,843; Juneau, 26,751; Sitka, 8,588; Ketchikan, 8,263; Kodiak, 6,365; Kenai, 4,028
Land area & (rank): 570,833 sq mi (1,478,458 sq km) (1)
Geographic center: 60 mi. NW of Mt. McKinley
Number of boroughs: 12
Largest borough (1990 census): Fairbanks North Star, 77,720
State forests: None
State parks: 5; 59 waysides and areas (3.3 million ac.)
1980 resident census population & (rank): 401,851 (50)
1990 resident census population, sex, & (rank): 550,043 (49). **Male:** 289,867; **Female:** 260,176. **White:** 415,492 (75.5%); **Black:** 22,451 (4.1%); **American Indian, Eskimo, or Aleut:** 85,698 (15.6%); **Asian or Pacific Islander:** 19,728 (3.6%); **Other race:** 6,674 (1.2%); **Hispanic:** 17,803 (3.2%). **1990 percent population under 18:** 31.3; **65 and over:** 4.1; **median age:** 29..4

1. Independent–Republican.

35

Vitus Bering, a Dane working for the Russians, and Alexei Chirikov discovered the Alaskan mainland and the Aleutian Islands in 1741. The tremendous land mass of Alaska—equal to one fifth of the continental U.S.—was unexplored in 1867 when Secretary of State William Seward arranged for its purchase from the Russians for $7,200,000. The transfer of the territory took place on Oct. 18, 1867. Despite a price of about two cents an acre, the purchase was widely ridiculed as "Seward's Folly." The first official census (1880) reported a total of 33,426 Alaskans, all but 430 being of aboriginal stock. The Gold Rush of 1898 resulted in a mass influx of more than 30,000 people. Since then, Alaska has returned billions of dollars' worth of products to the U.S.

In 1968, a large oil and gas reservoir near Prudhoe Bay on the Arctic Coast was found. The Prudhoe Bay reservoir, with an estimated recoverable 10 billion barrels of oil and 27 trillion cubic feet of gas, is twice as large as any other oil field in North America. The Trans-Alaska pipeline was completed in 1977 at a cost of $7.7 billion. On June 20, oil started flowing through the 800-mile-long pipeline from Prudhoe Bay to the port of Valdez.

Other industries important to Alaska's economy are fisheries, wood and wood products, and furs, and tourism.

Denali National Park and Mendenhall Glacier in North Tongass National Forest are of interest, as is the large totem pole collection at Sitka National Historical Park. The Katmai National Park includes the "Valley of Ten Thousand Smokes," an area of active volcanoes.

ARIZONA

Capital: Phoenix
Governor: Fife Symington, R
Organized as territory: Feb. 24, 1863
Entered Union & (rank): Feb. 14, 1912 (48)
Present constitution adopted: 1911
Motto: *Ditat Deus* (God enriches)
STATE SYMBOLS: flower: Flower of saguaro cactus (1931); **bird:** Cactus wren (1931); **colors:** Blue and old gold (1915); **song:** "Arizona March Song" (1919); **tree:** Palo Verde (1957); **neckwear,** Bolo tie (1973); **fossil,** Petrified wood (1988); **gemstone,** Turquoise (1974); **animals, mammal,** Ringtail; **reptile,** Arizona ridgenose rattlesnake; **fish,** Arizona trout; **amphibian,** Arizona tree frog (1986)
Nickname: Grand Canyon State
Origin of name: From the Indian "Arizonac," meaning "little spring"
10 largest cities (1990 census): Phoenix, 983,403; Tucson, 405,390; Mesa, 288,091; Glendale, 148,134; Tempe, 141,865; Scottsdale, 130,069; Chandler, 90,533; Yuma, 54,923; Peoria, 50,618; Flagstaff, 45,857
Land area & (rank): 113,508 sq mi. (293,986 sq km) (6)
Geographic center: In Yavapai Co., 55 mi. ESE of Prescott
Number of counties: 15
Largest county (1990 census): Maricopa, 2,122,101
State forests: None
State parks: 24
1980 resident census population & (rank): 2,718,215 (29)
1990 resident census population, sex, & (rank): 3,665,228 (24). **Male:** 1,810,691; **Female:** 1,854,537. **White:** 2,963,186 (80.8%); **Black:** 110,524 (3.0%); **American Indian, Eskimo, or Aleut:** 203,527 (5.6%); **Asian or Pacific Islander:** 55,206 (1.5%); **Other race:** 332,785 (9.1%); **Hispanic:** 688,338 (18.8%). **1990 percent population under 18:** 26.8; **65 and over:** 13.1; **median age:** 32.2

Marcos de Niza, a Spanish Franciscan friar, was the first European to explore Arizona. He entered the area in 1539 in search of the mythical Seven Cities of Gold. Although he was followed a year later by another gold seeker, Francisco Vásquez de Coronado, most of the early settlement was for missionary purposes. In 1776 the Spanish established Fort Tucson. In 1848, after the Mexican War, most of the Arizona territory became part of the U.S., and the southern portion of the territory was added by the Gadsden Purchase in 1853.

In 1973 the world's biggest dam, the New Cornelia Tailings, was completed near Ajo.

Arizona history is rich in legends of America's Old West. It was here that the great Indian chiefs Geronimo and Cochise led their people against the frontiersmen. Tombstone, Ariz., was the site of the West's most famous shoot-out—the gunfight at the O.K. Corral. Today, Arizona has the largest U.S. Indian population; more than 14 tribes are represented on 19 reservations.

Manufacturing has become Arizona's most important industry. Principal products include electrical, communications, and aeronautical items. The state produces over half the country's copper. Agriculture is also important to the state's economy.

State attractions include such famous scenery as the Grand Canyon, the Petrified Forest, and the Painted Desert. Hoover Dam, Lake Mead, Fort Apache, and the reconstructed London Bridge at Lake Havasu City are of particular interest.

ARKANSAS

Capital: Little Rock
Governor: Bill Clinton, D
Organized as territory: March 2, 1819
Entered Union & (rank): June 15, 1836 (25)
Present constitution adopted: 1874
Motto: *Regnat populus* (The people rule)
STATE SYMBOLS: flower, Apple Blossom (1901); **tree,** Pine (1939); **bird,** Mockingbird (1929); **insect,** Honeybee (1973); **song,** "Arkansas" (1963)
Nickname: Land of Opportunity
Origin of name: From the Quapaw Indians
10 largest cities (1990 census): Little Rock, 175,795; Fort Smith, 72,798; North Little Rock, 61,741; Pine Bluff, 57,140; Jonesboro, 46,535; Fayetteville, 42,099; Hot Springs, 32,462; Springdale, 29,941; Jacksonville, 29,101; West Memphis, 28,259
Land area & (rank): 52,078 sq mi. (134,883 sq km) (27)
Geographic center: In Pulaski Co., 12 mi. NW of Little Rock
Number of counties: 75
Largest county (1990 census): Pulaski, 349,660
State forests: None
State parks: 44
1980 resident census population & (rank): 2,286,435 (33)
1990 resident population, sex, & rank: 2,350,725 (33). **Male:** 1,133,076; **Female:** 1,217,649. **White:** 1,944,744 (82.7%); **Black:** 373,912 (15.9%); **American Indian, Eskimo, or Aleut:** 12,773 (0.5%); **Asian or Pacific Islander:** 12,530 (0.5%); **Other race:** 6,766 (0.3%); **Hispanic:** 19,876 (0.8%). **1990 percent population under 18:** 26.4; **65 and over:** 14.9; **median age:** 33.8.

Hernando de Soto, in 1541, was among the early European explorers to visit the territory. It was a Frenchman, Henri de Tonti, who in 1686 founded the first permanent white settlement—the Arkansas Post. In 1803 the area was acquired by the U.S. as part of the Louisiana Purchase.

Food products are the state's largest employing sector, with lumber and wood products a close second. Arkansas is also a leader in the production of cotton, rice, and soybeans. The state produces 97% of the nation's high-grade domestic bauxite ore—the source of aluminum. It also has the country's only active diamond mine; located near Murfreesboro, it is operated as a tourist attraction.

Hot Springs National Park, and Buffalo National River in the Ozarks are major state attractions.

Blanchard Springs Caverns, the Arkansas Territorial Restoration at Little Rock, and the Arkansas Folk Center in Mountain View are of interest.

CALIFORNIA

Capital: Sacramento
Governor: Pete Wilson, R
Entered Union & (rank): Sept. 9, 1850 (31)
Present constitution adopted: 1879
Motto: *Eureka* (I have found it)
STATE SYMBOLS: flower, Golden poppy (1903); **tree,** California redwoods (*Sequoia sempervirens & Sequoia gigantea)* (1937 & 1953); **bird,** California valley quail (1931); **animal,** California grizzly bear (1953); **fish,** California golden trout (1947); **colors,** Blue and gold (1951); **song,** "I Love You, California" (1951)
Nickname: Golden State
Origin of name: From a book, *Las Sergas de Esplandián,* by Garcia Ordóñez de Montalvo, c. 1500
10 largest cities (1990 census): Los Angeles, 3,485,398; San Diego, 1,110,549; San Jose, 782,248; San Francisco, 723,959; Long Beach, 429,433; Oakland, 372,242; Sacramento, 369,365; Fresno, 354,202; Santa Ana, 293,742; Anaheim, 266,406
Land area & (rank): 156,299 sq mi. (404,815 sq km) (3)
Geographic center: In Madera Co., 35 mi. NE of Madera
Number of counties: 58
Largest county (1990 census): Los Angeles, 8,863,164
State forests: 8 (70,283 ac.)
State parks and beaches: 180 (723,000 ac.)
1980 resident census population & (rank): 23,667,902 (1)
1990 resident population, sex, & (rank): 29,760,021 (1).
Male: 14,897,627; **Female:** 14,862,394. **White:** 20,524,327 (69.9%); **Black:** 2,208,801 (7.4%); **American Indian, Eskimo, or Aleut:** 242,164 (0.8%); **Asian or Pacific Islander,** 2,845,659 (9.6%); **Other race:** 3,939,070 (13.2%); **Hispanic,** 7,687,938 (25.8%). **1990 percent population under 18:** 26.0; **65 and over:** 10.5; **median age:** 31.5.

Although California was sighted by Spanish navigator Juan Rodríguez Cabrillo in 1542, its first Spanish mission (at San Diego) was not established until 1769. California became a U.S. Territory in 1847 when Mexico surrendered it to John C. Frémont. On Jan. 24, 1848, James W. Marshall discovered gold at Sutter's Mill, starting the California Gold Rush and bringing settlers to the state in large numbers.

In 1964, the U.S. Census Bureau estimated that California had become the most populous state, surpassing New York. California also leads the country in personal income and consumer expenditures.

Leading industries include manufacturing (transportation equipment, machinery, and electronic equipment), agriculture, biotechnology, and tourism. Principal natural resources include timber, petroleum, cement, and natural gas.

More immigrants settle in California than any other state—more than 30% of the nation's total in 1990.

Asian-Pacific Islanders led the influx.

Death Valley, in the southeast, is 282 feet below sea level, the lowest point in the nation; and Mt. Whitney (14,491 ft) is the highest point in the contiguous 48 states. Lassen Peak is one of two active U.S. volcanos outside of Alaska and Hawaii; its last eruptions were recorded in 1917. The General Sherman Tree in Sequoia National Park is estimated to be about 3,500 years old and a stand of bristlecone pine trees in the White Mountains may be over 4,000 years old.

Other points of interest include Yosemite National Park, Disneyland, Hollywood, the Golden Gate bridge, San Simeon State Park, and Point Reyes National Seashore.

COLORADO

Capital: Denver
Governor: Roy Romer, D
Organized as territory: Feb. 28, 1861
Entered Union & (rank): Aug. 1, 1876 (38)
Present constitution adopted: 1876
Motto: *Nil sine Numine* (Nothing without Providence)
STATE SYMBOLS: flower, Rocky Mountain columbine (1899); **tree,** Colorado blue spruce (1939); **bird,** Lark bunting (1931); **animal,** Rocky Mountain bighorn sheep (1961); **gemstone,** Aquamarine (1971); **colors,** Blue and white (1911); **song,** "Where the Columbines Grow" (1915); **fossil,** Stegosaurus (1991)
Nickname: Centennial State
Origin of name: From the Spanish, "ruddy" or "red"
10 largest cities (1990 census): Denver, 467,610; Colorado Springs, 281,140; Aurora, 222,103; Lakewood, 126,481; Pueblo, 98,640; Arvada, 89,235; Fort Collins, 87,758; Boulder, 83,312; Westminster, 74,625; Greeley, 60,536
Land area & (rank): 103,595 sq mi. (268,311 sq km) (8)
Geographic center: In Park Co., 30 mi. NW of Pikes Peak
Number of counties: 63
Largest county (1990 census): Denver, 467,610
State forests: 1 (71,000 ac.)
State parks: 44
1980 resident census population & (rank): 2,889,964 (28)
1990 resident census population, sex, & (rank): 3,294,394 (26). **Male:** 1,631,295; **Female:** 1,663,099. **White:** 2,095,474 (88.2%); **Black:** 133,146 (4.0%); **American Indian, Eskimo, or Aleut:** 27,776 (0.8%); **Asian or Pacific Islander,** 59,862 (1.8%); **Other race:** 168,136 (5.1%); **Hispanic,** 424,302 (12.9%). **1990 percent population under 18:** 26.1; **65 and over:** 10.0; **median age:** 32.5

First visited by Spanish explorers in the 1500s, the territory was claimed for Spain by Juan de Ulibarri in 1706. The U.S. obtained eastern Colorado as part of the Louisiana Purchase in 1803, the central portion in 1845 with the admission of Texas as a state, and the western part in 1848 as a result of the Mexican War.

Colorado has the highest mean elevation of any state, with more than 1,000 Rocky Mountain peaks over 10,000 feet high and 54 towering above 14,000 feet. Pikes Peak, the most famous of these mountains, was discovered by U.S. Army Lieut. Zebulon M. Pike in 1806.

Once primarily a mining and agricultural state, Colorado's economy is now driven by the service-producing industries, which provide jobs for more than four-fifths of the state's non-farm work force. In addition, tourism is extremely important to the state's economy. The ski industry accounts for approximately one-third of the state's tourism market. The main tourist attractions in the state include Rocky Mountain National Park, Curecanti National Recreation Area, Mesa Verde National Park, and the Great Sand Dunes and Dinosaur National Monuments.

The two primary facets of Colorado's manufacturing industry are advanced technology and defense.

The mining industry, which includes oil and gas, coal, and metal mining, was important to Colorado's economy, but it now employs only 1.3 percent of the state's workforce. Denver is home to companies that control half of the nation's gold production. The farm industry, which is primarily concentrated in livestock, is also an important element of the state's economy. The primary crops in Colorado are corn, hay, and wheat.

CONNECTICUT

Capital: Hartford
Governor: Lowell P. Weicker, Jr., ACP[1]
Entered Union & (rank): Jan. 9, 1788 (5)
Present constitution adopted: Dec. 30, 1965
Motto: *Qui transtulit sustinet* (He who transplanted still sustains)
STATE SYMBOLS: flower, mountain laurel (1907); **tree,** White Oak (1947); **animal,** Sperm whale (1975); **bird,** American robin (1943); **hero,** Nathan Hale (1985); **insect,** Praying mantis (1977); **mineral,** Garnet (1977); **song,** "Yankee Doodle" (1978); **ship,** USS Nautilus (SSN571) (1983)
Official designation: *Constitution State* (1959)
Nickname: Nutmeg State
Origin of name: From an Indian word (Quinnehtukqut) meaning "beside the long tidal river"
10 largest cities (1990 census): Bridgeport, 141,686; Hartford, 139,739; New Haven, 130,476; Waterbury, 108,961; Stamford, 108,056; Norwalk, 78,331; New Britain, 75,491; Danbury, 65,585; Bristol, 60,640; Meriden, 59,479
Land area & (rank): 4,872 sq mi. (12,618 km) (48)
Geographic center: In Hartford Co., at East Berlin
Number of counties: 8
Largest town (1990 census): West Hartford 60,110
State forests: 30 (139,377 ac.)
State parks: 89 (30,647 ac.)
1980 resident census population & (rank): 3,107,576 (25)
1990 resident population, sex, & (rank): 3,287,116 (27).
Male: 1,592,873; **Female:** 1,694,243. **White:** 2,859,353 (87.0%); **Black:** 274,269 (8.3%); **American Indian, Eskimo, or Aleut:** 6,654 (0.2%); **Asian or Pacific Islander:** 50,698 (1.5%); **Other race:** 96,142 (2.9%); **Hispanic:** 213,116 (6.5%). **1990 percent population under 18:** 22.8; **65 and over:** 13.6; **median age:** 34.4.

1. A Connecticut Party.

The Dutch navigator, Adriaen Block, was the first European of record to explore the area, sailing up the Connecticut River in 1614. In 1633, Dutch colonists built a trade and trading post near present-day Hartford, but soon lost control to English Puritans migrating south from the Massachusetts Bay Colony.

English settlements, established in the 1630s at Windsor, Wethersfield, and Hartford, united in 1639 to form the Connecticut Colony and adopted the *Fundamental Orders,* considered the world's first written constitution.

The colony's royal charter of 1662 was exceptionally liberal. When Gov. Edmund Andros tried to seize it in 1687, it was hidden in the Hartford Oak, commemorated in Charter Oak Place.

Connecticut played a prominent role in the Revolutionary War, serving as the Continental Army's major supplier. Sometimes called the "Arsenal of the Nation," the state became one of the most industrialized in the nation.

Today, Connecticut factories produce weapons, sewing machines, jet engines, helicopters, motors, hardware and tools, cutlery, clocks, locks, ball bearings, silverware, and submarines. Hartford, which has the oldest U.S. newspaper still being published—the *Courant,* established 1764—is the insurance capital of the nation.

Poultry, fruit, and dairy products account for the largest portion of farm income, and Connecticut shade-grown tobacco is acknowledged to be the nation's most valuable crop, per acre.

Connecticut is a popular resort area with its 250-mile Long Island Sound shoreline and many inland lakes. Among the major points of interest are Yale University's Gallery of Fine Arts and Peabody Museum. Other famous museums include the P.T. Barnum, Winchester Gun, and American Clock and Watch. The town of Mystic features a recreated 19th-century New England seaport and the Mystic Marinelife Aquarium.

DELAWARE

Capital: Dover
Governor: Michael N. Castle, R
Entered Union & (rank): Dec. 7, 1787 (1)
Present constitution adopted: 1897
Motto: Liberty and independence
STATE SYMBOLS: colors, Colonial blue and buff; **flower,** Peach blossom (1895); **tree,** American holly (1939); **bird,** Blue Hen chicken (1939); **insect,** Ladybug (1974); **fish,** Weakfish, *Cynoscion regalis* (1981); **song,** "Our Delaware"
Nicknames: Diamond State; First State; Small Wonder
Origin of name: From Delaware River and Bay; named in turn for Sir Thomas West, Lord De La Warr
10 largest cities (1990 census): Wilmington, 71,529; Dover, 27,630; Newark, 25,098; Milford, 6,040; Elsmere Town, 5,935; Seaford, 5,689; Smyrna Town, 5,213; New Castle 4,837; Middletown Town, 3,834; Georgetown Town, 3,732
Land area & (rank): 1,932 sq mi. (5,005 sq km) (49)
Geographic center: In Kent Co., 11 mi. S of Dover
Number of counties: 3
Largest county (1990 census): New Castle, 441,946
State forests: 3 (6,149 ac.)
State parks: 10
1980 resident census population & (rank): 594,338 (47)
1990 resident census population, sex, & (rank): 666,168 (46). **Male:** 322,968; **Female:** 343,200. **White:** 535,094 (80.3%); **Black:** 112,460 (16.9%); **American Indian, Eskimo, or Aleut:** 2,019 (0.3%); **Asian or Pacific Islander:** 9,057 (1.4%); **Other race:** 7,538 (1.1%); **Hispanic:** 15,820 (2.4%). **1990 percent population under 18:** 24.5; **65 and over:** 12.1; **median age:** 32.9.

Henry Hudson, sailing under the Dutch flag, is credited with Delaware's discovery in 1609. The following year, Capt. Samuel Argall of Virginia named Delaware for his colony's governor, Thomas West, Baron De La Warr. An attempted Dutch settlement failed in 1631. Swedish colonization began at Fort Christina (now Wilmington) in 1638, but New Sweden fell to Dutch forces led by New Netherlands' Gov. Peter Stuyvesant in 1655.

England took over the area in 1664 and it was transferred to William Penn as the southern Three Counties in 1682. Semiautonomous after 1704, Delaware fought as a separate state in the American Revolution and became the first state to ratify the constitution in 1787.

During the Civil War, although a slave state, Delaware did not secede from the Union.

In 1802, Éleuthère Irénée du Pont established a gunpowder mill near Wilmington that laid the foundation for Delaware's huge chemical industry. Delaware's manufactured products now also include vulcanized fiber, textiles, paper, medical supplies, metal products, machinery, machine tools, and automobiles.

Delaware also grows a great variety of fruits and vegetables and is a U.S. pioneer in the food-canning industry. Corn, soybeans, potatoes, and hay are important crops. Delaware's broiler chicken farms supply the big Eastern markets, fishing and dairy products are other important industries.

Points of interest include the Fort Christina Monument, Hagley Museum, Holy Trinity Church (erected in 1698, the oldest Protestant church in the United States still in use), and Winterthur Museum, in and near Wilmington; central New Castle, an almost unchanged late 18th-century capital; and the Delaware Museum of Natural History.

Popular recreation areas include Cape Henlopen, Delaware Seashore, Trapp Pond State Park, and Rehoboth Beach.

DISTRICT OF COLUMBIA

See listing at end of *50 Largest Cities of the United States.*

FLORIDA

Capital: Tallahassee
Governor: Lawton Chiles, D
Organized as territory: March 30, 1822
Entered Union & (rank): March 3, 1845 (27)
Present constitution adopted: 1969
Motto: In God we trust (1868)
STATE SYMBOLS: flower, Orange blossom (1909); **bird,** Mockingbird (1927); **song,** "Suwannee River" (1935)
Nickname: Sunshine State (1970)
Origin of name: From the Spanish, meaning "feast of flowers" (Easter)
10 largest cities (1990 census): Jacksonville (CC[1]), 672,971; Miami, 358,548; Tampa, 280,015; St. Petersburg, 238,629; Hialeah, 188,004; Orlando, 164,693; Fort Lauderdale, 149,377; Tallahassee, 124,773; Hollywood, 121,697; Clearwater, 98,784
Land area & (rank): 54,153 sq mi. (140,256 sq km) (26)
Geographic center: In Hernando Co., 12 mi. NNW of Brooksville
Number of counties: 67
Largest county (1990 census): Dade, 1,937,094
State forests: 3 (306,881 ac.)
State parks: 105 (215,820 ac.)
1980 resident census population & (rank): 9,746,324 (7)
1990 resident census population, sex, & (rank): 12,937,926 (4). **Male:** 6,261,719; **Female:** 6,676,207. **White:** 10,749,285 (83.1%); **Black:** 1,759,534 (13.6%); **American Indian, Eskimo, or Aleut:** 36,335 (0.3%); **Asian or Pacific Islander:** 154,302 (1.2%); **Other race:** 238,470 (1.8%); **Hispanic:** 1,574,143 (12.2%). **1990 percent population under 18:** 22.2; **65 and over:** 18.3; **median age:** 36.4.

1. Consolidated City (Coextensive with Duval County).

In 1513, Ponce De Leon, seeking the mythical "Fountain of Youth," discovered and named Florida, claiming it for Spain. Later, Florida would be held at different times by Spain and England until Spain finally sold it to the United States in 1819. (Incidentally, France established a colony named Fort Caroline in 1564 in the state that was to become Florida.)

Florida's early 19th-century history as a U.S. territory was marked by wars with the Seminole Indians that did not end until 1842, although a treaty was actually never signed.

One of the nation's fastest-growing states, Florida's population has gone from 2.8 million in 1950 to more than 12.9 million in 1990.

Florida's economy rests on a solid base of tourism (in 1989 the state entertained more than 41.7 million visitors from all over the world), manufacturing, and agriculture.

In recent years, oranges and grapefruit lead Florida's crop list, followed by vegetables, potatoes, melons, strawberries, sugar cane, dairy products, cattle and calves, and forest products.

Major tourist attractions are Miami Beach, Palm Beach, St. Augustine (founded in 1565, thus the oldest permanent city in the U.S.), Daytona Beach, and Fort Lauderdale on the East Coast. West Coast resorts include Sarasota, Tampa, Key West and St. Petersburg. Disney World, located on a 27,000-acre site near Orlando, is a popular attraction.

Also drawing many visitors are the NASA Kennedy Space Center's Spaceport USA, located in the town of Kennedy Space Center, Everglades National Park, and the Epcot Center.

GEORGIA

Capital: Atlanta
Governor: Zell Miller, D
Entered Union & (rank): Jan. 2, 1788 (4)
Present constitution adopted: 1977
Motto: Wisdom, justice, and moderation
STATE SYMBOLS: flower, Cherokee rose (1916); **tree,** Live oak (1937); **bird,** Brown thrasher (1935); **song,** "Georgia on My Mind" (1922)
Nicknames: Peach State, Empire State of the South
Origin of name: In honor of George II of England
10 largest cities (1990 census): Atlanta, 394,017; Columbus[1], 179,278; Savannah, 137,560; Macon, 106,612; Albany, 78,122; Roswell, 47,923; Athens, 45,734; Augusta, 44,639; Marietta, 44,129; Warner Robins, 43,726.
Land area & (rank): 58,910 sq mi. (152,577 sq km) (21)
Geographic center: In Twiggs Co., 18 mi. SE of Macon
Number of counties: 159
Largest county (1990 census): Fulton, 648,951
State forests: 25,258,000 ac. (67% of total state area)
State parks: 53 (42,600 ac.)
1980 resident census population & (rank): 5,463,105 (13)
1990 resident census population, sex, & (rank): 6,478,216 (11). **Male:** 3,144,503; **Female:** 3,333,713. **White:** 4,600,148 (71.0%); **Black:** 1,746,565 (27.0%); **American Indian, Eskimo, or Aleut:** 13,348 (0.2%); **Asian or Pacific Islander:** 75,781 (1.2%); **Other race:** 42,374 (0.7%); **Hispanic:** 108,922 (1.7%). **1990 percent population under 18:** 26.7; **65 and over:** 10.1; **median age:** 31.6.

1. Consolidated City (Coextensive with Muscogee County).

Hernando de Soto, the Spanish explorer, first traveled parts of Georgia in 1540. British claims later conflicted with those of Spain. After obtaining a royal charter, Gen. James Oglethorpe established the first permanent settlement in Georgia in 1733 as a refuge for English debtors. In 1742, Oglethorpe defeated Spanish invaders in the Battle of Bloody Marsh.

A Confederate stronghold, Georgia was the scene of extensive military action during the Civil War. Union General William T. Sherman burned Atlanta and destroyed a 60-mile wide path to the coast where he captured Savannah in 1864.

The largest state east of the Mississippi, Georgia is typical of the changing South with an ever-increasing industrial development. Atlanta, largest city in the state, is the communications and transportation center for the Southeast and the area's chief distributor of goods.

Georgia leads the nation in the production of paper and board, tufted textile products, and processed chicken. Other major manufactured products are transportation equipment, food products, apparel, and chemicals.

Important agricultural products are corn, cotton, tobacco, soybeans, eggs, and peaches. Georgia produces twice as many peanuts as the next leading state. From its vast stands of pine come more than half the world's resins and turpentine and 74.4% of the U.S. supply. Georgia is also a leader in the production of marble, kaolin, barite, and bauxite.

Principal tourist attractions in Georgia include the Okefenokee National Wildlife Refuge, Andersonville Prison Park and National Cemetery, Chickamauga and Chattanooga National Military Park, the Little White House at Warm Springs where Pres. Franklin D. Roosevelt died in 1945, Sea Island, the enormous Confederate Memorial at Stone Mountain, Kennesaw Mountain National Battlefield Park, and Cumberland Island National Seashore.

HAWAII

Capital: Honolulu (on Oahu)
Governor: John Waihee, D
Organized as territory: 1900
Entered Union & (rank): Aug. 21, 1959 (50)
Motto: *Ua Mau Ke Ea O Ka Aina I Ka Pono* (The life of the land is perpetuated in righteousness)
STATE SYMBOLS: flower, Hibiscus (yellow) 1988); **song,** "Hawaii Ponoi" (1967); **bird,** Nene (Hawaiian goose) (1957); **tree,** Kukui (Candlenut) (1959)
Nickname: Aloha State (1959)
Origin of name: Uncertain. The islands may have been named by Hawaii Loa, their traditional discoverer. Or they may have been named after Hawaii or Hawaiki, the traditional home of the Polynesians.
10 largest cities[1] (1990 census): Honolulu, 365,272; Hilo, 37,808; Kailua, 36,818; Kaneohe, 35,448; Waipahu, 31,435; Pearl City, 30,993; Waimalu, 29,967; Mililani Town, 29,359; Schofield Barracks, 19,597; Wahiawa, 17,386
Land area & (rank): 6,425 sq mi. (16,641 sq km) (47)
Geographic center: Between islands of Hawaii and Maui
Number of counties: 4 plus one non-functioning county (Kalawao)
Largest county (1990 census): Honolulu, 836,231
State parks and historic sites: 77
1980 resident census population & (rank): 964,691 (39)
1990 resident census population, sex, & (rank): 1,108,229 (40). **Male:** 563,891; **Female:** 544,338. **White:** 369,616 (33.4%); **Black:** 27,195 (2.5%); **American Indian, Eskimo, or Aleut:** 5,099 (0.5%); **Asian or Pacific Islander:** 685,236 (61.8%); **Other race:** 21,083 (1.9%);

Hispanic: 81,390 (7.3%). **1990 percent population under 18:** 25.3; **65 and over:** 11.3; **median age:** 32.6

1. Census Designated Place. There are no political boundaries to Honolulu or any other place, but statistical boundaries are assigned under state law.

First settled by Polynesians sailing from other Pacific islands between 300 and 600 A.D., Hawaii was visited in 1778 by British Captain James Cook who called the group the Sandwich Islands.

Hawaii was a native kingdom throughout most of the 19th century when the expansion of the vital sugar industry (pineapple came after 1898) meant increasing U.S. business and political involvement. In 1893, Queen Liliuokalani was deposed and a year later the Republic of Hawaii was established with Sanford B. Dole as president. Then, following its annexation in 1898, Hawaii became a U.S. Territory in 1900.

The Japanese attack on the naval base at Pearl Harbor on Dec. 7, 1941, was directly responsible for U.S. entry into World War II.

Hawaii, 2,397 miles west-southwest of San Francisco, is a 1,523-mile chain of islets and eight main islands—Hawaii, Kahoolawe, Maui, Lanai, Molokai, Oahu, Kauai, and Niihau. The Northwestern Hawaiian Islands, other than Midway, are administratively part of Hawaii.

The temperature is mild and Hawaii's soil is fertile for tropical fruits and vegetables. Cane sugar and pineapple are the chief products. Hawaii also grows coffee, bananas and nuts. The tourist business is Hawaii's largest source of outside income.

Hawaii's highest peak is Mauna Kea (13,796 ft.). Mauna Loa (13,679 ft.) is the largest volcanic mountain in the world in cubic content.

Among the major points of interest are Hawaii Volcanoes National Park (Hawaii), Haleakala National Park (Maui), Puuhonua o Honaunau National Historical Park (Hawaii), Polynesian Cultural Center (Oahu), the U.S.S. *Arizona* Memorial at Pearl Harbor, and Iolani Palace (the only royal palace in the U.S.), Bishop Museum, and Waikiki Beach (all in Honolulu).

IDAHO

Capital: Boise
Governor: Cecil D. Andrus, D
Organized as territory: March 3, 1863
Entered Union & (rank): July 3, 1890 (43)
Present constitution adopted: 1890
Motto: *Esto perpetua* (It is forever)
STATE SYMBOLS: flower, Syringa (1931); **tree,** White pine (1935); **bird,** Mountain bluebird (1931); **horse,** Appaloosa (1975); **gem,** Star garnet (1967); **song,** "Here We Have Idaho"; **folk dance,** Square Dance
Nicknames: Gem State; Spud State; Panhandle State
Origin of name: Unknown. It is an invented name and has no Indian translation meaning "Gem of the Mountains." Meaning of name, if any, is unknown.
10 largest cities (1990 census): Boise, 125,738; Pocatello, 46,080; Idaho Falls, 43,929; Nampa, 28,365; Lewiston, 28,082; Twin Falls, 27,591; Coeur d'Alene, 24,563, Moscow, 18,519; Caldwell, 18,400; Rexburg, 14,302
Land area & (rank): 82,412 sq mi. (213,449 sq km) (11)
Geographic center: In Custer Co., at Custer, SW of Challis
Number of counties: 44, plus small part of Yellowstone National Park
Largest county (1990 census): Ada, 205,775

State forests: 881,000 ac.
State parks: 21 (42,161 ac.)
1980 resident census population & (rank): 943,935 (41)
1990 resident census population, sex, & (rank):
1,006,749 (42). **Male:** 500,956; **Female:** 505,793. **White:** 950,451 (94.4%); **Black:** 3,370 (0.3%); **American Indian, Eskimo, or Aleut:** 13,780 (1.4%); **Asian or Pacific Islander:** 9,365 (0.9%); **Other race:** 29,783 (3.0%); **Hispanic:** 52,927 (5.3%). **1990 percent population under 18:** 30.6; **65 and over:** 12.0; **median age:** 31.5.

After its acquisition by the U.S. as part of the Louisiana Purchase in 1803, the region was explored by Meriwether Lewis and William Clark in 1805–06. Northwest boundary disputes with Great Britain were settled by the Oregon Treaty in 1846 and the first permanent U.S. settlement in Idaho was established by the Mormons at Franklin in 1860.

After gold was discovered on Orofino Creek in 1860, prospectors swarmed into the territory, but left little more than a number of ghost towns.

In the 1870s, growing white occupation of Indian lands led to a series of battles between U.S. forces and the Nez Percé, Bannock, and Sheepeater tribes.

Mining, lumbering, and irrigation farming have been important for years. Idaho produces more than one fifth of all the silver mined in the U.S. It also ranks high among the states in antimony, lead, cobalt, garnet, phosphate rock, vanadium, zinc, mercury, molybdenum, and gold.

Idaho's most impressive growth began when World War II military needs made processing agricultural products a big industry, particularly the dehydrating and freezing of potatoes. The state produces about one fourth of the nation's potato crop, as well as wheat, apples, corn, barley, sugar beets, and hops.

With the growth of winter sports, tourism now outranks mining in dollar revenue. Idaho's many streams and lakes provide fishing, camping, and boating sites. The nation's largest elk herds draw hunters from all over the world and the famed Sun Valley resort attracts thousands of visitors to its swimming and skiing facilities.

Other points of interest are the Craters of the Moon National Monument; Nez Percé National Historic Park, which includes many sites visited by Lewis and Clark; and the State Historical Museum in Boise.

ILLINOIS

Capital: Springfield
Governor: Jim Edgar, R
Organized as territory: Feb. 3, 1809
Entered Union & (rank): Dec. 3, 1818 (21)
Present constitution adopted: 1970
Motto: State sovereignty, national union
STATE SYMBOLS: flower, Violet (1908); **tree,** White oak (1973); **bird,** Cardinal (1929); **animal,** White-tailed deer (1982); **fish,** Bluegill (1987); **insect,** Monarch butterfly (1975); **song,** "Illinois" (1925); **mineral,** Fluorite (1965)
Nickname: Prairie State
Origin of name: From an Indian word and French suffix meaning "tribe of superior men"
10 largest cities (1990 census): Chicago, 2,783,726; Rockford, 139,426; Peoria, 113,504; Springfield, 105,227; Aurora, 99,581; Naperville, 85,351; Decatur, 83,885; Elgin, 77,010; Joliet, 76,836; Arlington Heights Village, 75,460
Land area & (rank): 55,645 sq mi. (144,120 sq km) (24)
Geographic center: In Logan County 28 mi. NE of

Springfield
Number of counties: 102
Largest county (1990 census): Cook, 5,105,067
Public use areas: 187 (275,000 ac.), incl. state parks, memorials, forests and conservation areas
1980 resident census population & (rank): 11,426,518 (5)
1990 resident census population, sex, & (rank):
11,430,602 (6). **Male:** 5,552,233; **Female:** 5,878,369. **White:** 8,952,978 (78.3%); **Black:** 1,694,273 (14.8%); **American Indian, Eskimo, or Aleut:** 21,836 (0.2%); **Asian or Pacific Islander:** 285,311 (2.5%); **Other race:** 476,204 (4.2%); **Hispanic:** 904,446 (7.9%). **1990 percent population under 18:** 25.8; **65 and over:** 12.6; **median age:** 32.8.

French explorers Marquette and Joliet, in 1673, were the first Europeans of record to visit the region. In 1699 French settlers established the first permanent settlement at Cahokia, near present-day East St. Louis.

Great Britain obtained the region at the end of the French and Indian War in 1763. The area figured prominently in frontier struggles during the Revolutionary War and in Indian wars during the early 19th century.

Significant episodes in the state's early history include the growing migration of Eastern settlers following the opening of the Erie Canal in 1825; the Black Hawk War, which virtually ended the Indian troubles in the area; and the rise of Abraham Lincoln from farm laborer to President-elect.

Today, Illinois stands high in manufacturing, coal mining, agriculture, and oil production. The sprawling Chicago district (including a slice of Indiana) is a great iron and steel producer, meat packer, grain exchange, and railroad center. Chicago is also famous as a Great Lakes port.

Illinois ranks first in the nation in export of agricultural products and second in hog production. An important dairying state, Illinois is also a leader in corn, oats, wheat, barley, rye, truck vegetables, and the nursery products.

The state manufactures a great variety of industrial and consumer products: railroad cars, clothing, furniture, tractors, liquor, watches, and farm implements are just some of the items made in its factories and plants.

Central Illinois is noted for shrines and memorials associated with the life of Abraham Lincoln. In Springfield are the Lincoln Home, the Lincoln Tomb, and the restored Old State Capitol. Other points of interest are the home of Mormon leader Joseph Smith in Nauvoo and, in Chicago: the Art Institute, Field Museum, Museum of Science and Industry, Shedd Aquarium, Adler Planetarium, Merchandise Mart, and Chicago Portage National Historic Site.

INDIANA

Capital: Indianapolis
Governor: Birch Evans Bayh III, D
Organized as territory: May 7, 1800
Entered Union & (rank): Dec. 11, 1816 (19)
Present constitution adopted: 1851
Motto: The Crossroads of America
STATE SYMBOLS: flower: Peony (1957); **tree,** Tulip tree (1931); **bird,** Cardinal (1933); **song,** "On the Banks of the Wabash, Far Away" (1913)
Nickname: Hoosier State
Origin of name: Meaning "land of Indians"

10 largest cities (1990 census): Indianapolis, 731,327; Fort Wayne, 173,072; Evansville, 126,272; Gary, 116,646; South Bend, 105,511; Hammond, 84,236; Muncie, 71,035; Bloomington, 60,633; Anderson, 59,459; Terre Haute, 57,483
Land area & (rank): 35,932 sq mi. (93,064 sq km) (38)
Geographic center: In Boone Co., 14 mi. NNW of Indianapolis
Number of Counties: 92
Largest county (1990 census): Marion, 797,159
State parks: 19 (54,126 ac.)
State memorials: 16 (941.977 ac.)
1980 resident census population & (rank): 5,490,224 (12)
1990 census population, sex, & (rank): 5,544,159 (14). **Male:** 2,688,281; **Female:** 2,855,878. **White:** 5,020,700 (90.6%); **Black:** 432,092 (7.8%); **American Indian, Eskimo, or Aleut:** 12,720 (0.2%); **Asian or Pacific Islander:** 37,617 (0.7%); **Other race:** 41,030 (0.7%); **Hispanic:** 98,788 (1.8%). **1990 percent population under 18:** 26.3; **65 and over:** 12.6; **median age:** 32.8.

First explored for France by La Salle in 1679–80, the region figured importantly in the Franco-British struggle for North America that culminated with British victory in 1763.

George Rogers Clark led American forces against the British in the area during the Revolutionary War and, prior to becoming a state, Indiana was the scene of frequent Indian uprisings until the victory of Gen. William Henry Harrison at Tippecanoe in 1811.

Indiana's 41-mile Lake Michigan waterfront—one of the world's great industrial centers—turns out iron, steel, and oil products. Products include automobile parts and accessories, mobile homes and recreational vehicles, truck and bus bodies, aircraft engines, farm machinery, and fabricated structural steel. Phonograph records, wood office furniture, and pharmaceuticals are also manufactured.

The state is a leader in agriculture with corn the principal crop. Hogs, soybeans, wheat, oats, rye, tomatoes, onions, and poultry also contribute heavily to Indiana's agricultural output. Much of the building limestone used in the U.S. is quarried in Indiana which is also a large producer of coal.

Wyandotte Cave, one of the largest in the U.S., is located in Crawford County in southern Indiana and West Baden and French Lick are well known for their mineral springs. Other attractions include Indiana Dunes National Lakeshore, Indianapolis Motor Speedway, Lincoln Boyhood National Memorial, and the George Rogers Clark National Historical Park.

IOWA

Capital: Des Moines
Governor: Terry E. Branstad, R
Organized as territory: June 12, 1838
Entered Union & (rank): Dec. 28, 1846 (29)
Present constitution adopted: 1857
Motto: Our liberties we prize and our rights we will maintain
STATE SYMBOLS: flower, Wild rose (1897); **bird,** Eastern goldfinch (1933); **colors,** Red, white, and blue (in state flag); **song,** "Song of Iowa"
Nickname: Hawkeye State
Origin of name: Probably from an Indian word meaning "I-o-w-a, this is the place," or "The Beautiful Land"
10 largest cities (1990 census): Des Moines, 193,187; Cedar Rapids, 108,751; Davenport, 95,333; Sioux City, 80,505; Waterloo, 66,467; Iowa City, 59,738; Dubuque, 57,546; Council Bluffs, 54,315; Ames, 47,198; Cedar Falls, 34,298
Land area & (rank): 55,965 sq mi. (144,950 sq km) (24)
Geographic center: In Story Co., 5 mi. NE of Ames
Number of counties: 99
Largest county (1990 census): Polk, 327,140
State forests: 5 (28,000 ac.)
State parks: 84 (49,237 ac.)
1980 resident census population & (rank): 2,913,808 (27)
1990 resident census population, sex, & (rank): 2,776,755 (30). **Male:** 1,344,802; **Female:** 1,431,953. **White:** 2,683,090 (96.6%); **Black:** 48,090 (1.7%); **American Indian, Eskimo, or Aleut:** 7,349 (0.3%); **Asian or Pacific Islander:** 25,476 (0.9%); **Other race:** 12,750 (0.5%); **Hispanic:** 32,647 (1.2%). **1990 percent population under 18:** 25.9; **65 and over:** 15.3; **median age:** 34.0

The first Europeans to visit the area were the French explorers, Father Jacques Marquette and Louis Joliet in 1673. The U.S. obtained control of the area in 1803 as part of the Louisiana Purchase.

During the first half of the 19th century, there was heavy fighting between white settlers and Indians. Lands were taken from the Indians after the Black Hawk War in 1832 and again in 1836 and 1837.

When Iowa became a state in 1846, its capital was Iowa City; the more centrally located Des Moines became the new capital in 1857. At that time, the state's present boundaries were also drawn.

Although Iowa produces a tenth of the nation's food supply, the value of Iowa's manufactured products is twice that of its agriculture. Major industries are food and associated products, non-electrical machinery, electrical equipment, printing and publishing, and fabricated products.

Iowa stands in a class by itself as an agricultural state. Its farms sell over $9 billion worth of crops and livestock annually. Iowa leads the nation in all livestock and hog marketings, with about 25% of the pork supply and 8% of the grain-fed cattle. Iowa's forests produce hardwood lumber, particularly walnut, and its mineral products include cement, limestone, sand, gravel, gypsum, and coal.

Tourist attractions include the Herbert Hoover birthplace and library near West Branch; the Amana Colonies; Fort Dodge Historical Museum, Fort, and Stockade; the Iowa State Fair at Des Moines in August; and the Effigy Mounds National Monument at Marquette, a prehistoric Indian burial site.

KANSAS

Capital: Topeka
Governor: Joan Finney, D
Organized as territory: May 30, 1854
Entered Union & (rank): Jan. 29, 1861 (34)
Present constitution adopted: 1859
Motto: *Ad astra per aspera* (To the stars through difficulties)
STATE SYMBOLS: flower, Sunflower (1903); **tree,** Cottonwood (1937); **bird,** Western meadowlark (1937); **animal,** Buffalo (1955); **song,** "Home on Range" (1947)
Nicknames: Sunflower State; Jayhawk State
Origin of name: From a Siouan word meaning "people of the south wind"
10 largest cities (1990 census): Wichita, 304,011; Kansas City, 149,767; Topeka, 119,883; Overland Park, 111,790; Lawrence, 65,608; Olathe, 63,352; Salina, 42,303; Hutchinson, 39,308; Leavenworth, 38,495; Shawnee, 37,993

Land area & (rank): 81,778 sq mi. (211,805 sq km) (13)
Geographic center: In Barton Co., 15 mi. NE of Great Bend
Number of counties: 105
Largest county (1990 census): Sedgwick, 403,662
State parks: 22 (14,394 ac.)
1980 resident census population & (rank): 2,363,679 (32)
1990 resident census population, sex, & (rank): 2,477,574 (32). **Male:** 1,214,645; **Female:** 1,262,929. **White:** 2,231,986 (90.1%); **Black:** 143,076 (5.8%); **American Indian, Eskimo, or Aleut:** 21,965 (0.9%); **Asian or Pacific Islander:** 31,750 (1.3%); **Other race:** 48,797 (2.0%); **Hispanic:** 93,670 (3.8%). **1990 percent population under 18:** 26.7; **65 and over:** 13.8; **median age:** 32.9.

Spanish explorer Francisco de Coronado, in 1541, is considered the first European to have traveled this region. La Salle's extensive land claims for France (1682) included present-day Kansas. Ceded to Spain by France in 1763, the territory reverted back to France in 1800 and was sold to the U.S. as part of the Louisiana Purchase in 1803.

Lewis and Clark, Zebulon Pike, and Stephen H. Long explored the region between 1803 and 1819. The first permanent settlements in Kansas were outposts—Fort Leavenworth (1827), Fort Scott (1842), and Fort Riley (1853)—established to protect travelers along the Santa Fe and Oregon Trails.

Just before the Civil War, the conflict between the pro- and anti-slavery forces earned the region the grim title "Bleeding Kansas."

Today, wheat fields, oil well derricks, herds of cattle, and grain storage elevators are chief features of the Kansas landscape. A leading wheat-growing state, Kansas also raises corn, sorghums, oats, barley, soy beans, and potatoes. Kansas stands high in petroleum production and mines zinc, coal, salt, and lead. It is also the nation's leading producer of helium.

Wichita is one of the nation's leading aircraft manufacturing centers, ranking first in production of private aircraft. Kansas City is an important transportation, milling, and meat-packing center.

Points of interest include the new Kansas Museum of History at Topeka, the Eisenhower boyhood home and the new Eisenhower Memorial Museum and Presidential Library at Abilene, John Brown's cabin at Osawatomie, recreated Front Street in Dodge City, Fort Larned (once the most important military post on the Santa Fe Trail), and Fort Leavenworth and Fort Riley.

Geographic center: In Marion Co., 3 mi. NNW of Lebanon
Number of counties: 120
Largest county (1990 census): Jefferson, population 664,937
State forests: 9 (44,173 ac.)
State parks: 43 (40,574 ac.)
1980 resident census population & (rank): 3,660,777 (23)
1990 resident census population, sex, & (rank): 3,685,296 (23). **Male:** 1,785,235; **Female:** 1,900,061. **White:** 3,391,832 (92.0%); **Black:** 262,907 (7.1%); **American Indian, Eskimo, or Aleut:** 5,769 (0.2%); **Asian or Pacific Islander:** 17,812 (0.5%); **Other race:** 6,976 (0.2%); **Hispanic:** 21,984 (0.6%). **1990 percent population below age 18:** 25.9; **65 and over:** 12.7; **median age:** 33.0.

Kentucky was the first region west of the Allegheny Mountains settled by American pioneers. James Harrod established the first permanent settlement at Harrodsburg in 1774; the following year Daniel Boone, who had explored the area in 1767, blazed the Wilderness Trail and founded Boonesboro.

Politically, the Kentucky region was originally part of Virginia, but early statehood was gained in 1792.

During the Civil War, as a slaveholding state with a considerable abolitionist population, Kentucky was caught in the middle of the conflict, supplying both Union and Confederate forces with thousands of troops.

In recent years, manufacturing has shown important gains, but agriculture and mining are still vital to Kentucky's economy. Kentucky prides itself on producing some of the nation's best tobacco, horses, and whiskey. Corn, soybeans, wheat, fruit, hogs, cattle, and dairy farming are also important.

Among the manufactured items produced in the state are furniture, aluminum ware, brooms, shoes, lumber products, machinery, textiles, and iron and steel products. Kentucky also produces significant amounts of petroleum, natural gas, fluorspar, clay, and stone. However, coal accounts for 90% of the total mineral income.

Louisville, the largest city, famed for the Kentucky Derby at Churchill Downs, is also the location of a large state university, whiskey distilleries, and cigarette factories. The Bluegrass country around Lexington is the home of some of the world's finest race horses. Other attractions are Mammoth Cave, the George S. Patton, Jr., Military Museum at Fort Knox, and Old Fort Harrod State Park.

KENTUCKY

Capital: Frankfort
Governor: Brereton C. Jones, D
Entered Union & (rank): June 1, 1792 (15)
Present constitution adopted: 1891
Motto: United we stand, divided we fall
STATE SYMBOLS: tree, Coffeetree; **flower,** Goldenrod; **bird,** Kentucky cardinal; **song,** "My Old Kentucky Home"
Nickname: Bluegrass State
Origin of name: From an Iroquoian word "Ken-tah-ten" meaning "land of tomorrow"
10 largest cities (1990 census): Louisville, 269,063; Lexington-Fayette, 225,366; Owensboro, 53,549; Covington, 43,264; Bowling Green, 40,641; Hopkinsville, 29,809; Paducah, 27,256; Frankfort, 25,968; Henderson, 25,945; Ashland, 23,622
Land area & (rank): 39,669 sq mi. (102,743 sq km) (37)

LOUISIANA

Capital: Baton Rouge
Governor: Edwin W. Edwards, D
Organized as territory: March 26, 1804
Entered Union & (rank): April 30, 1812 (18)
Present constitution adopted: 1974
Motto: Union, justice, and confidence
STATE SYMBOLS: flower, Magnolia (1900); **tree,** Bald cypress (1963); **bird,** Pelican (1958); **songs,** "Give Me Louisiana" and "You Are My Sunshine"
Nicknames: Pelican State; Sportsman's Paradise; Creole State; Sugar State
Origin of name: In honor of Louis XIV of France
10 largest cities (1990 census): New Orleans, 496,938; Baton Rouge, 219,531; Shreveport, 198,525; Lafayette, 94,440; Kenner, 72,033; Lake Charles, 70,580; Monroe, 54,909; Bossier City, 52,721; Alexandria, 49,188; New Iberia, 31,828

Land area & (rank): 44,521 sq mi. (115,309 sq km) (33)
Geographic center: In Avoyelles Parish, 3 mi. SE of Marksville
Number of parishes (counties): 64
Largest parish (1990 census): Jefferson, 448,306
State forests: 1 (8,000 ac.)
State parks: 30 (13,932 ac.)
1980 resident census population & (rank): 4,205,900 (19)
1990 resident census population, sex, & (rank):
4,219,973 (21). **Male:** 2,031,386; **Female:** 2,188,587.
White: 2,839,138 (67.3%); **Black:** 1,299,281 (30.8%);
American Indian, Eskimo, or Aleut: 18,541 (0.4%);
Asian or Pacific Islander: 41,099 (1.0%); **Other race:**
21,914 (0.5%); **Hispanic:** 93,044 (2.2%). **1990 percent population under 18:** 29.1; **65 and over:** 11.1; **median age:** 31.0.

Louisiana has a rich, colorful historical background. Early Spanish explorers were Piñeda, 1519; Cabeza de Vaca, 1528; and de Soto in 1541. La Salle reached the mouth of the Mississippi and claimed all the land drained by it and its tributaries for Louis XIV of France in 1682.

Louisiana became a French crown colony in 1731, was ceded to Spain in 1763, returned to France in 1800, and sold by Napoleon to the U.S. as part of the Louisiana Purchase (with large territories to the north and northwest) in 1803.

In 1815, Gen. Andrew Jackson's troops defeated a larger British army in the Battle of New Orleans, neither side aware that the treaty ending the War of 1812 had been signed.

As to total value of its mineral output, Louisiana is a leader in natural gas, salt, petroleum, and sulfur production. Much of the oil and sulfur comes from offshore deposits. The state also produces large crops of sweet potatoes, rice, sugar cane, pecans, soybeans, corn, and cotton.

Leading manufactures include chemicals, processed food, petroleum and coal products, paper, lumber and wood products, transportation equipment, and apparel.

Louisiana marshes supply most of the nation's muskrat fur as well as that of opossum, raccoon, mink, and otter, and large numbers of game birds.

Major points of interest include New Orleans with its French Quarter and Superdome, plantation homes near Natchitoches and New Iberia, Cajun country in the Mississippi delta region, Chalmette National Historical Park, and the state capital at Baton Rouge.

MAINE

Capital: Augusta
Governor: John R. McKernan, Jr., R
Entered Union & (rank): March 15, 1820 (23)
Present constitution adopted: 1820
Motto: *Dirigo* (I direct)
STATE SYMBOLS: flower, White pine cone and tassel (1895); **tree,** White pine tree (1945); **bird,** Chickadee (1927); **fish,** Landlocked salmon (1969); **mineral,** Tourmaline (1971); **song,** "State of Maine Song" (1937)
Nickname: Pine Tree State
Origin of name: First used to distinguish the mainland from the offshore islands. It has been considered a compliment to Henrietta Maria, Queen of Charles I of England. She was said to have owned the province of Mayne in France.
10 largest cities (1990 census): Portland, 64,358; Lewiston, 39,757; Bangor, 33,181; Auburn, 24,309; South

Portland, 23,163; Augusta, 21,325; Biddeford, 20,710; Waterville, 17,173; Westbrook, 16,121; Saco, 15,181
Land area & (rank): 30,995 sq mi. (80,277 sq km) (39)
Geographic center: In Piscataquis Co., 18 mi. N of Dover–Foxcroft
Number of counties: 16
Largest town (1990 census): Brunswick, 20,906
State forests: 1 (21,000 ac.)
State parks: 26 (247,627 ac.)
State historic sites: 18 (403 ac.)
1980 resident census population & (rank): 1,124,660 (38)
1990 resident census population, sex, & (rank):
1,227,928 (38). **Male:** 597,850; **Female:** 630,078. **White:**
1,208,360 (98.4%); **Black:** 5,138 (0.4%); **American Indian, Eskimo, or Aleut:** 5,998 (0.5%); **Asian or Pacific Islander:** 6,683: (0.5%); **Other race:** 1,749 (0.1%); **Hispanic:** 6,829 (0.6%).

John Cabot and his son, Sebastian, are believed to have visited the Maine coast in 1498. However, the first permanent English settlements were not established until more than a century later, in 1623.

The first naval action of the Revolutionary War occurred in 1775 when colonials captured the British sloop *Margaretta* off Machias on the Maine coast. In that same year, the British burned Falmouth (now Portland).

Long governed by Massachusetts, Maine became the 23rd state as part of the Missouri Compromise in 1820.

Maine produces 98% of the nation's low-bush blueberries. Farm income is also derived from apples, potatoes, dairy products, and vegetables, with poultry and eggs the largest items.

The state is one of the world's largest pulp-paper producers. It ranks fifth in boot-and-shoe manufacturing. With almost 89% of its area forested, Maine turns out wood products from boats to toothpicks.

Maine leads the world in the production of the familiar flat tins of sardines, producing more than 100 million of them annually. Lobstermen normally catch 80–90% of the nation's true total of lobsters.

A scenic seacoast, beaches, lakes, mountains, and resorts make Maine a popular vacationland. There are more than 2,500 lakes and 5,000 streams, plus 26 state parks, to attract hunters, fishermen, skiers, and campers.

Major points of interest are: Bar Harbor, Allagash National Wilderness Waterway, the Wadsworth-Longfellow House in Portland, Roosevelt Campobello International Park, and the St. Croix Island National Monument.

MARYLAND

Capital: Annapolis
Governor: William Donald Schaefer, D
Entered Union & (rank): April 28, 1788 (7)
Present constitution adopted: 1867
Motto: *Fatti maschii, parole femine* (Manly deeds, womanly words)
STATE SYMBOLS: flower, Black-eyed susan (1918); **tree,** White oak (1941); **bird,** Baltimore oriole (1947); **dog,** Chesapeake Bay retriever (1964); **fish,** Rockfish (1965); **crustacean,** Maryland Blue Crab (1989); **insect,** Baltimore checkerspot butterfly (1973); **boat,** Skipjack (1985); **sport,** Jousting (1962); **song,** "Maryland! My Maryland!" (1939)
Nicknames: Free State; Old Line State
Origin of name: In honor of Henrietta Maria (Queen of Charles I of England)

10 largest cities (1990 census): Baltimore, 736,014; Rockville, 44,835; Frederick, 40,148; Gaithersburg, 39,542; Bowie, 37,589; Hagerstown, 35,445; Annapolis, 33,187; Cumberland, 23,706; College Park, 21,927; Greenbelt, 21,096
Land area & (rank): 9,837 sq mi. (25,477 sq km) (42)
Geographic center: In Prince Georges Co., 4 1/2 mi. NW of Davidsonville
Number of counties: 23, and 1 independent city
Largest county (1990 census): Montgomery, 757,027
State forests: 13 (132,944 ac.)
State parks: 47 (87,670 ac.)
1980 resident census population & (rank): 4,216,975 (18)
1990 resident census population, sex, & (rank): 4,781,468 (19). **Male:** 2,318,671; **Female:** 2,462,797. **White:** 3,393,964 (71.0%); **Black:** 1,189,899 (24.9%); **American Indian, Eskimo, or Aleut:** 12,972 (0.3%); **Asian or Pacific Islander:** 139,719 (2.9%); **Other race:** 44,914 (0.9%); **Hispanic:** 125,102 (2.6%). **1990 percent population under 18:** 24.3; **65 and over:** 10.8; **median age:** 33.0

In 1608, Chesapeake Bay was explored by Capt. John Smith. Charles I granted a royal charter to Cecil Calvert, Lord Baltimore, in 1632 and English Roman Catholics landed on St. Clement's (now Blakistone Island) in 1634. Religious freedom, granted all Christians in the Toleration act passed by the Maryland assembly in 1649, was ended by a Puritan revolt, 1654–58.

From 1763 to 1767, Charles Mason and Jeremiah Dixon surveyed Maryland's northern boundary line with Pennsylvania. In 1791, Maryland ceded land to form the District of Columbia.

In 1814, when the British unsuccessfully tried to capture Baltimore, the bombardment of Fort McHenry inspired Francis Scott Key to write *The Star Spangled Banner.*

The Baltimore clipper ship trade developed during the 19th Century. The battles of South Mountain and Antietam (1862) and Monocacy (1864) were fought in this state.

In 1904, the Great Fire of Baltimore occurred. In 1937, the City of Greenbelt, a New Deal model community, was chartered.

Maryland is almost cut in two by the Chesapeake Bay, and the many estuaries and rivers create one of the longest waterfronts of any state. The Bay produces more seafood—oysters, crabs, clams, fin fish—than any comparable body of water. Important agricultural products, in order of cash value, are chickens, dairy products, cattle, soy beans, eggs, corn, hogs, vegetables, and tobacco. Maryland is a leader in vegetable canning. Sand, gravel, lime and cement, stone, coal, and clay are the chief mineral products.

Manufacturing industries produce missiles, airplanes, steel, clothing, and chemicals. Baltimore, home of The Johns Hopkins University and Hospital, ranks as the nation's second port in foreign tonnage. Annapolis, site of the U.S. Naval Academy, has one of the earliest state houses (1772–79) still in regular use by a State government.

Among the popular attractions in Maryland are the Fort McHenry National Monument, Harpers Ferry and Chesapeake and Ohio Canal, National Aquarium, and Maryland Science Center at Baltimore's Inner Harbor, National Historical Parks, Historic St. Mary's City restoration near Leonardtown, USS *Constellation* at Baltimore, U.S. Naval Academy in Annapolis, Goddard Space Flight Center at Greenbelt, Assateague Island National Seashore, Ocean City beach resort, and Catoctin Mountain, Ft. Frederick, and Piscataway parks.

MASSACHUSETTS

Capital: Boston
Governor: William F. Weld, R
Present constitution drafted: 1780 (oldest U.S. state constitution in effect today)
Entered Union & (rank): Feb. 6, 1788 (6)
Motto: *Ense petit placidam sub libertate quietem* (By the sword we seek peace, but peace only under liberty)
STATE SYMBOLS: flower, Mayflower (1918); **tree.** American elm (1941); **bird,** Chickadee (1941); **colors,** Blue and gold; **song,** "All Hail to Massachusetts" (1966); **beverage,** Cranberry juice (1970); **insect,** Ladybug (1974)
Nicknames: Bay State; Old Colony State
Origin of name: From two Indian words meaning "Great mountain place"
10 largest cities (1990 census): Boston, 574,283; Worcester, 169,759; Springfield, 156,983; Lowell, 103,439; New Bedford, 99,922; Cambridge, 95,802; Brockton, 92,788; Fall River, 92,703; Quincy, 84,985; Newton, 82,585
Land area & (rank): 7,824 sq mi. (20,265 sq km) (45)
Geographic center: In Worcester Co., in S part of city of Worcester
Number of counties: 14
Largest county (1990 census): Middlesex, 1,398,468
State forests and parks: 129 (242,000 ac.)[1]
1980 resident census population & (rank): 5,737,037 (11)
1990 resident census population, sex, & (rank): 6,016,425 (13). **Male:** 2,888,745; **Female:** 3,127,680. **White:** 5,405,374 (89.8%); **Black:** 300,130 (5.0%); **American Indian, Eskimo, or Aleut:** 12,241 (0.2%); **Asian or Pacific Islander:** 143,392 (2.4%); **Other race:** 155,288 (2.6%); **Hispanic:** 287,549 (4.8%). **1990 percent population under 18:** 22.5; **65 and over:** 13.6; **median age:** 33.6.

1. The Metropolitan District Commission, an agency of the Commonwealth serving municipalities in the Boston area, has about 14,000 acres of parkways and reservations under its jurisdiction.

Massachusetts has played a significant role in American history since the Pilgrims, seeking religious freedom, founded Plymouth Colony in 1620.

As one of the most important of the 13 colonies, Massachusetts became a leader in resisting British oppression. In 1773, the Boston Tea Party protested unjust taxation. The Minutemen started the American Revolution by battling British troops at Lexington and Concord on April 19, 1775.

During the 19th century, Massachusetts was famous for the vigorous intellectual activity of famous writers and educators and for its expanding commercial fishing, shipping, and manufacturing interests.

Massachusetts pioneered in the manufacture of textiles and shoes. Today, these industries have been replaced in importance by activity in the electronics and communications equipment fields.

The state's cranberry crop is the nation's largest. Also important are dairy and poultry products, nursery and greenhouse produce, vegetables, and fruit.

Tourism has become an important factor in the economy of the state because of its numerous recreational areas and historical landmarks.

Cape Cod has summer theaters, water sports, and an artists' colony at Provincetown. Tanglewood, in the Berkshires, features the summer concerts of the Boston Symphony.

Among the many other points of interest are Old Sturbridge Village, Minute Man National Historical Park between Lexington and Concord, and, in Boston: Old North Church, Old State House, Faneuil Hall, the USS *Constitution* and the John F. Kennedy Library.

MICHIGAN

Capital: Lansing
Governor: John M. Engler, R
Organized as territory: Jan. 11, 1805
Entered Union & (rank): Jan. 26, 1837 (26)
Present constitution adopted: April 1, 1963, (effective Jan. 1, 1964)
Motto: *Si quaeris peninsulam amoenam circumspice* (If you seek a pleasant peninsula, look around you)
STATE SYMBOLS: flower, Apple blossom (1897); **bird,** Robin (1931); **fishes,** Trout (1965), Brook trout (1988); **gem,** Isle Royal Greenstone (Chlorastrolite) (1972); **stone,** Petoskey stone (1965)
Nickname: Wolverine State
Origin of name: From two Indian words meaning "great lake"
10 largest cities (1990 census): Detroit, 1,027,974; Grand Rapids, 189,126; Warren, 144,864; Flint, 140,761; Lansing, 127,321; Sterling Heights, 117,810; Ann Arbor, 109,592; Livonia, 100,850; Dearborn, 89,286; Westland, 84,724
Land area & (rank): 56,954 sq mi. (147,511 sq km) (22)
Geographic center: In Wexford Co., 5 mi. NNW of Cadillac
Number of counties: 83
Largest county (1990 census): Wayne, 2,111,687
State parks and recreation areas: 92 (250,000 ac.)
1980 resident census population & (rank): 9,262,078 (8)
1990 resident census population, sex, & (rank): 9,295,297 (8). **Male:** 4,512,781; **Female:** 4,787,516. **White:** 7,756,086 (83.4%); **Black:** 1,291,706 (13.9%); **American Indian, Eskimo, or Aleut:** 55,638 (0.6%); **Asian or Pacific Islander:** 104,983 (1.1%); **Other race:** 86,983 (0.9%); **Hispanic:** 201,596 (2.2%). **1990 percent population under 18:** 26.5; **65 and over:** 11.9; **median age:** 32.6.

Indian tribes were living in the Michigan region when the first European, Etienne Brulé of France, arrived in 1618. Other French explorers, including Marquette, Joliet, and La Salle, followed, and the first permanent settlement was established in 1668 at Sault Ste. Marie. France was ousted from the territory by Great Britain in 1763, following the French and Indian War.

After the Revolutionary War, the U.S. acquired most of the region, which remained the scene of constant conflict between the British and U.S. forces and their respective Indian allies through the War of 1812.

Bordering on four of the five Great Lakes, Michigan is divided into Upper and Lower Peninsulas by the Straits of Mackinac, which link Lakes Michigan and Huron. The two parts of the state are connected by the Mackinac Bridge, one of the world's longest suspension bridges. To the north, connecting Lakes Superior and Huron are the busy Sault Ste. Marie Canals.

While Michigan ranks first among the states in production of motor vehicles and parts, it is also a leader in many other manufacturing and processing lines including prepared cereals, machine tools, air-plane parts, refrigerators, hardware, steel springs, and furniture.

The state produces important amounts of iron, copper, iodine, gypsum, bromine, salt, lime, gravel, and cement. Michigan's farms grow apples, cherries, pears, grapes, potatoes, and sugar beets and the 1987 value of its forest products was estimated at $3.2 billion. With over 36,000 miles of streams, some 11,000 lakes, and a 2,000 mile shoreline, Michigan is a prime area for both commercial and sport fishing.

Points of interest are the automobile plants in Dearborn, Detroit, Flint, Lansing, and Pontiac; Mackinac Island; Pictured Rocks and Sleeping Bear Dunes National Lakeshores, Greenfield Village in Dearborn; and the many summer resorts along both the inland and Great Lakes.

MINNESOTA

Capital: St. Paul
Governor: Arne Carlson, R
Organized as territory: March 3, 1849
Entered Union & (rank): May 11, 1858 (32)
Present constitution adopted: 1858
Motto: L'Etoile du Nord (The North Star)
STATE SYMBOLS: flower, Showy lady slipper (1902); **tree,** Red (or Norway) pine (1953); **bird,** Common loon (also called Great Northern Diver) (1961); **song,** "Hail Minnesota" (1945); **fish,** Walleye (1965); **mushroom,** Morel (1984)
Nicknames: North Star State; Gopher State; Land of 10,000 Lakes
Origin of name: From a Dakota Indian word meaning "sky-tinted water"
10 largest cities (1990 census): Minneapolis, 368,383; St. Paul, 272,235; Bloomington, 86,335; Duluth, 85,493; Rochester, 70,745; Brooklyn Park, 56,381; Coon Rapids, 52,978; Burnsville, 51,288; Plymouth, 50,889; St. Cloud, 48,812
Land area & (rank): 79,548 sq mi. (206,030 sq km) (14)
Geographic center: In Crow Wing Co., 10 mi. SW of Brainerd
Number of counties: 87
Largest county (1990 census): Hennepin, 1,032,431
State forests: 56 (3,200,000 ac.)
State parks: 66 (226,000 ac.)
1980 resident census population & (rank): 4,075,970 (21)
1990 resident census population, sex, & (rank): 4,375,099 (20). **Male:** 2,145,183; **Female:** 2,229,916. **White:** 4,130,395 (94.4%); **Black:** 94,944 (2.2%); **American Indian, Eskimo, or Aleut:** 49,909 (1.1%); **Asian or Pacific Islander:** 77,886 (1.8%); **Other race:** 21,965 (0.5%); **Hispanic:** 53,884 (1.2%). **1990 percent population under 18:** 26.7; **65 and over:** 12.5; **median age:** 32.5.

Following the visits of several French explorers, fur traders, and missionaries, including Marquette and Joliet and La Salle, the region was claimed for Louis XIV by Daniel Greysolon, Sieur Duluth, in 1679.

The U.S. acquired eastern Minnesota from Great Britain after the Revolutionary War and 20 years later bought the western part from France in the Louisiana Purchase of 1803. Much of the region was explored by U.S. Army Lt. Zebulon M. Pike before cession of the northern strip of Minnesota bordering Canada by Britain in 1818.

The state is rich in natural resources. A few square miles of land in the north in the Mesabi, Cuyuna, and Vermillion ranges, produce more than 75% of the nation's iron ore. The state's farms rank high in yields of corn, wheat, rye, alfalfa, and sugar beets. Other leading farm products include butter, eggs, milk, potatoes, green peas, barley, soy beans, oats, and livestock.

Minnesota's factory production includes nonelectrical machinery, fabricated metals, flour-mill products, plastics, electronic computers, scientific instruments, and processed foods. It is also one of the nation's leaders in the printing and paper products industries.

Minneapolis is the trade center of the Northwest; and the headquarters of the world's largest super computer and grain distributor. St. Paul is the nation's biggest publisher of calendars and law books. These "twin cities" are the nation's third largest trucking center. Duluth has the nation's largest inland harbor and now handles a significant amount of foreign trade. Rochester is the home of the Mayo Clinic, an internationally famous medical center.

Today, tourism is a major revenue producer in Minnesota, with arts, fishing, hunting, water sports, and winter sports bringing in millions of visitors each year.

Among the most popular attractions are the St. Paul Winter Carnival; the Tyrone Guthrie Theatre, the Institute of Arts, Walker Art Center, and Minnehaha Park, in Minneapolis; Boundary Waters Canal Area; Voyageurs National Park; North Shore Drive; and the Minnesota Zoological Gardens and the state's more than 10,000 lakes.

MISSISSIPPI

Capital: Jackson
Governor: Kirk Fordice, R
Organized as Territory: April 7, 1798
Entered Union & (rank): Dec. 10, 1817 (20)
Present constitution adopted: 1890
Motto: *Virtute et armis* (By valor and arms)
STATE SYMBOLS: flower, Flower or bloom of the magnolia or evergreen magnolia (1952); **tree,** Magnolia (1938); **bird,** Mockingbird (1944); **song,** "Go, Mississippi" (1962); **stone,** Petrified wood (1976); **fish,** Largemouth or black bass (1974); **insect,** Honeybee (1980); **shell,** Oyster shell (1974); **water mammal,** Bottlenosed dolphin or porpoise (1974); **fossil,** Prehistoric whale (1981); **land mammal,** White-tailed deer (1974); **waterfowl,** Wood duck (1974); **beverage,** Milk (1984)
Nickname: Magnolia State
Origin of name: From an Indian word meaning "Father of Waters"
10 largest cities (1990 census): Jackson, 196,637; Biloxi, 46,319; Greenville, 45,226; Hattiesburg, 41,882; Meridian, 41,036; Gulfport, 40,775; Tupelo, 30,685; Pascagoula, 25,899; Columbus, 23,799; Clinton, 21,847
Land area & (rank): 47,233 sq mi. (122,333 sq km) (31)
Geographic center: In Leake Co., 9 mi. WNW of Carthage
Number of counties: 82
Largest county (1990 census): Hinds, 254,441
State forests: 1 (1,760 ac.)
State parks: 27 (16,763 ac.)
1980 resident census population & (rank): 2,520,638 (31)
1990 resident census population, sex, & (rank): 2,573,216 (31). **Male:** 1,230,617; **Female:** 1,342,599. **White:** 1,633,461 (63.5%); **Black:** 915,057 (35.6%); **American Indian, Eskimo, or Aleut:** 8,525 (0.3%); **Asian or Pacific Islander:** 13,016 (0.5%); **Other race:** 3,157 (0.1%); **Hispanic:** 15,931 (0.6%). **1990 percent population under 18:** 29.0; **65 and over:** 12.5; **median age:** 31.2.

First explored for Spain by Hernando de Soto who discovered the Mississippi River in 1540, the region was later claimed by France. In 1699, a French group under Sieur d'Iberville established the first permanent settlement near present-day Biloxi.

Great Britain took over the area in 1763 after the French and Indian War, ceding it to the U.S. in 1783 after the Revolution. Spain did not relinquish its claims until 1798, and in 1810 the U.S. annexed West Florida from Spain, including what is now southern Mississippi.

For a little more than one hundred years, from shortly after the state's founding through the Great Depression, cotton was the undisputed king of Mississippi's largely agrarian economy. Over the last half-century, however, Mississippi has progressively deepened its commitment to diversification by balancing agricultural output with increased industrial activity.

Today, agriculture continues as a major segment of the state's economy. Soybeans have supplanted cotton as the largest crop—Mississippi is now third in cotton production—and the state's farmlands yield important harvests of corn, peanuts, pecans, rice, sugar cane, sweet potatoes, and hay, as well as poultry and eggs. Mississippi is also the world's leading producer of pond-raised catfish.

The state abounds in historical landmarks and is the home of the Vicksburg National Military Park. Other National Park Service areas are Brices Cross Roads National Battlefield Site, Tupelo National Battlefield, and part of Natchez Trace National Parkway. Pre-Civil War mansions are the special pride of Natchez, Oxford, Columbus, Vicksburg, and Jackson.

MISSOURI

Capital: Jefferson City
Governor: John D. Ashcroft, R
Organized as territory: June 4, 1812
Entered Union & (rank): Aug. 10, 1821 (24)
Present constitution adopted: 1945
Motto: *Salus populi suprema lex esto* (The welfare of the people shall be the supreme law)
STATE SYMBOLS: flower, Hawthorn (1923); **bird,** Bluebird (1927); **colors,** Red, white, and blue (1913); **song,** "Missouri Waltz" (1949); **fossil,** Crinoidea (1989); **musical instrument,** Fiddle (1987); **rock,** Mozarkite (1967); **mineral,** Galena (1967); **insect,** Honeybee (1985)
Nickname: Show-me State
Origin of name: Named after a tribe called Missouri Indians. "Missouri" means "town of the large canoes."
10 largest cities (1990 census): Kansas City, 435,146; St. Louis, 396,685; Springfield, 140,494; Independence, 112,301; St. Joseph, 71,852; Columbia, 69,101; St. Charles, 54,555; Florissant, 51,206; Lee's Summit, 46,418; St. Peter's, 45,779
Land area & (rank): 68,945 sq mi. (178,568 sq km) (18)
Geographic center: In Miller Co., 20 mi. SW of Jefferson City
Number of counties: 114, plus 1 independent city
Largest county (1990 census): St. Louis, 993,529
State forests and Tower sites: 134 (308,978 ac.)
State parks: 73 (105,325 ac.)[1]
1980 resident census population & (rank): 4,916,686 (15)
1990 resident census population, sex, & (rank): 5,117,073 (15). **Male:** 2,464,315; **Female:** 2,652,758. **White:** 4,486,228 (87.7%); **Black:** 548,208 (10.7%); **American Indian, Eskimo, or Aleut:** 19,835 (0.4%); **Asian or Pacific Islander:** 41,277 (0.8%); **Other race:**

21,525 (0.4%); **Hispanic:** 61,702 (1.2%). **1990 percent population under 18:** 25.7; **65 and over:** 14.0; **median age:** 33.5.

1. Includes 45 historic sites.

De Soto visited the Missouri area in 1541. France's claim to the entire region was based on La Salle's travels in 1682. French fur traders established Ste. Genevieve in 1735 and St. Louis was first settled in 1764.

The U.S. gained Missouri from France as part of the Louisiana Purchase in 1803, and the territory was admitted as a state following the Missouri Compromise of 1820. Throughout the pre-Civil War period and during the war, Missourians were sharply divided in their opinions about slavery and in their allegiances, supplying both Union and Confederate forces with troops. However, the state itself remained in the Union.

Historically, Missouri played a leading role as a gateway to the West, St. Joseph being the eastern starting point of the Pony Express, while the much-traveled Santa Fe and Oregon Trails began in Independence. Now a popular vacationland, Missouri has 11 major lakes and numerous fishing streams, springs, and caves. Bagnell Dam, across the Osage River in the Ozarks, completed in 1931, created one of the largest man-made lakes in the world, covering 65,000 acres of surface area.

Manufacturing, paced by the aerospace industry, provides more income and jobs than any other segment of the economy. Missouri is also a leading producer of transportation equipment, shoes, lead, and beer. Among the major crops are corn, soybeans, wheat, oats, barley, potatoes, tobacco, and cotton.

Points of interest include Mark Twain's boyhood home and Mark Twain Cave (Hannibal), the Harry S. Truman Library and Museum (Independence), the house where Jesse James was killed in St. Joseph, Jefferson National Expansion Memorial (St. Louis), and the Ozark National Scenic Riverway.

MONTANA

Capital: Helena
Governor: Stan Stephens, R
Organized as territory: May 26, 1864
Entered Union & (rank): Nov. 8, 1889 (41)
Present constitution adopted: 1972
Motto: *Oro y plata* (Gold and silver)
STATE SYMBOLS: flower, Bitterroot (1895); **tree,** Ponderosa pine (1949); **stones,** Sapphire and agate (1969); **bird,** Western meadowlark (1981); **song,** "Montana" (1945)
Nickname: Treasure State
Origin of name: Chosen from Latin dictionary by J. M. Ashley. It is a Latinized Spanish word meaning "mountainous."
10 largest cities (1990 census): Billings, 81,151; Great Falls, 55,097; Missoula, 42,918; Butte-Silver Bow[1], 33,941; Helena, 24,569; Bozeman, 22,660; Kalispell, 11,917; Anaconda-Deer Lodge County, 10,278; Havre, 10,201; Miles City, 8,461
Land area & (rank): 145,388 sq mi. (376,554 sq km) (4)
Geographic center: In Fergus Co., 12 mi. W of Lewistown
Number of counties: 56, plus small part of Yellowstone National Park
Largest county (1990 census): Yellowstone, 113,419
State forests: 7 (214,000 ac.)
State parks and recreation areas: 110 (18,273 ac.)

1980 resident census population & (rank): 786,690 (44)
1990 resident census population, sex, & (rank): 799,065 (44). **Male:** 395,769; **Female:** 403,296. **White:** 741,111 (92.7%); **Black:** 2,381 (0.3%); **American Indian, Eskimo, or Aleut:** 47,679 (6.0%); **Asian or Pacific Islander:** 4,259 (0.5%); **Other race:** 3,635 (0.5%); **Hispanic:** 12,174 (1.5%). **1990 percent population under 18:** 27.8; **65 and over:** 13.3; **median age:** 33.8.

1. Consolidated City.

First explored for France by François and Louis-Joseph Verendrye in the early 1740s, much of the region was acquired by the U.S. from France as part of the Louisiana Purchase in 1803. Before western Montana was obtained from Great Britain in the Oregon Treaty of 1846, American trading posts and forts had been established in the territory.

The major Indian wars (1867–1877) included the famous 1876 Battle of the Little Big Horn, better known as "Custer's Last Stand," in which Cheyennes and Sioux killed George A. Custer and more than 200 of his men in southeastern Montana.

Much of Montana's early history was concerned with mining with copper, lead, zinc, silver, coal, and oil as principal products.

Butte is the center of the area that once supplied half of the U.S. copper.

Fields of grain cover much of Montana's plains; it ranks high among the states in wheat and barley, with rye, oats, flaxseed, sugar beets, and potatoes other important crops. Sheep and cattle raising make significant contributions to the economy.

Tourist attractions include hunting, fishing, skiing, and dude ranching. Glacier National Park, on the Continental Divide, is a scenic and vacation wonderland with 60 glaciers, 200 lakes, and many streams with good trout fishing.

Other major points of interest include the Custer Battlefield National Monument, Virginia City, Yellowstone National Park, Museum of the Plains Indians at Browning, and the Fort Union Trading Post and Grant-Kohr's Ranch National Historic Sites.

NEBRASKA

Capital: Lincoln
Governor: Ben Nelson, D
Organized as territory: May 30, 1854
Entered Union & (rank): March 1, 1867 (37)
Present constitution adopted: Nov. 1, 1875 (extensively amended 1919–20)
Motto: Equality before the law
STATE SYMBOLS: flower, Goldenrod (1895); **tree,** Cottonwood (1972); **bird,** Western meadowlark (1929); **insect,** Honeybee (1975); **gemstone,** Blue agate (1967); **rock,** Prairie agate (1967); **fossil;** Mammoth (1967); **song,** "Beautiful Nebraska" (1967); **soil,** Typie Arguistolls, Holdrege Series (1979); **mammal,** Whitetail deer (1981)
Nicknames: Cornhusker State (1945); Beef State; The Tree Planter State (1895)
Origin of name: From an Oto Indian word meaning "flat water"
10 largest cities (1990 census): Omaha, 335,795; Lincoln, 191,972; Grand Island, 39,386; Bellevue, 30,982; Kearney, 24,396; Fremont, 23,680; Hastings, 22,837; North Platte, 22,605; Norfolk, 21,476; Columbus, 19,480
Land area & (rank): 76,644 sq mi. (198,508 sq km) (15)
Geographic center: In Custer Co., 10 mi. NW of Broken Bow

Number of counties: 93
Largest county (1990 census): Douglas, 416,444
State forests: None
State parks: 78 areas, historical and recreational; 7 major areas
1980 resident census population & (rank): 1,569,825 (35)
1990 resident census population, sex, & (rank):
1,578,385 (36). **Male:** 769,439; **Female:** 808,946. **White:** 1,480,558 (93.8%); **Black:** 57,404 (3.6%); **American Indian, Eskimo, or Aleut:** 12,410 (0.8%); **Asian or Pacific Islander:** 12,422 (0.8%); **Other race:** 15,591 (1.0%); **Hispanic:** 36,969 (2.3%). **1990 percent population under 18:** 27.2; **65 and over:** 14.1; **median age:** 33.0.

French fur traders first visited Nebraska in the early 1700s. Part of the Louisiana Purchase in 1803, Nebraska was explored by Lewis and Clark in 1804–06.

Robert Stuart pioneered the Oregon Trail across Nebraska in 1812–13 and the first permanent settlement was established at Bellevue in 1823. Western Nebraska was acquired by treaty following the Mexican War in 1848. The Union Pacific began its transcontinental railroad at Omaha in 1865. In 1937, Nebraska became the only state in the Union to have a unicameral (one-house) legislature. Members are elected to it without party designation.

Nebraska is a leading grain-producer with bumper crops of rye, corn, and wheat. More varieties of grass, valuable for forage, grow in this state than in any other in the nation.

The state's sizable cattle and hog industries make Dakota City and Lexington the nation's largest meat-packing center and the largest cattle markets in the world.

Manufacturing has become diversified in Nebraska, strengthening the state's economic base. Firms making electronic components, auto accessories, pharmaceuticals, and mobile homes have joined such older industries as clothing, farm machinery, chemicals, and transportation equipment. Oil was discovered in 1939 and natural gas in 1949.

Among the principal attractions are Agate Fossil Beds, Homestead, and Scotts Bluff National Monuments; Chimney Rock National Historic Site; a recreated pioneer village at Minden; SAC Museum at Bellevue; the Stuhr Museum of the Prairie Pioneer with 57 original 19th-century buildings near Grand Island; the Sheldon Memorial Art Gallery at the University of Nebraska in Lincoln; and the Lied Center for the Performing Arts located on the University of Nebraska campus in Lincoln.

NEVADA

Capital: Carson City
Governor: Robert J. Miller, D
Organized as territory: March 2, 1861
Entered Union & (rank): Oct. 31, 1864 (36)
Present constitution adopted: 1864
Motto: All for Our Country
STATE SYMBOLS: flower, Sagebrush (1959); **trees,** Single-leaf pinon (1953) and Bristlecone pine (1987); **bird,** Mountain bluebird (1967); **animal,** Desert bighorn sheep (1973); **colors,** Silver and blue (1983); **song,** "Home Means Nevada" (1933); **rock,** Sandstone (1987); **precious gemstone,** Virgin Valley Black Fire Opal (1987); **semiprecious gemstone,** Nevada Turquoise (1987); **grass,** Indian Ricegrass (1977); **metal,** Silver (1977); **fossil,** Ichthyosaur (1977); **fish,** Lahontan Cutthroat Trout (1981); **reptile,** Desert tortoise (1989)
Nicknames: Sagebrush State; Silver State; Battle-born

State
Origin of name: Spanish: "snowcapped"
10 largest cities (1990 census): Las Vegas, 258,295; Reno, 133,850; Henderson, 64,942; Sparks, 53,367; North Las Vegas, 47,707; Carson City, 40,443; Elko, 14,736; Boulder City, 12,567; Fallon, 6,438; Winnemucca, 6,134
Land area & (rank): 109,894 sq mi. (284,624 sq km) (7)
Geographic center: In Lander Co., 26 mi. SE of Austin
Number of counties: 16, plus 1 independent city
Largest county (1990 census): Clark, 741,459
State forests: None
State parks: 20 (150,000 ac., including leased lands)
1980 resident census population & (rank): 800,493 (43)
1990 resident census population, sex, & (rank):
1,201,833 (39). **Male:** 611,880; **Female:** 589,953. **White:** 1,012,695 (84.3%); **Black:** 78,771 (6.6%); **American Indian, Eskimo, or Aleut:** 19,637 (1.6%); **Asian or Pacific Islander:** 38,127 (3.2%); **Other race:** 52,603 (4.4%); **Hispanic:** 124,419 (10.4%). **1990 percent population under 18:** 24.7; **65 and over:** 10.6; **median age:** 33.3.

Trappers and traders, including Jedediah Smith, and Peter Skene Ogden, entered the Nevada area in the 1820s. In 1843–45, John C. Fremont and Kit Carson explored the Great Basin and Sierra Nevada.

In 1848 following the Mexican War, the U.S. obtained the region and the first permanent settlement was a Mormon trading post near present-day Genoa.

The driest state in the nation with an average annual rainfall of only about 7 inches,[1] much of Nevada is uninhabited, sagebrush-covered desert.

Nevada was made famous by the discovery of the fabulous Comstock Lode in 1859 and its mines have produced large quantities of gold, silver, copper, lead, zinc, mercury, barite, and tungsten. Oil was discovered in 1954. Gold now far exceeds all other minerals in value of production.

In 1931, the state created two industries, divorce and gambling. For many years, Reno and Las Vegas were the "divorce capitals of the nation." More liberal divorce laws in many states have ended this distinction, but Nevada is the gambling and entertainment capital of the U.S. State gambling taxes account for 61.3% of general fund tax revenues. Although Nevada leads the nation in per capita gambling revenue, it ranks only fourth in total gambling revenue.

Near Las Vegas, on the Colorado River, stands Hoover Dam, which impounds the waters of Lake Mead, one of the world's largest artificial lakes.

The state's agricultural crop consists mainly of hay, alfalfa seed, barley, wheat, and potatoes.

Nevada manufactures gaming equipment; lawn and garden irrigation devices; titanium products; seismic and machinery monitoring devices; and specialty printing.

Major resort areas flourish in Lake Tahoe, Reno, and Las Vegas. Recreation areas include those at Pyramid Lake, Lake Tahoe, and Lake Mead and Lake Mohave, both in Lake Mead National Recreation Area. Among the other attractions are Hoover Dam, Virginia City, and Great Basin National Park (includes Lehman Caves).

---

1. Wettest part of state receives about 40 inches of precipitation per year, while driest spot has less than four inches per year.

NEW HAMPSHIRE

Capital: Concord
Governor: Judd A. Gregg, R
Entered Union & (rank): June 21, 1788 (9)
Present constitution adopted: 1784
Motto: Live free or die
STATE SYMBOLS: flower, Purple lilac (1919); **tree,** White birch (1947); **bird,** Purple finch (1957); **songs,** "Old New Hampshire" (1949) and "New Hampshire, My New Hampshire" (1963)
Nickname: Granite State
Origin of name: From the English county of Hampshire
10 largest cities (1990 census): Manchester, 99,567; Nashua, 79,662; Concord, 36,006; Rochester, 26,630; Portsmouth, 25,925; Dover, 25,042; Keene, 22,430; Laconia, 15,743; Claremont, 13,902; Lebanon, 12,183
Land area & (rank): 8,993 sq mi. (23,292 sq km) (44)
Geographic center: In Belknap Co., 3 mi. E of Ashland
Number of counties: 10
Largest county (1990 census): Hillsborough, 336,073
State forests & parks: 175 (96,975 ac.)
1980 resident census population & (rank): 920,610 (42)
1990 resident census population, sex, & (rank): 1,109,252 (41). **Male:** 543,544; **Female:** 565,708. **White:** 1,087,433 (98.0%); **Black:** 7,198 (0.6%); **American Indian, Eskimo, or Aleut:** 2,134 (0.2%); **Asian or Pacific Islander:** 9,343 (0.8%); **Other race:** 3,144 (0.3%); **Hispanic:** 11,333 (1.0%). **1990 percent population under 18:** 25.1; **65 and over:** 11.3; **median age:** 32.8.

Under an English land grant, Capt. John Smith sent settlers to establish a fishing colony at the mouth of the Piscataqua River, near present-day Rye and Dover, in 1623. Capt. John Mason, who participated in the founding of Portsmouth in 1630, gave New Hampshire its name.

After a 38-year period of union with Massachusetts, New Hampshire was made a separate royal colony in 1679. As leaders in the revolutionary cause, New Hampshire delegates received the honor of being the first to vote for the Declaration of Independence on July 4, 1776. New Hampshire is the only state that ever played host at the formal conclusion of a foreign war when, in 1905, Portsmouth was the scene of the treaty ending the Russo-Japanese War.

Abundant water power early turned New Hampshire into an industrial state and manufacturing is the principal source of income in the state. The most important industrial products are electrical and other machinery, textiles, pulp and paper products, and stone and clay products.

Dairy and poultry farming and growing fruit, truck vegetables, corn, potatoes, and hay are the major agricultural pursuits.

Tourism, because of New Hampshire's scenic and recreational resources, now brings over $2.2 billion into the state annually.

Vacation attractions include Lake Winnipesaukee, largest of 1,300 lakes and ponds; the 724,000-acre White Mountain National Forest; Daniel Webster's birthplace near Franklin; Strawbery Banke, restored building of the original settlement at Portsmouth; and the famous "Old Man of the Mountain" granite head profile, the state's official emblem, at Franconia.

NEW JERSEY

Capital: Trenton
Governor: James J. Florio, D
Entered Union & (rank): Dec. 18, 1787 (3)
Present constitution adopted: 1947
Motto: Liberty and prosperity
STATE SYMBOLS: flower, Purple violet (1913); **bird,** Eastern goldfinch (1935); **insect,** Honeybee (1974); **tree,** Red oak (1950); **animal,** Horse (1977); **colors,** Buff and blue (1965)
Nickname: Garden State
Origin of name: From the Channel Isle of Jersey
10 largest cities (1990 census)[1]: Newark, 275,221; Jersey City, 228,537; Paterson, 140,891; Elizabeth, 110,002; Edison[2], 88,680; Trenton, 88,675; Camden, 87,492; East Orange, 73,552; Clifton, 71,742; Cherry Hill[2], 69,319
Land area & (rank): 7,468 sq mi. (19,342 sq km) (46)
Geographic center: In Mercer Co., 5 mi. SE of Trenton
Number of counties: 21
Largest county (1990 census): Bergen, 825,380
State forests: 11
State parks: 35 (67,111 ac.)
1980 resident census population & (rank): 7,364,823 (9)
1990 resident census population, sex, & (rank): 7,730,188 (9). **Male:** 3,735,685; **Female:** 3,994,503. **White:** 6,130,465 (79.3%); **Black:** 1,036,825 (13.4%); **American Indian, Eskimo, or Aleut:** 14,970 (0.2%); **Asian or Pacific Islander:** 272,521 (3.5%); **Other race:** 275,407 (3.6%); **Hispanic:** 739,861 (9.6%). **1990 percent population under 18:** 23.3; **65 and over:** 13.4; **median age:** 34.5.

---

1. These are the official 1990 census largest cities. However, the township of Woodbridge, 93,086, is also a legal municipality or city. 2. Census Designated Place.

New Jersey's early colonial history was involved with that of New York (New Netherlands), of which it was a part. One year after the Dutch surrender to England in 1664, New Jersey was organized as an English colony under Gov. Philip Carteret.

In the late 1600s the colony was divided between Carteret and William Penn; later it would be administered by the royal governor of New York. Finally, in 1738, New Jersey was separated from New York under its own royal governor, Lewis Morris.

Because of its key location between New York City and Philadelphia, New Jersey saw much fighting during the American Revolution.

Today, New Jersey, an area of wide industrial diversification, is known as the Crossroads of the East. Products from over 15,000 factories can be delivered overnight to almost 60 million people, representing 12 states and the District of Columbia. The greatest single industry is chemicals and New Jersey is one of the foremost research centers in the world. Many large oil refineries are located in northern New Jersey and other important manufactures are pharmaceuticals, instruments, machinery, electrical goods, and apparel.

Of the total land area, 37% is forested. Farmland is declining. In 1990 there were about 8,100 farms, with over 870,000 acres under harvest. The state ranks high in production of almost all garden vegetables. Tomatoes, asparagus, corn, and blueberries are important crops, and poultry farming and dairying make significant contributions to the state's economy.

Tourism is the second largest industry in New Jersey. The state has numerous resort areas on 127 miles of Atlantic coastline. In 1977, New Jersey voters approved legislation allowing legalized casino gambling in Atlantic City. Points of interest include the Walt Whitman House in Camden, the Delaware Water Gap, the Edison National Historic Site in West Orange, and Princeton University.

NEW MEXICO

Capital: Santa Fe
Governor: Bruce King, D
Organized as territory: Sept. 9, 1850
Entered Union & (rank): Jan. 6, 1912 (47)
Present constitution adopted: 1911
Motto: *Crescit eundo* (It grows as it goes)
STATE SYMBOLS: flower, Yucca (1927); **tree,** Piñon (1949); **animal,** Black bear (1963); **bird,** Roadrunner (1949); **fish,** Cutthroat trout (1955); **vegetables,** Chili and frijol (1965); **gem,** Turquoise (1967); **colors,** Red and yellow of old Spain (1925); **song,** "O Fair New Mexico" (1917); **Spanish language song,** "Asi Es Nuevo Méjico" (1971); **poem,** A Nuevo México (1991); **grass,** Blue gramma; **fossil,** Coelophysis; **cookie,** Bizcochito (1989); **insect,** Tarantula hawk wasp (1989)
Nicknames: Land of Enchantment; Sunshine State
Origin of name: From the country of Mexico
10 largest cities (1990 census): Albuquerque, 384,736; Las Cruces, 62,126; Santa Fe, 55,859; Roswell, 44,654; Farmington, 33,997; Rio Rancho, 32,505; Clovis, 30,954; Hobbs, 29,115; Alamogordo, 27,596; Carlsbad, 24,952
Land area & (rank): 121,335 sq mi. (314,258 sq km) (5)
Geographic center: In Torrance Co., 12 mi. SSW of Willard
Number of counties: 33
Largest county (1990 census): Bernalillo, 480,577
State-owned forested land: 933,000 ac.
State parks: 29 (105,012 ac.)
1980 resident census population & (rank): 1,302,894 (37)
1990 resident census population, sex, & (rank): 1,515,069 (37). **Male:** 745,253; **Female:** 769,816. **White:** 1,146,028 (75.6%); **Black:** 30,210 (2.0%); **American Indian, Eskimo, or Aleut:** 134,355 (8.9%); **Asian or Pacific Islander:** 14,124 (0.9%); **Other race:** 190,352 (12.6%); **Hispanic:** 579,224 (38.2%). **1990 percent population under 18:** 29.5; **65 and over:** 10.8; **median age:** 31.3.

Francisco Vásquez de Coronado, Spanish explorer searching for gold, traveled the region that became New Mexico in 1540–42. In 1598 the first Spanish settlement was established on the Rio Grande River by Juan de Onate and in 1610 Santa Fe was founded and made the capital of New Mexico.

The U.S. acquired most of New Mexico in 1848, as a result of the Mexican War, and the remainder in the 1853 Gadsden Purchase. Union troops captured the territory from the Confederates during the Civil War. With the surrender of Geronimo in 1886, the Apache Wars and most of the Indian troubles in the area were ended.

Since 1945, New Mexico has been a leader in energy research and development with extensive experiments conducted at Los Alamos Scientific Laboratory and Sandia Laboratories in the nuclear, solar, and geothermal areas.

Minerals are the state's richest natural resource and New Mexico is one of the U.S. leaders in output of uranium and potassium salts. Petroleum, natural gas, copper, gold, silver, zinc, lead, and molybdenum also contribute heavily to the state's income.

The principal manufacturing industries include food products, chemicals, transportation equipment, lumber, electrical machinery, and stone-clay-glass products. More than two thirds of New Mexico's farm income comes from livestock products, especially sheep. Cotton, pecans, and sorghum are the most important field crops. Corn, peanuts, beans, onions, chile, and lettuce are also grown.

Tourist attractions in New Mexico include the Carlsbad Caverns National Park, Inscription Rock at El Morro National Monument, the ruins at Fort Union, Billy the Kid mementos at Lincoln, the White Sands and Gila Cliff Dwellings National Monuments, and the Chaco Culture National Historical Park.

NEW YORK

Capital: Albany
Governor: Mario M. Cuomo, D
Entered Union & (rank): July 26, 1788 (11)
Present constitution adopted: 1777 (last revised 1938)
Motto: *Excelsior* (Ever upward)
STATE SYMBOLS: animal, Beaver (1975); **fish,** Brook trout (1975); **gem,** Garnet (1969); **flower,** Rose (1955); **tree,** Sugar maple (1956); **bird,** Bluebird (1970); **insect,** Ladybug (1989); **song,** "I Love New York" (1980)
Nickname: Empire State
Origin of name: In honor of the English Duke of York
10 largest cities (1990 census): New York, 7,322,564; Buffalo, 328,123; Rochester, 231,636; Yonkers, 188,082; Syracuse, 163,860; Albany, 101,082; Utica, 68,637; New Rochelle, 67,265; Mount Vernon, 67,153; Schenectady, 65,566
Land area & (rank): 47,377 sq mi. (122,707 sq km) (30)
Geographic center: In Madison Co., 12 mi. S of Oneida and 26 mi. SW of Utica
Number of counties: 62
Largest county (1990 census): Kings, 2,300,664
State forest preserves: Adirondacks, 2,500,000 ac.; Catskills, 250,000 ac.
State parks: 150 (250,000 ac.)
1980 resident census population & (rank): 17,558,072 (2)
1990 resident census population, sex, & (rank): 17,990,455 (2). **Male:** 8,625,673; **Female:** 9,364,782. **White:** 13,385,255 (74.4%); **Black:** 2,859,055 (15.9%); **American Indian, Eskimo, or Aleut:** 62,651 (0.3%); **Asian or Pacific Islander:** 693,760 (3.9%); **Other race:** 989,734 (5.5%); **Hispanic:** 2,214,026 (12.3%). **1990 percent population under 18:** 23.7; **65 and over:** 13.1; **median age:** 33.9,.

Giovanni da Verrazano, Italian-born navigator sailing for France, discovered New York Bay in 1524. Henry Hudson, an Englishman employed by the Dutch, reached the bay and sailed up the river now bearing his name in 1609, the same year that northern New York was explored and claimed for France by Samuel de Champlain.

In 1624 the first permanent Dutch settlement was established at Fort Orange (now Albany); one year later Peter Minuit is said to have purchased Manhattan Island from the Indians for trinkets worth about $24 and founded the Dutch colony of New Amsterdam (now New York City), which was surrendered to the English in 1664.

For a short time, New York City was the U.S. capital and George Washington was inaugurated there as first President on April 30, 1789.

New York's extremely rapid commercial growth may be partly attributed to Governor De Witt Clinton, who pushed through the construction of the Erie Canal (Buffalo to Albany), which was opened in 1825. Today, the 559-mile Governor Thomas E. Dewey Thruway connects New York City with Buffalo and with Connecticut, Massachusetts, and Pennsylvania express highways. Two toll-free superhighways, the Adirondack Northway (linking Albany with the Canadian border) and the North-South-Expressway (crossing central New York from the Pennsylvania border to the Thousand Islands) have been opened.

New York, with the great metropolis of New York City, is the spectacular nerve center of the nation. It is a leader in manufacturing, foreign trade, commercial and financial transactions, book and magazine publishing, and theatrical production.

New York City is not only a national but an international leader. A leading seaport, its John F. Kennedy International Airport is one of the busiest airports in the world. It is the largest manufacturing center in the country and its apparel industry is the city's largest manufacturing employer, with printing and publishing second.

Nearly all the rest of the state's manufacturing is done on Long Island, along the Hudson River north to Albany and through the Mohawk Valley, Central New York, and Southern Tier regions to Buffalo. The St. Lawrence seaway and power projects have opened the North Country to industrial expansion and have given the state a second seacoast.

The state ranks second in the nation in manufacturing with 1,192,400 employees in 1989. The principal industries are apparel, printing and publishing, leather products, instruments and electronic equipment.

The convention and tourist business is one of the state's most important sources of income.

New York farms are famous for raising cattle and calves, producing corn for grain, poultry, and the raising of vegetables and fruits. The state is a leading wine producer.

Among the major points of interest are Castle Clinton, Fort Stanwix, and Statue of Liberty National Monuments; Niagara Falls; U.S. Military Academy at West Point; National Historic Sites that include homes of Franklin D. Roosevelt at Hyde Park and Theodore Roosevelt in Oyster Bay and New York City; National Memorials, including Grant's Tomb and Federal Hall in New York City; Fort Ticonderoga; the Baseball Hall of Fame in Cooperstown; and the United Nations, skyscrapers, museums, theaters, and parks in New York City.

NORTH CAROLINA

Capital: Raleigh
Governor: James G. Martin, R
Entered Union & (rank): Nov. 21, 1789 (12)
Present constitution adopted: 1971
Motto: *Esse quam videri* (To be rather than to seem)
STATE SYMBOLS: flower, Dogwood (1941); **tree,** Pine (1963); **bird,** Cardinal (1943); **mammal,** Gray squirrel (1969); **insect,** Honeybee (1973); **reptile,** Turtle (1979); **gemstone,** Emerald (1973); **shell,** Scotch bonnet (1965); **historic boat,** Shad Boat (1987); **beverage,** Milk (1987); **rock,** Granite (1979); **dog,** Plott Hound (1989); **song,** "The Old North State" (1927); **colors,** Red and blue (1945)
Nickname: Tar Heel State
Origin of name: In honor of Charles I of England
10 largest cities (1990 census): Charlotte, 395,934; Raleigh, 207,951; Greensboro, 183,521; Winston-Salem, 143,485; Durham, 136,611; Fayetteville, 75,695; High Point, 69,496; Asheville, 61,607; Wilmington, 55,530; Gastonia, 54,732
Land area & (rank): 48,843 sq mi. (126,504 sq km) (29)
Geographic center: In Chatham Co., 10 mi. NW of Sanford
Number of counties: 100
Largest county (1990 census): Mecklenburg, 511,433
State forests: 1
State parks: 30 (125,000 ac.)
1980 resident census population & (rank): 5,881,766 (10)

1990 resident census population, sex, & (rank): 6,628,637 (10). **Male:** 3,214,290; **Female:** 3,414,347. **White:** 5,008,491 (75.6%); **Black:** 1,456,323 (22.0%); **American Indian, Eskimo, or Aleut:** 80,155 (1.2%); **Asian or Pacific Islander:** 52,166 (0.8%); **Other race:** 31,502 (0.5%); **Hispanic:** 76,726 (1.2%). **1990 percent population under 18:** 24.2; **65 and over:** 12.1; **median age:** 33.1.

English colonists, sent by Sir Walter Raleigh, unsuccessfully attempted to settle Roanoke Island in 1585 and 1587. Virginia Dare, born there in 1587, was the first child of English parentage born in America.

In 1653 the first permanent settlements were established by English colonists from Virginia near the Roanoke and Chowan Rivers.

The region was established as an English proprietary colony in 1663–65 and its early history was the scene of Culpepper's Rebellion (1677), the Quaker-led Cary Rebellion of 1708, the Tuscarora Indian War in 1711–13, and many pirate raids.

During the American Revolution, there was relatively little fighting within the state, but many North Carolinians saw action elsewhere. Despite considerable pro-Union, anti-slavery sentiment, North Carolina joined the Confederacy.

North Carolina is the nation's largest furniture, tobacco, brick, and textile producer. It holds second place in the Southeast in population and first place in the value of its industrial and agricultural production. This production is highly diversified, with metalworking, chemicals, and paper constituting enormous industries. Tobacco, corn, cotton, hay, peanuts, and truck and vegetable crops are of major importance. It is the country's leading producer of mica and lithium.

Tourism is also important, with travelers and vacationers spending more than $1 billion annually in North Carolina. Sports include year-round golfing, skiing at mountain resorts, both fresh and salt water fishing, and hunting.

Among the major attractions are the Great Smoky Mountains, the Blue Ridge National Parkway, the Cape Hatteras and Cape Lookout National Seashores, the Wright Brothers National Memorial at Kitty Hawk, Guilford Courthouse and Moores Creek National Military Parks, Carl Sandburg's home near Hendersonville, and the Old Salem Restoration in Winston-Salem.

NORTH DAKOTA

Capital: Bismarck
Governor: George A. Sinner, D
Organized as territory: March 2, 1861
Entered Union & (rank): Nov. 2, 1889 (39)
Present constitution adopted: 1889
Motto: Liberty and union, now and forever: one and inseparable
STATE SYMBOLS: tree, American elm (1947); **bird,** Western meadowlark (1947); **song,** "North Dakota Hymn" (1947)
Nickname: Sioux State; Flickertail State; Peace Garden State
Origin of name: From the Dakotah tribe, meaning "allies"
10 largest cities (1990 census): Fargo, 74,111; Grand Forks, 49,425; Bismarck, 49,256; Minot, 34,544; Dickinson, 16,097; Jamestown, 15,571; Mandan, 15,177; Williston, 13,131; West Fargo, 12,287; Wahpeton, 8,751

Land area & (rank): 70,665 sq mi. (183,022 sq km) (17)
Geographic center: In Sheridan Co., 5 mi. SW of
McClusky
Number of counties: 53
Largest county (1990 census): Cass, 102,874
State forests: None
State parks: 14 (14,922.6 ac.)
1980 resident census population & (rank): 652,717 (46)
1990 resident census population, sex, & (rank): 638,800
(47). **Male:** 318,201; **Female:** 320,599. **White:** 604,142
(94.6%); **Black:** 3,524 (0.6%); **American Indian, Eskimo, or Aleut:** 25,917 (4.1%); **Asian or Pacific Islander:**
3,462 (0.5%); **Other race:** 1,755 (0.3%); **Hispanic:** 4,665
(0.7%). **1990 percent population under 18:** 27.5; **65 and
over:** 14.3; **median age:** 32.4.

North Dakota was explored in 1738–40 by French
Canadians led by La Verendrye. In 1803, the U.S. acquired most of North Dakota from France in the Louisiana Purchase. Lewis and Clark explored the region
in 1804–06 and the first settlements were made at
Pembina in 1812 by Scottish and Irish families while
this area was still in dispute between the U.S. and
Great Britain.

In 1818, the U.S. obtained the northeastern part of
North Dakota by treaty with Great Britain and took
possession of Pembina in 1823.

North Dakota is the most rural of all the states,
with farms covering more than 90% of the land.
North Dakota ranks first in the Nation's production of
spring and durum wheat, and the state's coal and oil
reserves are plentiful.

Other agricultural products include barley, rye, sun-
flowers, dry edible beans, honey, oats, flaxseed, sugar
beets, and hay; beef cattle, sheep, and hogs.

Recently, manufacturing industries have grown, especially food processing and farm equipment. The
state also produces natural gas, lignite, salt, clay,
sand, and gravel.

The Garrison Dam on the Missouri River provides
extensive irrigation and produces 400,000 kilowatts
of electricity for the Missouri Basin areas.

Known for its waterfowl, grouse, and deer hunting
and bass, trout, and northern pike fishing, North Da-
kota has 20 state parks and recreation areas. Points of
interest include the International Peace Garden near
Dunseith, Fort Union Trading Post National Historic
Site, the State Capitol at Bismarck, the Badlands, and
Fort Lincoln, now a state park, from which Gen.
George Custer set out on his last campaign in 1876.

OHIO

Capital: Columbus
Governor: George V. Voinovich, R
Entered Union & (rank): March 1, 1803 (17)
Present constitution adopted: 1851
Motto: With God, all things are possible
STATE SYMBOLS: flower, Scarlet carnation (1904); **tree,**
Buckeye (1953); **bird,** Cardinal (1933); **insect,** Ladybug
(1975); **gemstone,** Flint (1965); **song,** "Beautiful Ohio"
(1969); **drink,** Tomato juice (1965)
Nickname: Buckeye State
Origin of name: From an Iroquoian word meaning "great
river"
10 largest cities (1990 census): Columbus, 632,910;
Cleveland, 505,616; Cincinnati, 364,040; Toledo, 332,943;
Akron, 223,019; Dayton, 182,044; Youngstown, 95,732;
Parma, 87,876; Canton, 84,161; Lorain, 71,245
Land area & (rank): 41,004 sq mi. (106,201 sq km) (35)

Geographic center: In Delaware Co., 25 mi. NNE of Co-
lumbus
Number of counties: 88
Largest county (1990 census): Cuyahoga, 1,412,140
State forests: 19 (172,744 ac.)
State parks: 71 (198,027 ac.)
1980 resident census population & (rank): 10,797,630 (6)
1990 resident census population, sex, & (rank):
10,847,115 (7). **Male:** 5,226,340; **Female:** 5,620,775.
White: 9,521,756 (87.8%); **Black:** 1,154,826 (10.6%);
American Indian, Eskimo, or Aleut: 20,358 (0.2%);
Asian or Pacific Islander: 91,179 (0.8%); **Other race:**
58,996 (0.5%); **Hispanic:** 139,696 (1.3%). **1990 percent
population under 18:** 25.8; **65 and over:** 13.0; **median
age:** 33.3.

First explored for France by La Salle in 1669, the
Ohio region became British property after the French
and Indian War. Ohio was acquired by the U.S. after
the Revolutionary War in 1783 and, in 1788, the first
permanent settlement was established at Marietta,
capital of the Northwest Territory.

The 1790s saw severe fighting with the Indians in
Ohio; a major battle was won by Maj. Gen. Anthony
Wayne at Fallen Timbers in 1794. In the War of
1812, Commodore Oliver H. Perry defeated the British in the Battle of Lake Erie on Sept. 10, 1813.

Ohio is one of the nation's industrial leaders, ranking third in the value of manufactured products. Important manufacturing centers are located in or near
Ohio's major cities. Akron is known for rubber; Canton for roller bearings; Cincinnati for jet engines and
machine tools; Cleveland for auto assembly and
parts, refining, and steel; Dayton for office machines,
refrigeration, and heating and auto equipment;
Youngstown and Steubenville for steel; and Toledo
for glass and auto parts.

The state's thousands of factories almost overshad-
ow its importance in agriculture and mining. Its fertile soil produces soybeans, corn, oats, grapes, and
clover. More than half of Ohio's farm receipts come
from dairying and sheep and hog raising. Ohio is the
top state in lime production and among the leaders in
coal, clay, salt, sand, and gravel. Petroleum, gypsum,
cement, and natural gas are also important.

Tourism is a valuable revenue producer, bringing
in over $3 billion annually. Attractions include the
Indian burial grounds at Mound City Group National
Monument, Perry's Victory International Peace Memorial, the Pro Football Hall of Fame at Canton, and
the homes of Presidents Grant, Taft, Hayes, Harding,
and Garfield.

OKLAHOMA

Capital: Oklahoma City
Governor: David Walters, D
Organized as territory: May 2, 1890
Entered Union & (rank): Nov. 16, 1907 (46)
Present constitution adopted: 1907
Motto: *Labor omnia vincit* (Labor conquers all things)
STATE SYMBOLS: flower, Mistletoe (1893); **tree,** Redbud
(1937); **bird,** Scissor-tailed flycatcher (1951); **animal,**
Bison (1972); **reptile,** Mountain boomer lizard (1969);
stone, Rose Rock (barite rose) (1968); **colors,** Green
and white (1915); **song,** "Oklahoma" (1953)
Nickname: Sooner State
Origin of name: From two Choctaw Indian words mean-
ing "red people"

10 largest cities (1990 census): Oklahoma City, 444,719; Tulsa, 367,302; Lawton, 80,561; Norman, 80,071; Broken Arrow, 58,043; Edmond, 52,315; Midwest City, 52,267; Enid, 45,309; Moore, 40,318; Muskogee, 37,708
Land area & (rank): 68,655 sq mi. (177,817 sq km) (19)
Geographic center: In Oklahoma Co., 8 mi. N of Oklahoma City
Number of counties: 77
Largest county (1990 census): Oklahoma, 599,611
State forests: None
State parks: 36 (57,487 ac.)
1980 resident census population & (rank): 3,025,290 (26)
1990 resident census population, sex, & (rank): 3,145,585 (28). **Male:** 1,530,819; **Female:** 1,614,766. **White:** 2,583,512 (82.1%); **Black:** 233,801 (7.4%); **American Indian, Eskimo, or Aleut:** 252,420 (8.0%); **Asian or Pacific Islander:** 33,563 (1.1%); **Other race:** 42,289 (1.3%); **Hispanic:** 86,160 (2.7%). **1990 percent population under 18:** 26.6; **65 and over:** 13.5; **median age:** 33.2.

Francisco Vásquez de Coronado first explored the region for Spain in 1541. The U.S. acquired most of Oklahoma in 1803 in the Louisiana Purchase from France; the Western Panhandle region became U.S. territory with the annexation of Texas in 1845.

Set aside as Indian Territory in 1834, the region was divided into Indian Territory and Oklahoma Territory on May 2, 1890. The two were combined to make a new state, Oklahoma, on Nov. 16, 1907.

On April 22, 1889, the first day homesteading was permitted, 50,000 people swarmed into the area. Those who tried to beat the noon starting gun were called "Sooners." Hence the state's nickname.

Oil made Oklahoma a rich state, but natural gas production has now surpassed it. Oil refining, meat packing, food processing, and machinery manufacturing (especially construction and oil equipment) are important industries.

Other minerals produced in Oklahoma include helium, gypsum, zinc, cement, coal, copper, and silver.

Oklahoma's rich plains produce bumper yields of wheat, as well as large crops of sorghum, hay, cotton, and peanuts. More than half of Oklahoma's annual farm receipts are contributed by livestock products, including cattle, dairy products, and broilers.

Tourist attractions include the National Cowboy Hall of Fame in Oklahoma City, the Will Rogers Memorial in Claremore, the Cherokee Cultural Center with a restored Cherokee village, the restored Fort Gibson Stockade near Muskogee, and the Lake Texoma recreation area, Pari-Mutual horse racing at Remington Park in Oklahoma City, and Blue Ribbon Downs in Sallisaw.

OREGON

Capital: Salem
Governor: Barbara Roberts, D
Organized as territory: Aug. 14, 1848
Entered Union & (rank): Feb. 14, 1859 (33)
Present constitution adopted: 1859
Motto: "Alis volat Propriis" ("She flies with her own wings") (1987)
STATE SYMBOLS: flower, Oregon grape (1899); **tree,** Douglas fir (1939); **animal,** Beaver (1969); **bird,** Western meadowlark (1927); **fish,** Chinook salmon (1961); **rock,** Thunderegg (1965); **colors,** Navy blue and gold (1959); **song,** "Oregon, My Oregon" (1927)
Nickname: Beaver State
Poet Laureate: William E. Stafford (1974)

Origin of name: Unknown. However, it is generally accepted that the name, first used by Jonathan Carver in 1778, was taken from the writings of Maj. Robert Rogers, an English army officer.
10 largest cities (1990 census): Portland, 437,319; Eugene, 112,669; Salem, 107,786; Gresham, 68,235; Beaverton, 53,310; Medford, 46,951; Corvallis, 44,757; Springfield, 44,683; Hillsboro, 37,520; Lake Oswego, 30,576
Land area & (rank): 96,184 sq mi. (249,117 sq km) (10)
Geographic center: In Crook Co., 25 mi. SSE of Prineville
Number of counties: 36
Largest county (1990 census): Multnomah, 583,887
State forests: 820,000 ac.
State parks: 240 (93,330 ac.)
1980 resident census population & (rank): 2,633,105 (30)
1990 resident census population, sex, & (rank): 2,842,321 (29). **Male:** 1,397,073; **Female:** 1,445,248. **White:** 2,636,787 (92.8%); **Black:** 46,178 (1.6%); **American Indian, Eskimo, or Aleut:** 38,496 (1.4%); **Asian or Pacific Islander:** 69,269 (2.4%); **Other race:** 51,591 (1.8%); **Hispanic:** 112,707 (4.0%). **1990 percent population under 18:** 25.5; **65 and over:** 13.8; **median age:** 34.5.

Spanish and English sailors are believed to have sighted the Oregon coast in the 1500s and 1600s. Capt. James Cook, seeking the Northwest Passage, charted some of the coastline in 1778. In 1792, Capt. Robert Gray, in the *Columbia,* discovered the river named after his ship and claimed the area for the U.S.

In 1805 the Lewis and Clark expedition explored the area and John Jacob Astor's fur depot, Astoria, was founded in 1811. Disputes for control of Oregon between American settlers and the Hudson Bay Company were finally resolved in the 1846 Oregon Treaty in which Great Britain gave up claims to the region.

Oregon has a $5.5 billion wood processing industry. Its salmon-fishing industry is one of the world's largest.

In agriculture, the state leads in growing peppermint, winter pears, fresh plums, prunes, blackberries, boysenberries, filberts, Blue Lake beans, and cover seed crops, and also raises strawberries, hops, wheat and other grains, sugar beets, potatoes, green peas, fiber flax, dairy products, livestock and poultry, apples, pears, and cherries. Oregon is the source of all the nickel produced in the U.S.

With the low-cost electric power provided by Bonneville Dam, McNary Dam, and other dams in the Pacific Northwest, Oregon has developed steadily as a manufacturing state. Leading manufactures are lumber and plywood, metalwork, machinery, aluminum, chemicals, paper, food packing, and electronic equipment.

Crater Lake National Park, Mount Hood, and Bonneville Dam on the Columbia are major tourist attractions. Oregon Dunes National Recreation Area has been established near Florence. Other points of interest include the Oregon Caves National Monument, Cape Perpetua in Siuslaw National Forest, Columbia River Gorge between The Dalles and Troutdale, and Hells Canyon.

PENNSYLVANIA

Capital: Harrisburg
Governor: Robert P. Casey, D
Entered Union & (rank): Dec. 12, 1787 (2)
Present constitution adopted: 1874
Motto: Virtue, liberty, and independence

STATE SYMBOLS: flower, Mountain laurel (1933); **tree,** Hemlock (1931); **bird,** Ruffled grouse (1931); **dog,** Great Dane (1965); **colors,** Blue and gold (1907); **song,** None
Nickname: Keystone State
Origin of name: In honor of Adm. Sir. William Penn, father of William Penn. It means "Penn's Woodland."
10 largest cities (1990 census): Philadelphia, 1,585,577; Pittsburgh, 369,879; Erie, 108,718; Allentown, 105,090; Scranton, 81,805; Reading, 78,380; Bethlehem, 71,428; Lancaster, 55,551; Harrisburg, 52,376; Altoona, 51,881
Land area & (rank): 44,888 sq mi. (116,260 sq km) (32)
Geographic center: In Centre Co., 2 1/2 mi. SW of Bellefonte
Number of counties: 67
Largest county (1990 census): Allegheny, 1,336,449
State forests: 1,930,108 ac.
State parks: 120 (297,438 ac.)
1980 resident census population & (rank): 11,863,895 (4)
1990 resident census population, sex, & (rank): 11,881,643 (5). **Male:** 5,694,265; **Female:** 6,187,378. **White:** 10,520,201 (88.5%); **Black:** 1,089,795 (9.2%); **American Indian, Eskimo, or Aleut:** 14,733 (0.1%); **Asian or Pacific Islander:** 137,438 (1.2%); **Other race:** 119,476 (1.0%); **Hispanic:** 232,262 (2.0%). **1990 percent population under 18:** 23.5; **65 and over:** 15.4; **median age:** 35.

Rich in historic lore, Pennsylvania territory was disputed in the early 1600s among the Dutch, the Swedes, and the English. England acquired the region in 1664 with the capture of New York and in 1681 Pennsylvania was granted to William Penn, a Quaker, by King Charles II.

Philadelphia was the seat of the federal government almost continuously from 1776 to 1800; there the Declaration of Independence was signed in 1776 and the U.S. Constitution drawn up in 1787. Valley Forge, of Revolutionary War fame, and Gettysburg, the turning-point of the Civil War, are both in Pennsylvania. The Liberty Bell is located in a glass pavilion across from Independence Hall in Philadelphia.

With the decline of the coal, steel and railroad industries, Pennsylvania's industry has diversified, though the state still leads the country in the production of specialty steel. Pennsylvania is a leader in the production of chemicals, food, and electrical machinery and produces 10% of the nations's cement. Also important are brick and tiles, glass, limestone, and slate. Data processing is also increasingly important.

Pennsylvania's nine million agricultural acres produce a wide variety of crops and its 55,535 farms are the backbone of the state's economy. Leading products are milk, poultry and eggs, a variety of fruits, sweet corn, potatoes, mushrooms, cheese, beans, hay, maple syrup, and even Christmas trees.

Pennsylvania has the largest rural population in the nation. The state's farmers sell more than $3 billion in crops and livestock annually and agribusiness and food-related industries account for another $35 billion in economic activity annually.

Tourists now spend approximately $6 billion in Pennsylvania annually. Among the chief attractions: the Gettysburg National Military Park, Valley Forge National Historical Park, Independence National Historical Park in Philadelphia, the Pennsylvania Dutch region, the Eisenhower farm near Gettysburg, and the Delaware Water Gap National Recreation Area.

RHODE ISLAND

Capital: Providence
Governor: Bruce Sundlun, D
Entered Union & (rank): May 29, 1790 (13)
Present constitution adopted: 1843
Motto: Hope
STATE SYMBOLS: flower, Violet (unofficial) (1968); **tree,** Red maple (official) (1964); **bird,** Rhode Island Red (official) (1954); **shell,** Quahog (official); **mineral,** Bowenite; **stone,** Cumberlandite; **colors,** Blue, white, and gold (in state flag); **song,** "Rhode Island" (1946)
Nickname: The Ocean State
Origin of name: From the Greek Island of Rhodes
10 largest cities (1990 census): Providence, 160,728; Warwick, 85,427; Cranston, 70,060; Pawtucket, 72,644; East Providence, 50,380; Woonsocket, 43,877; Newport, 28,227; Central Falls, 17,637
Land area & (rank): 1,055 sq mi. (2,732 sq km) (50)
Geographic center: In Kent Co., 1 mi. SSW of Crompton
Number of counties: 5
Largest town (1990 census): North Providence, 32,090
State forests: 11 (20,900 ac.)
State parks: 17 (8,200 ac.)
1980 resident census population & (rank): 947,154 (40)
1990 resident census population, sex, & (rank): 1,003,464 (43). **Male:** 481,496; **Female:** 521,968. **White:** 917,375 (91.4%); **Black:** 38,861 (3.9%); **American Indian, Eskimo, or Aleut:** 4,071 (0.4%); **Asian or Pacific Islander:** 18,325 (1.8%); **Other race:** 24,832 (2.5%); **Hispanic:** 45,752 (4.6%). **1990 percent population under 18:** 22.5; **65 and over:** 15.0; **median age:** 34.

From its beginnings, Rhode Island has been distinguished by its support for freedom of conscience and action, started by Roger Williams, who was exiled by the Massachusetts Bay Colony Puritans in 1636, and was the founder of the present state capital, Providence. Williams was followed by other religious exiles who founded Pocasset, now Portsmouth, in 1638 and Newport in 1639.

Rhode Island's rebellious, authority-defying nature was further demonstrated by the burnings of the British revenue cutters *Liberty* and *Gaspee* prior to the Revolution, by its early declaration of independence from Great Britain in May 1776, its refusal to participate actively in the War of 1812, and by Dorr's Rebellion of 1842, which protested property requirements for voting.

Rhode Island, smallest of the fifty states, is densely populated and highly industrialized. It is a primary center for jewelry manufacturing in the United States. Electronics, metal, plastic products, and boat and ship construction are other important industries. Non-manufacturing employment includes research in health and medical areas, and the ocean environment. Providence is a wholesale distribution center for New England.

Two of New England's fishing ports are at Galilee and Newport. Rural areas of the state support small-scale farming including grapes for local wineries, dairy, and poultry products.

Tourism is one of Rhode Island's largest industries, generating over a billion dollars a year in revenue.

Newport became famous as the summer capital of society in the mid-19th century. Touro Synagogue (1763) is the oldest in the U.S. Other points of interest include the Roger Williams National Memorial in Providence, Samuel Slater's Mill in Pawtucket, the General Nathanael Greene Homestead in Coventry and Block Island.

SOUTH CAROLINA

Capital: Columbia
Governor: Carroll A. Campbell, Jr., R
Entered Union & (rank): May 23, 1788 (8).
Present constitution adopted: 1895
Mottoes: *Animis opibusque parati* (Prepared in mind and resources) and *Dum spiro spero* (While I breathe, I hope)
STATE SYMBOLS: flower, Carolina yellow jessamine (1924); **tree,** Palmetto tree (1939); **bird,** Carolina wren (1948); **song,** "Carolina" (1911)
Nickname: Palmetto State
Origin of name: In honor of Charles I of England
10 largest cities (1990 census): Columbia, 98,052; Charleston, 80,414; North Charleston, 70,218; Greenville, 58,282; Spartanburg, 43,467; Sumter, 41,943; Rock Hill, 41,643; Mount Pleasant Town, 30,108; Florence, 29,813; Anderson, 26,184
Land area & (rank): 30,203 sq mi. (78,227 sq km) (40)
Geographic center: In Richland Co., 13 mi. SE of Columbia
Number of counties: 46
Largest county (1990 census): Greenville, 320,167
State forests: 4 (124,052 ac.)
State parks: 50 (61,726 ac.)
1980 resident census population & (rank): 3,121,820 (24)
1990 resident census population, sex, & (rank): 3,486,703 (25). **Male:** 1,688,510; **Female:** 1,798,193. **White:** 2,406,974 (69.0%); **Black:** 1,039,884 (29.8%); **American Indian, Eskimo, or Aleut:** 8,246 (0.2%); **Asian or Pacific Islander:** 22,382 (0.6%); **Other race:** 9,217 (0.3%); **Hispanic:** 30,551 (0.9%) **1990 percent population under 18:** 26.4; **65 and over:** 11.4; **median age: 32.0**

Following exploration of the coast in 1521 by De Gordillo, the Spanish tried unsuccessfully to establish a colony near present-day Georgetown in 1526 and the French also failed to colonize Parris Island near Fort Royal in 1562.

The first English settlement was made in 1670 at Albemarle Point on the Ashley River, but poor conditions drove the settlers to the site of Charleston (originally called Charles Town). South Carolina, officially separated from North Carolina in 1729, was the scene of extensive military action during the Revolution and again during the Civil War. The Civil War began in 1861 as South Carolina troops fired on federal Fort Sumter in Charleston Harbor and the state was the first to secede from the Union.

Once primarily agricultural, South Carolina has built so many large textile and other mills that today its factories produce eight times the output of its farms in cash value. Charleston makes asbestos, wood, pulp, and steel products; chemicals, machinery, and apparel are also important.

Farms have become fewer but larger in recent years. South Carolina grows more peaches than any other state except California; it ranks third in tobacco. Other farm products include cotton, peanuts, sweet potatoes, soybeans, corn, and oats. Poultry and dairy products are also important revenue producers.

Points of interest include Fort Sumter National Monument, Fort Moultrie, Fort Johnson, and aircraft carrier USS *Yorktown* in Charleston Harbor; the Middleton, Magnolia, and Cypress Gardens in Charleston; Cowpens National Battlefield; and the Hilton Head resorts.

SOUTH DAKOTA

Capital: Pierre
Governor: George S. Mickelson, R
Organized as territory: March 2, 1861
Entered Union & (rank): Nov. 2, 1889 (40)

Present constitution adopted: 1889
Motto: Under God the people rule
STATE SYMBOLS: flower, American pasqueflower (1903); **grass,** Western wheat grass (1970); **soil,** Houdek (1990); **tree,** Black Hills spruce (1947); **bird,** Ring-necked pheasant (1943); **insect,** Honeybee (1978); **animal,** Coyote (1949); **mineral stone,** Rose quartz (1966); **gemstone,** Fairburn agate (1966); **colors,** Blue and gold (in state flag); **song,** "Hail! South Dakota" (1943); **fish,** Walleye (1982); **musical instrument,** Fiddle (1989)
Nicknames: Sunshine State; Coyote State
Origin of name: Same as for North Dakota
10 largest cities (1990 census): Sioux Falls, 100,814; Rapid City, 54,523; Aberdeen, 24,927; Watertown, 17,592; Brookings, 16,270; Mitchell, 13,798; Pierre, 12,906; Yankton, 12,703; Huron, 12,448; Vermillion, 10,034
Land area & (rank): 75,952 sq mi. (196,715 sq km) (16)
Geographic center: In Hughes Co., 8 mi. NE of Pierre
Number of counties: 67 (64 county governments)
Largest county (1990 census): Minnehaha, 123,809
State forests: None[1]
State parks: 13 plus 39 recreational areas (87,269 ac.)[2]
1980 resident census population & (rank): 690,768 (45)
1990 resident census population, sex, & (rank): 696,004 (45). **Male:** 342,498; **Female:** 353,506. **White:** 637,515 (91.6%); **Black:** 3,258 (0.5%); **American Indian, Eskimo, or Aleut:** 50,575 (7.3%); **Asian or Pacific Islander:** 3,123 (0.4%); **Other race:** 1,533 (0.2%); **Hispanic:** 5,252 (0.8%). **1990 percent population under 18:** 28.5; **65 and over:** 14.7; **median age:** 32.5.

---

1. No designated state forests; about 13,000 ac. of state land is forestland. 2. Acreage includes 39 recreation areas and 80 roadside parks, in addition to 12 state parks.

Exploration of this area began in 1743 when Louis-Joseph and François Verendrye came from France in search of a route to the Pacific.

The U.S. acquired the region as part of the Louisiana Purchase in 1803 and it was explored by Lewis and Clark in 1804–06. Fort Pierre, the first permanent settlement, was established in 1817 and, in 1831, the first Missouri River steamboat reached the fort.

Settlement of South Dakota did not begin in earnest until the arrival of the railroad in 1873 and the discovery of gold in the Black Hills the following year.

Agriculture is the state's leading industry. South Dakota is a leading state in the production of rye, wheat, alfalfa, sunflower seed, flaxseed, and livestock.

South Dakota is the nation's second leading producer of gold and the Homestake Mine is the richest in the U.S. Other minerals produced include berylium, bentonite, granite, silver, petroleum, and uranium.

Processing of foods produced by farms and ranches is the largest South Dakota manufacturing industry, followed by lumber, wood products, and machinery, including farm equipment.

The Black Hills are the highest mountains east of the Rockies. Mt. Rushmore, in this group, is famous for the likenesses of Washington, Jefferson, Lincoln, and Theodore Roosevelt, which were carved in granite by Gutzon Borglum. A memorial to Crazy Horse is also being carved in granite near Custer.

Other tourist attractions include the Badlands; the World's Only Corn Palace in Mitchell; and the city of Deadwood where Wild Bill Hickok was killed in 1876 and where gambling was recently legalized to truly recapture the city's Old West flavor.

TENNESSEE

Capital: Nashville
Governor: Ned Ray McWerter, D
Entered Union & (rank): June 1, 1796 (16)
Present constitution adopted: 1870; amended 1953, 1960, 1966, 1972, 1978
Motto: "Agriculture and Commerce" (1987)
Slogan: "Tennessee—America at its best!" (1965)
STATE SYMBOLS: flower, Iris (1933); **tree,** Tulip poplar (1947); **bird,** Mockingbird (1933); **horse,** Tennessee walking horse; **animal,** Raccoon (1971); **wild flower,** Passion flower (1973); **song,** "Tennessee Waltz" (1965)
Nickname: Volunteer State
Origin of name: Of Cherokee origin; the exact meaning is unknown
10 largest cities (1990 census): Memphis, 610,337; Nashville-Davidson (CC[1]), 510,784; Knoxville, 165,121; Chattanooga, 152,466; Clarksville, 75,494; Johnson City, 49,381; Jackson, 48,949; Murfreesboro, 44,922; Kingsport, 36,365; Germantown, 32,893
Land area & (rank): 41,155 sq mi. (106,591 sq km) (34)
Geographic center: In Rutherford Co., 5 mi. NE of Murfreesboro
Number of counties: 95
Largest county (1990 census): Shelby, 826,330
State forests: 14 (155,752 ac.)
State parks: 21 (130,000 ac.)
1980 resident census population & (rank): 4,591,120 (17)
1990 resident census population, sex, & (rank): 4,877,185 (17). **Male:** 2,348,928; **Female:** 2,528,257. **White:** 4,048,068 (83.0%); **Black:** 778,035 (16.0%); **American Indian, Eskimo, or Aleut:** 10,039 (0.2%); **Asian or Pacific Islander:** 31,839 (0.7%); **Other race:** 9,204 (0.2%); **Hispanic:** 32,741 (0.7%). **1990 percent population under 18:** 24.9; **65 and over:** 12.7; **median age:** 33.6.

1. Consolidated City.

First visited by the Spanish explorer de Soto in 1540, the Tennessee area would later be claimed by both France and England as a result of the 1670s and 1680s explorations of Marquette and Joliet, La Salle, and the Englishmen James Needham and Gabriel Arthur.

Great Britain obtained the region following the French and Indian War in 1763 and it was rapidly occupied by settlers moving in from Virginia and the Carolinas.

During 1784–87, the settlers formed the "state" of Franklin, which was disbanded when the region was allowed to send representatives to the North Carolina legislature. In 1790 Congress organized the territory south of the Ohio River and Tennessee joined the Union in 1796.

Although Tennessee joined the Confederacy during the Civil War, there was much pro-Union sentiment in the state, which was the scene of extensive military action.

The state is now predominantly industrial; the majority of its population lives in urban areas. Among the most important products are chemicals, textiles, apparel, electrical machinery, furniture, and leather goods. Other lines include food processing, lumber, primary metals, and metal products. The state is known as the U.S. hardwood-flooring center and ranks first in the production of marble, zinc, pyrite, and ball clay.

Tennessee is one of the leading tobacco-producing states in the nation and its farming income is also derived from livestock and dairy products as well as corn, cotton, and soybeans.

With six other states, Tennessee shares the extensive federal reservoir developments on the Tennessee and Cumberland River systems. The Tennessee Valley Authority operates a number of dams and reservoirs in the state.

Among the major points of interest: the Andrew Johnson National Historic Site at Greenville, American Museum of Atomic Energy at Oak Ridge, Great Smoky Mountains National Park, The Hermitage (home of Andrew Jackson near Nashville), Rock City Gardens near Chattanooga, and three National Military Parks.

TEXAS

Capital: Austin
Governor: Ann Richards, D
Entered Union & (rank): Dec. 29, 1845 (28)
Present constitution adopted: 1876
Motto: Friendship
STATE SYMBOLS: flower, Bluebonnet (1901); **tree,** Pecan (1919); **bird,** Mockingbird (1927); **song,** "Texas, Our Texas" (1930); **fish,** Guadalupe bass (1989); **seashell,** Lightning whelk (1987)
Nickname: Lone Star State
Origin of name: From an Indian word meaning "friends"
10 largest cities (1990 census): Houston, 1,630,553; Dallas, 1,006,877; San Antonio, 935,933; El Paso, 515,342; Austin, 465,622; Fort Worth, 447,619; Arlington, 261,721; Corpus Christi, 257,453; Lubbock, 186,206; Garland, 180,650
Land area & (rank): 262,017 sq mi. (678,623 sq km) (2)
Geographic center: In McCulloch Co., 15 mi. NE of Brady
Number of counties: 254
Largest county (1990 census): Harris, 2,818,199
State forests: 4 (6,306 ac.)
State parks: 83 (64 developed)
1980 resident census population & (rank): 14,229,191 (3)
1990 resident census population, sex, & (rank): 16,986,510 (3). **Male:** 8,365,963; **Female:** 8,620,547. **White:** 12,774,762 (75.2%); **Black:** 2,021,632 (11.9%); **American Indian, Eskimo, or Aleut:** 65,877 (0.4%); **Asian or Pacific Islander:** 319,459 (1.9%); **Other race:** 1,804,780 (10.6%); **Hispanic:** 4,339,905 (25.5%). **1990 percent population under 18:** 28.5; **65 and over:** 10.1; **median age:** 30.8.

Spanish explorers, including Cabeza de Vaca and Coronado, were the first to visit the region in the 16th and 17th centuries, settling at Ysleta near El Paso in 1682. In 1685, La Salle established a short-lived French colony at Matagorda Bay.

Americans, led by Stephen F. Austin, began to settle along the Brazos River in 1821 when Texas was controlled by Mexico, recently independent from Spain. In 1836, following a brief war between the American settlers in Texas and the Mexican government, and famous for the battles of the Alamo and San Jacinto, the Independent Republic of Texas was proclaimed with Sam Houston as president.

After Texas became the 28th U.S. state in 1845, border disputes led to the Mexican War of 1846–48.

Today, Texas, second only to Alaska in land area, leads all other states in such categories as oil, cattle, sheep, and cotton. Possessing enormous natural resources, Texas is a major agricultural state and an industrial giant.

Sulfur, salt, helium, asphalt, graphite, bromine, natural gas, cement, and clays give Texas first place in mineral production. Chemicals, oil refining, food processing, machinery, and transportation equipment are among the major Texas manufacturing industries.

Texas ranches and farms produce beef cattle, poultry, rice, pecans, peanuts, sorghum, and an extensive variety of fruits and vegetables.

Millions of tourists spend well over $2 billion annually visiting more than 70 state parks, recreation areas, and points of interest such as the Gulf Coast resort area, the Lyndon B. Johnson Space Center in Houston, the Alamo in San Antonio, the state capital in Austin, and the Big Bend and Guadalupe Mountains National Parks.

UTAH

Capital: Salt Lake City
Governor: Norman H. Bangerter, R
Organized as territory: Sept. 9, 1850
Entered Union & (rank): Jan. 4, 1896 (45)
Present constitution adopted: 1896
Motto: Industry
STATE SYMBOLS: flower, Sego lily (1911); **tree,** Blue spruce (1933); **bird,** Seagull (1955); **emblem,** Beehive (1959); **song,** "Utah, We Love Thee" (1953)
Nickname: State
Origin of name: From the Ute tribe, meaning "people of the mountains"
10 largest cities (1990 census): Salt Lake City, 159,936; West Valley City, 86,976; Provo, 86,835; Sandy, 75,058; Orem, 67,561; Ogden, 63,909; Taylorsville-Bennion, 52,351; West Jordan, 42,892; Layton, 41,784; Bountiful, 36,659
Land area & (rank): 82,073 sq mi. (212,569 sq km) (12)
Geographic center: In Sanpete Co., 3 mi. N. of Manti
Number of counties: 29
Largest county (1990 census): Salt Lake, 725,956
National parks: 5
National monuments: 6
State parks/forests: 44 (64,097 ac.)
1980 resident census population & (rank): 1,461,037 (36)
1990 resident census population, sex, & (rank): 1,722,850 (35). **Male:** 855,759; **Female:** 867,091. **White:** 1,615,845 (93.8%); **Black:** 11,576 (0.7%); **American Indian, Eskimo, or Aleut:** 24,283 (1.4%); **Asian or Pacific Islander:** 33,371 (1.9%); **Other race:** 37,775 (2.2%); **Hispanic:** 84,597 (4.9%). **1990 percent population under 18:** 36.4; **65 and over:** 8.7; **median age:** 26.2.

The region was first explored for Spain by Franciscan friars, Escalante and Dominguez in 1776. In 1824 the famous American frontiersman Jim Bridger discovered the Great Salt Lake.

Fleeing the religious persecution encountered in eastern and middle-western states, the Mormons reached the Great Salt Lake in 1847 and began to build Salt Lake City. The U.S. acquired the Utah region in the treaty ending the Mexican War in 1848 and the first transcontinental railroad was completed with the driving of a golden spike at Promontory Summit in 1869.

Mormon difficulties with the federal government about polygamy did not end until the Mormon Church renounced the practice in 1890, six years before Utah became a state.

Rich in natural resources, Utah has long been a leading producer of copper, gold, silver, lead, zinc, and molybdenum. Oil has also become a major product; with Colorado and Wyoming, Utah shares what have been called the world's richest oil shale deposits.

Ranked eighth among the states in number of sheep in 1989, Utah also produces large crops of al-

falfa, winter wheat, and beans. Utah's farmlands and crops require extensive irrigation.

Utah's traditional industries of agriculture and mining are being complemented by increased tourism business and growing aerospace, biomedical, and computer-related businesses. Utah is home to computer software giants Novell and WordPerfect.

Utah is a great vacationland with 11,000 miles of fishing streams and 147,000 acres of lakes and reservoirs. Among the many tourist attractions are Arches, Bryce Canyon, Canyonlands, Capitol Reef, and Zion National Parks; Dinosaur, Natural Bridges, and Rainbow Bridge National Monuments; the Mormon Tabernacle in Salt Lake City; and Monument Valley.

VERMONT

Capital: Montpelier
Governor: Howard B. Dean, D
Entered Union & (rank): March 4, 1791 (14)
Present constitution adopted: 1793
Motto: Vermont, Freedom, and Unity
STATE SYMBOLS: flower, Red clover (1894); **tree,** Sugar maple (1949); **bird,** Hermit thrush (1941); **animal,** Morgan horse (1961); **insect,** Honeybee (1978); **song,** "Hail, Vermont!" (1938)
Nickname: Green Mountain State
Origin of name: From the French "vert mont," meaning "green mountain"
10 largest cities (1990 census): Burlington, 39,127; Rutland, 18,230; South Burlington, 12,809; Barre, 9,482; Essex Junction, 8,396; Montpelier, 8,247; St. Albans, 7,339; Winooski, 6,649; Newport, 4,434; Bellows Falls, 3,313
Land area & (rank): 9,273 sq mi. (24,017 sq km) (43)
Geographic center: In Washington Co., 3 mi. E of Roxbury
Number of counties: 14
Largest county (1990 census): Chittenden, 131,761
State forests: 34 (113,953 ac.)
State parks: 45 (31,325 ac.)
1980 resident census population & (rank): 511,456 (48)
1990 resident census population, sex, & (rank): 562,758 (48). **Male:** 275,492; **Female:** 287,266. **White:** 555,088 (98.6%); **Black:** 1,951 (0.3%); **American Indian, Eskimo, or Aleut:** 1,696 (0.3%); **Asian or Pacific Islander:** 3,215 (0.6%); **Other race:** 808 (0.1%); **Hispanic:** 3,661 (0.7%). **1990 percent population under 18:** 25.4; **65 and over:** 11.8; **median age:** 33.0.

The Vermont region was explored and claimed for France by Samuel de Champlain in 1609 and the first French settlement was established at Fort Ste. Anne in 1666. The first English settlers moved into the area in 1724 and built Fort Drummer on the site of present-day Brattleboro. England gained control of the area in 1763 after the French and Indian War.

First organized to drive settlers from New York out of Vermont, the Green Mountain Boys, led by Ethan Allen, won fame by capturing Fort Ticonderoga from the British on May 10, 1775, in the early days of the Revolution.

In 1777 Vermont adopted its first constitution abolishing slavery and providing for universal male suffrage without property qualifications. In 1791 Vermont became the first state after the original 13 to join the Union.

Vermont leads the nation in the production of monument granite, marble, and maple syrup. It is also a leader in the production of asbestos and talc.

In ratio to population, Vermont keeps more dairy cows than any other state. Vermont's soil is devoted to dairying, truck farming, and fruit growing because the rugged, rocky terrain discourages extensive farming.

Principal industrial products include electrical equipment, fabricated metal products, printing and publishing, and paper and allied products.

Tourism is a major industry in Vermont. Vermont's many famous ski areas include Stowe, Killington, Mt. Snow, Bromley, Jay Peak, and Sugarbush. Hunting and fishing also attract many visitors to Vermont each year. Among the many points of interest are the Green Mountain National Forest, Bennington Battle Monument, the Calvin Coolidge Homestead at Plymouth, and the Marble Exhibit in Proctor.

VIRGINIA

Capital: Richmond
Governor: L. Douglas Wilder, D
Entered Union & (rank): June 25, 1788 (10)
Present constitution adopted: 1970
Motto: *Sic semper tyrannis* (Thus always to tyrants)
STATE SYMBOLS: flower, American dogwood (1918); **bird,** Cardinal (1950); **dog,** American foxhound (1966); **shell,** Oyster shell (1974); **song,** "Carry Me Back to Old Virginia" (1940)
Nicknames: The Old Dominion; Mother of Presidents
Origin of name: In honor of Elizabeth "Virgin Queen" of England
10 largest cities (1990 census): Virginia Beach, 393,069; Norfolk, 261,229; Richmond, 203,056; Newport News, 170,045; Chesapeake, 151,976; Hampton, 133,793; Alexandria, 111,183; Portsmouth, 103,907; Roanoke, 96,907; Lynchburg, 66,049
Land area & (rank): 39,704 sq mi. (102,832 sq km) (36)
Geographic center: In Buckingham Co., 5 mi. SW of Buckingham
Number of counties: 95, plus 41 independent cities
Largest county (1990 census): Fairfax, 818,384
State forests: 8 (49,566 ac.)
State parks and recreational parks: 27, plus 3 in process of acquisition and/or development (42,722 ac.)[1]
1980 resident census population & (rank): 5,346,818 (14)
1990 resident census population, sex, & (rank): 6,187,358 (12). **Male:** 3,033,974; **Female:** 3,153,384. **White:** 4,791,739 (77.4%); **Black:** 1,162,994 (18.8%); **American Indian, Eskimo, or Aleut:** 15,282 (0.2%); **Asian or Pacific Islander:** 159,053 (2.6%); **Other race:** 58,290 (0.9%); **Hispanic:** 160,288 (2.6%). **1990 percent population under 18:** 24.3; **65 and over:** 10.7; **median age:** 32.6.

1. Does not include portion of Breaks Interstate Park (Va.-Ky., 1,200 ac.) which lies in Virginia.

The history of America is closely tied to that of Virginia, particularly in the Colonial period. Jamestown, founded in 1607, was the first permanent English settlement in North America and slavery was introduced there in 1619. The surrenders ending both the American Revolution (Yorktown) and the Civil War (Appomattox) occurred in Virginia. The state is called the "Mother of Presidents" because eight chief executives of the United States were born there.

Today, Virginia has a large number of diversified manufacturing industries including transportation equipment, textiles, food processing and printing. Other important lines are electronic and other electric equipment, chemicals, apparel, lumber and wood products, and furniture.

Agriculture remains an important sector in the Virginia economy and the state ranks among the leaders in the U.S. in tobacco, peanuts, apples, and tomatoes. Other crops include corn, vegetables, and barley. Famous for its turkeys and Smithfield hams, Virginia also has a large dairy industry.

Coal mining accounts for roughly 75% of Virginia's mineral output, and lime, kyanite, and stone are also mined.

Points of interest include Mt. Vernon and other places associated with George Washington; Monticello, home of Thomas Jefferson; Stratford, home of the Lees; Richmond, capital of the Confederacy and of Virginia; and Williamsburg, the restored Colonial capital.

The Chesapeake Bay Bridge-Tunnel spans the mouth of Chesapeake Bay, connecting Cape Charles with Norfolk. Consisting of a series of low trestles, two bridges and two mile-long tunnels, the complex is 18 miles (29 km) long. It was opened in 1964.

Other attractions are the Shenandoah National Park, Fredericksburg and Spotsylvania National Military Park, the Booker T. Washington birthplace near Roanoke, Arlington House (the Robert E. Lee Memorial), the Skyline Drive, and the Blue Ridge National Parkway.

WASHINGTON

Capital: Olympia
Governor: Booth Gardner, D
Organized as territory: March 2, 1853
Entered Union & (rank): Nov. 11, 1889 (42)
Present constitution adopted: 1889
Motto: *Al-Ki* (Indian word meaning "by and by")
STATE SYMBOLS: flower, Rhododendron (1949); **tree,** Western hemlock (1947); **bird,** Willow goldfinch (1951); **fish,** Steelhead trout (1969); **gem,** Petrified wood (1975); **colors,** Green and gold (1925); **song,** "Washington, My Home" (1959); **dance,** Square dance (1979)
Nicknames: Evergreen State; Chinook State
Origin of name: In honor of George Washington
10 largest cities (1990 census): Seattle, 516,259; Spokane, 177,196; Tacoma, 176,664; Bellevue, 86,874; Everett, 69,961; Yakima, 54,827; Bellingham, 42,155; Renton, 41,688
Land area & (rank): 66,511 sq mi (172,264 sq km) (20)
Geographic center: In Chelan Co., 10 mi. WSW of Wenatchee
Number of counties: 39
Largest county (1990 census): King, 1,507,319
State forest lands: 1,922,880 ac.
State parks: 202 (171,700 ac.)[1]
1980 resident census population & (rank): 4,132,156 (18)
1990 resident census population, sex, & (rank): 4,866,692 (18). **Male:** 2,413,747; **Female:** 2,452,945. **White:** 4,308,937 (88.5%); **Black:** 149,801 (3.1%); **American Indian, Eskimo, or Aleut:** 81,483 (1.7%); **Other race:** 115,513 (2.4%); **Hispanic:** 214,570 (4.4%). **1990 percent population under 18:** 25.9; **65 and over:** 11.8; **median age:** 33.1.

1. Parks and undeveloped areas administered by Parks and Recreation Dept. Game Dept. administers wildlife and recreation areas totaling 762,895 acres.

As part of the vast Oregon Country, Washington territory was visited by Spanish, American, and British explorers—Bruno Heceta for Spain in 1775, the American Capt. Robert Gray in 1792, and Capt. George Vancouver for Britain in 1792–94. Lewis and

Clark explored the Columbia River region and coastal areas for the U.S. in 1805–06.

Rival American and British settlers and conflicting territorial claims threatened war in the early 1840s. However, in 1846 the Oregon Treaty set the boundary at the 49th parallel and war was averted.

Washington is a leading lumber producer. Its rugged surface is rich in stands of Douglas fir, hemlock, ponderosa and white pine, spruce, larch, and cedar. The state holds first place in apples, blueberries, hops, and red raspberries and it ranks high in potatoes, winter wheat, pears, grapes, apricots, and strawberries. Livestock and livestock products make important contributions to total farm revenue and the commercial fishing catch of salmon, halibut, and bottomfish makes a significant contribution to the state's economy.

Manufacturing industries in Washington include aircraft and missiles, shipbuilding and other transportation equipment, lumber, food processing, metals and metal products, chemicals, and machinery.

The Columbia River contains one third of the potential water power in the U.S., harnessed by such dams as the Grand Coulee, one of the greatest power producers in the world. Washington has 90 dams throughout the state built for irrigation, power, flood control, and water storage. Its abundance of electrical power makes Washington the nation's largest producer of refined aluminum.

Among the major points of interest: Mt. Rainier, Olympic, and North Cascades. In 1980, Mount St. Helens, a peak in the Cascade Range in Southwestern Washington erupted on May 18th. Also of interest are National Parks; Whitman Mission and Fort Vancouver National Historic Sites; and the Pacific Science Center and Space Needle in Seattle.

WEST VIRGINIA

Capital: Charleston
Governor: Gaston Caperton, D
Entered Union & (rank): June 20, 1863 (35)
Present constitution adopted: 1872
Motto: *Montani semper liberi* (Mountaineers are always free)
STATE SYMBOLS: flower, Rhododendron (1903); **tree,** Sugar maple (1949); **bird,** Cardinal (1949); **animal,** Black bear (1973); **colors,** Blue and gold (official) (1863); **songs,** "West Virginia, My Home Sweet Home," "The West Virginia Hills," and "This Is My West Virginia" (adopted by Legislature in 1947, 1961, and 1963 as official state songs)
Nickname: Mountain State
Origin of name: Same as for Virginia
10 largest cities (1990 census): Charleston, 57,287; Huntington, 54,844; Wheeling, 34,882; Parkersburg, 33,862; Morgantown, 25,879; Weirton, 22,124; Fairmont, 20,210; Beckley, 18,296; Clarksburg, 18,059; Martinsburg, 14,073
Land area & (rank): 24,282 sq mi. (62,890 sq km) (41)
Geographic center: In Braxton Co., 4 mi. E of Sutton
Number of counties: 55
Largest county (1990 census): Kanawha, 207,619
State forests: 9 (79,081 ac.)
State parks: 34 (72,599 ac.)
1980 resident census population & (rank): 1,949,644 (34)
1990 resident census population, sex, & (rank): 1,793,477 (34). **Male:** 861,536; **Female:** 931,941. **White:** 1,725,523 (96.2%); **Black:** 56,295 (3.1%); **American Indian, Eskimo, or Aleut:** 2,458 (0.1%); **Asian or Pacific Islander:** 7,459 (0.4%); **Other race:** 1,742 (0.1%); **His-**

panic: 8,489 (0.5%). **1990 percent population under 18:** 24.7; **65 and over:** 15.0; **median age:** 35.4.

West Virginia's early history from 1609 until 1863 is largely shared with Virginia, of which it was a part until Virginia seceded from the Union in 1861. Then the delegates of 40 western counties formed their own government, which was granted statehood in 1863.

First permanent settlement dates from 1731 when Morgan Morgan founded Mill Creek. In 1742 coal was discovered on the Coal River, an event that would be of great significance in determining West Virginia's future.

The state usually ranks 3rd in total coal production with about 15% of the U.S. total. It also is a leader in steel, glass, aluminum, and chemical manufactures; natural gas, oil, quarry products, and hardwood lumber.

Major cash farm products are poultry and eggs, dairy products, apples, and feed crops. More than 75% of West Virginia is covered with forests.

Tourism is increasingly popular in mountainous West Virginia and visitors spent $2.475 billion in 1990. More than a million acres have been set aside in 34 state parks and recreation areas and in 9 state forests, and national forests.

Major points of interest include Harpers Ferry and New River Gorge National River, The Greenbrier and Berkeley Springs resorts, the scenic railroad at Cass, and the historic homes in the Eastern Panhandle.

WISCONSIN

Capital: Madison
Governor: Tommy G. Thompson, R
Organized as territory: July 4, 1836
Entered Union & (rank): May 29, 1848 (30)
Present constitution adopted: 1848
Motto: Forward
STATE SYMBOLS: flower, Wood violet (1949); **tree,** Sugar maple (1949); **grain,** corn (1990); **bird,** Robin (1949); **animal,** Badger; **"wild life" animal,** White-tailed deer (1957); **"domestic" animal,** Dairy cow (1971); **insect,** Honeybee (1977); **fish,** Musky (Muskellunge) (1955); **song,** "On Wisconsin"; **mineral,** Galena (1971); **rock,** Red Granite (1971); **symbol of peace:** Mourning Dove (1971); **soil,** Antigo Silt Loam (1983); **fossil,** Trilobite (1985); **dog,** American Water Spaniel (1986); **beverage,** Milk (1988)
Nickname: Badger State
Origin of name: French corruption of an Indian word whose meaning is disputed
10 largest cities (1990 census): Milwaukee, 628,088; Madison, 191,262; Green Bay, 96,466; Racine, 84,298; Kenosha, 80,352; Appleton, 65,695; West Allis, 63,221; Waukesha, 56,958; Eau Claire, 56,856; Oshkosh, 55,006
Land area & (rank): 54,426 sq mi. (140,964 sq km) (25)
Geographic center: In Wood Co., 9 mi. SE of Marshfield
Number of counties: 72
Largest county (1990 census): Milwaukee, 959,275
State forests: 9 (476,004 ac.)
State parks & scenic trails: 49 parks, 13 trails (66,185 ac.)
1980 resident census population & (rank): 4,705,767 (16)
1990 resident census population, sex, & (rank): 4,891,769 (16). **Male:** 2,392,935; **Female:** 2,498,834. **White:** 4,512,523 (92.2%); **Black:** 244,539 (5.0%); **American Indian, Eskimo, or Aleut:** 39,387 (0.8%); **Asian or Pacific Islander:** 53,583 (1.1%); **Other race:**

41,737 (0.9%); **Hispanic:** 93,194 (1.9%). **1980 percent population under 18:** 26.4; **65 and over:** 13.3; **median age:** 32.9.

The Wisconsin region was first explored for France by Jean Nicolet, who landed at Green Bay in 1634. In 1660 a French trading post and Roman Catholic mission were established near present-day Ashland.

Great Britain obtained the region in settlement of the French and Indian War in 1763; the U.S. acquried it in 1783 after the Revolutionary War. However, Great Britain retained actual control until after the War of 1812. The region was successively governed as part of the territories of Indiana, Illinois, and Michigan between 1800 and 1836, when it became a separate territory.

Wisconsin leads the nation in milk and cheese production. In 1989 the state ranked first in the number of milk cows (1,760,000) and produced 17.3% of the nation's total output of milk. Other important farm products are peas, beans, corn, potatoes, oats, hay, and cranberries.

The chief industrial products of the state are automobiles, machinery, furniture, paper, beer, and processed foods. Wisconsin ranks second among the 47 paper-producing states.

Wisconsin pioneered in social legislation, providing pensions for the blind (1907), aid to dependent children (1913), and old-age assistance (1925). In labor legislation, the state was the first to enact an unemployment compensation law (1932) and the first in which a workman's compensation law actually took effect. Wisconsin had the first state-wide primary-election law and the first successful income-tax law. In April 1984, Wisconsin became the first state to adopt the Uniform Marital Property Act. The act took effect on January 1, 1986.

The state has over 8,500 lakes, of which Winnebago is the largest. Water sports, ice-boating, and fishing are popular, as are skiing and hunting. Public parks and forests take up one seventh of the land, with 49 state parks, 9 state forests, 13 state trails, 3 recreational areas, and 2 national forests.

Among the many points of interest are the Apostle Islands National Lakeshore; Ice Age National Scientific Reserve; the Circus World Museum at Baraboo; the Wolf, St. Croix, and Lower St. Croix national scenic riverways; and the Wisconsin Dells.

WYOMING

Capital: Cheyenne
Governor: Michael J. Sullivan, D
Organized as territory: May 19, 1869
Entered Union & (rank): July 10, 1890 (44)
Present constitution adopted: 1890
Motto: Equal rights (1955)
STATE SYMBOLS: flower, Indian paintbrush (1917); **tree,** Cottonwood (1947); **bird,** Meadowlark (1927); **gemstone,** Jade (1967); **insignia,** Bucking horse (unofficial); **song,** "Wyoming" (1955)
Nickname: Equality State
Origin of name: From the Delaware Indian word, meaning "mountains and valleys alternating"; the same as the Wyoming Valley in Pennsylvania
10 largest cities (1990 census): Cheyenne, 50,008; Casper, 46,742; Laramie, 26,687; Rock Springs, 19,050; Gillette, 17,635; Sheridan, 13,900; Green River, 12,711; Evanston, 10,903; Rawlins, 9,380; Riverton, 9,202
Land area & (rank): 96,989 sq mi. (251,201 sq km) (9)
Geographic center: In Fremont Co., 58 mi. ENE of Lander
Number of counties: 23, plus Yellowstone National Park

Largest county (1990 census): Laramie, 73,142
State forests: None
State parks and historic sites: 17 (58,498 ac.)
1980 resident census population & (rank): 469,557 (49)
1990 resident census population, sex, & (rank): 453,588 (50). **Male:** 227,007; **Female:** 226,581. **White:** 427,061 (94.2%); **Black:** 3,606 (0.8%); **American Indian, Eskimo, or Aleut:** 9,479 (2.1%); **Asian or Pacific Islander:** 2.806 (0.6%); **Other race:** 10,636 (2.3%); **Hispanic:** 25,751 (5.7%). **1990 percent population under 18:** 29.9; **65 and over:** 10.4; **median age:** 32.0.

The U.S. acquired the territory from France as part of the Louisiana Purchase in 1803. John Colter, a fur-trapper, is the first white man known to have entered present Wyoming. In 1807 he explored the Yellowstone area and brought back news of its geysers and hot springs.

Robert Stuart pioneered the Oregon Trail across Wyoming in 1812–13 and, in 1834, Fort Laramie, the first permanent trading post in Wyoming, was built. Western Wyoming was obtained by the U.S. in the 1846 Oregon Treaty with Great Britain and as a result of the treaty ending the Mexican War in 1848.

When the Wyoming Territory was organized in 1869 Wyoming women became the first in the nation to obtain the right to vote. In 1925 Mrs. Nellie Tayloe Ross was elected first woman governor in the United States.

Wyoming's towering mountains and vast plains provide spectacular scenery, grazing lands for sheep and cattle, and rich mineral deposits.

Mining, particularly oil and natural gas, is the most important industry. In 1990, Wyoming led the nation in sodium carbonate (natrona) and bentonite production, and was second in uranium.

Wyoming ranks second among the states in wool production. In January 1989, its sheep numbered 837,000, exceeded only by Texas and California; it also had 1,330,000 cattle. Principal crops include wheat, oats, sugar beets, corn, potatoes, barley, and alfalfa.

Second in mean elevation to Colorado, Wyoming has many attractions for the tourist trade, notably Yellowstone National Park. Cheyenne is famous for its annual "Frontier Days" celebration. Flaming Gorge, the Fort Laramie National Historic Site, and Devils Tower and Fossil Butte National Monuments are other National points of interest.

1990 U.S. Population Center

The Center of Population is the place where an imaginary, flat, weightless, and rigid map of the United States would balance perfectly if all 248,709,873 residents were of identical weight. Based on the 1990 census, that balance point is at a spot of heavily wooded land in Crawford County, Mo., a little to the west of the former population center of DeSoto, Mo.

Each decade, after it tabulates the latest census, the Bureau of the Census calculates the center of population. The Center has moved in a southwesterly direction since the first census in 1790.

For the 1990 census, the bureau located that spot at latitude 37°52'20"N and longitude 91°12'55"W. The new center rests on property jointly-owned by three members of Ellisville, Missouri's Whitaker Family: Verla Faith, Terri and Randle L. In 1790, the year of the first census, the center was located near Chestertown, approximately 23 miles east of Baltimore on Maryland's eastern shore; the 1990 center is 818.6 miles from that site.

U.S. Territories and Outlying Areas

PUERTO RICO

(Commonwealth of Puerto Rico)
Governor: Rafael Hernández-Colón, Popular Democratic Party (1989)
Capital: San Juan
Land area: 3,459 sq mi. (8,959 sq km)
Song: "La Borinqueña"
1990 census population: 3,522,037
Language: Spanish (official), English is understood.
Literacy rate: 89%
Labor force (1988): 1,062,000; 23% government, 20% trade, 18% manufacturing, 4% agriculture, 35% other.
Ethnic divisions: Almost entirely Hispanic.
10 largest municipios (1990 census): San Juan, 437,745; Bayamón, 220,262; Ponce, 187,749; Carolina, 177,806; Caguas, 133,447; Mayagüez, 100,371; Arecibo, 93,385; Guaynabo, 92,886; Toa Baja, 89,454; Trujillo Alto, 61,120
Gross national product (FY 1988): $18.4 billion, per capita $5,574; real growth rate: 4.9%
Land use: 8% arable land; 9% permanent crops; 51% meadows and pastures; 25% forest and woodland; 7% other.
Environment: many small rivers and high central mountains ensure land is well watered; south coast relatively dry; fertile coastal plain belt in north.

Puerto Rico is an island about 100 miles long and 35 miles wide at the northeastern end of the Caribbean Sea. Columbus discovered the island on his second voyage to America in 1493. It is a self-governing Commonwealth freely and voluntarily associated with the U.S. Under its Constitution, a Governor and a Legislative Assembly are elected by direct vote for a four-year period. The judiciary is vested in a Supreme Court and lower courts established by law. The people elect a Resident Commissioner to the U.S. House of Representatives, where he has a voice but no vote. The island was formerly an unincorporated territory of the U.S. after being ceded by Spain as a result of the Spanish-American War.

The Commonwealth, established in 1952, has one of the highest standards of living in Latin America. Featuring Puerto Rican economic development is Operation Bootstrap. There are now over 1,600 manufacturing plants which have been created by this program. It has also greatly increased transportation and communications facilities, electric power, housing, and other industries.

The island's chief exports are chemicals, apparel, fish products and electronic products.

Puerto Rico is importantly located between the Dominican Republic and the Virgin Islands group along the Mona Passage—a key shipping lane to the Panama Canal. San Juan is one of the biggest and best natural harbors in the Caribbean.

GUAM

(Territory of Guam)
Governor: Joseph F. Ada
Capital: Agaña
Land area: 209 sq mi. (541 sq km)
1990 population prel.: 132,726
1989 net migration: 7 migrants per 1,000 population
Ethnic divisions: Chamorro, 50%; Filipino, 25%; Caucasian, 10%; Chinese, Japanese, Korean, and other, 15%
Language: English and Chamorro, most residents bilingual; Japanese also widely spoken
Literacy rate: 90%

Labor force (1990): 59,030; 32% government, 68% private
Gross national product (1988 est.): $1.0 billion, per capita $7,675; real growth rate 20%

Guam, the largest of the Mariana Islands, is independent of the trusteeship assigned to the U.S. in 1947. It was acquired by the U.S. from Spain in 1898 (occupied 1899) and was placed under the Navy Department.

In World War II, Guam was seized by the Japanese on Dec. 11, 1941; but on July 21, 1944, it was once more in U.S. hands.

On Aug. 1, 1950, President Truman signed a bill which granted U.S. citizenship to the people of Guam and established self-government. However, the people do not vote in national elections. In 1972 Guam elected its first delegate to the U.S. Congress. The Executive Branch of the Guam government is under the general supervision of the U.S. Secretary of the Interior. In November 1970, Guam elected its first Governor.

Currently, Guam is an unincorporated, organized territory of the United States. It is "unincorporated" because not all of the provisions of the U.S. constitution apply to the territory. It is an "organized" territory because the Congress provided the territory with an Organic Act in 1950 which organized the government much as a constitution would.

Guam's economy is based on two main sources of revenue: tourism and U.S. military spending (U.S. Naval and Air Force bases on Guam). Federal expenditures (most military) in 1989 amounted to more than $680 million, of which more than $300 million went for salaries and more than $100 million for purchases in the local economy.

U.S. VIRGIN ISLANDS

(Virgin Islands of the United States)
Governor: Alexander A. Farrelly
Capital: Charlotte Amalie (on St. Thomas)
1990 est. population: 96,947 (St. Croix, 45,399; St. Thomas, 47,083; St. John, 3,465)
Land area: 132 sq mi (342 sq km): St. Croix, 84 sq. mi. (218 sq km), St. Thomas, 32 sq mi (83 sq km), St. John, 20 sq mi. (52 sq km)
1989 net migration rate: –1 migrants per 1,000 population
Ethnic divisions: West Indian, 74% (45% born in the Virgin Islands and 29% born elsewhere in the West Indies), U.S. mainland, 13%; Puerto Rican, 5%; other, 8%; black, 80%, white, 15%, other, 5%; 14% of Hispanic origin.
Language: English (official), but Spanish and Creole are widely spoken.
Literacy rate: 90%
Labor force (1987): 45,000
Gross domestic product (1985): $1.03 billion, per capita $9,030
Aid: Western (non-U.S.) countries, official development assistance and other official flows, and bilateral commitments (1970–1987): $33.5 million.

The Virgin Islands, consisting of nine main islands and some 75 islets, were discovered by Columbus in 1493. Since 1666, England has held six of the main islands; the other three (St. Croix, St. Thomas, and St. John), as well as about 50 of the islets, were eventually acquired by Denmark, which named them the Danish West Indies. In 1917, these islands were purchased by the U.S. from Denmark for $25 million.

Congress granted U.S. citizenship to Virgin Islanders in 1927; and, in 1931, administration was transferred from the Navy to the Department of the Interior. Universal suffrage was given in 1936 to all persons who could read and write the English language. The Governor was elected by popular vote for the first time in 1970; previously he had been appointed by the President of the U.S. A unicameral 15-man legislature serves the Virgin Islands, and Congressional legislation gave the islands a non-voting Representative in Congress.

The "Constitution" of the Virgin Islands is the Revised Organic Act of 1954 in which the U.S. Congress defines the three branches of the territorial government, i.e., the Executive Branch, the Legislative Branch, and the Judicial Branch. Residents of the islands substantially enjoy the same rights as those enjoyed by mainlanders with one important exception: citizens of the U.S. who are residents may not vote in presidential elections.

Tourism is the primary economic activity, accounting for more than 70% of the GDP and 70% of employment. Tourist expenditures are estimated to be over $500 million annually. In 1990, 1,837,642 tourists arrived in the Virgin Islands; about two-thirds were day visitors on cruise ships. The manufacturing sector consists of textile, electronics, pharmaceutical, and watch assembly plants. The agricultural sector is small with most food imported. International business and financial services are a small but growing component of the economy. The world's largest petroleum refinery is at St. Croix.

AMERICAN SAMOA

(Territory of American Samoa)
Governor: Peter T. Coleman
Capital: Pago Pago
1990 census population: 46,638
1989 net migration rate: −11 migrants per 1,000 population
Ethnic divisions: Samoan (Polynesian) 90%; Caucasian, 2%; Tongan 2%; other 6%
Language: Samoan (closely related to Hawaiian and other Polynesian languages) and English; most people are bilingual
Literacy rate: 99%
Labor force (1990): 13,250
Land area: 77 sq mi (199 sq km)
Gross national product (1985): $190 million; per capita, $5,210
Aid (1989): $20.1 million in operational funds and $5.8 million in construction for capital-improvement projects from the U.S. Department of Interior.

American Samoa, a group of five volcanic islands and two coral atolls located some 2,600 miles south of Hawaii in the South Pacific Ocean, is an unincorporated, unorganized territory of the U.S., administered by the Department of the Interior.

By the Treaty of Berlin, signed Dec. 2, 1899, and ratified Feb. 16, 1900, the U.S. was internationally acknowledged to have rights extending over all the islands of the Samoa group east of longitude 171° west of Greenwich. On April 17, 1900, the chiefs of Tutuila and Aunu'u ceded those islands to the U.S. In 1904, the King and chiefs of Manu'a ceded the islands of Ofu, Olosega and Tau (composing the Manu'a group) to the U.S. Swains Island, some 214 miles north of Samoa, was included as part of the territory by Act of Congress March 4, 1925; and on Feb. 20, 1929, Congress formally accepted sovereignty over the entire group and placed the responsibility for administration in the hands of the President. From 1900 to 1951, by Presidential direction, the Department of the Navy governed the territory. On July 1, 1951, administration was transferred to the Department of the Interior. The first Constitution for the territory was signed on April 27, 1960, and was revised in 1967.

Congress has provided for a non-voting delegate to sit in the House of Representatives in 1981.

The people of American Samoa are U.S. nationals, not U.S. citizens. Like U.S. citizens, they owe allegiance to the United States.

Fish processing is the main economic activity. In 1988, American Samoa generated approximately $368 million worth of exports, almost exclusively by tuna canneries located in Pago Pago. The canneries are the second largest employer on the islands. Other principal products are fish, pet food, fish meal, mats, and handicrafts.

BAKER, HOWLAND, AND JARVIS ISLANDS

These Pacific islands were not to play a role in the extraterritorial plans of the U.S. until May 13, 1936. President F. D. Roosevelt, at that time, placed them under the control and jurisdiction of the Secretary of the Interior for administration purposes.

The three islands have a tropical climate with scant rainfall, constant wind, and a burning sun.

Baker Island is a saucer-shaped atoll with an area of approximately one square mile. It is about 1,650 miles from Hawaii.

Howland Island, 36 miles to the northwest, is approximately one and a half miles long and half a mile wide. It is a low-lying, nearly level, sandy, coral island surrounded by a narrow fringing reef.

Howland Island is related to the tragic disappearance of Amelia Earhart and Fred J. Noonan during the round-the-world flight in 1937. They left New Guinea on July 2, 1937, for Howland, but were never seen again.

Jarvis Island is several hundred miles to the east and is approximately one and three quarter miles long by one mile wide. It is a sandy coral island surrounded by a narrow fringing reef.

Baker, Howland, and Jarvis have been uninhabited since 1942. In 1974, these islands became part of the National Wildlife Refuge System, administered by the U.S. Fish & Wildlife Service, Department of the Interior.

CANTON AND ENDERBURY ISLANDS

Canton and Enderbury islands, the largest of the Phoenix group, are jointly administered by the U.S. and Great Britain after an agreement signed April 6, 1939. The status of Canton and Enderbury was the subject of negotiations between the U.S., U.K., and Gilbert Islands Governments in 1979. The negotiations resulted in the signing on September 20, 1979, of a Treaty of Friendship between the U.S. and the Republic of Kiribati. The Republic of Kiribati declared its independence on July 12, 1979.

Canton is triangular in shape and the largest of the eight islands of this group. It lies about 1,600 miles southwest of Hawaii and was discovered at the turn of the 18th century by U.S. whalers. After World War II it served as an aviation support facility, and later as a missile tracking station.

Enderbury is rectangular in shape and is 2.75 miles long by 1 mile wide. It is unpopulated and lies about 35 miles southeast of Canton.

JOHNSTON ATOLL

Johnston is a coral atoll about 700 miles southwest of Hawaii. It consists of four small islands—Johnston Island, Sand Island, Hikina Island, and Akau Island—which lie on a reef about 9 miles long in a north-east-southwest direction.

The atoll was discovered by Capt. Charles James Johnston of *H.M.S. Cornwallis* in 1807. In 1858 it was claimed by Hawaii, and later became a U.S. possession.

Johnston Atoll is a Naval Defense Sea Area and Airspace Reservation and is closed to the public. The administration of Johnston Atoll is under the jurisdiction of the Defense Nuclear Agency, Commander, Johnston Atoll (FCDNA), APO San Francisco, CA 96305.

KINGMAN REEF

Kingman Reef, located about 1,000 miles south of Hawaii, was discovered by Capt. E. Fanning in 1798, but named for Capt. W. E. Kingman, who rediscovered it in 1853. The reef, drying only on its northeast, east and southeast edges, is of atoll character. The reef is triangular in shape, with its apex northward; it is about 9.5 miles long, east and west, and 5 miles wide, north and south, within the 100-fathom curve. The island is uninhabited.

A United States possession, Kingman Reef is a Naval Defense Sea Area and Airspace Reservation, and is closed to the public. The Airspace Entry Control has been suspended, but is subject to immediate reinstatement without notice. No vessel, except those authorized by the Secretary of the Navy, shall be navigated in the area within the 3-mile limit.

MIDWAY ISLANDS

Midway Islands, lying about 1,150 miles west-northwest of Hawaii, were discovered by Captain N. C. Brooks of the Hawaiian bark *Gambia* on July 5, 1859, in the name of the United States. The atoll was formally declared a U.S. possession in 1867, and in 1903 Theodore Roosevelt made it a naval reservation. The island was renamed "Midway" by the U.S. Navy in recognition of its geographic location on the route between California and Japan.

Midway Islands consist of a circular atoll, 6 miles in diameter, and enclosing two islands. Eastern Island, on its southeast side, is triangular in shape, and about 1.2 miles long. Sand Island on its south side, is about 2.25 miles long in a northeast-southwest direction.

A National Wildlife Refuge was set up on Midway under an agreement with the Fish and Wildlife Service of the U.S. Dept. of the Interior.

The Midway Islands are within a Naval Defense Sea Area. The Navy Department maintains an installation and has jurisdiction over the atoll. Permission to enter the Naval Defense Sea Area must be obtained in advance from the Commander Third Fleet (N31), Pearl Harbor, HI 96860.

Midway has no indigenous population. It is currently populated with several U.S. military personnel.

WAKE ISLAND

Total area: 2.5 sq mi. (6.5 sq km)
Comparative size: about 11 times the size of The Mall in Washington, D.C.
Population (Jan. 1990): no indigenous inhabitants; temporary population consists of 11 U.S. Air Force personnel, 27 U.S. civilians, and 151 Thai contractors.
Economy: The economic activity is limited to providing services to U.S. military personnel and contractors on the island. All food and manufactured goods must be imported.

Wake Island, about halfway between Midway and Guam, is an atoll comprising the three islets of Wilkes, Peale, and Wake. They were discovered by the British in 1796 and annexed by the U.S. in 1899. The entire area comprises 3 square miles and has no native population. In 1938, Pan American Airways established a seaplane base and Wake Island has been used as a commercial base since then. On Dec. 8, 1941, it was attacked by the Japanese, who finally took possession on Dec. 23. It was surrendered by the Japanese on Sept. 4, 1945.

The President, acting pursuant to the Hawaii Omnibus Act, assigned responsibility for Wake to the Secretary of the Interior in 1962. The Department of Transportation exercised civil administration of Wake through an agreement with the Department of the Interior until June 1972, at which time the Department of the Air Force assumed responsibility for the Territory.

CAROLINE ISLANDS

The Caroline Islands, east of the Philippines and south of the Marianas, include the Yap, Truk, and the Palau groups and the islands of Ponape and Kusqie, as well as many coral atolls.

The islands are composed chiefly of volcanic rock, and their peaks rise 2,000 to 3,000 feet above sea level. Chief exports of the islands are copra, fish products, and handicrafts.

Formerly members of the U.S. Trust Territory of the Pacific, all of the group but Palau joined the Federated States of Micronesia.

MARIANA ISLANDS

(The Commonwealth of The Northern Mariana Islands)

Governor: Lorenzo I. De Leon Guerrero
1990 population: 43,345. The population of the Commonwealth of the Northern Mariana Islands (CNMI) is concentrated on the three largest inhabited islands: Saipan, the government seat and commerce center, 39,090; Rota, 2,311; and Tinian, 2,118. The CNMI's northern islands have a population of 36. Of the CNMI's total population, approximately 22,063 are registered aliens, a 670% increase since 1980.
Language: English is the official language, but Chamorro and Carolinian are the spoken native tongues. Japanese is also spoken in many of the hotels and shops, reflecting a heavy tourism industry.
Gross Island Product (1989): $512 million
Economy: The government of the CNMI benefits substantially from U.S. financial assistance. A seven-year financial agreement with the U.S.for the years 1986–1992 entitles the Commonwealth to $228 million for capital development, government operations, and special programs. In addition, the CNMI is eligible for categorical federal programs provided to the 50 states.

The Mariana Islands, east of the Philippines and south of Japan, include the islands of Guam, Rota, Saipan, Tinian, Pagan, Guguan, Agrihan, and Aguijan. Guam, the largest, is independent of the trusteeship, having been acquired by the U.S. from Spain in 1898. (For more information, *see* the entry on Guam in this section.) The remaining islands, referred to as the Commonwealth of the Northern Mariana Islands

(CNMI) became part of the United States pursuant to P.L. 94-241 as of November 3, 1986.

Tourism is the leading earning export with total visitor expenditures equaling about 37% of the GIP. Seventy-five percent of the tourists are Japanese.

Agricultural products are coffee, coconuts, fruits, tobacco, and cattle.

Trust Territory of the Pacific Islands

REPUBLIC OF PALAU

Capital: Koror
Total area: 177 sq mi (458 sq km)
Comparative size: slightly more than 2.5 times the size of Washington, D.C.
1990 population: 15,122, growth rate: 0.7%
Gross domestic product (1986): $31.6 million, per capita $2,260
Economy: The economy consists primarily of subsistence agriculture and fishing. Tourism provides some foreign exchange. The Government relies heavily on financial assistance from the United States.

Ethnic divisions: Palauans are a composite of Polynesian, Malayan, and Melanesian races.
Language: Palauan is the official language, though English is commonplace.

Palau is the last member of the Trust Territory of the Pacific Islands and is administered by the United States. The islands are located 528 mi. (850 km) southeast of the Philippines.

The islands vary geologically from the high mountainous main island of Babelthuap to low, coral islands usually fringed by large barrier reefs.

Tabulated Data on State Governments

	Governor		Legislature[1]					Highest Court[2]		
			Membership		Term, yrs.					
State	Term, years	Annual salary	U[3]	L[4]	U[3]	L[4]	Salaries of members[5]	Members	Term, years	Annual salary[4]
Alabama	4 [10]	70,222 [16]	35	105	4	4	50.00 per diem[21]	9	6	83,880 [6]
Alaska	4	81,648	20	40	4	2	22,872 per annum	5	([8])	99,504
Arizona	4	75,000	30	60	2	2	15,000 per annum	5	6	75,000
Arkansas	4	35,000	35	100	4	2	7,500 per annum	7	8	76,351 [6]
California	4	120,000 [30]	40	80	4 [35]	2 [36]	52,500 per annum	7	12	121,207 [6]
Colorado	4	70,000	35	65	4	2	17,500 per annum	7	10	84,000 [6, 25]
Connecticut	4	78,000	36	151	2	2	16,760 per biennium	7	8	96,647 [6]
Delaware	4 [9]	80,000	21	41	4	2	22,173 per annum	5	12	102,600
Florida	4 [10]	103,909	40	120	4	2	21,684 per annum	7	6	100,444
Georgia[10]	4	91,092	56	180	2	2	10,509 . per annum	7	6	92,778
Hawaii	4	94,780	25	51	4	2	27,000 per year	5	10	78,500 [6]
Idaho	4	75,000	42	84	2	2	12,000 per annum[5]	5	6	71,144 [6]
Illinois	4	93,266	59	118	4-2	2	35,661 per annum	7	10	93,266
Indiana	4 [10]	77,200	50	100	4	2	11,600 per annum	5	([24])	72,765
Iowa	4	72,500	50	100	4	2	16,600 per annum	9	8	72,900 [6]
Kansas	4	65,000	40	125	4	2	169 per diem[22]	7	6	59,143 [31]
Kentucky	4 [7]	79,255	38	100	4	2	100 per diem[22]	7	8	77,497 [6]
Louisiana	4	73,440	39	105	4	4	16,800 per annum	7	10	66,566
Maine	4	70,000 [16]	35	151	2	2	10,500 per annum[16]	7	7	77,300
Maryland	4 [10]	120,000	47	141	4	4	27,000 [5] per annum	7	10	99,000 [6]
Massachusetts	4	75,000	40	160	2	2	30,000 per annum	7	([13])	90,450 [6]
Michigan	4	106,690 [16]	38	110	4	2	45,450 [16] per annum[16]	7	8	106,610
Minnesota	4	109,053	67	134	4 [34]	2	27,979 [5] per annum[16]	7	6	89,052 [6]
Mississippi	4	63,000	52	122	4	4	10,000 per session[5]	9	8	76,000 [6]
Missouri	4 [10]	90,312	34	163	4	2	22,862 [5] per annum[5]	7	12	91,594
Montana	4	53,006	50	100	4	2	52.13 per diem[16]	7	8	56,452
Nebraska	4 [10]	65,000	49 [11]	—	4 [11]	—	12,000 per annum	7	6	77,000
Nevada	4	90,000	21	42	4	2	7,800 per biennium	5	6	85,000
New Hampshire	2	79,541	24	([12])	2	2	200 per biennium	5	([13])	88,200 [6]
New Jersey[28]	4 [10]	130,000	40	80	4 [14]	2	35,000 [32] per annum	7	7 [15]	112,000 [6]
New Mexico	4 [7]	90,000	42	70	4	2	75 per diem	5	8	75,000 [6]
New York	4	130,000	61	150	2	2	57,500 per annum	7	14	120,000 [6]
North Carolina	4 [9]	116,316 [16]	50	120	2	2	11,124 per annum[16]	7	8	84,456 [6]
North Dakota	4	65,200 [16]	53	106	4	2	90 per diem[16 23]	5	10	68,342 [6]
Ohio	4	100,000	33	99	4	2	38,483 [38] per annum	7	6	96,338
Oklahoma	4	70,000	48	101	4	2	32,000 [16] per annum	([19])	6	77,550 [6]
Oregon	4 [10]	75,000	30	60	4	2	937 [31] per annum	7	6	74,172 [6]
Pennsylvania	4 [10]	105,000	50	203	4	2	47,000 per annum	7	10	91,500
Rhode Island	2	69,900	50	100	2	2	5 per diem[17]	5	([18])	117,373

State	Governor		Legislature[1]					Highest Court[2]		
	Term, years	Annual salary	Member-ship U[3]	L[4]	Term, U[3]	yrs. L[4]	Salaries of members[5]		Mem-bers	Term, years	Annual salary[4]
South Carolina	4	99,960	46	124	4	2	10,400	per annum	5	10	91,163 [6]
South Dakota	4 [10]	63,232	35	70	2	2	8,000	per biennium	5	3 [27]	67,288
Tennessee	4	85,000	33	99	4	2	16,500	per annum	5	8	89,772 [26]
Texas	4	93,432	31	150	4	2	7,200 [5]	per annum	(20)	9	82,000
Utah	4	72,800	29	75	4	2	65	per diem[16]	5	(37)	80,300 [6]
Vermont	2	85,977	30	150	2	2	510	per week[29]	5	6	71,355 [6]
Virginia	4 [7]	108,000	40	100	4	2	17,640 [33]	per annum	7	12	99,709 [6]
Washington	4	99,600	49	98	4	2	19,900	per annum	9	6	89,300
West Virginia	4 [10]	72,000	34	100	4	2	6,500 [16]	per annum	5	12	55,000
Wisconsin	4	92,283	33	99	4	2	33,622	per annum	7	10	82,706
Wyoming	4	70,000	30	64	4	2	75 [16]	per diem[16]	5	8	66,500

1. General Assembly in Ark., Colo., Conn., Del., Ga., Ind., Ky., Md., Mo., N.C., Ohio, Pa., R.I., S.C., Tenn., Vt., Va., Legislative Assembly in N.D., Ore.; General Court in Mass., N.H.; Legislature in other states. Meets biennially in Calif., Ky., Me., Mont., Nev., N.J., N.C., N.D., Ore., Pa., Texas, Wash. Wyo Legislature meets annually. Regular general session on odd numbered years and a budget session on even numbered years. Ark. General Assembly meets every other year for 60 days in odd numbered years.; meets annually in other states. 2. Court of Appeals in Md., N.Y., Supreme Court of Virginia in Va., Supreme Judicial Court in Me., Mass.; Supreme Court in other states. 3. Upper house: Senate in all states. 4. Lower house: Assembly in Calif., Nev., N.Y., Wis.; House of Delegates in Md., Va., W.Va.; General Assembly in N.J.; House of Representatives in other states. 5. Does not include additional payments for expenses, mileage, special sessions, etc., or additional per diem payments beyond salary shown. 6. In some states, Chief Justice receives a higher salary. 7. Cannot succeed himself. 8. Appointed for 3 years; thereafter subject to approval or rejection on a nonpartisan ballot for 10-year term. 9. May serve only 2 terms, consecutive or otherwise. 10. May not serve 3rd consecutive term. 11. Unicameral legislature. 12. Constitutional number: 375-400. 13. Until 70 years old. 14. When term begins in Jan. of 2nd year following U.S. census, term shall be 2 years. 15. 2nd term receive tenure, mandatory retirement at 70. 16. Plus additional expenses. 17. For 60 days only. 18. Term of good behavior. 19. 9 members in Supreme Court, highest in civil cases; 5 in Court of Criminal Appeals. 20. 9 members in Supreme Court, highest in civil cases; 9 in Court of Criminal Appeals. 21. Five days a week when the Legislature is in session plus $2,280 per month in expenses. 22. When in session. 23. Plus $180 per month when not in session. 24. Appointed for 2 years; thereafter elected popularly for 10-year term. 25. Beginning FY 1993. 26. Adjusted annually according to increase in Consumer Price Index. 27. Subsequent terms, 8 years. 28. Governor has refused to accept the raise because of budget crisis. 29. To limit of $13,000 per biennium; $100 per diem for Special Session. 30. Governor remitted $6,000 for his salary to the state for current fiscal year. 31. Plus $400 monthly when not in session and per diem allowance when in session. 32. Each legislator receives $60,000 annually for appointment of personal staff aides. 33. Senate $18,000. 34. Every 10 years (the year after census) term is only for 2 years. 35. From 1991 onwards 2 terms or 8-year limit. 36. From 1991 onwards 3 terms or 6-year limit. 37. Appointed by governor. Up for re-election at first general election that takes place at least 3 years after appointment. After that, face a retention election every 10 years. 38. Senator's salary higher. NOTE: Salaries are rounded to nearest dollar. *Source:* Questionnaires to the states.

50 Largest Cities of the United States

(According to the 1990 Census.)

Data supplied by Bureau of the Census and by the cities in response to questionnaires. Ranking of 50 largest cities (April 1990 census data). Avg. daily temp.: *(County and City Data Book).*
NOTE: Persons of Hispanic origin may be of any race.

ALBUQUERQUE, N.M.

Incorporated as city: 1891
Mayor: Louis E. Saavedra
1980 population (1980 census) & (rank): 332,920 (44)
1990 census population, sex & (rank): 384,736 (38); % change, 15.6; **Male,** 186,584; **Female,** 198,152; **White,** 301,010; **Black,** 11,484 (3.0%); **American Indian, Eskimo, or Aleut,** 11,708 (3.0%); **Asian or Pacific Islander,** 6,660 (1.7%); **Other race,** 53.874; **Hispanic origin,** 132,706 (34.5%). **1990 percent population under 18:** 25.0%; **65 and over:** 11.1%; **median age:** 32.5.
Land area: 135 sq mi. (350 sq km)
Altitude: 4,958 ft.
Avg. daily temp: Jan., 34.8° F; July, 78.8° F
Location: Central part of state on Rio Grande River
County: Bernalillo
Churches: 211
City-owned parks: 160
Radio stations: 43 (AM, 19; FM, 24)

Television stations: 11
Chamber of Commerce: Greater Albuquerque Chamber of Commerce, 401 2nd St., N.W., Albuquerque, N.M. 87102. Albuquerque Hispano Chamber of Commerce, 1520 Central Ave., S.E., Albuquerque, N.M. 87106

ATLANTA, GA.

Incorporated as city: 1847
Mayor: Maynard Jackson
1980 population (1980 census) & (rank): 425,022 (29)
1990 census population, sex, & (rank): 394,017 (32); % change, −7.3; **Male,** 187,877; **Female,** 206,140; **White,** 122,327; **Black,** 264,262 (67.1%); **American Indian, Eskimo, or Aleut,** 563 (0.1%); **Asian or Pacific Islander,** 3,498 (0.9%); **Other race,** 3,367; **Hispanic origin,** 7,525 (1.9%). **1990 percent population under 18:** 24.1; **65 and over:** 11.3; **median age:** 31.5.
City land area: 136 sq mi. (352.2 sq km)

Altitude: Highest, 1,050 ft; lowest, 940
Avg. daily temp.: Jan., 41.9° F; July, 78.6° F
Location: In northwest central part of state, on Chatta-hoochee River
Counties: Fulton and DeKalb
Churches (18-county area): 1,500
City-owned parks: 277 (3,178 ac.)
Radio stations (18-county area): AM, 7; FM, 20
Television stations (18-county area): 7 commercial; 2 PBS
Chamber of Commerce: Atlanta Chamber of Commerce, 235 International Blvd., Atlanta, Ga. 30301; Information is gathered on the 18-county MSA

AUSTIN, TEX.

Incorporated as city: 1839
Mayor: Bruce Todd
1980 population (1980 census) & (rank): 345,890 (42)
1990 census population, sex, & (rank): 465,622 (27); % change, 34.6; **Male,** 232,473; **Female,** 233,149; **White,** 328,542; **Black,** 57,868 (12.4%); **American Indian, Eskimo, or Aleut:,** 1,756 (0.4%); **Asian or Pacific Islander,** 14,141 (3.0%); **Other race,** 63,315; **Hispanic origin,** 106,868 (23.0%). **1990 percent population under 18:** 23.1%; **65 and over:** 7.4%; **median age:** 28.9
Land area: 116 sq mi. (300 sq km)
Altitude: From 425 ft. to over 1000 ft. elevation
Avg. daily temp.: Jan., 49.1° F; July, 84.7° F
Location: In south central part of state, on the Colorado River
County: Seat of Travis Co.
Churches: 353 churches, representing 45 denominations
City-owned parks and playgrounds: 169 (11,800 ac.)
Radio stations: AM, 6; FM, 12
Television stations: 3 commercial; 1 PBS; 1 independent
Chamber of Commerce: Greater Austin Chamber of Commerce, P.O. Box 1967, Austin, Tex. 78767

BALTIMORE, MD.

Incorporated as city: 1797
Mayor: Kurt L. Schmoke
1980 population (1980 census) & (rank): 786,741 (10)
1990 census population, sex, & (rank): 736,014 (13); % change, −6.4; **Male,** 343,513; **Female,** 392,501; **White,** 287,753; **Black,** 435,768 (59.2%); **American Indian, Eskimo, or Aleut:** 2,555 (0.3%); **Asian or Pacific Islander:** 7,942 (1.1%); **Other race:** 1,996; **Hispanic origin:** 7,602 (1.0%). **1990 percent population under 18:** 24.4; **65 and over:** 13.7; **Median age:** 32.6.
Land area: 80.3 sq mi. (208 sq km)
Altitude: Highest, 490 ft; lowest, sea level
Avg. daily temp.: Jan., 35.5° F; July, 79.9° F
Location: On Patapsco River, about 12 mi. from Chesa-peake Bay
County: Independent city
Churches: Roman Catholic, 72; Jewish, 50; Protestant and others, 344
City-owned parks: 347 park areas and tracts (6,314 ac.)
Radio stations: AM, 10; FM, 11
Television stations: 7 (including Home Shopping Network)
Chamber of Commerce: Greater Baltimore Committee, 111 S. Calvert St., Ste. 1500, Baltimore, Md. 21202

BOSTON, MASS.

Incorporated as city: 1822
Mayor: Raymond L. Flynn
1980 population (1980 census) & (rank): 562,994 (20)
1990 census population, sex, & (rank): 574,283 (20); % change, 2.0; **Male,** 275,972; **Female,** 298,311; **White,** 360,875; **Black,** 146,945 (25.6%); **American Indian, Eskimo, or Aleut,** 1,884 (0.3%); **Asian or Pacific Islander,** 30,388 (5.3%); **Other race,** 34,191; **Hispanic origin,** 61,955 (10.8%). **1990 percent population under 18:** 19.1; **65 and over:** 11.5; **median age:** 30.3.
Land area: 47.2 sq mi. (122 sq km)
Altitude: Highest, 330 ft; lowest, sea level
Avg. daily temp.: Jan., 29.6° F; July, 73.5° F
Location: On Massachusetts Bay, at mouths of Charles and Mystic Rivers
County: Seat of Suffolk Co.
Churches: Protestant, 187; Roman Catholic, 72; Jewish, 28; others, 100
City-owned parks, playgrounds, etc.: 2,276.36 ac.
Radio stations: AM, 9; FM, 12
Television stations: 10
Chamber of Commerce: Boston Chamber of Commerce, 600 Atlantic Ave., Boston, Mass. 02210

BUFFALO, N.Y.

Incorporated as city: 1832
Mayor: James Griffin
1980 population (1980 census) & (rank): 357,870 (39)
1990 census population, sex, & (rank): 328,123 (50); % change, −8.3; **Male,** 153,050; **Female,** 175,073; **White,** 212,449; **Black,** 100,579 (30.7%); **American Indian, Eskimo, or Aleut:** 2,547 (0.8%); **Asian or Pacific Islander,** 3,261 (1.0%); **Other race,** 9,287; **Hispanic origin,** 16,129 (4.9%). **1990 percent population under 18:** 24.2%; **65 and over:** 14.8%; **median age:** 32.0.
Land area: 42.67 sq. mi. (109 sq. km)
Altitude: Highest 705 ft; lowest 571.84 ft
Avg. daily temp.: Jan., 23.5° F; July, 70.7° F
Location: At east end of Lake Erie, on Niagara River
County: Seat of Erie Co.
Churches: 60 denominations, with over 1,100 churches
County-owned parks: 9 public parks (3,000 ac.)
Radio stations: AM 10; FM 13
Television stations: 8 (plus reception from 3 Canadian stations)
Chamber of Commerce: Greater Buffalo Chamber of Commerce, 107 Delaware Avenue, Buffalo, N.Y. 14202

CHARLOTTE, N.C.

Incorporated as city: 1768
Mayor: Richard Vinroot
1980 population (1980 census) & (rank): 315,474 (47)
1990 census population, sex, & (rank): 395,934 (35); % change, 25.5; **Male,** 188,088; **Female,** 207,846; **White,** 259,760; **Black,** 125,827 (31.8%); **American Indian, Eskimo, or Aleut:** 1,425 (0.4%); **Asian or Pacific Islander:** 7,211 (1.8%); **Other race,** 1,711; **Hispanic origin,** 5,571 (1.4%). **1990 percent population under 18:** 24.2%; **65 and over:** 9.8%; **median age:** 32.1.
Land area: 175.59 sq mi. (455 sq km)
Altitude: 765 ft
Avg. daily temp.: Jan., 40.5° F; July, 78.5° F
Location: In the southern part of state near the border of South Carolina
County: Seat of Mecklenburg Co.
Churches: Protestant, over 400; Roman Catholic, 8; Jewish, 3; Greek Orthodox, 1

City-owned parks and parkways: 120
Radio stations: AM, 8; FM, 12
Television stations: 4 commercial; 2 PBS
Chamber of Commerce: Charlotte Chamber, P.O. Box 32785, Charlotte, N.C., 28232

CHICAGO, ILL.

Incorporated as city: 1837
Mayor: Richard M. Daley
1980 population (1980 census) & (rank): 3,005,072 (2)
1990 census population, sex, & (rank): 2,783,726 (3); % change, −7.4; **Male,** 1,334,705; **Female,** 1,449,021; **White,** 1,263,524; **Black,** 1,087,711 (39.1%); **American Indian, Eskimo, or Aleut,** 7,064 (0.3%); **Asian or Pacific Islander,** 104,118 (3.7%); **Other race,** 321,309; **Hispanic origin,** 545,852 (19.6%). **1990 percent population under 18:** 26.0%; **65 and over:** 11.9%; **median age:** 31.3.
Land area: 228.475 sq mi. (592 sq km)
Altitude: Highest, 672 ft; lowest, 578.5
Avg. daily temp.: Jan., 21.4° F; July, 73.0° F
Location: On lower west shore of Lake Michigan
County: Seat of Cook Co.
Churches: Protestant, 850; Roman Catholic, 252; Jewish, 51
City-owned parks: 563
Radio stations: AM, 17; FM, 23
Television stations: 12
Chamber of Commerce: Chicago Association of Commerce & Industry, 200 N. LaSalle, Chicago, Ill. 60601

CINCINNATI, OHIO

Incorporated as city: 1819
Mayor: David Mann
City Manager: Gerald Newfarmer
1980 population (1980 census) & (rank): 385,409 (32)
1990 census population, sex, & (rank): 364,040 (45); % change, −5.5; **Male,** 169,305; **Female,** 194,735; **White,** 220,285; **Black,** 138,1312 (37.9%); **American Indian, Eskimo, or Aleut,** 660 (0.2%); **Asian or Pacific Islander,** 4,030 (1.1%); **Other race,** 933; **Hispanic origin,** 2,386 (0.7%). **1990 percent population under 18:** 25.1%; **65 and over:** 13.9%; **median age:** 30.9.
Land area: 78.1 sq mi. (202 sq km)
Altitude: Highest, 960 ft; lowest, 441
Avg. daily temp.: Jan., 30.3° F; July, 76.1° F
Location: In southwestern corner of state on Ohio River
County: Seat of Hamilton Co.
Churches: 850
City-owned parks: 96 (4,345 ac.)
Radio stations: AM, 10; FM, 15 (Greater Cincinnati)
Television stations: 8
Chamber of Commerce: Cincinnati Chamber of Commerce, 441 Vine St. Suite 300, Cincinnati, Ohio 45202

CLEVELAND, OHIO

Incorporated as city: 1836
Mayor: Michael R. White
1980 population (1980 census) & (rank): 573,822 (18)
1990 census population, sex, & (rank): 505,616 (24); % change, −11.9; **Male,** 237,211; **Female,** 268,405; **White,** 250,234; **Black,** 235,405 (46.6%); **American Indian, Eskimo, or Aleut,** 1,562 (0.3%); **Asian or Pacific Is-**

lander, 5,115 (1.0%); **Other race,** 13,300; **Hispanic origin,** 23,197 (4.6%). **1990 percent population under 18:** 26.9; **65 and over:** 14.0; **median age:** 31.9.
Land area: 79 sq mi. (205 sq km)
Altitude: Highest, 1048 ft.; lowest, 573
Avg. daily temp.: Jan., 25.5° F; July, 71.6° F
Location: On Lake Erie at mouth of Cuyahoga River
County: Seat of Cuyahoga Co.
Churches: [1] Protestant, 980; Roman Catholic, 187; Jewish, 31; Eastern Orthodox, 22
City-owned parks: 41 (1,930 ac.)
Radio stations: AM, 15; FM, 17
Television stations: 7
Chamber of Commerce: Greater Cleveland Growth Association, 690 Huntington Building, Cleveland, Ohio 44115
1. PMSA.

COLUMBUS, OHIO

Incorporated as city: 1834
Mayor: Greg Lashutka
1980 population (1980 census) & (rank): 565,021 (19)
1990 census population, sex, & (rank): 632,910 (16); % change, 12.0; **Male,** 305,574; **Female,** 327,336; **White,** 471,025; **Black,** 142,748 (22.6%); **American Indian, Eskimo, or Aleut,** 1,469 (0.2%); **Asian or Pacific Islander,** 14,993 (2.4%); **Other race,** 2,675; **Hispanic origin,** 6,741 (1.1%). **1990 percent population under 18:** 23.7; **65 and over:** 9.2; **median age:** 29.4.
Land area: 196.151 sq mi. (508 sq km)
Altitude: Highest, 902 ft; lowest, 702
Avg. daily temp.: Jan., 27.1° F; July, 73.8° F
Location: In central part of state, on Scioto River
County: Seat of Franklin Co.
Churches: Protestant, 436; Roman Catholic, 62; Jewish, 5; Other, 8
City-owned parks: 200 (12,293 ac.)
Radio stations: AM, 10; FM, 15
Television stations: 8 commercial, 3 PBS
Chamber of Commerce: Columbus Area Chamber of Commerce, P.O. Box 1527, Columbus, Ohio 43216

DALLAS, TEX.

Incorporated as city: 1856
Mayor: Steve Bartlett
City Manager: Jan Hart
1980 population (1980 census) & (rank): 904,599 (7)
1990 census population, sex, & (rank): 1,006,877 (8); % change, 11.3; **Male,** 495,141; **Female,** 511,736; **White,** 556,760; **Black,** 296,994 (29.5%); **American Indian, Eskimo, or Aleut,** 4,792 (0.5%); **Asian or Pacific Islander,** 21,952 (2.2%); **Other race,** 126,379; **Hispanic origin,** 210,240 (20.9%). **1990 percent population under 18:** 25.0; **65 and over:** 9.7; **median age:** 30.6.
Land area: 378 sq mi. (979 sq km)
Altitude: Highest, 750 ft; lowest, 375
Avg. daily temp.: Jan., 45.0° F; July, 86.3° F
Location: In northeastern part of state, on Trinity River
County: Seat of Dallas Co.
Churches: 1,974 (in Dallas Co.)
City-owned parks: 296 (47,025 ac.)
Radio stations: AM, 19; FM, 30
Television stations: 10 commercial, 1 PBS
Chamber of Commerce: Dallas Chamber of Commerce, 1201 Elm, Dallas, Tex. 75270

DENVER, COLO.

Incorporated as city: 1861
Mayor: Wellington Webb
1980 population (1980 census) & (rank): 492,686 (24)
1990 census population, sex, & (rank): 467,610 (26); % change, –5.1; **Male,** 227,517; **Female,** 240,093; **White,** 337,198; **Black,** 60,046 (12.8%); **American Indian, Eskimo, or Aleut,** 5,381 (1.2%); **Asian or Pacific Islander,** 11,005 (2.4%); **Other race,** 53,980; **Hispanic origin,** 107,382 (23.0%); **1990 percent population under 18:** 22.0; **65 and over:** 13.9; **median age:** 33.9
Land area: 154.63 sq mi. (400.5 km)
Altitude: Highest, 5,494 ft; lowest, 5,140
Avg. daily temp.: Jan., 29.5° F; July, 73.3° F
Location: In northeast central part of state, on South Platte River
County: Contiguous boundaries with city of Denver
Churches:[1] Protestant, 859; Roman Catholic, 60; Jewish, 13
City-owned parks: 205 (4,166 ac.)
City-owned mountain parks: 40 (13,600 ac.)
Radio stations: AM, 23; FM, 20[1]
Television stations: 17[1]
Chamber of Commerce: Greater Denver Chamber of Commerce, 1445 Market Street, Denver, Colo. 80202
1. Metropolitan area.

DETROIT, MICH.

Incorporated as city: 1815
Mayor: Coleman A. Young
1980 population (1980 census) & (rank): 1,203,368 (6)
1990 census population, sex, & (rank): 1,027,974 (7); % change, –14.6; **Male,** 476,814; **Female,** 551,160; **White,** 222,316; **Black,** 777,916 (75.7%); **American Indian, Eskimo, or Aleut,** 3,655 (0.4%); **Asian or Pacific Islander,** 8,461 (0.8%); **Other race,** 15,626; **Hispanic origin,** 28,473 (2.8%); **1990 percent population under 18:** 29.4; **65 and over:** 12.2; **median age:** 30.8.
Land area: 143 sq mi. (370 sq km)
Altitude: Highest, 685 ft; lowest, 574
Avg. daily temp.: Jan., 23.4° F; July, 71.9° F
Location: In southeastern part of state, on Detroit River
County: Seat of Wayne Co.
Churches:[1] Protestant, 1,165; Roman Catholic, 89; Jewish, 2
City-owned parks: 56 parks (3,843 ac.); 393 sites (5,838 ac.)
Radio stations: AM, 27; FM, 30 (includes 3 in Windsor, Ont.)
Television stations: 8[2] (includes 1 in Windsor, Ont.)
Chamber of Commerce: Greater Detroit Chamber of Commerce, 622 W. Lafayette, Detroit, Mich. 48226
1. Six-county metropolitan area. 2. Within four counties of Metro Detroit.

EL PASO, TEX.

Incorporated as city: 1873
Mayor: Bill Tilney
1980 population (1980 census) & (rank): 425,259 (28)
1990 census population, sex, & (rank): 515,342 (22); % change, 21.2; **Male,** 247,163; **Female,** 268,179; **White,** 396,122; **Black,** 17,708 (3.4%); **American Indian, Eskimo, or Aleut,** 2,239 (0.4%); **Asian or Pacific Islander,** 5,956 (1.2%); **Other race,** 93,317; **Hispanic origin,** 355,669 (69.0%); **1990 percent population under 18:** 31.9; **65 and over:** 8.7; **median age:** 28.7
Land area: 247.4 sq mi. (641 sq km)

Altitude: 4,000 ft
Avg. daily temp.: Jan., 44.2° F; July, 82.5° F
Location: In far western part of state, on Rio Grande
County: Seat of El Paso Co.
Churches: Protestant, 320; Roman Catholic, 39; Jewish, 3; others, 20
City-owned parks: 116[1] (1,180 ac.)
Radio Stations: AM, 18; FM, 17
Television stations: 6
Chamber of Commerce: El Paso Chamber of Commerce, 10 Civic Center Plaza, El Paso, Tex. 79944
1. Includes 109 developed and 7 undeveloped parks.

FORT WORTH, TEX.

Incorporated as city: 1873
Mayor: Kay Granger
City Manager: David Ivory
1980 population (1980 census) & (rank): 385,164 (33)
1990 census population, sex, & (rank): 447,619 (28); % change, 16.2; **Male,** 220,268; **Female,** 227,351; **White,** 285,549; **Black,** 98,532 (22.0%); **American Indian, Eskimo, or Aleut,** 1,914 (0.4%); **Asian or Pacific Islander,** 8,910 (2.0%); **Other race,** 52,714; **Hispanic origin,** 87,345 (19.5%); **1990 percent population under 18:** 26.6; **65 and over:** 11.2; **median age:** 30.3.
Land area: 295.301 sq mi. (765 sq km)
Altitude: Highest, 780 ft; lowest, 520
Avg. daily temp.: Jan., 44.2° F; July, 82.5° F
Location: In north central part of state, on Trinity River
County: Seat of Tarrant Co.
Churches: 941, representing 72 denominations
City-owned parks: 171 (8,189 ac.; 3,500 ac. in Nature Center)
Radio stations: AM, 5; FM, 20
Television stations: 15 (9 local)
Chamber of Commerce: Fort Worth Chamber of Commerce, 777 Taylor Street, Suit 900, Fort Worth, Tex. 76102

FRESNO, CALIF.

Incorporated as city: 1885
Mayor: Karen Humphrey
City Manager: Michael A. Bierman
1980 population (1980 census) & (rank): 217,491 (65)
1990 census population, sex, & (rank): 354,202 (47); % change, 62.9; **Male,** 172,241; **Female,** 181,961; **White,** 209,604; **Black,** 29,409 (8.3%); **American Indian, Eskimo, or Aleut,** 3,729 (1.1%); **Asian or Pacific Islander,** 44,358 (12.5%); **Other race,** 67,102; **Hispanic origin,** 105,787 (29.9%); **1990 percent population under 18:** 31.7; **65 and over:** 10.1; **median age:** 28.4.
Land area: 99.38 sq mi. (257.39 sq km)
Altitude: 328 ft
Avg. daily temp.: Jan., 45.5° F; July, 81.0° F
Location: 184 miles southeast of San Francisco and 222 miles northwest of Los Angeles
County: Seat of Fresno County
Churches: 450 (approximate)
City-owned parks: 38 (690 ac.)
Radio stations: AM 11[1]; FM 13[1]; Bilingual 1
Television stations: 8[1]
Chamber of Commerce: Fresno County and City Chamber of Commerce, P.O. Box 1469, 2331 Fresno St., Fresno, CA 93716
1. Metropolitan area.

HONOLULU, HAWAII

Incorporated as city and county: 1907
Mayor: Frank F. Fasi
1980 population (1980 census) & (rank): 365,048 (36)
1990 census population, sex, & (rank): 365,272 (44)[1]; %
change, 0.1; **Male,** 180,357; **Female,** 184,915; **White,**
97,527; **Black,** 4,821 (1.3%); **American Indian, Eskimo,**
or Aleut, 1,126 (0.3%); **Asian or Pacific Islander,**
257,552 (70.5%); **Other race,** 4,246; **Hispanic origin,**
16,704 (4.6%). **1990 percent population under 18:** 19.1;
65 and over: 16.0; **median age:** 36.9.
Land area: 600 sq mi. (1,554 sq km)[1]
Altitude: Highest, 4,025 ft; lowest, sea level
Avg. daily temp.: Jan., 72.6° F; July, 80.1° F
Location: The city and county government's jurisdiction
includes the entire island of Oahu
Churches: Roman Catholic, 34; Buddhist, 35; Jewish, 2;
Protestant and others, 329
City-owned parks: 5,835 ac.
Radio stations: AM, 17; FM, 14
Television stations: 12
Chamber of Commerce: Chamber of Commerce of Ha-
waii, 735 Bishop St., Honolulu, Hawaii 96813
1. City and county area. The census bureau does not in-
clude the entire city and county in its census of Honolulu.
If it did, the 1990 census and rank would be 836,231 (12).

HOUSTON, TEX.

Incorporated as city: 1837
Mayor: Bob Lanier
1980 population (1980 census) & (rank): 1,595,138 (5)
1990 census population, sex, & (rank): 1,630,553 (4); %
change, 2.2; **Male,** 809,048; **Female,** 821,505; **White,**
859,069; **Black,** 457,990 (28.1%); **American Indian,**
Eskimo, or Aleut, 4,126 (0.3%); **Asian or Pacific Is-**
lander, 67,113 (4.1%); **Other race,** 242,255; **Hispanic**
origin, 450,483 (27.6%). **1990 percent population un-**
der 18: 26.7; **65 and over:** 8.3; **median age:** 30.4.
Land area: 581.44 sq mi. (1,506 sq km)
Altitude: Highest, 120 ft; lowest, sea level
Avg. daily temp.: Jan., 51.4° F; July, 83.1° F
Location: In southeastern part of state, near Gulf of
Mexico
County: Seat of Harris Co.
Churches: 1,750[2]
City-owned parks: 334 (32,500 ac.)
Radio stations: AM, 25; FM, 29[1]
Television stations: 10 commercial, 1 PBS
Poet Laureate: HUY-LUC Khoi Tien Bui
Chamber of Commerce: Greater Houston Partnership,
1100 Milam Building, 25th Fl., Houston, Tex. 77002
1. Includes annexations since 1970. 2. Harris County.

INDIANAPOLIS, IND.

Incorporated as city: 1832 (reincorporated 1838)
Mayor: Steve Goldsmith
1980 population (1980 census) & (rank): 711,539 (12)
1990 census population, sex, & (rank): 744,952 (12); %
change, 4.3; **Male,** 352,309; **Female,** 389,643; **White,**
564,447; **Black,** 166,031 (22.4%); **American Indian,**
Eskimo, or Aleut, 1,580 (0.2%); **Asian or Pacific Is-**
lander, 6,943 (0.9%); **Other race,** 2,951; **Hispanic ori-**
gin, 7,790 (1.0%). **1990 percent population under 18:**
25.6%; **65 and over:** 11.5; **median age:** 31.8.
Land area: 352 sq mi. (912 sq km)

Altitude: Highest, 840 ft; lowest, 700
Avg. daily temp.: Jan., 26.0 F; July, 75.1° F
Location: In central part of the state, on West Fork of
White River
County: Seat of Marion Co.
Churches: 1,200[1]
City-owned parks: 167 (10,753 ac.)
Radio stations: AM, 8[3]; FM, 17[3]
Television stations: 7[1]
Chamber of Commerce: Indianapolis Chamber of Com-
merce, 320 N Meridian St., Indianapolis, Ind. 46204
1. Marion County. 2. Consolidated city. 3. Metropolitan
area.

JACKSONVILLE, FLA.

Incorporated as city: 1822
Mayor: Ed Austin
1980 population (1980 census) & (rank)[1]: 571,003 (19)
1990 census population, sex, & (rank)[1]: 672,971 (15); %
change, 17.9; **Male,** 328,737; **Female,** 344,234; **White,**
489,604; **Black,** 163,902 (24.4%); **American Indian,**
Eskimo, or Aleut, 1,904 (0.3%); **Asian or Pacific Is-**
lander, 12,940 (1.9%); **Other race,** 4,621; **Hispanic ori-**
gin, 17,333 (2.6%). **1990 percent population under 18:**
25.9; **65 and over:** 10.7; **median age:** 31.5.
Land area: 759.6 sq mi. (1,967 sq km)
Altitude: Highest, 71 ft; lowest, sea level
Avg. daily temp.: Jan., 53.2° F; July, 81.3° F
Location: On St. Johns River, 20 miles from Atlantic
Ocean
County: Duval
Churches: Protestant, 771; Roman Catholic, 27; Jewish,
5; others, 21
City-owned parks and playgrounds: 138 (1,522 ac.)
Radio stations: AM, 13; FM, 15
Television stations: 6 commercial, 1 PBS
Chamber of Commerce: Jacksonville Area Chamber of
Commerce, Jacksonville, Fla. 32202
1. Consolidated city.

KANSAS CITY, MO.

Incorporated as city: 1850
Mayor: Emanuel Cleaver II
City Manager: David H. Olson
1980 population (1980 census) & (rank): 448,028 (27)
1990 census population, sex, & (rank): 435,146 (31); %
change, –2.9; **Male,** 206,965; **Female,** 228,181; **White,**
290,572; **Black,** 128,768 (29.6%); **American Indian,**
Eskimo, or Aleut, 2,144 (0.5%); **Asian or Pacific Is-**
lander, 5,239 (1.2%); **Other race,** 8,423; **Hispanic ori-**
gin, 17,017 (3.9%). **1990 percent population under 18:**
24.8; **65 and over:** 12.9; **median age:** 32.8.
Land area: 317 sq mi. (821 sq km)
Altitude: Highest, 1,014 ft; lowest, 722
Avg. daily temp.: Jan., 28.4° F; July, 80.9 F
Location: In western part of state, at juncture of Mis-
souri and Kansas Rivers
County: Located in Jackson, Clay, and Platte & Cass Co.
Churches: 1,100 churches of all denominations
City-owned parks and playgrounds: 180 (7,799 ac.)
Radio stations: AM, 15; FM, 14[1]
Television stations: 6[1]
Chamber of Commerce: Chamber of Commerce of
Greater Kansas City, 920 Main St., Kansas City, Mo.
64105
1. Metropolitan area.

LONG BEACH, CALIF.

Incorporated as city: 1888
Mayor: Ernie Kell
City Manager: James C. Hankla
1980 population (1980 census) & (rank): 361,498 (37)
1990 census population, sex, & (rank): 429,433 (32); **% change,** 18.8; **Male,** 216,685; **Female,** 212,748; **White,** 250,716; **Black,** 58,761 (13.7%); **American Indian, Eskimo, or Aleut,** 2,781 (0.6%); **Asian or Pacific Islander,** 58,266 (13.6%); **Other race,** 58,909; **Hispanic origin,** 101,419 (23.6%). **1990 percent population under 18:** 25.5; **65 and over:** 10.8; **median age:** 30.0.
Land area: 49.8 sq mi. (129 sq km)
Altitude: Highest, 170 ft; lowest, sea level
Avg. daily temp.: Jan., 55.2 F; July, 72.8° F
Location: On San Pedro Bay, south of Los Angeles
County: Los Angeles
Churches: 236
City-owned parks: 42 (1,182 ac.)
Radio stations: AM, 2; FM, 2
Television stations: 8 (metro area)
Chamber of Commerce: Long Beach Area Chamber of Commerce, One World Trade Center, Suite 350, Long Beach, CA 90831-0350

LOS ANGELES, CALIF.

Incorporated as city: 1850
Mayor: Tom Bradley
1980 population (1980 census) & (rank): 2,968,528 (3)
1990 census population, sex, & (rank): 3,485,398 (2); **% change,** 17.4; **Male,** 1,750,055; **Female,** 1,735,343; **White,** 1,841,182; **Black,** 487,674 (14.0%); **American Indian, Eskimo, or Aleut,** 16,379 (0.5%); **Asian or Pacific Islander,** 341,807 (9.8%); **Other race,** 798,356; **Hispanic origin,** 1,391,411 (39.9%). **1990 percent population under 18:** 24.8; **65 and over:** 10.0; **median age:** 30.7.
Land area: 467.4 sq mi. (1,210.57 sq km)
Altitude: Highest, 5,081 ft; lowest, sea level
Avg. daily temp.: Jan., 57.2° F; July, 74.1° F
Location: In southwestern part of state, on Pacific Ocean
County: Seat of Los Angeles Co.
Churches: 2,000 of all denominations
City-owned parks: 355 (15,357 ac.)
Radio stations: AM, 35; FM, 53
Television stations: 19
Chamber of Commerce: Los Angeles Chamber of Commerce, 404 S Bixel St., Los Angeles, Calif. 90017

MEMPHIS, TENN.

Incorporated as city: 1826
Mayor: W.W. Herenton
1980 population (1980 census) & (rank): 646,174 (14)
1990 census population, sex, & (rank): 610,337 (18); **% change,** –5.5; **Male,** 285,010; **Female,** 325,327; **White,** 268,960; **Black,** 334,737 (54.8%); **American Indian, Eskimo, or Aleut,** 960 (0.2%); **Asian or Pacific Islander,** 4,805 (0.8%); **Other race,** 1,235; **Hispanic origin,** 4,455 (0.7%). **1990 percent population under 18:** 26.9; **65 and over:** 12.2; **median age:** 31.5.
Land area: 281 sq mi. (728 sq km)
Altitude: Highest, 331 ft

Avg. daily temp.: Jan., 39.6° F; July, 82.1° F
Location: In southwestern corner of state, on Mississippi River
County: Seat of Shelby Co.
Churches: 800
Parks and playgrounds: 172 (5,363 ac.)
Radio stations: AM, 12; FM, 8
Television stations: 6
Chamber of Commerce: Memphis Area Chamber of Commerce, P.O. Box 224, Memphis, Tenn. 38103

MIAMI, FLA.

Incorporated as city: 1896
Mayor: Xavier L. Suarez
City manager: Cesar Odio
1980 population (1980 census) & (rank): 346,681 (41)
1990 census population, sex, & (rank): 358,548 (46); **% change,** 3.4; **Male,** 173,223; **Female,** 185,325; **White,** 235,358; **Black,** 98,207 (27.4%); **American Indian, Eskimo, or Aleut,** 545 (0.2%); **Asian or Pacific Islander,** 2,272 (0.6%); **Other race,** 22,166; **Hispanic origin,** 223,964 (62.5%). **1990 percent population under 18:** 23.0; **65 and over,** 16.6; **median age,** 36.0.
Land area: 34.3 sq mi. (89 sq km)
Water area: 19.5 sq mi.
Altitude: Average, 12 ft
Avg. daily temp.: Jan., 67.1° F; July, 82.4° F
Location: In southeastern part of state, on Biscayne Bay
County: Seat of Dade Co.
Churches: Protestant, 258; Roman Catholic, 12; Jewish, 4
City-owned parks: 103
Radio stations: AM, 9; FM, 9
Television stations: 8 commercial, 2 PBS
Chamber of Commerce: Greater Miami Chamber of Commerce, 1601 Biscayne Blvd., Miami, Fla. 33132

MILWAUKEE, WIS.

Incorporated as city: 1846
Mayor: John O. Norquist
1980 population (1980 census) & (rank): 636,297 (16)
1990 census population, sex, & (rank): 628,088 (17); **% change,** –1.3; **Male,** 296,837; **Female,** 331,251; **White,** 398,033; **Black,** 191,255 (30.5%); **American Indian, Eskimo, or Aleut,** 5,858 (0.9%); **Asian or Pacific Islander,** 11,817 (1.9%); **Other race,** 21,125; **Hispanic origin,** 39,409 (6.3%). **1990 percent population under 18:** 27.4; **65 and over:** 12.4; **median age:** 30.3.
Land area: 95.8 sq mi. (248 sq km)
Altitude: 580.60 ft
Avg. daily temp.: Jan., 18.7° F; July, 70.5° F
Location: In southeastern part of state, on Lake Michigan
County: Seat of Milwaukee Co.
Churches: 411
County-owned parks: 14,758 ac.
Radio stations: AM, 15; FM, 8
Television stations: 10
Chamber of Commerce: Metropolitan Milwaukee Association of Commerce, 828 N. Broadway, Milwaukee, Wis. 53202; Milwaukee Minority Chamber of Commerce, 2821 N. 4th St., Milwaukee, Wis. 53212; Hispanic Chamber of Commerce, 1125 W. National Ave., Milwaukee, Wis. 53204

MINNEAPOLIS, MINN.

Incorporated as city: 1867
Mayor: Donald M. Fraser
1980 population (1980 census) & (rank): 370,951 (34)
1990 census population, sex, & (rank): 368,383 (42); % change, –0.7; **Male,** 178,671; **Female,** 189,712; **White,** 288,967; **Black,** 47,948 (13.0%); **American Indian, Eskimo, or Aleut,** 12,335 (3.3%); **Asian or Pacific Islander,** 15,723 (4.3%); **Other race,** 3,410; **Hispanic origin,** 7,900 (2.1%). **1990 percent population under 18:** 20.6; **65 and over:** 13.0; **median age:** 31.7
Land area: 55.1 sq mi. (143 sq km)
Altitude: Highest, 945 ft; lowest, 695
Avg. daily temp.: Jan., 11.2° F; July, 73.1° F
Location: In southeast central part of state, on Mississippi River
County: Seat of Hennepin Co.
Churches: 419
City-owned parks: 153
Radio stations: AM, 17; FM, 15 (metro area)
Television stations: 6 (metro area)
Chamber of Commerce: Greater Minneapolis Chamber of Commerce, 15 S Fifth Street, Minneapolis, Minn. 55402

NASHVILLE-DAVIDSON, TENN.

Incorporated as city: 1806
Mayor: Phil Bredesen
1980 population (1980 census) & (rank)[1]: 477,811 (25)
1900 census population, sex, & (rank)[1]: 510,784 (23); % change, 6.9; **Male,** 242,492; **Female,** 268,292; **White,** 381,740; **Black,** 119,273 (23.4%); **American Indian, Eskimo, or Aleut,** 1,162 (0.2%); **Asian or Pacific Islander,** 7,081 (1.4%); **Other race,** 1,528; **Hispanic origin,** 4,775 (0.9%). **1900 percent population under 18:** 22.8; **65 and over:** 11.6; **median age:** 32.6.
Land area: 533 sq mi. (1,380 sq km)
Altitude: Highest, 1,100 ft; lowest, approx. 400 ft
Avg. daily temp.: Jan., 36.7° F; July, 76.6° F
Location: In north central part of state, on Cumberland River
County: Davidson
Churches: Protestant, 781; Roman Catholic, 18; Jewish, 3
City-owned parks: 76 (6,650 ac.)
Radio stations: AM, 11; FM, 8
Television stations: 7
Chamber of Commerce: Nashville Area Chamber of Commerce, 161 Fourth Ave. North, Nashville, Tenn. 37219
1. Consolidated city.

NEW ORLEANS, LA.

Incorporated as city: 1805
Mayor: Sidney J. Barthelemy
1980 population (1980 census) & (rank): 557,927 (21)
1990 census population, sex, & (rank): 496,938 (25); % change, –10.9; **Male,** 230,883; **Female,** 266,055; **White,** 173,554; **Black,** 307,728 (61.9%); **American Indian, Eskimo, or Aleut,** 759 (0.2%); **Asian or Pacific Islander,** 9,678 (1.9%); **Other race,** 5,219; **Hispanic origin,** 17,238 (3.5%). **1990 percent population under 18:** 27.5; **65 and over,** 13.0; **median age,** 31.6.
Land area: 199.4 sq mi. (516 sq km)
Altitude: Highest, 15 ft; lowest, –4
Avg. daily temp.: Jan., 52.4° F; July, 82.1° F
Location: In southeastern part of state, between Mississippi River and Lake Ponchartrain
Parish: Seat of Orleans Parish
Churches: 644
City-owned parks: 266 (4,460 ac.)
Radio stations: AM, 12; FM, 13
Television stations: 8
Chamber of Commerce: The Chamber/New Orleans and the River Region, 301 Camp Street, New Orleans, La. 70130

NEW YORK, N.Y.

Chartered as "Greater New York": 1898
Mayor: David N. Dinkins
Borough Presidents: Bronx, Fernando Ferrer; Brooklyn, Howard Golden; Manhattan, Ruth W. Messinger; Queens, Claire Shulman; Staten Island, Guy V. Molinari
1980 population (1980 census) & (rank): 7,071,639 (1)
1990 census population, sex, & (rank): 7,322,564 (1): % change, 3.5; **Male,** 3,437,687; **Female,** 3,884,877; **White,** 3,827,088; **Black,** 2,102,512 (28.7%); **American Indian, Eskimo, or Aleut,** 27,531 (0.4%); **Asian or Pacific Islander,** 512,719 (7.0%); **Other race,** 852,714; **Hispanic origin,** 1,783,511 (24.4%). **1990 percent population under 18:** 23.0; **65 and over:** 13.0; **median age:** 33.7.
Land area: 314.7 sq mi. (815 sq km) (Queens, 112.83; Brooklyn, 74.45; Staten Island, 60.06; Bronx, 43.63; Manhattan, 23.73)
Altitude: Highest, 410 ft; lowest, sea level
Avg. daily temp.: Jan., 31.8° F; July, 76.7° F
Location: In south of state, at mouth of Hudson River (also known as the North River as it passes Manhattan)
Counties: Consists of 5 counties: Bronx, Kings (Brooklyn), New York (Manhattan), Queens, Richmond (Staten Island)
Churches: Protestant, 1,766; Jewish, 1,256; Roman Catholic, 437; Orthodox, 66
City-owned parks: 1,701 (26,138 ac.)
Radio stations: AM, 13; FM, 18
Television stations: 6 commercial, 1 public
Chamber of Commerce: New York Chamber of Commerce and Industry, 65 Liberty St., New York, N.Y. 10005

OAKLAND, CALIF.

Incorporated as city: 1854
Mayor: Elihu Mason Harris
City Manager: Henry L. Gardner
1980 population (1980 census) & (rank): 339,337 (43)
1990 census popultion, sex, & (rank): 372,242 (39); % change, 9.7; **Male,** 178,824; **Female,** 193,418; **White,** 120,849; **Black,** 163,335 (43.9%); **American Indian, Eskimo, or Aleut,** 2,371 (0.6%); **Asian or Pacific Islander,** 54,931 (14.8%); **Other race,** 30,756; **Hispanic origin,** 51,711 (13.9%). **1990 percent population under 18,** 24.9; **65 and over,** 12.0; **median age:** 32.7.
Land area: 53.9 sq mi. (140 sq km)
Altitude: Highest, 1,700 ft; lowest, sea level
Avg. daily temp.: Jan., 49.0° F; July, 63.7° F
Location: In west central part of state, on east side of San Francisco Bay
County: Seat of Alameda Co.
Churches: 374, representing over 78 denominations in the City; over 500 churches in Alameda County
City-owned parks: 2,196 ac.
Radio stations: AM, 1

Television stations: 1 commercial
Chamber of Commerce: Oakland Chamber of Commerce, 475 Fourteenth St., Oakland, Calif. 94612-1903

OKLAHOMA CITY, OKLA.

Incorporated as city: 1890
Mayor: Ron Norick
City Manager: Don Brown
1980 population (1980 census) & (rank): 404,014 (31)
1990 census population, sex, & (rank): 444,719 (29); **% change,** 10.1; **Male,** 214,466; **Female,** 230,253; **White,** 332,539; **Black,** 71,064 (16.0%); **American Indian, Eskimo, or Aleut,** 18,794 (4.2%); **Asian or Pacific Islander,** 10,491 (2.4%); **Other race,** 11,831; **Hispanic origin,** 22,033 (5.0%). **1990 percent population under 18:** 26.0; **65 and over:** 11.9; **median age:** 32.4.
Land area: 623 sq mi. (1,614 sq km)
Altitude: Highest, 1,320 ft; lowest, 1,140
Avg. daily temp.: Jan., 35.9° F; July, 82.1° F
Location: In central part of state, on North Canadian River
County: Seat of Oklahoma Co.
Churches: Roman Catholic, 25; Jewish, 2; Protestant and others, 741
City-owned parks: 138 (3,944 ac.)
Radio stations: AM, 10; FM, 14
Television stations: 8
Chamber of Commerce: Oklahoma City Chamber of Commerce, 1 Santa Fe Plaza, Oklahoma City, Okla. 73102

OMAHA, NEB.

Incorporated as city: 1857
Mayor: P.J. Morgan
1980 population (1980 census) & (rank): 313,939 (48)
1990 census population, sex, & (rank): 335,795 (48); **% change,** 7.0; **Male,** 160,392; **Female,** 175,403; **White,** 281,603; **Black,** 43,989 (13.1%); **American Indian, Eskimo, or Aleut,** 2,274 (0.7%); **Asian or Pacific Islander,** 3,412 (1.0%); **Other race,** 4,517; **Hispanic origin,** 10,288 (3.1%). **1990 percent population under 18:** 25.4; **65 and over:** 12.9; **median age:** 32.2.
Land area: 102.98 sq mi. (267 sq km)
Altitude: Highest, 1,270 ft
Avg. daily temp.: Jan., 20.2° F; July, 77.7° F
Location: In eastern part of state, on Missouri River
County: Seat of Douglas Co.
Churches: Protestant, 246; Roman Catholic, 44; Jewish, 4
City-owned parks: 159 (over 7,000 ac.)
Radio stations: AM, 7; FM, 13
Television stations: 4
Chamber of Commerce: Omaha Chamber of Commerce, 1301 Harway St., Omaha, Neb. 68102

PHILADELPHIA, PA.

First charter as city: 1701
Mayor: Edward G. Rendall
1980 population (1980 census) & (rank): 1,688,210 (4)
1990 census population, sex, & (rank): 1,585,577 (5); **% change,** −6.1; **Male,** 737,763; **Female,** 848,586; **Black,** 631,936 (39.9%); **American Indian, Eskimo, or Aleut,** 3,454 (0.2%); **Asian or Pacific Islander,** 43,522 (2.7%); **Other race,** 58,079; **Hispanic**

origin, 89,193 (5.6%). **1990 percent population under 18:** 23.9; **65 and over:** 15.2; **median age:** 33.2.
Land area: 136 sq mi. (352 sq km)
Altitude: Highest, 440 ft; lowest, sea level
Avg. daily temp.: Jan., 31.2° F; July, 76.5° F
Location: In southeastern part of state, at junction of Schuylkill and Delaware Rivers
County: Seat of Philadelphia Co. (coterminous)
Churches: Roman Catholic, 133; Jewish, 55; Protestant and others, 830
City-owned parks: 630 (10,252 ac.)
Radio stations: AM, 40[1]; FM, 43[1]
Television stations: 14[1]
Chamber of Commerce: Philadelphia Chamber of Commerce, 1234 Market Street, Suite 1800, Philadelphia, Pa. 19107
1. PMSA.

PHOENIX, ARIZ.

Incorporated as city: 1881
Mayor: Paul Johnson
City Manager: Frank Fairbanks
1980 population (1980 census) & (rank): 789,704 (9)
1990 census population, sex, & (rank): 983,403 (9); **% change,** 24.5; **Male,** 487,589; **Female,** 495,814; **White,** 803,332; **Black,** 51,053 (5.2%); **American Indian, Eskimo, or Aleut,** 18,225 (1.9%); **Asian or Pacific Islander,** 16,303 (1.7%); **Other race,** 94,490; **Hispanic origin,** 197,103 (20.0%). **1990 percent population under 18:** 27.2; **65 and over,** 9.7; **median age,** 31.1.
Land area: 426.1 sq mi. (1,104 sq km)
Altitude: Highest, 2,740 ft.; lowest, 1,017
Avg. daily temp.: Jan., 52.3° F; July, 92.3° F
Location: In center of state, on Salt River
County: Seat of Maricopa Co.
City-owned parks: 140 (30,314 ac.)
Radio stations: AM, 22; FM, 18
Television stations: 9 commercial; 1 PBS
Chamber of Commerce: Phoenix Chamber of Commerce, 34 W. Monroe St., Phoenix, Ariz. 85003

PITTSBURGH, PA.

Incorporated as city: 1816
Mayor: Sophie Masloff
1980 population (1980 census) & (rank): 423,959 (30)
1990 census population, sex, & (rank): 369,879 (40); **% change,** −12.8; **Male,** 171,722; **Female,** 198,157; **White,** 266,791; **Black,** 95,362 (25.8%); **American Indian, Eskimo, or Aleut,** 671 (0.2%); **Asian or Pacific Islander,** 5,937 (1.6%); **Other race,** 1,118; **Hispanic origin,** 3,468 (0.9%). **1990 percent population under 18:** 19.8; **65 and over,** 17.9; **median age:** 34.6.
Land area: 55.5 sq mi. (144 sq km)
Altitude: Highest, 1,240 ft; lowest, 715
Avg. daily temp.: Jan., 26.7° F; July, 72.0° F
Location: In southwestern part of state, at beginning of Ohio River
County: Seat of Allegheny Co.
Churches: Protestant, 348; Roman Catholic, 86; Jewish, 28; Orthodox, 26
City-owned parks and playgrounds: 270 (2,572 ac.)
Radio stations: AM, 12; FM, 20
Television stations: 8
Chamber of Commerce: The Chamber of Commerce of Greater Pittsburgh, 3 Gateway Center, Pittsburgh, Pa. 15222

PORTLAND, ORE.

Incorporated as city: 1851
Mayor: John (Bud) Clark
1980 est. population (1980 census) & rank: 368,148 (35)
1990 census population, sex, & (rank): 437,319 (30); %
  change, 18.8; **Male,** 211,914; **Female,** 225,405; **White,**
  370,135; **Black,** 33,530 (7.7%); **American Indian, Eski-**
  mo, or Aleut, 5,399 (1.2%); **Asian or Pacific Islander,**
  23,185 (5.3%); **Other race,** 5,070; **Hispanic origin,**
  13,874 (3.2%). **1990 percent population under 18:** 21.9;
  65 and over, 14.6; **median age:** 34.5.
Land area: 136.7 sq mi. (354 sq km.)
Altitude: Highest, 1073 ft; lowest, sea level
Avg. daily temp.: Jan., 38.9° F; July, 67.7° F
Location: In northwestern part of the state on Willa-
  mette River
County: Seat of Multnomah Co.
Churches: Protestant, 450; Roman Catholic, 48; Jewish,
  9; Buddhist, 6; other, 190
City-owned parks: 200 (over 9,400 ac.)
Radio stations: AM: 14, FM: 14
Television stations: 5 commercial, 1 public
Chamber of Commerce: Portland Chamber of Com-
  merce, 221 NW 2nd Ave., Portland, Ore. 97209

SACRAMENTO, CALIF.

Incorporated as city: 1849
Mayor: Anne Rudin
1980 population (1980 census) & (rank): 275,741 (52)
1990 census population, sex, & (rank): 369,365 (41); %
  change, 34.0; **Male,** 178,737; **Female,** 190,628; **White,**
  221,963; **Black,** 56,521 (15.3%); **American Indian, Eski-**
  mo, or Aleut, 4,561 (1.2%); **Asian or Pacific Islander,**
  55,426 (15.0%); **Other race,** 30,894; **Hispanic origin,**
  60,007 (16.2%). **1990 percent population under 18:**
  26.2; **65 and over,** 12.1; **median age:** 31.8.
Land area: 98 sq mi. (254 sq km)
Avg. daily temp.: Jan., 47.1° F; July, 76.6° F
County: Seat of Sacramento Co.
City park & recreational facilities: 131+ (1,427+ ac.)
Television stations: 7
Chamber of Commerce: Sacramento Chamber of Com-
  merce, 917 7th St., Sacramento, Calif. 95814; West
  Sacramento Chamber of Commerce, 834-C Jefferson
  Blvd., Sacramento, Calif. 95691

ST. LOUIS, MO.

Incorporated as city: 1822
Mayor: Vincent Schoemehl, Jr.
1980 population (1980 census) & (rank): 452,801 (26)
1990 census population, sex, & (rank): 396,685 (34); %
  change, −12.4; **Male,** 180,680; **Female,** 216,005; **White,**
  202,085; **Black,** 188,408 (47.5%); **American Indian,**
  Eskimo, or Aleut, 950 (0.2%); **Asian or Pacific Island-**
  er, 3,733 (0.9%); **Other race,** 1,509; **Hispanic origin,**
  5,124 (1.3%). **1990 percent population under 18:** 25.2;
  65 and over: 16.6; **median age:** 32.8.
Land area: 61.4 sq mi. (159 sq km)
Altitude: Highest, 616 ft; lowest, 413
Avg. daily temp.: Jan., 28.8° F; July, 78.9° F
Location: In east central part of state, on Mississippi
  River
County: Independent city
Churches: 900[1]
City-owned parks: 89 (2,639 ac.)
Radio stations: AM, 21; FM 27[1]

Television stations: 6 commercial; 1 PBS
Chamber of Commerce: St. Louis Regional Commerce
  and Growth Association, 100 S. Fourth St., Ste. 500,
  St. Louis, Mo. 63102
1. Metropolitan area.

SAN ANTONIO, TEX.

Incorporated as city: 1837
Mayor: Nelson Wolff
City Manager: Alexander J. Briseno
1980 population (1980 census) & (rank): 785,940 (11)
1990 census population, sex, & (rank): 935,933 (10); %
  change, 19.1; **Male,** 450,695; **Female,** 485,238; **White,**
  676,082; **Black,** 65,884 (7.0%); **American Indian, Eski-**
  mo, or Aleut, 3,303 (0.4%); **Asian or Pacific Islander,**
  10,703 (1.1%); **Other race,** 179,961; **Hispanic origin,**
  520,282 (55.6%). **1990 percent population under 18:**
  29.0; **65 and over:** 10.5; **median age:** 29.8.
Land area: 341.23 sq mi. (884 sq km)
Altitude: 700 ft
Avg. daily temp.: Jan., 50.4° F; July, 84.6° F
Location: In south central part of state, on San Antonio
  River
County: Seat of Bexar Co.
City-owned parks: Approximately 6,385 ac.
Radio stations: AM, 19; FM, 19
Television stations: 9
Chamber of Commerce: Greater San Antonio Chamber
  of Commerce, P.O. Box 1628, 602 E Commerce, San
  Antonio, Tex. 78296

SAN DIEGO, CALIF.

Incorporated as city: 1850
Mayor: Maureen O'Connor
City Manager: Jack McGrory
1980 population (1980 census) & (rank): 875,538 (8)
1990 census population, sex, & (rank): 1,110,549 (6); %
  change, 26.8; **Male,** 566,464; **Female,** 544,085; **White,**
  745,406; **Black,** 104,261 (9.4%); **American Indian, Eski-**
  mo, or Aleut, 6,800 (0.6%); **Asian or Pacific Islander,**
  130,945 (11.8%); **Other race,** 123,137; **Hispanic origin,**
  229,519 (20.7%). **1990 percent population under 18:**
  23.1; **65 and over:** 10.2; **median age:** 30.5.
Land area: 330.7 sq miles (857 sq km)
Altitude: Highest, 1,591 ft; lowest, sea level
Avg. daily temp.: Jan., 56.8° F; July, 70.3° F
Location: In southwesternmost part of state, on San
  Diego Bay
County: Seat of San Diego Co.
Churches: Roman Catholic, 39; Jewish, 9; Protestant,
  334; Eastern Orthodox, 8; other, 18
City park and recreation facilities: 164 (17,207 ac.)
Radio stations: AM, 8; FM, 18
Television stations: 9
Chamber of Commerce: San Diego Chamber of Com-
  merce, 402 West Broadway, Suite 1000, San Diego,
  Calif. 92101

SAN FRANCISCO, CALIF.

Incorporated as city: 1850
Mayor: Frank Jordan
1980 population (1980 census) & (rank): 678,974 (13)
1990 census population, sex, & (rank): 723,959 (14); %
  change, 6.6; **Male,** 362,497; **Female,** 361,462; **White,**

387,783; **Black,** 79,039 (10.9%); **American Indian, Eskimo, or Aleut,** 3,456 (0.5%); **Asian or Pacific Islander,** 210,876 (29.1%); **Other race,** 42,805; **Hispanic origin,** 100,717 (13.9%). **1990 percent population under 18:** 16.1; **65 and over:** 14.6; **median age:** 35.8.
Land area: 46.1 sq mi. (120 sq km)
Altitude: Highest, 925 ft; lowest, sea level
Avg. daily temp.: Jan., 48.5° F; July, 62.2° F
Location: In northern part of state between Pacific Ocean and San Francisco Bay
County: Coextensive with San Francisco Co.
Churches: 540 of all denominations
City-owned parks and squares: 225
Radio stations: 29
Television stations: 10
Chamber of Commerce: Greater San Francisco Chamber of Commerce, 465 California St., San Francisco, Calif. 94104

SAN JOSE, CALIF.

Incorporated as city: 1850
Mayor: Susan Hammer
City Manager: Leslie R. White
1980 population (1980 census) & (rank): 629,400 (17)
1990 census population, sex, & (rank): 782,248 (11); % change, 24.3; **Male,** 397,709; **Female,** 384,539; **White,** 491,280; **Black,** 36,790 (4.7%); **American Indian, Eskimo, or Aleut,** 5,416 (0.7%); **Asian or Pacific Islander,** 152,815 (19.5%); **Other race,** 95,947; **Hispanic origin,** 208,388 (26.6%). **1990 percent population under 18:** 26.7; **65 and over:** 7.2; **median age:** 30.4.
Land area: 173.6 sq mi. (450 sq km)
Altitude: Highest, 4,372 ft.; lowest, sea level
Avg. daily temp.: Jan., 49.5° F; July, 68.8° F
Location: In northern part of state, on south San Francisco Bay, 50 miles south of San Francisco
County: Seat of Santa Clara County
Churches: 403
City-owned parks and playgrounds: 152 (3,136 ac.)
Radio stations: 14
Television stations: 4
Chamber of Commerce: San Jose Chamber of Commerce, One Paseo de San Antonio, San Jose, Calif. 95113

SEATTLE, WASH.

Incorporated as city: 1869
Mayor: Norman B. Rice
1980 population (1980 census) & (rank): 493,846 (23)
1990 census population, sex, & (rank): 516,259 (21); % change, 4.5; **Male,** 252,042; **Female,** 264,217; **White,** 388,858; **Black,** 51,948 (10.1%); **American Indian, Eskimo, or Aleut,** 7,326 (1.4%); **Asian or Pacific Islander,** 60,819 (11.8%); **Other race,** 7,308; **Hispanic origin,** 18,349 (3.6%). **1990 percent population under 18:** 16.5; **65 and over:** 15.2; **median age:** 34.9.
Land area: 144.6 sq mi. (375 sq km)
Altitude: Highest, 540 ft; lowest, sea level
Avg. daily temp.: Jan., 40.6° F; July, 65.3° F
Location: In west central part of state, on Puget Sound
County: Seat of King Co.
Churches: Roman Catholic, 36; Jewish, 13; Protestant and others, 535
City-owned parks, playgrounds, etc.: 278 (4,773.4 ac.)
Radio stations: AM, 22; FM, 26
Television stations: 3 commercial; 1 educational

Chamber of Commerce: Seattle Chamber of Commerce, 1200 One Union Square, Seattle, Wash. 98101

TOLEDO, OHIO

Incorporated as city: 1837
Mayor: John McHugh
City Manager: Thomas R. Hoover
1980 population (1980 census) & (rank): 354,635 (40)
1990 census population, sex, & (rank): 332,943 (49); % change, –6.1; **Male,** 157,941; **Female,** 175,002; **White,** 256,239; **Black,** 65,598 (19.7%); **Americn Indian, Eskimo, or Aleut,** 920 (0.3%); **Asian or Pacific Islander,** 3,487 (1.0%); **Other race,** 6,699; **Hispanic origin,** 13,207 (4.0%). **1990 percent population under 18:** 26.2; **65 and over:** 13.6; **median age:** 31.7.
Land area: 84.2 sq mi. (218 sq km)
Altitude: 630 ft
Avg. daily temp.: Jan., 23.1° F; July, 71.8° F
Location: In northwestern part of state, on Maumee River at Lake Erie
County: Seat of Lucas Co.
Churches: Protestant, 301; Roman Catholic, 55; Jewish, 4; others, 98
City-owned parks and playgrounds: 134 (2,650.90 ac.)
Radio stations: AM, 8; FM, 8
Television stations: 6
Chamber of Commerce: Toledo Area Chamber of Commerce, 218 Huron St., Toledo, Ohio 43604

TUCSON, ARIZ.

Incorporated as city: 1877
Mayor: George Miller
1980 population (1980 census) & (rank): 330,537 (45)
1990 census population, sex, & (rank): 405,390 (33); % change, 22.6; **Male,** 197,319; **Female,** 208,071; **White,** 305,055; **Black,** 17,366 (4.3%); **American Indian, Eskimo, or Aleut,** 6,464 (1.6%); **Asian or Pacific Islander,** 8,901 (2.2%); **Other race,** 67,604; **Hispanic origin,** 118,595 (29.3%). **1990 percent population under 18:** 24.5; **65 and over:** 12.6; **median age:** 30.6.
Land area: 156.04 sq mi. (404 sq km)
Altitude: 2,400 ft
Avg. daily temp.: Jan., 51.1° F; July, 86.2° F
Location: In southeastern part of state, on the Santa Cruz River
County: Seat of Pima Co.
Churches: Protestant, 325; Roman Catholic, 40; other, 74
City-owned parks and parkways: (25,349 ac.)
Radio stations: AM, 16; FM, 11
Television stations: 3 commercial; 1 educational; 3 other
Chamber of Commerce: Tucson Metropolitan Chamber of Commerce, P.O. Box 991, Tucson, Ariz. 85702

TULSA, OKLA.

Incorporated as city: 1898
Mayor: Rodger Randle
1980 population (1980 census) & (rank): 360,919 (38)
1990 census population, sex, & (rank): 367,302 (43); % change, 1.8; **Male,** 175,538; **Female,** 191,764; **White,** 291,444; **Black,** 49,825 (13.6%); **American Indian, Eskimo, or Aleut,** 17,091 (4.7%); **Asian or Pacific Islander,** 5,133 (1.4%); **Other race,** 3,809; **Hispanic origin,** 9,564 (2.6%). **1990 percent population under 18:** 24.4; **65 and over:** 12.7; **median age:** 33.1.
Land area: 192.459 sq mi. (499 sq km)

Altitude: 674 ft
Avg. daily temp.: Jan., 35.2° F; July, 83.2° F
Location: In northeastern part of state, on Arkansas River
County: Seat of Tulsa Co.
Churches: Protestant, 593; Roman Catholic, 32; Jewish, 2; others, 4
City parks and playgrounds: 113 (5,338 ac.)
Radio stations: AM, 7; FM, 8
Television stations: 5 commercial; 1 PBS; 1 cable
Chamber of Commerce: Metropolitan Tulsa Chamber of Commerce, 616 S Boston, Tulsa, Okla. 74119

VIRGINIA BEACH, VA.

Incorporated as city: 1963
Mayor: Meyera E. Obendorf
1980 population (1980 census) & (rank): 262,199 (56)
1990 census population, sex, & (rank): 393,069 (37); % change, 49.9; **Male,** 199,571; **Female,** 193,498; **White,** 316,408; **Black,** 54,671 (13.9%); **American Indian, Eskimo, or Aleut,** 1,384 (0.4%); **Asian or Pacific Islander,** 17,025 (4.3%); **Other race,** 3,581; **Hispanic origin,** 12,137 (3.1%); **1990 percent population under 18:** 28.0; **65 and over:** 5.9; **median age:** 28.9.
Land area: 258.7 sq mi. (670 sq km)
Altitude: 12 ft
Avg. daily temp.: Jan., 39.9° F; July, 78.4° F
Location: Southeastern most portion of state, on Atlantic coastline
County: None
Churches: Protestant, 159; Catholic, 8; Jewish, 4
City-owned parks: 151 (1,748 ac.)
Radio stations: AM 18, FM 22
Television stations: 4 commercial, 1 PBS, 1 cable
Chamber of Commerce: Hampton Roads Chamber of Commerce, 4512 Virginia Beach Blvd., Virginia Beach, Va., 23456

WASHINGTON, D.C.

Land ceded to Congress: 1788 by Maryland; 1789 by Virginia (retroceded to Virginia Sept. 7, 1846)
Seat of government transferred to D.C.: Dec. 1, 1800
Created municipal corporation: Feb. 21, 1871
Mayor: Sharon Pratt Dixon
Motto: *Justitia omnibus* (Justice to all)
Flower: American beauty rose
Tree: Scarlet oak
Origin of name: In honor of Columbus
1980 population (1980 census) & (rank): 638,432 (15)
1990 census population, sex, & (rank): 606,900 (19); % change, –4.9; **Male,** 282,970; **Female,** 323,930; **White,** 179,667; **Black,** 399,604 (65.8%); **American Indian, Eskimo,**

or Aleut, 1,466 (0.2%); **Asian or Pacific Islander,** 11,214 (1.8%); **Other race,** 14,949; **Hispanic origin,** 32,710 (5.4%)
Land area: 68.25 sq mi. (177 sq km)
Geographic center: Near corner of Fourth and L Sts., NW
Altitude: Highest, 420 ft; lowest, sea level
Avg. daily temp.: Jan., 35.2° F; July, 78.9° F
Location: Between Virginia and Maryland, on Potomac River
Churches: Protestant, 610; Roman Catholic, 132; Jewish, 9
City parks: 753 (7,725 ac.)
Radio stations: AM, 9; FM, 38
Television stations: 19
Board of Trade: Greater Washington Board of Trade, 1129 20th Street, N.W., Washington, D.C. 20036
Chamber of Commerce: D.C. Chamber of Commerce, 1319 F St., NW, Washington, D.C. 20004

The District of Columbia—identical with the City of Washington—is the capital of the United States and the first carefully planned capital in the world.

D.C. history began in 1790 when Congress directed selection of a new capital site, 100 miles square, along the Potomac. When the site was determined, it included 30.75 square miles on the Virginia side of the river. In 1846, however, Congress returned that area to Virginia, leaving the 68.25 square miles ceded by Maryland.

The city was planned and partly laid out by Major Pierre Charles L'Enfant, a French engineer. This work was perfected and completed by Major Andrew Ellicott and Benjamin Banneker, a freeborn black man, who was an astronomer and mathematician. In 1814, during the War of 1812, a British force fired the capital, and it was from the white paint applied to cover fire damage that the President's home was called the White House. This is a legend; proved to be untrue.

Until Nov. 3, 1967, the District of Columbia was administered by three commissioners appointed by the President. On that day, a government consisting of a mayor-commissioner and a 9-member Council, all appointed by the President with the approval of the Senate, took office. On May 7, 1974, the citizens of the District of Columbia approved a Home Rule Charter, giving them an elected mayor and 13-member council—their first elected municipal government in more than a century. The District also has one non-voting member in the House of Representatives and an elected Board of Education.

On Aug. 22, 1978, Congress passed a proposed constitutional amendment to give Washington, D.C., voting representation in the Congress. The amendment had to be ratified by at least 28 state legislatures within seven years to become effective. As of 1985 it died.

A petition asking for the District's admission to the Union as the 51st State was filed in Congress on September 9, 1983. The District is continuing this drive for statehood.

The Hispanic-Origin Population of States

California has the nation's largest Hispanic population. It increased sharply from 4,544,000 in 1980 to 7,688,000 in 1990, or by 69 percent. This exceeded the national Hispanic growth rate of 53 percent. California's Hispanic population in 1990 was larger than the total population of 42 states.

Three other states had Hispanic populations of more than 1 million in 1990: Texas (4.4 million), New York (2.2 million), and Florida (1.6 million).

The Hispanic-origin population is much more concentrated than the total population. A majority of the Hispanic population lived in just two states (California and Texas) in 1990.

The largest increase in Hispanic-origin population in the 1980-90 decade was in California (3,144,000), followed by Texas (1,354,000) and Florida (716,000). California alone accounted for 41% of Hispanic population growth in the United States during the decade while the ten states with the largest Hispanic growth together accounted for 89% of the increase.

Among the 15 states with Hispanic origin populations of 100,000 or more in 1980, the three states with the highest Hispanic growth rates in the 1980-90 decade were Massachusetts (104%), Florida (83%), and Washington (79%).

Largest Cities in the United States

(Over 100,000 population,)

City and State	1990 Population	Rank 1990	Rank 1980	City and State	1990 Population	Rank 1990	Rank 1980
New York, N.Y.	7,322,564	1	1	Corpus Christi, Tex.	257,453	64	60
Los Angeles, Calif.	3,485,398	2	3	St. Petersburg, Fla.	238,629	65	58
Chicago, Ill.	2,783,726	3	2	Rochester, N.Y.	231,636	66	57
Houston, Tex.	1,630,553	4	5	Jersey City, N.J.	228,537	67	61
Philadelphia, Pa.	1,585,577	5	4	Riverside, Calif.	226,505	68	84
San Diego, Calif.	1,110,549	6	8	Anchorage, Alaska	226,338	69	78
Detroit, Mich.	1,027,974	7	6	Lexington-Fayette, Ky.	225,366	70	68
Dallas, Tex.	1,006,877	8	7	Akron, Ohio	223,019	71	59
Phoenix, Ariz.	983,403	9	9	Aurora, Colo.	222,103	72	97
San Antonio, Tex.	935,933	10	11	Baton Rouge, La.	219,531	73	62
San Jose, Calif.	782,248	11	17	Stockton, Calif.	210,943	74	107
Indianapolis, Ind.[2]	741,952	12	12	Raleigh, N.C.	207,951	75	105
Baltimore, Md.	736,014	13	10	Richmond, Va.	203,056	76	64
San Francisco, Calif.	723,959	14	13	Shreveport, La.	198,525	77	67
Jacksonville, Fla.[2]	672,971	15	19	Jackson, Miss.	196,637	78	70
Columbus, Ohio	632,910	16	20	Mobile, Ala.	196,278	79	71
Milwaukee, Wis.	628,088	17	16	Des Moines, Iowa	193,187	80	74
Memphis, Tenn.	610,337	18	14	Lincoln, Nebr.	191,972	81	81
Washington, D.C.	606,900	19	15	Madison, Wis.	191,262	82	83
Boston, Mass.	574,283	20	21	Grand Rapids, Mich.	189,126	83	75
Seattle, Wash.	516,259	21	23	Yonkers, N.Y.	188,082	84	72
El Paso, Tex.	515,342	22	28	Hialeah, Fla.	188,004	85	108
Nashville-Davidson, Tenn.[2]	510,784	23	25	Montgomery, Ala.	187,106	86	76
Cleveland, Ohio	505,616	24	18	Lubbock, Tex.	186,206	87	79
New Orleans, La.	496,938	25	22	Greensboro, N.C.	183,521	88	100
Denver, Colo.	467,610	26	24	Dayton, Ohio	182,044	89	73
Austin, Tex.	465,622	27	42	Huntington Beach, Calif.	181,519	90	85
Fort Worth, Tex.	447,619	28	33	Garland, Tex.	180,650	91	115
Oklahoma City, Okla.	444,719	29	31	Glendale, Calif	180,038	92	114
Portland, Ore.	437,319	30	35	Columbus, Ga.[2]	179,278	93	86
Kansas City, Mo.	435,146	31	27	Spokane, Wash.	177,196	94	82
Long Beach, Calif.	429,433	32	37	Tacoma, Wash.	176,664	95	98
Tucson, Ariz.	405,390	33	45	Little Rock, Ark.	175,795	96	96
St. Louis, Mo.	396,685	34	26	Bakersfield, Calif.	174,820	97	152
Charlotte, N.C.	395,934	35	47	Fremont, Calif.	173,339	98	119
Atlanta, Ga.	394,017	36	29	Fort Wayne, Ind.	173,072	99	80
Virginia Beach, Va.	393,069	37	56	Arlington, Va.[3]	170,936	100	—
Albuquerque, N.M.	384,736	38	44	Newport News, Va.	170,045	101	109
Oakland, Calif.	372,242	39	43	Worcester, Mass.	169,759	102	91
Pittsburgh, Pa.	369,879	40	30	Knoxville, Tenn.	165,121	103	77
Sacramento, Calif.	369,365	41	52	Modesto, Calif.	164,730	104	147
Minneapolis, Minn.	368,383	42	34	Orlando, Fla.	164,693	105	124
Tulsa, Okla.	367,302	43	38	San Bernardino, Calif.	164,164	106	131
Honolulu, Hawaii[1]	365,272	44	36	Syracuse, N.Y.	163,860	107	87
Cincinnati, Ohio	364,040	45	32	Providence, R.I.	160,728	108	99
Miami, Fla.	358,548	46	41	Salt Lake City, Utah	159,936	109	90
Fresno, Calif.	354,202	47	65	Huntsville, Ala.	159,789	110	111
Omaha, Neb.	335,795	48	48	Amarillo, Tex.	157,615	111	106
Toledo, Ohio	332,943	49	40	Springfield, Mass.	156,983	112	103
Buffalo, N.Y.	328,123	50	39	Irving, Tex.	155,037	113	142
Wichita, Kan.	304,011	51	51	Chattanooga, Tenn.	152,466	114	88
Santa Ana, Calif.	293,742	52	69	Chesapeake, Va.	151,976	115	137
Mesa, Ariz.	288,091	53	102	Kansas City, Kan.	149,767	116	92
Colorado Springs, Colo.	281,140	54	66	Metairie, La.[3]	149,428	117	—
Tampa, Fla.	280,015	55	53	Fort Lauderdale, Fla.	149,377	118	101
Newark, N.J.	275,221	56	46	Glendale, Ariz.	148,134	119	—
St. Paul, Minn.	272,235	57	54	Warren, Mich.	144,864	120	93
Louisville, Ky.	269,063	58	49	Winston-Salem, N.C.	143,485	121	120
Anaheim, Calif.	266,406	59	63	Garden Grove, Calif.	143,050	122	127
Birmingham, Ala.	265,968	60	50	Oxnard, Calif.	142,216	123	145
Arlington, Tex.	261,721	61	94	Tempe, Ariz.	141,865	124	148
Norfolk, Va.	261,229	62	55	Bridgeport, Conn.	141,686	125	110
Las Vegas, Nev.	258,295	63	89	Paterson, N.J.	140,891	126	116
				Flint, Mich.	140,761	127	95

City and State	1990 Population	Rank 1990	Rank 1980	City and State	1990 Population	Rank 1990	Rank 1980
Springfield, Mo.	140,494	128	118	Overland Park, Kan.	111,790	165	—
Hartford, Conn.	139,739	129	117	Hayward, Calif.	111,498	166	—
Rockford, Ill.	139,426	130	113	Concord, Calif.	111,348	167	155
Savannah, Ga.	137,560	131	112	Alexandria, Va.	111,183	168	160
Durham, N.C.	136,611	132	168	Orange, Calif.	110,658	169	—
Chula Vista, Calif.	135,163	133	—	Santa Clarita, Calif.	110,642	170	—
Reno, Nev.	133,850	134	169	Irvine, Calif.	110,330	171	—
Hampton, Va.	133,793	135	128	Elizabeth, N.J.	110,002	172	150
Ontario, Calif.	133,179	136	—	Inglewood, Calif.	109,602	173	—
Torrance, Calif.	133,107	137	123	Ann Arbor, Mich.	109,592	174	146
Pomona, Calif.	131,723	138	—	Vallejo, Calif.	109,199	175	—
Pasadena, Calif.	131,591	139	134	Waterbury, Conn.	108,961	176	158
New Haven, Conn.	130,474	140	125	Salinas, Calif.	108,777	177	—
Scottsdale, Ariz.	130,069	141	—	Cedar Rapids, Iowa	108,751	178	141
Plano, Tex.	128,713	142	—	Erie, Pa.	108,718	179	130
Oceanside, Calif.	128,398	143	—	Escondido, Calif.	108,635	180	—
Lansing, Mich.	127,321	144	122	Stamford, Conn.	108,056	181	161
Lakewood, Colo.	126,481	145	138	Salem, Ore.	107,786	182	—
East Los Angeles, Calif.[3]	126,379	146	—	Citrus Heights, Calif.[3]	107,439	183	—
Evansville, Ind.	126,272	147	121	Abilene, Tex.	106,654	184	—
Boise, Idaho	125,738	148	162	Macon, Ga.	106,612	185	135
Tallahassee, Fla.	124,773	149	—	El Monte, Calif.	106,209	186	—
Paradise, Nev.[3]	124,682	150	—	South Bend, Ind.	105,511	187	143
Laredo, Tex.	122,899	151	—	Springfield, Ill.	105,227	188	171
Hollywood, Fla	121,697	152	129	Allentown, Pa.	105,090	189	156
Topeka, Kan.	119,883	153	132	Thousand Oaks, Calif.	104,352	190	—
Pasadena, Tex.	119,363	154	139	Portsmouth, Va.	103,907	191	154
Moreno Valley, Calif.	118,779	155	—	Waco, Tex.	103,590	192	166
Sterling Heights, Mich.	117,810	156	144	Lowell, Mass.	103,439	193	—
Sunnyvale, Calif.	117,229	157	149	Berkeley, Calif.	102,724	194	157
Gary, Ind.	116,646	158	104	Mesquite, Tex.	101,484	195	—
Beaumont, Tex.	114,323	159	133	Rancho Cucamonga, Calif.	101,409	196	—
Fullerton, Calif.	114,144	160	163	Albany, N.Y.	101,082	197	164
Peoria, Ill.	113,504	161	126	Livonia, Mich.	100,850	198	153
Santa Rosa, Calif.	113,313	162	—	Sioux Falls, S.D.	100,814	199	—
Eugene, Ore.	112,669	163	151	Simi Valley, Calif.	100,217	200	—
Independence, Mo.	112,301	164	140				

1. The estimates shown here are for Honolulu census designated place, which is treated as the city by the Census Bureau, rather than the Honolulu city/county governmental unit. 2. Consolidated city. 3. Census designated place. Data are latest Census Bureau report. *Source:* U.S. Department of Commerce, Bureau of the Census, April 1990.

The Nation's Ten Largest Counties

The 1990 census found 30 counties with populations over one million. Los Angeles County is the nation's largest, with 8.9 million people, followed by Cook (Chicago), with 5.1 million, and Harris (Houston), with 2.8 million. Others were San Diego County, 2.5 million; Orange County, Calif., 2.4 million; Kings County, N.Y., 2.3 million; Maricopa County, Ariz., and Wayne County, Mich., with 2.1 million; and Queens County, N.Y., and Dade County, Fla., with 1.9 million.

More than 45% of all counties lost population during the 1980s. Of the nation's 3,141 counties or equivalent areas, 1,420 declined compared with only 560 in the 1970s. A total of 1,369 lost population in the 1960s. Sixty-three percent of midwestern counties lost population from 1980 to 1990, as did 39% in the South, 30% in the West, and 27% in the Northeast.

Nine counties declined in population by more than 25% in the 1980s. They were Platte in Wyoming and Lake in Colorado (each −32%); Mineral in Colorado (−31%); Hall and Hemphill in Texas and Greenlee in Arizona (each −30%); McDowell in West Virginia (−29%); Shoshone in Idaho (−28%); and Dickens in Texas (−27%). Most of these reflect declines in mining and energy activities during the decade.

Eight counties more than doubled their population during the 1980s, including three each in Florida and Georgia. Flagler, Fla. (north of Daytona Beach) increased by 163% to 29,000, and Douglas, Colo. (suburban Denver) grew by 140% to 60,000. They were followed by Hernando, Fla., +127%; Camden, Ga., +126%; Matanuska-Susitna Borough, Alaska, +123%; Osceola, Fla., +119%; Fayette, Ga., +115%; and Gwinnett, Ga., +112%.

U.S. HISTORY & GOVERNMENT

THE DECLARATION OF INDEPENDENCE

In Congress, July 4, 1776

The unanimous Declaration of the thirteen united States of America.

When in the Course of human events it becomes necessary for one people to dissolve the political bands which have connected them with another, and to assume among the powers of the earth, the separate and equal station to which the Laws of Nature and of Nature's God entitle them, a decent respect to the opinions of mankind requires that they should declare the causes which impel them to the separation.

We hold these truths to be self-evident, that all men are created equal, that they are endowed by their Creator with certain unalienable Rights, that among these are Life, Liberty and the pursuit of Happiness.—That to secure these rights, Governments are instituted among Men, deriving their just powers from the consent of the governed,—That whenever any Form of Government becomes destructive of these ends, it is the Right of the People to alter or to abolish it, and to institute new Government, laying its foundation on such principles and organizing its powers in such form, as to them shall seem most likely to effect their Safety and Happiness. Prudence, indeed, will dictate that Governments long established should not be changed for light and transient causes; and accordingly all experience hath shewn that mankind are more disposed to suffer, while evils are sufferable, than to right themselves by abolishing the forms to which they are accustomed. But when a long train of abuses and usurpations, pursuing invariably the same Object evinces a design to reduce them under absolute Despotism, it is their right, it is their duty, to throw off such Government, and to provide new Guards for their future security.—Such has been the patient sufferance of these Colonies; and such is now the necessity which constrains them to alter their former Systems of Government. The history of the present King of Great Britain is a history of repeated injuries and usurpations, all having in direct object the establishment of an absolute Tyranny over these States. To prove this, let Facts be submitted to a candid world.

He has refused his Assent to Laws, the most wholesome and necessary for the public good.

He has forbidden his Governors to pass Laws of immediate and pressing importance, unless suspended in their operation till his Assent should be obtained; and when so suspended, he has utterly neglected to attend to them.

He has refused to pass other Laws for the accommodation of large districts of people, unless those people would relinquish the right of Representation in the Legislature, a right inestimable to them and formidable to tyrants only.

He has called together legislative bodies at places unusual, uncomfortable, and distant from the depository of their Public Records, for the sole purpose of fatiguing them into compliance with his measures.

He has dissolved Representative Houses repeatedly, for opposing with manly firmness his invasions on the rights of the people.

He has refused for a long time, after such dissolutions, to cause others to be elected; whereby the Legislative Powers, incapable of Annihilation, have returned to the People at large for their exercise; the State remaining in the mean time exposed to all the dangers of invasion from without, and convulsions within.

He has endeavoured to prevent the population of these States; for that purpose obstructing the Laws for Naturalization of Foreigners; refusing to pass others to encourage their migrations hither, and raising the conditions of new Appropriations of Lands.

He has obstructed the Administration of Justice, by refusing his Assent to Laws for establishing Judiciary Powers.

He has made Judges dependent on his Will alone, for the tenure of their offices, and the amount and payment of their salaries.

He has erected a multitude of New Offices, and sent hither swarms of Officers to harass our people, and eat out their substance.

He has kept among us, in times of peace, Standing Armies without the Consent of our legislatures.

He has affected to render the Military independent of and superior to the Civil Power.

He has combined with others to subject us to a jurisdiction foreign to our constitution, and unacknowledged by our laws; giving his Assent to their Acts of pretended Legislation:

For quartering large bodies of armed troops among us:

For protecting them, by a mock Trial, from punishment for any Murders which they should commit on the Inhabitants of these States:

For cutting off our Trade with all parts of the

NOTE: On April 12, 1776, the legislature of North Carolina authorized its delegates to the Continental Congress to join with others in a declaration of separation from Great Britain; the first colony to instruct its delegates to take the actual initiative was Virginia on May 15. On June 7, 1776, Richard Henry Lee of Virginia offered a resolution to the Congress to the effect "that these United Colonies are, and of right ought to be, free and independent States. . . ." A committee, consisting of Thomas Jefferson, John Adams, Benjamin Franklin, Robert R. Livingston, and Roger Sherman was organized to "prepare a declaration to the effect of the said first resolution." The Declaration of Independence was adopted on July 4, 1776.

Most delegates signed the Declaration August 2, but George Wythe (Va.) signed August 27; Richard Henry Lee (Va.), Elbridge Gerry (Mass.), and Oliver Wolcott (Conn.) in September; Matthew Thornton (N.H.), not a delegate until September, in November; and Thomas McKean (Del.), although present on July 4, not until 1781 by special permission, having served in the army in the interim.

world:

For imposing Taxes on us without our Consent:

For depriving us in many cases, of the benefits of Trial by Jury:

For transporting us beyond Seas to be tried for pretended offences:

For abolishing the free System of English Laws in a neighbouring Province, establishing therein an Arbitrary government, and enlarging its Boundaries so as to render it at once an example and fit instrument for introducing the same absolute rule into these Colonies:

For taking away our Charters, abolishing our most valuable Laws and altering fundamentally the Forms of our Governments:

For suspending our own Legislatures, and declaring themselves invested with power to legislate for us in all cases whatsoever.

He has abdicated Government here, by declaring us out of his Protection and waging War against us.

He has plundered our seas, ravaged our Coasts, burnt our towns, and destroyed the lives of our people.

He is at this time transporting large Armies of foreign Mercenaries to compleat the works of death, desolation, and tyranny, already begun with circumstances of Cruelty & Perfidy scarcely paralleled in the most barbarous ages, and totally unworthy the Head of a civilized nation.

He has constrained our fellow Citizens taken Captive on the high Seas to bear Arms against their Country, to become the executioners of their friends and Brethren, or to fall themselves by their Hands.

He has excited domestic insurrections amongst us, and has endeavoured to bring on the inhabitants of our frontiers, the merciless Indian Savages, whose known rule of warfare, is an undistinguished destruction of all ages, sexes and conditions.

In every stage of these Oppressions We have Petitioned for Redress in the most humble terms: Our repeated Petitions have been answered only by repeated injury. A Prince, whose character is thus marked by every act which may define a Tyrant, is unfit to be the ruler of a free people.

Nor have We been wanting in attentions to our Brittish brethren. We have warned them from time to time of attempts by their legislature to extend an unwarrantable jurisdiction over us. We have reminded them of the circumstances of our emigration and settlement here. We have appealed to their native justice and magnanimity, and we have conjured them by the ties of our common kindred to disavow these usurpations, which would inevitably interrupt our connections and correspondence. They too have been deaf to the voice of justice and of consanguinity. We must, therefore, acquiesce in the necessity, which denounces our Separation, and hold them, as we hold the rest of mankind, Enemies in War, in Peace Friends.

We, therefore, the Representatives of the United States of America, in General Congress, Assembled, appealing to the Supreme Judge of the world for the rectitude of our intentions, do, in the Name, and by Authority of the good People of these Colonies, solemnly publish and declare, That these United Colonies are, and of Right ought to be Free and Independent States; that they are Absolved from all Allegiance to the British Crown, and that all political connection between them and the State of Great Britain, is and ought to be totally dissolved; and that as Free and Independent States, they have full Power to levy War, conclude Peace, contract Alliances, establish Commerce, and to do all other Acts and Things which Independent States may of right do.—And for the support of this Declaration, with a firm reliance on the protection of Divine Providence, we mutually pledge to each other our Lives, our Fortunes and our sacred Honor.   —John Hancock

New Hampshire
Josiah Bartlett
Wm. Whipple
Matthew Thornton

Rhode Island
Step. Hopkins
William Ellery

Connecticut
Roger Sherman
Sam'el Huntington
Wm. Williams
Oliver Wolcott

New York
Wm. Floyd
Phil. Livingston
Frans. Lewis
Lewis Morris

New Jersey
Richd. Stockton
Jno. Witherspoon
Fras. Hopkinson
John Hart
Abra. Clark

Pennsylvania
Robt. Morris
Benjamin Rush
Benj. Franklin
John Morton
Geo. Clymer
Jas. Smith
Geo. Taylor
James Wilson
Geo. Ross

Massachusetts-Bay
Saml. Adams
John Adams
Robt. Treat Paine
Elbridge Gerry

Delaware
Caesar Rodney
Geo. Read
Tho. M'Kean

Maryland
Samuel Chase
Wm. Paca
Thos. Stone
Charles Carroll of Carrollton

Virginia
George Wythe
Richard Henry Lee
Th. Jefferson
Benj. Harrison
Ths. Nelson, Jr.
Francis Lightfoot Lee
Carter Braxton

North Carolina
Wm. Hooper
Joseph Hewes
John Penn

South Carolina
Edward Rutledge
Thos. Heyward, Junr.
Thomas Lynch, Junr.
Arthur Middleton

Georgia
Button Gwinnett
Lyman Hall
Geo. Walton

Constitution of the United States of America

(Historical text has been edited to conform to contemporary American usage.
The bracketed words are designations for your convenience; they are not part of the Constitution.)

The oldest federal constitution in existence was framed by a convention of delegates from twelve of the thirteen original states in Philadelphia in May, 1787, Rhode Island failing to send a delegate. George Washington presided over the session, which lasted until September 17, 1787. The draft (originally a preamble and seven Articles) was submitted to all thirteen states and was to become effective when ratified by nine states. It went into effect on the first Wednesday in March, 1789, having been ratified by New Hampshire, the ninth state to approve, on June 21, 1788. The states ratified the Constitution in the following order:

Delaware	December 7, 1787	South Carolina	May 23, 1788
Pennsylvania	December 12, 1787	New Hampshire	June 21, 1788
New Jersey	December 18, 1787	Virginia	June 25, 1788
Georgia	January 2, 1788	New York	July 26, 1788
Connecticut	January 9, 1788	North Carolina	November 21, 1789
Massachusetts	February 6, 1788	Rhode Island	May 29, 1790
Maryland	April 28, 1788		

[Preamble]

We the people of the United States, in order to form a more perfect Union, establish justice, insure domestic tranquility, provide for the common defence, promote the general welfare, and secure the blessings of liberty to ourselves and our posterity, do ordain and establish this Constitution for the United States of America.

Article I

Section 1

[Legislative powers vested in Congress.] All legislative powers herein granted shall be vested in a Congress of the United States, which shall consist of a Senate and House of Representatives.

Section 2

[Composition of the House of Representatives.—1.] The House of Representatives shall be composed of members chosen every second year by the people of the several States, and the electors in each State shall have the qualifications requisite for electors of the most numerous branch of the State Legislature.

[Qualifications of Representatives.—2.] No Person shall be a Representative who shall not have attained to the age of twenty-five years, and been seven years a citizen of the United States, and who shall not, when elected, be an inhabitant of that State in which he shall be chosen.

[Apportionment of Representatives and direct taxes—census.[1]—3.] (Representatives and direct taxes shall be apportioned among the several States which may be included within this Union, according to their respective numbers, which shall be determined by adding to the whole number of free persons, including those bound to service for a term of years, and excluding Indians not taxed, three fifths of all other persons.) The actual enumeration shall be made within three years after the first meeting of the Congress of the United States, and within every subsequent term of ten years, in such manner as they shall by law direct. The number of Representatives shall not exceed one for every thirty thousand, but each State shall have at least one Representative; and until such enumeration shall be made, the State of New Hampshire shall be entitled to choose three, Massachusetts eight, Rhode-Island and Providence Plantations one, Connecticut five, New York six, New Jersey four, Pennsylvania eight, Delaware one, Maryland six, Virginia ten, North Carolina five, South Carolina five, and Georgia three.

[Filling of vacancies in representation.—4.] When vacancies happen in the representation from any State, the Executive Authority thereof shall issue writs of election to fill such vacancies.

[Selection of officers; power of impeachment.—5.] The House of Representatives shall choose their Speaker and other officers; and shall have the sole power of impeachment.

Section 3[2]

[The Senate.—1.] The Senate of the United States shall be composed of two Senators from each State, chosen by the Legislature thereof, for six years; and each Senator shall have one vote.

[Classification of Senators; filling of vacancies.—2.] Immediately after they shall be assembled in consequence of the first election, they shall be divided as equally as may be into three classes. The seats of the Senators of the first class shall be vacated at the expiration of the second year, of the second class at the expiration of the fourth year, and of the third class at the expiration of the sixth year, so that one-third may be chosen every second year; and if vacancies happen by resignation, or otherwise, during the recess of the Legislature of any State, the Executive thereof may make temporary appointments (until the next meeting of the Legislature, which shall then fill such vacancies).

[Qualification of Senators.—3.] No person shall be a Senator who shall not have attained to the age of thirty years, and been nine years a citizen of the United States, and who shall not, when elected, be an inhabitant of that State for which he shall be chosen.

[Vice President to be President of Senate.—4.] The Vice President of the United States shall be President of the Senate, but shall have no vote, unless they be equally divided.

[Selection of Senate officers; President pro tempore.—5.] The Senate shall choose their other officers, and also a President pro tempore, in the absence of the Vice President, or when he shall exercise the office of President of the United States.

[Senate to try impeachments.—6.] The Senate

shall have the sole power to try all impeachments. When sitting for that purpose, they shall be on oath or affirmation. When the President of the United States is tried, the Chief Justice shall preside: and no person shall be convicted without the concurrence of two thirds of the members present.

[**Judgment in cases of Impeachment.—7.**] Judgment in cases of impeachment shall not extend further than to removal from office, and disqualification to hold and enjoy any office of honor, trust, or profit under the United States: but the party convicted shall nevertheless be liable and subject to indictment, trial, judgment and punishment, according to Law.

Section 4

[**Control of congressional elections.—1.**] The times, places, and manner of holding elections for Senators and Representatives, shall be prescribed in each State by the Legislature thereof; but the Congress may at any time by law make or alter such regulations, except as to the places of choosing Senators.

[**Time for assembling of Congress**[3]**—2.**] The Congress shall assemble at least once in every year, and such meeting shall be on the first Monday in December, unless they shall by law appoint a different day.

Section 5

[**Each house to be the judge of the election and qualifications of its members; regulations as to quorum.—1.**] Each House shall be the judge of the elections, returns, and qualifications of its own members, and a majority of each shall constitute a quorum to do business; but a smaller number may adjourn from day to day, and may be authorized to compel the attendance of absent members, in such manner, and under such penalties as each House may provide.

[**Each house to determine its own rules.—2.**] Each House may determine the rules of its proceedings, punish its members for disorderly behavior, and, with the concurrence of two thirds, expel a member.

[**Journals and yeas and nays.—3.**] Each House shall keep a journal of its proceedings, and from time to time publish the same, excepting such parts as may in their judgment require secrecy; and the yeas and nays of the members of either House on any question shall, at the desire of one fifth of those present, be entered on the journal.

[**Adjournment.—4.**] Neither House, during the session of Congress, shall, without the consent of the other, adjourn for more than three days, nor to any other place than that in which the two Houses shall be sitting.

Section 6

[**Compensation and privileges of members of Congress.—1.**] The Senators and Representatives shall receive a compensation for their services, to be ascertained by law, and paid out of the Treasury of the United States. They shall in all cases, except treason, felony, and breach of the peace, be privileged from arrest during their attendance at the session of their respective Houses, and in going to and returning from the same; and for any speech or debate in either House, they shall not be questioned in any other place.

[**Incompatible offices; exclusions.—2.**] No Senator or Representative shall, during the time for which he was elected, be appointed to any civil office under the authority of the United States, which shall have been created, or the emoluments whereof shall have been increased during such time; and no person holding any office under the United States shall be a member of either House during his continuance in office.

Section 7

[**Revenue bills to originate in House.—1.**] All bills for raising revenue shall originate in the House of Representatives; but the Senate may propose or concur with amendments as on other bills.

[**Manner of passing bills; veto power of President.—2.**] Every bill which shall have passed the House of Representatives and the Senate, shall, before it becomes a law, be presented to the President of the United States; if he approve he shall sign it, but if not he shall return it, with his objections to that House in which it shall have originated, who shall enter the objections at large on their journal, and proceed to reconsider it. If after such reconsideration two thirds of that House shall agree to pass the bill, it shall be sent, together with the objections, to the other House, by which it shall likewise be reconsidered, and if approved by two thirds of that House, it shall become a law. But in all such cases the votes of both Houses shall be determined by yeas and nays, and the names of the persons voting for and against the bill shall be entered on the journal of each house, respectively. If any bill shall not be returned by the President within ten days (Sundays excepted) after it shall have been presented to him, the same shall be a law, in like manner as if he had signed it, unless the Congress by their adjournment prevent its return, in which case it shall not be a law.

[**Concurrent orders or resolutions, to be passed by President.—3.**] Every order, resolution, or vote to which the concurrence of the Senate and House of Representatives may be necessary (except on a question of adjournment) shall be presented to the President of the United States; and before the same shall take effect, shall be approved by him, or being disapproved by him, shall be repassed by two thirds of the Senate and House of Representatives, according to the rules and limitations prescribed in the case of a bill.

Section 8

[**General powers of Congress.**[4]]

[**Taxes, duties, imposts, and excises.—1.**] The Congress shall have power to lay and collect taxes, duties, imposts and excises, to pay the debts and provide for the common defense and general welfare of the United States; but all duties, imposts and excises shall be uniform throughout the United States;

[**Borrowing of money.—2.**] To borrow money on the credit of the United States;

[**Regulation of commerce.—3.**] To regulate commerce with foreign nations, and among the several States, and with the Indian tribes;

[**Naturalization and bankruptcy.—4.**] To establish a uniform rule of naturalization, and uniform laws on the subject of bankruptcies throughout the United States;

[**Money, weights and measures.—5.**] To coin money, regulate the value thereof, and of foreign coin, and fix the standard of weights and measures;

[**Counterfeiting.—6.**] To provide for the punishment of counterfeiting the securities and current coin of the United States;

[**Post offices.—7.**] To establish post offices and post roads;

[**Patents and copyrights.—8.**] To promote the

progress of science and useful arts, by securing for limited times to authors and inventors the exclusive right to their respective writings and discoveries;

[**Inferior courts.—9.**] To constitute tribunals inferior to the Supreme Court;

[**Piracies and felonies.—10.**] To define and punish piracies and felonies committed on the high seas, and offences against the law of nations;

[**War; marque and reprisal.—11.**] To declare war, grant letters of marque and reprisal, and make rules concerning captures on land and water;

[**Armies.—12.**] To raise and support armies, but no appropriation of money to that use shall be for a longer term than two years;

[**Navy.—13.**] To provide and maintain a navy;

[**Land and naval forces.—14.**] To make rules for the government and regulation of the land and naval forces;

[**Calling out militia.—15.**] To provide for calling forth the militia to execute the laws of the Union, suppress insurrections, and repel invasions;

[**Organizing, arming, and disciplining militia.—16.**] To provide for organizing, arming, and disciplining, the militia, and for governing such part of them as may be employed in the service of the United States, reserving to the States, respectively, the appointment of the officers, and the authority of training the militia according to the discipline prescribed by Congress;

[**Exclusive legislation over District of Columbia.—17.**] To exercise exclusive legislation in all cases whatsoever, over such district (not exceeding ten miles square) as may, by cession of particular States, and the acceptance of Congress, become the seat of the Government of the United States, and to exercise like authority over all places purchased by the consent of the Legislature of the State in which the same shall be, for the erection of forts, magazines, arsenals, dock-yards, and other needful buildings;—And

[**To enact laws necessary to enforce Constitution.—18.**] To make all laws which shall be necessary and proper for carrying into execution the foregoing powers, and all other powers vested by this Constitution in the Government of the United States, or in any department or officer thereof.

Section 9

[**Migration or importation of certain persons not to be prohibited before 1808.—1.**] The migration or importation of such persons as any of the States now existing shall think proper to admit, shall not be prohibited by the Congress prior to the year one thousand eight hundred and eight, but a tax or duty may be imposed on such importation, not exceeding ten dollars for each person.

[**Writ of habeas corpus not to be suspended; exception.—2.**] The privilege of the writ of habeas corpus shall not be suspended, unless when in cases of rebellion or invasion the public safety may require it.

[**Bills of attainder and ex post facto laws prohibited.—3.**] No bill of attainder or ex post facto law shall be passed.

[**Capitation and other direct taxes.—4.**] No capitation, or other direct, tax shall be laid, unless in proportion to the census or enumeration herein before directed to be taken.[5]

[**Exports not to be taxed.—5.**] No tax or duty shall be laid on articles exported from any State.

[**No preference to be given to ports of any States; interstate shipping.—6.**] No preference shall be given by any regulation of commerce or revenue to the ports of one State over those of another: nor shall vessels bound to, or from, one State, be obliged to enter, clear, or pay duties in another.

[**Money, how drawn from treasury; financial statements to be published.—7.**] No money shall be drawn from the Treasury, but in consequence of appropriations made by law; and a regular statement and account of the receipts and expenditures of all public money shall be published from time to time.

[**Titles of nobility not to be granted; acceptance by government officers of favors from foreign powers.—8.**] No title of nobility shall be granted by the United States: and no person holding any office of profit or trust under them, shall, without the consent of the Congress, accept of any present, emolument, office, or title, of any kind whatever, from any king, prince, or foreign state.

Section 10

[**Limitations of the powers of the several States.—1.**] No State shall enter into any treaty, alliance, or confederation; grant letters of marque and reprisal; coin money; emit bills of credit; make any thing but gold and silver coin a tender in payment of debts; pass any bill of attainder, ex post facto law, or law impairing the obligation of contracts, or grant any title of nobility.

[**State imposts and duties.—2.**] No State shall, without the consent of the Congress, lay any imposts or duties on imports or exports, except what may be absolutely necessary for executing its inspection laws; and the net produce of all duties and imposts, laid by any State on imports or exports, shall be for the use of the Treasury of the United States; and all such laws shall be subject to the revision and control of the Congress.

[**Further restrictions on powers of States.—3.**] No State shall, without the consent of Congress, lay any duty of tonnage, keep troops, or ships of war in time of peace, enter into any agreement or compact with another state, or with a foreign power, or engage in war, unless actually invaded, or in such imminent danger as will not admit of delay.

Article II

Section 1

[**The President; the executive power.—1.**] The executive power shall be vested in a President of the United States of America. He shall hold his office during the term of four years, and, together with the Vice President, chosen for the same term, be elected, as follows

[**Appointment and qualifications of presidential electors.—2.**] Each State shall appoint, in such manner as the Legislature thereof may direct, a number of electors, equal to the whole number of Senators and Representatives to which the State may be entitled in the Congress: but no Senator or Representative, or person holding an office of trust or profit under the United States, shall be appointed an elector.

[**Original method of electing the President and Vice President.**[6]] (The electors shall meet in their respective States, and vote by ballot for two persons, of whom one at least shall not be an inhabitant of the same State with themselves. And they shall make a list of all the persons voted for, and of the number of votes for each; which list they shall sign and certify, and transmit sealed to the seat of the Government of the United States, directed to the President of the

Senate. The President of the Senate shall, in the presence of the Senate and House of Representatives, open all the certificates, and the votes shall then be counted. The person having the greatest number of votes shall be the President, if such number be a majority of the whole number of electors appointed; and if there be more than one who have such majority, and have an equal number of votes, then the House of Representatives shall immediately choose by ballot one of them for President; and if no person have a majority, then from the five highest on the list the said House shall in like manner choose the President. But in choosing the President, the votes shall be taken by States, the representation from each State having one vote; A quorum for this purpose shall consist of a member or members from two thirds of the States, and a majority of all the states shall be necessary to a choice. In every case, after the choice of the President, the person having the greatest number of votes of the electors shall be the Vice President. But if there should remain two or more who have equal votes, the Senate should choose from them by ballot the Vice President.)

[Congress may determine time of choosing electors and day for casting their votes.—3.] The Congress may determine the time of choosing the electors, and the day on which they shall give their votes; which day shall be the same throughout the United States.

[Qualifications for the office of President.[7]**—4.]** No person except a natural born citizen, or a citizen of the United States, at the time of the adoption of this Constitution, shall be eligible to the office of President; neither shall any person be eligible to that office who shall not have attained to the age of thirty-five years, and been fourteen years a resident within the United States.

[Filling vacancy in the office of President.[8]**—5.]** In case of the removal of the President from office, or of his death, resignation, or inability to discharge the powers and duties of the said office, the same shall devolve on the Vice President, and the Congress may by law provide for the case of removal, death, resignation or inability, both of the President and Vice President, declaring what officer shall then act as President, and such officer shall act accordingly, until the disability be removed, or a President shall be elected.

[Compensation of the President.—6.] The President shall, at stated times, receive for his services, a compensation, which shall neither be increased nor diminished during the period for which he shall have been elected, and he shall not receive within that period any other emolument from the United States, or any of them.

[Oath to be taken by the President.—7.] Before he enter on the execution of his office, he shall take the following oath or affirmation:—"I do solemnly swear (or affirm) that I will faithfully execute the office of President of the United States, and will to the best of my ability, preserve, protect, and defend the Constitution of the United States."

Section 2

[The President to be commander in chief of army and navy and head of executive departments; may grant reprieves and pardons.—1.] The President shall be Commander in Chief of the Army and Navy of the United States, and of the militia of the several States, when called into the actual service of the United States; he may require the opinion, in writing, of the principal officer in each of the executive departments, upon any subject relating to the duties of their respective offices, and he shall have power to grant reprieves and pardons for offences against the United States, except in cases of impeachment.

[President may, with concurrence of Senate, make treaties, appoint ambassadors, etc.; appointment of inferior officers, authority of Congress over.—2.] He shall have power, by and with the advice and consent of the Senate, to make treaties, provided two thirds of the Senators present concur; and he shall nominate, and by and with the advice and consent of the Senate, shall appoint ambassadors, other public ministers and consuls, judges of the Supreme Court, and all other officers of the United States, whose appointments are not herein otherwise provided for, and which shall be established by law: but the Congress may by law vest the appointment of such inferior officers, as they think proper, in the President alone, in the courts of law, or in the heads of departments.

[President may fill vacancies in office during recess of Senate.—3.] The President shall have power to fill up all vacancies that may happen during the recess of the Senate, by granting commissions which shall expire at the end of their session.

Section 3

[President to give advice to Congress; may convene or adjourn it on certain occasions; to receive ambassadors, etc.; have laws executed and commission all officers.] He shall from time to time give to the Congress information of the state of the Union, and recommend to their consideration such measures as he shall judge necessary and expedient; he may, on extraordinary occasions, convene both Houses, or either of them, and in case of disagreement between them, with respect to the time of adjournment, he may adjourn them to such time as he shall think proper; he shall receive ambassadors and other public ministers: he shall take care that the laws be faithfully executed, and shall commission all the officers of the United States.

Section 4

[All civil officers removable by impeachment.] The President, Vice President, and all civil officers of the United States shall be removed from office on impeachment for, and conviction of, treason, bribery, or other high crimes and misdemeanors.

Article III

Section 1

[Judicial powers; how vested; term of office and compensation of judges.] The judicial Power of the United States, shall be vested in one Supreme Court, and in such inferior courts as the Congress may from time to time ordain and establish. The judges, both of the supreme and inferior courts, shall hold their offices during good behavior, and shall, at stated times, receive for their services, a compensation, which shall not be diminished during their continuance in office.

Section 2

[Jurisdiction of Federal courts[9]**—1.]** The judicial power shall extend to all cases, in law and equity, arising under this Constitution, the laws of the United States, and treaties made, or which shall be made, under their authority; to all cases affecting ambassadors, other public ministers and consuls; to all cases of admiralty and maritime jurisdiction; to controversies to which the United States, shall be a party; to controversies between two or more States; between a State and citizens of another State; between citizens of different States; between citizens of the same State claiming lands under grants of different states, and between a State, or the citizens thereof, and foreign states, citizens, or subjects.

[Original and appellate jurisdiction of Supreme Court.—2.] In all cases affecting ambassadors, other public ministers and consuls, and those in which a State shall be party, the Supreme Court shall have original jurisdiction. In all the other cases before mentioned, the Supreme Court shall have appellate jurisdiction, both as to law and fact, with such exceptions, and under such regulations, as the Congress shall make.

[Trial of all crimes, except impeachment, to be by jury.—3.] The trial of all crimes, except in cases of impeachment, shall be by jury; and such trial shall be held in the State where the said crimes shall have been committed; but when not committed within any State, the trial shall be at such place or places as the Congress may by law have directed.

Section 3

[Treason defined; conviction of.—1.] Treason against the United States, shall consist only in levying war against them, or, in adhering to their enemies, giving them aid and comfort. No person shall be convicted of treason unless on the testimony of two witnesses to the same overt act, or on confession in open court.

[Congress to declare punishment for treason; proviso.—2.] The Congress shall have power to declare the punishment of treason, but no attainder of treason shall work corruption of blood, or forfeiture except during the life of the person attained.

Article IV

Section 1

[Each State to give full faith and credit to the public acts and records of other States.] Full faith and credit shall be given in each State to the public acts, records, and judicial proceedings of every other State. And the Congress may by general laws prescribe the manner in which such acts, records, and proceedings shall be proved, and the effect thereof.

Section 2

[Privileges of citizens.—1.] The citizens of each State shall be entitled to all privileges and immunities of citizens in the several States.

[Extradition between the several States.—2.] A person charged in any State with treason, felony, or other crime, who shall flee from justice, and be found in another State, shall on demand of the Executive authority of the State from which he fled, be delivered up, to be removed to the State having jurisdiction of the crime.

[Persons held to labor or service in one State, fleeing to another, to be returned.—3.] No person held to service or labor in one State, under the laws thereof, escaping into another, shall, in consequence of any law or regulation therein, be discharged from such service or labor, but shall be delivered up on claim of the party to whom such service or labor may be due.

Section 3

[New States.—1.] New States may be admitted by the Congress into this Union; but no new State shall be formed or erected within the jurisdiction of any other State; nor any State be formed by the junction of two or more States, or parts of States, without the consent of the Legislatures of the States concerned as well as of the Congress.

[Regulations concerning territory.—2.] The Congress shall have power to dispose of and make all needful rules and regulations respecting the territory or other property belonging to the United States; and nothing in this Constitution shall be so construed as to prejudice any claims of the United States, or of any particular State.

Section 4

[Republican form of government and protection guaranteed the several States.] The United States shall guarantee to every State in this Union a Republican form of government, and shall protect each of them against invasion; and on application of the Legislature, or of the Executive (when the Legislature cannot be convened) against domestic violence.

Article V

[Ways in which the Constitution can be amended.] The Congress, whenever two thirds of both Houses shall deem it necessary, shall propose amendments to this Constitution, or, on the application of the Legislatures of two thirds of the several States shall call a convention for proposing amendments, which, in either case, shall be valid to all intents and purposes, as part of this Constitution, when ratified by the Legislatures of three fourths of the several States, or by conventions in three fourths thereof, as the one or the other mode of ratification may be proposed by the Congress; provided that no amendment which may be made prior to the year one thousand eight hundred and eight shall in any manner affect the first and fourth clauses in the ninth Section of the first Article; and that no State, without its consent, shall be deprived of its equal suffrage in the Senate.

Article VI

[Debts contracted under the confederation secured.—1.] All debts contracted and engagements entered into, before the adoption of this Constitution, shall be as valid against the United States under this Constitution, as under the Confederation.

[Constitution, laws, and treaties of the United States to be supreme.—2.] This Constitution, and the laws of the United States which shall be made in pursuance thereof; and all treaties made, or which shall be made, under the authority of the United States, shall be the supreme law of the land; and the judges in every State shall be bound thereby, any thing in the Constitution or laws of any State to the

1. The clause included in parentheses is amended by the 14th Amendment, Section 2. 2. The first paragraph of this section and the part of the second paragraph included in parentheses are amended by the 17th Amendment. 3. Amended by the 20th Amendment, Section 2. 4. By the 16th Amendment, Congress is given the power to lay and collect taxes on income. 5. See the 16th Amendment. 6. This clause has been superseded by the 12th Amendment. 7. For qualifications of the Vice President, see 12th Amendment. 8. Amended by the 20th Amendment, Sections 3 and 4. 9. This section is abridged by the 11th Amendment. 10. See the 13th Amendment.

contrary notwithstanding.

[Who shall take constitutional oath; no religious test as to official qualification.—3.] The Senators and Representatives before mentioned, and the members of the several State Legislatures, and all executive and judicial officers, both of the United States and of the several States, shall be bound by oath or affirmation, to support this Constitution; but no religious test shall ever be required as a qualification to any office or public trust under the United States.

Article VII

[Constitution to be considered adopted when ratified by nine States.] The ratification of the conventions of nine States shall be sufficient for the establishment of this Constitution between the States so ratifying the same.

Done in convention by the unanimous consent of the States present the seventeenth day of September in the year of our Lord one thousand seven hundred and eighty seven and of the independence of the United States of America the Twelfth. In witness whereof we have hereunto subscribed our names.

GEORGE WASHINGTON
President and Deputy from Virginia

NEW HAMPSHIRE
John Langdon   Nicholas Gilman

MASSACHUSETTS
Nathaniel Gorham   Rufus King

CONNECTICUT
Wm. Saml. Johnson   Roger Sherman

NEW YORK
Alexander Hamilton

NEW JERSEY
Wil. Livingston   Wm. Paterson
David Brearley   Jona. Dayton

PENNSYLVANIA
B. Franklin   Thomas Mifflin
Robt. Morris   Geo. Clymer
Thos. FitzSimons   Jared Ingersoll
James Wilson   Gouv. Morris

DELAWARE
Geo. Read   Gunning Bedford Jun.
John Dickinson   Richard Bassett
Jaco. Broom

MARYLAND
James McHenry   Dan. of St. Thos. Jenifer
Danl. Carroll

VIRGINIA
John Blair   James Madison, Jr.

NORTH CAROLINA
Wm. Blount   Richd Dobbs Spaight
Hu. Williamson

SOUTH CAROLINA
J. Rutledge   Charles Cotesworth
Charles Pinckney   Pinckney
                                Pierce Butler

GEORGIA
William Few   Abr. Baldwin
Attest: William Jackson, Secretary

Amendments to the Constitution
of the United States

(Amendments I to X inclusive, popularly known as the Bill of Rights, were proposed and sent to the states by the first session of the First Congress. They were ratified Dec. 15, 1791.)

Article I

[Freedom of religion, speech, of the press, and right of petition.] Congress shall make no law respecting an establishment of religion, or prohibiting the free exercise thereof; or abridging the freedom of speech, or of the press; or the right of the people peaceably to assemble, and to petition the Government for a redress of grievances.

Article II

[Right of people to bear arms not to be infringed.] A well regulated militia, being necessary to the security of a free State, the right of the people to keep and bear arms, shall not be infringed.

Article III

[Quartering of troops.] No soldier shall, in time of peace be quartered in any house, without the consent of the owner, nor in time of war, but in a manner to be prescribed by law.

Article IV

[Persons and houses to be secure from unreasonable searches and seizures.] The right of the people to be secure in their persons, houses, papers, and effects, against unreasonable searches and seizures, shall not be violated, and no warrants shall issue, but upon probable cause, supported by oath or affirmation, and particularly describing the place to be searched, and the persons or things to be seized.

Article V

[Trials for crimes; just compensation for private property taken for public use.] No person shall be held to answer for a capital, or otherwise infamous crime, unless on a presentment or indictment of a Grand Jury, except in cases arising in the land or naval forces, or in the militia, when in actual service in time of war or public danger; nor shall any person be subject for the same offence to be twice put in jeopardy of life or limb; nor shall be compelled in any criminal case to be a witness, against himself, nor be deprived of life, liberty, or property, without due process of law; nor shall private property be taken for public use, without just compensation.

Article VI

[Civil rights in trials for crimes enumerated.] In all criminal prosecutions, the accused shall enjoy the right to a speedy and public trial, by an impartial jury of the State and district wherein the crime shall have been committed, which district shall have been previously ascertained by law, and to be informed of the nature and cause of the accusation; to be confronted with the witnesses against him; to have compulsory process for obtaining witnesses in his favor, and to have the assistance of counsel for his defense.

Article VII

[Civil rights in civil suits.] In suits at common law, where the value in controversy shall exceed twenty dollars, the right of trial by jury shall be preserved, and no fact tried by a jury, shall be otherwise re-examined in any court of the United States, than according to the rules of the common law.

Article VIII

[Excessive bail, fines, and punishments prohibited.] Excessive bail shall not be required, nor excessive fines imposed, nor cruel and unusual punishments inflicted.

Article IX

[Reserved rights of people.] The enumeration in the Constitution, of certain rights, shall not be construed to deny or disparage others retained by the people.

Article X

[Powers not delegated, reserved to states and people respectively.] The powers not delegated to the United States by the Constitution, nor prohibited by it to the States, are reserved to the States, respectively, or to the people.

Article XI

(The proposed amendment was sent to the states Mar. 5, 1794, by the Third Congress. It was ratified Feb. 7, 1795.)

[Judicial power of United States not to extend to suits against a State.] The judicial power of the United States shall not be construed to extend to any suit in law or equity, commenced or prosecuted against one of the United States by citizens of another State, or by citizens or subjects of any foreign state.

Article XII

(The proposed amendment was sent to the states Dec. 12, 1803, by the Eighth Congress. It was ratified July 27, 1804.)

[Present mode of electing President and Vice-President by electors.[1]] The electors shall meet in their respective states, and vote by ballot for President and Vice President, one of whom, at least, shall not be an inhabitant of the same state with themselves; they shall name in their ballots the person voted for as President, and in distinct ballots the person voted for as Vice President, and they shall make distinct lists of all persons voted for as President, and of all persons voted for as Vice President, and of the number of votes for each, which lists they shall sign and certify, and transmit sealed to the seat of the government of the United States, directed to the President of the Senate; the President of the Senate shall, in the presence of the Senate and House of Representatives, open all the certificates and the votes shall then be counted; the person having the greatest number of votes for President, shall be the President, if such number be a majority of the whole number of electors appointed; and if no person have such majority, then from the persons having the highest numbers not exceeding three on the list of those voted for as President, the House of Representatives shall choose immediately, by ballot, the President. But in choosing the President, the votes shall be taken by states, the representation from each State having one vote; a quorum for this purpose shall consist of a member or members from two thirds of the states, and a majority of all the states shall be necessary to a choice. And if the House of Representatives shall not choose a President whenever the right of choice shall devolve upon them, before the fourth day of March next following, then the Vice President shall act as President, as in the case of the death or other constitutional disability of the President. The person having the greatest number of votes as Vice President, shall be the Vice President, if such number be a majority of the whole number of electors appointed, and if no person have a majority, then from the two highest numbers on the list, the Senate shall choose the Vice President; a quorum for the purpose shall consist of two thirds of the whole number of Senators, and a majority of the whole number shall be necessary to a choice. But no person constitutionally ineligible to the office of President shall be eligible to that of Vice President of the United States.

Article XIII

(The proposed amendment was sent to the states Feb. 1, 1865, by the Thirty-eighth Congress. It was ratified Dec. 6, 1865.)

Section 1

[Slavery prohibited.] Neither slavery nor involuntary servitude, except as a punishment for crime whereof the party shall have been duly convicted, shall exist within the United States, or any place subject to their jurisdiction.

Section 2

[Congress given power to enforce this article.] Congress shall have power to enforce this article by appropriate legislation.

Article XIV

(The proposed amendment was sent to the states June 16, 1866, by the Thirty-ninth Congress. It was ratified July 9, 1868.)

Section 1

[Citizenship defined; privileges of citizens.] All persons born or naturalized in the United States, and subject to the jurisdiction thereof, are citizens of the United States and of the State wherein they reside. No State shall make or enforce any law which shall abridge the privileges or immunities of citizens of the United States; nor shall any State deprive any person of life, liberty, or property, without due process of law; nor deny to any person within its jurisdiction the equal protection of the laws.

Section 2

[**Apportionment of Representatives.**] Representatives shall be apportioned among the several States according to their respective numbers, counting the whole number of persons in each State, excluding Indians not taxed. But when the right to vote at any election for the choice of electors for President and Vice President of the United States, Representatives in Congress, the executive and judicial officers of a State, or the members of the Legislature thereof, is denied to any of the male inhabitants of such State, being twenty-one years of age, and citizens of the United States, or in any way abridged, except for participation in rebellion, or other crime, the basis of representation therein shall be reduced in the proportion which the number of such male citizens shall bear to the whole number of male citizens twenty-one years of age in such State.

Section 3

[**Disqualification for office; removal of disability.**] No person shall be a Senator or Representative in Congress, or elector of President and Vice President, or hold any office, civil or military, under the United States, or under any State, who, having previously taken an oath, as a member of Congress, or as an officer of the United States, or as a member of any State Legislature, or as an executive or judicial officer of any State, to support the Constitution of the United States, shall have engaged in insurrection or rebellion against the same, or given aid or comfort to the enemies thereof. But Congress may, by a vote of two thirds of each House, remove such disability.

Section 4

[**Public debt not to be questioned; payment of debts and claims incurred in aid of rebellion forbidden.**] The validity of the public debt of the United States, authorized by law, including debts incurred for payment of pensions and bounties for services in suppressing insurrection or rebellion, shall not be questioned. But neither the United States nor any State shall assume or pay any debt or obligation incurred in aid of insurrection or rebellion against the United States, or any claim for the loss or emancipation of any slave; but all such debts, obligations, and claims shall be held illegal and void.

Section 5

[**Congress given power to enforce this article.**] The Congress shall have power to enforce, by appropriate legislation, the provisions of this article.

Article XV

(The proposed amendment was sent to the states Feb. 27, 1869, by the Fortieth Congress. It was ratified Feb. 3, 1870.)

Section 1

[**Right of certain citizens to vote established.**] The right of citizens of the United States to vote shall not be denied or abridged by the United States or by any State on account of race, color, or previous condition of servitude.

Section 2

[**Congress given power to enforce this article.**] The Congress shall have power to enforce this article by appropriate legislation.

Article XVI

(The proposed amendment was sent to the states July 12, 1909, by the Sixty-first Congress. It was ratified Feb. 3, 1913.)

[**Taxes on income; Congress given power to lay and collect.**] The Congress shall have power to lay and collect taxes on incomes, from whatever source derived, without apportionment among the several States, and without regard to any census or enumeration.

Article XVII

(The proposed amendment was sent to the states May 16, 1912, by the Sixty-second Congress. It was ratified April 8, 1913.)

[**Election of United States Senators; filling of vacancies; qualifications of electors.**] The Senate of the United States shall be composed of two Senators from each State, elected by the people thereof, for six years; and each Senator shall have one vote. The electors in each State shall have the qualifications requisite for electors of the most numerous branch of the State Legislatures.

When vacancies happen in the representation of any State in the Senate, the executive authority of such State shall issue writs of election to fill such vacancies: Provided, that the legislature of any State may empower the executive thereof to make temporary appointment until the people fill the vacancies by election as the legislature may direct.

This amendment shall not be so construed as to affect the election or term of any Senator chosen before it becomes valid as part of the Constitution.

Article XVIII[2]

(The proposed amendment was sent to the states Dec. 18, 1917, by the Sixty-fifth Congress. It was ratified by three quarters of the states by Jan. 16, 1919, and became effective Jan. 16, 1920.)

Section 1

[**Manufacture, sale, or transportation of intoxicating liquors, for beverage purposes, prohibited.**] After one year from the ratification of this article the manufacture, sale, or transportation of intoxicating liquors within, the importation thereof into, or the exportation thereof from the United States and all territory subject to the jurisdiction thereof for beverage purposes is hereby prohibited.

Section 2

[**Congress and the several States given concurrent power to pass appropriate legislation to enforce this article.**] The Congress and the several States shall have concurrent power to enforce this article by appropriate legislation.

Section 3

[**Provisions of article to become operative, when adopted by three fourths of the States.**] This article shall be inoperative unless it shall have been ratified as an amendment to the Constitution by the legislatures of the several States, as provided in the Constitution, within seven years from the date of the submission hereof to the States by Congress.

Article XIX

(The proposed amendment was sent to the states June 4, 1919, by the Sixty-sixth Congress. It was ratified Aug. 18, 1920.)

[The right of citizens to vote shall not be denied because of sex.] The right of citizens of the United States to vote shall not be denied or abridged by the United States or by any State on account of sex.

[Congress given power to enforce this article.] Congress shall have power to enforce this article by appropriate legislation.

Article XX

(The proposed amendment, sometimes called the "Lame Duck Amendment," was sent to the states Mar. 3, 1932, by the Seventy-second Congress. It was ratified Jan. 23, 1933; but, in accordance with Section 5, Sections 1 and 2 did not go into effect until Oct. 15, 1933.)

Section 1

[Terms of President, Vice President, Senators, and Representatives.] The terms of the President and Vice President shall end at noon on the twentieth day of January, and the terms of Senators and Representatives at noon on the third day of January, of the years in which such terms would have ended if this article had not been ratified; and the terms of their successors shall then begin.

Section 2

[Time of assembling Congress.] The Congress shall assemble at least once in every year, and such meeting shall begin at noon on the third day of January, unless they shall by law appoint a different day.

Section 3

[Filling vacancy in office of President.] If, at the time fixed for the beginning of the term of the President, the President-elect shall have died, the Vice President-elect shall become President. If a President shall not have been chosen before the time fixed for the beginning of his term, or if the President-elect shall have failed to qualify, then the Vice President shall have qualified; and the Congress may by law provide for the case wherein neither a President-elect nor a Vice President-elect shall have qualified, declaring who shall then act as President, or the manner in which one who is to act shall be selected, and such person shall act accordingly until a President or Vice President shall have qualified.

Section 4

[Power of Congress in Presidential succession.] The Congress may by law provide for the case of the death of any of the persons from whom the House of Representatives may choose a President whenever the right of choice shall have devolved upon them, and for the case of the death of any of the persons from whom the Senate may choose a Vice President whenever the right of choice shall have devolved upon them.

Section 5

[Time of taking effect.] Sections 1 and 2 shall take effect on the 15th day of October following the ratification of this article.

Section 6

[Ratification.] This article shall be inoperative unless it shall have been ratified as an amendment to the Constitution by the legislatures of three fourths of the several States within seven years from the date of its submission.

Article XXI

(The proposed amendment was sent to the states Feb. 20, 1933, by the Seventy-second Congress. It was ratified Dec. 5, 1933.)

Section 1

[Repeal of Prohibition Amendment.] The eighteenth article of amendment to the Constitution of the United States is hereby repealed.

Section 2

[Transportation of intoxicating liquors.] The transportation or importation into any State, territory, or possession of the United States for delivery or use therein of intoxicating liquors, in violation of the laws thereof, is hereby prohibited.

Section 3

[Ratification.] This article shall be inoperative unless it shall have been ratified as an amendment to the Constitution by convention in the several States, as provided in the Constitution, within seven years from the date of the submission thereof to the States by the Congress.

Article XXII

(The proposed amendment was sent to the states Mar. 21, 1947, by the Eightieth Congress. It was ratified Feb. 27, 1951.)

Section 1

[Limit to number of terms a President may serve.] No person shall be elected to the office of the President more than twice, and no person who has held the office of President, or acted as President, for more than two years of a term to which some other person was elected President shall be elected to the office of the President more than once. But this article shall not apply to any person holding the office of President when this article was proposed by the Congress, and shall not prevent any person who may be holding the office of President, or acting as President, during the term within which this article becomes operative from holding the office of President or acting as President during the remainder of such term.

Section 2

[Ratification.] This article shall be inoperative unless it shall have been ratified as an amendment to the Constitution by the legislatures of three fourths of the several States within seven years from the date of its submission to the States by the Congress.

Article XXIII

(The proposed amendment was sent to the states June 16, 1960, by the Eighty-sixth Congress. It was ratified March 29, 1961.)

Section 1

[Electors for the District of Columbia.] The District constituting the seat of Government of the United States shall appoint in such manner as the Congress may direct: A number of electors of President and Vice President equal to the whole number of Senators and Representatives in Congress to which the District would be entitled if it were a State, but in no event more than the least populous State; they shall be in addition to those appointed by the States, but they shall be considered, for the purposes of the election of President and Vice President, to be electors appointed by a State; and they shall meet in the District and perform such duties as provided by the twelfth article of amendment.

Section 2

[Congress given power to enforce this article.] The Congress shall have the power to enforce this article by appropriate legislation.

Article XXIV

(The proposed amendment was sent to the states Aug. 27, 1962, by the Eighty-seventh Congress. It was ratified Jan. 23, 1964.)

Section 1

[Payment of poll tax or other taxes not to be prerequisite for voting in federal elections.] The right of citizens of the United States to vote in any primary or other election for President or Vice President, for electors for President or Vice President, or for Senator or Representative in Congress, shall not be denied or abridged by the United States or any State by reasons of failure to pay any poll tax or other tax.

Section 2

[Congress given power to enforce this article.] The Congress shall have the power to enforce this article by appropriate legislation.

Article XXV

(The proposed amendment was sent to the states July 6, 1965, by the Eighty-ninth Congress. It was ratified Feb. 10, 1967.)

Section 1

[Succession of Vice President to Presidency.] In case of the removal of the President from office or of his death or resignation, the Vice President shall become President.

Section 2

[Vacancy in office of Vice President.] Whenever there is a vacancy in the office of the Vice President, the President shall nominate a Vice President who shall take office upon confirmation by a majority vote of both Houses of Congress.

Section 3

[Vice President as Acting President.] Whenever the President transmits to the President pro tempore of the Senate and the Speaker of the House of Representatives his written declaration that he is unable to discharge the powers and duties of his office, and un-

til he transmits to them a written declaration to the contrary, such powers and duties shall be discharged by the Vice President as Acting President.

Section 4

[Vice President as Acting President.] Whenever the Vice President and a majority of either the principal officers of the executive departments or of such other body as Congress may by law provide, transmit to the President pro tempore of the Senate and the Speaker of the House of Representatives their written declaration that the President is unable to discharge the powers and duties of his office, the Vice President shall immediately assume the powers and duties of the office as Acting President.

Thereafter, when the President transmits to the President pro tempore of the Senate and the Speaker of the House of Representatives his written declaration that no inability exists, he shall resume the powers and duties of his office unless the Vice President and a majority of either the principal officers of the executive department or of such other body as Congress may by law provide, transmit within four days to the President pro tempore of the Senate and the Speaker of the House of Representatives their written declaration that the President is unable to discharge the powers and duties of his office. Thereupon Congress shall decide the issue, assembling within forty-eight hours for that purpose if not in session. If the Congress, within twenty-one days after receipt of the latter written declaration, or, if Congress is not in session, within twenty-one days after Congress is required to assemble, determines by two thirds vote of both Houses that the President is unable to discharge the powers and duties of his office, the Vice President shall continue to discharge the same as Acting President; otherwise, the President shall resume the powers and duties of his office.

Article XXVI

(The proposed amendment was sent to the states Mar. 23, 1971, by the Ninety-second Congress. It was ratified July 1, 1971.)

Section 1

[Voting for 18-year-olds.] The right of citizens of the United States, who are 18 years of age or older, to vote shall not be denied or abridged by the United States or by any state on account of age.

Section 2

[Congress given power to enforce this article.] The Congress shall have power to enforce this article by appropriate legislation.

1. Amended by the 20th Amendment, Sections 3 and 4. 2. Repealed by the 21st Amendment.

The White House

Source: Department of the Interior, U.S. National Park Service.

The White House, the official residence of the President, is at 1600 Pennsylvania Avenue in Washington, D.C. 20500. The site, covering about 18 acres, was selected by President Washington and Pierre Charles L'Enfant, and the architect was James Hoban. The design appears to have been influenced by Leinster House, Dublin, and James Gibb's *Book of Architecture.* The cornerstone was laid Oct. 13, 1792, and the first residents were President and Mrs. John Adams in November 1800. The building was fired by the British in 1814.

From December 1948 to March 1952, the interior of the White House was rebuilt, and the outer walls were strengthened.

The rooms for public functions are on the first floor; the second and third floors are used as the residence of the President and First Family. The most celebrated public room is the East Room, where formal receptions take place. Other public rooms are the Red Room, the Green Room, and the Blue Room. The State Dining Room is used for formal dinners. There are 132 rooms.

Other Historical Documents

The Mayflower Compact

On Sept. 6, 1620, the *Mayflower,* a sailing vessel of about 180 tons, started her memorable voyage from Plymouth, England, with about 100[1] pilgrims aboard, bound for Virginia to establish a private permanent colony in North America. Arriving at what is now Provincetown, Mass., on Nov. 11 (Nov. 21, new style calendar), 41 of the passengers signed the famous "Mayflower Compact" as the boat lay at anchor in that Cape Cod harbor. A small detail of the pilgrims, led by William Bradford, assigned to select a place for permanent settlement landed at what is now Plymouth, Mass., on Dec. 21 (n.s.).

The text of the compact follows:

In the name of God, Amen. We, whose names are underwritten, the Loyal Subjects of our dread Sovereign Lord, King *James,* by the Grace of God, of *Great Britain, France and Ireland,* King, *Defender of the Faith, &*
Having undertaken for the Glory of God, and Advancement of the Christian Faith, and the Honour of our King and Country, a voyage to plant the first colony in the northern Parts of Virginia; do by these Presents, solemnly and mutually in the Presence of God and one of another, covenant and combine ourselves together into a civil Body Politick, for our better Ordering and Preservation, and Furtherance of the Ends aforesaid; And by Virtue hereof to enact, constitute, and frame, such just and equal Laws, Ordinances, Acts, Constitutions and Offices, from time to time, as shall be thought most meet and convenient for the General good of the Colony; unto which we promise all due Submission and Obedience.
In Witness whereof we have hereunto subscribed our names at *Cape Cod* the eleventh of *November,* in the Reign of our Sovereign Lord, King *James* of *England, France* and *Ireland,* the eighteenth, and of *Scotland* the fifty-fourth. *Anno Domini,* 1620

John Carver	William Mullins	John Billington	Peter Brown
Digery Priest	Thomas English	Thomas Tinker	John Turner
William Brewster	John Howland	Samuel Fuller	Edward Tilly
Edmund Margesson	Stephen Hopkins	Richard Clark	John Craxton
John Alden	Edward Winslow	John Allerton	Thomas Rogers
George Soule	Gilbert Winslow	Richard Warren	John Goodman
James Chilton	Miles Standish	Edward Liester	Edward Fuller
Francis Cooke	Richard Bitteridge	William Bradford	Richard Gardiner
Moses Fletcher	Francis Eaton	Thomas Williams	William White
John Ridgate	John Tilly	Isaac Allerton	Edward Doten
Christopher Martin			

1. Historians differ as to whether 100, 101, or 102 passengers were aboard.

The Monroe Doctrine

The Monroe Doctrine was announced in President James Monroe's message to Congress, during his second term on Dec. 2, 1823, in part as follows:

"In the discussions to which this interest has given rise, and in the arrangements by which they may terminate, the occasion has been deemed proper for asserting as a principle in which rights and interests of the United States are involved, that the American continents, by the free and independent condition which they have assumed and maintain, are henceforth not to be considered as subjects for future colonization by any European power. . . . We owe it, therefore, to candor and to the amicable relations existing between the United States and those powers to declare that we should consider any attempt on their part to extend their system to any portion of this hemisphere as dangerous to our peace and safety. With the existing colonies or dependencies of any European power we have not interfered and shall not interfere. But with the governments who have declared their independence and maintain it, and whose independence we have, on great consideration and on just principles, acknowledged, we could not view any interposition for the purpose of oppressing them or controlling in any other manner their destiny by any European power in any other light than as the manifestation of an unfriendly disposition toward the United States."

The Star-Spangled Banner

Francis Scott Key, 1814

O say, can you see, by the dawn's early light,
What so proudly we hail'd at the twilight's last gleaming?
Whose broad stripes and bright stars, thro' the perilous fight,
O'er the ramparts we watch'd, were so gallantly streaming?
And the rockets' red glare, the bombs bursting in air,
Gave proof thro' the night that our flag was still there.
O say, does that star-spangled banner yet wave
O'er the land of the free and the home of the brave?

On the shore dimly seen thro' the mists of the deep,
Where the foe's haughty host in dread silence reposes,
What is that which the breeze, o'er the towering steep,
As it fitfully blows, half conceals, half discloses?
Now it catches the gleam of the morning's first beam,
In full glory reflected, now shines on the stream:
'T is the star-spangled banner: O, long may it wave
O'er the land of the free and the home of the brave!

And where is that band who so vauntingly swore
That the havoc of war and the battle's confusion,
A home and a country should leave us no more?
Their blood has wash'd out their foul footsteps' pollution.
No refuge could save the hireling and slave
From the terror of flight or the gloom of the grave:
And the star-spangled banner in triumph doth wave
O'er the land of the free and the home of the brave.

O thus be it ever when free-men shall stand
Between their lov'd home and the war's desolation;
Blest with vict'ry and peace, may the heav'n-rescued land
Praise the Pow'r that hath made and preserv'd us a nation!
Then conquer we must, when our cause it is just,
And this be our motto: "In God is our trust!"
And the star-spangled banner in triumph shall wave
O'er the land of the free and the home of the brave!

On Sept. 13, 1814, Francis Scott Key visited the British fleet in Chesapeake Bay to secure the release of Dr. William Beanes, who had been captured after the burning of Washington, D.C. The release was secured, but Key was detained on ship overnight during the shelling of Fort McHenry, one of the forts defending Baltimore. In the morning, he was so delighted to see the American flag still flying over the fort that he began a poem to commemorate the occasion. First published under the title "Defense of Fort M'Henry," and later as "The Star-Spangled Banner," the poem soon attained wide popularity as sung to the tune "To Anacreon in Heaven." The origin of this tune is obscure, but it may have been written by John Stafford Smith, a British composer born in 1750. "The Star-Spangled Banner" was officially made the National Anthem by Congress in 1931, although it had been already adopted as such by the Army and the Navy.

The Emancipation Proclamation

January 1, 1863

By the President of the United
States of America:

A Proclamation.
Whereas on the 22d day of September, A.D. 1862, a proclamation was issued by the President of the United States, containing, among other things, the following, to wit:
"That on the 1st day of January, A.D. 1863, all persons held as slaves within any State or designated part of a State the people whereof shall then be in rebellion against the United States shall be then, thenceforward, and forever free; and the executive government of the United States, including the military and naval authority thereof, will recognize and maintain the freedom of such persons and will do not act or acts to repress such persons, or any of them, in any efforts they may make for their actual freedom.
"That the executive will on the 1st day of January aforesaid, by proclamation, designate the States and parts of States, if any, in which the people thereof, respectively, shall then be in rebellion against the United States; and the fact that any State or the people thereof shall on that day be in good faith represented in the Congress of the United States by members chosen thereto at elections wherein a majority of the qualified voters of such States shall have participated shall, in the absence of strong countervailing testimony, be deemed conclusive evidence that such State and the people thereof are not then in rebellion against the United States."
Now, therefore, I, Abraham Lincoln, President of

the United States, by virtue of the power in me vested as Commander-in-Chief of the Army and Navy of the United States in time of actual armed rebellion against the authority and government of the United States, and as a fit and necessary war measure for suppressing said rebellion, do, on this 1st day of January, A.D. 1863, and in accordance with my purpose so to do, publicly proclaimed for the full period of one hundred days from the first day above mentioned, order and designate as the States and parts of States wherein the people thereof, respectively, are this day in rebellion against the United States the following, to wit:

Arkansas, Texas, Louisiana (except the parishes of St. Bernard, Plaquemines, Jefferson, St. John, St. Charles, St. James, Ascension, Assumption, Terrebonne, Lafourche, St. Mary, St. Martin, and Orleans, including the city of New Orleans), Mississippi, Alabama, Florida, Georgia, South Carolina, North Carolina, and Virginia (except the forty-eight counties designated as West Virginia, and also the counties of Berkeley, Accomac, Northhampton, Elizabeth City, York, Princess Anne, and Norfolk, including the cities of Norfolk and Portsmouth), and which excepted parts are for the present left precisely as if this proclamation were not issued.

And by virtue of the power and for the purpose aforesaid, I do order and declare that all persons held as slaves within said designated States and parts of States are, and henceforward shall be, free; and that the Executive Government of the United States, including the military and naval authorities thereof, will recognize and maintain the freedom of said persons.

And I hereby enjoin upon the people so declared to be free to abstain from all violence, unless in necessary self-defense; and I recommend to them that, in all cases when allowed, they labor faithfully for reasonable wages.

And I further declare and make known that such persons of suitable condition will be received into the armed service of the United States to garrison forts, positions, stations, and other places, and to man vessels of all sorts in said service.

And upon this act, sincerely believed to be an act of justice, warranted by the Constitution upon military necessity, I invoke the considerate judgment of mankind and the gracious favor of Almighty God.

The Confederate States of America

State	Seceded from Union	Readmitted to Union[1]	State	Seceded from Union	Readmitted to Union[1]
1. South Carolina	Dec. 20, 1860	July 9, 1868	7. Texas	March 2, 1861	March 30, 1870
2. Mississippi	Jan. 9, 1861	Feb. 23, 1870	8. Virginia	April 17, 1861	Jan. 26, 1870
3. Florida	Jan. 10, 1861	June 25, 1868	9. Arkansas	May 6, 1861	June 22, 1868
4. Alabama	Jan. 11, 1861	July 13, 1868	10. North Carolina	May 20, 1861	July 4, 1868
5. Georgia	Jan. 19, 1861	July 15, 1870[2]	11. Tennessee	June 8, 1861	July 24, 1866
6. Louisiana	Jan. 26, 1861	July 9, 1868			

1. Date of readmission to representation in U.S. House of Representatives. 2. Second readmission date. First date was July 21, 1868, but the representatives were unseated March 5, 1869. NOTE: Four other slave states—Delaware, Kentucky, Maryland, and Missouri—remained in the Union.

Lincoln's Gettysburg Address

The Battle of Gettysburg, one of the most noted battles of the Civil War, was fought on July 1, 2, and 3, 1863. On Nov. 19, 1863, the field was dedicated as a national cemetery by President Lincoln in a two-minute speech that was to become immortal. At the time of its delivery the speech was relegated to the inside pages of the papers, while a two-hour address by Edward Everett, the leading orator of the time, caught the headlines.

The following is the text of the address revised by President Lincoln from his own notes:

Fourscore and seven years ago our fathers brought forth on this continent a new nation conceived in liberty and dedicated to the proposition that all men are created equal. Now we are engaged in a great civil war testing whether that nation, or any nation so conceived and so dedicated, can long endure. We are met on a great battlefield of that war. We have come to dedicate a portion of that field as a final resting-place for those who here gave their lives that that nation might live. It is altogether fitting and proper that we should do this. But, in a larger sense, we cannot dedicate, we cannot consecrate, we cannot hallow this ground. The brave men, living and dead, who struggled here have consecrated it far above our poor power to add or detract. The world will little note nor long remember what we say here, but it can never forget what they did here. It is for us the living rather to be dedicated here to the unfinished work which they who fought here have thus far so nobly advanced. It is rather for us to be here dedicated to the great task remaining before us—that from these honored dead we take increased devotion to that cause for which they gave the last full measure of devotion—that we here highly resolve that these dead shall not have died in vain, that this nation under God shall have a new birth of freedom, and that government of the people, by the people, for the people shall not perish from the earth.

The Early Congresses

At the urging of Massachusetts and Virginia, the First Continental Congress met in Philadelphia on Sept. 5, 1774, and was attended by representatives of all the colonies except Georgia. Patrick Henry of Virginia declared: "The distinctions between Pennsylvanians, New Yorkers and New Englanders are no more. I am not a Virginian but an American." This Congress, which adjourned Oct. 26, 1774, passed intercolonial resolutions calling for extensive boycott by the colonies against British trade.

The following year, most of the delegates from the colonies were chosen by popular election to attend the Second Continental Congress, which assembled in Philadelphia on May 10. As war had already begun between the colonies and England, the chief problems before the Congress were the procuring of military supplies, the establishment of an army and proper defenses, the issuing of continental bills of credit, etc. On June 15, 1775, George Washington was elected to command the Continental army. Congress adjourned Dec. 12, 1776.

Other Continental Congresses were held in Baltimore (1776–77), Philadelphia (1777), Lancaster, Pa. (1777), York, Pa. (1777–78), and Philadelphia (1778–81).

In 1781, the Articles of Confederation, although establishing a league of the thirteen states rather than a strong central government, provided for the continuance of Congress. Known thereafter as the Congress of the Confederation, it held sessions in Philadelphia (1781–83), Princeton, N.J. (1783), Annapolis, Md. (1783–84), and Trenton, N.J. (1784). Five sessions were held in New York City between the years 1785 and 1789.

The Congress of the United States, established by the ratification of the Constitution, held its first meeting on March 4, 1789, in New York City. Several sessions of Congress were held in Philadelphia, and the first meeting in Washington, D.C., was on Nov. 17, 1800.

Presidents of the Continental Congresses

Name	Elected	Birth and Death Dates	Name	Elected	Birth and Death Dates
Peyton Randolph, Va.	9/5/1774	c.1721–1775	John Hanson, Md.	11/5/1781	1715–1783
Henry Middleton, S.C.	10/22/1774	1717–1784	Elias Boudinot, N.J.	11/4/1782	1740–1821
Peyton Randolph, Va.	5/10/1775	c.1721–1775	Thomas Mifflin, Pa.	11/3/1783	1744–1800
John Hancock, Mass.	5/24/1775	1737–1793	Richard Henry Lee, Va.	11/30/1784	1732–1794
Henry Laurens, S.C.	11/1/1777	1724–1792	John Hancock, Mass.[1]	11/23/1785	1737–1793
John Jay, N.Y.	12/10/1778	1745–1829	Nathaniel Gorham, Mass.	6/6/1786	1738–1796
Samuel Huntington, Conn.	9/28/1779	1731–1796	Arthur St. Clair, Pa.	2/2/1787	1734–1818
Thomas McKean, Del.	7/10/1781	1734–1817	Cyrus Griffin, Va.	1/22/1788	1748–1810

1. Resigned May 29, 1786, never having served, because of continued illness.

The Great Seal of the U.S.

On July 4, 1776, the Continental Congress appointed a committee consisting of Benjamin Franklin, John Adams, and Thomas Jefferson "to bring in a device for a seal of the United States of America." After many delays, a verbal description of a design by William Barton was finally approved by Congress on June 20, 1782. The seal shows an American bald eagle with a ribbon in its mouth bearing the device *E pluribus unum* (One out of many). In its talons are the arrows of war and an olive branch of peace. On the reverse side it shows an unfinished pyramid with an eye (the eye of Providence) above it. Although this description was adopted in 1782, the first drawing was not made until four years later, and no die has ever been cut.

The American's Creed

William Tyler Page

"I believe in the United States of America as a government of the people, by the people, for the people; whose just powers are derived from the consent of the governed; a democracy in a republic; a sovereign Nation of many sovereign States; a perfect union, one and inseparable; established upon those principles of freedom, equality, justice, and humanity for which American patriots sacrificed their lives and fortunes.

"I therefore believe it is my duty to my country to love it, to support its Constitution, to obey its laws, to respect its flag, and to defend it against all enemies."

NOTE: William Tyler Page, Clerk of the U.S. House of Representatives, wrote "The American's Creed" in 1917. It was accepted by the House on behalf of the American people on April 3, 1918.

U.S. Capitol

When the French architect and engineer Maj. Pierre L'Enfant first began to lay out the plans for a new Federal city (now Washington, D.C.), he noted that Jenkins' Hill, overlooking the area, seemed to be "a pedestal waiting for a monument." It was here that the U.S. Capitol would be built. The basic structure as we know it today evolved over a period of more than 150 years. In 1792 a competition was held for the design of a capitol building. Dr. William Thornton, a physician and amateur architect, submitted the winning plan, a simple, low-lying structure of classical proportions with a shallow dome. Later, internal modifications were made by Benjamin Henry Latrobe. After the building was burned by the British in 1814, Latrobe and architect Charles Bulfinch were responsible for its reconstruction. Finally, under Thomas Walter, who was Architect of the Capitol from 1851 to 1865, the House and Senate wings and the imposing cast iron dome topped with the Statue of Freedom were added, and the Capitol assumed the form we see today. It was in the old Senate chamber that Daniel Webster cried out, "Liberty and Union, now and forever, one and inseparable!" In Statuary Hall, which used to be the old House chamber, a small disk on the floor marks the spot where John

Quincy Adams was fatally stricken after more than 50 years of service to his country. A whisper from one side of this room can be heard across the vast space of the hall. Visitors can see the original Supreme Court chamber a floor below the Rotunda.

In addition to its historical association, the Capitol Building is also a vast artistic treasure house. The works of such famous artists as Gilbert Stuart, Rembrandt Peale, and John Trumbull are displayed on the walls. The Great Rotunda, with its 180-foot-(54.9-m-) high dome, is decorated with a massive fresco by Constantino Brumidi, which extends some 300 feet (90 m) in circumference. Throughout the building are many paintings of events in U.S. history and sculptures of outstanding Americans. The Capitol itself is situated on a 68-acre (27.5-ha) park designed by the 19th-century landscape architect Frederick Law Olmsted. There are free guided tours of the Capitol, which include admission to the House and Senate galleries. Those who wish to visit the visitors' gallery in either wing without taking the tour may obtain passes from their Senators or Congressmen. Visitors may ride on the monorail subway that joins the House and Senate wings of the Capitol with the Congressional office buildings.

Washington Monument

Construction of this magnificent Washington, D.C., monument, which draws some two million visitors a year, took nearly a century of planning, building, and controversy. Provision for a large equestrian statue of George Washington was made in the original city plan, but the project was soon dropped. After Washington's death it was taken up again, and a number of false starts and changes of design were made. Finally, in 1848, work was begun on the monument that stands today. The design, by architect Robert Mills, then featured an ornate base. In 1854, however, political squabbling and a lack of money brought construction to a halt. Work was resumed in 1880, and the monument was completed in 1884 and opened to the public in 1888. The tapered shaft, faced with white marble and rising from walls 15 feet thick (4.6 m) at the base was modeled after the obelisks of ancient Egypt. The monument, one of the tallest masonry constructions in the world, stands just over 555 feet (169 m). Memorial stones from the 50 States, foreign countries, and organizations line the interior walls. The top, reached only by elevator, commands a panoramic view of the city.

The Liberty Bell

The Liberty Bell was cast in England in 1752 for the Pennsylvania Statehouse (now named Independence Hall) in Philadelphia. It was recast in Philadelphia in 1753. It is inscribed with the words, "Proclaim liberty throughout all the land unto all the inhabitants thereof" (Lev. 25:10). The bell was rung on July 8, 1776, for the first public reading of the Declaration of Independence. Hidden in Allentown during the British occupation of Philadelphia, it was replaced in Independence Hall in 1778. The bell cracked on July 8, 1835, while tolling the death of Chief Justice John Marshall. In 1976 the Liberty Bell was moved to a special exhibition building near Independence Hall.

Arlington National Cemetery

Arlington National Cemetery occupies 612 acres in Virginia on the Potomac River, directly opposite Washington. This land was part of the estate of John Parke Custis, Martha Washington's son. His son, George Washington Parke Custis, built the mansion which later became the home of Robert E. Lee. In 1864, Arlington became a military cemetery. More than 216,000 servicemembers and their dependents are buried there. Expansion of the cemetery began in 1966, using a 180-acre tract of land directly east of the present site.

In 1921, an Unknown American Soldier of World War I was buried in the cemetery; the monument at the Tomb was opened to the public without ceremony in 1932. Two additional Unknowns, one from World War II and one from the Korean War, were buried May 30, 1958. The Unknown Serviceman of Vietnam was buried on May 28, 1984. The inscription carved on the Tomb of the Unknowns reads:

HERE RESTS IN
HONORED GLORY
AN AMERICAN
SOLDIER
KNOWN BUT TO GOD

History of the Flag

Source: Encyclopaedia Britannica.

The first official American flag, the Continental or Grand Union flag, was displayed on Prospect Hill, Jan. 1, 1776, in the American lines besieging Boston. It had 13 alternate red and white stripes, with the British Union Jack in the upper left corner.

On June 14, 1777, the Continental Congress adopted the design for a new flag, which actually was the Continental flag with the red cross of St. George and the white cross of St. Andrew replaced on the blue field by 13 stars, one for each state. No rule was made as to the arrangement of the stars, and while they were usually shown in a circle, there were various other designs. It is uncertain when the new flag was first flown, but its first official announcement is believed to have been on Sept. 3, 1777.

The first public assertion that Betsy Ross made the first Stars and Stripes appeared in a paper read before the Historical Society of Pennsylvania on March 14, 1870, by William J. Canby, a grandson. However, Mr. Canby on later investigation found no official documents of any action by Congress on the flag before June 14, 1777. Betsy Ross's own story, according to her daughter, was that Washington, Robert Morris, and George Ross, as representatives of Congress, visited her in Philadelphia in June 1776, showing her a rough draft of the flag and asking her if she could make one. However, the only actual record of the manufacture of flags by Betsy Ross is a voucher in Harrisburg, Pa., for 14 pounds and some shillings for flags for the Pennsylvania navy.

On Jan. 13, 1794, Congress voted to add two stars and two stripes to the flag in recognition of the admission of Vermont and Kentucky to the Union. By 1818, there were 20 states in the Union, and as it was obvious that the flag would soon become unwieldy, Congress voted April 18 to return to the original 13 stripes and to indicate the admission of a new state simply by the addition of a star the following July 4. The 49th star, for Alaska, was added July 4, 1959; and the 50th star, for Hawaii, was added July 4, 1960.

The first Confederate flag, adopted in 1861 by the Confederate convention in Montgomery, Ala., was called the Stars and Bars; but because of its similarity in colors to the American flag, there was much confusion in the Battle of Bull Run. To remedy this situation, Gen. G. T. Beauregard suggested a battle flag, which was used by the Southern armies throughout the war. The flag consisted of a red field on which was placed a blue cross of St. Andrew separated from the field by a white fillet and adorned with 13[1] white stars for the Confederate states. In May 1863, at Richmond, an official flag was adopted by the Confederate Congress. This flag was white and twice as long as wide; the union, two-thirds the width of the flag, contained the battle flag designed for Gen. Beauregard. A broad transverse stripe of red was added Feb. 4, 1865, so that the flag might not be mistaken for a signal of truce.

1. 11 states formally seceded, and unofficial groups in Kentucky and Missouri adopted ordinances of secession. On this basis, these two states were admitted to the Confederacy, although the official state governments remained in the Union.

The Pledge of Allegiance[1] to the Flag

"I pledge allegiance to the Flag of the United States of America, and to the Republic for which it stands, one Nation under God,[2] indivisible, with liberty and justice for all."

1. The original pledge was published in the Sept. 8, 1892, issue of *The Youth's Companion* in Boston. For years, the authorship was in dispute between James B. Upham and Francis Bellamy of the magazine's staff. In 1939, after a study of the controversy, the United States Flag Association decided that authorship be credited to Bellamy. 2. The phrase "under God" was added to the pledge on June 14, 1954.

The Statue of Liberty

The Statue of Liberty ("Liberty Enlightening the World") is a 225-ton, steel-reinforced copper female figure, 152 ft in height, facing the ocean from Liberty[1] Island in New York Harbor. The right hand holds aloft a torch, and the left hand carries a tablet upon which is inscribed: "July IV MDCCLXXVI."

The statue was designed by Frédéric Auguste Bartholdi of Alsace as a gift to the United States from the people of France to memorialize the alliance of the two countries in the American Revolution and their abiding friendship. The French people contributed the $250,000 cost.

The 150-foot pedestal was designed by Richard M. Hunt and built by Gen. Charles P. Stone, both Americans. It contains steel underpinnings designed by Alexander Eiffel of France to support the statue. The $270,000 cost was borne by popular subscription in this country. President Grover Cleveland accepted the statue for the United States on Oct. 28, 1886.

On Sept. 26, 1972, President Richard M. Nixon dedicated the American Museum of Immigration, housed in structural additions to the base of the stat-

1. Called Bedloe's Island prior to 1956.

ue. In 1984 scaffolding went up for a major restoration and the torch was extinguished on July 4. It was relit with much ceremony July 4, 1986 to mark its centennial.

On a tablet inside the pedestal is engraved the following sonnet, written by Emma Lazarus (1849–1887):

The New Colossus

Not like the brazen giant of Greek fame.
With conquering limbs astride from land to land;
Here at our sea-washed, sunset gates shall stand
A mighty woman with a torch, whose flame
Is the imprisoned lightning, and her name
Mother of Exiles. From her beacon-hand
Glows world-wide welcome; her mild eyes command
The air-bridged harbor that twin cities frame.
"Keep, ancient lands, your storied pomp!" cries she
With silent lips. "Give me your tired, your poor,
Your huddled masses yearning to breathe free,
The wretched refuse of your teeming shore.
Send these, the homeless, tempest-tost to me,
I lift my lamp beside the golden door!"

Firsts in America

This selection is based on our editorial judgment. Other sources may list different firsts.

Admiral in U.S. Navy: David Glasgow Farragut, 1866.

Air–mail route, first transcontinental: Between New York City and San Francisco, 1920.

Assembly, representative: House of Burgesses, founded in Virginia, 1619.

Bank established: Bank of North America, Philadelphia, 1781.

Birth in America to English parents: Virginia Dare, born Roanoke Island, N.C., 1587.

Black newspaper: *Freedom's Journal,* 1827, edited by John B. Russworm.

Black U.S. diplomat: Ebenezer D. Bassett, 1869, minister-resident to Haiti.

Black elected governor of a state: L. Douglas Wilder, Virginia, 1990.

Black elected to U.S. Senate: Hiram Revels, 1870, Mississippi.

Black elected to U.S. House of Representatives: Jefferson Long, Georgia, 1870.

Black associate justice of U.S. Supreme Court: Thurgood Marshall, Oct. 2, 1967.

Black U.S. cabinet minister: Robert C. Weaver, 1966, Secretary of the Department of Housing and Urban Development.

Botanic garden: Established by John Bartram in Philadelphia, 1728 and is still in existence in its original location.

Cartoon, colored: "The Yellow Kid," by Richard Outcault, in *New York World,* 1895.

College: Harvard, founded 1636.

College to confer degrees on women: Oberlin (Ohio) College, 1841.

College to establish coeducation: Oberlin (Ohio) College, 1833.

Electrocution of a criminal: William Kemmler in Auburn Prison, Auburn, N.Y., Aug. 6, 1890.

Five and Ten Cents Store: Founded by Frank Woolworth, Utica, N.Y., 1879 (moved to Lancaster, Pa., same year).

Fraternity: Phi Beta Kappa; founded Dec. 5, 1776, at College of William and Mary.

Law to be declared unconstitutional by U.S. Supreme Court: Judiciary Act of 1789. Case: *Marbury* v. *Madison,* 1803.

Library, circulating: Philadelphia, 1731.

Newspaper, illustrated daily: *New York Daily Graphic,* 1873.

Newspaper published daily: *Pennsylvania Packet and General Advertiser,* Philadelphia, Sept., 1784.

Newspaper published over a continuous period: *The Boston News–Letter,* April, 1704.

Newsreel: Pathé Frères of Paris, in 1910, circulated a weekly issue of their *Pathé Journal.*

Oil well, commercial: Titusville, Pa., 1859.

Panel quiz show on radio: *Information Please,* May 17, 1938.

Postage stamps issued: 1847.

Public School: Boston Latin School, Boston, 1635.

Railroad, transcontinental: Central Pacific and Union Pacific railroads, joined at Promontory, Utah, May 10, 1869.

Savings bank: The Provident Institute for Savings, Boston, 1816.

Science museum: Founded by Charleston (S.C.) Library Society, 1773.

Skyscraper: Home Insurance Co., Chicago, 1885 (10 floors, 2 added later).

Slaves brought into America: At Jamestown, Va., 1619, from a Dutch ship.

Sorority: Kappa Alpha Theta, at De Pauw University, 1870.

State to abolish capital punishment: Michigan, 1847.

State to enter Union after original 13: Vermont, 1791.

Steam–heated building: Eastern Hotel, Boston, 1845.

Steam railroad (carried passengers and freight): Baltimore & Ohio, 1830.

Strike on record by union: Journeymen Printers, New York City, 1776.

Subway: Opened in Boston, 1897.

"Tabloid" picture newspaper: *The Illustrated Daily News* (now *The Daily News*), New York City, 1919.

Vaudeville theater: Gaiety Museum, Boston, 1883.

Woman astronaut to ride in space: Dr. Sally K. Ride, 1983.

Woman astronaut to walk in space: Dr. Kathryn D. Sullivan, 1984.

Woman cabinet member: Frances Perkins, Secretary of Labor, 1933.

Woman candidate for President: Victoria Claflin Woodhull, nominated by National Woman's Suffrage Assn. on ticket of Nation Radical Reformers, 1872.

Woman candidate for Vice–President: Geraldine A. Ferraro, nominated on a major party ticket, Democratic Party, 1984.

Woman doctor of medicine: Elizabeth Blackwell; M.D. from Geneva Medical College of Western New York, 1849.

Woman elected governor of a state: Nellie Tayloe Ross, Wyoming, 1925.

Woman elected to U.S. Senate: Hattie Caraway, Arkansas; elected Nov., 1932.

Woman graduate of law school: Ada H. Kepley, Union College of Law, Chicago, 1870.

Woman member of U.S. House of Representatives: Jeannette Rankin; elected Nov., 1916.

Woman member of U.S. Senate: Rebecca Latimer Felton of Georgia; appointed Oct. 3, 1922.

Woman member of U.S. Supreme Court: Sandra Day O'Connor; appointed July 1981.

Woman suffrage granted: Wyoming Territory, 1869.

Written constitution: *Fundamental Orders of Connecticut,* 1639.

Presidents

Name and (party)[1]	Term	State of birth	Born	Died	Religion	Age at inaug.	Age at death
1. Washington (F)[2]	1789–1797	Va.	2/22/1732	12/14/1799	Episcopalian	57	67
2. J. Adams (F)	1797–1801	Mass.	10/30/1735	7/4/1826	Unitarian	61	90
3. Jefferson (DR)	1801–1809	Va.	4/13/1743	7/4/1826	Deist	57	83
4. Madison (DR)	1809–1817	Va.	3/16/1751	6/28/1836	Episcopalian	57	85
5. Monroe (DR)	1817–1825	Va.	4/28/1758	7/4/1831	Episcopalian	58	73
6. J. Q. Adams (DR)	1825–1829	Mass.	7/11/1767	2/23/1848	Unitarian	57	80
7. Jackson (D)	1829–1837	S.C.	3/15/1767	6/8/1845	Presbyterian	61	78
8. Van Buren (D)	1837–1841	N.Y.	12/5/1782	7/24/1862	Reformed Dutch	54	79
9. W. H. Harrison (W)[3]	1841	Va.	2/9/1773	4/4/1841	Episcopalian	68	68
10. Tyler (W)	1841–1845	Va.	3/29/1790	1/18/1862	Episcopalian	51	71
11. Polk (D)	1845–1849	N.C.	11/2/1795	6/15/1849	Methodist	49	53
12. Taylor (W)[3]	1849–1850	Va.	11/24/1784	7/9/1850	Episcopalian	64	65
13. Fillmore (W)	1850–1853	N.Y.	1/7/1800	3/8/1874	Unitarian	50	74
14. Pierce (D)	1853–1857	N.H.	11/23/1804	10/8/1869	Episcopalian	48	64
15. Buchanan (D)	1857–1861	Pa.	4/23/1791	6/1/1868	Presbyterian	65	77
16. Lincoln (R)[4]	1861–1865	Ky.	2/12/1809	4/15/1865	Liberal	52	56
17. A. Johnson (U)[5]	1865–1869	N.C.	12/29/1808	7/31/1875	(6)	56	66
18. Grant (R)	1869–1877	Ohio	4/27/1822	7/23/1885	Methodist	46	63
19. Hayes (R)	1877–1881	Ohio	10/4/1822	1/17/1893	Methodist	54	70
20. Garfield (R)[4]	1881	Ohio	11/19/1831	9/19/1881	Disciples of Christ	49	49
21. Arthur (R)	1881–1885	Vt.	10/5/1830	11/18/1886	Episcopalian	50	56
22. Cleveland (D)	1885–1889	N.J.	3/18/1837	6/24/1908	Presbyterian	47	71
23. B. Harrison (R)	1889–1893	Ohio	8/20/1833	3/13/1901	Presbyterian	55	67
24. Cleveland (D)[7]	1893–1897	—	—	—	—	55	—
25. McKinley (R)[4]	1897–1901	Ohio	1/29/1843	9/14/1901	Methodist	54	58
26. T. Roosevelt (R)	1901–1909	N.Y.	10/27/1858	1/6/1919	Reformed Dutch	42	60
27. Taft (R)	1909–1913	Ohio	9/15/1857	3/8/1930	Unitarian	51	72
28. Wilson (D)	1913–1921	Va.	12/28/1856	2/3/1924	Presbyterian	56	67
29. Harding (R)[3]	1921–1923	Ohio	11/2/1865	8/2/1923	Baptist	55	57
30. Coolidge (R)	1923–1929	Vt.	7/4/1872	1/5/1933	Congregationalist	51	60
31. Hoover (R)	1929–1933	Iowa	8/10/1874	10/20/1964	Quaker	54	90
32. F. D. Roosevelt (D)[3]	1933–1945	N.Y.	1/30/1882	4/12/1945	Episcopalian	51	63
33. Truman (D)	1945–1953	Mo.	5/8/1884	12/26/1972	Baptist	60	88
34. Eisenhower (R)	1953–1961	Tex.	10/14/1890	3/28/1969	Presbyterian	62	78
35. Kennedy (D)[4]	1961–1963	Mass.	5/29/1917	11/22/1963	Roman Catholic	43	46
36. L. B. Johnson (D)	1963–1969	Tex.	8/27/1908	1/22/1973	Disciples of Christ	55	64
37. Nixon (R)[8]	1969–1974	Calif.	1/9/1913	—	Quaker	56	—
38. Ford (R)	1974–1977	Neb.	7/14/1913	—	Episcopalian	61	—
39. Carter (D)	1977–1981	Ga.	10/1/1924	—	Southern Baptist	52	—
40. Reagan (R)	1981–1989	Ill.	2/6/1911	—	Disciples of Christ	69	—
41. Bush (R)	1989–	Mass.	6/12/24	—	Episcopalian	64	—

1. F—Federalist; DR—Democratic-Republican; D—Democratic; W—Whig; R—Republican; U—Union. 2. No party for first election. The party system in the U.S. made its appearance during Washington's first term. 3. Died in office. 4. Assassinated in office. 5. The Republican National Convention of 1864 adopted the name Union Party. It renominated Lincoln for President; for Vice President it nominated Johnson, a War Democrat. Although frequently listed as a Republican Vice President and President, Johnson undoubtedly considered himself strictly a member of the Union Party. When that party broke apart after 1868, he returned to the Democratic Party. 6. Johnson was not a professed church member; however, he admired the Baptist principles of church government. 7. Second nonconsecutive term. 8. Resigned Aug. 9, 1974.

Vice Presidents

Name and (party)[1]	Term	State of birth	Birth and death dates	President served under
1. John Adams (F)[2]	1789–1797	Massachusetts	1735–1826	Washington
2. Thomas Jefferson (DR)	1797–1801	Virginia	1743–1826	J. Adams
3. Aaron Burr (DR)	1801–1805	New Jersey	1756–1836	Jefferson
4. George Clinton (DR)[3]	1805–1812	New York	1739–1812	Jefferson and Madison
5. Elbridge Gerry (DR)[3]	1813–1814	Massachusetts	1744–1814	Madison
6. Daniel D. Tompkins (DR)	1817–1825	New York	1774–1825	Monroe
7. John C. Calhoun[4]	1825–1832	South Carolina	1782–1850	J. Q. Adams and Jackson
8. Martin Van Buren (D)	1833–1837	New York	1782–1862	Jackson
9. Richard M. Johnson (D)	1837–1841	Kentucky	1780–1850	Van Buren
10. John Tyler (W)[5]	1841	Virginia	1790–1862	W. H. Harrison
11. George M. Dallas (D)	1845–1849	Pennsylvania	1792–1864	Polk
12. Millard Fillmore (W)[5]	1849–1850	New York	1800–1874	Taylor
13. William R. King (D)[3]	1853	North Carolina	1786–1853	Pierce
14. John C. Breckinridge (D)	1857–1861	Kentucky	1821–1875	Buchanan

Name and (party)[1]	Term	State of birth	Birth and death dates	President served under
15. Hannibal Hamlin (R)	1861–1865	Maine	1809–1891	Lincoln
16. Andrew Johnson (U)[5]	1865	North Carolina	1808–1875	Lincoln
17. Schuyler Colfax (R)	1869–1873	New York	1823–1885	Grant
18. Henry Wilson (R)[3]	1873–1875	New Hampshire	1812–1875	Grant
19. William A. Wheeler (R)	1877–1881	New York	1819–1887	Hayes
20. Chester A. Arthur (R)[5]	1881	Vermont	1830–1886	Garfield
21. Thomas A. Hendricks (D)[3]	1885	Ohio	1819–1885	Cleveland
22. Levi P. Morton (R)	1889–1893	Vermont	1824–1920	B. Harrison
23. Adlai E. Stevenson (D)	1893–1897	Kentucky	1835–1914	Cleveland
24. Garrett A. Hobart (R)[3]	1897–1899	New Jersey	1844–1899	McKinley
25. Theodore Roosevelt (R)[5]	1901	New York	1858–1919	McKinley
26. Charles W. Fairbanks (R)	1905–1909	Ohio	1852–1918	T. Roosevelt
27. James S. Sherman (R)[3]	1909–1912	New York	1855–1912	Taft
28. Thomas R. Marshall (D)	1913–1921	Indiana	1854–1925	Wilson
29. Calvin Coolidge (R)[5]	1921–1923	Vermont	1872–1933	Harding
30. Charles G. Dawes (R)	1925–1929	Ohio	1865–1951	Coolidge
31. Charles Curtis (R)	1929–1933	Kansas	1860–1936	Hoover
32. John N. Garner (D)	1933–1941	Texas	1868–1967	F. D. Roosevelt
33. Henry A. Wallace (D)	1941–1945	Iowa	1888–1965	F. D. Roosevelt
34. Harry S. Truman (D)[5]	1945	Missouri	1884–1972	F. D. Roosevelt
35. Alben W. Barkley (D)	1949–1953	Kentucky	1877–1956	Truman
36. Richard M. Nixon (R)	1953–1961	California	1913–	Eisenhower
37. Lyndon B. Johnson (D)[5]	1961–1963	Texas	1908–1973	Kennedy
38. Hubert H. Humphrey (D)	1965–1969	South Dakota	1911–1978	Johnson
39. Spiro T. Agnew (R)[6]	1969–1973	Maryland	1918–	Nixon
40. Gerald R. Ford (R)[7]	1973–1974	Nebraska	1913–	Nixon
41. Nelson A. Rockefeller (R)[8]	1974–1977	Maine	1908–1979	Ford
42. Walter F. Mondale (D)	1977–1981	Minnesota	1928–	Carter
43. George Bush (R)	1981–1989	Massachusetts	1924–	Reagan
44. J. Danforth Quayle (R)	1989–	Indiana	1947–	Bush

1. F—Federalist; DR—Democratic-Republican; D—Democratic; W—Whig; R—Republican; U—Union. 2. No party for first election. The party system in the U.S. made its appearance during Washington's first term as President. 3. Died in office. 4. Democratic-Republican with J. Q. Adams; Democratic with Jackson. Calhoun resigned in 1832 to become a U.S. Senator. 5. Succeeded to presidency on death of President. 6. Resigned Oct. 10, 1973, after pleading no contest to Federal income tax evasion charges. 7. Nominated by Nixon on Oct. 12, 1973, under provisions of 25th Amendment. Confirmed by Congress on Dec. 6, 1973, and was sworn in same day. He became President Aug. 9, 1974, upon Nixon's resignation. 8. Nominated by Ford Aug. 20, 1974; confirmed by Congress on Dec. 19, 1974, and was sworn in same day.

Burial Places of the Presidents

President	Burial place	President	Burial place
Washington	Mt. Vernon, Va.	Grant	New York City
J. Adams	Quincy, Mass.	Hayes	Fremont, Ohio
Jefferson	Charlottesville, Va.	Garfield	Cleveland, Ohio
Madison	Montpelier Station, Va.	Arthur	Albany, N.Y.
Monroe	Richmond, Va.	Cleveland	Princeton, N.J.
J. Q. Adams	Quincy, Mass.	B. Harrison	Indianapolis, Ind.
Jackson	The Hermitage, nr. Nashville, Tenn.	McKinley	Canton, Ohio
		T. Roosevelt	Oyster Bay, N.Y.
Van Buren	Kinderhook, N.Y.	Taft	Arlington National Cemetery
W. H. Harrison	North Bend, Ohio	Wilson	Washington National Cathedral
Tyler	Richmond, Va.	Harding	Marion, Ohio
Polk	Nashville, Tenn.	Coolidge	Plymouth, Vt.
Taylor	Louisville, Ky.	Hoover	West Branch, Iowa
Fillmore	Buffalo, N.Y.	F. D. Roosevelt	Hyde Park, N.Y.
Pierce	Concord, N.H.	Truman	Independence, Mo.
Buchanan	Lancaster, Pa.	Eisenhower	Abilene, Kan.
Lincoln	Springfield, Ill.	Kennedy	Arlington National Cemetery
A. Johnson	Greeneville, Tenn.	L. B. Johnson	Stonewall, Tex.

"In God We Trust"

"In God We Trust" first appeared on U.S. coins after April 22, 1864, when Congress passed an act authorizing the coinage of a 2-cent piece bearing this motto. Thereafter, Congress extended its use to other coins. On July 30, 1956, it became the national motto.

Wives and Children of the Presidents

President	Wife's name	Year an place of wife's birth	Married	Wife died	Children of President[1] Sons	Daughters
Washington	Martha Dandridge Custis	1732, Va.	1759	1802	—	—
John Adams	Abigail Smith	1744, Mass.	1764	1818	3	2
Jefferson	Martha Wayles Skelton	1748, Va.	1772	1782	1	5
Madison	Dorothy "Dolley" Payne Todd	1768, N.C.	1794	1849	—	—
Monroe	Elizabeth "Eliza" Kortright	1768, N.Y.	1786	1830	—	2
J. Q. Adams	Louisa Catherine Johnson	1775, England	1797	1852	3	1
Jackson	Mrs. Rachel Donelson Robards	1767, Va.	1791	1828	—	—
Van Buren	Hannah Hoes	1788, N.Y.	1807	1819	4	—
W. H. Harrison	Anna Symmes	1775, N.J.	1795	1864	6	4
Tyler	Letitia Christian	1790, Va.	1813	1842	3	4
	Julia Gardiner	1820, N.Y.	1844	1889	5	2
Polk	Sarah Childress	1803, Tenn.	1824	1891	—	—
Taylor	Margaret Smith	1788, Md.	1810	1852	1	5
Fillmore	Abigail Powers	1798, N.Y.	1826	1853	1	1
	Caroline Carmichael McIntosh	1813, N.J.	1858	1881	—	—
Pierce	Jane Means Appleton	1806, N.H.	1834	1863	3	—
Buchanan	(Unmarried)	—	—	—	—	—
Lincoln	Mary Todd	1818, Ky.	1842	1882	4	—
A. Johnson	Eliza McCardle	1810, Tenn.	1827	1876	3	2
Grant	Julia Dent	1826, Mo.	1848	1902	3	1
Hayes	Lucy Ware Webb	1831, Ohio	1852	1889	7	1
Garfield	Lucretia Rudolph	1832, Ohio	1858	1918	5	2
Arthur	Ellen Lewis Herndon	1837, Va.	1859	1880	2	1
Cleveland	Frances Folsom	1864, N.Y.	1886	1947	2	3
B. Harrison	Caroline Lavinia Scott	1832, Ohio	1853	1892	1	1
	Mary Scott Lord Dimmick	1858, Pa.	1896	1948	—	1
McKinley	Ida Saxton	1847, Ohio	1871	1907	—	2
T. Roosevelt	Alice Hathaway Lee	1861, Mass.	1880	1884	—	1
	Edith Kermit Carow	1861, Conn.	1886	1948	4	1
Taft	Helen Herron	1861, Ohio	1886	1943	2	1
Wilson	Ellen Louise Axson	1860, Ga.	1885	1914	—	3
	Edith Bolling Galt	1872, Va.	1915	1961	—	—
Harding	Florence Kling DeWolfe	1860, Ohio	1891	1924	—	—
Coolidge	Grace Anna Goodhue	1879, Vt.	1905	1957	2	—
Hoover	Lou Henry	1875, Iowa	1899	1944	2	—
F. D. Roosevelt	Anna Eleanor Roosevelt	1884, N.Y.	1905	1962	5	1
Truman	Bess Wallace	1885, Mo.	1919	1982	—	1
Eisenhower	Mamie Geneva Doud	1896, Iowa	1916	1979	2	—
Kennedy	Jacqueline Lee Bouvier	1929, N.Y.	1953		—	2
L. B. Johnson	Claudia Alta "Lady Bird" Taylor	1912, Tex.	1934		—	2
Nixon	Thelma Catherine "Pat" Ryan	1912, Nev.	1940		—	2
Ford	Elizabeth "Betty" Bloomer Warren	1918, Ill.	1948		—	3	1
Carter	Rosalynn Smith	1928, Ga.	1946		—	3	1
Reagan	Jane Wyman	1914, Mo.	1940[2]		—	1[3]	1
	Nancy Davis	1921 (?)[4], N.Y.	1952		—	1	1
Bush	Barbara Pierce	1925, N.Y.	1945		—	4	2

1. Includes children who died in infancy. 2. Divorced in 1948. 3. Adopted. 4. Birthday officially given as 1923 but her high school and college records show 1921 for year of birth.

Elections

How a President Is Nominated and Elected

The National Conventions of both major parties are held during the summer of a presidential-election year. Earlier, each party selects delegates by primaries, conventions, committees, etc.

For their 1992 National Convention, the Republicans allow each state a base of 6 delegates at large; the District of Columbia, 14; Puerto Rico, 14; Guam and the Virgin Islands, 4 each. In addition, each state receives 3 district delegates for each representative it has in the House of Representatives, regardless of po-

litical affiliation. This did not apply to the District of Columbia, Puerto Rico, Guam and the Virgin Islands.

Each state is awarded additional delegates at large on the basis of having supported the Republican candidate for President in 1988 and electing Republican candidates for Senator, Governor, and U.S. Representative between 1988 and 1991 inclusive.

The number of delegates at the 1992 convention, to be held in Houston starting August 17, will be 2,206.[1]

Following is the apportionment of delegates:

Alabama	38	Florida	97	Kentucky	35	Montana	20	Ohio	83	Texas	121
Alaska	19	Georgia	52	Louisiana	38	Nebraska	24	Oklahoma	34	Utah	27
Arizona	37	Guam	4	Maine	22	Nevada	21	Oregon	23	Vermont	19
Arkansas	27	Hawaii	14	Maryland	42	N.H.	23	Pa.	90	V.I.	4
California	201	Idaho	22	Mass.	38	N. Jersey	60	P.R.	14	Virginia	54
Colorado	37	Illinois	85	Michigan	72	New Mexico	25	R.I.	15	Washington	35
Connecticut	35	Indiana	51	Minnesota	32	New York	100	S.C.	36	W. Va.	18
Delaware	19	Iowa	23	Mississippi	32	N.C.	57	S.D.	19	Wisconsin	35
D.C.	14	Kansas	30	Missouri	47	N.D.	17	Tennessee	45	Wyoming	20

1. Includes 4 delegates from American Samoa.

The Democrats base the number of delegates on a state's showing in the 1988 and 1990 elections. At the 1992 convention, to be held in New York starting July 13, there will be 4,313[1,2] delegates casting 4,282 votes. Following is the apportionment by states:

Alabama	62	Florida	160	Kentucky	62	Montana	22	Ohio	167	Texas	214
Alaska	18	Georgia	88	Louisiana	69	Nebraska	31	Oklahoma	52	Utah	28
Arizona	47	Guam	10[1]	Maine	30	Nevada	23	Oregon	53	Vermont	19
Arkansas	43	Hawaii	26	Maryland	80	N. H.	24	Pa.	188	V.I.	10[1]
California	382	Idaho	24	Mass.	107	New Jersey	117	P.R.	57	Virginia	92
Colorado	54	Illinois	183	Michigan	148	New Mexico	33	R.I.	28	Washington	80
Connecticut	61	Indiana	86	Minnesota	87	New York	268	S.C.	50	W. Va.	38
Delaware	19	Iowa	57	Mississippi	45	N.C.	93	S.D.	20	Wisconsin	91
D. C.	29	Kansas	42	Missouri	86	N.D.	20	Tennessee	77	Wyoming	19

1. Fractional votes. 2. Includes 22[1] delegates for Democrats Abroad and 10[1] for American Samoa. As of March 26, 1991.

The Conventions

At each convention, a temporary chairman is chosen. After a credentials committee seats the delegates, a permanent chairman is elected. The convention then votes on a platform, drawn up by the platform committee.

By the third or fourth day, presidential nominations begin. The chairman calls the roll of states alphabetically. A state may place a candidate in nomination or yield to another state.

Voting, again alphabetically by roll call of states, begins after all nominations have been made and seconded. A simple majority is required in each party, although this may require many ballots.

Finally, the vice-presidential candidate is selected. Although there is no law saying that the candidates *must* come from different states, it is, practically, necessary for this to be the case. Otherwise, according to the Constitution (*see* Amendment XII), electors from that state could vote for only one of the candidates and would have to cast their other vote for some person of another state. This could result in a presidential candidate's receiving a majority electoral vote and his running mate's failing to.

The Electoral College

The next step in the process is the nomination of electors in each state, according to its laws. These electors must not be Federal office holders. In the November election, the voters cast their votes for electors, not for President. In some states, the ballots include only the names of the presidential and vice-presidential candidates; in others, they include only names of the electors. Nowadays, it is rare for electors to be split between parties. The last such occurrence was in North Carolina in 1968[1]; the last before that, in Tennessee in 1948. On three occasions (1824, 1876, and 1888), the presidential candidate with the largest popular vote failed to obtain an electoral-vote majority.

Each state has as many electors as it has Senators and Representatives. For the 1988 election, the total electors were 538, based on 100 Senators, 435 Representatives, plus 3 electoral votes from the District of Columbia as a result of the 23rd Amendment to the Constitution.

On the first Monday after the second Wednesday in December, the electors cast their votes in their respective state capitols. Constitutionally they may vote for someone other than the party candidate but usually they do not since they are pledged to one party and its candidate on the ballot. Should the presidential or vice-presidential candidate die between the November election and the December meetings, the electors pledged to vote for him could vote for whomever they pleased. However, it seems certain that the national committee would attempt to get an agreement among the state party leaders for a replacement candidate.

The votes of the electors, certified by the states, are sent to Congress, where the president of the Senate opens the certificates and has them counted in the presence of both Houses on January 6. The new President is inaugurated at noon on January 20.

Should no candidate receive a majority of the electoral vote for President, the House of Representatives chooses a President from among the three highest candidates, voting, not as individuals, but as states, with a majority (now 26) needed to elect. Should no vice-presidential candidate obtain the majority, the Senate, voting as individuals, chooses from the highest two.

1. In 1956, 1 of Alabama's 11 electoral votes was cast for Walter B. Jones. In 1960, 6 of Alabama's 11 electoral votes and 1 of Oklahoma's 8 electoral votes were cast for Harry Flood Byrd. (Byrd also received all 8 of Mississippi's electoral votes.)

Presidential Elections, 1789 to 1988

For the original method of electing the President and the Vice President (elections of 1789, 1792, 1796, and 1800), see Article II, Section 1, of the Constitution. The election of 1804 was the first one in which the electors voted for President and Vice President on separate ballots. (See Amendment XII to the Constitution.)

Year	Presidential candidates	Party	Electoral vote	Year	Vice-presidential candidates	Party	Electoral vote
1789[1]	George Washington	(no party)	69	1796	John Adams	Federalist	71
	John Adams	(no party)	34		Thomas Jefferson	Dem.-Rep.	68
	Scattering	(no party)	35		Thomas Pinckney	Federalist	59
	Votes not cast		8		Aaron Burr	Dem.-Rep.	30
					Scattering		48
1792	George Washington	Federalist	132				
	John Adams	Federalist	77	1800[2]	Thomas Jefferson	Dem.-Rep.	73
	George Clinton	Anti-Federalist	50		Aaron Burr	Dem.-Rep.	73
	Thomas Jefferson	Anti-Federalist	4		John Adams	Federalist	65
	Aaron Burr	Anti-Federalist	1		Charles C. Pinckney	Federalist	64
	Votes not cast		6		John Jay	Federalist	1

Year	Presidential candidates	Party	Electoral vote	Vice-presidential candidates	Party	Electoral vote
1804	Thomas Jefferson	Dem.-Rep.	162	George Clinton	Dem.-Rep.	162
	Charles C. Pinckney	Federalist	14	Rufus King	Federalist	14
1808	James Madison	Dem.-Rep.	122	George Clinton	Dem.-Rep.	113
	Charles C. Pinckney	Federalist	47	Rufus King	Federalist	47
	George Clinton	Dem.-Rep.	6	John Langdon	Ind. (no party)	9
	Votes not cast		1	James Madison	Dem.-Rep.	3
				James Monroe	Dem.-Rep.	3
				Votes not cast		1
1812	James Madison	Dem.-Rep.	128	Elbridge Gerry	Dem.-Rep.	131
	De Witt Clinton	Federalist	89	Jared Ingersoll	Federalist	86
	Votes not cast		1	Votes not cast		1
1816	James Monroe	Dem.-Rep.	183	Daniel D. Tompkins	Dem.-Rep.	183
	Rufus King	Federalist	34	John E. Howard	Federalist	22
	Votes not cast		4	James Ross	Ind. (no party)	5
				John Marshall	Federalist	4
				Robert G. Harper	Ind. (no party)	3
				Votes not cast		4
1820	James Monroe	Dem-Rep	231	Daniel D. Tompkins	Dem.-Rep.	218
	John Quincy Adams	Ind. (no party)	1	Richard Stockton	Ind. (no party)	8
	Votes not cast		3	Daniel Rodney	Ind. (no party)	4
				Richard Rush	Ind. (no party)	1
				Robert G. Harper	Ind. (no party)	1
				Votes not cast		3
1824[3]	John Quincy Adams	(no party)	84	John C. Calhoun	(no party)	182
	Andrew Jackson	(no party)	99	Nathan Sanford	(no party)	30
	William H. Crawford	(no party)	41	Nathaniel Macon	(no party)	24
	Henry Clay	(no party)	37	Andrew Jackson	(no party)	13
				Martin Van Buren	(no party)	9
				Henry Clay	(no party)	2
				Votes not cast		1
1828	Andrew Jackson	Democratic	178	John C. Calhoun	Democratic	171
	John Quincy Adams	Natl. Rep.	83	Richard Rush	Natl. Rep.	83
				William Smith	Democratic	7
1832	Andrew Jackson	Democratic	219	Martin Van Buren	Democratic	189
	Henry Clay	Natl. Rep.	49	John Sergeant	Natl. Rep.	49
	John Floyd	Ind. (no party)	11	Henry Lee	Ind. (no party)	11
	William Wirt	Antimasonic[4]	7	Amos Ellmaker	Antimasonic	7
	Votes not cast		2	William Wilkins	Ind. (no party)	30
				Votes not cast		2

Year	Presidential candidates	Party	Electoral vote	Vice-presidential candidates	Party	Electoral vote
1836	Martin Van Buren	Democratic	170	Richard M. Johnson[5]	Democratic	147
	William H. Harrison	Whig	73	Francis Granger	Whig	77
	Hugh L. White	Whig	26	John Tyler	Whig	47
	Daniel Webster	Whig	14	William Smith	Ind. (no party)	23
	W. P. Mangum	Ind. (no party)	11			
1840	William H. Harrison[6]	Whig	234	John Tyler	Whig	234
	Martin Van Buren	Democratic	60	Richard M. Johnson	Democratic	48
				L. W. Tazewell	Ind. (no party)	11
				James K. Polk	Democratic	1
1844	James K. Polk	Democratic	170	George M. Dallas	Democratic	170
	Henry Clay	Whig	105	Theo. Frelinghuysen	Whig	105
1848	Zachary Taylor[7]	Whig	163	Millard Fillmore	Whig	163
	Lewis Cass	Democratic	127	William O. Butler	Democratic	127
1852	Franklin Pierce	Democratic	254	William R. King	Democratic	254
	Winfield Scott	Whig	42	William A. Graham	Whig	42
1856	James Buchanan	Democratic	174	John C. Breckinridge	Democratic	174
	John C. Fremont	Republican	114	William L. Dayton	Republican	114
	Millard Fillmore	American[8]	8	A. J. Donelson	American[8]	8
1860	Abraham Lincoln	Republican	180	Hannibal Hamlin	Republican	180
	John C. Breckinridge	Democratic	72	Joseph Lane	Democratic	72
	John Bell	Const. Union	39	Edward Everett	Const. Union	39
	Stephen A. Douglas	Democratic	12	H. V. Johnson	Democratic	12
1864	Abraham Lincoln[9]	Union[10]	212	Andrew Johnson	Union[15]	212
	George B. McClellan	Democratic	21	G. H. Pendleton	Democratic	21
1868	Ulysses S. Grant	Republican	214	Schuyler Colfax	Republican	214
	Horatio Seymour	Democratic	80	Francis P. Blair, Jr.	Democratic	80
	Votes not counted[11]		23	Votes not counted[11]		23

Year	Presidential candidates	Party	Electoral vote	Popular vote	Vice-presidential candidates and party
1872	Ulysses S. Grant	Republican	286	3,597,132	Henry Wilson—R
	Horace Greeley	Dem., Liberal Rep.	([12])	2,834,125	B. Gratz Brown—D, LR—(47)
	Thomas A. Hendricks	Democratic	42		Scattering—(19)
	B. Gratz Brown	Dem., Liberal Rep.	18		Votes not counted—(14)
	Charles J. Jenkins	Democratic	2		
	David Davis	Democratic	1		
	Votes not counted		17		
1876[13]	Rutherford B. Hayes	Republican	185	4,033,768	William A. Wheeler—R
	Samuel J. Tilden	Democratic	184	4,285,992	Thomas A. Hendricks—D
	Peter Cooper	Greenback	0	81,737	Samuel F. Cary—G
1880	James A. Garfield[14]	Republican	214	4,449,053	Chester A. Arthur—R
	Winfield S. Hancock	Democratic	155	4,442,035	William H. English—D
	James B. Weaver	Greenback	0	308,578	B. J. Chambers—G
1884	Grover Cleveland	Democratic	219	4,911,017	Thomas A. Hendricks—D
	James G. Blaine	Republican	182	4,848,334	John A. Logan—R
	Benjamin F. Butler	Greenback	0	175,370	A. M. West—G
	John P. St. John	Prohibition	0	150,369	William Daniel—P
1888	Benjamin Harrison	Republican	233	5,440,216	Levi P. Morton—R
	Grover Cleveland	Democratic	168	5,538,233	A. G. Thurman—D
	Clinton B. Fisk	Prohibition	0	249,506	John A. Brooks—P
	Alson J. Streeter	Union Labor	0	146,935	Charles E. Cunningham—UL
1892	Grover Cleveland	Democratic	277	5,556,918	Adlai E. Stevenson—D
	Benjamin Harrison	Republican	145	5,176,108	Whitelaw Reid—R
	James B. Weaver	People's[15]	22	1,041,028	James G. Field—Peo
	John Bidwell	Prohibition	0	264,133	James B. Cranfill—P

Year	Presidential candidates	Party	Electoral vote	Popular vote	Vice-presidential candidates and party
1896	William McKinley	Republican	271	7,035,638	Garret A. Hobart—R
	William J. Bryan	Dem., People's[15]	176	6,467,946	Arthur Sewall—D—(149)
					Thomas E. Watson—Peo—(27)
	John M. Palmer	Natl. Dem.	0	133,148	Simon B. Buckner—ND
	Joshua Levering	Prohibition	0	132,007	Hale Johnson—P
1900	William McKinley[16]	Republican	292	7,219,530	Theodore Roosevelt—R
	William J. Bryan	Dem., People's[15]	155	6,358,071	Adlai E. Stevenson—D, Peo
	Eugene V. Debs	Social Democratic	0	94,768	Job Harriman—SD
1904	Theodore Roosevelt	Republican	336	7,628,834	Charles W. Fairbanks—R
	Alton B. Parker	Democratic	140	5,084,491	Henry G. Davis—D
	Eugene V. Debs	Socialist	0	402,400	Benjamin Hanford—S
1908	William H. Taft	Republican	321	7,679,006	James S. Sherman—R
	William J. Bryan	Democratic	162	6,409,106	John W. Kern—D
	Eugene V. Debs	Socialist	0	402,820	Benjamin Hanford—S
1912	Woodrow Wilson	Democratic	435	6,286,214	Thomas R. Marshall—D
	Theodore Roosevelt	Progressive	88	4,126,020	Hiram Johnson—Prog
	William H. Taft	Republican	8	3,483,922	Nicholas M. Butler—R[17]
	Eugene V. Debs	Socialist	0	897,011	Emil Seidel—S
1916	Woodrow Wilson	Democratic	277	9,129,606	Thomas R. Marshall—D
	Charles E. Hughes	Republican	254	8,538,221	Charles W. Fairbanks—R
	A. L. Benson	Socialist	0	585,113	G. R. Kirkpatrick—S
1920	Warren G. Harding[18]	Republican	404	16,152,200	Calvin Coolidge—R
	James M. Cox	Democratic	127	9,147,353	Franklin D. Roosevelt—D
	Eugene V. Debs	Socialist	0	917,799	Seymour Stedman—S
1924	Calvin Coolidge	Republican	382	15,725,016	Charles G. Dawes—R
	John W. Davis	Democratic	136	8,385,586	Charles W. Bryan—D
	Robert M. LaFollette	Progressive, Socialist	13	4,822,856	Burton K. Wheeler—Prog S
1928	Herbert Hoover	Republican	444	21,392,190	Charles Curtis—R
	Alfred E. Smith	Democratic	87	15,016,443	Joseph T. Robinson—D
	Norman Thomas	Socialist	0	267,420	James H. Maurer—S
1932	Franklin D. Roosevelt	Democratic	472	22,821,857	John N. Garner—D
	Herbert Hoover	Republican	59	15,761,841	Charles Curtis—R
	Norman Thomas	Socialist	0	884,781	James H. Maurer—S
1936	Franklin D. Roosevelt	Democratic	523	27,751,597	John N. Garner—D
	Alfred M. Landon	Republican	8	16,679,583	Frank Knox—R
	Norman Thomas	Socialist	0	187,720	George Nelson—S
1940	Franklin D. Roosevelt	Democratic	449	27,244,160	Henry A. Wallace—D
	Wendell L. Willkie	Republican	82	22,305,198	Charles L. McNary—R
	Norman Thomas	Socialist	0	99,557	Maynard C. Krueger—S
1944	Franklin D. Roosevelt[19]	Democratic	432	25,602,504	Harry S. Truman—D
	Thomas E. Dewey	Republican	99	22,006,285	John W. Bricker—R
	Norman Thomas	Socialist	0	80,518	Darlington Hoopes—S
1948	Harry S. Truman	Democratic	303	24,179,345	Alben W. Barkley—D
	Thomas E. Dewey	Republican	189	21,991,291	Earl Warren—R
	J. Strom Thurmond	States' Rights Dem.	39	1,176,125	Fielding L. Wright—SR
	Henry A. Wallace	Progressive	0	1,157,326	Glen Taylor—Prog
	Norman Thomas	Socialist	0	139,572	Tucker P. Smith—S
1952	Dwight D. Eisenhower	Republican	442	33,936,234	Richard M. Nixon—R
	Adlai E. Stevenson	Democratic	89	27,314,992	John J. Sparkman—D
1956	Dwight D. Eisenhower	Republican	457	35,590,472	Richard M. Nixon—R
	Adlai E. Stevenson	Democratic	73[20]	26,022,752	Estes Kefauver—D
1960	John F. Kennedy[22]	Democratic	303	34,226,731	Lyndon B. Johnson—D
	Richard M. Nixon	Republican	219[21]	34,108,157	Henry Cabot Lodge—R

Year	Presidential candidates	Party	Electoral vote	Popular vote	Vice-presidential candidates and party
1964	Lyndon B. Johnson	Democratic	486	43,129,484	Hubert H. Humphrey—D
	Barry M. Goldwater	Republican	52	27,178,188	William E. Miller—R
1968	Richard M. Nixon	Republican	301	31,785,480	Spiro T. Agnew—R
	Hubert H. Humphrey	Democratic	191	31,275,166	Edmund S. Muskie—D
	George C. Wallace	American Independent	46	9,906,473	Curtis F. LeMay—AI
1972	Richard M. Nixon[23]	Republican	520[24]	47,169,911	Spiro T. Agnew—R
	George McGovern	Democratic	17	29,170,383	Sargent Shriver—D
	John G. Schmitz	American	0	1,099,482	Thomas J. Anderson—A
1976	Jimmy Carter	Democratic	297	40,830,763	Walter F. Mondale—D
	Gerald R. Ford	Republican	240[25]	39,147,973	Robert J. Dole—R
	Eugene J. McCarthy	Independent	0	756,631	None
1980	Ronald Reagan	Republican	489	43,899,248	George Bush—R
	Jimmy Carter	Democratic	49	36,481,435	Walter F. Mondale—D
	John B. Anderson	Independent	0	5,719,437	Patrick J. Lucey—I
1984	Ronald Reagan	Republican	525	54,455,075	George Bush—R
	Walter F. Mondale	Democratic	13	37,577,185	Geraldine A. Ferraro—D
1988	George H. Bush	Republican	426	48,886,097	J. Danforth Quayle—R
	Michael S. Dukakis	Democratic	111[26]	41,809,074	Lloyd Bentsen—D

1. Only 10 states participated in the election. The New York legislature chose no electors, and North Carolina and Rhode Island had not yet ratified the Constitution. 2. As Jefferson and Burr were tied, the House of Representatives chose the President. In a vote by states, 10 votes were cast for Jefferson, 4 for Burr; 2 votes were not cast. 3. As no candidate had an electoral-vote majority, the House of Representatives chose the President from the first three. In a vote by states, 13 votes were cast for Adams, 7 for Jackson, and 4 for Crawford. 4. The Antimasonic Party on Sept. 26, 1831, was the first party to hold a nominating convention to choose candidates for President and Vice-President. 5. As Johnson did not have an electoral-vote majority, the Senate chose him 33–14 over Granger, the others being legally out of the race. 6. Harrison died April 4, 1841, and Tyler succeeded him April 6. 7. Taylor died July 9, 1850, and Fillmore succeeded him July 10. 8. Also known as the Know-Nothing Party. 9. Lincoln died April 15, 1865, and Johnson succeeded him the same day. 10. Name adopted by the Republican National Convention of 1864. Johnson was a War Democrat. 11. 23 Southern electoral votes were excluded. 12. See Election of 1872 in *Unusual Voting Results*, page 122. 13. See Election of 1876 in *Unusual Voting Results*, page 122. 14. Garfield died Sept. 19, 1881, and Arthur succeeded him Sept. 20. 15. Members of People's Party were called Populists. 16. McKinley died Sept. 14, 1901, and Roosevelt succeeded him the same day. 17. James S. Sherman, Republican candidate for Vice President, died Oct. 30, 1912, and the Republican electoral votes were cast for Butler. 18. Harding died Aug. 2, 1923, and Coolidge succeeded him Aug. 3. 19. Roosevelt died April 12, 1945, and Truman succeeded him the same day. 20. One electoral vote from Alabama was cast for Walter B. Jones. 21. Sen. Harry F. Byrd received 15 electoral votes. 22. Kennedy died Nov. 22, 1963, and Johnson succeeded him the same day. 23. Nixon resigned Aug. 9, 1974, and Gerald R. Ford succeeded him the same day. 24. One electoral vote from Virginia was cast for John Hospers, Libertarian Party. 25. One electoral vote from Washington was cast for Ronald Reagan. 26. One electoral vote from West Virginia was cast for Lloyd Bentsen.

Characteristics of Voters in 1988 Presidential Election

(in thousands)

Characteristic	Persons of voting age	Persons reporting they voted Total	Percent	Persons reporting they did not vote	Characteristic	Persons of voting age	Persons reporting they voted Total	Percent	Persons reporting they did not vote
Male	84,531	47,704	56.4	36,826	North and West	117,373	69,129	58.9	48,243
Female	93,568	54,519	58.3	39,048	South	60,725	33,094	54.5	27,631
White	152,848	90,357	59.1	62,492	Education				
Black	19,692	10,144	51.5	9,548	8 years or less	19,145	7,025	36.7	12,120
Hispanic origin[1]	12,893	3,710	28.8	9,183	9–11 years	21,052	8,698	41.3	12,354
Age: 18–20	10,742	3,570	33.2	7,172	12 years	70,033	38,328	54.7	31,706
21–24	14,827	5,684	38.3	9,142	13–15 years	34,264	22,090	64.5	12,174
25–34	42,677	20,468	48.0	22,210	16 or more	33,604	26,083	77.6	7,521
35–44	35,186	21,550	61.2	13,636	Employed	113,836	66,510	58.4	47,327
45–54	24,277	16,170	66.6	8,107	Unemployed	5,809	2,243	38.6	3,565
55–64	21,585	14,964	69.3	6,621	Not in labor force	58,453	33,471	57.3	24,983
65–74	17,578	12,840	73.0	4,738	**Total**	**178,098**	**102,224**	**57.4**	**75,875**
75 and over	11,226	6,978	62.2	4,248					

1. Persons of Hispanic origin may be of any race. *Source:* Department of Commerce, Bureau of Commerce, Bureau of the Census, *Current Population Survey,* November 1988.

Cabinet Members

Although the Constitution made no provision for a President's advisory group, the heads of the three executive departments (State, Treasury, and War) and the Attorney General were organized by Washington into such a group; and by about 1793, the name "Cabinet" was applied to it. With the exception of the Attorney General up to 1870 and the Postmaster General from 1829 to 1872, Cabinet members have been heads of executive departments.

A Cabinet member is appointed by the President, subject to the confirmation of the Senate; and as his term is not fixed, he may be replaced at any time by the President. At a change in Administration, it is customary for him to tender his resignation, but he remains in office until a successor is appointed.

The table of Cabinet members lists only those members who actually served after being duly commissioned.

The dates shown are those of appointment. "Cont." indicates that the term continued from the previous Administration for a substantial amount of time.

With the creation of the Department of Transportation in 1966, the Cabinet consisted of 12 members. This figure was reduced to 11 when the Post Office Department became an independent agency in 1970 but, with the establishment in 1977 of a Department of Energy, became 12 again. Creation of the Department of Education in 1980 raised the number to 13. Creation of the Department of Veterans' Affairs in 1989 raised the number to 14.

WASHINGTON

Secretary of State	Thomas Jefferson 1789
	Edmund Randolph 1794
	Timothy Pickering 1795
Secretary of the Treasury	Alexander Hamilton 1789
	Oliver Wolcott, Jr. 1795
Secretary of War	Henry Knox 1789
	Timothy Pickering 1795
	James McHenry 1796
Attorney General	Edmund Randolph 1789
	William Bradford 1794
	Charles Lee 1795

J. ADAMS

Secretary of State	Timothy Pickering (Cont.)
	John Marshall 1800
Secretary of the Treasury	Oliver Wolcott, Jr. (Cont.)
	Samuel Dexter 1801
Secretary of War	James McHenry (Cont.)
	Samuel Dexter 1800
Attorney General	Charles Lee (Cont.)
Secretary of the Navy	Benjamin Stoddert 1798

JEFFERSON

Secretary of State	James Madison 1801
Secretary of the Treasury	Samuel Dexter (Cont.)
	Albert Gallatin 1801
Secretary of War	Henry Dearborn 1801
Attorney General	Levi Lincoln 1801
	Robert Smith 1805
	John Breckinridge 1805
	Caesar A. Rodney 1807
Secretary of the Navy	Benjamin Stoddert (Cont.)
	Robert Smith 1801

MADISON

Secretary of State	Robert Smith 1809
	James Monroe 1811
Secretary of the Treasury	Albert Gallatin (Cont.)
	George W. Campbell 1814
	Alexander J. Dallas 1814
	William H. Crawford 1816
Secretary of War	William Eustis 1809
	John Armstrong 1813
	James Monroe 1814
	William H. Crawford 1815
Attorney General	Caesar A. Rodney (Cont.)
	William Pinckney 1811
	Richard Rush 1814
Secretary of the Navy	Paul Hamilton 1809
	William Jones 1813
	B. W. Crowninshield 1814

MONROE

Secretary of State	John Quincy Adams 1817
Secretary of the Treasury	William H. Crawford (Cont.)
Secretary of War	John C. Calhoun 1817
Attorney General	Richard Rush (Cont.)
	William Wirt 1817

Secretary of the Navy	B. W. Crowninshield (Cont.)
	Smith Thompson 1818
	Samuel L. Southard 1823

J. Q. ADAMS

Secretary of State	Henry Clay 1825
Secretary of the Treasury	Richard Rush 1825
Secretary of War	James Barbour 1825
	Peter B. Porter 1828
Attorney General	William Wirt (Cont.)
Secretary of the Navy	Samuel L. Southard (Cont.)

JACKSON

Secretary of State	Martin Van Buren 1829
	Edward Livingston 1831
	Louis McLane 1833
	John Forsyth 1834
Secretary of the Treasury	Samuel D. Ingham 1829
	Louis McLane 1831
	William J. Duane 1833
	Roger B. Taney[3] 1833
	Levi Woodbury 1834
Secretary of War	John H. Eaton 1829
	Lewis Cass 1831
Attorney General	John M. Berrien 1829
	Roger B. Taney 1831
	Benjamin F. Butler 1833
Postmaster General[1]	William T. Barry 1829
	Amos Kendall 1835
Secretary of the Navy	John Branch 1829
	Levi Woodbury 1831
	Mahlon Dickerson 1834

VAN BUREN

Secretary of State	John Forsyth (Cont.)
Secretary of the Treasury	Levi Woodbury (Cont.)
Secretary of War	Joel R. Poinsett 1837
Attorney General	Benjamin F. Butler (Cont.)
	Felix Grundy 1838
	Henry D. Gilpin 1840
Postmaster General	Amos Kendall (Cont.)
	John M. Niles 1840
Secretary of the Navy	Mahlon Dickerson (Cont.)
	James K. Paulding 1838

W. H. HARRISON

Secretary of State	Daniel Webster 1841
Secretary of the Treasury	Thomas Ewing 1841
Secretary of War	John Bell 1841
Attorney General	John J. Crittenden 1841
Postmaster General	Francis Granger 1841
Secretary of the Navy	George E. Badger 1841

TYLER

Secretary of State	Daniel Webster (Cont.)
	Abel P. Upshur 1843
	John C. Calhoun 1844
Secretary of the Treasury	Thomas Ewing (Cont.)
	Walter Forward 1841

	John C. Spencer[3] 1843
	George M. Bibb 1844
Secretary of War	John Bell (Cont.)
	John C. Spencer 1841
	James M. Porter[3] 1843
	William Wilkins 1844
Attorney General	John J. Crittenden (Cont.)
	Hugh S. Legaré 1841
	John Nelson 1843
Postmaster General	Francis Granger (Cont.)
	Charles A. Wickliffe 1841
Secretary of the Navy	George E. Badger (Cont.)
	Abel P. Upshur 1841
	David Henshaw[3] 1843
	Thomas W. Gilmer 1844
	John Y. Mason 1844

POLK

Secretary of State	James Buchanan 1845
Secretary of the Treasury	Robert J. Walker 1845
Secretary of War	William L. Marcy 1845
Attorney General	John Y. Mason 1845
	Nathan Clifford 1846
	Isaac Toucey 1848
Postmaster General	Cave Johnson 1845
Secretary of the Navy	George Bancroft 1845
	John Y. Mason 1846

TAYLOR

Secretary of State	John M. Clayton 1849
Secretary of the Treasury	William M. Meredith 1849
Secretary of War	George W. Crawford 1849
Attorney General	Reverdy Johnson 1849
Postmaster General	Jacob Collamer 1849
Secretary of the Navy	William B. Preston 1849
Secretary of the Interior	Thomas Ewing 1849

FILLMORE

Secretary of State	Daniel Webster 1850
	Edward Everett 1852
Secretary of the Treasury	Thomas Corwin 1850
Secretary of War	Charles M. Conrad 1850
Attorney General	John J. Crittenden 1850
Postmaster General	Nathan K. Hall 1850
	Samuel D. Hubbard 1852
Secretary of the Navy	William A. Graham 1850
	John P. Kennedy 1852
Secretary of the Interior	Thos. M. T. McKennan 1850
	Alex. H. H. Stuart 1850

PIERCE

Secretary of State	William L. Marcy 1853
Secretary of the Treasury	James Guthrie 1853
Secretary of War	Jefferson Davis 1853
Attorney General	Caleb Cushing 1853
Postmaster General	James Campbell 1853
Secretary of the Navy	James C. Dobbin 1853
Secretary of the Interior	Robert McClelland 1853

BUCHANAN

Secretary of State	Lewis Cass 1857
	Jeremiah S. Black 1860
Secretary of the Treasury	Howell Cobb 1857
	Philip F. Thomas 1860
	John A. Dix 1861
Secretary of War	John B. Floyd 1857
	Joseph Holt 1861
Attorney General	Jeremiah S. Black 1857
	Edwin M. Stanton 1860
Postmaster General	Aaron V. Brown 1857
	Joseph Holt 1859
	Horatio King 1861
Secretary of the Navy	Isaac Toucey 1857
Secretary of the Interior	Jacob Thompson 1857

LINCOLN

Secretary of State	William H. Seward 1861
Secretary of the Treasury	Salmon P. Chase 1861
	William P. Fessenden 1864
	Hugh McCulloch 1865

Secretary of War	Simon Cameron 1861
	Edwin M. Stanton 1862
Attorney General	Edward Bates 1861
	James Speed 1864
Postmaster General	Montgomery Blair 1861
	William Dennison 1864
Secretary of the Navy	Gideon Welles 1861
Secretary of the Interior	Caleb B. Smith 1861
	John P. Usher 1863

A. JOHNSON

Secretary of State	William H. Seward (Cont.)
Secretary of the Treasury	Hugh McCulloch (Cont.)
Secretary of War	Edwin M. Stanton (Cont.)
	John M. Schofield 1868
Attorney General	James Speed (Cont.)
	Henry Stanbery 1866
	William M. Evarts 1868
Postmaster General	William Dennison (Cont.)
	Alexander W. Randall 1866
Secretary of the Navy	Gideon Welles (Cont.)
Secretary of the Interior	John P. Usher (Cont.)
	James Harlan 1865
	Orville H. Browning 1866

GRANT

Secretary of State	Elihu B. Washburne 1869
	Hamilton Fish 1869
Secretary of the Treasury	George S. Boutwell 1869
	William A. Richardson 1873
	Benjamin H. Bristow 1874
	Lot M. Morrill 1876
Secretary of War	John A. Rawlins 1869
	William W. Belknap 1869
	Alphonso Taft 1876
	James D. Cameron 1876
Attorney General	Ebenezer R. Hoar 1869
	Amos T. Akerman 1870
	George H. Williams 1871
	Edwards Pierrepont 1875
	Alphonso Taft 1876
Postmaster General	John A. J. Creswell 1869
	Marshall Jewell 1874
	James N. Tyner 1876
Secretary of the Navy	Adolph E. Borie 1869
	George M. Robeson 1869
Secretary of the Interior	Jacob D. Cox 1869
	Columbus Delano 1870
	Zachariah Chandler 1875

HAYES

Secretary of State	William M. Evarts 1877
Secretary of the Treasury	John Sherman 1877
Secretary of War	George W. McCrary 1877
	Alexander Ramsey 1879
Attorney General	Charles Devens 1877
Postmaster General	David M. Key 1877
	Horace Maynard 1880
	Richard W. Thompson 1877
	Nathan Goff, Jr. 1881
Secretary of the Interior	Carl Schurz 1877

GARFIELD

Secretary of State	James G. Blaine 1881
Secretary of the Treasury	William Windom 1881
Secretary of War	Robert T. Lincoln 1881
Attorney General	Wayne MacVeagh 1881
Postmaster General	Thomas L. James 1881
Secretary of the Navy	William H. Hunt 1881
Secretary of the Interior	Samuel J. Kirkwood 1881

ARTHUR

Secretary of State	James G. Blaine (Cont.)
	F. T. Frelinghuysen 1881
Secretary of the Treasury	William Windom (Cont.)
	Charles J. Folger 1881
	Walter Q. Gresham 1884
	Hugh McCulloch 1884
Secretary of War	Robert T. Lincoln (Cont.)
Attorney General	Wayne MacVeagh (Cont.)
	Benjamin H. Brewster 1881
Postmaster General	Thomas L. James (Cont.)

	Timothy O. Howe 1881
	Walter Q. Gresham 1883
	Frank Hatton 1884
Secretary of the Navy	William H. Hunt (Cont.)
	William E. Chandler 1882
Secretary of the Interior	Samuel J. Kirkwood (Cont.)
	Henry M. Teller 1882

CLEVELAND

Secretary of State	Thomas F. Bayard 1885
Secretary of the Treasury	Daniel Manning 1885
	Charles S. Fairchild 1887
Secretary of War	William C. Endicott 1885
Attorney General	Augustus H. Garland 1885
Postmaster General	William F. Vilas 1885
	Don M. Dickinson 1888
Secretary of the Navy	William C. Whitney 1885
Secretary of the Interior	Lucius Q. C. Lamar 1885
	William F. Vilas 1888
Secretary of Agriculture	Norman J. Colman 1889

B. HARRISON

Secretary of State	James G. Blaine 1889
	John W. Foster 1892
Secretary of the Treasury	William Windom 1889
	Charles Foster 1891
Secretary of War	Redfield Proctor 1889
	Stephen B. Elkins 1891
Attorney General	William H. H. Miller 1889
Postmaster General	John Wanamaker 1889
Secretary of the Navy	Benjamin F. Tracy 1889
Secretary of the Interior	John W. Noble 1889
Secretary of Agriculture	Jeremiah M. Rusk 1889

CLEVELAND

Secretary of State	Walter Q. Gresham 1893
	Richard Olney 1895
Secretary of the Treasury	John G. Carlisle 1893
Secretary of War	Daniel S. Lamont 1893
Attorney General	Richard Olney 1893
	Judson Harmon 1895
Postmaster General	Wilson S. Bissell 1893
	William L. Wilson 1895
Secretary of the Navy	Hilary A. Herbert 1893
Secretary of the Interior	Hoke Smith 1893
	David R. Francis 1896
Secretary of Agriculture	Julius Sterling Morton 1893

MCKINLEY

Secretary of State	John Sherman 1897
	William R. Day 1898
	John Hay 1898
Secretary of the Treasury	Lyman J. Gage 1897
Secretary of War	Russell A. Alger 1897
	Elihu Root 1899
Attorney General	Joseph McKenna 1897
	John W. Griggs 1898
	Philander C. Knox 1901
Postmaster General	James A. Gary 1897
	Charles E. Smith 1898
Secretary of the Navy	John D. Long 1897
Secretary of the Interior	Cornelius N. Bliss 1897
	Ethan A. Hitchcock 1898
Secretary of Agriculture	James Wilson 1897

T. ROOSEVELT

Secretary of State	John Hay (Cont.)
	Elihu Root 1905
	Robert Bacon 1909
Secretary of the Treasury	Lyman J. Gage (Cont.)
	Leslie M. Shaw 1902
	George B. Cortelyou 1907
Secretary of War	Elihu Root (Cont.)
	William H. Taft 1904
	Luke E. Wright 1908
Attorney General	Philander C. Knox (Cont.)
	William H. Moody 1904
	Charles J. Bonaparte 1906
Postmaster General	Charles E. Smith (Cont.)
	Henry C. Payne 1902
	Robert J. Wynne 1904
	George B. Cortelyou 1905

Secretary of the Navy	George von L. Meyer 1907
	John D. Long (Cont.)
	William H. Moody 1902
	Paul Morton 1904
	Charles J. Bonaparte 1905
	Victor H. Metcalf 1906
	Truman H. Newberry 1908
Secretary of the Interior	Ethan A. Hitchcock (Cont.)
	James R. Garfield 1907
Secretary of Agriculture	James Wilson (Cont.)
Secretary of Commerce	
and Labor	George B. Cortelyou 1903
	Victor H. Metcalf 1904
	Oscar S. Straus 1906

TAFT

Secretary of State	Philander C. Knox 1909
Secretary of the Treasury	Franklin MacVeagh 1909
Secretary of War	Jacob M. Dickinson 1909
	Henry L. Stimson 1911
Attorney General	George W. Wickersham 1909
Postmaster General	Frank H. Hitchcock 1909
Secretary of the Navy	George von L. Meyer 1909
Secretary of the Interior	Richard A. Ballinger 1909
	Walter L. Fisher 1911
Secretary of Agriculture	James Wilson (Cont.)
Secretary of Commerce	
and Labor	Charles Nagel 1909

WILSON

Secretary of State	William J. Bryan 1913
	Robert Lansing 1915
	Bainbridge Colby 1920
Secretary of the Treasury	William G. McAdoo 1913
	Carter Glass 1918
	David F. Houston 1920
Secretary of War	Lindley M. Garrison 1913
	Newton D. Baker 1916
Attorney General	James C. McReynolds 1913
	Thomas W. Gregory 1914
	A. Mitchell Palmer 1919
Postmaster General	Albert S. Burleson 1913
Secretary of the Navy	Josephus Daniels 1913
Secretary of the Interior	Franklin K. Lane 1913
	John B. Payne 1920
Secretary of Agriculture	David F. Houston 1913
	Edwin T. Meredith 1920
Secretary of Commerce	William C. Redfield 1913
	Joshua W. Alexander 1919
Secretary of Labor	William B. Wilson 1913

HARDING

Secretary of State	Charles E. Hughes 1921
Secretary of the Treasury	Andrew W. Mellon 1921
Secretary of War	John W. Weeks 1921
Attorney General	Harry M. Daugherty 1921
Postmaster General	Will H. Hays 1921
	Hubert Work 1922
	Harry S. New 1923
Secretary of the Navy	Edwin Denby 1921
Secretary of the Interior	Albert B. Fall 1921
	Hubert Work 1923
Secretary of Agriculture	Henry C. Wallace 1921
Secretary of Commerce	Herbert Hoover 1921
Secretary of Labor	James J. Davis 1921

COOLIDGE

Secretary of State	Charles E. Hughes (Cont.)
	Frank B. Kellogg 1925
Secretary of the Treasury	Andrew W. Mellon (Cont.)
Secretary of War	John W. Weeks (Cont.)
	Dwight F. Davis 1925
Attorney General	Harry M. Daughtery (Cont.)
	Harlan F. Stone 1924
	John G. Sargent 1925
Postmaster General	
	Harry S. New (Cont.)
Secretary of the Navy	Edwin Denby (Cont.)
	Curtis D. Wilbur 1924
Secretary of the Interior	Hubert Work (Cont.)
	Roy O. West 1928
Secretary of Agriculture	Henry C. Wallace (Cont.)
	Howard M. Gore 1924
	William M. Jardine 1925

Secretary of Commerce	Herbert Hoover (Cont.)
	William F. Whiting 1928
Secretary of Labor	James J. Davis (Cont.)

HOOVER

Secretary of State	Frank B. Kellogg (Cont.)
	Henry L. Stimson 1929
Secretary of the Treasury	Andrew W. Mellon (Cont.)
	Ogden L. Mills 1932
Secretary of War	James W. Good 1929
	Patrick J. Hurley 1929
Attorney General	William D. Mitchell 1929
Postmaster General	Walter F. Brown 1929
Secretary of the Navy	Charles F. Adams 1929
Secretary of the Interior	Ray Lyman Wilbur 1929
Secretary of Agriculture	Arthur M. Hyde 1929
Secretary of Commerce	Robert P. Lamont 1929
	Roy D. Chapin 1932
Secretary of Labor	James J. Davis (Cont.)
	William N. Doak 1930

F. D. ROOSEVELT

Secretary of State	Cordell Hull 1933
	E. R. Stettinius, Jr. 1944
Secretary of the Treasury	William H. Woodin 1933
	Henry Morgenthau, Jr. 1934
Secretary of War	George H. Dern 1933
	Harry H. Woodring 1936
	Henry L. Stimson 1940
Attorney General	Homer S. Cummings 1933
	Frank Murphy 1939
	Robert H. Jackson 1940
	Francis Biddle 1941
Postmaster General	James A. Farley 1933
	Frank C. Walker 1940
Secretary of the Navy	Claude A. Swanson 1933
	Charles Edison 1940
	Frank Knox 1940
	James Forrestal 1944
Secretary of the Interior	Harold L. Ickes 1933
Secretary of Agriculture	Henry A. Wallace 1933
	Claude R. Wickard 1940
Secretary of Commerce	Daniel C. Roper 1933
	Harry L. Hopkins 1938
	Jesse H. Jones 1940
	Henry A. Wallace 1945
Secretary of Labor	Frances Perkins 1933

TRUMAN

Secretary of State	E. R. Stettinius, Jr. (Cont.)
	James F. Byrnes 1945
	George C. Marshall 1947
	Dean Acheson 1949
Secretary of the Treasury	Henry Morgenthau, Jr. (Cont.)
	Frederick M. Vinson 1945
	John W. Snyder 1946
Secretary of Defense	James Forrestal 1947
	Louis A. Johnson 1949
	George C. Marshall 1950
	Robert A. Lovett 1951
Attorney General	Francis Biddle (Cont.)
	Tom C. Clark 1945
	J. Howard McGrath 1949
	James P. McGranery 1952
Postmaster General	Frank C. Walker (Cont.)
	Robert E. Hannegan 1945
	Jesse M. Donaldson 1947
Secretary of the Interior	Harold L. Ickes (Cont.)
	Julius A. Krug 1946
	Oscar L. Chapman 1949
Secretary of Agriculture	Claude R. Wickard (Cont.)
	Clinton P. Anderson 1945
	Charles F. Brannan 1948
Secretary of Commerce	Henry A. Wallace (Cont.)
	W. Averell Harriman 1946
	Charles Sawyer 1948
Secretary of Labor	Frances Perkins (Cont.)
	Lewis B. Schwellenbach 1945
	Maurice J. Tobin 1948
Secretary of War [2]	Henry L. Stimson (Cont.)
	Robert P. Patterson 1945
	Kenneth C. Royall 1947

Secretary of the Navy [2]	James Forrestal (Cont.)

EISENHOWER

Secretary of State	John Foster Dulles 1953
	Christian A. Herter 1959
Secretary of the Treasury	George M. Humphrey 1953
	Robert B. Anderson 1957
Secretary of Defense	Charles E. Wilson 1953
	Neil H. McElroy 1957
	Thomas S. Gates, Jr. 1959
Attorney General	Herbert Brownell, Jr. 1953
	William P. Rogers 1958
Postmaster General	Arthur E. Summerfield 1953
Secretary of the Interior	Douglas McKay 1953
	Frederick A. Seaton 1956
Secretary of Agriculture	Ezra Taft Benson 1953
Secretary of Commerce	Sinclair Weeks 1953
	Lewis L. Strauss[3] 1958
	Frederick H. Mueller 1959
Secretary of Labor	Martin P. Durkin 1953
	James P. Mitchell 1953
Secretary of Health, Education, and Welfare	Oveta Culp Hobby 1953
	Marion B. Folsom 1955
	Arthur S. Flemming 1958

KENNEDY

Secretary of State	Dean Rusk 1961
Secretary of the Treasury	C. Douglas Dillon 1961
Secretary of Defense	Robert S. McNamara 1961
Attorney General	Robert F. Kennedy 1961
Postmaster General	J. Edward Day 1961
	John A. Gronouski 1963
Secretary of the Interior	Stewart L. Udall 1961
Secretary of Agriculture	Orville L. Freeman 1961
Secretary of Commerce	Luther H. Hodges 1961
Secretary of Labor	Arthur J. Goldberg 1961
	W. Willard Wirtz 1962
Secretary of Health, Education, and Welfare	Abraham A. Ribicoff 1961
	Anthony J. Celebrezze 1962

L. B. JOHNSON

Secretary of State	Dean Rusk (Cont.)
Secretary of the Treasury	C. Douglas Dillon (Cont.)
	Henry H. Fowler 1965
	Joseph W. Barr[4] 1968
Secretary of Defense	Robert S. McNamara (Cont.)
	Clark M. Clifford 1968
Attorney General	Robert F. Kennedy (Cont.)
	N. de B. Katzenbach 1965
	Ramsey Clark 1967
Postmaster General	John A. Gronouski (Cont.)
	Lawrence F. O'Brien 1965
	W. Marvin Watson 1968
Secretary of the Interior	Stewart L. Udall (Cont.)
Secretary of Agriculture	Orville L. Freeman (Cont.)
Secretary of Commerce	Luther H. Hodges (Cont.)
	John T. Connor 1964
	A. B. Trowbridge 1967
	C. R. Smith 1968
Secretary of Labor	W. Willard Wirtz (Cont.)
Secretary of Health, Education, and Welfare	Anthony J. Celebrezze (Cont.)
	John W. Gardner 1965
	Wilbur J. Cohen 1968
Secretary of Housing and Urban Development	Robert C. Weaver 1966
	Robert C. Wood[4] 1969
Secretary of Transportation	Alan S. Boyd 1966

NIXON

Secretary of State	William P. Rogers 1969
	Henry A. Kissinger 1973
Secretary of the Treasury	David M. Kennedy 1969
	John B. Connally 1971
	George P. Shultz 1972
	William E. Simon 1974
Secretary of Defense	Melvin R. Laird 1969
	Elliot L. Richardson 1973
	James R. Schlesinger 1973
Attorney General	John N. Mitchell 1969

	Richard G. Kleindienst 1972
	Elliot L. Richardson 1973
	William B. Saxbe 1974
Postmaster General[5]	William M. Blount 1969
Secretary of the Interior	Walter J. Hickel 1969
	Rogers C. B. Morton 1971
Secretary of Agriculture	Clifford M. Hardin 1969
	Earl L. Butz 1971
Secretary of Commerce	Maurice H. Stans 1969
	Peter G. Peterson 1972
	Frederick B. Dent 1973
Secretary of Labor	George P. Shultz 1969
	James D. Hodgson 1970
	Peter J. Brennan 1973
Secretary of Health, Education, and Welfare	Robert H. Finch 1969
	Elliot L. Richardson 1970
	Caspar W. Weinberger 1973
Secretary of Housing and Urban Development	George Romney 1969
	James T. Lynn 1973
Secretary of Transportation	John A. Volpe 1969
	Claude S. Brinegar 1973

FORD

Secretary of State	Henry A. Kissinger (Cont.)
Secretary of the Treasury	William E. Simon (Cont.)
Secretary of Defense	James R. Schlesinger (Cont.)
	Donald H. Rumsfeld 1975
Attorney General	William B. Saxbe (Cont.)
	Edward H. Levi 1975
Secretary of the Interior	Rogers C. B. Morton (Cont.)
	Stanley K. Hathaway 1975
	Thomas S. Kleppe 1975
Secretary of Agriculture	Earl L. Butz (Cont.)
	John Knebel 1976
Secretary of Commerce	Frederick B. Dent (Cont.)
	Rogers C. B. Morton 1975
	Elliot L. Richardson 1976
Secretary of Labor	Peter J. Brennan (Cont.)
	John T. Dunlop 1975
	William J. Usery, Jr. 1976
Secretary of Health, Education, and Welfare	Caspar W. Weinberger (Cont.)
	F. David Mathews 1975
Secretary of Housing and Urban Development	James T. Lynn (Cont.)
	Carla A. Hills 1975
Secretary of Transportation	Claude S. Brinegar (Cont.)
	William T. Coleman, Jr. 1975

CARTER

Secretary of State	Cyrus R. Vance 1977
	Edmund S. Muskie 1980
Secretary of the Treasury	W. Michael Blumenthal 1977
	G. William Miller 1979
Secretary of Defense	Harold Brown 1977
Attorney General	Griffin B. Bell 1977
	Benjamin R. Civiletti 1979
Secretary of the Interior	Cecil D. Andrus 1977
Secretary of Agriculture	Bob S. Bergland 1977
Secretary of Commerce	Juanita M. Kreps 1977
	Philip M. Klutznick 1979
Secretary of Labor	F. Ray Marshall 1977
Secretary of Health and Human Services[6]	Joseph A. Califano, Jr. 1977
	Patricia Roberts Harris 1979
Secretary of Housing and Urban Development	Patricia Roberts Harris 1977

	Moon Landrieu 1979
Secretary of Transportation	Brock Adams 1977
	Neil E. Goldschmidt 1979
Secretary of Energy	James R. Schlesinger 1977
	Charles W. Duncan, Jr. 1979
Secretary of Education	Shirley Mount Hufstedler 1979

REAGAN

Secretary of State	Alexander M. Haig, Jr. 1981
	George P. Shultz 1982
Secretary of the Treasury	Donald T. Regan 1981
	James A. Baker 3rd 1985
	Nicholas F. Brady 1988
Secretary of Defense	Caspar W. Weinberger 1981
	Frank C. Carlucci 1987
Attorney General	William French Smith 1981
	Edwin Meese 3rd 1985
	Richard L. Thornburgh 1988
Secretary of the Interior	James G. Watt 1981
	William P. Clark 1983
	Donald P. Hodel 1985
Secretary of Agriculture	John R. Block 1981
	Richard E. Lyng 1986
Secretary of Commerce	Malcolm Baldrige 1981
	C. William Verity, Jr. 1987
Secretary of Labor	Raymond J. Donovan 1981
	William E. Brock 1985
	Ann Dore McLaughlin 1987
Secretary of Health and Human Services	Richard S. Schweiker 1981
	Margaret M. Heckler 1983
	Otis R. Bowen 1985
Secretary of Housing and Urban Development	Samuel R. Pierce, Jr. 1981
Secretary of Transportation	Andrew L. Lewis, Jr. 1981
	Elizabeth H. Dole 1983
	James H. Burnley 4th 1987
Secretary of Energy	James B. Edwards 1981
	Donald P. Hodel 1983
	John S. Herrington 1985
Secretary of Education	T. H. Bell 1981
	William J. Bennett 1985
	Lauro F. Cavazos 1988

BUSH

Secretary of State	James A. Baker 3d 1989
Secretary of the Treasury	Nicholas F. Brady (Cont.)
Secretary of Defense	Richard Cheney 1989
Attorney General	Richard L. Thornburgh (Cont.)
	William P. Barr (acting)
Secretary of the Interior	Manuel Lujan Jr. 1989
Secretary of Agriculture	Clayton K. Yeutter 1989
	Edward Madigan 1991
Secretary of Commerce	Robert A. Mosbacher Sr. 1989
	Barbara H. Franklin 1992
Secretary of Labor	Elizabeth H. Dole 1989
	Lynn Martin 1991
Secretary of Health and Human Services	Louis W. Sullivan 1989
Secretary of Housing and Urban Development	Jack F. Kemp 1989
Secretary of Transportation	Samuel K. Skinner 1989
Secretary of Energy	James D. Watkins 1989
Secretary of Education	Lauro F. Cavazos (Cont.)
	Lamar Alexander 1991
Secretary of Veterans Affairs	Edward J. Derwinski 1989

1. The Postmaster General did not become a Cabinet member until 1829. Earlier Postmasters General were: Samuel Osgood (1789), Timothy Pickering (1791), Joseph Habersham (1795), Gideon Granger (1801), Return J. Meigs, Jr. (1814), and John McLean (1823). 2. On July 26, 1947, the Departments of War and of the Navy were incorporated into the Department of Defense. 3. Not confirmed by the Senate. 4. Recess appointment. 5. The Postmaster General is no longer a Cabinet member. 6. Known as Department of Health, Education, and Welfare until May 1980.

Executive Departments and Agencies

Source: *Congressional Directory, 1991–1992*
Unless otherwise indicated, addresses shown are in Washington, D.C.

CENTRAL INTELLIGENCE AGENCY (CIA)
Washington, D.C. (20505).
 Established: 1947.
 Director: Robert M. Gates.
COUNCIL OF ECONOMIC ADVISERS (CEA)
Room 314, Old Executive Office Bldg. (20500).
 Members: 3.
 Established: Feb. 20, 1946.
 Chairman: Michael J. Boskin.
COUNCIL ON ENVIRONMENTAL QUALITY
722 Jackson Pl., N.W. (20503).
 Members: 3.
 Established: 1969.
 Chairman: Michael R. Deland.
NATIONAL SECURITY COUNCIL (NSC)
Old Executive Office Bldg. (20506).
 Members: 4.
 Established: July 26, 1947.
 Chairman: The President.
 Other members: Vice President; Secretary of State; Secretary of Defense.
OFFICE OF ADMINISTRATION
Old Executive Office Bldg. (20500).
 Established: Dec. 12, 1977.
 Director: Paul Bateman.
OFFICE OF MANAGEMENT AND BUDGET
Old Executive Office Bldg. (20503).
 Established: July 1, 1970.
 Director: Richard Darman.
OFFICE OF SCIENCE AND TECHNOLOGY POLICY
Executive Office Building (20506).
 Established: May 11, 1976.
 Director: D. Allan Bromley.
OFFICE OF THE UNITED STATES TRADE REPRESENTATIVE
600 17th St., N.W. (20506).
 Established: Jan. 15, 1963.
 Trade Representative: Carla A. Hills.
OFFICE OF POLICY DEVELOPMENT
1600 Pennsylvania Ave., N.W. (20500).
 Established: Jan. 21, 1981.
 Director: Charles E.M. Kolb.
OFFICE OF NATIONAL DRUG CONTROL POLICY
Suite 1011, 1825 Connecticut Ave., N.W. (20009).
 Established: March 13, 1989.
 Director: Robert Martinez.

Executive Departments

DEPARTMENT OF STATE
2201 C St., N.W. (20520).
 Established: 1781 as Department of Foreign Affairs; reconstituted, 1789, following adoption of Constitution; name changed to Department of State Sept. 15, 1789.
 Secretary: James A. Baker III.
 Deputy Secretary: Lawrence S. Eagleburger.
 Chief Delegate to U.N.: Thomas R. Pickering.
DEPARTMENT OF THE TREASURY
15th St. & Pennsylvania Ave., N.W. (20220).
 Established: Sept. 2, 1789.
 Secretary: Nicholas F. Brady.
 Deputy Secretary: John E. Robson.
 Treasurer of the U.S.: Catalina Vasquez Villalpando.
 Comptroller of the Currency: Vacancy.

DEPARTMENT OF DEFENSE
The Pentagon (20301).
 Established: July 26, 1947, as National Department Establishment; name changed to Department of Defense on Aug. 10, 1949. Subordinate to Secretary of Defense are Secretaries of Army, Navy, Air Force.
 Secretary: Richard Cheney.
 Deputy Secretary: Donald J. Atwood.
 Secretary of Army: Michael P.W. Stone
 Secretary of Navy: H. Lawrence Garrett III.
 Secretary of Air Force: Donald B. Rice.
 Commandant of Marine Corps: Gen. Alfred M. Gray.
 Joint Chiefs of Staff: Gen. Colin L. Powell, Chairman; Adm. Frank B. Kelso II, Navy; Gen. Merrill A. McPeak, Air Force; Gen. Gordon Russell Sullivan, Army; Lt. Gen. Carl E. Mundy, Jr., Marine Corps.
DEPARTMENT OF JUSTICE
Constitution Ave. between 9th & 10th Sts., N.W. (20530).
 Established: Office of Attorney General was created Sept. 24, 1789. Although he was one of original Cabinet members, he was not executive department head until June 22, 1870, when Department of Justice was established.
 Attorney General: William P. Barr (acting).
 Deputy Attorney General: Vacancy.
 Solicitor General: Kenneth W. Starr.
 Director of FBI: William Steele Sessions.
DEPARTMENT OF THE INTERIOR
C St. between 18th & 19th Sts., N.W. (20240).
 Established: March 3, 1849.
 Secretary: Manuel Lujan, Jr.
 Under Secretary: Frank A. Bracken.
DEPARTMENT OF AGRICULTURE
Independence Ave. between 12th & 14th Sts., S.W. (20250).
 Established: May 15, 1862. Administered by Commissioner of Agriculture until 1889, when it was made executive department.
 Secretary: Edward Madigan.
 Deputy Secretary: Ann M. Veneman.
DEPARTMENT OF COMMERCE
14th St. between Constitution Ave. & E St., N.W. (20230).
 Established: Department of Commerce and Labor was created Feb. 14, 1903. On March 4, 1913, all labor activities were transferred out of Department of Commerce and Labor and it was renamed Department of Commerce.
 Secretary: Barbara H. Franklin.
 Deputy Secretary: Rockwell Schnabel.
DEPARTMENT OF LABOR
200 Constitution Ave., N.W. (20210).
 Established: Bureau of Labor was created in 1884 under Department of the Interior; later became independent department without executive rank. Returned to bureau status in Department of Commerce and Labor, but on March 4, 1913, became independent executive department under its present name.
 Secretary: Lynn Morley Martin.
 Deputy Secretary: Roderick DeArment.
DEPARTMENT OF HEALTH AND HUMAN SERVICES[1]
200 Independence Ave., S.W. (20201).
 Established: April 11, 1953, replacing Federal Security Agency created in 1939.

Secretary: Louis W. Sullivan.
Surgeon General: Dr. Antonia Novello.
1. Originally Department of Health, Education and Welfare. Name changed in May 1980 when Department of Education was activated.

DEPARTMENT OF HOUSING AND URBAN DE-VELOPMENT
451 7th St., S.W. (20410).
Established: 1965, replacing Housing and Home Finance Agency created in 1947.
Secretary: Jack Kemp.
Under Secretary: Alfred A. Dellibovi.

DEPARTMENT OF TRANSPORTATION
400 7th St., S.W. (20590).
Established: Oct. 15, 1966, as result of Department of Transportation Act, which became effective April 1, 1967.
Secretary: Samuel K. Skinner.
Deputy Secretary: Elaine L. Chao.

DEPARTMENT OF ENERGY
1000 Independence Ave., S.W. (20585).
Established: Aug. 1977.
Secretary: James D. Watkins.
Deputy Secretary: W. Henson Moore.

DEPARTMENT OF EDUCATION
400 Maryland Avenue, S.W. (20202).
Established: Oct. 17, 1979.
Secretary: Lamar Alexander.
Under Secretary: Ted Sanders.

DEPARTMENT OF VETERANS' AFFAIRS
810 Vermont Avenue, N.W. (20420).
Established: March 15, 1989, replacing Veterans Administration created in 1930.
Secretary: Edward J. Derwinski.
Deputy Secretary: Anthony J. Principi.

Major Independent Agencies

ACTION
1100 Vermont Ave., N.W. (20525).
Established: July 1, 1971.
Director: Jane Kenny.

CONSUMER PRODUCT SAFETY COMMISSION
5401 Westbard Ave., Bethesda, Md. (20207).
Members: 5.
Established: Oct. 27, 1972.
Chairman: Jacqueline Jones-Smith.

ENVIRONMENTAL PROTECTION AGENCY (EPA)
401 M St., S.W. (20460).
Established: Dec. 2, 1970.
Administrator: William K. Reilly.

EQUAL EMPLOYMENT OPPORTUNITY COM-MISSION (EEOC)
1801 L St., N.W. (20507).
Members: 5.
Established: July 2, 1965.
Chairman: Evan J. Kemp, Jr.

FARM CREDIT ADMINISTRATION (FCA)
1501 Farm Credit Dr., McLean, Va. (22102).
Members: 13.
Established: July 17, 1916.
Chairman of Federal Farm Credit Board: Harold B. Steele.

FEDERAL COMMUNICATIONS COMMISSION (FCC)
1919 M St., N.W. (20554).
Members: 7.
Established: 1934.
Chairman: Alfred C. Silkes.

FEDERAL DEPOSIT INSURANCE CORPORATION (FDIC)
550 17th St., N.W. (20429).
Members: 3.
Established: June 16, 1933.

Chairman: L. William Seidman.

FEDERAL ELECTION COMMISSION (FEC)
999 E St., N.W. (20463).
Members: 6.
Established: 1974.
Chairman: John W. McGarry.

FEDERAL MARITIME COMMISSION
1100 L St., N.W. (20573).
Members: 5.
Established: Aug. 12, 1961.
Chairman: Christopher L. Koch.

FEDERAL MEDIATION AND CONCILIATION SERVICE (FMCS)
2100 K St., N.W. (20427).
Established: 1947.
Director: Bernard E. DeLury.

FEDERAL RESERVE SYSTEM (FRS), BOARD OF GOVERNORS OF
20th St. & Constitution Ave., N.W. (20551).
Members: 7.
Established: Dec. 23, 1913.
Chairman: Alan Greenspan.

FEDERAL TRADE COMMISSION (FTC)
Pennsylvania Ave. at 6th St., N.W. (20580).
Members: 5.
Established: Sept. 26, 1914.
Chairman: Janet D. Steiger.

GENERAL SERVICES ADMINISTRATION (GSA)
18th and F Sts., N.W. (20405).
Established: July 1, 1949.
Administrator: Richard G. Austin.

INTERSTATE COMMERCE COMMISSION (ICC)
12th St. & Constitution Ave., N.W. (20423).
Members: 7.
Established: Feb. 4, 1887.
Chairman: Edward Philbin.

NATIONAL AERONAUTICS AND SPACE ADMIN-ISTRATION (NASA)
600 Independence Ave. (20546).
Established: 1958.
Administrator: Vice Adm. Richard H. Truly (Ret.).

NATIONAL FOUNDATION ON THE ARTS AND THE HUMANITIES
1100 Pennsylvania Ave., N.W., (20506).
Established: 1965.
Chairmen: National Endowment for the Arts, John E. Frohnmayer; National Endowment for the Humanities, Lynne V. Cheney.

NATIONAL LABOR RELATIONS BOARD (NLRB)
1717 Pennsylvania Ave., N.W. (20570).
Members: 5.
Established: July 5, 1935.
Chairman: James M. Stephens.

NATIONAL MEDIATION BOARD
Suite 910, 1425 K St., N.W. (20572).
Members: 3.
Established: June 21, 1934.
Chairman: Joshua M. Javits.

NATIONAL SCIENCE FOUNDATION (NSF)
1800 G St., N.W. (20550).
Established: 1950.
Director: Walter E. Massey.

NATIONAL TRANSPORTATION SAFETY BOARD
800 Independence Ave., S.W. (20594).
Members: 5.
Established: April 1, 1975.
Chairman: James L. Kolstad (acting).

NUCLEAR REGULATORY COMMISSION (NRC)
Rockville, Md. (20852).
Members: 5.
Established: Jan. 19, 1975.
Chairman: Kenneth Carr.

OFFICE OF PERSONNEL MANAGEMENT (OPM)
1900 E St., N.W. (20415).
  Members: 3.
  Established: Jan. 1, 1979.
  Director: Constance B. Newman.
SECURITIES AND EXCHANGE COMMISSION (SEC)
450 5th St., N.W. (20549).
  Members: 5.
  Established: July 2, 1934.
  Chairman: Richard C. Breeden.
SELECTIVE SERVICE SYSTEM (SSS)
National Headquarters 1023 31st., N.W. (20435).
  Established: Sept. 16, 1940.
  Director: Gen. Samuel K. Lessey, Jr.
SMALL BUSINESS ADMINISTRATION (SBA)
409 3rd St., N.W. (20416).
  Established: July 30, 1953.
  Administrator: Patricia Saiki.
TENNESSEE VALLEY AUTHORITY (TVA)
400 West Summit Hill Drive, Knoxville, Tenn. (37902).
Washington office: Capitol Hill Office Bldg., 412 First St., S.E. (20444).
  Members of Board of Directors: 3.
  Established: May 18, 1933.
  Chairman: Marvin Runyon.
U.S. AGENCY FOR INTERNATIONAL DEVELOPMENT
520 21st St., N.W. (20523).
  Established: Oct. 1, 1979.
  Administrator: Ronald Roskens.
U.S. ARMS CONTROL AND DISARMAMENT AGENCY
520 21st St., N.W., (20451).
  Established: Sept. 26, 1961.
  Director: Ronald F. Lehman II.
U.S. COMMISSION ON CIVIL RIGHTS
1121 Vermont Avenue, N.W. (20425).
  Members: 8.
  Established: 1957.
  Chairman: Arthur A. Fletcher.
U.S. INFORMATION AGENCY
301 Fourth St., S.W. (20547).
  Established: Aug. 1, 1953. Reorganized April 1, 1978.
  Director: Henry E. Catto (acting).
U.S. INTERNATIONAL TRADE COMMISSION
500 E St., N.W. (20436).
  Members: 6.
  Established: Sept. 8, 1916.
  Chairman: Anne E. Brunsdale (acting).
U.S. POSTAL SERVICE
475 L'Enfant Plaza West, S.W. (20260).
  Postmaster General: Anthony M. Frank.
  Deputy Postmaster General: Michael S. Coughlin.
  Established: Office of Postmaster General and temporary post office system created in 1789. Act of Feb. 20, 1792, made detailed provisions for Post Office Department. In 1970 became independent agency headed by 11-member board of governors.

Other Independent Agencies

Administrative Conference of the United States—Suite 500, 2120 L St., N.W. (20037).
American Battle Monuments Commission—5127 Pulaski Bldg. 20 Massachusetts Ave., N.W. (20314).
Appalachian Regional Commission—1666 Connecticut Ave., N.W. (20235).
Board for International Broadcasting—Suite 400, 1201 Connecticut Ave., N.W. (20036).
Commission of Fine Arts—Pension Bldg. 441 F St., N.W. (20001).
Commodity Futures Trading Commission—2033 K St., N.W. (20581).
Export-Import Bank of the United States—811 Vermont Ave., N.W. (20571).
Federal Emergency Management Agency—500 C St., S.W. (20472).
Federal Home Loan Bank Board—1700 G St., N.W. (20552).
Federal Labor Relations Authority—500 C St., S.W. (20424).
Inter-American Foundation—1515 Wilson Blvd., Arlington, Va. (22209).
Merit Systems Protection Board—1120 Vermont Ave., N.W. (20419).
National Commission on Libraries and Information Science—Suite 310, 111 18th st., N.W. (20036).
National Credit Union Administration—1776 G St., N.W. (20456).
Occupational Safety and Health Review Commission—1825 K St., N.W. (20006).
Panama Canal Commission—Suite 550, 2000 L St., N.W. (20036).
Peace Corps—1990 K St., N.W. (20526).
Pension Benefit Guaranty Corporation—2020 K St., N.W. (20006).
Postal Rate Commission—Suite 300, 1333 H St., N.W. (20268).
President's Committee on Employment of the Handicapped—1111 20th St., N.W. (20036).
President's Council on Physical Fitness and Sports—450 5th St., N.W. (20001).
Railroad Retirement Board (RRB)—844 Rush St., Chicago, Ill. (60611); Washington Liaison Office: Suite 558, 2000 L St. (20036).
U.S. Parole Commission—Room 420, 5550 Friendship Blvd., Chevy Chase, Md. (20815).

Legislative Department

Architect of the Capitol—U.S. Capitol Building (20515).
General Accounting Office (GAO)—441 G St., N.W. (20548).
Government Printing Office (GPO)—North Capitol & H Sts., N.W. (20401).
Library of Congress—10 First St. S.E. (20540).
Office of Technology Assessment—600 Pennsylvania Ave., S.E. (20510).
United States Botanic Garden—Office of Director, 245 First St., S.W. (20024).

Quasi-Official Agencies

American National Red Cross—430 17th St., N.W. (20006).
Legal Services Corporation—400 Virginia Ave. S.W. (20024).
National Academy of Sciences, National Academy of Engineering, National Research Council, Institute of Medicine—2101 Constitution Ave., N.W. (20418).
National Railroad Passenger Corporation (Amtrak)—60 Massachusetts Ave., N.E. (20002).
Smithsonian Institution—1000 Jefferson Dr., S.W. (20560).

Congress of the United States

Composition of 101st and 102nd Congresses

	102nd Congress[2]				101st Congress[1]			
	Dem.	Rep.	Male	Female	Dem.	Rep.	Male	Female
Senate	57	43	98	2	55	45	98	2
House	269	165	407	29	257	176	406	27

1. One seat in House vacant in New Jersey and in Hawaii as of July 1, 1990. 2. There is one Independent member of the House.

The Senate

Senior Senator is listed first. The dates in the first column indicate period of service. The date given in parentheses after the Senator's name is year of birth. All terms are for six years and expire in January. Mailing address of Senators: The Senate, Washington, D.C. 20510.

ALABAMA
1979–97 Howell T. Heflin (D) (1921)
1987–93 Richard C. Shelby (D) (1934)
ALASKA
1968–97 Ted Stevens (R) (1923)
1981–93 Frank H. Murkowski (R) (1933)
ARIZONA
1977–95 Dennis DeConcini (D) (1937)
1987–93 John McCain (R) (1936)
ARKANSAS
1975–93 Dale Bumpers (D) (1925)
1979–97 David H. Pryor (D) (1934)
CALIFORNIA
1969–93 Alan Cranston (D) (1914)
1991–92 John Seymour (R) (1937)
COLORADO
1987–93 Timothy E. Wirth (D) (1939)
1991–97 Hank Brown (R) (1940)
CONNECTICUT
1981–93 Christopher J. Dodd (D) (1944)
1989–95 Joseph I. Lieberman (D) (1942)
DELAWARE
1971–95 William V. Roth, Jr. (R) (1921)
1973–97 Joseph R. Biden, Jr. (D) (1942)
FLORIDA
1987–93 Bob Graham (D) (1936)
1989–95 Connie Mack III (R) (1940)
GEORGIA
1972–97 Sam Nunn (D) (1938)
1987–93 Wyche Fowler, Jr. (D) (1940)
HAWAII
1963–93 Daniel K. Inouye (D) (1924)
1990–95 Daniel K. Akaka (D) (1924)
IDAHO
1981–93 Steven D. Symms (R) (1938)
1991–97 Larry E. Craig (R) (1945)
ILLINOIS
1981–93 Alan J. Dixon (D) (1927)
1985–97 Paul Simon (D) (1928)
INDIANA
1977–95 Richard G. Lugar (R) (1932)
1989–97 Dan Coats (R) (1943)
IOWA
1981–93 Charles E. Grassley (R) (1933)
1985–97 Tom Harkin (D) (1939)
KANSAS
1969–93 Robert J. Dole (R) (1923)
1978–97 Nancy Landon Kassebaum (R) (1932)
KENTUCKY
1974–93 Wendell H. Ford (D) (1924)
1985–97 Mitch McConnell (R) (1942)
LOUISIANA
1972–97 J. Bennett Johnson (D) (1932)
1987–93 John B. Breaux (D) (1944)
MAINE
1979–97 William S. Cohen (R) (1940)
1980–95 George J. Mitchell (D) (1933)

MARYLAND
1977–95 Paul Sarbanes (D) (1933)
1987–93 Barbara A. Mikulski (D) (1936)
MASSACHUSETTS
1962–95 Edward M. Kennedy (D) (1932)
1985–97 John F. Kerry (D) (1943)
MICHIGAN
1976–95 Donald W. Riegle, Jr. (D) (1938)
1979–97 Carl Levin (D) (1934)
MINNESOTA
1978–95 David F. Durenberger (R) (1934)
1991–97 Paul Wellstone (D) (1944)
MISSISSIPPI
1978–97 Thad Cochran (R) (1937)
1989–95 Trent Lott (R) (1941)
MISSOURI
1976–95 John C. Danforth (R) (1936)
1987–93 Christopher S. (Kit) Bond (R) (1939)
MONTANA
1978–97 Max Baucus (D) (1941)
1989–95 Conrad Burns (R) (1935)
NEBRASKA
1979–97 J. James Exon (D) (1921)
1989–95 Robert Kerrey (D) (1943)
NEVADA
1987–93 Harry M. Reid (D) (1939)
1989–95 Dick Bryan (D) (1937)
NEW HAMPSHIRE
1980–93 Warren B. Rudman (R) (1930)
1991–97 Robert C. Smith (R) (1941)
NEW JERSEY
1979–97 Bill Bradley (D) (1943)
1982–95 Frank R. Lautenberg (D) (1924)
NEW MEXICO
1973–97 Pete V. Domenici (R) (1932)
1983–95 Jeff Bingaman (D) (1943)
NEW YORK
1977–95 Daniel P. Moynihan (D) (1927)
1981–93 Alfonse M. D'Amato (R) (1937)
NORTH CAROLINA
1973–97 Jesse Helms (R) (1921)
1986–93 Terry Sanford (D) (1917)
NORTH DAKOTA
1960–95 Quentin N. Burdick (D) (1908)
1987–93 Kent Conrad (D) (1948)
OHIO
1974–93 John H. Glenn, Jr. (D) (1921)
1976–95 Howard M. Metzenbaum (D) (1917)
OKLAHOMA
1979–97 David L. Boren (D) (1941)
1981–93 Don Nickles (R) (1948)
OREGON
1967–97 Mark O. Hatfield (R) (1922)
1969–93 Bob Packwood (R) (1932)
PENNSYLVANIA
1981–93 Arlen Specter (R) (1930)
1991–95 Harris Wofford (D) (1926)

RHODE ISLAND
1961–97 Claiborne Pell (D) (1918)
1976–95 John H. Chafee (R) (1922)
SOUTH CAROLINA
1956–97 Strom Thurmond (R) (1902)
1966–93 Ernest F. Hollings (D) (1922)
SOUTH DAKOTA
1979–97 Larry Pressler (R) (1942)
1987–93 Thomas A. Daschle (D) (1947)
TENNESSEE
1977–95 James R. Sasser (D) (1936)
1985–97 Albert Gore, Jr. (D) (1948)
TEXAS
1971–95 Lloyd M. Bentsen (D) (1921)
1985–97 Phil Gramm (R) (1942)
UTAH
1974–93 E.J. (Jake) Garn (R) (1932)
1977–95 Orrin G. Hatch (R) (1934)

VERMONT
1975–93 Patrick J. Leahy (D) (1940)
1989–95 James M. Jeffords (R) (1934)
VIRGINIA
1979–97 John W. Warner (R) (1927)
1989–95 Charles Robb (D) (1939)
WASHINGTON
1987–93 Brock Adams (D) (1927)
1989–95 Slade Gorton (R) (1928)
WEST VIRGINIA
1959–95 Robert C. Byrd (D) (1918)
1985–97 John D. (Jay) Rockefeller IV (D) (1937)
WISCONSIN
1981–93 Robert W. Kasten, Jr. (R) (1942)
1989–95 Herbert Kohl (D) (1935)
WYOMING
1977–95 Malcolm Wallop (R) (1933)
1979–97 Alan K. Simpson (R) (1931)

The House of Representatives

The numerals indicate the Congressional Districts of the states; the designation AL means At Large. All terms end January 1993. Mailing address of Representatives: House of Representatives, Washington, D.C. 20515.

ALABAMA
(7 Representatives)
1. H.L. (Sonny) Callahan (R)
2. William L. Dickinson (R)
3. Glen Browder (D)
4. Thomas Bevill (D)
5. Bud Cramer (D)
6. Ben Erdreich (D)
7. Claude Harris (D)
ALASKA
(1 Representative)
AL Don Young (R)
ARIZONA
(5 Representatives)
1. John J. (Jay) Rhodes III (R)
2. Ed Pastor (D)
3. Bob Stump (R)
4. Jon Kyl (R)
5. Jim Kolbe (R)
ARKANSAS
(4 Representatives)
1. Bill Alexander (D)
2. Ray Thornton (D)
3. John Hammerschmidt (R)
4. Beryl Anthony (D)
CALIFORNIA
(45 Representatives)
1. Frank Riggs (R)
2. Wally Herger (R)
3. Robert T. Matsui (D)
4. Vic Fazio (D)
5. Nancy Pelosi (D)
6. Barbara Boxer (D)
7. George Miller (D)
8. Ronald V. Dellums (D)
9. Fortney H. (Pete) Stark (D)
10. Don Edwards (D)
11. Tom Lantos (D)
12. Thomas J. Campbell (R)
13. Norman Y. Mineta (D)
14. John Doolittle (D)
15. Gary Condit (D)
16. Leon E. Panetta (D)
17. Charles Pashayan, Jr. (R)
18. Richard H. Lehman (D)
19. Robert J. Lagomarsino (R)
20. William M. Thomas (R)
21. Elton Gallegly (R)
22. Carlos J. Moorhead (R)
23. Anthony C. Beilenson (D)
24. Henry A. Waxman (D)
25. Edward R. Roybal (D)
26. Howard L. Berman (D)
27. Mel Levine (D)
28. Julian C. Dixon (D)
29. Maxine Waters (D)
30. Matthew G. Martinez (D)
31. Mervyn M. Dymally (D)
32. Glenn M. Anderson (D)
33. David Dreier (R)
34. Esteban Edward Torres (D)
35. Jerry Lewis (R)
36. George E. Brown, Jr. (D)
37. Al McCandless (R)
38. Robert K. Dornan (R)
39. William E. Dannemeyer (R)
40. Christopher Cox (R)
41. Wiliam Lowery (R)
42. Dana Rohrabacher (R)
43. Ron Packard (R)
44. Randall Cunningham (R)
45. Duncan L. Hunter (R)
COLORADO
(6 Representatives)
1. Patricia Schroeder (D)
2. David E. Skaggs (D)
3. Ben Nighthorse Campbell (D)
4. Wayne Allard (R)
5. Joel Hefley (R)
6. Daniel L. Schaefer (R)
CONNECTICUT
(6 Representatives)
1. Barbara B. Kennelly (D)
2. Sam Gejdenson (D)
3. Rose DeLauro (D)
4. Christopher H. Shays (R)
5. Gary Franks (R)
6. Nancy L. Johnson (R)
DELAWARE
(1 Representative)
AL Thomas R. Carper (D)
FLORIDA
(19 Representatives)
1. Earl D. Hutto (D)
2. Pete Peterson (D)
3. Charles E. Bennett (D)
4. Craig James (R)
5. Bill McCollum (R)
6. Cliff Stearns (R)
7. Sam Gibbons (D)
8. C.W. Bill Young (R)
9. Michael Bilirakis (R)
10. Andy Ireland (R)
11. Jim Bacchus (D)
12. Tom Lewis (R)
13. Porter Goss (R)
14. Harry Johnston (D)
15. E. Clay Shaw, Jr. (R)
16. Larry Smith (D)
17. William Lehman (D)
18. Ileana Ros-Lehtineor (R)
19. Dante B. Fascell (D)
GEORGIA
(10 Representatives)
1. Robert Lindsay Thomas (D)
2. Charles Hatcher (D)
3. Richard Ray (D)
4. Ben Jones (D)
5. John Lewis (D)
6. Newt Gingrich (R)
7. George (Buddy) Darden (D)
8. J. Roy Rowland (D)
9. Edgar L. Jenkins (D)
10. Doug Barnard, Jr. (D)
HAWAII
(2 Representatives)
1. Neil Abercrombie (D)
2. Patsy Mink (D)
IDAHO
(2 Representatives)
1. Larry LaRocco (D)
2. Richard H. Stallings (D)
ILLINOIS
(22 Representatives)
1. Charles A. Hayes (D)
2. Gus Savage (D)
3. Marty Russo (D)
4. George Sangemeister (D)
5. William O. Lipinski (D)
6. Henry J. Hyde (R)
7. Cardiss Collins (D)
8. Dan Rostenkowski (D)
9. Sidney R. Yates (D)
10. John Edward Porter (R)
11. Frank Annunzio (D)
12. Philip M. Crane (R)
13. Harris W. Fawell (R)
14. J. Dennis Hastert (R)
15. Thomas Ewing (R)
16. John Cox Jr. (D)
17. Lane Evans (D)
18. Robert H. Michel (R)
19. Terry L. Bruce (D)
20. Richard Durbin (D)
21. Jerry Costello (D)
22. Glenn Poshard (D)
INDIANA
(10 Representatives)
1. Peter Visclosky (D)
2. Philip R. Sharp (D)
3. Tim Roemer (D)
4. Jill Long (D)
5. Jim Jontz (D)
6. Daniel Burton (R)
7. John T. Meyers (R)
8. Frank McCloskey (D)
9. Lee H. Hamilton (D)
10. Andrew Jacobs, Jr. (D)

IOWA
(6 Representatives)
1. Jim Leach (R)
2. Jim Nussel (R)
3. Dave R. Nagle (D)
4. Neal Smith (D)
5. Jim Ross Lightfoot (R)
6. Fred Grandy (R)

KANSAS
(5 Representatives)
1. Pat Roberts (R)
2. James Slattery (D)
3. Jan Meyers (R)
4. Dan Glickman (D)
5. Richard Nichols (R)

KENTUCKY
(7 Representatives)
1. Carroll Hubbard, Jr. (D)
2. William H. Natcher (D)
3. Romano L. Mazzoli (D)
4. Jim Bunning (R)
5. Harold Rogers (R)
6. Larry J. Hopkins (R)
7. Carl C. Perkins (D)

LOUISIANA
(8 Representatives)
1. Robert L. Livingston, Jr. (R)
2. William J. Jefferson (D)
3. W.J. (Billy) Tauzin (D)
4. Jim McCrery (R)
5. Thomas J. (Jerry) Huckaby (D)
6. Richard Baker (R)
7. Jimmy Hayes (D)
8. Clyde Holloway (R)

MAINE
(2 Representatives)
1. Tom Andrews (D)
2. Olympia J. Snowe (R)

MARYLAND
(8 Representatives)
1. Wayne Gilchrest (R)
2. Helen Delich Bentley (R)
3. Benjamin L. Cardin (D)
4. Thomas McMillen (D)
5. Steny H. Hoyer (D)
6. Beverly B. Byron (D)
7. Kweisi Mfume (D)
8. Constance A. Morella (R)

MASSACHUSETTS
(11 Representatives)
1. John Olver (D)
2. Richard Neal (D)
3. Joseph D. Early (D)
4. Barney Frank (D)
5. Chester G. Atkins (D)
6. Nicholas Mavroules (D)
7. Edward J. Markey (D)
8. Joseph P. Kennedy II (D)
9. Joe Moakley (D)
10. Gerry E. Studds (D)
11. Brian J. Donnelly (D)

MICHIGAN
(18 Representatives)
1. John Conyers, Jr. (D)
2. Carl D. Pursell (R)
3. Howard Wolpe (D)
4. Fred Upton (R)
5. Paul B. Henry (R)
6. Bob Carr (D)
7. Dale E. Kildee (D)
8. Bob Traxler (D)
9. Guy Vander Jagt (R)
10. David Camp (R)
11. Robert W. Davis (R)
12. David E. Bonior (D)
13. Barbara-Rose Collins (D)
14. Dennis M. Hertel (D)
15. William D. Ford (D)
16. John D. Dingell (D)
17. Sander M. Levin (D)

18. William S. Broomfield (R)

MINNESOTA
(8 Representatives)
1. Timothy J. Penny (D)
2. Vin Weber (R)
3. Jim Ramstad (R)
4. Bruce F. Vento (D)
5. Martin Sabo (D)
6. Gerry Sikorski (D)
7. Collin Peterson (D)
8. James L. Oberstar (D)

MISSISSIPPI
(5 Representatives)
1. Jamie L. Whitten (D)
2. Mike Espy (D)
3. G.V. (Sonny) Montgomery (D)
4. Michael Parker (D)
5. Gene Taylor (D)

MISSOURI
(9 Representatives)
1. William L. Clay (D)
2. Joan Horn (D)
3. Richard A. Gephardt (D)
4. Ike Skelton (D)
5. Alan Wheat (D)
6. E. Thomas Coleman (R)
7. Mel Hancock (R)
8. William Emerson (R)
9. Harold L. Volkmer (D)

MONTANA
(2 Representatives)
1. Pat Williams (D)
2. Ron Marlenee (R)

NEBRASKA
(3 Representatives)
1. Douglas K. Bereuther (R)
2. Peter Hoagland (D)
3. Bill Barrett (R)

NEVADA
(2 Representatives)
1. James H. Bilbray (D)
2. Barbara F. Vucanovich (R)

NEW HAMPSHIRE
(2 Representatives)
1. Bill Zeliff (R)
2. Dick Swett (D)

NEW JERSEY
(14 Representatives)
1. Robert Andrews (D)
2. William J. Hughes (D)
3. Frank Pallone (D)
4. Christopher H. Smith (R)
5. Marge Roukema (R)
6. Bernard J. Dwyer (D)
7. Matthew J. Rinaldo (R)
8. Robert A. Roe (D)
9. Robert G. Torricelli (D)
10. Donald Payne (D)
11. Dean A. Gallo (R)
12. Richard Zimmer (R)
13. H. James Saxton (R)
14. Frank Guarini (D)

NEW MEXICO
(3 Representatives)
1. Steve Schiff (R)
2. Joseph R. Skeen (R)
3. William Richardson (D)

NEW YORK
(34 Representatives)
1. George J. Hochbreuckner (D)
2. Thomas J. Downey (D)
3. Robert J. Mrazek (D)
4. Norman F. Lent (R)
5. Raymond J. McGrath (D)
6. Floyd H. Flake (D)
7. Gary L. Ackerman (D)

8. James H. Scheuer (D)
9. Thomas J. Manton (D)
10. Charles E. Schumer (D)
11. Edolphus Towns (D)
12. Major R. Owens (D)
13. Stephen J. Solarz (D)
14. Guy V. Molinari (R)
15. S. William Green (R)
16. Charles B. Rangel (D)
17. Ted Weiss (D)
18. Jose Serrano (D)
19. Elliott Engel (D)
20. Nita Lowey (D)
21. Hamilton Fish, Jr. (R)
22. Benjamin A. Gilman (R)
23. Michael McNulty (D)
24. Gerald B.H. Solomon (R)
25. Sherwood Boehlert (R)
26. David O'B. Martin (R)
27. James Walsh (R)
28. Matther F. McHugh (D)
29. Frank Horton (R)
30. Louise M. Slaughter (D)
31. L. William Paxon (R)
32. John L. LaFalce (D)
33. Henry J. Nowak (D)
34. Amory Houghton, Jr. (R)

NORTH CAROLINA
(11 Representatives)
1. Walter B. Jones (D)
2. Tim Valentine (D)
3. Martin Lancaster (D)
4. David E. Price (D)
5. Stephen L. Neal (D)
6. Howard Coble (R)
7. Charlie Rose (D)
8. W.G. (Bill) Hefner (D)
9. J. Alex McMillan (R)
10. Cass Ballenger (R)
11. Charles Taylor (R)

NORTH DAKOTA
(1 Representative)
AL Byron L. Dorgan (D)

OHIO
(21 Representatives)
1. Charles Luken (D)
2. Willis D. Gradison, Jr. (R)
3. Tony P. Hall (D)
4. Michael G. Oxley (R)
5. Paul Gillmor (R)
6. Bob McEwen (R)
7. David Hobson (R)
8. John Boehner (R)
9. Marcy Kaptur (D)
10. Clarence E. Miller (R)
11. Dennis E. Eckart (D)
12. John R. Kasich (R)
13. Don J. Pease (D)
14. Tom Sawyer (D)
15. Chalmers Wylie (R)
16. Ralph Regula (R)
17. James A. Traficant, Jr. (D)
18. Douglas Applegate (D)
19. Edward F. Feighan (D)
20. Mary Rose Oakar (D)
21. Louis Stokes (D)

OKLAHOMA
(6 Representatives)
1. James M. Inhofe (R)
2. Mike Synar (D)
3. Wesley W. Watkins (D)
4. Dave McCurdy (D)
5. Mickey Edwards (R)
6. Glenn English (D)

OREGON
(5 Representatives)
1. Les AuCoin (D)
2. Robert F. Smith (R)
3. Ronald L. Wyden (D)
4. Peter A. De Fazio (D)
5. Mike Kopetski (D)

PENNSYLVANIA
(23 Representatives)
1. Thomas M. Foglietta (D)
2. Lucien E. Blackwell (D)
3. Robert A. Borski (D)
4. Joseph P. Kolter (D)
5. Richard T. Schulze (R)
6. Gus Yatron (D)
7. Curt Weldon (R)
8. Peter H. Kostmayer (D)
9. E.G. Shuster (R)
10. Joseph M. McDade (R)
11. Paul E. Kanjorski (D)
12. John P. Murtha (D)
13. Lawrence Coughlin (R)
14. William J. Coyne (D)
15. Don Ritter (R)
16. Robert S. Walker (R)
17. George W. Gekas (R)
18. Rick Santorum (R)
19. William F. Goodling (R)
20. Joseph M. Gaydos (D)
21. Tom Ridge (R)
22. Austin J. Murphy (D)
23. William F. Clinger (R)

RHODE ISLAND
(2 Representatives)
1. Ronald Machtley (R)
2. Jack Reed (D)

SOUTH CAROLINA
(6 Representatives)
1. Arthur Ravenel, Jr. (R)
2. Floyd Spence (R)
3. Butler Derrick (D)
4. Elizabeth J. Patterson (D)
5. John M. Spratt, Jr. (D)
6. Robin Tallon (D)

SOUTH DAKOTA
(1 Representative)
AL Tim Johnson (D)

TENNESSEE
(9 Representatives)
1. James H. Quillen (R)
2. James Duncan (R)

3. Marilyn Lloyd (D)
4. James Cooper (D)
5. Robert Clement (D)
6. Bart Gordon (D)
7. Don Sundquist (R)
8. John Tanner (D)
9. Harold E. Ford (D)

TEXAS
(27 Representatives)
1. Jim Chapman (D)
2. Charles Wilson (D)
3. Sam Johnson (R)
4. Ralph M. Hall (D)
5. John Bryant (D)
6. Joe L. Barton (R)
7. William Archer (R)
8. Jack Fields (R)
9. Jack Brooks (D)
10. J.J. Pickle (D)
11. Chet Edwards (D)
12. Pete Green (D)
13. William Sarpalius (D)
14. Greg Laughlin (D)
15. E. (Kika) de la Garza (D)
16. Ronald D. Coleman (D)
17. Charles W. Stenholm (D)
18. Craig Washington (D)
19. Larry Combest (R)
20. Henry B. Gonzalez (D)
21. Lamar Smith (R)
22. Thomas D. Delay (R)
23. Albert G. Bustamante (D)
24. Martin Frost (D)
25. Michael A. Andrews (D)
26. Richard Armey (R)
27. Solomon P. Ortiz (D)

UTAH
(3 Representatives)
1. James V. Hansen (R)
2. Wayne Owens (D)
3. Bill Orton (D)

VERMONT
(1 Representative)
AL Bernie Sanders (Ind)

VIRGINIA
(10 Representatives)
1. Herbert H. Bateman (R)
2. Owen B. Pickett (D)
3. Thomas J. Bliley, Jr. (R)
4. Norman Sisisky (D)
5. L.F. Payne (D)
6. James R. Olin (D)
7. George F. Allen (R)
8. Jim Moran (D)
9. Frederick C. Boucher (D)
10. Frank R. Wolf (R)

WASHINGTON
(8 Representatives)
1. John R. Miller (R)
2. Al Swift (D)
3. Jolene Unsoeld (D)
4. Sid W. Morrison (R)
5. Thomas S. Foley (D)
6. Norman D. Dicks (D)
7. James McDermott (D)
8. Rodney Chandler (R)

WEST VIRGINIA
(4 Representatives)
1. Alan B. Mollohan (D)
2. Harley O. Staggers, Jr. (D)
3. Robert Wise (D)
4. Nick J. Rahall (D)

WISCONSIN
(9 Representatives)
1. Les Aspin (D)
2. Scott Klug (R)
3. Steve Gunderson (R)
4. Gerald D. Kleczka (D)
5. James Moody (D)
6. Thomas E. Petri (R)
7. David P. Obey (D)
8. Toby Roth (R)
9. F. James Sensenbrenner, Jr. (R)

WYOMING
(1 Representative)
AL Craig Thomas (R)

How a Bill Becomes a Law

When a Senator or a Representative introduces a bill, he sends it to the clerk of his house, who gives it a number and title. This is the _first reading,_ and the bill is referred to the proper committee.

The committee may decide the bill is unwise or unnecessary and _table_ it, thus killing it at once. Or it may decide the bill is worthwhile and hold hearings to listen to facts and opinions presented by experts and other interested persons. After members of the committee have debated the bill and perhaps offered amendments, a vote is taken; and if the vote is favorable, the bill is sent back to the floor of the house.

The clerk reads the bill sentence by sentence to the house, and this is known as the _second reading._ Members may then debate the bill and offer amendments. In the House of Representatives, the time for debate is limited by a _cloture rule,_ but there is no such restriction in the Senate for cloture, where 60 votes are required. This makes possible a _filibuster,_ in which one or more opponents hold the floor to defeat the bill.

The _third reading_ is by title only, and the bill is put to a vote, which may be voice or roll call, depending on the circumstances and parliamentary rules. Members who must be absent at the time but who wish to record their vote may be paired if each nega-

tive vote has a balancing affirmative one.

The bill then goes to the other house of Congress, where it may be defeated, or passed with or without amendments. If the bill is defeated, it dies. If it is passed with amendments, a joint Congressional committee must be appointed by both houses to iron out the differences.

After its final passage by both houses, the bill is sent to the President. If he approves, he signs it, and the bill becomes a law. However, if he disapproves, he _vetoes_ the bill by refusing to sign it and sending it back to the house of origin with his reasons for the veto. The objections are read and debated, and a roll-call vote is taken. If the bill receives less than a two-thirds vote, it is defeated and goes no farther. But if it receives a two-thirds vote or greater, it is sent to the other house for a vote. If that house also passes it by a two-thirds vote, the President's veto is _overridden,_ and the bill becomes a law.

Should the President desire neither to sign nor to veto the bill, he may retain it for ten days, Sundays excepted, after which time it automatically becomes a law without signature. However, if Congress has adjourned within those ten days, the bill is automatically killed, that process of indirect rejection being known as a _pocket veto._

Speakers of the House of Representatives

Dates served	Congress	Name and State	Dates served	Congress	Name and State
1789–1791	1	Frederick A. C. Muhlenberg (Pa.)	1869–1869	40	Theodore M. Pomeroy (N.Y.)[5]
1791–1793	2	Jonathan Trumbull (Conn.)	1869–1875	41–43	James G. Blaine (Me.)
1793–1795	3	Frederick A. C. Muhlenberg (Pa.)	1875–1876	44	Michael C. Kerr (Ind.)[6]
1795–1799	4–5	Jonathan Dayton (N.J.)[1]	1876–1881	44–46	Samuel J. Randall (Pa.)
1799–1801	6	Theodore Sedgwick (Mass.)	1881–1883	47	J. Warren Keifer (Ohio)
1801–1807	7–9	Nathaniel Macon (N.C.)	1883–1889	48–50	John G. Carlisle (Ky.)
1807–1811	10–11	Joseph B. Varnum (Mass.)	1889–1891	51	Thomas B. Reed (Me.)
1811–1814	12–13	Henry Clay (Ky.)[2]	1891–1895	52–53	Charles F. Crisp (Ga.)
1814–1815	13	Langdon Cheves (S.C.)	1895–1899	54–55	Thomas B. Reed (Me.)
1815–1820	14–16	Henry Clay (Ky.)[3]	1899–1903	56–57	David B. Henderson (Iowa)
1820–1821	16	John W. Taylor (N.Y.)	1903–1911	58–61	Joseph G. Cannon (Ill.)
1821–1823	17	Philip P. Barbour (Va.)	1911–1919	62–65	Champ Clark (Mo.)
1823–1825	18	Henry Clay (Ky.)	1919–1925	66–68	Frederick H. Gillett (Mass.)
1825–1827	19	John W. Taylor (N.Y.)	1925–1931	69–71	Nicholas Longworth (Ohio)
1827–1834	20–23	Andrew Stevenson (Va.)[4]	1931–1933	72	John N. Garner (Tex.)
1834–1835	23	John Bell (Tenn.)	1933–1934	73	Henry T. Rainey (Ill.)[7]
1835–1839	24–25	James K. Polk (Tenn.)	1935–1936	74	Joseph W. Byrns (Tenn.)[8]
1839–1841	26	Robert M. T. Hunter (Va.)	1936–1940	74–76	William B. Bankhead (Ala.)[9]
1841–1843	27	John White (Ky.)	1940–1947	76–79	Sam Rayburn (Tex.)
1843–1845	28	John W. Jones (Va.)	1947–1949	80	Joseph W. Martin, Jr. (Mass.)
1845–1847	29	John W. Davis (Ind.)	1949–1953	81–82	Sam Rayburn (Tex.)
1847–1849	30	Robert C. Winthrop (Mass.)	1953–1955	83	Joseph W. Martin, Jr. (Mass.)
1849–1851	31	Howell Cobb (Ga.)	1955–1961	84–87	Sam Rayburn (Tex.)[10]
1851–1855	32–33	Linn Boyd (Ky.)	1962–1971	87–91	John W. McCormack (Mass.)[11]
1855–1857	34	Nathaniel P. Banks (Mass.)	1971–1977	92–94	Carl Albert (Okla.)[12]
1857–1859	35	James L. Orr (S.C.)	1977–1987	95–99	Thomas P. O'Neill, Jr. (Mass.)[13]
1859–1861	36	Wm. Pennington (N.J.)	1987–1989	100–101	James C. Wright, Jr. (Tex.)[14]
1861–1863	37	Galusha A. Grow (Pa.)	1989–	101–	Thomas S. Foley (Wash.)
1863–1869	38–40	Schuyler Colfax (Ind.)			

1. George Dent (Md.) was elected Speaker pro tempore for April 20 and May 28, 1798. 2. Resigned during second session of 13th Congress. 3. Resigned between first and second sessions of 16th Congress. 4. Resigned during first session of 23rd Congress. 5. Elected Speaker and served the day of adjournment. 6. Died between first and second sessions of 44th Congress. During first session, there were two Speakers pro tempore: Samuel S. Cox (N.Y.), appointed for Feb. 17, May 12, and June 19, 1876, and Milton Sayler (Ohio), appointed for June 4, 1876. 7. Died in 1934 after adjournment of second session of 73rd Congress. 8. Died during second session of 74th Congress. 9. Died during third session of 76th Congress. 10. Died between first and second sessions of 87th Congress. 11. Not a candidate in 1970 election. 12. Not a candidate in 1976 election. 13. Not a candidate in 1986 election. 14. Resigned during first session of 101st Congress. *Source: Congressional Directory.*

Floor Leaders of the Senate

Democratic	Republican
Gilbert M. Hitchcock, Neb. (Min. 1919–20)	Charles Curtis, Kan. (Maj. 1925–29)
Oscar W. Underwood, Ala. (Min. 1920–23)	James E. Watson, Ind. (Maj. 1929–33)
Joseph T. Robinson, Ark. (Min. 1923–33, Maj. 1933–37)	Charles L. McNary, Ore. (Min. 1933–44)
Alben W. Barkley, Ky. (Maj. 1937–46, Min. 1947–48)	Wallace H. White, Jr., Me. (Min. 1944–47, Maj. 1947–48)
Scott W. Lucas, Ill. (Maj. 1949–50)	Kenneth S. Wherry, Neb. (Min. 1949–51)
Ernest W. McFarland, Ariz. (Maj. 1951–52)	Styles Bridges, N. H. (Min. 1951–52)
Lyndon B. Johnson, Tex. (Min. 1953–54, Maj. 1955–60)	Robert A. Taft, Ohio (Maj. 1953)
Mike Mansfield, Mont. (Maj. 1961–77)	William F. Knowland, Calif. (Maj. 1953–54, Min. 1955–58)
Robert C. Byrd, W. Va. (Maj. 1977–81, Min. 1981–86, Maj. 1987–88)	Everett M. Dirksen, Ill. (Min. 1959–69)
George John Mitchell, Me. (Maj. 1989–)	Hugh Scott, Pa. (Min. 1969–1977)
	Howard H. Baker, Jr., Tenn. (Min. 1977–81, Maj. 1981–84)
	Robert J. Dole, Kan. (Maj. 1985–86, Min. 1987–)

NOTE: Min. = Minority Leader; Maj. = Majority Leader. *Source:* United States Senate, Secretary for the Majority.

Members of the Supreme Court of the United States

Name; apptd. from	Service		Brith			
	Term	Yrs	Place	Date	Died	Religion
CHIEF JUSTICES						
John Jay, N.Y.	1789–1795	5	N.Y.	1745	1829	Episcopal
John Rutledge, S.C.	1795	0	S.C.	1739	1800	Church of England
Oliver Ellsworth, Conn.	1796–1800	4	Conn.	1745	1807	Congregational
John Marshall, Va.	1801–1835	34	Va.	1755	1835	Episcopal
Roger B. Taney, Md.	1836–1864	28	Md.	1777	1864	Roman Catholic
Salmon P. Chase, Ohio	1864–1873	8	N.H.	1808	1873	Episcopal
Morrison R. Waite, Ohio	1874–1888	14	Conn.	1816	1888	Episcopal
Melville W. Fuller, Ill.	1888–1910	21	Me.	1833	1910	Episcopal
Edward D. White, La.	1910–1921	10	La.	1845	1921	Roman Catholic
William H. Taft, Conn.	1921–1930	8	Ohio	1857	1930	Unitarian
Charles E. Hughes, N.Y.	1930–1941	11	N.Y.	1862	1948	Baptist
Harlan F. Stone, N.Y.	1941–1946	4	N.H.	1872	1946	Episcopal
Frederick M. Vinson, Ky.	1946–1953	7	Ky.	1890	1953	Methodist
Earl Warren, Calif.	1953–1969	15	Calif.	1891	1974	Protestant
Warren E. Burger, Va.	1969–1986	17	Minn.	1907	—	Presbyterian
William H. Rehnquist, Ariz.	1986–		Wis.	1924	—	Lutheran
ASSOCIATE JUSTICES						
James Wilson, Pa.	1789–1798	8	Scotland	1742	1798	Episcopal
John Rutledge, S.C.	1790–1791	1	S.C.	1739	1800	Church of England
William Cushing, Mass.	1790–1810	20	Mass.	1732	1810	Unitarian
John Blair, Va.	1790–1796	5	Va.	1732	1800	Presbyterian
James Iredell, N.C.	1790–1799	9	England	1751	1799	Episcopal
Thomas Johnson, Md.	1792–1793	0	Md.	1732	1819	Episcopal
William Paterson, N.J.	1793–1806	13	Ireland	1745	1806	Protestant
Samuel Chase, Md.	1796–1811	15	Md.	1741	1811	Episcopal
Bushrod Washington, Va.	1799–1829	30	Va.	1762	1829	Episcopal
Alfred Moore, N.C.	1800–1804	3	N.C.	1755	1810	Episcopal
William Johnson, S.C.	1804–1834	30	S.C.	1771	1834	Presbyterian
Brockholst Livingston, N.Y.	1807–1823	16	N.Y.	1757	1823	Presbyterian
Thomas Todd, Ky.	1807–1826	18	Va.	1765	1826	Presbyterian
Gabriel Duval, Md.	1811–1835	23	Md.	1752	1844	French Protestant
Joseph Story, Mass.	1812–1845	33	Mass.	1779	1845	Unitarian
Smith Thompson, N.Y.	1823–1843	20	N.Y.	1768	1843	Presbyterian
Robert Trimble, Ky.	1826–1828	2	Va.	1777	1828	Protestant
John McLean, Ohio	1830–1861	31	N.J.	1785	1861	Methodist-Epis.
Henry Baldwin, Pa.	1830–1844	14	Conn.	1780	1844	Trinity Church
James M. Wayne, Ga.	1835–1867	32	Ga.	1790	1867	Protestant
Philip P. Barbour, Va.	1836–1841	4	Va.	1783	1841	Episcopal
John Catron, Tenn.	1837–1865	28	Pa.	1786	1865	Presbyterian
John McKinley, Ala.	1837–1852	14	Va.	1780	1852	Protestant
Peter V. Daniel, Va.	1841–1860	18	Va.	1784	1860	Episcopal
Samuel Nelson, N.Y.	1845–1872	27	N.Y.	1792	1873	Protestant
Levi Woodbury, N.H.	1845–1851	5	N.H.	1789	1851	Protestant
Robert C. Grier, Pa.	1846–1870	23	Pa.	1794	1870	Presbyterian
Benjamin R. Curtis, Mass.	1851–1857	5	Mass.	1809	1874	(2)
John A. Campbell, Ala.	1853–1861	8	Ga.	1811	1889	Episcopal
Nathan Clifford, Maine	1858–1881	23	N.H.	1803	1881	(1)
Noah H. Swayne, Ohio	1862–1881	18	Va.	1804	1884	Quaker
Samuel F. Miller, Iowa	1862–1890	28	Ky.	1816	1890	Unitarian
David Davis, Ill.	1862–1877	14	Md.	1815	1886	(4)
Stephen J. Field, Calif.	1863–1897	34	Conn.	1816	1899	Episcopal
William Strong, Pa.	1870–1880	10	Conn.	1808	1895	Presbyterian
Joseph P. Bradley, N.J.	1870–1892	21	N.Y.	1813	1892	Presbyterian
Ward Hunt, N.Y.	1872–1882	9	N.Y.	1810	1886	Episcopal
John M. Harlan, Ky.	1877–1911	33	Ky.	1833	1911	Presbyterian
William B. Woods, Ga.	1880–1887	6	Ohio	1824	1887	Protestant
Stanley Matthews, Ohio	1881–1889	7	Ohio	1824	1889	Presbyterian
Horace Gray, Mass.	1882–1902	20	Mass.	1828	1902	(3)
Samuel Blatchford, N.Y.	1882–1893	11	N.Y.	1820	1893	Presbyterian
Lucius Q. C. Lamar, Miss.	1888–1893	5	Ga.	1825	1893	Methodist
David J. Brewer, Kan.	1889–1910	20	Asia Minor	1837	1910	Protestant
Henry B. Brown, Mich.	1890–1906	15	Mass.	1836	1913	Protestant
George Shiras, Jr., Pa.	1892–1903	10	Pa.	1832	1924	Presbyterian
Howell E. Jackson, Tenn.	1893–1895	2	Tenn.	1832	1895	Baptist
Edward D. White, La.	1894–1910	16	La.	1845	1921	Roman Catholic

Name; apptd. from	Service		Brith			
	Term	Yrs	Place	Date	Died	Religion
Rufus W. Peckham, N.Y.	1895–1909	13	N.Y.	1838	1909	Episcopal
Joseph McKenna, Calif.	1898–1925	26	Pa.	1843	1926	Roman Catholic
Oliver W. Holmes, Mass.	1902–1932	29	Mass.	1841	1935	Unitarian
William R. Day, Ohio	1903–1922	19	Ohio	1849	1923	Protestant
William H. Moody, Mass.	1906–1910	3	Mass.	1853	1917	Episcopal
Horace H. Lurton, Tenn.	1909–1914	4	Ky.	1844	1914	Episcopal
Charles E. Hughes, N.Y.	1910–1916	5	N.Y.	1862	1948	Baptist
Willis Van Devanter, Wyo.	1910–1937	26	Ind.	1859	1941	Episcopal
Joseph R. Lamar, Ga.	1910–1916	4	Ga.	1857	1916	Ch. of Disciples
Mahlon Pitney, N.J.	1912–1922	10	N.J.	1858	1924	Presbyterian
James C. McReynolds, Tenn.	1914–1941	26	Ky.	1862	1946	Disciples of Christ
Louis D. Brandeis, Mass.	1916–1939	22	Ky.	1856	1941	Jewish
John H. Clarke, Ohio	1916–1922	5	Ohio	1857	1945	Protestant
George Sutherland, Utah	1922–1938	15	England	1862	1942	Episcopal
Pierce Butler, Minn.	1923–1939	16	Minn.	1866	1939	Roman Catholic
Edward T. Sanford, Tenn.	1923–1930	7	Tenn.	1865	1930	Episcopal
Harlan F. Stone, N.Y.	1925–1941	16	N.H.	1872	1946	Episcopal
Owen J. Roberts, Pa.	1930–1945	15	Pa.	1875	1955	Episcopal
Benjamin N. Cardozo, N.Y.	1932–1938	6	N.Y.	1870	1938	Jewish
Hugo L. Black, Ala.	1937–1971	34	Ala.	1886	1971	Baptist
Stanley F. Reed, Ky.	1938–1957	19	Ky.	1884	1980	Protestant
Felix Frankfurter, Mass.	1939–1962	23	Austria	1882	1965	Jewish
William O. Douglas, Conn.	1939–1975	36	Minn.	1898	1980	Presbyterian
Frank Murphy, Mich.	1940–1949	9	Mich.	1890	1949	Roman Catholic
James F. Byrnes, S.C.	1941–1942	1	S.C.	1879	1972	Episcopal
Robert H. Jackson, Pa.	1941–1954	13	N.Y.	1892	1954	Episcopal
Wiley B. Rutledge, Iowa	1943–1949	6	Ky.	1894	1949	Unitarian
Harold H. Burton, Ohio	1945–1958	13	Mass.	1888	1964	Unitarian
Tom C. Clark, Tex.	1949–1967	17	Tex.	1899	1977	Presbyterian
Sherman Minton, Ind.	1949–1956	7	Ind.	1890	1965	Roman Catholic
John M. Harlan, N.Y.	1955–1971	16	Ill.	1899	1971	Presbyterian
William J. Brennan, Jr., N.J.	1956–1990	33	N.J.	1906	—	Roman Catholic
Charles E. Whittaker, Mo.	1957–1962	5	Kan.	1901	1973	Methodist
Potter Stewart, Ohio	1958–1981	23	Mich.	1915	1985	Episcopal
Byron R. White, Colo.	1962–	—	Colo.	1917	—	Episcopal
Arthur J. Goldberg, Ill.	1962–1965	2	Ill.	1908	—	Jewish
Abe Fortas, Tenn.	1965–1969	3	Tenn.	1910	1982	Jewish
Thurgood Marshall, N.Y.	1967–1991	24	Md.	1908	—	Episcopal
Harry A. Blackmun, Minn.	1970–	—	Ill.	1908	—	Methodist
Lewis F. Powell, Jr., Va.	1972–1987	15	Va.	1907	—	Presbyterian
William H. Rehnquist, Ariz.	1972–1986	14	Wis.	1924	—	Lutheran
John Paul Stevens, Ill.	1975–	—	Ill.	1920	—	Protestant
Sandra Day O'Connor, Ariz.	1981–	—	Tex.	1930	—	Episcopal
Antonin Scalia, D.C.	1986–	—	N.J.	1936	—	Roman Catholic
Anthony M. Kennedy, Calif.	1988–	—	Calif.	1936	—	n.a.
David H. Souter, N.H.	1990–	—	Mass.	1939	—	Episcopal
Clarence Thomas, D.C.	1991–	—	Ga.	1948	—	Episcopal

1. Congregational; later Unitarian. 2. Unitarian; then Episcopal. 3. Unitarian or Congregational. 4. Not a member of any church. NOTE: n.a. = not available.

U.S. Government

Black Elected Officials

Year	U.S. and State Legislatures[1]	City and County Offices[2]	Law Enforce- ment[3]	Education[4]	Total
1970 (Feb.)	182	715	213	362	1,472
1975 (Apr.)	299	1,878	387	939	3,503
1977 (July)	316	2,497	447	1,051	4,311
1978 (July)	316	2,595	454	1,138	4,503
1979 (July)	315	2,647	486	1,136	4,584
1980 (July)	326	2,832	526	1,206	4,890
1981 (July)	343	2,863	549	1,259	5,014
1982 (July)	342	2,951	563	1,259	5,115
1983 (July)	366	3,197	607	1,369	5,559
1984 (Jan.)	396	3,259	636	1,363	5,654
1985 (Jan.)	407	3,517	661	1,431	6,016 [5]
1986 (Jan.)	420	3,824	676	1,504	6,424 [5]
1987 (Jan.)	440	3,966	728	1,547	6,681
1988 (July)	436	4,105	738	1,550	6,829
1989 (Jan.)	448	4,406	759	1,612	7,225
1990 (Jan.)	447	4,499	769	1,655	7,370

1. Includes elected State administrators and governors. 2. County commissioners and councilmen, mayors, vice mayors, aldermen, regional officials, and other. 3. Judges, magistrates, constables, marshals, sheriffs, justices of the peace, and other. 4. Members of State education agencies, college boards, school boards, and other. 5. Includes Black elected officials in the Virgin Islands. *Source:* Joint Center for Political and Economic Studies, Washington, D.C., *Black Elected Officials: A National Roster,* Copyright.

Qualifications for Voting

The Supreme Court decision of March 21, 1972, declared lengthy requirements for voting in state and local elections unconstitutional and suggested that 30 days was an ample period. Most of the states have changed or eliminated their durational residency requirements to comply with the ruling, as shown.

NO DURATIONAL RESIDENCY REQUIREMENT

Alabama,[6] Arkansas, Connecticut,[13] Delaware,[12] District of Columbia,[16] Florida,[5] Georgia,[2] Hawaii,[2] Iowa,[6] Louisiana,[8] Maine, Maryland, Massachusetts,[3] Missouri,[4] Nebraska,[9] New Hampshire,[17] New Mexico,[7] North Carolina, Oklahoma, South Carolina,[22] South Dakota,[10] Tennessee,[20] Texas, Virginia, West Virginia,[2] Wyoming[2]

30-DAY RESIDENCY REQUIREMENT

Alaska,[18] Arizona,[11] Idaho,[17] Illinois, Indiana, Kentucky,[2] Michigan, Mississippi,[21] Montana, Nevada, New Jersey, New York, North Dakota,[3] Ohio, Pennsylvania, Rhode Island, Utah, Washington

OTHER

California,[19] Colorado,[1] Kansas, Minnesota[15] and Oregon, 20 days; Vermont, 17 days;[14] Wisconsin, 10 days

1. 32 days. 2. 30-day registration requirement. 3. No residency required to register to vote. 4. Must be registered by the fourth Wednesday prior to election. 5. 30-day registration requirement for national elections; 30-day for state elections. 6. 10-day registration requirement. In-person registration by 5 PM, eleven days before election date. 7. Must register 28 days before election. 8. 24 days prior to any election. 9. Registration requirement, 2nd Friday prior to elections. 10. 15-day registration requirement. 11. Residency in the state 29 days next preceding the election. 12. Must reside in Delaware and register by the last day that the books are open for registration. 13. Registration deadline 21st day before election; registration and party enrollment deadline the day before primary; unaffiliated voters may vote in Republican primaries for *some* offices. 14. Administrative cut-off date for processing applications. 15. Permits registration and voting on election day with approved ID. 16. Registration stops 30 days before any election and until 15 days after. Voters must inform Board of Elections of change of address within 30 days of moving. 17. Registration requirement, 10 days prior to elections. 18. If otherwise qualified but has not been a resident of the election district for at least 30 days preceding the date of a presidential election, is entitled to register and vote for presidential and vice   presidential candidates. 19. 29 days before an election. 20. Must be resident of state for a period of at least 20 days prior to registration. *Source: Information Please* questionnaires to the states. 21. 30 days registration required, 60 days if registration is by mail. 22. Registration certificate not valid for 30 days but if you move within the state you can vote in old precinct during the 30 days.

Unusual Voting Results

Election of 1872

The presidential and vice-presidential candidates of the Liberal Republicans and the northern Democrats in 1872 were Horace Greeley and B. Gratz Brown. Greeley died Nov. 29, 1872, before his 66 electors voted. In the electoral balloting for President, 63 of Greeley's votes were scattered among four other men, including Brown.

Election of 1876

In the election of 1876 Samuel J. Tilden, the Democratic candidate, received a popular majority but lacked one undisputed electoral vote to carry a clear majority of the electoral college. The crux of the problem was in the 22 electoral votes which were in dispute because Florida, Louisiana, South Carolina, and Oregon each sent in two sets of election returns. In the three southern states, Republican election boards threw out enough Democratic votes to certify the Republican candidate, Hayes. In Oregon, the Democratic governor disqualified a Republican elector, replacing him with a Democrat. Since the Senate was Republican and the House of Representatives Democratic, it seemed useless to refer the disputed returns to the two houses for solution. Instead Congress appointed an Electoral Commission with five representatives each from the Senate, the House, and the Supreme Court. All but one Justice was named, giving the Commission seven Republican and seven Democratic members. The naming of the fifth Justice was left to the other four. He was a Republican who first favored Tilden but, under pressure from his party, switched to Hayes, ensuring his election by the Commission voting 8 to 7 on party lines.

Minority Presidents

Fifteen candidates have become President of the United States with a popular vote less than 50% of the total cast. It should be noted, however, that in elections before 1872, presidential electors were not chosen by popular vote in all states. Adams' election in 1824 was by the House of Representatives, which chose him over Jackson, who had a plurality of both electoral and popular votes, but not a majority in the electoral college.

Besides Jackson in 1824, only two other candidates receiving the largest popular vote have failed to gain a majority in the electoral college—Samuel J. Tilden (D) in 1876 and Grover Cleveland (D) in 1888. The "minority" Presidents follow:

Vote Received by Minority Presidents

Year	President	Electoral Percent	Popular vote Percent
1824	John Q. Adams	31.8	29.8
1844	James K. Polk (D)	61.8	49.3
1848	Zachary Taylor (W)	56.2	47.3
1856	James Buchanan (D)	58.7	45.3
1860	Abraham Lincoln (R)	59.4	39.9
1876	Rutherford B. Hayes (R)	50.1	47.9
1880	James A. Garfield (R)	57.9	48.3
1884	Grover Cleveland (D)	54.6	48.8
1888	Benjamin Harrison (R)	58.1	47.8
1892	Grover Cleveland (D)	62.4	46.0
1912	Woodrow Wilson (D)	81.9	41.8
1916	Woodrow Wilson (D)	52.1	49.3
1948	Harry S. Truman (D)	57.1	49.5
1960	John F. Kennedy (D)	56.4	49.7
1968	Richard M. Nixon (R)	56.1	43.4

Annual Salaries of Federal Officials

President of the U.S.	$200,000[1]	Senators and Representatives	$125,100
Vice President of the U.S.	160,600[2]	President Pro Tempore of Senate	138,900
Cabinet members	138,900	Majority and Minority Leader of the Senate	138,900
Deputy Secretaries of State, Defense, Treasury	125,100	Majority and Minority Leader of the House	138,900
Deputy Attorney General	125,100	Speaker of the House	160,600
Secretaries of the Army, Navy, Air Force	125,100	Chief Justice of the United States	160,600
Under secretaries of executive departments	115,300	Associate Justices of the Supreme Court	153,600

1. Plus taxable $50,000 for expenses and a nontaxable sum (not to exceed $100,000 a year) for travel expenses. 2. Plus taxable $10,000 for expenses. NOTE: All salaries shown above are taxable. Data are as of September 1991. *Source:* Office of Personnel Management.

Order of Presidential Succession

1. The Vice President
2. Speaker of the House
3. President pro tempore of the Senate
4. Secretary of State
5. Secretary of the Treasury
6. Secretary of Defense
7. Attorney General
8. Secretary of the Interior
9. Secretary of Agriculture
10. Secretary of Commerce
11. Secretary of Labor
12. Secretary of Health and Human Services
13. Secretary of Housing and Urban Development
14. Secretary of Transportation
15. Secretary of Energy
16. Secretary of Education

NOTE: An official cannot succeed to the Presidency unless that person meets the Constitutional requirements.

The Military

Highest Ranking Officers in the Armed Forces

ARMY[1]
Generals; Colin L. Powell, Chairman of the Joint Chiefs of Staff; Gordon R. Sullivan, Chief of Staff; Robert Riscassi, Vice Chief of Staff; John R. Galvin, Supreme Allied Commander, Europe and Commander-in-Chief, U.S. European Command; Edwin H. Burba, Jr.; John W. Foss; George A. Joulwan; Crosbie E. Saint; Carl W. Stiner; William G.T. Tuttle, Jr.

AIR FORCE
Generals: Merril A. McPeak, Chief of Staff; Jimmie V. Adams; George L. Butler; Michael P.C. Carns; Hansford T. Johnson; Donald J. Kutyna; John M. Loh; James P. McCarthy; Charles C. McDonald; Robert C. Oaks; John A. Shaud; Ronald W. Yates.

1. On March 15, 1978, George Washington, the commander of the Continental Army in the American Revolution and our first President, was promoted posthumously to the newly-created rank of General of the Armies of the United States. Congress authorized this title to make it clear that Washington is the Army's senior general. *Source:* Department of Defense.

NAVY
Admirals: Frank B. Kelso II, Chief of Naval Operations; Leon A. Edney; Bruce DeMars; Jonathan T. Howe; Charles R. Larson; Jerome L. Johnson; Paul D. Miller; William D. Smith; Robert J. Kelly.

MARINE CORPS
Generals: Carl E. Mundy, Jr., Commandant of the Marine Corps; John R. Dailey, Assistant Commandant of the Marine Corps and Chief of Staff; Joseph P. Hoar.
Lieutenant Generals: William Keys, Walter Boomer, Robert Winglass, Royal Moore, Jr., Robert B. Johnston, Henry C. Stackpole, III, Martin Brandtner.

COAST GUARD
Admiral: Adm. J. William Kime, Commandant.
Vice Admirals: Vice Adm. Martin H. Daniell, Jr., Vice Commandant; Vice Adm. Howard B. Thorsen, Commander Atlantic Area; Vice Adm. A. Bruce Beren, Commander Pacific Area.

History of the Armed Services

Source: Department of Defense.

U.S. Army

On June 14, 1775, the Continental Congress "adopted" the New England Armies—a mixed force of volunteers besieging the British in Boston—appointing a committee to draft "Rules and regulations for the government of the Army" and voting to raise 10 rifle companies as a reinforcement. The next day, it appointed Washington commander-in-chief of the "Continental forces to be raised for the defense of liberty," and he took command at Boston on July 3, 1775. The Continental Army that fought the Revolution was our first national military organization, and hence the Army is the senior service. After the war, the army was radically reduced but enough survived to form a small Regular Army of about 700 men under the Constitution, a nucleus for expansion in the 1790s to successfully meet threats from the Indians and from France. From these humble beginnings, the U.S. Army has developed, normally expanding rapidly by absorbing citizen soldiers in wartime and contracting just as rapidly after each war.

U.S. Navy

The antecedents of the U.S. Navy go back to September 1775, when Gen. Washington commissioned 7 schooners and brigantines to prey on British supply vessels bound for the Colonies or Canada. On Oct. 13, 1775, a resolve of the Continental Congress called for the purchase of 2 vessels for the purpose of intercepting enemy transports. With its passage a Naval Committee of 7 men was formed, and they rapidly obtained passage of legislation calling for procurement of additional vessels. The Continental Navy was supplemented by privateers and ships operated as state navies, but soon after the British surrender it was disestablished.

In 1794, because of dissatisfaction with the payment of tribute to the Barbary pirates, Congress authorized construction of 6 frigates. The first, *United States,* was launched May 10, 1797, but the Navy still remained under the control of the Secretary of War until April 1798, when the Navy Department was created under the Secretary of the Navy with Cabinet rank.

U.S. Air Force

Until creation of the National Military Establishment in September 1947, which united the services under one department, military aviation was a part of the U.S. Army. In the Army, aeronautical operations came under the Signal Corps from 1907 to 1918, when the Army Air Service was established. In 1926, the Army Air Corps came into being and remained until 1941, when the Army Air Forces succeeded it as the Army's air arm. On Sept. 18, 1947, the U.S. Air Force was established as an independent military service under the National Military Establishment. At that time, the name "Army Air Forces" was abolished.

U.S. Coast Guard

Our country's oldest continuous seagoing service, the U.S. Coast Guard, traces its history back to 1790, when the first Congress authorized the construction of ten vessels for the collection of revenue. Known first as the Revenue Marine, and later as the Revenue Cutter Service, the Coast Guard received its present name in 1915 under an act of Congress combining the Revenue Cutter Service with the Life-Saving Service. In 1939, the Lighthouse Service was also consolidated with this unit. The Bureau of Marine Inspection and Navigation was transferred temporarily to the Coast Guard in 1942, permanently in 1946. Through its antecedents, the Coast Guard is one of the oldest organizations under the federal government and, until the Navy Department was established in 1798, served as the only U.S. armed force afloat. In times of peace, it operates under the Department of Transportation, serving as the nation's primary agency for promoting marine safety and enforcing federal maritime laws. In times of war, or on direction of the President, it is attached to the Navy Department.

U.S. Marine Corps

Founded in 1775 and observing its official birthday on Nov. 10, the U.S. Marine Corps was developed to serve on land, on sea, and in the air.

Marines have fought in every U.S. war. From an initial two battalions in the Revolution, the Corps reached a peak strength of six divisions and five aircraft wings in World War II. Its present strength is three active divisions and aircraft wings and a Reserve division/aircraft wing team. In 1947, the National Security Act set Marine Corps strength at not less than three divisions and three aircraft wings.

Service Academies

U.S. Military Academy

Source: U.S. Military Academy.

Established in 1802 by an act of Congress, the U.S. Military Academy is located on the west bank of the Hudson River some 50 miles north of New York City. To gain admission a candidate must first secure a nomination from an authorized source. These sources are:

Congressional Sources

Representatives
Senators
Other: Vice Presidential
   District of Columbia
   Puerto Rico
   Am. Samoa, Guam, Virgin Is.

Military-Service-Connected Sources

Presidential—Sons or daughers of active duty or re-
   tired service members
Enlisted members of Army
Enlisted members of Army Reserve/
   National Guard
Sons and daughters of deceased and disabled
   veterans
Honor military, naval schools
   and ROTC
Sons and daughters of persons awarded the
   Medal of Honor

Any number of applicants can meet the requirements for a *nomination* in these categories. *Appointments* (offers of admission), however, can only be made to a much smaller number, about 1,200 each year.

Candidates may be nominated for vacancies during the year preceding the day of admission, which occurs in early July. The best time to apply is during the junior year in high school.

Candidates must be citizens of the U.S., be unmarried, be at least 17 but not yet 22 years old on July 1 of the year admitted, have a secondary-school education or its equivalent, and be able to meet the academic, medical, and physical aptitude requirements.

Academic qualification is determined by an analysis of entire scholastic record, and performance on either the American College Testing (ACT) Assessment Program Test or the College Entrance Examination Board Scholastic Aptitude Test (SAT). Entrance requirements and procedures for appointment are described in the Admissions Bulletin, available without charge from Admissions, U.S. Military Academy, West Point, N.Y. 10996-1797.

Cadets are members of the Regular Army. As such they receive full scholarships and annual salaries from which they pay for their uniforms, textbooks, and incidental expenses. Upon successful completion of the four-year course, the graduate receives the degree of Bachelor of Science and is commissioned a second lieutenant in the Regular Army with a requirement to serve as an officer for a minimum of six years.

U.S. Naval Academy

Source: U.S. Naval Academy.

The Naval School, established in 1845 at Fort Severn, Annapolis, Md., was renamed the U.S. Naval Academy in 1850. A four-year course was adopted a year later.

The Superintendent is a rear admiral. A civilian academic dean heads the academic program. A captain heads the 4,300-man Brigade of Midshipmen and military, professional, and physical training. The faculty is half military and half civilian.

Graduates are awarded the Bachelor of Science or Bachelor of Science in Engineering and are commissioned as officers in the U.S. Navy or Marine Corps.

Midshipmen are nominated for an appointment from several official sources, which are summarized below. The numbers represent the total each nominator may have at the academy at any one time. Five each from the Vice President, U.S. Senators, U.S. Representatives, the delegate from Washington, D.C., and the Resident Commissioner of Puerto Rico. Delegates from Guam and the Virgin Islands nominate two each, with one each from the Governor of Puerto Rico, the delegate from American Samoa, and the Office of the Administrator of the Panama Canal Commission.

Annual nominations are from several other sources: Presidential nominations for 100 sons and daughters of career military personnel; 85 each from the regular Navy and Marine corps, and the Navy and Marine Corps reserve; 20 from NROTC/NJROTC/MCJROTC and Honor Military and Naval schools; 65 sons and daughters of disabled veterans or POWs, 600 qualified alternates; and an unlimited number of sons and daughters of Medal of Honor recipients.

To have basic eligibility for admission, candidates must be citizens of the U.S., of good moral character, at least 17 and not more than 22 years of age on July 1 of their entering year, and unmarried.

In order to be considered for admission, a candidate must obtain a nomination from one of the sources of appointments listed above. The Admissions Board at the Naval Academy examines the candidate's school record, College Board or ACT scores, recommendations from school officials, extracurricular activities, and evidence from other sources concerning his or her character, leadership potential, academic preparation, and physical fitness. Qualification for admission is based on all of the above factors.

Tuition, board, lodging, and medical and dental care are provided. Midshipmen receive over $500 a month for books, uniforms, and personal needs.

For general information or answers to specific questions, write: Director of Candidate Guidance, U.S. Naval Academy, Annapolis, Md. 21402-5018.

U.S. Air Force Academy

Source: U.S. Air Force Academy.

The bill establishing the Air Force Academy was signed by President Eisenhower on April 1, 1954. The first class of 306 cadets was sworn in on July 11, 1955, at Lowry Air Force Base, Denver, the Academy's temporary location. The Cadet Wing moved into the Academy's permanent home north of Colorado Springs, Colorado, in 1958.

Cadets receive four years of academic, military, and physical education to prepare them for leadership as officers in the Air Force. The Academy is authorized a total of 4,400 cadets. Each new class averages 1,400. The candidates for the Academy must be at least 17 but less than 22 on July 1 of the year for which they enter the Academy, must be a United States citizen, never married, and be able to meet the mental and physical requirements. A candidate is required to take the following examinations and tests: (1) the Service Academies' Qualifying Medical Examination; (2) either the American College Testing (ACT) Assessment Program test or the College Entrance Examination Board Scholastic Aptitude Test (SAT); and (3) a Physical Aptitude Examination.

Cadets receive their entire education at government expense and, in addition, are paid more than $500 per month base pay. From this sum, they pay for their uniforms, textbooks, tailoring, laundry, entertainment tickets, etc. Upon completion of the four-year program, leading to a Bachelor of Science degree, a cadet who meets the qualifications is commissioned a second lieutenant in the U.S. Air Force. Nearly 65 percent enter pilot or navigator training. For details on admissions, write: Director of Cadet Admissions (RRS), HQ USAF Academy, Colorado Springs, CO 80840-5651.

U.S. Coast Guard Academy

Source: U.S. Coast Guard Academy.

The U.S. Coast Guard Academy, New London, Conn., was founded on July 31, 1876, to serve as the "School of Instruction" for the Revenue Cutter Service, predecessor to the Coast Guard.

The J.C. Dobbin, a converted schooner, housed the first Coast Guard Academy, and was succeeded in 1878 by the barque Chase, a ship built for cadet training. First winter quarters were in a sail loft at New Bedford, Mass. The school was moved in 1900 to Arundel Cove, Md., to provide a more technical education, and in 1910 was moved back to New England to Fort Trumbull, New London, Conn. In 1932 the Academy moved to its present location in New London.

The Academy today offers a four-year curriculum for the professional and academic training of cadets, which leads to a Bachelor of Science degree and a commission as ensign in the Coast Guard.

The U.S. Coast Guard Academy is the only one of the five federal service academies that offers appointments solely on the basis of an annual nationwide competition; there are no congressional nominations or geographical quotas involved. Competition is open to any young American who meets the basic eligibility requirements, which consist of satisfactory Scholastic Aptitude Test (SAT) or American College Testing Program examination (ACT) results, high school standing, and leadership potential. Either the SAT or the ACT must be completed prior to or during the December test administration of the year of application. All cadets must have reached their 17th but not their 22nd birthday by July 1 of the year of entrance to the Academy. All cadets must pass a rigid medical examination before being accepted.

Women were first admitted to the Coast Guard Academy in 1976 and first graduated in 1980. Cadets must be unmarried upon entry and must remain unmarried until after graduation. As ensigns, they must serve a six-year obligation following graduation. Cadets receive a stipend to cover incidentals and uniform expenses. Meals and quarters are provided.

A catalog can be obtained by writing to: Director of Admissions, U.S. Coast Guard Academy, 15 Mohegan Ave., New London, Conn. 06320-4195, or call (203) 444-8501 or (800) 424-8883.

U.S. Merchant Marine Academy

Source: U.S. Merchant Marine Academy.

The U.S. Merchant Marine Academy, situated at Kings Point, N.Y., on the north shore of Long Island, was dedicated Sept. 30, 1943. It is maintained by the Department of Transportation under direction of the Maritime Administration.

The Academy has a complement of approximately 840 men and women representing every state, D.C., the Canal Zone, Puerto Rico, Guam, American Samoa, and the Virgin Islands. It is also authorized to admit up to 12 candidates from the Western Hemisphere and 30 other foreign students at any one time.

Candidates are nominated by Senators and members of the House of Representatives. Nominations to the Academy are governed by a state and territory quota system based on population and the results of the College Entrance Examination Board tests.

A candidate must be a citizen not less than 17 and not yet 22 years of age by July 1 of the year in which admission is sought. Fifteen high school credits, including 3 units in mathematics (from algebra, geometry and/or trigonometry), 1 unit in science (physics or chemistry) and 3 in English are required.

The course is four years and includes one year of practical training aboard a merchant ship. Study includes marine engineering, navigation, satellite navigation and communications, electricity, ship construction, naval science and tactics, economics, business, languages, history, etc.

Upon completion of the course of study, a graduate receives a Bachelor of Science degree, a license as a merchant marine deck or engineering officer, and a commission as an Ensign in the Naval Reserve.

U.S. Casualties in Major Wars

War	Branch of service	Numbers engaged	Battle deaths	Other deaths	Total deaths	Wounds not mortal	Total casualties[1]
Revolutionary War	Army	n.a.	4,044	n.a.	n.a.	6,004	n.a.
1775 to 1783	Navy	n.a.	342	n.a.	n.a.	114	n.a.
	Marines	n.a.	49	n.a.	n.a.	70	n.a.
	Total	**n.a.**	**4,435**	**n.a.**	**n.a.**	**6,188**	**n.a.**
War of 1812	Army	n.a.	1,950	n.a.	n.a.	4,000	n.a.
1812 to 1815	Navy	n.a.	265	n.a.	n.a.	439	n.a.
	Marines	n.a.	45	n.a.	n.a.	66	n.a.
	Total	**286,730**	**2,260**	**n.a.**	**n.a.**	**4,505**	**n.a.**
Mexican War	Army	n.a.	1,721	11,550	13,271	4,102	17,373
1846 to 1848	Navy	n.a.	1	n.a.	n.a.	3	n.a.
	Marines	n.a.	11	n.a.	n.a.	47	n.a.
	Total	**78,718**	**1,733**	**n.a.**	**n.a.**	**4,152**	**n.a.**
Civil War[2]	Army	2,128,948	138,154	221,374	359,528	280,040	639,568
1861 to 1865	Navy	84,415	2,112	2,411	4,523	1,710	6,233
	Marines		148	312	460	131	591
	Total	**2,213,363**	**140,414**	**224,097**	**364,511**	**281,881**	**646,392**
Spanish-American War	Army	280,564	369	2,061	2,430	1,594	4,024
1898	Navy	22,875	10	0	10	47	57
	Marines	3,321	6	0	6	21	27
	Total	**306,760**	**385**	**2,061**	**2,446**	**1,662**	**4,108**
World War I	Army	4,057,101	50,510	55,868	106,378	193,663	300,041
1917 to 1918	Navy	599,051	431	6,856	7,287	819	8,106
	Marines	78,839	2,461	390	2,851	9,520	12,371
	Total	**4,734,991**	**53,402**	**63,114**	**116,516**	**204,002**	**320,518**
World War II	Army[3]	11,260,000	234,874	83,400	318,274	565,861	884,135
1941 to 1946	Navy	4,183,466	36,950	25,664	62,614	37,778	100,392
	Marines	669,100	19,733	4,778	24,511	67,207	91,718
	Total	**16,112,566**	**291,557**	**113,842**	**405,399**	**670,846**	**1,076,245**
Korean War	Army	2,834,000	27,704	9,429	37,133	77,596	114,729
1950 to 1953	Navy	1,177,000	458	4,043	4,501	1,576	6,077
	Marine	424,000	4,267	1,261	5,528	23,744	29,272
	Air Force	1,285,000	1,200	5,884	7,084	368	7,452
	Total	**5,720,000**	**33,629**	**20,617**	**54,246**	**103,284**	**157,530**
War in Southeast Asia[4]	Army	4,386,000	30,904	7,270	38,174	96,802	134,976
	Navy[5]	1,842,000	1,634	916	2,552	4,178	6,730
	Marines	794,000	13,079	1,750	14,829	51,392	66,221
	Air Force	1,740,000	1,765	815	2,580	931	3,511
	Total	**8,744,000**	**47,382**	**10,753**	**58,135**	**153,303**	**211,438**

1. Excludes captured or interned and missing in action who were subsequently returned to military control. 2. Union forces only. Totals should probably be somewhat larger as data or disposition of prisoners are far from complete. Final Confederate deaths, based on incomplete returns, were 133,821, to which should be added 26,000–31,000 personnel who died in Union prisons. 3. Army data include Air Force. 4. As of Nov. 11, 1986. 5. Includes a small number of Coast Guard of which 5 were battle deaths. NOTE: All data are subject to revision. For wars before World War I, information represents best data from available records. However, due to incomplete records and possible difference in usage of terminology, reporting systems, etc., figures should be considered estimates. n.a. = not available. *Source:* Department of Defense.

Casualties in World War I

Country	Total mobilized forces	Killed or died[1]	Wounded	Prisoners or missing	Total Casualties
Austria-Hungary	7,800,000	1,200,000	3,620,000	2,200,000	7,020,000
Belgium	267,000	13,716	44,686	34,659	93,061
British Empire[2]	8,904,467	908,371	2,090,212	191,652	3,190,235
Bulgaria	1,200,000	87,500	152,390	27,029	266,919
France[2]	8,410,000	1,357,800	4,266,000	537,000	6,160,800
Germany	11,000,000	1,773,700	4,216,058	1,152,800	7,142,558
Greece	230,000	5,000	21,000	1,000	27,000
Italy	5,615,000	650,000	947,000	600,000	2,197,000
Japan	800,000	300	907	3	1,210
Montenegro	50,000	3,000	10,000	7,000	20,000
Portugal	100,000	7,222	13,751	12,318	33,291
Romania	750,000	335,706	120,000	80,000	535,706
Russia	12,000,000	1,700,000	4,950,000	2,500,000	9,150,000
Serbia	707,343	45,000	133,148	152,958	331,106
Turkey	2,850,000	325,000	400,000	250,000	975,000
United States	4,734,991	116,516	204,002	—	320,518

1. Includes deaths from all causes. 2. Official figures. NOTE: For additional U.S. figures, *see* the table on U.S. Casualties in Major Wars in this section.

Casualties in World War II

Country	Men in war	Battle deaths	Wounded
Australia	1,000,000	26,976	180,864
Austria	800,000	280,000	350,117
Belgium	625,000	8,460	55,513[1]
Brazil[2]	40,334	943	4,222
Bulgaria	339,760	6,671	21,878
Canada	1,086,343[7]	42,042[7]	53,145
China[3]	17,250,521	1,324,516	1,762,006
Czechoslovakia	—	6,683[4]	8,017
Denmark	—	4,339	—
Finland	500,000	79,047	50,000
France	—	201,568	400,000
Germany	20,000,000	3,250,000[4]	7,250,000
Greece	—	17,024	47,290
Hungary	—	147,435	89,313
India	2,393,891	32,121	64,354
Italy	3,100,000	149,496[4]	66,716
Japan	9,700,000	1,270,000	140,000
Netherlands	280,000	6,500	2,860
New Zealand	194,000	11,625[4]	17,000
Norway	75,000	2,000	—
Poland	—	664,000	530,000
Romania	650,000[5]	350,000[6]	—
South Africa	410,056	2,473	—
U.S.S.R.	—	6,115,000[4]	14,012,000
United Kingdom	5,896,000	357,116[4]	369,267
United States	16,112,566	291,557	670,846
Yugoslavia	3,741,000	305,000	425,000

1. Civilians only. 2. Army and Navy figures. 3. Figures cover period July 7, 1937–Sept. 2, 1945, and concern only Chinese regular troops. They do not include casualties suffered by guerrillas and local military corps. 4. Deaths from all causes. 5. Against Soviet Russia; 385,847 against Nazi Germany. 6. Against Soviet Russia; 169,822 against Nazi Germany. 7. National Defense Ctr., Canadian Forces Hq., Director of History. NOTE: The figures in this table are unofficial estimates obtained from various sources.

Merchant Marine Casualties in World War II

In 1988, the U.S. Government conferred official veterans status on those who served aboard oceangoing merchant ships in World War II. The officers and crews played a key role in transporting the troops and war material that enabled the United States and its allies to defeat the Axis powers.

During the war, merchant seamen died as a result of enemy attacks at a rate that proportionately exceeded all branches of the armed services, with the exception of the U.S. Marine Corps.

Enemy action sank more than 700 U.S.-flag merchant ships and claimed the lives of over 6,000 civilian seafarers. Untold thousands of additional seamen were wounded or injured during these attacks, and nearly 600 were made prisoners of war.

Veterans' Benefits

Although benefits of various kinds date back to Colonial days, veterans of World War I were the first to receive disability compensation, allotments for dependents, life insurance, and vocational rehabilitation. In the 1940's, these benefits were slowly broadened. On March 15, 1989, the Veterans Administration became the Department of Veterans Affairs.

The following benefits available to veterans require certain minimum periods of active duty during qualifying periods of service and generally are applicable only to those whose discharges are not dishonorable. Certain types of discharges are subject to special adjudication to determine eligibility.

For information or assistance in applying for veterans benefits, write, call, or visit a VA Regional Office. Consult your local telephone directory under United States Government, Department of Veterans Affairs (VA) for the address and telephone number. Toll-free telephone service is available in all 50 States.

Unemployment allowances. Every effort is being made to secure employment for Vietnam veterans. Unemployment benefits are administered by the U.S. Department of Labor.

Loan Guaranty. VA will guarantee loans for a variety of purposes, such as: to buy or build a home; to purchase a manufactured home with or without a lot; and to refinance a home presently owned and occupied by the veteran. When the purpose of a refinancing loan is to lower the interest rate on an existing guaranteed loan then prior occupancy by the veteran or spouse will suffice. VA will guarantee the lender against loss up to 50% on loans of $45,000 or less, the lesser of $36,000 or 40% (never less than $22,500) on loans of more than $45,000, and the lesser of $46,000 or 25% on loans of more than $144,000. On manufactured home loans, the amount of the guarantee is 40% of the loan to a maximum of $20,000. The interest rate may not exceed the maximum rate set by VA and in effect when the loan is made.

Compensation and rehabilitation benefits. These are available to those having some service-connected illness or disability.

Disability compensation. VA pays from $80 to $1,620 per month, and for specific conditions up to $4,628 per month, plus allowances for dependents, where the disability is rated 30% or more.

Vocational Rehabilitation. VA provides professional counseling, training and other assistance to help compensably service-disabled veterans, rated 20 percent or more, who have an employment handicap to achieve maximum independence in daily living and, to the extent possible, to obtain and maintain suitable employment. Generally, a veteran may receive up to 48 months of this assistance during the 12 years from the date he or she is notified of entitlement to VA compensation. All the expenses of a veteran's rehabilitation program are paid by VA. In addition, the veteran receives a subsistence allowance which varies based on the rate of training and number of dependents. For example, a single veteran training full time would receive $333 monthly.

Vocational Training for VA Pension Recipients. Veterans who are awarded pension during the period from February 1, 1985, through January 31, 1992, may participate in a program of vocational training essentially identical to that provided in VA's vocational rehabilitation program. Certain veterans awarded pension before February 1, 1985 may also participate in this program. Participants do not receive any direct payments, such as subsistence allowance, while in training.

Medical and dental care. This includes care in VA and, in certain instances, in non-VA, or other federal hospitals. It also covers outpatient treatment at a VA field facility or, in some cases, by an approved private physician or dentist. Full domiciliary care is also provided to veterans with low incomes. Nursing home care may be provided at certain VA medical facilities or in approved community nursing homes. Hospital and other medical care may also be provided for the spouse and child dependents of a veteran who is permanently and totally disabled due to a service-connected disability; or for survivors of a veteran who dies from a service-connected disability; or for survivors of a veteran who at the time of death had a total disability, permanent in nature, resulting from a service-connected disability. These latter benefits are usually provided in nonfederal facilities. Eligibility criteria for veterans' medical benefits vary. Veterans must agree to make a copayment for the care they receive from VA if their incomes exceed levels that vary with number of dependents and they do not have a service-connected disability or service in certain early war periods. Veterans and/or their dependents or survivors should always apply in advance. Contact the nearest VA medical facility.

Readjustment Counseling. VA provides readjustment counseling to veterans of the Vietnam Era in need of assistance in resolving post-war readjustment problems in the areas of employment, family, education, and personal readjustment including post-traumatic stress disorder. Services are provided at community-based Vet Centers and at VA Medical Centers in certain locations. Services include individual family and group counseling, employment and educational counseling, and assistance in obtaining referrals to various governmental and nongovernmental agencies with an interest in assisting Vietnam Era veterans. Contact the nearest Vet Center or VA facility to determine location of Vet Center.

Dependents' educational assistance. VA pays $404 a month for up to 45 months of schooling to spouses and children of veterans who died of service-connected causes or who were permanently and totally disabled from service-connected causes or died while permanently and totally disabled or who are currently missing in action, captured in the line of duty, or forcibly detained or interned in line of duty by a foreign power for more than 90 days. Students must usually be between 18 and 26.

Veterans readjustment education. Veterans and servicepersons who initially entered the military on or after Jan. 1, 1977, and before July 1, 1985, may receive educational assistance under a contributory plan. Individuals contribute $25 to $100 from military pay, up to a maximum of $2,700. This amount is matched by the Federal Government on a 2 for 1 basis. Participants, while on active duty, may make a lump sum contribution. Participants receive monthly payments for the number of months they contributed, or for 36 months, whichever is less. No initial enrollments are permitted after March 31, 1987.

Montgomery GI Bill. This Act provides education benefits for individuals entering the military after June 30, 1985. Servicepersons entering active duty after that date will have their basic pay reduced by $100 a month for the first 12 months of their service, unless they specifically elect not to participate in the program. Servicepersons eligible for post-Korean GI Bill benefits as of December 31, 1989, and who serve 3 years in active duty service after July 1, 1985, are also eligible for the new program, but will not have their basic pay reduced. Servicepersons who, after December 31, 1976, received commissions as officers from service academies or scholarship senior ROTC programs are not eligible for this program.

Active duty for three years (two years, if the initial obligated period of active duty is less than three years), or two years active duty plus four years in the Selected Reserve or National Guard will entitle an individual to $300 a month basic benefits. There is also a targeted, discretionary kicker of up to an additional $700 available. A supplemental benefit of up to an additional $300 with a targeted, discretionary kicker of up to $300 more is also available for certain additional active duty service.

An educational entitlement program is also available for members of the Selected Reserve. Eligibility applies to individuals who, after June 30, 1985 enlist, re-enlist, or extend an enlistment for a six-year period. Benefits may be paid to eligible members of the Selected Reserve who complete their initial period of active duty train ing. Full-time payments are $140 a month for 36 months.

Veterans' Benefits Improvement Act of 1989. Veterans awarded 100 percent disability compensation based upon unemployability during the period February 1, 1989, through January 31, 1992, for whom a vocational goal is feasible may participate in a rehabilitation program. Necessary training expenses, special equipment, etc., toward a definite job objective are paid for, plus a monthly allowance up to $333, with increased amounts for dependents, in addition to compensation. In addition, all veterans granted an unemployability rating before February 1, 1985, the start of the special program period, may receive special assistance in securing employment under the Vocational Rehabilitation Program. Any veteran with an unemployability rating who secures gainful employment during the special program period will be protected from reduction until such veteran has worked continuously for 12 months.

Pensions. Pension benefits are payable for wartime veterans permanently and totally disabled from non-service-connected causes. These benefits are based on need. Surviving spouses and children of wartime veterans have the same eligibility status, based on the veteran's honorable wartime service and their need.

Insurance. The VA life insurance programs have approximately 7.2 million policyholders with total coverage of about $216 billion. Detailed information on NSLI (National Service Life Insurance), USGLI (United States Government Life Insurance), and VMLI (Veterans Mortgage Life Insurance) may be obtained at any VA Office. Information regarding SGLI (Servicemen's Group Life Insurance) and VGLI (Veterans Group Life Insurance) may be obtained from the Office of Servicemen's Group Life Insurance, 213 Washington St., Newark, N.J. 07102

Burial benefits. Burial is provided in any VA national cemetery with available grave space to any deceased veteran of wartime or peacetime service, other than for training, who was discharged under conditions other than dishonorable. Also eligible for burial in a national cemetery are the veteran's spouse, widow, widower, minor children, and under certain conditions, unmarried adult children.

Headstone or marker. A government headstone or marker is furnished for any deceased veteran of wartime or peacetime service, other than for training, who was discharged under conditions other than dishonorable and is interred in a national, state veterans', or private cemetery. VA also will furnish markers to veterans' eligible dependents interred in a national or state veterans' cemetery.

The Medal of Honor

Often called the Congressional Medal of Honor, it is the Nation's highest military award for "uncommon valor" by men and women in the armed forces. It is given for actions that are above and beyond the call of duty in combat against an armed enemy. The medal was first awarded by the Army on March 25, 1863, and then by the Navy on April 3, 1863. In April 1991, President Bush awarded posthumously the Medal of Honor to World War I veteran, Army Cpl. Freddie Stowers. He was the first black soldier to receive the nation's highest honor for valor in either World War.

Recipients of the medal receive $200 per month for life, a right to burial at Arlington National Cemetary, admission for them or their children to a service academy if they qualify and quotas permit, and free travel on government aircraft to almost anywhere in the world, on a space-available basis.

In 1989, medals were restored to William F. Cody (Buffalo Bill) and four other scouts who had them revoked in 1917 due to a new ruling.

Law Enforcement and Crime

Rape Statistics

According to the latest *National Crime Survey (NCS) Report,* June 1991, an estimated 155,000 women were raped each year between 1973 and 1987. During this period, there were annually 1.6 rapes per 1,000 women age 12 or older, meaning that one out of every 600 women was raped each year. The average annual number of male victims reported to the NCS for those years was 13,200.

Almost two-thirds of all rapes occurred at night, and most rapes took place at the victim's home.

Black women were significantly more likely to be raped than white women, although a larger number of white women than the total of black, American Indian, Aleut, Eskimo, Asian, and Pacific Islander women were rape victims each year.

Hispanic and non-Hispanic women were equally likely to be raped.

Unemployed women were three times more likely and students one-and-one-half times more likely than women as a whole to be raped.

About half of all victims and almost three-quarters of black victims were in the lowest third of the income distribution.

Black women with low incomes were more likely to be raped than black women with medium or high incomes: they were also more likely to become victims than white women in any income category. Middle and upper-income women of all races had about the same chances of being raped.

According to the report, rapists and their victims were likely to be of the same race. In rapes with one offender, seven of every ten white victims were raped by a white offender, and eight out of ten black victims were raped by a black offender. In rapes with two or more offenders, victims and offenders were of the same race 49% of the time for white women and 72% for black women.

A previous study by the Bureau of Justice Statistics reported that although it is impossible to know exactly how many rapes go unreported, law enforcement agencies estimate that, for each reported rape, there are actually 1,200 rapes or attempted rapes that go unreported.

A February 1991 report entitled "Rape and Sexual Assault: Meeting the Crisis," a New York State Senate Republican study on sex crimes, noted that research indicates a vast majority of sexual attacks are planned in advance by the attacker. Moreover, the victim's attire and actions often have nothing at all to do with the attack itself. In other words, sex itself can often have little to do with the motivation for the attack. Rather, revenge, frustration, displaced anger, or power can often be the real factors behind a sexual attack.

Record Prison Population

According to the Bureau of Justice Statistics, the nation's prison population has increased by almost 134% since 1980. For every 100,000 U.S. residents in 1990 there were 293 prisoners with sentences greater than one year. At the end of 1990, a record number of 771,243 inmates were in state or federal prisons.

The imprisonment rate was highest in South Carolina with 451 per 100,000 residents, followed by Nevada with 444, and Louisiana with 427.

Record Number Under Care or Custody

At the end of 1989, an estimated 4.1 million adults or about one in every 46 were under the care or custody of a corrections agency. A record 2,520,000 adults in the United States were on probation and 456,479 were on parole. About 75% of all convicted offenders are being supervised in the community, not in prisons or jails.

During 1989, the greatest number of adult probationers were in the following states: Texas, 291,156; California, 285,018; Florida, 192,495; New York, 128,707; and Georgia with 125,441. The highest increase of persons on probation was in the West (9.4%) and the lowest increase was in the Northeast (1.2%).

Violent Crimes Against Teenagers

In April 1991, the Bureau of Justice Statistics reported that, each year from 1985 to 1988, youths age 12 to 19 were victims of 1.9 million rapes, robberies, and assaults. On an average every 1,000 teenagers experienced 67 violent crimes each year, compared to 26 violent crimes for every 1,000 persons age 20 or older. About half of these crimes occurred in school buildings, or school property, or on the street.

Recidivism of Prisoners

In April 1989, the Bureau of Justice Statistics released a special report on the recidivism of 108,580 persons in 11 states in 1983, representing more than half of all released state prisoners that year.

According to the study, an estimated 62.5% of the released prisoners had been rearrested for a felony or serious misdemeanor; 46.8% had been reconvicted; and 41.4% returned to prison or jail within three years after their release.

An estimated 67,898 of the prisoners were rearrested and charged with 326,746 new offenses by year-end 1986. More than 50,000 of the new charges were violent offenses, including 2,282 homicides, 1,451 kidnappings, 1,291 rapes, 2,262 other sexual assaults, 17,060 robberies, and 22,633 other assaults.

Released prisoners were often rearrested for the same type of crime for which they had served time in prison. Within three years, 31.9% of released burglars were rearrested for burglary; 24.8% of drug offenders were rearrested for a drug offense; and 19.6% of robbers were rearrested for robbery.

Released rapists were 10.5 times more likely than nonrapists to be rearrested for rape, and released murderers were about five times more likely than other offenders to be rearrested for homicide.

Estimated Arrests, 1990[1]

Murder and non–negligent manslaughter	22,990	Weapons—carrying, possession, etc.	221,200
Forcible rape	39,160	Prostitution and commercial vice	111,400
Robbery	167,990	Sex offenses, except forcible rape	
Aggravated assault	475,330	and prostitution	107,600
Burglary	432,600	Drug abuse violations	1,089,500
Larceny—theft	1,554,800	Gambling	19,300
Motor vehicle theft	211,300	Offenses against family and children	85,800
Arson	19,100	Driving under the influence	1,810,800
Total violent crime	705,500	Liquor laws	714,700
Total property crime	2,217,800	Drunkenness	910,100
Other assaults	1,014,100	Disorderly conduct	733,000
Forgery and counterfeiting	94,800	Vagrancy	38,500
Fraud	291,600	All other offenses, except traffic	3,267,800
Embezzlement	15,300	Curfew and loitering law violations	80,800
Stolen property—buying, receiving, possessing	165,200	Runaways	174,200
Vandalism	326,000	**Total**[2]	**14,195,100**

1. Arrest totals based on all reporting agencies and estimates for unreported areas. 2. Because of rounding, items may not add to totals. *Source:* Department of Justice, Federal Bureau of Investigation, *Uniform Crime Reports for the United States,* 1990, released 1991.

Number of Arrests by Sex and Age

	Male				Female			
	Total		Under 18		Total		Under 18	
Offense	1990	1989	1990	1989	1990	1989	1990	1989
Murder[1]	16,387	14,852	2,423	1,955	1,911	1,989	132	131
Forcible rape	30,630	27,796	4,546	4,229	336	325	82	97
Robbery	125,015	113,833	30,168	26,762	11,285	10,682	2,799	2,472
Aggravated assault	326,780	281,196	43,454	36,948	50,137	43,215	7,713	6,360
Burglary—breaking or entering	311,220	301,083	103,314	97,063	29,972	29,332	9,123	8,450
Larceny—theft	843,851	807,350	266,916	245,167	397,385	351,647	105,217	89,319
Motor vehicle theft	151,449	152,777	65,029	62,373	16,889	17,502	7,901	7,169
Arson	13,024	11,637	5,940	5,315	1,950	1,826	620	581
Violent crime[2]	498,812		80,591		63,669		10,726	
Other assaults	672,455	601,494	91,334	81,513	128,970	111,903	27,724	24,154
Forgery and counterfeiting	48,667	47,584	4,532	3,829	25,726	24,458	2,228	1,755
Fraud	156,120	140,787	6,629	6,305	123,656	116,831	2,839	2,655
Embezzlement	7,083	7,029	532	574	4,972	4,658	332	485
Stolen property—buying, receiving, possessing	115,864	113,096	30,813	28,972	15,792	15,106	3,274	2,901
Vandalism	228,872	201,279	95,070	82,112	27,686	24,949	8,684	8,094
Weapons—carrying, possessing, etc.	163,055	154,504	30,055	27,698	13,082	12,925	1,936	1,929
Prostitution and com- mercialized vice	32,770	25,483	587	490	58,323	57,315	694	709
Sex offenses, except forcible rape and prostitution	78,291	70,737	12,594	11,632	6,561	5,810	913	896
Drug abuse violations	723,329	825,247	57,457	73,379	145,826	161,102	7,283	9,565
Gambling	13,314	13,455	761	796	2,129	2,437	37	33
Offenses against family and children	54,216	42,724	1,700	1,181	11,776	9,366	911	656
Driving under the influence	1,213,216	1,054,789	13,567	11,981	117,690	147,565	2,205	1,930
Liquor laws	448,898	377,973	87,646	77,985	103,141	87,729	34,401	29,958
Drunkenness	644,594	543,426	16,379	13,187	71,910	58,270	2,965	2,666
Disorderly conduct	469,055	477,016	76,246	73,141	110,619	108,625	19,753	17,863
Vagrancy	27,307	24,008	2,116	1,822	3,930	3,063	415	322
All other offenses, except traffic	2,144,717	1,911,497	196,664	185,607	427,774	372,711	52,071	48,525
Curfew and loitering law violations	46,471	46,040	46,471	46,040	18,097	15,888	18,097	15,888
Runaways	60,189	52,067	60,189	52,067	77,966	65,978	77,966	65,978
Total	**9,181,930**	**8,440,759**	**1,355,638**	**1,260,123**	**2,068,153**	**1,863,207**	**398,904**	**351,541**

1. Includes non–negligent manslaughter. 2. Violent crimes are offenses of murder, forcible rape, robbery, and aggravated assault. NOTE: 10,206 agencies reporting; 1990 estimated population 193,507,000. *Source:* Department of Justice, Federal Bureau of Investigation, *Uniform Crime Reports for the United States, 1990,* released 1991.

Arrests by Race, 1990

Offense	White	Black	Other[1]	Total	Offense	White	Black	Other[1]	Total
Murder[2]	7,942	9,952	296	18,190	Sex offenses, except forcible rape and prostitution	65,798	16,271	1,542	83,611
Forcible rape	16,973	13,309	520	30,802					
Robbery	51,229	83,165	1,510	135,904					
Aggravated assault	223,952	143,540	6,380	373,872	Drug abuse violation	503,315	349,965	6,736	860,016
Burglary	230,310	101,855	5,931	338,096	Gambling	7,251	7,294	804	15,349
Larceny–theft	827,860	374,968	28,427	1,231,255	Offenses against family and children	42,469	19,602	2,535	64,606
Motor vehicle theft	99,821	64,526	3,561	167,908					
Arson	11,154	3,410	269	14,833					
Violent crime[3]	300,096	249,966	8,706	558,768	Driving under the influence	1,227,221	118,729	25,286	1,371,236
All other					Liquor laws	478,873	52,831	16,588	548,292
Other assaults	510,552	269,560	15,795	795,907	Drunkenness	566,075	130,226	17,298	713,599
Forgery and counterfeiting	47,330	24,839	958	73,127	Disorderly conduct	379,324	186,671	10,631	576,626
Fraud	180,671	90,708	2,120	273,499	Vagrancy	17,617	12,644	733	30,994
Embezzlement	7,900	3,816	190	11,906	All other offenses except traffic	1,619,001	886,880	49,622	2,555,503
Stolen property– buying, receiving, possessing	74,517	53,482	1,699	129,698					
Vandalism	191,269	57,253	4,751	253,273	Suspicion	7,462	10,125	159	17,746
Weapons– carrying, possession, etc.	102,228	69,331	2,772	174,331	Curfew and loitering law violations	50,721	11,379	2,160	64,260
Prostitution and commercial vice	54,345	35,398	1,155	90,898	Runaways	109,159	22,331	4,541	136,031
					Total	**7,712,339**	**3,224,060**	**214,969**	**11,151,368**

1. Includes American Indian, Alaskan Native, and Asian or Pacific Islander. 2. Includes non–negligent manslaughter. 3. Violent crimes are offenses of murder, forcible rape, robbery, and aggravated assault. NOTE: Figures represent arrests reported by 10,110 agencies serving a total 1990 population of 192,939,000 as estimated by FBI. *Source:* Department of Justice, Federal Bureau of Investigation, *Uniform Crime Reports for the United States, 1990,* released 1991.

Total Arrests, by Age Groups, 1990

Age	Arrests	Age	Arrests	Age	Arrests	Age	Arrests	Age	Arrests
Under 15	593,869	18	532,947	22	439,599	30–34	1,600,910	50–54	197,357
15	322,836	19	565,273	23	422,658	35–39	1,053,593	55 and over	283,435
16	390,418	20	526,051	24	423,683	40–44	622,896		
17	447,419	21	475,213	25–29	2,008,308	45–49	343,618	**Total**	**11,250,083**

NOTE: Based on reports furnished to the FBI by 10,206 agencies covering a 1990 estimated population of 193,507,000. *Source:* Department of Justice, Federal Bureau of Investigation, *Uniform Crime Reports for the United States, 1990,* released 1991.

Federal Prosecutions of Public Corruption: 1979 to 1988

(Prosecution of persons who have corrupted public office in violation of Federal Criminal Statutes. As of Dec. 31, 1988)

Prosecution status	1988	1987	1986	1985	1984	1983	1982	1981	1980	1979
Total:[1] Indicted	1,274	1,340	1,192	1,182	936	1,073	729	878	721	687
Convicted	1,067	1,075	1,027	997	934	972	671	730	552	555
Awaiting trial	288	368	246	256	269	222	186	231	213	187
Federal officials: Indicted	629	651	596	563	408	460[2]	158	198	123	128
Convicted	529	545	523	470	429	424[2]	147	159	131	115
Awaiting trial	86	118	83	90	77	58	38	23	16	21
State officials: Indicted	66	102	88	79	58	81	4	87	72	58
Convicted	69	76	71	66	52	65	43	66	51	32
Awaiting trial	14	26	24	20	21	26	18	36	28	30
Local officials: Indicted	276	246	232	248	203	270	257	244	247	212
Convicted	229	204	207	221	196	226	232	211	168	156
Awaiting trial	79	89	55	49	74	61	58	102	82	67

1. Includes individuals who are neither public officials nor employees, but who were involved with public officials or employees in violating the law, now shown separately. 2. Increases in the number indicted and convicted between 1982 and 1983 resulted from a greater focus on federal corruption nationwide and more consistent reporting of cases involving lower–level employees. NOTE: Figures are latest available. *Source:* U.S. Department of Justice, *Federal Prosecutions of Corrupt Public Officials, 1970–1980,* and *Report to Congress on the Activities and Operations of the Public Integrity Section,* annual.

U.S. District Courts—Criminal Cases Commenced and Defendants Disposed of, by Nature of Offense: 1985 and 1988

[For years ending June 30]

| | | | Disposition of Defendants, 1988 | | | | | | | 1985 | |
| | 1988 cases com-menced[1] | Not convicted | | Convicted[2] | | | Sentenced | | | | De-fend-ants |
Nature of offense		Total	Ac-quitted	Total	Guilty plea[3]	Court or jury	Im-prison-ment	Proba-tion	Fine and other	Cases com-menced[1]	dis-posed of
General offenses:											
Homicide	147	40	16	110	86	24	94	6	10	160	170
Robbery	1,283	131	27	1,064	927	137	990	72	2	1,236	1,387
Assault	617	163	37	436	338	98	267	138	31	552	555
Burglary	124	19	1	92	84	8	75	15	2	158	165
Larceny—theft	3,531	706	103	3,159	2,899	260	1,161	1,701	297	3,571	4,108
Embezzlement and fraud	9,433	1,571	240	9,609	8,736	873	4,004	5,334	271	7,912	9,044
Auto theft	293	59	14	323	291	32	224	92	7	300	461
Forgery, counterfeiting	1,674	293	39	1,777	1,666	111	853	910	14	2,118	2,372
Sex offenses	511	64	20	374	315	59	215	154	5	266	200
DAPCA[4]	10,291	2,588	420	13,162	11,044	2,118	9,983	3,042	137	6,690	11,177
Misc. general offenses	15,599	4,255	604	12,796	11,128	1,668	4,607	4,593	3,596	15,583	17,721
Total	**43,503**	**9,889**	**1,521**	**42,902**	**37,514**	**5,388**	**22,473**	**16,057**	**4,372**	**38,546**	**47,360**

1. Excludes transfers. 2. Convicted and sentenced. 3. Includes nolo contendere. 4. All marijuana, narcotics, and controlled substances under the Drug Abuse Prevention and Control Act. NOTE: Data are latest available. *Source: Statistical Abstract of the United States, 1990.*

Murder Victims by Weapons Used

| | | Weapons used or cause of death | | | | | | |
| Year | Murder victims, total | Guns | | Cutting or stabbing | Blunt object[1] | Strangu-lation, hands, fists, feet or pushing | Arson[3] | All other[2] |
		Total	Percent					
1965	8,773	5,015	57.2	2,021	505	894	226	112
1970	13,649	9,039	66.2	2,424	604	1,031	353	198
1971	16,183	10,712	66.2	3,017	645	1,295	314	200
1972	15,832	10,379	65.6	2,974	672	1,291	331	185
1973	17,123	11,249	65.7	2,985	848	1,445	173	423
1974	18,632	12,474	66.9	3,228	976	1,417	153	384
1975	18,642	12,061	64.7	3,245	1,001	1,646	193	496
1980	21,860	13,650	62.0	4,212	1,094	1,666	291	947
1981	20,053	12,523	62.4	3,886	1,038	1,469	258	658
1982	19,485	11,721	60.2	4,065	957	1,657	279	630
1983	18,673	10,895	58.0	4,075	1,062	1,656	216	769
1984	16,689	9,819	58.8	3,540	973	1,407	192	758
1985	17,545	10,296	58.7	3,694	972	1,491	243	849
1986	19,257	11,381	59.1	3,957	1,099	1,651	230	939
1987	17,963	10,612	59.1	3,643	1,045	1,525	200	938
1988	17,971	10,895	60.6	3,457	1,126	1,426	255	812
1989	18,954	11,832	62.4	3,458	1,128	1,416	234	886
1990	20,045	12,847	64.1	3,503	1,075	1,424	287	909

1. Refers to club, hammer, etc. 2. Includes poison, explosives, unknown, drowning, asphyxiation, narcotics, other means, and weapons not stated. 3. Before 1973, includes drowning. *Source:* Department of Justice, Federal Bureau of Investigation, *Uniform Crime Reports for the United States, 1990,* released 1991.

Crime Rates for Population Groups and Selected Cities, 1988

(offenses known to the police per 100,000 population, as of July 1)

Group and City	Violent Crime Mur-der	Violent Crime Forc-ible rape	Violent Crime Rob-bery	Violent Crime Aggra-vated assault	Violent Crime Total	Property crime Bur-glary—break-ing or enter-ing	Property crime Lar-ceny—theft	Property crime Motor vehicle theft	Property crime Total	Total all crimes
Total 7,434 cities	**10.5**	**47**	**318**	**462**	**836**	**1,539**	**3,967**	**788**	**6,295**	**7,130**
MSA's (Metropolitan Statistical Areas)	9	43	278	422	752	1,457	3,506	713	5,676	6,428
Other Cities	4	25	55	286	371	1,042	3,298	210	4,550	4,921
Rural Areas	5	18	15	141	180	672	973	114	1,759	1,938
Selected Cities:										
Baltimore	30.6	68	968	861	1,927	1,866	4,268	1,105	7,239	9,166
Chicago	22.0	(1)	968	1,202	(1)	1,739	4,295	1,503	7,537	(1)
Dallas	36.0	128	948	964	2,077	4,180	8,092	2,393	14,665	16,742
Detroit	57.9	133	1,194	989	2,375	2,958	3,981	2,772	9,711	12,085
Houston	25.5	70	582	471	1,149	2,908	4,491	1,763	9,163	10,311
Indianapolis	16.3	87	303	760	1,166	1,596	2,640	740	4,977	6,143
Los Angeles	21.6	59	770	1,111	1,961	1,499	3,531	1,685	6,714	8,676
Memphis	26.0	129	667	511	1,333	2,436	3,307	2,067	7,810	9,143
New York	25.8	46	1,179	967	2,218	1,731	4,199	1,633	7,562	9,780
Philadelphia	22.4	55	537	421	1,035	1,231	2,544	1,227	5,002	6,037
Phoenix	11.1	47	265	568	891	2,190	5,374	695	8,259	9,150
San Antonio	15.3	57	306	186	564	2,957	7,548	1,411	11,916	12,479
San Diego	13.4	36	298	506	854	1,634	4,278	2,247	8,159	9,013
San Francisco	12.2	60	646	560	1,278	1,346	4,863	1,270	7,479	8,757
Washington, D.C.	59.5	27	918	918	1,921	1,983	4,610	1,392	7,985	9,907

1. The rates for 1988 forcible rape, violent crime, and total crime are not shown because the forcible rape figures were not in accordance with national Uniform Crime Reporting guidelines. NOTE: Data are latest available. *Source: Statistical Abstract of the United States 1990.*

Percent of Firearms Usage in Selected Crimes, by Region: 1987–1989

Region	Murder[1] 1989	Murder[1] 1988	Murder[1] 1987	Aggravated assault 1989	Aggravated assault 1988	Aggravated assault 1987	Robbery 1989	Robbery 1988	Robbery 1987
Northeast	60.1	57.3	54.8	16.3	15.9	14.9	29.0	27.1	25.3
Midwest	58.8	59.0	57.7	23.6	23.1	24.4	33.0	33.4	32.6
South	65.8	64.4	62.9	25.3	26.3	25.6	39.2	40.8	39.7
West	61.6	59.2	56.4	19.5	18.4	17.7	32.4	33.1	33.8
U.S. Total	**62.4**	**60.7**	**59.1**	**21.5**	**21.1**	**21.4**	**33.2**	**33.4**	**33.0**

1. Murder includes non–negligent manslaughter. NOTE: Data are latest available. *Source:* U.S. Federal Bureau of Investigation, *Crime in the United States,* annual.

Reported Child Neglect and Abuse Cases: 1985 to 1987

Division	Percent change 1986–87	Total number of reports (1,000) 1987	Total number of reports (1,000) 1986	Total number of reports (1,000) 1985	Reports per 1,000 population 1987	Reports per 1,000 population 1986	Reports per 1,000 population 1985
New England	4.0	99.8	95.8	59.9	7.8	7.5	4.7
Middle Atlantic	6.3	242.5	228.1	152.2	6.5	6.1	4.1
North Central	−1.2	515.2	521.4	316.4	18.2	19.3	11.1
South Atlantic	−1.9	293.4	299.2	225.0	7.0	7.3	5.6
South Central	−3.0	302.4	311.7	249.9	14.8	15.1	12.9
Mountain	29.6	128.2	98.9	77.6	9.7	7.6	6.1
Pacific	6.1	443.7	418.3	218.4	12.1	11.7	6.2
U.S. Total	**2.6**	**2,025.2**	**1,973.4**	**1,299.4**	**8.3**	**8.2**	**5.4**

NOTE: Figures are latest available. *Source:* American Humane Association, *National Analysis of Official Child Neglect and Abuse Reporting,* annual.

Gang Violence: A National Problem

Source: National Institute of Justice Reports.

Gang violence is a growing problem across the Nation. It cuts across ethnic and cultural lines, involves youths and increasingly, adults, and is spreading at an alarming rate. It is responsible for an urban gang warfare that has resulted in drive-in shootings, turf battles, and killings of informers.

Two of the most violent youth gangs in America are the Los Angeles-based Crips and Bloods. Their activity in the Los Angeles sub-culture is well known and widely reported in the media. According to a recent Drug Enforcement Administration report, conflict between these two groups has escalated into open guerilla warfare. Youth gang members are readily armed with AK-47's, AK-15's, and other fully automatic weapons.

But more significant is the fact that the California gang members are spreading out into such areas as Shreveport, Louisiana; Kansas City, Missouri; and Seattle, Washington.

That the gang problem involves adults as well as juveniles is well documented. The average age of the gang homicide offender in Los Angeles is between 19 and 20 years of age; gang homicide reports from Chicago show that nearly 50% of the offenders are over the age of nineteen. Similarly, research by the Office of Juvenile Justice and Delinquency Prevention has shown that it is adults who adopt leadership roles and engage in the greatest violence: homicides, aggravated assaults, robberies, and drug trafficking. Their victims may include innocent members of the public, other gang members, and some professional community members such as police officers and teachers in schools. Prison gangs constitute a serious though separate problem as well, noticeably in Illinois, New York, California, and Texas.

Evidence further suggests that gang youths are particularly susceptible to being recruited into larger criminal organizations involved in drug trafficking. The link between organized crime and youth gangs, however, remains to be fully researched and reported.

A 1989 survey of law enforcement officials in 45 cities across the country produced the startling estimate of nearly 1,500 youth gangs nationwide, with more than 120,500 members.

African Americans and Hispanics make up 87% of gang membership, far in excess of their representation in the general population. Many of these gangs were involved in serious crimes. The rate of violent offenses for gang members was three times as high as that for non-gang delinquents.

But while African Americans and Hispanics seem to dominate in memberships in criminal gangs, the problem embraces other ethnic groups and cultures. Chinese, Vietnamese, Cambodian, and Laotian youth gangs have emerged in New York City, Chicago, and Los Angeles. In particular, recent news reports have detailed the involvement of Chinese youth gangs in a resurgent heroin trade in New York City.

In 1990, the number of gang homicides reached an all-time high of 329 in Los Angeles and 98 in Chicago, with gang homicide, as a proportion of total homicides, ranging from 11% in Chicago to 34% in Los Angeles.

Unfortunately, no national data on gangs or gang activity are collected; only gross estimates based on law enforcement perceptions are available in most cities. The definition of the term "gang" and what constitutes gang-related crimes varies from jurisdiction to jurisdiction, as well as in the research literature. This frequently renders problematic the development of laws and subsequent policies and strategies for dealing with the gang problem.

In order to meet this challenge, a new Office of Justice Programs study is now under way to fill in this important gap, and by coordinating their efforts with other concerned agencies will recommend effective ways to address this growing national problem.

Drug Offenses Rise Sharply

During 1989, the latest year complete Bureau of Justice Statistics are available, drug offenses accounted for 23% of the charges against the nearly 400,000 men and women held in local jails. Of all convicted jail inmates in 1989, more than four in ten said that they had been using an illegal drug during the month before committing the offense for which they were jailed. One in four had used heroin, cocaine, crack, LSD, or PCP that month.

Women were more likely than men and Hispanics were more likely than non-Hispanics to be jailed on drug charges. About a third of female and Hispanic inmates were in jail for drugs.

Of all jail inmates in 1989, 46% were on probation, parole, bail, or in some other criminal justice status at the time of their arrest. More than 75% had a prior sentence to probation, or incarceration, and at least a third were in jail for a violent offense or had previously been sentenced for a violent crime.

State courts convicted about 112,000 persons of felony drug trafficking in 1988, about 50% more than in 1986. The number of adults arrested for serious drug trafficking offenses was about 185,000 in 1986 and 290,000 in 1988.

Personal and Household Crimes Fall

Personal and household crimes declined from about 35.8 million in 1989 to about 34.8 million in 1990, a drop of one million. The over-all decline resulted from an 8% fall in the 1989 rate of personal thefts without direct contact between the victim and the offender.

About 95% of all personal thefts and about 66% of all cimes against persons involved such offenses as stealing personal belongings from public places or from an unattended automobile parked away from home.

There was a 19% increase in motor vehicle theft, the only crime to rise significantly in 1990. In all there were 1.4 million completed auto thefts and 770,000 attempted thefts—the highest number since the National Crime Survey began in 1977.

About 13.3 million personal and household crimes were reported to the police in 1990—not a statistically significant change from 1989.

Regional Crime Statistics

According to a National Crime Survey report published in July 1991, the West showed the highest victimization rate for both crimes of violence and crimes of theft. The Northeast had the lowest rates for these crimes, though the violent crime rate in the Midwest was only marginally higher than the rate in the Northeast. The South had a higher violent crime rate than the Midwest, but the rate of personal thefts was not measurably different.

Prisoners Under Sentence of Death

Characteristic	1988	1987	1986	Characteristic	1988	1987	1986
White	1,238	1,128	1,006	Marital status:			
Black and other	886	839	775	Never married	898	856	772
Under 20 years	11	10	19	Married	594	571	525
20–24 years	195	222	217	Divorced or separated[2]	632	557	484
25–34 years	1,048	969	872	Time elapsed since sentencing:			
35–54 years	823	744	639	Less than 12 months	293	295	293
55 years and over	47	39	34	12–47 months	812	804	757
				48–71 months	409	412	376
Schooling completed:				72 months and over	610	473	355
7 years or less	180	181	164	Legal status at arrest:			
8 years	184	183	174	Not under sentence	1,207	1,123[3]	992
9–11 years	692	650	577	On parole or probation	545[3]	480[3]	409[3]
12 years	657	591	515	In prison or escaped	93	91	82
More than 12 years	180	168	143	Unknown	279	290	298
Unknown	231	211	208	**Total**	**2,124**	**1,967**[1]	**1,781**

1. Revisions to the total number of prisoners were not carried to the characteristics except for race. 2. Includes widows, widowers, and unknown. 3. Includes 20 persons on mandatory conditional release, work release, leave, AWOL, or bail for 1986; 22 for 1987; 24 for 1988. NOTE: As of Dec. 31. Excludes prisoners under sentence of death confined in local correctional systems pending appeal or who had not been committed to prison. *Source:* U.S. Bureau of Justice Statistics, *Capital Punishment,* annual.

Methods of Execution[1]

State	Method	State	Method
Alabama[2]	Electrocution	Nevada[2]	Lethal injection
Alaska	No death penalty	New Hampshire[2]	Lethal injection
Arizona[2]	Lethal gas	New Jersey	Lethal injection[5]
Arkansas[2]	Lethal injection or electrocution	New Mexico	Lethal injection
California*	Lethal gas	New York	No death penalty
Colorado[2]	Lethal injection[7]	North Carolina[2]	Lethal gas or injection
Connecticut[2]	Electrocution	North Dakota	No death penalty
Delaware	Lethal injection[3]	Ohio[2]	Electrocution
D.C.	No death penalty	Oklahoma	Lethal injection
Florida	Electrocution	Oregon	Lethal injection[5]
Georgia[2]	Electrocution	Pennsylvania[2]	Lethal injection
Hawaii	No death penalty	Rhode Island	No death penalty
Idaho[2]	Lethal injection[9]	South Carolina[2]	Electrocution
Illinois	Lethal injection	South Dakota	Lethal injection
Indiana[2]	Electrocution	Tennessee[2]	Electrocution
Iowa	No death penalty	Texas[2]*	Lethal injection
Kansas	No death penalty	Utah[2]*	Firing squad or lethal injection
Kentucky[2]	Electrocution	Vermont	No death penalty
Louisiana[2]	Electrocution[10]	Virginia	Electrocution
Maine	No death penalty	Washington[2]*	Hanging or lethal injection
Maryland[2]	Lethal gas	West Virginia	No death penalty
Massachusetts*	No death penalty	Wisconsin	No death penalty
Michigan	No death penalty	Wyoming	Lethal injection
Minnesota	No death penalty	U.S. (Fed. Govt.)	(⁴)
Mississippi[2]	Lethal injection[8]	American Samoa	No death penalty
Missouri	Lethal injection	Guam	No death penalty
Montana[2]	Hanging, or lethal injection[6]	Puerto Rico	No death penalty
Nebraska[2]	Electrocution	Virgin Islands	No death penalty

1. On July 1, 1976, by a 7–2 decision, the U.S. Supreme Court upheld the death penalty as not being "cruel or unusual." However, in another ruling the same day, the Court, by a 5–4 vote, stated that states may not impose "mandatory" capital punishment on every person convicted of murder. These decisions left uncertain the fate of condemned persons throughout the U.S. On Oct. 4, the Court refused to reconsider its July ruling, which allows some states to proceed with executions of condemned prisoners. The first execution in this country since 1967 was in Utah on Jan. 17, 1977. Gary Mark Gilmore was executed by shooting. 2. Voted to restore death penalty after June 29, 1972, Supreme Court decision ruling capital punishment unconstitutional. 3. Prisoners originally sentenced to death prior to June 1986 may opt instead to hang. Those sentenced after June 1986 have no choice but lethal injection. 4. Is that of the state in which the execution takes place. 5. Death penalty has been passed, but not been used. 6. Defendant may choose between hanging and a lethal injection. 7. Applies to offenses committed on or after July, 1 1988. Prior to that date the method of execution is lethal gas. 8. Prisoners sentenced prior to July 1, 1984, shall be executed by lethal gas. 9. If the director of the Idaho Department of Corrections finds it impractical to carry out a lethal injection, he may instead use a firing squad. 10. Lethal injection for those individuals sentenced to death after January 1, 1991. *Source:* Questionnaires to the states. NOTE: An asterisk after the name of the state indicates non–reply.

Taxes

History of the Income Tax in the United States

Source: Deloitte & Touche

The nation had few taxes in its early history. From 1791 to 1802, the United States Government was supported by internal taxes on distilled spirits, carriages, refined sugar, tobacco and snuff, property sold at auction, corporate bonds, and slaves. The high cost of the War of 1812 brought about the nation's first sales taxes on gold, silverware, jewelry, and watches. In 1817, however, Congress did away with all internal taxes, relying on tariffs on imported goods to provide sufficient funds for running the Government.

In 1862, in order to support the Civil War effort, Congress enacted the nation's first income tax law. It was a forerunner of our modern income tax in that it was based on the principles of graduated, or progressive, taxation and of withholding income at the source. During the Civil War, a person earning from $600 to $10,000 per year paid tax at the rate of 3%. Those with incomes of more than $10,000 paid taxes at a higher rate. Additional sales and excise taxes were added, and an "inheritance" tax also made its debut. In 1866, internal revenue collections reached their highest point in the nation's 90-year history—more than $310 million, an amount not reached again until 1911.

The Act of 1862 established the office of Commissioner of Internal Revenue. The Commissioner was given the power to assess, levy, and collect taxes, and the right to enforce the tax laws through seizure of property and income and through prosecution. His powers and authority remain very much the same today.

In 1868, Congress again focused its taxation efforts on tobacco and distilled spirits and eliminated the income tax in 1872. It had a short-lived revival in 1894 and 1895. In the latter year, the U.S. Supreme Court decided that the income tax was unconstitutional because it was not apportioned among the states in conformity with the Constitution.

By 1913, with the 16th Amendment to the Constitution, the income tax had become a permanent fixture of the U.S. tax system. The amendment gave Congress legal authority to tax income and resulted in a revenue law that taxed incomes of both individuals and corporations. In fiscal year 1918, annual internal revenue collections for the first time passed the billion-dollar mark, rising to $5.4 billion by 1920. With the advent of World War II, employment increased, as did tax collections—to $7.3 billion. The withholding tax on wages was introduced in 1943 and was instrumental in increasing the number of taxpayers to 60 million and tax collections to $43 billion by 1945.

In 1981, Congress enacted the largest tax cut in U.S. history, approximately $750 billion over six years. The tax reduction, however, was offset by two tax acts, in 1982 and 1984, which attempted to raise approximately $265 billion.

On Oct. 22, 1986, President Reagan signed into law one of the most far-reaching reforms of the United States tax system since the adoption of the income tax. The Tax Reform Act of 1986, as it was called, attempted to be revenue neutral by increasing business taxes and correspondingly decreasing individual taxes by approximately $120 billion over a five-year period.

Following the yearly tradition of new tax acts which began in 1986, the President signed into law the Revenue Reconciliation Act of 1989 on December 19, 1989. As with the '87 and '88 acts, the 1989 act, while providing a number of substantive provisions, was small in comparison with the 1986 act.

Internal Revenue Service

The Internal Revenue Service (IRS), a bureau of the U.S. Treasury Department, is the federal agency charged with the administration of the tax laws passed by Congress. The IRS functions through a national office in Washington, 7 regional offices, 63 district offices, and 10 service centers.

Operations involving most taxpayers are carried out in the district offices and service centers. District offices are organized into Resources Management, Examination, Collection, Taxpayer Service, Employee Plans and Exempt Organizations, and Criminal Investigation. All tax returns are filed with the service centers, where the IRS computer operations are located.

IRS service centers are processing an ever increasing number of returns and documents. In 1990 the number of returns and supplemental documents processed totaled 201.7 million. This represented a 1% increase over 1989.

Prior to 1987, all tax return processing was performed by hand. This process was time consuming and costly. In an attempt to improve the speed and efficiency of the manual processing procedure, the IRS began testing an electronic return filing system beginning with the filing of 1985 returns.

The two most significant results of the test were that refunds for the electronically filed returns were issued more quickly and the tax processing error rate was significantly lower when compared to paper returns.

Electronic filing of individual income tax returns with refunds became an operational program in selected areas for the 1987 processing year. This program is continually expanding. In 1989 1,160,516 individual returns were electronically filed. In 1990 4,193,242 individual returns were filed electronically.

In addition to expanding the program for the electronic filing of individual returns, the IRS has also implemented programs for the electronic filing of partnership, fiduciary, and employee benefit plan returns.

Internal Revenue Service

	1990	1989	1988	1987	1986	1970
U.S. population (in thousands)	251,329	249,412	246,329	244,344	241,995	204,878
Number of IRS employees	111,858	114,758	114,873	102,188	95,880	68,683
Cost to govt. of collecting						
$100 in taxes	$0.52	$0.51	$0.54	$0.49	$0.49	$0.45
Tax per capita	$4,203.12	$4,062.84	$3,792.15	$3,627.22	$3,232.51	$955.31
Collections by principal sources (in thousands of dollars)						
Total IRS collections	$1,056,365,652	$1,013,322,133	$935,106,594	$886,290,590	$782,251,812	$195,722,096
Income and profits taxes						
Individual	540,228,408	515,731,504	473,666,566	465,452,486	416,568,384	103,651,585
Corporation	110,016,539	117,014,564	109,682,554	102,858,985	80,441,620	35,036,983
Employment taxes	367,219,321	345,625,586	318,038,990	277,000,469	244,374,767	37,449,188
Estate and gift taxes	11,761,939	8,973,146	7,784,445	7,667,670	7,194,956	3,680,076
Alcohol taxes	NOTE 4	NOTE 4	NOTE 4	11,097,677	5,647,485	4,746,382
Tobacco taxes	NOTE 4	NOTE 4	NOTE 4	NOTE 2	4,607,845	2,094,212
Manufacturers' excise taxes	NOTE 3	NOTE 3	NOTE 3	10,221,574	9,927,742	6,683,061
All other taxes	27,139,445	25,977,333	25,934,040	11,991,729	13,489,014	2,380,609

NOTE: For fiscal year ending September 30th. NOTE 2: Alcohol and tobacco tax collections are included in the "All other taxes" amount. NOTE 3: Manufacturers' excise taxes are included in the "All other taxes" amount. NOTE 4: Alcohol and tobacco tax collections are now collected and reported by the Bureau of Alcohol, Tobacco, and Firearms.

Auditing Tax Returns

Most taxpayers' contacts with the IRS arise through the auditing of their tax returns. The Service has been empowered by Congress to inquire about all persons who may be liable for any tax and to obtain for review the books and/or records pertinent to those taxpayers' returns. A wide-ranging audit operation is carried out in the 63 district offices by 15,350 field agents and 2,953 office auditors.

Selecting Returns for Audit

The primary method used by the IRS in selecting returns for audits is a computer program that measures the probability of tax error in each return. The data base (established by an in-depth audit of randomly selected returns in various income categories) consists of approximately 200–250 individual items of information taken from each return. These 200–250 variables individually or in combination are weighted as relative indicators of potential tax change. Returns are then scored according to the weights given the combinations of variables as they appear on each return. The higher the score, the greater the tax change potential. Other returns are selected for examination on the basis of claims for refund, multi-year audits, related return audits, and other audits initiated by the IRS as a result of informants' information, special compliance programs,

and the information document matching program.

In 1990, the IRS recommended additional tax and penalties on 883,319 returns, totaling $22 billion.

The Appeals Process

The IRS attempts to resolve tax disputes through an administrative appeals system. Taxpayers who, after audit of their tax returns, disagree with a proposed change in their tax liabilities are entitled to an independent review of their cases. Taxpayers are able to seek an immediate, informal appeal with the Appeals Office. If, however, the dispute arises from a field audit and the amount in question exceeds $10,000, a taxpayer must submit a written protest. Alternatively, the taxpayer can wait for the examiner's report and then request consideration by the Appeals Office and file a protest if necessary. Taxpayers may represent themselves or be represented by an attorney, accountant, or any other advisor authorized to practice before the IRS. Taxpayers can forego their right to the above process and await receipt of a deficiency notice. At this juncture, taxpayers can either (1) not pay the deficiency and petition the Tax Court by a required deadline or (2) pay the deficiency and file a claim for refund with the District Director's office. If the claim is not allowed, a suit for refund may be brought either in the District Court or the Claims Court within a specified period.

Federal Individual Income Tax

Tax Brackets—1991
Taxable Income

Joint return	Single Taxpayer	Rate
$0–$34,000	$0–$20,350	15%
34,001–82,150	20,351–49,300	28%
82,151 and up[1]	49,301 and up[1]	31%[2]

1. The deduction for personal exemptions is phased out as the taxpayer's gross income exceeds $150,000 (for a joint return) and $100,000 for single taxpayers. 2. The 31% rate is effectively increased because total otherwise allowable itemized deductions are reduced by 3% of the taxpayer's adjusted gross income in excess of $100,000.

The Federal individual income tax is levied on the world-wide income of U.S. citizens and resident aliens and on certain types of U.S. source income of non-residents. For a non-itemizer, "tax table income" is adjusted gross income (*see* below) less $2,150 for each personal exemption and the standard deduction (*see* below). If a taxpayer itemizes, tax table income is adjusted gross income minus total itemized deductions and personal exemptions. In addition, individuals may also be subject to the alternative minimum tax.

Who Must File a Return[1]

You must file a return and your gross income if you are: is at least:

Single (legally separated, divorced, or married living apart from spouse with dependent child) and are under 65	$5,500
Single (legally separated, divorced, or married living apart from spouse with dependent child) and are 65 or older	$6,350
A person who can be claimed as a dependent on your parent's return, and who has taxable dividends, interest, or other unearned income	$550
Head of household under age 65	$7,150
Head of household over age 65	$8,000
Married, filing jointly, living together at end of year (or at date of death of spouse), and both are under 65	$10,000
Married, filing jointly, living together at end of year (or at date of death of spouse), and one is 65 or older	$10,650
Married, filing jointly, living together at end of year (or at date of death of spouse), and both are 65 or older	$11,300
Married, filing separate return, or married but not living together at end of year	$2,150
Married, filing separate return, or married but not living together at end of year over age 65	$2,150

1. In 1991.

Adjusted Gross Income

Gross income consists of wages and salaries, unemployment compensation, tips and gratuities, interest, dividends, annuities, rents and royalties, up to 1/2 of Social Security Benefits if the recipient's income exceeds a base amount, and certain other types of income. Among the items excluded from gross income, and thus not subject to tax, are public assistance benefits and interest on exempt securities (mostly state and local bonds).

Adjusted gross income is determined by subtracting from gross income: alimony paid, penalties on early withdrawal of savings, payments to an I.R.A. (reduced proportionately based upon adjusted gross income levels if taxpayer is an active participant in an employer maintained retirement plan), payments to a Keogh retirement plan and self-employed health insurance payments (25% limit). Employee business expenses and job related moving expenses are now treated as itemized deductions.

Itemized Deductions

Taxpayers may itemize deductions or take the standard deduction. The standard deduction amounts for 1991 are as follows: Married filing jointly and surviving spouses $5,700; Heads of household $5,000; Single $3,400; and Married filing separate returns $2,850. Taxpayers who are age 65 or over or are blind are entitled to an additional standard deduction of $850 for single taxpayers and $650 for a married taxpayer.

In itemizing deductions, the following are major items that may be deducted in 1991: state and local income and property taxes, charitable contributions, employee moving expenses, medical expenses (exceeding 7.5% of adjusted gross income), casualty losses (only the amount over the $100 floor which exceeds 10% of adjusted gross income), mortgage interest, and miscellaneous deductions (deductible only to the extent by which cumulatively they exceed 2% of adjusted gross income).

Personal Exemptions

Personal exemptions are available to the taxpayer for himself, his spouse, and his dependents. The 1991 amount is $2,150 for each individual. Under the 1986 act, no exemption is allowed a taxpayer who can be claimed as a dependent on another taxpayer's return. Additional personal exemptions for taxpayers age 65 or over or blind have been eliminated.

Credits

Taxpayers can reduce their income tax liability by claiming the benefit of certain tax credits. Each dollar of tax credit offsets a dollar of tax liability. The following are a few of the available tax credits:

Certain low-income households with dependent children may claim an Earned Income Credit. The maximum Basic Earned Income Credit is $1,192 for taxpayers with one qualifying child and $1,235 for taxpayers with two or more qualifying children. In addition to the Basic Earned Income Credit, a taxpayer may also be eligible for a Health Insurance Credit which can be taken as a part of the total earned income credit. This maximum credit will be reduced if earned income or adjusted gross income exceeds $11,250, and the credit will be zero for families with incomes over $21,250. The earned income credit is a refundable credit.

A credit for Child and Dependent Care Expenses is available for amounts paid to care for a child or other dependent so that the taxpayer can work. The credit is between 20% and 30% (depending on adjusted gross income) of up to $2,400 of employment-related expenses for one qualifying child or dependent and up to $4,800 of expenses for two or more qualifying individuals.

The elderly and those under 65 who are retired under total disability may be entitled to a credit of up to $750 (if single) or $1,125 (if married and filing jointly). No credit is available if the taxpayer is single and has adjusted gross income of $17,500 or more, or $5,000 or more in nontaxable Social Security benefits. Similarly, the credit is unavailable to a married couple if their adjusted gross income exceeds $25,000 or if their nontaxable Social Security benefits equal or exceed $7,500.

Free Taxpayer Publications

The IRS publishes over 100 free taxpayer information publications on various subjects. One of these, Publication 910, *Guide to Free Tax Services*, is a catalog of the free services the IRS offers. You can order these publications and any tax forms or instructions you need by calling the IRS toll-free at 1-800-829-3676.

Federal Income Tax Comparisons

Taxes at Selected Rate Brackets After Standard Deductions and Personal Exemptions[1]

Adjusted gross income	Single return listing no dependents				Joint return listing two dependents			
	1991	1990	1989	1975	1991	1990	1989	1975
$ 10,000	$ 668	$ 705	$735	$ 1,506	$−1,235	$ −953[2]	$ −910[2]	$ 829
20,000	2,168	2,205	2,235	4,153	702	926	1,020	2,860
30,000	4,201	4,388	4,561	8,018	2,355	2,453	2,520	5,804
40,000	7,001	7,188	7,361	12,765	3,855	3,953	4,020	9,668
50,000	9,801	9,988	10,161	18,360	5,576	5,960	6,272	14,260

1. For comparison purposes, tax rate schedules were used. 2. Refund based on a basic earned income credit for families with dependent children.

Federal Corporation Taxes

Corporations are taxed under a graduated tax rate structure as shown in the chart. For tax years beginning on or after July 1, 1987, the benefits of the lower rates are phased out for corporations with taxable income between $100,000 and $335,000 and totally eliminated for corporations with income equal to or in excess of $335,000.

If the corporation qualifies, it may elect to be an S corporation. If it makes this election, the corporation will not (with certain exceptions) pay corporate tax on its income. Its income is instead passed through and taxed to its shareholders. There are several requirements a corporation must meet to qualify as an S corporation including having 35 or fewer shareholders, and having only one class of stock.

Tax Years Beginning on or After July 1, 1987

Taxable income	Tax rate
$0–$50,000	15%
$50,001–75,000	25
75,001–100,000	34
100,001–335,000	39
335,001 and up	34

State Corporation Income and Franchise Taxes

All states but Nevada, South Dakota, Washington, and Wyoming impose a tax on corporation net income. The majority of states impose the tax at flat rates ranging from 2.35% to 15%. Several states have adopted a graduated basis of rates for corporations.

Nearly all states follow the federal law in defining net income. However, many states provide for varying exclusions and adjustments.

A state is empowered to tax all of the net income of its domestic corporations. With regard to non-resi-

dent corporations, however, it may only tax the net income on business carried on within its boundaries. Corporations are, therefore, required to apportion their incomes among the states where they do business and pay a tax to each of these states. Nearly all states provide an apportionment to their domestic corporations, too, in order that they not be unduly burdened.

Several states tax unincorporated businesses separately.

Federal Estate and Gift Taxes

A Federal Estate Tax Return must be filed for the estate of every U.S. citizen or resident whose gross estate, if the decedent died in 1991, exceeds $600,000. An estate tax return must also be filed for the estate of a non-resident, if the value of his gross estate in the U.S. is more than $60,000 at the date of death. The estate tax return is due nine months after the date of death of the decedent, but a reasonable extension of time to file may be obtained for good reason.

Under the unified federal estate and gift tax structure, individuals who made taxable gifts during the calendar year are required to file a gift tax return by April 15 of the following year.

A unified credit of $192,800 (during 1991) is available to offset both estate and gift taxes. Any part of the credit used to offset gift taxes is not available to offset estate taxes. As a result, although they are still taxable as gifts, lifetime transfers no longer cushion the impact of progressive estate tax rates. Lifetime transfers and transfers made at death are combined for estate tax rate purposes.

Gift taxes are computed by applying the uniform rate schedule to lifetime taxable transfers (after deducting the unified credit) and subtracting the taxes payable for prior taxable periods. In general, estate taxes are computed by applying the uniform rate schedule to cumulative transfers and subtracting the gift taxes paid. An appropriate adjustment is made for taxes on lifetime transfers—such as certain gifts within three years of death—in a decedent's estate.

Among the deductions allowed in computing the amount of the estate subject to tax are funeral expenditures, administrative costs, claims and bequests to religious, charitable, and fraternal organizations or government welfare agencies, and state inheritance taxes. For transfers made after 1981 during life or death, there is an unlimited marital deduction.

An annual gift tax exclusion is provided that permits tax-free gifts to each donee of $10,000 for each year. A husband and wife who agree to treat gifts to third persons as joint gifts can exclude up to $20,000 a year to each donee. An unlimited exclusion for medical expenses and school tuition paid for the benefit of any donee is also available.

Federal Estate and Gift Taxes

Unified Rate Schedule, 1991[1]

If the net amount is:		Tentative tax is:		
From	To	Tax +	%	On excess over
$ 0	$ 10,000	$ 0	18	$ 0
10,001	20,000	1,800	20	10,000
20,001	40,000	3,800	22	20,000
40,001	60,000	8,200	24	40,000
60,001	80,000	13,000	26	60,000
80,001	100,000	18,200	28	80,000
100,001	150,000	23,800	30	100,000
150,001	250,000	38,800	32	150,000
250,001	500,000	70,800	34	250,000
500,001	750,000	155,800	37	500,000
750,001	1,000,000	248,300	39	750,000
1,000,001	1,250,000	345,800	41	1,000,000
1,250,001	1,500,000	448,300	43	1,250,000
1,500,001	2,000,000	555,800	45	1,500,000
2,000,001	2,500,000	780,800	49	2,000,000
2,500,001	3,000,000	1,025,800	53	2,500,000
3,000,001 and up	—	1,290,800	55	3,000,000

1. The estate and gift tax rates are combined in the single rate schedule effective for the estates of decedents dying, and for gifts made, after Dec. 31, 1976.

Recent Legislation

On November 5, 1990, the President signed into law the Revenue Reconciliation Act of 1990 ("the Act"). The emphasis of the Act was increased taxes on the wealthy. Changes imposed by the Act include:

Luxury Tax

A new 10% tax on the purchase of furs and jewelry (over $10,000), automobiles (over $30,000), boats and yachts (over $100,000), and airplanes (over $250,000) was imposed effective January 1, 1991.

Limitation on Itemized Deductions

Total otherwise allowable itemized deductions (other than medical expenses, casualty and theft losses, and investment interest) are reduced by 3% of a taxpayer's adjusted gross income in excess of $100,000. Total itemized deductions may not be reduced by more than 80%.

What if Your Tax Return is Examined?

Source: Internal Revenue Service.

If your return is selected for examination, it does not suggest that you are dishonest. The examination may or may not result in more tax. Your case may be closed without change. Or, you may receive a refund.

Many examinations are handled entirely by mail. For information on this, get Publication 1383, The Correspondence Process (Income Tax Accounts), available free by calling 1-800-829-3676. If the IRS notifies you that your examination is to be conducted through a face-to-face interview, or you request such an interview, you have the right to ask that the examination take place at a reasonable time and place that is convenient for both you and the IRS. If the time or place suggested by the IRS is not convenient, the examiner will try to work out something more suitable. However, in any case, the IRS makes the final determination of how, when, and where the examination will take place.

Throughout the examination, you may represent yourself, have someone else accompany you, or with proper written authorization, have someone represent you in your absence.

You may make a sound recording of the examination if you wish, provided you let the examiner know in advance so that he or she can do the same.

Repeat Examinations

The IRS tries to avoid repeat examinations of the same items, but this sometimes happens. If the IRS examined your tax return for the same items in either of the two previous years and proposed no change to your tax liability, you should contact the IRS as soon as possible so that the agency can see if it should discontinue the repeat examination.

Explanation of Changes

If the IRS proposes any changes to your return, they will explain the reasons for the changes. You should not hesitate to ask about anything that is unclear to you.

Interest

You must pay interest on additional tax that you owe. The interest is figured from the due date of the return. But if an IRS error caused a delay in your case, and this was grossly unfair, you may be entitled to a reduction in the interest. Only delays caused by procedural or mechanical acts that do not involve the exercise of judgment or discretion qualify. If you think the IRS caused such a delay, you should discuss it with the examiner and file a claim.

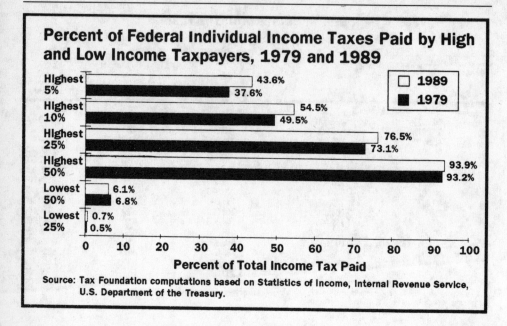

Percent of Federal Individual Income Taxes Paid by High and Low Income Taxpayers, 1979 and 1989

	1989	1979
Highest 5%	43.6%	37.6%
Highest 10%	54.5%	49.5%
Highest 25%	76.5%	73.1%
Highest 50%	93.9%	93.2%
Lowest 50%	6.1%	6.8%
Lowest 25%	0.7%	0.5%

☐ 1989
■ 1979

Percent of Total Income Tax Paid

Source: Tax Foundation computations based on Statistics of Income, Internal Revenue Service, U.S. Department of the Treasury.

Top Earners Still Pay Largest Share of Income Tax Bill

The top-earning ten percent of U.S. taxpayers paid nearly 55 percent of the Federal individual income tax bill in 1989, according to a Tax Foundation analysis of the recently released 1989 IRS tax return data. Despite all the major tax legislation witnessed over the decade of the 1980s, the fraction of income taxes collected for this top ten percent varied only slightly from year to year between 1979 and 1989 but inched steadily up during the decade.

After paying 49.5 percent of all Federal individual income taxes collected in 1979, these taxpayers, who now number 11.2 million, put a little more into the till most years until in 1989 they paid 54.5 percent. While their adjusted gross income (AGI) rose 89 percent from 1979 to 1989, their average tax payment rose even more—94 percent—and averaged $22,225 in 1989. Their AGI ranged down to $61,780, not exactly "fat cat" status. It still takes millions of middle- and upper-middle income taxpayers to pay the bulk of the total tax bill.

All segments of the top-earning half paid a larger share of the income tax bill over the course of the decade. The top five percent paid 43.6 percent in 1989, up from 37.6 in 1979; the top 25 percent paid 76.5 percent of the taxes paid in 1989, compared to 73.1 percent in 1979; and the top half increased its lion's share from 93.2 to 93.9 percent.

The lower half's share of income taxes paid dropped 11 percent over the decade. These taxpayers, whose AGI ranged from $18,851 down to zero in 1989, paid 6.1 percent of total taxes, down from 6.8 percent in 1979. The lowest 25 percent paid a slightly higher percentage of collections, up from .5 percent in 1979 to .7 percent in 1989.

Trends in Progressivity

The Federal income tax system has remained progressive. Top earners continue to pay a larger share of tax collections despite the alleged upper-income bias of the tax cuts and rate reductions under the Economic Recovery Tax Act of 1981 and the Tax Reform Act of 1986.

Growth in the income base itself has been increasing faster at the upper end of the income scale, resulting in increased income tax receipts from top earners. Naturally, this also results in a higher proportion of the entire population's income being taxed at the highest rate.

The 112 million returns filed for tax year 1989 reported an increase in AGI of $194 billion over 1988. The largest percentage gain in income was from Individual Retirement Account distributions, up 24.3 percent from 1988. Social Security benefits rose 22.4 percent, and taxable interest increased 15.5 percent. Salaries and wages, which constituted 71.6 percent of total positive income for 1989, rose 5.5 percent over 1988. All told, 1989 total individual income taxes rose $23.3 billion over 1988 for a record $439 billion take.

Taxpayer Rights

Source: Internal Revenue Service.

You have the right to have your personal and financial information kept confidential. You also have the right to know why the IRS is asking you for information, exactly how any information that you give will be used, and what might happen if you do not get the information.

Under the law, the IRS may share your tax information with State tax agencies with which the IRS has information exchange agreements, the Department of Justice and other federal agencies under strict legal guidelines, and certain foreign governments under tax treaty provisions.

State General Sales and Use Taxes[1]

State	Percent rate	State	Percent rate	State	Percent rate
Alabama	4	Kentucky	6	Ohio	5
Arizona	5	Louisiana	4	Oklahoma	4.5
Arkansas	4.5	Maine	5	Pennsylvania	5
California	4.75	Maryland	5	Rhode Island	7
Colorado	3	Massachusets	5	South Carolina	5
Connecticut	8	Michigan	4	South Dakota	4
D.C.	6	Minnesota	6	Tennessee	5.5
Florida	6	Mississippi	6	Texas	6.25
Georgia	4	Missouri	4.225	Utah	5
Hawaii	4	Nebraska	5	Vermont	5
Idaho	5	New Jersey	7	Virginia	3.5
Illinois	6.25	New Mexico	5	Washington	6.5
Indiana	5	New York	4	West Virginia	6
Iowa	4	North Carolina	3	Wisconsin	5
Kansas	4.25	North Dakota	5	Wyoming	3

1. Local and county taxes, if any, are additional. NOTE: Alaska, Delaware, Montana, New Hampshire, and Oregon have no state-wide sales and use taxes. *Source:* Questionnaires to the states.

Tax Freedom Day[1] by State

Calendar Years, 1990–91

State	Tax Freedom Day 1990	Tax Freedom Day 1991	Change from 1990 to 1991	State	Tax Freedom Day 1990	Tax Freedom Day 1991	Change from 1990 to 1991
Alabama	April 21	April 25	4	Montana	May 6	May 4	−2
Alaska	May 11	May 11	0	Nebraska	May 1	May 7	6
Arizona	May 2	May 7	5	Nevada	May 9	May 8	−1
Arkansas	April 22	April 26	4	New Hampshire	April 23	April 29	6
California	May 3	May 7	4	New Jersey	May 9	May 14	5
Colorado	April 28	May 2	4	New Mexico	May 4	May 7	3
Connecticut	May 11	May 17	6	New York	May 23	May 26	3
Delaware	May 18	May 21	3	North Carolina	May 1	May 3	2
Dist. of Columbia	May 21	May 26	5	North Dakota	May 5	May 6	1
Florida	May 2	May 4	2	Ohio	May 1	May 6	5
Georgia	April 27	May 3	6	Oklahoma	April 28	May 2	4
Hawaii	May 16	May 16	0	Oregon	May 5	May 10	5
Idaho	April 25	April 28	3	Pennsylvania	May 3	May 7	4
Illinois	May 6	May 9	3	Rhode Island	May 9	May 12	3
Indiana	April 28	May 2	4	South Carolina	April 26	May 1	5
Iowa	May 5	May 7	2	South Dakota	April 28	April 28	0
Kansas	May 1	May 5	4	Tennessee	April 25	April 29	4
Kentucky	April 25	April 29	4	Texas	May 2	May 5	3
Louisiana	April 28	May 4	6	Utah	May 2	May 1	−1
Maine	May 6	May 8	2	Vermont	May 11	May 10	−1
Maryland	May 8	May 11	3	Virginia	April 28	May 2	4
Massachusetts	May 3	May 8	5	Washington	May 9	May 10	1
Michigan	May 8	May 12	4	West Virginia	April 25	May 1	6
Minnesota	May 13	May 14	1	Wisconsin	May 8	May 11	3
Mississippi	April 19	April 24	5	Wyoming	May 2	May 6	4
Missouri	April 25	April 28	3	**U.S. Total**	**May 5**	**May 8**	**3**

1. Tax Freedom Day is the day on which the American taxpayer will have earned enough money to pay his 1991 total taxes. *Source:* Tax Foundation.

Taxes Dominate Average American's Budget

Based on the Government's budget for 1991, the Tax Foundation calculated that the federal tax bill for the average American family with two workers, earning $46,000 and two dependent children, to be $12,984. This 28.2% tax bite from the family's income will cover its direct and indirect federal taxes, but not state or local taxes.

Of the $12,984 that the typical family surrenders to Uncle Sam, nearly 80% will go to just four federal spending categories: Social Security, 32 cents from every dollar; National Defense, 20 cents out of each tax dollar; Interest on the National Debt, 14 cents per dollar; and Health Outlays (mainly Medicare and Medicaid), 13 cents of the family's tax dollar. These four alone will cost the typical family $10,251, or 79 cents of each tax dollar.

Property Tax Collections by State

Per Capita and Per $1,000 of Personal Income
Fiscal Years 1979 and 1989

State	Per capita property tax				Property tax per $1,000 of pers. income			
	Amount		Percent change	Rank 1989	Amount		Percent change	Rank 1989
	1979	1989			1979	1989		
Total	$295	$674	94.6 %	—	$38	$35	−7.5 %	—
Alabama	73	148	104.1	51	12	12	−0.4	51
Alaska	826	1,257	52.2	1	76	66	−12.8	1
Arizona	353	600	70.0	23	50	41	−18.1	19
Arkansas	125	211	68.0	49	21	17	−17.3	48
California	266	543	104.0	27	30	30	−2.1	33
Colorado	326	635	94.6	19	42	39	−7.3	22
Connecticut	456	1,003	119.8	5	51	44	−15.4	15
Delaware	165	276	67.1	44	19	16	−17.6	49
Florida	247	549	122.3	24	34	34	1.0	27
Georgia	209	444	111.8	33	31	30	−6.2	34
Hawaii	191	335	75.9	39	23	20	−13.3	43
Idaho	245	386	57.5	37	36	31	−14.4	31
Illinois	350	657	88.1	18	39	38	−4.3	23
Indiana	247	480	94.6	30	32	32	0.6	29
Iowa	339	624	84.1	20	42	43	0.5	17
Kansas	357	617	72.6	21	46	39	−13.8	21
Kentucky	131	228	74.8	48	20	18	−10.6	47
Louisiana	102	241	137.8	46	15	20	27.6	46
Maine	303	666	120.2	16	48	45	−7.4	13
Maryland	276	546	97.8	25	33	28	−13.9	36
Massachusetts	546	743	36.1	10	69	36	−47.9	24
Michigan	376	764	103.3	9	44	46	4.3	11
Minnesota	311	659	111.8	17	40	40	0.3	20
Mississippi	138	291	111.7	43	25	26	4.3	38
Missouri	205	318	54.9	41	28	21	−26.5	42
Montana	408	679	66.4	15	61	53	−12.7	6
Nebraska	389	698	79.4	14	52	47	−7.9	10
Nevada	355	386	8.8	36	40	23	−41.9	39
New Hampshire	426	1,058	148.5	3	59	56	−5.8	3
New Jersey	506	1,056	108.7	4	58	48	−16.7	9
New Mexico	131	180	37.0	50	20	15	−28.5	50
New York	482	929	92.9	6	58	48	−17.2	8
North Carolina	163	322	97.7	40	25	23	−8.4	40
North Dakota	257	441	71.4	34	36	34	−5.9	26
Ohio	260	476	83.0	31	33	31	−6.9	32
Oklahoma	149	267	78.9	45	21	20	−5.1	45
Oregon	366	795	117.4	8	47	54	16.5	4
Pennsylvania	230	467	103.4	32	30	29	−2.5	35
Rhode Island	399	737	84.7	11	53	44	−17.3	14
South Carolina	181	353	134.3	38	24	28	14.8	37
South Dakota	343	544	58.7	26	50	43	−14.3	16
Tennessee	155	296	90.9	42	24	22	−9.6	41
Texas	274	613	123.8	22	36	42	16.4	18
Utah	230	420	82.1	35	37	35	−5.3	25
Vermont	360	729	102.4	12	56	48	−12.8	7
Virginia	223	541	142.7	29	29	31	5.8	30
Washington	308	542	76.0	28	38	34	−10.6	28
West Virginia	131	237	81.7	47	20	20	0.5	44
Wisconsin	346	710	105.2	13	46	46	−1.1	12
Wyoming	513	870	69.6	7	63	63	0.4	2
Dist. of Columbia	323	1,117	263.8	2	32	54	69.7	5

Source: Department of Commerce, and Tax Foundation computations. Reprinted from *Tax Features*, May–June 1991.

Postal Regulations

Domestic Mail Service

First Class

First-class consists of letters and written and sealed matter. The rate is 29¢ for the first oz; 23¢ for each additional oz, or fraction of an oz, up to 11 oz. Pieces over 11 oz are subject to priority-mail (heavy pieces) rates. Single postcards, 19¢; double postcards, 38¢ (19¢ for each half). The post office sells prestamped single and double postal cards. Consult your postmaster for information on business-reply mail and presort rates.

The weight limit for first-class mail is 70 lb.

Weight not exceeding	Rates
1 oz	$ .29
2 oz	.52
3 oz	.75
4 oz	.98
5 oz	1.21
6 oz	1.44
7 oz	1.67
8 oz	1.90
9 oz	2.13
10 oz	2.36
11 oz	2.59
Over 11 ounces, *see* Priority Mail.	

Priority Mail (over 11 oz to 70 lb)

The zone rate applies to mailable matter over 11 oz of any class carried by air. Your local post office will supply free official zone tables appropriate to your location.

Airmail

First-class and priority mail receive airmail service.

Express Mail

Express Mail Service is available for any mailable article up to 70 lb in weight and 108 in. in combined length and girth, 7 days a week, 365 days a year. Call 800-333-8777 for pick-up service; there is a single charge of $4.50, no matter how many pieces. Flat rates: letter rate (up to 8 ounces), $9.95; up to 2 lb, $13.95; over 2 lb and up to 70 lb, consult your postmaster.

The flat-rate envelope (whatever the weight, the item goes for the same 2-lb rate) may be used by paying the appropriate 2-lb postage rate for the level of service desired. Other service features include: noon delivery between major business markets; merchandise and document reconstruction insurance; Express Mail shipping containers; shipment receipt; special collection boxes; and such options as return receipt service; COD service; waiver of signature; and pickup service.

Consult Postmaster for other Express Mail Services and rates.

The Postal Service will refund, upon application to originating office, the postage for any Express Mail shipments not meeting the service standard, except for those delayed by strike or work stoppage.

Second Class

Second-class mail is used primarily by newspapers, magazines, and other periodicals with second-class mailing privileges. For copies mailed by the public, the rate is the applicable Express Mail, Priority Mail, or single-piece first-, third- or fourth-class rate.

Third Class (under 16 oz)

Third-class mail is used for circulars, books, catalogs, printed matter, merchandise, seeds, cuttings, bulbs, roots, scions, and plants. There are two rate structures for this class, a single-piece and a bulk rate. Regular and special bulk rates are available only to authorized mailers—consult postmaster for details.

Third-Class, Single-Piece Rates

Weight not exceeding	Rates	Weight not exceeding	Rates
1 oz	$ .29	10 oz	$ 1.44
2 oz	.52	12 oz	1.56
3 oz	.75	14 oz	1.67
4 oz	.98	Over 14 oz but	
6 oz	1.21	less than 16 oz	1.79
8 oz	1.33		

Fourth Class (Parcel Post— 16 oz and over)

Fourth-class mail is used for merchandise, books, printed matter, and all other mailable matter not in first, second, or third class. Special fourth-class rates apply to books, library books, publications or records for the blind, and certain controlled-circulation publications.

Packages should be taken to your local post office, where the postage will be determined according to the weight of the package and the distance it is being sent. Information on weight and size limits for fourth-class mail may be obtained there.

Special Services

Registered Mail. When you use registered mail service, you are buying security—the safest way to send valuables. The full value of your mailing must be declared when mailed. You receive a receipt and the movement of your mail is controlled throughout the postal system. For an additional fee, a return receipt showing to whom, when, and where delivered may be obtained.

Fees for articles (in addition to postage)

Value			With insurance	Without insurance
$ 0.01	to	$ 100	$4.50	$4.40
100.01	to	500	4.85	4.70
500.01	to	1,000	5.25	5.05

For higher values, consult your postmaster.

Certified Mail. Certified mail service provides for a receipt to the sender and a record of delivery at the post office of address. No record is kept at the post office where mailed. It is for First-Class and Priority Mail only.

Fee in addition to postage, $1.00

Return Receipts. Available for COD, Express Mail, and certified, insured (for over $50), and registered mail. Requested at time of mailing:

Showing to whom and date delivered	$1.00
Showing to whom, date, and address where delivered	1.35
Requested after mailing:	
Showing to whom and date delivered	6.00

C.O.D. Mail. Maximum value for service is $600. Consult your postmaster for fees and conditions of mailing.

Insured Mail. Fees, in addition to postage, for coverage against loss or damage:

Liability			Fees
$ .01	to	$50	$ .75
$ 50.01	to	$100	1.60
$ 100.01	to	$200	2.40
$ 200.01	to	$300	3.50
$ 300.01	to	$400	4.60
$ 400.01	to	$500	5.40
$ 500.01	to	$600	6.20

Special Delivery. The payment of the special-delivery fee entitles mail to the most expeditious transportation and delivery. The fee is in addition to the regular postage.

	Weight/Fees		
Class of mail	Not more than 2 lb	More than 2 lb but not more than 10 lb	More than 10 lb
First–class	$7.65	$7.95	$8.55
All other classes	8.05	8.65	9.30

Special Handling. Payment of the special-handling fee entitles third- and fourth-class matter to the most expeditious handling and transportation, but not special delivery. The fee is in addition to the regular postage.

Weight	Fees
Not more than 10 lb	$1.80
More than 10 lb	2.50

Money Orders. Money orders are used for the safe transmission of money.

Amount of money order	Fees
$ .01 to $700	$1.00

Minimum Mail Sizes

All mail must be at least 0.007 in. thick and mail that is 1/4 in. or less in thickness must be at least 3 1/2 in. in height, at least 5 in. long, and rectangular in shape (except keys and identification devices). NOTE: Pieces greater than 1/4 in. thick can be mailed even if they measure less than 3 1/2 by 5 inches.

Adhesive Stamps Available

Purpose	Form	Prices and denomination
Regular postage	Single or sheet	1, 2, 3, 4, 5, 6, 7, 8, 9, 10, 15, 19, 20, 22, 23, 25, 28, 29, 30, 35, 40, 45, 50, 52, 65, 75¢, $1, $2, $2.90, $5, $9.95.
	Booklets	10 at 29 cents ($2.90) 20 at 29 cents ($5.80) 20 at 19 cents ($3.80)
	Coil of 100	19, 25, and 29¢ (dispenser and stamp affixer for use with these coils are also available).
	Coil of 500	1, 2, 3, 4, 5, 10, 15, 19, 20, 23, 25, 29¢, and $1.
	Coil of 3000	1, 2, 3, 4, 5, 10, 15, 19, 20, 23, 25, 29¢.
	Coil of 10,000	29¢.
International airmail postage	Single or sheet	40 and 50¢

Note: Denominations listed are currently in stock. Others may be available until supplies are exhausted.

Regular envelopes are available prestamped for 29¢ and 34¢ each (less than 500). For bulk prices, consult postmaster.

Single postcards are available prestamped for 19¢ each. Reply postcards (19¢ each half) are 38¢ each.

Non-Standard Mail

All first-class mail (except presort first-class and carrier route first-class weighing one ounce or less) and all single-piece rate third-class mail weighing one ounce or less is nonstandard (and subject to a 10¢ surcharge in addition to the applicable postage and fees) if any of the following dimensions are exceeded: length—11 1/2 inches; height—6 1/8 inches; thickness—1/4 inch, or the piece has a height to length (aspect) ratio which does not fall between 1 to 1.3 and 1 to 2.5 inclusive. (The aspect ratio is found by dividing the length by the height. If the answer is between 1.3 and 2.5 inclusive, the piece has a standard aspect ratio).

International Mail Service

Letters and Letter Packages

Items of mail containing personal handwritten or typewritten communications having the character of current correspondence must be sent as letters or letter packages. Unless prohibited by the country of destination, merchandise or other articles within the applicable weight and size limits may also be mailed at the letter rate of postage. Weight limit for all countries, 4 pounds. For rates, consult your local post office.

Letters and Letter Packages— Airmail Rates

All Countries other than Canada & Mexico

Weight not over	Rate	Weight not over	Rate
Oz		*Oz*	
0.5	$ 0.50	24.5	$19.28
1.0	0.95	25.0	19.67
1.5	1.34	25.5	20.06
2.0	1.73	26.0	20.45
2.5	2.12	26.5	20.84
3.0	2.51	27.0	21.23
3.5	2.90	27.5	21.62
4.0	3.29	28.0	22.01
4.5	3.68	28.5	22.40
5.0	4.07	29.0	22.79
5.5	4.46	29.5	23.18
6.0	4.85	30.0	23.57
6.5	5.24	30.5	23.96
7.0	5.63	31.0	24.35
7.5	6.02	31.5	24.74
8.0	6.41	32.0	25.13
8.5	6.80	33	25.52
9.0	7.19	34	25.91
9.5	7.58	35	26.30
10.0	7.97	36	26.69
10.5	8.36	37	27.08
11.0	8.75	38	27.47
11.5	9.14	39	27.86
12.0	9.53	40	28.25
12.5	9.92	41	28.64
13.0	10.31	42	29.03
13.5	10.70	43	29.42
14.0	11.09	44	29.81
14.5	11.48	45	30.20
15.0	11.87	46	30.59
15.5	12.26	47	30.98
16.0	12.65	48	31.37
16.5	13.04	49	31.76
17.0	13.43	50	32.15
17.5	13.82	51	32.54
18.0	14.21	52	32.93
18.5	14.60	53	33.32
19.0	14.99	54	33.71
19.5	15.38	55	34.10
20.0	15.77	56	34.49
20.5	16.16	57	34.88
21.0	16.55	58	35.27
21.5	16.94	59	35.66
22.0	17.33	60	36.05
22.5	17.72	61	36.44
23.0	18.11	62	36.83
23.5	18.50	63	37.22
24.0	18.89	64	37.61

Post and Postal Cards

Canada $0.30 All other—surface $0.35
Mexico $0.30 All other—air $0.40

Aerogrammes—$0.45 each.

Canada and Mexico—Surface Rates

All Countries other than Canada & Mexico

Weight not over	Canada	Mexico	Weight not over	Canada	Mexico
Lb	*Oz*			*Lb*	*Oz*		
0	0.5	$.40	$.35	0	10	2.47	2.65
0	1	.40	.45	0	11	2.70	2.90
0	1.5	.63	.55	0	12	2.93	3.15
0	2	.63	.65	1	0	3.25	4.15
0	3	.86	.90	1	8	3.85	6.15
0	4	1.09	1.15	2	0	4.45	8.15
0	5	1.32	1.40	2	8	5.38	10.15
0	6	1.55	1.65	3	0	6.31	12.15
0	7	1.78	1.90	3	8	7.24	14.15
0	8	2.01	2.15	4	0	8.17	16.15
0	9	2.24	2.40				

Weight Limit—4 Pounds*

Note: Mail paid at this rate receives First-Class service in the United States and air service in Canada and Mexico. *Registered letters to Canada may weigh up to 66 pounds. The rate for over 4 pounds to 66 pounds is $1.80 per pound or fraction of a pound.

Countries Other Than Canada and Mexico—Surface Rates

Letters and Letter Packages

Weight not over		Rate	Weight not over		Rate
Lb	*Oz*		*Lb*	*Oz*	
0	1	0.70	0	11	3.95
0	2	0.95	0	12	3.95
0	3	1.20	1	0	5.55
0	4	1.45	1	8	7.65
0	5	1.70	2	0	9.75
0	6	1.95	2	8	11.85
0	7	2.20	3	0	13.95
0	8	2.45	3	8	16.05
0	9	3.95	4	0	18.15
0	10	3.95			

Weight limit—4 pounds.

International Surface Parcel Post

Other Than Canada

Weight through lb	Mexico Central America, Caribbean Islands, Bahamas, Bermuda, St. Pierre and Miquelon	All other countries
2	$ 6.00	$ 6.55
	$1.85 each additional lb or fraction	$2.10 each additional lb or fraction

Consult your postmaster for weight/size limits of individual countries.

For other international services and rates consult your local postmaster.

Canada Surface Parcel Post

Up to 2 lb $4.85, $1.45 for each additional lb up to the maximum weight of 66 lb. Minimum weight is 1 lb.

International Money Order Fees

This service available only to certain countries. Consult post office. Fee: $3.00. Maximum amount for a single money order is $700.

United Nations Stamps

United Nations stamps are issued in three different currencies, namely, U.S. dollars, Swiss francs, and Austrian schillings. Stamps in all three currencies are available at face value at each of the U.N. Postal Administration offices in New York, Geneva, and Vienna. They may be purchased over the counter, by mail, or by opening a Customer Deposit Account.

Mail orders for mint (unused) stamps and postal stationery may be sent to the U.N. Postal Administration in New York, Geneva, and Vienna. Write to: United Nations Postal Administration, P.O. Box 5900, Grand Central Station, New York, N.Y. 10017.

How to Complain About a Postal Problem

When you have a problem with your mail service, complete a Consumer Service Card which is available from letter carriers and at post offices. This will help your postmaster respond to your problem. If you wish to telephone a complaint, a postal employee will fill out the card for you.

The Consumer Advocate represents consumers at the top management level in the Postal Service. If your postal problems cannot be solved by your local post office, then write to the Consumer Advocate. His staff stands ready to serve you.

Write to: The Consumer Advocate, U.S. Postal Service, Washington, D.C. 20260-6320. Or phone: 1-202-268-2284.

The Mail Order Merchandise Rule

The mail order rule adopted by the Federal Trade Commission in October 1975 provides that when you order by mail:

You must receive the merchandise when the seller says you will.

If you are not promised delivery within a certain time period, the seller must ship the merchandise to you no later than 30 days after your order comes in.

If you don't receive it shortly after that 30-day period, you can cancel your order and get your money back.

How the Rule Works

The seller must notify you if the promised delivery date (or the 30-day limit) cannot be met. The seller must also tell you what the new shipping date will be and give you the option to cancel the order and receive a full refund or agree to the new shipping date. The seller must also give you a free way to send back your answer, such as a stamped envelope or a postage-paid postcard. *If you don't answer, it means that you agree to the shipping delay.*

The seller must tell you if the shipping delay is going to be more than 30 days. You then can agree to the delay or, if you do not agree, the seller must return your money by the end of the first 30 days of the delay.

If you cancel a prepaid order, the seller must mail you the refund within seven business days. Where there is a credit sale, the seller must adjust your account within one billing cycle.

It would be impossible, however, for one rule to apply uniformly to such a varied field as mail order merchandising. For example, the rule does not apply to mail order photo finishing, magazine subscriptions, and other serial deliveries (except for the initial shipment); to mail order seeds and growing plants; to COD orders; or to credit orders where the buyer's account is not charged prior to shipment of the merchandise.

Authorized 2-Letter State Abbreviations

When the Post Office instituted the ZIP Code for mail in 1963, it also drew up a list of two-letter abbreviations for the states which would gradually replace the traditional ones in use. Following is the official list, including the District of Columbia, Guam, Puerto Rico, and the Virgin Islands (note that only capital letters are used):

Alabama	AL	Kentucky	KY	Ohio	OH
Alaska	AK	Louisiana	LA	Oklahoma	OK
Arizona	AZ	Maine	ME	Oregon	OR
Arkansas	AR	Maryland	MD	Pennsylvania	PA
California	CA	Massachusetts	MA	Puerto Rico	PR
Colorado	CO	Michigan	MI	Rhode Island	RI
Connecticut	CT	Minnesota	MN	South Carolina	SC
Delaware	DE	Mississippi	MS	South Dakota	SD
Dist. of Columbia	DC	Missouri	MO	Tennessee	TN
Florida	FL	Montana	MT	Texas	TX
Georgia	GA	Nebraska	NE	Utah	UT
Guam	GU	Nevada	NV	Vermont	VT
Hawaii	HI	New Hampshire	NH	Virginia	VA
Idaho	ID	New Jersey	NJ	Virgin Islands	VI
Illinois	IL	New Mexico	NM	Washington	WA
Indiana	IN	New York	NY	West Virginia	WV
Iowa	IA	North Carolina	NC	Wisconsin	WI
Kansas	KS	North Dakota	ND	Wyoming	WY

WORLD STATISTICS

GEOGRAPHY

Total area: 510,072,000 sq km; (196,887,792 sq. mi.); 361,132,000 sq km (139,396,952 sq mi.) (70.8%) is water and 148,940,000 sq km (57,490,840 sq mi.) (29.2%) is land

Comparative area: land area about 16 times the size of the U.S.

Land boundaries: 442,000 km (274,482 mi.)

Coastline: 359,000 km (222,939 mi.)

Maritime claims:
Contiguous zone: generally 24 nm, but varies from 4 nm to 24 nm
Continental shelf: generally 200 nm, but some are 200 meters in depth
Exclusive fishing zone: most are 200 nm, but varies from 12 nm to 200 nm
Extended economic zone: 200 nm, only Madagascar claims 150 nm
Territorial sea: generally 12 nm, but varies from 3 nm to 200 nm

Disputes: 13 international land boundary disputes—Argentina-Uruguay, Bangladesh-India, Brazil-Paraguay, Brazil-Uruguay, Cambodia-Vietnam, China-India, China-U.S.S.R., Ecuador-Peru, El Salvador-Honduras, French Guiana-Suriname, Guyana-Suriname, Guyana-Venezuela, Qatar-UAE

Climate: two large areas of polar climates separated by two rather narrow temperate zones from a wide equatorial band of tropical to subtropical climates

Terrain: highest elevation is Mt. Everest at 8,848 meters (29,108 ft) and lowest elevation is the Dead Sea at 392 meters (1,290 ft) below sea level; greatest ocean depth is the Marianas Trench at 10,924 meters (35,839 ft)

Natural resources: the oceans represent the last major frontier for the discovery and development of natural resources

Land use: 10% arable land; 1% permanent crops; 24% meadows and pastures; 31% forest and woodland; 34% other; includes 1.6% irrigated

Environment: large areas subject to severe weather (tropical cyclones), natural disasters (earthquakes, landslides, tsunamis, volcanic eruptions), industrial disasters, pollution (air, water, acid rain, toxic substances), loss of vegetation (overgrazing, deforestation, desertification), loss of wildlife resources, soil degradation, soil depletion, erosion

PEOPLE

Population: 5,384,000,000 (1991 est.), growth rate 1.7% (1990)

Birth rate: 27 births/1,000 population (1990)

Death rate: 9 deaths/1,000 population (1990)

Infant mortality rate: 70 deaths/1,000 live births (1990)

Life expectancy at birth: 60 years male, 64 years female (1990)

Total fertility rate: 3.4 children born/woman (1990)

Source: The World Factbook, 1990, published by the Directorate of Intelligence of the Central Intelligence Agency.

Literacy: 77% men; 66% women (1980)

Labor force: 1,939,000,000 (1984)

GOVERNMENT

Administrative divisions: 246 nations, dependencies, and geographic entities

Legal system: varies among each of the entities; 160 are parties to the United Nations International Court of Justice (ICJ) or World Court

Diplomatic representation: there are 166 members of the U.N.

ECONOMY

Overview: In 1989 the World economy grew at an estimated 3.0%, somewhat lower than the estimated 3.4% for 1988. The technologically advanced areas—North America, Japan, and Western Europe—together account for 65% of the gross world product (GWP) of $20.3 trillion; these developed areas grew in the aggregate at 3.5%. In contrast, the Communist (Second World) countries typically grew at between 0% and 2%, accounting for 23% of GWP. Experience in the developing countries continued mixed, with the newly industrializing countries generally maintaining their rapid growth, and many others struggling with debt, inflation, and inadequate investment. The years 1989 and 1990 saw remarkable political upheavals in the Communist countries, which presumably will dislocate economic production still further. The addition of nearly 100 million people a year to an already overcrowded globe will exacerbate the problems of pollution, desertification, underemployment, and poverty throughout the 1990s.

GWP (gross world product): $20.3 trillion, per capita $3,870; real growth rate 3.0% (1989 est.)

Inflation rate (consumer prices): 5% (1989 est.)

Exports: $2,694 billion (f.o.b. 1988); *commodities*—n.a.; *partners*—in value, about 70% of exports from industrial countries

Imports: $2,750 billion (c.i.f., 1988); *commodities*—n.a.; *partners*—in value, about 75% of imports by the industrial countries

External debt: $1,008 billion for less developed countries (1988 est.)

Industrial production: growth rate 5% (1989 est.)

Electricity: 2,838,680,000 kW capacity; 11,222,029 million kWh produced, 2,140 kWh per capita (1989)

Industries: chemicals, energy, machinery, electronics, metals, mining, textiles, food processing

DEFENSE FORCES

Branches: ground, maritime, and air forces at all levels of technology

Military manpower: 29.15 million persons in the defense forces of the World (1987)

Defense expenditures: 5.4% of GWP, or $1.1 trillion (1989 est.)

Area and Population by Country

Mid-1991 Estimates

Country	Area[1]	Population	Country	Area[1]	Population
Afghanistan	250,000	16,600,000	India	1,269,340	859,200,000
Albania	11,100	3,300,000	Indonesia	741,100	181,400,000
Algeria	919,590	26,000,000	Iran	636,290	58,600,000
Angola	481,350	8,500,000	Iraq	167,920	17,100,000
Antigua and Barbuda	170	100,000	Ireland	27,140	3,500,000
Argentina	1,068,300	32,700,000	Israel	8,020	4,900,000
Australia	2,967,900	17,500,000	Italy	116,310	57,700,000
Austria	32,370	7,700,000	Jamaica	4,240	2,500,000
Bahamas	5,380	300,000	Japan	143,750	123,800,000
Bahrain	240	500,000	Jordan	35,480	3,400,000
Bangladesh	55,600	116,600,000	Kenya	224,960	25,200,000
Barbados	170	300,000	Korea, North	46,540	21,800,000
Belgium	11,750	9,900,000	Korea, South	38,020	43,200,000
Belize	8,860	200,000	Kuwait	6,880	1,400,000
Benin	43,480	4,800,000	Laos	91,430	4,100,000
Bhutan	18,150	700,000	Lebanon	4,020	3,400,000
Bolivia	424,160	7,500,000	Lesotho	11,720	1,800,000
Botswana	231,800	1,300,000	Liberia	43,000	2,700,000
Brazil	3,268,470	153,300,000	Libya	679,360	4,400,000
Brunei	2,230	300,000	Luxembourg	990	400,000
Bulgaria	42,820	9,000,000	Madagascar	226,660	12,400,000
Burkina Faso	105,870	9,400,000	Malawi	45,750	9,400,000
Burundi	10,750	5,800,000	Malaysia	127,320	18,300,000
Cambodia	69,900	7,100,000	Maldives	120	200,000
Cameroon	183,570	11,400,000	Mali	478,760	8,300,000
Canada	3,851,790	26,800,000	Malta	120	400,000
Cape Verde	1,560	400,000	Mauritania	397,950	2,100,000
Central African Republic	240,530	3,000,000	Mauritius	790	1,100,000
Chad	495,750	5,100,000	Mexico	761,600	85,700,000
Chile	292,260	13,400,000	Mongolia	604,250	2,200,000
China, People's Republic of	3,705,390	1,151,300,000	Morocco	172,410	26,200,000
Colombia	439,730	33,600,000	Mozambique	309,490	16,100,000
Comoros	690	500,000	Myanmar	261,220	42,100,000
Congo	132,050	2,300,000	Namibia	318,260	1,500,000
Costa Rica	19,580	3,100,000	Nepal	54,360	19,600,000
Côte d'Ivoire	124,500	12,500,000	Netherlands	14,410	15,000,000
Cuba	44,420	10,700,000	New Zealand	103,740	3,500,000
Cyprus	3,570	700,000	Nicaragua	50,190	3,900,000
Czechoslovakia	49,370	15,700,000	Niger	489,190	8,000,000
Denmark	16,630	5,100,000	Nigeria	356,670	122,500,000
Djibouti	8,490	400,000	Norway	125,180	4,300,000
Dominica	290	100,000	Oman	82,030	1,600,000
Dominican Republic	18,810	7,300,000	Pakistan	310,400	117,500,000
Ecuador	109,480	10,800,000	Panama	29,760	2,500,000
Egypt	386,660	54,500,000	Papua New Guinea	178,260	3,900,000
El Salvador	8,260	5,400,000	Paraguay	157,050	4,400,000
Equatorial Guinea	10,830	400,000	Peru	496,220	22,000,000
Ethiopia	471,780	53,200,000	Philippines	115,830	62,300,000
Fiji	7,050	700,000	Poland	120,730	38,200,000
Finland	130,130	5,000,000	Portugal	35,550	10,400,000
France	211,210	56,700,000	Qatar	4,250	500,000
Gabon	103,350	1,200,000	Romania	91,700	23,400,000
Gambia	4,360	900,000	Rwanda	10,170	7,500,000
Germany	137,800	79,500,000	St. Lucia	240	200,000
Ghana	92,100	15,500,000	St. Vincent and the Grenadines	150	100,000
Greece	50,940	10,100,000	Saudi Arabia	830,000	15,500,000
Grenada	130	100,000	Senegal	75,750	7,500,000
Guatemala	42,040	9,500,000	Sierra Leone	27,700	4,300,000
Guinea	94,930	7,500,000	Singapore	220	2,800,000
Guinea-Bissau	13,950	1,000,000	Solomon Islands	10,980	300,000
Guyana	83,000	800,000	Somalia	246,200	7,700,000
Haiti	10,710	6,300,000	South Africa	471,440	40,600,000
Honduras	43,280	5,300,000	Spain	194,900	39,000,000
Hungary	35,920	10,400,000	Sri Lanka	26,330	17,400,000
Iceland	39,770	300,000	Sudan	967,490	25,900,000

Country	Area[1]	Population	Country	Area[1]	Population
Suriname	63,040	400,000	United Arab Emirates	32,280	2,400,000
Swaziland	6,700	800,000	United Kingdom	94,530	57,500,000
Sweden	173,730	8,600,000	United States	3,615,100	248,700,000
Switzerland	15,940	6,800,000	Uruguay	68,040	3,100,000
Syria	71,500	12,800,000	Vanuatu	5,700	200,000
Taiwan	12,460	20,500,000	Venezuela	352,140	20,100,000
Tanzania	364,900	26,900,000	Vietnam	127,240	67,600,000
Thailand	196,460	58,800,000	Western Samoa	1,100	200,000
Togo	21,930	3,800,000	Yemen	203,850	10,100,000
Trinidad and Tobago	1,980	1,300,000	Yugoslavia	98,760	23,900,000
Tunisia	63,170	8,400,000	Zaire	905,560	37,800,000
Turkey	301,380	58,500,000	Zambia	290,580	8,400,000
Uganda	91,140	18,700,000	Zimbabwe	150,800	10,000,000
U.S.S.R.	8,649,500	292,000,000			

1. Square miles. *Source: 1991 World Population Data Sheet,* Population Reference Bureau, Inc., Washington, D.C.

World's Largest Cities by Rank
(Estimated Mid-Year Population in Thousands)

Rank in 1990	City	1990	1995	2000	Average Annual Growth Rate (%) 1990–95	Area (square miles)
1.	Tokyo-Yokohama, Japan	26,952	28,447	29,971	1.08	1,089
2.	Mexico City, Mexico	20,207	23,913	27,872	3.37	522
3.	Sao Paulo, Brazil	18,052	21,539	25,354	3.53	451
4.	Seoul, South Korea	16,268	19,065	21,976	3.17	342
5.	New York, United States	14,622	14,638	14,648	0.02	1,274
6.	Osaka-Kobe-Kyoto, Japan	13,826	14,060	14,287	0.34	495
7.	Bombay, India	11,777	13,532	15,357	2.78	95
8.	Calcutta, India	11,663	12,885	14,088	1.99	209
9.	Buenos Aires, Argentina	11,518	12,232	12,911	1.20	535
10.	Rio de Janeiro, Brazil	11,428	12,786	14,169	2.25	260
11.	Moscow, Soviet Union	10,367	10,769	11,121	0.76	379
12.	Los Angeles, United States	10,060	10,414	10,714	0.69	1,110
13.	Manila, Philippines	9,880	11,342	12,846	2.76	188
14.	Cairo, Egypt	9,851	11,155	12,512	2.49	104
15.	Jakarta, Indonesia	9,588	11,151	12,804	3.02	76
16.	Tehran, Iran	9,354	11,681	14,251	4.44	112
17.	London, United Kingdom	9,170	8,897	8,574	−0.60	874
18.	Paris, France	8,709	8,764	8,803	0.13	432
19.	Delhi, India	8,475	10,105	11,849	3.52	138
20.	Karachi, Pakistan	7,711	9,350	11,299	3.85	190
21.	Lagos, Nigeria	7,602	9,799	12,528	5.08	56
22.	Essen, Germany	7,474	7,364	7,239	−0.30	704
23.	Shanghai, China	6,873	7,194	7,540	0.91	78
24.	Lima, Peru	6,578	7,853	9,241	3.54	120
25.	Chicago, United States	6,526	6,541	6,568	0.05	762
26.	Taipei, Taiwan	6,513	7,477	8,516	2.76	138
27.	Istanbul, Turkey	6,461	7,624	8,875	3.31	165
28.	Bangkok, Thailand	5,791	6,657	7,587	2.79	102
29.	Madras, India	5,743	6,550	7,384	2.63	115
30.	Beijing, China	5,736	5,865	5,993	0.44	151
31.	Bogota, Colombia	5,710	6,801	7,935	3.50	79
32.	Hong Kong, Hong Kong	5,656	5,841	5,956	0.64	23
33.	Santiago, Chile	5,275	5,812	6,294	1.94	128
34.	Pusan, South Korea	4,838	5,748	6,700	3.45	54
35.	Tianjin, China	4,804	5,041	5,298	0.96	49
36.	Milan, Italy	4,738	4,795	4,839	0.24	344
37.	Nagoya, Japan	4,736	5,017	5,303	1.15	307
38.	St. Petersburg, Soviet Union	4,667	4,694	4,738	0.12	139
39.	Bangalore, India	4,612	5,644	6,764	4.04	50
40.	Madrid, Spain	4,451	4,772	5,104	1.39	66
41.	Shenyang, China	4,248	4,457	4,684	0.96	39
42.	Lahore, Pakistan	4,236	4,986	5,864	3.26	57
43.	Dhaka, Bangladesh	4,224	5,296	6,492	4.52	32
44.	Barcelona, Spain	4,163	4,492	4,834	1.52	87

Rank in 1990	City	1990	1995	2000	Average Annual Growth Rate (%) 1990–95	Area (square miles)
45.	Manchester, United Kingdom	4,050	3,949	3,827	−0.50	357
46.	Philadelphia, United States	4,007	3,988	3,979	−0.10	471
47.	San Francisco, United States	3,958	4,104	4,214	0.72	428
48.	Baghdad, Iraq	3,941	4,566	5,239	2.94	97
49.	Belo Horizonte, Brazil	3,683	4,373	5,125	3.43	79
50.	Ho Chi Minh City, Vietnam	3,645	4,064	4,481	2.18	31
51.	Ahmadabad, India	3,595	4,200	4,837	3.11	32
52.	Kinshasa, Zaire	3,575	4,520	5,646	4.69	57
53.	Hyderabad, India	3,563	4,149	4,765	3.05	88
54.	Sydney, Australia	3,515	3,619	3,708	0.58	338
55.	Athens, Greece	3,468	3,670	3,866	1.13	116
56.	Miami, United States	3,421	3,679	3,894	1.45	448
57.	Guangzhou, China	3,330	3,485	3,652	0.91	79
58.	Guadalajara, Mexico	3,262	3,839	4,451	3.25	78
59.	Surabaya, Indonesia	3,205	3,428	3,632	1.35	43
60.	Caracas, Venezuela	3,188	3,338	3,435	0.92	54
61.	Wuhan, China	3,169	3,325	3,495	0.96	65
62.	Toronto, Canada	3,108	3,296	3,296	1.17	154
63.	Greater Berlin, Germany	3,022	3,018	3,006	−0.03	274
64.	Rome, Italy	3,021	3,079	3,129	0.38	69
65.	Porto Alegre, Brazil	3,015	3,541	4,109	3.22	231
66.	Detroit, United States	2,995	2,865	2,735	−0.89	468
67.	Naples, Italy	2,960	3,051	3,134	0.61	62
68.	Melbourne, Australia	2,907	2,946	2,968	0.27	327
69.	Alexandria, Egypt	2,899	3,114	3,304	1.43	35
70.	Montreal, Canada	2,896	2,996	3,071	0.68	164
71.	Casablanca, Morocco	2,891	3,327	3,795	2.81	35
72.	Monterrey, Mexico	2,837	3,385	3,974	3.53	77
73.	Rangoon, Burma	2,813	3,075	3,332	1.78	47
74.	Ankara, Turkey	2,782	3,263	3,777	3.19	55
75.	Kiev, Soviet Union	2,751	2,983	3,237	1.62	62
76.	Dallas, United States	2,743	2,972	3,257	1.60	419
77.	Singapore, Singapore	2,695	2,816	2,913	0.88	78
78.	Harbin, China	2,618	2,747	2,887	0.96	30
79.	Washington, United States	2,547	2,637	2,707	0.69	357
80.	Taegu, South Korea	2,529	3,201	4,051	4.71	(n.a.)
81.	Boston, United States	2,475	2,480	2,485	0.04	303
82.	Poona, India	2,447	2,987	3,647	3.99	(n.a.)
83.	Lisbon, Portugal	2,396	2,551	2,717	1.26	(n.a.)
84.	Tashkent, Soviet Union	2,365	2,640	2,947	2.20	(n.a.)
85.	Chengdu, China	2,349	2,465	2,591	0.96	25
86.	Chongqing, China	2,339	2,632	2,961	2.36	(n.a.)
87.	Vienna, Austria	2,313	2,474	2,647	1.35	(n.a.)
88.	Budapest, Hungary	2,301	2,313	2,335	0.10	138
89.	Houston, United States	2,298	2,456	2,651	1.33	310
90.	Salvador, Brazil	2,209	2,694	3,286	3.97	(n.a.)
91.	Birmingham, United Kingdom	2,170	2,130	2,078	−0.37	223
92.	Bucharest, Romania	2,150	2,214	2,271	0.59	52
93.	Havana, Cuba	2,109	2,218	2,333	1.01	(n.a.)
94.	Kanpur, India	2,076	2,356	2,673	2.53	(n.a.)

Source: U.S. Bureau of the Census, 1989, International Data Base. NOTE: For this table cities are defined as population clusters of continuous built-up area with a population density of at least 5,000 persons per square mile. The boundary of the city was determined by examining detailed maps of each city in conjunction with the most recent official population statistics. Exclaves of areas exceeding the minimum population density were added to the city if the intervening gap was less than one mile. To the extent practical, nonresidential areas such as parks, airports, industrial complexes, and water were excluded from the area reported for each city, thus making the population density reflective of the concentrations in the residential portions of the city. By using a consistent definition for the city, it is possible to make comparisons of the cities on the basis of total population, area, and population density.

Political and administrative boundaries were disregarded in determining the population of a city. Detroit includes Windsor, Canada.

The population of each city was projected based on the proportion each city was of its country total at the time of the last two censuses and projected country populations (U.S. Bureau of the Census 1989).

Population figures for the nine cities with (n.a.) in the area column were derived by a less precise method, not involving the use of detailed maps. In addition, three other cities (Abidjan, Côte d'Ivoire; Khartoum, Sudan; and Medan, Indonesia) were estimated to have at least 2,000,000 inhabitants as of midyear 1989. However, projections for these cities could not be prepared because the apparent growth rates indicate that data are not comparable. Thirty-four other cities are projected to have at least 2,000,000 inhabitants by midyear 2000.

Expectation of Life by Age and Sex for Selected Countries

| | | Average future lifetime in years at stated age | | | | | | | | | | | |
| | | Males | | | | | | Females | | | | | |
Country	Period	0	1	10	20	40	60	0	1	10	20	40	60
NORTH AMERICA													
U.S.	1986	71.30	71.10	62.40	52.80	34.50	18.00	78.30	78.00	69.20	59.40	40.20	22.50
Canada	1985–1987	73.02	72.64	63.87	54.26	35.51	18.40	79.79	79.33	70.52	60.71	41.27	23.24
Mexico	1979	62.10	—	—	—	—	—	66.00	—	—	—	—	—
Trinidad & Tobago	1980–1985	66.88	67.34	58.97	49.39	31.13	15.84	71.62	71.64	63.18	53.44	34.55	18.42
CENTRAL AND SOUTH AMERICA													
Brazil	1985–1990 [1]	62.30	—	—	—	—	—	67.50	—	—	—	—	—
Chile	1985–1990	68.05	68.43	59.87	50.27	32.30	16.84	75.05	75.29	66.69	56.93	37.81	20.58
Costa Rica	1985–1990 [1]	72.41	—	—	—	—	—	77.04	—	—	—	—	—
Ecuador	1985 [2]	63.39	67.12	60.43	51.16	33.57	17.76	67.59	70.64	63.09	54.51	36.32	19.43
Guatemala	1979–1980	55.11	59.09	54.38	45.55	30.56	16.57	59.43	62.98	58.74	49.79	33.01	17.50
Panama	1985–1990 [3]	70.15	70.92	63.00	53.58	35.43	18.80	74.10	74.65	66.62	57.03	38.28	20.81
Peru	1980–1985 [4]	56.77	62.32	57.21	48.13	30.97	15.41	66.50	65.67	60.48	51.34	33.82	17.07
Uruguay	1984–1986	68.43	69.67	61.03	51.40	32.68	16.65	74.88	75.89	67.24	57.46	38.27	21.01
Venezuela	1985 [4]	66.68	68.45	60.31	50.92	33.07	17.30	72.80	74.16	65.90	56.23	37.31	20.30
EUROPE													
Austria	1988 [5]	72.03	71.66	62.86	53.26	34.57	17.86	78.63	78.22	69.36	59.51	40.08	21.85
Belgium	1979–1982 [5]	70.04	69.99	61.26	51.64	32.98	16.26	76.79	76.61	67.88	58.08	38.82	20.93
Cyprus	1983–1987	73.90	73.91	65.14	55.47	36.48	19.27	77.82	77.61	68.85	58.99	39.43	21.12
Czechoslovakia	1986 [5]	67.31	67.35	58.61	48.91	30.19	14.58	74.69	74.53	65.72	55.88	36.46	18.71
Denmark[6]	1986–1987 [5]	71.80	71.40	62.60	52.90	34.10	17.40	77.60	77.20	68.40	58.50	39.10	21.70
Finland	1986 [5]	70.49	69.98	61.12	51.42	32.87	16.66	78.72	78.08	69.19	59.33	39.94	21.62
France	1987 [5]	72.03	71.69	62.91	53.24	34.76	18.41	80.27	79.79	70.99	61.16	41.84	23.67
Germany, East[7]	1987–1988 [5]	69.81	69.53	60.77	51.09	32.42	16.09	75.91	75.46	66.67	56.83	37.46	19.55
Germany, West[7]	1985–1987 [5]	71.81	71.52	62.73	53.01	34.07	17.26	78.37	77.97	69.15	59.30	39.87	21.72
Greece	1980 [5]	72.15	72.82	54.13	54.48	35.58	18.17	76.35	76.78	68.24	58.43	38.95	20.63
Hungary	1988	66.16	66.32	57.56	47.86	29.61	15.05	74.03	74.09	65.28	55.44	36.32	19.15
Ireland	1980–1982 [5]	70.14	69.94	61.25	51.58	32.63	15.90	75.62	75.35	66.58	56.75	37.26	19.54
Italy	1985 [5]	72.01	71.92	63.13	53.44	34.36	17.43	78.61	78.38	69.57	59.72	40.18	21.88
Netherlands	1985–1986 [5]	72.95	72.64	63.84	54.08	34.86	17.48	79.55	79.12	70.29	60.43	40.94	22.75
Norway	1987 [5]	72.75	72.42	63.33	53.96	35.08	17.94	79.55	79.16	70.32	60.47	40.93	22.70
Poland	1988	67.15	67.37	58.65	48.96	30.60	15.47	75.67	75.70	66.92	57.07	37.71	20.08
Portugal	1979–1982 [5]	68.35	69.10	60.66	51.31	33.09	16.74	75.20	75.72	67.17	57.46	38.27	20.29
Spain	1980–1982 [5]	72.52	72.54	63.88	54.20	35.35	18.39	78.61	78.44	69.73	59.91	40.46	22.13
Sweden	1987 [5]	74.16	73.66	64.80	55.06	36.12	18.73	80.15	79.60	70.73	60.86	41.39	23.07
Switzerland	1987–1989	73.90	73.50	64.70	55.00	36.40	19.00	80.70	80.20	71.40	61.60	42.20	23.70
U.S.S.R.	1986–1987	65.04	—	—	—	—	—	73.78	—	—	—	—	—
United Kingdom	1985–1987	71.90	71.66	62.86	53.13	33.98	16.80	77.64	77.27	68.45	58.60	39.10	21.16
Yugoslavia	1987–1989 [5]	68.43	69.26	60.66	50.96	32.25	16.28	74.25	75.03	66.39	56.57	37.21	19.39
ASIA													
Bangladesh	1988	56.91	63.66	58.73	49.53	31.58	15.50	55.97	61.50	57.26	48.30	31.44	15.76
India	1976–1980	52.50	58.60	54.80	45.80	28.30	14.10	52.10	58.60	56.60	47.80	31.20	15.90
Iran	1976	55.75	60.78	53.87	45.19	29.19	14.58	55.04	60.14	54.38	44.97	30.47	15.39
Israel[8]	1987	73.60	73.50	64.80	55.10	35.90	18.60	77.00	76.80	68.10	58.20	38.70	20.50
Japan	1988 [9]	75.54	—	66.15	56.40	37.24	19.78	81.30	—	71.84	61.96	42.44	23.88
Korea, South	1989	66.92	66.66	58.18	48.56	30.30	14.87	74.96	74.75	66.23	56.54	37.50	19.87
Pakistan	1976–1978	59.04	66.46	61.34	52.30	34.77	19.25	59.20	65.58	60.68	51.98	35.23	19.27
Sri Lanka	1981	67.78	68.99	60.99	51.64	33.19	17.74	71.66	72.67	64.75	55.36	36.96	19.57
Syria	1976–1979	63.77	66.92	59.88	50.69	32.74	16.16	64.70	67.06	60.14	50.90	32.84	16.23
AFRICA													
Egypt	1985–1990 [1]	59.29	—	—	—	—	—	61.97	—	—	—	—	—
Kenya	1985–1990 [1]	56.50	—	—	—	—	—	60.46	—	—	—	—	—
South Africa	1985–1990 [1]	57.51	—	—	—	—	—	63.48	—	—	—	—	—
OCEANIA													
Australia	1987 [5, 10]	73.03	72.75	63.97	54.35	35.60	18.27	79.46	79.05	70.22	60.40	40.97	22.76
New Zealand	1986–1988	71.03	70.94	62.24	52.75	34.09	17.12	77.27	77.02	68.27	58.50	39.21	21.47

1. Estimates prepared in the Population Division of the United Nations. 2. Excluding nomadic Indian tribes. 3. Excluding tribal Indian population numbering 62,187 in 1960. 4. Excluding Indian jungle population. 5. Complete life table. 6. Excluding the Faeroe Islands and Greenland. 7. Including relevant data relating to Berlin. No separate data have been supplied. 8. Including data for East Jerusalem and Israeli residents in certain other territories. 9. For Japanese nationals in Japan only. 10. Excluding full-blooded aborigines, estimated at 49,036 in June 1966. NOTE: Figures are latest available as of August 1991. *Source:* United Nations *Demographic Yearbook, 1989.*

Energy, Petroleum, and Coal, by Country

| Country | Energy consumed[1] (coal equiv.) | | | | Electric energy production[2] (bil. kwh) | | Crude petroleum production[3] (mil. metric tons) | | Coal production[4] (mil. metric tons) | |
| | Total (mil. metric tons) | | Per capita (kilograms) | | | | | | | |
	1987	1980	1987	1980	1987	1980	1987	1980	1987	1980
Algeria	33.3	24.8	1,441	1,327	13.4	7.1	33.1	47.4	(Z)[5]	(Z)
Argentina	59.5	49.3	1,912	1,746	52.2	39.7	22.0	25.3	.4	.4
Australia[6]	110.6	91.2	6,845	6,195	132.2	96.1	25.1	18.9	147.8	72.5
Austria	30.1	30.5	4,018	4,058	50.2	42.0	1.1	1.5	(Z)	(Z)
Bahrain	6.8	4.4	14,680	12,651	3.0	1.7	2.0	2.4	n.a.	n.a.
Bangladesh	6.9	3.8	64	44	5.9	2.7	(Z)	(Z)	(X)	(X)
Belgium	55.1	59.1	5,560	5,997	62.4	53.6	(X)	(X)	4.4[7]	6.3
Brazil	108.5	92.5	767	763	202.3	139.5	28.5	9.1	6.9	5.2
Bulgaria	53.1	47.3	5,912	5,254	43.5	34.8	.3[5]	.3[5]	.2	.3
Canada	256.5	254.2	9,915	10,547	496.3	377.5	75.2	70.4	32.7	20.2
Chile	11.8	11.4	938	1,025	15.6	11.8	1.3	1.6	1.6	1.0
China	800.8	562.8	749	571	497.3	300.6	134.1	105.9	928.0	595.8
Colombia	24.5	23.8	817	923	35.4	22.9	19.4	6.5	14.6	4.9
Cuba	14.5	13.6	1,442	1,394	13.6	9.9	.9	.3	(X)	(X)
Czechoslovakia	98.2	97.4	6,311	6,364	85.8	72.7	.1	.1	25.7[7]	28.3[7]
Denmark	27.4	26.9	5,346	5,254	29.4	27.1	4.6	.3	(X)	(X)
Ecuador	6.2	5.7	627	708	5.7	3.4	8.9	10.4	n.a.	(NA)
Egypt	33.8	20.1	674	488	32.5	18.9	45.2	29.4	(X)	(X)
Ethiopia	1.2	.9	28	27	.8	.7	(X)	(X)	n.a.	(NA)
Finland	28.1	26.4	5,692	5,514	53.5[8]	38.7[8]	(X)	(X)	(X)	(X)
France[9]	206.9	237.3	3,720	4,409	356.2[8]	246.4[8]	3.2	1.2	16.3[7]	20.2[7]
Germany, East	131.3	121.8	7,891	7,276	114.2	98.8	(Z)	.1	(Z)	(Z)
Germany, West	342.0	359.4	5,624	5,829	415.8	368.8	3.8[10]	4.6	82.4	94.5
Greece	24.5	20.1	2,452	2,088	30.1	22.7	1.1	(Z)	(X)	(X)
Hong Kong	10.6	7.3	1,891	1,448	23.8	12.6	n.a.	(NA)	(X)	(X)
Hungary	40.5	40.6	3,819	3,787	29.7	23.9	1.9	2.0	2.4[7]	3.1[7]
India	220.5	139.4	275	202	217.5	119.3	30.1	9.4	177.0	109.1
Indonesia	47.2	34.7	274	230	34.8	14.2	64.6	77.6	1.7	.3
Iran[11]	65.9	45.7	1,285	1,177	37.9	22.4	113.4	72.7	1.2[5]	.9[5]
Iraq	12.5	10.7	735	807	22.9	11.4	101.8	130.1	n.a.	(NA)
Ireland	12.5	11.1	3,462	3,268	12.6	10.9	(X)	(X)	(Z)	.1
Israel	12.2	8.8	2,794	2,273	17.5	12.5	(Z)	(Z)	(X)	(X)
Italy[12]	204.4	174.9	3,570	3,112	198.3	185.7	3.9	1.8	(Z)	(Z)[5]
Japan	456.1	434.8	3,741	3,726	699.0	577.5	.6[5]	.4	13.0	18.0
Korea, North	57.9	48.5	2,708	2,713	50.2	35.0	(X)	(X)	39.5[5]	36.0[5]
Korea, South	74.2	52.3	1,760	1,373	80.3	40.1	(X)	(X)	24.3	18.6
Kuwait[13]	17.1	6.9	9,191	5,019	18.4	9.4	61.4	84.1	n.a.	n.a.
Libya	11.0	7.3	3,023	2,456	14.3	4.8	46.8	88.3	(X)	(X)
Malaysia	20.8	12.2	1,283	882	17.4	10.2	24.3	13.2	(X)	(X)
Mexico	140.9	118.6	1,697	1,709	104.8[8]	67.0[8]	132.1	99.9	11.1	7.0
Morocco	7.8	6.4	336	319	7.1	4.9	(Z)[5]	(Z)	.8	.7
Myanmar	2.7	2.2	68	62	2.3	1.3	1.0	1.6	(Z)	(Z)
Netherlands	106.0	93.0	7,265	6,543	68.4	64.8	4.3	1.3	(Z)[5 14]	(Z)
New Zealand[18]	12.7	10.0	3,858	3,152	27.0	22.0	1.3	.3	2.1[5]	2.0
Nigeria	16.9	11.0	166	136	9.9	7.2	62.1	104.2	.1[5]	.2
Norway[15]	28.3	26.3	6,782	6,423	103.8	84.1	47.8	24.6	.4	.3
Pakistan	27.8	16.6	250	191	33.5	15.3	2.0	.5	2.4	1.5
Peru	11.7	12.0	564	693	14.2	9.8	8.8	9.6	.2[5]	.1[5]
Philippines	15.4	16.7	265	346	23.9	17.9	.3	.5	1.2	.3
Poland	181.5	176.8	4,810	4,935	145.8	121.9	.1	.3	193.0	193.1
Portugal	13.6	11.2	1,329	1,153	20.1	15.3	(X)	(X)	.3	.2
Romania	106.1	100.0	4,624	4,505	73.1	67.5	10.2[5]	11.5	8.8[5]	8.1
Saudi Arabia[13]	79.4	25.3	6,322	2,745	37.1	18.9	198.1	495.9	n.a.	n.a.
South Africa[16]	107.6	90.2	2,816	2,751	122.5	90.4	(X)	(X)	177.3	116.6
Soviet Union	1,867.2	1,473.1	6,634	5,549	1,664.9	1,293.9	624.0	603.2	519.1	492.9
Spain	81.9	88.4	2,106	2,359	133.2	110.5	1.6	1.6	14.5[7]	13.1[7]
Sudan	1.5	1.5	64	82	1.1	1.0	(X)	(X)	n.a.	n.a.
Sweden	41.8	44.5	5,004	5,376	146.6	96.7	(Z)	(Z)	(Z)	(Z)
Switzerland[17]	24.8	23.3	3,794	3,636	57.0[8]	48.1[8]	(X)	(X)	(X)	(X)
Syria	11.5	7.3	1,025	835	7.2	3.8	12.2	8.3	(X)	(X)
Taiwan[19]	n.a.	37.9	n.a.	2,127	n.a.	42.0	n.a.	.2	(X)	2.6
Tanzania	.9	.8	38	44	.9	.7	(X)	(X)	(Z)	(Z)
Thailand	26.3	17.3	493	372	30.0	15.1	1.0	(Z)	(Z)	(Z)
Trinidad and Tobago	7.1	7.5	5,770	6,992	3.3	2.0	8.1	11.0	n.a.	n.a.

Country	Energy consumed[1] (coal equiv.) Total (mil. metric tons) 1987	1980	Per capita (kilograms) 1987	1980	Electric energy production[2] (bil. kwh) 1987	1980	petroleum production[3] (mil. metric tons) 1987	1980	Crude Coal production[4] (mil. metric tons) 1987	1980
Tunisia	5.0	4.1	651	639	4.5	2.8	5.0	5.6	(X)	(X)
Turkey	52.4	31.9	998	718	44.4	23.3	2.6	2.3	3.5	3.6
United Arab Emirates	27.4	16.8	18,832	17,188	13.1	6.3	72.1	82.8	n.a.	n.a.
United Kingdom	290.8	271.0	5,107	4,850	300.2	284.9	117.6	78.9	104.4[7]	130.1[7]
United States	2,322.9	2,364.5	9,542	10,386	2,686[8]	2,354	418.6	424.2	761.1	710.4
Venezuela	55.1	49.0	3,018	3,140	54.7	35.9	95.5	114.8	.1	(Z)
Vietnam	7.4	6.6	118	122	5.3	3.8	n.a.	n.a.	5.6	5.2
Yugoslavia	56.7	48.0	2,423	2,152	80.8	59.4	3.9	4.2	.4	.4
Zaire	2.1	2.0	64	69	5.3	4.2	1.3[5]	1.0	(Z)[5]	.1
Zambia	1.9	2.3	248	403	8.5[8]	9.2	(X)	(X)	.5	.6
World, total	**9,653.6**	**8,544.3**	**1,921**	**1,919**	**10,467**	**8,247**	**2,787**	**2,979**	**3,334**	**2,728**

n.a. = not available. X = Not applicable. Z = Less than 50,000 metric tons. 1. Based on apparent consumption of coal, lignite, petroleum products, natural gas, and hydro, nuclear, and geothermal electricity. 2. Comprises production by utilities generating primarily for public use, and production by industrial establishments generating primarily for own use. Relates to production at generating centers, including station use and transmission losses. 3. Includes shale oil, but excludes natural gasoline. 4. Excludes lignite and brown coal, except as noted. 5. United Nations Statistical Office estimate. 6. For year ending June 30 of year shown. 7. Includes slurries. 8. Net production, i.e. excluding station use. 9. Includes Monaco. 10. Includes inputs other than crude petroleum and natural gas liquids. 11. For year ending March 20 of year shown. 12. Includes San Marino. 13. Includes share of production and consumption in the Neutral Zone. 14. Includes patent fuel and hard coal briquettes. 15. Includes Svalbard and Jan Mayen Islands. 16. Includes Botswana, Lesotho, Namibia, and Swaziland. 17. Includes Liechtenstein. 18. For year ending March 31 for year shown. 19. *Source:* U.S. Bureau of the Census. Data from Republic of China publications. *Source:* Except as noted, Statistical Office of the United Nations, New York, N.Y., *Energy Statistics Yearbook, 1986* (copyright). From: *Statistical Abstract of the United States, 1990.* NOTE: Data are most recent available.

Wheat, Rice, and Corn—Production for Selected Countries

(in thousands of metric tons)

Country	Wheat 1986	1985	1984	Rice 1986	1985	1984	Corn 1986	1985	1984
Argentina	8,900	8,700	13,220	405	410	476	12,400	11,530	9,500
Australia	17,356	16,127	18,666	687	864	632	228	291	238
Belgium[2]	1,265[1]	1,215	1,330	n.a.	n.a.	n.a.	58[1]	90[1]	53
Brazil	5,433	4,323	1,983	10,399	9,019	9,027	20,510	22,020	21,164
Canada	31,850	24,252	21,199	n.a.	n.a.	n.a.	6,694	7,472	7,024
China: Mainland[3]	89,002	85,812	87,817	177,000	171,417	181,193	65,560	64,056	73,600
Egypt	1,929	1,872	1,815	2,450[1]	2,310	2,236	3,801[1]	3,982[1]	3,170
France	26,587	28,890	32,977	60	62	36	10,792	12,409	10,493
Germany, West	10,406	9,866	10,223	n.a.	n.a.	n.a.	1,302	1,204	1,026
Greece	2,200	1,789	2,308	102	103	92	2,070	1,948	2,091
Hungary	5,803	6,578	7,392	44	38	33	7,214	6,818	6,686
India	46,885	44,069	45,476	90,000	96,306	87,553	8,000	6,890	8,442
Indonesia	n.a.	n.a.	n.a.	39,275	39,033	38,136	5,767	4,330	5,288
Iran	7,128	6,661	5,500[3]	1,569	1,523	1,600	50[3]	50[1]	50[1]
Iraq	1,100[1]	1,406	471	145[1]	149	109	36[1]	41	30
Italy	9,070	8,516	10,057	1,082	1,123	1,009	6,560	6,309	6,672
Japan	876	874	741	14,559	14,578	14,848	1	2	2
Korea, South	5[1]	11	17	7,790	7,855	7,970	113	132	133
Mexico	4,772	5,207	4,505	523	809	484	12,154	13,957	12,910
Myanmar	246	206	214	15,000[3]	15,219	14,255	350[3]	323	303
Pakistan	13,923	11,703	10,882	5,241	4,437	4,973	1,067	1,009	1,028
Soviet Union	92,300	78,100	68,600	2,600	2,570	2,720	12,500	14,400	13,600
Sweden	1,714	1,338	1,776	n.a.	n.a.	n.a.	n.a.	n.a.	n.a.
Thailand	n.a.	n.a.	n.a.	19,100	20,264	19,905	4,197	4,934	4,226
United Kingdom	13,874	12,046	14,970	n.a.	n.a.	n.a.	1[3]	1[3]	1[3]
United States	56,792	65,999	70,618	6,097	6,120	6,296	209,632	225,478	194,928
Vietnam	n.a.	n.a.	n.a.	16,197	15,875	15,506	600[1]	600	525
Yugoslavia	4,776	4,859	5,595	48	36	36	12,502	9,896	11,312
World, total	**535,842**	**506,034**	**516,457**	**475,533**	**474,728**	**470,284**	**480,609**	**488,325**	**452,753**

1. Unofficial figure. 2. Includes Luxembourg. 3. FAO estimate. NOTES: Rice data cover rough and paddy. Data for each country pertain to the calendar year in which all or most of the crop was harvested. n.a. = not available. *Source:* Food and Agriculture Organization of the United Nations, Rome, Italy, 1986. *FAO Production Yearbook, vol. 40* (copyright). From: *Statistical Abstract of the United States, 1990.* NOTE: Data are most recent available.

Wheat, Rice and Corn Exports and Imports, 1985–1987

(in thousands of metric tons. Countries listed are the 10 leading exporters or importers in 1987)

Exporters	1985	1986	1987	Importers	1985	1986	1987
WHEAT				**WHEAT**			
United States	24,810	24,555	30,638	Soviet Union	20,309	15,745	18,097
Canada	17,007	15,957	22,140	China: Mainland	6,135	6,883	14,050
Australia	15,704	16,109	14,789	Japan	5,510	5,620	5,476
France	16,943	13,367	14,220	Egypt	4,524	4,329	5,162
Argentina	9,583	4,021	4,197	Italy	4,534	5,259	4,617
United Kingdom	1,886	3,987	4,122	South Korea	2,986	3,449	4,121
West Germany	1,045	2,143	2,262	Iran	2,144	1,908	3,600
Soviet Union	1,250	1,181	1,480	Iraq	2,096	2,185	2,900
Hungary	2,002	1,670	1,281	Brazil	4,041	2,255	2,749
Sweden	626	466	691	Poland	1,703	1,662	2,343
RICE				**RICE**			
Thailand	4,062	4,524	4,443	Iran	539	493	800
United States	1,940	2,392	2,472	Soviet Union	321	493	599
Pakistan	719	1,316	1,240	China: Mainland	213	326	559
China: Mainland	1,046	1,123	1,202	Iraq	500	550	524
Italy	727	676	610	Vietnam	422	500	450
Myanmar	452	636	486	Ivory Coast	342	361	401
India	250	200	350	Nigeria	356	320	400
North Korea	200	200	225	Saudi Arabia	428	375	381
Uruguay	242	270	204	Hong Kong	378	368	373
Australia	341	178	186	Senegal	336	378	307
CORN				**CORN**			
United States	44,033	27,099	40,906	Japan	14,225	14,653	16,504
France	4,456	5,799	6,305	Soviet Union	16,600	7,236	9,238
Argentina	7,069	7,411	3,963	China: Mainland	3,108	3,659	5,249
China: Mainland	6,338	5,642	3,917	South Korea	3,406	3,671	4,566
South Africa	400	1,800	2,350	Mexico	1,726	1,704	3,603
Thailand	2,752	3,981	1,628	Egypt	1,907	2,028	2,200
Yugoslavia	900	1,798	1,166	Netherlands	2,374	1,977	1,760
Belgium-Luxembourg	656	364	604	Belgium-Luxembourg	1,930	1,466	1,729
Spain	2	60	459	United Kingdom	1,455	1,482	1,471
Greece	209	580	368	Malaysia	1,182	1,204	1,302

Source: U.S. Dept. of Agriculture, Economic Research Service. Data from Food and Agriculture Organization of the United Nations, Rome, Italy, *FOA Trade Yearbook.* From *Statistical Abstract of the United States 1990.* NOTE: Data are most recent available.

Passenger Car Production[1]

(in thousands, monthly averages)

Country	1989	1988	1987	1986	1985	1984	1983
Argentina[2]	—	10.4	13.0	11.7	9.6	11.9	11.0
Australia[2]	27.7	26.2	25.2	26.5	31.8	28.4	30.3
Austria	0.6	0.6	0.6	0.6	0.6	0.6	0.5
Brazil[2]	26.1	32.9	33.1	39.9	38.3	55.5	57.1
Canada	82.0	84.0	67.5	88.4	89.6	86.1	80.9
Czechoslovakia	15.7	13.7	14.5	15.4	15.2	15.0	14.9
France	284.5	261.5	248.5	227.7	232.0	242.5	269.0
Germany, East	18.2	18.2	18.1	18.2	17.5	16.8	15.7
Germany, West	378.6	359.1	361.7	356.1	347.1	315.3	322.9
India	14.8	14.5	12.9	10.8	7.8	7.3	5.7
Italy	164.2	157.0	142.7	136.9	112.8	119.7	116.3
Japan	697.5	683.3	657.6	650.9	637.1	589.4	596.0
Korea, South[2]	70.6	72.3	64.8	38.1	21.8	13.9	10.7
Mexico[2]	37.9	29.0	19.0	16.5	23.8	20.6	17.8
Netherlands	11.2	10.0	10.4	9.9	9.0	9.1	8.9
Poland	23.8	24.5	24.5	24.2	23.6	23.2	22.4
Romania	—	—	10.8	10.3	11.2	10.4	7.5
Spain	141.3	131.3	119.3	108.2	101.4	94.8	92.5
Sweden	—	—	34.7	34.6	33.4	26.2	31.2
U.S.S.R.	—	105.1	108.3	109.9	111.0	110.6	109.6
United Kingdom	108.3	102.2	95.2	84.9	87.3	75.8	87.1
United States[3]	567.3	592.1	590.4	626.3	666.8	635.2	565.1
Yugoslavia	26.0[2]	25.8[2]	25.8[2]	17.5	19.1	15.6	14.0

1. Vehicles built on imported chassis or assembled from imported parts are excluded except for those countries marked. 2. Including assembly. 3. Factory sales. *Source:* United Nations, *Monthly Bulletin of Statistics, January 1991.*

Meat—Production by Country

(in thousands of metric tons)

Country	1980	1985	1987, est.	Country	1980	1985	1987, est.
Argentina	3,220	3,077	2,951	Mexico	2,044	2,289	2,125
Australia[1]	2,332	2,086	2,373	Poland	2,397	2,192	2,502
Brazil	3,115	3,045	3,003	Soviet Union	12,698	14,050	15,210
China	12,664	18,443	20,136	United Kingdom	2,305	2,419	2,440
France	3,823	3,733	3,853	United States	17,680	17,874	17,564
Italy	2,305	2,462	2,413	West Germany	4,759	4,845	5,095
Japan	1,893	2,087	2,155	**World, total**	**104,535**	**115,537**	**119,724**

1. Year ending June 30. NOTE: Covers beef and veal (incl. buffalo meat), pork (incl. bacon and ham), and mutton and lamb (incl. goat meat). Refers to meat from animals slaughtered within the national boundaries irrespective of origin of animals, and relates to commercial and farm slaughter. In terms of carcass weight. Excludes lard, tallow, and edible offals. NOTE: Data are most recent available. *Source:* Statistical Office of the United Nations, New York, NY, *Statistical Yearbook.* (Copyright.) From: *Statistical Abstract of the United States 1990.*

Crude Steel Production and Consumption

| | Production (mil. metric tons) | | | Consumption | | | | | |
| | | | | Total (mil. metric tons) | | | Per capita (kilograms) | | |
Country	1987	1986	1985	1987	1986	1985	1987	1986	1985
Argentina	3.6	3.1	2.7	3.0	n.a.	n.a.	95	n.a.	n.a.
Australia	6.1	6.7	6.3[1]	5.8	5.8	5.8	354	363	366
Austria	0.2	0.2	0.3	1.7	2.1	1.8	229	274	235
Bangladesh	0.1	0.1	0.1	0.5	0.3	0.5	5	3	5
Belgium	9.8	9.7	10.7	2.5	0.7	2.8[2]	244	64	275[2]
Brazil	12.0	11.3	11.4	14.0	n.a.	n.a.	99	n.a.	n.a.
Bulgaria	3.0	3.0	2.9	3.4	2.3	3.0	381	258	336
Canada	14.6	14.0	13.4	13.0	11.4	11.9	507	443	471
China: Mainland	56.3	52.2	46.8	69.7	66.2	66.6	64	64	63
Czechoslovakia	15.4	15.1	15.0	11.0	10.3	11.0	703	665	709
France	17.7	17.6	18.8	14.4	14.2	14.2	259	257	258
Germany, East	8.2	8.0	7.9	9.7	4.1	9.5	581	249	574
Germany, West	35.9	36.7	40.1	28.0	28.1	29.3	457	460	481
Greece	0.9	0.9	1.0	1.9	1.7	1.6	189	175	164
India	12.0	11.3	11.0	16.0	n.a.	n.a.	20	n.a.	n.a.
Italy	22.7	22.7	23.7	22.8	20.6	20.7	397	360	362
Japan	97.9	97.6	104.4	71.0	60.3	66.7	582	496	553
Korea, North	6.5	6.5	6.5	6.8	9.2	8.4	316	441	413
Korea, South	2.6	4.1	4.9	13.0	n.a.	n.a.	308	n.a.	n.a.
Mexico	7.0	6.9	7.2	7.6	8.1	8.3	93	102	105
Netherlands	1.8	3.0	3.4	3.9	3.7	4.4	263	254	305
Nigeria	0.2	0.2	0.3	0.8	0.5	0.9	8	5	9
Poland	15.6	15.7	14.8	15.9	15.0	15.2	422	400	409
Romania	13.9	13.5	13.0	n.a.	10.4	10.9	n.a.	451	480
South Africa	8.9	8.0	8.5	6.3	n.a.	n.a.	164	n.a.	n.a.
Soviet Union	161.9	160.6	154.7	164.6	n.a.	n.a.	582	n.a.	n.a.
Spain	11.5	12.0	14.6	8.3	8.0	9.9	214	208	257
Sweden	4.7	4.7	4.8	3.5	3.4	3.2	421	406	384
Turkey	7.0	6.0	4.7	7.7	n.a.	n.a.	149	n.a.	n.a.
United Kingdom	17.2	14.5	15.5	14.7	12.9	14.4	259	227	254
United States	80.9	74.0	80.1[3]	102.9	89.3	107.3	417	370	448
Venezuela	3.7	3.4	3.1	4.1	3.7	3.2	227	208	186
Yugoslavia	1.9	2.0	2.0	4.0	5.1	5.1	170	218	221
World	**681.1**	**665.0**	**673.5**	**n.a.**	**n.a.**	**n.a.**	**n.a.**	**n.a.**	**n.a.**

1. Year ending June 30. 2. Luxembourg included with Belgium. 3. Excludes steel for castings made in foundries operated by companies not producing ingots. n.a. = not available. NOTE: Production data cover both ingots and steel for castings and exclude wrought (puddled) iron. Consumption data represent apparent consumption (i.e. production plus imports minus exports) and do not take into account changes in stock. *Source:* Statistical Office of the United Nations, New York, NY, *Statistical Yearbook.* (Copyright.) From *Statistical Abstract of the United States 1990.* NOTE: Figures are latest available.

Value of Exports and Imports

(in millions of U.S. dollars)

Country	Exports[1]	Imports[1]	Country	Exports[1]	Imports[1]
Afghanistan	$238[2]	$798[2]	Libya	$6,683[3]	$5,879[3]
Algeria	8,164[3]	7,396[3]	Madagascar	312[2]	340[2]
Argentina	9,579[2]	4,204[2]	Malawi	418	573
Australia	39,659	38,847	Malaysia	29,418	29,261
Austria	41,881	50,017	Mali	271[2]	500[2]
Bahamas	2,786[2]	3,001[2]	Malta	858[2]	1,505[2]
Bahrain	2,689[2]	2,866[2]	Mauritania	437[2]	222[2]
Bangladesh	1,305[2]	3,524[2]	Mauritius	987[2]	1,326[2]
Barbados	209	705	Mexico	22,819[2]	23,633[2]
Belgium-Luxembourg	118,295	120,067	Morocco	3,308[2]	5,492[2]
Benin	167[4]	288[4]	Myanmar	325	261
Bolivia	900	715	Netherlands	131,839	126,195
Brazil	34,392[2]	18,281[2]	New Zealand	9,435	9,489
Bulgaria	13,428	13,089	Nicaragua	300[5]	923[5]
Burkina Faso	142[3]	489[3]	Nigeria	8,138[2]	3,419[2]
Burundi	75	236	Norway	34,072	26,905
Cameroon	924[3]	1,271[3]	Oman	3,933[2]	2,255[2]
Canada	126,995	116,461	Pakistan	5,522	7,356
Cape Verde	7[2]	112[2]	Panama	321	1,489
Central African Republic	134[2]	150[2]	Papua-New Guinea	1,281[2]	1,355[2]
Chile	8,580	7,272	Paraguay	1,163[2]	695[2]
Colombia	5,739[2]	5,010[2]	Peru	3,274	2,455
Congo	751[3]	544[3]	Phillipines	8,186	12,206
Costa Rica	1,362[2]	1,743[2]	Poland	13,627	8,160
Côte d'Ivoire	2,792[3]	2,100[3]	Portugal	16,348	25,072
Cuba	5,518[3]	7,579[3]	Qatar	3,541[6]	1,139[6]
Cyprus	956	2,558	Romania	6,095	9,249
Czechoslovakia	11,882	13,106	Rwanda	101[3]	369[3]
Denmark	35,112	31,766	Saudi Arabia	28,369[2]	21,153[2]
Dominican Republic	924	1,964	Senegal	606[5]	1,023[5]
Ecuador	2,722	1,862	Sierra Leone	138[2]	189[2]
Egypt	2,234	9,202	Singapore	52,729	60,787
El Salvador	412	902	Solomon Islands	75[2]	114[2]
Ethiopia	446[3]	1,075[3]	Somalia	104[5]	132[5]
Fiji	233	735	Spain	55,640	87,694
Finland	26,743	27,110	Sri Lanka	1,912	2,634
France	209,996	233,163	Sudan	509[3]	1,060[3]
Gabon	1,288[5]	732[5]	Suriname	301[5]	294[5]
Gambia	40[5]	127[5]	Sweden	57,423	54,580
Germany, East	17,334[2]	17,778[2]	Switzerland	63,884	69,869
Germany, West	406,483	349,417	Syria	3,006[2]	2,097[2]
Ghana	1,014[3]	907[3]	Tanzania	337[3]	1,495[3]
Greece	7,543[2]	16,126[2]	Thailand	22,972	32,746
Guatemala	1,108[2]	1,654[2]	Togo	242[3]	487[3]
Guyana	167[6]	248[6]	Tonga	9[2]	57[2]
Haiti	200[3]	344[3]	Trinidad	2,049	1,222
Honduras	869[3]	933[3]	Tunisia	3,595	5,550
Hungary	9,707	8,764	Turkey	11,626[2]	15,799[2]
Iceland	1,401[2]	1,395[2]	Uganda	274[3]	544[3]
India	17,787	23,396	U.S.S.R.	104,177	120,651
Indonesia	25,675	21,837	United Arab Emirates	15,837[8]	6,422[8]
Iran	19,975[7]	9,738[7]	U.K.	185,976	224,938
Iraq	21,431[7]	7,257[7]	U.S.	393,893	516,575
Ireland	23,778	20,716	Uruguay	1,599[2]	1,203[2]
Israel	11,576	15,104	Vanuatu	20[3]	71[3]
Italy	168,680	180,105	Venezuela	12,983[2]	6,881[2]
Jamaica	1,119	1,848	Western Samoa	12[2]	67[2]
Japan	286,949	234,800	Yemen	101[5]	1,378[5]
Jordan	922	2,603	Yugoslavia	14,312	18,890
Kenya	1,054	2,227	Zaire	1,249[2]	849[2]
Korea, South	65,016	69,844	Zambia	1,347[2]	873[2]
Kuwait	11,476[2]	6,303[2]	Zimbabwe	1,420[5]	1,043[5]
Liberia	382[5]	308[5]			

1. 1990 unless otherwise indicated. 2. 1989. 3. 1988. 4. 1984. 5. 1987. 6. 1985. 7. 1979. 8. 1986. *Source:* United Nations, *Monthly Bulletin of Statistics,* July 1991.

WORLD GEOGRAPHY

Explorations and Discoveries

(All years are A.D. unless B.C. is specified.)

Country or place	Event	Explorer or discoverer	Date
AFRICA			
Sierra Leone	Visited	Hanno, Carthaginian seaman	c. 520 B.C.
Zaire River (Congo)	Mouth discovered	Diogo Cão, Portuguese	c. 1484
Cape of Good Hope	Rounded	Bartolomeu Diaz, Portuguese	1488
Gambia River	Explored	Mungo Park, Scottish explorer	1795
Sahara	Crossed	Dixon Denham and Hugh Clapperton, English explorers	1822–23
Zambezi River	Discovered	David Livingstone, Scottish explorer	1851
Sudan	Explored	Heinrich Barth, German explorer	1852–55
Victoria Falls	Discovered	Livingstone	1855
Lake Tanganyika	Discovered	Richard Burton and John Speke, British explorers	1858
Zaire River (Congo)	Traced	Sir Henry M. Stanley, British explorer	1877
ASIA			
Punjab (India)	Visited	Alexander the Great	327 B.C.
China	Visited	Marco Polo, Italian traveler	c. 1272
Tibet	Visited	Odoric of Pordenone, Italian monk	c. 1325
Southern China	Explored	Niccolò dei Conti, Venetian traveler	c. 1440
India	Visited (Cape route)	Vasco da Gama, Portuguese navigator	1498
Japan	Visited	St. Francis Xavier of Spain	1549
Arabia	Explored	Carsten Niebuhr, German explorer	1762
China	Explored	Ferdinand Richthofen, German scientiest	1868
Mongolia	Explored	Nikolai M. Przhevalsky, Russian explorer	1870–73
Central Asia	Explored	Sven Hedin, Swedish scientist	1890–1908
EUROPE			
Shetland Islands	Visited	Pytheas of Massilia (Marseille)	c. 325 B.C.
North Cape	Rounded	Ottar, Norwegian explorer	c. 870
Iceland	Colonized	Norwegian noblemen	c. 890–900
NORTH AMERICA			
Greenland	Colonized	Eric the Red, Norwegian	c. 985
Labrador; Nova Scotia(?)	Discovered	Leif Ericson, Norse explorer	1000
West Indies	Discovered	Christopher Columbus, Italian	1492
North America	Coast discovered	Giovanni Caboto (John Cabot), for British	1497
Pacific Ocean	Discovered	Vasco Núñez de Balboa, Spanish explorer	1513
Florida	Explored	Ponce de León, Spanish explorer	1513
Mexico	Conquered	Hernando Cortés, Spanish adventurer	1519–21
St. Lawrence River	Discovered	Jacques Cartier, French navigator	1534
Southwest U. S.	Explored	Francisco Coronado, Spanish explorer	1540–42
Colorado River	Discovered	Hernando de Alarcón, Spanish explorer	1540
Mississippi River	Discovered	Hernando de Soto, Spanish explorer	1541
Frobisher Bay	Discovered	Martin Frobisher, English seaman	1576
Maine Coast	Explored	Samuel de Champlain, French explorer	1604

Country or place	Event	Explorer or discoverer	Date
Jamestown, Va.	Settled	John Smith, English colonist	1607
Hudson River	Explored	Henry Hudson, English navigator	1609
Hudson Bay (Canada)	Discovered	Henry Hudson	1610
Baffin Bay	Discovered	William Baffin, English navigator	1616
Lake Michigan	Navigated	Jean Nicolet, French explorer	1634
Arkansas River	Discovered	Jacques Marquette and Louis Jolliet, French explorers	1673
Mississippi River	Explored	Sieur de La Salle, French explorer	1682
Bering Strait	Discovered	Vitus Bering, Danish explorer	1728
Alaska	Discovered	Vitus Bering	1741
Mackenzie River (Canada)	Discovered	Sir Alexander Mackenzie, Scottish–Canadian explorer	1789
Northwest U. S.	Explored	Meriwether Lewis and William Clark	1804–06
Northeast Passage (Arctic Ocean)	Navigated	Nils Nordenskjöld, Swedish explorer	1879
Greenland	Explored	Robert Peary, American explorer	1892
Northwest Passage	Navigated	Roald Amundsen, Norwegian explorer	1906
SOUTH AMERICA			
Continent	Visited	Columbus, Italian	1498
Brazil	Discovered	Pedro Alvarez Cabral, Portuguese	1500
Peru	Conquered	Francisco Pizarro, Spanish explorer	1532–33
Amazon River	Explored	Francisco Orellana, Spanish explorer	1541
Cape Horn	Discovered	Willem C. Schouten, Dutch navigator	1615
OCEANIA			
Papua New Guinea	Visited	Jorge de Menezes, Portuguese explorer	1526
Australia	Visited	Abel Janszoon Tasman, Dutch navigator	1642
Tasmania	Discovered		
Australia	Explored	John McDouall Stuart, English explorer	1828
Australia	Explored	Robert Burke and William Wills, Australian explorers	1861
New Zealand	Sighted (and named)	Abel Janszoon Tasman	1642
New Zealand	Visited	James Cook, English navigator	1769
ARCTIC, ANTARCTIC, AND MISCELLANEOUS			
Ocean exploration	Expedition	Magellan's ships circled globe	1519–22
Galápagos Islands	Visited	Diego de Rivadeneira, Spanish captain	1535
Spitsbergen	Visited	Willem Barents, Dutch navigator	1596
Antarctic Circle	Crossed	James Cook, English navigator	1773
Antarctica	Discovered	Nathaniel Palmer, U. S. whaler (archipelago) and Fabian Gottlieb von Bellingshausen, Russian admiral (mainland)	1820–21
Antarctica	Explored	Charles Wilkes, American explorer	1840
North Pole	Reached	Robert E. Peary, American explorer	1909
South Pole	Reached	Roald Amundsen, Norwegian explorer	1911

The Continents

A continent is defined as a large unbroken land mass completely surrounded by water, although in some cases continents are (or were in part) connected by land bridges.

The hypothesis first suggested late in the 19th century was that the continents consist of lighter rocks that rest on heavier crustal material in about the same manner that icebergs float on water. That the rocks forming the continents are lighter than the material below them and under the ocean bottoms is now established. As a consequence of this fact, Alfred Wegener (for the first time in 1912) suggested that the continents are slowly moving, at a rate of about one yard per century, so that their relative positions are not rigidly fixed. Many geologists that were originally skeptical have come to accept this theory of Continental Drift.

When describing a continent, it is important to remember that there is a fundamental difference between a deep ocean, like the Atlantic, and shallow seas, like the Baltic and most of the North Sea, which are merely flooded portions of a continent. Another and entirely different point to remember is that political considerations have often overridden geographical facts when it came to naming continents.

Geographically speaking, Europe, including the British Isles, is a large western peninsula of the continent of Asia; and many geographers, when referring to Europe and Asia, speak of the Eurasian Continent. But traditionally, Europe is counted as a separate continent, with the Ural and the Caucasus mountains forming the line of demarcation between Europe and Asia.

To the south of Europe, Asia has an odd-shaped peninsula jutting westward, which has a large number of political subdivisions. The northern section is taken up by Turkey; to the south of Turkey there are Syria, Iraq, Israel, Jordan, Saudi Arabia, and a number of smaller Arab countries. All this is part of Asia. Traditionally, the island of Cyprus in the Mediterranean is also considered to be part of Asia, while the island of Crete is counted as European.

The large islands of Java, Borneo, and Sumatra and the smaller islands near them are counted as part of "tropical Asia," while New Guinea is counted as related to Australia. In the case of the Americas, the problem arises as to whether they should be considered one or two continents. There are good arguments on both sides, but since there is now a land bridge between North and South America (in the past it was often flooded) and since no part of the sea east of the land bridge is deep ocean, it is more logical to consider the Americas as one continent.

Politically, based mainly on history, the Americas are divided into North America (from the Arctic to the Mexican border), Central America (from Mexico to Panama, with the Caribbean islands), and South America. Greenland is considered a section of North America, while Iceland is traditionally counted as a European island because of its political ties with the Scandinavian countries.

The island groups in the Pacific are often called "Oceania," but this name does *not* imply that scientists consider them the remains of a continent.

The seven continents are North America, South America, Europe, Asia, Africa, Australia, and Antarctica.

Volcanoes of the World

About 500 volcanoes have had recorded eruptions within historical times. Almost two thirds of these are in the Northern Hemisphere. Most volcanoes occur at the boundaries of the earth's crustal plates, such as the famous "Ring of Fire" that surrounds the Pacific Ocean plate. Of the world's active volcanoes, about 60% are along the perimeter of the Pacific, about 17% on mid-oceanic islands, about 14% in an arc along the south of the Indonesian islands, and about 9% in the Mediterranean area, Africa, and Asia Minor. Many of the world's volcanoes are submarine and have unrecorded eruptions.

Pacific "Ring of Fire"

NORTHWEST
Japan: At least 33 active vents.

Aso (5,223 ft; 1,592 m), on Kyushu, has one of the largest craters in the world.

Asama (over 8,300 ft; 2,530 m), on Honshu, is continuously active; violent eruption in 1783.

Azuma (nearly 7,700 ft; 2,347 m), on Honshu, erupted in 1900.

Chokai (7,300 ft; 2,225 m), on Honshu, erupted in 1974 after having been quiescent since 1861.

Fujiyama (Fujisan) (12,385 ft; 3,775 m), on Honshu, southwest of Tokyo. Symmetrical in outline, snow-covered. Regarded as a sacred mountain.

On-take (3,668 ft; 1,118 m), on peninsula of Kyushu. Strong smoke emissions and explosions began November 1973 and continued through 1974.

Mt. Unzen (4,500 ft; 1,371 m), on Kyushu erupted on June 3, 1991. Last eruption was in 1792.

U.S.S.R.: Kamchatka peninsula, 14–18 active volcanoes. Klyuchevskaya (Kluchev) (15,500 ft; 4,724 m) reported active in 1974.

Kurile Islands: At least 13 active volcanoes and several submarine outbreaks.

SOUTHWEST
New Zealand: Mount Tarawera (3,645 ft; 1,112 m), on North Island, had a severe eruption in 1886 that destroyed the famous Pink and White sinter terraces of Rotomahana, a hot lake.

Ngauruhoe (7,515 ft; 2,291 m), on North Island, emits steam and vapor constantly. Erupted 1974.

Papua New Guinea: Karkar Island (4,920 ft; 1,500 m). Mild eruptions 1974.

Philippine Islands: About 100 eruptive centers; Hibok Hibok, on Camiguin, erupted September 1950 and again in December 1951, when about 750 were reported killed or missing; eruptions continued during 1952–53.

Taal (4,752 ft; 1,448 m), on Luzon. Major eruption in 1965 killed 190; erupted again, 1968.

Mt. Pinatubo (4,795 ft; 1,462 m), on Luzon erupted on June 10, 1991. Last major eruption in 1380.

Volcano Islands: Mount Suribachi (546 ft; 166 m), on Iwo Jima. A sulfurous steaming volcano. Raising of U.S. flag over Mount Suribachi was one of the dramatic episodes of World War II.

NORTHEAST
Alaska: Mount Wrangell (14,163 ft; 4,317 m) and Mount Katmai (about 6,700 ft; 2,042 m). On June 6, 1912, a violent eruption (Nova Rupta) of Mount Katmai occurred, during which the "Valley of Ten Thousand Smokes" was formed.

Aleutian Islands: There are 32 active vents known and numerous inactive cones. Akutan Island (over 4,000 ft; 1,220 m) erupted in 1974, with ash and debris rising over 300 ft.

Great Sitkin (5,741 ft; 1,750 m). Explosive activity February-September 1974, accompanied by earthquake originating at volcano that registered 2.3 on Richter scale.

Augustine Island: Augustine volcano (4,000 ft; 1,220 m) erupted March 27, 1986. It last erupted in 1976.

California, Oregon, Washington: Lassen Peak (10,453 ft; 3,186 m) in California is one of two observed active volcanoes in the U.S. outside Alaska and Hawaii. The last period of activity was 1914–17. Mt. St. Helens (9,677 ft; 2,950 m) in the Cascade Range of southwest Washington became active on March 27, 1980, and erupted on May 18 after being inactive since 1857. From April 15 through May 1, 1986, weak activity began for the first time in two years. Other mountains of volcanic origin include Mount Shasta (California), Mount Hood (Oregon), Mount Mazama (Oregon)—the mountain containing Crater Lake, Mount Rainier (Washington), and Mount Baker (Washington), which has been steaming since

Continued on page 164

The Pacific Ocean "Ring of Fire"

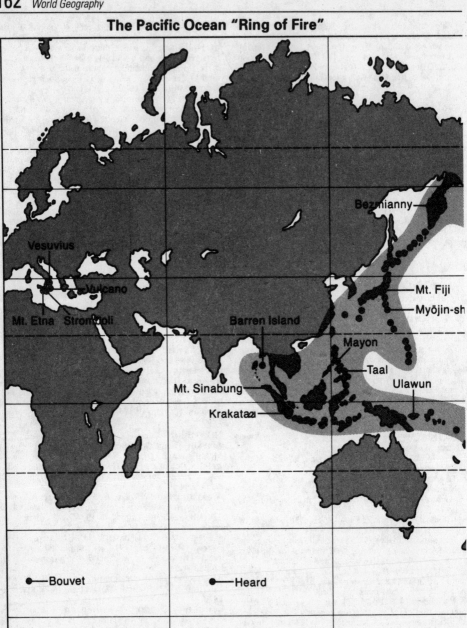

Bezmianny

Vesuvius

Mt. Fiji

Vulcano

Myōjin-sh

Mt. Etna Stromboli

Barren Island

Mayon

Taal

Mt. Sinabung

Ulawun

Krakataa

●—Bouvet   ●—Heard

Earthquake Fatalities Rose in 1990

Source: U.S. Department of the Interior, U.S. Geological Survey.

According to the U.S. Geological Survey, over 52,000 people were killed in earthquakes during 1990, almost reaching the ten-year total of over 57,000 deaths for the 1980s. None of the fatalities were in the United States. An estimated 50,000 of those deaths resulted from an Iranian earthquake on June 21.

During the past three decades, the worldwide death toll from earthquakes has averaged about 30,000 people a year.

Sixty-eight significant earthquakes occurred throughout the world in 1990, six more than the annual average during the 1980s. The USGS defines significant earthquakes as those that register 6.5 or

Source: U.S. Department of the Interior, U.S. Geological Survey.

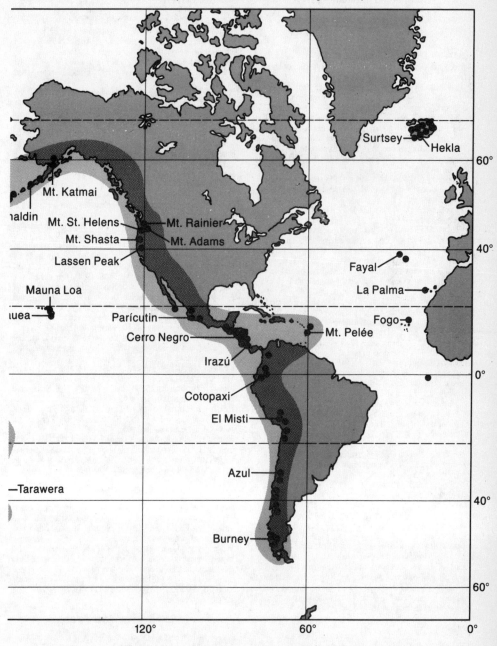

larger in magnitude, or smaller earthquakes that cause casualties or significant damage. Forty of the significant earthquakes in 1990 occurred in the world's most prolific earthquake zone—the Ring of Fire rimming the Pacific Ocean.

The strongest earthquake in the world in 1990 occurred July 16 on Luzon Island in the Philippines, registering a magnitude of 7.8 and leaving more than 1,600 people dead.

According to the USGS, there are probably several million earthquakes occurring each year, but most are so small or occur in such remote areas that they are undetected even by the most sensitive instruments in the world.

(Continued from page 161)

October 1975, but gives no sign of an impending eruption.

SOUTHEAST

Chile and Argentina: About 25 active or potentially active.

Colombia: Huila (nearly 18,900 ft; 5,760 m), a vapor-emitting volcano, and Tolima (nearly 18,500 ft; 5,640 m). Eruption of Puracé (15,600 ft; 4,755 m) in 1949 killed 17 people. Nevado del Ruiz (16,200 ft; 4,938 m.), erupted Nov. 13, 1985, sending torrential floods of mud and water engulfing the town of Armero and killing more than 22,000 people.

Ecuador: Cayambe (nearly 19,000 ft; 5,791 m). Almost on the equator.

Cotopaxi (19,344 ft; 5,896 m). Perhaps highest active volcano in the world. Possesses a beautifully formed cone.

Reventador (11,434 ft; 3,485 m). Observed in active state in late 1973.

El Salvador: Izalco ("beacon of Central America") (7,830 ft; 2,387 m) first appeared in 1770 and is still growing (erupted in 1950, 1956; last erupted in October-November 1966). San Salvador (6,187 ft; 1,886 m) had a violent eruption in 1923. Conchagua (about 4100 ft; 1,250 m) erupted with considerable damage early in 1947.

Guatemala: Santa Maria Quezaltenango (12,361 ft; 3,768 m). Frequent activity between 1902–08 and 1922–28 after centuries of quiescence. Most dangerously active vent of Central America. Other volcanoes include Tajumulco (13,814 ft; 4,211 m) and Atitlán (11,633 ft; 3,546 m).

Mexico: Boquerón ("Big Mouth"), on San Benedicto, about 250 mi. south of Lower California. Newest volcano in Western Hemisphere, discovered September 1952.

Colima (about 14,000 ft; 4,270 m), in group that has had frequent eruptions.

Orizaba (Citlaltépetl) (18,701 ft; 5,700 m).

Parícutin (7,450 ft; 2,270 m). First appeared in February 1943. In less than a week, a cone over 140 ft high developed with a crater one quarter mile in circumference. Cone grew more than 1,500 ft (457 m) in 1943. Erupted 1952.

Popocatépetl (17,887 ft; 5,452 m). Large, deep, bell-shaped crater. Not entirely extinct; steam still escapes.

El Chinchonal (7,300 ft; 1,005.6 m) about 15 miles from Pichucalco. Long inactive, it erupted in March 1982.

Nicaragua: Volcanoes include Telica, Coseguina, and Momotombo. Between Momotombo on the west shore of Lake Managua and Coseguina overlooking the Gulf of Fonseca, there is a string of more than 20 cones, many still active. One of these, Cerro Negro, erupted in July 1947, with considerable damage and loss of life, and again in 1971.

Concepción (5,100 ft; 1,555 m). Ash eruptions 1973–74.

Mid-oceanic Islands

Canary Islands: Pico de Teide (12,192 ft; 3,716 m), on Tenerife.

Cape Verde Islands: Fogo (nearly 9,300 ft; 2,835 m). Severe eruption in 1857; quiescent until 1951.

Caribbean: La Soufrière (4,813 ft; 1,467 m), on Basse-Terre, Guadeloupe. Also called La Grande Soufrière. Violent activity in July-August 1976 caused evacuation of 73,000 people; renewed activity in April 1977 again caused thousands to flee their homes.

La Soufrière (4,048 ft; 1,234 m), on St. Vincent. Major eruption in 1902 killed over 1,000 people. Eruptions over 10-day period in April 1979 caused evacuation of northern two thirds of island.

Comoros: One volcano, Karthala (nearly 8,000 ft; 2,440 m), is visible for over 100 miles. Last erupted in 1904.

Hawaii: Mauna Loa ("Long Mountain") (13,680 ft; 4,170 m), on Hawaii, discharges from its high side vents more lava than any other volcano. Largest volcanic mountain in the world in cubic content. Area of crater is 3.7 sq mi. Violent eruption in June 1950, with lava pouring 25 miles into the ocean. Last major eruption in March 1984.

Mauna Kea (13,796 ft; 4,205 m), on Hawaii. Highest mountain in state.

Kilauea (4,090 ft; 1,247 m) is a vent in the side of Mauna Loa, but its eruptions are apparently independent. One of the most spectacular and active craters. Crater has an area of 4.14 sq mi. Earthquake in July 1975 caused major eruption. Eruptions began in September 1977 and reached a height of 980 ft (300 m). Activity ended Oct. 1. Became active again in January 1983, exploding in earnest in March 1983 forming the volcanic cone Pu'u O which has erupted periodically ever since. By May 1990, the lava flow had traveled 20 miles, obliterating the community of Kalapana on the southeast coast. By summer it had reached the Pacific Ocean.

Iceland: At least 25 volcanoes active in historical times. Very similar to Hawaiian volcanoes. Askja (over 4,700 ft; 1,433 m) is the largest. Hekla, one of the most active volcanoes in Iceland, erupted on Jan. 17, 1990 after 10 years of repose.

Lesser Antilles (West Indian Islands): Mount Pelée (over 4,500 ft; 1,370 m), northwestern Martinique. Eruption in 1902 destroyed town of St. Pierre and killed approximately 40,000 people.

Réunion Island (east of Madagascar): Piton de la Fournaise (Le Volcan) (8,610 ft; 2,624 m). Large lava flows. Last erupted in 1972.

Samoan archipelago: Savai'i Island had an eruption in 1905 that caused considerable damage. Niuafoo (Tin Can), in the Tonga Islands, has a crater that extends 6,000 feet below and 600 feet above water.

Indonesia

Sumatra: Ninety volcanoes have been discovered; 12 are now active. The most famous, Krakatau, is a small volcanic island in the Sunda Strait. Numerous volcanic discharges occurred in 1883. One extremely violent explosion caused the disappearance of the highest peak and the northern part of the island. Fine dust was carried around the world in the upper atmosphere. Over 36,000 persons lost their lives in resultant tidal waves that were felt as far away as Cape Horn. Active in 1972.

Mediterranean Area

Italy: Mount Etna (10,902 ft; 3,323 m), eastern Sicily. Two new craters formed in eruptions of February-March 1947. Worst eruption in 50 years occurred November 1950–January 1951. Erupted again in 1974, 1975, 1977, 1978, 1979, and 1983.

Stromboli (about 3,000 ft; 914 m), Lipari Islands (north of Sicily). Called "Lighthouse of the Mediterranean." Reported active in 1971.

Mount Vesuvius (4,200 ft; 1,280 m), southeast of Naples. Only active volcano on European mainland. Pompeii buried by an eruption, A.D. 79.

Antarctica

The discovery of two small active volcanoes in 1982 brings to five the total number known on Antarctica. The new ones, 30 miles apart, are on the Weddell Sea side of the Antarctic Peninsula. The largest, Mount Erebus (13,000 ft; 3,962 m), rises from McMurdo Sound. Mount Melbourne (9,000 ft; 2,743 m) is in Victoria Land. The fifth, off the northern tip of the Antarctic Peninsula, is a crater known as Deception Island.

Principal Types of Volcanoes

(*Source:* U.S. Dept. of Interior, Geological Survey.)

The word "volcano" comes from the little island of Vulcano in the Mediterranean Sea off Sicily. Centuries ago, the people living in this area believed that Vulcano was the chimney of the forge of Vulcan—the blacksmith of the Roman gods. They thought that the hot lava fragments and clouds of dust erupting from Vulcano came from Vulcan's forge. Today, we know that volcanic eruptions are not supernatural but can be studied and interpreted by scientists.

Geologists generally group volcanoes into four main kinds—cinder cones, composite volcanoes, shield volcanoes, and lava domes.

Cinder Cones

Cinder cones are the simplest type of volcano. They are built from particles and blobs of congealed lava ejected from a single vent. As the gas-charged lava is blown violently into the air, it breaks into small fragments that solidify and fall as cinders around the vent to form a circular or oval cone. Most cinder cones have a bowl-shaped crater at the summit and rarely rise more than a thousand feet or so above their surroundings. Cinder cones are numerous in western North America as well as throughout other volcanic terrains of the world.

Composite Volcanoes

Some of the Earth's grandest mountains are composite volcanoes—sometimes called *stratovolcanoes.* They are typically steep-sided, symmetrical cones of large dimension built of alternating layers of lava flows, volcanic ash, cinders, blocks, and bombs and may rise as much as 8,000 feet above their bases. Some of the most conspicuous and beautiful mountains in the world are composite volcanoes, including Mount Fuji in Japan, Mount Cotopaxi in Ecuador, Mount Shasta in California, Mount Hood in Oregon, and Mount St. Helens and Mount Rainier in Washington.

Most composite volcanoes have a crater at the summit which contains a central vent or a clustered group of vents. Lavas either flow through breaks in the crater wall or issue from fissures on the flanks of the cone. Lava, solidified within the fissures, forms *dikes* that act as ribs which greatly strengthen the cone.

The essential feature of a composite volcano is a conduit system through which magma from a reservoir deep in the Earth's crust rises to the surface. The volcano is built up by the accumulation of material erupted through the conduit and increases in size as lava, cinders, ash, etc., are added to its slopes.

Shield Volcanoes

Shield volcanoes, the third type of volcano, are built almost entirely of fluid lava flows. Flow after flow pours out in all directions from a central summit vent, or group of vents, building a broad, gently sloping cone of flat, domical shape, with a profile much like that of a warrior's shield. They are built up slowly by the accretion of thousands of flows of highly fluid basaltic (from *basalt,* a hard, dense dark volcanic rock) lava that spread widely over great distances, and then cool as thin, gently dipping sheets. Lavas also commonly erupt from vents along fractures (rift zones) that develop on the flanks of the cone. Some of the largest volcanoes in the world are shield volcanoes. In northern California and Oregon, many shield volcanoes have diameters of 3 or 4 miles and heights of 1,500 to 2,000 feet. The Hawaiian Islands are composed of linear chains of these volcanoes, including Kilauea and Mauna Loa on the island of Hawaii.

In some shield-volcano eruptions, basaltic lava pours out quietly from long fissures instead of central vents and floods the surrounding countryside with lava flow upon lava flow, forming broad plateaus. Lava plateaus of this type can be seen in Iceland, southeastern Washington, eastern Oregon, and southern Idaho.

Lava Domes

Volcanic or lava domes are formed by relatively small, bulbous masses of lava too viscous to flow any great distance; consequently, on extrusion, the lava piles over and around its vent. A dome grows largely by expansion from within. As it grows its outer surface cools and hardens, then shatters, spilling loose fragments down its sides. Some domes form craggy knobs or spines over the volcanic vent, whereas others form short, steep-sided lava flows known as "coulees." Volcanic domes commonly occur within the craters or on the flanks of large composite volcanoes. The nearly circular Novarupta Dome that formed during the 1912 eruption of Katmai Volcano, Alaska, measures 800 feet across and 200 feet high. The internal structure of this dome—defined by layering of lava fanning upward and outward from the center—indicates that it grew largely by expansion from within. Mount Pelée in Martinique, West Indies, and Lassen Peak and Mono domes in California, are examples of lava domes.

Submarine Volcanoes

Submarine volcanoes and volcanic vents are common features on certain zones of the ocean floor. Some are active at the present time and, in shallow water, disclose their presence by blasting steam and rock-debris high above the surface of the sea. Many others lie at such great depths that the tremendous weight of the water above them results in high, confining pressure and prevents the formation and release of steam and gases. Even very large, deepwater eruptions may not disturb the ocean floor.

The famous black sand beaches of Hawaii were created virtually instantaneously by the violent interaction between hot lava and sea water.

Plate-Tectonics Theory—The Lithosphere Plates of the Earth

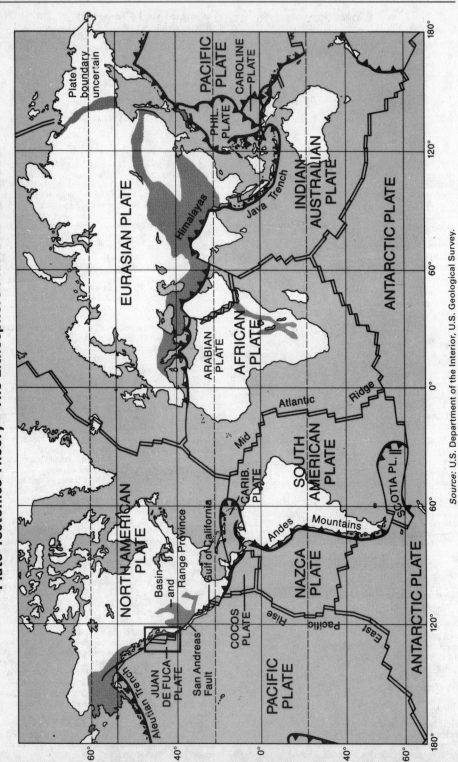

Source: U.S. Department of the Interior, U.S. Geological Survey.

World Population, Land Areas, and Elevations

Area	Estimated population, mid-1991	Approximate Land area sq mi.	Percent of total land area	Population density per sq mi.	Elevation, feet	
					Highest	Lowest
WORLD	5,384,000,000	58,433,000	100.0	92.1 [1]	Mt. Everest, Asia, 29,108	Dead Sea, Asia, 1,290 below sea level
ASIA, incl. Philippines, Indonesia, and European and Asiatic Turkey; excl. Asiatic U.S.S.R	3,155,000,000	10,644,000	18.2	296.4	Mt. Everest, Tibet-Nepal, 29,108	Dead Sea, Israel-Jordan, 1,290 below sea level
AFRICA	677,000,000	11,707,000	20.0	57.8	Mt. Kilimanjaro, Tanzania, 19,340	Lake Assal, Djibouti, 571 below sea level
NORTH AMERICA, including Hawaii, Central America, and Caribbean region	430,000,000	9,360,000	16.0	45.9	Mt. McKinley; Alaska, 20,320	Death Valley, Calif., 282 below sea level
SOUTH AMERICA	302,000,000	6,883,000	11.8	43.9	Mt. Aconcagua, Arg.-Chile, 23,034	Valdes Peninsula, 131 below sea level
ANTARCTICA	—	6,000,000	10.3	—	Vinson Massif, Sentinel Range, 16,863	Sea level
EUROPE, incl. Iceland; excl. European U.S.S.R. and European Turkey	502,000,000	1,905,000	3.3	263.5	Mont Blanc, France, 15,781	Sea level
OCEANIA, incl. Australia, New Zealand, Melanesia, Micronesia, and Polynesia [2]	27,000,000	3,284,000	5.6	8.2	Wilhelm, Papua New Guinea, 14,793	Lake Eyre, Australia, 38 below sea level
U.S.S.R., both European and Asiatic	292,000,000	8,647,000	14.8	33.8	Communism Peak, Pamir, 24,590	Caspian Sea, 96 below sea level

1. In computing density per square mile, the area of Antarctica is omitted. 2. Although Hawaii is geographically part of Oceania, its population is included in the population figure for North America. *Source:* Population Reference Bureau, Inc.

Plate-Tectonics Theory

(*Source:* U.S. Dept. of the Interior, Geological Survey.)

According to the generally accepted "plate-tectonics" theory, scientists believe that the Earth's surface is broken into a number of shifting slabs or plates, which average about 50 miles in thickness. These plates move relative to one another above a hotter, deeper, more mobile zone at average rates as great as a few inches per year. Most of the world's active volcanoes are located along or near the boundaries between shifting plates and are called "plate-boundary" volcanoes. However, some active volcanoes are not associated with plate boundaries, and many of these so-called "intra-plate" volcanoes form roughly linear chains in the interior of some oceanic plates. The Hawaiian Islands provide perhaps the best example of an "intra-plate" volcanic chain, developed by the northwest-moving Pacific plate passing over an inferred "hot spot" that initiates the magma-generation and volcano-formation process. The peripheral areas

of the Pacific Ocean Basin, containing the boundaries of several plates, are dotted by many active volcanoes that form the so-called "Ring of Fire." The "Ring" provides excellent examples of "plate-boundary" volcanoes, including Mount St. Helens.

The accompanying figure on page 166 shows the boundaries of lithosphere plates that are active at present. The double lines indicate zones of spreading from which plates are moving apart. The lines with barbs show zones of underthrusting (subduction), where one plate is sliding beneath another. The barbs on the lines indicate the overriding plate. The single line defines a strike-slip fault along which plates are sliding horizontally past one another. The stippled areas indicate a part of a continent, exclusive of that along a plate boundary, which is undergoing active extensional, compressional, or strike-slip faulting.

The Severity of an Earthquake

(*Source:* U.S. Dept. of the Interior, Geological Survey.)

The Richter Magnitude Scale

The Richter magnitude scale was developed in 1935 by Charles F. Richter of the California Institute of Technology as a mathematical device to compare the size of earthquakes. The magnitude of an earthquake is determined from the logarithm of the amplitude of waves recorded by seismographs. Adjustments are included in the magnitude formula to compensate for the variation in the distance between the various seismographs and the epicenter of the earthquakes. On the Richter Scale, magnitude is expressed in whole numbers and decimal fractions. For example, a magnitude of 5.3 might be computed for a moderate earthquake, and a strong earthquake might be rated as magnitude 6.3.

Because of the logarithmic basis of the scale, each whole-number increase in magnitude represents a tenfold increase in measured amplitude; as an estimate of energy, each whole number step in the magnitude scale corresponds to the release of about 31 times more energy than the amount associated with the preceding whole number value.

Earthquakes with magnitudes of about 2.0 or less are usually called microearthquakes; they are not commonly felt by people and are generally recorded only on local seismographs. Events with magnitudes of about 4.5 or greater—there are several thousand such shocks annually—are strong enough to be recorded by sensitive seismographs all over the world.

Great earthquakes, such as the 1906 Good Friday earthquake in San Francisco, have magnitudes of 8.0 or higher. On the average, one earthquake of such size occurs somewhere in the world each year. Although the Richter Scale has no upper limit, the largest known shocks have had magnitudes in the 8.8 to 8.9 range.

The Richter Scale is not used to express damage. An earthquake in a densely populated area which results in many deaths and considerable damage may have the same magnitude as a shock in a remote area that does nothing more than frighten the wildlife. Large-magnitude earthquakes that occur beneath the oceans may not even be felt by humans.

The Modified Mercalli Intensity Scale

The effect of an earthquake on the Earth's surface is called the intensity. The intensity scale consists of a series of certain key responses such as people awakening, movement of furniture, damage to chimneys, and finally—total destruction. Although numerous *intensity scales* have been developed over the last several hundred years to evaluate the effects of earthquakes, the one currently used in the United States is the Modified Mercalli (MM) Intensity Scale. It was developed in 1931 by the American seismologists Harry Wood and Frank Neumann. This scale, composed of 12 increasing levels of intensity that range from imperceptible shaking to catastrophic destruction, is designated by Roman numerals. It does not have a mathematical basis; instead it is an arbitrary ranking based on observed effects.

The Modified Mercalli Intensity value assigned to a specific site after an earthquake has a more mean-ingful measure of severity to the nonscientist than the magnitude because intensity refers to the effects actually experienced at that place. After the occurrence of widely-felt earthquakes, the Geological Survey mails questionnaires to postmasters in the disturbed area requesting the information so that intensity values can be assigned. The results of this postal canvass and information furnished by other sources are used to assign an intensity value, and to compile isoseismal maps that show the extent of various levels of intensity within the felt area. The maximum observed intensity generally occurs near the epicenter.

The *lower* numbers of the intensity scale generally deal with the manner in which the earthquake is felt by people. The *higher* numbers of the scale are based on observed structural damage. Structural engineers usually contribute information for assigning intensity values of VIII or above.

The Mexico City earthquake on September 19, 1985, was assigned an intensity of IX on the Mercalli Scale.

The following is an abbreviated description of the 12 levels of Modified Mercalli intensity.

I. Not felt except by a very few under especially favorable conditions.

II. Felt only by a few persons at rest, especially on upper floors of buildings. Delicately suspended objects may swing.

III. Felt quite noticeably by persons indoors, especially on upper floors of buildings. Many people do not recognize it as an earthquake. Standing motor cars may rock slightly. Vibration similar to the passing of a truck. Duration estimated.

IV. Felt indoors by many, outdoors by few during the day. At night, some awakened. Dishes, windows, doors disturbed; walls make cracking sound. Sensation like heavy truck striking building. Standing motor cars rocked noticeably.

V. Felt by nearly everyone; many awakened. Some dishes, windows broken. Unstable objects overturned. Pendulum clocks may stop.

VI. Felt by all, many frightened. Some heavy furniture moved; a few instances of fallen plaster. Damage slight.

VII. Damage negligible in buildings of good design and construction; slight to moderate in well-built ordinary structures; considerable damage in poorly built or badly designed structures; some chimneys broken.

VIII. Damage slight in specially designed structures; considerable damage in ordinary substantial buildings with partial collapse. Damage great in poorly built structures. Fall of chimneys, factory stacks, columns, monuments, walls. Heavy furniture overturned.

IX. Damage considerable in specially designed structures; well-designed frame structures thrown out of plumb. Damage great in substantial buildings, with partial collapse. Buildings shifted off foundations.

X. Some well-built wooden structures destroyed; most masonry and frame structures destroyed with foundations. Rails bent.

XI. Few, if any (masonry) structures remain standing. Bridges destroyed. Rails bent greatly.

XII. Damage total. Lines of sight and level are distorted. Objects thrown into the air.

Latitude and Longitude of World Cities

(and time corresponding to 12:00 noon, eastern standard time)

City	Lat. °	Lat. ′	Long. °	Long. ′	Time
Aberdeen, Scotland	57	9 n	2	9 w	5:00 p.m.
Adelaide, Australia	34	55 s	138	36 e	2:30 a.m.[1]
Algiers	36	50 n	3	0 e	6:00 p.m.
Amsterdam	52	22 n	4	53 e	6:00 p.m.
Ankara, Turkey	39	55 n	32	55 e	7:00 p.m.
Asunción, Paraguay	25	15 s	57	40 w	1:00 p.m.
Athens	37	58 n	23	43 e	7:00 p.m.
Auckland, New Zealand	36	52 s	174	45 e	5:00 a.m.[1]
Bangkok, Thailand	13	45 n	100	30 e	midnight[1]
Barcelona	41	23 n	2	9 e	6:00 p.m.
Belém, Brazil	1	28 s	48	29 w	2:00 p.m.
Belfast, Northern Ireland	54	37 n	5	56 w	5:00 p.m.
Belgrade, Yugoslavia	44	52 n	20	32 e	6:00 p.m.
Berlin	52	30 n	13	25 e	6:00 p.m.
Birmingham, England	52	25 n	1	55 w	5:00 p.m.
Bogotá, Colombia	4	32 n	74	15 w	12:00 noon
Bombay	19	0 n	72	48 e	10:30 p.m.
Bordeaux, France	44	50 n	0	31 w	6:00 p.m.
Bremen, W. Germany	53	5 n	8	49 e	6:00 p.m.
Brisbane, Australia	27	29 s	153	8 e	3:00 a.m.[1]
Bristol, England	51	28 n	2	35 w	5:00 p.m.
Brussels	50	52 n	4	22 e	6:00 p.m.
Bucharest	44	25 n	26	7 e	7:00 p.m.
Budapest	47	30 n	19	5 e	6:00 p.m.
Buenos Aires	34	35 s	58	22 w	2:00 p.m.
Cairo	30	2 n	31	21 e	7:00 p.m.
Calcutta	22	34 n	88	24 e	10:30 p.m.
Canton, China	23	7 n	113	15 e	1:00 a.m.[1]
Cape Town, South Africa	33	55 s	18	22 e	7:00 p.m.
Caracas, Venezuela	10	28 n	67	2 w	1:00 p.m.
Cayenne, French Guiana	4	49 n	52	18 w	1:00 p.m.
Chihuahua, Mexico	28	37 n	106	5 w	11:00 a.m.
Chongqing, China	29	46 n	106	34 e	1:00 a.m.[1]
Copenhagen	55	40 n	12	34 e	6:00 p.m.
Córdoba, Argentina	31	28 s	64	10 w	2:00 p.m.
Dakar, Senegal	14	40 n	17	28 w	5:00 p.m.
Darwin, Australia	12	28 s	130	51 e	2:30 a.m.[1]
Djibouti	11	30 n	43	3 e	8:00 p.m.
Dublin	53	20 n	6	15 w	5:00 p.m.
Durban, South Africa	29	53 s	30	53 e	7:00 p.m.
Edinburgh, Scotland	55	55 n	3	10 w	5:00 p.m.
Frankfurt	50	7 n	8	41 e	6:00 p.m.
Georgetown, Guyana	6	45 n	58	15 w	1:15 p.m.
Glasgow, Scotland	55	50 n	4	15 w	5:00 p.m.
Guatemala City, Guatemala	14	37 n	90	31 w	11:00 a.m.
Guayaquil, Ecuador	2	10 s	79	56 w	12:00 noon
Hamburg	53	33 n	10	2 e	6:00 p.m.
Hammerfest, Norway	70	38 n	23	38 e	6:00 p.m.
Havana	23	8 n	82	23 w	12:00 noon
Helsinki, Finland	60	10 n	25	0 e	7:00 p.m.
Hobart, Tasmania	42	52 s	147	19 e	3:00 a.m.[1]
Iquique, Chile	20	10 s	70	7 w	1:00 p.m.
Irkutsk, U.S.S.R.	52	30 n	104	20 e	1:00 a.m.[1]
Jakarta, Indonesia	6	16 s	106	48 e	0:30 a.m.[1]
Johannesburg, South Africa	26	12 s	28	4 e	7:00 p.m.
Kingston, Jamaica	17	59 n	76	49 w	12:00 noon
Kinshasa, Zaire	4	18 s	15	17 e	6:00 p.m.
La Paz, Bolivia	16	27 s	68	22 w	1:00 p.m.
Leeds, England	53	45 n	1	30 w	5:00 p.m.
Lima, Peru	12	0 s	77	2 w	2:00 noon
Lisbon	38	44 n	9	9 w	5:00 p.m.
Liverpool, England	53	25 n	3	0 w	5:00 p.m.
London	51	32 n	0	5 w	5:00 p.m.
Lyons, France	45	45 n	4	50 e	6:00 p.m.
Madrid	40	26 n	3	42 w	6:00 p.m.
Manchester, England	53	30 n	2	15 w	5:00 p.m.
Manila	14	35 n	120	57 e	1:00 a.m.[1]
Marseilles, France	43	20 n	5	20 e	6:00 p.m.
Mazatlán, Mexico	23	12 n	106	25 w	10:00 a.m.
Mecca, Saudi Arabia	21	29 n	39	45 e	8:00 p.m.
Melbourne	37	47 s	144	58 e	3:00 a.m.[1]
Mexico City	19	26 n	99	7 w	11:00 a.m.
Milan, Italy	45	27 n	9	10 e	6:00 p.m.
Montevideo, Uruguay	34	53 s	56	10 w	2:00 p.m.
Moscow	55	45 n	37	36 e	8:00 p.m.
Munich, Germany	48	8 n	11	35 e	6:00 p.m.
Nagasaki, Japan	32	48 n	129	57 e	2:00 a.m.[1]
Nagoya, Japan	35	7 n	136	56 e	2:00 a.m.[1]
Nairobi, Kenya	1	25 s	36	55 e	8:00 p.m.
Nanjing (Nanking), China	32	3 n	118	53 e	1:00 a.m.[1]
Naples, Italy	40	50 n	14	15 e	6:00 p.m.
Newcastle-on-Tyne, Eng.	54	58 n	1	37 w	5:00 p.m.
Odessa, U.S.S.R.	46	27 n	30	48 e	8:00 p.m.
Osaka, Japan	34	32 n	135	30 e	2:00 a.m.[1]
Oslo	59	57 n	10	42 e	6:00 p.m.
Panama City, Panama	8	58 n	79	32 w	12:00 noon
Paramaribo, Surinam	5	45 n	55	15 w	1:30 p.m.
Paris	48	48 n	2	20 e	6:00 p.m.
Peking	39	55 n	116	25 e	1:00 a.m.[1]
Perth, Australia	31	57 s	115	52 e	1:00 a.m.[1]
Plymouth, England	50	25 n	4	5 w	5:00 p.m.
Port Moresby, Papua New Guinea	9	25 s	147	8 e	3:00 a.m.[1]
Prague	50	5 n	14	26 e	6:00 p.m.
Reykjavik, Iceland	64	4 n	21	58 w	4:00 p.m.
Rio de Janeiro	22	57 s	43	12 w	2:00 p.m.
Rome	41	54 n	12	27 e	6:00 p.m.
Salvador, Brazil	12	56 s	38	27 w	2:00 p.m.
St. Petersburg	59	56 n	30	18 e	8:00 p.m.
Santiago, Chile	33	28 s	70	45 w	1:00 p.m.
Sao Paulo, Brazil	23	31 s	46	31 w	2:00 p.m.
Shanghai, China	31	10 n	121	28 e	1:00 a.m.[1]
Singapore	1	14 n	103	55 e	0:30 a.m.[1]
Sofia, Bulgaria	42	40 n	23	20 e	7:00 p.m.
Stockholm	59	17 n	18	3 e	6:00 p.m.
Sydney, Australia	34	0 s	151	0 e	3:00 a.m.[1]
Tananarive, Madagascar	18	50 s	47	33 e	8:00 p.m.
Teheran, Iran	35	45 n	51	45 e	8:30 p.m.
Tokyo	35	40 n	139	45 e	2:00 a.m.[1]
Tripoli, Libya	32	57 n	13	12 e	7:00 p.m.
Venice	45	26 n	12	20 e	6:00 p.m.
Veracruz, Mexico	19	10 n	96	10 w	11:00 a.m.
Vienna	48	14 n	16	20 e	6:00 p.m.
Vladivostok, U.S.S.R.	43	10 n	132	0 e	3:00 a.m.[1]
Warsaw	52	14 n	21	0 e	6:00 p.m.
Wellington, New Zealand	41	17 s	174	47 e	5:00 a.m.[1]
Yangon, Myanmar	16	50 n	96	0 e	11:30 p.m.
Zürich	47	21 n	8	31 e	6:00 p.m.

1. On the following day.

Highest Mountain Peaks of the World

(For U.S. peaks, see Index)

Mountain peak	Range	Location	Height feet	meters
Everest	Himalayas	Nepal-Tibet	29,108[1]	8,872
Godwin Austen (K-2)	Karakoram	Kashmir	29,064	8,858
Kanchenjunga	Himalayas	Nepal-Sikkim	28,208	8,598
Lhotse	Himalayas	Nepal-Tibet	27,890	8,501
Makalu	Himalayas	Tibet-Nepal	27,790	8,470
Dhaulagiri I	Himalayas	Nepal	26,810	8,172
Manaslu	Himalayas	Nepal	26,760	8,156
Cho Oyu	Himalayas	Nepal	26,750	8,153
Nanga Parbat	Himalayas	Kashmir	26,660	8,126
Annapurna I	Himalayas	Nepal	26,504	8,078
Gasherbrum I	Karakoram	Kashmir	26,470	8,068
Broad Peak	Karakoram	Kashmir	26,400	8,047
Gasherbrum II	Karakoram	Kashmir	26,360	8,033
Gosainthan	Himalayas	Tibet	26,291	8,013
Gasherbrum III	Karakoram	Kashmir	26,090	7,952
Annapurna II	Himalayas	Nepal	26,041	7,937
Gasherbrum IV	Karakoram	India	26,000	7,925
Kangbachen	Himalayas	Nepal	25,925	7,902
Gyachung Kang	Himalayas	Nepal	25,910	7,897
Himal Chuli	Himalayas	Nepal	25,895	7,893
Disteghil Sar	Karakoram	Kashmir	25,868	7,885
Nuptse	Himalayas	Nepal	25,850	7,829
Kunyang Kish	Karakoram	Kashmir	25,760	7,852
Dakum (Peak 29)	Himalayas	Nepal	25,760	7,852
Masherbrum	Karakoram	Kashmir	25,660	7,821
Nanda Devi	Himalayas	India	25,645	7,817
Chomolonzo	Himalayas	Nepal-Tibet	25,640	7,815
Rakaposhi	Karakoram	Kashmir	25,550	7,788
Batura	Karakoram	Kashmir	25,540	7,785
Kanjut Sar	Karakoram	Kashmir	25,460	7,760
Kamet	Himalayas	India-Tibet	25,447	7,756
Namche Barwa	Himalayas	Tibet	25,445	7,756
Dhaulagiri II	Himalayas	Nepal	25,427	7,750
Saltoro Kangri	Karakoram	India	25,400	7,742
Gurla Mandhata	Himalayas	Tibet	25,355	7,728
Ulugh Muztagh	Kunlun	Tibet	25,341	7,724
Trivor	Karakoram	Kashmir	25,330	7,721
Jannu	Himalayas	Nepal	25,294	7,710
Tirich Mir	Hindu Kush	Pakistan	25,230	7,690
Saser Kangri	Karakoram	India	25,170	7,672
Makalu II	Himalayas	Nepal	25,130	7,660
Chogolisa	Karakoram	India	25,110	7,654
Dhaulagiri IV	Himalayas	Nepal	25,064	7,639
Fang	Himalayas	Nepal	25,013	7,624
Kula Kangri	Himalayas	Bhutan	24,783	7,554
Changtse	Himalayas	Tibet	24,780	7,553
Muztagh Ata	Muztagh Ata	China	24,757	7,546
Skyang Kangri	Himalayas	Kashmir	24,750	7,544
Communism Peak	Pamir	U.S.S.R.	24,590	7,495
Victory Peak	Pamir	U.S.S.R.	24,406	7,439
Sia Kangri	Himalayas	Kashmir	24,340	7,419
Chamlang	Himalayas	Nepal	24,012	7,319
Alung Gangri	Himalayas	Tibet	23,999	7,315
Chomo Lhari	Himalayas	Tibet-Bhutan	23,996	7,314
Muztagh (K-5)	Kunlun	China	23,891	7,282
Amne Machin	Kunlun	China	23,490	7,160
Gaurisankar	Himalayas	Népal-Tibet	23,440	7,145
Lenin Peak	Pamir	U.S.S.R.	23,405	7,134
Korzhenevski Peak	Pamir	U.S.S.R.	23,310	7,105
Kangto	Himalayas	Tibet	23,260	7,090
Dunagiri	Himalayas	India	23,184	7,066
Pauhunri	Himalayas	India-Tibet	23,180	7,065
Aconcagua	Andes	Argentina-Chile	23,034	7,021
Revolution Peak	Pamir	U.S.S.R.	22,880	6,974
Kangchenjhan	Himalayas	India	22,700	6,919
Siniolchu	Himalayas	India	22,620	6,895

Mountain peak	Range	Location	Height feet	Height meters
Ojos des Salado	Andes	Argentina-Chile	22,588	6,885
Bonete	Andes	Argentina-Chile	22,546	6,872
Simvuo	Himalayas	India	22,346	6,811
Tup	Andes	Argentina	22,309	6,800
Kungpu	Himalayas	Bhutan	22,300	6,797
Falso-Azufre	Andes	Argentina-Chile	22,277	6,790
Moscow Peak	Pamir	U.S.S.R.	22,260	6,785
Veladero	Andes	Argentina	22,244	6,780
Pissis	Andes	Argentina	22,241	6,779
Mercedario	Andes	Argentina-Chile	22,211	6,770
Huascarán	Andes	Peru	22,198	6,766
Tocorpuri	Andes	Bolivia-Chile	22,162	6,755
Karl Marx Peak	Pamir	U.S.S.R.	22,067	6,726
Llullaillaco	Andes	Argentina-Chile	22,057	6,723
Libertador	Andes	Argentina	22,047	6,720
Kailas	Himalayas	Tibet	22,027	6,714
Lingtren	Himalayas	Nepal-Tibet	21,972	6,697
Incahuasi	Andes	Argentina-Chile	21,719	6,620
Carnicero	Andes	Peru	21,689	6,611
Kurumda	Pamir	U.S.S.R.	21,686	6,610
Garmo Peak	Pamir	U.S.S.R.	21,637	6,595
Sajama	Andes	Bolivia	21,555	6,570
Ancohuma	Andes	Bolivia	21,490	6,550
El Muerto	Andes	Argentina-Chile	21,456	6,540
Nacimiento	Andes	Argentina	21,302	6,493
Illimani	Andes	Bolivia	21,184	6,457
Antofalla	Andes	Argentina-Chile	21,129	6,440
Coropuña	Andes	Peru	21,079	6,425
Cuzco (Ausangate)	Andes	Peru	20,995	6,399
Toro	Andes	Argentina-Chile	20,932	6,380
Parinacota	Andes	Bolivia-Chile	20,768	6,330
Chimboraso	Andes	Ecuador	20,702	6,31
Salcantay	Andes	Peru	20,575	6,271
General Manuel Belgrano	Andes	Argentina	20,505	6,250
Chañi	Andes	Argentina	20,341	6,200
Caca Aca	Andes	Bolivia	20,328	6,196
McKinley	Alaska	Alaska	20,320	6,194
Vudor Peak	Pamir	U.S.S.R.	20,118	6,132
Condoriri	Andes	Bolivia	20,095	6,125
Solimana	Andes	Peru	20,069	6,117
Nevada	Andes	Argentina	20,023	6,103

1. Mt. Everest grows about 1 centimeter (.394 inch) higher each year.

Oceans and Seas

Name	Area sq mi.	Area sq km	Average depth feet	Average depth meters	Greatest known depth feet	Greatest known depth meters	Place greatest known depth
Pacific Ocean	64,000,000	165,760,000	13,215	4,028	36,198	11,033	Mariana Trench
Atlantic Ocean	31,815,000	82,400,000	12,880	3,926	30,246	9,219	Puerto Rico Trough
Indian Ocean	25,300,000	65,526,700	13,002	3,963	24,460	7,455	Sunda Trench
Arctic Ocean	5,440,200	14,090,000	3,953	1,205	18,456	5,625	77° 45′ N; 175° W
Mediterranean Sea[1]	1,145,100	2,965,800	4,688	1,429	15,197	4,632	Off Cape Matapan, Greece
Caribbean Sea	1,049,500	2,718,200	8,685	2,647	22,788	6,946	Off Cayman Islands
South China Sea	895,400	2,319,000	5,419	1,652	16,456	5,016	West of Luzon
Bering Sea	884,900	2,291,900	5,075	1,547	15,659	4,773	Off Buldir Island
Gulf of Mexico	615,000	1,592,800	4,874	1,486	12,425	3,787	Sigsbee Deep
Okhotsk Sea	613,800	1,589,700	2,749	838	12,001	3,658	146° 10′ E; 46° 50′ N
East China Sea	482,300	1,249,200	617	188	9,126	2,782	25° 16′ N; 125° E
Hudson Bay	475,800	1,232,300	420	128	600	183	Near entrance
Japan Sea	389,100	1,007,800	4,429	1,350	12,276	3,742	Central Basin
Andaman Sea	308,100	797,700	2,854	870	12,392	3,777	Off Car Nicobar Island
North Sea	222,100	575,200	308	94	2,165	660	Skagerrak
Red Sea	169,100	438,000	1,611	491	7,254	2,211	Off Port Sudan
Baltic Sea	163,000	422,200	180	55	1,380	421	Off Gotland

1. Includes Black Sea and Sea of Azov. NOTE: For Caspian Sea, *see* Large Lakes of World elsewhere in this section.

World's Greatest Man-Made Lakes[1]

Name of dam	Location	Millions of cubic meters	Thousands of acre-feet	Year completed
Owen Falls	Uganda	204,800	166,000	1954
Kariba	Zimbabwe	181,592	147,218	1959
Bratsk	U.S.S.R.	169,270	137,220	1964
High Aswan (Sadd-el-Aali)	Egypt	168,000	136,200	1970
Akosombo	Ghana	148,000	120,000	1965
Daniel Johnson	Canada	141,852	115,000	1968
Guri (Raul Leoni)	Venezuela	136,000	110,256	1986
Krasnoyarsk	U.S.S.R.	73,300	59,425	1967
Bennett W.A.C.	Canada	70,309	57,006	1967
Zeya	U.S.S.R.	68,400	55,452	1978
Cabora Bassa	Mozambique	63,000	51,075	1974
LaGrande 2	Canada	61,720	50,037	1982
LaGrande 3	Canada	60,020	48,659	1982
Ust'-Ilimsk	U.S.S.R.	59,300	48,075	1980
Volga-V.I. Lenin	U.S.S.R.	58,000	47,020	1955
Caniapiscau	Canada	53,790	43,608	1981
Poti (Chapetón)	Argentina	53,700	43,535	UC
Upper Wainganga	India	50,700	41,103	1987
São Felix	Brazil	50,600	41,022	1986
Bukhtarma	U.S.S.R.	49,740	40,325	1960
Atatürk (Karababa)	Turkey	48,700	39,482	1990
Cerros Colorados	Argentina	48,000	38,914	1973
Irkutsk	U.S.S.R.	46,000	37,290	1956
Tucuruí	Brazil	36,375	29,489	1984
Vilyuy	U.S.S.R.	35,900	29,104	1967
Sanmenxia	China	35,400	28,700	1960
Hoover	Nevada/Arizona	35,154	28,500	1936
Sobridinho	Brazil	34,200	27,726	1981
Glen Canyon	Arizona	33,304	27,000	1964
Jenpeg	Canada	31,790	25,772	1975

1. Formed by construction of dams. NOTE: UC = under construction, *Source:* Department of the Interior, Bureau of Reclamation and *International Water Power and Dam Construction.*

Large Lakes of the World

Name and location	Area		Length		Maximum depth	
	sq mi.	km	mi.	km	feet	meters
Caspian Sea, U.S.S.R.-Iran[1]	152,239	394,299	745	1,199	3,104	946
Superior, U.S.-Canada	31,820	82,414	383	616	1,333	406
Victoria, Tanzania-Uganda	26,828	69,485	200	322	270	82
Aral, U.S.S.R.	25,659	66,457	266	428	223	68
Huron, U.S.-Canada	23,010	59,596	247	397	750	229
Michigan, U.S.	22,400	58,016	321	517	923	281
Tanganyika, Tanzania-Zaire	12,700	32,893	420	676	4,708	1,435
Baikal, U.S.S.R.	12,162	31,500	395	636	5,712	1,741
Great Bear, Canada	12,000	31,080	232	373	270	82
Nyasa, Malawi-Mozambique-Tanzania	11,600	30,044	360	579	2,316	706
Great Slave, Canada	11,170	28,930	298	480	2,015	614
Chad,[2] Chad-Niger-Nigeria	9,946	25,760	—	—	23	7
Erie, U.S.-Canada	9,930	25,719	241	388	210	64
Winnipeg, Canada	9,094	23,553	264	425	204	62
Ontario, U.S.-Canada	7,520	19,477	193	311	778	237
Balkash, U.S.S.R.	7,115	18,428	376	605	87	27
Ladoga, U.S.S.R.	7,000	18,130	124	200	738	225
Onega, U.S.S.R.	3,819	9,891	154	248	361	110
Titicaca, Bolivia-Peru	3,141	8,135	110	177	1,214	370
Nicaragua, Nicaragua	3,089	8,001	110	177	230	70
Athabaska, Canada	3,058	7,920	208	335	407	124
Rudolf, Kenya	2,473	6,405	154	248	—	—
Reindeer, Canada	2,444	6,330	152	245	—	—
Eyre, South Australia	2,400 [3]	6,216	130	209	varies	varies
Issyk-Kul, U.S.S.R.	2,394	6,200	113	182	2,297	700
Urmia,[2] Iran	2,317	6,001	81	130	49	15
Torrens, South Australia	2,200	5,698	130	209	—	—
Vänern, Sweden	2,141	5,545	87	140	322	98

Name and location	Area		Length		Maximum depth	
	sq mi.	km	mi.	km	feet	meters
Winnipegosis, Canada	2,086	5,403	152	245	59	18
Mobutu Sese Seko, Uganda	2,046	5,299	100	161	180	55
Nettilling, Baffin Island, Canada	1,950	5,051	70	113	—	—
Nipigon, Canada	1,870	4,843	72	116	—	—
Manitoba, Canada	1,817	4,706	140	225	22	7
Great Salt, U.S.	1,800	4,662	75	121	15/25	5/8
Kioga, Uganda	1,700	4,403	50	80	about 30	9
Koko-Nor, China	1,630	4,222	66	106	—	—

1. The Caspian Sea is called "sea" because the Romans, finding it salty, named it *Mare Caspium*. Many geographers, however, consider it a lake because it is land-locked. 2. Figures represent high-water data. 3. Varies with the rainfall of the wet season. It has been reported to dry up almost completely on occasion.

Principal Rivers of the World

(For other U.S. rivers, see Index)

River	Source	Outflow	Approx. length	
			miles	km
Nile	Tributaries of Lake Victoria, Africa	Mediterranean Sea	4,180	6,690
Amazon	Glacier-fed lakes, Peru	Atlantic Ocean	3,912	6,296
Mississippi-Missouri-Red Rock	Source of Red Rock, Montana	Gulf of Mexico	3,880	6,240
Yangtze Kiang	Tibetan plateau, China	China Sea	3,602	5,797
Ob	Altai Mts., U.S.S.R.	Gulf of Ob	3,459	5,567
Huang Ho (Yellow)	Eastern part of Kunlan Mts., west China	Gulf of Chihli	2,900	4,667
Yenisei	Tannu-Ola Mts., western Tuva, U.S.S.R.	Arctic Ocean	2,800	4,506
Paraná	Confluence of Paranaiba and Grande rivers	Río de la Plata	2,795	4,498
Irtish	Altai Mts., U.S.S.R.	Ob River	2,758	4,438
Zaire (Congo)	Confluence of Lualab and Luapula rivers, Zaire	Atlantic Ocean	2,716	4,371
Heilong (Amur)	Confluence of Shilka (U.S.S.R.) and Argun (Manchuria) rivers	Tatar Strait	2,704	4,352
Lena	Baikal Mts., U.S.S.R.	Arctic Ocean	2,652	4,268
Mackenzie	Head of Finlay River, British Columbia, Canada	Beaufort Sea (Arctic Ocean)	2,635	4,241
Niger	Guinea	Gulf of Guinea	2,600	4,184
Mekong	Tibetan highlands	South China Sea	2,500	4,023
Mississippi	Lake Itasca, Minnesota	Gulf of Mexico	2,348	3,779
Missouri	Confluence of Jefferson, Gallatin, and Madison rivers, Montana	Mississippi River	2,315	3,726
Volga	Valdai plateau, U.S.S.R.	Caspian Sea	2,291	3,687
Madeira	Confluence of Beni and Maumoré rivers, Bolivia-Brazil boundary	Amazon River	2,012	3,238
Purus	Peruvian Andes	Amazon River	1,993	3,207
São Francisco	Southwest Minas Gerais, Brazil	Atlantic Ocean	1,987	3,198
Yukon	Junction of Lewes and Pelly rivers, Yukon Territory, Canada	Bering Sea	1,979	3,185
St. Lawrence	Lake Ontario	Gulf of St. Lawrence	1,900	3,058
Rio Grande	San Juan Mts., Colorado	Gulf of Mexico	1,885	3,034
Brahmaputra	Himalayas	Ganges River	1,800	2,897
Indus	Himalayas	Arabian Sea	1,800	2,897
Danube	Black Forest, Germany	Black Sea	1,766	2,842

River	Source	Outflow	Approx. length	
			miles	km
Euphrates	Confluence of Murat Nehri and Kara Su rivers, Turkey	Shatt-al-Arab	1,739	2,799
Darling	Central part of Eastern Highlands, Australia	Murray River	1,702	2,739
Zambezi	11°21'S, 24°22'E, Zambia	Mozambique Channel	1,700	2,736
Tocantins	Goiás, Brazil	Pará River	1,677	2,699
Murray	Australian Alps, New South Wales	Indian Ocean	1,609	2,589
Nelson	Head of Bow River, western Alberta, Canada	Hudson Bay	1,600	2,575
Paraguay	Mato Grosso, Brazil	Paraná River	1,584	2,549
Ural	Southern Ural Mts., U.S.S.R.	Caspian Sea	1,574	2,533
Ganges	Himalayas	Bay of Bengal	1,557	2,506
Amu Darya (Oxus)	Nicholas Range, Pamir Mts., U.S.S.R.	Aral Sea	1,500	2,414
Japurá	Andes, Colombia	Amazon River	1,500	2,414
Salween	Tibet, south of Kunlun Mts.	Gulf of Martaban	1,500	2,414
Arkansas	Central Colorado	Mississippi River	1,459	2,348
Colorado	Grand County, Colorado	Gulf of California	1,450	2,333
Dnieper	Valdai Hills, U.S.S.R.	Black Sea	1,419	2,284
Ohio-Allegheny	Potter County, Pennsylvania	Mississippi River	1,306	2,102
Irrawaddy	Confluence of Nmai and Mali rivers, northeast Burma	Bay of Bengal	1,300	2,092
Orange	Lesotho	Atlantic Ocean	1,300	2,092
Orinoco	Serra Parima Mts., Venezuela	Atlantic Ocean	1,281	2,062
Pilcomayo	Andes Mts., Bolivia	Paraguay River	1,242	1,999
Xi Jiang (Si Kiang)	Eastern Yunnan Province, China	China Sea	1,236	1,989
Columbia	Columbia Lake, British Columbia, Canada	Pacific Ocean	1,232	1,983
Don	Tula, R.S.F.S.R., U.S.S.R.	Sea of Azov	1,223	1,968
Sungari	China-North Korea boundary	Amur River	1,215	1,955
Saskatchewan	Canadian Rocky Mts.	Lake Winnipeg	1,205	1,939
Peace	Stikine Mts., British Columbia, Canada	Great Slave River	1,195	1,923
Tigris	Taurus Mts., Turkey	Shatt-al-Arab	1,180	1,899

Highest Waterfalls of the World

Waterfall	Location	River	Height	
			feet	meters
Angel	Venezuela	Tributary of Caroni	3,281	1,000
Tugela	Natal, South Africa	Tugela	3,000	914
Cuquenán	Venezuela	Cuquenán	2,000	610
Sutherland	South Island, N.Z.	Arthur	1,904	580
Takkakaw	British Columbia	Tributary of Yoho	1,650	503
Ribbon (Yosemite)	California	Creek flowing into Yosemite	1,612	491
Upper Yosemite	California	Yosemite Creek, tributary of Merced	1,430	436
Gavarnie	Southwest France	Gave de Pau	1,384	422
Vcttisfoss	Norway	Mörkedola	1,200	366
Widows' Tears (Yosemite)	California	Tributary of Merced	1,170	357
Staubbach	Switzerland	Staubbach (Lauterbrunnen Valley)	984	300

Waterfall	Location	River	Height feet	Height meters
Middle Cascade (Yosemite)	California	Yosemite Creek, tributary of Merced	909	277
King Edward VIII	Guyana	Courantyne	850	259
Gersoppa	India	Sharavati	829	253
Kaieteur	Guyana	Potaro	822	251
Skykje	Norway	In Skykjedal (valley of Inner Hardinger Fjord)	820	250
Kalambo	Tanzania-Zambia	—	720	219
Fairy (Mount Rainier Park)	Washington	Stevens Creek	700	213
Trummelbach	Switzerland	Trummelbach (Lauterbrunnen Valley)	700	213
Aniene (Teverone)	Italy	Tiber	680	207
Cascata delle Marmore	Italy	Velino, tributary of Nera	650	198
Maradalsfos	Norway	Stream flowing into Ejkisdalsvand (lake)	643	196
Feather	California	Fall River	640	195
Maletsunyane	Lesotho	Maletsunyane	630	192
Bridalveil (Yosemite)	California	Yosemite Creek	620	189
Multnomah	Oregon	Multnomah Creek, tributary of Columbia	620	189
Vøringsfos	Norway	Bjoreia	597	182
Nevada (Yosemite)	California	Merced	594	181
Skjeggedal	Norway	Tysso	525	160
Marina	Guyana	Tributary of Kuribrong, tributary of Potaro	500	152
Tequendama	Colombia	Funza, tributary of Magdalena	425	130
King George's	Cape of Good Hope, South Africa	Orange	400	122
Illilouette (Yosemite)	California	Illilouette Creek, tributary of Merced	370	113
Victoria	Rhodesia-Zambia boundary	Zambezi	355	108
Handöl	Sweden	Handöl Creek	345	105
Lower Yosemite	California	Yosemite	320	98
Comet (Mount Rainier Park)	Washington	Van Trump Creek	320	98
Vernal (Yosemite)	California	Merced	317	97
Virginia	Northwest Territories, Canada	South Nahanni, tributary of Mackenzie	315	96
Lower Yellowstone	Wyoming	Yellowstone	310	94

NOTE: Niagara Falls (New York-Ontario), though of great volume, has parallel drops of only 158 and 167 feet.

Large Islands of the World

Island	Location and status	Area sq mi.	Area sq km
Greenland	North Atlantic (Danish)	839,999	2,175,597
New Guinea	Southwest Pacific (Irian Jaya, Indonesian, west part; Papua New Guinea, east part)	316,615	820,033
Borneo	West mid-Pacific (Indonesian, south part, Brunei and Malaysian, north part)	286,914	743,107
Madagascar	Indian Ocean (Malagasy Republic)	226,657	587,042
Baffin	North Atlantic (Canadian)	183,810	476,068
Sumatra	Northeast Indian Ocean (Indonesian)	182,859	473,605
Honshu	Sea of Japan-Pacific (Japanese)	88,925	230,316
Great Britain	Off coast of NW Europe (England, Scotland, and Wales)	88,758	229,883
Ellesmere	Arctic Ocean (Canadian)	82,119	212,688
Victoria	Arctic Ocean (Canadian)	81,930	212,199
Celebes	West mid-Pacific (Indonesian)	72,986	189,034
South Island	South Pacific (New Zealand)	58,093	150,461
Java	Indian Ocean (Indonesian)	48,990	126,884
North Island	South Pacific (New Zealand)	44,281	114,688

Island	Location and status	Area	
		sq mi.	sq km
Cuba	Caribbean Sea (republic)	44,218	114,525
Newfoundland	North Atlantic (Canadian)	42,734	110,681
Luzon	West mid-Pacific (Philippines)	40,420	104,688
Iceland	North Atlantic (republic)	39,768	102,999
Mindanao	West mid-Pacific (Philippines)	36,537	94,631
Ireland	West of Great Britain (republic, south part; United Kingdom, north part)	32,597	84,426
Hokkaido	Sea of Japan—Pacific (Japanese)	30,372	78,663
Hispaniola	Caribbean Sea (Dominican Republic, east part; Haiti, west part)	29,355	76,029
Tasmania	South of Australia (Australian)	26,215	67,897
Sri Lanka (Ceylon)	Indian Ocean (republic)	25,332	65,610
Sakhalin (Karafuto)	North of Japan (U.S.S.R.)	24,560	63,610
Banks	Arctic Ocean (Canadian)	23,230	60,166
Devon	Arctic Ocean (Canadian)	20,861	54,030
Tierra del Fuego	Southern tip of South America (Argentinian, east part; Chilean, west part)	18,605	48,187
Kyushu	Sea of Japan—Pacific (Japanese)	16,223	42,018
Melville	Arctic Ocean (Canadian)	16,141	41,805
Axel Heiberg	Arctic Ocean (Canadian)	15,779	40,868
Southampton	Hudson Bay (Canadian)	15,700	40,663

Principal Deserts of the World

Desert	Location	Approximate size	Approx. elevation, ft
Atacama	North Chile	400 mi. long	7,000–13,500
Black Rock	Northwest Nevada	About 1,000 sq mi.	2,000–8,500
Colorado	Southeast California from San Gorgonio Pass to Gulf of California	200 mi. long and a maximum width of 50 mi.	Few feet above to 250 below sea level
Dasht-e-Kavir	Southeast of Caspian Sea, Iran	—	2,000
Dasht-e-Lūt	Northeast of Kerman, Iran	—	1,000
Gobi (Shamo)	Covers most of Mongolia	500,000 sq mi.	3,000–5,000
Great Arabian	Most of Arabia	1,500 mi. long	—
An Nafud (Red Desert)	South of Jauf	400 mi. by avg of 140 mi.	3,000
Dahna	Northeast of Nejd	400 mi. by 30 mi.	—
Rub' al-Khali	South portion of Nejd	Over 200,000 sq. mi.	—
Syrian (Al-Hamad)	North of lat. 30°N	—	1,850
Great Australian	Western portion of Australia	About one half the continent	600–1,000
Great Salt Lake	West of Great Salt Lake to Nevada—Utah boundary	About 110 mi. by 50 mi.	4,500
Kalahari	South Africa—South-West Africa	About 120,000 sq mi.	Over 3,000
Kara Kum (Desert of Kiva)	Southwest Turkmen, U.S.S.R.	115,000 sq mi.	—
Kyzyl Kum	Uzbek and Kazakh, U.S.S.R.	Over 100,000 sq. mi.	160 near Lake Aral to 2,000 in southeast
Libyan	Libya, Egypt, Sudan	Over 500,000 sq. mi.	—
Mojave	North of Colorado Desert and south of Death Valley, southeast California	15,000 sq mi.	2,000
Nubian	From Red Sea to great west bend of the Nile, Sudan	—	2,500
Painted Desert	Northeast Arizona	Over 7,000 sq mi.	High plateau, 5,000
Sahara	North Africa to about lat. 15°N and from Red Sea to Atlantic Ocean	3,200 mi. greatest length along lat. 20°N; area over 3,500,000 sq mi.	440 below sea level to 11,000 above; avg elevation, 1,400–1,600
Takla Makan	South central Sinkiang, China	Over 100,000 sq mi.	—
Thar (Indian)	Pakistan-India	Nearly 100,000 sq mi.	Over 1,000

Interesting Caves and Caverns of the World

Aggtelek. In village of same name, northern Hungary. Large stalactitic cavern about 5 miles long.

Altamira Cave. Near Santander, Spain. Contains animal paintings (Old Stone Age art) on roof and walls.

Antiparos. On island of same name in the Grecian Archipelago. Some stalactites are 20 ft long. Brilliant colors and fantastic shapes.

Blue Grotto. On island of Capri, Italy. Cavern hollowed out in limestone by constant wave action. Now half filled with water because of sinking coast. Name derived from unusual blue light permeating the cave. Source of light is a submerged opening, light passing through the water.

Carlsbad Caverns. Southeast New Mexico. Largest underground labyrinth yet discovered. Three levels: 754, 900, and 1,320 ft below the surface.

Fingal's Cave. On island of Staffa off coast of western Scotland. Penetrates about 200 ft inland. Contains basaltic columns almost 40 ft high.

Ice Cave. Near Dobsina, Czechoslovakia. Noted for its beautiful crystal effects.

Jenolan Caves. In Blue Mountain plateau, New South Wales, Australia. Beautiful stalactitic formations.

Kent's Cavern. Near Torquay, England. Source of much information on Paleolithic man.

Luray Cavern. Near Luray, Va. Has large stalactitic and stalagmitic columns of many colors.

Mammoth Cave. Limestone cavern in central Kentucky. Cave area is about 10 miles in diameter but has over 300 miles of irregular subterranean passageways at various levels. Temperature remains fairly constant at 54°F.

Peak Cavern or Devil's Hole. Derbyshire, England. About 2,250 ft into a mountain. Lowest part is about 600 ft below the surface.

Postojna (Postumia) Grotto. Near Postumia in Julian Alps, about 25 miles northeast of Trieste. Stalactitic cavern, largest in Europe. Piuca (Pivka) River flows through part of it. Caves have numerous beautiful stalactites.

Singing Cave. Iceland. A lava cave; name derived from echoes of people singing in it.

Wind Cave. In Black Hills of South Dakota. Limestone caverns with stalactites and stalagmites almost entirely missing. Variety of crystal formations called "boxwork."

Wyandotte Cave. In Crawford County, southern Indiana. A limestone cavern with five levels of passages; one of the largest in North America. "Monumental Mountain," approximately 135 ft high, is believed to be one of the world's largest underground "mountains."

UNITED NATIONS

The 166 Members of the United Nations

Country	Joined U.N.[1]	Country	Joined U.N.[1]	Country	Joined U.N.[1]
Afghanistan	1946	Germany	1973	Niger	1960
Albania	1955	Ghana	1957	Nigeria	1960
Algeria	1962	Greece	1945	Norway	1945
Angola	1976	Grenada	1974	Oman	1971
Antigua and Barbuda	1981	Guatemala	1945	Pakistan	1947
Argentina	1945	Guinea	1958	Panama	1945
Australia	1945	Guinea-Bissau	1974	Papua New Guinea	1975
Austria	1955	Guyana	1966	Paraguay	1945
Bahamas	1973	Haiti	1945	Peru	1945
Bahrain	1971	Honduras	1945	Philippines	1945
Bangladesh	1974	Hungary	1955	Poland	1945
Barbados	1966	Iceland	1946	Portugal	1955
Belgium	1945	India	1945	Qatar	1971
Belize	1981	Indonesia	1950	Romania	1955
Benin	1960	Iran	1945	Rwanda	1962
Bhutan	1971	Iraq	1945	St. Kitts and Nevis	1983
Bolivia	1945	Ireland	1955	St. Lucia	1979
Botswana	1966	Israel	1949	St. Vincent and the Grenadines	1980
Brazil	1945	Italy	1955	São Tomé and Príncipe	1975
Brunei	1984	Jamaica	1962	Saudi Arabia	1945
Bulgaria	1955	Japan	1956	Senegal	1960
Burkina Faso	1960	Jordan	1955	Seychelles	1976
Burundi	1962	Kenya	1963	Sierra Leone	1961
Byelorussian S.S.R.	1945	Korea, North	1991	Singapore	1965
Cambodia	1955	Korea, South	1991	Solomon Islands	1978
Cameroon	1960	Kuwait	1963	Somalia	1960
Canada	1945	Laos	1955	South Africa	1945
Cape Verde	1975	Latvia	1991	Spain	1955
Central African Republic	1960	Lebanon	1945	Sri Lanka	1955
Chad	1960	Lesotho	1966	Sudan	1956
Chile	1945	Liberia	1945	Suriname	1975
China[2]	1945	Libya	1955	Swaziland	1968
Colombia	1945	Liechtenstein	1990	Sweden	1946
Comoros	1975	Lithuania	1991	Syria	1945
Congo	1960	Luxembourg	1945	Tanzania	1961
Costa Rica	1945	Madagascar	1960	Thailand	1946
Côte d'Ivoire	1960	Malawi	1964	Togo	1960
Cuba	1945	Malaysia	1957	Trinidad and Tobago	1962
Cyprus	1960	Maldives	1965	Tunisia	1956
Czechoslovakia	1945	Mali	1960	Turkey	1945
Denmark	1945	Malta	1964	Uganda	1962
Djibouti	1977	Marshall Islands	1991	Ukrainian S.S.R.	1945
Dominica	1978	Mauritania	1961	U.S.S.R.	1945
Dominican Republic	1945	Mauritius	1968	United Arab Emirates	1971
Ecuador	1945	Mexico	1945	United Kingdom	1945
Egypt	1945	Micronesia	1991	United States	1945
El Salvador	1945	Mongolia	1961	Uruguay	1945
Equatorial Guinea	1968	Morocco	1956	Vanuatu	1981
Estonia	1991	Mozambique	1975	Venezuela	1945
Ethiopia	1945	Myanmar	1948	Vietnam	1977
Fiji	1970	Namibia	1990	Western Samoa	1976
Finland	1955	Nepal	1955	Yemen, Republic of	1947
France	1945	Netherlands	1945	Yugoslavia	1945
Gabon	1960	New Zealand	1945	Zaire	1960
Gambia	1965	Nicaragua	1945	Zambia	1964
				Zimbabwe	1980

1. The U.N. officially came into existence on Oct. 24, 1945. 2. On Oct. 25, 1971, the U.N. voted membership to the People's Republic of China, which replaced the Republic of China (Taiwan) in the world body.

Six Official Languages Used by U.N.

There are six official working languages recognized by the United Nations. They are Chinese, English, French, Russian, and Spanish, which have been in use since the world body was organized, and Arabic, which was added by the General Assembly in 1973 and by the Security Council in 1982.

Preamble of the United Nations Charter

The Charter of the United Nations was adopted at the San Francisco Conference of 1945. The complete text may be obtained by writing to the United Nations Sales Section, United Nations, New York, N.Y. 10017, and enclosing $1.

We the peoples of the United Nations determined to save succeeding generations from the scourge of war, which twice in our lifetime has brought untold sorrow to mankind, and

To reaffirm faith in fundamental human rights, in the dignity and worth of the human person, in the equal rights of men and women and of nations large and small, and

To establish conditions under which justice and respect for the obligations arising from treaties and other sources of international law can be maintained, and

To promote social progress and better standards of life in larger freedom, and for these ends

To practice tolerance and live together in peace with one another as good neighbors, and

To unite our strength to maintain international peace and security, and

To insure, by the acceptance of principles and the institution of methods, that armed force shall not be used, save in the common interest, and

To employ international machinery for the promotion of the economic and social advancement of all peoples, have resolved to combine our efforts to accomplish these aims.

Accordingly, our respective Governments, through representatives assembled in the city of San Francisco, who have exhibited their full powers found to be in good and due form, have agreed to the present Charter of the United Nations and do hereby establish an international organization to be known as the United Nations.

Principal Organs of the United Nations

Secretariat

This is the directorate on U.N. operations, apart from political decisions. All members contribute to its upkeep. Its staff of over 6,000 specialists is recruited from member nations on the basis of as wide a geographical distribution as possible. The staff works under the Secretary-General, whom it assists and advises.

Secretaries-General

Javier Pérez de Cuéllar, Peru, Jan. 1, 1982.
Kurt Waldheim, Austria, Jan. 1, 1972, to Dec. 31, 1981.
U Thant, Burma, Nov. 3, 1961, to Dec. 31, 1971.
Dag Hammarskjöld, Sweden, April 11, 1953, to Sept. 17, 1961.
Trygve Lie, Norway, Feb. 1, 1946, to April 10, 1953.

General Assembly

The General Assembly is the world's forum for discussing matters affecting world peace and security, and for making recommendations concerning them. It has no power of its own to enforce decisions.

The Assembly is composed of the 51 original member nations and those admitted since, a total of 166. Each nation has one vote. On important questions including international peace and security, a two-thirds majority of those present and voting is required. Decisions on other questions are made by a simple majority.

The Assembly's agenda can be as broad as the Charter. It can make recommendations to member nations, the Security Council, or both. Emphasis is given on questions relating to international peace and security brought before it by any member, the Security Council, or nonmembers.

The Assembly also maintains a broad program of international cooperation in economic, social, cultural, educational, and health fields, and for assisting in human rights and freedoms.

Among other duties, the Assembly has functions relating to the trusteeship system, and considers and approves the U.N. Budget. Every member contributes to operating expenses according to its means.

Security Council

The Security Council is the primary instrument for establishing and maintaining international peace. Its main purpose is to prevent war by settling disputes between nations.

Under the Charter, the Council is permitted to dispatch a U.N. force to stop aggression. All member nations undertake to make available armed forces, assistance, and facilities to maintain international peace and security.

Any member may bring a dispute before the Security Council or the General Assembly. Any nonmember may do so if it accepts the charter obligations of pacific settlement.

The Security Council has 15 members. There are five permanent members: the United States, the Soviet Union, Britain, France, and China; and 10 temporary members elected by the General Assembly for two-year terms, from five different regions of the world.

Voting on procedural matters requires a nine-vote majority to carry. However, on questions of substance, the vote of each of the five permanent members is required.

Current temporary members are (term expires Dec. 31, 1991): Cuba, Yemen, Côte d'Ivoire, Romania, and Zaire; (term expires Dec. 31, 1992): Austria, Belgium, Ecuador, India, and Zimbabwe.

Economic and Social Council

This council is composed of 54 members elected by the General Assembly to 3-year terms. It works closely with the General Assembly as a link with groups formed within the U.N. to help peoples in such fields as education, health, and human rights. It insures that there is no overlapping and sets up commissions to deal with economic conditions and collect facts and figures on conditions over the world. It issues studies and reports and may make recommendations to the Assembly and specialized agencies.

Functional Commissions

Statistical Commission; Population Commission; Commission for Social Development; Commission on Human Rights; Commission on the Status of Women; Commission on Narcotic Drugs.

Regional Commissions

Economic Commission for Europe (ECE); Economic and Social Commission for Asia and the Pacific (ESCAP); Economic Commission for Latin America and the Caribbean (ECLAC); Economic Commission for Africa (ECA); Economic and Social Commission for Western Asia (ESCWA).

Trusteeship Council

This council supervises territories administered by various nations and placed under an international trusteeship system by the United Nations. Each nation is charged with developing the self-government of the territory and preserving and advancing the cultural, political, economic, and other forms of welfare of the people.

The Trusteeship Council is currently composed of 5 members: 1 member—the United States—that administers a trust territory, and 4 members—China, France, the Soviet Union, and the United Kingdom—that are permanent members of the Security Council but do not administer trust territories.

The following countries ceased to be administering members because of the independence of territories they had administered: Italy and France in 1960, Belgium in 1962, New Zealand and the United Kingdom in 1968 and Australia in 1975. France and the U.K. became nonadministering members.

As of December 1985, there was only one trust territory: the Trust Territory of the Pacific Islands (administered by the United States).

International Court of Justice

The International Court of Justice sits at The Hague, the Netherlands. Its 15-judge bench was established to hear disputes among states, which must agree to accept its verdicts. Its judges, charged with administering justice under international law, deal with cases ranging from disputes over territory to those concerning rights of passage.

Following are the members of the Court and the years in which their terms expire on Feb. 5:

President: Sir Robert Yewdall Jennings, United Kingdom (1994 as president; 2000 term)
Vice President: Shigeru Oda, Japan (1994)
Taslim Olawale Elias, Nigeria (1994)
Jens Evensen, Norway (1994)
Ni Zhengyu, China (1994)
Manfred Lachs, Poland (1994)
Roberto Ago, Italy (1997)
Mohamed Shahabuddeen, Guyana (1997)
Stephen Schwebel, United States (1997)
Mohammed Bedjaoui, Algeria (1997)
Nikolai Tarassov, U.S.S.R. (1997)
Gilbert Guillaume, France (2000)
Andres Aguilar, Venezuela (2000)
Raymond Ranjeva, Madagascar (2000)
Christopher Gregory Weeramantry, Sri Lanka (2000)

Agencies of the United Nations

INTL. ATOMIC ENERGY AGENCY (IAEA)

Established: Statute for IAEA, approved on Oct. 26, 1956, at a conference held at U.N. Headquarters, New York, came into force on July 29, 1957. The Agency is under the aegis of the U.N., but unlike the following, it is not a specialized agency.

Purpose: To promote the peaceful uses of atomic energy; to ensure that assistance provided by it or at its request or under its supervision or control is not used in such a way as to further any military purpose.

Headquarters: Vienna International Center, P.O. Box 100, A 1400 Vienna, Austria

FOOD AND AGRICULTURE ORGANIZATION OF THE UNITED NATIONS (FAO)

Established: October 16, 1945, when constitution became effective.

Purpose: To raise nutrition levels and living standards; to secure improvements in production and distribution of food and agricultural products.

Headquarters: Via delle Terme di Caracalla, 00100, Rome, Italy.

GENERAL AGREEMENT ON TARIFFS AND TRADE (GATT)

Established: Jan. 1, 1948.

Purpose: An International Trade Organization (ITO) was originally planned. Although this agency has not materialized, some of its objectives have been embodied in an international commercial treaty, the General Agreement on Tariffs and Trade. Its purpose is to sponsor trade negotiations.

Headquarters: Centre William Rappard, 154 Rue de Lausanne, CH-1211, Geneva 21, Switzerland.

INTERNATIONAL BANK FOR RECONSTRUCTION AND DEVELOPMENT (IBRD) (WORLD BANK)

Established: December 27, 1945, when Articles of Agreement drawn up at Bretton Woods Conference in July 1944 came into force. Began operations on June 25, 1946.

Purpose: To assist in reconstruction and development of economies of members by facilitating capital investment and by making loans to governments and furnishing technical advice.

Headquarters: 1818 H St., N.W., Washington, D.C. 20433.

INTL. CIVIL AVIATION ORGANIZATION (ICAO)

Established: April 4, 1947, after working as a provisional organization since June 1945.

Purpose: To study problems of international civil aviation; to establish international standards and regulations; to promote safety measures, uniform regulations for operation, simpler procedures at international borders, and the use of new technical methods and equipment. It has evolved standards for meteorological services, traffic control, communications, radio beacons and ranges, search and rescue organization, and other facilities. It has brought about much simplification of customs, immigration, and public health regulations as they apply to international air transport. It drafts international air law conventions, and is concerned with economic aspects of air travel.

Headquarters: 1000 Sherbrooke St. West, Montreal, Quebec, H3A 2R2, Canada.

INTL. DEVELOPMENT ASSOCIATION (IDA)

Established: Sept. 24, 1960. An affiliate of the World Bank, IDA has the same officers and staff as the Bank.

Purpose: To further economic development of its members by providing finance on terms which bear less heavily on balance of payments of members than those of conventional loans.

Headquarters: 1818 H St., N.W., Washington, D.C. 20433.

INTERNATIONAL FINANCE CORPORATION (IFC)

Established: Charter of IFC came into force on July 20, 1956. Although IFC is affiliated with the World Bank, it is a separate legal entity, and its funds are entirely separate from those of the Bank. However, membership in the Corporation is open only to Bank members.

Purpose: To further economic development by encouraging the growth of productive private enterprise in its member countries, particularly in the less developed areas; to invest in productive private enterprises in association with private investors, without government guarantee of repayment where sufficient private capital is not available on reasonable terms; to serve as a clearing house to bring together investment opportunities, private capital (both foreign and domestic), and experienced management.

Headquarters: 1818 H St., N.W., Washington, D.C. 20433.

INTERNATIONAL FUND FOR AGRICULTURAL DEVELOPMENT (IFAD)

Established: June 18, 1976. Began operations in December 1977.

Purpose: To mobilize additional funds for agricultural and rural development in developing countries through projects and programs directly benefiting the poorest rural populations.

Headquarters: 107 Via del Serafico, 00142, Rome, Italy.

INTERNATIONAL LABOR ORGANIZATION (ILO)

Established: April 11, 1919, when constitution was adopted as Part XIII of Treaty of Versailles. Became specialized agency of U.N. in 1946.

Purpose: To contribute to establishment of lasting peace by promoting social justice; to improve labor conditions and living standards through international action; to promote economic and social stability. The U.S. withdrew from the ILO in 1977 and resumed membership in 1980.

Headquarters: 4, route des Morillons, CH-1211 Geneva 22, Switzerland.

INTERNATIONAL MARITIME ORGANIZATION (IMO)

Established: March 17, 1958.

Purpose: To give advisory and consultative help to promote international cooperation in maritime navigation and to encourage the highest standards of safety and navigation. Its aim is to bring about a uniform system of measuring ship tonnage; systems now vary widely in different parts of the world. Other activities include cooperation with other U.N. agencies on matters affecting the maritime field.

Headquarters: 4 Albert Embankment, London SE 1 7SR England.

INTERNATIONAL MONETARY FUND (IMF)

Established: Dec. 27, 1945, when Articles of Agreement drawn up at Bretton Woods Conference in July 1944 came into force. Fund began operations on March 1, 1947.

Purpose: To promote international monetary cooperation and expansion of international trade; to promote exchange stability; to assist in establishment of multilateral system of payments in respect of currency transactions between members.

Headquarters: 700 19th St., N.W., Washington, D.C. 20431.

INTERNATIONAL TELECOMMUNICATION UNION (ITU)

Established: 1865. Became specialized agency of U.N. in 1947.

Purpose: To extend technical assistance to help members keep up with present day telecommunication needs; to standardize communications equipment and procedures; to lower costs. It also works for orderly sharing of radio frequencies and makes studies and recommendations to benefit its members.

Headquarters: Place des Nations, CH-1211 Geneva 20, Switzerland.

UNITED NATIONS EDUCATIONAL, SCIENTIFIC, AND CULTURAL ORGANIZATION (UNESCO)

Established: Nov. 4, 1946, when twentieth signatory to constitution deposited instrument of acceptance with government of U.K.

Purpose: To promote collaboration among nations through education, science, and culture in order to further justice, rule of law, and human rights and freedoms without distinction of race, sex, language, or religion.

Headquarters: UNESCO House. 7, Place de Fontenoy, 75700 Paris, France.

UNITED NATIONS INDUSTRIAL DEVELOPMENT ORGANIZATION (UNIDO)

Established: Nov. 17, 1966. Became specialized agency of the U.N. in 1985.

Purpose: To promote and accelerate the industrialization of the developing countries.

Headquarters: UNIDO, Vienna International Centre, P.O. Box 300, A-1400 Vienna, Austria.

UNIVERSAL POSTAL UNION (UPU)

Established: Oct. 9, 1874. Became specialized agency of U.N. in 1947.

Purpose: To facilitate reciprocal exchange of correspondence by uniform procedures by all UPU members; to help governments modernize and speed up mailing procedures.

Headquarters: Weltpoststrasse 4, CH-3000 Berne 15, Switzerland.

WORLD HEALTH ORGANIZATION (WHO)

Established: April 7, 1948, when 26 members of the U.N. had accepted its constitution, adopted July 22, 1946, by the International Health Conference in New York City.

Purpose: To aid attainment by all people of highest possible level of health.

Headquarters: 20 Avenue Appia, CH-1211 Geneva 27, Switzerland.

WORLD INTELLECTUAL PROPERTY ORGANIZATION (WIPO)

Established: April 26, 1970, when its Convention came into force. Originated as International Bureau of Paris Union (1883) and Berne Union (1886), later succeeded by United International Bureau for the Protection of Intellectual Property (BIRPI). Became a specialized agency of the U.N. in December 1974.

Purpose: To promote legal protection of intellectual property, including artistic and scientific works, artistic performances, sound recordings, broadcasts, inventions, trademarks, industrial designs, and commercial names.

Headquarters: 34 Chemin des Colombettes, 1211 Geneva 20, Switzerland.

WORLD METEOROLOGICAL ORGANIZATION (WMO)

Established: March 23, 1950, succeeding the International Meteorological Organization, a non-governmental organization founded in 1878.

Purpose: To promote international exchange of weather reports and maximum standardization of observations; to help developing countries establish weather services for their own economic needs; to fill gaps in observation stations; to promote meteorological investigations affecting jet aircraft, satellites, energy resources, etc.

Headquarters: 41, Avenue Giuseppe Motta, CH-1211 Geneva 2, Switzerland.

COUNTRIES OF THE WORLD

Countries of the World by Groupings

NORTH AMERICA
Canada: 4, 11, 13
Mexico: 1, 14
United States: 1, 4, 13, 14

SOUTH AMERICA
Argentina: 1, 14, 15
Bolivia: 1, 14, 15
Brazil: 1, 14
Chile: 1, 14
Colombia: 1, 14
Ecuador: 1, 3, 14, 15
Guyana: 1, 11, 15
Paraguay: 1, 14
Peru: 1, 14, 15
Suriname: 1, 15
Uruguay: 1, 14
Venezuela: 1, 3, 14

CENTRAL AMERICA
Belize: 11, 15
Costa Rica: 1, 14
El Salvador: 1, 14
Guatemala: 1, 14
Honduras: 1, 14
Nicaragua: 1, 14, 15
Panama: 1, 14, 15

CARIBBEAN REGION
Antigua and Barbuda: 11
Bahamas: 11
Barbados: 1, 11, 15
Cuba: 15
Dominica: 1, 11
Dominican Republic: 1, 14
Grenada: 1, 11, 15
Haiti: 1, 14
Jamaica: 1, 11, 15
St. Lucia: 1, 11, 15
St. Vincent and the Grenadines: 11
Trinidad and Tobago: 1, 11, 14, 15

EUROPE
Albania
Andorra
Austria: 10, 13
Belgium: 4, 9, 13
Bulgaria: 8

Cyprus: 11
Czechoslovakia: 8
Denmark: 4, 9, 13
Finland: 10 (assoc. mem.), 13
France: 4, 9, 13
Germany, East: 8
Germany, West: 4, 9, 13
Greece: 4, 9, 13
Hungary: 8
Iceland: 4, 10, 13
Ireland: 9, 13
Italy: 4, 9, 13
Liechtenstein
Luxembourg: 4, 9, 13
Malta: 11, 15
Monaco
Netherlands: 4, 9, 13
Norway: 4, 10, 13
Poland: 8
Portugal: 4, 9, 10, 13
Romania: 8
San Marino
Spain: 4, 9, 13
Sweden: 10, 13
Switzerland: 10, 13
U.S.S.R.: 8
United Kingdom: 4, 6, 9, 11, 13
Vatican City State
Yugoslavia: 15

MIDDLE EAST
Bahrain: 7, 15
Iran: 3, 15
Iraq: 3, 7, 15
Israel: 15
Jordan: 7, 15
Kuwait: 3, 7, 15
Lebanon: 7, 15
Oman: 7, 15
Qatar: 3, 7, 15
Saudi Arabia: 3, 7, 15
Syria: 7, 15
Turkey: 4, 6, 13
United Arab Emirates: 3, 7, 15
Yemen, People's Democratic Republic of: 7, 15
Yemen Arab Republic: 7, 15

FAR EAST
China, People's Republic of
China, Republic of
Japan: 13
Korea, North: 15
Korea, South
Mongolia
Philippines: 5

SOUTHEAST ASIA
Cambodia
Indonesia: 3, 5, 15
Laos: 15
Malaysia: 5, 11, 15
Singapore: 5, 11, 15
Thailand: 5
Vietnam: 15

SOUTH ASIA
Afghanistan: 15
Bangladesh: 11, 15
Bhutan: 15
Burma
India: 11, 15
Maldives: 15
Nepal: 15
Pakistan: 15
Sri Lanka: 11, 15

OCEANIA
Australia: 11
Fiji: 11
Kiribati: 11
Nauru: 11[1]
New Zealand: 11, 13
Papua New Guinea: 11
Solomon Islands: 11
Tonga: 11
Tuvalu: 11[1]
Vanuatu (New Hebrides)
Western Samoa: 11

AFRICA
Algeria: 2, 3, 7, 15
Angola: 2, 15
Benin: 2, 12, 15
Bophuthatswana
Botswana: 2, 11, 15
Burundi: 2, 15

Cameroon: 2, 12, 15
Cape Verde: 2, 15
Central African Republic: 2, 15
Chad: 2, 12, 15
Comoro Islands: 2, 15
Congo: 2, 15
Côte d'Ivoire: 2, 12, 15
Djibouti: 7, 15
Egypt: 2, 7, 15
Equatorial Guinea: 2, 15
Ethiopia: 2, 15
Gabon: 2, 3, 15
Gambia: 2, 11, 12, 15
Ghana: 2, 11, 12, 15
Guinea: 12, 15
Guinea-Bissau: 2, 12, 15
Kenya: 2, 11, 15
Lesotho: 2, 11, 15
Liberia: 2, 12, 15
Libya: 2, 3, 7, 15
Madagascar: 2, 15
Malawi: 2, 11, 15
Mali: 2, 12, 15
Mauritania: 2, 7, 12, 15
Mauritius: 2, 11, 15
Morocco: 2, 7, 15
Mozambique: 2, 15
Niger: 2, 12, 15
Nigeria: 2, 3, 11, 12, 15
Rwanda: 2, 15
São Tomé and Príncipe: 2, 15
Senegal: 2, 12, 15
Seychelles: 11, 15
Sierra Leone: 2, 11, 12, 15
Somalia: 2, 7, 15
South Africa, Rep. of: 15
Sudan: 2, 7, 15
Swaziland: 2, 11, 15
Tanzania: 2, 11, 15
Togo: 2, 12, 15
Transkei
Tunisia: 2, 7, 15
Uganda: 2, 11, 15
Upper Volta: 2, 12, 15
Venda
Zaire: 2, 15
Zambia: 2, 11, 15
Zimbabwe: 2, 11, 15

1. Special status.

AFGHANISTAN

Republic of Afghanistan
President: Dr. Najibullah (November 1987)
Area: 250,000 sq mi. (647,500 sq km).
Population (est. mid-1991): 16,600,000 (Average annual rate of natural increase: 2.6%); birth rate: 48/1000; infant mortality rate: 182/1000; density per square mile: 67
Capital: Kabul
Largest cities (est. 1983): Kabul, 750,000; Kandahar, 225,000; Herat, 150,000
Monetary unit: Afghani
Languages: Pushtu, Dari Persian, other Turkic and minor languages
Religion: Islam (Sunni, 74%; Shiite, 25%; other 1%)
National name: Jamhouri Afghanistan
Literacy rate: 12%
Economic summary: Gross domestic product (1989): $3 billion, $200 per capita. Average annual growth rate (1989 est.): .0%. Arable land: 12%; labor force: 4,980,000. Principal agricultural products: wheat, cotton, fruits, nuts, wool. Labor force in industry: 10.2%. Major industrial products: carpets and textiles. Natural resources: natural gas, oil, coal, copper, sulfur, lead, zinc, iron, salt, precious and semi-precious stones. Exports: fresh and dried fruits, nuts, natural gas, carpets. Imports: petroleum products and food supplies. Major trading partners: U.S.S.R., former Soviet bloc countries, Japan, and China.

Geography. Afghanistan, approximately the size of Texas, lies wedged between the U.S.S.R., China, Pakistan, and Iran. The country is split east to west by the Hindu Kush mountain range, rising in the east to heights of 24,000 feet (7,315 m). With the exception of the southwest, most of the country is covered by high snow-capped mountains and is traversed by deep valleys.

Government. Previously a Marxist "people's republic", a new republic was established following constitutional changes in 1986 and new reforms brought up by Dr. Najibullah after his election as president. Presently a coalition government is functioning under the Premiership of Mr. Fazelhaq Khaliqyar and an effort is being made towards expanding the base of this government through new democratic reforms.

History. Darius I and Alexander the Great were the first conquerors to use Afghanistan as the gateway to India. Islamic conquerors arrived in the 7th century and Genghis Khan and Tamerlane followed in the 13th and 14th centuries.

In the 19th century, Afghanistan became a battleground in the rivalry of imperial Britain and Czarist Russia for the control of Central Asia. The Afghan Wars (1838–42 and 1878–81) fought against the British by Dost Mohammed and his son and grandson ended in defeat.

Afghanistan regained autonomy by the Anglo-Russian agreement of 1907 and full independence by the Treaty of Rawalpindi in 1919. Emir Amanullah founded the kingdom in 1926.

After a coup in 1978, Noor Taraki's attempts to create a Marxist state with Soviet aid brought armed resistance from conservative Muslim opposition.

Taraki was succeeded by Prime Minister Hafizullah Amin. Amin was replaced by Babrak Karmal, who had called for Soviet troops under a mutual defense treaty. Pakistan and other Moslem nations called for a U.N. Security Council session and charged that Amin had been executed on Dec. 27 by Soviet troops already present in Kabul. The Council's call for immediate withdrawal of Soviet troops was vetoed by the U.S.S.R. on Jan. 8, 1980.

The Soviet invasion was met with unanticipated fierce resistance from the Afghan population, resulting in a bloody war. Soviet troops had to fight Afghan tribesmen who called themselves "mujahedeen," or "holy warriors." In the early fighting, many of the guerrillas were armed only with flintlock rifles, but later they acquired more modern weapons, including rockets that they used to attack Soviet installations.

In April 1988, the U.S.S.R., U.S.A., Afghanistan, and Pakistan signed accords calling for an end to outside aid to the warring factions, in return for Soviet withdrawal by 1989. This took place in February of that year but the U.S. and the U.S.S.R. have continued to aid the warring Communist and mujahedeen factions.

At the beginning of April 1991 the rebels scored a psychologically important victory in taking the garrison town of Khost.

ALBANIA

The Republic of Albania
President: Ramiz Alia (1991)
Prime Minister: Ylli Bufi (1991)
Area: 11,100 sq mi. (28,748 sq km)
Population (est. mid-1991): 3,300,000 (average annual rate of natural increase: 1.9%); birth rate: 25/1000; infant mortality rate: 25.2/1000; density per square mile: 299
Capital and largest city (est. 1983): Tiranë, 206,100
Monetary unit: Lek
Language: Albanian, Greek
Religions (1980): Sunni Moslem, 99.1%; Roman Catholic, 0.5%; other, 0.4%
Literacy rate 75%
Economic summary: Gross national product (1989 est.): $3.8 billion. Average annual growth rate (1970–78): 4.2%. Per capita income: $1,200. Arable land: 21%; labor force: 1,500,000 (1987). Principal agricultural products: wheat, corn, potatoes, sugar beets, cotton, tobacco. Labor force in industry and commerce: 40%. Major industrial products: textiles, timber, construction materials, fuels, semi-processed minerals. Exports: minerals, metals, fuels, foodstuffs, agricultural materials. Imports: machinery, equipment, and spare parts, minerals, metals, fuels, construction materials, foodstuffs. Major trading partners: Greece, Yugoslavia, Czechoslovakia, Poland, Hungary, Bulgaria, Romania, Germany, France, Italy

Geography. Albania is situated on the eastern shore of the Adriatic Sea, with Yugoslavia to the north and east and Greece to the south. Slightly larger than Maryland, it is a mountainous country, mostly over 3,000 feet (914 m) above sea level, with a narrow, marshy coastal plain crossed by several rivers. The centers of population are contained in the interior mountain plateaus and basins.

Government. A multi-party system was installed in March 1991 when free elections were held. Albania's first non-Communist Cabinet was approved June 12, 1991. The Cabinet members are barred from holding office when new elections are held in May or June 1992.

History. Albania proclaimed its independence on Nov. 28, 1912, after a history of Roman, Byzantine, and Turkish domination.

Largely agricultural, Albania is one of the poorest countries in Europe. A battlefield in World War I, after the war it became a republic in which a conservative Moslem landlord, Ahmed Zogu, proclaimed himself President in 1925, and then proclaimed himself King Zog I in a monarchy in 1928. He ruled until Italy annexed Albania in 1939. Communist guerrillas under Enver Hoxha seized power in 1944, near the end of World War II.

His regime closed all of the nation's 2,169 churches and mosques in 1967 in a move to make Albania "the first atheist state in the world."

Hoxha was succeeded by Ramiz Alia, 59, who had been President since 1982.

The elections in March 1991 gave the Communists a decisive majority. But a general strike and street demonstrations soon forced the all-Communist cabinet to resign. A nonpartisan caretaker cabinet was soon appointed.

ALGERIA

Democratic and Popular Republic of Algeria
President: Vacant
Prime Minister: Sidi Ahmed Ghozali (1991)
Area: 919,595 sq mi. (2,381,751 sq km)
Population (est. mid-1991): 26,000,000 (average annual rate of natural increase: 2.7%); birth rate: 35/1000; infant mortality rate: 74/1000; density per square mile: 28
Capital: Algiers
Largest cities (est. 1987): Algiers, 1,483,000; Oran, 590,000; Constantine, 438,000; Annaba, 310,000
Monetary unit: Dinar
Languages: Arabic (official), French, Berber dialects
Religion: 99% Islam (Sunni)
National name: République Algérienne Democratique et Populaire—El Djemhouria El Djazaïria Demokratia Echaabia
Literacy rate: 52%
Economic summary: Gross domestic product (1988): $54.1 billion, $2,235 per capita. Real growth rate: −1.8%. Arable land: 3%; labor force: 3,700,000. Principal products: wheat, barley, oats, wine, citrus fruits, olives, livestock. Labor force in industry: 40%. Major products: petroleum, gas, petrochemicals, fertilizers, iron and steel, textiles, transport equipment. Natural resources: petroleum, natural gas, iron ore, phosphates, lead, zinc, mercury, uranium. Exports: petroleum and gas, iron, wine, phosphates. Imports: food, capital and consumer goods. Major trading partners: U.S., Germany, France, Italy, Belgium, Netherlands, Canada.

Geography. Nearly four times the size of Texas, Algeria is bordered on the west by Morocco and on the east by Tunisia and Libya. To the south are Mauritania, Mali, and Niger. Low plains cover small areas near the Mediterranean coast, with 68% of the country a plateau between 2,625 and 5,250 feet (800 and 1,600 m) above sea level. The highest point is Mount Tahat in the Sahara, which rises 9,850 feet (3,000 m).

Government. Algeria is governed by the President, whose term runs for 5 years. A new Constitution was approved on Feb. 23, 1989. A National Popular Assembly of 295 members exercises legislative power, serving for a five-year term. The National Liberation

Front, which led the struggle for independence from France, is the only legal party.

History. As ancient Numidia, Algeria became a Roman colony at the close of the Punic Wars (145 B.C.). Conquered by the Vandals about A.D. 440, it fell from a high state of civilization to virtual barbarism, from which it partly recovered after invasion by the Moslems about 650.

In 1492 the Moors and Jews, who had been expelled from Spain, settled in Algeria. Falling under Turkish control in 1518, Algiers served for three centuries as the headquarters of the Barbary pirates. The French took Algeria in 1830 and made it a part of France in 1848.

On July 5, 1962, Algeria was proclaimed independent. In October 1963, Ahmed Ben Bella was elected President. He began to nationalize foreign holdings and aroused opposition. He was overthrown in a military coup on June 19, 1965, by Col. Houari Boumediène, who suspended the Constitution and sought to restore financial stability.

Boumediène died in December 1978 after a long illness. Chadli Bendjedid, Secretary-General of the National Liberation Front, took the presidency in a smooth transition of power. On July 4, 1979, he released from house arrest former President Ahmed Ben Bella, who had been confined for 14 years since his overthrow.

Nationwide riots in 1988 led the government to introduce democratic reforms. In 1990 numerous political parties appeared. President Bendjedid's originally scheduled parliamentary elections for June 1991 were postponed after violent demonstrations arose in Algiers. Such national voting would be the first multiparty election since independence.

ANDORRA

Principality of Andorra
Episcopal Co-Prince: Msgr. Juan Martí y Alanís, Bishop of Seo de Urgel, Spain (1971)
French Co-Prince: François Mitterrand, President of France (1981)
Head of Government: Josep Pintat Solans (1984)
Area: 175 sq mi. (453 sq km)
Population (est. 1990): 49,974 (average annual growth rate: 2.2%); density per square mile: 282
Capital (est. 1986): Andorra la Vella, 15,639
Monetary units: French franc and Spanish peseta
Languages: Catalán (official); French, Spanish
Religion: Roman Catholic
National names: Les Vallées d'Andorre-Valls d'Andorra
Literacy rate 100%
Economic summary: Arable land: 2%; labor force: NA. Principal products: oats, barley, cattle, sheep. Major products: tobacco products and electric power; tourism. Natural resources: water power, mineral water. Major trading partners: Spain and France.

Geography. Andorra lies high in the Pyrenees Mountains on the French-Spanish border. The country is drained by the Valira River.

Government. A General Council of 28 members, elected for four years, chooses the First Syndic and Second Syndic. In 1976 the Andorran Democratic Party, the principality's first political party, was formed.

History. An autonomous and semi-independent co-principality, Andorra has been under the joint suzerainty of the French state and the Spanish bishops of Urgel since 1278.

In 1990 Andorra approved a customs union treaty with the E.C. permitting free movement of industrial goods between the two, but Andorra would apply the E.C.'s external tariffs to third countries.

ANGOLA

People's Republic of Angola
President: José Eduardo dos Santos (1979)
Area: 481,350 sq mi. (1,246,700 sq km)
Population (est. mid-1991): 8,500,000 (average annual rate of natural increase: 2.8); birth rate: 47/1000; infant mortality rate: 132/1000; density per square mile: 18
Capital and largest city (est. 1983): Luanda, 525,000
Monetary unit: Kwanza
Languages: Bantu, Portuguese (official)
Religions: 47% Indigenous, 38% Roman Catholic, 15% Protestant (est.)
Literacy rate: 41%
Economic summary: Gross domestic product (1988 est.): $5.0 billion, per capita $600; real growth rate 9.2%. Arable land: 2%. Labor force: 2,783,000; Labor force in industry: 15%. Principal agricultural products: coffee, sisal, corn, cotton, sugar, tobacco, bananas, cassava. Major industrial products: oil, diamonds, processed fish, tobacco, textiles, cement, processed food and sugar, brewing. Natural resources: diamonds, gold, iron, oil. Exports: oil, coffee, diamonds, fish and fish products, iron ore, timber, corn. Imports: machinery and electrical equipment, bulk iron, steel and metals, textiles, clothing, food. Major trading partners: Brazil, U.S.S.R., Cuba, Portugal, U.S.

Geography. Angola, more than three times the size of California, extends for more than 1,000 miles (1,609 km) along the South Atlantic in southwestern Africa. Zaire is to the north and east, Zambia to the east, and South-West Africa (Namibia) to the south. A plateau averaging 6,000 feet (1,829 m) above sea level rises abruptly from the coastal lowlands. Nearly all the land is desert or savanna, with hardwood forests in the northeast.

Government. President José Eduardo dos Santos heads the only official party, the Popular Movement for the Liberation of Angola–Workers Party, which in 1990 discarded its official Marxism-Leninism in favor of democratic socialism. Large areas in the east and south are held by the Union for the Total Independence of Angola (Unita), led by Jonas Savimbi.

The Popular Movement won out over Savimbi's group and a third element in an internal struggle after Portugal granted its former colony independence on Nov. 11, 1975. Elections promised at the time of independence have never taken place, and the government relies heavily on Soviet support and Cuban troops, while Savimbi receives aid from South Africa and the U.S.

History. Discovered by the Portuguese navigator Diego Cao in 1482, Angola became a link in trade with India and the Far East. Later it was a major source of slaves for Portugal's New World colony of Brazil. Development of the interior began after the Treaty of Berlin in 1885 fixed the colony's borders, and British and Portuguese investment pushed mining, railways, and agriculture.

Following World War II, independence movements began but were sternly suppressed by military force. The April revolution of 1974 brought about a reversal of Portugal's policy, and the next year President Francisco da Costa Gomes signed an agreement to grant independence to Angola. The plan called for election of a constituent assembly and a settlement of differences by the MPLA and the National Front for the Liberation of Angola (FNLA) and the National Union for the Total Independence of Angola (UNITA).

The Organization of African Unity recognized the MPLA government led by Agostinho Neto on Feb. 11, 1976, and the People's Republic of Angola became the 47th member of the organization.

Although militarily victorious, Neto's regime had yet to consolidate its power in opposition strongholds in the east and south.

In March 1977 and May 1978, Zairean refugees in Angola invaded Zaire's Shaba Province, bringing charges by Zairean President Mobutu Sese Seko that the unsucessful invasions were Soviet-backed with Angolan help. Angola, the U.S.S.R., and Cuba denied complicity.

Neto died in Moscow of cancer on Sept. 10, 1979. The Planning Minister, José Eduardo dos Santos, was named President.

The South-West Africa People's Organization, or SWAPO, the guerrillas fighting for the independence of the disputed territory south of Angola also known as Namibia, fought from bases in Angola and the South African armed forces also maintained troops there both to fight the SWAPO guerrillas and to assist the UNITA guerrillas against Angolan and Cuban troops.

In December 1988, Angola, Cuba, and South Africa signed agreements calling for Cuban withdrawal from Angola and South African withdrawal from Namibia by July 1991 and independence for Namibia. An agreement that would mark a ceasefire and lead to multiparty elections was signed in early 1991.

ANTIGUA AND BARBUDA

Sovereign: Queen Elizabeth II (1952)
Governor-General: Sir Wilfred E. Jacobs (1981)
Prime Minister: Vere C. Bird, Sr. (1976)
Area: 171 sq mi. (442 sq km)
Population (est. mid-1991): 100,000 (average annual growth rate: .8%); birth rate: 14/1000; infant mortality rate: 22/1000; density per square mile: 377
Capital and largest city (est. 1983): St. John's, 30,000
Monetary unit: East Caribbean dollar
Language: English
Religions: Anglican and Roman Catholic
Literacy rate: 90% (est.)
Member of Commonwealth of Nations
Economic summary: Gross domestic product (1989 est.): $353.5 million., per capita $5,500; real growth rate 6.2%. Arable land: 18%; Labor force: 30,000; Labor force in industry: 7% (1983); principal products: cotton, bananas, coconuts, cucumbers, mangoes. Major industry: tourism. Exports: petroleum products, manufactures, machinery and transport equipment. Imports: fuel, food, machinery. Major trading partners: U.K., U.S.

Geography. Antigua, the larger of the two main islands located 295 miles (420 km) south-southeast of San Juan, P.R., is low-lying except for a range of hills in the south that rise to their highest point at Boggy Peak (1,330 ft; 405 m). As a result of its relative flatness, Antigua suffers from cyclical drought, despite a mean annual rainfall of 44 inches. Barbuda is a coral island, well-wooded.

Government. Executive power is held by the Cabinet, presided over by Prime Minister Vere C. Bird, Sr. A 17-member Parliament is elected by universal suffrage. The Antigua Labour Party, led by Prime Minister Bird, holds 15 seats and the remaining two are held by an independent member, H. Frank, and the United National Democratic Party.

History. Antigua was discovered by Christopher Columbus in 1493 and named for the Church of Santa Maria la Antigua in Seville. Colonized by Britain in 1632, it joined the West Indies Federation in 1958. With the breakup of the Federation, it became one of the West Indies Associated States in 1967, self-governing in internal affairs. Full independence was granted Nov. 1, 1981.

Minister of Public Works, Vere Bird, Jr. was removed from office following disclosure that Israeli guns and ammunition had been delivered to Colombia's drug cartel through Antigua.

ARGENTINA

Argentine Republic
President: Carlos S. Menem (1989)
Area: 1,072,067 sq mi. (2,776,654 sq km)
Population (est. mid-1991): 32,700,000 (average annual rate of natural increase: 1.2%); birth rate: 21/1000; infant mortality rate: 31/1000; density per square mile: 31
Capital: Buenos Aires
Largest cities (est. 1983): Buenos Aires, 3,000,000; Córdoba, 1,000,000; Rosario, 950,000; La Plafa, 450,000; San Miguel de Tucumán, 400,000
Monetary unit: Austral
Language: Spanish, English, Italian, German, French
Religion: Predominantly Roman Catholic (nominally)
National name: República Argentina
Literacy rate 94%
Economic summary: Gross national product (1989 est.): $68.8 billion; $2,160 per capita; real growth rate: –5.5%. Arable land: 9%; labor force: 11,500,000. Principal products: grains, oilseeds, livestock products. Labor force in industry: 31%. Major products: processed foods, motor vehicles, consumer durables, textiles, chemicals. Natural resources: minerals, lead, zinc, tin, copper, iron, manganese, oil, uranium. Exports: meats, corn, wheat, wool, hides and industrial products (durables, textiles, airplanes etc.). Imports: machinery, fuel and lubricating oils, iron and steel, chemical products. Major trading partners: U.S., Brazil, Italy, Germany, Netherlands, Soviet Union, France, Bolivia.

Geography. With an area slightly less than one third of the United States and second in South America only to its eastern neighbor, Brazil, in size and population, Argentina is a plain, rising from the Atlantic to the Chilean border and the towering Andes peaks. Aconcagua (23,034 ft.; 7,021 m) is the highest peak in the world outside Asia. It is bordered also by Bolivia and Paraguay on the north, and by Uruguay on the east.

The northern area is the swampy and partly wooded Gran Chaco, bordering on Bolivia and Paraguay. South of that are the rolling, fertile pampas, rich for agriculture and grazing and supporting most of the population. Next southward is Patagonia, a region of cool, arid steppes with some wooded and fertile sections.

Government. Argentina is a federal union of 22 provinces, one national territory, and the Federal District. Under the Constitution of 1853 (restored by a Constituent National Convention in 1957), the President and Vice President are elected every six years by popular vote through an electoral college. The President appoints his Cabinet. The Vice President presides over the Senate but has no other powers. The Congress consists of two houses: a 46-member Senate and a 254-member Chamber of Deputies.

History. Discovered in 1516 by Juan Díaz de Solis, Argentina developed slowly under Spanish colonial rule. Buenos Aires was settled in 1580; the cattle industry was thriving as early as 1600.

Invading British forces were expelled in 1806–07, and when Napoleon conquered Spain, the Argentinians set up their own government in the name of the Spanish King in 1810. On July 9, 1816, independence was formally declared.

As in World War I, Argentina proclaimed neutrality at the outbreak of World War II, but in the closing phase declared war on the Axis on March 27, 1945, and became a founding member of the United Nations. Juan D. Perón, an army colonel, emerged as the strongman of the postwar era, winning the Presidential elections of 1946 and 1951.

Opposition to Perón's increasing authoritarianism led to a coup by the armed forces that sent Perón into exile in 1955. Argentina entered a long period of military dictatorships with brief intervals of constitutional government.

The former dictator returned to power in 1973 and his wife was elected Vice-President.

After Peron's death in 1974, his widow became the hemisphere's first woman chief of state, but was deposed in 1976 by a military junta.

In December 1981. Lt. Gen. Leopoldo Galtieri, commander of the army, was named president.

On April 2, 1982, Galtieri landed thousands of troops on the Falkland Islands and reclaimed the Malvinas, their Spanish name, as national territory. By May 21, 5,000 British marines and paratroops landed from the British armada, and regained control of the islands.

Galtieri resigned three days after the surrender of the island garrison on June 14. Maj. Gen. Reynaldo Bignone, took office as President on July 1.

In the presidential election of October 1983, Raúl Alfonsín, leader of the middle-class Radical Civic Union, handed the Peronist Party its first defeat since its founding.

Among the enormous problems facing Alfonsín after eight years of mismanagement under military rule was a $45-billion foreign debt, the developing world's third largest. After cliff-hanging negotiations with American, European, and Japanese banks representing the country's private creditors, the Alfonsín government agreed on June 29, 1984, to pay $350 million in overdue interest and was moving toward austerity measures.

With the arrears mounting at the rate of $150 million a month, the debt to foreign creditors mounted to $48 billion by mid-1985, and more than $1 billion was past due. On June 11, the Alfonsín government reached agreement with the International Monetary Fund on an austerity program designed to put Argentina into a position to pay its way internationally and keep current with its debt obligations. The agreement opened the door for up to $1.2 billion of new loans to Argentina.

Three days later, on June 14, President Alfonsín announced an "economy of war" to bring the inflation rate down. The program combined the creation of a new currency—the austral, meaning southern—to replace the peso, wage and price controls and a halt to the government's deficit spending. In April 1986, the austral was devalued to spur exports.

Twin economic problems of growing unemployment and quadruple-digit inflation led to a Peronist victory in the elections of May 1989. Inflation of food prices led to riots that induced Alfonsín to step down in June 1989, six months early, in favor of the Peronist, Carlos Menem.

On the eve of a visit by President Bush a group of army leaders and their followers attempted an uprising on December 3, 1990. The rebels attacked important military buildings in the capital in an apparent attempt to take control of the army. Most commanders, however, stood by the legitimate government, and the insurrection was suppressed in less than 24 hours.

AUSTRALIA

Commonwealth of Australia
Sovereign: Queen Elizabeth II (1952)
Governor-General: William Hayden (1989)
Prime Minister: Paul Keating (1991)
Area: 2,966,150 sq mi. (7,682,300 sq km)
Population (est. mid-1991): 17,500,000 (average annual rate of natural increase: 0.8%); birth rate: 14/1000; infant mortality rate: 24.3/1000; density per square mile: 6
Capital (est. 1988): Canberra, 297,300
Largest cities (1990): Sydney, 3,656,900; Melbourne, 3,080,000; Brisbane, 1,301,700; Adelaide, 1,049,100; Perth, 1,193,100
Monetary unit: Australian dollar
Language: English
Religions: 26.1% Anglican, 26.0% Roman Catholic, 24.3% other Christian
Literacy rate: 98.5%
Member of Commonwealth of Nations
Economic summary: Gross national product (1989 est.): $240.8 billion, per capita $14,380; real growth rate 4.1%. Arable land: 6%; labor force: 6%. Principal products: wool, meat, cereals, sugar, sheep, cattle, dairy products. Labor force: 7,700,000; Labor force in manufacturing and industry: 16.2% (1987). Major products: machinery, motor vehicles, iron and steel, chemicals. Natural resources: iron ore, bauxite, zinc, lead, tin, coal, oil, gas, copper, nickel, uranium. Exports: wheat, wool, coal. Imports: meat; iron ore; capital equipment. Major trading partners: Japan, U.S., U.K., New Zealand, Germany, South Korea, Singapore.

Geography. The continent of Australia, with the island state of Tasmania, is approximately equal in area to the United States (excluding Alaska and Hawaii), and is nearly 50% larger than Europe (excluding the U.S.S.R.).

Mountain ranges run from north to south along the east coast, reaching their highest point in Mount Kos-

ciusko (7,308 ft; 2,228 m). The western half of the continent is occupied by a desert plateau that rises into barren, rolling hills near the west coast. It includes the Great Victoria Desert to the south and the Great Sandy Desert to the north. The Great Barrier Reef, extending about 1,245 miles (2,000 km), lies along the northeast coast.

The island of Tasmania (26,178 sq mi.; 67,800 sq km) is off the southeastern coast.

Government. The Federal Parliament consists of a bicameral legislature. The House of Representatives has 148 members elected for three years by popular vote. The Senate has 76 members elected by popular vote for six years. One half of the Senate is elected every three years. Voting is compulsory at 18. Supreme federal judicial power is vested in the High Court of Australia in the Federal Courts, and in the State Courts invested by Parliament with Federal jurisdiction. The High Court consists of seven justices, appointed by the Governor-General in Council. Each of the states has its own judicial system.

History. Dutch, Portuguese, and Spanish ships sighted Australia in the 17th century; the Dutch landed at the Gulf of Carpentaria in 1606. Australia was called New Holland, Botany Bay, and New South Wales until about 1820.

Captain James Cook, in 1770, claimed possession for Great Britain. A British penal colony was set up at what is now Sydney, then Port Jackson, in 1788, and about 161,000 transported English convicts were settled there until the system was suspended in 1839.

Free settlers established six colonies: New South Wales (1786), Tasmania (then Van Diemen's Land) (1825), Western Australia (1829), South Australia (1834), Victoria (1851), and Queensland (1859).

The six colonies became states and in 1901 federated into the Commonwealth of Australia with a Constitution that incorporated British parliamentary tradition and U.S. federal experience. Australia became known for liberal legislation: free compulsory education, protected trade unionism with industrial conciliation and arbitration, the "Australian" ballot facilitating selection, the secret ballot, women's suffrage, maternity allowances, and sickness and old age pensions.

In the election of 1983, Robert Hawke, head of the Labor Party, became Prime Minister. The Labor government was reelected in a Federal election in December 1984.

Prime Minister Hawke survived a challenge to his leadership of the ruling Labor party in early June 1991 from Paul Keating, who thereafter resigned his positions as deputy p.m. and treasurer. A small cabinet reshuffle followed.

Australian External Territories

Norfolk Island (13 sq mi.; 36.3 sq km) was placed under Australian administration in 1914. Population in 1988 was about 1,800.

The Ashmore and Cartier Islands (.8 sq mi.), situated in the Indian Ocean off the northwest coast of Australia, came under Australian administration in 1934. In 1938 the islands were annexed to the Northern Territory. On the attainment of self-government by the Northern Territory in 1978, the islands which are uninhabited were retained as Commonwealth Territory.

The Australian Antarctic Territory (2,360,000 sq mi.; 6,112,400 sq km), comprises all the islands and territories, other than Adélie Land, situated south of lat. 60°S and lying between long. 160° to 45°E. It came under Australian administration in 1936.

Heard Island and the McDonald Islands (158 sq mi.; 409.2 sq km), lying in the sub-Antarctic, were placed under Australian administration in 1947. The islands are uninhabited.

Christmas Island (52 sq mi.; 134.7 sq km) is situated in the Indian Ocean. It came under Australian administration in 1958. Population in 1988 was about 2,000.

Coral Sea Islands (400,000 sq mi.; 1,036,000 sq km, but only a few sq mi. of land) became a territory of Australia in 1969. There is no permanent population on the islands.

AUSTRIA

Republic of Austria
President: Kurt Waldheim (1986)
Chancellor: Franz Vranitzky (1986)
Area: 32,375 sq mi. (83,851 sq km)
Population (est. mid-1991): 7,700,000 (average annual rate of natural increase: 0.1%); birth rate: 12/1000; infant mortality rate: 7.9/1000; density per square mile: 239
Capital: Vienna
Largest cities (est. 1983): Vienna, 1,550,000; Graz, 240,000; Linz, 200,000; Salzburg, 135,000; Innsbruck, 115,000; Klagenfurt, 85,000
Monetary unit: Schilling
Language: German
Religion: Roman Catholic, 85%
Literacy rate: 98%
National name: Republik Österreich
Economic summary: Gross domestic product (1989 est.): $103.2 billion; per capita $13,600; real growth rate 4.2%. Arable land: 17%. Labor force: 3,037,000; 56.4% in services; principal agricultural products: livestock, forest products, grains, sugar beets, potatoes. Principal products: iron and steel, chemicals, machinery, paper and pulp. Natural resources: iron ore, petroleum, timber, magnesite, aluminum, coal, lignite, cement, copper, hydropower. Exports: iron and steel products, timber, paper, textiles, chemical products. Imports: machinery, chemicals, foodstuffs, textiles and clothing, petroleum. Major trading partners: Germany, Italy, Switzerland, U.S., Eastern Europe.

Geography. Slightly smaller than Maine, Austria includes much of the mountainous territory of the eastern Alps (about 75% of the area). The country contains many snowfields, glaciers, and snowcapped peaks, the highest being the Grossglockner (12,530 ft; 3,819 m). The Danube is the principal river. Forests and woodlands cover about 40% of the land area.

Almost at the heart of Europe, Austria has as its neighbors Italy, Switzerland, Germany, Czechoslovakia, Hungary, Yugoslavia, and Liechtenstein.

Government. Austria is a federal republic composed of nine provinces (Bundesländer), including Vienna. The President is elected by the people for a term of six years. The bicameral legislature consists of the Bundesrat, with 58 members chosen by the provincial assemblies, and the Nationalrat, with 183 members popularly elected for four years. Presidency of the Bundesrat revolves every six months, going to the provinces in alphabetical order.

History. Settled in prehistoric times, the Central European land that is now Austria was overrun in pre-Roman times by various tribes, including the Celts. Charlemagne conquered the area in 788 and encouraged colonization and Christianity. In 1252, Ottokar, King of Bohemia, gained possession, only to lose the territories to Rudolf of Hapsburg in 1278. Thereafter, until World War I, Austria's history was largely that of its ruling house, the Hapsburgs.

Austria emerged from the Congress of Vienna in 1815 as the Continent's dominant power. The *Ausgleich* of 1867 provided for a dual sovereignty, the empire of Austria and the kingdom of Hungary, under Francis Joseph I, who ruled until his death on Nov. 21, 1916. He was succeeded by his grandnephew, Charles I.

During World War I, Austria-Hungary was one of the Central Powers with Germany, Bulgaria, and Turkey, and the conflict left the country in political chaos and economic ruin. Austria, shorn of Hungary, was proclaimed a republic in 1918, and the monarchy was dissolved in 1919.

A parliamentary democracy was set up by the Constitution of Nov. 10, 1920. To check the power of Nazis advocating union with Germany, Chancellor Engelbert Dolfuss in 1933 established a dictatorship, but was assassinated by the Nazis on July 25, 1934. Kurt von Schuschnigg, his successor, struggled to keep Austria independent but on March 12, 1938, German troops occupied the country, and Hitler proclaimed its *Anschluss* (union) with Germany, annexing it to the Third Reich.

After World War II, the U.S. and Britain declared the Austrians a "liberated" people. But the Russians prolonged the occupation. Finally Austria concluded a state treaty with the U.S.S.R. and the other occupying powers and regained its independence on May 15, 1955. The second Austrian republic, established Dec. 19, 1945, on the basis of the 1920 Constitution (amended in 1929), was declared by the federal parliament to be permanently neutral.

On June 8, 1986, former UN Secretary-General Kurt Waldheim was elected to the ceremonial office of President in a campaign marked by controversy over his alleged links to Nazi war-crimes in Yugoslavia.

To the relief of all four political parties President Waldheim announced in June 1991 that he would not seek reelection in 1992. Despite its neutrality Austria permitted the U.S. military to fly aircraft over Austrian airspace during the Persian Gulf war.

BAHAMAS

Commonwealth of the Bahamas
Sovereign: Queen Elizabeth II (1952)
Governor-General: Sir Henry M. Taylor (1988)
Prime Minister: Lynden O. Pindling (1967)
Area: 5,380 sq mi. (13,939 sq km)
Population (1991 census): 254,685 (average annual rate of natural increase: 1.3%); birth rate: 18/1000; infant mortality rate: 22.3/1000; density per square mile: 47
Capital and largest city (1991 census): Nassau, 171,542
Monetary unit: Bahamian dollar
Language: English

Religions: Baptist, 29%; Anglican, 23%; Roman Catholic, 22%, others
Literacy rate: 95%
Member of Commonwealth of Nations
Economic summary: Gross domestic product (1988 est.): $2.4 billion; $9,875 per capita; real growth rate 2.0%. Labor force: 132,600; Principal agricultural products: fruits, vegetables. Major industrial products: fish, refined petroleum, pharmaceutical products; tourism. Natural resources: salt, aragonite, timber. Exports: rum, crawfish, pharmaceuticals, cement. Imports: foodstuffs, manufactured goods, fuels. Major trading partners: U.S., U.K., Nigeria, Canada, Iran.

Geography. The Bahamas are an archipelago of about 700 islands and 2,400 uninhabited islets and cays lying 50 miles off the east coast of Florida. They extend from northwest to southeast for about 760 miles (1,223 km). Only 22 of the islands are inhabited; the most important is New Providence (80 sq mi.; 207 sq km), on which Nassau is situated. Other islands include Grand Bahama, Abaco, Eleuthera, Andros, Cat Island, San Salvador (or Watling's Island), Exuma, Long Island, Crooked Island, Acklins Island, Mayaguana, and Inagua.

The islands are mainly flat, few rising above 200 feet (61 m). There are no fresh water streams. There are several large brackish lakes on several islands including Inagua and New Providence.

Government. The Bahamas moved toward greater autonomy in 1968 after the overwhelming victory in general elections of the Progressive Liberal Party, led by Prime Minister Lynden O. Pindling. The black leader's party won 29 seats in the House of Assembly to only 7 for the predominantly white United Bahamians, who had controlled the islands for decades before Pindling became Premier in 1967.

With its new mandate from the 85%-black population, Pindling's government negotiated a new Constitution with Britain under which the colony became the Commonwealth of the Bahama Islands in 1969. On July 10, 1973, The Bahamas became an independent nation as the Commonwealth of the Bahamas. The islands established diplomatic relations with Cuba in 1974.

In the 1987 election, Pindling's Progressive Liberal Party won 31 of 49 seats in Parliament; the Free National Movement, 16.

The PLP majority rose to 32 seats when Perry Christie reentered the party upon accepting a ministerial portfolio.

History. The islands were reached by Columbus in October 1492, and were a favorite pirate area in the early 18th century. The Bahamas were a crown colony from 1717 until they were granted internal self-government in 1964.

BAHRAIN

State of Bahrain
Emir: Sheik Isa bin-Sulman al-Khalifa (1961)
Prime Minister: Sheik Khalifa bin Sulman al-Khalifa (1970)
Area: 240 sq mi. (620 sq km)
Population (est. mid-1991): 500,000 (average annual rate of natural increase: 2.3%); birth rate: 27/1000; infant mortality rate: 24/1000; density per square mile: 2,243

Capital (est. 1982): Manama, 150,000
Monetary unit: Bahrain dinar
Languages: Arabic (official), English, Farsi, Urdu
Religion: Islam
Literacy rate : 40%
Economic summary: Gross domestic product (1987): $3.5 billion, $7,550 per capita; real growth rate (1988): 0%. Labor force (1982): 140,000; labor force in industry and commerce: 85%. Principal products: eggs, vegetables, fruits. Major products: oil, fish. Natural resources: oil, fish. Exports: oil, aluminum, fish. Imports: machinery, oil-industry equipment, motor vehicles, foodstuffs. Major trading partners: Saudi Arabia, U.S., U.K., Japan.

Geography. Bahrain is an archipelago in the Persian Gulf off the coast of Saudi Arabia. The islands for the most part are level expanses of sand and rock.

Government. A new Constitution was approved in 1973. It created the first elected parliament in the country's history. Called the National Council, it consisted of 30 members elected by male citizens for four-year terms, plus up to 16 Cabinet ministers as ex-officio members. In August 1975, the Emir dissolved the National Council.

History. A sheikdom that passed from the Persians to the al-Khalifa family from Arabia in 1782, Bahrain became, by treaty, a British protectorate in 1820. It has become a major Middle Eastern oil center and, through use of oil revenues, is one of the most developed of the Persian Gulf sheikdoms. The Emir, Sheik Isa bin-Sulman al-Khalifa, who succeeded to the post in 1961, is a member of the original ruling family. Bahrain announced its independence on Aug. 14, 1971.

Expanded use of Bahrain for Allied forces during the Persian Gulf war was granted.

BANGLADESH

People's Republic of Bangladesh
President: Shahabuddin Ahmed
Prime Minister: Khaleda Zia (1991)
Vice President: Moudud Ahmed (1989)
Area: 55,598 sq mi. (143,998 sq km)
Population (est. mid-1991): 116,600,000 (average annual rate of natural increase: 2.4%); birth rate: 37/1000; infant mortality rate: 120/1000; density per square mile: 2,097
Capital and largest city (est 1986): Dhaka, 4,470,000
Monetary unit: Taka
Principal languages: Bangla (official), English
Religions: Islam, (official) 83%; Hindu, 16%
Literacy rate: 29%
Member of Commonwealth of Nations
Economic summary: Gross domestic product (FY89 est.): $20.6 billion, per capita $180; real growth rate 2.1%. Arable land: 67%. Principal products: rice, jute, tea, sugar, potatoes, beef. Labor force: 35,100,000, 11% in industry and commerce. Major industrial products: jute goods, textiles, sugar, fertilizer, paper, processed foods. Natural resources: natural gas, uranium, timber. Exports: jute, tea, leather, garments. Imports: food grains, fuels, raw cotton, manufactured goods. Major trading partners: U.S., Japan, Middle East, Europe.

Geography. Bangladesh, on the northern coast of the Bay of Bengal, is surrounded by India, with a small common border with Burma in the southeast. It is approximately the size of Wisconsin. The country is low-lying riverine land traversed by the many branches and tributaries of the Ganges and Brahmaputra rivers. Elevations averages less than 600 feet (183 m) above sea level. Tropical monsoons and frequent floods and cyclones inflict heavy damage in the delta region.

Government. Khalida Zia, widow of assassinated President Ziaur Rahman, and her Bangladesh Nationalist Party won the election of late-February 1991. The BNP gained just enough seats in the 330-seat parliament to form a government.

History. The former East Pakistan was part of imperial British India until Britain withdrew in 1947. The two Pakistans were united by religion (Islam), but their peoples were separated by culture, physical features, and 1,000 miles of Indian territory. Bangladesh consists primarily of East Bengal (West Bengal is part of India and its people are primarily Hindu) plus the Sylhet district of the Indian state of Assam. For almost 25 years after independence from Britain, its history was as part of Pakistan (*see* Pakistan).

The East Pakistanis unsuccessfully sought greater autonomy from West Pakistan. The first general elections in Pakistani history, in December 1970, saw virtually all 171 seats of the region (out of 300 for both East and West Pakistan) go to Sheik Mujibur Rahman's Awami League.

Attempts to write an all-Pakistan Constitution to replace the military regime of Gen. Yahya Khan failed. Yahya put down a revolt in March 1971. An estimated one million Bengalis were killed in the fighting or later slaughtered. Ten million more took refuge in India.

In December 1971, India invaded East Pakistan, routed the West Pakistani occupation forces, and created Bangladesh. In February 1974, Pakistan agreed to recognize the independence of Bangladesh.

On March 24, 1982, Gen. Hossain Mohammad Ershad, army chief of staff, took control in a bloodless coup. Ershad assumed the office of President in 1983.

Gen. Ershad resigned on December 6, 1990 amidst protests and numerous allegations of corruption. During his nine-year tenure as president, the country's foreign debt went from $3 billion to $10 billion.

BARBADOS

Sovereign: Queen Elizabeth II
Governor-General: Dame Nita Barrow (June 1990)
Prime Minister: L. Erskine Sandiford (1987)
Area: 166 sq. mi. (431 sq km)
Population (est. mid-1991): 300,000; growth rate: .7%.; birth rate: 16;/1000 infant mortality rate: 9/1000; density per square mile: 1,548
Capital and largest city (est. 1988): Bridgetown, 102,000
Monetary unit: Barbados dollar
Language: English
Religions: Anglican, 70%; Methodist, 9%; Roman Catholic, 4%
Literacy rate: 99%
Member of Commonwealth of Nations
Economic summary: Gross domestic product (1988 est.): $1.3 billion, per capita $5,250; real growth rate (1989 est.) 3.7%). Arable land: 77%. Principal products: sugar cane, subsistence foods. Labor force: 112,300; 37% services and government. Major industrial prod-

ucts: light manufactures, sugar milling, tourism. Exports: sugar and sugar cane byproducts, clothing, electrical parts. Imports: foodstuffs, crude oil, manufactured goods. Major trading partners: U.S., Caribbean nations, U.K., Canada.

Geography. An island in the Atlantic about 300 miles (483 km) north of Venezuela, Barbados is only 21 miles long (34 km) and 14 miles across (23 km) at its widest point. It is circled by fine beaches and narrow coastal plains. The highest point is Mount Hillaby (1,105 ft; 337 m) in the north central area.

Government. The Barbados legislature dates from 1627. It is bicameral, with a Senate of 21 appointed members and an Assembly of 28 elected members. The major political parties are the Democratic Labor Party (18 seats in Assembly), led by Prime Minister L. Erskine Sandiford; Barbados Labor Party (10 seats), led by Henry Deb. Forde and National Democratic Party (0 seats) led by Richie Haynes.

History. Barbados, with a population 90% black, was settled by the British in 1627. It became a crown colony in 1885. It was a member of the Federation of the West Indies from 1958 to 1962. Britain granted the colony independence on Nov. 30, 1966, and it became a parliamentary democracy.

While retaining membership in the Commonwealth of Nations and economic ties with Britain, Barbados seeks broader economic and political relations with Western Hemisphere countries and in particular the developing nations of the Caribbean.

Prime Minister Sandiford handily won a second five-year term as a result of parliamentary elections in January 1991.

BELGIUM

Kingdom of Belgium
Sovereign: King Baudouin I (1951)
Prime Minister: Wilfried Martens (1981)
Area: 11,781 sq mi. (30,513 sq km)
Population (est. mid-1991): 9,900,000 (average annual rate of natural increase: .1%); birth rate: 12/1000; infant mortality rate: 8.6/1000; density per square mile: 842
Capital: Brussels
Largest cities (est. 1987): Brussels, 970,346; Antwerp, 479,748; Ghent, 233,856; Charleroi, 209,395; Liège, 200,891; Bruges, 117,755
Monetary Unit: Belgian franc
Languages: Flemish, 56%; French, 32%; bilingual (Brussels), 11%; German, 1%.
Religion: Roman Catholic, 75%
National name: Royaume de Belgique—Koninkrijk van België
Literacy rate: 98%
Economic summary: Gross domestic product (1989): $136 billion, per capita $13,700; real growth rate 4.5%). Arable land: 24%. Principal products: livestock, poultry, grain, sugar beets, flax, tobacco, potatoes, vegetables, fruits. Labor force: 4,000,000; 37% in industry. Major products: fabricated metal, iron and steel, machinery, textiles, chemicals, food processing. Exports: (Belg.-Luxembourg Econ. Union) iron and steel products, chemicals, pharmaceuticals, textile products. Imports: (Belg.-Luxembourg Econ. Union) nonelectrical machinery, motor vehicles, textiles, chemicals, fuels. Major trading partners: European Communities, U.S., Eastern Europe.

Geography. A neighbor of France, Germany, the Netherlands, and Luxembourg, Belgium has about 40 miles of seacoast on the North Sea at the Strait of Dover. In area, it is approximately the size of Maryland. The northern third of the country is a plain extending eastward from the seacoast. North of the Sambre and Meuse Rivers is a low plateau; to the south lies the heavily wooded Ardennes plateau, attaining an elevation of about 2,300 feet (700 m).

The Schelde River, which rises in France and flows through Belgium, emptying into the Schelde estuaries, enables Antwerp to be an ocean port.

Government. Belgium, a parliamentary democracy under a constitutional monarch, consists of nine provinces. Its bicameral legislature has a Senate, with its 181 members elected for four years—106 by general election, 50 by provincial councillors and 25 by the Senate itself. The 212-member Chamber of Representatives is directly elected for four years by proportional representation. There is universal suffrage, and those who do not vote are fined.

Belgium joined the North Atlantic Alliance in 1949 and is a member of the European Community. NATO and the European Community have their headquarters in Brussels.

The sovereign, Baudouin I, was born Sept. 7, 1930, the son of King Leopold III and Queen Astrid. He became King on July 17, 1951, after the abdication of his father. He married Doña Fabiola de Mora y Aragón on Dec. 15, 1960. Since he has no children, his brother, Prince Albert, is heir to the throne.

History. Belgium occupies part of the Roman province of Belgica, named after the Belgae, a people of ancient Gaul. The area was conquered by Julius Caesar in 57–50 B.C., then was overrun by the Franks in the 5th century. It was part of Charlemagne's empire in the 8th century, then in the next century was absorbed into Lotharingia and later into the Duchy of Lower Lorraine. In the 12th century it was partitioned into the Duchies of Brabant and Luxembourg, the Bishopric of Liège, and the domain of the Count of Hainaut, which included Flanders.

In the 16th century, Belgium, with most of the area of the Low Countries, passed to the Duchy of Burgundy and was the marriage portion of Archduke Maximilian of Hapsburg and the inheritance of his grandson, Charles V, who incorporated it into his empire. Then, in 1555, they were united with Spain.

By the treaty of Utrecht in 1713, the country's sovereignty passed to Austria. During the wars that followed the French Revolution, Belgium was occupied and later annexed to France. But with the downfall of Napoleon, the Congress of Vienna in 1815 gave the country to the Netherlands. The Belgians revolted in 1830 and declared their independence.

Germany's invasion of Belgium in 1914 set off World War I. The Treaty of Versailles (1919) gave the areas of Eupen, Malmédy, and Moresnet to Belgium. Leopold III succeeded Albert, King during World War I, in 1934. In World War II, Belgium was overwhelmed by Nazi Germany, and Leopold III was made prisoner. When he attempted to return in 1950, Socialists and Liberals revolted. He abdicated July 16, 1951, and his son, Baudouin, became King the next day.

Despite the increasingly strong divisions between the French- and Flemish-speaking communities, a Christian Democrat-Liberal coalition that took office in December 1981 came close to setting a record for longevity among the 32 governments that had ruled Belgium since World War II. Headed by Prime Minis-

ter Wilfried Martens—the fifth government he had led since 1979—it survived several serious political challenges, including the implementation of an unpopular economic austerity program in 1983 and the deployment of NATO cruise missiles in March 1985.

Strife between French and Flemish speakers almost toppled the government in 1986 and 1987. Belgian dithering during the Persian Gulf war saw an outpour of criticism from foreign and domestic sources but proved no danger to the Martens government.

BELIZE

Sovereign: Queen Elizabeth II (1952)
Governor-General: Dame Minita Gordon (1981)
Prime Minister: George Price (1989)
Area: 8,867 sq mi. (22,965 sq km)
Population (est. mid-1991): 200,000 (average annual rate of natural increase: 3.3%); birth rate: 38/1000; infant mortality rate: 35/1000.; density per sq mi.: 27
Capital (1989): Belmopan, 8,000
Largest city (1989): Belize City, 70,000
Monetary unit: Belize dollar
Languages: English (official) and Spanish, Maya, Carib
Religions: 60% Roman Catholic, 40% Protestant
Literacy rate: 93% (est.)
Member of Commonwealth of Nations
Economic summary: Gross domestic product (1989 est.): $225.6 million, per capita $1,285; real growth rate 6%). Arable land: 2%. Principal products: sugar cane, citrus fruits, corn, molasses, rice, bananas, livestock. Labor force: 51,500; 10.3% in manufacturing. Major products: timber, processed foods, furniture, rum, soap. Natural resources: timber, fish. Exports: sugar, molasses, clothing, lumber, citrus fruits, fish. Imports: fuels, transportation equipment, foodstuffs, textiles, machinery. Major trading partners: U.S., U.K., Trinidad and Tobago, Canada, Netherlands Antilles, Mexico.

Geography. Belize (formerly British Honduras) is situated on the Caribbean Sea south of Mexico and east and north of Guatemala. In area, it is about the size of New Hampshire. Most of the country is heavily forested with various hardwoods. Mangrove swamps and cays along the coast give way to hills and mountains in the interior. The highest point is Victoria Peak, 3,681 feet (1,122 m).

Government. Formerly the colony of British Honduras, Belize became a fully independent commonwealth on Sept. 21, 1981, after having been self-governing since 1964. Executive power is nominally wielded by Queen Elizabeth II through an appointed Governor-General but effective power is held by the Prime Minister, who is responsible to a 28-member parliament elected by universal suffrage.

History. Once a part of the Mayan empire, the area was deserted until British timber cutters began exploiting valuable hardwoods in the 17th century. Efforts by Spain to dislodge British settlers, including a major naval attack in 1798, were defeated. The territory was formally named a British colony in 1862 but administered by the Governor of Jamaica until 1884.

Guatemala has long made claims to the territory. A tentative agreement was reached between Britain, Belize, and Guatemala in March 1981 that would offer access to the Caribbean through Belizean territory for Guatemala. The agreement broke down, however.

The prime minister and his People's United Party easily defeated the opposition United Democratic Party in the general elections of Septemebr 1989. Cordial talks held in July 1990 between the Guatemalan president and Prime Minister Price raised hopes of settling a long-standing border dispute between the two countries.

BENIN

Republic of Benin
President: Nicephore Soglo (1991)
Area: 43,483 sq mi. (112,622 sq km)
Population (est. mid-1991): 4,800,000 (average annual rate of natural increase: 3.0%); birth rate: 49/1000; infant mortality rate: 90/1000; density per square mile: 110
Capital (est. 1984): Porto-Novo, 208,000
Largest city (est. 1982): Cotonou, 490,000
Monetary unit: Franc CFA
Ethnic groups: Fons and Adjas, Baribas, Yorubas, Mahis
Languages: French, African languages
Religions: indigenous, 70%; Christian, 15%; Islam, 15%
National name: Republique Populaire du Benin
Literacy rate (1981): 25.9%
Economic summary: Gross domestic product (1988): $1.7 billion. per capita $335; real growth rate 1.8%. Arable land: 12%. Principal products: oil palms, peanuts, cotton, coffee, tobacco, corn, rice, livestock, fish. Labor force: 1,900,000; less than 2% industry. Major industrial products: processed palm oil, palm kernel oil, textiles, beverages. Natural resources: low-grade iron ore, limestone, some offshore oil. Exports: palm and agricultural products. Imports: beverages, tobacco, consumer goods, fuels, foodstuffs, machinery. Major trading partners: France and other Western European countries, Japan, U.S.

Geography. This West African nation on the Gulf of Guinea, between Togo on the west and Nigeria on the east, is about the size of Tennessee. It is bounded also by Burkina Faso and Niger on the north. The land consists of a narrow coastal strip that rises to a swampy, forested plateau and then to highlands in the north. A hot and humid climate blankets the entire country.

Government. The change in name from Dahomey to Benin was announced by President Mathieu Kerekou on November 30, 1975. Benin commemorates an African kingdom that flourished in the 17th century. At the same time, Kerekou announced the formation of a political organization, the Party of the People's Revolution of Benin, to mark the first anniversary of his declaration of a "new society" guided by Marxist-Leninist principles. Kérékou repudiated Marxism-Leninism in 1989.

History. One of the smallest and most densely populated states in Africa, Benin was annexed by the French in 1893. The area was incorporated into French West Africa in 1904. It became an autonomous republic within the French Community in 1958, and on Aug. 1, 1960, was granted its independence within the Community.

Gen. Christophe Soglo deposed the first president, Hubert Maga, in an army coup in 1963. He dismissed the civilian government in 1965, proclaiming himself chief of state. A group of young army officers seized power in December 1967, deposing Soglo. They promulgated a new Constitution in 1968.

In December 1969, Benin had its fifth coup of the decade, with the army again taking power. In May 1970, a three-man presidential commission was created to take over the government. The commission had a six-year term; each member serves as president for two years. Maga turned over power as scheduled to Justin Ahomadegbe in May 1972, but six months later yet another army coup ousted the triumvirate and installed Lt. Col. Mathieu Kerekou as President.

Student protests and widespread strikes in 1989 and 1990 moved Benin toward multiparty democracy. In March 1991 Prime Minister Soglo won the first free presidential election.

BHUTAN

Kingdom of Bhutan
Ruler: King Jigme Singye Wangchuk (1972)
Area: 18,000 sq mi. (46,620 sq km)
Population (est. mid-1991): 700,000 (average annual rate of natural increase: 2.0%); birth rate: 39/1000; infant mortality rate: 142/1000; density per square mile: 37
Capital (est. 1984): Thimphu, 30,000
Monetary unit: Ngultrum
Language: Dzongkha (official)
Religions: Buddhist, 75%; Hindu, 25%
National name: Druk-yul
Literacy rate: 15%
Economic summary: Gross domestic product (1988 est.): $273 million, per capita $199; real growth rate 6.3%. Arable land: 3%. Labor force in agriculture: 95%. Principal products: rice, barley, wheat, potatoes, fruit. Major industrial product: cement. Natural resources: timber, hydroelectric power. Exports: cardamom, gypsum, timber, handicrafts, cement, fruit. Imports: fuels, machinery, vehicles. Major trading partner: India.

Geography. Mountainous Bhutan, half the size of Indiana, is situated on the southeast slope of the Himalayas, bordered on the north and east by Tibet and on the south and west by India. The landscape consists of a succession of lofty and rugged mountains running generally from north to south and separated by deep valleys. In the north, towering peaks reach a height of 24,000 feet (7,315 m).

Government. Bhutan is a constitutional monarchy. The King rules with a Council of Ministers and a Royal Advisory Council. There is a National Assembly (Parliament), which meets semiannually, but no political parties.

History. British troops invaded the country in 1865 and negotiated an agreement under which Britain undertook to pay an annual allowance to Bhutan on condition of good behavior. A treaty with India in 1949 increased this subsidy and placed Bhutan's foreign affairs under Indian control.

In the 1960s, Bhutan undertook modernization, abolishing slavery and the caste system, emancipating women and enacting land reform. In 1985, Bhutan made its first diplomatic links with non-Asian countries.

Although there were no serious threats to his authority, the King in 1990 took measures to isolate his people further from foreign, Western influences.

BOLIVIA

Republic of Bolivia
President: Jaime Paz Zamora (1989)
Area: 424,162 sq mi. (1,098,581 sq km)
Population (est. mid-1991): 7,500,000 (average annual rate of natural increase: 2.6%; birth rate: 38/1000; infant mortality rate: 93/1000; density per square mile: 18
Judicial capital (est. 1985): Sucre, 86,609
Administrative capital (est. 1985): La Paz, 992,592
Largest cities (est. 1985): Santa Cruz, 441,717; Cochabamba, 317,251; Oruro, 178,393
Monetary unit: Boliviano
Languages: Spanish, Quechua, Aymara
Religion: Roman Catholic, 94%
National name: República de Bolivia
Literacy rate: 63%
Economic summary: Gross national product (1988): $4.6 billion, $660 per capita, real growth rate 2.8%. Arable land: 3%. Labor force in agriculture: 50%. Principal products: potatoes, corn, rice, sugar cane, bananas, coffee. Labor force in manufacturing: 10%. Major products: refined petroleum, processed foods, tin, textiles, clothing. Natural resources: petroleum, natural gas, tin, lead, zinc, copper, tungsten, bismuth, antimony, gold, sulfur, silver, iron ore. Exports: tin, lead, zinc, silver, antimony, coffee, sugar, cotton, soya beans, leather, citrus, natural gas. Imports: foodstuffs, petroleum, consumer goods, capital goods. Major trading partners: U.S., Argentina, U.K.

Geography. Landlocked Bolivia, equal in size to California and Texas combined, lies to the west of Brazil. Its other neighbors are Peru and Chile on the west and Argentina and Paraguay on the south.

The country is a low alluvial plain throughout 60% of its area toward the east, drained by the Amazon and Plata river systems. The western part, enclosed by two chains of the Andes, is a great plateau—the Altiplano, with an average altitude of 12,000 feet (3,658 m). More than 80% of the population lives on the plateau, which also contains La Paz. At an altitude of 11,910 feet (3,630 m), it is the highest capital city in the world.

Lake Titicaca, half the size of Lake Ontario, is one of the highest large lakes in the world, at an altitude of 12,507 feet (3,812 m). Islands in the lake hold ruins of the ancient Incas.

Government. The Bolivian Constitution provides for a democratic, representative, unitary republic, with a government made up of three branches: legislative, executive, and judicial. Executive power is exercised by the president, elected by a direct vote for a four-year term. Legislative power is vested in the National Congress, consisting of the Chamber of Deputies and the Senate. Judicial power is in the hands of the Supreme Court.

History. Famous since Spanish colonial days for its mineral wealth, modern Bolivia was once a part of the ancient Incan Empire. After the Spaniards defeated the Incas in the 16th century, Bolivia's predominantly Indian population was reduced to slavery. The country won its independence in 1825 and was named after Simón Bolívar, the famed liberator.

Harassed by internal strife, Bolivia lost great slices of territory to three neighbor nations. Several thousand square miles and its outlet to the Pacific were taken by Chile after the War of the Pacific (1879–84). In 1903 a piece of Bolivia's Acre province, rich in rubber, was ceded to Brazil. And in 1938, after a war with Paraguay, Bolivia gave up

claim to nearly 100,000 square miles of the Gran Chaco.

In 1965 a guerrilla movement mounted from Cuba and headed by Maj. Ernesto (Ché) Guevara began a revolutionary war. With the aid of U.S. military advisers, the Bolivian army, helped by the peasants, smashed the guerrilla movement, wounding and capturing Guevara on Oct. 8, 1967, and shooting him to death the next day.

Faltering steps toward restoration of civilian government were halted abruptly on July 17, 1980, when Gen. Luis Garcia Meza Tejada seized power. A series of military leaders followed before the military moved, in 1982, to return the government to civilian rule. Hernán Siles Zuazo was inaugurated President on Oct. 10, 1982.

Under Siles' left-of-center government, the country was regularly shut down by work stoppages, the bulk of Bolivia's natural resources—natural gas, gold, lithium, potassium and tungsten—were either sold on the black market or left in the ground, the country had the lowest per-capita income in South America, and inflation approached 3,000 percent. In 1985, the 73-year-old Siles decided he was unable to carry on and quit a year early.

No candidate won a majority in the elections in 1985 and Victor Paz Estensoro, 77, was picked by Congress to become President.

As in 1985 the inconclusive presidential election of 1989 was decided in Congress, where the second place finisher Bánzer threw his support to Paz Zamora, who finished third, in exchange for naming a majority of the new cabinet.

In January 1991 the government started a crop substitution plan aimed at reducing the cultivation of coca plants.

BOPHUTHATSWANA

See South Africa

BOTSWANA

Republic of Botswana
President: Quett K.J. Masire (1980)
Area: 231,800 sq mi. (600,360 sq km)
Population (est. mid-1991): 1,300,000 (average annual rate of natural increase: 2.7%); birth rate: 37/1000; infant mortality rate: 63/1000; density per square mile: 5
Capital and largest city (est. 1984): Gaborone, 79,000
Monetary unit: Pula
Languages: English, Setswana
Religions: Christian, 48%; traditional, 49%
Member of Commonwealth of Nations
Literacy rate: 60%
Economic summary: Gross domestic product (FY88): $1.87 billion, per capita $1,600; real growth rate 8.4%. Arable land: 2%. Principal products: livestock, sorghum, corn, millet, cowpeas, beans. Labor force: 400,000; 163,000 formal sector employees, most others involved in cattle raising and subsistence agriculture. Major industrial products: diamonds, copper, nickel, salt, soda ash, potash, coal, frozen beef; tourism. Natural resources: diamonds, copper, nickel, salt, soda ash, potash, coal, natural gas. Exports: diamonds, cattle, animal products, copper, nickel. Imports: foodstuffs, vehicles, textiles, petroleum products. Major trading partners: South Africa, U.K., U.S., Switzerland.

Geography. Twice the size of Arizona, Botswana is
in south central Africa, bounded by Namibia, Zambia, Zimbabwe, and South Africa. Most of the country is near-desert, with the Kalahari occupying the
western part of the country. The eastern part is hilly,
with salt lakes in the north.

Government. The Botswana Constitution provides,
in addition to the unicameral National Assembly, for
a House of Chiefs, which has a voice on bills affecting tribal affairs. There is universal suffrage. The major political parties are the Democratic Party (29 of
34 elective seats in 36-man Legislative Assembly),
led by President Quett Masire; National Front (4
seats), led by Kenneth Koma; People's Party (1 seat),
led by Kenneth Nkhwa.

History. Botswana is the land of the Batawana tribes,
which, when threatened by the Boers in Transvaal,
asked Britain in 1885 to establish a protectorate over
the country, then known as Bechuanaland. In 1961,
Britain granted a Constitution to the country. Self-
government began in 1965, and on Sept. 30, 1966,
the country became independent. Since 1975, it has
been an associate member of the European Common
Market.

In connection with the release of Nelson Mandela
in South Africa Botswana freed 16 detained members
of South African liberation movements in February
1990.

BRAZIL

Federative Republic of Brazil
President: Fernando Affonso Collor de Mello (1990)
Area: 3,286,470 sq mi. (8,511,957 sq km)
Population (est. mid-1991): 153,300,000 (average annual
rate of natural increase: 1.9%); birth rate: 27/1000;
infant mortality rate: 63/1000; density per square mile:
47
Capital (est. 1985): Brasilia, 1,576,657
Largest cities (est. 1985): São Paulo, 10,099,086; Rio de
Janeiro, 5,615,149; Salvador, 1,811,367; Belo Horizonte,
2,122,073; Recife, 1,289,627; Porto Alegre, 1,275,483
Monetary unit: Novo cruzado
Language: Portuguese
Religion: Roman Catholic, 90% (nominal)
National name: República Federativa de Brasil
Literacy rate: 76%
Economic summary: Gross national product (1989 est.):
$377 billion, per capita $2,500; real growth rate 3%.
Arable land: 7%. Principal products: coffee, sugar
cane, oranges, cocoa, soybeans, tobacco, cattle. Labor force (1988 est.): 57,000,000; 27% in industry. Major industrial products: steel, chemicals, petrochemicals, machinery, motor vehicles, cement, lumber.
Natural resources: iron ore, manganese, bauxite,
nickel, other industrial metals, hydropower, timber.
Exports: coffee, iron ore, soybeans, sugar, beef, transport equipment, footwear, orange juice. Imports:
crude oil, capital goods, chemical products, foodstuffs,
coal. Major trading partners: U.S., Japan, Saudi Arabia, Africa.

Geography. Brazil covers nearly half of South
America, extends 2,965 miles (4,772 km)
north-south, 2,691 miles (4,331 km), east-west, and
borders every nation on the continent except Chile
and Ecuador. It is the fifth largest country in the
world, ranking after the U.S.S.R., Canada, China, and
the U.S.

More than a third of Brazil is drained by the Amazon and its more than 200 tributaries. The Amazon is
navigable for ocean steamers to Iquitos, Peru, 2,300
miles (3,700 km) upstream. Southern Brazil is
drained by the Plata system—the Paraguay, Uruguay,
and Paraná Rivers. The most important stream entirely within Brazil is the São Francisco, navigable for
1,000 miles (1,903 km), but broken near its mouth by
the 275-foot (84 m) Paulo Afonso Falls.

Government. The military took control in 1964,
ousting the last elected civilian President and installing a series of military men (with the Congress ratifying the junta's choice). Election of a civilian President by the 686-member electoral college took place
in January 1985.

A new constitution in 1988 provided for the president to be elected for a five-year term through direct,
compulsory and secret suffrage. The National Congress maintains a bicameral structure—a Senate,
whose members serve eight-year terms, and a Chamber of Deputies, elected for four-year terms.

History. Brazil is the only Latin American nation
deriving its language and culture from Portugal.
Adm. Pedro Alvares Cabral claimed the territory for
the Portuguese in 1500. He brought to Portugal a cargo of wood, pau-brasil, from which the land received
its name. Portugal began colonization in 1532 and
made the area a royal colony in 1549.

During the Napoleonic wars, King João VI, then
Prince Regent, fled the country in 1807 in advance of
the French armies and in 1808 set up his court in Rio
de Janeiro. João was drawn home in 1820 by a revolution, leaving his son as Regent. When Portugal
sought to reduce Brazil again to colonial status, the
prince declared Brazil's independence on Sept. 7,
1822, and became Pedro I, Emperor of Brazil.

Harassed by his parliament, Pedro I abdicated in
1831 in favor of his five-year-old son, who became
Emperor in 1840 as Pedro II. The son was a popular
monarch, but discontent built up and, in 1889, following a military revolt, he had to abdicate. Although
a republic was proclaimed, Brazil was under two military dictatorships during the next four years. A revolt permitted a gradual return to stability under civilian Presidents.

The President during World War I, Wenceslau
Braz, cooperated with the Allies and declared war on
Germany.

In World War II, Brazil cooperated with the Western Allies, welcoming Allied air bases, patrolling the
South Atlantic, and joining the invasion of Italy after
declaring war on the Axis.

Gen. João Baptista de Oliveira Figueiredo, became
President in 1979 and pledged a return to democracy
in 1985.

The electoral college's choice of Tancredo Neves
on Jan. 15, 1985, as the first civilian President since
1964 brought a nationwide wave of optimism, but the
75-year-old President-elect was hospitalized and underwent a series of intestinal operations. The civilian
government was inaugurated on schedule on March
15, but only Neves' Vice Presidential running mate,
José Sarney, was sworn in, and he was widely dis-
trusted because he had previously been a member of
the governing military regime's political party. When
Neves died on April 21, Sarney became President.

Economically, Brazil's $93-billion foreign debt was
the Third World's largest, and inflation reached a
staggering 229% annual rate in 1984, almost double
the 115% rate in 1983.

Collor de Mello won the election of late 1989 and took office in March 1990 despite his lack of support from a major party. In the campaign he pledged to lower the chronic hyperinflation following the path of free-market economics. Yet an economic recession still saw the inflation rate running at about 400% during the president's first year in office. On the other hand, his program has helped reduce the destruction of the rain forest, and he has successfully faced down the military. Progress has also been slow in renegotiating the payment terms on Brazil's huge foreign debt.

BRUNEI DARUSSALAM

State of Brunei Darussalam
Sultan: Hassanal Bolkiah
Area: 2,226 sq mi. (5,765 sq km)
Population (est. mid-1991): 300,000 (annual rate of natural increase: 2.5%); birth rate: 29/1000; infant mortality rate: 7/1000; density per square mile: 119
Capital and largest city (est. 1987): Bandar Seri Begawan, 56,300
Monetary unit: Brunei dollar
Ethnic groups: 64% Malay, 20% Chinese, 16% other
Languages: Malay (official), Chinese, English
Religions: Islam (official religion), 60%; Christian, 8%; Buddhist and local, 32%
Literacy rate: 45%
Member of Commonwealth of Nations
Economic summary: Gross domestic product (1989 est.): $3.3 billion, per capita $9,600; real growth rate 2.5%. Arable land: 1%; principle agricultural products: fruit, rice, pepper, buffaloes. Labor force: 89,000; 50.4% in production of oil, natural gas and construction. major industrial products: crude petroleum, liquified natural gas. Natural resources: petroleum, natural gas, timber. Exports: crude petroleum, liquified natural gas. Imports: machinery, transport equipment, manufactured goods, foodstuffs. Major trading partners: Japan, U.S., U.K., Singapore.

Geography. About the size of Delaware, Brunei is an independent sultanate on the northwest coast of the island of Borneo in the South China Sea, wedged between the Malaysian states of Sabah and Sarawak. Three quarters of the thinly populated country is covered with tropical rain forest; there are rich oil and gas deposits.

Government. Sultan Hassanal Bolkiah is ruler of the state, a former British protectorate which became fully sovereign and independent on New Year's Day, 1984, presiding over a Privy Council and Council of Ministers appointed by himself. The Constitution provides for a three-tiered system of indirect elections, but the last elections were held in 1965. The only known opposition leader is in exile. In 1985, the Brunei National Democratic Party (BDNP) was formed but was dissolved by the sultan in 1988.

History. Brunei (pronounced broon-eye) was a powerful state from the 16th to the 19th century, ruling over the northern part of Borneo and adjacent island chains. But it fell into decay and lost Sarawak in 1841, becoming a British protectorate in 1888 and a British dependency in 1905.

The Sultan regained control over internal affairs in 1959, but Britain retained responsibility for the state's defense and foreign affairs until the end of 1983,

when the sultanate became fully independent.

Sultain Bolkiah was crowned in 1968 at the age of 22, succeeding his father, Sir Omar Ali Saifuddin, who had abdicated. During his reign, exploitation of the rich Seria oilfield has made the sultanate wealthy.

Warning against opposition to his government, the Islamic religion and himself, the sultan in 1990 said that the laws of the sultanate would be restructured into conformity with Islamic law.

BULGARIA

Republic of Bulgaria
Prime Minister: Dimitar Popov (1990)
President: Zhelyu Zhelev (1990)
Area: 42,823 sq mi. (110,912 sq km)
Population (est. mid-1991): 9,000,000 (average annual rate of natural increase: 0.1%); birth rate:13/1000; infant mortality rate: 13.6/1000; density per square mile: 210
Capital: Sofia
Largest cities (est. 1986): Sofia, 1,114,962; Plovdiv, 342,131; Varna, 302,211; Ruse, 183,746; Burgas, 182,570
Monetary unit: Lev
Language: Bulgarian
Religions: Bulgarian Orthodox, 90%; Muslim, Catholic, Protestant, Judaic, Armeno-Gerogorian
National name: Narodna Republika Bulgariya
Literacy rate: 95%
Economic summary: Gross national product (1989 est.): $51.2 billion, per capita $5,710; real growth rate –0.1%. Arable land: 34%. Principal products: grains, tobacco, fruits, vegetables. Labor force: 4,300,000, 33% in industry. Major products: processed agricultural products, machinery, electronics, chemicals. Natural resources: metals, minerals, timber. Exports: machinery and transport equipment, fuels, minerals, raw materials, agricultural products. Imports: machinery and transportation equipment, fuels, raw materials, metals, agricultural raw materials. Major trading partners: U.S.S.R., Eastern European countries, EEC.

Geography. Two mountain ranges and two great valleys mark the topography of Bulgaria, a country the size of Tennessee. Situated on the Black Sea in the eastern part of the Balkan peninsula, it shares borders with Yugoslavia, Romania, Greece, and Turkey. The Balkan belt crosses the center of the country, almost due east-west, rising to a height of 6,888 feet (2,100 m). The Rhodope, Rila and Pirin mountains straightens out along the western and southern border. Between the two ranges, is the valley of the Maritsa, Bulgaria's principal river. Between the Balkan range and the Danube, which forms most of the northern boundary with Romania, is the Danubian tableland.

Southern Dobruja, a fertile region of 2,900 square miles (7,511 sq km), below the Danube delta, is an area of low hills, fens, and sandy steppes.

Government. The 1971 Constitution was radically amended in 1990. The National Assembly, consisting of 400 members elected June 1990 is the legislative body. It elects the President of the Republic and the Council of Ministers.

History. The first Bulgarians, a tribe of wild horsemen akin to the Huns, crossed the Danube from the north in A.D. 679 and subjugated the Slavic population of Moesia. They adopted a Slav dialect and Slavic customs and twice conquered most of the Balkan peninsula between 893 and 1280. After the Serbs subjected their kingdom in 1330, the Bulgars gradually fell prey to the Turks, and from 1396 to 1878 Bulgaria was a Turkish province. In 1878, Russia forced Turkey to give the country its independence; but the European powers, fearing that Bulgaria might become a Russian dependency, intervened. By the Treaty of Berlin in 1878, Bulgaria became autonomous under Turkish sovereignty.

In 1887, Prince Ferdinand of Saxe-Coburg-Gotha was elected ruler of Bulgaria; on Oct. 5, 1908, he declared the country independent and took the title of Tsar.

Bulgaria joined Germany in World War I and lost. On Oct. 3, 1918, Tsar Ferdinand abdicated in favor of his son, Tsar Boris III. Boris assumed dictatorial powers in 1934–35. When Hitler awarded Bulgaria southern Dobruja, taken from Romania in 1940, Boris joined the Nazis in war the next year and occupied parts of Yugoslavia and Greece. Later the Germans tried to force Boris to send his troops against the Russians. Boris resisted and died under mysterious circumstances on Aug. 28, 1943. Simeon II, infant son of Boris, became nominal ruler under a regency. Russia declared war on Bulgaria on Sept. 5, 1944. An armistice was agreed to three days later, after Bulgaria had declared war on Germany. Russian troops streamed in the next day and under an informal armistice a coalition "Fatherland Front" cabinet was set up under Kimon Georgiev.

A Soviet-style people's Republic was established in 1947 and Bulgaria acquired the reputation of being the most slavishly loyal to Moscow of all the East European Communist countries.

Zhikov resigned in 1989 after 35 years in power. His successor, Peter Mladenov, purged the Politburo, ended the Communist monopoly on power and held free elections in May 1990 that led to a surprising victory for the Communists, renamed the Bulgarian Socialist Party. Mladenov was forced to resign in July 1990.

In January 1991 a coalition government of all major political groups was formed embarking on a program of tight monetary policy and committed to political pluralism and reforms aimed at creating a market economy.

BURKINA FASO

Chairman of the Popular Front: Blaise Compaore (1987)
Area: 105,870 sq mi. (274,200 sq km)
Population (est. mid-1991): 9,400,000 (average annual rate of natural increase: 3.3%); birth rate: 50/1000; infant mortality rate: 121/1000; density per square mile: 88
Capital and largest city (est. 1990): Ouagadougou, 500,000
Monetary unit: Franc CFA
Ethnic groups: Mossis, Bobos, Lobis, Fulanis
Languages: French, tribal languages
Religions: Animist, 65%; Islam, 25%; Roman Catholic, 10%
National name: Burkina Faso
Literacy rate: 13.2%

Economic summary: Gross domestic product (1988): $1.43 billion, per capita $170; real growth rate 7.7%. Arable land: 10%. Labor force in agriculture: 82%. Principal products: millet, sorghum, corn, rice, livestock, peanuts, sugar cane, cotton. Major industrial products: processed agricultural products, light industrial items, brick, brewed products. Natural resources: manganese, limestone, marble, gold, uranium, bauxite, copper. Exports: oilseeds, cotton, live animals, gold. Imports: textiles, food and consumer goods, transport equipment, machinery, fuels. Major trading partners: E.C., Taiwan, Côte d'Ivoire, Africa, U.S.

Geography. Slightly larger than Colorado, Burkina Faso, formerly known as Upper Volta, is a landlocked country in West Africa. Its neighbors are the Côte d'Ivoire, Mali, Niger, Benin, Togo, and Ghana. The country consists of extensive plains, low hills, high savannas, and a desert area in the north.

Government. The former French colony has been governed by a series of military leaders since a coup in November 1980 overthrew the last elected president.

History. The country, called Upper Volta by the French, consists chiefly of the lands of the Mossi Empire, where France established a protectorate over the Kingdom of Ouagadougou in 1897. Upper Volta became a separate colony in 1919, was partitioned among Niger, the Sudan, and the Ivory Coast in 1933 and was reconstituted in 1947. An autonomous republic within the French Community, it became independent on Aug. 5, 1960.

President Maurice Yameogo was deposed on Jan. 3, 1966, by a military coup led by Col. Sangoulé Lamizana, who dissolved the National Assembly and suspended the Constitution. Constitutional rule returned in 1978 with the election of an Assembly and a presidential vote in June in which Gen. Lamizana won by a narrow margin over three other candidates.

On Nov. 25, 1980, there was a bloodless coup which placed Gen. Lamizana under house arrest. Col. Sayé Zerbo took charge as the President of the Military Committee of Reform for National Progress. Maj. Jean-Baptiste Ouedraogo toppled Zerbo in another coup on Nov. 7, 1982. Captain Thomas Sankara, in turn, deposed Ouedraogo a year later. His government changed the country's name on Aug. 3, 1984, to Burkina Faso (the "land of upright men") to sever ties with its colonial past. He was overthrown and killed by Blaise Compaore in 1987.

In June 1991 voters approved a draft constitution providing for three branches of government and presidential elections every seven years. The government has promised a multiparty democracy.

BURMA

See Myanmar

BURUNDI

Republic of Burundi
President: Maj. Pierre Buyoya (1987)
Prime Minister: Adrien Sibomana (1988)
Area: 10,747 sq mi. (27,834 sq km)
Population (est. mid-1991): 5,800,000 (average annual rate of natural increase: 3.2%); birth rate: 47/1000; infant mortality rate: 111/1000; density per square mile: 543

Capital and largest city (1986): Bujumbura, 272,600
Monetary unit: Burundi franc
Languages: Kirundi and French (official), Swahili
Religions: Roman Catholic, 62%; Protestant, 5%; indigenous, 32%
National name: Republika Y'Uburundi
Literacy rate: 33.8%
Economic summary: Gross domestic product (1988): $1.3 billion, per capita $255; real growth rate 2.8%. Arable land: 43%; Principal agricultural products: coffee, tea, cotton, bananas, sorghum. Labor force: 1,900,000 (1983 est.); 93% in agriculture. Major industrial products: light consumer goods. Natural resources: nickel, uranium, rare earth oxide, peat, cobalt, copper, unexploited platinum, vanadium. Exports: coffee, tea, cotton, hides and skins. Imports: food, petroleum products, capital goods, consumer goods. Major trading partners: U.S., Western Europe, Asia.

Geography. Wedged among Tanzania, Zaire, and Rwanda in east central Africa, Burundi occupies a high plateau divided by several deep valleys. It is equal in size to Maryland.

Government. Legislative and executive power is vested in the president.

Burundi's first Constitution, approved July 11, 1974, placed UPRONA (Unity and National Progress), the only political party, in control of national policy.

History. Burundi was once part of German East Africa. An integrated society developed among the Watusi, a tall, warlike people and nomad cattle raisers, and the Bahutu, a Bantu people, who were subject farmers. Belgium won a League of Nations mandate in 1923, and subsequently Burundi, with Rwanda, was transferred to the status of a United Nations trust territory.

In 1962, Burundi gained independence and became a kingdom under Mwami Mwambutsa IV. His son deposed him in 1966 to rule as Ntaré V. He was overthrown by Premier Micombero.

One of Africa's worst tribal wars, which became genocide, occurred in Burundi in April 1972, following the return of Ntare V. He was given a safe-conduct promise in writing by President Micombero but was "judged and immediately executed" by the Burundi leader. His return was apparently attended by an invasion of exiles of Burundi's Hutu tribe. Whether Hutus living in Burundi joined the invasion is unclear, but after it failed, the victorious Tutsis proceeded to massacre some 100,000 persons in six weeks, with possibly 100,000 more slain by summer.

On Nov. 1, 1976, Lt. Col. Jean-Baptiste Bagaye led a coup and assumed the presidency. He suspended the Constitution, and announced that a 30-member Supreme Revolutionary Council would be the governing body.

Bagaza was elected head of the only legal political party in 1979 and was overthrown as party chieftain in 1987.

Intertribal massacres in 1988 led the government to issue a Charter of National Unity, granting the country's three ethnic groups equal rights.

CAMBODIA

President: Prince Norodom Sihanouk (1991)
Prime Minister: Son Sann (1982)
Area: 69,884 sq mi. (181,000 sq km)

Population (est. mid-1991): 7,100,000 (average annual rate of natural increase: 2.2%); birth rate: 38/1000; infant mortality rate: 125/1000; density per square mile: 102
Capital and largest city (est. 1980 for metropolitan area): Phnom Penh, 500,000
Monetary unit: Riel
Ethnic groups: Khmer, 90%; Chinese, 5%; other minorities 5%
Languages: Khmer (official), French
Religion: Theravada Buddhist, 5% others
Literacy rate: 48%
Economic summary: Gross domestic product (1989 est.): $890 million, per capita $130; real growth rate 0%. Arable land: 16%. Principal agricultural products: rice, rubber, corn. Labor force: 2.5–3.0 million; 80% in agriculture. Major industrial products: fish, wood and wood products, milled rice, rubber, cement. Natural resources: timber, gemstones, iron ore, manganese, phosphate. Exports: natural rubber, rice, pepper, wood. Imports: foodstuffs, fuel, consumer goods. Major trading partners: Vietnam, U.S.S.R., Eastern Europe, Japan, India.

Geography. Situated on the Indochinese peninsula, Cambodia is bordered by Thailand and Laos on the north and Vietnam on the east and south. The Gulf of Siam is off the western coast. The country, the size of Missouri, consists chiefly of a large alluvial plain ringed in by mountains and on the east by the Mekong River. The plain is centered on Lake Tonle Sap, which is a natural storage basin of the Mekong.

Government. A bloodless coup toppled Prince Sihanouk in 1970. It was led by Lon Nol and Prince Sisowath Sirik Matak, Sihanouk's cousin. Sihanouk moved to Peking to head a government-in-exile. On Oct. 9, 1970, Lon Nol proclaimed himself President.

The Lon Nol regime was overthrown in April 1975 by Pol Pot, a leader of the Communist Khmer Rouge forces, who instituted a xenophobic reign of terror. Pol Pot was in turn ousted on Jan. 8, 1979, by Vietnamese forces. A new government led by Heng Samrin was installed.

History. Cambodia came under Khmer rule about A.D. 600. Under the Khmers, magnificent temples were built at Angkor. The Khmer kingdom once ruled over most of Southeast Asia, but attacks by the Thai and the Vietnamese almost annihilated the empire until the French joined Cambodia, Laos, and Vietnam into French Indochina.

Under Norodom Sihanouk, enthroned in 1941, and particularly under Japanese occupation during World War II, nationalism revived. After the ouster of the Japanese, the Cambodians sought independence, but the French returned in 1946, granting the country a Constitution in 1947 and independence within the French Union in 1949. Sihanouk won full military control during the French--Indochinese War in 1953. He abdicated in 1955 in favor of his parents, remaining head of the government, and when his father died in 1960, became chief of state without returning to the throne. In 1963, he sought a guarantee of Cambodia's neutrality from all parties to the Vietnam War.

On March 18, 1970, while Sihanouk was abroad trying to get North Vietnamese and the Vietcong out of border sanctuaries near Vietnam, anti-Vietnamese riots occurred, and Sihanouk was overthrown.

North Vietnamese and Vietcong units in border sanctuaries began moving deeper into Cambodia, threatening rapid overthrow of the new regime headed by Lon Nol. President Nixon sent South Vietnamese and U.S. troops across the border on April

30. U.S. ground forces, limited to 30-kilometer penetration, withdrew by June 30.

The Vietnam peace agreement of 1973 stipulated withdrawal of foreign forces from Cambodia, but fighting continued between Hanoi-backed insurgents and U.S.-supplied government troops. U.S. air support for the government forces was ended by Congress on Aug. 15, 1973.

Fighting reached a quick climax early in 1975, as government troops fell back in bitter fighting, Lon Nol fled by air April 1, leaving the government under the interim control of Premier Long Boret. On April 16, the government's capitulation ended the five-year war, but not the travails of war-ravaged Cambodia.

A new Constitution was proclaimed in December 1975, establishing a 250-member People's Assembly, a State Presidium headed by Pol Pot, and a Supreme Judicial Tribunal. Samphan replaced Sihanouk as head of state in April 1976, and the former monarch was a virtual prisoner until 1979.

In the next two years, from 2 million to 4 million Cambodians are estimated to have died under the brutality of the Pol Pot regime. Border clashes with Vietnam developed into a Vietnamese invasion and by the end of 1978 the Pol Pot government appeared to be collapsing.

Phnom Penh was captured on Jan. 8 and retreating Pol Pot forces and 40,000 refugees were driven into Thailand by May.

At a meeting in Kuala Lumpur, Malaysia, on June 22, 1982, Sihanouk formed an alliance with Son Sann, his former prime minister, and Khieu Samphan, Pol Pot's representative, to oppose the Heng Samrin regime installed by Vietnam.

While Sihanouk remained in exile, about 9,000 noncommunist troops loyal to him and another 15,000 under Son Sann joined about 35,000 communist Pol Pot forces fighting the 170,000 Vietnamese troops supporting the Heng Samrin government. The Cambodian insurgents suffered a major defeat in March 1985 when Vietnamese forces overran their camps in Cambodia and forced them into Thailand.

The Vietnamese plan originally called for them to withdraw by early 1990 and negotiate a political settlement. The main issues were the level of inclusion of the Khmer Rouge, with their record of atrocities, in any new government, the organization and powers of the interim government pending new elections and the role of the United Nations in the transition.

The talks, however, stalled through 1990 on into 1991 with no clear resolution in sight. A continuation of the mid-1991 ceasefire appeared shaky as the warring parties alleged violations by their opponents.

CAMEROON

Republic of Cameroon
President: Paul Biya (1988)
Area: 183,569 sq mi. (475,442 sq km)
Population (est. mid-1991): 11,400,000 (average annual rate of natural increase: 2.6%); birth rate: 42/1000; infant mortality rate: 123/1000; density per square mile: 62
Capital: Yaoundé
Largest cities (est. 1985): Douala, 852,700; Yaoundé, 583,500
Monetary unit: Franc CFA
Languages: French and English (both official); 24 major African language groups

Religions: 51% indigenous beliefs, 33% Christian, 16% Muslim
National name: République du Cameroun
Literacy rate: 56.2%
Economic summary: Gross domestic product (1988): $12.9 billion, per capita $955; real growth rate −8.6%. Arable land: 13%. principal products: coffee, cocoa, timber, corn, peanuts. Labor force in agriculture: 74.4%. Major industrial products: crude oil, small manufacturing, consumer goods, aluminum. Natural resources: timber, some oil, bauxite, hydropower potential. Exports: cocoa, coffee, timber, aluminum, petroleum. Imports: machines and electrical equipment, transport equipment, chemical products, consumer goods. Major trading partners: France, U.S., Western European nations.

Geography. Cameroon is a West African nation on the Gulf of Guinea, bordered by Nigeria, Chad, the Central African Republic, the Congo, Equatorial Guinea, and Gabon. It is nearly twice the size of Oregon.

The interior consists of a high plateau, rising to 4,500 feet (1,372 m), with the land descending to a lower, densely wooded plateau and then to swamps and plains along the coast. Mount Cameroon (13,350 ft.; 4,069 m), near the coast, is the highest elevation in the country. The main rivers are the Benue, Nyong, and Sanaga.

Government. After a 1972 plebiscite, a unitary nation was formed out of East and West Cameroon to replace the former Federal Republic. A Constitution was adopted, providing for election of a president every five years and of a 120-seat National Assembly (later increased to 180), whose nominal five-year term can be extended or shortened by the president. The Cameroon People's Democratic Movement is the only political party.

History. The Republic of Cameroon is inhabited by Hamitic and Semitic peoples in the north, where Islam is the principal religion, and by Bantu peoples in the central and southern regions, where native animism prevails. The tribes were conquered by many invaders.

The land escaped colonial rule until 1884, when treaties with tribal chiefs brought the area under German domination. After World War I, the League of Nations gave the French a mandate over 80% of the area, and the British 20% adjacent to Nigeria. After World War II, when the country came under a U.N. trusteeship in 1946, self-government was granted, and the Cameroun People's Union emerged as the dominant party by campaigning for reunification of French and British Cameroon and for independence. Accused of being under Communist control, it waged a campaign of revolutionary terror from 1955 to 1958, when it was crushed. In British Cameroon, unification was pressed also by the leading party, the Kamerun National Democratic Party, led by John Foncha.

France set up Cameroon as an autonomous state in 1957, and the next year its legislative assembly voted for independence by 1960. In 1959 a fully autonomous government of Cameroon was formed under Ahmadou Ahidjo. Cameroon became an independent republic on Jan. 1, 1960.

Although hesitantly President Biya in the face of repeated calls and demonstrations in 1990 endorsed multiparty democracy. Most political prisoners have been freed, and the country has implemented some basic structural changes in the economy, winning praise from the IMF.

CANADA

Sovereign: Queen Elizabeth II (1952)
Governor General: Raymond John Hnatyshyn (1990)
Prime Minister: Brian Mulroney (1984)
Area: 3,851,809 sq mi. (9,976,186 sq km)
Population (est. mid-1991): 26,832,000 (average annual rate of natural increase: 0.7%); birth rate: 15/1000; infant mortality rate: 7.2/1000; density per square mile: 7
Capital: Ottawa, Ont.
Largest cities (1986 census; metropolitan areas): Toronto, 3,427,168; Montreal, 2,921,357; Vancouver, 1,380,729; Ottawa, 819,263; Edmonton, 785,465; Calgary, 671,326; Winnipeg, 625,304; Quebec, 603,627; Hamilton, 557,029; St. Catherines-Niagara, 343,258
Monetary Unit: Canadian dollar
Languages: English, French
Religions: 46% Roman Catholic, 16% United Church, 10% Anglican
Literacy rate: 99%
Economic Summary: Gross national product (1989 est.): $513.6 billion, per capita $19,600; real growth rate 1%. Arable land: 7.47%. Principal products; wheat, barley, oats, livestock. Labor force (1990): 13,681,000; 75% in manufacturing. Major industrial products; transportation equipment, petroleum, chemicals, wood products. Exports: wheat, petroleum, lumber and wood products, ores, motor vehicles. Imports: electronic equipment, chemicals, processed foods, beverages. Major trading partners: U.S., Japan, U.K., U.S.S.R., Germany, Mexico, South Korea.

Geography. Covering most of the northern part of the North American continent and with an area larger than that of the United States, Canada has an extremely varied topography. In the east the mountainous maritime provinces have an irregular coastline on the Gulf of St. Lawrence and the Atlantic. The St. Lawrence plain, covering most of southern Quebec and Ontario, and the interior continental plain, covering southern Manitoba and Saskatchewan and most of Alberta, are the principal cultivable areas. They are separated by a forested plateau rising from lakes Superior and Huron.

Westward toward the Pacific, most of British Columbia, Yukon, and part of western Alberta are covered by parallel mountain ranges including the Rockies. The Pacific border of the coast range is ragged with fiords and channels. The highest point in Canada is Mount Logan (19,850 ft; 6,050 m), which is in the Yukon.

Canada has an abundance of large and small lakes. In addition to the Great Lakes on the U.S. border, there are 9 others that are more than 100 miles long (161 km) and 35 that are more than 50 miles long (80 km). The two principal river systems are the Mackenzie and the St. Lawrence. The St. Lawrence, with its tributaries, is navigable for over 1,900 miles (3,058 km).

Government. Canada, a self-governing member of the Commonwealth of Nations, is a federation of 10 provinces (Alberta, British Columbia, Manitoba, New Brunswick, Newfoundland, Nova Scotia, Ontario, Prince Edward Island, Quebec, and Saskatchewan) and two territories (Northwest Territories and Yukon) whose powers were spelled out in the British North America Act of 1867. With the passing of the Constitution Act of 1981, the act and the Constitutional amending power were transferred from the British government to Canada so that the Canadian Constitution is now entirely in the hands of the Canadians.

Actually the Governor General acts only with the advice of the Canadian Prime Minister and the Cabinet, who also sit in the federal Parliament. The Parliament has two houses: a Senate of 104 members appointed for life, and a House of Commons of 295 members apportioned according to provincial population. Elections are held at least every five years or whenever the party in power is voted down in the House of Commons or considers it expedient to appeal to the people. The Prime Minister is the leader of the majority party in the House of Commons—or, if no single party holds a majority, the leader of the party able to command the support of a majority of members of the House. Laws must be passed by both houses of Parliament and signed by the Governor General in the Queen's name.

The 10 provincial governments are nominally headed by Lieutenant Governors appointed by the federal government, but the executive power in each actually is vested in a Cabinet headed by a Premier, who is leader of the majority party. The provincial legislatures are composed of one-house assemblies whose members are elected for four-year terms. They are known as Legislative Assemblies, except in Newfoundland, where it is the House of Assembly, and in Quebec, where it is the National Assembly.

The judicial system consists of a Supreme Court in Ottawa (established in 1875), with appellate jurisdiction, and a Supreme Court in each province, as well as county courts with limited jurisdiction in most of the provinces. The Governor General in Council appoints these judges.

History. The Norse explorer Leif Ericson probably reached the shores of Canada (Labrador or Nova Scotia) in A.D. 1000, but the history of the white man in the country actually began in 1497, when John Cabot, an Italian in the service of Henry VII of England, reached Newfoundland or Nova Scotia. Canada was taken for France in 1534 by Jacques Cartier. The actual settlement of New France, as it was then called, began in 1604 at Port Royal in what is now Nova Scotia; in 1608, Quebec was founded. France's colonization efforts were not very successful, but French explorers by the end of the 17th century had penetrated beyond the Great Lakes to the western prairies and south along the Mississippi to the Gulf of Mexico. Meanwhile, the English Hudson's Bay Company had been established in 1670. Because of the valuable fisheries and fur trade, a conflict developed between the French and English; in 1713, Newfoundland, Hudson Bay, and Nova Scotia (Acadia) were lost to England.

Population by Provinces and Territories

Province	1981 (Census)	1991 (March Estimate)
Alberta	2,237,724	2,501,400
British Columbia	2,744,467	3,185,900
Manitoba	1,026,241	1,092,600
New Brunswick	696,403	725,600
Newfoundland	567,681	571,600
Nova Scotia	847,442	897,500
Ontario	8,625,107	9,840,300
Prince Edward Island	122,506	129,900
Quebec	6,438,403	6,811,800
Saskatchewan	968,313	995,300
Northwest Territories	45,471	54,000
Yukon Territory	23,153	26,500
Total	**24,343,181**	**26,832,400**

Source: Statistics Canada.

Canadian Governors General and Prime Ministers Since 1867

Term of Office	Governor General	Term	Prime Minister	Party
1867–1868	Viscount Monck[1]	1867–1873	Sir John A. MacDonald	Conservative
1869–1872	Baron Lisgar	1873–1878	Alexander Mackenzie	Liberal
1872–1878	Earl of Dufferin	1878–1891	Sir John A. MacDonald	Conservative
1878–1883	Marquess of Lorne	1891–1892	Sir John J. C. Abbott	Conservative
1883–1888	Marquess of Lansdowne	1892–1894	Sir John S. D. Thompson	Conservative
1888–1893	Baron Stanley of Preston	1894–1896	Sir Mackenzie Bowell	Conservative
1893–1898	Earl of Aberdeen	1896	Sir Charles Tupper	Conservative
1898–1904	Earl of Minto	1896–1911	Sir Wilfrid Laurier	Liberal
1904–1911	Earl Grey	1911–1917	Sir Robert L. Borden	Conservative
1911–1916	Duke of Connaught	1917–1920	Sir Robert L. Borden	Unionist
1916–1921	Duke of Devonshire	1920–1921	Arthur Meighen	Unionist
1921–1926	Baron Byng of Vimy	1921–1926	W. L. Mackenzie King	Liberal
1926–1931	Viscount Willingdon	1926	Arthur Meighen	Conservative
1931–1935	Earl of Bessborough	1926–1930	W. L. Mackenzie King	Liberal
1935–1940	Baron Tweedsmuir	1930–1935	Richard B. Bennett	Conservative
1940–1946	Earl of Athlone	1935–1948	W. L. Mackenzie King	Liberal
1946–1952	Viscount Alexander	1948–1957	Louis S. St. Laurent	Liberal
1952–1959	Vincent Massey	1957–1963	John G. Diefenbaker	Conservative
1959–1967	George P. Vanier	1963–1968	Lester B. Pearson	Liberal
1967–1973	Roland Michener	1968–1979	Pierre Elliott Trudeau	Liberal
1974–1979	Jules Léger	1979–1980	Charles Joseph Clark	Conservative
1979–1984	Edward R. Schreyer	1980–1984	Pierre Elliott Trudeau	Liberal
1984–1990	Jeanne Sauvé	1984–1984	John Turner	Liberal
1990–	Raymond John Hnatyshyn	1984–	Brian Mulroney	Conservative

1. Became Governor General of British North America in 1861.

During the Seven Years' War (1756–63), England extended its conquest, and the British Maj. Gen. James Wolfe won his famous victory over Gen. Louis Montcalm outside Quebec on Sept. 13, 1759. The Treaty of Paris in 1763 gave England control.

At that time the population of Canada was almost entirely French, but in the next few decades, thousands of British colonists emigrated to Canada from the British Isles and from the American colonies. In 1849, the right of Canada to self-government was recognized. By the British North America Act of 1867, the Dominion of Canada was created through the confederation of Upper and Lower Canada, Nova Scotia, and New Brunswick. Prince Edward Island joined the Dominion in 1873.

In 1869 Canada purchased from the Hudson's Bay Company the vast middle west (Rupert's Land) from which the provinces of Manitoba (1870), Alberta, and Saskatchewan (1905) were later formed. In 1871, British Columbia joined the Dominion. The country was linked from coast to coast in 1885 by the Canadian Pacific Railway.

During the formative years between 1866 and 1896, the Conservative Party, led by Sir John A. MacDonald, governed the country, except during the years 1873–78. In 1896, the Liberal Party took over and, under Sir Wilfrid Laurier, an eminent French Canadian, ruled until 1911.

By the Statute of Westminster in 1931 the British Dominions, including Canada, were formally declared to be partner nations with Britain, "equal in status, in no way subordinate to each other," and bound together only by allegiance to a common Crown.

Newfoundland became Canada's 10th province on March 31, 1949, following a plebiscite. Canada includes two territories—the Yukon Territory, the area north of British Columbia and east of Alaska, and the Northwest Territories, including all of Canada north of 60° north latitude except Yukon and the northernmost sections of Quebec and Newfoundland. This area includes all of the Arctic north of the mainland, Norway having recognized Canadian sovereignty over the Svendrup Islands in the Arctic in 1931.

The Liberal Party, led by William Lyon Mackenzie King, dominated Canadian politics from 1921 until 1957, when it was succeeded by the Progressive Conservatives. The Liberals, under the leadership of Lester B. Pearson, returned to power in 1963. Pearson remained Prime Minister until 1968, when he retired and was replaced by a former law professor, Pierre Elliott Trudeau. Trudeau maintained Canada's defensive alliance with the United States, but began moving toward a more independent policy in world affairs.

Trudeau's election was considered in part a response to the most serious problem confronting the country, the division between French- and English-speaking Canadians, which had led to a separatist movement in the predominantly French province of Quebec. Trudeau, himself a French Canadian, supported programs for bilingualism and an increased measure of provincial autonomy, although he would not tolerate the idea of separatism. In 1974, the provincial government voted to make French the official language of Quebec.

Conflicts over the law establishing French as the dominant language in Quebec, particularly in schooling, kept separatism as a national issue, but by-elections in 1977 produced easy victories for Trudeau's ruling Liberals in four Quebec seats in the national legislature.

Economic problems appeared to take precedence over politics in 1978, as the Sun Life Assurance Company of Canada, the nation's largest insurance firm, announced that it would move its headquarters from Montreal to Toronto. Sun Life was the first business to cite the language law as the reason for its departure.

Despite Trudeau's removal of price and wage controls in 1978, continuing inflation and a high rate of unemployment caused him to delay elections until May 22, 1979. The delay gave Trudeau no advantage—the Progressive Conservatives under Charles Joseph Clark defeated the Liberals everywhere except in Quebec, New Brunswick, and Newfoundland.

Clark took office as the head of Canada's fifth minority government in the last 20 years.

His government collapsed after only six months when a motion to defeat the Tory budget carried by 139–133 on Dec. 13, 1979. On the same day, the Quebec law making French the exclusive official language of the province—an issue which had been expected to provide Clark's first major internal test—was voided by the Canadian Supreme Court.

In national elections Feb. 18, 1980, the resurgent Liberals under Trudeau scored an unexpectedly big victory.

Resolving a dispute that had occupied Trudeau since the beginning of his tenure, Queen Elizabeth II, in Ottawa on April 17, 1982, signed the Constitution Act, cutting the last legal tie between Canada and Britain. Since 1867, the British North America Act required British Parliament approval for any Canadian constitutional change.

The new charter was approved by the federal House of Commons, 246–24, on Dec. 2, 1981, and by a 59–23 vote of the Senate six days later. The Constitution retains Queen Elizabeth as Queen of Canada and keeps Canada's membership in the Commonwealth.

Ending an era, Trudeau retired on June 30, 1984, after 16 years as prime minister, except for the nine-month interruption in 1979–80.

His successor as Liberal Party leader and Prime Minister, John N. Turner, called an early election for a new Parliament after polls showed the Liberals had made a big comeback from the last months of Trudeau's term, despite Canada's continuing recession and 11.2% unemployment, the highest in 40 years.

In the national election on Sept. 4, 1984, the Progressive Conservative Party scored an overwhelming victory, fundamentally changing the country's political landscape. The Conservatives, led by Brian Mulroney, a 45-year-old corporate lawyer, won the highest political majority in Canadian history, Mulroney was sworn in as Canada's 18th Prime Minister on Sept. 17.

The dominant foreign issue was a free trade pact with the U.S., a treaty bitterly opposed by the Liberal and New Democratic parties. The conflict led to elections in Nov. 1988 that solidly re-elected Mulroney and gave him a mandate to proceed with the agreement.

The issue of separatist sentiments in French-speaking Quebec flared up again in 1990 with the failure of the Meech Lake accord. The accord was designed to ease the Quebecers' fear of losing their identity within the English-speaking majority by giving Quebec constitutional status as a "distinct society." The dominant issues during 1991 have been "Whither Canada?" and the continuing effort for a North American free trade zone.

CAPE VERDE

Republic of Cape Verde
President: Antonio Mascarenhas Monteiro (1991)
Premier: Maj. Pedro Pires (1975)

Area: 1,557 sq mi. (4,033 sq km)
Population: (est. mid-1991): 400,000 (average annual rate of natural increase: 3.2%); birth rate: 40/1000; infant mortality rate: 44/1000; density per square mile: 246
Capital (est. 1982): Praia, 37,676
Largest city (est. 1982): Mindelo, 50,000
Monetary unit: Cape Verdean escudo
Language: Portuguese, Criuolo
Religion: Roman Catholic fused with indigenous beliefs
National name: República de Cabo Verde
Literacy rate: 37%
Economic summary: Gross domestic product (1987): $158 million, per capita $494; real growth rate 6.1%. Arable land: 9%. Labor force in agriculture: 57%. Principal agricultural products: bananas, corn, sugar cane, beans. Major industry: fishing, salt mining. Natural resources: salt, siliceous rock. Exports: fish, bananas, salt. Imports: petroleum, foodstuffs, consumer goods, industrial products. Major trading partners: Portugal, Angola, Algeria, Belgium/Luxembourg, Italy, Netherlands, Spain, France, U.S., Germany.

Geography: Cape Verde, only slightly larger than Rhode Island, is an archipelago in the Atlantic 385 miles (620 km) west of Dakar, Senegal.

The islands are divided into two groups: Barlavento in the north, comprising Santo Antão (291 sq mi.; 754 sq km), Boa Vista (240 sq mi.; 622 sq km), São Nicolau (132 sq mi.; 342 sq km), São Vicente (88 sq mi.; 246 sq km), Sal (83 sq mi.; 298 sq km), and Santa Luzia (13 sq mi.; 34 sq km); and Sotavento in the south, consisting of São Tiago (383 sq mi.; 992 sq km), Fogo (184 sq mi.; 477 sq km), Maio (103 sq mi.; 267 sq km), and Brava (25 sq mi.; 65 sq km). The islands are mostly mountainous, with the land deeply scarred by erosion. There is an active volcano on Fogo.

Government. The islands became independent on July 5, 1975, under an agreement negotiated with Portugal in 1974. Elections of January 13, 1991 resulted in the ruling African Party for the Independence of Cape Verde losing its majority in the 79-seat parliament. The big winner was the Movement for Democracy, whose candidate, Antonio Monteiro, won the subsequent presidential election on February 17. These were the first free elections since independence in 1975.

History. Uninhabited upon their discovery in 1456, the Cape Verde islands became part of the Portuguese empire in 1495. A majority of their modern inhabitants are of mixed Portuguese and African ancestry. A coaling station developed during the 19th century on the island of São Vicente has grown in recent years to an oil and gasoline storage depot for ships and aircraft.

CENTRAL AFRICAN REPUBLIC

Head of Government: Gen. André Kolingba (1986)
Area: 241,313 sq mi. (625,000 sq km)
Population (est. mid-1991): 3,000,000 (average annual rate of natural increase: 2.6%); birth rate: 44/1000; infant mortality rate: 141/1000; density per square mile: 12
Capital and largest city (est. 1985): Bangui, 473,000
Monetary unit: Franc CFA
Ethnic groups: Baya, Banda, Sara, Mandjia, M'boum, M'Baka, 6,500 Europeans

Languages: French (official), Sangho, Arabic, Hansa, Swahili
Religions: 24% indigenous beliefs, 50% Protestant and Roman Catholic with animist influence, 15% Muslim, 11% other
National name: République Centrafricaine
Literacy rate: 33%
Economic summary: Gross domestic product (1988 est.): $1.27 billion, per capita $453; real growth rate 2.0%. Arable land: 3%. Principal products: cotton, coffee, peanuts, food crops, livestock. Labor force (1986 est.): 775,413; 85% in agriculture. Major industrial products: timber, textiles, soap, cigarettes, diamonds, processed food, brewed beverages. Natural resources: diamonds, uranium, timber. Exports: diamonds, cotton, timber, coffee. Imports: machinery and electrical equipment, petroleum products, textiles. Major trading partners: France, Japan, U.S., Western Europe, Algeria, Yugoslavia.

Geography. Situated about 500 miles north (805 km) of the equator, the Central African Republic is a landlocked nation bordered by Cameroon, Chad, the Sudan, Zaire, and the Congo. Twice the size of New Mexico, it is covered by tropical forests in the south and semidesert land in the east. The Ubangi and Shari are the largest of many rivers.

Government. On Dec. 4, 1976, the Central African Republic became the Central African Empire. Marshal Jean-Bédel Bokassa, who had ruled the republic since he took power in a military coup Dec. 31, 1965, was declared Emperor Bokassa I. He was overthrown in a coup on Sept. 20, 1979. Former President David Dacko, returned to power and changed the country's name back to the Central African Republic. An army coup on Sept. 1, 1981, deposed Dacko and suspended the Constitution and all political parties. A Military Committee of National Redress was set up to run the country. A new constitution was enacted on Nov. 21, 1986 that extended Kolingba's term another six years and allowed for parliamentary elections in which the Centrafrican Democratic Assembly would be the only party.

History. As the colony of Ubangi-Shari, what is now the Central African Republic was united with Chad in 1905 and joined with Gabon and the Middle Congo in French Equatorial Africa in 1910. After World War II a rebellion in 1946 forced the French to grant self-government. In 1958 the territory voted to become an autonomous republic within the French Community, but on Aug. 13, 1960, President David Dacko proclaimed the republic's independence from France.

Dacko undertook to move the country into Peking's orbit, but was overthrown in a coup on Dec. 31, 1965, by the then Col. Jean-Bédel Bokassa, Army Chief of Staff. In August 1977, the U.S. State Department protested the Emperor's jailing of American and British newsmen.

Politically rather tranquil, relations with Sudan were restored in 1990 after a one-year severance. Falling coffee and timber prices worldwide weakened the economy.

CHAD

Republic of Chad
President: Gen. Idriss Deby (1991)
Prime Minister: Ousmane Gam

Area: 495,752 sq mi. (1,284,000 sq km)
Population (est. mid-1991): 5,100,000 (average annual rate of natural increase, 2.5%); birth rate: 44/1000; infant mortality rate: 127/1000; density per square mile: 10
Capital and largest city (est. 1991): N'Djamena, 500,000
Monetary unit: Franc CFA
Ethnic groups: Baguirmiens, Kanembous, Saras, Massas, Arabs, Toubous, others
Languages: French and Arabic (official), many tribal languages
Religions: Islam, 44%; Christian, 33%; traditional, 23%
National name: République du Tchad
Literacy rate: 25.3%
Economic summary: Gross domestic product (1990): $800 million, per capita $150; real growth rate 3%. Arable land: 2%; principal agricultural products: cotton, cattle, sugar, subsistence crops. Labor force in agriculture: 85%. Major products: livestock and livestock products, beer, food processing, textiles, cigarettes. Natural resources: petroleum, unexploited uranium, kaolin. Exports: cotton, livestock and animal products, fish. Imports: food, motor vehicles and parts, petroleum products, machinery, cement, textiles. Major trading partners: France, Nigeria, U.S., Cameroon.

Geography. A landlocked country in north central Africa, Chad is about 85% the size of Alaska. Its neighbors are Niger, Libya, the Sudan, the Central African Republic, Cameroon, and Nigeria. Lake Chad, from which the country gets its name, lies on the western border with Niger and Nigeria. In the north is a desert that runs into the Sahara.

Government. Hissen Habré was overthrown by Gen. Idriss Deby in December 1990.

History. Chad was absorbed into the colony of French Equatorial Africa, as part of Ubangi-Shari, in 1910. France began the country's development after 1920, when it became a separate colony. In 1946, French Equatorial Africa was admitted to the French Union. By referendum in 1958 the Chad territory became an autonomous republic within the French Union.

A movement led by the first Premier and President, François (later Ngarta) Tombalbaye, achieved complete independence on Aug. 11, 1960.

Tombalbaye was killed in the 1975 coup and was succeeded by Gen. Félix Malloum, who faced a Libyan-financed rebel movement throughout his tenure in office. A ceasefire backed by Libya, Niger, and the Sudan early in 1978 failed to end the fighting.

Nine rival groups meeting in Lagos, Nigeria, in March 1979 agreed to form a provisional government headed by Goukouni Oueddei, a former rebel leader. Fighting broke out again in Chad in March 1980, when Defense Minister Hissen Habré challenged Goukouni and seized the capital. By the year's end, Libyan troops supporting Goukouni recaptured N'djamena, and Libyan President Muammar el-Qaddafi, in January 1981, proposed a merger of Chad with Libya.

The Libyan proposal was rejected and Libyan troops withdrew from Chad but in 1983 poured back into the northern part of the country in support of Goukouni. France, in turn, sent troops into southern Chad in support of Habré.

A Qaddafi-Goukouni break in Nov. 1986 led to the defection of his troops. Government troops then launched an offensive in early 1987 that drove the Libyans out of most of the country.

After the overthrow of Habré's government, Deby, a former defense minister, declared himself president, dissolved the legislature (elected the previous July), and suspended the constitution. He has, however, promised a multiparty democracy despite a widespread belief about Libyan backing.

CHILE

Republic of Chile
President: Patricio Aylwin (1990)
Area: 292,132 sq mi. (756,622 sq km)
Population (est. mid-1991): 13,400,000 (average annual rate of natural increase: 1.8%); birth rate: 23/1000; infant mortality rate: 18.9/1000; density per square mile: 46
Capital: Santiago
Largest cities (est. 1986): Santiago, 4,804,200; Valparaiso, 277,900; Concepción, 292,700; Antofagasta, 203,100; Talcahuano, 229,500; Temuco, 215,400
Monetary unit: Peso
Language: Spanish
Religion: Roman Catholic, 89%; Protestant, 11%; small Jewish and Muslim populations.
National name: República de Chile
Literacy rate: 94%
Economic summary: Gross domestic product (1990): $27.8 billion; $2,111 per capita; 2.1% real growth rate. Arable land: 7%. Principal products: wheat, corn, sugar beets, vegetables, wine, livestock. Labor force: 31.3% in industry. Major industrial products: processed fish, iron and steel, pulp, paper. Natural resources: copper, timber, iron ore, nitrates. Exports: copper, iron ore, paper and wood products, fruits. Imports: wheat, vehicles, petroleum, capital goods, spare parts, raw materials. Major trading partners: U.S., Japan, European Community, Brazil.

Geography. Situated south of Peru and west of Bolivia and Argentina, Chile fills a narrow 1,800-mile (2,897 km) strip between the Andes and the Pacific. Its area is nearly twice that of Montana.

One third of Chile is covered by the towering ranges of the Andes. In the north is the mineral-rich Atacama Desert, between the coastal mountains and the Andes. In the center is a 700-mile-long (1,127 km) valley, thickly populated, between the Andes and the coastal plateau. In the south, the Andes border on the ocean.

At the southern tip of Chile's mainland is Punta Arenas, the southernmost city in the world, and beyond that lies the Strait of Magellan and Tierra del Fuego, an island divided between Chile and Argentina. The southernmost point of South America is Cape Horn, a 1,390-foot (424-m) rock on Horn Island in the Wollaston group, which belongs to Chile. Chile also claims sovereignty over 482,628 sq mi (1,250,000 sq km) of Antarctic territory.

The Juan Fernández Islands, in the South Pacific about 400 miles (644 km) west of the mainland, and Easter Island, about 2,000 miles (3,219 km) west, are Chilean possessions.

Government. Under the 1980 Constitution, the President serves an eight-year term (with the exception of the 1990–1994 term). There is a bicameral legislature which opened its first session in 1990.

History. Chile was originally under the control of the Incas in the north and the fierce Araucanian people in the south. In 1541, a Spaniard, Pedro de Valdivia, founded Santiago. Chile won its independence from Spain in 1818 under Bernardo O'Higgins and an Argentinian, José de San Martin. O'Higgins, dictator until 1823, laid the foundations of the modern state with a two-party system and a centralized government.

The dictator from 1830 to 1837, Diego Portales, fought a war with Peru in 1836–39 that expanded Chilean territory. The Conservatives were in power from 1831 to 1861. Then the Liberals, winning a share of power for the next 30 years, disestablished the church and limited presidential power. Chile fought the War of the Pacific with Peru and Bolivia from 1879 to 1883, winning Antofagasta, Bolivia's only outlet to the sea, and extensive areas from Peru. A revolt in 1890 led by Jorge Montt overthrew, in 1891, José Balmaceda and established a parliamentary dictatorship that existed until a new Constitution was adopted in 1925. Industrialization began before World War I and led to the formation of Marxist groups.

Juan Antonio Ríos, President during World War II, was originally pro-Nazi but in 1944 led his country into the war on the side of the U.S.

A small abortive army uprising in 1969 raised fear of military intervention to prevent a Marxist, Salvador Allende Gossens, from taking office after his election to the presidency on Sept. 4, 1970. Dr. Allende was the first President in a non-Communist country freely elected on a Marxist-Leninist program.

Allende quickly established relations with Cuba and the People's Republic of China and nationalized several American companies.

Allende's overthrow and death in an army assault on the presidential palace in September 1973 ended a 46-year era of constitutional government in Chile.

The takeover was led by a four-man junta headed by Army Chief of Staff Augusto Pinochet Ugarte, who assumed the office of President.

Committed to "exterminate Marxism," the junta embarked on a right-wing dictatorship. It suspended parliament, banned political activity, and broke relations with Cuba.

In 1977, Pinochet, in a speech marking his fourth year in power, promised elections by 1985 if conditions warranted. Earlier, he had abolished DINA, the secret police, and decreed an amnesty for political prisoners.

Pinochet was inaugurated on March 11, 1981, for an eight-year term as President, at the end of which, according to the Constitution adopted six months earlier, the junta would nominate a civilian as successor, although Pinochet announced that he might serve another eight-year term. He stepped down in January 1990 in favor of Patricio Aylwin who was elected Dec. 1989 as the head of a 17-party coalition. President Aylwin in April 1990 charged a commission to examine evidence concerning the disappearance of political prisoners during the early years of Pinochet's rule. In September 1990 the opposition Renovacion Nacional party named a shadow cabinet in a move interpreted as a sign of further democratic consolidation.

CHINA

People's Republic of China
President: Gen. Yang Shangkun (1988)
Premier: Li Peng (1987)
Area: 3,691,521 sq mi. (9,561,000 sq km)[1]
Population (est. mid-1991): 1,151,300,000 (average rate of natural increase: 1.4%); birth rate: 21/1000; infant mortality rate: 33/1000; density per square mile: 311
Capital: Beijing
Largest cities (est. 1983): Shanghai, 11,940,000; Beijing (Peking) 9,330,000; Tianjin (Tientsin) 7,850,000; Canton, 6,840,000; Wuhan, 5,940,000; Shenyang (Mukden), 5,210,000; Nanjing (Nanking), 4,560,000; Chongqing (Chungking), 3,890,000; Harbin; 3,730,000
Monetary unit: Yuan
Languages: Chinese, Mandarin, also local dialects
Religions: Officially atheist but traditional religion contains elements of Confucianism, Taoism, Buddhism
National name: Zhonghua Renmin Gongheguo
Literacy rate: over 75%
Economic summary: Gross national product (1988); $350 billion; $320 per capita; 11% real growth rate. Arable land: 10%. Principal products: rice, wheat, grains, cotton. Labor force: 513,000,000; 61.1% in agriculture. Major industrial products: iron and steel, textiles, armaments, petroleum. Natural resources: coal, natural gas, limestone, marble, metals, hydropower potential. Exports: agricultural products, oil, minerals, metals, manufactured goods. Imports: grains, chemical fertilizer, steel, industrial raw materials, machinery and equipment. Major trading partners: Japan, Hong Kong, U.S., Germany, Singapore, U.S.S.R.

1. Including Manchuria and Tibet.

Geography. China, which occupies the eastern part of Asia, is slightly larger in area than the U.S. Its coastline is roughly a semicircle. The greater part of the country is mountainous, and only in the lower reaches of the Yellow and Yangtze Rivers are there extensive low plains.

The principal mountain ranges are the Tien Shan, to the northwest; the Kunlun chain, running south of the Taklimakan and Gobi Deserts; and the Trans-Himalaya, connecting the Kunlun with the borders of China and Tibet. Manchuria is largely an undulating plain connected with the north China plain by a narrow lowland corridor. Inner Mongolia contains the relatively fertile southern and eastern portions of the Gobi. The large island of Hainan (13,500 sq mi.; 34,380 sq km) lies off the southern coast.

Hydrographically, China proper consists of three great river systems. The northern part of the country is drained by the Yellow River (Huang Ho), 2,109 miles long (5,464 km) and mostly unnavigable. The central part is drained by the Chang Jiang (Yangtze Kiang), the third longest river in the world 2,432 miles (6,300 km). The Zhujiang (Si Kiang) in the south is 848 miles long (2,197 km) and navigable for a considerable distance. In addition, the Amur (1,144 sq mi.; 2,965 km) forms part of the northeastern boundary.

Government. With 2,978 deputies, elected for four-year terms by universal suffrage, the National People's Congress is the chief legislative organ. A State Council has the executive authority. The Congress elects the Premier and Deputy Premiers. All ministries are under the State Council, headed by the Premier.

The Communist Party controls the government.

History. By 2000 B.C. the Chinese were living in the Huang Ho basin, and they had achieved an advanced stage of civilization by 1200 B.C. The great philosophers Lao-tse, Confucius Mo Ti, and Mencius lived during the Chou dynasty (1122–249 B.C.). The warring feudal states were first united under Emperor Ch'in Shih Huang Ti, during whose reign (246–210 B.C.) work was begun on the Great Wall. Under the Han dynasty (206 B.C.–A.D. 220), China prospered and traded with the West.

In the T'ang dynasty (618–907), often called the golden age of Chinese history, painting, sculpture, and poetry flourished, and printing made its earliest known appearance.

The Mings, last of the native rulers (1368–1644), overthrew the Mongol, or Yuan, dynasty (1280–1368) established by Kublai Khan. The Mings in turn were overthrown in 1644 by invaders from the north, the Manchus.

China closely restricted foreign activities, and by the end of the 18th century only Canton and the Portuguese port of Macao were open to European merchants. Following the Anglo-Chinese War of 1839–42, however, several treaty ports were opened, and Hong Kong was ceded to Britain. Treaties signed after further hostilities (1856–60) weakened Chinese sovereignty and removed foreigners from Chinese jurisdiction. The disastrous Chinese-Japanese War of 1894–95 was followed by a scramble for Chinese concessions by European powers, leading to the Boxer Rebellion (1900), suppressed by an international force.

The death of the Empress Dowager Tzu Hsi in 1908 and the accession of the infant Emperor Hsüan T'ung (Pu-Yi) were followed by a nation-wide rebellion led by Dr. Sun Yat-sen, who became first President of the Provisional Chinese Republic in 1911. The Manchus abdicated on Feb. 12, 1912. Dr. Sun resigned in favor of Yuan Shih-k'ai, who suppressed the republicans but was forced by a serious rising in 1915–16 to abandon his intention of declaring himself Emperor. Yuan's death in June 1916 was followed by years of civil war between rival militarists and Dr. Sun's republicans.

Nationalist forces, led by Gen. Chiang Kai-shek and with the advice of Communist experts, soon occupied most of China, setting up a Kuomintang regime in 1928. Internal strife continued, however, and Chiang broke with the Communists.

An alleged explosion on the South Manchurian Railway on Sept. 18, 1931, brought invasion of Manchuria by Japanese forces, who installed the last Manchu Emperor, Henry Pu-Yi, as nominal ruler of the puppet state of "Manchukuo." Japanese efforts to take China's northern provinces in July 1937 were resisted by Chiang, who meanwhile had succeeded in uniting most of China behind him. Within two years, however, Japan seized most of the ports and railways. The Kuomintang government retreated first to Hankow and then to Chungking, while the Japanese set up a puppet government at Nanking headed by Wang Jingwei.

Japan's surrender in 1945 touched off civil war between Nationalist forces under Chiang and Communist forces led by Mao Zedong, the party chairman. Despite U.S. aid, the Chiang forces were overcome by the Maoists, backed by the Soviet bloc, and were expelled from the mainland. The Mao regime, established in Peking as the new capital, proclaimed the People's Republic of China on Oct. 1, 1949, with Zhou Enlai as Premier.

After the Korean War began in June 1950, China led the Communist bloc in supporting North Korea, and on Nov. 26, 1950, the Mao regime intervened openly.

Provinces and Regions of China

Name	Area (sq mi.)	Area (sq km)	Capital
Provinces			
Anhui (Anhwei)	54,015	139,900	Hefei (Hofei)
Fujian (Fukien)	47,529	123,100	Fuzhou (Fukien)
Gansu (Kansu)	137,104	355,100	Lanzhou (Lanchow)
Guangdong (Kwangtung)	76,100	197,100	Canton
Guizhou (Kweichow)	67,181	174,000	Guiyang (Kweiyang)
Hainan	13,200	34,300	Haikou
Hebei (Hopei)	81,479	211,030	Shijiazhuang (Shitikiachwang)
Heilongjiang (Heilungkiang)[1]	178,996	463,600	Harbin
Henan (Honan)	64,479	167,000	Zhengzhou (Chengchow)
Hubei (Hupeh)	72,394	187,500	Wuhan
Hunan	81,274	210,500	Changsha
Jiangsu (Kiangsu)	40,927	106,000	Nanjing (Nanking)
Jiangxi (Kiangsi)	63,629	164,800	Nanchang
Jilin (Kirin)[1]	72,201	187,000	Changchun
Liaoning[1]	53,301	138,050	Shenyang
Quinghai (Chinghai)	278,378	721,000	Xining (Sining)
Shaanxi (Shensi)	75,598	195,800	Xian (Sian)
Shandong (Shantung)	59,189	153,300	Jinan (Tsinan)
Shanxi (Shansi)	60,656	157,100	Taiyuan
Sichuan (Szechwan)	219,691	569,000	Chengdu (Chengtu)
Yunnan	168,417	436,200	Kunming
Zhejiang (Chekiang)	39,305	101,800	Hangzhou (Hangchow)
Autonomous Region			
Guangxi Zhuang (Kwangsi Chuang)	85,096	220,400	Nanning
Nei Monggol (Inner Mongolia)[1]	454,633	1,177,500	Hohhot (Huhehot)
Ningxia Hui	30,039	77,800	Yinchuan (Yinchwan)
Xinjiang Uygur (Sinkiang Uighur)[1]	635,829	1,646,800	Urumqi (Urumchi)
Xizang (Tibet)	471,660	1,221,600	Lhasa

1. Together constitute (with Taiwan) what has been traditionally known as Outer China, the remaining territory forming the historical China Proper. NOTE: Names are in Pinyin, with conventional spelling in parentheses.

In 1958, Mao undertook the "Great Leap Forward" campaign, which combined the establishment of rural communes with a crash program of village industrialization. These efforts also failed, causing Mao to lose influence to Liu Shaoqi, who became President in 1959, to Premier Zhou, and to Party Secretary Deng Xiaoping.

China exploded its first atomic (fission) bomb in 1964 and produced a fusion bomb in 1967.

Mao moved to Shanghai, and from that base he and his supporters waged what they called a Cultural Revolution. In the spring of 1966 the Mao group formed Red Guard units dominated by youths and students, closing the schools to free the students for agitation.

The Red Guards campaigned against "old ideas, old culture, old habits, and old customs." Often they were no more than uncontrolled mobs, and brutality was frequent. Early in 1967 efforts were made to restore control. The Red Guards were urged to return home. Schools started opening.

Persistent overtures by the Nixon Administration resulted in the dramatic announcement in July that Henry Kissinger, President Richard M. Nixon's national security adviser, had secretly visited Peking and reached agreement on a visit by the President to China.

The movement toward reconciliation, which signaled the end of the U.S. containment policy toward China, provided irresistible momentum for Chinese admission to the U.N. Despite U.S. opposition to expelling Taiwan (Nationalist China), the world body overwhelmingly ousted Chiang in seating Peking.

President Nixon went to Peking for a week early in 1972, meeting Mao as well as Zhou. The summit ended with a historic communiqué on February 28, in which both nations promised to work toward improved relations.

In 1973, the U.S. and China agreed to set up "liaison offices" in each other's capitals, which constituted de facto diplomatic relations. Full diplomatic relations were barred by China as long as the U.S. continued to recognize Nationalist China.

On Jan. 8, 1976, Zhou died. His successor, Vice Premier Deng Xiaoping was supplanted within a month by Hua Guofeng, former Minister of Public Security. Hua became permanent Premier in April. In October he was named successor to Mao as Chairman of the Communist Party.

After Mao died on Sept. 10, a campaign against his widow, Jiang Qing, and three of her "radical" colleagues began. The "Gang of Four" was denounced for having undermined the party, the government, and the economy.

Jiang was brought to trial in 1980 and sentenced on Jan. 25, 1981, to die within two years unless she showed repentance, in which case she would be imprisoned for life.

At the Central Committee meeting of 1977, Deng was reinstated as Deputy Premier, Chief of Staff of the Army, and member of the Central Committee of the Politburo.

At the same time, Jiang Qing, Wang Hongwen, Zhang Chunqiao, and Yao Wenyuan—the notorious "Gang of Four"—were removed from all official posts and banished from the party.

In May 1978, expulsion of ethnic Chinese by Vietnam produced an open rupture. Peking sided with Cambodia in the border fighting that flared between Vietnam and Cambodia, charging Hanoi with aggression.

On Aug. 12, 1978, China and Japan signed a treaty of peace and friendship. Peking and Washington then announced that they would open full diplomatic relations on Jan. 1, 1979 and the Carter Administration abrogated the Taiwan defense treaty. Deputy Premier Deng sealed the agreement with a visit to the United States that coincided with the opening of embassies in both capitals on March 1.

On Deng's return from the U.S. Chinese troops invaded Vietnam to avenge alleged violations of Chinese territory. The action was seen as a reaction to Vietnam's invasion of Cambodia.

The first People's Congress in five years confirmed Zhao Ziyang, an economic planner, as Premier replacing Hua Guofeng, who had held the post since 1976.

After the Central Committee meeting of June 27–29, 1981, Hu Yaobang, a Deng protégé, was elevated to the party chairmanship, replacing Hua Guofeng. Deng became chairman of the military commission of the central committee, giving him control over the army. The committee's 215 members concluded the session with a statement holding Mao Zedong responsible for the "grave blunder" of the Cultural Revolution.

Under Deng Xiaoping's leadership, meanwhile, China's Communist idealogy was almost totally reinterpreted and sweeping economic changes were set in motion in the early 1980s. The Chinese scrapped the personality cult that idolized Mao Zedong, muted Mao's old call for class struggle and exportation of the Communist revolution, and imported Western technology and management techniques to replace the Marxist tenets that retarded modernization.

Also under Deng's leadership, the Chinese Communists worked out an arrangement with Britain for the future of Hong Kong after 1997. The flag of China will be raised but the territory will retain its present social, economic and legal system.

The removal of Hu Yaobang as party chairman in January 1987 was a sign of a hard-line resurgence. He was replaced by former Premier Zhao Ziyang. Conflict between hard-liners and moderates continued and reached a violent climax in 1989. Student demonstrations calling for accelerated liberalization were crushed by military force in June, resulting in several hundred deaths. This was followed by a purge of moderates, including party leader Zhao Ziyang, who was replaced with Jiang Zemin.

In January 1991 a Chinese court convicted and sentenced eight, including the country's leading human rights advocate, to prison for terms of two to seven years for "counterrevolutionary propaganda and incitement." Two additional dissidents were sentenced to 13 years in prison in connection with the Tiananmen protests. Nevertheless, the National People's Congress in April appointed two new deputy prime ministers Zou Jiahua, generally regarded as hard-line, and Zhu Rongji, regarded as reformist.

COLOMBIA

Republic of Colombia
President: César Gaviria Trujillo (1990)
Population (est. mid-1991): 33,600,000 (average annual rate of natural increase, 2.0%); birth rate: 26/1000;

infant mortality rate: 37/1000; density per square mile: 76
Capital: Bogotá
Largest cities (est. 1985): Bogotá, 4,208,000; Medellín, 2,069,000; Cali, 1,654,000; Baranquilla, 1,120,000; Bucaramanga, 545,000; Cartagena, 530,000
Monetary unit: Peso
Language: Spanish
Religion: 95% Roman Catholic
National name: República de Colombia
Literacy rate (1985): 88%, Indians about 40%
Economic summary: Gross domestic product (1988): $35.4 billion, per capita $1,110; real growth rate 3.7%. Arable land: 4%. Principal products: coffee, bananas, rice, corn, sugar cane, cotton, tobacco, oilseeds. Labor force: 11,000,000; 21% in industry. Major products: textiles, processed food, beverages, chemicals, cement. Natural resources: petroleum, natural gas, coal, iron ore, nickel, gold, silver. Exports: coffee, fuel oil, cotton, bananas. Imports: machinery, paper products, chemical products, metals and metal products, transportation equipment. Major trading partners: U.S., E.C., Japan, Venezuela, Netherlands, Brazil, Sweden.

Geography. Colombia, in the northwestern part of South America, is the only country on that continent that borders on both the Atlantic and Pacific Oceans. It is nearly equal to the combined areas of California and Texas.

Through the western half of the country, three Andean ranges run north and south, merging into one at the Ecuadorean border. The eastern half is a low, jungle-covered plain, drained by spurs of the Amazon and Orinoco, inhabited mostly by isolated, tropical-forest Indian tribes. The fertile plateau and valley of the eastern range are the most densely populated parts of the country.

Government. Colombia's President, who appoints his own Cabinet, serves for a four-year term. The Senate, the upper house of Congress, has 114 members elected for four years by direct vote. The House of Representatives of 199 members is directly elected for four years.

History. Spaniards in 1510 founded Darien, the first permanent European settlement on the American mainland. In 1538 the Spaniards established the colony of New Granada, the area's name until 1861. After a 14-year struggle, in which Simón Bolívar's Venezuelan troops won the battle of Boyacá in Colombia on Aug. 7, 1819, independence was attained in 1824. Bolívar united Colombia, Venezuela, Panama, and Ecuador in the Republic of Greater Colombia (1819–30), but lost Venezuela and Ecuador to separatists. Bolívar's Vice President, Francisco de Paula Santander, founded the Liberal Party as the Federalists while Bolívar established the Conservatives as the Centralists.

Santander's presidency (1832–36) re-established order, but later periods of Liberal dominance (1849–57 and 1861–80), when the Liberals sought to disestablish the Roman Catholic Church, were marked by insurrection and even civil war. Rafael Nuñez, in a 15-year-presidency, restored the power of the central government and the church, which led in 1899 to a bloody civil war and the loss in 1903 of Panama over ratification of a lease to the U.S. of the Canal Zone. For 21 years, until 1930, the Conservatives held power as revolutionary pressures built up.

The Liberal administrations of Enrique Olaya Herrera and Alfonso López (1930–38) were marked by social reforms that failed to solve the country's problems, and in 1946, insurrection and banditry broke out, claiming hundreds of thousands of lives by 1958. Laureano Gómez (1950–53); the Army Chief of Staff, Gen. Gustavo Rojas Pinilla (1953–56), and a military junta (1956–57) sought to curb disorder by repression.

Government efforts to stamp out the Movement of April 19 (M–19), an urban guerrilla organization, intensified in 1981 with the capture of some of the leaders. A general amnesty offered to the organization failed to bring an end to the movement. The Liberals won a solid majority in 1982, but a party split enabled Belisario Betancur Cuartas, the Conservative candidate, to win the presidency on May 31. After his inauguration, he ended the state of siege that had existed almost continuously for 34 years and renewed the general amnesty of 1981.

In an official war against drug trafficking Colombia became a public battleground with bombs, killings and kidnapping. In 1989 a leading presidential candidate, Luis Carlos Galán, was murdered. In an effort to quell the terror President Gaviria proposed lenient punishment in exchange for surrender by the leading drug dealers. In addition in 1991 the constitutional convention voted to ban extradition. In June the most violent trafficker, Pablo Escobar, surrendered.

COMOROS

Federal Islamic Republic of the Comoros
President: Said Mohammed Djohar (1989)
Area: 690 sq mi. (1,787 sq km)
Population (est. 1991): 500,000 (average annual rate of natural increase 3.5%); birth rate: 47/1000; infant mortality rate: 92/1000; density per square mile: 687
Capital and largest city (est. 1980): Moroni (on Grande Comoro), 20,000
Monetary unit: Franc CFA
Languages: Shaafi Islam, Malagasu, French
Religions: Sunni Muslim, 86%; Roman Catholic, 14%.
National name: République Fédéral Islamique des Comores
Literacy rate (1981): 15%
Economic summary: Gross national product (1988 est.): $207 million, per capita $475; real growth rate 0.1%. Arable land: 35%. Labor force: 140,000 (1982); 80% in agriculture. Principal agricultural products: perfume essences, copra, coconuts, cloves, vanilla, cassava, bananas. Major industrial products: perfume distillations. Exports: perfume essences, vanilla, copra, cloves. Imports: foodstuffs, cement, petroleum products, consumer goods. Major trading partners: France, Germany, U.S., Africa, Pakistan.

Geography. The Comoros Islands—Grande Comoro, Anjouan, Mohéli, and Mayotte (which retains ties to France)—are an archipelago of volcanic origin in the Indian Ocean between Mozambique and Madagascar.

Government. Democratic elections were held in March 1990. The interim president Said Djohar won from among a field of eight candidates. The constitution dates from October 1, 1978, and the country is an Islamic republic with a 42-member unicameral legislature.

History. Under French rule since 1886, the Comoros declared themselves independent July 6, 1975. However, Mayotte, with a Christian majority, voted against joining the other, mainly Islamic, islands, in the move to independence and remains French.

A month after independence, Justice Minister Ali Soilih staged a coup with the help of mercenaries, overthrowing the new nation's first president, Ahmed Abdallah. He was overthrown on May 13, 1978, when a small boatload of French mercenaries, some of whom had aided him three years earlier, seized government headquarters. These mercenaries assassinated Abdallah in a coup attempt in 1989. They were forced to leave by French military pressure.

CONGO

Republic of the Congo
President: Col. Denis Sassou-Neguessou (1979)
Prime Minister: Pierre Moussa (1990)
Area: 132,046 sq mi. (342,000 sq km)
Population (est. mid-1991): 2,300,000 (average annual rate of natural increase: 3.0%); birth rate: 43/1000; infant mortality rate: 112/1000. Density per sq mile: 17
Capital and largest city (est. 1984): Brazzaville, 595,102
Monetary unit: Franc CFA
Ethnic groups: About 15 Bantu groups, Europeans
Languages: French, Lingala, Kikongo, others
Religions: 50% Christian, 48% animist, 2% Muslim
National name: République Populaire du Congo
Literacy rate: 62.9%
Economic summary: Gross domestic product (1988 est.): $2.2 billion, per capita $1,000; real growth rate –3%. Arable land: 2%. Principal agricultural products: cassava, rice, corn, peanuts, coffee, cocoa. Labor force: 79,100; 75% in agriculture. Major industrial products: crude oil, cigarettes, cement, beverages, milled sugar. Natural resources: wood, potash, petroleum, natural gas. Exports: oil, lumber, tobacco, wood, coffee. Imports: foodstuffs, consumer goods, intermediate manufactures, capital equipment. Major trading partners: France, U.S., Italy, Spain, Brazil, Germany.

Geography. The Congo is situated in west Central Africa astride the Equator. It borders on Gabon, Cameroon, the Central African Republic, Zaire, and the Angola exclave of Cabinda, with a short stretch of coast on the South Atlantic. Its area is nearly three times that of Pennsylvania.

Most of the inland is tropical rain forest, drained by tributaries of the Zaire (Congo) River, which flows south along the eastern border with Zaire to Stanley Pool. The narrow coastal plain rises to highlands separated from the inland plateaus by the 200-mile-wide Niari River Valley, which gives passage to the coast.

Government. Since the coup of September 1968 the country has been governed by a military regime. The Congolese Labor Party is the only party.

History. The inhabitants of the former French Congo, mainly Bantu peoples with Pygmies in the north, were subjects of several kingdoms in earlier times.

The Frenchman Pierre Savorgnan de Brazza signed a treaty with Makoko, ruler of the Bateke people, in 1880, which established French control. The area, with Gabon and Ubangi-Shari, was constituted the colony of French Equatorial Africa in 1910. It joined Chad in supporting the Free French cause in World War II. The Congo proclaimed its independence without leaving the French Community in 1960.

Maj. Marien Ngouabi, head of the National Council of the Revolution, took power as president on Jan. 1, 1969. He was sworn in for a second five-year term in 1975. A visit to Moscow by Ngouabi in March ended with the signing of a Soviet-Congolese economic and technical aid pact.

A four-man commando squad assassinated Ngouabi in Brazzaville on March 18, 1977.

Col. Joachim Yhombi-Opango, Army Chief of Staff, assumed the presidency on April 4. In June, the new government agreed to resume diplomatic relations with the U.S., ending a 12-year rift. Yombhi-Opango resigned on Feb. 4, 1979, and was replaced by Col. Denis Sassou-Neguessou.

In July 1990 the leaders of the ruling party voted to end the one-party system. A national political conference, hailed as a model for sub-Saharan Africa, in 1991 renounced Marxism, rewrote the constitution and scheduled the country's first free elections for 1992.

Except for the military dictatorship of Tomás Guardia from 1870 to 1882, Costa Rica has enjoyed one of the most democratic governments in Latin America.

Rodrigo Carazo Odio, leader of a four-party coalition called the Unity Party, won the presidency in February 1978. His tenure was marked by a disastrous decline in the economy. Luis Alberto Monge Alvarez, a former union organizer and cofounder of the National Liberation Party, swept to victory in the Feb. 7, 1982, national elections.

On Feb. 2, 1986, Oscar Arias Sanchez won the national elections on a neutralist platform. Arias initiated a policy of preventing contra usage of Costa Rican territory. Rafael Calderón won the presidential election of February 4, 1990 with 51% of the vote, his party winning 29 seats in the Assembly. Calderón promised to continue the economic policies of the previous administration.

COSTA RICA

Republic of Costa Rica
President: Rafael Calderón Fournier (1990)
Area: 19,652 sq mi. (50,898 sq km)
Population (est. mid-1991): 3,100,000 (average annual rate of natural increase: 2.4%); birth rate: 28/1000; infant mortality rate: 13.9/1000; density per square mile: 159
Capital and largest city (est. 1984): San José, 278,500
Monetary unit: Colón
Language: Spanish
Religion: 95% Roman Catholic
National name: República de Costa Rica
Literacy rate (1984): 93%
Economic summary: Gross domestic product (1988): $4.7 billion, per capita $1,630; real growth rate 3.8%. Arable land: 6%. Principal products: bananas, coffee, sugar cane, rice, corn, livestock. Labor force: 868,300; 35.1% in industry and commerce. Major products: processed foods, textiles and clothing, construction materials, fertilizer. Natural resource: hydropower potential. Exports: coffee, bananas, beef, sugar, cocoa. Imports: machinery, chemicals, foodstuffs, fuels, fertilizer. Major trading partners: U.S., Central American countries, Germany, Japan, United Kingdom.

Geography. This Central American country lies between Nicaragua to the north and Panama to the south. Its area slightly exceeds that of Vermont and New Hampshire combined.

Most of Costa Rica is tableland, from 3,000 to 6,000 feet (914 to 1,829 m) above sea level. Cocos Island (10 sq mi.; 26 sq km), about 300 miles (483 km) off the Pacific Coast, is under Costa Rican sovereignty.

Government. Under the 1949 Constitution, the president and the one-house Legislative Assembly of 57 members are elected for terms of four years.

The army was abolished in 1949. There is a civil guard and a rural guard.

History. Costa Rica was inhabited by 25,000 Indians when Columbus discovered it and probably named it in 1502. Few of the Indians survived the Spanish conquest, which began in 1563. The region was administered as a Spanish province. Costa Rica achieved independence in 1821 but was absorbed for two years by Agustín de Iturbide in his Mexican Empire. It was established as a republic in 1848.

COTE D'IVOIRE

Republic of Côte d'Ivoire
President: Félix Houphouët-Boigny (1960)
Area: 124,502 sq mi. (322,462 sq km)
Population (est. mid-1991): 12,500,000 (average annual rate of natural increase: 3.5%); birth rate: 50/1000; infant mortality rate: 96/1000; density per square mile: 100
Capital: Yamoussoukro[1]
Monetary unit: Franc CFA
Ethnic groups: 60 different groups: principals are Baoule, Bete, Senoufou, Malinke, Agni
Languages: French and African languages (Diaula esp.)
Religions: 63% indigenous, 12% Christian, 25% Islam
National name: République de la Côte d'Ivoire
Literacy rate: 42.7%
Economic summary: Gross domestic product (1988): $10 billion, per capita $900; real growth rate –6.4%. Arable land: 9%; Labor force: 5,718,000; over 85% in agriculture. Principal products: coffee, cocoa, corn, beans, timber. Major industrial products: food, wood, refined oil, textiles, fertilizer. Natural resources: diamonds, iron ore, crude oil, manganese, cobalt, bauxite, copper. Exports: coffee, cocoa, tropical woods. Imports: raw materials, consumer goods, fuels. Major trading partners: France, U.S., Western European countries, Nigeria.

1. Not recognized by U.S. which recognizes Abidjan.

Geography. Côte d'Ivoire, in western Africa on the Gulf of Guinea, is a little larger than New Mexico. Its neighbors are Liberia, Guinea, Mali, Burkina Faso, and Ghana.

The country consists of a coastal strip in the south, dense forests in the interior, and savannas in the north. Rainfall is heavy, especially along the coast.

Government. The government is headed by a President who is elected every five years by popular vote, together with a National Assembly of 175 members.

History. Côte d'Ivoire attracted both French and Portuguese merchants in the 15th century. French traders set up establishments early in the 19th century, and in 1842, the French obtained territorial concessions from local tribes, gradually extending their influence along the coast and inland. The area was organized as a territory in 1893, became an autonomous republic in the French Union after World War II, and achieved independence on Aug. 7, 1960.

Côte d'Ivoire formed a customs union in 1959 with Dahomey (Benin), Niger, and Burkina Faso.

Falling cocoa and coffee prices made this nation the largest per capita debtor in Africa. Massive protests by students, farmers and professionals forced the president to legalize opposition parties and hold the first contested presidential election. In October 1990 Houphouët-Boigny won 81% of the vote. In the first multiparty legislative elections in November the president's Democratic Party won 163 of the 175 seats.

CUBA

Republic of Cuba
President: Fidel Castro Ruz (1976)
Area: 44,218 sq mi. (114,524 sq km)
Population (est. mid-1991): 10,700,000 (average annual rate of natural increase: 1.1%); birth rate: 18/1000; infant mortality rate: 10.7/1000; density per square mile: 243
Capital: Havana
Largest cities (est. 1986): Havana, 2,013,746; Santiago de Cuba, 358,764; Camaguëy, 260,782; Holguin, 194,728; Santa Clara, 178,278
Monetary unit: Peso
Language: Spanish
Religion: at least 85% nominally Roman Catholic before Castro assumed power
National name: República de Cuba
Literacy rate: 98.5%
Economic summary: Gross national product (1989 est.): $20.9 billion, per capita $2,000; real growth rate –1%. Arable land: 23%. Principal products: sugar, tobacco, coffee, rice, fruits. Labor force: 3,300,000; 29% in industry. Major products: processed sugar and tobacco, refined oil products, textiles, chemicals, paper and wood products, metals, consumer products. Natural resources: metals, primarily nickel, timber. Exports: coffee, sugar, nickel, shellfish, tobacco. Imports: capital goods, industrial raw materials, petroleum, foodstuffs. Major trading partners: U.S.S.R., Eastern European countries, China.

Geography. The largest island of the West Indies group (equal in area to Pennsylvania), Cuba is also the westernmost—just west of Hispaniola (Haiti and the Dominican Republic), and 90 miles (145 km) south of Key West, Fla., at the entrance to the Gulf of Mexico.

The island is mountainous in the southeast and south central area (Sierra Maestra). Elsewhere it is flat or rolling.

Government. Since 1976, elections have been held every five years to elect the National Assembly, which in turn elects the 31-member Council of States, its President, First Vice-President, five Vice-Presidents, and Secretary. Fidel Castro is President of the Council of State and of the government and First Secretary of the Communist Party of Cuba, the only political party.

History. Arawak Indians inhabiting Cuba when Columbus discovered the island in 1492 died off from diseases brought by sailors and settlers. By 1511, Spaniards under Diego Velásquez were founding settlements that served as bases for Spanish exploration. Cuba soon after served as an assembly point for treasure looted by the conquistadores, attracting French and English pirates.

Black slaves and free laborers were imported to work sugar and tobacco plantations, and waves of chiefly Spanish immigrants maintained a European character in the island's culture. Early slave rebellions and conflicts between colonials and Spanish rulers laid the foundation for an independence movement that turned into open warfare from 1867 to 1878. The poet, José Marti, in 1895 led the struggle that finally ended Spanish rule, thanks largely to U.S. intervention in 1898 after the sinking of the battleship *Maine* in Havana harbor.

A treaty in 1899 made Cuba an independent republic under U.S. protection. The U.S. occupation, which ended in 1902, suppressed yellow fever and brought large American investment. From 1906 to 1909, Washington invoked the Platt Amendment to the treaty, which gave it the right to intervene in order to suppress any revolt. U.S. troops came back in 1912 and again in 1917 to restore order. The Platt Amendment was abrogated in 1934.

Fulgencio Batista, an army sergeant, led a revolt in 1934 that overthrew the regime of President Gerado Machado.

Batista's Cuba was a police state. Corrupt officials took payoffs from American gamblers who operated casinos, demanded bribes from Cubans for various public services and enriched themselves with raids on the public treasury. Dissenters were murdered and their bodies dumped in gutters.

Fidel Castro Ruz, a hulking, bearded attorney in his 30s, landed in Cuba on Christmas Day 1956 with a band of 12 fellow revolutionaries, evaded Batista's soldiers, and set up headquarters in the jungled hills of the Sierra Maestra range. By 1958 his force had grown to about 2,000 guerrillas, for the most part young and middle class. Castro's brother, Raul, and Ernesto (Ché) Guevara, an Argentine physician, were his top lieutenants. Businessmen and landowners who opposed the Batista regime gave financial support to the rebels. The United States, meanwhile, cut off arms shipments to Batista's army.

The beginning of the end for Batista came when the rebels routed 3,000 government troops and captured Santa Clara, capital of Las Villas province 150 miles from Havana, and a trainload of Batista reinforcements refused to get out of their railroad cars. On New Year's Day 1959, Batista flew to exile in the Dominican Republic and Castro took over the government. Crowds cheered the revolutionaries on their seven-day march to the capital.

The United States initially welcomed what looked like the prospect for a democratic Cuba, but a rude awakening came within a few months when Castro established military tribunals for political opponents, jailed hundreds, and began to veer leftward. Castro disavowed Cuba's 1952 military pact with the United States. He confiscated U.S. investments in banks and industries and seized large U.S. landholdings, turning them first into collective farms and then into Soviet-type state farms. The United States broke relations with Cuba on Jan. 3, 1961. Castro thereupon forged an alliance with the Soviet Union.

From the ranks of the Cuban exiles who had fled to the United States, the Central Intelligence Agency recruited and trained an expeditionary force, numbering less than 2,000 men, to invade Cuba, with the expectation that the invasion would spark an uprising of the Cuban populace against Castro. The invasion was planned under the Eisenhower administration and President John F. Kennedy gave the go-ahead for it in the first months of his administration, but rejected a CIA proposal for U.S. planes to provide air support. The landing at the Bay of Pigs on April 17, 1961, was a fiasco. Not only did the invaders fail to receive any support from the populace, but Castro's tanks and artillery made short work of the small force.

A Soviet attempt to change the global power balance by installing in Cuba medium-range missiles—capable of striking targets in the United States with nuclear warheads—provoked a crisis between the superpowers in 1962 that had the potential of touching off World War III. After a visit to Moscow by Cuba's war minister, Raul Castro, work began secretly on the missile launching sites.

Denouncing the Soviets for "deliberate deception," President Kennedy on Oct. 22 announced that the U.S. navy would enforce a "quarantine" of shipping to Cuba and search Soviet bloc ships to prevent the missiles themselves from reaching the island. After six days of tough public statements on both sides and secret diplomacy, Soviet Premier Nikita Khrushchev on Oct. 28 ordered the missile sites dismantled, crated and shipped back to the Soviet Union, in return for a U.S. pledge not to attack Cuba. Limited diplomatic ties were re-established on Sept. 1, 1977.

Emigration increased dramatically after April 1, 1980, when Castro, irritated by the granting of asylum to would-be refugees by the Peruvian embassy in Havana, removed guards and allowed 10,000 Cubans to swarm into the embassy grounds.

As an airlift began taking the refugees to Costa Rica, Castro opened the port of Mariel to a "freedom flotilla" of ships and yachts from the United States, many of them owned or chartered by Cuban-Americans to bring out relatives. More than 125,000 Cubans poured out of Mariel in a mass exodus. It wasn't until after they had reached the United States that it was discovered that the regime had opened prisons and mental hospitals to permit criminals, homosexuals and others unwanted in Cuba to join the refugees.

For most of President Ronald Reagan's first term, U.S.-Cuban relations were frozen, with Secretary of State Alexander Haig calling Havana the "source" of troubles in Central America. But late in 1984, an agreement was reached between the two countries. Cuba would take back more than 2,700 Cubans who had come to the United States in the Mariel exodus but were not eligible to stay in the country under U.S. immigration law because of criminal or psychiatric disqualification. The United States, in exchange, would reinstitute regular immigration for Cubans to the United States. Castro cancelled it when the U.S. began the Radio Marti broadcasts in May 1985 to bring a non-Communist view to the Cuban people.

In the face of sweeping changes in Eastern Europe and the Soviet Union itself, Cuba has reaffirmed its adherence to Marxism-Leninism. Its economy, furthermore, already under strain, remains heavily indebted to continuing Soviet aid. The last of the Cuban troops left Angola in May 1991, thereby ending a presence begun in 1975 and costing an official count of 2,100 Cuban lives.

CYPRUS

Republic of Cyprus
President: Dr. George Vassiliou (1988)
Area: 3,572 sq mi (9,251 sq km)
Population (est. mid-1991): 700,000 (average annual rate of natural increase: 1.0%); birth rate: 18/1000; infant mortality rate: 11/1000; density per square mile: 200
Capital and largest city: Nicosia, 123,298

Monetary unit: Cyprus pound
Languages: Greek, Turkish, English
Religions: Greek Orthodox, 80%; Islam, 18%; Maronite Latin, 2%
National name: Kypriaki Dimokratia—Kibris Cumhuriyeti
Member of Commonwealth of Nations
Literacy rate (1981): 99%
Economic summary: Gross domestic product (1990 est.): $5.2 billion, per capita $9,000; real growth rate 6.9%. Arable land: 40%. Principal products: vine products, citrus, potatoes, other vegetables. Labor force: 251,406 (in Greek area); 33% in industry. Major products: beverages, footwear, clothing, cement, asbestos mining. Natural resources: copper, asbestos, gypsum, timber, marble, clay, salt. Exports: citrus, potatoes, grapes, wine, cement, clothing. Imports: consumer goods, petroleum and lubricants, food and feed grains, machinery. Major trading partners: U.K., Middle East, North Africa, E.C. (61% exports), U.S., Japan

Geography. The third largest island in the Mediterranean (one and one half times the size of Delaware), Cyprus lies off the southern coast of Turkey and the western shore of Syria. Most of the country consists of a wide plain lying between two mountain ranges that cross the island. The highest peak is Mount Olympus at 6,406 feet (1,953 m).

Government. Under the republic's Constitution, for the protection of the Turkish minority the vice president as well as three of the 10 Cabinet ministers must be from the Turkish community, while the House of Representatives is elected by each community separately, 70% Greek Cypriote and 30% Turkish Cypriote representatives.

The Greek and Turkish communities are self-governing in questions of religion, education, and culture. Other governmental matters are under the jurisdiction of the central government. Each community is entitled to a Communal Chamber.

The Greek Communal Chamber, which had 23 members, was abolished in 1965 and its function was absorbed by the Ministry of Education. The Turkish Communal Chamber, however, has continued to function.

History. Cyprus was the site of early Phoenician and Greek colonies. For centuries its rule passed through many hands. It fell to the Turks in 1571, and a large Turkish colony settled on the island.

In World War I, on the outbreak of hostilities with Turkey, Britain annexed the island. It was declared a crown colony in 1925.

For centuries the Greek population, regarding Greece as its mother country, has sought self-determination and reunion with it *(enosis)*. The resulting quarrel with Turkey threatened NATO. Cyprus became an independent nation on Aug. 16, 1960, with Britain, Greece, and Turkey as guarantor powers.

Archbishop Makarios, president since 1959, was overthrown July 15, 1974, by a military coup led by the Cypriot National Guard. The new regime named Nikos Giorgiades Sampson as president and Bishop Gennadios as head of the Cypriot Church to replace Makarios. The rebels were led by rightist Greek officers who supported *enosis*.

Diplomacy failed to resolve the crisis. Turkey invaded Cyprus by sea and air July 20, 1974, asserting its right to protect the Turkish Cypriote minority.

Geneva talks involving Greece, Turkey, Britain, and the two Cypriote factions failed in mid-August, and the Turks subsequently gained control of 40% of the island. Greece made no armed response to the superior Turkish force, but bitterly suspended military participation in the NATO alliance.

The tension continued after Makarios returned to become President on Dec. 7, 1974. He offered self-government to the Turkish minority, but rejected any solution "involving transfer of populations and amounting to partition of Cyprus."

Turkish Cypriots proclaimed a separate state under Rauf Denktash in the northern part of the island in Nov. 1983, and proposed a "biregional federation."

Makarios died on Aug. 3, 1977, and Spyros Kyprianou was elected to serve the remainder of his term. Kyprianou was subsequently re-elected in 1978, 1983, and 1985. In 1988, George Vassiliou defeated Kyprianou.

On the other hand, talks in New York in 1990 between Vassiliou and Denktash ended in failure. The latter went home espousing a harder than ever line and won a presidential election in his portion of the island.

CZECHOSLOVAKIA

Czech and Slovak Federative Republic
President: Vaclav Havel (1989)
Premier: Marian Calfa (1989)
Area: 49,374 sq mi. (127,896 sq km)
Population (est. mid-1991): 15,700,000 (average annual rate of natural increase: 0.2%); birth rate: 13/1000; infant mortality rate: 11.3/1000; density per square mile: 318
Capital: Prague
Largest cities (est. 1989): Prague, 1,206,098; Bratislava, 429,743; Brno, 388,084; Ostrava, 329,587; Kosice, 229,175
Monetary unit: Koruna
Languages: Czech, Slovak
Religions: Roman Catholic, 50%; Protestant, 20%; Orthodox, 2%; other, 28%
National name: Ceská a Slovenská Federatívní Republika
Literacy rate (1981): 99%
Economic summary: Gross national product (1989 est.): $123.2 billion, per capita $7,878; real growth rate 1.0%. Arable land: 40%. Principal products: grains, potatoes, sugar beets, hops, fruit, hogs, cattle, poultry. Labor force: 8,200,000 (1987); 36.9% in industry. Major products: iron and steel, machinery and equipment, cement, sheet glass, motor vehicles, armaments, chemicals, ceramics. Natural resources: coal, timber, lignite, uranium, magnesite. Exports: machinery, chemicals, industrial consumer goods. Imports: machinery, equipment, fuels, raw materials, food, consumer goods. Major trading partners: U.S.S.R. and Eastern Europe, Yugoslavia, Germany, Austria, U.S.

Geography. Czechoslovakia lies in central Europe, a neighbor of Germany, Poland, the U.S.S.R., Hungary, and Austria. It is equal in size to New York State. The principal rivers—the Elbe, Danube, Oder, and Vetava—are vital commercially to this landlocked country, for both waterborne commerce and agriculture, which flourishes in fertile valleys irrigated by these rivers and their tributaries.

Government. Since 1969 the supreme organ of the state has been the Federal Assembly, which has two equal chambers: the Chamber of People, with 150 deputies, and the Chamber of Nations, with 150 deputies. The chief executive is the President, who is elected by the Federal Assembly for a two-year term. The Premier and his Cabinet are appointed by the President but are responsible to the Federal Assembly.

History. Probably about the 5th century A.D., Slavic tribes from the Vistula basin settled in the region of modern Czechoslovakia. Slovakia came under Magyar domination. The Czechs founded the kingdom of Bohemia, the Premyslide dynasty, which ruled Bohemia and Moravia from the 10th to the 16th century. One of the Bohemian kings, Charles IV, Holy Roman Emperor, made Prague an imperial capital and a center of Latin scholarship. The Hussite movement founded by Jan Hus (1369?–1415) linked the Slavs to the Reformation and revived Czech nationalism, previously under German domination. A Hapsburg, Ferdinand I, ascended the throne in 1526. The Czechs rebelled in 1618. Defeated in 1620, they were ruled for the next 300 years as part of the Austrian Empire.

In World War I, Czech and Slovak patriots, notably Thomas G. Masaryk and Milan Stefanik, promoted Czech-Slovak independence from abroad while their followers fought against the Central Powers. On Oct. 28, 1918, Czechoslovakia proclaimed itself a republic. Shortly thereafter Masaryk was unanimously elected first President.

Hitler provoked the country's German minority in the Sudetenland to agitate for autonomy. At the Munich Conference on Sept. 30, 1938, France and the U.K., seeking to avoid World War II, agreed that the Nazis could take the Sudetenland. Dr. Eduard Benes, who had succeeded Masaryk, resigned on Oct. 5, 1938, and fled to London. Czechoslovakia became a state within the German orbit and was known as Czecho-Slovakia. In March 1939, the Nazis occupied the country.

Soon after Czechoslovakia was liberated in World War II and the government returned in April 1945, it was obliged to cede Ruthenia to the U.S.S.R. In 1946, a Communist, Klement Gottwald, formed a six-party coalition Cabinet. Pressure from Moscow increased until Feb. 23–25, 1948, when the Communists seized complete control in a coup. Following constituent assembly elections in which the Communists and their allies were unopposed, a new Constitution was adopted.

The "people's democracy" was converted into a "socialist" state by a new Constitution adopted June 11, 1960.

After the death of Stalin and the relaxing of Soviet controls, Czechoslovakia witnessed a nationalist awakening. In 1968 conservative Stalinists were driven from power and replaced by more liberal, reform-minded Communists.

Soviet military maneuvers on Czechoslovak soil in May 1968 were followed in July by a meeting of the U.S.S.R. with Poland, Bulgaria, East Germany, and Hungary in Warsaw that demanded an accounting, which Prague refused. Czechoslovak-Soviet talks on Czechoslovak territory, at Cierna, in late July led to an accord. But the Russians charged that the Czechoslovaks had reneged on pledges to modify their policies, and on Aug. 20–21, troops of the five powers, estimated at 600,000, executed a lightning invasion and occupation.

Soviet secret police seized the top Czechoslovak leadership and detained it for several days in Moscow. But Soviet efforts to establish a puppet regime failed. President Ludvik Svoboda negotiated an accord providing for a gradual troop withdrawal in return for "normalization" of political policy.

Czechoslovakia signed a new friendship treaty with the U.S.S.R. that codified the "Brezhnev doctrine," under which Russia can invade any Eastern European socialist nation that threatens to leave the satellite camp.

Anti-government demonstrations reached a head in 1990 when the brutal suppression of a protest on November 17 led to massive popular protests against the Husak regime. Members of the opposition formed the Civic Forum, which pushed for democratization. Marian Colfa became the country's first non-Communist Premier since 1948. Opposition leader Vaclav Havel was elected President on December 29. Opposition groups won a majority in both legislative chambers in the elections of June 1990.

During 1991 strains further developed between the Czech and Slovak regions that threatened to sunder the country in two. In January Czechoslovakia's application to join the Council of Europe was approved unanimously, and the nation moved cautiously toward dismantling the state-run economy. In that month 85% of prices were freed, and the state began the process of auctioning off all state-owned stores. The last Soviet troops left as provided for in negotiations in June 1991.

DENMARK

Kingdom of Denmark
Sovereign: Queen Margrethe II (1972)
Prime Minister: Poul Schlüter (1982)
Area: 16,631 sq mi. (43,075 sq km)[1]
Population (est. mid-1991): 5,100,000 (average annual rate of natural increase: 0.0%); birth rate: 12/1000; infant mortality rate: 8.4/1000; density per square mile: 309
Capital: Copenhagen
Largest cities (est. 1985): Copenhagen, 1,358,540; Aarhus, 252,071; Odense, 171,468; Alborg, 154,750
Monetary unit: Krone
Language: Danish, Faroese, Greenlandic, small German-speaking minority
Religion: 97% Evangelical Lutheran
National name: Kongeriget Danmark
Literacy rate: 99%
Economic summary: Gross domestic product (1990): $125.7 billion; $24,500 per capita; real growth rate, 1.75%. Arable land: 61%. Principal products: meat, dairy products, fish, grains. Labor force: 2,760,000; 34% in industry. Major products: processed foods, machinery and equipment, textiles. Natural resources: crude oil, natural gas, fish, salt, limestone. Exports: meat and dairy products, fish, industrial machinery, chemical products, transportation equipment. Imports: machinery and equipment, transport equipment, petroleum, chemicals, grains and foodstuffs, textiles, paper. Major trading partners: Germany, Sweden, U.K., U.S., Norway, Japan.

1. Excluding Faeroe Islands and Greenland.

Geography. Smallest of the Scandinavian countries (half the size of Maine), Denmark occupies the Jutland peninsula, which extends north from Germany between the tips of Norway and Sweden. To the west is the North Sea and to the east the Baltic.

The country also consists of several Baltic islands; the two largest are Sjaelland, the site of Copenhagen, and Fyn. The narrow waters off the north coast are called the Skagerrak and those off the east, the Kattegat.

Government. Denmark has been a constitutional monarchy since 1849. Legislative power is held jointly by the Sovereign and parliament. The Constitution of 1953 provides for a unicameral parliament called the Folketing, consisting of 179 popularly elected members who serve for four years. The Cabinet is presided over by the Sovereign, who appoints the Prime Minister.

The Sovereign, Queen Margrethe II, was born April 16, 1940, and became Queen—the first in Denmark's history—Jan. 15, 1972, the day after her father, King Frederik IX, died at 72 in the 25th year of his reign. Margrethe was the eldest of his three daughters (by Princess Ingrid of Sweden). The nation's Constitution was amended in 1953 to permit her to succeed her father in the absence of a male heir to the throne. (Denmark was ruled six centuries ago by Margrethe I, but she was never crowned Queen since there was no female right of succession.)

History. Denmark emerged with establishment of the Norwegian dynasty of the Ynglinger in Jutland at the end of the 8th century. Danish mariners played a major role in the raids of the Vikings, or Norsemen, on Western Europe and particularly England. The country was Christianized by St. Ansgar and Harald Blaatand (Bluetooth)—the first Christian king—in the 10th century. Harald's son, Sweyn, conquered England in 1013. His son, Canute the Great, who reigned from 1014 to 1035, united Denmark, England, and Norway under his rule; the southern tip of Sweden was part of Denmark until the 17th century. On Canute's death, civil war tore the country until Waldemar I (1157–82) re-established Danish hegemony over the north.

In 1282, the nobles won the Great Charter, and Eric V was forced to share power with parliament and a Council of Nobles. Waldemar IV (1340–75) restored Danish power, checked only by the Hanseatic League of north German cities allied with ports from Holland to Poland. His daughter, Margrethe, in 1397 united under her rule Denmark, Norway, and Sweden. But Sweden later achieved autonomy and in 1523, under Gustavus I, independence.

Denmark supported Napoleon, for which it was punished at the Congress of Vienna in 1815 by the loss of Norway to Sweden. In 1864, Bismarck, together with the Austrians, made war on the little country as an initial step in the unification of Germany. Denmark was neutral in World War I.

In 1940, Denmark was invaded by the Nazis. King Christian X reluctantly cautioned his countrymen to accept the occupation, but there was widespread resistance against the Nazis. In 1944, Iceland declared its independence from Denmark, ending a union that had existed since 1380.

Liberated by British troops in May 1945, the country staged a fast recovery in both agriculture and manufacturing and was a leader in liberalizing trade. It joined the United Nations in 1945 and NATO in 1949.

The Social Democrats largely ran Denmark after the war but were ousted in 1973 in an election dominated by protests against high taxes.

Disputes over economic policy led to elections in 1981 that led to Poul Schlüter coming to power in early 1982. Further disputes over his pro-NATO posture led to elections in May, 1988 that marginally confirmed his position. A dispute over tax reform led the calling of an election in December 1990, after which a Conservative-Liberal coalition government was formed, though it controlled only 61 of the 179 seats in parliament.

Outlying Territories of Denmark

FAEROE ISLANDS

Status: Autonomous part of Denmark
Lagmand (President): Jogran Sundstein (1989)
Area: 540 sq mi. (1,399 sq km)
Population (1989): 47,283 (average annual growth rate:
.9%); density per square mile: 87
Capital (est. 1982): Thorshavn, 12,750
Monetary unit: Faeroese krone
Literacy rate: 99%
Economic summary: Gross domectic product (1989 est.):
$662 million, per capita $14,000; real growth rate 3%.
Arable land: 2%; principal agricultural products:
sheep, vegetables. Labor force: 17,585, largely engaged in fishing manufacturing, transportation and
commerce. Major industrial products: fish, ships,
handicrafts. Exports: fish and fish products. Imports:
machinery and transport equipment, foodstuffs, petroleum and petroleum products. Major trading partners: Denmark, U.S., U.K., Germany, Canada, France,
Japan.

This group of 18 islands, lying in the North Atlantic about 200 miles (322 km) northwest of the Shetland Islands, joined Denmark in 1386 and has since
been part of the Danish kingdom. The islands were
occupied by British troops during World War II, after
the German occupation of Denmark.

The Faeroes have home rule under a bill enacted in
1948; they also have two representatives in the Danish Folketing.

GREENLAND

Status: Autonomous part of Denmark
Premier: Lars Emil Johansen (1991)
Area: 840,000 sq mi. (incl. 708,069 sq mi. covered by ice-
cap) (2,175,600 sq km)
Population (1989): 55,415 (growth rate: 12%)
Capital (est. 1982): Godthaab, 10,000
Monetary unit: Krone
Literacy rate: 99%
Economic summary: Gross national product (1988): $500
million, per capita $9,000; real growth rate 5%. Arable
land: 0%; principal agricultural products: hay, sheep,
garden produce. Labor force: 22,800, largely engaged
in fishing, hunting, sheep breeding. Major industries:
fish processing, lead and zinc processing, handicrafts.
Natural resources: metals, cryolite, iron ore, coal,
uranium, fish. Exports: fish and fish products, metalic
ores and concentrates. Imports: petroleum and petroleum products, machinery and transport equipment,
foodstuffs. Major trading partners: Denmark, U.S.,
Germany, Sweden, Japan, Norway.

Greenland, the world's largest island, was colonized in 985–86 by Eric the Red. Danish sovereignty,
which covered only the west coast, was extended
over the whole island in 1917. In 1941 the U.S.
signed an agreement with the Danish minister in
Washington, placing it under U.S. protection during
World War II but maintaining Danish sovereignty. A
definitive agreement for the joint defense of Greenland within the framework of NATO was signed in
1951. A large U.S. air base at Thule in the far north
was completed in 1953.

Under 1953 amendments to the Danish Constitution, Greenland became part of Denmark, with two
representatives in the Danish Folketing. On May 1,
1979, Greenland gained home rule, with its own local

parliament (Landsting), replacing the Greenland Provincial Council.

In February 1982, Greenlanders voted to withdraw
from the European Community, which they had
joined as part of Denmark in 1973. Danish Premier
Anker Jørgensen said he would support the request,
but with reluctance.

An election in early March 1991 gave the Siumut
Party 11 of the 27 available seats. The early election
was called after a scandal allegedly involving over-
spending by government officials on entertainment.

DJIBOUTI

Republic of Djibouti
President: Hassan Gouled Aptidon (1977)
Prime Minister: Barkat Gourad Hamadou (1978)
Area: 8,490 sq mi. (22,000 sq km)
Population (est. mid-1991): 400,000 (average annual rate
of natural increase: 2.9%); birth rate: 46/1000; infant
mortality rate: 117/1000; density per square mile: 50
Capital (est. 1980): Djibouti, 200,000
Monetary unit: Djibouti franc
Languages: Arabic, French, Afar, Somali
Religions: Muslim, 94%; Christian, 6%
National name: Jumhouriyya Djibouti
Literacy rate: 20%
Economic summary: Gross domestic product (1986):
$333 million, $1,070 per capita; real growth rate –.7%.
Arable land: 0%; principal agricultural products: goats,
sheep, camels. Labor force: NA. Industries: small-
scale enterprises such as dairy products and mineral-
water bottling. Exports: hides, skins, coffee (in transit
from Ethiopia). Imports: petroleum, transport equipment, foodstuffs. Major trading partners: Middle East,
Africa, Europe, Bahrain, Asia.

Geography. Djibouti lies in northeastern Africa on
the Gulf of Aden at the southern entrance to the Red
Sea. It borders on Ethiopia and Somalia. The country,
the size of Massachusetts, is mainly a stony desert,
with scattered plateaus and highlands.

Government. On May 8, 1977, the population of
the French Territory of the Afars and Issas voted by
more than 98% for independence. Voters also approved a 65-member interim Constituent Assembly.
France transferred sovereignty to the new nation of
Djibouti on June 27. Later in the year it became a
member of the Organization of African Unity and the
Arab League. The People's Progress Assembly is the
only legal political party.

History. The territory that is now Djibouti was acquired by France between 1843 and 1886 by treaties
with the Somali sultans. Small, arid, and sparsely
populated, Djibouti is important chiefly because of
the capital city's port, the terminal of the Djibou-
ti-Addis Ababa railway that carries 60% of Ethiopia's
foreign trade.

Originally known as French Somaliland, the colony
voted in 1958 and 1967 to remain under French rule.
It was renamed the Territory of the Afars and Issas in
1967 and took the name of its capital city on attaining independence.

The two principal opposition groups in exile
banded to form a common front in early 1990. The
divisive state of affairs in Somalia caused nervous-
ness in Djibouti lest a large wave of refugees flee
into the country.

DOMINICA

Commonwealth of Dominica
President: Sir Clarence Seignoret (1985)
Prime Minister: Mary Eugenia Charles (1980)
Area: 290 sq mi. (751 sq km)
Population: (1990): 87,800 (average annual rate of natural increase: 2.9%); birth rate: 26/1000; infant mortality rate: 13/1000; density per square mile: 297
Capital and largest city (est. 1981): Roseau, 20,000
Monetary unit: East Caribbean dollar
Languages: English and French patois
Religions: Roman Catholic, Anglican, Methodist
Member of Commonwealth of Nations
Literacy rate: 80% (est.)
Economic summary: Gross domestic product (1988 est.): $137 million, per capita $1,408; real growth rate 5.6%. Arable land: 9%. Principal products: bananas, citrus fruits, coconuts, cocoa. Labor force: 25,000; 32% in industry and commerce (1984). Major industries: agricultural processing; tourism. Exports: bananas, coconuts, grapefruit, soap, galvanized sheets. Imports: food, oils and fats, chemicals, fuels and lubricants. Major trading partners: U.K., Caribbean countries, U.S.

Geography. Dominica is an island of the Lesser Antilles in the Caribbean south of Guadeloupe and north of Martinique.

Government. Dominica is a republic, with a president elected by the House of Assembly as head of state and a prime minister appointed by the president on the advice of the Assembly. The Freedom Party (11 of 21 seats in the Assembly) is led by Prime Minister Mary Eugenia Charles. The Opposition United Workers Party holds six seats and the United Dominica Labor Party holds four seats.

History. Discovered by Columbus in 1493, Dominica was claimed by Britain and France until 1815, when Britain asserted sovereignty. Dominica, along with other Windward Isles, became a self-governing member of the West Indies Associated States in free association with Britain in 1967.

Dissatisfaction over the slow pace of reconstruction after Hurricane David struck the island in September 1979 brought a landslide victory for the Freedom Party in July 1980. The vote gave the prime ministership to Mary Eugenia Charles, a strong advocate of free enterprise. The Freedom Party won again in 1985 elections, giving Miss Charles a second five-year term as prime minister. She and her party won a third term in elections on May 28, 1990, though with a greatly reduced mandate. The Freedom party retained only 11 seats in the Assembly.

DOMINICAN REPUBLIC

President: Joaquin Balaguer (1986)
Area: 18,704 sq mi. (48,442 sq km)
Population (est. mid-1991): 7,300,000 (average annual rate of natural increase: 2.3%); birth rate: 30/1000; infant mortality rate: 61/1000; density per square mile: 389
Capital: Santo Domingo
Largest cities (est. 1983): Santo Domingo, 1,410,000; Santiago de los Caballeros, 285,000
Monetary unit: Peso
Language: Spanish
Religion: 95% Roman Catholic

National name: República Dominicana
Literacy rate: 74%
Economic summary: Gross domestic product (1988): $5.1 billion, $790 per capita, 0.5% real growth rate. Arable land: 23%. Principal agricultural products: sugar cane, coffee, cocoa, tobacco. Labor force (1986): 2,300,000–2,600,000; 18% in industry. Major industries: tourism, sugar processing, ferronickel and gold mining, textiles, cement, tobacco. Natural resources: nickel, bauxite, gold, silver. Exports: sugar, coffee, cocoa, gold, ferronickel. Imports: foodstuffs, petroleum, cotton and fabrics, chemicals, and pharmaceuticals. Major trading partners: U.S., including Puerto Rico.

Geography. The Dominican Republic in the West Indies, occupies the eastern two thirds of the island of Hispaniola, which it shares with Haiti. Its area equals that of Vermont and New Hampshire combined.

Crossed from northwest to southeast by a mountain range with elevations exceeding 10,000 feet (3,048 m), the country has fertile, well-watered land in the north and east, where nearly two thirds of the population lives. The southwest part is arid and has poor soil, except around Santo Domingo.

Government. The president is elected by direct vote every four years. Legislative powers rest with a Senate and a Chamber of Deputies, both elected by direct vote, also for four years. All citizens must vote when they reach 18 years of age, or even earlier if they are married.

History. The Dominican Republic was discovered by Columbus in 1492. He named it La Española, and his son, Diego, was its first viceroy. The capital, Santo Domingo, founded in 1496, is the oldest European settlement in the Western Hemisphere. Spain ceded the colony to France in 1795, and Haitian blacks under Toussaint L'Ouverture conquered it in 1801.

In 1808 the people revolted and the next year captured Santo Domingo, setting up the first republic. Spain regained title to the colony in 1814. In 1821 the people overthrew Spanish rule, but in 1822 they were reconquered by the Haitians. They revolted again in 1844, threw out the Haitians, and established the Dominican Republic, headed by Pedro Santana. Uprisings and Haitian attacks led Santana to make the country a province of Spain from 1861 to 1865. The U.S. Senate refused to ratify a treaty of annexation. Disorder continued until the dictatorship of Ulíses Heureaux; in 1916, when disorder broke out again, the U.S. sent in a contingent of marines, who remained until 1934.

A sergeant in the Dominican army trained by the marines, Rafaél Leonides Trujillo Molina, overthrew Horacio Vásquez in 1930 and established a dictatorship that lasted until his assassination 31 years later.

A new Constitution was adopted in 1962, and the first free elections since 1924 put Juan Bosch, a leftist leader, in office. However, a right-wing military coup replaced Bosch with a civilian triumvirate.

Leftists rebelled April 24, 1965, and President Lyndon Johnson sent in marines and troops. After an OAS ceasefire request May 6, a compromise installed Hector Garcia-Godoy as provisional president. Joaquin Balaguer won in free elections in 1966 against Bosch, and a peacekeeping force of 9,000 U.S. troops and 2,000 from other countries withdrew. Balaguer restored political and economic stability.

In 1978, the army suspended the counting of ballots when Balaguer trailed in a fourth-term bid. After a warning from President Jimmy Carter, however, Balaguer accepted the victory of Antonio Guzmán of the opposition Dominican Revolutionary Party.

Salvador Jorge Blanco of the Dominican Revolutionary Party was elected President on May 16, 1982, defeating Balaguer and Bosch. Austerity measures imposed by the International Monetary Fund, including sharply higher prices for food and gasoline, provoked rioting in the spring of 1984 that left more than 50 dead.

Saying he feared they would provoke "some kind of revolution," Blanco dragged his feet about putting into effect further IMF demands for higher prices and taxes and devaluation of the peso, and came within weeks of defaulting on several big loans.

Balaguer was elected President in May 1986 and aimed economic policy at diversifying the economy. On May 16, 1990 Balaguer won a sixth presidential term in elections following a non-violent campaign. In its wake Juan Bosch resigned as head of his Dominican Liberation Party.

ECUADOR

Republic of Ecuador
President: Rodrigo Borja Cevallos (1988)
Area: 109,484 sq mi. (270,670 sq km)
Population (est. mid-1991): 10,800,000 (average annual rate of natural increase: 2.4%); birth rate: 31/1000; infant mortality rate: 58/1000; density per square mile: 95
Capital: Quito
Largest cities (est. 1987): Guayaquil, 1,572,615; Quito, 1,137,705; Cuenca, 201,490
Monetary unit: Sucre
Languages: Spanish, Quéchua
Religion: Roman Catholic, 95%
National name: República del Ecuador
Literacy rate: 85%
Economic summary: Gross domestic product (1989). $9.8 billion, $935 per capita; .5% real growth rate. Arable land: 6%; principal agricultural products: bananas, cocoa, coffee, sugar cane, manioc, plantains, potatoes, rice. Labor force (1982): 2,800,000; 21% in manufacturing; major industries: food processing, textiles, chemicals, fishing, timber, petroleum. Exports: petroleum, coffee, bananas, cocoa products, shrimp, fish products. Imports: transport equipment, vehicles, machinery, chemicals, petroleum. Major trading partners: U.S., Latin America, EEC, Caribbean, Japan.

Geography. Ecuador, equal in area to Nevada, is in the northwest part of South America fronting on the Pacific. To the north is Colombia and to the east and south is Peru. Two high and parallel ranges of the Andes, traversing the country from north to south, are topped by tall volcanic peaks. The highest is Chimborazo at 20,577 feet (6,272 m).

The Galápagos Islands (or Colón Archipelago) (3,029 sq mi.; 7,845 sq km) in the Pacific Ocean about 600 miles (966 km) west of the South American mainland, became part of Ecuador in 1832.

Government. A 1978 Constitution returned Ecuador to civilian government after eight years of military rule. The President is elected to a term of four years and a House of Representatives of 71 members is popularly elected for the same period.

History. The tribes in the northern highlands of Ecuador formed the Kingdom of Quito around A.D. 1000. It was absorbed, by conquest and marriage, into the Inca Empire. Pizarro conquered the land in 1532, and through the 17th century a thriving colony was built by exploitation of the Indians. The first revolt against Spain occurred in 1809. Ecuador then joined Venezuela, Colombia, and Panama in a confederacy known as Greater Colombia.

On the collapse of this union in 1830, Ecuador became independent. Subsequent history was one of revolts and dictatorships; it had 48 presidents during the first 131 years of the republic. Conservatives ruled until the Revolution of 1895 ushered in nearly a half century of Radical Liberal rule, during which the church was disestablished and freedom of worship, speech, and press was introduced.

A three-man military junta which had taken power in a 1976 coup, agreed to a free presidential election on July 16, 1978. Jaime Roldós Aguilera won the runoff on April 29, 1979.

The 40-year-old President died in the crash of a small plane May 24, 1981. Vice President Osvaldo Hurtado Larrea became President. León Febres Cordero, was installed President in August 1984. Combined opposition parties won a majority in the 71-member Congress large enough to block significant action, a majority increased in the June 1986 elections.

Problems with the military plagued Febres in 1986–87, and he faced two rebellions.

In 1988, Rodrigo Borja was elected President. He was also able to form a coalition in the House, confirming a leftward shift in the government and promising smoother executive-legislative relations.

Ecuador has been trying to keep out of the drug trafficking trade, which has plagued its neighbors.

EGYPT

Arab Republic of Egypt
President: Hosni Mubarak (1981)
Premier: Dr. Atef Sedky (1986)
Area: 386,900 sq. mi. (1,002,000 sq km)
Population (est. mid-1991): 54,500,000 (average annual rate of natural increase: 2.9%); birth rate: 38/1000; infant mortality rate: 73/1000; density per square mile: 141
Capital: Cairo
Largest cities (est. 1987): Cairo, 12,560,000; (1986 est.): Alexandria, 2,893,000; Giza, 1,670,800; Shubra el Kheima, 533,300; El Mahalla el Kubra, 385,300
Monetary unit: Egyptian pound
Language: Arabic
Religions: Islam, 94%; Christian (mostly Coptic), 6%
Literacy rate: 45%
Economic summary: Gross domestic product (1989 est.): $38.3 billion; $700 per capita; 1.0% real growth rate. Arable land: 3%. Principal agricultural products: cotton, wheat, rice, corn, beans. Labor force: 15,000,000; 20% in privately owned services and manufacturing. Major industries: textiles, food processing, tourism, chemicals, petroleum, construction, cement, metals. Natural resources: crude oil, natural gas, iron ore, phosphates, manganese, limestone, gypsum, talc, asbestos, lead, zinc. Exports: cotton, petroleum, yarn, textiles. Imports: foodstuffs, machinery, fertilizers, woods. Major trading partners: U.S., Western Europe, Japan, Eastern Europe.

Geography. Egypt, at the northeast corner of Africa on the Mediterranean Sea, is bordered on the west by Libya, on the south by the Sudan, and on the east by the Red Sea and Israel. It is nearly one and one half times the size of Texas.

The historic Nile flows through the eastern third of the country. On either side of the Nile valley are desert plateaus, spotted with oases. In the north, toward the Mediterranean, plateaus are low, while south of Cairo they rise to a maximum of 1,015 feet (309 m) above sea level. At the head of the Red Sea is the Sinai Peninsula, between the Suez Canal and Israel.

Navigable throughout its course in Egypt, the Nile is used largely as a means of cheap transport for heavy goods. The principal port is Alexandria.

The Nile delta starts 100 miles (161 km) south of the Mediterranean and fans out to a sea front of 155 miles between the cities of Alexandria and Port Said. From Cairo north, the Nile branches into many streams, the principal ones being the Damietta and the Rosetta.

Except for a narrow belt along the Mediterranean, Egypt lies in an almost rainless area, in which high daytime temperatures fall quickly at night.

Government. Executive power is held by the President, who is elected every six years and can appoint one or more Vice Presidents.

The National Democratic Party, led by President Hosni Mubarak, is the dominant political party. Elections on Nov. 29, 1990 confirmed its huge majority. There is also one opposition party and some independents. The major opposition parties boycotted the elections.

History. Egyptian history dates back to about 4000 B.C., when the kingdoms of upper and lower Egypt, already highly civilized, were united. Egypt's "Golden Age" coincided with the 18th and 19th dynasties (16th to 13th centuries B.C.), during which the empire was established. Persia conquered Egypt in 525 B.C.; Alexander the Great subdued it in 332 B.C.; and then the dynasty of the Ptolemies ruled the land until 30 B.C., when Cleopatra, last of the line, committed suicide and Egypt became a Roman province. From 641 to 1517 the Arab caliphs ruled Egypt, and then the Turks took it for their Ottoman Empire.

Napoleon's armies occupied the country from 1798 to 1801. In 1805, Mohammed Ali, leader of a band of Albanian soldiers, became Pasha of Egypt. After completion of the Suez Canal in 1869, the French and British took increasing interest in Egypt.

British troops occupied Egypt in 1882, and British resident agents became its actual administrators, though it remained under nominal Turkish sovereignty. In 1914, this fiction was ended, and Egypt became a protectorate of Britain.

Egyptian nationalism forced Britain to declare Egypt an independent, sovereign state on Feb. 28, 1922, although the British reserved rights for the protection of the Suez Canal and the defense of Egypt. In 1936, by an Anglo-Egyptian treaty of alliance, all British troops and officials were to be withdrawn, except from the Suez Canal Zone. When World War II started, Egypt remained neutral. British imperial troops finally ended the Nazi threat to Suez in 1942 in the battle of El Alamein, west of Alexandria.

In 1951, Egypt abrogated the 1936 treaty and the 1899 Anglo-Egyptian condominium of the Sudan (*See* Sudan). Rioting and attacks on British troops in the Suez Canal Zone followed, reaching a climax in January 1952. The army, led by Gen. Mohammed Na-

guib, seized power on July 23, 1952. Three days later, King Farouk abdicated in favor of his infant son. The monarchy was abolished and a republic proclaimed on June 18, 1953, with Naguib holding the posts of Provisional President and Premier. He relinquished the latter in 1954 to Gamal Abdel Nasser, leader of the ruling military junta. Naguib was deposed seven months later and Nasser confirmed as President in a referendum on June 23, 1956.

Nasser's policies embroiled his country in continual conflict. In 1956, the U.S. and Britain withdrew their pledges of financial aid for the building of the Aswan High Dam. In reply, Nasser nationalized the Suez Canal and expelled British oil and embassy officials. Israel, barred from the Canal and exasperated by terrorist raids, invaded the Gaza Strip and the Sinai Peninsula. Britain and France, after demanding Egyptian evacuation of the Canal Zone, attacked Egypt on Oct. 31, 1956. Worldwide pressure forced Britain, France, and Israel to halt the hostilities. A U.N. emergency force occupied the Canal Zone, and all troops were evacuated in the spring of 1957.

On Feb. 1, 1958, Egypt and Syria formed the United Arab Republic, which was joined by Yemen in an association known as the United Arab States. However, Syria withdrew from the United Arab Republic in 1961 and Egypt dissolved its ties with Yemen in the United Arab States.

On June 5, 1967, Israel invaded the Sinai Peninsula, the East Bank of the Jordan River, and the zone around the Gulf of Aqaba. A U.N. ceasefire on June 10 saved the Arabs from complete rout.

Nasser declared the 1967 cease-fire void along the Canal in April 1969 and began a war of attrition. The U.S. peace plan of June 19, 1970, resulted in Egypt's agreement to reinstate the cease-fire for at least three months, (from August) and to accept Israel's existence within "recognized and secure" frontiers that might emerge from U.N.-mediated talks. In return, Israel accepted the principle of withdrawing from occupied territories.

Then, on Sept. 28, 1970, Nasser died, at 52, of a heart attack. The new President was Anwar el-Sadat, an associate of Nasser and a former newspaper editor.

The Aswan High Dam, whose financing by the U.S.S.R. was its first step into Egypt, was completed and dedicated in January 1971.

In July 1972, Sadat ordered the expulsion of Soviet "advisors and experts" from Egypt because the Russians had not provided the sophisticated weapons he felt were needed to retake territory lost to Israel in 1967.

The fourth Arab-Israeli war broke out Oct. 6, 1973, while Israelis were commemorating Yom Kippur, the Jewish high holy day. Egypt swept deep into the Sinai, while Syria strove to throw Israel off the Golan Heights.

A U.N.-sponsored truce was accepted on October 22. In January 1974, both sides agreed to a settlement negotiated by U.S. Secretary of State Henry A. Kissinger that gave Egypt a narrow strip along the entire Sinai bank of the Suez Canal. In June, President Nixon made the first visit by a U.S. President to Egypt and full diplomatic relations were established. The Suez Canal was cleared and reopened on June 5, 1975.

Kissinger pursued "shuttle diplomacy" between Cairo and Jerusalem to extend areas of agreement. Israel yielded on three points—the possession of the Mitla and Giddi passes in the Sinai and the Abu Rudeis oil field in the peninsula—and both sides committed themselves to annual renewal of the U.N. peacekeeping force in the Sinai.

In the most audacious act of his career, Sadat flew to Jerusalem at the invitation of Prime Minister Menachem Begin and pleaded before Israel's Knesset on Nov. 20, 1977, for a permanent peace settlement. The Arab world reacted with fury—only Morocco, Tunisia, Sudan, and Oman approved.

Egypt and Israel signed a formal peace treaty on March 26, 1979. The pact ended 30 years of war and established diplomatic and commercial relations.

Egyptian and Israeli officials met in the Sinai desert on April 26, 1979, to implement the peace treaty calling for the phased withdrawal of occupation forces from the peninsula. By mid-1980, two thirds of the Sinai was transferred, but progress here was not matched in the negotiation of Arab autonomy in the Gaza Strip and the West Bank.

Sadat halted further talks in August 1980 because of continued Israeli settlement of the West Bank. On October 6 1981, Sadat was assassinated by extremist Muslim soldiers at a parade in Cairo. Vice President Hosni Mubarak, a former Air Force chief of staff, was confirmed by the parliament as president the next day.

Although feared unrest in Egypt did not occur in the wake of the assassination, and Israel completed the return of the Sinai to Egyptian control on April 25, 1982, Mubarak was unable to revive the autonomy talks. Israel's invasion of Lebanon in June imposed a new strain on him, and brought a marked cooling in Egyptian-Israeli relations, but not a disavowal of the peace treaty.

During 1985, pressures by Moslem fundamentalists to implement Islamic law in Egypt increased. In response, the government began putting all mosques under control of the minister for religious endowments.

While President Mubarak's stand during the Persian Gulf war won wide praise in the West, domestically this position proved far less popular. President Bush proposed writing-off Egypt's large debt to the U.S., but the Congress balked at such a large forgiveness.

Suez Canal. The Suez Canal, in Egyptian territory between the Arabian Desert and the Sinai Peninsula, is an artificial waterway about 100 miles (161 km) long between Port Said on the Mediterranean and Suez on the Red Sea. Construction work, directed by the French engineer Ferdinand de Lesseps, was begun April 25, 1859, and the Canal was opened Nov. 17, 1869. The cost was 432,807,882 francs. The concession was held by an Egyptian joint stock company, *Compagnie Universelle du Canal Maritime de Suez,* in which the British government held 353,504 out of a total of 800,000 shares. The concession was to expire Nov. 17, 1968, but the company was nationalized July 26, 1956, by unilateral action of the Egyptian government.

The Canal was closed in June 1967 after the Arab-Israeli conflict. With the help of the U.S. Navy, work was begun on clearing the Canal in 1974, after the cease-fire ending the Arab-Israeli war. It was reopened to traffic June 5, 1975.

EL SALVADOR

Republic of El Salvador
President: Alfredo Cristiani (1989)
Area: 8,260 sq mi. (21,393 sq km)
Population (est. mid-1991): 5,400,000 (average annual rate of natural increase: 2.7%); birth rate: 35/100; infant mortality rate: 55/1000; density per square mile: 656
Capital: San Salvador
Largest cities (est. 1985): San Salvador, 459,902; Santa Ana, 137,879; Mejicanos, 91,465; San Miguel, 88,520
Monetary unit: Colón
Language: Spanish
Religion: Roman Catholic
National name: República de El Salvador
Literacy rate: 65%
Economic summary: Gross domestic product (1989 est.): $5.5 billion; $1,020 per capita; 0.9% real growth rate. Arable land: 27%. Principal products: coffee, cotton, corn, sugar, rice, sorghum. Labor force: 1,700,000; 15% in manufacturing. Major products: processed foods, clothing and textiles, petroleum products. Natural resources: hydro- and geothermal power, crude oil. Exports: coffee, cotton, sugar, shrimp. Imports: machinery, construction materials, petroleum, foodstuffs, fertilizer. Major trading partners: U.S., Guatemala, Japan, Germany, Mexico, Venezuela.

Geography. Situated on the Pacific coast of Central America, El Salvador has Guatemala to the west and Honduras to the north and east. It is the smallest of the Central American countries, its area equal to that of Massachusetts, and the only one without an Atlantic coastline.

Most of the country is a fertile volcanic plateau about 2,000 feet (607 m) high. There are some active volcanoes and many scenic crater lakes.

Government. A new Constitution enacted in 1983 vests executive power in a President elected for a nonrenewable, five-year term, and legislative power in a 60-member National Assembly elected by universal suffrage and proportional representation. Judicial power is vested in a Supreme Court, composed of a President and eleven magistrates elected by the Assembly, and subordinate courts.

History. Pedro de Alvarado, a lieutenant of Cortés, conquered El Salvador in 1525. El Salvador, with the other countries of Central America, declared its independence from Spain on Sept. 15, 1821, and was part of a federation of Central American states until that union was dissolved in 1838. Its independent career for decades thereafter was marked by numerous revolutions and wars against other Central American republics.

On Oct. 15, 1979, a junta deposed the President, Gen. Carlos Humberto Romero, seeking to halt increasingly violent clashes between leftist and rightist forces.

On Dec. 4, 1980, three American nuns and an American lay worker were killed in an ambush near San Salvador, causing the Carter Administration to suspend all aid pending an investigation. The naming of José Napoleón Duarte, a moderate civilian, as head of the governing junta brought a resumption of U.S. aid.

Defying guerrilla threats, voters on March 28, 1982, elected a rightist majority to a constituent assembly that dismissed Duarte and replaced him with a centrist physician, Dr. Alvaro Alfredo Magaña. The rightist majority repealed the laws permitting expropriation of land, and critics charged that the land-reform program begun under Duarte was dead.

In an election closely monitored by American and other foreign observers, Duarte was elected President in May 1984.

Duarte's Christian Democratic Party scored an unexpected electoral triumph in national legislative and municipal elections held in March 1985, a winning majority in the new National Assembly. The rightist parties that had been dominant in the previous Constituent Assembly demanded that the vote be nullified, but the army high command rejected their assertion the voting had been fraudulent.

At the same time, U.S. officials said that while the rebels still were far from being defeated, there had been marked improvement in the effectiveness of government troops in the civil war against antigovernment guerrillas that has been waged mainly in the countryside. Talks with the rebels broke down in September 1986. Duarte's inability to find solutions led to the rightwing ARENA party controlling half the seats in the National Assembly, in the elections of March, 1988. The decisive victory of Alfredo Christiani, the ARENA candidate for president, gives the right-wing party effective control of the country, given their political control of most of the municipalities.

U.N.-mediated ceasefire talks in Mexico between the government and rebel forces ended in June 1991 without an agreement, although progress was reportedly made. The 11-year-old civil war has claimed an estimated 75,000 lives.

EQUATORIAL GUINEA

Republic of Equatorial Guinea
President: Col. Teodoro Obiang Nguema Mbasogo (1979)
Prime Minister: Capt. Cristino Seriche Bioko
Area: 10,830 sq mi. (28,051 sq km)
Population (mid-1991): 400,000 (average annual rate of natural increase: 2.6%); birth rate: 43/1000; infant mortality rate: 118/1000; density per square mile: 35
Capital and largest city (est. 1983): Malabo, 37,500
Monetary unit: CFA Franc
Languages: Spanish, pidgin English, Fang, Bubi, Ibo
Religions: Roman Catholic, Protestant, traditional
National name: República de Guinea Ecuatorial
Literacy rate: 40%
Economic summary: Gross national product (1987): $103 million, $293 per capita. Arable land: 8%. Principal products: cocoa, wood, coffee; rice, yams. Natural resource: wood, crude oil. Exports: cocoa, wood, coffee. Imports: petroleum, foodstuffs, textiles, machinery. Major trading partners: Spain, Italy, France, the Netherlands.

Geography. Equatorial Guinea, formerly Spanish Guinea, consists of Rio Muni (10,045 sq mi.; 26,117 sq km), on the western coast of Africa, and several islands in the Gulf of Guinea, the largest of which is Bioko (formerly Fernando Po) (785 sq mi.; 2,033 sq km). The other islands are Annobón, Corisco, Elobey Grande, and Elobey Chico. The total area is twice that of Connecticut.

Government. The Constitution of 1973 was suspended after a coup on Aug. 3, 1979. A Supreme Military Council, headed by the president, exercises all power. Political parties were banned until Aug. 1987.

History. Fernando Po and Annobón came under Spanish control in 1778. From 1827 to 1844, with Spanish consent, Britain administered Fernando Po, but in the latter year Spain reclaimed the island. Río Muni was given to Spain in 1885 by the Treaty of Berlin.

Negotiations with Spain led to independence on

Oct. 12, 1968.

In 1969, anti-Spanish incidents in Río Muni, including the tearing down of a Spanish flag by national troops, caused 5,000 Spanish residents to flee for their safety, and diplomatic relations between the two nations became strained. A month later, President Masie Nguema Biyogo Negue Ndong charged that a coup had been attempted against him. He seized dictatorial powers and arrested 80 opposition politicians and even several of his Cabinet ministers and the secretary of the National Assembly.

A coup on Aug. 3, 1979, deposed Masie, and a junta led by Lieut. Col. Teodoro Obiang Nguema Mbasogo took over the government. Obiang expelled Soviet technicians and reinstated cooperation with Spain.

In an effort to rehabilitate the country's cocoa production the World Bank devised and was putting into effect a new plan. Spain agreed to provide major economic assistance for the period 1990–93 including help in completing a national television system.

ESTONIA

Republic of Estonia
President: Arnold Ruutel (1990)
Prime Minister: Edgar Savisaar (1990)
Area: 18,370 sq mi. (47,549 sq km)
Population (1990): 1.5 million (Estonians, 61.5%; Russians, 30.3%; Ukrainians, 3.1%; Byelorussians, 1.8%; Finns, 1.1%); (avg. annual growth rate, ethnic Estonians: 1.6%); density per square mile: 82
Capital and largest city (1990): Tallinn, 506,000. Other important cities: Tartu, Kohtla-Järve, Narva, and Pärnu
Monetary unit: Ruble, Estonian currency to be created
Languages: Estonian is official; also Russian
Religions (1937): Lutheran, 78%; Orthodox, 19%
National name: Esti
Literacy: (n.a., there was a high literacy rate before the Soviet occupation)
Economic survey (1989): Gross national product: n.a. Per capita income: $6,240. Labor force (1987): urban areas, 72%, rural, 28%. Major industries: oil shale processing (World's No. 2 producer), mineral fertilizers, wood processing, pulp, and peat. Fishing, farming, and shipbuilding are also important. Trade: exports to over 30 countries, (sold for rubles to Moscow, who exported the products to West for hard currency).

Geography: Estonia borders on the Baltic Sea in the west, the gulfs of Riga and Finland in the southwest and north, respectively, Latvia in the south, and Russia in the east. It is mainly a lowland country with numerous lakes. Lake Chudskoye is the largest and is important to the fishing and shipping industries.

Government: Transitional, from a Moscow-directed occupation government to an anticipated Western-style democratic government.

History: Born out of World War I, this small Baltic state enjoyed a mere two short decades of independence before it was absorbed again by its powerful neighbor, Russia. In the 13th century, the Estonians had been conquered by the Teutonic Knights of Germany, who reduced them to serfdom. In 1521, the Swedes took over, and the power of the German (Balt) landowning class was curbed somewhat. But after 1721, when Russia succeeded Sweden as the ruling power, the Estonians were subjected to a double bondage—the Balts and the tsarist officials. The oppression lasted until the closing months of World War I, when Estonia finally achieved independence.

Shortly after the start of World War II, the nation was occupied by Russian troops and was incorporated as the 16th republic of the U.S.S.R. in 1940. Germany occupied the nation from 1941 to 1944, when it was retaken by the Russians. Most of the nations of the world, including the United States and Great Britain, never recognized the Soviet incorporation of Estonia.

Soon after Lithuania's declaration of independence from the Soviet Union in March 1990, the Estonian congress renamed its country on May 8 and omitted the words "Soviet Socialist" and adopted the former (1918) Coat of Arms of the Republic of Estonia. Thereafter, the government cautiously promoted national autonomy.

After the attempted Soviet coup to remove President Gorbachev failed, Estonia formally declared its independence from the U.S.S.R. on August 20, 1991. Recognition by European and other countries followed, and on Sept. 2, 1991, President Bush announced that the United States was giving full diplomatic recognition to the Baltic nations. The Soviet Union recognized Estonia's independence on September 6 and it received UN membership on Sept. 17, 1991.

ETHIOPIA

People's Democratic Republic of Ethiopia
President: Meles Zenawi (1991)
Prime Minister: Hailu Yemenu (1989)
Area: 472,432 sq mi. (1,223,600 sq km)
Population (est. mid-1991): 53,200,000 (average annual rate of natural increase: 2.9%); birth rate: 49/1000; infant mortality rate: 130/1000; density per square mile: 113
Capital: Addis Ababa
Largest cities (est. 1984): Addis Ababa, 1,423,111; Asmara, 275,385
Monetary unit: Birr
Languages: Amharic (official), Galligna, Tigrigna
Religions: Ethiopian Orthodox, 35–40%; Islam, 40–45%; animist, 15-20%; other, 5%
Literacy rate: 55.2%
Economic summary: Gross domestic product (FY89 est.): $6.6 billion; $130 per capita; 4.5% real growth rate. Arable land: 12%. Principal products: coffee, barley, wheat, corn, sugar cane, cotton, oilseeds, livestock. Major industrial products: cement, textiles, processed foods, refined oil. Natural resources: potash, gold, platinum, copper. Exports: coffee, hides and skins, oilseeds. Imports: petroleum, foodstuffs. Major trading partners: U.S.S.R., U.S., Germany, Italy, Japan, Djibouti, South Yemen.

Geography. Ethiopia is in east central Africa, bordered on the west by the Sudan, the east by Somalia and Djibouti, the south by Kenya, and the north by the Red Sea. It is nearly three times the size of California.

Over its main plateau land, Ethiopia has several high mountains, the highest of which is Ras Dashan at 15,158 feet (4,620 m). The Blue Nile, or Abbai, rises in the northwest and flows in a great semicircle east, south, and northwest before entering the Sudan.

Its chief reservoir, Lake Tana, lies in the northwestern part of the plateau.

Government. On Feb. 22, 1987, a new constitution came into effect. It established a Communist civilian government with a national assembly. A provisional government was formed in Addis Adaba in early July 1991. The leader of the separatist organization in control of Eritrea attended as an observer.

History. Black Africa's oldest state, Ethiopia can trace 2,000 years of recorded history. Its now deposed royal line claimed descent from King Menelik I, traditionally believed to have been the son of the Queen of Sheba and King Solomon. The present nation is a consolidation of smaller kingdoms that owed feudal allegiance to the Ethiopian Emperor.

Hamitic peoples migrated to Ethiopia from Asia Minor in prehistoric times. Semitic traders from Arabia penetrated the region in the 7th century B.C. Its Red Sea ports were important to the Roman and Byzantine Empires. Coptic Christianity came to the country in A.D. 341, and a variant of that communion became Ethiopia's state religion.

Ancient Ethiopia reached its peak in the 5th century, then was isolated by the rise of Islam and weakened by feudal wars. Modern Ethiopia emerged under Emperor Menelik II, who established its independence by routing an Italian invasion in 1896. He expanded Ethiopia by conquest.

Disorders that followed Menelik's death brought his daughter to the throne in 1917, with his cousin, Tafari Makonnen, as Regent, heir presumptive, and strongman. When the Empress died in 1930, Tafari was crowned Emperor Haile Selassie I.

As Regent, Haile Selassie outlawed slavery. As Emperor, he worked for centralization of his diffuse realm, in which 70 languages are spoken, and for moderate reform. In 1931, he granted a Constitution, revised in 1955, that created a parliament with an appointed Senate and an elected Chamber of Deputies, and a system of courts. But basic power remained with the Emperor.

Bent on colonial empire, fascist Italy invaded Ethiopia on Oct. 3, 1935, forcing Haile Selassie into exile in May 1936. Ethiopia was annexed to Eritrea, then an Italian colony, and Italian Somaliland to form Italian East Africa, losing its independence for the first time in recorded history. In 1941, British troops routed the Italians, and Haile Selassie returned to Addis Ababa.

In August 1974, the Armed Forces Committee nationalized Haile Selassie's palace and estates and directed him not to leave Addis Ababa. On Sept. 12, 1974, he was deposed after nearly 58 years as Regent and Emperor. The 82-year-old "Lion of Judah" was placed under guard. Parliament was dissolved and the Constitution suspended.

On Aug. 27, 1975, Haile Selassie died in a small apartment in his former Addis Ababa palace where he had been treated as a state prisoner. He was 83.

Lt. Col. Mengistu Haile Mariam was named head of state Feb. 2, 1977, to replace Brig. Gen. Teferi Benti, who was killed in a factional fight of the Dirgue after having ruled since 1974. The government was losing its fight to hold Eritrea and in the southeastern region of Ogaden, Somali guerrillas backed by Somali regular forces threatened the ancient city of Harar. In October, the U.S.S.R. announced it would end military aid to Somalia and henceforth back its new ally, Ethiopia. This, together with the intervention of Cuban troops in Ogaden, turned the tide for Mengistu. By March 1978, the badly beaten

Somalis had retreated to their homeland. This brought an end to large-scale fighting with Somalia, but border skirmishing continued intermittently.

A Communist regime was formally proclaimed on Sept. 10, 1984, with Mengistu as party leader.

Ethiopia became a Marxist state with forced collectivization and relocation of peasants. A cut-off of Soviet aid led to mass animosity, and a rebel offensive began in February 1991. Mengistu resigned and fled the country in May. A group called the Ethiopian People's Revolutionary Democratic Front seized the capital. Also in May a separatist guerrilla organization, the Eritrean People's Liberation Front, took control of the province of Eritrea. The two groups agreed in early July that Eritrea would have an internationally supervised referendum on independence, though probably not for two years to allow for a measure of stability.

FIJI

Republic of Fiji
President: Ratu Sir Penaia Ganilau (1987)
Prime Minister: Ratu Sir Kamisese Mara (1987)
Area: 7,078 sq mi. (18,333 sq km)
Population (est. mid-1991): 700,000 (average annual rate of natural increase: 2.0%); birth rate: 24/1000 infant mortality rate: 21/1000; density per square mile: 104
Capital (1985): Suva (on Viti Levu), 75,000
Monetary unit: Fiji dollar
Languages: Fijian, Hindustani, English
Religions: Christian, 50%; Hindu, 41%; Islam, 8%
Literacy rate: 80%
Economic summary: Gross domestic product (1989 est.): $1.32 billion; $1,750 per capita; real growth rate 12.5%. Arable land: 8%. Principal products: sugar, copra, rice, ginger. Labor force: 176,000; 60% subsistence agriculture; 40% wage earners. Major industrial products: refined sugar, gold, lumber. Natural resources: timber, fish, gold, copper. Exports: sugar, copra, processed fish, lumber. Imports: foodstuffs, machinery, manufactured goods, fuels, chemicals. Major trading partners: U.S., Australia, Japan, New Zealand.

Geography. Fiji consists of more than 330 islands in the southwestern Pacific Ocean about 1,960 miles (3,152 km) from Sydney, Australia. The two largest islands are Viti Levu (4,109 sq mi.; 10,642 sq km) and Vanua Levu (2,242 sq mi.; 5,807 sq km). The island of Rotuma (18 sq mi.; 47 sq km), about 400 miles (644 km) to the north, is a province of Fiji. Overall, Fiji is nearly as large as New Jersey.

The largest islands in the group are mountainous and volcanic, with the tallest peak being Mount Victoria (4,341 ft; 1,323 m) on Viti Levu. The islands in the south have dense forests on the windward side and grasslands on the leeward.

Government. Military coup leader Major General Sitiveni Rabuka formerly declared Fiji a republic on Oct. 6, 1987. A civilian interium government was established in December 1987. General elections are expected to be held in July 1992.

History. In 1874, an offer of cession by the Fijian chiefs was accepted, and Fiji was proclaimed a possession and dependency of the British Crown.

During World War II, the archipelago was an important air and naval station on the route from the U.S. and Hawaii to Australia and New Zealand.

Fiji became independent on Oct. 10, 1970. The next year it joined the five-island South Pacific Forum, which intends to become a permanent regional group to promote collective diplomacy of the newly independent members.

In Oct., 1987, then Brig. Gen. Sitiveni Rabuka, the coup leader, declared Fiji a republic and removed it from the British Commonwealth.

Rabuka resigned from the cabinet in 1990, and a new constitution came into effect in July that ensured ethnic Fijians a majority of seats in the parliament. Opposition parties condemned this provision and vowed not to participate in elections held under this constitution.

FINLAND

Republic of Finland
President: Mauno H. Koivisto (1982)
Premier: Esko Aho (1991)
Area: 130,119 sq mi. (337,009 sq km)
Population (est. mid-1991): 5,000,000 (average annual rate of natural increase: 0.3%); birth rate: 13/1000; infant mortality rate: 5.8/1000; density per square mile: 38
Capital: Helsinki
Largest cities (est. 1987): Helsinki, 487,749; Tampere, 170,097; Espoo, 162,106; Turku, 160,974
Monetary unit: Markka
Languages: Finnish, Swedish
Religions: Evangelical Lutheran, 97%; Eastern Orthodox, 1.8%
National name: Suomen Tasavalta—Republiken Finland
Literacy rate: almost 100%
Economic summary: Gross domestic product (1989 est.): $74.4 billion; $15,000 per capita; 4.6% real growth rate. Arable land: 8%. Principal products: dairy and meat products, cereals, sugar beets, potatoes. Labor force: 2,556,000; 22.9% mining and manufacturing. Major products: metal manufactures, forestry and wood products, refined copper, ships, electronics. Natural resource: timber. Exports: timber, paper and pulp, ships, machinery, clothing, footwear. Imports: petroleum and petroleum products, chemicals, transportation equipment, machinery, textile yarns, foodstuffs, fodder grain. Major trading partners: Germany, Sweden, U.S.S.R., U.K., U.S.

Geography. Finland stretches 700 miles (1,127 km) from the Gulf of Finland on the south to Soviet Petsamo, north of the Arctic Circle. The U.S.S.R. extends along the entire eastern frontier while Norway is on her northern border and Sweden lies on her western border. In area, Finland is three times the size of Ohio.

Off the southwest coast are the Aland Islands, controlling the entrance to the Gulf of Bothnia. Finland has more than 200,000 lakes.

The Swedish-populated Aland Islands (581 sq mi.; 1,505 sq km) have an autonomous status under a law passed in 1921.

Government. The president, chosen for six years by the popularly elected Electoral College of 301 members, appoints the Cabinet. The one-chamber Diet, the Eduskunta, consists of 200 members elected for four-year terms by proportional representation.

History. At the end of the 7th century, the Finns came to Finland from their Volga settlements, taking the country from the Lapps, who retreated northward. The Finns' repeated raids on the Scandinavian coast impelled Eric IX, the Swedish King, to conquer the country in 1157 and bring it into contact with Western Christendom. By 1809 the whole of Finland was conquered by Alexander I of Russia, who set up Finland as a Grand Duchy.

The first period of Russification (1809–1905) resulted in a lessening of the powers of the Finnish Diet. The Russian language was made official, and the Finnish military system was superseded by the Russian. The pace of Russification was intensified from 1908 to 1914. When Russian control was weakened as a consequence of the March Revolution of 1917, the Diet on July 20, 1917, proclaimed Finland's independence, which became complete on Dec. 6, 1917.

Finland rejected Soviet territorial demands, and the U.S.S.R. attacked on Nov. 30, 1939. The Finns made an amazing stand of three months and finally capitulated, ceding 16,000 square miles (41,440 sq km) to the U.S.S.R. Under German pressure, the Finns joined the Nazis against Russia in 1941, but were defeated again and ceded the Petsamo area to the U.S.S.R. In 1948, a 20-year treaty of friendship and mutual assistance was signed by the two nations and renewed for another 20 years in 1970.

After 25 years in office, President Urho K. Kekkonen resigned in October 1981 because of ill health. Premier Mauno Koivisto, leader of the Social Democratic Party, was elected President on Jan. 26, 1982, winning decisively over a conservative rival with support from Finnish Communists.

Elections in March 1991 made the Center Party the largest single party in parliament. A center-right coalition government was formed that in June decided to peg the markka to the Ecu and thereby slowly intergate the Finnish economy into that of Western Europe.

FRANCE

French Republic
President: François Mitterrand (1981)
Premier: Edith Cresson (1991)
Area: 211,208 sq mi. (547,026 sq km)
Population (est. mid-1991): 56,700,000 (average annual rate of natural increase: 0.4%); birth rate: 14/1000; infant mortality rate: 7.2/1000; density per square mile: 268
Capital: Paris
Largest cities (est. 1983): Paris, 2,150,000; (1982 est.): Marseilles, 868,435; Lyons, 410,455; Toulouse, 344,917; Nice, 331,165; Nantes, 237,789; Strasbourg, 247,068; Bordeaux, 201,965
Monetary unit: Franc
Language: French, declining regional dialects
Religion: Roman Catholic, 90%
National name: République Française
Literacy rate: 99%
Economic summary: Gross domestic product (1989 est.): $819.6 billion; $14,600 per capita; 3.4% real growth rate. Arable land: 32%. Principal products: cereals, feed grains, livestock and dairy products, wine, fruits, vegetables, potatoes. Labor force: 24,170,000; 31.3% industry. Major products: chemicals, automobiles, processed foods, iron and steel, aircraft, textiles, clothing. Natural resources: coal, iron ore, bauxite,

fish, forests. Exports: textiles and clothing, chemicals, machinery and transport equipment, agricultural products. Imports: machinery, crude petroleum, chemicals, agricultural products. Major trading partners: Germany, Italy, U.S., Belgium-Luxembourg, U.K., Netherlands.

Geography. France (80% the size of Texas) is second in size to the U.S.S.R. among Europe's nations. In the Alps near the Italian and Swiss borders is Europe's highest point—Mont Blanc (15,781 ft; 4,810 m). The forest-covered Vosges Mountains are in the northeast, and the Pyrenees are along the Spanish border.

Except for extreme northern France, which is part of the Flanders plain, the country may be described as four river basins and a plateau. Three of the streams flow west—the Seine into the English Channel, the Loire into the Atlantic, and the Garonne into the Bay of Biscay. The Rhône flows south into the Mediterranean. For about 100 miles (161 km), the Rhine is France's eastern border.

West of the Rhône and northeast of the Garonne lies the central plateau, covering about 15% of France's area and rising to a maximum elevation of 6,188 feet (1,886 m). In the Mediterranean, about 115 miles (185 km) east-southeast of Nice, is Corsica (3,367 sq mi.; 8,721 sq km).

Government. The president is elected for seven years by universal suffrage. He appoints the premier, and the Cabinet is responsible to Parliament. The president has the right to dissolve the National Assembly or to ask Parliament for reconsideration of a law. The Parliament consists of two houses: the National Assembly and the Senate.

History. The history of France, as distinct from ancient Gaul, begins with the Treaty of Verdun (843), dividing the territories corresponding roughly to France, Germany, and Italy among the three grandsons of Charlemagne. Julius Caesar had conquered part of Gaul in 57–52 B.C., and it remained Roman until Franks invaded it in the 5th century.

Charles the Bald, inheritor of *Francia Occidentalis*, founded the Carolingian dynasty, which ruled over a kingdom increasingly feudalized. By 987, the crown passed to Hugh Capet, a princeling who controlled only the Ile-de-France, the region surrounding Paris. For 350 years, an unbroken Capetian line added to its domain and consolidated royal authority until the accession in 1328 of Philip VI, first of the Valois line. France was then the most powerful nation in Europe, with a population of 15 million.

The missing pieces in Philip's domain were the French provinces still held by the Plantagenet kings of England, who also claimed the French crown. Beginning in 1338, the Hundred Years' War eventually settled the contest. English longbows defeated French armored knights at Crécy (1346) and the English also won the second landmark battle at Agincourt (1415), but the final victory went to the French at Castillon (1453).

Absolute monarchy reached its apogee in the reign of Louis XIV (1643–1715), the Sun King, whose brilliant court was the center of the Western world.

Revolution plunged France into a blood bath beginning in 1789 and ending with a new authoritarianism under Napoleon Bonaparte, who had successfully defended the infant republic from foreign attack and then made himself First Consul in 1799 and Emperor in 1804.

Rulers of France

Name	Born	Ruled[1]
CAROLINGIAN DYNASTY		
Pepin the Short	c. 714	751–768
Charlemagne[2]	742	768–814
Louis I the Debonair[3]	778	814–840
Charles I the Bald[4]	823	840–877
Louis II the Stammerer	846	877–879
Louis III[5]	c. 863	879–882
Carloman[5]	?	879–884
Charles II the Fat[6]	839	884–887 [7]
Eudes (Odo), Count of Paris	?	888–898
Charles III the Simple[8]	879	893–923 [9]
Robert I[10]	c. 865	922–923
Rudolf (Raoul), Duke of Burgundy	?	923–936
Louis IV d'Outremer	c. 921	936–954
Lothair	941	954–986
Louis V the Sluggard	c. 967	986–987
CAPETIAN DYNASTY		
Hugh Capet	c. 940	987–996
Robert II the Pious[11]	c. 970	996–1031
Henry I	1008	1031–1060
Philip I	1052	1060–1108
Louis VI the Fat	1081	1108–1137
Louis VII the Young	c.1121	1137–1180
Philip II (Philip Augustus)	1165	1180–1223
Louis VIII the Lion	1187	1223–1226
Louis IX (St. Louis)	1214	1226–1270
Philip III the Bold	1245	1270–1285
Philip IV the Fair	1268	1285–1314
Louis X the Quarreler	1289	1314–1316
John I[12]	1316	1316
Philip V the Tall	1294	1316–1322
Charles IV the Fair	1294	1322–1328
HOUSE OF VALOIS		
Philip VI	1293	1328–1350
John II the Good	1319	1350–1364
Charles V the Wise	1337	1364–1380
Charles VI the Well–Beloved	1368	1380–1422
Charles VII	1403	1422–1461
Louis XI	1423	1461–1483
Charles VIII	1470	1483–1498
Louis XII the Father of the People	1462	1498–1515
Francis I	1494	1515–1547
Henry II	1519	1547–1559
Francis II	1544	1559–1560
Charles IX	1550	1560–1574
Henry III	1551	1574–1589
HOUSE OF BOURBON		
Henry IV of Navarre	1553	1589–1610
Louis XIII	1601	1610–1643
Louis XIV the Great	1638	1643–1715
Louis XV the Well–Beloved	1710	1715–1774
Louis XVI	1754	1774–1792 [13]
Louis XVII (Louis Charles de France)[14]	1785	1793–1795

Name	Born	Ruled[1]
FIRST REPUBLIC		
National Convention	—	1792–1795
Directory (Directoire)	—	1795–1799
CONSULATE		
Napoleon Bonaparte[15]	1769	1799–1804
FIRST EMPIRE		
Napoleon I	1769	1804–1815 [16]
RESTORATION OF HOUSE OF BOURBON		
Louis XVIII le Désiré	1755	1814–1824
Charles X	1757	1824–1830 [17]
BOURBON-ORLEANS LINE		
Louis Philippe ("Citizen King")	1773	1830–1848 [18]
SECOND REPUBLIC		
Louis Napoleon[19]	1808	1848–1852
SECOND EMPIRE		
Napoleon III (Louis Napoleon)	1808	1852–1870 [20]
THIRD REPUBLIC (PRESIDENTS)		
Louis Adolphe Thiers	1797	1871–1873
Marie E. P. M. de MacMahon	1808	1873–1879
François P. J. Grévy	1807	1879–1887
Sadi Carnot	1837	1887–1894
Jean Casimir–Périer	1847	1894–1895
François Félix Faure	1841	1895–1899
Émile Loubet	1838	1899–1906
Clement Armand Fallières	1841	1906–1913
Raymond Poincaré	1860	1913–1920
Paul E. L. Deschanel	1856	1920–1920
Alexandre Millerand	1859	1920–1924
Gaston Doumergue	1863	1924–1931
Paul Doumer	1857	1931–1932
Albert Lebrun	1871	1932–1940
VICHY GOVERNMENT (CHIEF OF STATE)		
Henri Philippe Pétain	1856	1940–1944
PROVISIONAL GOVERNMENT (PRESIDENTS)		
Charles de Gaulle	1890	1944–1946
Félix Gouin	1884	1946–1946
Georges Bidault	1899	1946–1947
FOURTH REPUBLIC (PRESIDENTS)		
Vincent Auriol	1884	1947–1954
René Coty	1882	1954–1959
FIFTH REPUBLIC (PRESIDENTS)		
Charles de Gaulle	1890	1959–1969
Georges Pompidou	1911	1969–1974
Valéry Giscard d'Estaing	1926	1974–1981
François Mitterrand	1916	1981–

1. For Kings and Emperors through the Second Empire, year of end of rule is also that of death, unless otherwise indicated. 2. Crowned Emperor of the West in 800. His brother, Carloman, ruled as King of the Eastern Franks from 768 until his death in 771. 3. Holy Roman Emperor 814–840. 4. Holy Roman Emperor 875–877 as Charles II. 5. Ruled jointly 879–882. 6. Holy Roman Emperor 881–887 as Charles III. 7. Died 888. 8. King 893–898 in opposition to Eudes. 9. Died 929. 10. Not counted in regular line of Kings of France by some authorities. Elected by nobles but killed in Battle of Soissons. 11. Sometimes called Robert I. 12. Posthumous son of Louis X; lived for only five days. 13. Executed 1793. 14. Titular King only. He died in prison according to official reports, but many pretenders appeared during the Bourbon restoration. 15. As First Consul, Napoleon held the power of government. In 1804, he became Emperor. 16. Abdicated first time June 1814. Re–entered Paris March 1815, after escape from Elba; Louis XVIII fled to Ghent. Abdicated second time June 1815. He named as his successor his son, Napoleon II, who was not acceptable to the Allies. He died 1821. 17. Died 1836. 18. Died 1850. 19. President; became Emperor in 1852. 20. Died 1873.

The Congress of Vienna (1815) sought to restore the pre-Napoleonic order in the person of Louis XVIII, but industrialization and the middle class, both fostered under Napoleon, built pressure for change, and a revolution in 1848 drove Louis Phillipe, last of the Bourbons, into exile.

A second republic elected as its president Prince Louis Napoleon, a nephew of Napoleon I, who declared the Second Empire in 1852 and took the throne as Napoleon III. His opposition to the rising power of Prussia ignited the Franco-Prussian War (1870–71), ending in his defeat and abdication.

A new France emerged from World War I as the continent's dominant power. But four years of hostile occupation had reduced northeast France to ruins. The postwar Third Republic was plagued by political instability and economic chaos.

From 1919, French foreign policy aimed at keeping Germany weak through a system of alliances, but it failed to halt the rise of Adolf Hitler and the Nazi war machine. On May 10, 1940, mechanized Nazi troops attacked, and, as they approached Paris, Italy joined with Germany. The Germans marched into an undefended Paris and Marshal Henri Philippe Pétain signed an armistice June 22. France was split into an occupied north and an unoccupied south, the latter becoming a totalitarian state with Pétain as its chief.

Allied armies liberated France in August 1944. The French Committee of National Liberation, formed in Algiers in 1943, established a provisional government in Paris headed by Gen. Charles de Gaulle. The Fourth Republic was born Dec. 24, 1946.

The Empire became the French Union; the National Assembly was strengthened and the presidency weakened; and France joined the North Atlantic Treaty Organization. A war against communist insurgents in Indochina was abandoned after the defeat at Dien Bien Phu. A new rebellion in Algeria threatened a military coup, and on June 1, 1958, the Assembly invited de Gaulle to return as premier with extraordinary powers. He drafted a new Constitution for a Fifth Republic, adopted Sept. 28, which strengthened the presidency and reduced legislative power. He was elected president Dec. 21.

De Gaulle took France out of the NATO military command in 1967 and expelled all foreign-controlled troops from the country. He later went on to attempt to achieve a long-cherished plan of regional reform. This, however, aroused wide opposition. He decided to stake his fate on a referendum. At the voting in April 1969, the electorate defeated the plan.

His successor Georges Pompidou continued the de Gaulle policies of seeking to expand France's influence in the Mideast and Africa, selling arms to South Africa (despite the U.N. embargo), to Libya, and to Greece, and in 1971 he endorsed British entry into the Common Market.

Socialist François Mitterrand attained a stunning victory in the May 10, 1981, Presidential election over the Gaullist alliance that had held power since 1958.

The victors immediately moved to carry out campaign pledges to nationalize major industries, halt nuclear testing, suspend nuclear power plant construction, and impose new taxes on the rich. On Feb. 11, 1982, the nationalization bills became law.

The Socialists' policies during Mitterrand's first two years created a 12% inflation rate, a huge trade deficit, and devaluations of the franc. In early 1983, Mitterrand, embarked on an austerity program to control inflation and reduce the trade deficit. He increased taxes and slashed government spending. A halt in economic growth, declining purchasing power

for the average Frenchman, and an increase in unemployment to 10% followed. Mitterrand sank lower and lower in the opinion polls.

In March, 1986, a center-right coalition led by Jacques Chirac won a slim majority in legislative elections. Chirac became Premier initiating a period of "co-habitation" between him and the Socialist President, Mitterrand, a cooperation marked by sparring over Chirac's plan to denationalize major industries and effect a harder line on security issues and on New Caledonia.

Mitterrand's decisive reelection in May, 1987, led to Chirac being replaced as Premier by Michel Rocard, a Socialist. Mitterrand called legislative elections for June, 1987 that gave the Socialists a plurality.

Relations, however, cooled with Rocard, and in May 1991 he was replaced with Edith Cresson, France's first female prime minister and like Mitterrand a Socialist. Almost immediately upon taking office she faced a number of economic and social problems that threatened to cut short any honeymoon period. In June France announced it would sign the 1968 Nuclear Nonproliferation Treaty.

Overseas Departments

Overseas Departments elect representatives to the National Assembly, and the same administrative organization as that of mainland France applies to them.

FRENCH GUIANA (including ININI)

Status: Overseas Department
Prefect: Jacques Dewatre (1986)
Area: 35,126 sq mi. (90,976 sq km)
Population (est. mid 1990): 94,702 (average annual growth rate: 3.2%)
Capital (est. 1982): Cayenne, 37,097
Monetary unit: Franc
Language: French
Religion: Roman Catholic
Literacy rate: 73%
Economic summary: Gross domestic product (1982): $210 million; $3,230 per capita. Arable land: NEGL%; principal agricultural products: rice, cassava, bananas, sugar cane. Labor force: 23,265; 21.2% in industry. Major industrial products: timber, rum, rosewood essence, gold mining, processed shrimp. Natural resources: bauxite, timber, cinnabar, kaolin. Exports: shrimp, timber, rum, rosewood essence. Imports: food, consumer and producer goods, petroleum. Major trading partners: U.S., France, Japan.

French Guiana, lying north of Brazil and east of Suriname on the northeast coast of South America, was first settled in 1604. Penal settlements, embracing the area around the mouth of the Maroni River and the Iles du Salut (including Devil's Island), were founded in 1852; they have since been abolished.

During World War II, French Guiana at first adhered to the Vichy government, but the Free French took over in 1943. French Guiana accepted in 1958 the new Constitution of the French Fifth Republic and remained an Overseas Department of the French Republic.

GUADELOUPE

Status: Overseas Department
Prefect: Yves Bonnet (1986)
Area: 687 sq mi. (1,779 sq km)
Population (est. mid-1991): 300,000 (average annual growth rate: 1.4%); birth rate: 21/1000; infant mortality rate: 13/1000
Capital (est. 1983): Basse-Terre, 35,000
Largest city (est. 1982): Pointe-à-Pitre, 50,000
Monetary unit: Franc
Language: French, Creole patois
Religions: Roman Catholic
Literacy rate: over 70%
Economic summary: Gross domestic product (1987): $1.1 billion; $3,300 per capita; n.a. real growth rate. Arable land: 18%; principal agricultural products: sugar cane, bananas, eggplant, flowers. Labor force: 120,000; 25.8% industry. Major industries: construction, public works, sugar, rum, tourism. Exports: sugar, rum, bananas. Imports: foodstuffs, clothing, consumer goods, construction materials, petroleum products. Major trading partner: France.

Guadeloupe, in the West Indies about 300 miles (483 km) southeast of Puerto Rico, was discovered by Columbus in 1493. It consists of the twin islands of Basse-Terre and Grande-Terre and five dependencies—Marie-Galante, Les Saintes, La Désirade, St. Barthélemy, and the northern half of St. Martin. The volcano Soufrière (4,813 ft; 1,467 m), also called La Grande Soufrière, is the highest point on Guadeloupe. Violent activity in 1976 and 1977 caused thousands to flee their homes.

French colonization began in 1635. In 1958, Guadeloupe voted in favor of the new Constitution of the French Fifth Republic and remained an Overseas Department of the French Republic.

MARTINIQUE

Status: Overseas Department
Prefect: Edouard LaCroix (1986)
Area: 431 sq mi. (1,116 sq km)
Population (est. mid-1991): 300,000 (average annual growth rate: 1.3%); birth rate: 19/1000; infant mortality rate: 11/1000
Capital (est. 1984): Fort-de-France, 97,814
Monetary unit: Franc
Languages: French, Creole patois
Religion: Roman Catholic
Literacy rate: over 70%
Economic summary: Gross domestic product (1984): $1.3 billion, $3.650 per capita. Average annual growth rate n.a. Arable land: 10%; principal agricultural products: sugar cane, bananas, rum, pineapples. Labor force: 100,000; 31.7% in service industry. Major industries: sugar, rum, refined oil, cement, tourism. Natural resources: coastal scenery and beaches. Exports: bananas, refined petroleum products, rum, sugar, pineapples. Imports: foodstuffs, clothing and other consumer goods, petroleum products, construction materials. Major trading partners: France, U.S.

Martinique, lying in the Lesser Antilles about 300 miles (483 km) northeast of Venezuela, was probably discovered by Columbus in 1502 and was taken for France in 1635. Following the Franco-German armistice of 1940, it had a semiautonomous status until 1943, when authority was relinquished to the Free French. The area, administered by a Prefect assisted by an elected council, is represented in the French Parliament. In 1958, Martinique voted in favor of the new Constitution of the French Fifth Republic and remained an Overseas Department of the French Republic.

RÉUNION

Status: Overseas Department
Prefect: Jean Anciaux (1986)
Area: 970 sq mi. (2,510 sq km)
Population (est. mid-1991): 600,000 (average annual growth rate, 1.7%); birth rate: 22/1000; infant mortality rate: 13/1000
Capital (est. 1986): Saint-Denis, 109,072
Monetary unit: Franc
Languages: French, Creole
Religion: Roman Catholic
Economic summary: Gross domestic product (1985): $2.4 billion; $4,290 per capita; real growth rate 9% (1987 est.). Arable land: 20%; principal agricultural products: rum, vanilla, bananas, perfume plants. Major industrial products: rum, cigarettes, processed sugar. Exports: sugar, perfume essences, rum, molasses. Imports: manufactured goods, foodstuffs, beverages, machinery and transportation equipment, petroleum products. Major trading partners: France, Mauritius, Bahrain, South Africa, Italy.

Discovered by Portuguese navigators in the 16th century, the island of Réunion, then uninhabited, was taken as a French possession in 1642. It is located about 450 miles (724 km) east of Madagascar, in the Indian Ocean. In 1958, Réunion approved the Constitution of the Fifth French Republic and remained an Overseas Department of the French Republic.

ST. PIERRE AND MIQUELON

Status: Overseas Department
Prefect: Bernard Leurguin (1986)
Area: 93 sq mi. (242 sq km)
Population (est. 1989): 6,303; .4% growth rate.
Capital (est. 1981): Saint Pierre, 5,800
Economic summary: Major industries: fishing, canneries. Exports: fish, pelts. Imports: meat, clothing, fuel, electrical equipment, machinery, building materials. Major trading partners: Canada, France, U.S., U.K., Netherlands.

The sole remnant of the French colonial empire in North America, these islands were first occupied by the French in 1604. Their only importance arises from proximity to the Grand Banks, located 10 miles south of Newfoundland, making them the center of the French Atlantic cod fisheries. On July 19, 1976, the islands became an Overseas Department of the French Republic.

Overseas Territories

Overseas Territories are comparable to Departments, except that their administrative organization includes a locally-elected government.

FRENCH POLYNESIA

Status: Overseas Territory
High Commissioner: Bernard Gerard (1986)
Area: 1,544 sq mi. (4,000 sq km)
Population (mid-1991): 200,000 (average annual growth rate: 2.5%); birth rate: 30/1000; infant mortality rate: 20/1000
Monetary unit: Pacific financial community franc
Language: French

Religions: Protestant, 55%; Roman Catholic, 32%
Capital (est. 1983): Papeete (on Tahiti), 23,496
Economic summary: Gross national product (1986): $2.24
billion. Average annual growth rate n.a. Per capita
income (1986): $6,400. Principal agricultural product:
copra. Major industries: tourism, maintenance of
French nuclear test base. Exports: coconut products,
mother of pearl, vanilla. Imports: fuels, foodstuffs,
equipment. Major trading partners: France, U.S.

The term French Polynesia is applied to the scattered French possessions in the South Pacific—Man-
gareva (Gambier), Makatea, the Marquesas Islands,
Rapa, Rurutu, Rimatara, the Society Islands, the Tua-
motu Archipelago, Tubuai, Raivavae, and the island
of Clipperton—which were organized into a single
colony in 1903. There are 120 islands, of which 25
are uninhabited.

The High Commissioner is assisted by a Council of
Government and a popularly elected Territorial Assembly. The principal and most populous island—Tahiti, in the Society group—was claimed as French in
1768. In 1958, French Polynesia voted in favor of the
new Constitution of the French Fifth Republic and
remained an Overseas Territory of the French Republic. The natives are mostly Maoris.

The Pacific Nuclear Test Center on the atoll of
Mururoa, 744 miles (1,200 km) from Tahiti, was
completed in 1966.

MAYOTTE

Status: Territorial collectivity
Prefect: Guy DuPuis (1986)
Area: 146 sq mi. (378 sq km)
Population (est. 1985): 66,282
Capital (est. 1985): Dzaoudzi, 5,675
Principal products: vanilla, ylang-ylang, coffee, copra

The most populous of the Comoro Islands in the
Indian Ocean, with a Christian majority, Mayotte
voted in 1974 and 1976 against joining the other, predominantly Moslem islands, in declaring themselves
independent. It continues to retain its ties to France.

NEW CALEDONIA AND DEPENDENCIES

Status: Overseas Territory
High Commissioner: Ferdinand Wibaux (1986)
Area: 7,374 sq mi. (19,103 sq km)[1]
Population (mid-1991): 200,000 (average annual growth
rate: 1.9%); birth rate: 24/1000; infant mortality rate:
21/1000
Capital (est. 1983): Nouméa, 60,112
Monetary unit: Pacific financial community franc
Languages: French, Melanesian and Polynesian dialects
Religion: Roman Catholic, 60%; Protestant, 30%
Literacy rate: Not known
Economic summary: Gross national product (1989 est):
$860 million; average annual growth rate 2.4%; per
capita income $5,810. Principal agricultural products:
coffee, copra, beef, wheat, vegetables. Major industrial product: nickel. Natural resources: nickel, chromite, iron ore. Exports: nickel, chrome. Imports: minerals, fuels, machinery, electrical equipment,
foodstuffs. Major trading partners: France, Japan,
U.S., Australia.

1. Including dependencies.

New Caledonia (6,466 sq mi.; 16,747 sq km),
about 1,070 miles (1,722 km) northeast of Sydney,
Australia, was discovered by Capt. James Cook in
1774 and annexed by France in 1853. The government also administers the Isle of Pines, the Loyalty
Islands (Uvéa, Lifu, and Maré), the Belep Islands, the
Huon Island group, and Chesterfield Islands.

The natives are Melanesians; about one third of the
population is white and one fifth Indochinese and
Javanese. The French National Assembly on July 31,
1984, voted a bill into law that granted internal autonomy to New Caledonia and opened the way to
possible eventual independence. This touched off ethnic tensions and violence between the natives and the
European settlers, with the natives demanding full independence and sovereignty while the settlers wanted
to remain part of France. In June, 1988, France resumed direct administration of the territory and promised a referendum on self-determination in 1998. This
was agreed to by organizations representing the natives and the French settlers.

SOUTHERN AND ANTARCTIC LANDS

Status: Overseas Territory
Administrator: Claude Corbier
Area: 3,004 sq mi. (7,781 sq km, excluding Adélie Land)
Capital: Port-au-Français

This territory is uninhabited except for the personnel of scientific bases. It consists of Adélie Land
(166,752 sq mi.; 431,888 sq km) on the Antarctic
mainland and the following islands in the southern
Indian Ocean: the Kerguelen and Crozet archipelagos
and the islands of Saint-Paul and New Amsterdam.

WALLIS AND FUTUNA ISLANDS

Status: Overseas Territory
Administrator Superior: Roger Dumec (1988)
Area: 106 sq mi. (274 sq km)
Population (July 1990): 14,910
Capital (1980): Wallis (on Uvea), 600

The two islands groups in the South Pacific between Fiji and Samoa were settled by French missionaries at the beginning of the 19th century. A protectorate was established in the 1880s. Following a
referendum by the Polynesian inhabitants, the status
was changed to that of an Overseas Territory in 1961.

GABON

Gabonese Republic
President: Omar Bongo (1967)
Premier: Oyé Mba Casimir (1990)
Area: 103,346 sq mi. (267,667 sq km)
Population (est. mid-1991): 1,200,000 (average annual
rate of natural increase: 2.3%); birth rate: 39/1000;
infant mortality rate: 103/1000; density per square
mile: 12
Capital and largest city (est. 1983): Libreville, 257,000
Monetary unit: Franc CFA
Ethnic groups: Bateke, Obamba, Bakota, Shake,
Pongwés, Adumas, Chiras, Punu, and Lumbu
Languages: French (official) and Bantu dialects
Religions: Roman Catholic, 65%, Protestant, 19%
National name: République Gabonaise
Member of French Community
Literacy rate: 61.6%
Economic summary: Gross domestic product (1989): $3.2
billion; $3,000 per capita; real growth rate 0%. Arable

land: 1%. Principal products: cocoa, coffee, wood, palm oil. Labor force: 120,000 salaried; 30% in industry and commerce. Major products: petroleum, natural gas, processed wood, manganese, uranium. Natural resources: wood, petroleum, iron ore, manganese, uranium. Exports: crude petroleum, wood and wood products, minerals. Imports: mining and road-building machinery, electrical equipment, foodstuffs, textiles, transport vehicles. Major trading partners: France, U.S. Germany.

Geography. This West African land with the Atlantic as its western border is also bounded by Equatorial Guinea, Cameroon, and the Congo. Its area is slightly less than Colorado's.

From mangrove swamps on the coast, the land becomes divided plateaus in the north and east and mountains in the north. Most of the country is covered by a dense tropical forest.

Government. The president is elected for a seven-year term. Legislative powers are exercised by a 120-seat National Assembly, which is elected for a seven-year term. After his conversion to Islam in 1973, President Bongo changed his given name, Albert Bernard, to Omar. The Rassemblement Social Démocrate Gabonais is led by President Bongo. He was re-elected without opposition in 1973 and in 1980.

History. Little is known of Gabon's history, even in oral tradition, but Pygmies are believed to be the original inhabitants. Now there are many tribal groups in the country, the largest being the Fang people who constitute a third of the population.

Gabon was first visited by the Portuguese navigator Diego Cam in the 15th century. In 1839, the French founded their first settlement on the left bank of the Gabon Estuary and gradually occupied the hinterland during the second half of the 19th century. It was organized as a French territory in 1888 and became an autonomous republic within the French Union after World War II and an independent republic on Aug. 17, 1960.

Following strikes and riots the president called a national conference in March 1990. In May it adopted a transitional constitution legalizing political parties and calling for free elections. When these took place in September riots arising out of charges of irregularities caused the disqualification of the results. A subsequent round gave the ruling party a victory, but by a narrow margin.

GAMBIA

Republic of the Gambia
President: Sir Dawda K. Jawara (1970)
Area: 4,093 sq mi. (10,600 sq km)
Population (est. mid-1991): 900,000 (average annual rate of natural increase: 2.6%); birth rate: 47/1000; infant mortality rate: 143/1000; density per square mile: 203
Capital (est. 1983): Banjul, 44,188
Monetary unit: Dalasi
Languages: Native tongues, English (official)
Religions: Islam, 90%, Christian, 9%, traditional, 1%
Member of Commonwealth of Nations
Literacy rate: 25.1%
Economic summary: Gross domestic product (FY89 est.): $195 million; $250 per capita; 4.6% real growth rate. Arable land: 16%. Principal products: peanuts, rice, palm kernels. Labor force: 400,000; 18.9% in industry,

commerce and services. Major industrial products: processed peanuts, fish, and hides. Natural resources: fish. Exports: peanuts and peanut products, fish. Imports: foodstuffs, fuel, machinery, transport equipment. Major trading partners: U.S., E.C., Asia.

Geography. Situated on the Atlantic coast in westernmost Africa and surrounded on three sides by Senegal, Gambia is twice the size of Delaware. The Gambia River flows for 200 miles (322 km) through Gambia on its way to the Atlantic. The country, the smallest on the continent, averages only 20 miles (32 km) in width.

Government. The president's five-year term is linked to the 35-member unicameral House of Representatives, from which he appoints his Cabinet members and the vice president.

The major political party is the People's Progressive Party (27 seats in House of Representatives), led by President Jawara.

History. During the 17th century, Gambia was settled by various companies of English merchants. Slavery was the chief source of revenue until it was abolished in 1807. Gambia became a crown colony in 1843 and an independent nation within the Commonwealth of Nations on Feb. 18, 1965.

Full independence was approved in a 1970 referendum, and on April 24 of that year Gambia proclaimed itself a republic.

President Dawda K. Jawara won overwhelming re-election to his fifth term on May 5, 1982. Although insisting on his commitment to a multiparty system President Jawara held talks in 1990 with the opposition National Convention Party about the possibility of a party merger.

GERMANY

Federal Republic of Germany
President: Richard von Weizsäcker (1984)
Chancellor: Helmut Kohl (1982)
Area: 137,838 sq mi. (357,000 sq km)
Population (Jan. 1991): 78,700,000 (average annual growth rate: 0%; birth rate: 11/1000; infant mortality rate: 7.5/1000; density per square mile: 571
Capital (est. 1990): Berlin, 3,410,000; seat of parliament and government: Bonn[1], 279,000 (1988)
Largest cities (1989 est.): Hamburg, 1,597,500; Munich, 1,206,400; Cologne, 934,400; Frankfurt, 623,700; Essen, 620,000; Dortmund, 584,600; Dusseldorf, 564,400; Stuttgart, 560,100; Bremen, 533,800; Dresden, 501,400; Leipzig, 530,000; Hanover, 497,200
Monetary unit: Deutsche Mark
Language: German
Religions: Protestant, 49%; Roman Catholic, 45%
National name: Bundesrepublik Deutschland
Literacy rate: 99%
Economic summary: Preliminary GNP, West Germany (1990): $1,579 billion; $24,980 est. per capita; GNP 3.6 real growth rate. Arable land: 30%. Principal products: grains, potatoes, sugar beets. Labor force: 27,790,000; 41.6% in industry. Major products: chemicals, machinery, vehicles. Natural resources: iron ore, timber, coal. Exports: machines and machine tools, chemicals, motor vehicles, iron and steel products. Imports: manufactured and agricultural products, raw materials, fuels. Major trading partners: France, Netherlands, Belgium-Luxembourg, Italy, U.S., U.K.
East Germany (1989): $159.5 billion; $9,679 per capita. Arable land: 45%; principal products: grains, potatoes, sugar beets, meat and dairy products. Labor force:

8,960,000; 37.5% in industry; major products: steel, chemicals, machinery, electrical and precision engineering products. Natural resources: brown coal, potash, bauxite. Exports: machinery and equipment, chemical products, textiles, clothing. Imports: raw materials, fuels, agricultural products, machinery and equipment

1. At present, seat of government will eventually move to Berlin.

Geography. The Federal Republic of Germany occupies the western half of the central European area historically regarded as German. This was the part of Germany occupied by the United States, Britain, and France after World War II, when the eastern half of prewar Germany was split roughly between a Soviet-occupied zone, which became the German Democratic Republic, and an area annexed by Poland. After being divided for more than four decades, the two Germanys were reunited on Oct. 3, 1990. The united Federal Republic is about the size of Montana.

Germany's neighbors are France, Belgium, Luxembourg, and the Netherlands on the west, Switzerland and Austria on the south, Czechoslovakia and Poland on the east, and Denmark on the north.

The northern plain, the central hill country, and the southern mountain district constitute the main physical divisions of West Germany, which is slightly smaller than Oregon. The Bavarian plateau in the southwest averages 1,600 feet (488 m) above sea level, but it reaches 9,721 feet (2,962 m) in the Zugspitze Mountains, the highest point in the country.

Important navigable rivers are the Danube, rising in the Black Forest and flowing east across Bavaria into Austria, and the Rhine, which rises in Switzerland and flows across the Netherlands in two channels to the North Sea and is navigable by ocean-going and coastal vessels as far as Cologne. The Elbe, which also empties into the North Sea, is navigable within Germany for smaller vessels. The Weser, flowing into the North Sea, and the Main and Mosel (Moselle), both tributaries of the Rhine, are also important. In addition, the Oder and Neisse Rivers form the border with Poland.

Government. Under the Constitution of May 23, 1949, the Federal Republic was established as a parliamentary democracy. The Parliament consists of the Bundesrat, an upper chamber representing and appointed by the Länder, or states, and the Bundestag, a lower house elected for four years by universal suffrage. A federal assembly composed of Bundestag deputies and deputies from the state parliaments elects the President of the Republic for a five-year term; the Bundestag alone chooses the Chancellor, or Prime Minister. Each of the 16 Länder have a legislature popularly elected for a four-year or five-year term.

The major political parties are the Christian Democratic Union-Christian Social Union (319 of 662 seats in the Bundestag), led by Chancellor Helmut Kohl; Social Democratic Party (239 seats) led by Björn Engleholm; and the Free Democratic Party (78 seats), led by Otto Count Larbsdorff, the Alliance 90/Greens (8 seats) and Party of Democratic Socialism (17 seats). Kohl's government is a coalition with the Free Democrats.

History. Immediately before the Christian era, when the Roman Empire had pushed its frontier to the Rhine, what is now Germany was inhabited by several tribes believed to have migrated from Central Asia between the 6th and 4th centuries B.C. One of these tribes, the Franks, attained supremacy in western Europe under Charlemagne, who was crowned Holy Roman Emperor A.D. 800. By the Treaty of Verdun (843), Charlemagne's lands east of the Rhine were ceded to the German Prince Louis. Additional territory acquired by the Treaty of Mersen (870) gave Germany approximately the area it maintained throughout the Middle Ages. For several centuries after Otto the Great was crowned King in 936, the German rulers were also usually heads of the Holy Roman Empire.

Relations between state and church were changed by the Reformation, which began with Martin Luther's 95 theses, and came to a head in 1547, when Charles V scattered the forces of the Protestant League at Mühlberg. Freedom of worship was guaranteed by the Peace of Augsburg (1555), but a Counter Reformation took place later, and a dispute over the succession to the Bohemian throne brought on the Thirty Years' War (1618–48), which devastated Germany and left the empire divided into hundreds of small principalities virtually independent of the Emperor.

Meanwhile, Prussia was developing into a state of considerable strength. Frederick the Great (1740–86) reorganized the Prussian army and defeated Maria Theresa of Austria in a struggle over Silesia. After the defeat of Napoleon at Waterloo (1815), the struggle between Austria and Prussia for supremacy in Germany continued, reaching its climax in the defeat of Austria in the Seven Weeks' War (1866) and the formation of the Prussian-dominated North German Confederation (1867).

The architect of German unity was Otto von Bismarck, a conservative, monarchist, and militaristic Prussian Junker who had no use for "empty phrase-making and constitutions." From 1862 until his retirement in 1890 he dominated not only the German but also the entire European scene. He unified all Germany in a series of three wars against Denmark (1864), Austria (1866), and France (1870–71), which many historians believe were instigated and promoted by Bismarck in his zeal to build a nation through "blood and iron."

On Jan. 18, 1871, King Wilhelm I of Prussia was proclaimed German Emperor in the Hall of Mirrors at Versailles. The North German Confederation, created in 1867, was abolished, and the Second German Reich, consisting of the North and South German states, was born. With a powerful army, an efficient bureaucracy, and a loyal bourgeoisie, Chancellor Bismarck consolidated a powerful centralized state.

Wilhelm II dismissed Bismarck in 1890 and embarked upon a "New Course," stressing an intensified colonialism and a powerful navy. His chaotic foreign policy culminated in the diplomatic isolation of Germany and the disastrous defeat in World War I (1914–18).

The Second German Empire collapsed following the defeat of the German armies in 1918, the naval mutiny at Kiel, and the flight of the Kaiser to the Netherlands on November 10. The Social Democrats, led by Friedrich Ebert and Philipp Scheidemann, crushed the Communists and established a moderate republic with Ebert as President.

The Weimar Constitution of 1919 provided for a President to be elected for seven years by universal suffrage and a bicameral legislature, consisting of the Reichsrat, representing the states, and the Reichstag, representing the people. It contained a model Bill of Rights. It was weakened, however, by a provision that enabled the President to rule by decree.

Rulers of Germany and Prussia

Name	Born	Ruled[1]	Name	Born	Ruled[1]
KINGS OF PRUSSIA			**GERMAN FEDERAL REPUBLIC (WEST) (CHANCELLORS)**		
Frederick I[2]	1657	1701–1713	Konrad Adenauer	1876	1949–1963
Frederick William I	1688	1713–1740	Ludwig Erhard	1897	1963–1966
Frederick II the Great	1712	1740–1786	Kurt Georg Kiesinger	1904	1966–1969
Frederick William II	1744	1786–1797	Willy Brandt	1913	1969–1974
Frederick William III	1770	1797–1840	Helmut Schmidt	1918	1974–1984
Frederick William IV	1795	1840–1861	Helmut Kohl	1930	1984–1990
William I	1797	1861–1871 [3]			
			GERMAN DEMOCRATIC REPUBLIC (EAST)		
EMPERORS OF GERMANY			Wilhelm Pieck[5]	1876	1949–1960
William I	1797	1871–1888	Walter Ulbricht[8]	1893	1960–1973
Frederick III	1831	1888–1888	Willi Stoph[9]	1914	1973–1976
William II	1859	1888–1918 [4]	Erich Honecker[9]	1912	1976–1989
			Egon Krenz[9]	1937	1989–1989
HEADS OF THE REICH			Manfred Gerlach[9]		1989–1990
Friedrich Ebert[5]	1871	1919–1925	Sabine Bergman–Pohl[9]		1990–1990
Paul von Hindenburg[5]	1847	1925–1934			
Adolf Hitler[6][7]	1889	1934–1945	**GERMAN FEDERAL REPUBLIC CHANCELLORS**		
Karl Doenitz[6]	1891	1945–1945	Helmut Kohl	1930	1991–

1. Year of end of rule is also that of death, unless otherwise indicated. 2. Was Elector of Brandenburg (1688–1701) as Frederick III. 3. Became Emperor of Germany in 1871. 4. Died 1941. 5. President. 6. Führer. 7. Named Chancellor by President Hindenburg in 1933. 8. Chairman of Council of State. Died 1973. 9. Chairman of Council of State.

President Ebert died Feb. 28, 1925, and on April 26, Field Marshal Paul von Hindenburg was elected president.

The mass of Germans regarded the Weimar Republic as a child of defeat, imposed upon a Germany whose legitimate aspirations to world leadership had been thwarted by a world conspiracy. Added to this were a crippling currency debacle, a tremendous burden of reparations, and acute economic distress.

Adolf Hitler, an Austrian war veteran and a fanatical nationalist, fanned discontent by promising a Greater Germany, abrogation of the Treaty of Versailles, restoration of Germany's lost colonies, and destruction of the Jews. When the Social Democrats and the Communists refused to combine against the Nazi threat, President Hindenburg made Hitler chancellor on Jan. 30, 1933.

With the death of Hindenburg on Aug. 2, 1934, Hitler repudiated the Treaty of Versailles and began full-scale rearmament. In 1935 he withdrew Germany from the League of Nations, and the next year he reoccupied the Rhineland and signed the anti-Comintern pact with Japan, at the same time strengthening relations with Italy. Austria was annexed in March 1938. By the Munich agreement in September 1938 he gained the Czech Sudetenland, and in violation of this agreement he completed the dismemberment of Czechoslovakia in March 1939. But his invasion of Poland on Sept. 1, 1939, precipitated World War II.

On May 8, 1945, Germany surrendered unconditionally to Allied and Soviet military commanders, and on June 5 the four-nation Allied Control Council became the *de facto* government of Germany.

At the Berlin (or Potsdam) Conference (July 17–Aug. 2, 1945) President Truman, Premier Stalin, and Prime Minister Clement Attlee of Britain set forth the guiding principles of the Allied Control Council. They were Germany's complete disarmament and demilitarization, destruction of its war potential, rigid control of industry, and decentralization of the political and economic structure. Pending final determination of territorial questions at a peace conference, the three victors agreed in principle to the ultimate transfer of the city of Königsberg (now Kaliningrad) and its adjacent area to the U.S.S.R. and to the administration by Poland of former German territories lying generally east of the Oder-Neisse Line.

For purposes of control Germany was divided in 1945 into four national occupation zones, each headed by a Military Governor.

The Western powers were unable to agree with the U.S.S.R. on any fundamental issue. Work of the Allied Control Council was hamstrung by repeated Soviet vetoes; and finally, on March 20, 1948, Russia walked out of the Council. Meanwhile, the U.S. and Britain had taken steps to merge their zones economically (Bizone); and on May 31, 1948, the U.S., Britain, France, and the Benelux countries agreed to set up a German state comprising the three Western Zones.

The U.S.S.R. reacted by clamping a blockade on all ground communications between the Western Zones and Berlin, an enclave in the Soviet Zone. The Western Allies countered by organizing a gigantic airlift to fly supplies into the beleaguered city, assigning 60,000 men to it. The U.S.S.R. was finally forced to lift the blockade on May 12, 1949.

The Federal Republic of Germany was proclaimed on May 23, 1949, with its capital at Bonn. In free elections, West German voters gave a majority in the Constituent Assembly to the Christian Democrats, with the Social Democrats largely making up the opposition. Konrad Adenauer became chancellor, and Theodor Heuss of the Free Democrats was elected first president.

When the Federal Republic of Germany was established in West Germany, the East German states adopted a more centralized constitution for the Democratic Republic of Germany, and it was put into effect on Oct. 7, 1949. The U.S.S.R. thereupon dissolved its occupation zone but Soviet troops remained. The Western Allies declared that the East German Republic was a Soviet creation undertaken without self-determination and refused to recognize it. It was recognized only within the Soviet bloc.

The area that was occupied by East Germany, as well as adjacent areas in Eastern Europe, consists of Mecklenburg, Brandenburg, Lusatia, Saxony, and Thuringia. Soviet armies conquered the five territories by 1945. In the division of 1945 they were allot-

THE BERLIN WALL (1961–1990)

Major anti-Communist riots broke out in East Berlin in June 1953 and, on Aug. 13, 1961, the Soviet Sector was sealed off by a Communist-built wall, 26 1/2 miles (43 km) long, running through the city. It was built to stem the flood of refugees seeking freedom in the West, 200,000 having fled in 1961 before the wall was erected.

On Nov. 9, 1989, several weeks after the resignation of East Germany's long-time Communist leader, Erich Honecker, the wall's designer and chief defender, the East German government opened its borders to the West and allowed thousands of its citizens to pass freely through the Berlin Wall. They were cheered and greeted by thousands of West Berliners, and many of the jubilant newcomers celebrated their new freedom by climbing on top of the hated wall.

The following day, East German troops began dismantling parts of the wall. It was ironic that this wall was built to keep the citizens from leaving and, 28 years later, it was being dismantled for the same reason.

On Nov. 22, new passages were opened at the north and south of the Brandenburg Gate in an emotional ceremony attended by Chancellor Helmut Kohl of West Germany and Chancellor Hans Modrow of East Germany. The opening of the Brandenburg Gate climaxed the ending of the barriers that had divided the German people since the end of World War II. By the end of 1990, the entire wall had been removed.

ted to the U.S.S.R. Soviet forces created a State controlled by the secret police with a single party, the Socialist Unity (Communist) Party. The Russians appropriated East German plants to restore their war-ravaged industry.

By 1973, normal relations were established between East and West Germany and the two states entered the United Nations.

The 25-year diplomatic hiatus between East Germany and the U.S. ended Sept. 4, 1974, with the establishment of formal relations.

Agreements in Paris in 1954 giving the Federal Republic full independence and complete sovereignty came into force on May 5, 1955. Under it, West Germany and Italy became members of the Brussels treaty organization created in 1948 and renamed the Western European Union. West Germany also became a member of NATO. In 1955 the U.S.S.R. recognized the Federal Republic. The Saar territory, under an agreement between France and West Germany, held a plebiscite and despite economic links to France voted to rejoin West Germany. It became a state of West Germany on Jan. 1, 1957.

In 1963, Chancellor Adenauer concluded a treaty of mutual cooperation and friendship with France and then retired. He was succeeded by his chief inner-party critic, Ludwig Erhard, who was followed in 1966 by Kurt Georg Kiesinger. He, in turn, was succeeded in 1969 by Willy Brandt, former mayor of West Berlin.

The division between West Germany and East Germany was intensified when the Communists erected the Berlin Wall in 1961. In 1968, the East German Communist leader, Walter Ulbricht, imposed restrictions on West German movements into West Berlin. The Soviet-bloc invasion of Czechoslovakia in August 1968 added to the tension.

A treaty with the U.S.S.R. was signed in Moscow in August 1970 in which force was renounced and respect for the "territorial integrity" of present European states declared.

Three months later, West Germany signed a similar treaty with Poland, renouncing force and setting Poland's western border as the Oder-Neisse Line. It subsequently resumed formal relations with Czechoslovakia in a pact that "voided" the Munich treaty that gave Nazi Germany the Sudetenland.

Brandt, winner of a Nobel Peace Prize for his for-eign policies, was forced to resign in 1974 when an East German spy was discovered to be one of his top staff members. Succeeding him was a moderate Social Democrat, Helmut Schmidt.

Helmut Schmidt, Brandt's successor as chancellor, staunchly backed U.S. military strategy in Europe nevertheless, staking his political fate on the strategy of placing U.S. nuclear missiles in Germany unless the Soviet Union reduced its arsenal of intermediate missiles.

The chancellor also strongly opposed nuclear freeze proposals and won 2–1 support for his stand at the convention of Social Democrats in April. The Free Democrats then deserted the Socialists after losing ground in local elections and joined with the Christian Democrats to unseat Schmidt and install Helmut Kohl as chancellor in 1982.

Kohl's tenure has seen a dwindling of the nuclear freeze issue after the deployment of the U.S. missiles. U.S.-Soviet negotiations in 1987 produced a treaty setting up the removal of medium- and short-range missiles from Europe. An economic upswing in 1986 led to Kohl's re-election.

The fall of the Communist government in East Germany left only Soviet objections to German reunification to be dealt with. This was resolved in July 1990. Soviet objections to a reunified Germany belonging to NATO were dropped in return for German promises to reduce their military and engage in wide-ranging economic cooperation with the Soviet Union.

In ceremonies beginning on the evening of Tuesday, Oct. 2, 1990, and continuing throughout the next day, the German Democratic Republic acceded to the Federal Republic and Germany became a united and sovereign state for the first time since 1945. Some one million people gathered at midnight Oct. 2 at the Reichstag in Berlin. At midnight, a replica of the Liberty Bell, a gift from the United States, rang, and unity was officially proclaimed.

Following unification, the Federal Republic became the second largest country in Europe, after the Soviet Union. A reunited Berlin serves as the official capital, although the government will initially remain in Bonn.

During the national election campaign of late 1990 the central issue remained the cost of unification, including the modernization of the former East German economy. The ruling Christian Democrats promised no tax increases would be needed, while the opposition Social Democrats argued that this was mere wishful thinking.

In the December 2 election the Christian Democrats emerged as the strongest group, taking 43.8% of the vote. Analysts generally considered the vote to be an expression of thanks and support to the Chancellor for his forceful drive for political unity. The Party of Democratic Socialism, formerly the Communist Party, won 17 seats in Parliament.

The new Parliament convened in January 1991 re-electing Helmut Kohl chancellor. Nevertheless it soon became clear that previous official estimates of the cost and time required to absorb eastern Germany were considerably understated. The number of failed enterprises in the east continued to grow, and the exodus of personnel to western Germany ceased to abate.

On June 20, 1991 the German Parliament officially voted in favor of moving the seat of the federal government to Berlin, although given the huge expense of such a move it would be done slowly and require 12 years before Berlin would be a fully functional federal capital.

In foreign affairs Germany signed treaties with Poland establishing and guaranteeing permanent borders. During the Persian Gulf crisis Germany was criticized for what was viewed as its less than full support for the allied cause.

GHANA

Republic of Ghana
Chairman of Provisional National Defense Council:
  Flight Lt. Jerry John Rawlings (1981)
Area: 92,100 sq mi. (238,537 sq km)
Population (est. mid-1991): 15,500,000 (average annual rate of natural increase: 3.2%); birth rate: 44/1000; infant mortality rate: 86/1000; density per square mile: 168
Capital: Accra
Largest cities (est. 1984): Accra, 859,600; Kumasi, 348,900; Tamale, 136,800
Monetary unit: Cedi
Languages: English (official), Native tongues (Brong Ahafo, Twi, Fanti, Ga, Ewe, Dagbani)
Religions: indigenous belief, 38%; Islam, 30%; Christian, 24%
Literacy rate: 53.2%
Member of Commonwealth of Nations
Economic summary: Gross national product (1988): $5.2 billion; $400 per capita; 6% real growth rate. Arable land: 5%. Principal products: cocoa, coconuts, coffee, cassava, yams, rice, rubber. Labor force: 3,700,000; 18.7% in industry. Major products: mining products, cocoa products, aluminum. Natural resources: gold, industrial diamonds, bauxite, manganese, timber, fish. Exports: cocoa beans and products, gold, timber, tuna, bauxite, and aluminum. Imports: petroleum, consumer goods, foods, intermediate goods, capital equipment. Major trading partners: U.K., U.S., Germany, France, Japan, South Korea.

Geography. A West African country bordering on the Gulf of Guinea, Ghana has Côte d'Ivoire to the west, Burkina Faso to the north, and Togo to the east. It compares in size to Oregon.

The coastal belt, extending about 270 miles (435 km), is sandy, marshy, and generally exposed. Behind it is a gradually widening grass strip. The forested plateau region to the north is broken by ridges and hills. The largest river is the Volta.

Government. Ghana returned to military rule after two years of constitutional government when Flight Lt. Jerry Rawlings, who led a coup in 1979 and stepped down voluntarily, seized power on Dec. 31, 1981. Rawlings heads a Provisional National Defense Council, which exercises all power.

History. Created an independent country on March 6, 1957, Ghana is the former British colony of the Gold Coast. The area was first seen by Portuguese traders in 1470. They were followed by the English (1553), the Dutch (1595), and the Swedes (1640). British rule over the Gold Coast began in 1820, but it was not until after quelling the severe resistance of the Ashanti in 1901 that it was firmly established. British Togoland, formerly a colony of Germany, was incorporated into Ghana by referendum in 1956. As the result of a plebiscite, Ghana became a republic on July 1, 1960.

Premier Kwame Nkrumah attempted to take leadership of the Pan-African Movement, holding the All-African People's Congress in his capital, Accra, in 1958 and organizing the Union of African States with Guinea and Mali in 1961. But he oriented his country toward the Soviet Union and China and built an autocratic rule over all aspects of Ghanaian life.

In February 1966, while Nkrumah was visiting Peking and Hanoi, he was deposed by a military coup led by Gen. Emmanuel K. Kotoka.

A series of military coups followed and on June 4, 1979, Flight Lieutenant Jerry Rawlings overthrew Lt. Gen. Frederick Akuffo's military rule on June 4, 1979. Rawlings permitted the election of a civilian president to go ahead as scheduled the following month, and Hilla Limann, candidate of the People's National Party, took office. Charging the civilian government with corruption and repression, Rawlings staged another coup on Dec. 31, 1981. As chairman of the Provisional National Defense Council, Rawlings instituted an austerity program and reduced budget deficits.

On July 11, 1985, a relative of Rawlings, Michael Agbotui Soussoudis, 39, and Sharon M. Scranage, 29, who had been a low-level clerk in the Central Intelligence Agency station in the West African country, were arrested in the United States on espionage charges.

The movement toward multiparty democracy also found expression in Ghana. A new Movement for Freedom and Justice campaigned for democracy. As a member of the Economic Community of West African States Ghana contributed to a peacekeeping force in Liberia.

GREECE

Hellenic Republic
President: Constantine Karamanlis (1990)
Premier: Constantine Mitsotakis (1990)
Area: 50,961 sq mi. (131,990 sq km)
Population (est. mid-1991): 10,100,000 (average annual rate of natural increase: 0.1%); birth rate: 10/1000; infant mortality rate: 9.8/1000; density per square mile: 197
Capital: Athens
Largest cities (1981 census): Athens, 3,027,000; Salonika, 720,000; Patras, 150,000; Larissa, 102,000; Heraklion, 111,000; Volos, 107,000.

Monetary unit: Drachma
Language: Greek
Religion: Greek Orthodox
National name: Elliniki Dimokratia
Literacy rate: 95%
Economic summary: Gross domestic product (1989 est.): $56.3 billion; $5,605 per capita; 2.3% real growth rate. Arable land: 23%. Principal products: grains, fruits, vegetables, olives, olive oil, tobacco, cotton, livestock, dairy products. Labor force: 3,860,000; 20% in manufacturing and mining. Major products: textiles, chemicals, food processing. Natural resources: bauxite, lignite, magnesite, crude oil, marble. Exports: manufactured goods, food and live animals, fuels and lubricants, raw materials. Imports: machinery and automotive equipment, petroleum, consumer goods, chemicals, foodstuffs. Major trading partners: Germany, Italy, France, U.S.A., U.K.

Geography. Greece, on the Mediterranean Sea, is the southernmost country on the Balkan Peninsula in southern Europe. It is bordered on the north by Albania, Yugoslavia, and Bulgaria; on the west by the Ionian Sea; and on the east by the Aegean Sea and Turkey. It is slightly smaller than Alabama.

North central Greece, Epirus, and western Macedonia all are mountainous. The main chain of the Pindus Mountains rises to 10,256 feet (3,126 m) in places, separating Epirus from the plains of Thessaly. Mt. Olympus, rising to 9,570 feet (2,909 m) in the north near the Aegean Sea, is the highest point in the country. Greek Thrace is mostly a lowland region separated from European Turkey by the lower Evros River.

Among the many islands are the Ionian group off the west coast; the Cyclades group to the southeast; other islands in the eastern Aegean, including the Dodecanese Islands, Euboea, Lesbos, Samos, and Chios; and Crete, the fourth largest Mediterranean island.

Government. A referendum in December 1974, five months after the collapse of a military dictatorship, ended the Greek monarchy and established a republic. Ceremonial executive power is held by the president; the Premier heads the government and is responsible to a 300-member unicameral Parliament.

History. Greece, with a recorded history going back to 766 B.C., reached the peak of its glory in the 5th century B.C., and by the middle of the 2nd century B.C., it had declined to the status of a Roman province. It remained within the Eastern Roman Empire until Constantinople fell to the Crusaders in 1204.

In 1453, the Turks took Constantinople, and by 1460 Greece was a Turkish province. The insurrection made famous by the poet Lord Byron broke out in 1821, and in 1827 Greece won independence with sovereignty guaranteed by Britain, France, and Russia.

The protecting powers chose Prince Otto of Bavaria as the first king of modern Greece in 1832 to reign over an area only slightly larger than the Peloponnese Peninsula. Chiefly under the next king, George I, chosen by the protecting powers in 1863, Greece acquired much of its present territory. During his 57-year reign, a period in which he encouraged parliamentary democracy, Thessaly, Epirus, Macedonia, Crete, and most of the Aegean islands were added from the disintegrating Turkish empire. An unsuccessful war against Turkey after World War I brought down the monarchy, to be replaced by a republic in 1923.

Two military dictatorships and a financial crisis brought George II back from exile, but only until 1941, when Italian and German invaders defeated tough Greek resistance. After British and Greek troops liberated the country in October 1944, Communist guerrillas staged a long campaign in which the government received U.S. aid under the Truman Doctrine, the predecessor of the Marshall Plan.

A military junta seized power in April 1967, sending young King Constantine II into exile December 14. Col. George Papadopoulos, as premier, converted the government to republican form in 1973 and as President ended martial law. He was moving to restore democracy when he was ousted in November of that year by his military colleagues. The regime of the "colonels," which had tortured its opponents and scoffed at human rights, resigned July 23, 1974, after having bungled an attempt to seize Cyprus.

Former Premier Karamanlis returned from exile to become premier of Greece's first civilian government since 1967.

On Jan. 1, 1981, Greece became the 10th member of the European Community.

Double-digit inflation and scandals in the Socialist government led to them losing their majority in the elections of June 1989. The opposition New Democracy Party did not gain a majority, however, leading to the creation of a NDP-Communist coalition that initiated an investigation of the scandals. The coalition government was short-lived. Elections in April 1990 finally gave the conservative New Democracy Party a one-seat majority in parliament. Soon afterwards Karamanlis, the founder of that party, was elected president by parliament.

GRENADA

State of Grenada
Sovereign: Queen Elizabeth II
Governor General: Paul Scoon (1978)
Prime Minister: Nicholas Braithwaite (1990)
Area: 133 sq mi. (344 sq km)
Population (est. mid-1991): 100,000 (average annual growth rate, 2.9%); birth rate: 37/1000; infant mortality rate: 30/1000; density per square mile: 634
Capital and largest city (est. 1981): St. George's, 4,800
Monetary unit: East Caribbean dollar
Ethnic groups: Blacks and Indians
Language: English
Religions: Roman Catholic, 64%; Anglican, 21%
Member of Commonwealth of Nations
Literacy rate: 85%
Economic summary: Gross domestic product (1988 est.): $129.7 million; $1,535 per capita; 5% real growth rate. Arable land: 15%. Principal products: spices, cocoa, bananas. Exports: nutmeg, cocoa beans, bananas, mace. Imports: foodstuffs, machinery, manufactured goods, petroleum. Labor force: 36,000; 31% in services. Major trading partners: U.K., Trinidad and Tobago, U.S., Japan, Canada.

Geography. Grenada (the first "a" is pronounced as in "gray") is the most southerly of the Windward Islands, about 100 miles (161 km) from the South American coast. It is a volcanic island traversed by a mountain range, the highest peak of which is Mount St. Catherine (2,756 ft.; 840 m).

Government. A Governor-General represents the sovereign, Elizabeth II. The Prime Minister is the head of government, chosen by a 15-member House of Representatives elected by universal suffrage every five years.

History. Grenada was discovered by Columbus in 1498. After more than 200 years of British rule, most recently as part of the West Indies Associated States, it became independent Feb. 7, 1974, with Eric M. Gairy as Prime Minister.

Prime Minister Maurice Bishop, a protégé of Cuba's President Castro, was killed in a military coup on Oct. 19, 1983. At the request of five members of the Organization of Eastern Caribbean States, President Reagan ordered an invasion of Grenada on Oct. 25 involving over 1,900 U.S. troops and a small military force from Barbados, Dominica, Jamaica, St. Lucia, and St. Vincent. The troops met strong resistance from Cuban military personnel on the island.

A centrist coalition led by Herbert A. Blaize, a 66-year-old lawyer, won 14 of the 15 seats in Parliament in an election in December 1984, and Blaize became Prime Minister.

None of the four main parties won a clear victory in the election of March 1990. Negotiations led to the National Democratic Congress forming a government with the support of several members from other parties.

GUATEMALA

Republic of Guatemala
President: Jorge Serrano (1991)
Area: 42,042 sq mi. (108,889 sq km)
Population (est. mid-1991): 9,500,000 (average annual rate of natural increase: 3.0%); birth rate: 38/1000; infant mortality rate: 62/1000; density per square mile: 225
Capital and largest city (est. 1982): Guatemala City, 1,250,000
Monetary unit: Quetzal
Languages: Spanish, Indian dialects
Religion: Roman Catholic, Protestant, Mayan.
National name: República de Guatemala
Literacy rate: 50%
Economic summary: Gross domestic product (1990 est.): $12.8 billion; $1,250 per capita; 3.5% real growth rate. Arable land: 12%. Principal products: corn, beans, coffee, cotton, cattle, sugar, bananas, fruits and vegetables. Labor force: 2,500,000; 14% in manufacturing. Principal products: sugar, textiles and clothing, furniture, chemicals, petroleum, metals, rubber. Natural resources: nickel, crude oil, rare woods, fish, chicle. Exports: bananas, cardamom. Imports: manufactured products, machinery, transportation equipment, chemicals, fuels. Major trading partners: U.S., Central American nations, Caribbean, Mexico.

Geography. The northernmost of the Central American nations, Guatemala is the size of Tennessee. Its neighbors are Mexico on the north, west, and east and Belize, Honduras, and El Salvador on the east. The country consists of two main regions—the cool highlands with the heaviest population and the tropical area along the Pacific and Caribbean coasts. The principal mountain range rises to the highest elevation in Central America and contains many volcanic peaks. Volcanic eruptions are frequent.

The Petén region in the north contains important resources and archaeological sites of the Mayan civilization.

Government. On January 14, 1991 Jorge Serrano was sworn in as president, the first transfer of power from one elected civilian to another. Gustavo Espina, a businessman, was also sworn in as vice president.

Both the President and the Congress are elected for five-year terms and the President may not be re-elected.

History. Once the site of the ancient Mayan civilization, Guatemala, conquered by Spain in 1524, set itself up as a republic in 1839. From 1898 to 1920, the dictator Manuel Estrada Cabrera ran the country, and from 1931 to 1944, Gen. Jorge Ubico Castaneda was the strongman. In 1944 the National Assembly elected Gen. Federico Ponce president, but he was overthrown in October. In December, Dr. Juan José Arévalo was elected as the head of a leftist regime that continued to press its reform program. Jacobo Arbenz Guzmán, administration candidate with leftist leanings, won the 1950 elections.

Arbenz expropriated the large estates, including plantations of the United Fruit Company. With covert U.S. backing, a revolt was led by Col. Carlos Castillo Armas, and Arbenz took refuge in Mexico. Castillo Armas became president but was assassinated in 1957. Constitutional government was restored in 1958, and Gen. Miguel Ydigoras Fuentes was elected president.

A wave of terrorism, by left and right, began in 1967, and in August 1968 U.S. Ambassador John Gordon Mein was killed when he resisted kidnappers. Fear of anarchy led to the election in 1970 of Army Chief of Staff Carlos Araña Osorio, who had put down a rural guerrilla movement at the cost of nearly 3,000 lives. Araña, surprisingly, pledged social reforms when he took office. Another military candidate, Gen. Kjell Laugerud, won the presidency in 1974 amid renewed political violence.

The administration of Gen. Romeo Lucas Garcia, elected president in 1978, ended in a coup by a three-man military junta on March 23, 1982. Lucas Garcia was charged by Amnesty International with responsibility for at least 5,000 political murders in a reign of brutality and corruption that brought a cutoff of U.S. military aid in 1978. Hopes for improvement under the junta faded when Gen. José Efraín Ríos Montt took sole power in June.

President Oscar Mejía Victores, another general, seized power from Rios Montt in an August 1983 coup and pledged to turn over power to an elected civilian President in 1985. A constituent assembly was elected on July 1, 1984, to write a new Constitution.

President Serrano's election was noteworthy for, among other things, he became the first Protestant president in Latin America, and his candidacy at first received hardly any public notice.

GUINEA

Republic of Guinea
President: Brig. Gen. Lansana Conté (1984)
Area: 94,925 sq mi. (245,857 sq km)
Population (est. mid-1991): 7,500,000 (average annual rate of natural increase: 2.6%); birth rate: 47/1000; infant mortality rate: 147/1000; density per square mile: 79
Capital and largest city (est. 1983): Conakry, 656,000
Monetary unit: Guinean franc
Languages: French (official), native tongues (Malinké, Susu, Fulani)
Religions: Islam, 85%; 5% indigenous, 1.5% Christian
National name: République de Guinée
Literacy rate: 20% in French, 48% in local languages
Economic summary: Gross domestic product (1988): $2.5 billion, $350 per capita; real growth rate 5.0%. Arable

land: 6%. Principal agricultural products: rice, cassava, millet, corn, coffee, bananas, pineapples. Labor force: 2,400,000 (1983); 11% in industry and commerce. Major industrial products: bauxite, alumina, light manufactured and processed goods, diamonds. Natural resources: bauxite, iron ore, diamonds, gold, water power. Exports: bauxite, alumina, diamonds, pineapples, bananas, coffee. Imports: petroleum, machinery, transport equipment, foodstuffs, textiles. Major trading partners: U.S., U.S.S.R., France, Germany.

Geography. Guinea, in West Africa on the Atlantic, is also bordered by Guinea-Bissau, Senegal, Mali, the Ivory Coast, Liberia, and Sierra Leone. Slightly smaller than Oregon, the country consists of a coastal plain, a mountainous region, a savanna interior, and a forest area in the Guinea Highlands. The highest peak is Mount Nimba at 5,748 ft (1,752 m).

Government. Military government headed by President Lansana Conté, who promoted himself from colonel to brigadier general after a 1984 coup. Although President Conté announced in 1989 that Guinea would move to a multiparty democracy, later details proved the plan disappointing.

History. Previously part of French West Africa, Guinea achieved independence by rejecting the new French Constitution, and on Oct. 2, 1958, became an independent state with Sékou Touré as president. Touré led the country into being the first avowedly Marxist state in Africa. Diplomatic relations with France were suspended in 1965, with the Soviet Union replacing France as the country's chief source of economic and technical assistance.

Prosperity came in 1960 after the start of exploitation of bauxite deposits. Touré was re-elected to a seven-year term in 1974 and again in 1981.

After 26 years as President, Touré died in the United States in March 1984, following surgery. A week later, a military regime headed by Col. Lansana Conté took power with a promise not to shed any more blood after Touré's harsh rule. Conté became President and his co-conspirator in the coup, Col. Diara Traoré, became Prime Minister, but Conté later demoted Traoré to Education Minister. Traoré tried to seize power on July 4, 1985, while Conté was out of the country, but his attempted coup was crushed by troops loyal to Conté.

Along with Sierra Leone and Nigeria, Guinea sent a peacekeeping force to Liberia in August 1990. With Nigeria Guinea deployed troops to Sierra Leone in 1991 to repel invading rebels from Liberia.

Economic summary: Gross national product (1986): $168 million; $170 per capita; real growth rate –.6%. Arable land: 9%. Principal products: palm kernels, cotton, rice, cashew nuts, peanuts. Labor force: 403,000 (est.). Major industries: food processing, beer, soft drinks. Natural resources: unexploited deposits of bauxite, petroleum, phosphates; fish and timber. Exports: peanuts, cashews, fish, palm kernels. Imports: foodstuffs, manufactured goods, fuels, transportation equipment. Major trading partners: Portugal, Spain, and other European countries.

Geography. A neighbor of Senegal and Guinea in West Africa, on the Atlantic coast, Guinea-Bissau is about half the size of South Carolina.

The country is a low-lying coastal region of swamps, rain forests, and mangrove-covered wetlands, with about 25 islands off the coast. The Bijagos archipelago extends 30 miles (48 km) out to sea. Internal communications depend mainly on deep estuaries and meandering rivers, since there are no railroads. Bissau, the capital, is the main port.

Government. After the overthrow of Louis Cabral in November 1980, the nine-member Council of the Revolution formed an interm government. In 1982, they formed a new government consisting of the President, 2 Vice-Presidents, 18 ministers and 10 state secretaries.

History. Guinea-Bissau was discovered in 1446 by the Portuguese Nuno Tristao, and colonists in the Cape Verde Islands obtained trading rights in the territory. In 1879 the connection with the Cape Verde Islands was broken. Early in the 1900s the Portuguese managed to pacify some tribesmen, although resistance to colonial rule remained.

The African Party for the Independence of Guinea-Bissau and Cape Verde was founded in 1956 and several years later began guerrilla warfare that grew increasingly effective. By 1974 the rebels controlled most of the countryside, where they formed a government that was soon recognized by scores of countries. The military coup in Portugal in April 1974 brightened the prospects for freedom, and in August the Lisbon government signed an agreement granting independence to the province as of Sept. 10. The new republic took the name Guinea-Bissau.

In November 1980, Prémier João Bernardo Vieira headed a coup that deposed Luis Cabral, President since 1974. A Revolutionary Council assumed the powers of government, with Vieira as its head. A dispute with Senegal over territorial waters erupted in April 1990 when Senegal stopped three Guinea-Bissau ships.

GUINEA-BISSAU

Republic of Guinea-Bissau
President of the Council of State: João Bernardo Vieira (1980)
Area: 13,948 sq mi. (36,125 sq km)
Population (est. mid-1991): 1,000,000 (average annual rate of natural increase: 2.0%); birth rate: 43/1000; infant mortality rate: 151/1000; density per square mile: 71
Capital and largest city (est. 1980): Bissau, 110,000
Monetary unit: Guinea-Bissau peso
Language: Portugese Criolo, African languages
Religions: traditional, 65%; Islam, 30%; Christian, 5%
National name: República da Guiné-Bissau
Literacy rate: 34% (1986)

GUYANA

Cooperative Republic of Guyana
President: Desmond Hoyte (1985)
Area: 83,000 sq mi. (214,969 sq km)
Population (est. mid-1991): 800,000 (average annual rate of natural increase: 1.8%); birth rate: 25/1000; infant mortality rate: 52/1000; density per square mile: 10
Capital and largest city (est. 1981): Georgetown, 200,000
Monetary unit: Guyana dollar
Languages: English (official), Amerindian dialects
Religions: Hindu, 34%; Protestant, 18%; Islam, 9%; Roman Catholic, 18%; Anglican, 16%
Member of Commonwealth of Nations

Literacy rate: 85%
Economic summary: Gross domestic product (1988 est.): $323 million; $420 per capita; –3.0% real growth rate. Arable land: 3%. Principal products: sugar, rice. Labor force: 268,000; 44.5% industry and commerce. Major products: bauxite, alumina. Natural resources: bauxite, gold, diamonds, hardwood timber, shrimp. Exports: sugar, bauxite, rice, timber, shrimp, gold, molasses, rum. Imports: petroleum, food, machinery. Major trading partners: U.K., U.S., Canada.

Geography. Guyana is situated on the northern coast of South America east of Venezuela, west of Suriname, and north of Brazil. The country consists of a low coastal area and the Guiana Highlands in the south. There is an extensive north-south network of rivers. Guyana is the size of Idaho.

Government. Guyana, formerly British Guiana, proclaimed itself a republic on Feb. 23, 1970, ending its tie with Britain while remaining in the Commonwealth.

Guyana has a unicameral legislature, the National Assembly, with 53 members directly elected for five-year terms and 12 elected by local councils. A 24-member Cabinet is headed by the President.

History. British Guiana won internal self-government in 1952. The next year the People's Progressive Party, headed by Cheddi B. Jagan, an East Indian dentist, won the elections and Jagan became Prime Minister. British authorities deposed him for alleged Communist connections. A coalition ousted Jagan in 1964, installing a moderate Socialist, Forbes Burnham, a black, as Prime Minister. On May 26, 1966, the country became an independent member of the Commonwealth and resumed its traditional name, Guyana.

After ruling Guyana for 21 years, Burnham died on Aug. 6 1985, in a Guyana hospital after a throat operation. Desmond Hoyte, the country's Prime Minister succeeded him under the Guyanese constitution.

On January 8, 1991 Guyana became the 35th member of the Organization of American States.

HAITI

Republic of Haiti
President: Rev. Jean-Bertrand Aristide (1991)
Area: 10,714 sq mi. (27,750 sq km)
Population (est. mid-1991): 6,300,000 (average annual rate of natural increase: 2.3%); birth rate: 45/1000; infant mortality rate: 107/1000; density per square mile: 587
Capital and largest city (est. 1984): Port-au-Prince, city, 461,464; urban area, 738,342
Monetary unit: Gourde
Languages: French, Creole
Religion: Roman Catholic, 80%; Protestant, 10%
National name: République d'Haïti
Literacy rate: 23%
Economic summary: Gross domestic product (1988 est.): $2.4 billion; $380 per capita; 0.3% real growth rate. Arable land: 20%. Principal products: coffee, sugar cane, rice, corn, sorghum. Labor force: 2,300,000; 9% in industry. Major products: refined sugar, textiles, flour, cement, light assembly products. Natural resource: bauxite. Exports: coffee, light industrial products, sugar, cocoa, sisal. Imports: machines and manufactures, food and beverages, petroleum products, fats and oils, chemicals. Major trading partner: U.S.

Geography. Haiti, in the West Indies, occupies the western third of the island of Hispaniola, which it shares with the Dominican Republic. About the size of Maryland, Haiti is two thirds mountainous, with the rest of the country marked by great valleys, extensive plateaus, and small plains. The most densely populated region is the Cul-de-Sac plain near Port-au-Prince.

History. Discovered by Columbus, who landed at Môle Saint Nicolas on Dec. 6, 1492, Haiti in 1697 became a French possession known as Saint Domingue. An insurrection among a slave population of 500,000 in 1791 ended with a declaration of independence by Pierre-Dominique Toussaint l'Ouverture in 1801. Napoleon Bonaparte suppressed the independence movement, but it eventually triumphed in 1804 under Jean-Jacques Dessalines, who gave the new nation the aboriginal name Haiti.

Its prosperity dissipated in internal strife as well as disputes with neighboring Santo Domingo during a succession of 19th-century dictatorships, a bankrupt Haiti accepted a U.S. customs receivership from 1905 to 1941. Direct U.S. rule from 1915 to 1934 brought a measure of stability and a population growth that made Haiti the most densely populated nation in the hemisphere.

In 1949, after four years of democratic rule by President Dumarsais Estimé, dictatorship returned under Gen. Paul Magloire, who was succeeded by François Duvalier in 1957.

Duvalier established a dictatorship based on secret police, known as the "Ton-ton Macoutes," who gunned down opponents of the regime. Duvalier's son, Jean-Claude, or "Baby Doc," succeeded his father in 1971 as ruler of the poorest nation in the Western Hemisphere. Duvalier fled the country in 1986 after strong unrest.

Following the election of December 6, 1990 which he won, Jean-Bertrand Aristide, a Roman Catholic priest, was sworn in as president on February 7, 1991—the country's first freely elected chief executive. Aristide was outsted by a military coup in the fall of 1991.

Government. A republic with a bicameral assembly consisting of an upper house or Senate and a lower house, the House of Deputies. The National Assembly consists of 27 senate seats and 83 deputies. The army stopped the first scheduled elections in November and army-sponsored elections led to the election of Leslie Manigat in Jan., 1988. He was overthrown in June 1988 in a military coup led by Namphy, after the former attempted to dismiss him. He was in turn overthrown by Lt. Gen. Prosper Avril.

The ruling council that took power upon the exile of Duvalier was criticized for the inclusion of former Duvalier aides.

Anti-government protests aginst the Avril governments crackdown on opposition leaders forced Avril to resign. Ertha-Trovillot, a former Supreme Court Justice, became President in March 1990.

HONDURAS

Republic of Honduras
President: Rafael L. Callejas (1990)
Area: 43,277 sq mi. (112,088 sq km)
Population (est. mid-1991): 5,300,000 (average annual rate of natural increase: 3.1%); birth rate: 39/1000; infant mortality rate: 48/1000; density per square mile: 122
Capital and largest city (1985): Tegucigalpa, 571,400

Monetary unit: Lempira
Languages: Spanish, some Indian dialects, English in Bay Islands Department
Religion: Roman Catholic
National name: República de Honduras
Literacy rate: 56%
Economic summary: Gross domestic product (1988): $4.4 billion; $890 per capita; 4.0% real growth rate. Arable land: 14%. Principal products: bananas, coffee, timber, beef, shrimp, citrus. Labor force: 1,300,000; 9% in manufacturing. Major industrial products: processed agricultural products, textiles and clothing, wood products. Natural resources: timber, gold, silver, copper, lead, zinc, iron ore, antimony. Exports: bananas, coffee, lumber, shrimp and lobster, minerals. Imports: manufactured goods, machinery, transportation equipment, chemicals, petroleum. Major trading partners: U.S., Caribbean countries, Western Europe, Japan, Latin America.

Geography. Honduras, in the north central part of Central America, has a 400-mile (644-km) Caribbean coastline and a 40-mile (64-km) Pacific frontage. Its neighbors are Guatemala to the west, El Salvador to the south, and Nicaragua to the east. Honduras is slightly larger than Tennessee. Generally mountainous, the country is marked by fertile plateaus, river valleys, and narrow coastal plains.

Government. The President serves a four-year term. There is a 134-member National Congress.

History. Columbus discovered Honduras on his last voyage in 1502. Honduras, with four other countries of Central America, declared its independence from Spain in 1821 and was part of a federation of Central American states until 1838. In that year it seceded from the federation and became a completely independent country.

In July 1969, El Salvador invaded Honduras after Honduran landowners had deported several thousand Salvadorans. The fighting left 1,000 dead and tens of thousands homeless. By threatening economic sanctions and military intervention, the OAS induced El Salvador to withdraw.

Although parliamentary democracy returned with the election of Roberto Suazo Córdova as President in 1982 after a decade of military rule, Honduras faced severe economic problems and tensions along its border with Nicaragua. "Contra" rebels, waging a guerrilla war against the Sandinista regime in Nicaragua, used Honduras as a training and staging area. At the same time, the United States used Honduras as a site for military exercises and built bases to train both Honduran and Salvadoran troops.

In the first democratic transition of power since 1932 Rafael Callejas became president in January 1990. The immediate task was to deal with a deficit caused in part by reduced U.S. aid and the previous government's fiscal policies. The IMF would not grand new loans to the country owing to its arrears on repayment of previous loans.

HUNGARY

Republic of Hungary
President: Arpad Goncz (1990)
Premier: József Antall (1990)
Area: 35,919 sq mi. (93,030 sq km)

Population (1990 census): 10,375,000 (average annual rate of natural increase: –0.2%); birth rate: 12/1000; infant mortality rate: 15.7/1000; density per square mile: 289
Capital: Budapest
Largest cities (1989): Budapest, 2,113,645; Debrecen, 219,151; Miskolc, 207,826; Szeged, 189,484; Pécs, 183,082; Györ, 183,082.
Monetary unit: Forint
Language: Magyar
Religions: Roman Catholic, 67.5%; Protestant, 25%; atheist and others, 7.5%
National name: Magyar Köztársaság
Literacy rate: 99%
Economic summary: Gross national product (1989 est.): $64.6 billion; $6,108 per capita; –1.3% real growth rate. Arable land: 54%. Principal products: corn, wheat, potatoes, sugar beets, sun flowers, livestock, dairy products. Labor force: 4,860,000; 30.9% in industry. Major products: steel, chemicals, pharmaceuticals, textiles, transport equipment. Natural resources: bauxite, coal, natural gas. Exports: machinery and tools, industrial and consumer goods, raw materials. Imports: machinery and transport, fuels, chemical products, manufactured consumer goods. Major trading partners: U.S.S.R., Eastern Europe.

Geography. This central European country the size of Indiana is bordered by Austria to the west, Czechoslovakia to the north, the U.S.S.R. and Romania to the east, and Yugoslavia to the south.

Most of Hungary is a fertile, rolling plain lying east of the Danube River and drained by the Danube and Tisza rivers. In the extreme northwest is the Little Hungarian Plain. South of that area is Lake Balaton (250 sq mi.; 648 sq km).

Government. Hungary is a Republic with legislative power vested in the unicameral National Assembly, whose 386 members are elected directly for four-year terms. The National Assembly elects the President. The supreme body of state power is the 21-member Presidential Council elected by the National Assembly. The supreme administrative body is the Council of Ministers, headed by the Premier.

The major political parties are the Socialist Party, the Hungarian Democratic Forum, the Alliance of Free Democrats, the Independent Socialist Party and the Independent Smallholder's Party.

History. About 2,000 years ago, Hungary was part of the Roman provinces of Pannonia and Dacia. In A.D. 896 it was invaded by the Magyars, who founded a kingdom. Christianity was accepted during the reign of Stephen I (St. Stephen) (997–1038).

The peak of Hungary's great period of medieval power came during the reign of Louis I the Great (1342–82), whose dominions touched the Baltic, Black, and Mediterranean seas.

War with the Turks broke out in 1389, and for more than 100 years the Turks advanced through the Balkans. When the Turks smashed a Hungarian army in 1526, western and northern Hungary accepted Hapsburg rule to escape Turkish occupation. Transylvania became independent under Hungarian princes. Intermittent war with the Turks was waged until a peace treaty was signed in 1699.

After the suppression of the 1848 revolt against Hapsburg rule, led by Louis Kossuth, the dual monarchy of Austria-Hungary was set up in 1867.

The dual monarchy was defeated with the other Central Powers in World War I. After a short-lived republic in 1918, the chaotic Communist rule of 1919 under Béla Kun ended with the Romanians occupying

Budapest on Aug. 4, 1919. When the Romanians left, Adm. Nicholas Horthy entered the capital with a national army. The Treaty of Trianon of June 4, 1920, cost Hungary 68% of its land and 58% of its population. Meanwhile, the National Assembly had restored the legal continuity of the old monarchy; and, on March 1, 1920, Horthy was elected Regent.

Following the German invasion of Russia on June 22, 1941, Hungary joined the attack against the Soviet Union, but the war was not popular and Hungarian troops were almost entirely withdrawn from the eastern front by May 1943. German occupation troops set up a puppet government after Horthy's appeal for an armistice with advancing Soviet troops on Oct. 15, 1944, had resulted in his overthrow. The German regime soon fled the capital, however, and on December 23 a provisional government was formed in Soviet-occupied eastern Hungary. On Jan. 20, 1945, it signed an armistice in Moscow. Early the next year, the National Assembly approved a constitutional law abolishing the thousand-year-old monarchy and establishing a republic.

By the Treaty of Paris (1947), Hungary had to give up all territory it had acquired since 1937 and to pay $300 million reparations to the U.S.S.R., Czechoslovakia, and Yugoslavia. In 1948 the Communist Party, with the support of Soviet troops seized control. Hungary was proclaimed a People's Republic and one-party state in 1949. Industry was nationalized, the land collectivized into state farms, and the opposition terrorized by the secret police.

The terror, modeled after that of the U.S.S.R., reached its height with the trial of Jozsef Cardinal Mindszenty, Roman Catholic primate. He confessed to fantastic charges under duress of drugs or brainwashing and was sentenced to life imprisonment in 1949. Protests were voiced in all parts of the world.

On Oct. 23, 1956, anti-Communist revolution broke out in Budapest. To cope with it, the Communists set up a coalition government and called former Premier Imre Nagy back to head it. But he and most of his ministers were swept by the logic of events into the anti-Communist opposition, and he declared Hungary a neutral power, withdrawing from the Warsaw Treaty and appealing to the United Nations for help.

One of his ministers, János Kádár, established a counter-regime and asked the U.S.S.R. to send in military power. Soviet troops and tanks suppressed the revolution in bloody fighting after 190,000 people had fled the country and Mindszenty, freed from jail, had taken refuge in the U.S. Embassy.

Kádár was succeeded as Premier, but not party secretary, by Gyula Kallai in 1965. Continuing his program of national reconciliation, Kádár emptied prisons, reformed the secret police, and eased travel restrictions.

Hungary developed the reputation of being the freest East European state.

Relations with the U.S. improved in 1972 when World War II debt claims between the two nations were settled. On Jan. 6, 1978, the U.S. returned to Hungary, over anti-Communist protests, the 977-year-old crown of St. Stephen, held at Fort Knox since World War II.

A reform movement in the late-1980s led to the disbanding of the party militia, the withdrawal of political cells from factories and offices, and free multi-party elections. The new Parliament elected Arpad Goncz, who had been jailed for his role in the 1956 uprising, as interim President.

Following local and parliamentary elections in October 1990, Jozsef Antall's Hungarian Democratic

Forum and its conservative coalition parties held 60% of the parliamentary seats. The last Soviet troops left Hungary in June 1991, thereby ending almost 47 years of military presence.

ICELAND

Republic of Iceland
President: Mrs. Vigdis Finnbogadottir (1980)
Prime Minister: David Oddsson (1991)
Area: 39,709 sq mi. (102,846 sq km)
Population (Dec. 1990): 255,000 (average annual rate of natural increase: 1.1%); birth rate: 18/1000; infant mortality rate: 5.3/1000; density per square mile: 7
Capital and largest city (1988): Reykjavik, 95,799
Monetary unit: M.N. króna
Language: Icelandic
Religion: Evangelical Lutheran
National name: Lydveldid Island
Literacy rate: 100%
Economic summary: Gross domestic product (1988): $5.9 billion; $24,031 per capita; −1.8% real growth rate. Arable land: NEGL%; principal agricultural products: livestock, potatoes and turnips. Labor force: 134,429; 55.4% in commerce, finance and services. Major products: processed aluminum, fish. Natural resources: fish, diatomite, hydroelectric and geothermal power. Exports: fish, animal products, aluminum, diatomite. Imports: petroleum products, machinery and transportation equipment, food, textiles. Major trading partners: European Communities (EC) countries, European Free Trade Association (EFTA) countries, U.S., Japan, and U.S.S.R.

1. Including some offshore islands.

Geography. Iceland, an island about the size of Kentucky, lies in the north Atlantic Ocean east of Greenland and just touches the Arctic Circle. It is one of the most volcanic regions in the world.

Small fresh-water lakes are to be found throughout the island, and there are many natural phenomena, including hot springs, geysers, sulfur beds, canyons, waterfalls, and swift rivers. More than 13% of the area is covered by snowfields and glaciers, and most of the people live in the 7% of the island comprising fertile coastlands.

Government. The president is elected for four years by popular vote. Executive power resides in the prime minister and his Cabinet. The Althing (Parliament) is composed of 63 members.

History. Iceland was first settled shortly before 900, mainly by Norse. A Constitution drawn up about 930 created a form of democracy and provided for an Althing, or General Assembly.

In 1262–64, Iceland came under Norwegian rule and passed to ultimate Danish control through the formation of the Union of Kalmar in 1483. In 1874, Icelanders obtained their own Constitution. In 1918, Denmark recognized Iceland as a separate state with unlimited sovereignty but still nominally under the Danish king.

On June 17, 1944, after a popular referendum, the Althing proclaimed Iceland an independent republic.

The British occupied Iceland in 1940, immediately after the German invasion of Denmark. In 1942, the U.S. took over the burden of protection. Iceland refused to abandon its neutrality in World War II and thus forfeited charter membership in the United Nations, but it cooperated with the Allies throughout the conflict. Iceland joined the North Atlantic Treaty Organization in 1949.

Iceland unilaterally extended its territorial waters from 12 to 50 nautical miles in 1972, precipitating a running dispute with Britain known as the "cod war."

An agreement calling for registration of all British trawlers fishing within 200 miles of Iceland and a 24-hour time limit on incursions was finally reached in 1976.

Elections to the Althing in April 1991 gave the opposition Independence Party 26 of the 63 seats, up from 18. Prime Minister Hermannson resigned allowing David Oddsson of the Independence Party to enter into talks with the Social Democrats about a coalition government. None of the parties is interested in Iceland pursuing membership in the E.C., although it is a member of the European Free Trade Association.

INDIA

Republic of India
President: Ramaswamy Venkataraman (1987)
Prime Minister: P.V. Narasimha Rao (1991)
Area: 1,229,737 sq mi. (3,185,019 sq km)
Population (est. mid-1991): 859,200,000 (average annual rate of natural increase: 2.0%); birth rate: 31/1000; infant mortality rate: 91/1000; density per square mile: 677
Capital (1980 census): New Delhi, 619,417
Largest cities (1981 est.): Calcutta, 9,194,018; Greater Bombay, 8,243,405; Delhi, 5,729,283; Madras, 4,289,347; Bangalore, 2,921,751; Ahmedabad, 2,548,057; Kanpur, 1,639,064
Monetary unit: Rupee
Principal languages: Hindi (official), English (official), Bengali, Gujarati, Kashmiri, Malayalam, Marathi, Oriya, Punjabi, Tamil, Telugu, Urdu, Kannada, Assamese (all recognized by the Constitution)
Religions: Hindu, 82.6%; Islam, 11.4%; Christian, 2.4%; Sikh, 2%
National name: Bharat
Literacy rate: 36%
Member of Commonwealth of Nations
Economic summary: Gross national product (1989 est.): $333 billion; $400 per capita; 5.0% real growth rate. Arable land: 55%. Principal products: rice, wheat, oilseeds, cotton, tea, opium poppy (for pharmaceuticals). Labor force: 284,400,000; 67% in agriculture. Major industrial products: jute, processed food, steel, machinery, transport machinery, cement. Natural resources: iron ore, coal, manganese, mica, bauxite, limestone, textiles. Exports: tea, coffee, iron ore, fish products, manufactures. Imports: petroleum, edible oils, textiles, clothing, capital goods. Major trading partners: U.S., U.S.S.R., Japan, E.C., Middle East

Geography. One third the area of the United States, the Republic of India occupies most of the subcontinent of India in south Asia. It borders on China in the northeast. Other neighbors are Pakistan on the west, Nepal and Bhutan on the north, and Burma and Bangladesh on the east.

The country contains a large part of the great Indo-Gangetic plain, which extends from the Bay of Bengal on the east to the Afghan frontier on the Arabian Sea on the west. This plain is the richest and most densely settled part of the subcontinent. Another distinct natural region is the Deccan, a plateau of 2,000 to 3,000 feet (610 to 914 m) in elevation, occupying the southern portion of the subcontinent.

Forming a part of the republic are several groups of islands—the Laccadives (14 islands) in the Arabian Sea and the Andamans (204 islands) and the Nicobars (19 islands) in the Bay of Bengal.

India's three great river systems, all rising in the Himalayas, have extensive deltas. The Ganges flows south and then east for 1,540 miles (2,478 km) across the northern plain to the Bay of Bengal; part of its delta, which begins 220 miles (354 km) from the sea, is within the republic. The Indus, starting in Tibet, flows northwest for several hundred miles in the Kashmir before turning southwest toward the Arabian Sea; it is important for irrigation in Pakistan. The Brahmaputra, also rising in Tibet, flows eastward, first through India and then south into Bangladesh and the Bay of Bengal.

Government. India is a federal republic. It is also a member of the Commonwealth of Nations, a status defined at the 1949 London Conference of Prime Ministers, by which India recognizes Queen as head of the Commonwealth. Under the Constitution effective Jan. 26, 1950, India has a parliamentary type of government.

The constitutional head of the state is the President, who is elected every five years. He is advised by the Prime Minister and a Cabinet based on a majority of the bicameral Parliament, which consists of a Council of States (Rajya Sabha), representing the constituent units of the republic and a House of the People (Lok Sabha), elected every five years by universal suffrage.

History. The Aryans, or Hindus, who invaded India between 2400 and 1500 B.C. from the northwest found a land already well civilized. Buddhism was founded in the 6th century B.C. and spread through northern India.

In 1526, Moslem invaders founded the great Mogul empire, centered on Delhi, which lasted, at least in name, until 1857. Akbar the Great (1542–1605) strengthened this empire and became the ruler of a greater portion of India than had ever before acknowledged the suzerainty of one man. The long reign of his great-grandson, Aurangzeb (1658–1707), represents both the culmination of Mogul power and the beginning of its decay.

Vasco da Gama, the Portuguese explorer, visited India first in 1498, and for the next 100 years the Portuguese had a virtual monopoly on trade with the subcontinent. Meanwhile, the English founded the East India Company, which set up its first factory at Surat in 1612 and began expanding its influence, fighting the Indian rulers and the French, Dutch, and Portuguese traders simultaneously.

Bombay, taken from the Portuguese, became the seat of English rule in 1687. The defeat of French and Islamic armies by Lord Clive in the decade ending in 1760 laid the foundation of the British Empire in India. From then until 1858, when the administration of India was formally transferred to the British Crown following the Sepoy Mutiny of native troops in 1857, the East India Company suppressed native uprisings and extended British rule.

After World War I, in which the Indian states sent more than 6 million troops to fight beside the Allies, Indian nationalist unrest rose to new heights under the leadership of a little Hindu lawyer, Mohandas K. Gandhi, called Mahatma Gandhi. His tactics called for nonviolent revolts against British authority. He soon became the leading spirit of the All-India Congress Party, which was the spearhead of revolt. In

1919 the British gave added responsibility to Indian officials, and in 1935 India was given a federal form of government and a measure of self-rule.

In 1942, with the Japanese pressing hard on the eastern borders of India, the British War Cabinet tried and failed to reach a political settlement with nationalist leaders. The Congress Party took the position that the British must quit India. In 1942, fearing mass civil disobedience, the government of India carried out widespread arrests of Congress leaders, including Gandhi.

Gandhi was released in 1944 and negotiations for a settlement were resumed. Finally, in February 1947, the Labor government announced its determination to transfer power to "responsible Indian hands" by June 1948 even if a Constitution had not been worked out.

Lord Mountbatten as Viceroy, by June 1947, achieved agreement on the partitioning of India along religious lines and on the splitting of the provinces of Bengal and the Punjab, which the Moslems had claimed.

The Indian Independence Act, passed quickly by the British Parliament, received royal assent on July 18, 1947, and on August 15 the Indian Empire passed into history.

Jawaharlal Nehru, leader of the Congress Party, was made Prime Minister. Before an exchange of populations could be arranged, bloody riots occurred among the communal groups, and armed conflict broke out over rival claims to the princely state of Jammu and Kashmir. Peace was restored only with the greatest difficulty. In 1949 a Constitution, along the lines of the U.S. Constitution, was approved making India a sovereign republic. Under a federal structure the states were organized on linguistic lines.

The dominance of the Congress Party contributed to stability. In 1956 the republic absorbed the former French settlements. Five years later, it forcibly annexed the Portuguese enclaves of Goa, Damao, and Diu.

Nehru died in 1964. His successor, Lal Bahadur Shastri, died on Jan. 10, 1966. Nehru's daughter, Indira Gandhi, became Prime Minister, and she continued his policy of nonalignment.

In 1971 the Pakistani Army moved in to quash the independence movement in East Pakistan that was supported by clandestine aid from India, and some 10 million Bengali refugees poured across the border into India, creating social, economic, and health problems. After numerous border incidents, India invaded East Pakistan and in two weeks forced the surrender of the Pakistani army. East Pakistan was established as an independent state and renamed Bangladesh.

In the summer of 1975, the world's largest democracy veered suddenly toward authoritarianism when a judge in Allahabad, Mrs. Gandhi's home constituency, found her landslide victory in the 1971 elections invalid because civil servants had illegally aided her campaign. Amid demands for her resignation, Mrs. Gandhi decreed a state of emergency on June 26 and ordered mass arrests of her critics, including all opposition party leaders except the Communists.

In 1976, India and Pakistan formally renewed diplomatic relations.

Despite strong opposition to her repressive measures and particularly the resentment against compulsory birth control programs, Mrs. Gandhi in 1977 announced parliamentary elections for March. At the same time, she freed most political prisoners.

The landslide victory of Morarji R. Desai unseated Mrs. Gandhi and also defeated a bid for office by her son, Sanjay.

Mrs. Gandhi staged a spectacular comeback in the elections of January 1980.

In 1984, Mrs. Gandhi ordered the Indian Army to root out a band of Sikh holy men and gunmen who were using the holiest shrine of the Sikh religion, the Golden Temple in Amritsar, as a base for terrorist raids in a violent campaign for greater political autonomy in the strategic Punjab border state. As many as 1,000 people were reported killed in the June 5–6 battle, including Jarnall Singh Bhindranwale, the Khomeini-like militant leader, and 93 soldiers. The perceived sacrilege to the Golden Temple kindled outrage among many of India's 14 million Sikhs and brought a spasm of mutinies and desertions by Sikh officers and soldiers in the army.

On Oct. 31, 1984, Mrs. Gandhi was assassinated by two men identified by police as Sikh members of her bodyguard. The ruling Congress I Party chose her second son, Rajiv Gandhi, to succeed her as Prime Minister.

One week after the resignation of Prime Minister Shekhar, India's president in March 1991 called for national elections, the tenth in its history and the second in less than two years. While at an election rally on May 22 former prime minister Rajiv Gandhi was assassinated. Final phases of the election were postponed a month. When they were resumed the Congress Party and its allies won 236 seats in the lower house, 20 short of a majority. P.V. Narasimha Rao was chosen to form a new government over a strong challenge from within the Congress Party. Ailing with a poor heart, he is widely regarded as a caretaker prime minister.

Native States. Most of the 560-odd native states and subdivisions of pre-1947 India acceded to the new nation, and the central government pursued a vigorous policy of integration. This took three forms: merger into adjacent provinces, conversion into centrally administered areas, and grouping into unions of states. Finally, under a controversial reorganization plan effective Nov. 1, 1956, the unions of states were abolished and merged into adjacent states, and India became a union of 15 states and 8 centrally administered areas. A 16th state was added in 1962, and in 1966, the Punjab was partitioned into two states.

Resolution of the territorial dispute over Kashmir grew out of peace negotiations following the two-week India-Pakistan war of 1971. After sporadic skirmishing, an accord reached July 3, 1972, committed both powers to withdraw troops from a temporary cease-fire line after the border was fixed. Agreement on the border was reached Dec. 7, 1972.

In April 1975, the Indian Parliament voted to make the 300-year-old kingdom of Sikkim a full-fledged Indian state, and the annexation took effect May 16.

Situated in the Himalayas, Sikkim was a virtual dependency of Tibet until the early 19th century. Under an 1890 treaty between China and Great Britain, it became a British protectorate, and was made an Indian protectorate after Britain quit the subcontinent.

INDONESIA

Republic of Indonesia
President: Suharto (1969)[1]
Area: 735,268 sq mi. (1,904,344 sq km)[2]
Population (est. mid-1991): 181,400,000 (average annual rate of natural increase: 1.7%); birth rate: 25/1000; infant mortality rate: 73/1000; density per square mile: 245

Capital: Jakarta
Largest cities (est. 1983): Jakarta, 7,636,000; Surabaja, 2,289,000; Bandung, 1,602,000; Medan, 1,966,000; Semarang, 1,269,000
Monetary unit: Rupiah
Languages: Bahasa Indonesia (official), Dutch, English, and more than 60 regional languages
Religions: Islam, 88%; Christian, 9%; Hindu, 2%; other, 1%
National name: Republik Indonesia
Literacy rate: 62%
Economic summary: Gross national product (1989 est.): $80 billion; $430 per capita; 5.7% real growth rate. Arable land: 8%. Principal products: rice, cassava, peanuts, rubber, coffee. Labor force: 67,000,000; 10% in manufacturing. Major products: petroleum, timber, textiles, cement, fertilizer, rubber. Natural resources: oil, timber, nickel, natural gas, tin, bauxite, copper. Exports: petroleum and liquid natural gas, timber, rubber, coffee, textiles. Imports: chemicals, machinery, manufactured goods. Major trading partners: Japan, U.S., Singapore, E.C.

1. General Suharto served as Acting President of Indonesia from 1967 to 1969. 2. Includes West Irian (former Netherlands New Guinea), renamed Irian Jaya in March 1973 (159,355 sq mi.; 412,731 sq km), and former Portuguese Timor (5,763 sq mi.; 14,925 sq km), annexed in 1976.

Geography. Indonesia is part of the Malay archipelago in Southeast Asia with an area nearly three times that of Texas. It consists of the islands of Sumatra, Java, Madura, Borneo (except Sarawak and Brunei in the north), the Celebes, the Moluccas, Irian Jaya, and about 30 smaller archipelagos, totaling 13,677 islands, of which about 6,000 are inhabited. Its neighbor to the north is Malaysia and to the east Papua New Guinea.

A backbone of mountain ranges extends throughout the main islands of the archipelago. Earthquakes are frequent, and there are many active volcanoes.

Government. The President is elected by the People's Consultative Assembly, whose 1000 members include the functioning legislative arm, the 500-member House of Representatives. Meeting at least once every five years, the Assembly has broad policy functions. The House, 100 of whose members are appointed by the President, meets at least once annually. General Suharto was elected unopposed to a fifth five-year term in 1988.

History. Indonesia is inhabited by Malayan and Papuan peoples ranging from the more advanced Javanese and Balinese to the more primitive Dyaks of Borneo. Invasions from China and India contributed Chinese and Indian admixtures.

During the first few centuries of the Christian era, most of the islands came under the influence of Hindu priests and traders, who spread their culture and religion. Moslem invasions began in the 13th century, and most of the area was Moslem by the 15th. Portuguese traders arrived early in the 16th century but were ousted by the Dutch about 1595. After Napoleon subjugated the Netherlands homeland in 1811, the British seized the islands but returned them to the Dutch in 1816. In 1922 the islands were made an integral part of the Netherlands kingdom.

During World War II, Indonesia was under Japanese military occupation with nominal native self-government. When the Japanese surrendered to the Allies, President Sukarno and Mohammed Hatta, his Vice President, proclaimed Indonesian independence from the Dutch on Aug. 17, 1945. Allied troops—mostly British Indian troops—fought the nationalists until the arrival of Dutch troops. In November 1946, the Dutch and the Indonesians reached a draft agreement contemplating formation of a Netherlands-Indonesian Union, but differences in interpretation resulted in more fighting between Dutch and Indonesian forces.

On Nov. 2, 1949, Dutch and Indonesian leaders agreed upon the terms of union. The transfer of sovereignty took place at Amsterdam on Dec. 27, 1949. In February 1956 Indonesia abrogated the Union with the Netherlands and in August 1956 repudiated its debt to the Netherlands. In 1963, Netherlands New Guinea was transferred to Indonesia and renamed West Irian. In 1973 it became Irian Jaya.

Hatta and Sukarno, the co-fathers of Indonesian independence, split after it was achieved over Sukarno's concept of "guided democracy." Under Sukarno, the country's leading political figure for almost a half century, the Indonesian Communist Party gradually gained increasing influence.

After an attempted coup was put down by General Suharto, the army chief of staff, and officers loyal to him, thousands of Communist suspects were sought out and killed all over the country. Suharto took over the reins of government, gradually eased Sukarno out of office, and took full power in 1967.

Suharto permitted national elections, which moved the nation back to representative government. He also ended hostilities with Malaysia. Under President Suharto, Indonesia has been strongly anticommunist. It also has been politically stable and has made progress in economic development.

Indonesia invaded the former Portuguese half of the island of Timor in 1975, and annexed the territory in 1976. On a visit to Jakarta in July 1984, Secretary of State George P. Shultz expressed concern about reports of human rights abuses being carried out by Indonesian forces in East Timor. More than 100,000 Timorese, a sixth of the mostly Catholic population, were reported to have died from famine, disease, and fighting since the annexation.

Relations with China were normalized in 1990. The army has recently expressed the need for change in the political system. The government has also attempted to liberalize and diversify the economy, relying less on oil export revenue. Indonesia is a member of OPEC.

IRAN

Islamic Republic of Iran
President: Hashemi Rafsanjani (1989)
Area: 636,293 sq mi. (1,648,000 sq km)
Population (est. mid-1991): 58,600,000 (average annual rate of natural increase: 3.3%); birth rate: 41/1000; infant mortality rate: 43/1000; density per square mile: 92
Capital: Teheran
Largest cities (est. 1986): Teheran, 6,037,658; Isfahan, 1,422,308; Mashed, 2,038,388; Tabriz, 1,566,932
Monetary unit: Rial
Languages: Farsi (Persian), Kurdish, Arabic
Religions: Shi'ite Moslem, 95%; Sunni Moslem, 4%
Literacy rate: 48% (est.)
Economic summary: Gross national product (1989): $97.6 billion; $1,800 per capita; real growth rate 0–1%. Arable land: 8%. Principal products: wheat, barley, rice, sugar beets, cotton, dates, raisins, sheep, goats. Labor force: 15,400,000; 21% in manufacturing. Major

products: crude and refined oil, textiles, petrochemicals, cement, processed foods, steel and copper fabrication. Natural resources: oil, gas, iron, copper. Exports: petroleum, carpets. Imports: machinery, military supplies, foodstuffs, pharmaceuticals. Major trading partners: Japan, Germany, Netherlands, U.K., Italy, Spain, Turkey.

Geography. Iran, a Middle Eastern country south of the Caspian Sea and north of the Persian Gulf, is three times the size of Arizona. It shares borders with Iraq, Turkey, the U.S.S.R., Afghanistan, and Pakistan.

In general, the country is a plateau averaging 4,000 feet (1,219 m) in elevation. There are also maritime lowlands along the Persian Gulf and the Caspian Sea. The Elburz Mountains in the north rise to 18,603 feet (5,670 m) at Mt. Damavend. From northwest to southeast, the country is crossed by a desert 800 miles (1,287 km) long.

Government. The Pahlavi dynasty was overthrown on Feb. 11, 1979, by followers of the Ayatollah Ruhollah Khomeini. After a referendum endorsed the establishment of a republic, Khomeini drafted a Constitution calling for a President to be popularly elected every four years, an appointed Prime Minister, and a unicameral National Consultative Assembly, popularly elected every four years. A constitutional amendment in 1989 eliminated the post of Prime Minister.

Khomeini also instituted a Revolutionary Council to insure the adherence to Islamic principles in all phases of Iranian life. The Council formally handed over its powers to the Assembly after the organization of the legislature in July 1980, but continued to exercise power behind the scenes.

History. Oil-rich Iran was called Persia before 1935. Its key location blocks the lower land gate to Asia and also stands in the way of traditional Russian ambitions for access to the Indian Ocean. After periods of Assyrian, Median, and Achaemenidian rule, Persia became a powerful empire under Cyrus the Great, reaching from the Indus to the Nile at its zenith in 525 B.C. It fell to Alexander in 331–30 B.C. and to the Seleucids in 312–02 B.C., and a native Persian regime arose about 130 B.C. Another Persian regime arose about A.D. 224, but it fell to the Arabs in 637. In the 12th century, the Mongols took their turn ruling Persia, and in the early part of the 18th century, the Turks occupied the country.

An Anglo-Russian convention of 1907 divided Persia into two spheres of influence. British attempts to impose a protectorate over the entire country were defeated in 1919. Two years later, Gen. Reza Pahlavi seized the government and was elected hereditary Shah in 1925. Subsequently he did much to modernize the country and abolished all foreign extraterritorial rights.

Increased pro-Axis activity led to Anglo-Russian occupation of Iran in 1941 and deposition of the Shah in favor of his son, Mohammed Reza Pahlavi.

Ali Razmara became premier in 1950 and pledged to restore efficient and honest government, but he was assassinated after less than nine months in office and Mohammed Mossadegh took over. Mossadegh was ousted in August 1953, by Fazollah Zahedi, whom the Shah had named premier.

Opposition to the Shah spread, despite the imposition of martial law in September 1978, and massive demonstrations demanded the return of the exiled Ayatollah Ruhollah Khomeini. Riots and strikes continued despite the appointment of an opposition leader, Shahpur Bakhtiar, as premier on Dec. 29. The Shah and his family left Iran on Jan. 16, 1979, for a "vacation," leaving power in the hands of a regency council.

Khomeini returned on Feb. 1 to a nation in turmoil as military units loyal to the Shah continued to support Bakhtiar and clashed with revolutionaries. Khomeini appointed Mehdi Bazargan as premier of the provisional government and in two days of fighting, revolutionaries forced the military to capitulate on Feb. 11.

The new government began a program of nationalization of insurance companies, banks, and industries both locally and foreign-owned. Oil production fell amid the political confusion.

Khomeini, ignoring opposition, proceeded with his plans for revitalizing Islamic traditions. He urged women to return to the veil, or chador; banned alcohol and mixed bathing, and prohibited music from radio and television broadcasting, declaring it to be "no different from opium."

Revolutionary militants invaded the U.S. Embassy in Teheran on Nov. 4, 1979, seized staff members as hostages, and precipitated an international crisis.

Khomeini refused all appeals, even a unanimous vote by the U.N. Security Council demanding immediate release of the hostages.

Iranian hostility toward Washington was reinforced by the Carter administration's economic boycott and deportation order against Iranian students in the U.S., the break in diplomatic relations and ultimately an aborted U.S. raid in April aimed at rescuing the hostages.

As the first anniversary of the embassy seizure neared, Khomeini and his followers insisted on their original conditions: guarantee by the U.S. not to interfere in Iran's affairs, cancellation of U.S. damage claims against Iran, release of $8 billion in frozen Iranian assets, an apology, and the return of the assets held by the former imperial family.

These conditions were largely met and the 52 American hostages were released on Jan. 20, ending 444 days in captivity.

From the release of the hostages onward, President Bani-Sadr and the conservative clerics of the dominant Islamic Republican Party clashed with growing frequency. He was stripped of his command of the armed forces by Khomeini on June 6 and ousted as President on June 22. On July 24, Prime Minister Mohammed Ali Rajai was elected overwhelmingly to the Presidency.

Rajai and Prime Minister Mohammed Javad Bahonar were killed on Aug. 30 by a bomb in Bahonar's office. Hojatolislam Mohammed Ali Khamenei, a clergyman, leader of the Islamic Republican Party and spokesman for Khomeini, was elected President on Oct. 2, 1981.

The sporadic war with Iraq regained momentum in 1982, as Iran launched an offensive in March and regained much of the border area occupied by Iraq in late 1980. Khomeini rejected Iraqi bids for a truce, insisting that Iraq's President Saddam Hussein must leave office first.

Iran continued to be at war with Iraq well into 1988. Although Iraq expressed its willingness to cease fighting, Iran stated that it would not stop the war until Iraq agreed to make payment for war damages to Iran, and punish the Iraqi government leaders involved in the conflict.

On July 20, 1988, Khomeini, after a series of Iranian military reverses, agreed to ceasefire negotiations with Iraq. A cease-fire went into effect Aug. 20, 1988.

Khomeini died in June 1989.

By early 1991 the Islamic Revolution appeared to have lost much of its militancy. Attempting to revive a stagnant economy President Rafsanjani took measures to decentralize the command system and introduce free-market mechanisms. Seeking better relations with the West, and hopefully its money, Iran began making overtures to the European Community.

IRAQ

Republic of Iraq
President: Saddam Hussein (1979)
Area: 167,920 sq mi. (434,913 sq km)
Population (est. mid-1991): 17,100,000 (average annual rate of natural increase: 2.7%); birth rate: 41/1000; infant mortality rate: 69/1000; density per square mile: 102
Capital: Baghdad
Largest cities (est. 1985): Baghdad, 4,648,609; Basra, 616,700; Mosul, 570,926
Monetary unit: Iraqi dinar
Languages: Arabic (official) and Kurdish
Religions: Islam, 97%; Christian or other, 3%
National name: Al Jumhouriya Al Iraqia
Literacy rate: 55–65% (est.)
Economic summary: Gross national product (1989 est.): $35 billion, $1,940 per capita; 5% real growth rate. Arable land: 12%. Principal products: dates, livestock, wheat, barley, cotton, rice. Labor force: 3,400,000 (1984); 28% in industry. Major products: petroleum, chemicals, textiles, construction materials. Natural resources: oil, natural gas, phosphates, sulfur. Exports: petroleum and refined products, machinery, chemicals, dates. Imports: manufactured goods, food. Major trading partners: France, Italy, Japan, Germany, Brazil, U.K., U.S., Turkey, U.S.S.R.

Geography. Iraq, a triangle of mountains, desert, and fertile river valley, is bounded on the east by Iran, on the north by Turkey, the west by Syria and Jordan, and the south by Saudi Arabia and Kuwait. It is twice the size of Idaho.

The country has arid desertland west of the Euphrates, a broad central valley between the Euphrates and Tigris, and mountains in the northeast. The fertile lower valley is formed by the delta of the two rivers, which join about 120 miles (193 km) from the head of the Persian Gulf. The gulf coastline is 26 miles (42 km) long. The only port for seagoing vessels is Basra, which is on the Shatt-al-Arab River near the head of the Persian Gulf.

Government. Since the coup d'etat of July 1968, Iraq has been governed by the Arab Ba'ath Socialist Party through a Council of Command of the Revolution headed by the President. There is also a Council of Ministers headed by the President.

History. From earliest times Iraq was known as Mesopotamia—the land between the rivers—for it embraces a large part of the alluvial plains of the Tigris and Euphrates.

An advanced civilization existed by 4000 B.C. Sometime after 2000 B.C. the land became the center of the ancient Babylonian and Assyrian empires. It was conquered by Cyrus the Great of Persia in 538 B.C., and by Alexander in 331 B.C. After an Arab conquest in A.D. 637–40, Baghdad became capital of the ruling caliphate. The country was cruelly pillaged by the Mongols in 1258, and during the 16th, 17th, and 18th centuries was the object of repeated Turkish-Persian competition.

Nominal Turkish suzerainty imposed in 1638 was replaced by direct Turkish rule in 1831. In World War I, an Anglo-Indian force occupied most of the country, and Britain was given a mandate over the area in 1920. The British recognized Iraq as a kingdom in 1922 and terminated the mandate in 1932 when Iraq was admitted to the League of Nations. In World War II, Iraq generally adhered to its 1930 treaty of alliance with Britain, but in 1941, British troops were compelled to put down a pro-Axis revolt led by Premier Rashid Ali.

Iraq became a charter member of the Arab League in 1945, and Iraqi troops took part in the Arab invasion of Palestine in 1948.

Faisal II, born on May 2, 1935, succeeded his father, Ghazi I, who was killed in an automobile accident on April 4, 1939. Faisal and his uncle, Crown Prince Abdul-Ilah, were assassinated in August 1958 in a swift revolutionary coup that brought to power a military junta headed by Abdul Karem Kassim. Kassim, in turn, was overthrown and killed in a coup staged March 8, 1963, by the Ba'ath Socialist Party.

Abdel Salam Arif, a leader in the 1958 coup, staged another coup in November 1963, driving the Ba'ath members of the revolutionary council from power. He adopted a new constitution in 1964. In 1966, he, two Cabinet members, and other supporters died in a helicopter crash. His brother, Gen. Abdel Rahman Arif, assumed the presidency, crushed the opposition, and won an indefinite extension of his term in 1967. His regime was ousted in July 1968 by a junta led by Maj. Gen. Ahmed Hassan al-Bakr.

A long-standing dispute over control of the Shatt al-Arab waterway between Iraq and Iran broke into full-scale war on Sept. 20, 1980. Iraqi planes attacked Iranian airfields and the Abadan refinery, and Iraqi ground forces moved into Iran.

Despite the smaller size of its armed forces, Iraq took and held the initiative by seizing Abadan and Khurramshahr together with substantial Iranian territory by December and beating back Iranian counterattacks in January. Peace efforts by the Islamic nations, the nonaligned, and the United Nations failed as 1981 wore on and the war stagnated.

In 1982, the Iraqis fell back to their own country and dug themselves in behind sandbagged defensive fortifications. With massive firepower, they turned back wave after wave of attacking Iranian troops and revolutionary guards, many of them in their teens. From the beginning of the war in September 1980 to September 1984, foreign military analysts estimated that more than 100,000 Iranians and perhaps 50,000 Iraqis had been killed.

The Iraqis clearly wanted to end the war, but the Iranians refused. In March of 1985, Iraq apparently won the largest battle of the long war, crushing a major Iranian offensive in the southern marshes in a week of heavy fighting.

In February 1986, Iranian forces gained on two fronts; but Iraq retook most of the lost ground in 1988 and the war continued a stalemate. In August, Iraq and Iran agreed to hold direct talks after a cease-fire takes effect.

In July 1990, President Hussein claimed that Kuwait was flooding world markets with oil and forcing down prices. A mediation attempt by Arab leaders failed, and on Aug. 2, 1990, over this and territorial claims, Iraqi troops invaded Kuwait and set up a puppet government.

After the Gulf War, Saddam Hussein was still in power. The UN Security Council affirmed an embargo against military supplies to that country and a trade embargo was still in place, pending claims of compensation for damage to Kuwait.

IRELAND

President: Mary Robinson (1990)
Taoiseach (Prime Minister): Charles J. Haughey (1987)
Area: 27,136 sq mi. (70,282 sq km)
Population (est. mid-1991): 3,600,000 (average annual rate of natural increase: 0.6%); birth rate: 15/1000; infant mortality rate: 7.5/1000; density per square mile: 133
Capital: Dublin
Largest cities (est. 1982): Dublin, 550,000; Cork, 140,000; Limerick, 60,000
Monetary unit: Irish pound (punt)
Languages: Irish, English
Religions: Roman Catholic, 94%; Anglican, 4%; other, 2%
National name: Ireland or Eire in the Irish language
Literacy rate: 99%
Economic summary: Gross national product (1989 est.): $31.4 billion; $8,900 per capita; 4.3% real growth rate. Arable land: 14%. Principal products: cattle and dairy products, pigs, poultry and eggs, sheep and wool, horses, barley, sugar beets. Labor force: 1,310,000; 19.1% in manufacturing and construction. Major products: processed foods, brews, textiles, clothing, chemicals, pharmaceuticals, machinery, transportation equipment, glass and crystal. Natural resources: zinc, lead, natural gas, crude oil, barite, copper, gypsum, limestone, dolomite, peat, silver. Exports: livestock, dairy products, machinery, chemicals, data processing equipment. Imports: food, anrmtal feed, chemicals, petroleum products, machinery, textile clothing. Major trading partners: U.K., Western European countries, U.S.

Geography. Ireland is situated in the Atlantic Ocean and separated from Britain by the Irish Sea. Half the size of Arkansas, it occupies the entire island except for the six counties which make up Northern Ireland.

Ireland resembles a basin—a central plain rimmed with mountains, except in the Dublin region. The mountains are low, with the highest peak, Carrantuohill in County Kerry, rising to 3,415 feet (1,041 m).

The principal river is the Shannon, which begins in the north central area, flows south and southwest for about 240 miles (386 km), and empties into the Atlantic.

Government. Ireland is a parliamentary democracy. The National Parliament (Oireachtas) consists of the president and two Houses, the House of Representatives (Dáil éireann) and the Senate (Seanad éireann), whose members serve for a maximum term of five years. The House of Representatives has 166 members elected by proportional representation; the Senate has 60 members of whom 11 are nominated by the prime minister, 6 by the universities and the remaining 43 from five vocational panels. The prime minister (Taoiseach), who is the head of government, is appointed by the president on the nomination of the House of Representatives, to which he is responsible.

History. In the Stone and Bronze Ages, Ireland was inhabited by Picts in the north and a people called the Erainn in the south, the same stock, apparently, as in all the isles before the Anglo-Saxon invasion of Britain. About the fourth century B.C., tall, red-haired Celts arrived from Gaul or Galicia. They subdued and assimilated the inhabitants and established a Gaelic civilization.

By the beginning of the Christian Era, Ireland was divided into five kingdoms—Ulster, Connacht, Leinster, Meath, and Munster. St. Patrick introduced Christianity in 432 and the country developed into a center of Gaelic and Latin learning. Irish monasteries, the equivalent of universities, attracted intellectuals as well as the pious and sent out missionaries to many parts of Europe and, some believe, to North America.

Norse depredations along the coasts, starting in 795, ended in 1014 with Norse defeat at the Battle of Clontarf by forces under Brian Boru. In the 12th century, the Pope gave all Ireland to the English Crown as a papal fief. In 1171, Henry II of England was acknowledged "Lord of Ireland," but local sectional rule continued for centuries, and English control over the whole island was not reasonably absolute until the 17th century. By the Act of Union (1801), England and Ireland became the "United Kingdom of Great Britain and Ireland."

A steady decline in the Irish economy followed in the next decades. The population had reached 8.25 million when the great potato famine of 1846–48 took many lives and drove millions to emigrate to America. By 1921 it was down to 4.3 million.

In the meantime, anti-British agitation continued along with demands for Irish home rule. The advent of World War I delayed the institution of home rule and resulted in the Easter Rebellion in Dublin (April 24–29, 1916), in which Irish nationalists unsuccessfully attempted to throw off British rule. Guerrilla warfare against British forces followed proclamation of a republic by the rebels in 1919.

The Irish Free State was established as a dominion on Dec. 6, 1922, with the six northern counties as part of the United Kingdom. Ireland was neutral in World War II.

In 1948, Eamon de Valera, American-born leader of the Sinn Fein, who had won establishment of the Free State in 1921 in negotiations with Britain's David Lloyd George, was defeated by John A. Costello, who demanded final independence from Britain. The Republic of Ireland was proclaimed on April 18, 1949. It withdrew from the Commonwealth but in 1955 entered the United Nations. Since 1949 the prime concern of successive governments has been economic development.

Through the 1960s, two antagonistic currents dominated Irish politics. One sought to bind the wounds of the rebellion and civil war. The other was the effort of the outlawed extremist Irish Republican Army to bring Northern Ireland into the republic. Despite public sympathy for unification of Ireland, the Dublin government dealt rigorously with IRA guerrillas caught inside the republic's borders.

In the elections of June 11, 1981, Garret M. D. FitzGerald, leader of the Fine Gael, was elected Prime Minister by 81 to 78 with the support of 15 Labor Party members and one independent Socialist added to his own party's 65 members.

FitzGerald resigned Jan. 27, 1982, after his presentation of an austerity budget aroused the opposition of independents who had backed him previously. Former Prime Minister Haughey was sworn in on March 9 and presented a budget with nearly a $1 billion deficit, with additional public spending aimed at stimulating the lagging economy. FitzGerald was re-elected Prime Minister on Dec. 14, 1982 but was unable to solve the problem of unemployment and the elections of 1987 brought Haughey back into power on March 10.

Three candidates vied in the November 1990 presidential election. Although Brian Lenihan of Fianna Fail led in the first round, Mary Robinson, supported by the Labour Party and the Workers Party, won the second round with 52.8% of the vote, becoming the first non-Fianna Fail president since 1945. In local elections of June 1991 the Fianna Fail Party suffered heavy losses.

ISRAEL

State of Israel
President: Chaim Herzog (1988)
Prime Minister: Yitzhak Shamir (1988) (term ends Nov., 1992)
Area: 8,020 sq mi. (20,772 sq km)
Population (est. mid-1991): 4,900,000[1] (average annual rate of natural increase: 1.6%); birth rate: 22/1000; infant mortality rate: 10/1000; density per square mile: 606
Capital: Jerusalem[2]
Largest cities (1989): Jerusalem, 493,500[3]; Tel Aviv, 317,800; Haifa, 222,600
Monetary unit: Shekel
Languages: Hebrew, Arabic, English
Religions: Judaism, 83%; Islam, 13.1%; Christian, 2.3%; Druze, 1.6%
National name: Medinat Yisra'el
Literacy rate: 88% Jews, 70% Arabs
Economic summary: Gross national product (1989): $51.8 billion; $11,296 per capita; 1.5% real growth rate. Arable land: 17%. Principal products: citrus and other fruits, vegetables, beef, dairy and poultry products. Labor force: (1989): 1,348,000; 22.8% in industry, mining and manufacturing. Major products: processed foods, cut diamonds, clothing and textiles, chemicals, metal products, transport and electrical equipment, high-technology electronics. Natural resources: sulfur, copper, phosphates, potash, bromine. Exports: polished diamonds, citrus and other fruits, clothing and textiles, processed foods, high technology products, computerized medical equipment, military hardware, fertilizer and chemical products. Imports: rough diamonds, chemicals, oil, machinery, iron and steel, cereals, textiles, vehicles, ships. Major trading partners: U.S., Germany, U.K., Switzerland, France, Italy, Belgium, Luxembourg.

1. Includes West Bank, Gaza Strip, East Jerusalem. 2. Not recognized by U.S. which recognizes Tel Aviv. 3. Includes East Jerusalem.

Geography. Israel, slightly smaller than Massachusetts, lies at the eastern end of the Mediterranean Sea. It is bordered by Egypt on the west, Syria and Jordan on the east, and Lebanon on the north. Northern Israel is largely a plateau traversed from north to south by mountains and broken by great depressions, also running from north to south.

The maritime plain of Israel is remarkably fertile.

The southern Negev region, which comprises almost half the total area, is largely a wide desert steppe area. The National Water Project irrigation scheme is now transforming it into fertile land. The Jordan, the only important river, flows from the north through Lake Hule (Waters of Merom) and Lake Kinneret (Sea of Galilee or Sea of Tiberias), finally entering the Dead Sea, 1,290 feet (393 m) below sea level. This "sea," which is actually a salt lake (394 sq mi.; 1,020 sq km), has no outlet, its water balance being maintained by evaporation.

Government. Israel, which does not have a written constitution, has a republican form of government headed by a president elected for a five-year term by the Knesset. He may serve no more than two terms. The Knesset has 120 members elected by universal suffrage under proportional representation for four years. The government is administered by the Cabinet, which is headed by the prime minister.

The Knesset decided in June 1950 that Israel would acquire a constitution gradually through the years by the enactment of fundamental laws. Israel grants automatic citizenship to every Jew who desires to settle within its borders, subject to control of the Knesset.

History. Palestine, cradle of two great religions and homeland of the modern state of Israel, was known to the ancient Hebrews as the "Land of Canaan." Palestine's name derives from the Philistines, a people who occupied the southern coastal part of the country in the 12th century B.C.

A Hebrew kingdom established in 1000 B.C. was later split into the kingdoms of Judah and Israel; they were subsequently invaded by Assyrians, Babylonians, Egyptians, Persians, Macedonians, Romans, and Byzantines. The Arabs took Palestine from the Byzantine Empire A.D. 634–40. With the exception of a Frankish Crusader kingdom from 1099 to 1187, Palestine remained under Moslem rule until the 20th century (Turkish rule from 1516), when British forces under Gen. Sir Edmund Allenby defeated the Turks and captured Jerusalem Dec. 9, 1917. The League of Nations granted Britain a mandate to govern Palestine, effective in 1923.

Jewish colonies—Jews from Russia established one as early as 1882—multiplied after Theodor Herzl's 1897 call for a Jewish state. The Zionist movement received official approval with the publication of a letter Nov. 2, 1917, from Arthur Balfour, British Foreign Secretary, to Lord Rothschild, a British Jewish leader. Balfour promised support for the establishment of a Jewish homeland in Palestine on the understanding that the civil and religious rights of non-Jewish Palestinians would be safeguarded.

A 1937 British proposal called for an Arab and a Jewish state separated by a mandated area incorporating Jerusalem and Nazareth. Arabs opposed this, demanding a single state with minority rights for Jews, and a 1939 British White Paper retreated, offering instead a single state with further Jewish immigration to be limited to 75,000. Although the White Paper satisfied neither side, further discussion ended on the outbreak of World War II, when the Jewish population stood at nearly 500,000, or 30% of the total. Illegal and legal immigration during the war brought the Jewish population to 678,000 in 1946, compared with 1,269,000 Arabs. Unable to reach a compromise, Britain turned the problem over to the United Nations in 1947, which on November 29 voted for partition—despite strong Arab opposition.

Britain did not help implement the U.N. decision and withdrew on expiration of its mandate May 14, 1948. Zionists had already seized control of areas designated as Jewish, and, on the day of British departure, the Jewish National Council proclaimed the State of Israel.

U.S. recognition came within hours. The next day, Jordanian and Egyptian forces invaded the new nation. At the cease-fire Jan. 7, 1949, Israel increased its original territory by 50%, taking western Galilee, a broad corridor through central Palestine to Jerusalem, and part of modern Jerusalem. (In April 1950, Jordan annexed areas of eastern and central Palestine that had been designated for an Arab state, together with the old city of Jerusalem).

Chaim Weizmann and David Ben-Gurion became Israel's first president and prime minister. The new government was admitted to the U.N. May 11, 1949.

The next clash with Arab neighbors came when Egypt nationalized the Suez Canal in 1956 and barred Israeli shipping. Coordinating with an Anglo-French force, Israeli troops seized the Gaza Strip and drove through the Sinai to the east bank of the Suez Canal, but withdrew under U.S. and U.N. pressure. In 1967, Israel threatened retaliation against Syrian border raids, and Syria asked Egyptian aid. Egypt demanded the removal of U.N. peace-keeping forces from Suez, staged a national mobilization, closed the Gulf of Aqaba, and moved troops into the Sinai. Starting with simultaneous air attacks against Syrian, Jordanian, and Egyptian air bases on June 5, Israel during a six-day war totally defeated its Arab enemies. Expanding its territory by 200%, Israel at the cease-fire held the Golan Heights, the West Bank of the Jordan River, the Old City, and all of the Sinai and the east bank of the Suez Canal.

Israel insisted that Jerusalem remain a unified city and that peace negotiations be conducted directly, something the Arab states had refused to do because it would constitute a recognition of their Jewish neighbor.

Egypt's President Gamal Abdel Nasser renounced the 1967 cease-fire in 1969 and began a "war of attrition" against Israel, firing Soviet artillery at Israeli forces on the east bank of the canal. Nasser died of a heart attack on Sept. 28, 1970, and was succeeded by Anwar el-Sadat.

In the face of Israeli reluctance even to discuss the return of occupied territories, the fourth Mideast war erupted Oct. 6, 1973, with a surprise Egyptian and Syrian assault on the Jewish high holy day of Yom Kippur. Initial Arab gains were reversed when a cease-fire took effect two weeks later, but Israel suffered heavy losses in manpower.

U.S. Secretary of State Henry A. Kissinger arranged a disengagement of forces on both the Egyptian and Syrian fronts. Geneva talks, aimed at a lasting peace, foundered, however, when Israel balked at inclusion of the Palestine Liberation Organization, a group increasingly active in terrorism directed against Israel.

A second-stage Sinai withdrawal signed by Israel and Egypt in September 1975 required Israel to give up the strategic Mitla and Gidi passes and to return the captured Abu Rudeis oil fields. Egypt guaranteed passage of Israeli cargoes through the reopened Suez Canal, and both sides renounced force in the settlement of disputes. Two hundred U.S. civilian technicians were stationed in a widened U.N buffer zone to monitor and warn either side of truce violations.

A dramatic breakthrough in the tortuous history of Mideast peace efforts occurred Nov. 9, 1977, when Egypt's President Sadat declared his willingness to go anywhere to talk peace. Prime Minister Menachem Begin on Nov. 15 extended an invitation to the Egyptian leader to address the Knesset. Sadat's arrival in Israel four days later raised worldwide hopes. But optimism ebbed even before Begin was invited to Ismailia by Sadat, December 25–26.

An Israeli peace plan unveiled by Begin on his return, and approved by the Knesset, offered to end military administration in the West Bank and the Gaza Strip, with a degree of Arab self-rule but no relinquishment of sovereignty by Israel. Sadat severed talks on Jan. 18 and, despite U.S. condemnation, Begin approved new West Bank settlements by Israelis.

A PLO raid on Israel's coast on March 11, 1978, killed 30 civilians and provoked a full-scale invasion of southern Lebanon by Israel three days later to attack PLO bases. Israel withdrew three months later, turning over strongpoints to Lebanese Christian militia wherever possible rather than to a U.N. peacekeeping force installed in the area.

On March 14, 1979, after a visit by Carter, the Knesset approved a final peace treaty, and 12 days later Begin and Sadat signed the document, together with Carter, in a White House ceremony. Israel began its withdrawal from the Sinai on May 25 by handing over the coastal town of El Arish and the two countries opened their border on May 29.

One of the most difficult periods in Israel's history began with a confrontation with Syria over the placing by Syria of Soviet surface-to-air missiles in the Bekaa Valley of Lebanon in April 1981. President Reagan dispatched Philip C. Habib to prevent a clash. While Habib was seeking a settlement, Begin ordered a bombing raid against an Iraqi nuclear reactor on June 7, invoking the theory of preemptive self-defense because he said Iraq was planning to make nuclear weapons to attack Israel.

Although Israel withdrew its last settlers from the Sinai in April 1982 and agreed to a Sinai "peace patrol" composed of troops from four West European nations, the fragile peace engineered by Habib in Lebanon was shattered on June 9 by a massive Israeli assault on southern Lebanon. The attack was in retaliation for what Israel charged was a PLO attack that critically wounded the Israeli ambassador to London six days earlier.

Israeli armor swept through UNIFIL lines in southern Lebanon, destroyed PLO strongholds in Tyre and Sidon, and reached the suburbs of Beirut on June 10. As Israeli troops ringed Moslem East Beirut, where 5,000 PLO guerrillas were believed trapped, Habib sought to negotiate a safe exit for them.

A U.S.-mediated accord between Lebanon and Israel, signed on May 17, 1983, provided for Israeli withdrawal from Lebanon. Israeli withdrawal was conditioned on withdrawal of Syrian troops from the Bekaa Valley, however, and the Syrians refused to leave. Israel eventually withdrew its troops from the Beirut area, but kept them in southern Lebanon. Lebanon, under pressure from Syria, canceled the accord in March 1984.

Prime Minister Begin resigned on Sept. 15, 1983. On Oct. 10, Likud Party stalwart Yitzhak Shamir was elected Prime Minister.

After a close election, the two major parties worked out a carefully balanced power-sharing agreement and the Knesset, on Sept. 14, 1984 approved a national unity government including both the Labor Alignment and the Likud bloc.

In one hopeful development, the coalition government declared an economic emergency on July 1 and imposed sweeping austerity measures intended to break the country's 260% inflation. Key elements were an 18.8% devaluation of the shekel, price increases in such government-subsidized products as gasoline, dismissal of 9,000 government employees, government spending cuts and a wage and price freeze. By the end of Peres' term in October, 1986, the shekel had been revalued and stabilized and inflation was down to less than 20%.

Differences in the approach to take to peace talks started to strain the government in 1987.

In Dec. 1987, riots by Gazan Palestinians led to the current general uprising throughout the occupied territories which consists of low-level violence and civil disobedience. As a consequence, in 1988 the PLO formally declared an independent state. Also, in response to their ostensible recognition of Israel in that year, the U.S. established low-level diplomatic contacts with the PLO.

A deadlock in the elections of Dec. 1988 led to a continuation of the Likud-Labor national unity government. This collapsed in 1990, leading to Shamir forming a right-wing coalition that included the religious parties.

The relaxation of Soviet emigration rules resulted in a massive wave of Jews entering Israel. Citing for one the severe housing shortage, but probably owing as much to political considerations, Israel embarked on constructing new settlements in the West Bank, angering the U.S. Hopes for quick progress on a general Israel-Arab peace after the Persian Gulf War dimmed as many parties to the dispute resumed traditional stances. Opposition leader Shimon Peres expressed disagreement with the official position concerning the settlements. The *intifada* appeared to be losing strength, and the Israelis sensed they were gaining the upperhand.

ITALY

Italian Republic
President: Francesco Cossiga (1985)
Premier: Giulio Andreotti (1989)
Area: 116,500 sq mi. (301,278 sq km)
Population (est. mid-1991): 57,700,000 (average annual rate of natural increase: .1%); birth rate: 10/1000; infant mortality rate: 8.8/1000; density per square mile: 496
Capital: Rome
Largest cities (1984): Rome, 2,826,733; Milan, 1,535,722; Naples, 1,206,955; Turin, 1,049,997; Genoa, 738,099; Palermo, 716,149; Bologna, 442,307; Florence, 435,698; Catania, 377,707; Bari, 368,216.
Monetary unit: Lira
Language: Italian
Religion: Roman Catholic, almost 100%
National name: Repubblica Italiana
Literacy rate: 93%
Economic summary: Gross national product (1990): $1,050 billion; $18,420 per capita; 2.7% real growth rate. Arable land: 32%. Principal products: grapes, olives, citrus fruits, vegetables, wheat, corn. Labor force: 23,670,000; 37.9% in industry. Major products: machinery, iron and steel, autos, textiles, shoes,

chemicals. Natural resources: mercury, potash, sulfur, fish, gas, marble. Exports: textiles, wearing apparel, metals, transport equipment, chemicals. Imports: petroleum, industrial machinery, chemicals, food, metals. Major trading partners: United States, E.C., OPEC

Geography. Italy is a long peninsula shaped like a boot bounded on the west by the Tyrrhenian Sea and on the east by the Adriatic. Slightly larger than Arizona, it has for neighbors France, Switzerland, Austria, and Yugoslavia.

Approximately 600 of Italy's 708 miles (1,139 km) of length are in the long peninsula that projects into the Mediterranean from the fertile basin of the Po River. The Apennine Mountains, branching off from the Alps between Nice and Genoa, form the peninsula's backbone, and rise to a maximum height of 9,560 feet (2,912 m) at the Gran Sasso d'Italia (Corno). The Alps form Italy's northern boundary.

Several islands form part of Italy. Sicily (9,926 sq mi.; 25,708 sq km) lies off the toe of the boot, across the Strait of Messina, with a steep and rockbound northern coast and gentler slopes to the sea in the west and south. Mount Etna, an active volcano, rises to 10,741 feet (3,274 m), and most of Sicily is more than 500 feet (3,274 m) in elevation. Sixty-two miles (100 km) southwest of Sicily lies Pantelleria (45 sq mi.; 117 sq km), and south of that are Lampedusa and Linosa. Sardinia (9,301 sq mi.; 24,090 sq km), which is just south of Corsica and about 125 miles (200 km) west of the mainland, is mountainous, stony, and unproductive.

Italy has many northern lakes, lying below the snow-covered peaks of the Alps. The largest are Garda (143 sq mi.; 370 sq km), Maggiore (83 sq mi.; 215 sq km), and Como (55 sq mi.; 142 sq km).

The Po, the principal river, flows from the Alps on Italy's western border and crosses the Lombard plain to the Adriatic.

Government. The president is elected for a term of seven years by Parliament in joint session with regional representatives. The president nominates the premier and, upon the premier's recommendations, the members of the Cabinet. Parliament is composed of two houses: a Senate with 315 elective members and a Chamber of Deputies of 630 members elected by the people for a five-year term.

History. Until A.D. 476, when the German Odoacer became head of the Roman Empire in the west, the history of Italy was largely the history of Rome. From A.D. 800 on, the Holy Roman Emperors, Popes, Normans, and Saracens all vied for control over various segments of the Italian peninsula. Numerous city states, such as Venice and Genoa, and many small principalities flourished in the late Middle Ages.

In 1713, after the War of the Spanish Succession, Milan, Naples, and Sardinia were handed over to Austria, which lost some of its Italian territories in 1735. After 1800, Italy was unified by Napoleon, who crowned himself King of Italy in 1805; but with the Congress of Vienna in 1815, Austria once again became the dominant power in Italy.

Austrian armies crushed Italian uprisings in 1820–1821, and 1831. In the 1830s Giuseppe Mazzini, brilliant liberal nationalist, organized the Risorgimento (Resurrection), which laid the foundation for Italian unity.

Disappointed Italian patriots looked to the House of Savoy for leadership. Count Camille di Cavour (1810–61), Premier of Sardinia in 1852 and the architect of a united Italy, joined England and France in the Crimean War (1853–56), and in 1859, helped France in a war against Austria, thereby obtaining Lombardy. By plebiscite in 1860, Modena, Parma, Tuscany, and the Romagna voted to join Sardinia. In 1860, Giuseppe Garibaldi conquered Sicily and Naples and turned them over to Sardinia. Victor Emmanuel II, King of Sardinia, was proclaimed King of Italy in 1861.

Allied with Germany and Austria-Hungary in the Triple Alliance of 1882, Italy declared its neutrality upon the outbreak of World War I on the ground that Germany had embarked upon an offensive war. In 1915, Italy entered the war on the side of the Allies.

Benito (Il Duce) Mussolini, a former Socialist, organized discontented Italians in 1919 into the Fascist Party to "rescue Italy from Bolshevism." He led his Black Shirts in a march on Rome and, on Oct. 28, 1922, became premier. He transformed Italy into a dictatorship, embarking on an expansionist foreign policy with the invasion and annexation of Ethiopia in 1935 and allying himself with Adolf Hitler in the Rome-Berlin Axis in 1936. He was executed by Partisans on April 28, 1945 at Dongo on Lake Como.

Following the overthrow of Mussolini's dictatorship and the armistice with the Allies (Sept. 3, 1943), Italy joined the war against Germany as a co-belligerent. King Victor Emmanuel III abdicated May 9, 1946, and left the country after having installed his son as King Humbert II. A plebiscite rejected monarchy, however, and on June 13, King Humbert followed his father into exile.

The peace treaty of Sept. 15, 1947, required Italian renunciation of all claims in Ethiopia and Greece and the cession of the Dodecanese to Greece and of five small Alpine areas to France. Much of the Istrian Peninsula, including Fiume and Pola, went to Yugoslavia.

The Trieste area west of the new Yugoslav territory was made a free territory (until 1954, when the city and a 90-square-mile zone were transferred to Italy and the rest to Yugoslavia).

Scandal brought the long reign of the Christian Democrats to an end when Italy's 40th premier since World War II, Arnaldo Forlani, was forced to resign in the wake of disclosure that many high-ranking Christian Democrats and civil servants belonged to a secret Masonic lodge known as "P-2."

When the Socialists deserted the coalition, Forlani was forced to resign on May 26, 1981, leaving to Giovanni Spadolini of the small Republican Party the task of forming a new government. He was succeeded by Amintore Fanfani, a Christian Democrat, the following year. Bettino Craxi, a Socialist, became Premier in 1983.

Craxi was forced to resign on June 27, 1986 following the loss of a key secret-ballot vote in Parliament. After a month of political wrangling, Craxi was able to form a new government on condition that his term end in March, 1987.

In early February 1991 the Italian Communist Party officially changed its name to the Democratic Party of the Left. Though still the second largest party, it has three bitter factions. A political crisis in March led Prime Minister Andreotti to fashion a new coalition in April, Italy's 50th postwar government. The new cabinet represented the same five parties as the previous one. After four days, however, the small Republican Party quit its three relatively low-level appointments.

JAMAICA

Sovereign: Queen Elizabeth II
Governor-General: Hon. Edward Zacca (Acting April 1991)
Prime Minister: Michael Manley (1989)
Area: 4,411 sq mi. (11,424 sq km)
Population (est. mid-1991): 2,500,000 (average annual rate of natural increase: 1.9%); birth rate: 25/1000; infant mortality rate: 18/1000; density per square mile: 587
Capital and largest city (est. 1982): Kingston, 104,000
Monetary unit: Jamaican dollar
Language: English
Religions: Protestant, 71%; Roman Catholic, 10%; Rastafarian, 7%
Member of Commonwealth of Nations
Literacy rate: 74%
Economic summary: Gross domestic product (1990): $1.85 billion; $1,100 per capita; 3.8% real growth rate. Arable land: 19%. Principal products: sugar cane, citrus fruits, bananas, coffee, potatoes, livestock. Labor force: 728,700; 28% in industry and commerce. Major products: bauxite, textiles, processed foods, light manufactures. Natural resources: bauxite, gypsum. Exports: alumina, bauxite, sugar, bananas. Imports: fuels, machinery, consumer goods, construction goods, food. Major trading partners: U.S., U.K., Canada, Venezuela.

Geography. Jamaica is an island in the West Indies, 90 miles (145 km) south of Cuba and 100 miles (161 km) west of Haiti. It is a little smaller than Connecticut.

The island is made up of a plateau and the Blue Mountains, a group of volcanic hills, in the east. Blue Mountain (7,402 ft.; 2,256 m) is the tallest peak.

Government. The legislature is a 60-member House of Representatives elected by universal suffrage and an appointed Senate of 21 members. The Prime Minister is appointed by the Governor-General and must, in the Governor-General's opinion, be the person best able to command the confidence of a majority of the members of the House of Representatives.

History. Jamaica was inhabited by Arawak Indians when Columbus discovered it in 1494 and named it St. Iago. It remained under Spanish rule until 1655, then became a British possession. The island prospered from wealth brought by buccaneers to their base, Port Royal, the capital, until the city disappeared in the sea in 1692 after an earthquake. The Arawaks died off from disease and exploitation, and slaves, mostly black, were imported to work sugar plantations. Abolition of the slave trade (1807), emancipation of the slaves (1833), and a gradual drop in sugar prices led to depressed economic conditions that resulted in an uprising in 1865.

The following year Jamaica's status was changed to that of a colony, and conditions improved considerably. Introduction of banana cultivation made the island less dependent on the sugar crop for its well-being.

On May 5, 1953, Jamaica attained internal autonomy, and in 1958 it led in organizing the West Indies Federation. This effort at Caribbean unification failed. A nationalist labor leader, Sir Alexander Bustamente, led a campaign for withdrawal from the Federation. As the result of a popular referendum in 1961, Jamaica became independent on Aug. 6, 1962.

Michael Manley became Prime Minister in 1972 and initiated a socialist program and in 1977, the government bought 51% of the Kaiser and Reynolds bauxite operations.

The Labor Party defeated Manley's People's National Party in 1980 and its capitalist-oriented leader, Edward P.G. Seaga, became Prime Minister. He instituted measures to encourage private investment.

Like other Caribbean countries, Jamaica was hard-hit by the 1981–82 recession. By 1984, austerity measures that Seaga instituted in the hope of bringing the economy back into balance included elimination of government subsidies. Devaluation of the Jamaican dollar made Jamaican products more competitive on the world market and Jamaica achieved record growth in tourism and agriculture. Manufacturing also grew. But at the same time, the cost of many foods went up 50% to 75% and thousands of Jamaicans fell deeper into poverty.

The PNP decisively won local elections in mid-July, 1987, signaling a weakening in Seaga's position. In 1989, Manley swept back into power with a clear-cut victory. He indicated that he would pursue more centrist policies than he did in his previous administration.

The PNP again decisively won local elections in March 1990. Nevertheless Seaga retained his leadership position in the Labor Party at its annual conference in June.

JAPAN

Emperor: Akihito (1989)
Prime Minister: Kiichi Miyazawa (1991)
Area: 145,874 sq mi. (377,815 sq km)
Population (est. mid-1991): 123,800,000 (average annual rate of natural increase: .3%); birth rate: 10/1000; infant mortality rate: 4.5/1000; density per square mile: 849
Capital: Tokyo
Largest cities (1990): Tokyo, 8,163,000; Yokohama, 3,220,000; Osaka, 2,624,000; Nagoya, 2,155,000; Sapporo, 1,672,000; Kobe, 1,477,000; Kyoto, 1,461,000; Fukuoka, 1,237,000; Kawasaki, 1,174,000; Hiroshima, 1,086,000; Kitakyushi, 1,026,000
Monetary unit: Yen
Language: Japanese
Religions: Shintoist, Buddhist
National name: Nippon
Literacy rate: 99%
Economic summary: Gross national product (1989): $2,920 billion; $23,730 per capita; 4.8% real growth rate. Arable land: 13%. Principal products: rice, vegetables, fruits, sugar beets. Labor force: 63,330,000; 33% in manufacturing. Major products: machinery and equipment, metals and metal products, textiles, autos, consumer electronics, chemicals, electrical and electronic equipment. Natural resource: fish. Exports: machinery and equipment, automobiles, metals and metal products, consumer electronics. Imports: fossil fuels, metal ore, raw materials, foodstuffs. Major trading partners: U.S., Middle East, Western Europe, Southeast Asia

Geography. An archipelago extending more than 1,744 miles (2,790 km) from northeast to southwest in the Pacific, Japan is separated from the east coast of Asia by the Sea of Japan. It is approximately the size of Montana.

Japan's four main islands are Honshu, Hokkaido, Kyushu, and Shikoku. The Ryukyu chain to the southwest was U.S.-occupied and the Kuriles to the northeast are Russian-occupied. The surface of the main islands consists largely of mountains separated by narrow valleys. There are about 60 more or less active volcanoes, of which the best-known is Mount Aso. Mount Fuji, seen on postcards, is not active.

Government. Japan's Constitution, promulgated on Nov. 3, 1946, replaced the Meiji Constitution of 1889. The 1946 Constitution, sponsored by the U.S. during its occupation of Japan, brought fundamental changes to the Japanese political system, including the abandonment of the Emperor's divine rights. The Diet (Parliament) consists of a House of Representatives of 511 members, elected for four years, and a House of Councilors of 252 members, half of whom are elected every three years for six-year terms. Executive power is vested in the Cabinet, which is headed by a Prime Minister, nominated by the Diet from its members.

On Jan. 7, 1989, Emperor Hirohito, Japan's longest-reigning monarch died and was succeeded by his son, Akihito (born 1933). He was married in 1959 to Michiko Shoda (the first time a crown prince married a commoner). They have two sons, Hiro and Aya, and a daughter, Nori.

History. A series of legends attributes creation of Japan to the sun goddess, from whom the later emperors were allegedly descended. The first of them was Jimmu Tenno, supposed to have ascended the throne in 660 B.C.

Recorded Japanese history begins with the first contact with China in the 5th century A.D. Japan was then divided into strong feudal states, all nominally under the Emperor, but with real power often held by a court minister or clan. In 1185, Yoritomo, chief of the Minamoto clan, was designated Shogun (Generalissimo) with the administration of the islands under his control. A dual government system—Shogun and Emperor—continued until 1867.

First contact with the West came about 1542, when a Portuguese ship off course arrived in Japanese waters. Portuguese traders, Jesuit missionaries, and Spanish, Dutch, and English traders followed. Suspicious of Christianity and of Portuguese support of a local Japanese revolt, the shoguns prohibited all trade with foreign countries; only a Dutch trading post at Nagasaki was permitted. Western attempts to renew trading relations failed until 1853, when Commodore Matthew Perry sailed an American fleet into Tokyo Bay.

Japan now quickly made the transition from a medieval to a modern power. Feudalism was abolished and industrialization was speeded. An imperial army was established with conscription. The shogun system was abolished in 1868 by Emperor Meiji, and parliamentary government was established in 1889. After a brief war with China in 1894–95, Japan acquired Formosa (Taiwan), the Pescadores Islands, and part of southern Manchuria. China also recognized the independence of Korea (Chosen), which Japan later annexed (1910).

In 1904–05, Japan defeated Russia in the Russo-Japanese War, gaining the territory of southern Sakhalin (Karafuto) and Russia's port and rail rights in Manchuria. In World War I Japan seized Germany's Pacific islands and leased areas in China. The Treaty of Versailles then awarded it a mandate over the islands.

At the Washington Conference of 1921–22, Japan agreed to respect Chinese national integrity. The series of Japanese aggressions that was to lead to the nation's downfall began in 1931 with the invasion of Manchuria. The following year, Japan set up this area as a puppet state, "Manchukuo," under Emperor

Henry Pu-Yi, last of China's Manchu dynasty. On Nov. 25, 1936, Japan joined the Axis by signing the anti-Comintern pact. The invasion of China came the next year and the Pearl Harbor attack on the U.S. on Dec. 7, 1941.

Japan surrendered formally on Sept. 2, 1945, aboard the battleship *Missouri* in Tokyo Bay after atomic bombs had hit Hiroshima and Nagasaki. Southern Sakhalin and the Kurile Islands reverted to the U.S.S.R., and Formosa (Taiwan) and Manchuria to China. The Pacific islands remained under U.S. occupation. General of the Army Douglas MacArthur was appointed Supreme Commander for the Allied Powers on Aug. 14, 1945.

A new Japanese Constitution went into effect in 1947. In 1949, many of the responsibilities of government were returned to the Japanese. Full sovereignty was granted to Japan by the Japanese Peace Treaty in 1951.

The treaty took effect on April 28, 1952, when Japan returned to full status as a nation. It was admitted into the United Nations in 1958.

Following the visit of Prime Minister Eisaku Sato to Washington in 1969, the U.S. agreed to return Okinawa and other Ryukyu Islands to Japan in 1972, and both nations renewed the security treaty in 1970.

When President Nixon opened a dialogue with Peking in 1972, Prime Minister Kakuei Tanaka, who succeeded Sato in 1972, quickly established diplomatic relations with the mainland Chinese and severed ties with Formosa.

Suzuki was defeated in 1982 by Yasuhiro Nakasone who is considered pro-Western and better relations with the United States have ensued. Despite some opposition to his pro-Western policies in general, his Liberal Democratic party won decisively in the elections of July 7, 1986 and he was granted another year beyond his four-year limit which would have expired in October, 1986. Noboru Takeshita succeeded him in November 1987.

In 1989, an influence-peddling scandal shook the LDP and led to Takeshita's resignation. He was succeeded by Sousuke Uno, who also resigned in scandal.

The general election of July 1989 for the upper house of parliament scored a loss for the ruling Liberal Democratic Party, the first in 35 years. The following month, however, the party's president, Toshiki Kaifu, was elected prime minister. He stressed the need for the government to rid itself of scandal.

Kaifu pledged to provide $9 billion to the U.S. to help defray the expense of the latter's operations in the Persian Gulf. Kaifu's general stance in support of the U.S. drew considerable domestic criticism. The government attempted to push legislation that would have permitted Japan to send a military contingent to the Gulf in noncombat roles. This was defeated amid public outcry against it.

During Soviet President Gorbachev's visit to Tokyo in April 1991 he and Prime Minister Kaifu attempted to resolve a territorial dispute arising out of the last days of World War II. No breakthrough resulted, and the issue still remained at an impasse. President Gorbachev was also unable to convince Japan to grant sizable aid or to engage in large-scale economic cooperation.

JORDAN
The Hashemite Kingdom of Jordan
Ruler: King Hussein I (1952)
Prime Minister: Taher Masri (1991)
Area: 34,573 sq mi (89,544 sq km) excludes West Bank
Population (est. mid-1991): 3,400,000 (average annual rate of natural increase: 4.1%); birth rate: 46/1000; infant mortality rate: 38/1000; density per square mile: 105
Capital: Amman
Largest cities (est. 1986): Amman, 972,000; Zarka, 392,220; Irbid, 271,000; Salt, 134,100
Monetary unit: Jordanian dinar
Languages: Arabic, English
Religions: Islam (Sunni), 92%; Christian, 8%
National name: Al Mamlaka al Urduniya al Hashemiyah
Literacy rate: 79% (est.)
Economic summary: Gross national product (1989): $6.2 billion; $1,760 per capita; 0% real growth rate (1986). Arable land: 4%. Principal products: wheat, fruits, vegetables, olive oil. Labor force: 572,000 (1988); 20% in manufacturing and mining. Major exports: phosphate, refined petroleum products, cement. Natural resources: phosphate, potash. Exports: phosphates, fruits, and vegetables, shale oil, fertilizer. Imports: petroleum products, textiles, capital goods, motor vehicles, foodstuffs. Major trading partners: U.S., Japan, Saudi Arabia, Iraq, E.C.

Geography. The Middle East kingdom of Jordan is bordered on the west by Israel and the Dead Sea, on the north by Syria, on the east by Iraq, and on the south Saudi Arabia. It is comparable in size to Indiana.

Arid hills and mountains make up most of the country. The southern section of the Jordan River flows through the country.

Government. Jordan is a constitutional monarchy with a bicameral parliament.

The upper house consists of 40 members appointed by the king and the lower house is composed of 80 members elected by popular vote. The Constitution guarantees freedom of religion, speech, press, association, and private property.

Political parties were legalized in 1991.

History. In biblical times, the country that is now Jordan contained the lands of Edom, Moab, Ammon, and Bashan. In A.D. 106 it became part of the Roman province of Arabia and in 633–36 was conquered by the Arabs.

Taken from the Turks by the British in World War I, Jordan (formerly known as Transjordan) was separated from the Palestine mandate in 1920, and in 1921, placed under the rule of Abdullah ibn Hussein.

In 1923, Britain recognized Jordan's independence, subject to the mandate. In 1946, grateful for Jordan's loyalty in World War II, Britain abolished the mandate. That part of Palestine occupied by Jordanian troops was formally incorporated by action of the Jordanian Parliament in 1950.

King Abdullah was assassinated in 1951. His son Talal was deposed as mentally ill the next year. Talal's son Hussein, born Nov. 14, 1935, succeeded him.

From the beginning of his reign, Hussein had to steer a careful course between his powerful neighbor to the west, Israel, and rising Arab nationalism, frequently a direct threat to this throne. Riots erupted when he joined the Central Treaty Organization (the Baghdad Pact) in 1955, and he incurred further unpopularity when Britain, France, and Israel attacked the Suez Canal in 1956, forcing him to place his army under nominal command of the United Arab Republic of Egypt and Syria.

The 1961 breakup of the UAR eased Arab national pressure on Hussein, who was the first to recognize Syria after it reclaimed its independence. Jordan was swept into the 1967 Arab-Israeli war, however, and lost the old city of Jerusalem and all of its territory west of the Jordan river, the West Bank. Embittered Palestinian guerrilla forces virtually took over sections of Jordan in the aftermath of defeat, and open warfare broke out between the Palestinians and government forces in 1970.

Despite intervention of Syrian tanks, Hussein's Bedouin army defeated the Palestinians, suffering heavy casualties. A U.S. military alert and Israeli armor massed on the Golan Heights contributed psychological weight, but the Jordanians alone drove out the Syrians and invited the departure of 12,000 Iraqui troops who had been in the country since the 1967 war. Ignoring protests from other Arab states, Hussein by mid-1971 crushed Palestinian strength in Jordan and shifted the problem to Lebanon, where many of the guerrillas had fled.

In October 1974, Hussein concurred in an Arab summit resolution calling for an independent Palestinian state and endorsing the Palestine Liberation Organization as the "sole legitimate representative of the Palestinian people." This apparent reversal of policy changed with the growing disillusion of Arab states with the P.L.O., however, and by 1977 Hussein referred again to the unity of people on both banks of the Jordan.

As Egypt and Israel neared final agreement on a peace treaty early in 1979, Hussein met with Yassir Arafat, the PLO leader, on March 17 and issued a joint statement of opposition. Although the U.S. pressed Jordan to break Arab ranks on the issue, Hussein elected to side with the great majority, cutting ties with Cairo and joining the boycott against Egypt.

In September 1980, Jordan declared itself with Iraq in its conflict with Iran and, despite threats from Syria, opened ports to war shipments for Iraq.

In 1988, Hussein formally renounced all claims to the West Bank, thus implicitly acknowledging Palestinian claims to statehood and torpedoing USA-sponsored efforts at a Palestinian confederation with Jordan.

Jordan's stance during the Persian Gulf war strained relations with the U.S. and led to the termination of aid to the former. The signing of a national charter by King Hussein and leaders of the main political groups in June 1991 meant political parties were permitted in exchange for acceptance of the constitution and the monarchy. Also that month Palestinian Taher Masri was named prime minister. American-educated Masri was interpreted as an effort to regain U.S. favor.

KENYA

Republic of Kenya
President: Daniel arap Moi (1978)
Area: 224,960 sq mi. (582,646 sq km)
Population (est. mid-1991): 25,200,000 (average annual rate of natural increase: 3.5%); birth rate: 46/1000; infant mortality rate: 62/1000; density per square mile: 112
Capital: Nairobi
Largest cities (est. 1990): Nairobi, 1,200,000; Mombasa, 800,000
Monetary unit: Kenyan shilling

Languages: English (official), Swahili (national), and several other languages spoken by 40 ethnic groups
Religions: Protestant, 38%; Roman Catholic, 28%; traditional, 26%; Islam, 6%
Literacy rate: 59.2%
Member of Commonwealth of Nations
National name: Jamhuri ya Kenya
Economic summary: Gross domestic product (1989 est.): $8.5 billion; $360 per capita; 4.9% real growth rate. Arable land: 3%. Principal products: coffee, sisal, tea, pineapples, livestock. Labor force: 9,003,000; 22% (1987 est.) in industry and commerce. Major products: textiles, processed foods, consumer goods, refined oil. Natural resources: gold, limestone, minerals, wildlife. Exports: coffee, tea, refined petroleum. Imports: machinery, transport equipment, crude oil, iron and steel products. Major trading partners: Western European countries, Far East, U.S., Africa, Middle East

Geography. Kenya lies on the equator in east central Africa on the coast of the Indian Ocean. It is twice the size of Nevada. Kenya's neighbors are Tanzania, Uganda, the Sudan, Ethiopia, and Somalia.

In the north, the land is arid; the southwestern corner is in the fertile Lake Victoria Basin; and a length of the eastern depression of Great Rift Valley separates western highlands from those that rise from the lowland coastal strip. Large game reserves have been developed.

Government. Under its Constitution Kenya has a one-house National Assembly of 188 members, elected for five years by universal suffrage and 12 nominated and 2 ex-officio, for a total of 202. Since 1969, the president has been chosen by a general election.

The Kenya African National Union (KANU), led by the president, is the only political party allowed.

President died in his sleep on Aug. 22, 1978. Vice President Daniel arap Moi was elected to succeed him on Oct. 10.

History. Kenya, formerly a British colony and protectorate, was made a crown colony in 1920. The whites' domination of the rich plateau area, the White Highlands, long regarded by the Kikiyu people as their territory, was a factor leading to native terrorism, called the Mau Mau movement, in 1952. In 1954 the British began preparing the territory for African rule and independence. In 1961 Jomo Kenyatta was freed from banishment to become leader of the Kenya African National Union.

Internal self-government was granted in 1963; Kenya became independent on Dec. 12, 1963, with Kenyatta the first president.

Moi's tenure has been marked by a consolidation of power which has included the harassment of political opponents, the banning of secret ballots, and his declaration that KANU was more powerful than the Assembly or the courts.

Calls for electoral reform leading particularly to multiparty democracy resounded repeatedly from different quarters during 1990.

KIRIBATI

Republic of Kiribati
President: Ieremia Tabai (1979)
Area: 277 sq mi. (717 sq km)
Population (est. 1989): 68,828 (average annual growth rate: 1.5%); density per square mile: 245
Capital (1985): Tarawa, 21,393

Monetary unit: Australian dollar
Language: English
Religions: Roman Catholic, 48%; Protestant, 45%
Member of Commonwealth of Nations
Literacy rate: 90%
Economic summary: Gross domestic product (1989): $34 million; $500 per capita; 0% real growth rate. Arable land: NEGL%: Principal agricultural products: copra, vegetables. Exports: fish, copra. Imports: foodstuffs, fuel, transportation equipment. Major trading partners: New Zealand, Australia, Japan, American Samoa, U.K., U.S.

Geography. Kiribati, formerly the Gilbert Islands, consists of three widely separated main groups of Southwest Pacific islands, the Gilberts on the equator, the Phoenix Islands to the east, and the Line Islands further east. Ocean Island, producer of phosphates until it was mined out in 1981, is also included in the two million square miles of ocean, which give Kiribati an important fishery resource.

Government. The president holds executive power. The legislature consists of a House Assembly with 39 members.

History. A British protectorate since 1892, the Gilbert and Ellice Islands became a colony in 1915–16. The two island groups were separated in 1975 and given internal self-government.

Tarawa and others of the Gilbert group were occupied by Japan during World War II. Tarawa was the site of one of the bloodiest battles in U.S. Marine Corps history when Marines landed in November 1943 to dislodge the Japanese defenders.

Princess Anne, representing Queen Elizabeth II, presented the independence documents to the new government on July 12, 1979.

Suffering a huge trade deficit, the nation recently has drawn on its monetary reserves. Similar to other South Pacific island-nations Kiribati is fearful of the effect of global warming on sea levels.

KOREA, NORTH

Democratic People's Republic of Korea
President: Marshal Kim Il Sung (1972)
Premier: Yong Hyong Muk (1989)
Area: 46,768 sq mi. (121,129 sq km)
Population (est. mid-1991): 21,800,000 (average annual rate of natural increase: 1.8%); birth rate: 24/1000; infant mortality rate: 30/1000; density per square mile: 469
Capital and largest city (est. 1982): Pyongyang, 1,500,000
Monetary unit: Won
Language: Korean
Religions: atheist, 68%; traditional, 16%
National name: Choson Minjujuui Inmin Konghwaguk
Literacy rate: 95% (est.)
Economic summary: Gross national product (1989): $28 billion; $1,240 per capita; 3% real growth rate. Arable land: 18%. Principal products: corn, rice, vegetables. Labor force: 9,615,000; 64% nonagricultural. Major industrial products: machines, electric power, chemicals, textiles, processed food, metallurgical products. Natural resources: coal, iron ore, hydroelectric power. Exports: minerals, metallurgical products, agricultural products. Imports: machinery and equipment, petroleum, grain, coking coal. Major trading partners: U.S.S.R., China, Japan.

Geography. Korea is a 600-mile (966 km) peninsula jutting from Manchuria and China (and a small portion of the U.S.S.R.) into the Sea of Japan and the Yellow Sea off eastern Asia. North Korea occupies an area slightly smaller than Pennsylvania north of the 38th parallel.

The country is almost completely covered by a series of north-south mountain ranges separated by narrow valleys. The Yalu River forms part of the northern border with Manchuria.

Government. The elected Supreme People's Assembly, as the chief organ of government, chooses a Presidium and a Cabinet. The Cabinet, which exercises executive authority, is subject to approval by the Assembly and the Presidium.

The Korean Workers (Communist) Party, led by President Kim Il Sung, is the only political party.

History. According to myth, Korea was founded in 2333 B.C. by Tangun. In the 17th century, it became a vassal of China and was isolated from all but Chinese influence and contact until 1876, when Japan forced Korea to negotiate a commercial treaty, opening the land to the U. S. and Europe. Japan achieved control as the result of its war with China (1894–95) and with Russia (1904–05) and annexed Korea in 1910. Japan developed the country but never won over the Korean nationalists.

After the Japanese surrender in 1945, the country was divided into two occupation zones, the U.S.S.R. north of and the U.S. south of the 38th parallel. When the cold war developed between the U.S. and U.S.S.R., trade between the zones was cut off. In 1948, the division between the zones was made permanent with the establishment of separate regimes in the north and south. By mid-1949, the U.S. and U.S.S.R. withdrew all troops. The Democratic People's Republic of Korea (North Korea) was established on May 1, 1948. The Communist Party, headed by Kim Il Sung, was established in power.

On June 25, 1950, the North Korean army launched a surprise attack on South Korea. On June 26, the U.N. Security Council condemned the invasion as aggression and ordered withdrawal of the invading forces. On June 27, President Harry S. Truman ordered air and naval units into action to enforce the U.N. order. The British government did the same, and soon a multinational U.N. command was set up to aid the South Koreans. The North Korean invaders took Seoul and pushed the South Koreans into the southeast corner of their country.

Gen. Douglas MacArthur, U.N. commander, made an amphibious landing at Inchon on September 15 behind the North Korean lines, which resulted in the complete rout of the North Korean army. The U.N. forces drove north across the 38th parallel, approaching the Yalu River. Then Communist China entered the war, forcing the U.N. forces into headlong retreat. Seoul was lost again, then regained; ultimately the war stabilized near the 38th parallel but dragged on for two years while the belligerents negotiated. An armistice was agreed to on July 27, 1953.

In July 1990, North and South Korea signed a historic agreement to meet in September and discuss the easing of political and military confrontations.

Since that time talks have continued repeatedly on and off.

Formerly strenuously opposed to separate membership for the two Koreas in the U.N., the North in May 1991 announced it would, albeit reluctantly, apply for such membership.

KOREA, SOUTH

Republic of Korea
President: Roh Tae Woo (1987)
Premier: Chung Won Shik (1991)
Area: 38,031 sq mi. (98,500 sq km)
Population (est. mid-1991): 43,200,000 (average annual rate of natural increase: 0.9%); birth rate: 15/1000; infant mortality rate: 23/1000; density per square mile: 1,136
Capital: Seoul
Largest cities (est. 1989): Seoul, 10,500,000; Pusan, 3,650,700; Taegu, 2,000,200; Inchon, 1,600,000
Monetary unit: Won
Language: Korean
Religions: strong Confucian tradition, Christian, 28%; Buddhist,
National name: Taehan Min'guk
Literacy rate: over 90%
Economic summary: Gross national product (1989): $200 billion; $4,600 per capita; 6.5% real growth rate. Arable land: 21%. Principal products: rice, barley. Labor force: 16,900,000; 27% in mining and manufacturing. Major products: clothing and textiles, processed foods, automobiles, steel, electronics equipment. Natural resources: molybdenum, lead, tungsten, graphite, coal, hydropower. Exports: Textiles, automobiles, electric and electronics, ships, and steel. Imports: oil, grains, chemicals, machinery, electronics. Major trading partners: U.S., Japan.

Geography. Slightly larger than Indiana, South Korea lies below the 38th parallel on the Korean peninsula. It is mountainous in the east; in the west and south are many harbors on the mainland and offshore islands.

Government. Constitutional amendments enacted in Sept. 1987 called for direct election of a President, who would be limited to a single five-year term, and increased the powers of the National Assembly *vis a vis* the President.

The National Assembly was expanded from 276 to 299 seats, filled by proportional representation.

History. South Korea came into being in the aftermath of World War II as the result of a 1945 agreement making the 38th parallel the boundary between a northern zone occupied by the U.S.S.R. and a southern zone occupied by U.S. forces. (For details, *see* North Korea.)

Elections were held in the U.S. zone in 1948 for a national assembly, which adopted a republican Constitution and elected Syngman Rhee president. The new republic was proclaimed on August 15 and was recognized as the legal government of Korea by the U.N. on Dec. 12, 1948.

On June 25, 1950, South Korea was attacked by North Korean Communist forces. U.S. armed intervention was ordered on June 27 by President Harry S. Truman, and on the same day the U.N. invoked military sanctions against North Korea. Gen. Douglas MacArthur was named commander of the U.N. forces. U.S. and South Korean troops fought a heroic holding action but, by the first week of August, they had been forced back to a 4,000-square-mile beachhead in southeast Korea.

There they stood off superior North Korean forces until September 15, when a major U.N. amphibious attack was launched far behind the Communist lines at Inchon, port of Seoul. By September 30, U.N. forces were in complete control of South Korea. They then invaded North Korea and were nearing the Man-

churian and Siberian borders when several hundred thousand Chinese Communist troops entered the conflict in late October. U.N. forces were then forced to retreat below the 38th parallel.

On May 24, 1951, U.N. forces recrossed the parallel and had made important new inroads into North Korea when truce negotiations began on July 10. An armistice was finally signed at Panmunjom on July 27, 1953, leaving a devastated Korea in need of large-scale rehabilitation.

The U.S. and South Korea signed a mutual-defense treaty on Oct. 1, 1953.

Rhee, president since 1948, resigned in 1960 in the face of rising disorders. PoSun Yun was elected to succeed him, but political instability continued. In 1961, Gen. Park Chung Hee took power and subsequently built up the country. The U.S. stepped up military aid, building up South Korea's armed forces to 600,000 men. The South Koreans sent 50,000 troops to Vietnam, at U.S. expense.

Park's assassination on Oct. 26, 1979, by Kim Jae Kyu, head of the Korean Central Intelligence Agency, brought a liberalizing trend as Choi Kyu Hah, the new President, freed imprisoned dissidents. The release of opposition leader Kim Dae jung in February 1980 generated anti-government demonstrations that turned into riots by May. Choi resigned on Aug. 16. Chun Doo Wha, head of a military Special Committee for National Security Measures, was the sole candidate as the electoral college confirmed him as President on Aug. 27.

Elected to a full seven-year term on Feb. 11, Chun had visited Washington on Feb. 2 to receive President Reagan's assurance that U.S. troops would remain in South Korea.

Debate over the Presidential succession in 1988 was the main dispute in 1986–87 with Chun wanting election by the electoral college and the opposition demanding a direct popular vote, charging that Chun could manipulate the college. On April 13, 1987, Chun declared a close on the debate but when, in June, he appointed Roh Toe Woo, the DJP chairman as his successor, violent protests broke out. Roh, and later, Chun, agreed that direct elections should be held. A split in the opposition led to Roh's election on Dec. 16, 1987, with 36.6% of the vote.

Weeks of anti-government protests in May 1991 led to the resignation of then-Prime Minister Ro Ja Bong.

In April President Gorbachev of the Soviet Union became the first Soviet leader to visit South Korea in a bid to win help for his country's own economic problems. At roughly the same time the Soviet Union announced it would not oppose South Korea's application for U.N. membership.

KUWAIT

State of Kuwait
Emir: Sheik Jaber al-Ahmad al-Sabah (1977)
Prime Minister: Sheik Sa'ad Abdullah al-Salim (1978)
Area: 6,880 sq mi. (17,820 sq km)
Population (est. mid-1991): 1,400,000 (average annual rate of natural increase: 3.0%); birth rate: 32/1000; infant mortality rate: 16/1000; density per square mile: 204
Capital (est. 1990): Kuwait, 151,060
Largest city (est. 1980): Hawalli, 152,402
Monetary unit: Kuwaiti dinar
Languages: Arabic and English

Religions: Islam
National name: Dawlat al Kuwayt
Literacy rate: about 71%
Economic summary: Gross domestic product (1988): $20.5 billion; $10,500 per capita; 5% real growth rate. Labor force: 566,000 (1986); 45% in services. Major products: crude and refined oil, petrochemicals, building materials, salt. Natural resources: petroleum, fish, shrimp. Exports: crude and refined petroleum, shrimp. Imports: foodstuffs, automobiles, building materials, machinery, textiles. Major trading partners: U.S., Japan, Italy, Germany, U.K..

Geography. Kuwait is situated northeast of Saudi Arabia at the northern end of the Persian Gulf, south of Iraq. It is slightly larger than Hawaii. The low-lying land is mainly sandy and barren.

Government. Sheik Jaber al-Ahmad al-Sabah rules as Emir of Kuwait and appoints the Prime Minister, who appoints his Cabinet (Council of Ministers). The National Assembly was suspended on July 3, 1986. There are no political parties in Kuwait.

History. Kuwait obtained British protection in 1897 when the Sheik feared that the Turks would take over the area. In 1961, Britain ended the protectorate, giving Kuwait independence, but agreed to give military aid on request. Iraq immediately threatened to occupy the area and Sheik Sabah al-Salem al-Sabah called in British troops in 1961. Soon afterward the Arab League sent in troops, replacing the British. The prize was oil.

Oil was discovered in the 1930s. Kuwait proved to have 20% of the world's known oil resources. It has been a major producer since 1946, the world's second largest oil exporter. The Sheik, who gets half the profits, devotes most of them to the education, welfare, and modernization of his kingdom. In 1966, Sheik Sabah designated a relative, Jaber al-Ahmad al-Sabah, as his successor.

By 1968, the sheikdom had established a model welfare state, and it sought to establish dominance among the sheikdoms and emirates of the Persian Gulf.

A worldwide decline in the price of oil reduced Kuwait's oil income from $18.4 billion in 1980 to only $9 billion in 1984. During the same period Kuwait's support for Iraq in its war with Iran sparked terrorist attacks in Kuwait by radical Shiite Moslem supporters of Iran's Ayatollah Khomeini. The risk of Iranian attack prompted Kuwait to obtain U.S. protection for its tankers in 1987.

In May 1985, a suicide bomber drove into the motorcade of Sheik Jaber al-Ahmed al-Sabah, the ruler. The Sheik escaped with minor cuts and bruises.

In July 1990, Iraq President Hussein blamed Kuwait for falling oil prices. After a failed Arab mediation attempt to solve the dispute peacefully, Iraq invaded Kuwait on Aug. 2, 1990, and set up a pro-Iraqi provisional government.

A coalition of Arab and Western military forces drove Iraqi troops from Kuwait in February 1991. The Emir returned to his country from Saudi Arabia in mid-March. In his first address after that he promised parliamentary elections but gave no precise date. Martial law, in effect since the end of the Gulf war, ended in late June.

LAOS
Lao People's Democratic Republic
President (acting): Phuomi Vongvichit (1986)
Chairman of the Council of Ministers: Kaysone Phomvihane (1975)
Area: 91,429 sq mi. (236,800 sq km)
Population (est. mid-1991): 4,100,000 (average annual rate of natural increase: 2.2%); birth rate: 37/1000; infant mortality rate: 124/1000; density per square mile: 45
Capital and largest city (est. 1984): Vientiane, 200,000
Monetary unit: Kip
Languages: Lao (official), French, English
Religions: Buddhist, 85%; animist and other, 15%
Literacy rate: 85%
Economic summary: Gross domestic product: (1989 est.): $585 million; $150 per capita; 3% real growth rate. Arable land: 4%. Principal products: rice, corn, vegetables. Labor force: 1–1.5 million; 85–90% in agriculture. Major industrial products: tin, timber, electric power. Natural resources: tin, timber, hydroelectric power. Exports: electric power, forest products, tin concentrates, coffee. Imports: rice, foodstuffs, petroleum products, machinery, transport equipment. Major trading partners: Thailand, Malaysia, Vietnam, U.S.S.R., Japan, France, U.S.

Geography. A landlocked nation in Southeast Asia occupying the northwestern portion of the Indochinese peninsula, Laos is surrounded by China, Vietnam, Cambodia, Thailand, and Burma. It is twice the size of Pennsylvania.

Laos is a mountainous country, especially in the north, where peaks rise above 8,000 feet (2,438 m). Dense forests cover the northern and eastern areas. The Mekong River, which forms the boundary with Burma and Thailand, flows entirely through the country for 300 miles (483 km) of its course.

Government. Laos is a people's democratic republic with executive power in the hands of the premier. The monarchy was abolished Dec. 2, 1975, when the Pathet Lao ousted a coalition government and King Sisavang Vatthana abdicated. The King was appointed "Supreme Adviser" to the President, the former Prince Souphanouvong. Former Prince Souvanna Phouma, Premier since 1962, was made an "adviser" to the government. The Lao People's Revolutionary Party (Pathet Lao), led by Chairman Kaysone Phomvihane, is the only political party.

History. Laos became a French protectorate in 1893, and the territory was incorporated into the union of Indochina. A strong nationalist movement developed during World War II, but France reestablished control in 1946 and made the King of Luang Prabang constitutional monarch of all Laos. France granted semiautonomy in 1949 and then, spurred by the Viet Minh rebellion in Vietnam, full independence within the French Union in 1950. In 1951, Prince Souphanouvong organized the Pathet Lao, a Communist independence movement, in North Vietnam. The Viet Minh in 1953 established the Pathet Lao in power at Samneua. Viet Minh and Pathet Lao forces invaded central Laos, and civil war resulted.

By the Geneva agreements of 1954 and an armistice of 1955, two northern provinces were given the Pathet Lao, the royal regime the rest. Full sovereignty was given the kingdom by the Paris agreements of Dec. 29, 1954. In 1957, Prince Souvanna Phouma, the royal Premier, and the Pathet Lao leader, Prince Souphanouvong, the Premier's half-brother, agreed to reestablishment of a unified government, with Pathet Lao participation and integration of Pathet Lao forces into the royal army. The agreement broke down in 1959, and armed conflict broke out again.

In 1960, the struggle became three-way as Gen. Phoumi Nosavan, controlling the bulk of the royal army, set up in the south a pro-Western revolutionary government headed by Prince Boun Gum. General Phoumi took Vientiane in December, driving Souvanna Phouma into exile in Cambodia. The Soviet bloc supported Souvanna Phouma. In 1961, a cease-fire was arranged and the three princes agreed to a coalition government headed by Souvanna Phouma.

But North Vietnam, the U.S. (in the form of Central Intelligence Agency personnel), and China remained active in Laos after the settlement. North Vietnam used a supply line (Ho Chi Minh trail) running down the mountain valleys of eastern Laos into Cambodia and South Vietnam, particularly after the U.S.-South Vietnamese incursion into Cambodia in 1970 stopped supplies via Cambodian seaports.

An agreement, reached in 1973 revived coalition government. The Communist Pathet Lao seized complete power in 1975, installing Souphanouvong as president and Kaysone Phomvihane as premier. Since then other parties and political groups have been moribund and most of their leaders have fled the country.

In July 1985, Laos agreed to help the United States search for U.S. servicemen missing since the Indochina war.

In 1985, border clashes between Laos and Thailand intensified, with over 120 skirmishes reported in 1984 and 1985.

Basically in step with Vietnam's policy of economic but not political reform, Laos has recently dropped all reference to itself as a socialist state. In addition to implementing market-oriented policies, the country has passed laws governing property, inheritance and contracts.

LATVIA

The Republic of Latvia
President: Anatolijs Gorbunovos (1990)
Prime Minister: Ivars Jodmanis
Area: 25,400 sq mi. (65,786 sq km)
Population (1990): 2,700,000 (Latvian, 53%; Russian, 33%; Ukrainians, Byelorussians, other 14%); density per square mile: 106
Capital and largest city (1990): Riga, 915,000. Other important cities: Daugavpils, 127,000; Liepaja, 114,000
Monetary unit: Ruble (from 1940–1991). Will convert to "Lat" in mid-1992.
Language: Latvian
Religions: Lutheran, Catholic, and Baptist
National name: Latvija
Literacy: very high
Economic survey: Most industrialized of the Baltic states. Gross national product and per capita income: n.a. Natural resources: Peat, sapropel, timber, limestone, dolomite, and clay. Major industries: Machinery and metalworking, electrical equipment, agricultural engineering, light industry, timber and paper, building materials, and chemicals and pharmaceuticals. Latvia also has a large dairy industry. About 80% of trade is with the Soviet Union; other countries are Poland, Germany, Sweden, and Czechoslovakia.

Geography: Latvia borders Estonia on the north, Lithuania in the south, the Baltic Sea with the Gulf of Riga in the west, Russia in the east, and Byelorussia in the southeast. Latvia is largely a fertile lowland with numerous lakes and hills to the east.

Government: Latvia is a parliamentary democracy.

History: Descended from Aryan stock, the Latvians were early tribesmen who settled along the Baltic Sea and, lacking a central government, fell an easy prey to more powerful peoples. The German Teutonic knights first conquered them in the 13th century and ruled the area, consisting of Livonia and Courland, until 1562.

Poland conquered the territory in 1562 and ruled until 1795 in Courland; control of Livonia was disputed between Sweden and Poland from 1562 to 1629. Sweden controlled Livonia from 1629 to 1721. Russia took over Livonia in the latter year and Courland after the third partition of Poland in 1795.

From that time until 1918, the Latvians remained Russian subjects, although they preserved their language, customs, and folklore. The Russian Revolution of 1917 gave them their opportunity for freedom, and the Latvian republic was proclaimed on Nov. 18, 1918.

The republic lasted little more than 20 years. It was occupied by Russian troops in 1939 and incorporated into the Soviet Union in 1940. German armies occupied the nation from 1941 to 1943–44, when they were driven out by the Russians. Most countries, including the United States, refused to recognize the Soviet annexation of Latvia.

In September 1989, the Central Committee of the Soviet Communist Party accused the independence movements of the three Baltic republics of trying to disintegrate the cohesion of the Soviet Union and warned them of "impending disaster." Despite continued threats from the Kremlin, the leaders of the movements continued to protest and demand a peaceful transition to self-determination.

When the coup against Soviet President Mikhail Gorbachev failed, the Baltic nations saw a historic opportunity to free themselves from Soviet domination and, following the actions of Lithuania and Estonia, Latvia declared its independence on Aug. 21, 1991.

European and most other nations quickly recognized their independence, and on Sept. 2, 1991, President Bush announced full diplomatic recognition for Latvia, Estonia, and Lithuania. The Soviet Union recognized Latvia's independence on September 6, and UN membership followed on Sept. 17, 1991.

LEBANON

Republic of Lebanon
President: Elias Hrawi (1989)
Premier: Omar Karami
Area: 4,015 sq mi. (10,400 sq km)
Population (est. mid-1991): 3,400,000 (average annual rate of natural increase: 2.1%); birth rate: 28/1000; infant mortality rate: 48/1000; density per square mile: 843
Capital: Beirut
Largest cities (est. 1990): Beirut, 1,100,000; Tripoli, 240,000; Sidon, 110,000; Tyre, 60,000; Zahleh, 55,000
Monetary unit: Lebanese pound
Languages: Arabic (official), French, English
Religions: Islam, 75% (5 sects); Christian, 25% (11 sects); Judaism Negl. % (1 sect)
National name: Al-Joumhouriya al-Lubnaniya
Literacy rate: 75%

Economic summary: Gross domestic product (1989 est.): $2.3 billion. Per capita income: $700; Arable land: 21%; principal products: citrus fruits, vegetables, potatoes, tobacco, olives, hemp. Labor force: 650,000; 79% in industry, commerce and services. Major products: processed foods, textiles, cement, chemicals, refined oil. Exports: fruits, vegetables, textiles. Imports: metals, machinery, foodstuffs. Major trading partners: U.S., Western European and Arab countries.

Geography. Lebanon lies at the eastern end of the Mediterranean Sea north of Israel and west of Syria. It is four fifths the size of Connecticut.

The Lebanon Mountains, which parallel the coast on the west, cover most of the country, while on the eastern border is the Anti-Lebanon range. Between the two lies the Bekaa Valley, the principal agricultural area.

Government. Lebanon is governed by a President, elected by Parliament for a six-year term, and a Cabinet of Ministers appointed by the President but responsible to Parliament.

The unicameral Parliament has 108 members elected for a four-year term by universal suffrage and chosen by proportional division of religious groups.

History. After World War I, France was given a League of Nations mandate over Lebanon and its neighbor Syria, which together had previously been a single political unit in the Ottoman Empire. France divided them in 1920 into separate colonial administrations, drawing a border that separated predominantly Moslem Syria from the kaleidoscope of religious communities in Lebanon in which Maronite Christians were then dominant. After 20 years of the French mandate regime, Lebanon's independence was proclaimed on Nov. 26, 1941, but full independence came in stages. Under an agreement between representatives of Lebanon and the French National Committee of Liberation, most of the powers exercised by France were transferred to the Lebanese government on Jan. 1, 1944. The evacuation of French troops was completed in 1946.

Civil war broke out in 1958, with Moslem factions led by Kamal Jumblat and Saeb Salam rising in insurrection against the Lebanese government headed by President Camille Chamoun, a Maronite Christian. At Chamoun's request, President Eisenhower on July 15 sent U.S. troops to reestablish the government's authority.

Clan warfare between various factions in Lebanon goes back centuries. The hodgepodge includes Maronite Christians, who since independence have dominated the government; Sunni Moslems, who have prospered in business and shared political power; the Druse, a secretive Islamic splinter group; and at the bottom of the heap until recently, Shiite Moslems.

A new—and bloodier—Lebanese civil war that broke out in 1975 resulted in the addition of still another ingredient in the brew—the Syrians. In the fighting between Lebanese factions, 40,000 Lebanese were estimated to have been killed and 100,000 wounded between March 1975 and November 1976. At that point, a Syrian-dominated Arab Deterrent Force intervened and brought large-scale fighting to a halt.

Palestinian guerrillas staging raids on Israel from Lebanese territory drew punitive Israeli raids on Lebanon, and two large-scale Israeli invasions. The Israelis withdrew in June after the U.N. Security Council created a 6,000-man peacekeeping force for the area, called UNIFIL. As they departed, the Israelis turned their strongpoints over to a Christian militia that they had organized, instead of to the U.N. force.

The second Israeli invasion came on June 6, 1982, and this time it was a total one. It was in response to an assassination attempt by Palestinian terrorists on the Israeli ambassador in London.

A U.S. special envoy, Philip C. Habib, negotiated the dispersal of most of the PLO to other Arab nations and Israel pulled back some of its forces. The violence seemed to have come to an end when, on Sept. 14, Bashir Gemayel, the 34-year-old President-elect, was killed by a bomb that destroyed the headquarters of his Christian Phalangist Party.

The day after Gemayel's assassination, Israeli troops moved into west Beirut in force. On Sept. 17 it was revealed that Christian militiamen had massacred hundreds of Palestinians in two refugee camps but Israel denied responsibility.

On Sept. 20, Amin Gemayel, older brother of Bashir Gemayel, was elected President by the parliament.

The massacre in the refugee camps prompted the return of a multinational peacekeeping force composed of U.S. Marines and British, French, and Italian soldiers. Their mandate was to support the central Lebanese government, but they soon found themselves drawn into the struggle for power between different Lebanese factions. During their stay in Lebanon, 260 U.S. Marines and about 60 French soldiers were killed, most of them in suicide bombings of the Marine and French Army compounds on Oct. 23, 1983. The multinational force left in the spring of 1984.

During 1984, Israeli troops remained in southern Lebanon and Syrian troops remained in the Bekaa Valley. By the third anniversary of the invasion, June 6, 1985, all Israeli troops had withdrawn except for several hundred "advisers" to a Christian militia trained and armed by the Israelis.

Events since the Israeli withdrawal included Shiite-PLO fighting resulting from PLO attempts to reestablish its old power base in areas now held by Shiite militia.

In July 1986, Syrian observers took position in Beirut to monitor a peacekeeping agreement. The agreement broke down and fighting between Shiite and Druze militia in West Beirut became so intense that Syrian troops moved in force in February 1987, suppressing militia resistance.

Amin Gemayel's Presidency expired on Sept. 23, 1988. The impossibility of setting up elections led Gemayel to designate a government under army chief Gen. Michael Aoun. Aoun's government was rejected by Prime Minister Selim al-Hoss who established a rival government in Muslim West Beirut.

In October 1989, Lebanese Christian and Moslem deputies approved a tentative peace accord and the new National Assembly selected a President. Christian leader Aoun, charging that the accord didn't place enough pressure on the Syrians to withdraw, refused to recognize the new government.

In early 1991 the Lebanese government, backed by Syria, attempted to regain control over the south and disband all private militias, thereby ending the 16-year civil war. This led in July to clashes with PLO guerrillas, who on July 4 agreed to hand over their weapons. Israel, however, announced it would not withdraw from its self-proclaimed security zone in the south, as Beirut had hoped.

LESOTHO

Kingdom of Lesotho
Sovereign: King Letsie III (1990)
Chairman, Military Council and Council of Ministers:
Col. E.P. Ramaemba (Head of Government)
Area: 11,720 sq mi. (30,355 sq km)
Population (est. mid-1991): 1,800,000 (average annual
rate of natural increase: 2.9%); birth rate: 41/1000;
infant mortality rate: 95/1000; density per square mile:
156
Capital and largest city (est. 1990): Maseru, 109,382
Monetary unit: Loti
Languages: English and Sesotho (official); also Zulu and
Xhosa
Religions: Roman Catholic, 44%; Lesotho Evangelical
Church, 30%; Anglican, 12%
Member of Commonwealth of Nations
Literacy rate: 59% (1989)
Economic summary: Gross domestic product (1989FY
est.): $412 million; $245 per capita; 8.2% real growth
rate. Arable land: 10%. Principal products: corn,
wheat, sorghum, barley. Labor force: 689,000; 86.2% in
subsistence agriculture. Natural resources: diamonds.
Exports: wool, mohair, wheat, cattle, hides and skins.
Imports: foodstuffs, building materials, clothing, vehicles, machinery. Major trading partner: South Africa.

Geography. Mountainous Lesotho, the size of Maryland, is surrounded by the Republic of South Africa
in the east central part of that country except for
short borders on the east and south with two discontinuous units of the Republic of Transkei. The Drakensberg Mountains in the east are Lesotho's principal chain. Elsewhere the region consists of rocky
tableland.

Government. A military regime and constitutional
monarchy. The king has no legislative or executive
powers. The executive branch consists of the monarch, chairman of the Military Council, and the
Council of Ministers (cabinet).

History. Lesotho (formerly Basutoland) was constituted a native state under British protection by a
treaty signed with the native chief Moshesh in 1843.
It was annexed to Cape Colony in 1871, but in 1884
it was restored to direct control by the Crown.
The colony of Basutoland became the independent
nation of Lesotho on Oct. 4, 1966.
In the 1970 elections, Ntsu Mokhehle, head of the
Basutoland Congress Party, claimed a victory, but Jonathan declared a state of emergency, suspended the
Constitution, and arrested Mokhehle. The major issue
in the election was relations with South Africa, with
Jonathan for close ties to the surrounding white nation, while Mokhehle was for a more independent
policy. Jonathan jailed 45 opposition politicians, declared the King had "technically abdicated" by siding
with the opposition party, exiled him to the Netherlands, and named his Queen and her seven-year-old
son as Regent.
The King returned after a compromise with Jonathan in which the new Constitution would name him
head of state but forbid his participation in politics.
After the King refused to approve the replacements
in February 1990 of individuals dismissed by Lekhanya, the latter stripped the King of his executive
power. Then in early March Lekhanya sent the King
into exile. In November the King was dethroned, and
his son was sworn in as King Letsie III.

LIBERIA

Republic of Liberia
President: Amos Sawyer (interim) (1990)
Area: 43,000 sq mi. (111,370 sq km)
Population (est. mid-1991): 2,700,000 (average annual
rate of natural increase: 3.2%); birth rate: 47/1000;
infant mortality rate: 134/1000; density per square
mile: 63
Capital and largest city (est. 1984): Monrovia, 425,000
Monetary unit: Liberian dollar
Languages: English (official) and tribal dialects
Religions: traditional, 70%; Christian, 10%; Islam, 20%
Literacy rate: 35%
Economic summary: Gross domestic product (1988):
$988 million; $395 per capita; 1.5% real growth rate.
Arable land: 1%. Principal products: rubber, rice, palm
oil, cassava, coffee, cocoa. Labor force: 510,000; 4.5%
in industry and commerce. Major products: iron ore,
diamonds, processed rubber, processed food, construction materials. Natural resources: iron ore, gold,
timber, diamonds. Exports: iron ore, rubber, timber,
coffee. Imports: machinery, petroleum products,
transport equipment, foodstuffs. Major trading partners: U.S., E.C., Netherlands, Japan, China.

Geography. Lying on the Atlantic in the southern
part of West Africa, Liberia is bordered by Sierra
Leone, Guinea, and Côte d'Ivoire. It is comparable in
size to Tennessee.
Most of the country is a plateau covered by dense
tropical forests, which thrive under an annual rainfall
of about 160 inches a year.

Government. A five-nation West African peacekeeping force installed an interim government in October 1990 and in November made Amos Sawyer interim president. The National Patriotic Front led by
Charles Taylor controls most of the country.

History. Liberia was founded in 1822 as a result of
the efforts of the American Colonization Society to
settle freed American slaves in West Africa. In 1847,
it became the Free and Independent Republic of Liberia.
The government of Africa's first republic was modeled after that of the United States, and Joseph J.
Roberts of Virginia was elected the first president. He
laid the foundations of a modern state and initiated
efforts, never too successful but pursued for more
than a century, to bring the aboriginal inhabitants of
the territory to the level of the emigrants. The English-speaking descendants of U.S. blacks, known as
Americo-Liberians, were the intellectual and ruling
class. The indigenous inhabitants, divided, constitute
99% of the population.
After 1920, considerable progress was made toward opening up the interior, a process that was
spurred in 1951 by the establishment of a 43-mile
(69-km) railroad to the Bomi Hills from Monrovia.
In July 1971, while serving his sixth term as president, William V. S. Tubman died following surgery
and was succeeded by his long-time associate, Vice
President William R. Tolbert, Jr.
Tolbert was ousted in a military coup carried out
April 12, 1980, by army enlisted men led by Master
Sgt. Samuel K. Doe. Tolbert and 27 other high officials were executed. Doe and his colleagues based
their action on the grievances of "native" Liberians
against corruption and misrule by the Americo-Liberians who had ruled the country since its founding.

A rebellion led by Charles Taylor, a former Doe aide, started in December 1989 and, by mid-July 1990, had taken most of Liberia's key population and economic centers and surrounded the capital.

A West African peacekeeping force intervened in Liberia and effectively partitioned the country into two zones: One, containing the capital of Monrovia, led by President Sawyer, is backed by virtually all West African nations. The other, led by Mr. Taylor, constitutes about 95% of the territory. The two leaders reached an accord to set aside their differences in June 1990.

LIBYA

Socialist People's Libyan Arab Jamahiriya
Head of State: Col. Muammar el-Qaddafi (1969)
Secretary of the General People's Committee: Abuzeid Omar Dorda (1990)
Area: 679,536 sq mi. (1,759,998 sq km)
Population (est. mid-1991): 4,400,000 (average annual rate of natural increase: 3.1%); birth rate: 37/1000; infant mortality rate: 64/1000; density per square mile: 6
Capital: Tripoli
Largest cities (est. 1980): Tripoli, 587,400; Benghazi, 267,700
Monetary unit: Libyan dinar
Language: Arabic
Religion: Islam
National name: Al-Jumhuria al-Arabia al-Libya
Literacy rate: 50–60%
Economic summary: Gross national product (1988 est.): $20 billion, $5,410 per capita; real growth rate: 0%. Arable land: 1%. Principal products: wheat, barley, olives, dates, citrus fruits, peanuts. Labor force: 1,000,000; 31% in industry. Major products: petroleum, processed foods, textiles, handicrafts. Natural resources: petroleum, natural gas. Exports: petroleum, peanuts, hides. Imports: machinery, foodstuffs, manufactured goods. Major trading partners: Italy, Germany, U.K., France, Spain, Japan.

Geography. Libya stretches along the northeastern coast of Africa between Tunisia and Algeria on the west and Egypt on the east; to the south are the Sudan, Chad, and Niger. It is one sixth larger than Alaska.

A greater part of the country lies within the Sahara. Along the Mediterranean coast and farther inland is arable plateau land.

Government. In a bloodless coup d'etat on Sept. 1, 1969, the military seized power in Libya. King Idris I, who had ruled since 1951, was deposed and the Libyan Arab Republic proclaimed. The official name was changed in 1977 to the Socialist People's Libyan Arab Jamahiriya. The Revolutionary Council that had governed since the coup was renamed the General Secretariat of the General People's Congress. The Arab Socialist Union Organization is the only political party.

History. Libya was a part of the Turkish dominions from the 16th century until 1911. Following the outbreak of hostilities between Italy and Turkey in that year, Italian troops occupied Tripoli; Italian sovereignty was recognized in 1912.

Libya was the scene of much desert fighting during World War II. After the fall of Tripoli on Jan. 23, 1943, it came under Allied administration. In 1949, the U.N. voted that Libya should become independent by 1952.

Discovery of oil in the Libyan Desert promised financial stability and funds for economic development.

The Reagan Administration, accusing Libya of supporting international terrorism, closed the Libyan embassy in Washington on May 6, 1981.

On Aug. 19, 1981, two U.S. Navy F-14's shot down two Soviet-made SU-22's of the Libyan air force that had attacked them in air space above the Gulf of Sidra, claimed by Libya but held to be international by the U.S. In December, Washington asserted that Libyan "hit squads" had been dispatched to the U.S. and security was drastically tightened around President Reagan and other officials. Reagan requested remaining American citizens to leave Libya and nearly all did by Dec. 15. When the Mobil Oil Company abandoned its operations in April 1982, only four U.S. firms were still in Libya, using Libyan or third-country personnel.

Qaddafi's troops also supported rebels in Chad but suffered major military reverses in 1987.

On March 24, 1986, U.S. and Libyan forces skirmished in the Gulf of Sidra, with two Libyan patrol boats being sunk.

On April 14, after a Libyan-backed attack on a West Berlin disco in which two people, including an American serviceman, were killed, Reagan ordered an air raid on Libyan military installations.

A two-year-old U.S. covert policy to destabilize the Libyan government with U.S.-trained Libyan ex-P.O.W.s ended in failure in December 1990 when a Libyan-supplied guerrilla force assumed power in Chad, where the commandos were based, and asked the band to leave. Exiled Prince Idris in March 1991 said he would take control of the paramilitary group, although finding a place of exile for them proved difficult.

LIECHTENSTEIN

Principality of Liechtenstein
Ruler: Prince Hans Adam (1989)
Prime Minister: Hans Brunhart (1978)
Area: 61 sq mi. (157 sq km)
Population (mid-1991): 30,000 (average annual growth rate: 0.7%); birth rate: 13/1000; infant mortality rate: 2.7/1000; density per square mile: 468
Capital and largest city (est. 1986): Vaduz, 4,920
Monetary unit: Swiss franc
Language: German
Religions: Roman Catholic, 82.7%; Protestant, 7.1%; other 10.2%
Literacy rate: 100%
Economic summary: Gross national product: $405 million; $15,000 per capita (1984). Arable land: 25%; Labor force in agriculture: 4%. Principal products: livestock, vegetables, corn, wheat, potatoes, grapes. Labor force: 12,258; 54.4% in industry, trade and building. Major products: electronics, metal products, textiles, ceramics, pharmaceuticals, food products, precision instruments. Natural resource: hydroelectric power. Exports: small specialty machinery, dental products, stamps, hardware, pottery. Imports: machinery, processed foods, metal goods, textiles, motor vehicles. Major trading partners: Switzerland and other Western European countries.

Geography. Tiny Liechtenstein, not quite as large as Washington, D.C., lies on the east bank of the Rhine River south of Lake Constance between Austria and Switzerland. It consists of low valley land and Alpine peaks. Falknis (8,401 ft; 2,561 m) and Naatkopf (8,432 ft; 2,570 m) are the tallest.

Government. The Constitution of 1921, amended in 1972, provides for a legislature, the Landtag, of 25 members elected by direct male suffrage.

History. Founded in 1719, Liechtenstein was a member of the German Confederation from 1815 to 1866, when it became an independent principality. It abolished its army in 1868 and has managed to stay neutral and undamaged in all European wars since then. In a referendum on July 1, 1984, male voters granted women the right to vote, a victory for Prince Hans Adam.

In 1990 the government announced plans to revise the country's banking laws.

LITHUANIA

Republic of Lithuania
President: Vytautas Landsbergis (1990)
Prime Minister: Gediminas Vatnorius (1991)
Area: 25,174 sq mi. (64,445 sq km)
Population (1989): 3,690,000 (Lithuanian, 80.1%; Russian, 8.6%); density per square mile: 82
Capital and largest city: Vilnius, 582,000
Monetary unit: Ruble; Lithuanian currency will replace it
Languages: Lithuanian
Religion (1939): Catholic, 85%
National name: Lietuva
Literacy: very high
Economic survey: Gross national product: n.a. Per capita income (1989): $3,000. Labor force: 1,653,000. Employment: Industry and construction, 40%; agriculture and forestry, 20%. Lithuania has many mineral resources. About 55% of trade is with the Soviet Union. Also trades with Germany, Great Britain, Belgium, Denmark, Poland, Cuba, Czechoslovakia, and Hungary.

Geography: Lithuania is situated on the eastern shore of the Baltic Sea and borders Latvia on the north, Russia on the east, and Poland on the south. It is a country of gently rolling hills, many forests, rivers and streams, and lakes. Its principal natural resource is agricultural land.

Government: Lithuania is a parliamentary democracy. The head of state is the chairman of the Supreme Council (parliament). The president chooses the prime minister with the approval of the parliament.

History: Southernmost of the three Baltic states, Lithuania in the Middle Ages was a grand duchy joined to Poland through royal marriage. Poles and Lithuanians merged forces to defeat the Teutonic knights of Germany at Tannenberg in 1410 and extended their power far into Russian territory. In 1795, however, following the third partition of Poland, Lithuania fell into Russian hands and did not regain its independence until 1918, toward the end of the first World War.

The republic was occupied by the Soviet Union in 1939 and annexed outright the following year. From 1940 to 1944 it was occupied by German troops and then was retaken by Russia. Western countries, including the United States, never recognized the Russian annexation of Lithuania.

Nineteen eighty-eight saw a re-emergence of the Lithuanian independence movement. On March 11,

1990, Vytautas Landsbergis, the non-communist head of the largest Lithuanian popular movement (Sajudis) was elected president, and his party swept the Lithuanian parliament. On the same day, the Supreme Council rejected Soviet rule and declared the restoration of Lithuania's independence, the first Baltic republic to take this action.

Confrontation with the Soviet Union ensued along with economic sanctions, but they were lifted after which the Lithuanian government agreed to freeze its declaration. However, the growing split with Moscow led to increasing popular demands for self-determination.

After an abortive coup to depose Soviet President Mikhail Gorbachev, President Landsbergis called his country's independence a formality.

Lithuania's independence was quickly recognized by major European and other nations, and on Sept. 2, 1991, President Bush announced full diplomatic recognition for the Baltic republics. The Soviet Union finally recognized the independence of the Baltic states on September 6. UN admittance followed on Sept. 17, 1991.

LUXEMBOURG

Grand Duchy of Luxembourg
Ruler: Grand Duke Jean (1964)
Premier: Jacques Santer (1984)
Area: 999 sq mi. (2,586 sq km)
Population (est. mid-1991): 400,000 (average annual rate of natural increase: 0.2%); birth rate: 12/1000; infant mortality rate: 9.9/1000; density per square mile: 391
Capital and largest city (est. 1982): Luxembourg, 80,000
Monetary unit: Luxembourg franc
Languages: Luxermbourgish, French, German
Religion: Mainly Roman Catholic
National name: Grand-Duché de Luxembourg
Literacy rate: 100%
Economic summary: Gross national product (1989 est.): $6.3 billion; $17,200 per capita; 4% real growth rate. Arable land: 24%. Principal products: livestock, dairy products, wine. Labor force: 161,000; 24.7% in industry. Major products: banking, steel, processed food, chemicals, metal products, tires, glass. Natural resource: Iron ore. Exports: steel, chemicals, rubber products, glass, aluminum. Imports: minerals, metals, foodstuffs, consumer goods. Major trading partners: European Common Market countries.

Geography. Luxembourg is a neighbor of Belgium on the west, West Germany on the east, and France on the south. The Ardennes Mountains extend from Belgium into the northern section of Luxembourg.

Government. Luxembourg's unicameral legislature, the Chamber of Deputies, consists of 59 members elected for five years.

History. Sigefroi, Count of Ardennes, an offspring of Charlemagne, was Luxembourg's first sovereign ruler. In 1060, the country came under the rule of the House of Luxembourg. From the 15th to the 18th century, Spain, France, and Austria held it in turn. The Congress of Vienna in 1815 made it a Grand Duchy and gave it to William I, King of the Netherlands. In 1839 the Treaty of London ceded the western part of Luxembourg to Belgium.

The eastern part, continuing in personal union with the Netherlands and a member of the German Confederation, became autonomous in 1848 and a neutral territory by decision of the London Conference of 1867, governed by its Grand Duke. Germany occupied the duchy in World Wars I and II. Allied troops liberated the enclave in 1944.

In 1961, Prince Jean, son and heir of Grand Duchess Charlotte, was made head of state, acting for his mother. She abdicated in 1964, and Prince Jean became Grand Duke. Grand Duchess Charlotte died in 1985.

By a customs union between Belgium and Luxembourg, which came into force on May 1, 1922, to last for 50 years, customs frontiers between the two countries were abolished. On Jan. 1, 1948, a customs union with Belgium and the Netherlands (Benelux) came into existence. On Feb. 3, 1958, it became an economic union.

The Luxembourg-based Bank of Credit and Commerce International in 1990 pleaded guilty to charges of money laundering from drug trafficking.

MADAGASCAR
Democratic Republic of Madagascar
President and Head of State: Didier Ratsiraka (1975)
Prime Minister: Lt. Col. Victor Ramahatra (1988)
Area: 226,660 sq mi. (587,050 sq km)
Population (est. mid-1991): 12,400,000 (average annual rate of natural increase: 3.2%); birth rate: 45/1000; infant mortality rate: 115/1000; density per square mile: 55
Capital and largest city (est. 1983): Antananarivo, 700,000
Monetary unit: Malagasy franc
Languages: Malagasy, French
Ethnic groups: Merina (or Hova), Betsimisaraka, Betsileo, Tsimihety, Antaisaka, Sakalava, Antandroy
Religions: traditional, 52%; Christian, 41%; Islam, 7%
National name: Repoblika Demokratika Malagasy
Literacy rate: 67.5%
Economic summary: Gross domestic product (1988): $1.7 billion; $155 per capita; 2.2% real growth rate. Arable land: 4%. Principal products: rice, livestock, coffee, vanilla, sugar, cloves, cassava, beans, bananas. Labor force: 4,900,000; 90% in subsistence agriculture. Major industrial products: processed food, textiles, assembled automobiles, soap, cement. Natural resources: graphite, chromium, bauxite, semiprecious stones. Exports: coffee, cloves, vanilla, sugar, petroleum products. Imports: consumer goods, foodstuffs, crude petroleum. Major trading partners: France, U.S., Japan, E.C.

Geography. Madagascar lies in the Indian Ocean off the southeast coast of Africa opposite Mozambique. The world's fourth-largest island, it is twice the size of Arizona. The country's low-lying coastal area gives way to a central plateau. The once densely wooded interior has largely been cut down.

Government. The Constitution of Dec. 30, 1975, approved by referendum following a military coup, provides for direct election by universal suffrage of a president for a seven-year term, a Supreme Council of the Revolution as a policy-making body, a unicameral People's National Assembly of 137 members (elected for five-year terms), and a military Committee for Development. The new constitution followed a period of martial rule that began with the suspension of the republic's original bicameral legislature in 1972.

A decree of March 1990 permitted the formation of political parties. Three new groupings immediately appeared.

History. The present population is of black and Malay stock, with perhaps some Polynesian, called Malagasy. The French took over a protectorate in 1885, and then in 1894–95 ended the monarchy, exiling Queen Rànavàlona III to Algiers. A colonial administration was set up, to which the Comoro Islands were attached in 1908, and other territories later. In World War II, the British occupied Madagascar, which retained ties to Vichy France.

An autonomous republic within the French Community since 1958, Madagascar became an independent member of the Community in 1960. In May 1973, an army coup led by Maj. Gen. Gabriel Ramanantsoa ousted Philibert Tsiranana, president since 1959.

With unemployment and inflation both high, Ramanantsoa resigned Feb. 5, 1975. His leftist-leaning successor, Interior Minister Richard Ratsimandrava, an Army lieutenant colonel, was killed six days later by a machine-gun ambush in Antananarivo, the capital.

On June 15, 1975, Comdr. Didier Ratsiraka was named President. He announced that he would follow a socialist course and, after nationalizing banks and insurance companies, declared all mineral resources nationalized.

An attempted coup in May 1990 was soon put down with a loss of five lives, according to official sources.

MALAWI
Republic of Malawi
President: Hastings Kamuzu Banda (1966)
Area: 45,747 sq mi. (118,484 sq km)
Population (est. mid-1991): 9,400,000 (average annual rate of natural increase: 3.4%); birth rate: 52/1000; infant mortality rate: 136/1000; density per square mile: 206
Capital (est. 1986): Lilongwe, 202,900
Largest city (est. 1986): Blantyre, 378,100
Monetary unit: Kwacha
Languages: English and Chichewa (National); also Tombuka
Religions: Christian, 75%; Islam, 20%; traditional, 5%
Member of Commonwealth of Nations
Literacy rate: 41.2%
Economic summary: Gross domestic product (1988): $1.4 billion; $180 per capita; growth rate: 3.6%. Arable land: 25%. Principal products: tobacco, tea, sugar, corn, cotton. Labor force: 428,000 wage earners; 16% in manufacturing. Major products: food, tobacco, cement, processed wood, consumer goods. Natural resources: limestone, uranium, coal, bauxite. Exports: tobacco, sugar, tea. Imports: transport equipment, food, petroleum, consumer goods. Major trading partners: U.K., U.S., Japan, Germany, South Africa.

Geography. Malawi is a landlocked country the size of Pennsylvania in southeastern Africa, surrounded by Mozambique, Zambia, and Tanzania. Lake Malawi, formerly Lake Nyasa, occupies most of the country's eastern border. The north-south Rift Valley is flanked by mountain ranges and high plateau areas.

Government. Under a Constitution that came into effect on July 6, 1966, the president is the sole head of state; there is neither a prime minister nor a vice president. The National Assembly has 107 members.

There is only one national party—the Malawi Congress Party led by President Hastings K. Banda, who was designated President for life in 1970.

History. The first European to make extensive explorations in the area was David Livingstone in the 1850s and 1860s. In 1884, Cecil Rhodes's British South African Company received a charter to develop the country. The company came into conflict with the Arab slavers in 1887–89. After Britain annexed the Nyasaland territory in 1891, making it a protectorate in 1892, Sir Harry Johnstone, the first high commissioner, using Royal Navy gunboats, wiped out the slavers.

Nyasaland became the independent nation of Malawi on July 6, 1964. Two years later, it became a republic within the Commonwealth of Nations.

Dr. Hastings K. Banda, Malawi's first Prime Minister, became its first President. He pledged to follow a policy of "discretionary nonalignment." Banda alienated much of black Africa by maintaining good relations with South Africa. He argued that his landlocked country had to rely on South Africa for access to the sea and trade.

In recent years this country's problems have been more economic than political. Malawi's main export crop, tobacco, has sharply dropped in price on world markets producing dramatically lowered foreign earnings.

MALAYSIA

Paramount Ruler: Azlan Muhibuddin Shah, Sultan of Perak (1989)
Prime Minister: D.S. Mahathir bin Mohamed (1981)
Area: 128,328 sq mi. (332,370 sq km)
Population (est. mid-1991): 18,300,000 (average annual rate of natural increase: 2.5%); birth rate: 29/1000; infant mortality rate: 29/1000; density per square mile: 143
Capital: Kuala Lumpur
Largest cities (est. 1980 by U.N.): Kuala Lumpur, 1,000,000; George Town (Pinang), 300,000; Ipoh, 275,000
Monetary unit: Ringgit
Languages: Malay (official), Chinese, Tamil, English
Ethnic divisions: 59% Malay and other indigenous; 32% Chinese; 9% Indian
Religions: Malays nearly all Muslim, Chinese predominantly Buddhists, Indians predominantly Hindu
Member of Commonwealth of Nations
Literacy rate: 65%
Economic summary: Gross domestic product (1989 est.): $37.9 billion; $2,270 per capita; 7.7% real growth rate. Arable land: 3%. Principal products: rice, rubber, palm products. Labor force: 6,800,000; 17% in manufacturing. Major industrial products: processed rubber, timber, and palm oil, tin, petroleum, light manufactures, electronics equipment. Natural resources: tin, oil, copper, timber. Exports: natural rubber, palm oil, tin, timber, petroleum. Imports: food, crude oil, capital equipment, chemicals. Major trading partners: Japan, Singapore, U.S., Western European countries.

Geography. Malaysia is at the southern end of the Malay Peninsula in southeast Asia. The nation also includes Sabah and Sarawak on the island of Borneo to the southeast. Its area slightly exceeds that of New Mexico.

Most of Malaysia is covered by dense jungle and swamps, with a mountain range running the length of the peninsula. Extensive forests provide ebony, sandalwood, teak, and other woods.

Government. Malaysia is a sovereign constitutional monarchy within the Commonwealth of Nations. The Paramount Ruler is elected for a five-year term by the hereditary rulers of the states from among themselves. He is advised by the prime minister and his cabinet. There is a bicameral legislature. The Senate, whose role is comparable more to that of the British House of Lords than to the U.S. Senate, has 68 members, partly appointed by the Paramount Ruler to represent minority and special interests, and partly elected by the legislative assemblies of the various states.

The House of Representatives, is made up of 180 members, who are elected for five-year terms.

History. Malaysia came into existence on Sept. 16, 1963, as a federation of Malaya, Singapore, Sabah (North Borneo), and Sarawak. In 1965, Singapore withdrew from the federation. Since 1966, the 11 states of former Malaya have been known as West Malaysia, and Sabah and Sarawak have been known as East Malaysia.

The Union of Malaya was established April 1, 1946, being formed from the Federated Malay States of Negri Sembilan, Pahang, Perak, and Selangor; the Unfederated Malay States of Johore, Kedah, Kelantan, Perlis, and Trengganu; and two of the Straits Settlements—Malacca and Penang. The Malay states had been brought under British administration during the late 19th and early 20th centuries.

It became the Federation of Malaya on Feb. 1, 1948, and the Federation attained full independence within the Commonwealth of Nations in 1957.

Sabah, constituting the extreme northern portion of the island of Borneo, was a British protectorate administered under charter by the British North Borneo Company from 1881 to 1946, when it assumed the status of a colony. It was occupied by Japanese troops from 1942 to 1945.

Sarawak extends along the northwestern coast of Borneo for about 500 miles (805 km). In 1841, part of the present territory was granted by the Sultan of Brunei to Sir James Brooke. Sarawak continued to be ruled by members of the Brooke family until the Japanese occupation.

From 1963, when Malaysia became independent, it was the target of guerrilla infiltration from Indonesia, but beat off invasion attempts. In 1966, when Sukarno fell and the Communist Party was liquidated in Indonesia, hostilities ended.

In the late 1960s, the country was torn by communal rioting directed against Chinese and Indians, who controlled a disproportionate share of the country's wealth. Beginning in 1968, the government moved to achieve greater economic balance through a rural development program.

Malaysia felt the impact of the "boat people" fleeing Vietnam early in 1978. Because the refugees were mostly ethnic Chinese, the government was apprehensive about any increase of a minority that previously had been the source of internal conflict in the country. In April 1988, it announced that starting in April 1989 it would accept no more refugees.

General elections were held in October 1990 producing another victory for Prime Minister Mahathir and his Barisan National coalition, which won 127 of the 180 parliamentary seats. Although still more than the two-thirds majority needed to pass constitutional amendments, this total is down from the previous 133 seats.

MALDIVES

Republic of Maldives
President: Maumoon Abdul Gayoom (1978)
Area: 115 sq mi. (298 sq km)
Population (1990 census): 213,215 (average annual rate of natural increase: 3.7%); birth rate: 46/1000; infant mortality rate: 72/1000; density per square mile: 1,951
Capital and largest city (1990): Malé, 55,130
Monetary unit: Maldivian rufiyaa
Language: Dhivehi
Religion: Islam
Literacy rate: 36%
Economic summary: Gross domestic product (1988): $136 million; $670 per capita; 9.2% real growth rate. Arable land: 10%. Principal agricultural products: coconuts, corn, sweet potatoes. Labor force: 66,000; 80% in fishing. Major products: fish, processed coconuts, handicraft. Natural resource: fish. Export: fish, clothing. Imports: intermediate and capital goods, consumer goods, petroleum products. Major trading partners: Sri Lanka, Thailand, Western Europe, Japan.

Geography. The Republic of Maldives is a group of atolls in the Indian Ocean about 417 miles (671 km) southwest of Sri Lanka. Its 1,190 coral islets stretch over an area of 35,200 square miles (90,000 sq km). With concerns over global warming and the shrinking of the polar ice caps, Maldives felt directly threatened as none of its islands rises more than six feet above sea level.

Government. The 11-member Cabinet is headed by the president. The Majlis (Parliament) is a unicameral legislature consisting of 48 members. Eight of these are appointed by the president. The others are elected for five-year terms, 2 from the capital island of Malé and 2 from each of the 19 administrative atolls.
There are no political parties in the Maldives.

History. The Maldives (formerly called the Maldive Islands) are inhabited by an Islamic seafaring people. Originally the islands were under the suzerainty of Ceylon. They came under British protection in 1887 and were a dependency of the then colony of Ceylon until 1948. The independence agreement with Britain was signed July 26, 1965.
For centuries a sultanate, the islands adopted a republican form of government in 1952, but the sultanate was restored in 1954. In 1968, however, as the result of a referendum, a republic was again established in the islands.
Ibrahim Nasir, president since 1968, was removed from office by the Majlis in November 1978 and replaced by Maumoon Abdul Cayoom. A national referendum confirmed the new leader.

MALI

Republic of Mali
President of the Republic: Lt. Col. Amadou (1991)
Area: 478,819 sq mi. (1,240,142 sq km)
Population (est. mid-1991): 8,300,000 (average annual rate of natural increase: 3%); birth rate: 51/1000; infant mortality rate: 116/1000; density per square mile: 17
Capital and largest city (est. 1981): Bamako, 750,000
Monetary unit: Franc CFA
Ethnic groups: Bambara, Peul, Soninke, Malinke, Songhai, Dogon, Senoufo, Minianka, Berbers, and Moors
Languages: French (official), African languages
Religions: Islam, 90%; traditional, 9%; Christian, 1%
National name: République de Mali
Literacy rate: 18%
Economic summary: Gross domestic product (1988 est.): $1.94 billion; $220 per capita; –0.9% real growth rate. Arable land: 2%; Principal agricultural products: millet, corn, rice, cotton, peanuts, livestock. Labor force: 2,666,000; 80% in agriculture. Major industrial products: consumer goods, phosphates, gold, fish. Natural resources: bauxite, iron ore, manganese, phosphate, salt, limestone, gold. Exports: livestock, peanuts, dried fish, cotton, skins. Imports: textiles, vehicles, petroleum products, machinery, sugar, cereals. Major trading partners: Western Europe.

Geography. Most of Mali, in West Africa, lies in the Sahara. A landlocked country four fifths the size of Alaska, it is bordered by Guinea, Senegal, Mauritania, Algeria, Niger, Burkina Faso, and the Côte d'Ivoire.
The only fertile area is in the south, where the Niger and Senegal Rivers provide irrigation.

Government. The army overthrew the government on Nov. 19, 1968, and formed a provisional government. The Military Committee of National Liberation consists of 14 members and forms the decision-making body.
In late 1969 an attempted coup was foiled, and Lt. Moussa Traoré, president of the Military Committee took over as chief of state and later as head of government, ousting Capt. Yoro Diakité as Premier.
Soldiers promising a multiparty democracy overthrew the dictatorship of General Traoré in March 1991.

History. Subjugated by France by the end of the 19th century, this area became a colony in 1904 (named French Sudan in 1920) and in 1946 became part of the French Union. On June 20, 1960, it became independent and, under the name of Sudanese Republic, was federated with the Republic of Senegal in the Mali Federation. However, Senegal seceded from the Federation on Aug. 20, 1960, and the Sudanese Republic then changed its name to the Republic of Mali on September 22.
In the 1960s, Mali concentrated on economic development, continuing to accept aid from both Soviet bloc and Western nations, as well as international agencies. In the late 1960s, it began retreating from close ties with China. But a purge of conservative opponents brought greater power to President Modibo Keita, and in 1968 the influence of the Chinese and their Malian sympathizers increased. By a treaty signed in Peking in 1968, China agreed to help build a railroad from Mali to Guinea, providing Mali with vital access to the sea.
Mali, with Mauritania, the Côte d'Ivoire, Senegal, Dahomey (Benin), Niger, and Burkina Faso signed a treaty establishing the Economic Community for West Africa.
Mali and Burkina Faso fought a brief border war from December 25 to 29, 1985.
The leader of the March 1991 coup, Lieut. Col. Amadou Toumani Touré, promised the army would return to the barracks. There were at least 59 casualties after the overnight coup, which France welcomed. A failed coup attempt by Major Lamine Diabira, a member of the ruling council, resulted in his arrest in July.

MALTA

Republic of Malta
President: Dr. Vincent Tabone (1989)
Prime Minister: Edward Fenech Adami (1987)
Area: 122 sq mi. (316 sq km)
Population (est. mid-1991): 400,000 (average annual rate of natural increase: 0.8%); birth rate: 16/1000; infant mortality rate: 10.4/1000; density per square mile: 2,873
Capital (est. 1987): Valetta, 9,300
Largest city (est. 1987): Birkirkara, 20,300
Monetary unit: Maltese lira
Languages: Maltese and English
Religion: Roman Catholic
National name: Malta
Member of Commonwealth of Nations
Literacy rate: 83%
Economic summary: Gross domestic product (1989): $1.99 billion; $5,645 per capita; 4.9% real growth rate. Arable land: 38%. Principal products: potatoes, wheat, barley, citrus, vegetables, hogs, poultry. Labor force: 125,674; 24% in manufacturing. Major products: textiles, beverages, processed foods, clothing, footwear, tobacco. Natural resources: limestone, salt. Exports: textiles, clothing, footwear. Imports: foods, petroleum, raw material. Major trading partners: Germany, U.K., Italy, U.S.

Geography. The five Maltese islands—with a combined land area smaller than Philadelphia—are in the Mediterranean about 60 miles (97 km) south of the southeastern tip of Sicily.

Government. The government is headed by a Prime Minister, responsible to a 69-member House of Representatives elected by universal suffrage.

The major political parties are the Nationalists (35 of 69 seats in the House,) led by Prime Minister Dr. Dr. Edward Fenech-Adami; Malta Labor Party (34 seats), led by Carmelo Mifsud Bonnici.

History. The strategic importance of Malta was recognized by the Phoenicians, who occupied it, as did in their turn the Greeks, Carthaginians, and Romans. The apostle Paul was shipwrecked there in A.D. 58.

The Knights of St. John (Malta), who obtained the three habitable Maltese islands of Malta, Gozo, and Comino from Charles V in 1530, reached their highest fame when they withstood an attack by superior Turkish forces in 1565.

Napoleon seized Malta in 1798, but the French forces were ousted by British troops the next year, and British rule was confirmed by the Treaty of Paris in 1814.

Malta was heavily attacked by German and Italian aircraft during World War II, but was never invaded by the Axis.

Malta became an independent nation on Sept. 21, 1964, and a republic Dec. 13, 1974, but remained in the British Commonwealth. The Governor-General, Sir Anthony Mamo, was sworn in as first president and Dom Mintoff became prime minister.

After 13 years in office, Mintoff resigned as Prime Minister on Dec. 22, 1984, giving way to chosen successor, Carmelo Mifsud Bonnici, who had been Senior Deputy Prime Minister. Fenech Adami's election in 1987 ended 16 years of Labor rule.

Malta applied for membership in the E.C. in July 1990 and expects to be admitted in the next enlargement.

MARSHALL ISLANDS

Republic of the Marshall Islands
President: Amata Kabua
Total land area: 70 sq mi (181.3 sq km), includes the atolls of Bikini, Eniwetok, and Kwajalein
Comparative land area: slightly larger than Washington, D.C.
1990 population: 43,417, growth rate: 3.2%
Capital: Majuro
Government: Constitutional government in free association with the United States
Ethnic divisions: almost entirely Micronesian
Language: Both Marshallese and English are official languages. Marshallese is a dialect of the Malayo-Polynesian family
Religion: predominantly Christian, mostly Protestant
Net migration rate (1990): –1 migrant/1000 population
Economy: Gross domestic product (1989): $64 million; $1,500 per capita. Total exports from the Marshall Islands are some $2 million annually, of which copra products account for some 90 percent. Agriculture, marine resources, and tourism are the top development priorities for the Republic of the Marshall Islands (RMI). The government of the RMI is the largest employer with some 2,000 workers. Direct U.S. aid under the Compact of Free Association accounts for some two-thirds of the RMI's 1990 budget of $69 million. The United States and Japan are major trading partners.

The Government of the United States and the RMI signed a Compact of Free Association on October 15, 1986, which became effective as of October 21, 1986. The termination of the Trusteeship Agreement became effective on November 3, 1986. The Marshall Islands were admitted to the United Nations on Sept. 17, 1991.

The Marshall Islands, east of the Carolines, are divided into two chains: the western or Ralik group, including the atolls Jaluit, Kwajalein, Wotho, Bikini, and Eniwetok; and the eastern or Ratak group, including the atolls Mili, Majuro, Maloelap, Wotje, and Likiep. The islands are of the coral-reef type and rise only a few feet above sea level.

Bikini and Eniwetok were the scene of several atom-bomb tests after World War II. In April 1977, some 55 original inhabitants, the forerunner of 450 returnees, were resettled after an absence of 30 years.

MAURITANIA

Islamic Republic of Mauritania
Chief of State and Head of Government: Col. Maaouye Ould Sidi Ahmed Taya (1984)
Area: 397,953 sq mi. (1,030,700 sq km)
Population (est. mid-1991): 2,100,000 (average annual rate of natural increase: 2.8%); birth rate: 46/1000; infant mortality rate: 122/1000; density per square mile: 5
Capital and largest city (est. 1981): Nouakchott, 175,000
Monetary unit: Ouguiya
Ethnic groups: Moors, Black/moor mix, 70%; Blacks, 30%.
Languages: Arabic (official) and French
Religion: Islam
National name: République Islamique de Mauritanie
Literacy rate: 17%
Economic summary: Gross domestic product (1988): $1.0 billion; $520 per capita; 3.6% real growth rate. Arable land: 1%; Principal agricultural products: livestock, millet, maize, wheat, dates, rice. Labor force: 465,000

(1981 est.); 45,000 wage earners; 14% in industry and commerce. Major industrial products: iron ore, processed fish. Natural resources: copper, iron ore, gypsum, fish. Exports: iron ore, fish, gum arabic, gypsum. Imports: foodstuffs, petroleum, capital goods. Major trading partners: E.C., Japan, Côte d'Ivoire.

Geography. Mauritania, three times the size of Arizona, is situated in northwest Africa with about 350 miles (592 km) of coastline on the Atlantic Ocean. It is bordered by Morocco on the north, Algeria and Mali on the east, and Senegal on the south.

The country is mostly desert, with the exception of the fertile Senegal River valley in the south and grazing land in the north.

Government. An Army coup on July 10, 1978, deposed Moktar Ould Daddah, who had been President since Mauritania's independence in 1960. President Mohammed Khouna Ould Haldala, who seized power in the 1978 coup, was in turn deposed in a Dec. 12, 1984, coup by army chief of staff Maaouye Ould Sidi Ahmed Taya, who assumed the title of President.

History. Mauritania was first explored by the Portuguese. The French organized the area as a territory in 1904.

Mauritania became an independent nation on Nov. 28, 1960, and was admitted to the United Nations in 1961 over the strenuous opposition of Morocco, which claimed the territory. With Moors, Arabs, Berbers, and blacks frequently in conflict, the government in the late 1960s sought to make Arab culture dominant to unify the land.

Mauritania acquired administrative control of the southern part of the former Spanish Sahara when the colonial administration withdrew in 1975, under an agreement with Morocco and Spain. Mauritanian troops moved into the territory but encountered resistance from the Polisario Front, a Saharan independence movement backed by Algeria. The task of trying to pacify the area proved a heavy burden. Mauritania signed a peace agreement with the Polisario insurgents in August 1979, withdrew from the territory and renounced territorial claims.

Increased military spending and rising casualties in Western Sahara contributed to the discontent that brought down the civilian government of Ould Daddah in 1978. A succession of military rulers has followed.

In 1989 Mauritania fought a border war with Senegal. In January 1990 Arabic was made the official language of government. Although the country voted in the U.N. to support the embargo against Iraq, the government actually leaned the other way.

MAURITIUS

Sovereign: Queen Elizabeth II
Governor-General: Sir Veerasamy Ringadoo (1986)
Prime Minister: Aneerood Jugnauth (1982)
Area: 787 sq mi. (2,040 sq km)
Population (est. mid-1991): 1,100,000 (average annual rate of natural increase: 1.4%); birth rate: 20/1000; infant mortality rate: 22.7/1000; density per square mile: 1,368
Capital and largest city (est. 1980): Port Louis, 155,000
Monetary unit: Mauritian rupee
Languages: English (official), French, Creole, Hindi, Urdu, Chinese
Religions: Hindu, 51%, Christian, 30%; Islam, 17%; other, 2%

Member of Commonwealth of Nations
Literacy rate: 82.8%
Economic summary: Gross domestic product (1988): $1.9 billion; $1,910 per capita; 6.3% real growth rate. Arable land: 54%. Principal products: sugar cane, tea. Labor force: 335,000; 22% in manufacturing. Major products: processed sugar, wearing apparel, chemical products, textiles. Natural resources: fish. Exports: sugar, light manufactures, textiles. Imports: foodstuffs, manufactured goods. Major trading partners: E.C., S. Africa, U.S.

Geography. Mauritius is a mountainous island in the Indian Ocean east of Madagascar.

Government. Mauritius is a member of the British Commonwealth, with Queen Elizabeth II as head of state. She is represented by a governor-general, who chooses the prime minister from the unicameral Legislative Assembly. The Legislative Assembly has 70 members, 62 of whom are elected by direct suffrage. The remaining 8 are chosen from among the unsuccessful candidates.

History. After a brief Dutch settlement, French immigrants who came in 1715 gave the name of Isle de France to the island and established the first road and harbor infrastructure, as well as the sugar industry, under the leadership of Gov. Mahe de Labourdonnais. Negroes from Africa and Madagascar came as slaves to work in the cane fields. In 1810, the British captured the island and in 1814, by the Treaty of Paris, it was ceded to Great Britain along with its dependencies.

Indian immigration which followed the abolition of slavery in 1835 changed rapidly the fabric of Mauritian society, and the country flourished with the increased cultivation of sugar cane.

Mauritius became independent on March 12, 1968.

The Labor Party government of Sir Seewoosagur Ramgoolam, who had ruled Mauritius since independence, was toppled in a 1982 election by the Movement Militant Mauricien, which had campaigned for recovery of Diego Garcia island, separated from Mauritius during the colonial period and leased by Britain to the United States for a naval base. But an Alliance Party coalition, including the Labor Party, regained power at the end of 1983 and brought back Ramgoolam as Prime Minister. He was succeeded by Aneerood Jugnauth of his party in 1982.

A transformation of the nation from a constitutional monarchy into a republic was attempted in mid-1990 on the understanding that opposition party leader Paul Bérenger would be named president. Public dissent for the move, however, arose, and the required parliamentary vote was never taken.

MEXICO

United Mexican States
President: Carlos Salinas de Gortari (1988)
Area: 761,600 sq mi. (1,972,547 sq km)
Population (est. mid-1991): 85,700,000 (average annual rate of natural increase: 2.3%); birth rate: 29/1000; infant mortality rate: 43/1000; density per square mile: 113
Capital: Federal District (Mexico City)
Largest cities (1989): Federal District, 19,479,000; Guadalajara, 3,186,500; Monterey, 2,858,800; Puebla, 1,707,000; Leon, 1,006,700

Monetary unit: Peso
Languages: Spanish, Indian languages
Religion: nominally Roman Catholic, 97%; Protestant, 3%
Official name: Estados Unidos Mexicanos
Literacy rate: 88%
Economic summary: Gross domestic product (1989): $187.0 billion; $2,165 per capita; 2.5% real growth rate. Arable land: 12%;principal products: corn, cotton, fruits, wheat, beans, coffee, tomatoes, rice. Labor force: 26,100,000 (1988); 12.8% in manufacturing. Major products: processed foods, chemicals, basic metals and metal products, petroleum. Natural resources: petroleum, silver, copper, gold, lead, zinc, natural gas, timber. Exports: cotton, cattle, shrimp, coffee, petroleum, petroleum products, engines. Imports: grain, metal manufactures, agricultural machinery, electrical equipment. Major trading partners: U.S., Japan, Western European countries.

Geography. The United States' neighbor to the south, Mexico is about one fifth its size. Baja California in the west, an 800-mile (1,287-km) peninsula, forms the Gulf of California. In the east are the Gulf of Mexico and the Bay of Campeche, which is formed by Mexico's other peninsula, the Yucatán.

The center of Mexico is a great, high plateau, open to the north, with mountain chains on east and west and with ocean-front lowlands lying outside of them.

Government. The President, who is popularly elected for six years and is ineligible to succeed himself, governs with a Cabinet of secretaries. Congress has two houses—a 400-member Chamber of Deputies, elected for three years, and a 64-member Senate, elected for six years.

Each of the 31 states has considerable autonomy, with a popularly elected governor, a legislature, and a local judiciary. The President of Mexico appoints the mayor of the Federal District.

History. At least two civilized races—the Mayas and later the Toltecs—preceded the wealthy Aztec empire, conquered in 1519–21 by the Spanish under Hernando Cortés. Spain ruled for the next 300 years until 1810 (the date was Sept. 16 and is now celebrated as Independence Day), when the Mexicans first revolted. They continued the struggle and finally won independence in 1821.

From 1821 to 1877, there were two emperors, several dictators, and enough presidents and provisional executives to make a new government on the average of every nine months. Mexico lost Texas (1836), and after defeat in the war with the U.S. (1846–48) it lost the area comprising the present states of California, Nevada, and Utah, most of Arizona and New Mexico, and parts of Wyoming and Colorado.

In 1855, the Indian patriot Benito Juárez began a series of liberal reforms, including the disestablishment of the Catholic Church, which had acquired vast property. A subsequent civil war was interrupted by the French invasion of Mexico (1861), the crowning of Maximilian of Austria as Emperor (1864), and then his overthrow and execution by forces under Juárez, who again became President in 1867.

The years after the fall of the dictator Porfirio Diaz (1877–80 and 1884–1911) were marked by bloody political-military strife and trouble with the U.S., culminating in the punitive expedition into northern Mexico (1916–17) in unsuccessful pursuit of the revolutionary Pancho Villa. Since a brief period of civil war in 1920, Mexico has enjoyed a period of gradual

agricultural, political, and social reforms. Relations with the U.S. were again disturbed in 1938 when all foreign oil wells were expropriated. Agreement on compensation was finally reached in 1941.

The last year of José López Portillo's presidency was shadowed by economic problems caused by falling oil prices.

Miguel de la Madrid Hurtado, candidate of the ruling Partido Revolucionario Institucional, won the July 4 election for a six-year term.

During 1983 and 1984, Mexico suffered its worst financial crisis in 50 years, leading to critically high unemployment and an inability to pay its foreign debt. The collapse of oil prices in 1986 cut into Mexico's export earnings and worsened the situation.

Although the ruling Institutional Revolutionary Party's candidate, Carlos Salinas de Gortari, won the presidential election of 1988, the opposition parties on the left and the right showed unprecedented strength. This continued in mid-1989 when the ruling PRI acknowledged an unprecedented defeat in a gubernatorial election.

In the economic sphere Mexico decided to apply for membership in the Organization for Economic Cooperation & Development and talks began on a comprehensive North American free-trade agreement. The national telephone company was privatized, and the government in 1990 announced it would reprivatize the banks nationalized in 1982.

MICRONESIA

The Federated States of Micronesia
President: Bailey Olter
Vice President: Jacob Nena
Total area: 271 sq mi (703 sq km). Land area, same (includes islands of Pohnpei, Truk, Yap, and Kosrae.
Population (1990): 104,937, growth rate (1990): 2.6%
Capital: Kolonia (on the island of Pohnpei. A new capital is being built about 6.2 miles (10 km) southwest in the Palikir valley.
Government: A constitutional government in free association with the United States since November 1986.
Ethnic divisions: Nine ethnic Micronesian and Polynesian groups.
Language: English is the official and common language; major indigenous languages are Trukese, Pohnpeian, Yapase, and Kosrean.
Gross national product (1989 est.): $150 million, per capita $1,500
Economy: Financial assistance from the U.S. is the primary source of revenue, with the U.S. pledged to spend $1 billion in the islands in the 1990s. Micronesia also earns about $4 million a year in fees from foreign fishing concerns. Economic activity consists primarily of subsistence farming and fishing.
Unemployment rate: 80%
Aid: Under the terms of the Compact of Free Association, the U.S. will provide $1.3 billion in grand aid during the period 1986–2001.

On April 2, 1947, the United Nations Security Council created the Trust Territory of the Pacific Islands under which the Northern Mariana, Caroline, and Marshall Islands were placed under the administration of the United States. These islands comprised what is now called the Federated States of Micronesia and only the Republic of Palau is still administered as a Trust Territory. Micronesia was admitted to the United Nations on September 17, 1991.

The Micronesian islands vary geologically from high mountainous islands to low, coral atolls; volcanic outcroppings on Pohnpei, Kosrae, and Truk. The climate is tropical with heavy, year-round rainfall. The islands are located 3,200 miles (5,150 km) west-southwest of Honolulu in the North Pacific Ocean, about three-quarters of the way between Hawaii and Indonesia.

MONACO

Principality of Monaco
Ruler: Prince Rainier III (1949)
Minister of State: Jacques Dupont (1991)
Area: 0.73 sq mi. (465 acres)
Population (1989): 28,188 (average annual growth rate: .9%)
Density per square mile: 38,356.2
Capital: Monaco-Ville
Monetary unit: French franc
Languages: French, Monégasque, Italian
Religion: Roman Catholic, 95%
National name: Principauté de Monaco
Literacy rate: 99%

Geography. Monaco is a tiny, hilly wedge driven into the French Mediterranean coast nine miles east of Nice.

Government. Prince Albert of Monaco gave the principality a Constitution in 1911, creating a National Council of 18 members popularly elected for five years. The head of government is the Minister of State.

Prince Rainier III, born May 31, 1923, succeeded his grandfather, Louis II, on the latter's death, May 9, 1949. Rainier was married April 18, 1956, to Grace Kelly, U.S. actress. A daughter, Princess Caroline Louise Marguerite, was born on Jan. 23, 1957 (married to Philippe Junot June 28, 1978 and divorced in 1980; married to Stefano Casiraghi Dec. 29, 1983, and gave birth to three children; Casiraghi died in a boating accident October, 1990); a son, Prince Albert Louis Pierre, on March 14, 1958; and Princess Stéphanie Marie Elisabeth, on Feb. 1, 1965. Princess Grace died Sept. 14, 1982, of injuries received the day before when the car she was driving went off the road near Monte Carlo. She was 52.

The special significance attached to the birth of descendants to Prince Rainier stems from a clause in the Treaty of July 17, 1919, between France and Monaco stipulating that in the event of vacancy of the Crown, the Monégasque territory would become an autonomous state under a French protectorate.

The National and Democratic Union (all 18 seats in National Council), led by Auguste Medecin, is the only political party.

History. The Phoenicians, and after them the Greeks, had a temple on the Monacan headland honoring Hercules. From *Monoikos,* the Greek surname for this mythological strong man, the principality took its name. After being independent for 800 years, Monaco was annexed to France in 1793 and was placed under Sardinia's protection in 1815. In 1861, it went under French guardianship but continued to be independent.

By a treaty in 1918, France stipulated that the French government be given a veto over the succession to the throne.

Monaco is a little land of pleasure with a tourist business that runs as high as 1.5 million visitors a year. It had popular gaming tables as early as 1856. Five years later, a 50-year concession to operate the games was granted to François Blanc, of Bad Homburg. This concession passed into the hands of a private company in 1898.

Monaco's practice of providing a tax shelter for French businessmen resulted in a dispute between the countries. When Rainier refused to end the practice, France retaliated with a customs tax. In 1967, Rainier took control of the Société des Bains de Mer, operator of the famous Monte Carlo gambling casino, in a program to increase hotel and convention space.

A series of robberies in 1989 led Prince Rainier to appoint a new police commissioner. With the recent tragedies in the royal family speculation has centered on Rainier's grooming of his son Prince Albert to assume the duties of chief of state.

MONGOLIA

Mongolian People's Republic
Chairman of Presidium of the Great People's Khural (President): Punsalmaagiin Ochirbat (1990)
Prime Minister: Dashün Byambasuren (1990)
Area: 604,250 sq mi. (1,565,000 sq km)
Population (est. mid-1991): 2,200,000 (average annual rate of natural increase: 2.7%); birth rate: 36/1000; infant mortality rate: 64/1000; density per square mile: 4
Capital and largest city (est. 1990): Ulan Bator, 550,000
Monetary unit: Tugrik
Language: Mongolian
Religion: predominantly Tibetan Buddhist; Islam about 4%
National name: Bugd Nairamdakh Mongol Ard Uls
Literacy rate: 90% (est.)
Economic summary: Gross domestic product (1989 est.): $1.06 billion; $532 per capita; 3.6% real growth rate. Arable land: 1%. Principal agricultural products: livestock, wheat, potatoes, forage, barley. Major industrial products: coal, copper and molybdenum concentrate. Natural resources: coal, copper, molybdenum, iron, oil, lead, gold, and tungsten. Exports: livestock, animal products, wool, nonferrous metals. Imports: machinery and equipment, fuels, industrial consumers goods, chemicals, building materials, sugar, tea. Major trading partners: U.S.S.R., China, Japan.

Geography. Mongolia lies in eastern Asia between Soviet Siberia on the north and China on the south. It is slightly larger than Alaska.

The productive regions of Mongolia—a tableland ranging from 3,000 to 5,000 feet (914 to 1,524 m) in elevation—are in the north, which is well drained by numerous rivers, including the Hovd, Onon, Selenga, and Tula.

Much of the Gobi Desert falls within Mongolia.

Government. The Mongolian People's Republic is a socialist state. The highest organ of state power is the Great People's Hural (Parliament), which is elected for a term of four years and is convened once a year. The powers of the Great People's Hural include the adoption of or making amendments to the constitution, the election of the Baga Hural (standing legislature), the president and vice-president, appointment of the prime minister, the general public prosecutor, and the chief justice of the Supreme Court. In 1990, the Mongolian People's Revolutionary Party, led by Budragchaagiin Dashyondon, gave up its constitutional monopoly on power. Other political parties are the Mongolian Democratic Party, Social Democratic Party, National Progress Party, Party of the Greens, and the Free Labor Party.

History. The Mongolian People's Republic, formerly known as Outer Mongolia, is a Soviet satellite. It contains the original homeland of the historic Mongols, whose power reached its zenith during the 13th century under Kublai Khan. The area accepted Manchu rule in 1689, but after the Chinese Revolution of 1911 and the fall of the Manchus in 1912, the northern Mongol princes expelled the Chinese officials and declared independence under the Khutukhtu, or "Living Buddha."

In 1921, Soviet troops entered the country and facilitated the establishment of a republic by Mongolian revolutionaries in 1924 after the death of the last Living Buddha. China, meanwhile, continued to claim Outer Mongolia but was unable to back the claim with any strength. Under the 1945 Chinese-Russian Treaty, China agreed to give up Outer Mongolia, which, after a plebiscite, became a nominally independent country.

Allied with the U.S.S.R. in its dispute with China, Mongolia has mobilized troops along its borders since 1968 when the two powers became involved in border clashes on the Kazakh-Sinkiang frontier to the west and on the Amur and Ussuri Rivers. A 20-year treaty of friendship and cooperation, signed in 1966, entitled Mongolia to call upon the U.S.S.R. for military aid in the event of invasion.

Free elections were held in August 1990 that produced a multiparty government, though still largely Communist. As a result Mongolia has decided to move toward a market economy with the first step being the auctioning off of many shops and service firms in late June 1991.

MOROCCO

Kingdom of Morocco
Ruler: King Hassan II (1961)
Prime Minister: Azzedine Laraki (1986)
Area: 172,413 sq mi. (446,550 sq km)
Population (est. mid-1991): 26,200,000 (average annual rate of natural increase: 2.5%); birth rate: 34/1000; infant mortality rate: 75/1000; density per square mile: 152
Capital: Rabat
Largest cities: Casablanca, 3,500,000; Rabat-Sale, 1,000,000; Fez, 600,000; Marrakesh, 500,000; Laayoune, 100,000
Monetary unit: Dirham
Languages: Arabic, French, Berber dialects, Spanish
Religions: Islam, 98.7%, Christian, 1.1%; Jewish, 0.2%
National name: al-Mamlaka al-Maghrebia
Literacy rate: 28%
Economic summary: Gross domestic product (1989): $22.5 billion; $800 per capita; 3.4% real growth rate. Arable land: 20%. Products: barley, wheat, citrus fruits, vegetables. Labor force: approx. 7,000,000; 15% in industry. Major products: textiles, processed food, phosphates, leather goods. Natural resources: phosphates, lead, manganese, fisheries. Exports: phosphates, citrus fruits, vegetables, canned fruits and vegetables, canned fish, carpets. Imports: capital

goods, fuels, foodstuffs, raw materials, consumer goods. Major trading partners: E.C., U.S.S.R., Japan, U.S.

Geography. Morocco, about one tenth larger than California, is just south of Spain across the Strait of Gibraltar and looks out on the Atlantic from the northwest shoulder of Africa. Algeria is to the east and Mauritania to the south.

On the Atlantic coast there is a fertile plain. The Mediterranean coast is mountainous. The Atlas Mountains, running northeastward from the south to the Algerian frontier, average 11,000 feet (3,353 m) in elevation.

Government. The King, after suspending the 1962 Constitution and dissolving Parliament in 1965, promulgated a new Constitution in 1972. He continued to rule by decree until June 3, 1977, when the first free elections since 1962 took place. The 306-member Chamber of Deputies has 204 elected seats, with the balance chosen by local councils and groups.

History. Morocco was once the home of the Berbers, who helped the Arabs invade Spain in A.D. 711 and then revolted against them and gradually won control of large areas of Spain for a time after 739.

The country was ruled successively by various native dynasties and maintained regular commercial relations with Europe, even during the 17th and 18th centuries when it was the headquarters of the famous Salé pirates. In the 19th century, there were frequent clashes with the French and Spanish. Finally, in 1904, France and Spain divided Morocco into zones of French and Spanish influence, and these were established as protectorates in 1912.

Meanwhile, Morocco had become the object of big-power rivalry, which almost led to a European war in 1905 when Germany attempted to gain a foothold in the rich mineral country. By terms of the Algeciras Conference (1906), Morocco was internationalized economically, and France's privileges were limited.

The Tangier Statute, concluded by Britain, France, and Spain in 1923, created an international zone at the port of Tangier, permanently neutralized and demilitarized. In World War II, Spain occupied the zone, ostensibly to ensure order, but was forced to withdraw in 1945.

Sultan Mohammed V was deposed by the French in 1953 and replaced by his uncle, but nationalist agitation forced his return in 1955. On his death on Feb. 26, 1961, his son, Hassan, became King.

France and Spain recognized the independence and sovereignty of Morocco in 1956. Later the same year, the Tangier international zone was abolished.

In 1975, tens of thousands of Moroccans crossed the border into Spanish Sahara to back their government's contention that the northern part of the territory was historically part of Morocco. At the same time, Mauritania occupied the southern half of the territory in defiance of Spanish threats to resist such a takeover. Abandoning its commitment to self-determination for the territory, Spain withdrew, and only Algeria protested.

When Mauritania signed a peace treaty with the Algerian-backed Polisario Front in August 1979, Morocco occupied and assumed administrative control of the southern part of the Western Sahara, in addition to the northern part it already occupied. Under pressure from other African leaders, Hassan agreed in mid-1981 to a cease-fire with a referendum under international supervision to decide the fate of the Sahara territory, but the referendum was never carried out.

King Hassan, startled the Reagan Administration in mid-August 1984 by signing a treaty of union with Col. Muammar el-Qaddafi, the Libyan leader.

King Hassan became the second Arab leader to meet with an Israeli leader when, on July 21, 1986, Israeli Prime Minister Shimon Peres came to Morocco. Libyan criticism of the meeting led to King Hassan's abrogation of the treaty with Libya.

Morocco became the first Arab state to condemn the 1990 Iraqi invasion of Kuwait and promised to send an 1,100-men contingent to Saudi Arabia. Public opinion, however, as evidenced by sanctioned marches in Rabat, mounted against Moroccan involvement and demanded withdrawal from the U.S.-led alliance. The official policy remained that the presence of Moroccan troops was exclusively meant to help defend Saudi Arabia.

FRELIMO was organized in 1963. Guerrilla activity had become so extensive by 1973 that Portugal was forced to dispatch 40,000 troops to fight the rebels. A cease-fire was signed in September 1974, when Portugal agreed to grant Mozambique independence.

On Jan. 25, 1985, Mozambique's celebration of a decade of independence from Portugal was not a happy one. The government was locked in a five-year-old, stalemated, paralyzing war with anti-government guerrillas, known as the MNR, backed by the white minority government in South Africa.

President Chissano decided to abandon Marxism-Leninism in 1989. A new constitution was drafted calling for three branches of government and granting civil liberties. The civil war, however, continued through 1990, though hopes for a peaceful settlement emerged in 1991.

MOZAMBIQUE

Republic of Mozambique
President: Joaquim Chissano (1986)
Prime Minister: Dr. Mario Machungo (1986)
Area: 303,073 sq mi. (799,380 sq km)
Population (est. mid-1991): 16,100,000 (average annual rate of natural increase: 2.7%); birth rate: 45/1000; infant mortality rate: 136/1000; density per square mile: 52
Capital and largest city (est. mid-1986): Maputo, 882,800
Monetary unit: Metical
Languages: Portuguese (official), Bantu languages
Religions: traditional, 60%; Christian, 30%; Islam, 10%
National name: República Popular de Moçambique
Literacy rate: 38%
Economic summary: Gross national product (1988): $1.6 billion; per capita less than $110; 5% real growth rate. Arable land: 4%. Principal agricultural products: cotton, cashew nuts, sugar, tea, shrimp. Labor force: 90% in agriculture. Major products: processed foods, petroleum products, beverages, textiles, tobacco. Natural resources: coal, titanium. Exports: cashew nuts, sugar, shrimp, copra, citrus. Imports: refined petroleum, food, clothing, farm equipment. Major trading partners: U.S., Western Europe, Japan, U.S.S.R.

Geography. Mozambique stretches for 1,535 miles (2,470 km) along Africa's southeast coast. It is nearly twice the size of California. Tanzania is to the north; Malawi, Zambia, and Zimbabwe to the west; and South Africa and Swaziland to the south.

The country is generally a low-lying plateau broken up by 25 sizable rivers that flow into the Indian Ocean. The largest is the Zambezi, which provides access to central Africa. The principal ports are Maputo and Beira, which is the port for Zimbabwe.

Government. After having been under Portuguese colonial rule for 470 years, Mozambique became independent on June 25, 1975. The first President, Samora Moises Machel, headed the National Front for the Liberation of Mozambique (FRELIMO) in its 10-year guerrilla war for independence. He died in a plane crash on Oct. 19, 1986, and was succeeded by his Foreign Minister, Joaquim Chissano.

History. Mozambique was discovered by Vasco da Gama in 1498, although the Arabs had penetrated into the area as early as the 10th century. It was first colonized in 1505, and by 1510, the Portuguese had control of all the former Arab sultanates on the east African coast.

MYANMAR

Union of Myanmar
Head of State (Chairman): Gen. Saw Maung (1988)
Area: 261,220 sq mi. (676,560 sq km)
Population (est. mid-1991): 42,100,000 (average annual rate of natural increase: 1.9%); birth rate: 32/1000; infant mortality rate: 95/1000; density per square mile: 161
Capital: Yangon
Largest cities (est. 1983): Yangon, 2,458,712; Mandalay, 532,895; Moulmein, 219,991; Bassein, 144,092
Monetary unit: Kyat
Language: Burmese, minority languages
Religions: Buddhist, 85%; animist, Islam, Christian, or other, 15%
National name: Pyidaungsu Myanmar Naingngandau
Literacy rate: 78%
Economic summary: Gross domestic product (FY 1988): $11.0 billion; $280 per capita; 0.2% (FY1988 est.) real growth rate. Arable land: 15%. Principal products: oilseed, pulses, sugar cane, corn, rice. Labor force: 16,036,000; 14.3% in industry. Major products: textiles, footwear, processed agricultural products, wood and wood products, refined petroleum. Natural resources: timber, tin, antimony, zinc, copper, precious stones, crude oil and natural gas. Exports: rice, teak, oilseeds, metals, rubber, gems. Imports: machinery, transportation equipment, chemicals, food products. Major trading partners: Japan, E.C., China, Southeast Asia.

Geography. Myanmar occupies the northwest portion of the Indochinese peninsula. India lies to the northwest and China to the northeast. Bangladesh, Laos, and Thailand are also neighbors. The Bay of Bengal touches the southwestern coast.

Slightly smaller than Texas, the country is divided into three natural regions: the Arakan Yoma, a long, narrow mountain range forming the barrier between Myanmar and India; the Shan Plateau in the east, extending southward into Tenasserim; and the Central Basin, running down to the flat fertile delta of the Irrawaddy in the south. This delta contains a network of intercommunicating canals and nine principal river mouths.

Government. On March 2, 1962, the government of U Nu was overthrown and replaced by a Revolutionary Council, which assumed all power in the state. Gen. U Ne Win, as chairman of the Revolutionary Council, became the chief executive. In 1972, Ne Win and his colleagues resigned their military titles. In 1974, Ne Win dissolved the Revolutionary Council and became President under the new Constitution. He voluntarily relinquished the presidency on Nov. 9, 1981.

History. In 1612, the British East India Company sent agents to Burma, but the Burmese long resisted efforts of British traders, and Dutch and Portuguese as well, to establish posts on the Bay of Bengal. By the Anglo-Burmese War in 1824–26 and two following wars, the British East India Company expanded to the whole of Burma by 1886. Burma was annexed to India. It became a separate colony in 1937.

During World War II, Burma was a key battleground; the 800-mile Burma Road was the Allies' vital supply line to China. The Japanese invaded the country in December 1941, and by May 1942 had occupied most of it, cutting off the Burma Road. After one of the most difficult campaigns of the war, Allied forces liberated most of Burma prior to the Japanese surrender in August 1945.

Burma became independent on Jan. 4, 1948. In 1951 and 1952 the Socialists achieved power, and Burma became the first Asian country to introduce social legislation.

In 1968, after the government had made headway against the Communist and separatist rebels, the military regime adopted a policy of strict nonalignment and followed "the Burmese Way" to socialism. But the insurgents continued active.

In July 1988, Ne Win announced his resignation from the Burmese Socialist Program Party (BSPP), the only legal political party.

The civilian government was overthrown in Sept. 1988 by a military junta led by General Saw Maung, an associate of U Ne Win. He changed the name of the party to the National Unity Party.

The new government held elections in May 1990 and the opposition National League for Democracy won in a landslide despite its leaders being in jail or under house arrest.

Since then these leaders have been kept incommunicado, and the military government has consolidated its power. A coalition government-in-exile was formed in December 1990, but no foreign government has recognized it.

NAMIBIA

President: Sam Nujoma (1990)
Status: Independent Country
Area: 318,261 sq mi. (824,296 sq km)
Population (mid-1991): 1,500,000 (average annual growth rate: 3.1%); birth rate: 43/1000; infant mortality rate: 102/1000; density per square mile: 5
Capital (est. 1980): Windhoek, 85,000
Summer capital (est. 1980): Swakopmund, 17,500
Monetary unit: South African rand[1]
Languages: Afrikaans, German, English (all official), several indigenous
Religion: Predominantly Christian
National name: Republic of Namibia
Literacy rate: 58%
Economic summary: Gross national product (1987): $1.54 billion; $1,245 per capita; 2.9% real growth rate. Arable land: 1%. Principal products: corn, millet, sorghum, livestock. Labor force: 500,000; 19% in industry and commerce. Major products: canned meat, dairy products, tanned leather, textiles, clothing. Natural resources: diamonds, copper, lead, zinc, uranium, fish. Exports: diamonds, copper, lead, zinc, beef cattle, karakul pelts. Imports: construction materials, fertilizer, grain, foodstuffs. Major trading partner: South Africa.

1. Namibian dollar to replace rand in 1992–93.

Geography. Namibia, bounded on the north by An-gola and Zambia and on the east by Botswana and South Africa, was discovered for Europeans by the Portuguese explorer Diaz in the late 15th century. It is for the most part a portion of the high plateau of southern Africa with a general elevation of from 3,000 to 4,000 feet.

Government. Namibia became independent in 1990 after its new constitution was ratified. A multi-party democracy with an independent judiciary was established.

History. The territory became a German colony in 1884 but was taken by South African forces in 1915, becoming a South African mandate by the terms of the Treaty of Versailles in 1920.

South Africa's application for incorporation of the territory was rejected by the U.N. General Assembly in 1946 and South Africa was invited to prepare a trusteeship agreement instead. By a law passed in 1949, however, the territory was brought into much closer association with South Africa—including representation in its Parliament.

In 1969, South Africa extended its laws to the mandate over the objection of the U.N., particularly its black African members. When South Africa refused to withdraw them, the Security Council condemned it.

Under a 1974 Security Council resolution, South Africa was required to begin the transfer of power to the Namibians by May 30, 1975, or face U.N. action, but 10 days before the deadline Prime Minister Balthazar J. Vorster rejected U.N. supervision. He said, however, that his government was prepared to negotiate Namibian independence, but not with the South-West African People's Organization, the principal black separatist group. Meanwhile, the all-white legislature of South-West Africa eased several laws on apartheid in public places.

Despite international opposition, the Turnhalle Conference in Windhoek drafted a constitution to organize an interim government based on racial divisions, a proposal overwhelmingly endorsed by white voters in the territory in 1977. At the urging of ambassadors of the five Western members of the Security Council—the U.S., Britain, France, West Germany, and Canada—South Africa on June 11 announced rejection of the Turnhalle constitution and acceptance of the Western proposal to include the South-West Africa People's Organization (SWAPO) in negotiations.

Although negotiations continued between South Africa, the western powers, neighboring black African states, and internal political groups, there was still no agreement on a final independence plan. A new round of talks aimed at resolving the 18-year-old conflict ended in a stalemate on July 25, 1984.

As policemen wielding riot sticks charged demonstrators in a black, South-West Africa township, South Africa handed over limited powers to a new, multiracial administration in the former German colony on June 17, 1985. Installation of the new government ended South Africa's direct rule, but South Africa retained an effective veto over the new government's decisions along with responsibility for the territory's defense and foreign policy, and South Africa's efforts to quell the insurgents seeking independence continued.

An agreement between South Africa, Angola, and Cuba arranged for elections for a Constituent Assembly in Nov. 1989 to establish a new government. SWAPO won 57% of the vote, a majority but not enough to dictate a constitution unilaterally. In February 1990, SWAPO leader Sam Nujoma was elected President and took office when Namibia became independent on March 21, 1990.

On March 14, 1991 delegations from Namibia and South Africa met to discuss the future ownership of Walvis Bay, the chief port along Namibia's coast but which South Africa retained after Namibia's independence. The talks broke off, however, after only a few hours.

NAURU

Republic of Nauru
President: Bernard Dowiyogo (1989)
Area: 8.2 sq mi. (21 sq km)
Population (mid-1989): 9,053 (average annual growth rate: 1.7%)
Density per square mile: 1,086
Capital: Yaren
Monetary unit: Australian dollar
Languages: Nauruan and English
Religions: Protestant, 58%; Roman Catholic, 24%; Confucian and Taoist, 8%
Special relationship within the Commonwealth of Nations
Literacy rate: 99%
Economic summary: Gross national product (1989): more than $90 million; $10,000 per capita. Major industrial products: phosphates. Natural resources: phosphates. Exports: phosphates. Imports: foodstuffs, fuel, machinery. Major trading partners: Australia, New Zealand, U.K., Japan.

Geography. Nauru (pronounced NAH oo roo) is an island in the Pacific just south of the equator, about 2,500 miles (4,023 km) southwest of Honolulu.

Government. Legislative power is invested in a popularly elected 18-member Parliament, which elects the President from among its members. Executive power rests with the President, who is assisted by a five-member Cabinet.

History. Nauru was annexed by Germany in 1888. It was placed under joint Australian, New Zealand, and British mandate after World War I, and in 1947 it became a U.N. trusteeship administered by the same three powers. On Jan. 31, 1968, Nauru became an independent republic.

In elections on December 9, 1989, Bernard Dowiyogo was elected and took office three days later.

NEPAL

Kingdom of Nepal
Ruler: King Birendra Bir Bikram Shah Deva (1972)
Prime Minister: Girija Prasad Koirala (1991)
Area: 54,463 sq mi. (141,059 sq km)
Population (mid-1991): 19,600,000 (average annual rate of natural growth: 2.5%); birth rate: 42/1000; infant mortality rate: 112/1000; density per square mile: 361
Capital and largest city (est. 1980): Katmandu, 400,000
Monetary unit: Nepalese rupee
Languages: Nepali (official), Newari, Bhutia, Maithali
Religions: Hindu, 90%; Buddhist, 5%; Islam, 3%
Literacy rate: 20%
Economic summary: Gross domestic product (FY89): $2.9 billion; $158 per capita; 1.5% real growth rate.

Arable land: 17%. Labor force: 4,100,000; 93% in agriculture. Principal products: rice, maize, wheat, millet, jute, sugar cane, oilseed, potatoes. Labor force in industry: 2%. Major products: sugar, textiles, jute, cigarettes, cement. Natural resources: water, timber, hydroelectric potential. Exports: clothing, carpets, leather goods, grain. Imports: petroleum products, fertilizer, machinery. Major trading partners: India, Japan, U.S., Europe.

Geography. A landlocked country the size of Arkansas, lying between India and the Tibetan Autonomous Region of China, Nepal contains Mount Everest (29,108 ft; 8,872 m), the tallest mountain in the world. Along its southern border, Nepal has a strip of level land that is partly forested, partly cultivated. North of that is the slope of the main section of the Himalayan range, including Everest and many other peaks higher than 20,000 feet (6,096 m).

Government. In November, 1990, King Birendra promulgated a new constitution and introduced a multiparty democracy in Nepal. In the May elections of 1991, the Nepali Congress Party won an absolute majority and Mr. Girija Prasad Koirala became the Prime Minister.

History. The Kingdom of Nepal was unified in 1768 by King Prithwi Narayan Shah. A commercial treaty was signed with Britain in 1792, and in 1816, after more than a year's hostilities, the Nepalese agreed to allow British residents to live in Katmandu, the capital. In 1923, Britain recognized the absolute independence of Nepal. Between 1846 and 1951, the country was ruled by the Rana family, which always held the office of prime minister. In 1951, however, the King took over all power and proclaimed a constitutional monarchy.

Mahendra Bir Bikram Shah became King in 1955. After Mahendra, who had ruled since 1955, died of a heart attack in 1972, Prince Birendra, at 26, succeeded to the throne.

In the first election in 22 years, on May 2, 1980, voters approved the continued autocratic rule by the King with the advice of a partyless Parliament. The King, however, permitted the election of a new legislature, in May 1986, to which the Prime Minister and Cabinet are responsible.

A dispute with India over the renewal of a trade and transit treaty led to India closing most of the border crossings, causing severe economic disruption.

In 1990 the pro-democracy movement forced King Birendra to lift the ban on political parties and appoint an opposition leader to head an interim government as Prime Minister.

The first free election in three decades provided a victory for the liberal Nepali Congress Party in 1991, although the Communists made a strong showing.

THE NETHERLANDS

Kingdom of the Netherlands
Sovereign: Queen Beatrix (1980)
Premier: Ruud Lubbers (1982)
Area: 16,041 sq mi. (41,548 sq km)
Population (est. mid-1991): 15,000,000 (average annual rate of natural increase: 0.8%); birth rate: 13/1000; infant mortality rate: 6.8/1000; density per square mile: 1,044

Capital: Amsterdam; seat of government: The Hague
Largest cities: Amsterdam, 694,656; Rotterdam, 576,218;
's-Gravenhage, 444,000; Utrecht, 230,738; Eidhoven,
191,500
Monetary unit: Guilder
Language: Dutch
Religions: Roman Catholic, 36%; Protestant, 27%; other,
4%; unaffiliated, 33%
National name: Koninkrijk der Nederlanden
Literacy rate: 99%
Economic summary: Gross national product (1990):
$221.8 billion; $28,000 per capita income; 4.2% real
growth rate. Arable land; 25%. Principal products:
wheat, barley, sugar beets, potatoes, meat and dairy
products. Labor force: 6,955,000; 28.2% in manufacturing and construction. Major products: metal fabrication, electrical machinery and equipment, chemicals,
electronic equipment, petroleum, fishing. Exports:
foodstuffs, natural gas, chemicals, metal products,
textiles. Imports: raw materials, consumer goods,
transportation equipment, food products, crude petroleum. Major trading partners: Germany, Belgium,
France, U.K., U.S.

Geography. The Netherlands, on the coast of the
North Sea, has West Germany to the east and Belgium to the south. It is twice the size of New Jersey.
Part of the great plain of north and west Europe,
the Netherlands has maximum dimensions of 190 by
160 miles (360 by 257 km) and is low and flat except
in Limburg in the southeast, where some hills rise to
300 feet (92 m). About half the country's area is below sea level, making the famous Dutch dikes a requisite to the use of much land. Reclamation of land
from the sea through dikes has continued through recent times.
All drainage reaches the North Sea, and the principal rivers—Rhine, Maas (Meuse), and Schelde—
have their sources outside the country. The Rhine is
the most heavily used waterway in Europe.

Government. The Netherlands and its former colony of the Netherlands Antilles form the Kingdom of
the Netherlands.
The Netherlands is a constitutional monarchy with
a bicameral Parliament. The Upper Chamber has 75
members elected for six years by representative bodies of the provinces, half of the members retiring
every three years. The Lower Chamber has 150 members elected by universal suffrage for four years. The
two Chambers have the right of investigation and in-
terpellation; the Lower Chamber can initiate legislation and amend bills.
The Sovereign, Queen Beatrix Wilhelmina Arm-
gard, born Jan. 31, 1938, was married on March 10,
1966, to Claus von Amsberg, a former West German
diplomat. The marriage drew public criticism because
of the bridegroom's service in the German army during World War II. In 1967, Beatrix gave birth to a
son, Willem-Alexander Claus George Ferdinand, the
first male heir to the throne since 1884. She also has
two other sons, Johan Friso Bernhard Christian David, born in 1968, and Constantijn Christof Frederik
Aschwin, born the next year.

History. Julius Caesar found the low-lying Netherlands inhabited by Germanic tribes—the Nervii, Fri-
sii, and Batavi. The Batavi on the Roman frontier did
not submit to Rome's rule until 13 B.C., and then only
as allies.
A part of Charlemagne's empire in the 8th and 9th
centuries A.D., the area later passed into the hands of

Burgundy and the Austrian Hapsburgs, and finally in
the 16th century came under Spanish rule.
When Philip II of Spain suppressed political liberties and the growing Protestant movement in the
Netherlands, a revolt led by William of Orange broke
out in 1568. Under the Union if Utrecht (1579), the
seven northern provinces became the Republic of the
United Netherlands.
The Dutch East India Company was established in
1602, and by the end of the 17th century Holland
was one of the great sea and colonial powers of Europe.
The nation's independence was not completely established until after the Thirty Years' War (1618–48),
after which the country's rise as a commercial and
maritime power began. In 1814, all the provinces of
Holland and Belgium were merged into one kingdom,
but in 1830 the southern provinces broke away to
form the Kingdom of Belgium. A liberal Constitution
was adopted by the Netherlands in 1848.
In spite of its neutrality in World War II, the Netherlands was invaded by the Nazis in May 1940, and
the East Indies were later taken by the Japanese. The
nation was liberated in May 1945. In 1948, after a
reign of 50 years, Queen Wilhelmina resigned and
was succeeded by her daughter Juliana.
In 1949, after a four-year war, the Netherlands
granted independence to the East Indies, which became the Republic of Indonesia. In 1963, it turned
over the western half of New Guinea to the new nation, ending 300 years of Dutch presence in Asia. Attainment of independence by Suriname on Nov. 25,
1975, left the Dutch Antilles as the Netherlands' only
overseas territory.
Prime Minister Van Agt lost his narrow majority in
elections on May 26, 1981, in which the major issue
was the deployment of U.S. cruise missiles on Dutch
soil. Public opposition to the missiles forced the
Netherlands, along with Belgium, to reverse its position in 1982 despite the Prime Minister's personal
support for the NATO decision to deploy the new
weapons in Western Europe. Van Agt lost his centrist
coalition in May 1982 in a dispute over economic
policy, and was succeeded by Ruud Lubbers as Premier.
Lubbers formed his third government, a center-left
coalition, in November 1989. The Netherlands participated in the Persian Gulf war by sending two marine
frigates to the Gulf.

Netherlands Autonomous Countries

NETHERLANDS ANTILLES

Status: Part of the Kingdom of the Netherlands
Governor: Mr. J. M. Saleh (1990)
Premier: Maria Liberia Peters
Area: 313 sq mi. (800 sq km)
Population (mid-1991): 200,000 (average annual growth
rate: 1.2%); birth rate: 18/1000; infant mortality rate:
13.9/1000
Capital (est. 1978): Willemstad, 152,000
Literacy rate: 95%
Economic summary: Gross national product (1988 est.):
$1.0 billion; $5,500 per capita; 3% real growth rate.
Arable land: 8%. Principal agricultural products: aloes,
sorghum, peanuts. Labor force: 89,000; 28% industry
and commerce (1983). Major industries: oil refining,
tourism. Natural resource: phosphate. Export: petroleum products. Imports: crude petroleum, food. Major
trading partners: U.S., Venezuela.

Geography. The Netherlands Antilles comprise two groups of Caribbean islands 500 miles (805 km) apart: one, about 40 miles (64 km) off the Venezuelan coast, consists of Curaçao (173 sq mi.; 448 sq km), Bonaire (95 sq mi.; 246 sq km), the other, lying to the northeast, consists of three small islands with a total area of 34 square miles (88 sq km).

Government. There is a constitutional government formed by the Governor and Cabinet and an elected Legislative Council. The area has complete autonomy in domestic affairs.

ARUBA

Status: Part of the Kingdom of the Netherlands
Governor: F. B. Tromp
Prime Minister: Nelson Oduber
Area: 75 sq mi. (193 sq km)
Population: (est. mid-1988): 62,322 (average annual growth rate: 0.29%)
Capital: (1986): Oranjestad, 19,800
Literacy rate: 95%
Economic summary: Gross national product (1988 est.): $620 million. Real growth rate: 16.7%. Per capita income, $10,000. Little agriculture. Major industries: tourism, light manufacturing (tobacco, beverages, consumer goods.

Geography. Aruba, an island slightly larger than Washington D.C., lies 18 miles (28.9 km) off the coast of Venezuela in the southern Caribbean.

Government. The governmental structure comprises the Governor, appointed by the Queen for a term of six years; the Legislature consisting of 21 members elected by universal suffrage for terms not exceeding four years; and the Council of Ministers, presided over by the Prime Minister, which holds executive power.

NEW ZEALAND

Sovereign: Queen Elizabeth II
Governor-General: Dame Catherine Tizard (1990)
Prime Minister: Hon. Jon Bolger (1990)
Area: 103,884 sq mi. (269,062 sq km) (excluding dependencies)
Population (est. mid-1991): 3,500,000 (average annual growth rate: 0.9%; birth rate: 17/1000; infant mortality rate: 10.6/1000; density per square mile: 33
Capital: Wellington
Largest cities (1989): Auckland, 850,900; Wellington, 324,600; Christchurch, 301,500
Monetary unit: New Zealand dollar
Languages: English, Maori
Religions: Christian, 81%; none or unspecified, 18%; Hindu, Confucian, and other, 1%
Member of Commonwealth of Nations
Literacy rate: 99%
Economic summary: Gross domestic product (1989): $41 billion; $12,555 per capita; real growth rate 2.4%. Arable land: 2%. Principal products: wool, meat, dairy products, livestock. Labor force: 1,591,900: 19.8% in manufacturing. Major products: processed foods, textiles, machinery, transport equipment, wood and paper products, financial services. Natural resources: forests, natural gas, iron ore, coal, gold. Exports:

meat, dairy products, wool. Imports: consumer goods, petroleum, motor vehicles, industrial equipment. Major trading partners: Japan, Australia, E.C., U.S.

Geography. New Zealand, about 1,250 miles (2,012 km) southeast of Australia, consists of two main islands and a number of smaller, outlying islands so scattered that they range from the tropical to the antarctic. The country is the size of Colorado.

New Zealand's two main components are North Island and South Island, separated by Cook Strait, which varies from 16 to 190 miles (26 to 396 km) in width. North Island (44,281 sq mi.; 114,688 sq km) is 515 miles (829 km) long and volcanic in its south-central part. This area contains many hot springs and beautiful geysers. South Island (58,093 sq mi.; 150,461 sq km) has the Southern Alps along its west coast, with Mount Cook (12,349 ft; 3,764 m) the highest point.

The largest of the outlying islands are the Auckland Islands (234 sq mi.; 606 sq km), Campbell Island (44 sq mi.; 114 sq km), the Antipodes Islands (24 sq mi.; 62 sq km), and the Kermadec Islands (13 sq mi.; 34 sq km).

Government. New Zealand was granted self-government in 1852, a full parliamentary system and ministries in 1856, and dominion status in 1907. The Queen is represented by a Governor-General, and the Cabinet is responsible to a unicameral Parliament of 97 members, who are elected by popular vote for three years.

History. New Zealand was discovered and named in 1642 by Abel Tasman, a Dutch navigator. Captain James Cook explored the islands in 1769. In 1840, Britain formally annexed them.

From the first, the country has been in the forefront in instituting social welfare legislation. It adopted old age pensions (1898); a national child welfare program (1907); social security for the aged, widows, and orphans, along with family benefit payments; minimum wages; a 40-hour week and unemployment and health insurance (1938); and socialized medicine (1941).

In September 1990 Prime Minister Geoffrey Palmer resigned in the face of a threatened no-confidence vote. He was succeeded by Mike Moore. In the general elections of late October the opposition National Party captured 49% of the vote, winning a 39-seat majority in Parliament. Shortly after becoming the new prime minister, Jim Bolger, abandoning campaign promises, in an effort to revive the economy began severe cutbacks in government social benefits, reductions in health-care coverage and introduced legislation to weaken the country's strong labor unions.

Cook Islands and Overseas Territories

The Cook Islands (93 sq mi.; 241 sq km) were placed under New Zealand administration in 1901. They achieved self-governing status in association with New Zealand in 1965. Population in 1978 was about 19,600. The seat of government is on Rarotonga Island.

The island's chief exports are citrus juice, clothing, canned fruit, and pineapple juice. Nearly all of the trade is with New Zealand.

Niue (100 sq mi.; 259 sq km) was formerly administered as part of the Cook Islands. It was placed under separate New Zealand administration in 1901 and achieved self-governing status in association with New Zealand in 1974. The capital is Alofi. Population in 1980 was about 3,300.

Niue exports passion fruit, copra, plaited ware, honey, and limes. Its principal trading partner is New Zealand.

The Ross Dependency (160,000 sq mi.; 414,400 sq km), an Antarctic region, was placed under New Zealand administration in 1923.

Tokelau (4 sq mi.; 10 sq km) was formerly administered as part of the Gilbert and Ellice Islands colony. It was placed under New Zealand administration in 1925. Its population is about 1,600.

NICARAGUA

Republic of Nicaragua
President: Violeta Barrios de Chamorro (1990)
Area: 50,180 sq mi. (130,000 sq km)
Population (mid-1991): 3,900,000 (average annual rate of natural increase: 3.4%); birth rate: 42/1000; infant mortality rate: 62/1000; density per square mile: 77
Capital and largest city (est. 1985): Managua, 682,111
Monetary unit: Cordoba
Language: Spanish
Religion: Roman Catholic, 95%; Protestant, 5%
National name: República de Nicaragua
Literacy rate: 88%
Economic summary: Gross domestic product (1989 est.): $1.7 billion; $470 per capita; real growth rate –5.0% (1988). Arable land: 9%. Principal products: cotton, coffee, sugar cane, rice, corn, beans, cattle. Labor force: 1,086,000; 13% in industry (1986). Major products: processed foods, chemicals, metal products, clothing and textiles, beverages, footwear. Natural resources: timber, fisheries, gold, silver, copper, tungsten, lead, zinc. Exports: coffee, cotton, seafood, bananas, sugar, meat, chemicals. Imports: machinery, chemicals, food, clothing, petroleum. Major trading partners: Mexico, Germany, Japan, France, U.S., Central America, Caribbean.

Geography. Largest but most sparsely populated of the Central American nations, Nicaragua borders on Honduras to the north and Costa Rica to the south. It is slightly larger than New York State.

Nicaragua is mountainous in the west, with fertile valleys. A plateau slopes eastward toward the Caribbean.

Two big lakes—Nicaragua, about 100 miles long (161 km), and Managua, about 38 miles long (61 km)—are connected by the Tipitapa River. The Pacific coast is volcanic and very fertile. The Caribbean coast, swampy and indented, is aptly called the "Mosquito Coast."

Government. After an election on Nov. 4, 1984, Daniel Ortega began a six-year term as President on Jan. 10, 1985. He was defeated in general elections held in Feb. 1990 by Violeta Chamorro.

History. Nicaragua, which established independence in 1838, was first visited by the Spaniards in 1522. The chief of the country's leading Indian tribe at that time was called Nicaragua, from whom the nation derived its name. A U.S. naval force intervened in 1909 after two American citizens had been executed, and a few U.S. Marines were kept in the country from 1912 to 1925. The Bryan-Chamorro Treaty of 1916 (terminated in 1970) gave the U.S. an option on a canal route through Nicaragua, and naval bases. Disorder after the 1924 elections brought in the marines again.

A guerrilla leader, Gen. César Augusto Sandino, began fighting the occupation force in 1927. He fought the U.S. troops until their withdrawal in 1933. They trained Gen. Anastasio (Tacho) Somoza García to head a National Guard. In 1934, Somoza assassinated Sandino and overthrew the Liberal President Juan Batista Sacassa, establishing a military dictatorship with himself as president. He spurred the economic development of the country, meanwhile enriching his family through estates in the countryside and investments in air and shipping lines. On his assassination in 1956, he was succeeded by his son Luis, who alternated with trusted family friends in the presidency until his death in 1967. Another son, Maj. Gen. Anastasio Somoza Debayle, became President in 1967.

Sandinista guerrillas, leftists who took their name from Gen. Sandino, launched an offensive in May 1979. After seven weeks of fighting, Somoza fled the country on July 17, 1979. The Sandinistas assumed power on July 19, promising to maintain a mixed economy, a non-aligned foreign policy, and a pluralist political system. However, the prominence of Cuban President Fidel Castro at the celebration of the first anniversary of the revolution and a five-year delay in holding elections increased debate over the true political color of the Sandinistas.

On Jan. 23, 1981, the Reagan Administration suspended U.S. aid, charging that Nicaragua, with the aid of Cuba and the Soviet Union, was supplying arms to rebels in El Salvador. The Sandinistas denied the charges. Later that year, Nicaraguan guerrillas known as "contras," began a war to overthrow the Sandinistas.

The elections were finally held on Nov. 4, 1984, with Daniel Ortega Saavedra, the Sandinista junta coordinator, winning 63% of the votes cast for President. He began a six-year term on Jan. 10, 1985.

In October 1985, Nicaragua suspended civil liberties and in June 1986, the U.S. Congress voted $100 million in aid, military and non-military, to the contras.

The war intensified in 1986–87, with the resupplied contras establishing themselves inside the country. Negotiations sponsored by the Contadora (neutral Latin American) nations, but a peace plan sponsored by Arias, the Costa Rican president, led to a treaty signed by the Central American leaders in August 1987, that called for an end to outside aid to guerrillas and negotiations between hostile parties. Congress later cut off military aid to the contras. Although the two sides agreed to a cease-fire in March 1988, further negotiations were inconclusive.

In 1989, an accord established a one-year advance in general elections to Feb. 1990. It also called for easing press restrictions and the release of political prisoners and the disbanding of the contras.

Violetta Chamorro, owner of the opposition paper *La Prensa,* led a broad anti-Sandinista coalition to victory in the presidential and legislative elections, ending 11 years of Sandinista rule.

After a year in office Pres. Chamorro found herself besieged. Business groups were dissatisfied with the pace of reforms; Sandinistas with what they regarded as the dismantling of their earlier achievements and they threatened to take up arms again. In Feb. 1991 the president brought the military under her direct command.

NIGER

Republic of Niger
Chief of State: Gen. Ali Saibou (1987)
Area: 489,206 sq mi. (1,267,044 sq km)
Population (est. mid-1991): 8,000,000 (average annual rate of natural increase: 3.3%); birth rate: 51/1000; infant mortality rate: 124/1000; density per square mile: 16
Capital and largest city (est. 1983): Niamey, 399,100
Monetary unit: Franc CFA
Ethnic groups: Hausa, 54%; Djerma and Songhai, 24%; Peul, 11%
Languages: French (official); Hausa, Songhai; Arabic
Religions: Islam, 80%; Animist and Christian, 20%
National name: République du Niger
Literacy rate: 13.9%
Economic summary: Gross domestic product (1988 est.): $2.4 billion; $330 per capita; 7.1% real growth rate. Arable land: 3%. Principal products: peanuts, cotton, livestock, millet, sorghum, cassava, rice. Labor force: 2,500,000 (1982); 90% in agriculture. Major industrial products: uranium, cement, bricks, light industrial products. Natural resources: uranium, coal, iron ore, tin, phosphates. Exports: uranium, cowpeas, livestock, hides, skins. Imports: fuels, machinery, transport equipment, foodstuffs, consumer goods. Major trading partners: France, Nigeria, Japan, Algeria, U.S.

Geography. Niger, in West Africa's Sahara region, is four-fifths the size of Alaska. It is surrounded by Mali, Algeria, Libya, Chad, Nigeria, Benin, and Burkina Faso.

The Niger River in the southwest flows through the country's only fertile area. Elsewhere the land is semiarid.

Government. After a military coup on April 15, 1974, Gen. Seyni Kountché suspended the Constitution and instituted rule by decree. Previously, the President was elected by direct universal suffrage for a five-year term and a National House of Assembly of 50 members was elected for the same term. He died on Nov. 10, 1987, and Col. Saibou, his Chief of Staff, succeeded him.

Demonstrations and strikes in 1990 eventually led to amending the constitution so as to permit a multi-party system. Three underground parties quickly emerged.

History. Niger was incorporated into French West Africa in 1896. There were frequent rebellions, but when order was restored in 1922, the French made the area a colony. In 1958, the voters approved the French Constitution and voted to make the territory an autonomous republic within the French Community. The republic adopted a Constitution in 1959 and the next year withdrew from the Community, proclaiming its independence.

The 1974 army coup ousted President Hamani Diori, who had held office since 1960. He was charged with having mishandled relief for the terrible drought that had devastated Niger and five neighboring sub-Saharan nations for several years. An estimated 2 million people were starving in Niger, but 200,000 tons of imported food, half U.S.-supplied, substantially ended famine conditions by the year's end. The new President, Lt. Col. Seyni Kountché, Chief of Staff of the army, installed a 12-man military government. A predominantly civilian government was formed by Kountché in 1976.

NIGERIA

Federal Republic of Nigeria
President: Gen. Ibrahim Badamasi Babangida (1985)
Area: 356,700 sq mi. (923,853 sq km)
Population (est. mid-1991): 122,500,000 (average annual rate of natural increase: 2.8%); birth rate: 44/1000; infant mortality rate: 119/1000; density per square mile: 343
Capital: Lagos
Largest cities (est. 1983): Lagos, 1,097,000; Ibadan, 1,060,000; Ogbomosho, 527,400; Kano, 487,100
Monetary unit: Naira
Languages: English (official) Hausa, Yoruba, Ibo
Religions: Islam, 50%; Christian, 40%; indigenous, 10%
Member of Commonwealth of Nations
Literacy rate: 42.4%
Economic summary: Gross national product (1989): $30.0 billion; $270 per capita; real growth rate 4%. Arable land: 31%. Principal products: peanuts, rubber, cocoa, grains, fish, yams, cassava, livestock. Labor force: 42,844,000; 19% in industry;. Major products: crude oil, natural gas, coal, tin, processed rubber, cotton, petroleum, hides, textiles, cement, chemicals. Natural resources: petroleum, tin, columbite, iron ore, coal, limestone, lead. Exports: oil, cocoa, palm products, rubber. Imports: consumer goods, capital equipment, raw materials, chemicals. Major trading partners: Western European countries, U.S.

Geography. Nigeria, one-third larger than Texas and black Africa's most populous nation, is situated on the Gulf of Guinea in West Africa. Its neighbors are Benin, Niger, Cameroon, and Chad.

The lower course of the Niger River flows south through the western part of the country into the Gulf of Guinea. Swamps and mangrove forests border the southern coast; inland are hardwood forests.

Government. After 12 years of military rule, a new Constitution re-established democratic government in 1979, but it lasted four years. The military again took over from the democratically elected civilian government on Dec. 31, 1983.

Adopting a U.S.-style constitution the military has pledged to return to the barracks. Two political parties are permitted—the National Republican Convention and the Social Democratic Party. Presidential elections are scheduled for October 1992.

History. Between 1879 and 1914, private colonial developments by the British, with reorganizations of the Crown's interest in the region, resulted in the formation of Nigeria as it exists today. During World War I, native troops of the West African frontier force joined with French forces to defeat the German garrison in the Cameroons.

Nigeria became independent on Oct. 1, 1960.

Organized as a loose federation of self-governing states, the independent nation faced an overwhelming task of unifying a country with 250 ethnic and linguistic groups.

Rioting broke out again in 1966, the military commander was seized, and Col. Yakubu Gowon took power. Also in that year, the Moslem Hausas in the north massacred the predominantly Christian Ibos in the east, many of whom had been driven from the north. Thousands of Ibos took refuge in the Eastern Region. The military government there asked Ibos to return to the region and, in May 1967, the assembly voted to secede from the federation and set up the Republic of Biafra. Civil war broke out.

In January 1970, after 31 months of civil war, Biafra surrendered to the federal government.

Gowon's nine-year rule was ended in 1975 by a bloodless coup that made Army Brigadier Muritala Rufai Mohammed the new chief of state. Mohammed was assassinated the next year 1976 by a group of seven young officers, who failed to seize control of the government.

The return of civilian leadership was established with the election of Alhaji Shehu Shagari, as president in 1979.

A coup on December 31, 1983, restored military rule. The military regime headed by Maj. Gen. Mohammed Buhari was overthrown in a bloodless coup on Aug. 27, 1985, led by Maj. Gen. Ibrahim Babangida, who proclaimed himself president.

He has promised to return to civilian rule in 1992.

NORWAY

Kingdom of Norway
Sovereign: King Harald V (1991)
Prime Minister: Gro Harlem Brundtland (1991)
Area: 125,049 sq mi. (323,877 sq km)
Population (est. 1991): 4,300,000 (average annual growth rate: 0.3%); birth rate: 14/1000; infant mortality rate: 8/1000; density per square mile: 34
Capital: Oslo
Largest cities (1990): Oslo, 457,818; Bergen, 211,866; Trondheim, 137,408; Stavanger, 97,716
Monetary unit: Krone
Language: Norwegian
Religion: Evangelical Lutheran (state), 94%; other Protestant and Roman Catholic, 4%
National name: Kongeriket Norge
Literacy rate: 100%
Economic summary: Gross domestic product (1989 est.): $75.8 billion; $17,900 per capita; 5.7% real growth rate. Arable land: 3%. Principal products: dairy products, livestock, grain, potatoes, furs, wool. Labor force: 2,164,000; 16.6% in mining and manufacturing. Major products: oil and gas, fish, pulp and paper, ships, aluminum, iron, steel, nickel, fertilizers, transportation equipment, hydroelectric power, petrochemicals. Natural resources: fish, timber, hydroelectric power, ores, oil, gas. Exports: oil, natural gas, fish products, ships, pulp and paper, aluminum. Imports: machinery, fuels and lubricants, transportation equipment, chemicals foodstuffs, and clothing. Major trading partners: U.K., Sweden, Germany, U.S., Denmark, Netherlands, Japan.

Geography. Norway is situated in the western part of the Scandinavian peninsula. It extends about 1,100 miles (1,770 km) from the North Sea along the Norwegian Sea to more than 300 miles (483 km) above the Arctic Circle, the farthest north of any European country. It is slightly larger than New Mexico. Sweden borders on most of the eastern frontier, with Finland and the U.S.S.R. in the northeast.

Nearly 70% of Norway is uninhabitable and covered by mountains, glaciers, moors, and rivers. The hundreds of deep fiords that cut into the coastline give Norway an overall oceanfront of more than 12,000 miles (19,312 km). Nearly 50,000 islands off the coast form a breakwater and make a safe coastal shipping channel.

Government. Norway is a constitutional hereditary monarchy. Executive power is vested in the King together with a Cabinet, or Council of State, consisting of a Prime Minister and at least seven other members. The Storting, or Parliament, is composed of 165 members elected by the people under proportional representation. The Storting discusses and votes on political and financial questions, but divides itself into two sections (Lagting and Odelsting) to discuss and pass on legislative matters. The King cannot dissolve the Storting before the expiration of its term.

The sovereign is Harald V, born in 1937, son of Olav V and Princess Martha of Sweden. He succeeded to the throne upon the death of his father in January 1991. He married Sonja Haraldsen, a daughter of a merchant, in 1968.

History. Norwegians, like the Danes and Swedes, are of Teutonic origin. The Norsemen, also known as Vikings, ravaged the coasts of northwestern Europe from the 8th to the 11th century.

In 1815, Norway fell under the control of Sweden. The union of Norway, inhabited by fishermen, sailors, merchants, and peasants, and Sweden, an aristocratic country of large estates and tenant farmers, was not a happy one, but it lasted for nearly a century. In 1905, the Norwegian Parliament arranged a peaceful separation and invited a Danish prince to the Norwegian throne—King Haakon VII. A treaty with Sweden provided that all disputes be settled by arbitration and that no fortifications be erected on the common frontier.

When World War I broke out, Norway joined with Sweden and Denmark in a decision to remain neutral and to cooperate in the joint interest of the three countries. In World War II, Norway was invaded by the Germans on April 9, 1940. It resisted for two months before the Nazis took over complete control. King Haakon and his government fled to London, where they established a government-in-exile. Maj. Vidkun Quisling, whose name is now synonymous with traitor or fifth columnist, was the most notorious Norwegian collaborator with the Nazis. He was executed by the Norwegians on Oct. 24, 1945.

Despite severe losses in the war, Norway recovered quickly. The country led the world in social experimentation. A neighbor of the U.S.S.R., Norway sought to retain good relations with the Soviet Union without losing its identity with the West. It entered the North Atlantic Treaty Organization in 1949.

The Conservative government of Jan Syse resigned in October 1990 over the issue of Norway's future relationship to the E.C. A minority Labor government headed by Gro Brundtland was installed a few days later. The new government promised to be "flexible" in negotiating with the E.C., including allowing changes in the so-called concession laws, which protect Norwegian sovereignty over domestic resources and industry. Norway is a member of the European Free Trade Association.

Dependencies of Norway

Svalbard (24,208 sq mi.; 62,700 sq km), in the Arctic Ocean about 360 miles north of Norway, consists of the Spitsbergen group and several smaller islands, including Bear Island, Hope Island, King Charles Land, and White Island (or Gillis Land). It came under Norwegian administration in 1925. The population in 1986 was 3,942 of which 1,387 were Norwegians.

Bouvet Island (23 sq mi.; 60 sq km), in the South Atlantic about 1,600 miles south-southwest of the Cape of Good Hope, came under Norwegian administration in 1928.

Jan Mayen Island (147 sq mi.; 380 sq km), in the Arctic Ocean between Norway and Greenland, came under Norwegian administration in 1929.

Peter I Island (96 sq mi.; 249 sq km), lying off Antarctica in the Bellinghausen Sea, came under Norwegian administration in 1931.

Queen Maud Land, a section of Antarctica, came under Norwegian administration in 1939.

OMAN

Sultanate of Oman
Sultan: Qabus Bin Said (1970)
Area: 82,030 sq mi. (212,458 sq km)[1]
Population (est. mid-1991): 1,600,000 (average annual rate of natural increase: 3.8%); birth rate: 46/1000; infant mortality rate: 40/1000; density per square mile: 19
Capital and largest city (est. 1981): Muscat, 70,000
Monetary unit: Omani rial
Language: Arabic (official); also English and Indian languages
Religion: Islam, 86%
National name: Saltonat Uman
Literacy rate: 20%
Economic summary: Gross domestic product (1987 est.): $7.8 billion; $6,006 per capita; –3.0% real growth rate. Principal agricultural products: dates, fruit, cereal, livestock. Labor force: 430,000; 60% in agriculture. Major industries: petroleum drilling, fishing, construction. Natural resources: oil, marble, copper, limestone. Exports: oil. Imports: machinery and transport equipment, food, manufactured goods, livestock, lubricants. Major trading partners: U.K., U.S., Germany, Japan, Korea, Thailand.

1. Excluding the Kuria Muria Islands.

Geography. Oman is a 1,000-mile-long (1,700-km) coastal plain at the southeastern tip of the Arabian peninsula lying on the Arabian Sea and the Gulf of Oman. The interior is a plateau. The country is the size of Kansas.

Government. The Sultan of Oman (formerly called Muscat and Oman), an absolute monarch, is assisted by a council of ministers, six specialized councils, a consultative council and personal advisers.
There are no political parties.

History. Although Oman is an independent state under the rule of the Sultan, it has been under British protection since the early 19th century.
Muscat, the capital of the geographical area known as Oman, was occupied by the Portuguese from 1508 to 1648. Then it fell to Persian princes and later was regained by the Sultan.
In a palace coup on July 23, 1970, the Sultan, Sa'id bin Taimur, who had ruled since 1932, was overthrown by his son, who promised to establish a modern government and use new-found wealth to aid the people of this very isolated state.
The formation of a new consultative council, ex-

cluding government officials, was announced in November 1990.

PAKISTAN

Islamic Republic of Pakistan
President: Gulam Ishaq Khan (1988)
Prime Minister: Mian Mohammad Nawaz Sharif (1990)
Area: 310,400 sq mi. (803,936 sq km)[1]
Population (est. mid-1991): 117,500,000 (average annual growth rate: 3%); birth rate: 43/1000; infant mortality rate: 112/1000; density per square mile: 379
Capital (1981 census): Islamabad, 201,000
Largest cities (1981 census for metropolitan area): Karachi, 5,208,100; Lahore, 2,952,700; Faisalabad, (Lyallpur) 1,920,000; Rawalpindi, 920,000; Hyderabad, 795,000
Monetary unit: Pakistan rupee
Principal languages: Urdu (national), English (official), Punjabi, Sindhi, Pashtu, and Baluchi
Religions: Islam, 97%; Hindu, Christian, Buddhist, Parsi
Literacy rate: 26%
Economic summary: Gross national product (FY89): $43.2 billion; $409 per capita; 5.1% real growth rate. Arable land: 26%. Principal products: wheat, rice, cotton, sugarcane. Labor force: 28,900,000; 13% in mining and manufacturing. Major products: cotton textiles, processed foods, petroleum products, construction materials. Natural resources: natural gas, limited petroleum, iron ore. Exports: cotton, rice, textiles, clothing. Imports: edible oil, crude oil, machinery, chemicals, transport equipment. Major trading partners: U.S., E.C., Japan.

1. Excluding Kashmir and Jammu.

Geography. Pakistan is situated in the western part of the Indian subcontinent, with Afghanistan and Iran on the west, India on the east, and the Arabian Sea on the south.
Nearly twice the size of California, Pakistan consists of towering mountains, including the Hindu Kush in the west, a desert area in the east, the Punjab plains in the north, and an expanse of alluvial plains. The 1,000-mile-long (1,609 km) Indus River flows through the country from the Kashmir to the Arabian Sea.

Government. Pakistan is a federal republic with a bicameral legislature—a 217-member National Assembly and an 87-member Senate.

History. Pakistan was one of the two original successor states to British India. For almost 25 years following independence in 1947, it consisted of two separate regions East and West Pakistan, but now comprises only the western sector. It consists of Sind, Baluchistan, the former North-West Frontier Province, western Punjab, the princely state of Bahawalpur, and several other smaller native states.
The British became the dominant power in the region in 1797 following Lord Clive's military victory, but rebellious tribes kept the northwest in turmoil. In the northeast, the formation of the Moslem League in 1906 estranged the Moslems from the Hindus. In 1930, the league, led by Mohammed Ali Jinnah, demanded creation of a Moslem state wherever Moslems were in the majority. He supported Britain during the war. Afterward, the league received almost a unanimous Moslem vote in 1946 and Britain agreed to the formation of Pakistan as a separate dominion.

Pakistan was proclaimed a republic March 23, 1956. Iskander Mirza, then Governor General, was elected Provisional President and H. S. Suhrawardy became the first non-Moslem League Prime Minister.

The election of 1970 set the stage for civil war when Sheik Muuibur told East Pakistanis to stop paying taxes to the central government. West Pakistan troops moved in and fighting began. The independent state of Bangladesh, or Bengali nation, was proclaimed March 26, 1971.

The intervention of Indian troops protected the new state and brought President Yahya Kahn down. Bhutto took over and accepted Bangladesh as an independent entity.

Diplomatically, 1976 saw the resumption of formal relations between India and Pakistan.

Pakistan's first elections under civilian rule took place in March 1977 and provoked bitter opposition protest when Bhutto's party was declared to have won 155 of the 200 elected seats in the 216-member National Assembly. A rising tide of violent protest and political deadlock led to a military takeover on July 5. Gen. Mohammed Zia ul-Haq became Chief Martial Law Administrator.

Bhutto was tried and convicted for the 1974 murder of a political opponent, and despite worldwide protests was executed on April 4, 1979, touching off riots by his supporters. Zia declared himself President on Sept. 16, 1978, a month after Fazel Elahi Chaudhry left office upon the completion of his 5-year term.

A measure of representative government was restored with the election of a new National Assembly in February 1985, although leaders of opposition parties were banned from the election and it was unclear what powers Zia would yield to the legislature.

On December 30, 1985, Zia ended martial law. In May 1988, Zia deposed Prime Minister Mohammed Junejo and dissolved the National Assembly on the grounds that they had not moved quickly enough to establish Islamic law or deal with ethnic strife.

On August 19, 1988, President Zia was killed in a midair explosion of a Pakistani Air Force plane.

Elections at the end of 1988 brought longtime Zia opponent Benazir Bhutto, daughter of Zulfikar Bhutto, into office as Prime Minister.

In August 1990, Pakistan's President dismissed Prime Minister Bhutto on charges of corruption and incompetence and dissolved parliament. Sharif's coalition, the Islamic Democratic Alliance, won the elections of October 1990. Fulfilling a campaign promise, parliament decreed in May 1991 that Islamic law would take precedence over civil legislation. The opposition charged that the bill is undemocratic and would promote sectarianism.

PANAMA

Republic of Panama
President: Guillermo Endara Galimany (1990)
Area: 29,761 sq mi. (77,082 sq km)
Population (est. mid-1991): 2,500,000 (average annual rate of natural increase: 2.1%); birth rate: 26/1000; infant mortality rate: 22/1000; density per square mile: 83
Capital and largest city (est. 1987): Panama City, 440,000
Monetary unit: Balboa
Language: Spanish (official); many bilingual in English
Religions: Roman Catholic, over 93%; Protestant, 6%
National name: República de Panamá

Literacy rate: 90%
Economic summary: Gross domestic product (1989 est.): $3.9 billion; $1,648 per capita; real growth rate –7.5%. Arable land: 6%. Principal products: bananas, corn, sugar, rice, coffee. Labor force: 770,472 (1987); 10.5% in manufacturing and mining. Major industrial products: refined petroleum, sugar, cement, paper products. Natural resources: copper, mahogany, shrimp. Exports: bananas, refined petroleum, sugar, shrimp, coffee. Imports: petroleum, manufactured goods, machinery and transportation equipment, food. Major trading partners: U.S., Central America and the Caribbean, Western Europe, Mexico.

Geography. The southernmost of the Central American nations, Panama is south of Costa Rica and north of Colombia. The Panama Canal bisects the isthmus at its narrowest and lowest point, allowing passage from the Caribbean Sea to the Pacific Ocean.

Panama is slightly smaller than South Carolina. It is marked by a chain of volcanic mountains in the west, moderate hills in the interior, and a low range on the east coast. There are extensive forests in the fertile Caribbean area.

Government. Panama is a centralized republic. The executive power is vested in the president and two vice presidents who exercise power jointly with a cabinet of 12 ministers of state appointed by the president. Presidents and vice presidents are elected for five-year terms and may not succeed themselves. The legislative function is exercised through the National Assembly. The legislators are elected for five-year terms by direct vote and can be reelected.

History. Visited by Columbus in 1502 on his fourth voyage and explored by Balboa in 1513, Panama was the principal transshipment point for Spanish treasure and supplies to and from South and Central America in colonial days. In 1821, when Central America revolted against Spain, Panama joined Colombia, which already had declared its independence. For the next 82 years, Panama attempted unsuccessfully to break away from Colombia. After U.S. proposals for canal rights over the narrow isthmus had been rejected by Colombia, Panama proclaimed its independence with U.S. backing in 1903.

For canal rights in perpetuity, the U.S. paid Panama $10 million and agreed to pay $250,000 each year, increased to $430,000 after devaluation of the U.S. dollar in 1933 and was further increased under a revised treaty signed in 1955. In exchange, the U.S. got the Canal Zone—a 10-mile-wide strip across the isthmus—and a considerable degree of influence in Panama's affairs.

In 1968, Dr. Arnulfo Arias was elected President for the third time in three decades. And for the third time, he was thrown out of office by the military. A two-man junta, Col. José M. Pinilla and Col. Bolivar Urrutia, took control. They were ousted by Gen. Omar Torrijos Herrera, who named a new junta, with Demetrio Lakas Bahas as President.

Panama and the U.S. agreed in 1974 to negotiate the eventual reversion of the canal to Panama, despite strongly expressed opposition in the U.S. Congress. The texts of two treaties—one governing the transfer of the canal and the other guaranteeing its neutrality after transfer—were negotiated by August 1977 and were signed by Pres. Omar Torrijos Herara and President Carter in Washington on September 7. A Panamanian referendum approved the treaties by more than two thirds on October 23, but further changes were insisted upon by the U.S. Senate.

The principal change was a reservation specifying that despite the neutrality treaty's specification that only Panama shall maintain forces in its territory after transfer of the canal Dec. 31, 1999, the U.S. should have the right to use military force to keep the canal operating if it should become obstructed. The Senate approved the treaties in March-April 1978. On June 16, Carter and Torrijos exchanged instruments of ratification in Panama City.

The death of Torrijos in a plane crash on July 31, 1981, left a power vacuum. President Aristides Royo, named by Torrijos in 1978 to a six-year term, clashed with the leadership of the National Guard and was unable to harmonize factions within the ruling Democratic Revolutionary Party. On July 30, 1982, Royo resigned in favor of Vice President Ricardo de la Espriella.

Nicolas Ardito Barletta, Panama's first directly elected President in 16 years, was inaugurated on Oct. 11, 1984, for a five-year term. He lacked the necessary support to solve the country's economic crisis and resigned September 28, 1985. He was replaced by Vice President Eric Arturo Delvalle.

In June 1986, reports surfaced that the behind-the-scenes strongman, Gen. Manuel Noriega, was involved in drug trafficking and the murder of an opposition leader. In 1987, Noriega was accused by his ex-Chief of Staff of assassinating Torrijos in 1981. He was indicted in the U.S. for drug trafficking but when Delvalle attempted to fire him, he forced the National Assembly to replace Delvalle with Manuel Solis Palma. Despite protests and U.S. economic sanctions, Noriega remained in power.

The crisis continued when Noriega called presidential elections for when the current term expired. Despite massive fraud by Noriega, the opposition seemed headed to a landslide. Noriega annulled the elections and suppressed protests by the opposition.

In December 1989, the Assembly named Noriega the "maximum leader" and declared the U.S. and Panama to be in a state of war. A further series of incidents led to a U.S. invasion overthrowing Noriega, who was brought to the U.S. to stand trial for drug trafficking. Guillermo Endara, who probably would have won the election suppressed by Noriega, was instated as President.

A military revolt in December 1990 was easily suppressed, although the leaders eluded capture. The U.S. has pledged to use its troops in Panama if necessary to foil any coup attempt. In May 1991, the Christian Democratic Party, until then largest in the National Assembly, quit the government and went into opposition.

Panama Canal. First conceived by the Spaniards in 1524, when King Charles V of Spain ordered a survey of a waterway across the Isthmus, a construction concession was granted by the Colombian government in 1878 to St. Lucien N. B. Wyse, representing a French company. Two years later, the French Canal Company, inspired by Ferdinand de Lesseps, began construction of what was to have been a sea-level canal. The effort ended in bankruptcy nine years later and the United States ultimately paid the French $40 million for their rights and assets.

The U.S. project, built on territory controlled by the United States, and calling for the creation of an interior lake connected to both oceans by locks, got under way in 1904. Completed in 1914, the Canal is 50.7 miles long and lifts ships 85 feet above sea level through a series of three locks on the Pacific and Atlantic sides. Enlarged in later years, each lock now measures 1,000 feet in length, 110 feet in width, and 40 feet in depth of water.

PAPUA NEW GUINEA

Sovereign: Queen Elizabeth II
Governor General: Sir Serei Eri
Prime Minister: Rabbie Namaliu (1988)
Area: 178,704 sq mi. (462,840 sq km)
Population (est. mid-1991): 3,900,000 (average annual rate of natural increase: 2.3%); birth rate: 34/1000; infant mortality rate: 59/1000; density per square mile: 22
Capital and largest city (est. 1986): Port Moresby, 145,000
Monetary unit: Kina
Languages: English, Melanesian pidgin, Hiri Motu, and 717 distinct native languages
Religions: over half Christian, remainder indigenous
Member of Commonwealth of Nations
Literacy rate: 32%
Economic summary: Gross domestic product (1988 est.): $3.26 billion; $890 per capita; 1.2% real growth rate. Principal products: coffee, copra, palm oil, cocoa, tea, coconuts. Labor force (1980): 1,660,000; 9% industry and commerce. Major industrial products: coconut oil, plywood, wood chips, gold, silver. Natural resources: copper, gold, silver, timber, natural gas. Exports: gold, copper, coffee, palm oil, copra, timber. Imports: food, machinery, transport equipment, fuels. Major trading partners: Australia, U.K., Japan, Germany, Singapore, New Zealand, U.S.

Geography. Papua New Guinea occupies the eastern half of the island of New Guinea, just north of Australia, and many outlying islands. The Indonesian province of Irian Jaya is to the west. To the north and east are the islands of Manus, New Britain, New Ireland, and Bougainville, all part of Papua New Guinea.

Papua New Guinea is about one-tenth larger than California. Its mountainous interior has only recently been explored. The high-plateau climate is temperate, in contrast to the tropical climate of the coastal plains. Two major rivers, the Sepik and the Fly, are navigable for shallow-draft vessels.

Government. Papua New Guinea attained independence Sept. 16, 1975, ending a United Nations trusteeship under the administration of Australia. Parliamentary democracy was established by a Constitution that invests power in a 109-member national legislature.

History. The eastern half of New Guinea was first visited by Spanish and Portuguese explorers in the 16th century, but a permanent European presence was not established until 1884, when Germany declared a protectorate over the northern coast and Britain took similar action in the south. Both nations formally annexed their protectorates and, in 1901, Britain transferred its rights to a newly independent Australia. Australian troops invaded German New Guinea in World War I and retained control under a League of Nations mandate that eventually became a United Nations trusteeship, incorporating a territorial government in the southern region, known as Papua.

Australia granted limited home rule in 1951 and, in 1964, organized elections for the first House of Assembly. Autonomy in internal affairs came nine years later.

In February 1990 guerrillas of the Bougainville Revolutionary Army (BRA) attacked plantations, forcing the evacuation of numerous workers. In May the BRA declared Bougainville's independence, whereupon the government blockaded the island until January 1991.

PARAGUAY

Republic of Paraguay
President: Gen. Andres Rodriguez (1989)
Area: 157,047 sq mi. (406,752 sq km)
Population (est. mid-1991): 4,400,000 (average annual rate of natural increase: 2.8%); birth rate: 34/1000; infant mortality rate: 41/1000; density per square mile: 28
Capital and largest city (est. 1985): Asunción, 477,000
Monetary unit: Guaraní
Languages: Spanish (official), Guaraní
Religion: Roman Catholic, 90%
National name: República del Paraguay
Literacy rate: 81%
Economic summary: Gross domestic product (1989 est.): $8.9 billion; $1,970 per capita; 5.2% real growth rate. Arable land: 20%. Principal products: soybeans, cotton, timber, cassava, tobacco, corn, rice, sugar cane. Labor force: 1,300,000; 34% in industry and commerce. Major products: packed meats, crushed oilseeds, beverages, textiles, light consumer goods, cement. Natural resources: iron ore, timber, manganese, limestone, hydropower. Exports: cotton, soybeans, meat products, timber, coffee, tung oil. Imports: fuels and lubricants, machinery and motors, motor vehicles, beverages, tobacco, foodstuffs. Major trading partners: Argentina, Brazil, U.S., E.C., Japan.

Geography. California-size Paraguay is surrounded by Brazil, Bolivia, and Argentina in south central South America. Eastern Paraguay, between the Paraná and Paraguay Rivers, is upland country with the thickest population settled on the grassy slope that inclines toward the Paraguay River. The greater part of the Chaco region to the west is covered with marshes, lagoons, dense forests, and jungles.

Government. The President is elected by popular vote for five years. The legislature is bicameral, consisting of a Senate of 30 members and a Chamber of Representatives of 60 members. There is also a Council of State, whose members are nominated by the government.

History. In 1526 and again in 1529, Sebastian Cabot explored Paraguay when he sailed up the Paraná and Paraguay Rivers. From 1608 until their expulsion from the Spanish dominions in 1767, the Jesuits maintained an extensive establishment in the south and east of Paraguay. In 1811, Paraguay revolted against Spanish rule and became a nominal republic under two Consuls.

Actually, Paraguay was governed by three dictators during the first 60 years of independence. The third, Francisco López, waged war against Brazil and Argentina in 1865–70, a conflict in which the male population was almost wiped out. A new Constitution in 1870, designed to prevent dictatorships and internal strife, failed to do so, and not until 1912 did a period of comparative economic and political stability begin.

After World War II, politics became particularly unstable.

Stroessner ruled under a state of siege until 1965, when the dictatorship was relaxed and exiles returned. The Constitution was revised in 1967 to permit Stroessner to be re-elected.

Although oil exploration begun by U.S. companies in the Chaco boreal in 1974 was fruitless, Paraguay found prosperity in another form of energy when construction started in 1978 on the Itaipu Dam on the Parana River as a joint Paraguayan-Brazilian project.

The Stroessner regime was criticized by the U.S. State Department during the Carter administration as a violator of human rights, but unlike Argentina and Uruguay, Paraguay did not suffer cuts in U.S. military aid.

The government was forced to devalue the guarani as a condition for IMF help for the ailing economy.

Stroessner was overthrown by an army leader, Gen. Andres Rodriguez, in 1989. Rodriguez won in Paraguay's first multi-candidate elections in decades. He has promised to hand over power to an elected civilian successor in 1993.

Foreign Minister Luis Argaña was dismissed following condemnation of a speech in July 1990 in which he said that the ruling party would hold on to political power by a new revolution if necessary.

PERU

Republic of Peru
President: Alberto Fujimori (1990)
Premier: Dr. Carlos Torres y Torres Lara (1991)
Area: 496,222 sq mi. (1,285,216 sq km)
Population (est. mid-1991): 22,000,000 (average annual rate of natural increase: 2.3%); birth rate: 31/1000; infant mortality rate: 76/1000; density per square mile: 44
Capital: Lima
Largest cities (est. 1987): Lima, 5,330,800; Arequipa, 572,000; Callao, 545,000; Trujillo, 476,000; Chiclayo, 379,000
Monetary unit: Nuevo Sol (1991)
Languages: Spanish, Quéchua, Aymara, and other native languages
Religion: Roman Catholic
National name: República del Perú
Literacy rate: est. 80%
Economic summary: Gross domestic product (1989 est.): $18.9 billion; $880 per capita; real growth rate –12.2%. Arable land: 3%. Principal products: wheat, potatoes, beans, rice, sugar, cotton, coffee. Labor force: 6,800,000 (1986); 19% in industry (1988 est.). Major products: processed minerals, fish meal, refined petroleum, textiles. Natural resources: silver, gold, iron, copper, fish, petroleum, timber. Exports: copper, fish products, cotton, sugar, coffee, lead, silver, zinc, oil, iron ore. Imports: machinery, foodstuffs, chemicals, pharmaceuticals. Major trading partners: U.S., Japan, Western European and Latin American countries.

Geography. Peru, in western South America, extends for nearly 1,500 miles (2,414 km) along the Pacific Ocean. Colombia and Ecuador are to the north, Brazil and Bolivia to the east, and Chile to the south.

Five-sixths the size of Alaska, Peru is divided by the Andes Mountains into three sharply differentiated zones. To the west is the coastline, much of it arid, extending 50 to 100 miles (80 to 160 km) inland. The mountain area, with peaks over 20,000 feet (6,096 m), lofty plateaus, and deep valleys, lies centrally. Beyond the mountains to the east is the heavily forested slope leading to the Amazonian plains.

Government. The President, elected by universal suffrage for a five-year term, holds executive power. A Senate of 60 members and a Chamber of Deputies of 180 members, both elected for five-year terms, share legislative power.

History. Peru was once part of the great Incan empire and later the major vice-royalty of Spanish South America. It was conquered in 1531–33 by Francisco Pizarro. On July 28, 1821, Peru proclaimed its independence, but the Spanish were not finally defeated until 1824. For a hundred years thereafter, revolutions were frequent, and a new war was fought with Spain in 1864–66.

Peru emerged from 20 years of dictatorship in 1945 with the inauguration of President José Luis Bustamente y Rivero after the first free election in many decades. But he served for only three years and was succeeded in turn by Gen. Manual A. Odria, Manuel Prado y Ugarteche, and Fernando Belaúnde Terry. On Oct. 3, 1968, Belaúnde was overthrown by Gen. Juan Velasco Alvarado.

Velasco nationalized the nation's second biggest bank and turned two large newspapers over to Marxists in 1970, but he also allowed a new agreement with a copper-mining consortium of four American firms.

In 1975, Velasco was replaced in a bloodless coup by his Premier, Gen. Francisco Morales Bermudez, who promised to restore civilian government. In elections held on May 18, 1980, Belaunde Terry, the last previous civilian President and the candidate of the conservative parties that have traditionally ruled Peru, was elected President again. By the end of his five-year term in 1985, the country was in the midst of acute economic and social crisis.

But Peru's fragile democracy survived this period of stress and when he left office in 1985 Belaunde Terry was the first elected President to turn over power to a constitutionally elected successor since 1945.

In the June run-off to the April 1990 elections Alberto Fujimori won 56.5% of the vote. A newcomer to national politics, Fujimori is the son of Japanese immigrants. The new Cabinet included representatives from the entire political spectrum as well as the military. Nevertheless, two guerrilla groups working separately declared war on the government. Adding to its problems Peru faced a cholera epidemic in 1991, which struck more than 200,000 people, devastating the tourist industry and straining the economy further.

THE PHILIPPINES

Republic of the Philippines
President: Corazon C. Aquino (1986)
Vice President: Salvador H. Laurel (1986)
Area: 115,830 sq mi. (300,000 sq km)
Population (est. mid-1991): 62,300,000 (average annual rate of natural increase: 2.6%); birth rate: 33/1000; infant mortality rate: 54/1000; density per square mile: 538
Capital: Manila
Largest cities (est. 1984): Manila, 1,728,400[1]; Quezon City, 1,326,000; Cebu, 552,200
Monetary unit: Peso
Languages: Filipino (based on Tagalog), English; regional languages: Tagalog, Ilocano, Cebuano, others
Religions: Roman Catholic, 83%; Islam, 3%; Protestant, 9%; Buddhist and other, 3%
National name: Republika ng Pilipinas
Literacy rate: 88% (est.)
Economic summary: Gross domestic product (1989): $40.5 billion; $625 per capita; 5.2% real growth rate. Arable land: 26%. Principal products: rice, corn, coco-nuts, sugar cane, bananas, pineapple. Labor force: 22,889,000; 20% in industry and commerce. Major products: textiles, pharmaceuticals, chemicals, food processing, electronics assembly. Natural resources: forests, crude oil, metallic and non-metallic minerals. Exports: electrical equipment, coconut products, chemicals, logs and lumber, copper concentrates, nickel. Imports: petroleum, industrial equipment, raw materials. Major trading partners: U.S., Japan, E.C.

1. Metropolitan area population is 7,500,000.

Geography. The Philippine Islands are an archipelago of over 7,000 islands lying about 500 miles (805 km) off the southeast coast of Asia. The overall land area is comparable to that of Arizona. The northernmost island, Y'Ami, is 65 miles (105 km) from Taiwan, while the southernmost, Saluag, is 40 miles (64 km) east of Borneo.

Only about 7% of the islands are larger than one square mile, and only one third have names. The largest are Luzon in the north (40,420 sq mi.; 104,687 sq km), Mindanao in the south (36,537 sq mi.; 94,631 sq km), Samar (5,124 sq mi.; 13,271 sq km).

The islands are of volcanic origin, with the larger ones crossed by mountain ranges. The highest peak is Mount Apo (9,690 ft; 2,954 m) on Mindanao.

Government. On February 2, 1987, the Filipino people voted for a new Constitution that established a 24-seat Senate and a 250-seat House of Representatives and gave President Aquino a six-year term. It limits the powers of the President, who can't be re-elected.

History. Fernando Magellan, the Portuguese navigator in the service of Spain, discovered the Philippines in 1521. Twenty-one years later, a Spanish exploration party named the group of islands in honor of Prince Philip, later Philip II of Spain. Spain retained possession of the islands for the next 350 years.

The Philippines were ceded to the U.S. in 1899 by the Treaty of Paris after the Spanish-American War. Meanwhile, the Filipinos, led by Emilio Aguinaldo, had declared their independence. They continued guerrilla warfare against U.S. troops until the capture of Aguinaldo in 1901. By 1902, peace was established except among the Moros.

The first U.S. civilian Governor-General was William Howard Taft (1901–04). The Jones Law (1916) provided for the establishment of a Philippine Legislature composed of an elective Senate and House of Representatives. The Tydings-McDuffie Act (1934) provided for a transitional period until 1946, at which time the Philippines would become completely independent.

Under a Constitution approved by the people of the Philippines in 1935, the Commonwealth of the Philippines came into being, with Manuel Quezon y Molina as President.

On Dec. 8, 1941, the Philippines were invaded by Japanese troops. Following the fall of Bataan and Corregidor, Quezon established a government-in-exile, which he headed until his death in 1944. He was succeeded by Vice President Sergio Osmeña.

U.S. forces led by Gen. Douglas MacArthur reinvaded the Philippines in October 1944 and, after the liberation of Manila in February 1945, Osmeña re-established the government.

The Philippines achieved full independence on July 4, 1946. Manual A. Roxas y Acuña was elected first president. Subsequent presidents have been Elpidio Quirino (1948–53), Ramón Magsaysay (1953–57).

Carlos P. García (1957–61), Diosdado Macapagal (1961–65), Ferdinand E. Marcos (1965–86).

The Philippines was one of six nations criticized by the U.S. State Department for human-rights violations in a report made public in 1977, although the department recommended continuing aid because of the importance of U.S. bases in the Philippines.

Marcos, who had freed the last of the national leaders still in detention, former Senator Benigno S. Aquino, Jr., in 1980 and permitted him to go to the United States, ended eight years of martial law on January 17, 1981.

Despite having been warned by First Lady Imelda Marcos that he risked being killed if he came back, opposition leader Aquino returned to the Philippines from self-exile on Aug. 21, 1983. He was shot to death as he was being escorted from his plane by military police at Manila International Airport. The government contended the assassin was a small-time hoodlum allegedly hired by communists, who was in turn shot dead by Filipino troops, but there was widespread suspicion that the Marcos government was involved in the murder.

The assassination sparked huge anti-government rallies and violent clashes between demonstrators and police, which continued intermittently through most of 1984, and helped the fragmented opposition parties score substantial gains in the May 14, 1984, elections for a National Assembly with greater power than a previous interim parliament.

On Jan. 23, 1985, one of Marcos' closest associates, Gen. Fabian C. Ver, the armed forces chief of staff, and 25 others were charged with the 1983 assassination of Aquino. Their trial dragged on through most of the year, with defense attorneys charging the evidence against Ver and the other defendants was fabricated.

In an attempt to re-secure American support, Marcos set Presidential elections for Feb. 7, 1986. After Ver's acquittal, and with the support of the Catholic church, Corazon Aquino, widow of Benigno Aquino, declared her candidacy. Marcos was declared the winner but the vote was widely considered to be rigged and anti-Marcos protests continued. The defection of Defense Minister Juan Enrile and Lt. Gen. Fidel Ramos signaled an end of military support for Marcos, who fled into exile in the U.S. on Feb. 25, 1986.

The Aquino government survived coup attempts by Marcos supporters and other right-wing elements including one, in November, by Enrile. Legislative elections on May 11, 1987, gave pro-Aquino candidates a large majority.

Negotiations on renewal of leases for U.S. military bases threatened to sour relations between the two countries. The volcanic eruptions from Mount Pinatubo, however, severely damaged Clark Air Base. In July 1991 the U.S. decided simply to abandon the base.

President Aquino faced a difficult year passing from one crisis or problem to another compounded by international events and natural disasters.

POLAND

Republic of Poland
President: Lech Walesa (1990)
Prime Minister: Jan Olszewski (1991)
Area: 120,727 sq mi. (312,683 sq km)
Population (est. mid-1991): 38,200,000 (average annual rate of natural increase: .5%); birth rate: 15/1000; infant mortality rate: 15.9/1000; density per square mile: 316

Capital: Warsaw
Largest cities (est. 1986): Warsaw, 1,659,400; Lodz, 847,900; Krakow, 740,100; Wroclaw, 637,200; Poznan, 575,100; Gdansk, 464,600; Szczecin, 392,300
Monetary unit: Zloty
Language: Polish
Religions: Roman Catholic, 95%; Russian Orthodox, Protestant, and other, 5%
National name: Rzeczpospolita Polska
Literacy rate: 98%
Economic summary: Gross national product (1989 est.): $172.4 billion; $4,565 per capita; –1.6% real growth rate. Arable land: 46%. Principal products: rye, rapeseed, potatoes, hogs and other livestock. Labor force: 17,128,000 (1988); 36.5% in industry and construction. Major products: iron and steel, chemicals, textiles, processed foods, machine building. Natural resources: coal, sulfur, copper, natural gas. Exports: coal, machinery and equipment, industrial products. Imports: machinery and equipment, fuels, raw materials, agricultural and food products. Major trading partners: U.S.S.R., Germany, Czechoslovakia.

Geography. Poland, a country the size of New Mexico in north central Europe, borders on East Germany to the west, Czechoslovakia to the south, and the U.S.S.R. to the east. In the north is the Baltic Sea.

Most of the country is a plain with no natural boundaries except the Carpathian Mountains in the south and the Oder and Neisse Rivers in the east. Other major rivers, which are important to commerce, are the Vistula, Warta, and Bug.

Government. The 1952 Constitution describes Poland as the Republic of Poland. The supreme organ of state authority is the Sejm (Parliament), which is composed of 460 members elected for four years.

A 100-seat Senate was established in 1989. A new constitution is scheduled to be passed in 1992, the 200th anniversary of Poland's pre-partition constitution.

History. Little is known about Polish history before the 11th century, when King Boleslaus I (the Brave) ruled over Bohemia, Saxony, and Moravia. Meanwhile, the Teutonic knights of Prussia conquered part of Poland and barred the latter's access to the Baltic. The knights were defeated by Wladislaus II at Tannenberg in 1410 and became Polish vassals, and Poland regained a Baltic shoreline. Poland reached the peak of power between the 14th and 16th centuries, scoring military successes against the Russians and Turks. In 1683, John III (John Sobieski) turned back the Turkish tide at Vienna.

An elective monarchy failed to produce strong central authority, and Prussia and Austria were able to carry out a first partition of the country in 1772, a second in 1792, and a third in 1795. For more than a century thereafter, there was no Polish state, but the Poles never ceased their efforts to regain their independence.

Poland was formally reconstituted in November 1918, with Marshal Josef Pilsudski as Chief of State. In 1919, Ignace Paderewski, the famous pianist and patriot, became the first premier. In 1926, Pilsudski seized complete power in a coup and ruled dictatorially until his death on May 12, 1935, when he was succeeded by Marshal Edward Smigly-Rydz.

Despite a 10-year nonaggression pact signed in 1934, Hitler attacked Poland on Sept. 1, 1939. Russian troops invaded from the east on September 17, and on September 28 a German-Russian agreement divided Poland between Russia and Germany. Wladyslaw Raczkiewicz formed a government-in-exile in France, which moved to London after France's defeat in 1940.

All of Poland was occupied by Germany after the Nazi attack on the U.S.S.R. in June 1941.

The legal Polish government soon fell out with the Russians, and, in 1944, a Communist-dominated Polish Committee of National Liberation received Soviet recognition. Moving to Lublin after that city's liberation, it proclaimed itself the Provisional Government of Poland. Some former members of the Polish government in London joined with the Lublin government to form the Polish Government of National Unity, which Britain and the U.S. recognized.

On Aug. 2, 1945, in Berlin, President Harry S. Truman, Joseph Stalin, and Prime Minister Clement Attlee of Britain established a new *de facto* western frontier for Poland along the Oder and Neisse Rivers. (The border was finally agreed to by West Germany in a nonagression pact signed Dec. 7, 1970.) On Aug. 16, 1945, the U.S.S.R. and Poland signed a treaty delimiting the Soviet-Polish frontier. Under these agreements, Poland was shifted westward. In the east it lost 69,860 square miles (180,934 sq km) with 10,772,000 inhabitants; in the west it gained (subject to final peace-conference approval) 38,986 square miles (100,973 sq km) with a prewar population of 8,621,000.

A New Constitution in 1952 made Poland a "people's democracy" of the Soviet type. In 1955, Poland became a member of the Warsaw Treaty Organization, and its foreign policy became identical with that of the U.S.S.R. The government undertook persecution of the Roman Catholic Church as a remaining source of opposition.

Wladyslaw Gomulka was elected leader of the United Workers (Communist) Party in 1956. He denounced the Stalinist terror, ousted many Stalinists, and improved relations with the church. Most collective farms were dissolved, and the press became freer.

A strike that began in shipyards and spread to other industries in August 1980 produced a stunning victory for workers when the economically hard-pressed government accepted for the first time in a Marxist state the right of workers to organize in independent unions.

Led by Solidarity, a free union founded by Lech Walesa, workers launched a drive for liberty and improved conditions. A national strike for a five-day week in January 1981 led to the dismissal of Premier Pinkowski and the naming of the fourth Premier in less than a year, Gen. Wojciech Jaruzelski.

Antistrike legislation was approved on Dec. 2 and martial law declared on Dec. 13, when Walesa and other Solidarity leaders were arrested. Ten days later, President Reagan ordered sanctions against the Polish government, stopping food shipments and cutting commercial air traffic. The sanctions were lifted in early 1987.

Martial law was formally ended in 1984 but the government retained emergency powers. On July 21, 1984, the Parliament marked the 40th anniversary of Communist rule in Poland by enacting an amnesty bill authorizing the release of 652 political prisoners—virtually all except for those charged with high treason, espionage, and sabotage—and 35,000 common criminals. On September 10, 1986, the government freed all 225 remaining political prisoners.

Increasing opposition to the government because of the failing economy led to a new wave of strikes in 1988. Unable to totally quell the dissent, it relegalized Solidarity and allowed them to compete in elections.

Solidarity won a stunning victory, taking almost all the seats in the Senate and all of the 169 seats they were allowed to contest in the Sejm. This has given them substantial influence in the new government. Taduesz Mazowiecki was appointed prime minister.

The presidential election of 1990 was essentially a three-way race between Mazowiecki, Solidarity-leader Lech Walesa and an almost unknown businessman Stanislaw Tyminski. In the second round Walesa received 74% of the vote.

Well into 1991 the parliament was still controlled by former Communists. A new election bill was held up until July 1 when President Walesa reluctantly signed it, charging the bill would lead to a weak legislature.

PORTUGAL

Republic of Portugal
President: Mario Soares (1986)
Prime Minister: Anibal Cavaco Silva (1987)
Area: 35,550 sq mi. (92,075 sq km)
Population (est. mid-1991): 10,400,000 (average annual rate of natural increase: 0.2%); birth rate: 12/1000; infant mortality rate: 12.1/1000; density per square mile: 292
Capital: Lisbon
Largest cities (est. 1985): Lisbon, 827,800; Opporto, 344,500
Monetary unit: Escudo
Language: Portuguese
Religion: Roman Catholic 97%, 1% Protestant, 2% other
National name: República Portuguesa
Literacy rate: 83%
Economic summary: Gross domestic product (1989 est.): $72.1 billion; $6,900 per capita; 3.5% real growth rate. Arable land: 32%. Principal products: grains, potatoes, olives, wine grapes. Labor force: 4,605,700; 35% in industry. Major products: textiles, footwear, wood pulp, paper, cork, metal products, refined oil, chemicals, canned fish, wine. Natural resources: fish, cork, tungsten, iron ore. Exports: cotton, textiles, cork and cork products, canned fish, wine, timber and timber products, resin. Imports: petroleum, cotton, food-grains, industrial machinery, iron and steel, chemicals. Major trading partners: Western European countries, U.S.

Geography. Portugal occupies the western part of the Iberian Peninsula, bordering on the Atlantic Ocean to the west and Spain to the north and east. It is slightly smaller than Indiana.

The country is crossed by many small rivers, and also by three large ones that rise in Spain, flow into the Atlantic, and divide the country into three geographic areas. The Minho River, part of the northern boundary, cuts through a mountainous area that extends south to the vicinity of the Douro River. South of the Douro, the mountains slope to the plains about the Tejo River. The remaining division is the southern one of Alentejo.

The Azores, stretching over 340 miles (547 km) in the Atlantic, consist of nine islands divided into three groups, with a total area of 902 square miles (2,335 sq km). The nearest continental land is Cape da Roca, Portugal, about 900 miles (1,448 km) to the east. The Azores are an important station on Atlantic air routes, and Britain and the U.S. established air bases there during World War II. Madeira, consisting of two inhabited islands, Madeira and Porto Santo, and two groups of uninhabited islands, lie in the Atlantic about 535 miles (861 km) southwest of Lisbon. The Madeiras are 307 square miles (796 sq km) in area.

Government. The Constitution of 1976, revised in 1982, provides for popular election of a President for a five-year term and for a legislature, the Assembly of the Republic, for four years.

History. Portugal was a part of Spain until it won its independence in the middle of the 12th century. King John I (1385–1433) unified his country at the expense of the Castilians and the Moors of Morocco. The expansion of Portugal was brilliantly coordinated by John's son, Prince Henry the Navigator. In 1488, Bartolomew Diaz reached the Cape of Good Hope, proving that the Far East was accessible by sea. In 1498, Vasco da Gama reached the west coast of India. By the middle of the 16th century, the Portuguese Empire was in West and East Africa, Brazil, Persia, Indochina, and Malaya.

In 1581, Philip II of Spain invaded Portugal and held it for 60 years, precipitating a catastrophic decline of Portuguese commerce. Courageous and shrewd explorers, the Portuguese proved to be inefficient and corrupt colonizers. By the time the Portuguese dynasty was restored in 1640, Dutch, English, and French competitors began to seize the lion's share of the world's colonies and commerce. Portugal retained Angola and Mozambique in Africa, and Brazil (until 1822).

The corrupt King Carlos, who ascended the throne in 1889, made Joao Franco the Premier with dictatorial power in 1906. In 1908, Carlos and his heir were shot dead on the streets of Lisbon. The new King, Manoel II, was driven from the throne in the Revolution of 1910 and Portugal became a French-style republic.

Traditionally friendly to Britain, Portugal fought in World War I on the Allied side in Africa as well as on the Western Front. Weak postwar governments and a revolution in 1926 brought Antonio Oliveira Salazar to power. He kept Portugal neutral in World War II but gave the Allies naval and air bases after 1943.

Portugal lost the tiny remnants of its Indian empire—Goa, Daman, and Diu—to Indian military occupation in 1961, the year an insurrection broke out in Angola. For the next 13 years, Salazar, who died in 1970, and his successor, Marcello Caetano, fought independence movements amid growing world criticism. Leftists in the armed forces, weary of a losing battle, launched a successful revolution on April 25, 1974.

In late 1985, a PSP-PSD split ended the Soares coalition government. Cavaco Silva, an advocate of free-market economics, was the Social Democratic candidate. His party emerged with a plurality, unseating the Socialists.

In July 1987, the governing Social Democratic Party was swept back into office with 50.22% of the popular vote, giving Portugal its first majority Government since democracy was restored in 1974.

Mario Soares easily won a second five-year term as president in January 1991 elections.

Portuguese Overseas Territory

After the April 1974 revolution, the military junta moved to grant independence to the territories, beginning with Portuguese Guinea in September 1974, which became the Republic of Guinea-Bissau.

Mozambique and Angola followed, leaving only Portuguese Timor and Macao of the former empire. Despite Lisbon's objections, Indonesia annexed Timor.

MACAO

Status: Territory
Governor: Francisco Nabo (1990)
Area: 6 sq mi. (15.5 sq km)
Population (est. mid-1991): 400,000 (average annual growth rate: 1.4%); birth rate: 17/1000; infant mortality rate: 10/1000
Capital (1970 census): Macao, 241,413
Monetary unit: Patacá
Literacy rate (1981): almost 100% among Portuguese and Macanese, no data on Chinese
Economic summary: Gross domestic product (1989 est.): $2.7 billion, $6,300 per capita; real growth rate 5%. Principal agricultural products: rice and vegetables. Major agricultural products: clothing, textiles, plastics, furniture. Exports: textiles, clothing, toys. Imports: raw materials, foodstuffs, capital goods. Major trading partners: Hong Kong, China, U.S., Germany, France.

Macao comprises the peninsula of Macao and the two small islands of Taipa and Colôane on the South China coast, about 35 miles (53 km) from Hong Kong. Established by the Portuguese in 1557, it is the oldest European outpost in the China trade, but Portugal's sovereign rights to the port were not recognized by China until 1887. The port has been eclipsed in importance by Hong Kong, but it is still a busy distribution center and also has an important fishing industry. Portugal will return Macao to China in 1999.

Carlos Melancia resigned as governor in September 1990 after being accused of accepting a bribe from a German firm doing consulting work for a planned airport.

QATAR

State of Qatar
Emir: Sheikh Khalifa bin Hamad al-Thani (1972)
Area: 4,000 sq mi. (11,437 sq km)
Population (est. mid-1991): 500,000 (average annual rate of natural increase: 2.5%); birth rate: 27/1000; infant mortality rate: 24/1000; density per square mile: 122
Capital (est. 1990): Doha, 300,000
Monetary unit: Qatari riyal
Language: Arabic; English is also widely spoken
Religion: Islam, 95%
Literacy rate: 40%
Economic summary: Gross national product (1987): $5.4 billion; $17,070 per capita; 9% real growth rate. Labor force: 104,000. Major industrial product: oil. Natural resources: oil, gas. Export: oil. Imports: foodstuffs, animal and vegetable oils, chemicals, machinery and equipment. Major trading partners: Japan, Western Europe, U.S., Australia, Arab countries.

Geography. Qatar occupies a small peninsula that extends into the Persian Gulf from the east side of the Arabian Peninsula. Saudi Arabia is to the west and the United Arab Emirates to the south. The country is mainly barren.

Government. Qatar, one of the Arabian Gulf states, lies between Bahrain and United Arab Emirates. For a long time, it was under Turkish protection, but in 1916, the Emir accepted British protection. After the discovery of oil in the 1940s and its exploitation in the 1950s and 1960s, political unrest spread to the sheikhdoms. Qatar declared its independence in 1971.

The next year the current Sheikh, Khalifa bin Hamad al-Thani, ousted his cousin in a bloodless coup.

History. The emir agreed to the deployment of Arab and Western forces in Qatar following the Iraqi invasion of Kuwait. Also at this time a number of Palestinians were expelled for fear of their support of the PLO's pro-Iraqi position.

ROMANIA

Romania
President: Ion Iliescu (1990)
Premier: Petre Roman
Area: 91,700 sq mi. (237,500 sq km)
Population (est. mid-1991): 23,400,000 (average annual rate of natural increase: 0.5%); birth rate: 16/1000; infant mortality rate: 26.9/1000; density per square mile: 255
Capital: Bucharest
Largest cities (est. July 1, 1986): Bucharest, 2,014,359 (1987); Brasov, 351,493; Constanta, 327,676; Timisoara, 325,272; Iasi, 313,060; Cluj-Napoca, 310,017; Galati, 295,372
Monetary unit: Leu
Languages: Romanian, Magyar
Religions: Romanian Orthodox, 80%; Roman Catholic, 6%; 4% others
National name: România
Literacy rate: 98%
Economic summary: Gross national product (1989 est.): $79.8 billion; $3,445 per capita; –1.5% real growth rate. Arable land: 43%. Principal products: corn, wheat, livestock. Labor force: 10,690,000; 34% in industry. Major products: timber, metal production and processing, chemicals, food processing, petroleum. Natural resources: oil, timber, natural gas, coal, iron ore. Exports: machinery, minerals and metals, foodstuffs, lumber, fuel, manufactures. Imports: machinery, minerals, fuels, agricultural products, consumer goods. Major trading partners: U.S.S.R., Germany, E.C., U.S., China.

Geography. A country in southeastern Europe slightly smaller than Oregon, Romania is bordered on the west by Hungary and Yugoslavia, on the north and east by the U.S.S.R., on the east by the Black Sea, and on the south by Bulgaria.

The Carpathian Mountains divide Romania's upper half from north to south and connect near the center of the country with the Transylvanian Alps, running east and west.

North and west of these ranges lies the Transylvanian plateau, and to the south and east are the plains of Moldavia and Walachia. In its last 190 miles (306 km), the Danube River flows through Romania only. It enters the Black Sea in northern Dobruja, just south of the border with the Soviet Union.

Government. After the overthrow of Nicolae Ceausescu's Communist government at the end of 1989, an interim-government was headed by the National Salvation Front. The sweeping victory of the NSF in May 1990 elections gave the NSF a popular mandate for retaining power yet its legitimacy remains questionable in the eyes of many Romanians.

History. Most of Romania was the Roman province of Dacia from about A.D. 100 to 271. From the 6th to the 12th century, wave after wave of barbarian conquerors overran the native Daco-Roman population. By the

16th century, the main Romanian principalities of Moldavia and Walachia had become satellites within the Ottoman Empire, although they retained much independence. After the Russo-Turkish War of 1828–29, they became Russian protectorates. The nation became a kingdom in 1881 after the Congress of Berlin.

King Ferdinand ascended the throne in 1914. At the start of World War I, Romania proclaimed its neutrality, but later joined the Allied side and in 1916 declared war on the Central Powers. The armistice of Nov. 11, 1918, gave Romania vast territories from Russia and the Austro-Hungarian Empire.

The gains of World War I, making Romania the largest Balkan state, included Bessarabia, Transylvania, and Bukovina. The Banat, a Hungarian area, was divided with Yugoslavia.

In 1925, Crown Prince Carol renounced his rights to the throne, and when King Ferdinand died in 1927, Carol's son, Michael (Mihai) became King under a regency. However, Carol returned from exile in 1930, was crowned King Carol II, and gradually became a powerful political force in the country. In 1938, he abolished the democratic Constitution of 1923.

In 1940, the country was reorganized along Fascist lines, and the Fascist Iron Guard became the nucleus of the new totalitarian party. On June 27, the Soviet Union occupied Bessarabia and northern Bukovina. By the Axis-dictated Vienna Award of 1940, two-fifths of Transylvania went to Hungary, after which Carol dissolved Parliament and granted the new premier, Ion Antonescu, full power. He abdicated and again went into exile.

Romania subsequently signed the Axis Pact on Nov. 23, 1940, and the following June joined in Germany's attack on the Soviet Union, reoccupying Bessarabia. Following the invasion of Romania by the Red Army in August 1944, King Michael led a coup that ousted the Antonescu government. An armistice with the Soviet Union was signed in Moscow on Sept. 12, 1944.

A Communist-dominated government bloc won elections in 1946, Michael abdicated on Dec. 30, 1947, and Romania became a "people's republic." In 1955, Romania joined the Warsaw Treaty Organization and the United Nations. A decade later, with the adoption of a new Constitution emphasizing national autonomy, and especially after Nicolae Ceausescu came to power in 1967, Bucharest became an increasingly dissident voice in the Soviet bloc. Despite his liberal international record, at home Ceausescu harshly suppressed dissidents calling for freedom of expression in the wake of the Helsinki agreements.

An army-assisted rebellion in Dec. 1989 led to Ceausescu's overthrow. He was tried and executed. Elections in May 1990 led to the head of the interim government, Ion Iliescu, being elected President.

The government remains torn between introducing free-market reforms and its pledges to hold down unemployment and reduce shortages. While some, though few, measures have been implemented, price reforms in November 1990 led to strikes and demonstrations. The opposition remains weak and fragmented.

RWANDA

Republic of Rwanda
President: Maj. Gen. Juvénal Habyarimana (1973)
Area: 10,169 sq mi. (26,338 sq km)
Population (est. mid-1991): 7,500,000 (average annual rate of natural increase: 3.4%); birth rate: 51/1000; infant mortality rate: 117/1000; density per square mile: 739

Capital and largest city (1990): Kigali, 300,000
Monetary unit: Rwanda franc
Languages: Kinyarwanda and French
Religions: Roman Catholic, 56%; Protestant, 18%; Islam, 1%; indigenous and other, 25%
National name: Republika y'u Rwanda
Literacy rate: 46.6%
Economic summary: Gross domestic product (1988 est.): $2.3 billion; $325 per capita; real growth rate –2.5%. Arable land: 29%. Principal products: coffee, tea, bananas, yams, beans. Labor force 3,600,000; in industry: 2%. Major products: processed foods, light consumer goods, minerals. Natural resources: gold, cassiterite, wolfram. Exports: coffee, tea, tungsten, tin, pyrethrum. Imports: textiles, foodstuffs, machinery, and equipment. Major trading partners: Belgium, Germany, Kenya, Japan, France, U.S.

Geography. Rwanda, in east central Africa, is surrounded by Zaire, Uganda, Tanzania, and Burundi. It is slightly smaller than Maryland.

Steep mountains and deep valleys cover most of the country. Lake Kivu in the northwest, at an altitude of 4,829 feet (1,472 m) is the highest lake in Africa. Extending north of it are the Virunga Mountains, which include Volcan Karisimbi (14,187 ft; 4,324 m), Rwanda's highest point.

Government. Grégoire Kayibanda was President from 1962 until he was overthrown in a bloodless coup on July 5, 1973, by the military led by Gen. Juvénal Habyarimana.

In a plebiscite in December 1978, Habyarimana was elected to a five-year term as president and a new constitution adopted that provides for an elected Assembly and a single official party, the National Revolutionary Development Movement.

In 1988, Habyarimana was elected to a third five-year term.

The constitution was revised in 1991 to implement a multiparty system and schedule new elections.

History. Rwanda, which was part of German East Africa, was first visited by European explorers in 1854. During World War I, it was occupied in 1916 by Belgian troops. After the war, it became a Belgian League of Nations mandate, along with Burundi, under the name of Ruanda-Urundi. The mandate was made a U.N. trust territory in 1946. Until the Belgian Congo achieved independence in 1960, Ruanda-Urundi was administered as part of that colony.

Ruanda became the independent nation of Rwanda on July 1, 1962.

Rebel forces battled with government troops for control of parts of the country during late 1990 and early 1991.

ST. KITTS AND NEVIS

Federation of St. Kitts and Nevis
Sovereign: Queen Elizabeth II
Governor General: Sir Clement Athelston Arrindell (1985)
Prime Minister: Kennedy Alphonse Simmonds (1980)
Area: St. Kitts 65 sq mi. (169 sq km); Nevis 35 sq mi. (93 sq km)
Total population (est. mid-1991): 40,000 (average annual rate of natural increase: 1.1%); birth rate: 21/1000; infant mortality rate: 23/1000
Capital: Basseterre (on St. Kitts), 19,000
Largest town on Nevis: Charlestown, 1,771

Monetary unit: East Caribbean dollar
Economic summary: Gross domestic product (1988 est.): $119 million; $3,240 per capita; 6% real growth rate. Arable land: 22%. Principal agricultural products: sugar, rice, yams. Labor force: 20,000 (1981). Major industries: tourism, sugar processing, salt extraction. Exports: sugar, manufactures, postage stamps. Imports: foodstuffs, manufactured goods, machinery, fuels. Major trading partners: U.S., U.K., Japan, Trinidad and Tobago, Canada.

St. Christopher-Nevis, preferably St. Kitts and Nevis, was formerly part of the West Indies Associated States which were established in 1967 and consisted of Antigua and St. Kitts-Nevis-Anguilla of the Leeward Islands, and Dominica, Grenada, St. Lucia, and St. Vincent of the Windward Islands. Statehood for St. Vincent was held up until 1969 because of local political uncertainties. Anguilla's association with St. Christopher-Nevis ended in 1980.

Two members of the Leeward group—the British Virgin Islands and Montserrat—did not become Associated States.

St. Christopher-Nevis, now St. Kitts and Nevis, became independent on September 19, 1983.

Hurricane Hugo in 1989 inflicted such damage that the sugar crop was sharply reduced in 1990. Tourism and construction, however, have successfully rebounded.

ST. LUCIA

Sovereign: Queen Elizabeth II
Governor-General: (acting) Stanislaus A. James (1989)
Prime Minister: John Compton (1982)
Area: 238 sq mi. (616 sq km)
Population (est. mid-1991): 150,000 (average annual rate of natural increase: 1.6%); birth rate: 21/1000; infant mortality rate: 17.7/1000; density per square mile: 630
Capital (est. 1972): Castries, 45,000
Monetary unit: East Caribbean dollar
Languages: English and patois
Religions: Roman Catholic, 90%; Protestant, 7%; Anglican, 3%
Member of Commonwealth of Nations
Literacy rate: 90%
Economic summary: Gross domestic product (1988 est.): $172 million; $1,258 per capita; 6.8% real growth rate. Arable land: 8%. Principal products: bananas, coconuts, cocoa, citrus fruit. Major industrial products: clothing, assembled electronics, beverages. Exports: bananas, cocoa. Imports: foodstuffs, machinery and equipment, fertilizers, petroleum products. Major trading partners: U.K., U.S., Caribbean countries, Japan.

Geography. One of the Windward Isles of the Eastern Caribbean, St. Lucia lies just south of Martinique. It is of volcanic origin. A chain of wooded mountains runs from north to south, and from them flow many streams into fertile valleys.

Government. A Governor-General represents the sovereign, Queen Elizabeth II. A Prime Minister is head of government, chosen by a 17-member House of Assembly elected by universal suffrage for a maximum term of five years.

History. Discovered by Spain in 1503 and ruled by Spain and then France, St. Lucia became a British territory in 1803. With other Windward Isles, St. Lucia was granted home rule in 1967 as one of the West Indies Associated States. On Feb. 22, 1979, St. Lucia achieved full independence in ceremonies boycotted by the opposition St. Lucia Labor Party, which had advocated a referendum before cutting ties with Britain.

Unrest and a strike by civil servants forced Prime Minister John Compton to hold elections in July, in which his United Workers Party lost its majority for the first time in 15 years.

A Labor Party government was ousted in turn by Compton and his followers, in elections in May 1982.

Formerly dependent on a single crop, bananas, St. Lucia has sought to lower its chronic unemployment and payments deficit. The government provided tax incentives to a U.S. corporation, Amerada Hess, to facilitate location of a $150-million oil refinery and transshipment terminal on the island.

Desmond Fostin, the minister of communications and works, resigned in February 1990 amid charges of corruption in his ministry.

ST. VINCENT AND THE GRENADINES

Sovereign: Queen Elizabeth II
Governor-General: David Jack (1989)
Prime Minister: James Mitchell (1984)
Area: 150 sq mi. (389 sq km)
Population (est. mid-1991): 100,000 (average annual rate of natural increase: 1.6%); birth rate: 23/1000; infant mortality rate: 21.7/1000; density per square mile: 760
Capital and largest city (est. 1984): Kingstown, 18,378
Monetary unit: East Caribbean dollar
Language: English, some French patois
Religions: Anglican, 47%; Methodist, 28%; Roman Catholic, 13%
Member of Commonwealth of Nations
Literacy rate: 82%
Economic summary: Gross domestic product (1988): $160.5 million; $1,413 per capita; 8.4% real growth rate. Arable land: 38%. Principal products: bananas, arrowroot, coconuts. Labor Force: 67,000 (1984 est.). Major industry: food processing. Exports: bananas, arrowroot, copra. Imports: foodstuffs, machinery and equipment, chemicals, fuels, minerals. Major trading partners: U.K., U.S., Canada, Caribbean nations.

Geography. St. Vincent, chief island of the chain, is 18 miles (29 km) long and 11 miles (18 km) wide. One of the Windward Islands in the Lesser Antilles, it is 100 miles (161 km) west of Barbados. The island is mountainous and well forested. The Grenadines, a chain of nearly 600 islets with a total area of only 17 square miles (27 sq km), extend for 60 miles (96 km) from northeast to southwest between St. Vincent and Grenada, southernmost of the Windwards.

St. Vincent is dominated by the volcano La Soufrière, part of a volcanic range running north and south, which rises to 4,048 feet (1,234 m). The volcano erupted over a 10-day period in April 1979, causing the evacuation of the northern two-thirds of the island. (There is also a volcano of the same name on Basse-Terre, Guadeloupe, which became violently active in 1976 and 1977.)

Government. A Governor-General represents the sovereign, Queen Elizabeth II. A Prime Minister, elected by a 15-member unicameral legislature, holds executive power.

History. Discovered by Columbus in 1498, and alternately claimed by Britain and France, St. Vincent became a British colony by the Treaty of Paris in 1783. The islands won home rule in 1969 as part of the West Indies Associated States and achieved full independence Oct. 26, 1979. Prime Minister Milton Cato's government quelled a brief rebellion Dec. 8, 1979, attributed to economic problems following the eruption of La Soufrière in April 1979. Unlike a 1902 eruption which killed 2,000, there was no loss of life but widespread losses to agriculture.

Recently unemployment has become a major problem as well as the burgeoning debt and trade deficit.

SAN MARINO

Most Serene Republic of San Marino
Co-Regents: Two selected every six months by Grand and General Council
Area: 23.6 sq mi. (62 sq km)
Population (mid-1989): 22,980 (average annual growth rate: 0.6%)
Density per square mile: 974.6
Capital and largest city (est. 1982 for metropolitan area): San Marino, 4,500
Monetary unit: Italian lira
Language: Italian
Religion: Roman Catholic
National name: Repubblica di San Marino
Literacy rate: 97%
Economic summary: Gross national product: NA. Arable land: 17%. Principal products: wheat and other grains, grapes, olives, cheese. Labor force: approx. 4,300. Major industrial products: textiles, leather, cement, wine, olive oil. Exports: building stone, lime, chestnuts, wheat, hides, baked goods. Imports: manufactured consumer goods. Major trading partner: Italy.

Geography. One-tenth the size of New York City, San Marino is surrounded by Italy. It is situated in the Apennines, a little inland from the Adriatic Sea near Rimini.

Government. The country is governed by two co-regents. Executive power is exercised by ten ministers. In 1959, the Grand Council granted women the vote. San Marino is a member of the Conference on Security and Cooperation in Europe.

History. According to tradition, San Marino was founded about A.D. 350 and had good luck for centuries in staying out of the many wars and feuds on the Italian peninsula. It is the oldest republic in the world.

A person born in San Marino remains a citizen and can vote no matter where he lives.

The Communist Party underwent a metamorphosis becoming the Democratic Progressive Party, symbolized by a dove of peace.

SÃO TOMÉ AND PRÍNCIPE

Democratic Republic of São Tomé and Príncipe
President: Miguel Trovoada (1991)
Prime Minister: Celestino Rocha da Costa (1988)
Area: 370 sq mi. (958 sq km)
Population (est. mid-1991): 100,000 (average annual growth rate: 2.5%); birth rate: 35/1000; infant mortality rate: 71.9/1000; density per square mile: 345

Capital and largest city (est. 1984): São Tomé, 34,997
Monetary unit: Dobra
Language: Portuguese
Religions: Roman Catholic, Evangelical Protestant, Seventh-Day Adventist
Literacy rate: 50% (est.)
Economic summary: Gross domestic product (1986): $37.9 million; $340 per capita; 1.8% annual growth rate. Arable land: 1%. Principal agricultural products: cocoa, copra, coconuts, palm oil, coffee, bananas. Labor force: 21,096 (1981): mostly in subsistence agriculture. Major industrial products: shirts, soap, beer, processed fish and shrimp. Exports: cocoa, coffee, copra, palm oil. Imports: textiles, machinery, electrical equipment, fuels, food products. Major trading partners: Netherlands, Portugal, Germany, U.S., China.

Geography. The tiny volcanic islands of São Tomé and Príncipe lie in the Gulf of Guinea about 150 miles (240 km) off West Africa. São Tomé (about 330 sq mi.; 859 sq km) is covered by a dense mountainous jungle, out of which have been carved large plantations. Príncipe (about 40 sq mi.; 142 sq km) consists of jagged mountains. Other islands in the republic are Pedras Tinhosas and Rolas.

Government. The Constitution grants supreme power to a People's Assembly composed of members elected for four years. In 1990 a referendum approved a new constitution paving the way for a multi-party democracy.

History. São Tomé and Príncipe were discovered by Portuguese navigators in 1471 and settled by the end of the century. Intensive cultivation by slave labor made the islands a major producer of sugar during the 17th century but output declined until the introduction of coffee and cacao in the 19th century brought new prosperity. The island of São Tomé was the world's largest producer of cacao in 1908 and the crop is still the most important. An exile liberation movement was formed in 1953 after Portuguese landowners quelled labor riots by killing several hundred African workers.

The Portuguese revolution of 1974 brought the end of the overseas empire and the new Lisbon government transferred power to the liberation movement on July 12, 1975.

President Pinto da Costa's ruling party was defeated in multi-party elections in January 1991. A former prime minister and dissident Miguel Trovoada was elected president in March after the withdrawal of the two other candidates.

SAUDI ARABIA

Kingdom of Saudi Arabia
Ruler and Prime Minister: King Fahd bin 'Abdulaziz (1982)
Area: 865,000 sq mi. (2,250,070 sq km)
Population (est. mid-1991): 15,500,000 (average annual rate of natural increase: 3.4%); birth rate: 42/1000; infant mortality rate: 71/1000; density per square mile: 19
Capital: Riyadh
Largest cities (est. 1980): Jeddah, 1,500,000; Riyadh, 1,250,000; Mecca, 750,000
Monetary unit: Riyal
Language: Arabic
Religion: Islam, 100%
National name: Al-Mamlaka al-'Arabiya as-Sa'udiya
Literacy rate: 52%

Economic summary: Gross domestic product (1988): $73 billion; $4,720 per capita; 3.2% real growth rate. Arable land: 1%. Principal products: dates, grains, livestock. Labor force: 4,200,000; about 60% are foreign workers; 28% in industry and oil. Major products: petroleum, cement, plastic products, steel. Natural resources: oil, natural gas, iron ore. Exports: petroleum and petroleum products. Imports: manufactured goods, transport equipment, construction materials, processed food. Major trading partners: U.S., Germany, Great Britain and other Western European countries, South Korea, Taiwan, Japan.

Geography. Saudi Arabia occupies most of the Arabian Peninsula, with the Red Sea and the Gulf of Aqaba to the west, the Arabian Gulf to the east. Neighboring countries are Jordan, Iraq, Kuwait, Qatar, the United Arab Emirates, the Sultanate of Oman, and Yemen.

A narrow coastal plain on the Red Sea rims a mountain range that spans the length of the western coastline. These mountains gradually rise in elevation from north to south. East of these mountains is a massive plateau which slopes gently downward toward the Arabian Gulf. Part of this plateau is covered by the world's largest continuous sand desert, the Rub Al-Khali, or Empty Quarter. Saudi Arabia's oil region lies primarily along the Arabian Gulf.

Government. Saudi Arabia is a monarchy based on the Sharia (Islamic law), as revealed in the Koran (the holy book) and the Hadith (teachings and sayings of the prophet Mohammed). A Council of Ministers was formed in 1953, which acts as a Cabinet under the leadership of the King. There are 20 Ministries.

Royal and ministerial decrees account for most of the promulgated legislation, treaties, and conventions. There are no political parties.

History. Mohammed united the Arabs in the 7th century, and his followers, led by the caliphs, founded a great empire, with its capital at Medina. Later, the caliphate capital was transferred to Damascus and then Baghdad, but Arabia retained its importance because of the holy cities of Mecca and Medina. In the 16th and 17th centuries, the Turks established at least nominal rule over much of Arabia, and in the middle of the 18th century, it was divided into separate principalities.

The Kingdom of Saudi Arabia is almost entirely the creation of King Ibn Saud (1882–1953). A descendant of earlier Wahabi rulers, he seized Riyadh, the capital of Nejd, in 1901 and set himself up as leader of the Arab nationalist movement. By 1906 he had established Wahabi dominance in Nejd. He conquered Hejaz in 1924–25, consolidating it and Nejd into a dual kingdom in 1926. In 1932, Hejaz and Nejd became a single kingdom, which was officially named Saudi Arabia. A year later the region of Asir was incorporated into the kingdom.

Oil was discovered in 1936, and commercial production began during World War II. Saudi Arabia was neutral until nearly the end of the war, but it was permitted to be a charter member of the United Nations. The country joined the Arab League in 1945 and took part in the 1948–49 war against Israel.

On Ibn Saud's death in 1953, his eldest son, Saud, began an 11-year reign marked by an increasing hostility toward the radical Arabism of Egypt's Gamal Abdel Nasser. In 1964, the ailing Saud was deposed and replaced by the Premier, Crown Prince Faisal, who gave vocal support but no military help to Egypt in the 1967 Mideast war.

Faisal's assassination by a deranged kinsman in 1975 shook the Middle East, but failed to alter his kingdom's course. His successor was his brother, Prince Khalid. Khalid gave influential support to Egypt during negotiations on Israeli withdrawal from the Sinai desert.

King Khalid died of a heart attack June 13, 1982, and was succeeded by his half-brother, Prince Fahd bin 'Abdulaziz, 60, who had exercised the real power throughout Khalid's reign. King Fahd, a pro-Western modernist, chose his 58-year-old half-brother, Abdullah, as Crown Prince.

Saudi Arabia and the smaller, oil-rich Arab states on the Persian Gulf, fearful that they might become Ayatollah Ruhollah Khomeini's next targets if Iran conquered Iraq, made large financial contributions to the Iraqi war effort. They began being dragged into the conflict themselves in the spring of 1984, when Iraq and Iran extended their ground war to attacks on Gulf shipping. First, Iraq attacked tankers loading at Iran's Kharg Island terminal with air-to-ground missiles, then Iran struck back at tankers calling at Saudi Arabia and other Arab countries.

At the same time, cheating by other members of the Organization of Petroleum Exporting Countries, competition from nonmember oil producers, and conservation efforts by consuming nations combined to drive down the world price of oil. Saudi Arabia has one-third of all known oil reserves, but falling demand and rising production outside OPEC combined to reduce its oil revenues from $120 billion in 1980 to $43 billion in 1984 to less the $25 billion in 1985, threatening the country with domestic unrest and undermining its influence in the Gulf area.

Saudi Arabia broke relations with Iran in April 1988 over the issues of riots by Iranian pilgrims in Mecca in July, 1987 and Iranian naval attacks on Saudi vessels in the Persian Gulf.

Following the invasion of Kuwait in August 1990, Saudi Arabia allowed the U.S. to station military forces there ("Operation Desert Shield") to defend its territory against possible Iraqi invasion.

Diplomatic relations with the U.S.S.R. and China were established in 1990, and in November of that year promises were made to revive long-dormant plans for a consultative council. Oil production rose, and government spending substantially increased.

SENEGAL

Republic of Senegal
President: Abdou Diouf (1981)
Area: 75,954 sq mi. (196,722 sq km)
Population (est. mid-1991): 7,500,000 (average annual rate of natural increase: 2.8%); birth rate: 46/1000; infant mortality rate: 87/1000; density per square mile: 99
Capital and largest city (est. 1982): Dakar, 975,000
Monetary unit: Franc CFA
Ethnic groups: Wolofs, Sereres, Peuls, Tukulers, and others
Languages: French (official); Wolof, Serer, other ethnic dialects
Religions: Islam, 92%; indigenous, 6%; Christian, 2%
National name: République du Sénégal
Literacy rate: 28.1%
Economic summary: Gross domestic product (1988 est.): $5 billion; $680 per capita; 5.1% real growth rate. Arable land: 27%. Principal products: peanuts, millet, corn, rice, sorghum. Labor force: 2,509,000; 77% subsistence agriculture workers. Major industrial products: processed food, phosphates, refined petroleum, cement, and fish. Natural resources: fish, phosphate,

iron ore. Exports: peanuts, phosphate rock, canned fish, petroleum products. Imports: foodstuffs, consumer goods, machinery, transport equipment, petroleum. Major trading partners: U.S., France, Western European countries, African neighbors.

Geography. The capital of Senegal, Dakar, is the westernmost point in Africa. The country, slightly smaller than South Dakota, surrounds Gambia on three sides and is bordered on the north by Mauritania, on the east by Mali, and on the south by Guinea and Guinea-Bissau.

Senegal is mainly a low-lying country, with a semidesert area in the north and northeast and forests in the southwest. The largest rivers include the Senegal in the north and the Casamance in the south tropical climate region.

Government. There is a National Assembly of 120 members, elected every five years. There is universal suffrage and a constitutional guarantee of equality before the law.

History. The Portuguese had some stations on the banks of the Senegal River in the 15th century, and the first French settlement was made at Saint-Louis about 1650. The British took parts of Senegal at various times, but the French gained possession in 1840 and organized the Sudan as a territory in 1904. In 1946, together with other parts of French West Africa, Senegal became part of the French Union. On June 20, 1960, it became an independent republic federated with the Sudanese Republic in the Mali Federation, from which it withdrew two months later.

In 1973, Senegal joined with six other states to create the West African Economic Community.

Pres. Diouf continues his commitment to the austerity measures imposed by the IMF. Senegal's border war with Mauritania still smolders as does the territorial waters dispute with Guinea-Bissau.

SEYCHELLES

Republic of Seychelles
President: France-Albert René (1977)
Area: 175 sq mi. (453 sq km)
Population (est. mid-1991): 100,000 (average annual rate of natural increase: 1.6%); birth rate: 24/1000; infant mortality rate: 18.1/1000; density per square mile: 638
Capital: Victoria, 24,000
Monetary unit: Seychelles rupee
Languages: English and French (official); Creole
Religions: Roman Catholic, 90%; Anglican, 8%
Member of Commonwealth of Nations
Literacy rate: 60%
Economic summary: Gross domestic product (1988 est.): $255 million; $3,720 per capita; 6.2% real growth rate. Arable land: 4%. Principal products: vanilla, coconuts, cinnamon. Labor force: 27,700; 31% in industry and commerce. Major products: processed coconut and vanilla, coir rope. Exports: cinnamon, fish, copra. Imports: food, tobacco, manufactured goods, machinery, petroleum products, transport equipment. Major trading partners: U.K., France, Japan, Pakistan, Reunion, South Africa.

Geography. Seychelles consists of an archipelago of about 100 islands in the Indian Ocean northeast of Madagascar. The principal islands are Mahé (55 sq mi.; 142 sq km), Praslin (15 sq mi.; 38 sq km), and La Digue (4 sq mi.; 10 sq km). The Aldabra, Farquhar, and Desroches groups are included in the territory of the republic.

Government. Seized from France by Britain in 1810, the Seychelles Islands remained a colony until June 29, 1976. The state is an independent republic within the Commonwealth.

On June 5, 1977, Prime Minister Albert René ousted the islands' first President, James Mancham, suspending the Constitution and the 25-member National Assembly. Mancham, whose "lavish spending" and flamboyance were cited by René in seizing power, charged that Soviet influence was at work. The new president denied this and, while more left than his predecessor, pledged to keep the Seychelles in the nonaligned group of countries.

An unsuccessful attempted coup against René attracted international attention when a group of 50 South African mercenaries posing as rugby players attacked the Victoria airport on Nov. 25, 1981. They caused extensive damage before they hijacked an Air India plane and returned to South Africa, where all but five were freed. Only after widespread international protest did the Pretoria government, which denied any responsibility for the attack, reverse the decision and order all the mercenaries tried as hijackers.

Recently experiencing a large trade deficit, partly to supply the tourist industry, the country for this and other reasons has decided to put a ceiling on the number of tourists permitted.

SIERRA LEONE

Republic of Sierra Leone
President: Maj. Gen. Joseph Saidu Momoh (1985)
Area: 27,700 sq mi. (71,740 sq km)
Population (est. mid-1991): 4,300,000 (average annual rate of natural increase: 2.7%); birth rate: 48/1000; infant mortality rate: 147/1000; density per square mile: 154
Capital and largest city (est. 1985): Freetown, 500,000
Monetary unit: Leone
Languages: English (official), Mende, Temne, Krio
Religions: Islam, 30%; indigenous, 30%; Christian, 10%; other, 30%
Member of Commonwealth of Nations
Literacy rate: 31%
Economic summary: Gross domestic product (FY87): $965 million; $250 per capita; real growth rate 1.8%. Arable land: 25%; principal products: coffee, cocoa, palm kernels, rice. Labor force: 1,369,000 (est.); 19% in industry. Major products: diamonds, bauxite, rutile, beverages, cigarettes, textiles, footwear. Natural resources: diamonds, bauxite, iron ore. Exports: diamonds, rutile, bauxite, cocoa, coffee. Imports: food, petroleum products, capital goods. Major trading partners: U.K., U.S., Western European countries, Japan.

Geography. Sierra Leone, on the Atlantic Ocean in West Africa, is half the size of Illinois. Guinea, in the north and east, and Liberia, in the south, are its neighbors.

Mangrove swamps lie along the coast, with wooded hills and a plateau in the interior. The eastern region is mountainous.

Government. Sierra Leone became an independent nation on April 27, 1961, and declared itself a republic on April 19, 1971.

Sierra Leone became a one party state under the aegis of the All People's Congress Party in April 1978.

History. The coastal area of Sierra Leone was ceded to English settlers in 1788 as a home for blacks discharged from the British armed forces and also for runaway slaves who had found asylum in London. The British protectorate over the hinterland was proclaimed in 1896.

After elections in 1967, the British Governor-General replaced Sir Albert Margai, head of SLPP, which had held power since independence, with Dr. Stevens, head of APC, as prime minister. The Army took over the government; then another coup in April 1968 restored civilian rule and put the military leaders in jail.

A coup attempt early in 1971 by the army commander was apparently foiled by loyal army officers, but the then Prime Minister Stevens called in troops of neighboring Guinea's army, under a 1970 mutual defense pact, to guard his residence. After perfunctorily blaming the U.S. for the coup attempt, Stevens switched Governors-General, changed the Constitution, and ended up with a republic, of which he was first president. He was accused of taking "sweeping dictatorial powers," but was re-elected in 1978. Dr. Stevens' picked successor, Major-General Joseph Saidu Momoh was elected unopposed on Oct. 1, 1985.

A number of organizations in the last year have voiced support for the introduction of multiparty democracy, but President Momoh has opposed the idea.

SINGAPORE

Republic of Singapore
Prime Minister: Goh Chok Tong (1990)
Area: 220 sq mi. (570 sq km)
Population (est. mid-1991): 2,800,000 (average annual rate of natural increase: 1.3%); birth rate: 18/1000; infant mortality rate: 6.6/1000; density per square mile: 12,307
Capital (est. mid-1988): Singapore, 2,600,000
Monetary unit: Singapore dollar
Languages: Malay, Chinese (Mandarin), Tamil, English
Religions: Islam, Christian, Buddhist, Hindu, Taoist
Member of Commonwealth of Nations
Literacy rate: 90%
Economic summary: Gross domestic product (1989 est.): $27.5 billion; $10,300 per capita; 9.2% real growth rate. Arable land: 4%. Principal products: poultry, rubber, copra, vegetables, fruits. Labor force: 1,324,700; 34.4% in industry. Major industries: petroleum refining, ship repair, electronics, financial services, biotechnology. Exports: petroleum products, rubber, manufactured goods, electronics, computers and computer peripherals. Imports: capital equipment, manufactured goods, petroleum. Major trading partners: U.S., Malaysia, E.C., Japan.

Geography. The Republic of Singapore consists of the main island of Singapore, off the southern tip of the Malay Peninsula between the South China Sea and the Indian Ocean, and 58 nearby islands.

There are extensive mangrove swamps extending inland from the coast, which is broken by many inlets.

Government. There is a Cabinet, headed by the Prime Minister, and a Parliament of 81 members elected by universal suffrage.

The People's Action Party, led by Prime Minister Goh Chok Tong, is the ruling political party in Parliament, holding all but one seat.

History. Singapore, founded in 1819 by Sir Stamford Raffles, became a separate crown colony of Britain in 1946, when the former colony of the Straits Settlements was dissolved. The other two settlements—Penang and Malacca—were transferred to the Union of

Malaya, and the small island of Labuan was transferred to North Borneo. The Cocos (or Keeling) Islands were transferred to Australia in 1955 and Christmas Island in 1958.

Singapore attained full internal self-government in 1959. On Sept. 16, 1963, it joined Malaya, Sabah (North Borneo), and Sarawak in the Federation of Malaysia. It withdrew from the Federation on Aug. 9, 1965, and proclaimed itself a republic the next month.

Long-time Prime Minister Lee Kuan Yew stepped down in late November 1990 in order, he said, to make way for a younger team. He remained, however, in the government as a cabinet minister.

SOLOMON ISLANDS

Sovereign: Queen Elizabeth II
Governor-General: Sir George Lepping (1988)
Prime Minister: Solomon Mamaloni (1989)
Area: 11,500 sq mi. (29,785 sq km)
Population (est. mid-1991): 300,000 (average annual rate of natural increase: 3.5%); birth rate: 40/1000; infant mortality rate: 39/1000; density per square mile: 32
Capital and largest city (est. 1986): Honiara (on Guadalcanal), 30,499
Monetary unit: Solomon Islands dollar
Languages: English, Pidgin, 70 other languages and dialects
Religions: Anglican; Roman Catholic; South Seas Evangelical; Seventh-Day Adventist, United (Methodist) Church, other Protestant
Member of British Commonwealth
Literacy rate: 60%
Economic summary: Gross domestic product (1988): $156 million; $500 per capita; 4.3% real growth rate. Arable land: 1%. Principal agricultural products: coconuts, palm oil, rice, cocoa, yams, pigs. Labor force: 23,448; 7% in construction, manufacturing and mining. Major industrial products: processed fish, copra. Natural resources: fish, timber, gold, bauxite. Exports: fish, timber, copra, palm oil. Imports: machinery and transport equipment, foodstuffs, fuel. Major trading partners: Japan, Australia, U.K., Thailand, Singapore.

Geography. Lying east of New Guinea, this island nation consists of the southern islands of the Solomon group: Guadalcanal, Malaita, Santa Isabel, San Cristóbal, Choiseul, New Georgia, and numerous smaller islands.

Government. After 85 years of British rule, the Solomons achieved independence July 7, 1978. The Crown is represented by a Governor-General and legislative power is vested in a unicameral legislature of 38 members, led by the Prime Minister.

History. Discovered in 1567 by Alvaro de Mendana, the Solomons were not visited again for about 200 years. In 1886, Great Britain and Germany divided the islands between them. In 1914, Australian forces took over the German islands and the Solomons became an Australian mandate in 1920. In World War II, most of the islands were occupied by the Japanese. American forces landed on Guadalcanal on Aug. 7, 1942. The islands were the scene of several important U.S. naval and military victories. Although surviving a vote of no-confidence the prime minister resigned from his party and was forced to take five opposition members into his cabinet.

SOMALIA

Somali Democratic Republic
President: Ali Mahdi Mohammed (interim 1991)
Prime Minister: Omar Artan Qalib (1991)
Area: 246,199 sq mi. (637,655 sq km)
Population (est. mid-1991): 7,700,000 (average annual rate of natural increase: 2.9%); birth rate: 49/1000; infant mortality rate: 127/1000; density per square mile: 31
Capital and largest city (est. 1982): Mogadishu, 700,000
Monetary unit: Somali shilling
Language: Somali (official), Arabic, English, Italian
Religion: Islam (Sunni)
National name: Al Jumhouriya As-Somalya al-Dimocradia
Literacy rate: 11.6% (government est.)
Economic summary: Gross domestic product (1988): $1.7 billion; $210 per capita; –1.4% real growth rate. Arable land: 2%. Principal products: livestock, bananas, sorghum, cereals, sugar cane, maize. Labor force: 2,200,000; very few are skilled laborers. A few small industries: sugar refining, textiles, petroleum refining. Natural resources: uranium. Exports: livestock, skins and hides, bananas. Imports: textiles, cereals, construction materials and equipment, petroleum products. Major trading partners: Saudi Arabia, Italy, U.S., U.K.

Geography. Somalia, situated in the Horn of Africa, lies along the Gulf of Aden and the Indian Ocean. It is bounded by Djibouti in the northwest, Ethiopia in the west, and Kenya in the southwest. In area it is slightly smaller than Texas.

Generally arid and barren, Somalia has two chief rivers, the Shebelle and the Juba.

Government. Maj. Gen. Mohamed Siad Barre took power on Oct. 21, 1969, in a coup that established a Supreme Revolutionary Council as the governing body, replacing a parliamentary government. On July 1, 1976, Barre dissolved the Council, naming its members to the Somali Socialist Party, organized that day as the nation's only legal political party. In December 1979, a 171-member People's Assembly was elected under a new Constitution adopted in August. The Assembly confirmed Barre as President for a six-year term. He was re-elected in 1986.

History. From the 7th to the 10th century, Arab and Persian trading posts were established along the coast of present-day Somalia. Nomadic tribes occupied the interior, occasionally pushing into Ethiopian territory. In the 16th century, Turkish rule extended to the northern coast and the Sultans of Zanzibar gained control in the south.

After British occupation of Aden in 1839, the Somali coast became its source of food. The French established a coaling station in 1862 at the site of Djibouti and the Italians planted a settlement in Eritrea. Egypt, which for a time claimed Turkish rights in the area, was succeeded by Britain. By 1920, a British protectorate and an Italian protectorate occupied what is now Somalia. The British ruled the entire area after 1941, with Italy returning in 1950 to serve as United Nations trustee for its former territory.

In mid-1960, Britain and Italy granted independence to their respective sectors, enabling the two to join as the Republic of Somalia on July 1. Somalia broke diplomatic relations with Britain in 1963 when the British granted the Somali-populated Northern Frontier District of Kenya to the Republic of Kenya.

On Oct. 15, 1969, President Abdi Rashid Ali Sher-marke was assassinated and the army seized power, dissolving the legislature and arresting all government leaders. Maj. Gen. Mohamed Siad Barre, as President of a renamed Somali Democratic Republic, leaned heavily toward the U.S.S.R.

In 1977, Somalia openly backed rebels in the east-ernmost area of Ethiopia, the Ogaden desert, which had been seized by Ethiopia at the turn of the century.

Somalia acknowledged defeat in an eight-month war against the Ethiopians, having lost much of its 32,000-man army and most of its tanks and planes.

A U.S. announcement on Jan. 9, 1980, that bases for U.S. ships and planes in the Indian Ocean would be sought in Somalia, Oman, and Kenya, brought a request from Somalia for $1 billion worth of modern arms and an equal amount of economic aid. In August, an agreement was signed giving the U.S. use of military bases in Somalia in return for $25 million in military aid in 1981 and more in subsequent years. In 1988, guerrillas in the north went on the offensive and threatened the northern regional capital.

President Siad Barre fled the country in late January 1991. His departure left Somalia in the hands of a number of clan-based guerrilla groups, none of which trust each other. The installation of Ali Mahdi Mohammed in the capital by the United Somali Congress, based on the Hawye clan, as interim president won the disapproval of other groups. Most of the south is controlled by the Somali Patriotic Movement.

SOUTH AFRICA

Republic of South Africa
President: F.W. de Klerk (1989)
Area: 471,440 sq mi. (1,221,030 sq km)
Population (est. mid-1991): 40,600,000 (average annual rate of natural increase: 2.7%); birth rate: 35/1000; infant mortality rate: 52/1000; density per square mile: 86
Administrative capital: Pretoria
Legislative capital: Cape Town
Judicial capital: Bloemfontein
Largest metropolitan areas: Cape Peninsula (Cape Town and surroundings), 1,911,500; Johannesburg/Rand-burg, 1,609,500; East Rand (Springs, Germiston and surroundings), 1,038,000; Durban/Pinetown/Inanda, 982,075; Pretoria/Wonderboom/Shoshanguve, 822,900
Monetary unit: Rand
Languages: English, Afrikaans (official); Xhosa, Zulu, other African tongues
Religions: Christian; Hindu; Islam
National name: Republic of South Africa
Literacy rate: 99% (whites), 50% blacks (govt. est.)
Economic summary: Gross domestic product (1988): $83.5 billion; $2,380 per capita; 3.2% real growth rate. Arable land: 11.6%. Principal products: corn, wool, wheat, sugar cane, fruits, vegetables. Labor force: 11,000,000; 29% in industry and commerce. Major products: gold, chromium, diamonds, assembled automobiles, machinery, textiles, iron and steel, chemicals, fertilizer. Natural resources: gold, diamonds, platinum, uranium, coal, iron ore, phosphates, manganese. Exports: gold, diamonds, minerals and metals, food, chemicals. Imports: motor vehicle parts, machinery, metals, chemicals, textiles, scientific instruments. Major trading partners: U.S., Germany, other E.C., Japan, U.K., Hong Kong.

Geography. South Africa, on the continent's southern tip, is washed by the Atlantic Ocean on the west and by the Indian Ocean on the south and east. Its neighbors are Namibia in the northwest, Zimbabwe and Botswana in the north, and Mozambique and Swaziland in the northeast. The kingdom of Lesotho forms an enclave within the southeastern part of South Africa. Bophuthatswana, Transkei, Ciskei, and Venda are independent states within South Africa, which occupies an area nearly three times that of California.

The country has a high interior plateau, or veld, nearly half of which averages 4,000 feet (1,219 m) in elevation.

There are no important mountain ranges, although the Great Escarpment, separating the veld from the coastal plain, rises to over 11,000 feet (3,350 m) in the Drakensberg Mountains in the east. The principal river is the Orange, rising in Lesotho and flowing westward for 1,300 miles (2,092 km) to the Atlantic.

The southernmost point of Africa is Cape Agulhas, located in Cape Province about 100 miles (161 km) southeast of the Cape of Good Hope.

Government. A new Constitution in 1984 created a new office of Executive State President, with potentially authoritarian powers. Pieter W. Botha, Prime Minister since 1978, was sworn in as President on Sept. 14, 1984. The President has the power to act at his own discretion (e.g. appoint cabinet members) as well as power that has to be exercised in consultation with the cabinet (e.g. declare war, ratify treaties).

Negotiations are to be initiated between parliamentary and non–parliamentary organizations with the ultimate purpose of establishing a constitution for a non-racial and democratic South Africa based on universal franchise. With regard to the participation in the negotiation process by the six independent homelands and the four independent states within the borders of South Africa, their individual governments will independently decide whether to take part in the negotiations or not and/or whether their states will form part of a unified South Africa once a new constitution has been effected.

The new Constitution brought whites, Indians, and coloreds (mixed-race) into a racially divided Parliament made up of three separate chambers for different racial groups. It provides for selection of the President by an Electoral College made up of representatives from the three chambers. Ten "Bantu-stans," or black homelands, have unicameral legislatures elected by black voters.

History. The Dutch East India Company landed the first settlers on the Cape of Good Hope in 1652, launching a colony that by the end of the 18th century numbered only about 15,000. Known as Boers or Afrikaners, speaking a Dutch dialect known as Afrikaans, the settlers as early as 1795 tried to establish an independent republic.

After occupying the Cape Colony in that year, Britain took permanent possession in 1814 at the end of the Napoleonic wars, bringing in 5,000 settlers. Anglicization of government and the freeing of slaves in 1833 drove about 12,000 Afrikaners to make the "great trek" north and east into African tribal territory, where they established the republics of the Transvaal and the Orange Free State.

The discovery of diamonds in 1867 and gold nine years later brought an influx of "outlanders" into the republics and spurred Cecil Rhodes to plot annexation. Rhodes's scheme of sparking an "outlander" rebellion to which an armed party under Leander Starr Jameson would ride to the rescue misfired in

1895, forcing Rhodes to resign as prime minister of the Cape colony. What British expansionists called the "inevitable" war with the Boers eventually broke out on Oct. 11, 1899.

The defeat of the Boers in 1902 led in 1910 to the Union of South Africa, composed of four provinces, the two former republics and the old Cape and Natal colonies. Louis Botha, a Boer, became the first Prime Minister.

Jan Christiaan Smuts brought the nation into World War II on the Allied side against Nationalist opposition, and South Africa became a charter member of the United Nations in 1945, but refused to sign the Universal Declaration of Human Rights. Apartheid—racial separation—dominated domestic politics as the Nationalists gained power and imposed greater restrictions on Bantus, Coloreds, and Asians.

Afrikaner hostility to Britain triumphed in 1961 with the declaration on May 31 of the Republic of South Africa and the severing of ties with the Commonwealth. Nationalist Prime Minister H. F. Verwoerd's government in 1963 asserted the power to restrict freedom of those who opposed rigid racial laws. Three years later, amid increasing racial tension and criticism from the outside world, Verwoerd was assassinated. His Nationalist successor, Balthazar J. Vorster, launched a campaign of conciliation toward conservative black African states, offering development loans and trade concessions.

A scandal led to Vorster's resignation on June 4, 1978. Pieter W. Botha succeeded him as Prime Minister, and became President on Sept. 14, 1984.

Protests against apartheid by militant blacks, beginning in the latter half of 1984, led to a state of emergency being declared twice. The first, on July 20, 1985, covered 36 cities and towns and gave the police powers to make arrests without warrants and to detain people indefinitely. The second, declared on June 12, 1986, covered the whole nation. It gave the police a similar extension of powers and banned "subversive" press reports. It was extended for another year in June 1988.

Elections on May 7, 1987, increased the power of Botha's Nationalist party while enabling the far-right Conservative Party to replace the liberal Progressives as the official opposition. The results of the whites-only vote indicated a strong conservative reaction against Botha's policy of limited reform.

A stroke led Botha to step down as leader of his party in 1989 in favor of Frederick de Klerk. De Klerk has accelerated the pace of reform. He unbanned the African National Congress, the principal anti-apartheid organization, and released Nelson Mandela, the ANC deputy chief, after 27 1/2 years imprisonment. Negotiations between the government and the ANC have commenced.

On June 5, 1991 the parliament scrapped the country's apartheid laws concerning property ownership. On June 17 the parliament did the same for the Population Registration Act of 1950, which classified all South Africans at birth by race.

President Bush in early July announced the U.S. was lifting its economic sanctions.

BOPHUTHATSWANA

Republic of Bophuthatswana
President: Kgosi Lucas Mangope (1977)
Area: 15,573 sq mi. (40,333 sq km)
Population (est. 1988): 1,300,000 (average annual growth rate: 2.8%)
Density per square mile: 83.5
Capital: Mmabatho

Largest city (est. 1987): Mabopane, 100,000
Monetary unit: South African rand
Languages: Setswana, English, Afrikaans
Religions: Methodist, Lutheran, Anglican, Presbyterian, Dutch Reformed, Roman Catholic, A.M.E.

Geography. Bophuthatswana consists of six discontinuous areas within the boundaries of South Africa. Most of them share a common border with Botswana.

Government. The republic has a 108-member Legislative Assembly, three quarters of whom are elected and the other 24 nominated by regional authorities. President Mangope's Democratic Party is the majority party.

History. Bophuthatswana was given independence by South Africa on Dec. 6, 1977, following Transkei as the second "homeland" to opt for independence. The new state and Transkei are recognized only by South Africa and each other.

Mangope, as chief minister in the pre-independence period, sought linkage of the seven units into a consolidated area, and has succeeded because Marico Corridor and adjoining farmers have been added and many more farms will be released. A second issue, the citizenship of Batswana in South Africa who wished to remain South African nationals, was settled by enabling them to have citizenship in South African homelands not yet independent.

About two-thirds of the population of Bophuthatswana live permanently in Bophuthatswana and thousands commute daily to South Africa.

Economy. Bophuthatswana is richer than many other South African homelands, as it has more than half of the republic's platinum deposits. All foreign trade is included with South Africa's, and it is economically interdependent at present with that country.

CISKEI

Republic of Ciskei
Head of State: Brig. Gen. Oupa Gqozo (1990)
Area: 3,282 sq mi. (8,500 sq km)
Population (est. 1982): 675,000
Density per square mile: 205.7
Capital (est. 1980): Zwelitsha, 30,750
Largest city (est. 1981): Mdantsane, 159,000
Monetary unit: South African rand
Languages: Xhosa (official) and English
Religions: Methodist, Lutheran, Anglican, and Bantu Christian

Geography. Ciskei is surrounded by South Africa on three sides, with the Indian Ocean on the south. From a subtropical coastal strip, the land rises through grasslands to the mountainous escarpment that edges the South African interior plateau.

Government. Ruled by a military council installed after Gen Oupa Gqozo seized power in a March 1990 coup. South Africa's State President retains the power to legislate by proclamation and has veto power over the budget.

History. Oral tradition ascribes the origin of the Cape Nguni peoples to the central lakes area of Africa. They arrived in what is now Ciskei in the mid-17th century. White settlers from the Cape Colony first entered the territory a century later, but the Dutch East India Colony sought unsuccessfully to discourage white penetration. Nine wars between whites and the inhabitants, by now known as Xhosas, occurred between 1779 and 1878.

A Ciskeian territorial authority was established in 1961, with 84 chiefs and an executive council exercising limited self-government. In 1972, 20 elected members were added to the legislative assembly and a chief minister and six cabinet members elected by the assembly to function as an executive.

A proposed Constitution was approved by referendum on Oct. 30, 1980, and independence ceremonies held on Dec. 4. No government outside South Africa recognized the new state.

Economy. A subsistence agricultural economy has been superseded by commuter and migratory labor, which accounted for 64% of national income in 1977. There is some light industry and a potential for exploitation of limestone and other minerals.

TRANSKEI

Republic of Transkei
President: Chief Tutor N. Ndamase (1986)
Head of Military Council: Maj. Gen. Bantu Holomisa (1987)
Area: 15,831 sq mi. (41,002 sq km)
Population (est. 1986): 3,609,962 (growth rate: 2.2%)
Density per square mile: 151.6
Capital (est. 1989): Umtala, 57,796
Monetary unit: South African rand
Languages: English, Xhosa, Southern Sotho
Religions: Christian, 66%; tribal, 24%
Economic summary: Gross domestic product: $150 million. Per capita income: $86. Principal agricultural products: tea, corn, sorghum, dry beans. Major industrial products: timber, textiles. Natural resource: timber. Exports: timber, tea, sacks. Imports: foodstuffs, machines, equipment. Major trading partner: South Africa.

Geography. Transkei occupies three discontinuous enclaves within southeast South Africa that add up to twice the size of Massachusetts. It has a 270-mile (435 km) coastline on the Indian Ocean. The capital, Umtala, is connected by rail to the South African port of East London, 100 miles (161 km) to the southwest.

Government. Transkei was granted independence by South Africa as of Oct. 26, 1976. A constitution called for organization of a parliament composed of 77 chiefs and 75 elected members, with a ceremonial president and executive power in the hands of a prime minister.

The Organization of African States and the chairman of the United Nations Special Committee Against Apartheid denounced the new state as a sham and urged governments not to recognize it.

History. British rule was established over the Transkei region between 1866 and 1894, and the Transkeian Territories were formed in 1903. Under the Native Land Act of 1913, the Territories were reserved for black occupation. In 1963, Transkei was given internal self-government and a legislature that elected Paramount Chief Kaiser Matanzima as Chief Minister, a post he retained in elections in 1968 and 1973. Instability led to a coup in Dec. 1987.

Economy. Some 60% of Transkei is cultivated, producing corn, wheat, beans, and sorghum. Grazing is important. Some light industry has been established.

VENDA

Republic of Venda
Chairman of the Council of National Unity: Col. Gabriel Mutheiwana Ramushwana (1990)

Area: 2,510 sq mi. (6,500 sq km)
Population (est. 1982): 400,000 (average annual growth rate: 2.4%)
Density per square mile: 214.5
Capital: Thohoyandou
Largest town (est. 1980): Makearela, 2,500
Monetary unit: South African rand
Languages: Venda, English, Afrikaans
Religions: Christian, tribal
Economic summary: Gross domestic product: $156 million. Per capita income: $312. Principal agricultural products: meat, tea, fruit, sisal, corn. Major industrial products: timber, graphite, magnetite.

Geography. Venda is composed of two noncontiguous territories in northeast South Africa with a total area of about half that of Connecticut. It is mountainous but fertile, well-watered land, with a climate ranging from tropical to subtropical.

Government. The third of South Africa's homelands to be granted independence, Venda became a separate republic on Sept. 13, 1979, unrecognized by any government other than South Africa and its sister homelands, Transkei and Bophuthatswana. The President is popularly elected. An 84-seat legislature is half elected, half appointed.

History. The first European reached Venda in 1816, but the isolation of the area prevented its involvement in the wars of the 19th century between blacks and whites and with other tribes. Venda came under South African administration after the Boer War in 1902. Limited home rule was granted in 1962. Chief Patrick R. Mphephu, leader of one of the 27 tribes that historically made up the Venda nation, became Chief Minister of the interim government in 1973 and President upon independence in 1979. There has been a military regime in power since April 5, 1990.

SOVIET UNION

Union of Soviet Socialist Republics
President: Mikhail S. Gorbachev (1990)
Vice President: Gennady Yanayev (1990)
Prime Minister: Ivan Silayev (1991)
Area[1]: 8,580,545 sq mi. (22,223,509 sq km)
Population (est. 1991[1]): 284,110,000 (average annual rate of natural increase: .8%); birth rate: 18/1000; infant mortality rate: 23/1000; density per square mile[1]: 33.1
Capital: Moscow
Largest cities (1989): Moscow, 8,769,000; St. Petersburg, 4,456,000; Kiev, 2,587,000; Tashkent, 2,073,000; Baku, 1,757,000; Kharkov, 1,611,000; Minsk, 1,589,000; Novosibirsk, 1,436,000; Nizhny Novgorod, 1,438,000; Sverdlovsk, 1,367,000; Tbilisi, 1,260,000; Kuybyshev, 1,257,000; Dnepropetrovsk, 1,179,000
Monetary unit: Ruble
Languages: Russian, Ukranian, Uzbek, Byelorussian, Kazak, Tatar
Religions: Russian Orthodox (predominant), 20%; Islam, 10%; Roman Catholic, Protestant, Georgian Orthodox, Armenian Orthodox, 7%; Jewish, less than 1%; atheist 60% (est.)
National name: Soyuz Sovyetskikh Sotsialisticheskikh Respublik
Literacy rate: 99%
Economic summary[2]: Gross national product (1989 est.): $2,659 billion; $9,211 per capita; 1.4% real growth rate.

Arable land: 10%. Principal products: wheat, rye, corn, oats, potatoes, sugar beets, cotton and flax, cattle, pigs, sheep. Labor force: 152,300,000 civilians; 80% in industry. Major products: ferrous and nonferrous metals, fuels and power, building materials, chemicals, machinery. Natural resources: fossil fuels, water power, timber, manganese, lead, zinc, nickel, mercury, potash, phosphate. Exports: petroleum and petroleum products, natural gas, machinery and equipment, manufactured goods. Imports: grain, machinery and equipment, foodstuffs, steel products, consumer manufactures. Major trading partners: E. European countries; E.C., U.S., Cuba, China.

1. Does not include the total areas and population of the former Baltic republics. 2. Includes former Baltic republics.

Geography. The U.S.S.R. is the largest unbroken political unit in the world, occupying more than one-seventh of the land surface of the globe. The greater part of its territory is a vast plain stretching from eastern Europe to the Pacific Ocean. This plain, relieved only occasionally by low mountain ranges (no tably the Urals), consists of three zones running east and west: the frozen marshy tundra of the Arctic; the more temperate forest belt; and the steppes or prairies to the south, which in southern Soviet Asia become sandy deserts.

The topography is more varied in the south, particularly in the Caucasus between the Caspian and Black Seas, and in the Tien-Pamir mountain system bordering Afghanistan, Sinkiang, and Mongolia. Mountains (Stanovoi and Kolyma) and great rivers (Amur, Yenisei, Lena) also break up the sweep of the plain in Siberia.

In the west, the major rivers are the Volga, Dnieper, Don, Kama, and Southern Bug.

Government. The creation of a new supreme legislature—the 2,250-member Congress of People's Deputies—was approved at the 19th Communist Party Conference, which opened on June 28, 1988. It elected Gorbachev as President in 1990.

Following the abortive coup, the Congress in September 1991 established a transitional government consisting of an executive State Council and two subordinate bodies: a reconstituted parliament and an Inter-Republic Economic Committee. The State Council, led by President Gorbachev, consists of himself and leaders of the ten participating republics. The still vague plan for a new parliament calls for a Council of Republics, wherein each republic is allotted one vote, and a lower-house Council of Union, in which each republic's number of delegates and voting power is in proportion to its population. The Economic Committee, according to the tentative plan, is to oversee the running of the economy on a daily basis. Its leadership and membership are yet to be determined.

At present the State Council is charged with governing the country until the adoption of a new constitution and a new union treaty, which may in turn alter the above arrangement. By accepting the transitional plans the Congress of People's Deputies effectively voted to disband their organization.

History. Tradition says the Viking Rurik came to Russia in A.D. 862 and founded the first Russian dynasty in Novgorod. The various tribes were united by the spread of Christianity in the 10th and 11th centuries; Vladimir "the Saint" was converted in 988. During the 11th century, the grand dukes of Kiev held such centralizing power as existed. In 1240, Kiev was destroyed by the Mongols, and the Russian territory

was split into numerous smaller dukedoms, early dukes of Moscow extended their dominions through their office of tribute collector for the Mongols.

In the late 15th century, Duke Ivan III acquired Novgorod and Tver and threw off the Mongol yoke. Ivan IV, the Terrible (1533–84), first Muscovite Tsar, is considered to have founded the Russian state. He crushed the power of rival princes and boyars (great landowners), but Russia remained largely medieval until the reign of Peter the Great (1689–1725), grandson of the first Romanov Tsar, Michael (1613–45). Peter made extensive reforms aimed at westernization and, through his defeat of Charles XII of Sweden at the Battle of Poltava in 1709, he extended Russia's boundaries to the west.

Catherine the Great (1762–96) continued Peter's westernization program and also expanded Russian territory, acquiring the Crimea and part of Poland. During the reign of Alexander I (1801–25), Napoleon's attempt to subdue Russia was defeated (1812–13), and new territory was gained, including Finland (1809) and Bessarabia (1812). Alexander originated the Holy Alliance, which for a time crushed Europe's rising liberal movement.

Alexander II (1855–81) pushed Russia's borders to the Pacific and into central Asia. Serfdom was abolished in 1861, but heavy restrictions were imposed on the emancipated class. Revolutionary strikes following Russia's defeat in the war with Japan forced Nicholas II (1894–1917) to grant a representative national body (Duma), elected by narrowly limited suffrage. It met for the first time in 1906, little influencing Nicholas in his reactionary course.

World War I demonstrated tsarist corruption and inefficiency and only patriotism held the poorly equipped army together for a time. Disorders broke out in Petrograd (renamed Leningrad now St. Petersburg) in March 1917, and defection of the Petrograd garrison launched the revolution. Nicholas II was forced to abdicate on March 15, 1917, and he and his family were killed by revolutionists on July 16, 1918.

A provisional government under the successive premierships of Prince Lvov and a moderate, Alexander Kerensky, lost ground to the radical, or Bolshevik, wing of the Socialist Democratic Labor Party. On Nov. 7, 1917, the Bolshevik revolution, engineered by N. Lenin[1] and Leon Trotsky, overthrew the Kerensky government and authority was vested in a Council of People's Commissars, with Lenin as Premier.

The humiliating Treaty of Brest-Litovsk (March 3, 1918) concluded the war with Germany, but civil war and foreign intervention delayed Communist control of all Russia until 1920. A brief war with Poland in 1920 resulted in Russian defeat.

The Union of Soviet Socialist Republics was established as a federation on Dec. 30, 1922.

The death of Lenin on Jan. 21, 1924, precipitated an intraparty struggle between Joseph Stalin, General Secretary of the party, and Trotsky, who favored swifter socialization at home and fomentation of revolution abroad. Trotsky was dismissed as Commissar of War in 1925 and banished from the Soviet Union in 1929. He was murdered in Mexico City on Aug. 21, 1940, by a political agent.

Stalin further consolidated his power by a series of purges in the late 1930s, liquidating prominent party leaders and military officers. Stalin assumed the premiership May 6, 1941.

1. N. Lenin was the pseudonym taken by Vladimir Ilich Ulyanov. It is sometimes given as Nikolai Lenin or V. Lenin.

Republics of the U.S.S.R.

Republic and Capital	Area sq mi.	Population 1989 census (thousands)
Russian S.F.S.R. (Moscow)	6,592,800	147,400
Ukraine (Kiev)	233,100	51,707
Kazakhstan (Alma-Ata)	1,049,200	16,536
Byelorussia (Minsk)	80,200	10,200
Uzbekistan (Tashkent)	172,700	19,905
Georgia (Tbilisi)	26,900	5,443
Azerbaijan (Baku)	33,400	7,038
Moldavia (Kishinyov)	13,000	4,338
Kirghizia (Pishpek)	76,600	4,290
Tadzhikistan (Dushanbe)	55,300	5,109
Armenia (Yerevan)	11,500	3,288
Turkmenistan (Ashkhabad)	188,500	3,534

Soviet foreign policy, at first friendly toward Germany and antagonistic toward Britain and France and then, after Hitler's rise to power in 1933, becoming anti-Fascist and pro-League of Nations, took an abrupt turn on Aug. 24, 1939, with the signing of a nonaggression pact with Nazi Germany. The next month, Moscow joined in the German attack on Poland, seizing territory later incorporated into the Ukrainian and Byelorussian S.S.R.'s. The war with Finland, 1939–40, added territory to the Karelian S.S.R. set up March 31, 1940; the annexation of Bessarabia and Bukovina from Romania became part of the new Moldavian S.S.R. on Aug. 2, 1940; and the annexation of the Baltic republics of Estonia, Latvia, and Lithuania in June 1940 (never recognized by the U.S.) created the 14th, 15th, and 16th Soviet Republics. The illegal annexation of the Baltic republics was never recognized by the U.S. for the 51 years leading up to Soviet recognition of Estonia, Latvia and Lithuania's independence on September 6, 1991. (The number of so-called "Union" republics was reduced to 15 in 1956 when the Karelian S.S.R. became one of the 20 Autonomous Soviet Socialist Republics based on ethnic groups.)

The Soviet-German collaboration ended abruptly with a lightning attack by Hitler on June 22, 1941, which seized 500,000 square miles of Russian territory before Soviet defenses, aided by U.S. and British arms, could halt it. The Soviet resurgence at Stalingrad from November 1942 to February 1943 marked the turning point in a long battle, ending in the final offensive of January 1945.

Then, after denouncing a 1941 nonaggression pact with Japan in April 1945, when Allied forces were nearing victory in the Pacific, the Soviet Union declared war on Japan on Aug. 8, 1945, and quickly occupied Manchuria, Karafuto, and the Kurile islands.

The U.S.S.R. built a cordon of Communist states running from Poland in the north to Albania and Bulgaria in the south, including East Germany, Czechoslovakia, Hungary, and Romania, composed of the territories Soviet troops occupied at the war's end. With its Eastern front solidified, the Soviet Union launched a political offensive against the non-Communist West, moving first to block the Western access to Berlin. The Western powers countered with an airlift, completed unification of West Germany, and organized the defense of Western Europe in the North Atlantic Treaty Organization.

Stalin died on March 6, 1953, and was succeeded the next day by G. M. Malenkov as Premier. His chief rivals for power—Lavrenti P. Beria (chief of the secret police), Nikolai A. Bulganin, and Lazar M. Kaganovich—were named first deputies. Beria was purged in July and executed on Dec. 23, 1953.

The new power in the Kremlin was Nikita S. Khrushchev, First Secretary of the party.

Khrushchev formalized the Eastern European system into a Council for Mutual Economic Assistance (Comecon) and a Warsaw Pact Treaty Organization as a counterweight to NATO.

In its technological race with the U.S., the Soviet Union exploded a hydrogen bomb in 1953, developed an intercontinental ballistic missile by 1957, sent the first satellite into space (Sputnik I) in 1957, and put Yuri Gagarin in the first orbital flight around the earth in 1961.

Khrushchev's downfall stemmed from his decision to place Soviet nuclear missiles in Cuba and then, when challenged by the U.S., backing down and removing the weapons. He was also blamed for the ideological break with China after 1963.

Khrushchev was forced into retirement on Oct. 15, 1964, and was replaced by Leonid I. Brezhnev as First Secretary of the Party and Aleksei N. Kosygin as Premier.

President Nixon visited the U.S.S.R. for summit talks in May 1972, concluding agreements on strategic-arms limitation and a declaration of principles on future U.S.-Soviet relations.

President Carter, actively pursuing both human rights and disarmament, joined with the Soviet Union in September 1977 to declare that the SALT I accord, which would have expired Oct. 1 without further action, be maintained in effect while the two sides sought a new agreement (SALT II).

Brezhnev's 1977 election to the presidency followed publication of a new Constitution supplanting the one adopted in 1936. It specified the dominance of the Communist Party, previously unstated.

Carter and the ailing Brezhnev signed the SALT II treaty in Vienna on June 18, 1979, setting ceilings on each nation's arsenal of intercontinental ballistic missiles. Doubts about Senate ratification grew, and became a certainty on Dec. 27, when Soviet troops invaded Afghanistan. Despite protests from the Moslem and Western worlds, Moscow insisted that Afghan President Hafizullah Amin had asked for aid in quelling a rebellion.

In the face of evidence that Amin had been liquidated by Soviet advisers before the troops arrived, the Soviet Union vetoed a Security Council resolution on Jan. 7, 1980, that called for a withdrawal. Carter ordered a freeze on grain exports and high-technology equipment.

On Jan. 20, Carter called for a world boycott of the Summer Olympic Games scheduled for Moscow. The boycott, less than complete, nevertheless marred the first Olympics to be held in Moscow as the United States, Canada, Japan, and to a partial extent all the western allies except France and Italy shunned the event.

The Soviet Union maintained a stony defense in the face of criticism from Western Europe and the U.S., and a summit meeting of 37 Islamic nations that unanimously condemned the "imperialist invasion" of Afghanistan.

Despite the tension between Moscow and Washington, Strategic Arms Reduction Talks (START) began in Geneva between U.S. and Soviet delegations in mid-1982. Negotiations on intermediate missile reduction also continued in Geneva.

On November 10, 1982, Soviet radio and television announced the death of Leonid Brezhnev. Yuri V. Andropov, who formerly headed the K.G.B., was chosen to succeed Brezhnev as General Secretary. By

Rulers of Russia Since 1533

Name	Born	Ruled[1]	Name	Born	Ruled[1]
Ivan IV the Terrible	1530	1533–1584	Alexander II	1818	1855–1881
Theodore I	1557	1584–1598	Alexander III	1845	1881–1894
Boris Godunov	c.1551	1598–1605	Nicholas II	1868	1894–1917 [7]
Theodore II	1589	1605–1605			
Demetrius I[2]	?	1605–1606	**PROVISIONAL GOVERNMENT**		
Basil IV Shuiski	?	1606–1610 [3]	**(PREMIERS)**		
"Time of Troubles"	—	1610–1613	Prince Georgi Lvov	1861	1917–1917
Michael Romanov	1596	1613–1645	Alexander Kerensky	1881	1917–1917
Alexis I	1629	1645–1676			
Theodore III	1656	1676–1682	**POLITICAL LEADERS**		
Ivan V[4]	1666	1682–1689 [5]	N. Lenin	1870	1917–1924
Peter I the Great[4]	1672	1682–1725	Aleksei Rykov	1881	1924–1930
Catherine I	c.1684	1725–1727	Vyacheslav Molotov	1890	1930–1941
Peter II	1715	1727–1730	Joseph Stalin[8]	1879	1941–1953
Anna	1693	1730–1740	Georgi M. Malenkov	1902	1953–1955
Ivan VI	1740	1740–1741 [6]	Nikolai A. Bulganin	1895	1955–1958
Elizabeth	1709	1741–1762	Nikita S. Khrushchev	1894	1958–1964
Peter III	1728	1762–1762	Leonid I. Brezhnev	1906	1964–1982
Catherine II the Great	1729	1762–1796	Yuri V. Andropov	1914	1982–1984
Paul I	1754	1796–1801	Konstantin U. Chernenko	1912	1984–1985
Alexander I	1777	1801–1825	Mikhail S. Gorbachev	1931	1985–1991
Nicholas I	1796	1825–1855			

1. For Tsars through Nicholas II, year of end of rule is also that of death, unless otherwise indicated. 2. Also known as Pseudo–Demetrius. 3. Died 1612. 4. Ruled jointly until 1689, when Ivan was deposed. 5. Died 1696. 6. Died 1764. 7. Killed 1918. 8. General Secretary of Communist Party, 1924–53.

mid-June 1983, Andropov had assumed all of Brezhnev's three titles.

The Soviet Union broke off both the START talks and the parallel negotiations on European-based missiles in November 1983 in protest against the deployment of medium-range U.S. missiles in Western Europe.

After months of illness, Andropov died in February 1984. Konstantin U. Chernenko, a 72-year-old party stalwart who had been close to Brezhnev, succeeded him as General Secretary and, by mid-April, had also assumed the title of President. In the months following Chernenko's assumption of power, the Kremlin took on a hostile mood toward the West of a kind rarely seen since the height of the cold war 30 years before. Led by Moscow, all the Soviet bloc countries except Romania boycotted the 1984 Summer Olympic Games in Los Angeles—tit-for-tat for the U.S.-led boycott of the 1980 Moscow Games, in the view of most observers.

After 13 months in office, Chernenko died on March 10, 1985. He had been ill much of the time and left only a minor imprint on Soviet history.

Chosen to succeed him as Soviet leader was Mikhail S. Gorbachev, at 54 the youngest man to take charge of the Soviet Union since Stalin. Under Gorbachev, the Soviet Union began its long-awaited shift to a new generation of leadership. Unlike his immediate predecessors, Gorbachev did not also assume the title of President but wielded power from the post of party General Secretary. In a surprise move, Gorbachev elevated Andrei Gromyko, 75, for 28 years the Soviet Union's stony-faced Foreign Minister, to the largely ceremonial post of President. He installed a younger man with no experience in foreign affairs, Eduard Shevardnadze, 57, as Foreign Minister.

A new round of U.S. Soviet arms reduction negotiations began in Geneva in March 1985, this time involving three types of weapons systems.

The Soviet Union took much criticism in early 1986 over the April 24 meltdown at the Chernobyl nuclear plant and its reluctance to give out any information on the accident.

In June 1987, Gorbachev obtained the support of the Central Committee for proposals that would loosen some government controls over the economy and in June 1988, an unusually open party conference approved several resolutions for changes in the structure of the Soviet system. These included a shift of some power from the Party to local soviets, a ten-year limit on the terms of elected government and party officials, and an alteration in the office of the President to give it real power in domestic and foreign policy. Gorbachev was elected President in 1989. The elections to the Congress were the first competitive elections in the Soviet Union since 1917. Dissident candidates won a surprisingly large minority although pro-Government deputies maintained a strong lock on the Supreme Soviet.

Glasnost took a new turn when Lithuania declared its independence. The central government responded with an economic blockade. After a stalemate, Lithuania suspended, but didn't revoke, its declaration in return for a lifting of the blockade.

The possible beginning of the fragmentation of the Communist party took place when Boris Yeltsin, leader of the Russian S.S.R. who urges faster reform, left the Communist party along with other radicals.

In March 1991 the Soviet people were asked to vote on a referendum on national unity engineered by President Gorbachev. The resultant victory for the federal government was tempered by the separate approval in Russia for the creation of a popularly-elected republic presidency. In addition, six republics boycotted the vote.

The bitter election contest for the Russian presidency principally between Yeltsin and a Communist loyalist resulted in a major victory for Yeltsin. He took the oath of office for the new position on July 10.

Reversing his relative hard-line position adopted in the autumn of 1990, Gorbachev together with leaders of nine Soviet republics signed an accord, called the Union Treaty, which was meant to preserve the unity of the nation. In exchange the federal government would have turned over control of industrial and natural resources to the individual republics.

An attempted coup d'état took place on August 19 orchestrated by a group of eight senior officials calling itself the State Committee on the State of Emergency. Boris Yeltsin, held up in the Russian Parliament building, defiantly called for a general strike. The next day huge crowds demonstrated in Leningrad, and Yeltsin supporters fortified barricades surrounding the Parliament building. On August 21 the coup committee disbanded, and at least some of its members attempted to flee Moscow. The Soviet Parliament formally reinstated Gorbachev as President. Two days later he resigned from his position as General Secretary of the Communist Party and recommended that its Central Committee be disbanded. On August 29 the Parliament approved the suspension of all Communist Party activities pending an investigation of its role in the failed coup.

SPAIN

Kingdom of Spain
Ruler: King Juan Carlos I (1975)
Prime Minister: Felipe González Márquez (1982)
Area: 194,884 sq mi. (504,750 km)[1]
Population (est. mid-1991): 39,000,000 (average annual growth rate: 0.2%); birth rate: 11/1000; infant mortality rate: 8.3/1000; density per square mile: 200
Capital: Madrid
Largest cities (est. 1987): Madrid, 3,158,800; Barcelona, 1,752,627; Valencia, 774,748; Seville, 645,817
Monetary unit: Peseta
Languages: Spanish, Basque, Catalan, Galician
Religion: Roman Catholic, 99%
National name: Reino de España
Literacy rate: 97%
Economic summary: Gross national product (1989 est.): $398.7 billion; $10,100 per capita; 4.8% real growth rate. Arable land: 31%. Principal products: cereals, vegetables, citrus fruits, wine, olives and olive oil, livestock. Labor force: 14,621,000; 24% in industry. Major products: processed foods, textiles, footwear, petro-chemicals, steel, automobiles, ships. Natural resources: coal, lignite, water power, uranium, mercury, pyrites, fluorspar, gypsum, iron ore, zinc, lead, tungsten, copper. Exports: foodstuffs, live animals, wood, footwear, machinery, chemicals. Imports: machinery and transportation equipment, chemicals, petroleum, timber, iron, steel. Major trading partners: Western European nations, U.S., Middle Eastern countries.

---

1. Including the Balearic and Canary Islands.

Geography. Spain occupies 85% of the Iberian Peninsula in southwestern Europe, which it shares with Portugal; France is to the northeast, separated by the Pyrenees. The Bay of Biscay lies to the north, the Atlantic Ocean to the west, and the Mediterranean Sea to the south and east: Africa is less than 10 miles (16 km) south at the Strait of Gibraltar.

A broad central plateau slopes to the south and east, crossed by a series of mountain ranges and river valleys.

Principal rivers are the Ebro in the northeast, the Tajo in the central region, and the Guadalquivir in the south.

Off Spain's east coast in the Mediterranean are the Balearic Islands (1,936 sq mi.; 5,014 sq km), the largest of which is Majorca. Sixty miles (97 km) west of Africa are the Canary Islands (2,808 sq mi.; 7,273 sq km).

Government. King Juan Carlos I (born Jan. 5, 1938) succeeded Generalissimo Francisco Franco Bahamonde as Chief of State Nov. 27, 1975.

The Cortes, or Parliament, consists of a Chamber of Deputies of 350 members and a Senate of 208, all elected by universal suffrage. The new Cortes, replacing one that was largely appointed or elected by special constituencies, was organized under a constitution adopted by referendum Dec. 6, 1978.

History. Spain, originally inhabited by Celts, Iberians, and Basques, became a part of the Roman Empire in 206 B.C., when it was conquered by Scipio Africanus. In A.D. 412, the barbarian Visigothic leader Ataulf crossed the Pyrenees and ruled Spain, first in the name of the Roman emperor and then independently. In 711, the Moslems under Tariq entered Spain from Africa and within a few years completed the subjugation of the country. In 732, the Franks, led by Charles Martel, defeated the Moslems near Poitiers, thus preventing the further expansion of Islam in southern Europe. Internal dissension of Spanish Islam invited a steady Christian conquest from the north.

Aragon and Castile were the most important Spanish states from the 12th to the 15th century, consolidated by the marriage of Ferdinand II and Isabella I in 1469. The last Moslem stronghold, Granada, was captured in 1492. Roman Catholicism was established as the official state religion and the Jews (1492) and the Moslems (1502) expelled.

In the era of exploration, discovery, and colonization, Spain amassed tremendous wealth and a vast colonial empire through the conquest of Peru by Pizarro (1532–33) and of Mexico by Cortés (1519–21). The Spanish Hapsburg monarchy became for a time the most powerful in the world.

In 1588, Philip II sent his Invincible Armada to invade England, but its destruction cost Spain its supremacy on the seas and paved the way for England's colonization of America. Spain then sank rapidly to the status of a second-rate power and never again played a major role in European politics. Its colonial empire in the Americas and the Philippines vanished in wars and revolutions during the 18th and 19th centuries.

In World War I, Spain maintained a position of neutrality. In 1923, Gen. Miguel Primo de Rivera became dictator. In 1930, King Alfonso XIII revoked the dictatorship, but a strong antimonarchist and republican movement led to his leaving Spain in 1931. The new Constitution declared Spain a workers' republic, broke up the large estates, separated church and state, and secularized the schools. The elections held in 1936 returned a strong Popular Front majority, with Manuel Azaña as President.

On July 18, 1936, a conservative army officer in Morocco, Francisco Franco Bahamonde, led a mutiny against the government. The civil war that followed lasted three years and cost the lives of nearly a million people. Franco was aided by Fascist Italy and Nazi Germany, while Soviet Russia helped the Loyalist side. Several hundred leftist Americans served in the Abraham Lincoln Brigade on the side of the republic. The war ended when Franco took Madrid on March 28, 1939.

Franco became head of the state, national chief of the Falange Party (the governing party), and Premier and Caudillo (leader). In a referendum in 1947, the Spanish people approved a Franco-drafted succession law declaring Spain a monarchy again. Franco, however, continued as Chief of State.

In 1969, Franco and the Cortes designated Prince Juan Carlos Alfonso Victor María de Borbón (who married Princess Sophia of Greece on May 14, 1962) to become King of Spain when the provisional government headed by Franco came to an end. He is the grandson of Alfonso XIII and the son of Don Juan, pretender to the throne.

Franco died of a heart attack on Nov. 20, 1975, after more than a year of ill health, and Juan Carlos was proclaimed King seven days later.

Over strong rightist opposition, the government legalized the Communist Party in advance of the 1977 elections. Premier Adolfo Suaraz Gonzalez's Union of the Democratic Center, a coalition of a dozen centrist and rightist parties, claimed 34.3% of the popular vote in the election.

Under pressure from Catalonian and Basque nationalists, Suárez granted home rule to these regions in 1979, but centrists backed by him did poorly in the 1980 elections for local assemblies in the two areas. Economic problems persisted, along with new incidents of terrorism, and Suárez resigned on Jan. 29, 1981 and was succeeded by Leopoldo Calvo Sotelo.

With the overwhelming election of Prime Minister Felipe González Márquez and his Spanish Socialist Workers Party in the Oct. 20, 1982, parliamentary elections, the Franco past was finally buried. The thrust of González, a pragmatic moderate, was to modernize rather than radicalize Spain.

A treaty admitting Spain, along with Portugal, to the European Economic Community took effect on Jan. 1, 1986. Later that year, in June, Spain voted to remain in NATO, but outside of its military command.

A cabinet reshuffle in March 1991 effectively meant a shift to the right with a left-wing deputy being replaced by a moderate. Nationwide regional and municipal elections in May produced a setback for the ruling Socialist Party.

SRI LANKA

Democratic Socialist Republic of Sri Lanka
President: Ranasinghe Premadasa (1988)
Prime Minister: Hondoval D. B. Wijetunga (1989)
Area: 25,332 sq mi. (65,610 sq km)
Population (est. mid-1991): 17,400,000 (average annual rate of natural increase: 1.5%); birth rate: 21/1000; infant mortality rate: 19.4/1000; density per square mile: 688
Capital: Sri Jayewardenepura Kotte (Colombo)
Largest cities (est. 1990): Colombo, 1,262,000; Kandy, 200,000; Jafna, 250,000; Galle, 170,000
Monetary unit: Sri Lanka rupee
Languages: Sinhala, Tamil, English
Religions: Buddhist, 69%; Hindu, 15%; Islam, 8%; Christian, 8%
Member of Commonwealth of Nations
Literacy rate: 87%
Economic summary: Gross domestic product (1989): $7 billion; $416 per capita; 6.25% real growth rate (1990). Arable land: 16%. Principal products: tea, coconuts, rubber, rice, spices. Labor force: 6,600,000; 13.3% in mining and manufacturing. Major products: processed rubber, tea, coconuts, textiles, cement, refined petroleum. Natural resources: limestone, graphite, gems. Exports: textiles, tea, rubber, petroleum products, gems and jewelry. Imports: petroleum, machinery, transport equipment, sugar. Major trading partners: Egypt, Iraq, Saudi Arabia, U.S., U.K., Germany, Japan, Singapore, India.

Geography. An island in the Indian Ocean off the southeast tip of India, Sri Lanka is about half the size of Alabama. Most of the land is flat and rolling;

mountains in the south central region rise to over 8,000 feet (2,438 m).

Government. Ceylon became an independent country in 1948 after British rule and reverted to the traditional name (resplendent island) on May 22, 1972. A new Constitution was adopted in 1978, replacing that of 1972.

The new Constitution set up the National State Assembly, a 168-member unicameral legislature that serves for six years unless dissolved earlier.

History. Following Portuguese and Dutch rule, Ceylon became an English crown colony in 1798. The British developed coffee, tea, and rubber plantations and granted six Constitutions between 1798 and 1924. The Constitution of 1931 gave a large measure of self-government.

Ceylon became a self-governing dominion of the Commonwealth of Nations in 1948.

Presidential elections were held in December 1982, and won by J.R. Jayewardene.

Tension between the Tamil minority and the Sinhalese majority continued to build and erupted in bloody violence in 1983 that has grown worse since. There are about 2.6 million Tamils in Sri Lanka, while the Sinhalese make up about three-quarters of the 17-million population. Tamil extremists are fighting for a separate nation.

Negotiations broke down in late 1986. A string of Tamil atrocities in early 1987 brought on a government offensive in May-June against guerilla base areas.

The civil war continued during 1990 after a 13-month cease-fire collapsed. The president ruled month to month. The Tamil guerrillas announced a unilateral cease-fire to take effect on January 1, 1991, and the government, too, suspended operations. The cease-fire broke down ten days later. In the early months of 1991 the rebel forces suffered severe casualties.

India had sent soldiers in July 1987 to help enforce an accord granting the Tamil minority limited autonomy. The agreement failed, and Indian troops withdrew at the end of 1989.

SUDAN

Republic of the Sudan
Prime Minister: Brig. Omar Hassam Ahmed Bashir (1989)
Area: 967,491 sq mi. (2,505,802 sq km)
Population (est. mid-1991): 25,900,000 (average annual rate of natural increase: 2.9%); birth rate: 44/1000; infant mortality rate: 104/1000; density per square mile: 27
Capital: Khartoum
Largest cities (est. 1988): Khartoum, 817,000; Omdurman, 527,000; Port Sudan, 207,000
Monetary unit: Sudanese pound
Languages: Arabic, English, tribal dialects
Religions: Islam, 70% (Sunni); indigenous, 20%; Christian, 5%
National name: Jamhuryat es-Sudan
Literacy rate: 31% (1986)
Economic summary: Gross domestic product (FY89 est.): $8.5 billion; $340 per capita (FY87); 7% real growth rate. Arable land: 5%. Principal products: cotton, oil seeds, gum arabic, sorghum, wheat, millet, sheep. Labor force: 8,500,000, 10% in industry and commerce. Major products: cement, textiles, pharmaceuticals, shoes, soap, refined petroleum. Natural resources: crude oil, some iron ore, copper, chrome, industrial

metals. Exports: cotton, peanuts, gum arabic, sesame. Imports: petroleum products, machinery and equipment, medicines and chemicals. Major trading partners: Western Europe, Saudi Arabia, Eastern Europe, Japan, U.S.

Geography. The Sudan, in northeast Africa, is the largest country on the continent, measuring about one fourth the size of the United States. Its neighbors are Chad and the Central African Republic on the west, Egypt and Libya on the north, Ethiopia on the east, and Kenya, Uganda, and Zaire on the south. The Red Sea washes about 500 miles of the eastern coast.

The country extends from north to south about 1,200 miles (1,931 km) and west to east about 1,000 miles (1,609 km). The northern region is a continuation of the Libyan Desert. The southern region is fertile, abundantly watered, and, in places, heavily forested. It is traversed from north to south by the Nile, all of whose great tributaries are partly or entirely within its borders.

Government. On January 31, 1991, a criminal code became law that applied Islamic law in the predominantly Moslem north, but not in the more Christian south. The ruling military council passed a decree on February 4 dividing the country into nine states each administered by a governor and a cabinet of ministers.

History. The early history of the Sudan (known as the Anglo-Egyptian Sudan between 1898 and 1955) is linked with that of Nubia, where a powerful local kingdom was formed in Roman times with its capital at Dongola. After conversion to Christianity in the 6th century, it joined with Ethiopia and resisted Mohammedanization until the 14th century. Thereafter the area was broken up into many small states until 1820–22, when it was conquered by Mohammed Ali, Pasha of Egypt. Egyptian forces were evacuated during the Mahdist revolt (1881–98), but the Sudan was reconquered by the Anglo-Egyptian expeditions of 1896–98, and in 1899 became an Anglo-Egyptian condominium, which was reaffirmed by the Anglo-Egyptian treaty of 1936.

Egypt and Britain agreed in 1953 to grant self-government to the Sudan under an appointed Governor-General. An all-Sudanese Parliament was elected in November-December 1953, and an all-Sudanese government was formed. In December 1955, the Parliament declared the independence of the Sudan, which, with the approval of Britain and Egypt, was proclaimed on Jan. 1, 1956.

In October 1969, Maj. Gen. Gaafar Mohamed Nimeiri, the president of the Council for the Revolution, took over as prime minister. He was elected the nation's first president in 1971.

In 1976, a third coup was attempted against Nimeiri. Nimeiri accused President Muammar el Qaddafi of Libya of having instigated the attempt and broke relations with Libya.

On April 6, 1985, while out of the country on visits to the United States and Egypt, Nimeiri lost power in the same way he gained it 16 years previously—by a military coup headed by his Defense Minister, Gen. Abdel Rahman Siwar el-Dahab.

Among the problems that the new government faced were a debilitating civil war with rebels in the south of the country, other sectarian and tribal conflicts, and a famine.

The government's inability to cope with the war led to disaffections within the army and a military coup in June 1989.

The U.N. estimates that over seven million people in Sudan are threatened with famine as a result of the second successive year of extreme drought and the seven-year civil war. The change to a federal system inaugurated at the beginning of 1991 was part of an attempt to end the war.

SURINAME

Republic of Suriname
President: Johan Kraag (1990)
Vice President and Prime Minister: Henck Aaron (1988)
Area: 63,251 sq mi. (163,820 sq km)
Population (est. mid-1991): 400,000 (average annual rate of natural increase: 2%); birth rate: 26/1000; infant mortality rate: 31/1000; density per square mile: 7
Capital and largest city (est. 1982): Paramaribo, 100,000
Monetary unit: Suriname guilder
Languages: Dutch, Surinamese (lingua franca), English also widely spoken
Religions: Protestant, 25.2%; Roman Catholic, 22.8%; Hindu, 27.4%; Islam, 19.6%; indigenous, about 5%
Literacy rate: 65%
Economic summary: Gross domestic product (1988 est.): $1.27 billion; $3,215 per capita; real growth rate 3.6%. Arable land: NEGL %. Principal products: rice. Labor force: 104,000 (1984). Major products: aluminum, alumina, processed foods, lumber. Natural resources: bauxite, iron ore, timber, fish, shrimp. Exports: bauxite, alumina, aluminum, rice, shrimp, lumber and wood products. Imports: capital equipment, petroleum, cotton, foodstuffs, consumer goods.Major trading partners: U.S., Trinidad, Netherlands, Norway.

Geography. Suriname lies on the northeast coast of South America, with Guyana to the west, French Guiana to the east, and Brazil to the south. It is about one-tenth larger than Michigan. The principal rivers are the Corantijn on the Guyana border, the Marowijne in the east, and the Suriname, on which the capital city of Paramaribo is situated. The Tumuc-Humac Mountains are on the border with Brazil.

Government. Suriname, formerly known as Dutch Guiana, became an independent republic on Nov. 25, 1975. Elections in November 1987 gave the Front for Democracy and Development coalition an overwhelming majority in the 51-seat National Assembly. The coalition elected Shankar and Aaron as President and Vice-President in January 1988.

A draft constitution approved in September 1987 gave the military a continuing behind-the-scenes role in the government.

History. England established the first European settlement on the Suriname River in 1650 but transferred sovereignty to the Dutch in 1667 in the Treaty of Breda, by which the British acquired New York. Colonization was confined to a narrow coastal strip, and until the abolition of slavery in 1863, African slaves furnished the labor for the plantation economy. After 1870, laborers were imported from British India and the Dutch East Indies.

In 1948, the colony was integrated into the Kingdom of the Netherlands and two years later was granted full home rule in other than foreign affairs and defense. After race rioting over unemployment and inflation, the Netherlands offered complete independence in 1973. Henck A. E. Aaron, leader of a coalition of Creole (Surinamese of African descent) parties, advocated independence, while Jaggernath

Lachmon, leader of the Surinamese of East Indian descent, urged delay.

During much of the 1980s Suriname has been under the control of Lieut. Col. Dési Bouterse, who in late December 1990 resigned as commander of the armed forces. The following night Pres. Shenkar was ousted in a bloodless coup. A few days later interim president Johan Krug acted to reinstate Bouterse.

In March 1991 insurgent leader Ronny Brunswijk pledged to end his four-year rebellion. In May national elections gave two parties favoring stronger ties to the Netherlands more than a two-thirds majority.

SWAZILAND

Kingdom of Swaziland
Ruler: King Mswati III (1986)
Prime Minister: Obed Dlamini (1989)
Area: 6,704 sq mi. (17,363 sq km)
Population (est. mid-1991): 800,000 (average annual rate of natural increase: 3.1%); birth rate: 46/1000; infant mortality rate: 101/1000; density per square mile: 122
Capital (est. 1986): Mbabane, 40,000
Monetary unit: Lilangeni
Languages: English and Swazi (official)
Religions: Christian, 60%; indigenous, 40%
Member of Commonwealth of Nations
Literacy rate: 67.9%
Economic summary: Gross national product (1989 est.): $539 million; $750 per capita; 5.7% real growth rate. Arable land: 8%. Principal products: corn, livestock, sugar cane, citrus fruits, cotton, sorghum, peanuts. Labor force: 195,000; about 92,000 wage earners with 14% in manufacturing. Major products: milled sugar, ginned cotton, processed meat and wood. Natural resources: asbestos, diamonds. Exports: sugar, wood pulp, asbestos, citrus fruits. Imports: motor vehicles, transport equipment, petroleum products, foodstuffs, chemicals. Major trading partners: South Africa, U.K., U.S.

Geography. Swaziland, 85% the size of New Jersey, is surrounded by South Africa and Mozambique. The country consists of a high veld in the west and a series of plateaus descending from 6,000 feet (1,829 m) to a low veld of 1,500 feet (457 m).

Government. In 1967, a new Constitution established King Sobhuza II as head of state and provided for an Assembly of 24 members elected by universal suffrage, together with a Senate of 12 members—half appointed by the Assembly and half by the King. In 1973, the King renounced the Constitution, suspended political parties, and took total power for himself. In 1977, he replaced the Parliament with an assembly of tribal leaders. The Parliament reconvened in 1979.

History. Bantu peoples migrated southwest to the area of Mozambique in the 16th century. A number of clans broke away from the main body in the 18th century and settled in Swaziland. In the 19th century they organized as a tribe, partly because they were in constant conflict with the Zulu. Their ruler, Mswazi, applied to the British in the 1840s for help against the Zulu. The British and the Transvaal governments guaranteed the independence of Swaziland in 1881.

South Africa held Swaziland as a protectorate from 1894 to 1899, but after the Boer War, in 1902, Swaziland was transferred to British administration. The Paramount Chief was recognized as the native authority in 1941.

In 1963, the territory was constituted a protectorate, and on Sept. 6, 1968, it became the independent nation of Swaziland.

King Sobhuza died in August 1982.

A substantial drug trade has developed with South Africa.

SWEDEN

Kingdom of Sweden
Sovereign: King Carl XVI Gustaf (1973)
Prime Minister: Ingvar Carlsson (1986)
Area: 173,800 sq mi. (449,964 sq km)
Population (est. mid-1991): 8,600,000 (average annual rate of natural increase: 0.3%); birth rate: 14/1000; infant mortality rate: 5.8/1000; density per square mile: 50
Capital: Stockholm
Largest cities (est. 1986): Stockholm, 1,435,000; Göteborg, 704,000; Malmö, 458,000
Monetary unit: Krona
Language: Swedish
Religions: Evangelical Lutheran, 93.5%; Roman Catholic, 1%; other, 5.5%
National name: Konungariket Sverige
Literacy rate: 99%
Economic summary: Gross domestic product (1989 est.): $132.7 billion; $15,700 per capita; 2.1% real growth rate. Arable land: 7%. Principal agricultural products: dairy products, grains, sugar beets, potatoes. Labor force: 4,526,000 (1989); 22% in mining and manufacturing. Major products: iron and steel, precision equipment, wood pulp and paper products, automobiles. Natural resources: forests, iron ore, hydroelectric power, zinc, uranium. Exports: machinery, motor vehicles, wood pulp, paper products, iron and steel products. Imports: machinery, petroleum, yarns, foodstuffs, iron and steel, chemicals. Major trading partners: Norway, Germany, U.K., Denmark, U.S.

Geography. Sweden occupies the eastern part of the Scandinavian peninsula, with Norway to the west, Finland and the Gulf of Bothnia to the east, and Denmark and the Baltic Sea in the south. Sweden is the fourth largest country in Europe and is one-tenth larger than California.

The country slopes eastward and southward from the Kjölen Mountains along the Norwegian border, where the peak elevation is Kebnekaise at 6,965 feet (2,123 m) in Lapland. In the north are mountains and many lakes. To the south and east are central lowlands and south of them are fertile areas of forest, valley, and plain.

Along Sweden's rocky coast, chopped up by bays and inlets, are many islands, the largest of which are Gotland and Öland.

Government. Sweden is a constitutional monarchy. Under the 1975 Constitution, the Riksdag is the sole governing body. The prime minister is the political chief executive.

In 1967, agreement was reached on part of a new Constitution after 13 years of work. It provided for a single-house Riksdag of 350 members (later amended to 349 seats) to replace the 104-year old bicameral Riksdag. The members are popularly elected for three years. Ninety-two present members of the Riksdag are women.

The King, Carl XVI Gustaf, was born April 30, 1946, and succeeded to the throne Sept. 19, 1973, on the death at 90 of his grandfather, Gustaf VI Adolf. Carl Gustaf was married on June 19, 1976, to Silvia Sommerlath, a West German commoner. They have three children:

Princess Victoria, born July 14, 1977; Prince Carl Philip, born May 13, 1979; and Princess Madeleine, born June 10, 1982. Under the new Act of Succession, effective Jan. 1, 1980, the first child of the reigning monarch, regardless of sex, is heir to the throne.

History. The earliest historical mention of Sweden is found in Tacitus' *Germania*, where reference is made to the powerful king and strong fleet of the Suiones. Toward the end of the 10th century, Olaf Sköttkonung established a Christian stronghold in Sweden. Around 1400, an attempt was made to unite the northern nations into one kingdom, but this led to bitter strife between the Danes and the Swedes.

In 1520, the Danish King, Christian II, conquered Sweden and in the "Stockholm Bloodbath" put leading Swedish personalities to death. Gustavus Vasa (1523–60) broke away from Denmark and fashioned the modern Swedish state.

Sweden played a leading role in the second phase (1630–35) of the Thirty Years' War (1618–48). By the Treaty of Westphalia (1648), Sweden obtained western Pomerania and some neighboring territory on the Baltic. In 1700, a coalition of Russia, Poland, and Denmark united against Sweden and by the Peace of Nystad (1721) forced it to relinquish Livonia, Ingria, Estonia, and parts of Finland.

Sweden emerged from the Napoleonic Wars with the acquisition of Norway from Denmark and with a new royal dynasty stemming from Marshal Jean Bernadotte of France, who became King Charles XIV (1818–44). The artificial union between Sweden and Norway led to an uneasy relationship, and the union was finally dissolved in 1905.

Sweden maintained a position of neutrality in both World Wars.

An elaborate structure of welfare legislation, imitated by many larger nations, began with the establishment of old-age pensions in 1911. Economic prosperity based on its neutralist policy enabled Sweden, together with Norway, to pioneer in public health, housing, and job security programs.

Forty-four years of Socialist government were ended in 1976 with the election of a conservative coalition headed by Thorbjörn Fälldin, a 50-year-old sheep farmer.

Fälldin resigned on Oct. 5, 1978, when his conservative parties partners demanded less restrictions on nuclear power, and his successor, Ola Ullsten, resigned a year later after failing to achieve a consensus on the issue. Returned to office by his coalition partners, Fälldin said he would follow the course directed by a national referendum. On March 23, 1980, voters backed the development of 12 nuclear plants and use of them for at least 25 years to supply 40% of national energy needs while the search for alternative sources continued.

Olof Palme and the Socialists were returned to power in the election of 1982.

In February 1986, Palme was killed by an unknown assailant.

Spiraling inflation coupled with its already high cost of living moved the government in 1990 to act on an austerity package that seriously shook the electorate's confidence in the long-ruling Social Democrats. In July 1991 Sweden formally filed an application for membership in the European Community.

SWITZERLAND

Swiss Confederation

President: Flavio Cotti (1991)
Vice President: René Felber (1991)
Area: 15,941 sq mi. (41,288 sq km)
Population (est. mid-1991): 6,800,000 (average annual rate of natural increase: 0.3%); birth rate: 12/1000; infant mortality rate: 7.3/1000; density per square mile: 424
Capital: Bern
Largest cities (1989): Zurich, 342,900; Basel, 169,600; Geneva, 165,400; Bern, 134,400; Lausanne, 122,600
Monetary unit: Swiss franc
Languages: German, 65%; French, 18%; Italian, 10%; Romansch, 1%
Religions: Roman Catholic, 49%; Protestant, 48%
National name: Schweiz/Suisse/Svizzera/Svizra
Literacy rate: 99%
Economic summary: Gross national product (1989 est.): $119.5 billion; $17,800 per capita; 3.0% real growth rate. Arable land: 10%. Principal products: cheese and other dairy products, livestock. Labor force: 3,220,000; 39% in industry and crafts;. Major products: watches and clocks, precision instruments, machinery, chemicals, pharmaceuticals, textiles. Natural resources: water power, timber, salt. Exports: machinery and equipment, precision instruments, textiles, foodstuffs, metal products. Imports: transport equipment, foodstuffs, chemicals, textiles, construction material. Major trading partners: U.S., E.C., Japan

Geography. Switzerland, in central Europe, is the land of the Alps. Its tallest peak is the Dufourspitze at 15,203 feet (4,634 m) on the Swiss side of the Italian border, one of 10 summits of the Monte Rose massif in the Apennines. The tallest peak in all of the Alps, Mont Blanc (15,771 ft; 4,807 m), is actually in France.

Most of Switzerland comprises a mountainous plateau bordered by the great bulk of the Alps on the south and by the Jura Mountains on the northwest. About one-fourth of the total area is covered by mountains and glaciers.

The country's largest lakes—Geneva, Constance (Bodensee), and Maggiore—straddle the French, German-Austrian, and Italian borders, respectively.

The Rhine, navigable from Basel to the North Sea, is the principal inland waterway. Other rivers are the Aare and the Rhône.

Switzerland, twice the size of New Jersey, is surrounded by France, West Germany, Austria, Liechtenstein, and Italy.

Government. The Swiss Confederation consists of 23 sovereign cantons, of which three are divided into six half-cantons. Federal authority is vested in a bicameral legislature. The Ständerat, or State Council, consists of 46 members, two from each canton. The lower house, the Nationalrat, or National Council, has 200 deputies, elected for four-year terms.

Executive authority rests with the Bundesrat, or Federal Council, consisting of seven members chosen by parliament. The parliament elects the President, who serves for one year and is succeeded by the Vice President. The federal government regulates foreign policy, railroads, postal service, and the national mint. Each canton reserves for itself important local powers.

A constitutional amendment adopted in 1971 by referendum gave women the vote in federal elections and the right to hold federal office. An equal rights amendment was passed in a national referendum June

14, 1981, barring discrimination against women under canton as well as federal law.

A referendum in March 1990 gave 18-year olds the right to vote in federal elections. A similar referendum failed to pass in 1979.

History. Called Helvetia in ancient times, Switzerland in the Middle Ages was a league of cantons of the Holy Roman Empire. Fashioned around the nucleus of three German forest districts of Schwyz, Uri, and Unterwalden, the Swiss Confederation slowly added new cantons. In 1648 the Treaty of Westphalia gave Switzerland its independence from the Holy Roman Empire.

French revolutionary troops occupied the country in 1798 and named it the Helvetic Republic, but Napoleon in 1803 restored its federal government. By 1815, the French- and Italian-speaking peoples of Switzerland had been granted political equality.

In 1815, the Congress of Vienna guaranteed the neutrality and recognized the independence of Switzerland. In the revolutionary period of 1847, the Catholic cantons seceded and organized a separate union called the *Sonderbund.* In 1848 the new Swiss Constitution established a union modeled upon that of the U.S. The Federal Constitution of 1874 established a strong central government while maintaining large powers of control in each canton.

National unity and political conservatism grew as the country prospered from its neutrality. Its banking system became the world's leading repository for international accounts. Strict neutrality was its policy in World Wars I and II. Geneva was the seat of the League of Nations (later the European headquarters of the United Nations) and of a number of international organizations.

In 1971, the Swiss Supreme Court ruled that Swiss banks must show U.S. tax officials records of U.S. citizens suspected of tax fraud, thus significantly modifying a 1934 law that had seemed to forbid any bank disclosures.

SYRIA

Syrian Arab Republic
President: Hafez al-Assad (1971)
Premier: Mahmoud al-Zubi (1987)
Area: 71,498 sq mi. (185,180 sq km)
Population (est. mid-1991): 12,800,000 (average annual rate of natural increase: 3.8%); birth rate: 43/1000; infant mortality rate: 37/1000; density per square mile: 179
Capital: Damascus
Largest cities (est. 1987): Damascus, 1,292,000; Aleppo, 1,216,000; Homs, 431,000; Hama, 214,000; Latakia, 241,000
Monetary unit: Syrian pound
Language: Arabic
Religions: Islam, 90%; Christian, 10%
National name: Al-Jamhouriya al Arabiya As-Souriya
Literacy rate: 49%
Economic summary: Gross domestic product (1989 est.): $18.5 billion, $1,540 per capita; –2% real growth rate. Arable land: 28%. Principal products: Cotton, wheat, barley, lentils, sheep, goats. Labor force: 2,400,000; 32% in industry. Major products: textiles, phosphate, petroleum, processed food. Natural resources: chrome, manganese, asphalt, iron ore, rock salt, phosphate, oil, gypsum. Exports: petroleum, textiles, phosphates. Imports: machinery and metal products, fuels,

foodstuffs. Major trading partners: Italy, Romania, U.S.S.R., U.S., Iran, Libya, France, Germany.

Geography. Slightly larger than North Dakota, Syria lies at the eastern end of the Mediterranean Sea. It is bordered by Lebanon and Israel on the west, Turkey on the north, Iraq on the east, and Jordan on the south.

Coastal Syria is a narrow plain, in back of which is a range of coastal mountains, and still farther inland a steppe area. In the east is the Syrian Desert, and in the south is the Jebel Druze Range. The highest point in Syria is Mount Hermon (9,232 ft; 2,814 m) on the Lebanese border.

Government. Syria's first permanent Constitution was approved in 1973, replacing a provisional charter that had been in force for 10 years. It provided for an elected People's Council as the legislature.

In the first election in 10 years, in 1973, the Ba'ath Arab Socialist Party of President Hafez al-Assad, running on a unified National Progressive ticket with the Communist and Socialist parties, won 70% of the vote and a commensurate proportion of the seats in the People's Assembly. In 1977 and 1981 elections, the ruling Ba'athists won by similar margins.

History. Ancient Syria was conquered by Egypt about 1500 B.C., and after that by Hebrews, Assyrians, Chaldeans, Persians, and Greeks. From 64 B.C. until the Arab conquest in A.D. 636, it was part of the Roman Empire except during brief periods. The Arabs made it a trade center for their extensive empire, but it suffered severely from the Mongol invasion in 1260 and fell to the Ottoman Turks in 1516. Syria remained a Turkish province until World War I.

A secret Anglo-French pact of 1916 put Syria in the French zone of influence. The League of Nations gave France a mandate over Syria after World War I, but the French were forced to put down several nationalist uprisings. In 1930, France recognized Syria as an independent republic, but still subject to the mandate. After nationalist demonstrations in 1939, the French High Commissioner suspended the Syrian Constitution. In 1941, British and Free French forces invaded Syria to eliminate Vichy control. During the rest of World War II, Syria was an Allied base.

Again in 1945, nationalist demonstrations broke into actual fighting, and British troops had to restore order. Syrian forces met a series of reverses while participating in the Arab invasion of Palestine in 1948. In 1958, Egypt and Syria formed the United Arab Republic, with Gamal Abdel Nasser of Egypt as President. However, Syria became independent again on Sept. 29, 1961, following a revolution.

In the war of 1967, Israel quickly vanquished the Syrian army. Before acceding to the U.N. cease-fire, the Israeli forces took over control of the fortified Golan Heights commanding the Sea of Galilee.

Syria joined Egypt in attacking Israel in October 1973 in the fourth Arab-Israeli war, but was pushed back from initial successes on the Golan Heights to end up losing more land. However, in the settlement worked out by U.S. Secretary of State Henry A. Kissinger in 1974, the Syrians recovered all the territory lost in 1973 and a token amount of territory, including the deserted town of Quneitra, lost in 1967.

Syrian troops, in Lebanon since 1976 as part of an Arab peacekeeping force whose other members subsequently departed, intervened increasingly during 1980 and 1981 on the side of Moslem Lebanese in their clashes with Christian militants supported by Israel. When Israeli jets shot down Syrian helicopters operating in Lebanon in April 1981, Syria moved Soviet-built surface-to-air (SAM 6) missiles into Lebanon's Bekaa Valley. Israel demanded that the missiles be removed because they violated a 1976 understanding between the governments. The demand, backed up by bombing raids, prompted the Reagan Administration to send veteran diplomat Philip C. Habib as a special envoy to avert a new conflict between the nations.

Habib's carefully engineered cease-fire was shattered by a new Israeli invasion in June 1982, when Israeli aircraft bombed Bekaa Valley missile sites, claiming to destroy all of them along with 25 Syrian planes that had sought to defend the sites. On the ground, Syrian army units were driven back by Israeli armor along the Lebanese coast. The Syrians, who were equipped with Soviet weapons, were outfought everywhere by U.S.-equipped Israelis.

Nevertheless, while the Israelis overran most of the rest of Lebanon, the Syrians retained their positions in the Bekaa Valley. Over the next three years, as the Israelis gradually withdrew their forces, the Syrians remained. As the various Lebanese factions fought each other, the Syrians became the dominant force in the country, both militarily and politically.

The first Arab country to condemn Iraq's invasion of Kuwait, Syria sent troops to help defend Saudi Arabia from possible Iraq attack. After the Gulf war hope for peace negotiations between Israel and Arab states, particularly Syria, rose then floundered.

In 1990 President Assad ruled out any possibility of legalizing opposition political parties.

TAIWAN

Republic of China
President: Li Teng-hui (1988)
Premier: Hao Po-ts'un (1991)
Area: 13,895 sq mi. (35,988 sq km)
Population (est. mid-1991): 20,500,000 (average annual rate of natural increase: 1.1%); birth rate: 16/1000; infant mortality rate: 6.2/1000; density per square mile: 1,644
Capital: Taipei
Largest cities (1991): Taipei, 2,724,829; Kaohsiung, 1,398,667; Tai Chung, 764,651; Tainan, 685,390; Chilung (Keelung), 353,594
Monetary unit: New Taiwan dollar
Languages: Chinese (Mandarin) and various dialects
Religions: mixture of Buddhist, Confucian, and Taoist, 93%; Christian, 4.5%; other, 2.5%
Literacy rate: 94%
Economic summary: Gross national product (1990): $161.7 billion. Real growth rate (1990): 5.29%. Per capita income (1990): $7,332. Arable land: 24%; principal products: rice, yams, sugar cane, bananas, pineapples, citrus fruits. Labor force: 7,880,000; 41% in industry; major products: textiles, clothing, chemicals, processed foods, electronic equipment, cement, ships, plywood. Natural resources: coal, natural gas, limestone, marble. Exports: textiles, electrical machinery, plywood. Imports: machinery, basic metals, crude oil, chemicals. Major trading partners: U.S., Japan, Hong Kong, Germany.

Geography. The Republic of China today consists of the island of Taiwan, an island 100 miles (161 km) off the Asian mainland in the Pacific; two off-shore islands, Quemoy and Matsu; and the nearby islets of the Pescadores chain. It is slightly larger than the combined areas of Massachusetts and Connecticut.

Taiwan is divided by a central mountain range that runs from north to south, rising sharply on the east coast and descending gradually to a broad western plain, where cultivation is concentrated.

Government. The President and the Vice President are elected by the National Assembly for a term of six years. There are five major governing bodies called Yuans: Executive, Legislative, Judicial, Control, and Examination. Taiwan's internal affairs are administered by the Taiwan Provincial Government under the supervision of the Provincial Assembly, which is popularly elected.

The majority and ruling party is the Kuomintang (KMT) (Nationalist Party) led by President Li Tenghui. The main opposition party is the Democratic Progressive Party (DPP).

History. Taiwan was inhabited by aborigines of Malayan descent when Chinese from the areas now designated as Fukien and Kwangtung began settling it beginning in the 7th century, becoming the majority.

The Portuguese explored the area in 1590, naming it The Beautiful (Formosa). In 1624 the Dutch set up forts in the south, the Spanish in the North. The Dutch threw out the Spanish in 1641 and controlled the island until 1661, when the Chinese General Koxinga took it over, established an independent kingdom, and expelled the Dutch. The Manchus seized the island in 1683 and held it until 1895, when it passed to Japan after the first Sino-Japanese War. Japan developed and exploited it, and it was heavily bombed by American planes during World War II, after which it was restored to China.

After the defeat of its armies on the mainland, the Nationalist Government of Generalissimo Chiang Kai-shek retreated to Taiwan in December 1949. With only 15% of the population consisting of the 1949 immigrants, Chiang dominated the island, maintaining a 600,000-man army in the hope of eventually recovering the mainland. Japan renounced its claim to the island by the San Francisco Peace Treaty of 1951.

By stationing a fleet in the Strait of Formosa the U.S. prevented a mainland invasion in 1953.

The "China seat" in the U.N., which the Nationalists held with U.S. help for over two decades was lost in October 1971, when the People's Republic of China was admitted and Taiwan ousted by the world body.

Chiang died at 87 of a heart attack on April 5, 1975. His son, Chiang Ching-kuo, continued as Premier and dominant power in the Taipei regime. He assumed the presidency in 1978, and Sun Yun-hsuan became Premier.

President Carter's announcement that the U.S. would recognize only the People's Republic of China after Jan. 1, 1979, and that the U.S. defense treaty with the Nationalists would end aroused protests in Taiwan and in the U.S. Congress. Against Carter's wishes, Congress, in a bill governing future relations with Taiwan, guaranteed U.S. action in the event of an attack on the island. The legislation also provided for the continuation of trade and other relations through an American Institute in Taipei, housed in the former American Embassy.

Although the U.S. had assured Taiwan of continuing arms aid, a communiqué on Aug. 17, 1982, signed by Washington and Peking and promising a gradual reduction of such aid, cast a shadow over Taiwan.

Martial law was lifted in 1987. In April 1991 President Li Teng-hui formally declared an end to emergency rule yet without abandoning his government's claim to be the sole legitimate government of China. All deputies in the National Assembly must retire by the end of 1991.

TANZANIA

United Republic of Tanzania
President: Ali Hassan Mwinyi (1985)
Prime Minister: John Malecela (1990)
Area: 364,879 sq mi. (945,037 sq km)[1]
Population (est. mid-1991): 26,900,000 (average annual rate of natural increase: 3.7%); birth rate: 50/1000; infant mortality rate: 102/1000; density per square mile: 74
Capital and largest city (est. 1984): Dar es Salaam, 1,400,000
Monetary unit: Tanzanian shilling
Languages: Swahili, English, local languages
Religions: Christian, 33%; Islam, 33%; indigenous beliefs, 33%
Member of Commonwealth of Nations
Literacy rate: 79%
Economic summary: Gross domestic product (1989 est.): $5.92 billion; $235 per capita; 4.5% real growth rate. Arable land: 5%. Principal products: tobacco, corn, cassava, wheat, cotton, coffee, sisal, cashew nuts, pyrethrum, cloves. Labor force: 732,200; 10% in industry and commerce. Major industrial products: textiles, wood products, refined oil, processed agricultural products, diamonds, cement, fertilizer. Natural resources: hydroelectric potential, phosphates, iron and coal. Exports: coffee, cotton, sisal, diamonds, cloves, cashew nuts. Imports: manufactured goods, machinery and transport equipment, crude oil, foodstuffs. Major trading partners: Germany, U.K., U.S., Iran, Japan.

1. Including Zanzibar.

Geography. Tanzania is in East Africa on the Indian Ocean. To the north are Uganda and Kenya; to the west, Burundi, Rwanda, and Zaire; and to the south, Mozambique, Zambia, and Malawi. Its area is three times that of New Mexico.

Tanzania contains three of Africa's best-known lakes—Victoria in the north, Tanganyika in the west, and Nyasa in the south. Mount Kilimanjaro in the north, 19,340 feet (5,895 m), is the highest point on the continent.

Government. Under the republican form of government, Tanzania has a President elected by universal suffrage who appoints the Cabinet ministers. The 244-member National Assembly is composed of 119 elected members from the mainland, 50 elected from Zanzibar, 10 members appointed by the President (from both Tanganyika and Zanzibar), 5 national members (elected by the National Assembly after nomination by various national institutions), 20 members elected by Zanzibar's House of Representatives, 25 Regional Commissioners sitting as *ex officio* members, and 15 seats reserved for women (elected by the National Assembly).

The Tanganyika African National Union, the only authorized party on the mainland, and the Afro-Shirazi Party, the only party in Zanzibar and Pemba, merged in 1977 as the Revolutionary Party (Chama Cha Mapinduzi) and elected Julius K. Nyerere as its head.

History. Arab traders first began to colonize the area in A.D. 700. Portuguese explorers reached the coastal regions in 1500 and held some control until the 17th century, when the Sultan of Oman took power. With what are now Burundi and Rwanda, Tanganyika became the colony of German East Africa in 1885. After World War I, it was administered by Britain under a League of Nations mandate and later as a U.N. trust territory.

Although not mentioned in old histories until the 12th century, Zanzibar was believed always to have had connections with southern Arabia. The Portuguese made it one of their tributaries in 1503 and later established a trading post, but they were driven out by Arabs from Oman in 1698. Zanzibar was declared independent of Oman in 1861 and, in 1890, it became a British protectorate.

Tanganyika became independent on Dec. 9, 1961; Zanzibar, on Dec. 10, 1963. On April 26, 1964, the two nations merged into the United Republic of Tanganyika and Zanzibar. The name was changed to Tanzania six months later.

An invasion by Ugandan troops in November 1978 was followed by a counterattack in January 1979, in which 5,000 Tanzanian troops were joined by 3,000 Ugandan exiles opposed to President Idi Amin. Within a month, full-scale war developed.

Nyerere kept troops in Uganda in open support of former Ugandan President Milton Obote, despite protests from opposition groups, until the national elections in December 1980. Although Obote asked that the Tanzanians remain after his victory in order to control guerrilla resistance, Nyerere ordered their withdrawal in May 1981, citing the $1-million-a-month drain on his precarious finances.

In November 1985, Nyerere stepped down as President. Ali Hassan Myinyi, his Vice-President, succeeded him. Nyerere remained chairman of the party. Nyerere resigned as head of the party in August 1990, being replaced by President Mwinyi. Running unopposed Mwinyi was elected president in October. Shortly thereafter plans were announced to study the benefits of instituting a multiparty democracy.

THAILAND

Kingdom of Thailand
Ruler: King Bhumibol Adulyadej (1946)
Prime Minister: Anand Panyarachun (1991)
Area: 198,455 sq mi. (514,000 sq km)
Population (est. mid-1991): 58,800,000 (average annual rate of natural increase: 1.3%); birth rate: 20/1000; infant mortality rate: 39/1000; density per square mile: 296
Capital and largest city (est. 1984): Bangkok, 5,174,682
Monetary unit: Baht
Languages: Thai (Siamese), Chinese, English
Religions: Buddhist, 95.5%; Islam, 4%
National name: Thailand
Literacy rate: 82%
Economic summary: Gross national product (1989 est.): $64.5 billion; $1,160 per capita; 10.8% real growth rate. Arable land: 34%. Principal products: rice, rubber, corn, tapioca, sugar, coconuts. Labor force: 26,000,000; 11% in industry and commerce. Major products: processed food, textiles, furniture, cement, tin, tungsten, jewelry. Natural resources: fish, natural gas, forests, fluorite, tin, tungsten. Exports: rice, tapioca, fishing products, tin, textiles, jewelry. Imports: machinery and parts, petroleum products, iron and steel, electrical appliances, chemicals. Major trading partners: Japan, U.S., Singapore, Malaysia, Netherlands, U.K., Hong Kong, Germany.

Geography. Thailand occupies the western half of the Indochinese peninsula and the northern two-thirds of the Malay peninsula in southeast Asia. Its neighbors are Myanmar on the west and north, Laos on the north and northeast, Cambodia on the east, and Malaysia on the south. Thailand is about the size of France.

Most of the population is supported in the fertile central alluvial plain, which is drained by the Chao Phraya River and its tributaries.

Government. King Bhumibol Adulyadej, who was born Dec. 5, 1927, second son of Prince Mahidol of Songkhla, succeeded to the throne on June 9, 1946, when his brother, King Ananda Mahidol, died of a gunshot wound. He was married on April 28, 1950, to Queen Sirikit; their son, Vajiralongkorn, born July 28, 1952, is the Crown Prince.

History. The Thais first began moving down into their present homeland from the Asian continent in the 6th century A.D. and by the end of the 13th century ruled most of the western portion. During the next 400 years, the Thais fought sporadically with the Cambodians and the Burmese. The British obtained recognition of paramount interest in Thailand in 1824, and in 1896 an Anglo-French accord guaranteed the independence of Thailand.

A coup in 1932 changed the absolute monarchy into a representative government with universal suffrage. After five hours of token resistance on Dec. 8, 1941, Thailand yielded to Japanese occupation and became one of the springboards in World War II for the Japanese campaign against Malaya.

After the fall of its pro-Japanese puppet government in July 1944, Thailand pursued a policy of passive resistance against the Japanese, and after the Japanese surrender, Thailand repudiated the declaration of war it had been forced to make against Britain and the U.S. in 1942.

Thailand's major problem in the late 1960s was suppressing guerrilla action by Communist invaders in the north.

Although Thailand had received $2 billion in U.S. economic and military aid since 1950 and had sent troops (paid by the U.S.) to Vietnam while permitting U.S. bomber bases on its territory, the collapse of South Vietnam and Cambodia in the spring of 1975 brought rapid changes in the country's diplomatic posture.

At the Thai government's insistence, the U.S. agreed to withdraw all 23,000 U.S. military personnel remaining in Thailand by March 1976. Diplomatic relations with China were established in 1975. Meanwhile, overtures toward an accommodation with the new regime in South Vietnam were initiated.

After three years of civilian government ended with a military coup on Oct. 6, 1976, Thailand reverted to military rule. Political parties, banned after the coup, gained limited freedom in 1980. The same year, the National Assembly elected Gen. Prem Tinsulanonda as prime minister. General elections on April 18, 1983, and July 27, 1986, resulted in Prem continuing as prime minister over a coalition government.

Refugees from Laos, Cambodia, and Vietnam flooded into Thailand in 1978 and 1979, and despite efforts by the United States and other Western countries to resettle them, a total of 130,000 Laotian and Vietnamese refugees were living in camps along the Cambodian border in mid-1980. A drive by Vietnamese occupation forces on western Cambodian areas loyal to the Pol Pot government, culminating in invasions of Thai territory in late June, drove an estimated 100,000 Cambodians across the line as refugees, adding to the 200,000 of their countrymen already in Thailand. The total of 430,000 were being fed by United Nations and church relief organizations but the Thai government complained of the burden of their presence.

On April 3, 1981, a military coup against the Prem government failed. Another coup attempt on Sept. 9, 1985, was crushed by loyal troops after 10 hours of fighting in Bangkok. Four persons were killed and about 60 wounded.

General elections in 1988 led to Prem stepping down in favor of Chatichai Choonharan.

In February 1991 a nonviolent military coup led by Gen. Suchinda Krapayoon overthrew the democratic government charging corruption. The junta leaders declaring a state of emergency and martial law dismissed the houses of Parliament and abolished the Constitution. The following week the military appointed a well-known businessman and former ambassador, Anand Panyarachun to serve as interim prime minister. Under terms of an interim constitution the junta serves as an equal partner in an administration otherwise dominated by experienced technocrats and diplomats.

TOGO

Republic of Togo
President: Gen. Gnassingbé Eyadema (1967)
Area: 21,925 sq mi. (56,785 sq km)
Population (est. mid-1991): 3,800,000 (average annual rate of natural increase: 3.7%); birth rate: 50/1000; infant mortality rate: 112/1000; density per square mile: 174
Capital and largest city (est. 1982): Lomé, 285,000
Monetary unit: Franc CFA
Languages: Ewé, Mina (south), Kabyé, Cotocoli (north), French (official), and many dialects
Religions: indigenous beliefs, 70%; Christian, 20%; Islam, 10%
National name: République Togolaise
Literacy rate: 40.7%
Economic summary: Gross domestic product (1988 est.): $1.35 billion; $405 per capita; 4.1% real growth rate. Arable land: 25%. Principal products: yams, cotton, millet, sorghum, cocoa, coffee, rice. Labor force: 78% in agriculture. Major products: phosphate, textiles, processed food. Natural resources: marble, phosphate, limestone. Exports: phosphate, cocoa, coffee. Imports: consumer goods, fuels, machinery, foodstuffs. Major trading partners: E.C., Japan, U.S., Africa.

Geography. Togo, twice the size of Maryland, is on the south coast of West Africa bordering on Ghana to the west, Burkina Faso to the north and Benin to the east.

The Gulf of Guinea coastline, only 32 miles long (51 km), is low and sandy. The only port is at Lomé. The Togo hills traverse the central section.

Government. The government of Nicolas Grunitzky was overthrown in a bloodless coup on Jan. 13, 1967, led by Lt. Col. Etienne Eyadema (now Gen. Gnassingbé Eyadema). A National Reconciliation Committee was set up to rule the country. In April, however, Eyadema dissolved the Committee and took over as President. In December 1979, a 67-member National Assembly was voted in by national referendum. The Assembly of the Togolese People is the only political party.

History. Freed slaves from Brazil were the first traders to settle in Togo. Established as a German colony (Togoland) in 1884, the area was split between the British and the French as League of Nations mandates after World War I and subsequently administered as U.N. trusteeships. The British portion voted for incorporation with Ghana.

Togo became independent on April 27, 1960.

Although several independent candidates were elected to the Assembly in March 1990, two opposition leaders were arrested in October. Violent student protests led to further arrests. Sympathy strikes broke out, and the government announced plans to draft a new constitution.

TONGA

Kingdom of Tonga
Sovereign: King Taufa'ahau Tupou IV (1965)
Prime Minister: Prince Fatafehi Tu'ipelehake (1965)
Area: 290 sq mi. (751 sq km)
Population (mid-1989): 100,465 (average annual growth rate: 0.8%)
Density per square mile: 344
Capital (est. 1986): Nuku'alofa, 28,899
Monetary unit: Pa'anga
Languages: Tongan, English
Religions: Christian; Free Wesleyan Church claims over 30,000 adherents
Member of Commonwealth of Nations
Literacy rate: 90–95%
Economic summary: Gross domestic product (FY89 est.): $86 million; $850 per capita; 3.6% real growth rate. Arable land: 25%. Principal products: vanilla, coffee, ginger, black pepper, coconuts, bananas, copra. Labor force: 70% in agriculture. Major industrial products: copra, desiccated coconut. Natural resources: fish. Exports: copra, coconut products, bananas. Imports: foodstuffs, machinery and transport equipment, fuels, chemicals, building materials. Major trading partners: New Zealand, Australia, Fiji, U.S., Japan, E.C.

Geography. Situated east of the Fiji Islands in the South Pacific, Tonga (also called the Friendly Islands) consists of some 150 islands, of which 36 are inhabited. Most of the islands contain active volcanic craters; others are coral atolls.

Government. Tonga is a constitutional monarchy. Executive authority is vested in the Sovereign, a Privy Council, and a Cabinet headed by the Prime Minister. Legislative authority is vested in the Legislative Assembly. Nine seats are reserved for commoners; the others filled by appointees of the king.

History. The present dynasty of Tonga was founded in 1831 by Taufa'ahau Tupou, who took the name George I. He consolidated the kingdom by conquest and in 1875 granted a Constitution.

In 1900, his great-grandson, George II, signed a treaty of friendship with Britain, and the country became a British protected state. The treaty was revised in 1959.

Tonga became independent on June 4, 1970.

General elections in 1990 were won by reformists charging the government with corruption.

TRANSKEI

See South Africa

TRINIDAD AND TOBAGO

Republic of Trinidad and Tobago
President: Noor Hassanali (1987)
Prime Minister: A.N.R. Robinson (1986)
Area: 1,980 sq mi. (5,128 sq km)

Population (est. mid-1991): 1,300,000 (average annual rate of natural increase: 1.6%); birth rate: 23/1000; infant mortality rate: 11.4/1000; density per square mile: 649
Capital and largest city (est. 1981): Port-of-Spain, 125,000
Monetary unit: Trinidad and Tobago dollar
Languages: English (official); Hindi, French, Spanish
Religions: Christian, 49.3%; Hindu, 23%; Islam, 6%; unknown, 21.7%
Member of Commonwealth of Nations
Literacy rate: 98%
Economic summary: Gross domestic product (1988 est.): $3.75 billion; $3,070 per capita; –2.0% real growth rate. Arable land: 14%. Principal products: sugar cane, cocoa, coffee, citrus. Labor force: 463,900; 14.8% in manufacturing, mining, and quarrying. Major industrial products: petroleum, processed food, cement; tourism. Natural resources: petroleum, natural gas, asphalt. Exports: petroleum, chemicals, fertilizer. Imports: raw materials, capital goods, consumer goods. Major trading partners: U.S., Caribbean, Latin America, Western Europe.

Geography. Trinidad and Tobago lies in the Caribbean Sea off the northeast coast of Venezuela. The area of the two islands is slightly less than that of Delaware.

Trinidad, the larger, is mainly flat and rolling, with mountains in the north that reach a height of 3,085 feet (940 m) at Mount Aripo. Tobago is heavily forested with hardwood trees.

Government. The legislature consists of a 24-member Senate and a 36-member House of Representatives.

The political parties are the National Alliance for Reconstruction, led by Prime Minister A.N.R. Robinson (33 seats in the House of Representatives); People's National Movement (3 seats).

History. Trinidad was discovered by Columbus in 1498 and remained in Spanish possession, despite raids by other European nations, until it capitulated to the British in 1797 during a war between Britain and Spain.

Trinidad was ceded to Britain in 1802, and in 1899 it was united with Tobago as a colony. From 1958 to 1962, Trinidad and Tobago was a part of the West Indies Federation, and on Aug, 31, 1962, it became independent.

On Aug. 1, 1976, Trinidad and Tobago cut its ties with Britain and became a republic, remaining within the Commonwealth and recognizing Queen Elizabeth II only as head of that organization.

In an attempted coup on July 27, 1990 the prime minister and 54 others were taken hostage. The rebels surrendered, and the hostages freed on August 1. Although the coup had no popular support, 30 people lost their lives.

TUNISIA

Republic of Tunisia
President: Gen. Zine al-Abidine Ben Ali (1987)
Prime Minister: Hamed Karoui (1989)
Area: 63,379 sq mi. (164,152 sq km)
Population (est. mid-1991): 8,400,000 (average annual rate of natural increase: 2.2%); birth rate: 29/1000; infant mortality rate: 48/1000; density per square mile: 132
Capital and largest city (est. 1981): Tunis, 600,000
Monetary unit: Tunisian dinar
Languages: Arabic, French
Religion: Islam (Sunni), 98%; Christian, 1%; Jewish, less than 1%

National name: Al-Joumhouria Attunisia
Literacy rate: 62% (est.)
Economic summary: Gross domestic product (1989 est.): $8.7 billion; $1,105 per capita; 3.1% real growth rate. Arable land: 20%. Principal products: wheat, olives, oranges, grapes, dates. Labor force: 2,250,000; 32% in agriculture. Major industrial products: textiles, leather, chemical fertilizers, petroleum, phosphate, iron ore. Natural resources: oil, phosphates, iron ore, lead, zinc. Exports: petroleum, phosphates, and chemicals. Imports: machinery and equipment, consumer goods, foodstuffs. Major trading partners: E.C., U.S.S.R., Middle East, U.S.

Geography. Tunisia, at the northernmost bulge of Africa, thrusts out toward Sicily to mark the division between the eastern and western Mediterranean Sea. Twice the size of South Carolina, it is bordered on the west by Algeria and by Libya on the south.

Coastal plains on the east rise to a north-south escarpment which slopes gently to the west. Saharan in the south, Tunisia is more mountainous in the north, where the Atlas range continues from Algeria.

Government. Executive power is vested by the Constitution in the president, elected for five years and eligible for re-election to two additional terms. Legislative power is vested in a House of Deputies elected by universal suffrage.

In 1975, the National Assembly amended the Constitution to make Habib Bourguiba president for life. At 71, Bourguiba was re-elected to a fourth five-year term when he ran unopposed in 1974. He was deposed by Gen. Zine Ben Ali in 1987. Ben Ali was elected to a five-year term in April 1989.

History. Tunisia was settled by the Phoenicians and Carthaginians in ancient times. Except for an interval of Vandal conquest in A.D. 439–533, it was part of the Roman Empire until the Arab conquest of 648–69. It was ruled by various Arab and Berber dynasties until the Turks took it in 1570–74. French troops occupied the country in 1881, and the Bey signed a treaty acknowledging a French protectorate.

Nationalist agitation forced France to grant internal autonomy to Tunisia in 1955 and to recognize Tunisian independence and sovereignty in 1956. The Constituent Assembly deposed the Bey on July 25, 1957, declared Tunisia a republic, and elected Habib Bourguiba as president.

Bourguiba maintained a pro-Western foreign policy that earned him enemies. Tunisia refused to break relations with the U.S. during the Israeli-Arab war in June 1967.

Tunisia ended its traditionally neutral role in the Arab world when it joined with the majority of Arab League members to condemn Egypt for concluding a peace treaty with Israel.

Developments in 1986–87 were characterized by a consolidation of power by the 84-year-old Bourguiba and his failure to arrange for a successor. This issue was settled when the then-Prime Minister, Gen. Ben Ali, deposed Bourguiba.

In a surprise move to Western observers President Ben Ali in 1990 expressed his disapproval of U.S.-led actions leading up to the Gulf war. The foreign minister was dismissed, presumably over this issue. Relations between Tunisia and Libya improved, and an attempt was made to improve relations with the European Community.

TURKEY

Republic of Turkey
President: Turgut Ozal (1989)
Prime Minister: Suleyman Demirel (1991)
Area: 300,947 sq mi. (incl. 9,121 in Europe) (779,452 sq km)
Population (est. mid-1991): 58,500,000 (average annual rate of natural increase: 2.2%); birth rate: 30/1000; infant mortality rate: 62/1000; density per square mile: 194
Capital: Ankara
Largest cities (1985 census): Istanbul, 5,858,558; Ankara, 3,462,880; Izmir, 2,316,843; Adana, 1,757,102; Bursa, 1,327,762; Gaziantep, 953,859
Monetary unit: Turkish Lira
Language: Turkish
Religion: Islam (mostly Sunni), 98%
National name: Türkiye Cumhuriyeti
Literacy rate: 70%
Economic summary: Gross domestic product (est. 1989): $75 billion; $1,350 per capita; 1.8% real growth rate. Arable land: 20%. Principal products: cotton, tobacco, cereals, sugar beets, fruits, olives. Labor force: 18,800,000; 14% in industry. Major products: textiles, coal, minerals, processed foods, steel, petroleum. Natural resources: coal, chromite, copper, borate, sulfur. Exports: cotton, tobacco, fruits, nuts, livestock products, textiles. Imports: crude oil, machinery, transport equipment, metals, mineral fuels, fertilizer, chemicals. Major trading partners: Germany, Iraq, France, Italy, U.S., U.K., Iran, Japan.

Geography. Turkey is at the northeastern end of the Mediterranean Sea in southeast Europe and southwest Asia. To the north is the Black Sea and to the west the Aegean Sea. Its neighbors are Greece and Bulgaria to the west, the U.S.S.R. to the north, Iran to the east, and Syria and Iraq to the south. Overall, it is a little larger than Texas.

The Dardanelles, the Sea of Marmara, and the Bosporus divide the country.

Turkey in Europe comprises an area about equal to the state of Massachusetts. It is hilly country drained by the Maritsa River and its tributaries.

Turkey in Asia, or Anatolia, about the size of Texas, is roughly a rectangle in shape with its short sides on the east and west. Its center is a treeless plateau rimmed by mountains.

Government. The President is elected by the Grand National Assembly for a seven-year term and is not eligible for re-election.

In a military coup on Sept. 12, 1980, led by Gen. Kenan Evren, the Chief of General Staff, Premier Süleyman Demirel was ousted, the Grand National Assembly dissolved, and the Constitution suspended. Demirel, former Premier Bülent Ecevit, and some 100 legislators and political figures were detained, but later released. Martial law was declared and all political parties were dissolved. New elections were held in 1983 and a new Assembly was established.

The Prime Minister and his Council of Ministers hold the executive power although the President has the right to veto legislation.

History. The Ottoman Turks first appeared in the early 13th century in Anatolia, subjugating Turkish and Mongol bands pressing against the eastern borders of Byzantium. They gradually spread through the Near East and Balkans, capturing Constantinople in 1453 and storming the gates of Vienna two centuries later. At its height, the Ottoman Empire stretched from the Persian Gulf to western Algeria.

Defeat of the Turkish navy at Lepanto by the Holy League in 1571 and failure of the siege of Vienna heralded the decline of Turkish power. By the 18th century, Russia was seeking to establish itself as the protector of Christians in Turkey's Balkan territories. Russian ambitions were checked by Britain and France in the Crimean War (1854–56), but the Russo-Turkish War (1877–78) gave Bulgaria virtual independence and Romania and Serbia liberation from their nominal allegiance to the Sultan.

Turkish weakness stimulated a revolt of young liberals known as the Young Turks in 1909. They forced Sultan Abdul Hamid to grant a constitution and install a liberal government. Reforms were no barrier to further defeats, however, in a war with Italy (1911–12) and the Balkan Wars (1912–13). Under the influence of German military advisors, Turkey signed a secret alliance with Germany on Aug. 2, 1914, that led to a declaration of war by the Allied powers and the ultimate humiliation of the occupation of Turkish territory by Greek and other Allied troops.

In 1919, the new Nationalist movement, headed by Mustafa Kemal, was organized to resist the Allied occupation and, in 1920, a National Assembly elected him President of both the Assembly and the government. Under his leadership, the Greeks were driven out of Smyrna, and other Allied forces were withdrawn.

The present Turkish boundaries (with the exception of Alexandretta, ceded to Turkey by France in 1939) were fixed by the Treaty of Lausanne (1923) and later negotiations. The caliphate and sultanate were separated, and the sultanate was abolished in 1922. On Oct. 29, 1923, Turkey formally became a republic, with Mustafa Kemal, who took the name Kemal Atatürk, as its first President. The caliphate was abolished in 1924, and Atatürk proceeded to carry out an extensive program of reform, modernization, and industrialization.

Gen. Ismet İnönü was elected to succeed Atatürk in 1938 and was re-elected in 1939, 1943, and 1946. Defeated in 1950, he was succeeded by Celâl Bayar. In 1939, a mutual assistance pact was concluded with Britain and France. Neutral during most of World War II Turkey, on Feb. 23, 1945, declared war on Germany and Japan, but took no active part in the conflict.

Turkey became a full member of NATO in 1952. Turkey invaded Cyprus by sea and air July 20, 1974, following the failure of diplomatic efforts to resolve the crisis caused by the ouster of Archbishop Makarios.

Talks in Geneva involving Greece, Turkey, Britain, and Greek Cypriot and Turkish Cypriot leaders broke down in mid-August. Turkey unilaterally announced a cease-fire August 16, after having gained control of 40% of the island. Turkish Cypriots established their own state in the north on Feb. 13, 1975.

In July 1975, after a 30-day warning, Turkey took over control of all the U.S. installations except the big joint defense base at Incirlik, which it reserved for "NATO tasks alone."

The establishment of military government in September 1980 stopped the slide toward anarchy and brought some improvement in the economy.

A Constituent Assembly, consisting of the six-member National Security Council and members appointed by them, drafted a new Constitution that was approved by an overwhelming (91.5%) majority of the voters in a Nov. 6, 1982, referendum. Prime Minister Turgut Özal's Motherland Party came to power in parliamentary elections held in late 1983. Özal was re-elected in November 1987.

During the Persian Gulf war Turkey allowed use of its military bases by the U.S.-led forces principally for air attacks on Iraq. This caused much concern over possible retaliation by Iraq. Despite NATO assurances of protection Turkey openly expressed doubts of the sincerity of such pledges from certain NATO members, particularly Germany.

In the aftermath of the war Turkey kept its borders closed to the flood of Kurds seeking to escape northern Iraq.

The ruling Anap Party chose a new leader in June 1991, Mesut Yilmaz, who reorganized the government, replacing 20 members of the former cabinet.

TUVALU

Sovereign: Queen Elizabeth II
Governor-General: Tupua Leupena (1986)
Prime Minister: Bikenibeu Paeniu (1989)
Area: 10 sq mi. (26 sq km)
Population (mid-1989): 8,624 (average annual growth rate: 1.7%)
Density per square mile: 848
Capital and largest city (est. 1981): Funafuti, 2,500
Monetary unit: Australian dollar
Languages: Tuvaluan, English
Member of the Commonwealth of Nations
Literacy rate: less than 50%
Economic summary: Gross national product (1989 est.): $4.6 million; $530 per capita. Principal agricultural products: copra and coconuts. Export: copra. Imports: food, fuels, machinery. Major trading partners: Australia, Fiji, New Zealand.

Geography. Formerly the Ellice Islands, Tuvalu consists of nine small islands scattered over 500,000 square miles of the western Pacific, just south of the equator.

Government. Official executive power is vested in a Governor-General, representing the Queen, who is appointed by her on the recommendation of the Tuvalu government. Actual executive power lies with a Prime Minister, who is responsible to a House of Assembly composed of eight elected members.

History. The Ellice Islands became a British protectorate in 1892 and were annexed by Britain in 1915–16 as part of the Gilbert and Ellice Islands Colony. The Ellice Islands were separated in 1975, given home rule, and renamed Tuvalu. Full independence was granted on Sept. 30, 1978.

Prime Minister Paeniu's emphasis since his election in September 1989 has been on opening the economy and making the country more self-sufficient.

UGANDA

Republic of Uganda
President: Yoweri Museveni (1986)
Prime Minister: George Kosmas Adyebo (1991)
Area: 91,459 sq mi. (236,880 sq km)
Population (est. mid-1991): 18,700,000 (average annual rate of natural increase: 3.5%); birth rate: 52/1000; infant mortality rate: 107/1000; density per square mile: 205
Capital and largest city (est. 1980): Kampala, 458,000
Monetary unit: Ugandan shilling
Languages: English (official), Swahili, Luganda, Ateso, Luo
Religions: Christian, 66%; Islam, 16%

Member of Commonwealth of Nations
Literacy rate: 57.3%
Economic summary: Gross domestic product (1988): $4.9 billion; $300 per capita; 6.1% real growth rate. Arable land: 23%. Principal products: coffee, tea, cotton, sugar. Labor force: 4,500,000 (est.); 94% in subsistence activities. Major industrial products: sugar, beer, tobacco, cotton textiles, cement. Natural resources: copper, cobalt, limestone, salt. Exports: coffee, cotton, tea. Imports: petroleum products, machinery, transport equipment, metals, food. Major trading partners: U.S., U.K., Kenya, Italy, France, Spain.

Geography. Uganda, twice the size of Pennsylvania, is in east Africa. It is bordered on the west by Zaire, on the north by the Sudan, on the east by Kenya, and on the south by Tanzania and Rwanda.

The country, which lies across the Equator, is divided into three main areas—swampy lowlands, a fertile plateau with wooded hills, and a desert region. Lake Victoria forms part of the southern border.

Government. The country has been run by the National Resistance Movement (NRM) since January, 1986.

History. Uganda was first visited by European explorers as well as Arab traders in 1844. An Anglo-German agreement of 1890 declared it to be in the British sphere of influence in Africa, and the Imperial British East Africa Company was chartered to develop the area. The company did not prosper financially, and in 1894 a British protectorate was proclaimed.

Uganda became independent on Oct. 9, 1962.

Sir Edward Mutesa was elected the first President and Milton Obote the first Prime Minister of the newly independent country. With the help of a young army officer, Col. Idi Amin, Prime Minister Obote seized control of the government from President Mutesa four years later.

On Jan. 25, 1971, Col. Amin deposed President Obote. Obote went into exile in Tanzania. Amin expelled Asian residents and launched a reign of terror against Ugandan opponents, torturing and killing tens of thousands. In 1976, he had himself proclaimed President for Life. In 1977, Amnesty International estimated that 300,000 may have died under his rule, including church leaders and recalcitrant cabinet ministers.

After Amin held military exercises on the Tanzanian border, angering Tanzania's President Julius Nyerere, a combined force of Tanzanian troops and Ugandan exiles loyal to former President Obote invaded Uganda and chased Amin into exile.

After a series of interim administrations, President Obote led his People's Congress Party to victory in 1980 elections that opponents charged were rigged.

On July, 27, 1985, army troops staged a coup taking over the government. Obote fled into exile. The military regime installed Gen. Tito Okello as chief of state.

The National Resistance Army (NRA), an anti-Obote group led by Yoweri Musevni, kept fighting after being excluded from the new regime. They seized Kampala on January 29, 1986, and Musevni was declared President but strife still continues in the northern part of the country.

President Museveni was chosen chairman of the Organization of African Unity in July 1990 only to be charged with complicity three months later in the Rwandan civil war.

UNION OF SOVIET SOCIALIST REPUBLICS

See Soviet Union

UNITED ARAB EMIRATES

President: Sheik Zayed Bin Sultan Al-Nahayan (1971)
Prime Minister: Sheik Maktum ibn Rashid al-Maktum (1990)
Area: 32,000 sq mi. (82,880 sq km)
Population (est. mid-1991): 2,400,000 (average annual rate of natural increase: 2.7%); birth rate: 30/1000; infant mortality rate: 23/1000; density per square mile: 74
Capital and largest city (est. 1981): Abu Dhabi, 225,000
Monetary unit: Dirham
Language: Arabic; Farsi and English widely spoken
Religion: Islam (Sunni, 80%; Shiite, 16%); other, 4%
Literacy rate: 68%
Economic summary: Gross national product (1989): $23.3 billion, $11,680 per capita; real growth rate –2.1%. Arable land: NEGL%. Principal products: vegetables, dates, poultry, fish. Labor force: 580,000 (1986 est.) 80% is foreign; 85% in industry and commerce. Major products: fish, light manufactures, petroleum, construction materials. Natural resource: oil. Exports: petroleum, dates, fish. Imports: consumer goods, food. Major trading partners: Japan, Western Europe, U.S.

Geography. The United Arab Emirates, in the eastern part of the Arabian Peninsula, extends along part of the Gulf of Oman and the southern coast of the Persian Gulf. The nation is the size of Maine. Its neighbors are Saudi Arabia in the west and south, Qatar in the north, and Oman in the east. Most of the land is barren and sandy.

Government. The United Arab Emirates was formed in 1971 by seven emirates known as the Trucial States—Abu Dhabi (the largest), Dubai, Sharjah, Ajman, Fujairah, Ras al Khaimah and Umm al-Qaiwain.

The loose federation allows joint policies in foreign relations, defense, and development, with each member state keeping its internal local system of government headed by its own ruler. A 40-member legislature consists of eight seats each for Abu Dhabi and Dubai, six seats each for Ras al Khaimah and Sharjah, and four each for the others. It is a member of the Arab League.

History. Originally the area was inhabited by a seafaring people who were converted to Islam in the seventh century. Later, a dissident sect, the Carmathians, established a powerful sheikdom, and its army conquered Mecca. After the sheikdom disintegrated, its people became pirates.

Threatening the sultanate of Muscat and Oman early in the 19th century, the pirates provoked the intervention of the British, who in 1820 enforced a partial truce and in 1853 a permanent truce. Thus what had been called the Pirate Coast was renamed the Trucial Coast.

After a long illness the vice president and ruler of Dubai died. He was succeeded by his son Sheik Maktum, who in November 1990 was appointed prime minister.

UNITED KINGDOM

United Kingdom of Great Britain and Northern Ireland
Sovereign: Queen Elizabeth II (1952)
Prime Minister: John Major (1990)
Area: 94,247 sq mi. (244,100 sq km)
Population (mid-1990): 57,500,000 (average annual rate of natural increase: 0.2%); birth rate: 14/1000; infant mortality rate: 8.4/1000; density per square mile: 609

Rulers of England and Great Britain

Name	Born	Ruled[1]	Name	Born	Ruled[1]
SAXONS[2]			**HOUSE OF YORK**		
Egbert[3]	c.775	828–839	Edward IV	1442	1461–1483 [5]
Ethelwulf	?	839–858	Edward V	1470	1483–1483
Ethelbald	?	858–860	Richard III	1452	1483–1485
Ethelbert	?	860–866			
Ethelred I	?	866–871	**HOUSE OF TUDOR**		
Alfred the Great	849	871–899	Henry VII	1457	1485–1509
Edward the Elder	c.870	899–924	Henry VIII	1491	1509–1547
Athelstan	895	924–939	Edward VI	1537	1547–1553
Edmund I the Deed-doer	921	939–946	Jane (Lady Jane Grey)[6]	1537	1553–1553
Edred	c.925	946–955	Mary I ("Bloody Mary")	1516	1553–1558
Edwy the Fair	c.943	955–959	Elizabeth I	1533	1558–1603
Edgar the Peaceful	943	959–975			
Edward the Martyr	c.962	975–979	**HOUSE OF STUART**		
Ethelred II the Unready	968	979–1016	James I[7]	1566	1603–1625
Edmund II Ironside	c.993	1016–1016	Charles I	1600	1625–1649
DANES			**COMMONWEALTH**		
Canute	995	1016–1035	Council of State	—	1649–1653
Harold I Harefoot	c.1016	1035–1040	Oliver Cromwell[8]	1599	1653–1658
Hardecanute	c.1018	1040–1042	Richard Cromwell[8]	1626	1658–1659 [9]
SAXONS			**RESTORATION OF HOUSE OF**		
Edward the Confessor	c.1004	1042–1066	**STUART**		
Harold II	c.1020	1066–1066	Charles II	1630	1660–1685
			James II	1633	1685–1688 [10]
HOUSE OF NORMANDY			William III[11]	1650	1689–1702
William I the Conqueror	1027	1066–1087	Mary II[11]	1662	1689–1694
William II Rufus	c.1056	1087–1100	Anne	1665	1702–1714
Henry I Beauclerc	1068	1100–1135			
Stephen of Boulogne	c.1100	1135–1154	**HOUSE OF HANOVER**		
			George I	1660	1714–1727
HOUSE OF PLANTAGENET			George II	1683	1727–1760
Henry II	1133	1154–1189	George III	1738	1760–1820
Richard I Coeur de Lion	1157	1189–1199	George IV	1762	1820–1830
John Lackland	1167	1199–1216	William IV	1765	1830–1837
Henry III	1207	1216–1272	Victoria	1819	1837–1901
Edward I Longshanks	1239	1272–1307			
Edward II	1284	1307–1327	**HOUSE OF SAXE-COBURG[12]**		
Edward III	1312	1327–1377	Edward VII	1841	1901–1910
Richard II	1367	1377–1399 [4]			
			HOUSE OF WINDSOR[12]		
HOUSE OF LANCASTER			George V	1865	1910–1936
Henry IV Bolingbroke	1367	1399–1413	Edward VIII	1894	1936–1936 [13]
Henry V	1387	1413–1422	George VI	1895	1936–1952
Henry VI	1421	1422–1461 [5]	Elizabeth II	1926	1952–

1. Year of end of rule is also that of death, unless otherwise indicated. 2. Dates for Saxon kings are still subject of controversy. 3. Became King of West Saxons in 802; considered (from 828) first King of all England. 4. Died 1400. 5. Henry VI reigned again briefly 1470–71. 6. Nominal Queen for 9 days; not counted as Queen by some authorities. She was beheaded in 1554. 7. Ruled in Scotland as James VI (1567–1625). 8. Lord Protector. 9. Died 1712. 10. Died 1701. 11. Joint rulers (1689–1694). 12. Name changed from Saxe–Coburg to Windsor in 1917. 13. Was known after his abdication as the Duke of Windsor, died 1972.

Capital: London, England
Largest cities (est. 1990): London, 9,170,000; Manchester, 4,050,000; Birmingham, 2,170,000; (est. mid. 1987) Glasgow, 715,621; Leeds, 709,000; Sheffield, 532,300; Liverpool, 476,000; Bradford, 462,500; Edinburgh, 438,232; Bristol, 384,400
Monetary unit: Pound sterling (£)
Languages: English, Welsh, Scots Gaelic
Religions: Church of England (established church); Church of Wales (disestablished); Church of Scotland (established church—Presbyterian); Church of Ireland (disestablished); Roman Catholic; Methodist; Congregational; Baptist; Jewish
Literacy rate: 99%

Economic summary: Gross domestic product (1989 est.): $818.0 billion; $14,300 per capita; 2.3% real growth rate. Arable land: 29%. Principal products: wheat, barley, potatoes, sugar beets, livestock, dairy products. Labor force: 28,120,000; 23.6% in manufacturing and construction. Major industrial products: machinery and transport equipment, metals, processed food, paper, textiles, chemicals, clothing. Natural resources: coal, oil, gas. Exports: machinery, transport equipment, chemicals, petroleum. Imports: foodstuffs, machinery, manufactured goods, semifinished goods. Major trading partners: Western European nations, U.S.

Geography. The United Kingdom, consisting of England, Wales, Scotland, and Northern Ireland, is twice the size of New York State. England, in the southeast part of the British Isles, is separated from Scotland on the north by the granite Cheviot Hills; from them the Pennine chain of uplands extends south through the center of England, reaching its highest point in the Lake District in the northwest. To the west along the border of Wales—a land of steep hills and valleys—are the Cambrian Mountains, while the Cotswolds, a range of hills in Gloucestershire, extend into the surrounding shires.

The remainder of England is plain land, though not necessarily flat, with the rocky sand-topped moors in the southwest, the rolling downs in the south and southeast, and the reclaimed marshes of the low-lying fens in the east central districts.

Scotland is divided into three physical regions—the Highlands, the Central Lowlands, containing two-thirds of the population, and the Southern Uplands. The western Highland coast is intersected throughout by long, narrow sea-lochs, or fiords. Scotland also includes the Outer and Inner Hebrides and other islands off the west coast and the Orkney and Shetland Islands off the north coast.

Wales is generally hilly; the Snowdon range in the northern part culminates in Mount Snowdon (3,560 ft, 1,085 m), highest in both England and Wales.

Important rivers flowing into the North Sea are the Thames, Humber, Tees, and Tyne. In the west are the Severn and Wye, which empty into the Bristol Channel and are navigable, as are the Mersey and Ribble.

Government. The United Kingdom is a constitutional monarchy, with a Queen and a Parliament that has two houses: the House of Lords with about 830 hereditary peers, 26 spiritual peers, about 270 life peers and peeresses, and 9 law-lords, who are hereditary, or life, peers, and the House of Commons, which has 650 popularly elected members. Supreme legislative power is vested in Parliament, which sits for five years unless sooner dissolved.

The executive power of the Crown is exercised by the Cabinet, headed by the Prime Minister. The latter, normally the head of the party commanding a majority in the House of Commons, is appointed by the Sovereign, with whose consent he or she in turn appoints the rest of the Cabinet. All ministers must be members of one or the other house of Parliament; they are individually and collectively responsible to the Crown and Parliament. The Cabinet proposes bills and arranges the business of Parliament, but it depends entirely on the votes in the House of Commons. The Lords cannot hold up "money" bills, but they can delay other bills for a maximum of one year.

By the Act of Union (1707), the Scottish Parliament was assimilated with that of England, and Scotland is now represented in Commons by 71 members. The Secretary of State for Scotland, a member of the Cabinet, is responsible for the administration of Scottish affairs.

Ruler. Queen Elizabeth II, born April 21, 1926, elder daughter of King George VI and Queen Elizabeth, succeeded to the throne on the death of her father on Feb. 6, 1952; married Nov. 20, 1947, to Prince Philip, Duke of Edinburgh, born June 10, 1921; their children are Prince Charles[1] (heir presumptive), born Nov. 14, 1948; Princess Anne, born Aug. 15, 1950; Prince Andrew, born Feb. 19, 1960; and Prince Edward, born March 10, 1964. The Queen's sister is Princess Margaret, born Aug. 21, 1930. Prince William Arthur Philip Louis, son of the Prince and Princess of Wales and second in line to the throne, was born June 21, 1982. A

Area and Population of United Kingdom

Subdivision	Area sq mi.	Area sq km	Population (Est. 1988)
England and Wales	58,381	151,207	50,393,000
Scotland	30,414	78,772	5,074,000
Northern Ireland	5,452	14,121	1,598,100
Total	**94,247**	**244,100**	**57,065,400**

second son, Prince Henry Charles Albert David, was born Sept. 15, 1984, and is third in line.

History. Roman invasions of the 1st century B.C. brought Britain into contact with the Continent. When the Roman legions withdrew in the 5th century A.D., Britain fell easy prey to the invading hordes of Angles, Saxons, and Jutes from Scandinavia and the Low Countries. Seven large kingdoms were established, and the original Britons were forced into Wales and Scotland. It was not until the 10th century that the country finally became united under the kings of Wessex. Following the death of Edward the Confessor (1066), a dispute about the succession arose, and William, Duke of Normandy, invaded England, defeating the Saxon King, Harold II, at the Battle of Hastings (1066). The Norman conquest introduced Norman law and feudalism.

The reign of Henry II (1154–89), first of the Plantagenets, saw an increasing centralization of royal power at the expense of the nobles, but in 1215 John (1199–1216) was forced to sign the Magna Carta, which awarded the people, especially the nobles, certain basic rights. Edward I (1272–1307) continued the conquest of Ireland, reduced Wales to subjection, and made some gains in Scotland. In 1314, however, English forces led by Edward II were ousted from Scotland after the Battle of Bannockburn. The late 13th and early 14th centuries saw the development of a separate House of Commons with tax-raising powers.

Edward III's claim to the throne of France led to the Hundred Years' War (1338–1453) and the loss of almost all the large English territory in France. In England, the great poverty and discontent caused by the war were intensified by the Black Death, a plague that reduced the population by about one-third. The Wars of the Roses (1455–85), a struggle for the throne between the House of York and the House of Lancaster, ended in the victory of Henry Tudor (Henry VII) at Bosworth Field (1485).

During the reign of Henry VIII (1509–47), the Church in England asserted its independence from the Roman Catholic Church. Under Edward VI and Mary, the two extremes of religious fanaticism were reached, and it remained for Henry's daughter, Elizabeth I (1558–1603), to set up the Church of England on a moderate basis. In 1588, the Spanish Armada, a fleet sent out by Catholic King Philip II of Spain, was defeated by the English and destroyed during a storm. During Elizabeth's reign, England became a world power.

Elizabeth's heir was a Stuart—James VI of Scotland—who joined the two crowns as James I (1603–25). The Stuart kings incurred large debts and

---

1. The title Prince of Wales, which is not inherited, was conferred on Prince Charles by his mother on July 26, 1958. The investiture ceremony took place on July 1, 1969. The previous Prince of Wales was Prince Edward Albert, who held the title from 1911 to 1936 before he became Edward VIII.

British Prime Ministers Since 1770

Name	Term	Name	Term
Lord North (Tory)	1770–1782	William E. Gladstone (Liberal)	1886–1886
Marquis of Rockingham (Whig)	1782–1782	Marquis of Salisbury (Conservative)	1886–1892
Earl of Shelburne (Whig)	1782–1783	William E. Gladstone (Liberal)	1892–1894
Duke of Portland (Coalition)	1783–1783	Earl of Rosebery (Liberal)	1894–1895
William Pitt, the Younger (Tory)	1783–1801	Marquis of Salisbury (Conservative)	1895–1902
Henry Addington (Tory)	1801–1804	Earl Balfour (Conservative)	1902–1905
William Pitt, the Younger (Tory)	1804–1806	Sir H. Campbell–Bannerman (Liberal)	1905–1908
Baron Grenville (Whig)	1806–1807	Herbert H. Asquith (Liberal)	1908–1915
Duke of Portland (Tory)	1807–1809	Herbert H. Asquith (Coalition)	1915–1916
Spencer Perceval (Tory)	1809–1812	David Lloyd George (Coalition)	1916–1922
Earl of Liverpool (Tory)	1812–1827	Andrew Bonar Law (Conservative)	1922–1923
George Canning (Tory)	1827–1827	Stanley Baldwin (Conservative)	1923–1924
Viscount Goderich (Tory)	1827–1828	James Ramsay MacDonald (Labor)	1924–1924
Duke of Wellington (Tory)	1828–1830	Stanley Baldwin (Conservative)	1924–1929
Earl Grey (Whig)	1830–1834	James Ramsay MacDonald (Labor)	1929–1931
Viscount Melbourne (Whig)	1834–1834	James Ramsay MacDonald (Coalition)	1931–1935
Sir Robert Peel (Tory)	1834–1835	Stanley Baldwin (Coalition)	1935–1937
Viscount Melbourne (Whig)	1835–1841	Neville Chamberlain (Coalition)	1937–1940
Sir Robert Peel (Tory)	1841–1846	Winston Churchill (Coalition)	1940–1945
Earl Russell (Whig)	1846–1852	Clement R. Attlee (Labor)	1945–1951
Earl of Derby (Tory)	1852–1852	Sir Winston Churchill (Conservative)	1951–1955
Earl of Aberdeen (Coalition)	1852–1855	Sir Anthony Eden (Conservative)	1955–1957
Viscount Palmerston (Liberal)	1855–1858	Harold Macmillan (Conservative)	1957–1963
Earl of Derby (Conservative)	1858–1859	Sir Alec Frederick Douglas–Home	
Viscount Palmerston (Liberal)	1859–1865	(Conservative)	1963–1964
Earl Russell (Liberal)	1865–1866	Harold Wilson (Labor)	1964–1970
Earl of Derby (Conservative)	1866–1868	Edward Heath (Conservative)	1970–1974
Benjamin Disraeli (Conservative)	1868–1868	Harold Wilson (Labor)	1974–1976
William E. Gladstone (Liberal)	1868–1874	James Callaghan (Labor)	1976–1979
Benjamin Disraeli (Conservative)	1874–1880	Margaret Thatcher (Conservative)	1979–1990
William E. Gladstone (Liberal)	1880–1885	John Major (Conservative)	1990–
Marquis of Salisbury (Conservative)	1885–1886		

were forced either to depend on Parliament for taxes or to raise money by illegal means. In 1642, war broke out between Charles I and a large segment of the Parliament; Charles was defeated and executed in 1649, and the monarchy was then abolished. After the death in 1658 of Oliver Cromwell, the Lord Protector, the Puritan Commonwealth fell to pieces and Charles II was placed on the throne in 1660. The struggle between the King and Parliament continued, but Charles II knew when to compromise. His brother, James II (1685–88), possessed none of his ability and was ousted by the Revolution of 1688, which confirmed the primacy of Parliament. James's daughter, Mary, and her husband, William of Orange, were now the rulers.

Queen Anne's reign (1702–14) was marked by the Duke of Marlborough's victories against France at Blenheim, Oudenarde, and Malplaquet in the War of the Spanish Succession. England and Scotland meanwhile were joined by the Act of Union (1707). Upon the death of Anne, the distant claims of the elector of Hanover were recognized, and he became King of Great Britain and Ireland as George I.

The unwillingness of the Hanoverian kings to rule resulted in the formation by the royal ministers of a Cabinet, headed by a Prime Minister, which directed all public business. Abroad, the constant wars with France expanded the British Empire all over the globe, particularly in North America and India. This imperial growth was checked by the revolt of the American colonies (1775–81).

Struggles with France broke out again in 1793 and during the Napoleonic Wars, which ended at Waterloo in (1815).

The Victorian era, named after Queen Victoria (1837–1901), saw the growth of a democratic system of government that had begun with the Reform Bill of 1832. The two important wars in Victoria's reign were the Crimean War against Russia (1853–56) and the Boer War (1899–1902), the latter enormously extending Britain's influence in Africa.

Increasing uneasiness at home and abroad marked the reign of Edward VII (1901–10). Within four years after the accession of George V in 1910, Britain entered World War I when Germany invaded Belgium. The nation was led by coalition Cabinets, headed first by Herbert Asquith and then, starting in 1916, by the Welsh statesman David Lloyd George. Postwar labor unrest culminated in the general strike of 1926.

King Edward VIII succeeded to the throne on Jan. 20, 1936, at his father's death, but abdicated on Dec. 11, 1936 (in order to marry an American divorcee, Wallis Warfield Simpson) in favor of his brother, who became George VI.

The efforts of Prime Minister Neville Chamberlain to stem the rising threat of Nazism in Germany failed with the German invasion of Poland on Sept. 1, 1939, which was followed by Britain's entry into World War II on September 3. Allied reverses in the spring of 1940 led to Chamberlain's resignation and the formation of another coalition war Cabinet by the Conservative leader, Winston Churchill, who led Britain through most of World War II. Churchill resigned shortly after V-E Day, May 7, 1945, but then formed a "caretaker" government that remained in office until after the parliamentary elections in July, which the Labor Party won overwhelmingly. The government formed by Clement R. Attlee began a moderate socialist program.

In 1951, Churchill again became Prime Minister at the head of a Conservative government. George VI died Feb. 6, 1952, and was succeeded by his daughter Elizabeth II.

Churchill stepped down in 1955 in favor of Sir Anthony Eden, who resigned on grounds of ill health in 1957, and was succeeded by Harold Macmillan and Sir Alec Douglas-Home. In 1964, Harold Wilson led the Labor Party to victory.

A lagging economy brought the Conservatives back to power in 1970. Prime Minister Edward Heath won Britain's admission to the European Community.

Margaret Thatcher became Britain's first woman Prime Minister as the Conservatives won 339 seats on May 3, 1979.

An Argentine invasion of the Falkland Islands on April 2, 1982, involved Britain in a war 8,000 miles from the home islands. Although Argentina had long claimed the Falklands, known as the Malvinas in Spanish, negotiations were in progress until a month before the invasion. The Thatcher government responded to the invasion with a 40-ship task force, which sailed from Portsmouth on April 5. U.S. efforts to settle the dispute failed and United Nations efforts collapsed as the Argentine military government ignored Security Council resolutions calling for a withdrawal of its forces.

When more than 11,000 Argentine troops on the Falklands surrendered on June 14, 1982, Mrs. Thatcher declared her intention to garrison the islands indefinitely, together with a naval presence.

In the general election of June 9, 1983, Prime Minister Thatcher and her Conservative party won a landslide victory over the Laborites and other opponents.

Although there were continuing economic problems and foreign policy disputes, an upswing in the economy in 1986–87 led Thatcher to call elections for June 11 in which she won a near-unprecedented third consecutive term.

Through much, if not all, of 1990 the Conservatives were losing the confidence of the electorate. The unpopularity of her poll tax together with an uncompromising position toward further European integration eroded support within her own party. When John Major won the Conservative Party leadership in November, Mrs. Thatcher resigned, paving the way for the Queen to ask Mr. Major to form a government. In the ensuing months the prime minister has revamped the nation's tax system.

NORTHERN IRELAND

Status: Part of United Kingdom
Secretary of State: Thomas Jeremy King
Area: 5,452 sq mi. (14,121 sq km)
Population (est. 1988): 1,598,100
Density per square mile: 279.7
Capital and largest city (est. mid-1987): Belfast, 303,800
Monetary unit: British pound sterling
Languages: English, Gaelic
Religions: Roman Catholic, 28%; Presbyterian, 22.9%; Church of Ireland, 19%; Methodist, 4%

Geography. Northern Ireland comprises the counties of Antrim, Armagh, Down, Fermanagh, Londonderry, and Tyrone, which make up predominantly Protestant Ulster and form the northern part of the island of Ire-

land, westernmost of the British Isles. It is slightly larger than Connecticut.

Government. Northern Ireland is an integral part of the United Kingdom (it has 12 representatives in the British House of Commons), but under the terms of the government of Ireland Act in 1920, it had a semiautonomous government. But in 1972, after three years of internal strife which resulted in over 400 dead and thousands injured, Britain suspended the Ulster parliament. The Ulster counties became governed directly from London after an attempt to return certain powers to an elected Assembly in Belfast.

The Northern Ireland Assembly was dissolved in 1975 and a Constitutional Convention was elected to write a Constitution acceptable to Protestants and Catholics. The convention failed to reach agreement and closed down the next year.

History. Ulster was part of Catholic Ireland until the reign of Elizabeth I (1558–1603) when, after crushing three Irish rebellions, the crown confiscated lands in Ireland and settled in Ulster the Scot Presbyterians who became rooted there. Another rebellion in 1641–51, crushed as brutally by Oliver Cromwell, resulted in the settlement of Anglican Englishmen in Ulster. Subsequent political policy favoring Protestants and disadvantaging Catholics encouraged further settlement in Northern Ireland.

But the North did not separate from the South until William Gladstone presented in 1886 his proposal for home rule in Ireland as a means of settling the Irish Question. The Protestants in the North, although they had grievances like the Catholics in the South, feared domination by the Catholic majority. Industry, moreover, was concentrated in the north and dependent on the British market.

When World War I began, civil war threatened between the regions. Northern Ireland, however, did not become a political entity until the six counties accepted the Home Rule Bill of 1920. This set up a semiautonomous Parliament in Belfast and a Crown-appointed Governor advised by a Cabinet of the Prime Minister and eight ministers, as well as a 12-member representation in the House of Commons in London.

As the Republic of Ireland gained its sovereignty, relations improved between North and South, although the Irish Republican Army, outlawed in recent years, continued the struggle to end the partition of Ireland. In 1966–69, communal rioting and street fighting between Protestants and Catholics occurred in Londonderry, fomented by extremist nationalist Protestants, who feared the Catholics might attain a local majority, and by Catholics demonstrating for civil rights.

Rioting, terrorism, and sniping killed more than 2,200 people from 1969 through 1984 and the religious communities, Catholic and Protestant, became hostile armed camps. British troops were brought in to separate them but themselves became a target of Catholics.

In 1973, a new British charter created a 78-member Assembly elected by proportional representation that gave more weight to Catholic strength. It created a Province Executive with committee chairmen of the Assembly heading all government departments except law enforcement, which remained under London's control. Assembly elections in 1973 produced a majority for the new Constitution that included Catholic assemblymen.

Ulster's leaders agreed in 1973 to create an 11-member Executive Body with six seats assigned to

Unionists (Protestants) and four to members of Catholic parties. Unionist leader Brian Faulkner headed the Executive. Also agreed to was a Council of Ireland, with 14 seats evenly divided between Dublin and Belfast, which could act only by unanimous vote.

Although the Council lacked real authority, its creation sparked a general strike by Protestant extremists in 1974. The two-week strike caused Faulkner's resignation from the Executive and resumption of direct rule from London.

In April 1974, London instituted a new program that responded to some Catholic grievances, but assigned more British troops to cut off movement of arms and munitions to Ulster's violence-racked cities.

Violence continued unabated, with new heights reached early in 1976 when the British government announced the end of special privileges for political prisoners in Northern Ireland. British Prime Minister James Callaghan visited Belfast in July and pledged that Ulster would remain part of the United Kingdom unless a clear majority wished to separate.

In October 1977, the 1976 Nobel Prize for Peace was awarded to Mairead Corrigan and Betty Williams for their campaign for peace in Northern Ireland. Intermittent violence continued, however, and on Aug. 27, 1979, an I.R.A. bomb killed Earl Mountbatten as he was sailing off southern Ireland.

New talks aimed at a restoration of home rule in Northern Ireland began and quickly ended in January 1980. In May, Mrs. Thatcher met with the new Prime Minister of the Irish Republic, Charles Haughey, but she insisted that the future of Ulster must be decided only by its people and the British Parliament. Haughey declared that an internal solution "cannot and will not succeed."

On November 15, 1985, Mrs. Thatcher signed an agreement with Irish Prime Minister Garrett Fitzgerald giving Ireland a consultative role in the affairs of Northern Ireland. It was met with intense disapproval by the Ulster Unionists.

Talks began in June 1991 between leaders of four major Ulster political parties. The hope was that these talks would lead to some degree of home rule in Northern Ireland. On July 3, however, they collapsed.

Dependencies of the United Kingdom

ANGUILLA

Status: Dependency
Governor: B. G. Canty (1989)
Area: 35 sq mi. (91 sq km)
Population (U.N. est. 1988): 8,000
Monetary unit: East Caribbean dollar
Literacy: 80%

Anguilla was originally part of the West Indies Associated States as a component of St. Kitts-Nevis-Anguilla.

In 1967, Anguilla declared its independence from the St. Kitts-Nevis-Anguilla federation. Britain however, did not recognize this action. In February 1969, Anguilla voted to cut all ties with Britain and become an independent republic. In March, Britain landed troops on the island and, on March 30, a truce was signed. In July 1971, Anguilla became a dependency of Britain and two months later Britain ordered the withdrawal of all its troops.

A new Constitution for Anguilla, effective in February 1976, provides for separate administration and a government of elected representatives. The Associated State of St. Kitts-Nevis-Anguilla ended Dec. 19, 1980.

BERMUDA

Status: Self-governing dependency
Governor: Sir Desmond Langley (1988)
Premier: John Swan (1982)
Area: 20 sq mi. (52 sq km)
Population (mid-1989): 58,238 (average annual growth rate: 0.2%)
Capital (1989): Hamilton, 2,000
Monetary unit: Bermuda dollar
Literacy rate: 98%
Economic summary: Gross domestic product (1989 est.): $1.3 billion; $23,000 per capita; 2.0% real growth rate. Arable land: 0%. Principal agricultural products: bananas, vegetables, citrus fruits, dairy products. Labor force: 32,000; 47% clerical and in services. Major industrial products: structural concrete, paints, pharmaceuticals. Natural resource: limestone. Exports: semi-tropical produce, light manufactures. Imports: foodstuffs, fuel, machinery. Major trading partners: U.S., U.K., Canada.

Bermuda is an archipelago of about 360 small islands, 580 miles (934 km) east of North Carolina. The largest is (Great) Bermuda, or Long Island. Discovered by Juan de Bermúdez, a shipwrecked Spaniard, early in the 16th century, the islands were settled in 1612 by an offshoot of the Virginia Company and became a crown colony in 1684.

In 1940, sites on the islands were leased for 99 years to the U.S. for air and navy bases. Bermuda is also the headquarters of the West Indies and Atlantic squadron of the Royal Navy.

In 1968, Bermuda was granted a new Constitution, its first Prime Minister, and autonomy, except for foreign relations, defense, and internal security. The predominantly white United Bermuda Party has retained power in four elections against the opposition—the black-led Progressive Laborites—although Bermuda's population is 60% black. Serious rioting occurred in December 1977 after two blacks were hanged for a series of murders, including the 1973 assassination of the Governor, Sir Richard Sharples, and British troops were summoned to restore order.

BRITISH ANTARCTIC TERRITORY

Status: Dependency
High Commissioner: William Hugh Fullerton (1988)
Area: 500,000 sq mi. (1,395,000 sq km)
Population (1986): no permanent residents

The British Antarctic Territory consists of the South Shetland Islands, South Orkney Islands, and nearby Graham Land on the Antarctic continent, largely uninhabited. They are dependencies of the British crown colony of the Falkland Islands but received a separate administration in 1962, being governed by a British-appointed High Commissioner who is Governor of the Falklands.

BRITISH INDIAN OCEAN TERRITORY

Status: Dependency
Commissioner and Administrator: R. Edis
Administrative headquarters: Victoria, Seychelles
Area: 85 sq mi. (220 sq km)

This dependency, consisting of the Chagos Archipelago and other small island groups, was formed in 1965 by agreement with Mauritius and the Seychelles. There is no permanent civilian population in the territory.

BRITISH VIRGIN ISLANDS

Status: Dependency
Governor: Mark Herdman (1986)
Area: 59 sq mi. (153 sq km)
Population (mid-1989): 12,124 (growth rate: 1.1%)
Capital (est. 1986): Road Town (on Tortola): 2,479
Monetary unit: U.S. dollar

Some 36 islands in the Caribbean Sea northeast of Puerto Rico and west of the Leeward Islands, the British Virgin Islands are economically interdependent with the U.S. Virgin Islands to the south. They were formerly part of the administration of the Leeward Islands. They received a separate administration in 1956 as a crown colony. In 1967 a new Constitution was promulgated that provided for a ministerial system of government headed by the Governor. The principal islands are Tortola, Virgin Gorda, Anegada, and Jost Van Dyke.

CAYMAN ISLANDS

Status: Dependency
Governor: Alan James Scott (1987)
Area: 100 sq mi. (259 sq km)
Population (census 1989): 25,535
Capital (1989): George Town (on Grand Cayman), 12,972
Monetary unit: Cayman Islands dollar

This dependency consists of three islands—Grand Cayman (76 sq mi.; 197 sq km), Cayman Brac (22 sq mi.; 57 sq km), and Little Cayman (20 sq mi.; 52 sq km)—situated about 180 miles (290 km) northwest of Jamaica. They were dependencies of Jamaica until 1959, when they became a unit territory within the Federation of the West Indies. In 1962, upon the dissolution of the Federation, the Cayman Islands became a British dependency.

The islands' chief export is turtle products.

CHANNEL ISLANDS

Status: Crown dependencies
Lieutenant Governor of Jersey: Air Marshall Sir John Sutton (1990)
Lieutenant Governor of Guernsey: Lt. Gen. Sir Michael Wilkins (1990)
Area: 120 sq mi. (311 sq km)
Population (1988): 133,960
Capital of Jersey: St. Helier
Capital of Guernsey: St. Peter Port
Monetary units: Guernsey pound; Jersey pound

This group of islands, lying in the English Channel off the northwest coast of France, is the only portion of the Duchy of Normandy belonging to the English Crown, to which it has been attached since the conquest of 1066. It was the only British possession occupied by Germany during World War II.

For purposes of government, the islands are divided into the Bailiwick of Jersey (45 sq mi.; 117 sq km) and the Bailiwick of Guernsey (30 sq mi.; 78 sq km), including Alderney (3 sq mi.; 7.8 sq km), Sark (2 sq mi.; 5.2 sq km), Herm, Jethou, etc. The islands are administered according to their own laws and customs by local governments. Acts of Parliament in London are not binding on the islands unless they are specifically mentioned. The Queen is represented in each Bailiwick by a Lieutenant Governor.

FALKLAND ISLANDS AND DEPENDENCIES

Status: Dependency
Governor: William Hugh Fullerton (1988)
Chief Executive: R. Sampson
Area: 4,700 sq mi. (12,173 sq km)
Population est. (mid-1989): 1,943 (growth rate: .5%)
Capital (est. 1986): Stanley (on East Falkland), 1,231
Monetary unit: Falkland Island pound

This sparsely inhabited dependency consists of a group of islands in the South Atlantic, about 250 miles (402 km) east of the South American mainland. The largest islands are East Falkland and West Falkland. Dependencies are South Georgia Island (1,450 sq mi.; 3,756 sq km), the South Sandwich Islands, and other islets. Three former dependencies—Graham Land, the South Shetland Islands, and the South Orkney Islands—were established as a new British dependency, the British Antarctic Territory, in 1962.

The chief industry is sheep raising and, apart from the production of wool, hides and skins, and tallow, there are no known resources. The whaling industry is carried on from South Georgia Island.

The chief export is wool.

GIBRALTAR

Status: Self-governing dependency
Governor: Admiral Sir Derek Reffell
Chief Minister: J. Bossano
Area: 2.25 sq mi. (5.8 sq km)
Population (1989): 30,689 (growth rate: .2%)
Monetary unit: Gibraltar pound
Literacy rate: 99% (est.)
Economic summary: Gross national product (FY85 est.): $129 million; $4,450 per capita. Exports: re-exports of tobacco, petroleum, wine. Imports: manufactured goods, fuels, foodstuffs. Major trading partners: U.K., Morocco, Portugal, Netherlands, Spain, U.S.

Gibraltar, at the south end of the Iberian Peninsula, is a rocky promontory commanding the western entrance to the Mediterranean. Aside from its strategic importance, it is also a free port, naval base, and coaling station. It was captured by the Arabs crossing from Africa into Spain in A.D. 711. In the 15th century, it passed to the Moorish ruler of Granada and later became Spanish. It was captured by an Anglo-Dutch force in 1704 during the War of the Spanish Succession and passed to Great Britain by the Treaty of Utrecht in 1713. Most of the inhabitants of Gibraltar are of Spanish, Italian, and Maltese descent.

Spanish efforts to recover Gibraltar culminated in a referendum in 1967 in which the residents voted overwhelmingly to retain their link with Britain. Spain sealed Gibraltar's land border in 1969 and did not open communications until April 1980, after the two governments had agreed to solve their dispute in keeping with a United Nations resolution calling for restoration of the "Rock" to Spain.

HONG KONG

Status: Dependency
Governor: Sir David Wilson (1987)
Area: 398 sq mi. (1,031 sq km)
Population (est. mid-1991): 5,900,000 (average annual rate of natural increase: 0.7%); birth rate: 12/1000; infant mortality rate: 7.4/1000; density per square mile: 14,584
Capital (1976 census): Victoria (Hong Kong Island), 501,700
Monetary unit: Hong Kong dollar
Literacy rate: 75%
Economic summary: Gross domestic product (1989): $57 billion; $10,000 per capita; 3% real growth rate. Arable land: 7%. Principal products: vegetables, rice, dairy products. Labor force: 2,640,000; 35.8% in manufacturing. Major industrial products: textiles, clothing, toys, transistor radios, watches, electronic components. Exports: clothing, textiles, toys, watches, electrical appliances, footwear. Imports: raw materials, transport equipment, food. Major trading partners: U.S., U.K., Japan, Germany, China, Taiwan.

The crown colony of Hong Kong comprises the island of Hong Kong (32 sq mi.; 83 sq km), Stonecutters' Island, Kowloon Peninsula, and the New Territories on the adjoining mainland. The island of Hong Kong, located at the mouth of the Pearl River about 90 miles (145 km) southeast of Canton, was ceded to Britain in 1841.

Stonecutters' Island and Kowloon were annexed in 1860, and the New Territories, which are mainly agricultural lands, were leased from China in 1898 for 99 years. Hong Kong was attacked by Japanese troops Dec. 7, 1941, and surrendered the following Christmas. It remained under Japanese occupation until August 1945.

After two years of painstaking negotiation, authorities of Britain and the People's Republic of China agreed in 1984 that Hong Kong would return to Chinese sovereignty on June 30, 1997, when Britain's lease on the New Territories expires. They also agreed that the vibrant capitalist enclave on China's coast would retain its status as a free port and its social, economic, and legal system as a special administrative region of China. Current laws will remain basically unchanged.

Under a unique "One Country, Two Systems" arrangement, the Chinese government promised that Hong Kong's lifestyle would remain unchanged for 50 years, and that freedoms of speech, press, assembly, association, travel, right to strike, and religious belief would be guaranteed by law. However, the chief executive and some of the legislature will be appointed by Beijing.

Hong Kong will continue to have its own finances and issue its own travel documents, and Peking will not levy taxes.

The crackdown by hard-liners in China has led to apprehension that Hong Kong's autonomy won't be respected.

ISLE OF MAN

Status: Self-Governing Crown Dependency
Lieutenant Governor: Air Marshall Sir Laurence Jones
Area: 227 sq mi. (588 sq km)
Population (mid-1989): 64,728 (growth rate: .2%)
Capital (1986): Douglas, 20,368
Monetary unit: Isle of Man pound

Situated in the Irish Sea, equidistant from Scotland, Ireland, and England, the Isle of Man is administered according to its own laws by a government composed of the Lieutenant Governor, a Legislative Council, and a House of Keys, one of the most ancient legislative assemblies in the world.

The chief exports are beef and lamb, fish, and livestock.

LEEWARD ISLANDS

See British Virgin Islands; Montserrat

MONTSERRAT

Status: Dependency
Governor: David Taylor (1990)
Area: 38 sq mi. (98 sq km)
Population (mid-1989): 12,428 (growth rate: .3%)
Capital (est. 1988): Plymouth, 3,000
Monetary unit: East Caribbean dollar

The island of Montserrat is in the Lesser Antilles of the West Indies. Until 1956, it was a division of the Leeward Islands. It did not join the West Indies Associated States established in 1967.

The chief exports are cattle, potatoes, cotton, lint, recapped tires, mangoes, and tomatoes.

PITCAIRN ISLAND

Status: Dependency
Governor: David Joseph Moss
Island Magistrate: B. Young
Area: 1.75 sq mi. (4.5 sq km)
Population (April 1990): 65 (growth rate: 0%)
Capital: Adamstown

Pitcairn Island, in the South Pacific about midway between Australia and South America, consists of the island of Pitcairn and the three uninhabited islands of Henderson, Duicie, and Oeno. The island of Pitcairn was settled in 1790 by British mutineers from the ship *Bounty,* commanded by Capt. William Bligh. It was annexed as a British colony in 1838. Overpopulation forced removal of the settlement to Norfolk Island in 1856, but about 40 persons soon returned.

The colony is governed by a 10-member Council presided over by the Island Magistrate, who is elected for a three-year term.

ST. HELENA

Status: Dependency
Governor: Robert F. Stimson (1988)
Area: 120 sq mi. (310 sq km)
Population (mid-1989): 7,200 (growth rate: .6%)
Capital (1987): Jamestown, 1,330
Monetary unit: Pound sterling

St. Helena is a volcanic island in the South Atlantic about 1,100 miles (1,770 km) from the west coast of Africa. It is famous as the place of exile of Napoleon (1815–21).

It was taken for England in 1659 by the East India Company and was brought under the direct government of the Crown in 1834.

St. Helena has two dependencies: Ascension (34 sq mi.; 88 sq km), an island about 700 miles (1,127 km) northwest of St. Helena; and Tristan da Cunha (40 sq mi.; 104 sq km), a group of six islands about 1,500 miles (2,414 km) south-southwest of St. Helena.

TURKS AND CAICOS ISLANDS

Status: Dependency
Governor: Michael Bradley (1987)
Area: 193 sq mi. (500 sq km)
Population (mid-1989): 9,531 (growth rate: 2.4%)
Capital (est. 1988): Grand Turk, 4,500
Monetary unit: U.S. dollar

These two groups of islands are situated at the southeast end of the Bahamas. The principal islands in the Turks group are Grand Turk and Salt Cay; the principal ones in the Caicos group are South Caicos, East Caicos, Middle (or Grand) Caicos, North Caicos, Providenciales, and West Caicos.

The Turks and Caicos Islands were dependencies of Jamaica until 1959, when they became a unit territory within the Federation of the West Indies. In 1962, when Jamaica became independent, the Turks and Caicos became a British crown colony. The present Constitution has been in force since 1969.

Chief exports in 1974 were crayfish (73%) and conch (25%).

VIRGIN ISLANDS

See British Virgin Islands

UNITED STATES

The United States of America
President: George Bush (1989)
Area: 3,540,939 sq mi. (9,171,032 sq km)
Population (1990 census): 248,709,873 (% change 1980–1990: +9.80). White: 199,686,070 (80.3%); Black: 29,986,060 (12.1%); American Indian, Eskimo, or Aleut: 1,959,234 (0.8%); Asian or Pacific Islander: 7,273,662 (2.9%); Other Race: 9,804,847 (3.9%); Hispanic Origin[1]: 22,354,059 (9.0%)
Density per square mile: 70.2
Capital (1990 census): Washington, D.C., 606,900
Largest cities (1990 census): New York, 7,322,564; Los Angeles, 3,485,398; Chicago, 2,783,726; Houston, 1,630,553; Philadelphia, 1,585,577; San Diego, 1,110,549; Detroit, 1,027,974; Dallas, 1,006,877; Phoenix, 983,403; San Antonio, 935,933
Monetary unit: Dollar
Languages: predominantly English, sizable Spanish-speaking minority
Religions: Protestant, 61%; Roman Catholic, 25%; Jewish, 2%; other, 5%; none, 7%
Literacy rate: 99%
Economic summary: Gross national product (1990): $5,465.1 billion; per capita (1990): $21,974; real growth rate: 2.9%. Arable land: 20%. Principal products: corn, wheat, barley, oats, sugar, potatoes, soybeans, fruits, beef, veal, pork. Labor force: 125,557,000. Major industrial products: petroleum products, fertilizers, cement, pig iron and steel, plastics and resins, newsprint, motor vehicles, machinery, natural gas, electricity. Natural resources: coal, oil, copper, gold, silver, minerals, timber. Exports: machinery, chemicals, aircrafts, military equipment, cereals, motor vehicles, grains. Imports: crude and partly refined petroleum, machinery, automobiles. Major trading partners: Canada, Japan.

1. Persons of Hispanic origin can be of any race.

Government. The president is elected for a four-year term and may be re-elected only once. In 1991, the bicameral Congress consisted of the 100-member Senate (57 Democrats, 43 Republicans), elected to a six-year term with one-third of the seats becoming vacant every two years, and the 435-member House of Representatives (269 Democrats, 165 Republicans, 1 Independent), elected every two years. The minimum voting age is 18.

URUGUAY

Oriental Republic of Uruguay
President: Luis Alberto Lacalle (1990)
Area: 68,040 sq mi. (176,224 sq km)
Population (est. mid-1991): 3,100,000 (average annual rate of natural increase: 0.8%); birth rate: 18/1000; infant mortality rate: 21.9/1000; density per square mile: 46
Capital and largest city (est. 1982): Montevideo, 1,325,000
Monetary unit: Peso
Language: Spanish
Religion: Roman Catholic, 66%; Protestant, 2%; Jewish, 2%
National name: Republica Oriental del Uruguay
Literacy rate: 94%
Economic summary: Gross domestic product (1989 est.): $8.8 billion, $2,950 per capita; 1% real growth rate. Arable land: 8%. Principal products: livestock, grains, Labor force: 1,300,000; 19% in manufacturing;. Major products: processed meats, wool and hides, textiles, shoes, handbags and leather wearing apparel, cement, refined petroleum. Natural resources: hydroelectric power potential. Exports: meat, hides, wool, fish. Imports: crude petroleum, transportation equipment, chemicals, machinery, metals. Major trading partners: U.S., Brazil, Argentina, Germany.

Geography. Uruguay, on the east coast of South America south of Brazil and east of Argentina, is comparable in size to the State of Washington.

The country consists of a low, rolling plain in the south and a low plateau in the north. It has a 120-mile (193 km) Atlantic shore line, a 235-mile (378 km) frontage on the Rio de la Plata, and 270 miles (435 km) on the Uruguay River, its western boundary.

Government. After elections in November 1984, Julio Maria Sanguinetti was inaugurated as President on March 1, 1985, ending 12 years of military rule. Under the Constitution, Presidents serve a single five-year term. The bicameral Congress, dissolved by the military in 1973, also was restored in 1985.

History. Juan Díaz de Solis, a Spaniard, discovered Uruguay in 1516, but the Portuguese were first to settle it when they founded Colonia in 1680. After a long struggle, Spain wrested the country from Portugal in 1778. Uruguay revolted against Spain in 1811, only to be conquered in 1817 by the Portuguese from Brazil. Independence was reasserted with Argentine help in 1825, and the republic was set up in 1828.

Independence, however, did not restore order, and a revolt in 1836 touched off nearly 50 years of factional strife, with occasional armed intervention from Argentina and Brazil.

Uruguay, made prosperous by meat and wool exports, founded a welfare state early in the 20th century. A decline began in the 1950s as successive governments struggled to maintain a large bureaucracy and costly social benefits. Economic stagnation and political frustration followed.

A military coup ousted the civilian government in 1973. The military dictatorship that followed used fear and terror to demoralize the population, taking thousands of political prisoners, probably the highest proportion of citizens jailed for political reasons anywhere in the world.

After ruling for 12 years, the military regime permitted election of a civilian government in November 1984 and relinquished rule in March 1985.

Luis Lacalle became president in March 1990, becoming the first Blanco Party member to assume that office in 23 years. His position, however, became contingent upon accepting four members of the opposition Colorados party into his cabinet.

VANUATU

Republic of Vanuatu
President: Fred Timakata (1989)
Prime Minister: Fr. Walter Lini (1980)
Area: 5,700 sq mi. (14,763 sq km)
Population (est. mid-1991): 200,000 (average annual rate of natural increase: 3.1%); birth rate: 36/1000; infant mortality rate: 36/1000; density per square mile: 30
Capital (est. 1987): Port Vila, 15,100
Monetary unit: Vatu
Religions: Presbyterian, 47%; Roman Catholic, 15%; Anglican, 15%; other Christian, 10%; Animist, 9%
Literacy rate: 10–20% (est.)
Economic Summary: Gross domestic product (1987 est.): $120 million, $820 per capita; real growth rate: 0.7%. Arable land: 1%. Principal agricultural products: copra, cocoa, coffee. Exports: copra, cocoa, coffee, frozen fish. Imports: food, machinery. Major trading partners: France, New Zealand, Japan, Australia, Netherlands.

Geography. Formerly known as the New Hebrides, Vanuatu is an archipelago of some 80 islands lying between New Caledonia and Fiji in the South Pacific. Largest of the islands is Espiritu Santo (875 sq mi.; 2,266 sq km); others are Efate, Malekula, Malo, Pentecost, and Tanna. The population is largely Melanesian of mixed blood.

Government. The constitution by which Vanuatu achieved independence on July 30, 1980, vests executive authority in a President, elected by an electoral college for a five-year term. A unicameral legislature of 39 members exercises legislative power.

History. The islands were discovered by Pedro Fernandes de Queiros of Portugal in 1606 and were charted and named by the British navigator James Cook in 1774. Conflicting British and French interests were resolved by a joint naval commission that administered the islands from 1887. A condominium government was established in 1906.

The islands' plantation economy, based on imported Vietnamese labor, was prosperous until the 1920s, when markets for its products declined. The New Hebrides escaped Japanese occupation in World War II and the French population was among the first to support the Gaullist Free French movement.

A brief rebellion by French settlers and plantation workers on Espiritu Santo led by Jimmy Stevens in May 1980 threatened the scheduled independence of the islands. Britain sent a company of Royal Marines and France a contingent of 50 policemen to quell the revolt, which the new government said was financed by the Phoenix Foundation, a right-wing U.S. group. With the British and French forces replaced by soldiers from Papua New Guinea, independence ceremonies took place on July 30. The next month it was reported that Stevens had been arrested and the revolt quelled.

On the tenth anniversary of independence in 1990 prime minister Lini called for a reexamination of the constitution and existing institutions, claiming that they were forged under colonialism.

VATICAN CITY STATE

Ruler: Pope John Paul II (1978)
Area: 0.17 sq mi. (0.44 sq km)
Population (mid-1989): 755
Density per square mile: 4,424
Monetary unit: Lira
Languages: Latin and Italian
Religion: Roman Catholic
National name: Stato della Città del Vaticano

Geography. The Vatican City State is situated on the Vatican hill, on the right bank of the Tiber River, within the commune of Rome.

Government. The Pope has full legal, executive, and judicial powers. Executive power over the area is in the hands of a Commission of Cardinals appointed by the Pope. The College of Cardinals is the Pope's chief advisory body, and upon his death the cardinals elect his successor for life. The cardinals themselves are created for life by the Pope.

In the Vatican the central administration of the Roman Catholic Church throughout the world (Holy See) is carried on by the Secretariat of State, nine Congregations, three tribunals, twelve councils, and five offices. In its diplomatic relations, the Holy See is represented by the Papal Secretary of State.

History. The Vatican City State, sovereign and independent, is the survivor of the papal states that in 1859 comprised an area of some 17,000 square miles (44,030 sq km). During the struggle for Italian unification, from 1860 to 1870, most of this area became part of Italy.

By an Italian law of May 13, 1871, the temporal power of the Pope was abrogated, and the territory of the Papacy was confined to the Vatican and Lateran palaces and the villa of Castel Gandolfo. The Popes consistently refused to recognize this arrangement and, by the Lateran Treaty of Feb. 11, 1929, between the Vatican and the Kingdom of Italy, the exclusive dominion and sovereign jurisdiction of the Holy See over the city of the Vatican was again recognized, thus restoring the Pope's temporal authority over the area.

The first session of Ecumenical Council Vatican II was opened by John XXIII on Oct. 11, 1962, to plan and set policies for the modernization of the Roman Catholic Church. Pope Paul VI continued the Council, opening the second session on Sept. 29, 1963.

On Aug. 26, 1978, Cardinal Albino Luciani was chosen by the College of Cardinals to succeed Paul VI, who had died of a heart attack on Aug. 6. The new Pope, who took the name John Paul I, was born on Oct. 17, 1912, at Forno di Canale in Italy.

Only 34 days after his election, John Paul I died of a heart attack, ending the shortest reign in 373 years. On Oct. 16, Cardinal Karol Wojtyla, 58, was chosen Pope and took the name John Paul II.

A visit to the Irish Republic and to the United States in September and October 1979, followed by a 12-nation African tour in May 1980 and a visit in July to Brazil, the most populous Catholic nation, further established John Paul's image as a "people's" Pope. On May 13, 1981, a Turkish terrorist shot the Pope in St. Peter's Square, the first assassination attempt against the Pontiff in modern times. Mehmet Ali Agca was sentenced on July 22 to life imprisonment by an Italian Court.

The Pontiff traveled to Britain and Argentina in 1982. He also made a visit to Poland.

On June 3, 1985, the Vatican and Italy ratified a new church-state treaty, known as a concordat, replacing the Lateran Pact of 1929. The new accord affirmed the independence of Vatican City but ended a number of privileges the Catholic Church had in Italy, including its status as the state religion. The treaty ended Rome's status as a "sacred city."

Relations, diplomatic and ecclesiastical, with Eastern Europe have improved dramatically with the fall of communism. Relations with the Soviet Union, while improving, have not yet reached the ambassadorial level.

VENEZUELA

Republic of Venezuela
President: Carlos Andrés Pérez (1989)
Area: 352,143 sq mi. (912,050 sq km)
Population (est. mid-1991): 20,100,000 (average annual rate of natural increase: 2.3%); birth rate: 28/1000; infant mortality rate: 23.3/1000; density per square mile: 57
Capital: Caracas
Largest cities (est. 1981 for metropolitan area): Caracas, 3,000,000; Maracaibo, 890,000; Valencia, 616,000; Barquisimento, 498,000
Monetary unit: Bolivar
Language: Spanish, Indian dialects in interior
Religion: Roman Catholic
National name: Republica de Venezuela
Literacy rate: 85.6%
Economic summary: Gross domestic product (1989 est.): $52 billion; $2,700 per capita; –8.1% real growth rate. Arable land: 3. Principal products: rice, coffee, corn, sugar, bananas, dairy and meat products. Labor force: 5,800,000; 28% in industry; principal products: refined petroleum products, iron and steel, cement, textiles, transport equipment. Natural resources: petroleum, natural gas, iron ore, hydroelectric power. Exports: petroleum, iron ore. Imports: industrial machinery and equipment, manufactures, chemicals, foodstuffs. Major trading partners: U.S., Japan, Germany, Brazil, Italy.

Geography. Venezuela, a third larger than Texas, occupies most of the northern coast of South America

on the Caribbean Sea. It is bordered by Colombia to the west, Guyana to the east, and Brazil to the south.

Mountain systems break Venezuela into four distinct areas: (1) the Maracaibo lowlands; (2) the mountainous region in the north and northwest; (3) the Orinoco basin, with the llanos (vast grass-covered plains) on its northern border and great forest areas in the south and southeast; (4) the Guiana Highlands, south of the Orinoco, accounting for nearly half the national territory. About 80% of Venezuela is drained by the Orinoco and its tributaries.

Government. Venezuela is a federal republic consisting of 20 states, the Federal District, two territories and 72 islands in the Caribbean. There is a bicameral Congress, the 50 members of the Senate and the 201 members of the Chamber of Deputies being elected by popular vote to five-year terms. The President is also elected for five years. He must be a Venezuelan by birth and over 30 years old. He is not eligible for re-election until 10 years after the end of his term.

History. Columbus discovered Venezuela on his third voyage in 1498. A subsequent Spanish explorer gave the country its name, meaning "Little Venice." There were no important settlements until Caracas was founded in 1567. Simón Bolívar, who led the liberation of much of the continent from Spain, was born in Caracas in 1783. With Bolívar taking part, Venezuela was one of the first South American colonies to revolt against Spain, in 1810, but it was not until 1821 that independence was won. Federated at first with Colombia and Ecuador, the country set up a republic in 1830 and then sank for many decades into a condition of revolt, dictatorship, and corruption.

From 1908 to 1935, Gen. Juan Vicente Gómez ruled tyrannically, picking satellites to alternate with him in the presidential palace. Thereafter, there was a struggle between democratic forces and those backing a return to strong-man rule. Dr. Rómulo Betancourt and the liberal Acción Democrática Party won a majority of seats in a constituent assembly to draft a new Constitution in 1946. A well-known writer, Rómulo Gallegos, candidate of Betancourt's party, easily won the presidential election of 1947. But, the army ousted Gallegos the next year and instituted a military junta.

The country overthrew the dictatorship in 1958 and thereafter enjoyed democratic government. Rafael Caldera Rodríguez, President from 1969 to 1974, legalized the Communist Party and established diplomatic relations with Moscow.

Venezuela and neighboring Guyana in 1970 called a 12-year moratorium on their border dispute (Venezuela claimed 50,000 square miles of Guyana's 83,000). In 1974, President Carlos Andrés Perez took office.

In 1976, Venezuela nationalized 21 oil companies, mostly subsidiaries of U.S. firms, offering compensation of $1.28 billion. Oil income in that year was $9.9 billion, and although production decreased 2.2%, revenue remained at the same level in 1977 because of higher prices, largely financing an ambitious social welfare program.

Despite difficulties at home, Pérez continued to play an active foreign role in extending economic aid to Latin neighbors, in backing the human-rights policy of President Carter, and in supporting Carter's return of the Panama Canal to Panama.

Opposition Christian Democrats capitalized on

Pérez's domestic problems to elect Luis Herrera Campíns President in Venezuela's fifth consecutive free election, on Dec. 3, 1978.

Herrera Campins at first supported U.S. policy in Central America, lining up behind the government of El Salvador but he later shifted toward a "political solution" that would include the insurgents. In March 1982, he assailed Reagan's policy as "interventionist."

When the Falklands war broke out, Venezuela became one of the most vigorous advocates of the Argentine cause and one of the sharpest critics of the U.S. decision to back Britain.

Jaime Lusinchi of the Democratic Action party won the country's sixth consecutive free election, on Dec. 4, 1983, and was inaugurated President in March 1984.

In the presidential election of December 1988 former president Carlos Andres Perez of the Democratic Action party easily won. Upon assuming office President Perez introduced an economic austerity program.

VIETNAM

Socialist Republic of Vietnam
President: Vo Chi Cong (1987)
Premier: Vo Van Kiet (1991)
Area: 127,246 sq mi. (329,566 sq km)
Population (est. mid-1991): 67,600,000 (average annual rate of natural increase: 2.3%); birth rate: 32/1000; infant mortality rate: 44/1000; Density per square mile: 531
Capital: Hanoi
Largest cities (est. 1979): Ho Chi Minh City (Saigon),[1] 3,450,000; Hanoi, 2,600,000; Haiphong, 1,280,000; (est. 1973): Da Nang, 492,200; Nha Trang, 216,200; Qui Nho'n, 213,750; Hué 209,000
Monetary unit: Dong
Languages: Vietnamese (official), French, English, Khmer, Chinese
Religions: Buddhist, Roman Catholic, Islam, Taoist, Confucian, Animist
National name: Công Hòa Xa Hôi Chú Nghia Viêt Nam
Literacy rate: 78%
Economic summary: Gross national product (1989 est.): $14.2 billion; $215 per capita; 8% real growth rate. Arable land: 22%. Principal products: rice, rubber, fruits and vegetables, corn, sugar cane, fish. Labor force: 35,000,000 (1989 est.). Major industrial products: processed foods, textiles, cement, chemical fertilizers, glass, tires. Natural resources: phosphates, forests, coal. Exports: agricultural products, coal, minerals. Imports: petroleum, steel products, railroad equipment, chemicals, medicines, raw cotton, fertilizer, grain. Major trading partners: U.S.S.R., Singapore, Japan, Eastern Europe.

1. Includes suburb of Cholon.

Geography. Vietnam occupies the eastern and southern part of the Indochinese peninsula in Southeast Asia, with the South China Sea along its entire coast. China is to the north and Laos and Cambodia to the west. Long and narrow on a north-south axis, Vietnam is about twice the size of Arizona.

The Mekong River delta lies in the south and the Red River delta in the north. Heavily forested mountain and plateau regions make up most of the country.

Government. Less than a year after the capitulation of the former Republic of Vietnam (South Vietnam) on April 30, 1975, a joint National Assembly convened with 249 deputies representing the North and 243 representing the South. The Assembly set July 2, 1976, as the official reunification date. Hanoi became the capital, with North Vietnamese President Ton Duc Thang becoming President of the new Socialist Republic of Vietnam and North Vietnamese Premier Pham Van Dong becoming its head of government. By 1981, the National Assembly had increased to 496 members. Truong Chinh succeeded Thang in 1981.

Dang Cong san Vietnam (Communist Party), led by General Secretary Nguyen Van Linh, is the ruling political party. There are also the Socialist Party and the Democratic Party.

History. The Vietnamese are descendants of Mongoloid nomads from China and migrants from Indonesia. They recognized Chinese suzerainty until the 15th century, an era of nationalistic expansion, when Cambodians were pushed out of the southern area of what is now Vietnam.

A century later, the Portuguese were the first Europeans to enter the area. France established its influence early in the 19th century and within 80 years conquered the three regions into which the country was then divided—Cochin-China in the south, Annam in the center, and Tonkin in the north.

France first unified Vietnam in 1887, when a single governor-generalship was created, followed by the first physical links between north and south—a rail and road system. Even at the beginning of World War II, however, there were internal differences among the three regions.

Japan took over military bases in Vietnam in 1940 and a pro-Vichy French administration remained until 1945. A veteran Communist leader, Ho Chi Minh, organized an independence movement known as the Vietminh to exploit a confused situation. At the end of the war, Ho's followers seized Hanoi and declared a short-lived republic, which ended with the arrival of French forces in 1946.

Paris proposed a unified government within the French Union under the former Annamite emperor, Bao Dai. Cochin-China and Annam accepted the proposal, and Bao Dai was proclaimed emperor of all Vietnam in 1949. Ho and the Vietminh withheld support, and the revolution in China gave them the outside help needed for a war of resistance against French and Vietnamese troops armed largely by the U.S.

A bitter defeat at Dien Bien Phu in northwest Vietnam on May 5, 1954, broke the French military campaign and brought the division of Vietnam at the conference of Geneva that year.

In the new South, Ngo Dinh Diem, Premier under Bao Dai, deposed the monarch in 1955 and established a republic with himself as President. Diem used strong U.S. backing to create an authoritarian regime that suppressed all opposition but could not eradicate the Northern-supplied Communist Viet Cong.

Skirmishing grew into a full-scale war, with escalating U.S. involvement. A military coup, U.S.-inspired in the view of many, ousted Diem Nov. 1, 1963, and a kaleidoscope of military governments followed. The most savage fighting of the war occurred in early 1968, during the Tet holidays.

Although the Viet Cong failed to overthrow the Saigon government, U.S. public reaction to the apparently endless war forced a limitation of U.S. troops to

550,000 and a new emphasis on shifting the burden of further combat to the South Vietnamese. Ho Chi Minh's death on Sept. 3, 1969, brought a quadrumvirate to replace him but no flagging in Northern will to fight.

U.S. bombing and invasion of Cambodia in the summer of 1970—an effort to destroy Viet Cong bases in the neighboring state—marked the end of major U.S. participation in the fighting. Most American ground troops were withdrawn from combat by mid-1971 as heavy bombing of the Ho Chi Minh trail from North Vietnam appeared to cut the supply of men and matériel to the South.

Secret negotiations for peace by Secretary of State Henry A. Kissinger with North Vietnamese officials during 1972 after heavy bombing of Hanoi and Haiphong brought the two sides near agreement in October. When the Northerners demanded the removal of the South's President Nguyen Van Thieu as their price, President Nixon ordered the "Christmas bombing" of the North. The conference resumed and a peace settlement was signed in Paris on Jan. 27, 1973. It called for release of all U.S. prisoners, withdrawal of U.S. forces, limitation of both sides' forces inside South Vietnam, and a commitment to peaceful reunification.

Despite Chinese and Soviet endorsement, the agreement foundered. U.S. bombing of Communist-held areas in Cambodia was halted by Congress in August 1973, and in the following year Communist action in South Vietnam increased.

An armored attack across the 17th parallel in January 1975 panicked the South Vietnamese army and brought the invasion within 40 miles of Saigon by April 9. Thieu resigned on April 21 and fled, to be replaced by Vice President Tran Van Huong, who quit a week later, turning over the office to Gen. Duong Van Minh. "Big Minh" surrendered Saigon on April 30, ending a war that took 1.3 million Vietnamese and 56,000 American lives, at the cost of $141 billion in U.S. aid.

On May 3, 1977, the U.S. and Vietnam opened negotiations in Paris to normalize relations. One of the first results was the withdrawal of U.S. opposition to Vietnamese membership in the United Nations, formalized in the Security Council on July 20. Two major issues remained to be settled, however: the return of the bodies of some 2,500 U.S. servicemen missing in the war and the claim by Hanoi that former President Nixon had promised reconstruction aid under the 1973 agreement. Negotiations failed to resolve these issues.

The new year also brought an intensification of border clashes between Vietnam and Cambodia and accusations by China that Chinese residents of Vietnam were being subjected to persecution. Peking cut off all aid and withdrew 800 technicians.

By June, 133,000 ethnic Chinese were reported to have fled Vietnam, and a year later as many as 500,000 of the 1.8 million Vietnamese of Chinese ancestry were believed to have escaped.

Half of them had gone by land or sea to China. Tens of thousands more had survived boat passage to Thailand, Malaysia, Indonesia, or Hong Kong. U.S. officials said 100,000 may have died. Survivors said they had paid up to $5,000 in bribes to leave Vietnam, and U.S. and British officials charged Hanoi with a deliberate extortion policy.

Hanoi was undoubtedly preoccupied with a continuing war in Cambodia, where 60,000 Vietnamese troops were aiding the Heng Samrin regime in suppressing the last forces of the pro-Chinese Pol Pot

regime. In early 1979, Vietnam was conducting a two-front war, defending its northern border against a Chinese invasion and at the same time supporting its army in Cambodia.

Despite Hanoi's claims of total victory, resistance in Cambodia continued through 1984. Vietnam's second conflict, on its border with China, also flared sporadically.

The Hanoi government agreed in July 1984 to resume technical talks with U.S. officials on the possible whereabouts of the 2,490 Americans still listed as missing, most of them believed dead. In August 1985, the North Vietnamese turned over to an American team 26 numbered crates described as containing the remains of 26 U.S. servicemen.

Economic troubles continued, with the government seeking to reschedule its $1.4-billion foreign hard-currency debt, owed mainly to Japan and the International Monetary Fund. In late 1987, a shuffle of the Vietnamese Politburo brought in new leaders who are expected to slightly relax the government grip on the economy and crack down on corruption within the party.

In 1988, Vietnam also began limited troop withdrawals from Laos and Cambodia. Aid from Eastern Europe dropped considerably although in January 1991 the Soviet Union signed a $1 billion trade agreement with Vietnam, which has resisted the pressure for political reform.

WESTERN SAMOA

Independent State of Western Samoa
Head of State: Malietoa Tanumafili II (1962)
Prime Minister: Tofilau Eti Alesana (1988)
Area: 1,093 sq mi. (2,831 sq km)
Population (est. mid-1991): 200,000 (average annual growth rate: 2.8%; birth rate: 34/1000; infant mortality rate: 47/1000; density per square mile: 172
Capital and largest city (1980): Apia, 50,000
Monetary unit: Tala
Languages: Samoan and English
Religions: Christian, 99.7%
National name: Samoa i Sísifo
Member of Commonwealth of Nations
Literacy rate: 90%
Economic summary: Gross domestic product (1989 est.): $112 million; $615 per capita; 0.2% real growth rate. Arable land: 19%. Principal products: copra, coconuts, cocoa, bananas, taro, yams. Labor force: 37,000; 22,000 employed in agriculture (1983 est.). Major industrial products: timber, processed food, fish. Natural resource: timber. Exports: copra, cocoa, coconut oil and cream, timber. Imports: food, manufactured goods, machinery. Major trading partners: New Zealand, Australia, U.S., Fiji, Japan.

Geography. Western Samoa, the size of Rhode Island, is in the South Pacific Ocean about 2,200 miles (3,540 km) south of Hawaii midway to Sydney, Australia, and about 800 miles (1,287 km) northeast of Fiji. The larger islands in the Samoan chain are mountainous and of volcanic origin. There is little level land except in the coastal areas, where most cultivation takes place.

Government. Western Samoa has a 47-member Legislature, consisting mainly of the titleholders (chiefs) of family groups, with two non-title members. All members are elected by universal suffrage. When the present Head of State dies, successors will be elected by the Legislature for five-year terms.

History. The Samoan islands were discovered in the 18th century and visited by Dutch and French traders. Toward the end of the 19th century, conflicting interests of the U.S., Britain, and Germany resulted in a treaty signed in 1899. It recognized the paramount interests of the U.S. in those islands east of 171° west longitude (American Samoa) and Germany's interests in the other islands (Western Samoa); the British withdrew in return for recognition of their rights in Tonga and the Solomons.

New Zealand occupied Western Samoa in 1914, and was granted a League of Nations mandate. In 1947, the islands became a U.N. trust territory administered by New Zealand.

Western Samoa became independent on Jan. 1, 1962.

The damage caused by a cyclone in early 1990 worsened the island's already ailing economy.

REPUBLIC OF YEMEN

President: Ali Abdullah Salen
Prime Minister: Haidar Abu Bakr al-Attas
Area: 203,850 sq mi. (527,970 sq km)
Population (est. mid-1991): 10,100,000 (average annual rate of natural increase: 3.5%); birth rate: 51/1000; infant mortality rate: 121/1000; density per square mile: 49
Capital: San'a', 427,185
Monetary unit: Both Dinar and Rial
Largest cities: San'a', 427,185; Aden, 365,000
Language: Arabic
Religion: Islam (Sunni and Shiite)
Literacy rate: 20%
Economic summary: Gross national product (North Yemen) (1988 est.): $5.5 billion, $820 per capita; real growth rate 19.7%; Gross national product (South Yemen) (1988 est.): $1.2 billion. $495 per capita, real growth rate 5.2%; Principal agricultural products: wheat, sorghum, cattle, sheep, cotton, fruits, coffee, dates. Principal industrial products: crude and refined oil, textiles, leather goods, handicrafts, fish. Exports: cotton, coffee, hides, vegetables, dried fish; Imports: textiles, manufactured consumer goods, foodstuffs, sugar, grain, flour. Major trading partners: U.K., U.S.S.R., Japan, Saudi Arabia, Australia, U.S.

Geography. Formerly known as the states of Yemen and the Yemen Arab Republic, the Republic of Yemen occupies the southwestern tip of the Arabian Peninsula on the Red Sea opposite Ethiopia, and extends along the southern part of the Arabian Peninsula on the Gulf of Aden and the Indian Ocean. Saudi Arabia is to the north and Oman is to the east. The country is about the size of France.

It has a 700-mile (1,130-km) narrow coastal plain in the south that gives way to a mountainous region and then a plateau area. Some of the interior highlands in the west attain a height of 12,000 feet (3,660 m).

Government. Parliamentary. There is a five-man ruling Presidential Council consisting of the President, Vice-President, and three other members. They are Salem Saleh Mohammed, the former deputy to the new vice-president, Abdel-Karim al-Arshi, former speaker of Yemen's parliament, and Abdel-Aziz Abdulghani, former Prime Minister of the Yemen Arab Republic. Elections are planned for the end of 1992.

History. The history of Yemen dates back to the Minaean kingdom (1200–650 B.C.). It accepted Islam in A.D. 628, and in the 10th century came under the control of the Rassite dynasty of the Zaidi sect. The Turks occupied the area from 1538 to 1630 and from 1849 to 1918. The sovereign status of Yemen was confirmed by treaties signed with Saudi Arabia and Britain in 1934.

Yemen joined the Arab League in 1945 and established diplomatic relations with the U.S. in 1946.

In 1962, a military revolt of elements favoring President Gamal Abdel Nasser of Egypt broke out. A ruling junta proclaimed a republic, and Yemen became an international battleground, with Egypt and the U.S.S.R. supporting the revolutionaries, and King Saud of Saudi Arabia and King Hussein of Jordan the royalists. The civil war continued until the war between the Arab states and Israel broke out in June 1967. Nasser had to pull out many of his troops and agree to a cease-fire and withdrawal of foreign forces. The war finally ended with the defeat of the royalists in mid-1969.

The People's Republic of Southern Yemen was established Nov. 30, 1967, when Britain granted independence to the Federation of South Arabia. This Federation consisted of the state (once the colony) of Aden and 16 of the 20 states of the Protectorate of South Arabia (once the Aden Protectorate). The four states of the Protectorate that did not join the Federation later became part of Southern Yemen.

The Republic of Yemen was established on May 23, 1990, when pro-western Yemen and Marxist Yemen Arab Republic merged after 300 years of separation to form the new nation. The union had been approved by both governments in November 1989.

The new president, Ali Abdullah Salen of Yemen, was elected by the parliaments of both countries. The parliaments also chose South Yemen's Ali Salem al-Baidh, secretary general of the ruling socialist party, to be the new vice-president.

Since unification a coalition of the People's Congress Party, which ruled in the north, and the Yemen Socialist Party, which ruled in the south, has governed the country. Because of its tight organization the Socialist Party, despite its Marxism, has flourished and become entrenched in the running of the government.

YUGOSLAVIA

Socialist Federal Republic of Yugoslavia
President: Stipe Mesic (1991)
President of Federal Executive Council (Premier): Ante Marković (1989)
Area: 98,766 sq mi. (255,804 sq km)
Population (est. mid-1991): 23,900,000 (average annual rate of natural increase: 0.5%); birth rate: 14/1000; infant mortality rate: 24.3/1000; density per square mile: 242
Capital: Belgrade
Largest cities (est. 1982): Belgrade, 1,250,000; Zagreb, 765,000; Skopje, 505,000; Sarajevo, 450,000; Ljubljana, 255,000; Split, 200,000
Monetary unit: Dinar
Languages: Serbo-Croatian, Slovene, Macedonian (all official)

Religions: Eastern Orthodox, 50%; Roman Catholic, 30%; Islam, 9%; Protestant, 1%; other, 10%
National name: Socijalisticka Federativna Republika Jugoslavija
Literacy rate: 90.5%
Economic summary: Gross national product (1989 est.): $129.5 billion, $5,464 per capita; –1% real growth rate. Arable land: 28%. Principal products: corn, wheat, tobacco, sugar beets. Labor force: 9,600,000; 27% in mining and manufacturing. Major products: wood, processed food, nonferrous metals, machinery, textiles. Natural resources: coal, timber, copper, iron, lead, zinc, bauxite. Exports: leather goods, textiles, machinery. Imports: machinery, chemicals, iron, and steel. Major trading partners: U.S.S.R., E.C., U.S., Czechoslovakia.

Geography. Yugoslavia fronts on the eastern coast of the Adriatic Sea opposite Italy. Its neighbors are Austria, Italy, and Hungary to the north, Romania and Bulgaria to the east, and Greece and Albania to the south. It is slightly larger than Wyoming.

About half of Yugoslavia is mountainous. In the north, the Dinaric Alps rise abruptly from the sea and progress eastward as a barren limestone plateau called the Karst. Montenegro is a jumbled mass of mountains, containing also some grassy slopes and fertile river valleys. Southern Serbia, too, is mountainous. A rich plain in the north and northeast, drained by the Danube, is the most fertile area of the country.

Government. Yugoslavia is a federal republic composed of six socialist republics—Serbia (which includes the provinces of Vojvodina and Kosovo), Croatia, Slovenia, Bosnia-Herzegovina, Macedonia, and Montenegro. Actual administration is carried on by the Federal Executive Council and its secretaries.

The League of Communists and the Socialist Alliance of the Working People are the major political parties.

History. Yugoslavia was formed Dec. 4, 1918, from the patchwork of Balkan states and territories where World War I began with the assassination of Archduke Ferdinand of Austria at Sarajevo on June 28, 1914. The new Kingdom of Serbs, Croats, and Slovenes included the former kingdoms of Serbia and Montenegro; Bosnia-Herzegovina, previously administered jointly by Austria and Hungary; Croatia-Slavonia, a semi-autonomous region of Hungary; and Dalmatia, formerly administered by Austria. King Peter I of Serbia became the first monarch, his son acting as Regent until his accession as Alexander I on Aug. 16, 1921.

Croatian demands for a federal state forced Alexander to assume dictatorial powers in 1929 and to change the country's name to Yugoslavia. Serbian dominance continued despite his efforts, amid the resentment of other regions. A Macedonian associated with Croatian dissidents assassinated Alexander in Marseilles, France, on Oct. 9, 1934, and his cousin, Prince Paul, became Regent for the King's son, Prince Peter.

Paul's pro-Axis policy brought Yugoslavia to sign the Axis Pact on March 25, 1941, and opponents overthrew the government two days later. On April 6 the Nazis occupied the country, and the young King and his government fled. Two guerrilla armies —the Chetniks under Draza Mihajlovic supporting the monarchy and the Partisans under Tito (Josip Broz) leaning toward the U.S.S.R.—fought the Nazis for the duration of the war. In 1943, Tito established an Executive National Committee of Liberation to function as a provisional government.

Tito won the election held in the fall of 1945, as monarchists boycotted the vote. A new Assembly abolished the monarchy and proclaimed the Federal People's Republic of Yugoslavia, with Tito as Prime Minister.

Ruthlessly eliminating opposition, the Tito government executed Mihajlovic in 1946. With Soviet aid, Tito annexed the greater part of Italian Istria under the 1947 peace treaty with Italy but failed in his claim to the key port of Trieste. Zone B of the former free territory of Trieste went to Yugoslavia in 1954.

Tito broke with the Soviet bloc in 1948 and Yugoslavia has since followed a middle road, combining orthodox Communist control of politics and general overall economic policy with a varying degree of freedom in the arts, travel, and individual enterprise. Tito, who became President in 1953 and President for life under a revised Constitution adopted in 1963, played a major part in the creation of a "non-aligned" group of states, the so-called "third world."

The Marshal supported his one-time Soviet mentors in their quarrel with Communist China, but even though he imprisoned the writer Mihajlo Mihajlov and other dissenters at home, he criticized Soviet repression of Czechoslovakia in 1968.

Tito's death on May 4, 1980, three days before his 88th birthday, removed from the scene the last World War II leader. A rotating presidency designed to avoid internal dissension was put into effect immediately, and the feared clash of Yugoslavia's multiple nationalities and regions appeared to have been averted. A collective presidency, rotated annually among the six republics and two autonomous provinces of the federal republic, continued to govern according to a constitutional change made in 1974.

Demonstrations by ethnic Albanians in Kosovo for freedom from Serb rule were met with a forcible response from Serb authorities under the direction of Serb leader Slobodan Miloslovic. Miloslovic has mobilized Serb sentiment not only against the Albanians but also against the central government, raising the spectre of further divisiveness within Yugoslavia. In 1990, elections in the states of Croatia and Slovenia were won by parties advocating greater autonomy.

In May 1991 Croatian voters supported a referendum calling for their republic to become an independent nation. A similar referendum passed in December in Slovenia. In June the respective parliaments in both republics passed declarations of independence. Tensions mounted almost immediately in Yugoslavia, and civil war loomed imminent. Although some fighting did break out, a compromise was accepted in July deferring Slovenia's independence for three months in exchange for talks on a new federal structure.

ZAIRE

Republic of Zaire
President: Mobutu Sese Seko (1965)
Prime Minister: Nguza Karl-i-Bond (1991)
Area: 905,365 sq mi. (2,344,885 sq km)
Population (est. mid-1991): 37,800,000 (average annual rate of natural increase: 3.1%); birth rate: 46/1000; infant mortality rate: 83/1000; density per square mile: 42

Capital: Kinshasa
Largest cities (est. 1984): Kinshasa, 2,653,558; Lubumbashi, 543,268; Mbuji-Mayi, 423,363; Kananga, 290,898
Monetary unit: Zaire
Languages: French (official), English, Bantu dialects, mainly Swahili, Lingala, Ishiluba, and Kikongo
Religions: Roman Catholic 50%, Protestant 20%, Kimbanguist 10%, Islam 10%; syncretic and traditional, 10%
Ethnic groups: Bantu, Sudanese, Nilotics, Pygmies, Hamites
National name: République du Zaïre
Literacy rate: 55% male, 37% female
Economic summary: Gross domestic product (1988): $6.5 billion; $195 per capita; 2.8% real growth rate. Arable land: 3%. Principal products: coffee, palm oil, rubber, quinine, cassava, bananas, plantains, vegetables, fruits. Labor force: 15,000,000; 13% in industry. Major industrial products: processed and unprocessed minerals, consumer goods. Natural resources: copper, cobalt, zinc, industrial diamonds, manganese, tin, gold, silver, bauxite, iron, coal, crude oil, hydroelectric potential. Exports: copper, cobalt, diamonds, petroleum, coffee. Imports: consumer goods, foodstuffs, mining and other machinery, transport equipment. Major trading partners: Belgium, France, U.S., Germany.

Geography. Zaire is situated in west central Africa and is bordered by the Congo, the Central African Republic, the Sudan, Uganda, Rwanda, Burundi, Tanzania, Zambia, Angola, and the Atlantic Ocean. It is one quarter the size of the U.S.

The principal rivers are the Ubangi and Bomu in the north and the Zaire (Congo) in the west, which flows into the Atlantic. The entire length of Lake Tanganyika lies along the eastern border with Tanzania and Burundi.

Government. Under the Constitution approved by referendum in 1967 and amended in 1974, the third Constitution since 1960, the president and a unicameral Legislature are elected by universal suffrage for five-year terms.

In 1971, the government proclaimed that the Democratic Republic of the Congo would be known as the Republic of Zaire, since the Congo River's name had been changed to the Zaire. In addition, President Joseph D. Mobutu took the name Mobutu Sese Seko and Katanga Province became Shaba.

There is only one political party: the Popular Movement of the Revolution, led by President Mobutu. However, in April 1990, Mobutu lifted the ban on opposition parties.

History. Formerly the Belgian Congo, this territory was inhabited by ancient Negrito peoples (Pygmies), who were pushed into the mountains by Bantu and Nilotic invaders. The American correspondent Henry M. Stanley navigated the Congo River in 1877 and opened the interior to exploration. Commissioned by King Leopold II of the Belgians, Stanley made treaties with native chiefs that enabled the King to obtain personal title to the territory at the Berlin Conference of 1885.

Criticism of forced labor under royal exploitation prompted Belgium to take over administration of the Congo, which remained a colony until agitation for independence forced Brussels to grant freedom on June 30, 1960. Moise Tshombe, Premier of the then

Katanga Province seceded from the new republic on July 11, and another mining province, South Kasai, followed. Belgium sent paratroopers to quell the civil war, and with President Joseph Kasavubu and Premier Patrice Lumumba of the national government in conflict, the United Nations flew in a peacekeeping force.

Kasavubu staged an army coup in 1960 and handed Lumumba over to the Katangan forces. A U.N. investigating commission found that Lumumba had been killed by a Belgian mercenary in the presence of Tshombe. Dag Hammarskjold, U.N. Secretary-General, died in a plane crash en route to a peace conference with Tshombe on Sept. 17, 1961.

U.N. Secretary-General U Thant submitted a national reconciliation plan in 1962 that Tshombe rejected. Tshombe's troops fired on the U.N. force in December, and in the ensuing conflict Tshombe capitulated on Jan. 14, 1963. The peacekeeping force withdrew, and, in a complete about-face, Kasavubu named Tshombe Premier to fight a spreading rebellion. Tshombe used foreign mercenaries and, with the help of Belgian paratroops airlifted by U.S. planes, defeated the most serious opposition, a Communist-backed regime in the northeast.

Kasavubu abruptly dismissed Tshombe in 1965 and was himself ousted by Gen. Joseph-Desiré Mobutu, Army Chief of Staff. The new President nationalized the Union Minière, the Belgian copper mining enterprise that had been a dominant force in the Congo since colonial days. The plane carrying the exiled Tshombe was hijacked in 1967 and he was held prisoner in Algeria until his death from a heart attack was announced June 29, 1969.

Mobutu eliminated opposition to win election in 1970 to a term of seven years, which was renewed in a 1977 election. He invited U.S., South African, and Japanese investment to replace Belgian interests. In 1975, he nationalized much of the economy, barred religious instruction in schools, and decreed the adoption of African names.

On March 8, 1977, invaders from Angola calling themselves the Congolese National Liberation Front pushed into Shaba and threatened the important mining center of Kolwezi. France and Belgium responded to Mobutu's pleas for help with weapons, but the U.S. gave only nonmilitary supplies.

In April, France flew 1,500 Moroccan troops to Shaba to defeat the invaders, who were, Mobutu charged, Soviet-inspired, and Cuban-led. U.S. intelligence sources, however, confirmed Soviet and Cuban denials of any participation and identified the rebels as former Katanga gendarmes who had fled to Angola after their 1963 defeat.

On May 15, 1978, a new assault from Angola resulted in the capture of Kolwezi and the death of 100 whites and 300 blacks. In this second invasion, France and Belgium intervened directly as 1,000 Foreign Legion paratroopers repelled the Katangese and 1,750 Belgian soldiers helped evacuate 2,000 Europeans. The U.S. supplied 18 air transports for both the troop movement and the evacuation.

In April 1990 Mobutu announced he intended to introduce multiparty democracy, but that elections in January 1991 would reduce the number of political parties to two besides his own. Opposition leaders denounced the scheme as giving Mobutu's party an unfair advantage.

A national conference was scheduled for July 1991, but in June three opposition groups announced a boycott and that they would form a parallel government of national union. The conference was postponed.

ZAMBIA

Republic of Zambia
President: Frederick Chiluba (1991)
Prime Minister: Gen. Malimba Masheke (1989)
Area: 290,586 sq mi. (752,618 sq km)
Population (est. mid-1991): 8,400,000 (average annual rate of natural increase: 3.8%); birth rate: 51/1000; infant mortality rate: 76/1000; density per square mile: 29
Capital: Lusaka
Largest cities (est. 1982): Lusaka, 650,000; Kitwe, 345,000; Ndola, 325,000; Chingola, 195,000
Monetary unit: Kwacha
Languages: English and local dialects
Religions: Christian, 50–75%; Islam and Hindu, 1%; remainder indigenous beliefs
Member of Commonwealth of Nations
Literacy rate: 75.7%
Economic summary: Gross domestic product (1988): $4 billion; $530 per capita; real growth rate 6.7%. Arable land: 7%. Principal products: corn, tobacco, rice, sugar cane. Labor force: 2,455,000; 6% in mining, manufacturing and construction. Major products: copper, textiles, chemicals, zinc, fertilizers. Natural resources: copper, zinc, lead, cobalt, coal. Exports: copper, zinc, lead, cobalt, tobacco. Imports: manufactured goods, machinery and transport equipment, foodstuffs. Major trading partners: Western Europe, Japan, South Africa, U.S.

Geography. Zambia, a landlocked country in south central Africa, is about one-tenth larger than Texas. It is surrounded by Angola, Zaire, Tanzania, Malawi, Mozambique, Zimbabwe, Botswana, and Namibia (formerly South-West Africa). The country is mostly a plateau that rises to 8,000 feet (2,434 m) in the east.

Government. Zambia (formerly Northern Rhodesia) is governed by a president, elected by universal suffrage, and a Legislative Assembly, consisting of 125 members elected by universal suffrage and up to 10 additional members nominated by the president.

In December 1990 President Kenneth Kaunda signed constitutional amendments legalizing opposition political parties.

History. Empire builder Cecil Rhodes obtained mining concessions in 1889 from King Lewanika of the Barotse and sent settlers to the area soon thereafter. It was ruled by the British South Africa Company, which he established, until 1924, when the British government took over the administration.

From 1953 to 1964, Northern Rhodesia was federated with Southern Rhodesia and Nyasaland in the Federation of Rhodesia and Nyasaland. On Oct. 24, 1964, Northern Rhodesia became the independent nation of Zambia.

Kenneth Kaunda, the first president, kept Zambia within the Commonwealth of Nations. The country's economy, dependent on copper exports, was threatened when Rhodesia declared its independence from British rule in 1965 and defied U.N. sanctions, which Zambia supported, an action that deprived Zambia of its trade route through Rhodesia. The U.S., Britain, and Canada organized an airlift in 1966 to ship gasoline into Zambia. In 1967, Britain agreed to finance new trade routes for Zambia.

Kaunda visited China in 1967, and China later agreed to finance a 1,000-mile railroad from the copper fields to Dar es Salaam in Tanzania. A pipeline was opened in 1968 from Ndola in Zambia's copper belt to the Indian Ocean at Dar es Salaam, ending the three-year oil drought.

In 1969, Kaunda announced the nationalization of the foreign copper-mining industry, with Zambia to take 51% (over $1 billion, estimated), and an agreement was reached with the companies on payment. He then announced a similar takeover of foreign oil producers.

Zambia suffered heavy damage from bombing raids by the former Rhodesian air force on Zimbabwean guerrilla bases and on its transportation links. These actions, combined with falling prices for copper and cobalt, forced Kaunda to declare a state of economic austerity in January 1981.

With a soaring debt and inflation rate the government in 1990 turned to the International Monetary Fund and the World Bank, with whom an agreement was reached in exchange for economic reforms. Soaring prices in June 1990 led to riots in Lusaka, resulting in a number of killings. Mounting domestic pressure forced Kaunda to move Zambia toward multi-party democracy.

ZIMBABWE

Republic of Zimbabwe
Executive President: Robert Mugabe (1987)
Area: 150,698 sq mi. (390,308 sq km)
Population (est. mid-1991): 10,000,000 (average annual rate of natural increase: 3.1%); birth rate: 41/1000; infant mortality rate: 61/1000; density per square mile: 66
Capital: Harare
Largest cities (est. 1983 for metropolitan area): Harare, 681,000; Bulawayo, 429,000
Monetary unit: Zimbabwean dollar
Languages: English (official), Ndebele, Shona
Religions: Christian, 25%; Animist, 24%; Syncretic, 50%
Literacy rate: 74%
Economic summary: Gross domestic product (1988 est.): $4.6 billion; $470 per capita; 5.3% real growth rate. Arable land: 7%. Principal agricultural products: tobacco, corn, sugar, cotton, livestock. Labor force: 3,100,000; 10% in mining, manufacturing, and construction. Major products: steel, textiles, chemicals, vehicles, gold, copper. Natural resources: gold, copper, chrome, nickel, tin, asbestos. Exports: gold, tobacco, asbestos, copper, meat, chrome, nickel, corn, sugar. Imports: machinery, petroleum products, transport equipment. Major trading partners: South Africa, E.C., U.S.

Geography. Zimbabwe, a landlocked country in south central Africa, is slightly smaller than California. It is bordered by Botswana on the west, Zambia on the north, Mozambique on the east, and South Africa on the south.

A high veld up to 6,000 feet (1,829 m) crosses the country from northeast to southwest. This is flanked by a somewhat lower veld that contains ranching country. Tropical forests that yield hardwoods lie in the southeast.

In the north, on the border with Zambia, is the 175-mile-long (128-m) Kariba Lake, formed by the Kariba Dam across the Zambezi River. It is the site of one of the world's largest hydroelectric projects.

Government. An amendment to the Constitution in October 1987 created the position of Executive President that would combine Presidential and Prime Ministerial functions. Prime Minister Mugabe was the sole candidate and was elected to this post December 30. On December 22, the long negotiated

ZANU-ZAPU merger was promulgated with ZAPU head Joshua Nkomo becoming a Vice President of the renamed ZANU(PF). In August 1987, the Parliament voted to abolish the 20 whites-only seats that had existed since 1980. The remaining 80 members selected replacements who were obliged to support Mugabe's ZANU party.

In March 1990, a constitutional amendment adopted a 150-seat unilateral legislature (House of Assembly) in place of the old bicameral one.

History. Zimbabwe was colonized by Cecil Rhodes's British South Africa Company at the end of the 19th century. In 1923, European settlers voted to become the self-governing British colony of Southern Rhodesia rather than merge with the Union of South Africa. After a brief federation with Northern Rhodesia and Nyasaland in the post-World War II period, Southern Rhodesia chose to remain a colony when its two partners voted for independence in 1963.

On Nov. 11, 1965, the white-minority government of Rhodesia unilaterally declared its independence from Britain.

In 1967, the U.N. imposed mandatory sanctions against Rhodesia. The country moved slowly toward meeting the demands of black Africans. The white-minority regime of Prime Minister Ian Smith withstood British pressure, economic sanctions, guerrilla attacks, and a right-wing assault.

On March 1, 1970, Rhodesia formally proclaimed itself a republic, and within the month nine nations, including the U.S., closed their consulates there.

Heightened guerrilla war and a withdrawal of South African military aid—particularly helicopters—marked the beginning of the collapse of Smith's 11 years of resistance in the spring of 1976. Under pressure from South Africa, Smith agreed with the U.S. that majority rule should come within two years.

In the fall, Smith met with black nationalist leaders in Geneva. The meeting broke up six weeks later when the Rhodesian Premier insisted that whites must retain control of the police and armed forces during the transition to majority rule. A British proposal called for Britons to take over these powers.

Divisions between Rhodesian blacks—Bishop Abel Muzorewa of the African National Congress and Ndabaningi Sithole as moderates versus Robert Mugabe and Joshua Nkomo of the Patriotic Front as advocates of guerrilla force—sharpened in 1977 and no agreement was reached. In July, with white residents leaving in increasing numbers and the economy showing the strain of war, Smith rejected outside mediation and called for general elections in order to work out an "internal solution" of the transfer of power.

On March 3, 1978, Smith, Muzorewa, Sithole, and Chief Jeremiah Chirau signed an agreement to trans-fer power to the black majority by Dec. 31, 1978. They constituted themselves an Executive Council, with chairmanship rotating but Smith retaining the title of Prime Minister. Blacks were named to each cabinet ministry, serving as co-ministers with the whites already holding these posts. African nations and the Patriotic Front leaders immediately denounced the action, but Western governments were more reserved, although none granted recognition to the new regime.

White voters ratified a new constitution on Jan. 30, 1979, enfranchising all blacks, establishing a black majority Senate and Assembly, and changing the country's name to Zimbabwe Rhodesia.

Muzorewa agreed to negotiate with Mugabe and Nkomo in British-sponsored talks beginning Sept. 9. By December, all parties accepted a new draft constitution, a cease-fire, and a period of British administration pending a general election.

In voting completed on Feb. 29, 1980, Mugabe's ZANU-Patriotic Front party won 57 of the 80 Assembly seats reserved for blacks. In an earlier vote on Feb. 14, the Rhodesian Front won all 20 seats reserved for whites in the Assembly.

At a ceremony on April 18, Prince Charles of Britain handed to President-elect Rev. Canaan Banana the symbols of independence.

On April 18, 1980, Britain formally recognized the independence of Zimbabwe.

In January 1981, Mugabe dismissed Nkomo as Home Minister and his onetime rival left the government in protest. At the same time, the Prime Minister discharged Edgar Z. Tekere, Manpower and Planning Minister, who had been tried and acquitted of the murder of a white farmer.

Mugabe survived both tests and scored an unprecedented triumph when, in response to his appeal for economic aid, Western nations pledged $1.8 billion for the next three years.

The 1985 harvest was good in Zimbabwe and the country could feed itself. But political turmoil and civil strife continued. In what Western analysts viewed as a free and fair election, President Mugabe's African National Union increased its sizeable majority in the House of Assembly but Mugabe was frustrated because it did not win the 70 seats he sought to cement one-party rule. After the election, Mugabe cracked down on Nkomo's ZAPU-Patriotic Front party.

In April 1990, Mugabe was re-elected and his ZANU(PF) party given virtual unanimity in the Assembly.

In December 1990 the parliament voted by 113 to 3 to amend the original 1980 constitution to allow the compulsory acquisition of white-owned farmland at government-set prices. Indeed, white farmers would have no judiciary recourse.

BUSINESS & THE ECONOMY

Facing the "Totally New and Dynamic"

An interview with Peter Drucker by Edward Reingold

Q. In the remaining years of the 20th century . . .

A. We are already deep in the new century, a century that is fundamentally different from the one we still assume we live in. Although most everyone has a sense of deep unease with prevailing political and economic policies, whether in the U.S. or Japan or West Germany or England or Eastern Europe. Things somehow don't fit, and there is a clear sign that while we don't yet see the new [era], we know the old one is no longer right, no longer congruent. For 500 years the century mark has been almost irrelevant; the new century has always begun at least 25 years earlier.

Q. What kind of new century are we in, then?

A. In this 21st century world of dynamic political change, the significant thing is that we are in a post-business society. Business is still very important, and greed is as universal as ever; but the values of people are no longer business values, they are professional values. Most people are no longer part of the business society; they are part of the knowledge society. If you go back to when your father was born and mine, knowledge was an ornament, a luxury—and now it is the very center. We worry if the kids don't do as well in math tests as others. No earlier civilization would have dreamed of paying any attention to something like this. The greatest changes in our society are going to be in education.

Q. This is a result of advanced technology, is it not?

A. Every major change in educational technology changes not only how we learn but also what we learn. Just as the printed book totally changed the curriculum of the schools, so are the computer and tape recorder and video. The printed book is primarily a tool for adults. The new tools are for children; they fit the way children learn best. We now know how to make the accumulated wisdom of the human race relevant again. We should know that the old approach to education is theoretical and unsound. We still believe that teaching and learning are two sides of the same coin, but we ought to realize that they are not; one learns a subject, and one teaches a person. The process is increasingly going to shift to self-teaching on the basis of new technology because we now have these self-teaching tools.

Q. You call this a post-business society, but predatory takeovers and greenmail are still with us.

A. Yes. There is an old proverb that says if you don't have gravediggers you need vultures. And with management of large corporations being accountable to no one for the past 30 years, you need vultures. The vultures are the raiders who have come to clean up. But the cost to society of the hostile takeover is extremely high. It totally demoralizes a company, and above all it demoralizes middle management, the people who actually do the work.

Q. But don't you think there can be reasonable benefits even from a hostile takeover?

A. Let me say there is absolutely no doubt that a good many of these conglomerates need to be unbundled, need to be split up. Many managements have been building empires without economic justification, just fo the sake, well, partly of having a big company, and partly for the sake of dealmaking. I will tell you a secret: dealmaking beats working. Dealmaking is exciting and fun, and working is grubby. Running anything is primarily an enormous amount of grubby detail work and very little excitement, so dealmaking is kind of romantic, sexy. That's why you have deals that make no sense. There's also another rule that says if you can't run this business, buy another one. There are a lot of companies around that need to be restructured and split up, that never had a justification for being.

Q. Then what are the implications for U.S. business competing in the world economy in the new century?

A. For a hundred years, we have had basically a European-based American foreign policy. Now the world economy is moving very fast toward regions rather than nations. The Soviet empire is unraveling. In North America the only question is whether Mexico will join in; Canada has basically already integrated with the U.S.

In Asia one of the big question marks is whether the Japanese will succeed—they are certainly trying—in creating a Far Eastern trading bloc that would include Korea, Taiwan, Singapore, Hong Kong and, I think, Thailand. The question is whether China will go along. After all, the old Japanese co-prosperity sphere basically was built around the development potential of the coastal cities of Shanghai and Canton.

Q. So the world of the 21st century is split into competing trading groups: Europe, North America and Asia?

A. Yes, and the activities of three big trading blocs will have political consequences. I think we are already in the midst of this, and the pattern is not going to be fair trade or protectionism but reciprocity.

Q. That's a bad word to the Japanese.

A. Very bad, and quite rightfully so. Reciprocity is a two-way street, and that is not the Japanese way of doing business. It is a threat to them. But in some ways Japanese industry is way ahead of the government.

Q. You mean by exporting manufacturing to the U.S. and the E.C.?

A. Yes. For example, those big car-carrying ships landing in San Pedro or Rotterdam are going to be as obsolete as the steam locomotive.

Q. How do you envision the new living patterns in the years ahead?

A. The city as we know it is obsolete. It is a 19th century product based on our 19th century ability to move people. Moving ideas and information then was more difficult, and the great inventions of the 19th century were the streetcar and the post office. Today we have an incredible ability to move ideas and information, but the movement of people is grinding to a standstill.

Q. And what happens to cities? Do they become ghost towns?

A. I don't think you can foretell the shape of the city of tomorrow, but what you can say is that the city of the 19th century reached its pinnacle, its apogee, in the 20th, in the 1980s, with an enormous building boom all over the world. This also happened in the great cathedral-building era a millennium ago. But nobody would build a monastery for 600 Benedictine monks anymore. I think we have seen the last outburst of the city as we know it.

Q. Then what will we do in the cities?

A. I don't know what the function of the city will be. Look, the medieval cathedral functioned more as a town cultural center, school and governmental center than as a church most of the year. Nobody lived in Chartres. I do not see our cities as ghost towns so much as a congeries of ghettos—the city is already becoming a place where only the very rich, the very young, and the very poor live. The middle class works in the city, but doesn't live there. Those enormous central offices we have built in the post-World War II period are, I think very largely going to be counterproductive. The clerical work will move out. Our largest single pool of labor in the years ahead will be older people and part-time employees, and they aren't going to commute four hours to work. This is soon going to be a problem all over the world.

Q. Do you think we and our institutions are ready to cope with what you call "new Realities?"

A. Many are still stuck in the world of 1960. What we face now is totally new and dynamic—and we are quite unprepared for it.

Consumer Price Indexes

(1982–84 = 100)

Year	All items	En-ergy	Food	Shel-ter	Apparel[1]	Trans-porta-tion	Medical care	Fuel oil	Electric-ity	Utility (gas)	Tele-phone	Com-modi-ties
1960	29.6	22.4	30.0	25.2	45.7	29.8	22.3	13.5	29.9	17.6	58.3	33.6
1970	38.8	25.5	39.2	35.5	59.2	37.5	34.0	16.5	31.8	19.6	58.7	41.7
1975	53.8	42.1	59.8	48.8	72.5	50.1	47.5	34.9	50.0	31.1	71.7	58.2
1980	82.4	86.0	86.8	81.0	90.9	83.1	74.9	87.7	75.8	65.7	77.7	86.0
1988	118.3	89.3	118.2	127.1	115.4	108.7	138.6	75.8	111.5	94.5	116.0	111.5
1989	124.0	100.9	125.1	132.8	118.6	114.1	149.3	n.a.	n.a.	n.a.	n.a.	n.a.
1990	130.7	104.5	132.4	140.0	124.1	120.5	162.8	n.a.	n.a.	n.a.	n.a.	n.a.

1. Includes upkeep. *Source: Monthly Labor Review, July 1991.*

Consumer Price Index for All Urban Consumers

(1982–84 = 100)

Group	March 1991	March 1990	Group	March 1991	March 1990
All items	135.0	128.7	Fuel oil, coal, bottled gas	99.3	91.5
Food	135.8	131.5	House operation[1]	115.7	112.8
Alcoholic beverages	142.2	127.8	House furnishings	107.5	106.9
Apparel and upkeep	128.8	125.4	Transportation	122.3	116.8
Men's and boys' apparel	123.0	119.3	Medical care	173.7	158.7
Women's and girls' apparel	129.5	126.8	Personal care	133.6	129.0
Footwear	120.8	116.9	Tobacco products	197.6	175.1
Housing, total	132.6	126.8	Entertainment	136.7	130.9
Rent	142.0	136.5	Personal and educational		
Gas and electricity	110.8	107.9	expenses	179.3	166.3

1. Combines house furnishings and operation. *Source:* Department of Labor, Bureau of Labor Statistics.

Per Capita Personal Income

Year	Amount	Year	Amount	Year	Amount	Year	Amount	Year	Amount
1935	$474	1965	$2,773	1976	6,402	1981	10,949	1986	14,597
1945	1,223	1970	3,893	1977	7,043	1982	11,480	1987	15,471
1950	1,501	1973	4,980	1978	7,729	1983	12,098	1988	16,491
1955	1,881	1974	5,428	1979	8,638	1984	13,114	1989	17,594
1960	2,219	1975	$5,851	1980	$9,910	1985	$13,896	1990[1]	18,685

1. Preliminary. *Source:* Department of Commerce, Bureau of Economic Analysis.

Total Family Income
(figures in percent)

Income range	White 1989	White 1985	White 1975	Black 1989	Black 1985	Black 1975	Hispanic[1] 1989	Hispanic[1] 1985	Hispanic[1] 1975
Families (thousands)[2]	56,590	54,991	49,873	7,470	6,921	5,586	4,840	4,206	2,499
Under $5,000	2.6	3.3	2.2	11.2	11.6	6.9	6.7	7.0	5.6
$5,000 to $9,999	5.1	6.5	6.3	14.7	16.8	18.3	11.9	15.6	13.8
$10,000 to $14,999	7.5	8.5	8.8	12.6	12.8	14.7	12.1	14.0	14.9
$15,000 to $24,999	16.4	18.8	19.7	19.5	21.8	23.2	21.9	22.6	25.3
$25,000 to $34,999	16.8	18.2	20.5	14.4	14.4	16.4	16.5	16.5	19.4
$35,000 to $49,999	20.7	20.6	22.7	13.7	13.1	13.7	16.2	13.5	14.1
$50,000 to $74,999	18.7	16.0	14.3	10.2	7.6	5.8	10.2	8.6	5.4
$75,000 to $99,999	6.9	4.7	3.3	2.8	1.3	0.8	2.9	1.5	0.9
$100,000 and over	5.3	3.3	2.1	0.8	0.6	0.3	1.6	0.8	0.6
Median income	$35,975	$32,051	$31,374	$20,209	$18,455	$19,304	$23,446	$20,919	$21,002

1. Persons of Hispanic origin may be of any race. 2. As of March 1990. *Source:* Department of Commerce, Bureau of the Census.

Median Weekly Earnings of Full-Time Workers by Occupation and Sex

Occupation	Men Number of workers (in thousands)	Men Median weekly earnings	Women Number of workers (in thousands)	Women Median weekly earnings	Total Number of workers (in thousands)	Total Median weekly earnings
Managerial and prof. specialty	12,145	$754	10,632	$520	22,778	$622
Executive, admin, and managerial	6,274	766	4,742	500	11,016	620
Professional specialty	5,871	743	5,891	548	11,762	623
Technical, sales, and admin. support	9,481	497	15,870	337	25,351	383
Technicians and related support	1,704	578	1,371	417	3,075	496
Sales occupations	4,600	502	3,496	299	8,095	404
Administrative support, incl. clerical	3,178	450	11,003	336	14,181	355
Service occupations	4,415	327	4,444	234	8,859	273
Private household	23	(1)	298	169	321	171
Protective service	1,429	496	187	443	1,616	488
Service, except private household and protective	2,963	284	3,959	235	6,922	255
Precision production, craft, and repair	9,992	492	851	315	10,843	481
Mechanics and repairers	3,637	478	145	413	3,781	477
Construction trades	3,402	482	39	(1)	3,441	480
Other precision production, craft, and repair	2,953	514	668	305	3,621	487
Operators, fabricators, and laborers	11,235	383	3,701	265	14,936	345
Machine operators, assemblers, and inspectors	4,458	392	2,793	262	7,251	332
Transportation and material moving occupations	3,873	419	231	325	4,104	415
Handlers, equipment cleaners, helpers, and laborers	2,904	313	677	260	3,581	304
Farming, forestry, and fishing	1,199	268	125	208	1,324	263

1. Data not shown where base is less than 100,000. NOTE: Figures are for the fourth quarter of 1990. *Source:* U.S. Department of Labor, Bureau of Labor Statistics, "Employment and Earnings," January 1991.

Consumer Credit
(installment credit outstanding; in billions of dollars, not seasonally adjusted)

Holder	1990	1989	1988	1987	1986	1985	1980	1975
Commercial banks	347.5	342.8	324.8	287.2	266.8	245.1	147.0	82.9
Finance companies	137.5	140.8	146.2	141.1	134.7	111.9	62.2	32.7
Credit unions	92.9	93.1	88.3	81.0	77.1	72.7	44.0	25.7
Retailers[1]	43.6	44.2	48.4	46.0	43.3	42.9	28.7	18.2
Other[2]	50.4	61.2	67.1	64.4	60.0	53.8	20.1	9.2
Total[3]	748.3	730.9	674.8	619.7	581.9	526.4	302.1	168.7

1. Excludes 30-day charge credit held by retailers, oil and gas companies, and travel and entertainment companies. 2. Includes mutual savings banks, savings and loan associations, and gasoline companies. 3. Beginning 1989, outstanding balances of pools upon which securities have been issued; these balances are no longer on the balance sheets for the loan originators. Data are *not* available historically. *Source:* Federal Reserve Bulletin.

The Public Debt

	Gross debt				Gross debt	
Year	Amount (in millions)	Per capita	Year		Amount (in millions)	Per capita
1800 (Jan. 1)	$ 83	$ 15.87	1950		$256,087[1]	$1,688.30
1860 (June 30)	65	2.06	1955		272,807[1]	1,650.63
1865	2,678	75.01	1960		284,093[1]	1,572.31
1900	1,263	16.60	1965		313,819[1]	1,612.70
1920	24,299	228.23	1970		370,094[1]	1,807.09
1925	20,516	177.12	1975		533,189	2,496.90
1930	16,185	131.51	1980		907,701	3,969.55
1935	28,701	225.55	1985		1,823,103	7,598.51
1940	42,968	325.23	1989		2,857,431	11,452.12
1945	258,682	1,848.60	1990		3,233,313	12,823,28

1. Adjusted to exclude issues to the International Monetary Fund and other international lending institutions to conform to the budget presentation. *Source:* Department of the Treasury, Financial Management Service.

Gross National Product or Expenditure[1]

(in billions)

Holder	1990	1989	1988	1987	1985	1980	1970	1960	1950
Gross national product	5,465.1	$5,200.8	$4,880.6	$4,524.3	$4,014.9	$2,732.0	$1,015.5	515.3	288.3
GNP in constant (1982) dollars	4,157.3	4,117.7	4,024.4	3,853.7	3,618.7	3,187.1	2,416.2	1,665.3	1,203.7
Personal consumption expenditures	3,657.3	3,450.1	3,235.1	3,010.8	2,629.0	1,732.6	640.0	330.7	192.1
Durable goods	480.3	474.6	455.2	421.0	372.2	219.3	85.7	43.5	30.8
Nondurable goods	1,193.7	1,130.0	1,052.3	998.1	911.2	681.4	270.3	153.2	98.2
Services	1,983.3	1,845.5	1,727.6	1,591.7	1,345.6	831.9	284.0	134.0	63.2
Gross private domestic investment	741.0	771.2	750.3	699.9	643.1	437.0	148.8	78.2	55.1
Residential	222.0	231.0	232.4	226.4	188.8	122.5	40.5	26.3	20.5
Nonresidential	524.1	511.9	487.2	444.3	442.9	322.8	105.2	48.8	27.8
Change in business inventories	−5.0	28.3	30.6	29.3	11.3	−8.3	3.1	3.1	6.8
Net export of goods and services	−31.2	−46.1	−73.7	−112.6	−78.0	32.1	8.5	5.9	2.2
Government purchases	1,098.1	1,025.6	968.9	926.1	820.8	530.3	218.2	100.6	38.8
Federal	424.0	400.0	381.3	381.6	355.2	208.1	98.8	54.4	19.1
National defense	313.6	301.1	298.0	294.8	259.1	142.7	76.8	45.3	14.3
Other	110.4	98.9	83.3	86.8	96.1	65.4	22.0	9.1	4.8
State and local	674.1	625.6	587.6	544.5	465.6	322.2	119.4	46.1	19.8

1. Current dollars except as noted. *Source:* Department of Commerce, Bureau of Economic Analysis.

Producer Price Indexes by Major Commodity Groups

(1982 = 100)

Commodity	1990	1989	1985	1980	1975	1970
All commodities	116.3	112.2	103.2	89.8	58.4	38.1
Farm products	112.2	110.7	95.1	102.9	77.0	45.8
Processed foods and feeds	121.9	117.8	103.5	95.9	72.6	44.6
Textile products and apparel	114.9	112.3	102.9	89.7	67.4	52.4
Hides, skins, and leather products	141.7	136.3	108.9	94.7	56.5	42.0
Fuels and related products and power	82.2	72.9	91.4	82.8	35.4	15.3
Chemicals and allied products	123.6	123.1	103.7	89.0	62.0	35.0
Rubber and plastic products	113.6	112.6	101.9	90.1	62.2	44.9
Lumber and wood products	129.7	126.7	106.6	101.5	62.1	39.9
Pulp, paper, and allied products	141.3	137.8	113.3	86.3	59.0	37.5
Metals and metal products	123.0	124.1	104.4	95.0	61.5	38.7
Machinery and equipment	120.7	117.4	107.2	86.0	57.9	40.0
Furniture and household durables	119.1	116.9	107.1	90.7	67.5	51.9
Nonmetallic mineral products	114.7	112.6	108.6	88.4	54.4	35.3
Transportation equipment	121.5	117.7	107.9	82.9	56.7	41.9
Miscellaneous products	n.a.	n.a.	109.4	93.6	53.4	39.8

NOTE: n.a. = not available. *Source:* Department of Commerce, Bureau of Economic Analysis, *Survey of Current Businesses, July 1991.*

Weekly Earnings[1] of Full-Time Women Workers

Major occupation group	1990 weekly earnings	% Men's weekly earnings
Managerial and professional specialty	$511	69.9
Executive, administrative, and managerial	485	65.4
Professional specialty	534	74.2
Technical, sales, and administrative support	332	66.9
Technicians and related support	417	73.2
Sales occupations	292	57.8
Administrative support, including clerical	332	75.5
Service occupations	230	71.9
Precision production, craft, and repair	316	64.8
Operators, fabricators, and laborers	262	69.3
Machine operators, assemblers, and inspectors	260	66.5
Transportation and material moving	314	75.1
Handlers, equipment cleaners, helpers, and laborers	250	81.2
Farming, forestry, and fishing	216	82.1
Total; all occupations	**348**	**71.8**

1. Median usual weekly earnings. Half the workers earn more and half the workers usually earn less each week. *Source:* U.S. Department of Labor, Bureau of Labor Statistics.

Median Family Income

(in current dollars)

Year	Income	Percent change	Year	Income	Percent change
1970	$9,867	—	1985	27,144	5.0
1980	21,023	6.9	1986	28,236	4.0
1981	22,388	6.5	1987	29,744	5.3
1982	23,433	4.7	1988	30,992	4.0
1983	24,580	4.9	1989	32,448	4.5
1984	25,948	5.1	1990	33,956	4.4

Source: U.S. Department of Labor, Bureau of Labor Statistics, *Employment and Earnings.*

Expenditures for New Plant and Equipment[1]

(in billions of dollars)

Year	Manufacturing	Transportation[2]	Total nonmanufacturing	Total
1950	$7.73	$2.87	$18.08	$25.81
1955	12.50	3.10	24.58	37.08
1960	16.36	3.54	32.63	48.99
1965	25.41	5.66	45.39	70.79
1970	36.99	7.17	69.16	106.15
1975	53.66	9.95	108.95	162.60
1980	112.60	13.56	205.48	318.08
1984	139.61	13.44	278.77	418.38
1985	152.88	14.57	302.05	454.93
1986	137.95	15.05	309.16	447.11
1987	141.06	15.07	320.45	461.51
1988	163.45	16.63	344.77	508.22
1989	183.80	18.84	380.13	563.93
1990	192.78	21.59	399.52	592.31

1. Data exclude agriculture. 2. Transportation is included in total nonmanufacturing. NOTE: This series was revised in April 1991. *Source:* Department of Commerce, Bureau of the Census.

New Housing Starts[1] and Mobile Homes Shipped

(in thousands)

Year	No. of units started	Year	No. of units started	Year	Mobile homes shipped
1900	189	1970	1,469	1965	216
1910	387	1975	1,171	1970	401
1920	247	1980	1,313	1975	213
1925	937	1982	1,072	1980	222
1930	330	1983	1,712	1983	296
1935	221	1984	1,756	1984	295
1940	603	1985	1,745	1985	284
1945	326	1986	1,807	1986	244
1950	1,952	1987	1,623	1987	233
1955	1,646	1988[2]	1,488	1988	218
1960[1]	1,296	1989	1,376	1989	198
1965	1,510	1990	1,193	1990	188

1. Prior to 1960, starts limited to nonfarm housing; from 1960 on, figures include farm housing. 2. As of 1988 data for housing starts no longer includes public housing starts and only includes private housing starts. *Sources:* Department of Commerce, Housing Construction Statistics, 1900–1965, and Construction Reports, Housing Starts, 1970–83; Manufactured Housing Institute, 1965–76; National Conference of States on Building Codes and Standards.

Life Insurance in Force

(in millions of dollars)

As of Dec. 31	Ordinary	Group	Industrial	Credit	Total
1915	$16,650	$100	$4,279	—	$21,029
1930	78,756	9,801	17,693	$73	106,413
1945	101,550	22,172	27,675	365	151,762
1950	149,071	47,793	33,415	3,844	234,168
1955	216,812	101,345	39,682	14,493	373,332
1960	341,881	175,903	39,563	29,101	586,448
1965	499,638	308,078	39,818	53,020	900,554
1970	734,730	551,357	38,644	77,392	1,402,123
1980	1,760,474	1,579,355	35,994	165,215	3,541,038
1985	3,247,289	2,561,595	28,250	215,973	6,053,107
1989	4,939,964	3,469,498	24,446	260,107	8,694,015
1990	5,366,982	3,753,506	24,071	248,038	9,392,597

Source: American Council of Life Insurance.

Farm Indexes

(1977 = 100)

Year	Prices paid by farmers[1]	Prices rec'd by farmers[2]	Ratio
1950	37	56	151
1955	40	51	128
1960	44	52	118
1965	49	54	115
1970	56	60	109
1975	90	101	113
1980	138	134	97
1985	162	128	79
1989	178	147	83
1990	184	150	82

1. Commodities, interest, and taxes and wage rates. 2. All crops and livestock. *Source:* Department of Agriculture, National Agricultural Statistics Service.

Estimated Annual Retail and Wholesale Sales by Kind of Business
(in millions of dollars)

Kind of business	1990	1989	Kind of business	1990	1989
Retail trade, total	1,807,219	1,741,748	Electrical goods	116,901	112,919
Building materials, hardware, garden			Hardware, plumbing, heating, and		
supplies, and mobile home dealers	92,524	92,700	supplies	44,922	44,047
Automotive dealers	381,961	383,596	Machinery, equipment, supplies	264,382	251,122
Furniture, home furnishings,			Sporting, recreational, photographic		
and equipment stores	92,983	91,493	and hobby goods, toys, supplies	25,234	24,553
General merchandise group stores	211,933	204,387	Metals and minerals except petroleum	90,871	86,937
Food stores	362,410	345,069	Miscellaneous durable goods	72,546	71,588
Gasoline service stations	131,725	117,791	Nondurable goods, total	914,139	885,994
Apparel and accessory stores	94,731	91,426	Paper and paper products	51,454	50,015
Eating and drinking places	182,044	173,894	Drugs, drug proprietaries, and		
Drug and proprietary stores	68,557	62,495	druggists' sundries	47,247	43,040
Liquor stores	20,813	20,033	Apparel, piece goods, & notions	64,186	59,035
Merchant wholesale trade, total	1,790,321	1,728,059	Groceries and related products	238,513	242,684
Durable goods, total	876,182	842,065	Beer, wine, distilled alcoholic		
Motor vehicles and automotive			beverages	44,651	42,925
parts and supplies	174,981	163,614	Farm-product raw materials	122,406	129,499
Furniture and home furnishings	30,251	29,720	Chemical and allied products	41,936	37,584
Lumber and other construction			Petroleum and petroleum products	154,211	140,677
materials	56,094	57,565	Miscellaneous nondurable goods	149,535	140,535

Source: Department of Commerce, Bureau of the Census.

Shareholders in Public Corporations

Characteristic	1990	1985	1983	1981	1980	1975	1970
Individual shareholders (thousands)	51,440	47,040	42,360	32,260	30,200	25,270	30,850
Adult shareowner incidence in population	1 in 4	1 in 4	1 in 4	1 in 5	1 in 5	1 in 6	1 in 4
Median household income	$43,800	$36,800	$33,200	$29,200	$27,750	$19,000	$13,500
Adult shareowners with household							
income: under $10,000 (thousands)	n.a.	2,151	1,460	2,164	1,742	3,420	8,170
$10,000 and over (thousands)	n.a.	40,999	36,261	26,913	25,715	19,970	20,130
$15,000 and over (thousands)	42,920	39,806	33,665	24,376	22,535	15,420	12,709
$25,000 and over (thousands)	38,230	32,690	25,086	17,547	15,605	6,642	4,114
$50,000 and over (thousands)	17,910	11,321	7,918	5,457	3,982	1,216	n.a.
Adult female shareowners (thousands)	17,750	17,547 [1]	20,385	14,154	13,696	11,750	14,290
Adult male shareowners (thousands)	30,220	27,446 [1]	19,226	15,785	14,196	11,630	14,340
Median age	43	44	45	46	46	53	48

NOTE: 1990 results are not strictly comparable with previous studies because of differences in methodologies. 1. Revised to correspond to 1990 methodology. n.a. = not available. *Source:* New York Stock Exchange.

50 Most Active Stocks in 1990

Stock	Share volume	Stock	Share volume	Stock	Share volume
Morris (Philip) (7)	448,780,400	BankAmerica		Unisys Corporation (24)	152,646,600
American Tel. & Tel. (1)	358,179,700	Corporation (21)	179,387,800	Eli Lilly	148,810,800
Int'l Business Machines (2)	341,426,800	Baxter International (27)	178,760,100	Amoco Corporation (47)	147,651,300
General Electric (4)	325,881,200	McDonald's Corporation (20)	177,803,900	Mobil Corporation (36)	146,740,600
Citicorp (14)	323,847,700	Texas Utilities (15)	177,751,400	Motorola Inc.	146,448,100
Federal National		du Pont de Nemours	177,135,800	Archer-Daniels-Midland	146,026,100
Mortgage (30)	282,286,900	Ford Motor (10)	172,246,000	Computer Associates	
American Express (13)	274,643,100	Toys "R" Us	171,965,300	International (32)	144,765,000
Exxon Corporation (5)	246,706,800	Texaco Inc. (3)	167,135,200	Glaxo Holdings	144,220,200
General Motors (12)	243,767,300	Merck & Co. (25)	166,707,800	Digital Equipment (29)	140,010,100
Boeing Company (35)	234,405,000	Coca-Cola Company (50)	165,831,900	Global Marine	139,482,400
Wal-Mart Stores	227,087,600	Dow Chemical (31)	162,559,900	Variety Corporation	138,794,900
Waste Management	221,898,000	COMPAQ Computer (48)	161,092,650	Pfizer Inc.	136,131,300
Bristol-Myers Squibb (16)	218,107,600	GTE Corp.	160,635,200	Schlumberger Limited	135,547,300
Eastman Kodak (8)	208,754,000	USX Corporation (9)	158,890,600	Tandem Computers	132,079,500
Chase Manhattan Corp. (41)	204,899,600	Limited, Inc.	155,931,700	Procter & Gamble	131,496,500
United Telecommunications	192,424,000	Upjohn Company (22)	153,357,000	Unocal Corporation	131,439,300
PepsiCo, Inc. (46)	186,391,100	Johnson & Johnson	153,245,600		

NOTE: 1989 ranking in parentheses, if among top 50. *Source:* New York Stock Exchange.

Geographic Distribution of Shareowners of Public Corporations

Metropolitan Area	Individuals	Households	Metropolitan area	Individuals	Households
New York	2,470,000	1,630,000	Pittsburgh	450,000	300,000
Los Angeles	1,850,000	1,230,000	Denver	440,000	290,000
Chicago	1,610,000	1,070,000	San Jose	420,000	280,000
Detroit	1,240,000	820,000	Cincinnati	410,000	270,000
Philadelphia	1,100,000	720,000	Riverside-San Bernardino	410,000	270,000
Washington D.C.	1,000,000	670,000	Bergan-Passaic, N.J.	400,000	270,000
Boston	940,000	620,000	Milwaukee	400,000	270,000
Houston	880,000	580,000	Kansas City	390,000	260,000
Nassau-Suffolk, N.Y.	750,000	500,000	Seattle	380,000	260,000
Dallas	670,000	440,000	Fort Worth	370,000	240,000
Phoenix	650,000	430,000	Fort Lauderdale	360,000	240,000
St. Louis	640,000	420,000	Columbus	330,000	220,000
Anaheim	630,000	420,000	Portland	310,000	210,000
Atlanta	630,000	410,000	Sacramento	310,000	210,000
Minneapolis	620,000	410,000	Hartford	310,000	210,000
Newark	600,000	400,000	Indianapolis	280,000	190,000
Cleveland	540,000	360,000	Norfolk	280,000	180,000
Baltimore	520,000	350,000	New Orleans	270,000	180,000
San Francisco	490,000	330,000	Orlando	270,000	180,000
Oakland	490,000	320,000	Charlotte	240,000	160,000
Tampa	480,000	320,000	Middlesex, N.J.	230,000	150,000
Miami	470,000	310,000	San Antonio	230,000	150,000
San Diego	450,000	300,000			

Source: New York Stock Exchange.

New York Stock Exchange Seat Sales for Cash, 1990

Month	Price High	Price Low	Number	Month	Price High	Price Low	Number
January	$400,000	$365,000	3	July	$385,000	$370,000	2
February	360,000	351,000	3	August	330,000	301,000	7
March	360,000	—	1	September	301,000	—	1
April	410,000	390,000	4	October	295,000	—	1
May	410,000	—	1	November	265,000	250,000	2
June	430,000	400,000	2	December	295,000	—	1

NOTE: In addition, there were 12 private seat sales, ranging from a high of $400,000 and a low of $260,000; and 2 EX—OTR private sales. *Source:* New York Stock Exchange.

Largest Businesses, 1990

(in millions of dollars)

Source: FORTUNE © 1991 The Time Inc. Magazine Company. All rights reserved.

50 LARGEST INDUSTRIAL CORPORATIONS

	Sales	Assets
General Motors	126,017.0	180,236.5
Exxon	105,885.0	87,707.0
Fort Motor	98,274.7	173,662.7
Int'l Business Machines	69,018.0	87,568.0
Mobil	58,770.0	41,665.0
General Electric	58,414.0	153,884.0
Philip Morris	44,323.0	46,569.0
Texaco	41,235.0	25,975.0
E.I. Du Pont De Nemours	39,839.0	38,128.0
Chevron	39,262.0	35,089.0
Chrysler	30,868.0	46,374.0
Amoco	28,277.0	32,209.0
Boeing	27,595.0	14,591.0
Shell Oil	24,423.0	28,496.0
Procter & Gamble	24,376.0	18,487.0
Occidental Petroleum	21,947.0	19,743.0
United Technologies	21,783.2	15,918.3
Dow Chemical	20,005.0	23,953.0
USX	19,462.0	17,268.0
Eastman Kodak	19,075.0	24,125.0
Atlantic Richfield	18,819.0	23,864.0
Xerox	18,382.0	31,495.0
Pepsico	17,802.7	17,143.4
McDonnell Douglas	16,351.0	14,965.0
Conagra	15,517.7	4,804.2
Tenneco	14,893.0	19,034.0
Phillips Petroleum	14,032.0	12,130.0
RJR Nabisco Holdings	13,879.0	32,915.0
Hewlett-Packard	13,233.0	11,395.0
Digital Equipment	13,084.5	11,654.8
Minnesota Minning & Mfg.	13,021.0	11,079.0
International Paper	12,960.0	13,669.0
Westinghouse Electric	12,915.0	22,033.0
Georgia-Pacific	12,665.0	12,060.0

Rockwell International	12,442.5	9,738.1
Allied-Signal	12,396.0	10,456.0
Sun	11,909.0	9,000.0
Sara Lee	11,652.0	7,636.4
Caterpillar	11,540.0	11,951.0
Goodyear Tire & Rubber	11,453.1	8,963.6
Johnson & Johnson	11,232.0	9,506.0
Motorola	10,885.0	8,742.0
Aluminum Co. of America	10,865.1	11,413.2
Anheuser-Busch	10,750.6	9,634.3
Unocal	10,740.0	9,762.0
Bristol-Myers Squibb	10,509.0	9,215.0
Coca-Cola	10,406.3	9,278.2
General Dynamics	10,182.0	6,573.0
Unisys	10,111.3	10,288.6
Lockheed	9,977.0	6,860.0

25 LARGEST RETAILING COMPANIES

	Sales	Assets
Sears Roebuck	55,971.7	96,252.8
Wal-Mart Stores	32,601.6	11,388.9
Kmart	32,080.0	13,899.0
American Stores	22,155.5	7,244.7
Kroger	20,261.0	4,118.5
J.C. Penney	17,410.0	12,325.0
Safeway	14,873.6	4,739.1
Dayton Hudson	14,739.0	8,524.0
Great Atlantic & Pacific Tea	11,164.2	2,831.6
May Department Stores	11,027.0	8,295.0
Woolworth	9,789.0	4,305.0
Winn-Dixie	9,744.5	1,732.7
Melville	8,686.8	3,662.2
Albertson's	8,218.6	2,013.5
Southland	8,037.1	2,799.0
R.H. Macy	7,266.8	6,483.3
McDonald's	6,639.6	10,667.5
Supermarkets General Holdings	6,126.0	2,438.8
Walgreen	6,063.0	1,913.6
Publix Super Markets	5,820.7	1,475.7
Food Lion	5,584.5	1,559.5
Toys "R" Us	5,521.2	3,582.4
Price	5,428.8	1,210.1
Vons	5,333.9	1,712.8
The Limited	5,253.5	2,871.9

10 LARGEST TRANSPORTATION COMPANIES

	Operating revenues	Assets
United Parcel Service	13,628.6	8,176.1
AMR	11,803.6	13,353.6
UAL	11,160.1	7,993.8
Delta Air Lines	8,582.2	7,227.0
CSX	8,306.0	12,804.0
NWA	7,257.1	7,273.3
Union Pacific	7,059.2	13,078.4
Federal Express	7,026.2	5,675.1
USAir Group	6,562.8	6,574.2
Continental Airlines Holdings	6,283.6	3,415.4

10 LARGEST DIVERSIFIED FINANCIAL COMPANIES

	Assets	Revenues
American Express	137,682.0	24,332.0
Federal Nat'l Mortgage Ass'n	133,113.0	12,612.0
Salomon	109,877.0	8,946.0
Aetna Life & Casualty	89,300.7	19,428.3
Merrill Lynch	68,129.5	11,213.4
CIGNA	63,691.0	18,344.0
American International Group	58,143.1	15,702.1
Travelers Corp.	55,356.0	12,150.0
Morgan Stanley Group	53,526.5	5,869.6
ITT	49,043.0	20,604.0

10 LARGEST LIFE INSURANCE COMPANIES

	Assets	Premium and annuity income
Prudential of America	133,456.0	24,108.2
Metropolitan Life	103,228.4	19,527.4
Aetna Life	52,342.6	9,591.4
Equitable Life Assurance	50,301.6	4,029.8
Teachers Insurance & Annuity	49,894.1	2,978.9
New York Life	39,876.3	7,709.6
Connecticut General Life	37,407.3	4,418.7
John Hancock Mutual Life	33,749.5	6,822.8
Travelers	33,027.6	4,866.1
Northwestern Mutual Life	31,377.1	4,166.2

10 LARGEST COMMERCIAL BANKS

	Assets	Deposits
Citicorp	216,986.0	142,452.0
BankAmerica Corp.	110,728.0	92,321.0
Chase Manhattan Corp.	98,064.0	70,713.0
J.P. Morgan & Co.	93,103.0	37,557.0
Security Pacific Corp.	84,731.0	58,191.0
Chemical Banking Corp.	73,019.0	48,951.0
NCNB Corp.	65,284.5	50,222.0
Bankers Trust New York Corp.	63,596.0	28,588.0
Manufacturers Hanover Corp.	61,530.0	40,196.0
Wells Fargo & Co.	56,198.5	42,685.0

10 LARGEST UTILITIES

	Assets	Operating revenues
GTE	33,769.0	18,374.0
Bellsouth	30,206.8	14,436.0
Bell Atlantic	27,998.5	12,298.0
US West	27,050.2	9,957.3
NYNEX	26,650.7	13,585.3
Southwestern Bell	22,195.5	9,112.9
Pacific Gas & Electric	21,958.4	9,597.5
American Information Tech.	21,715.1	10,662.5
Pacific Telesis Group	21,581.0	9,716.0
Southern	19,955.0	8,003.0

New Business Concerns and Business Failures

Formations and failures	1988[1]	1987	1986	1985	1984	1983	1982	1980
Business formations								
Index, net formations (1967 = 100)	124.1	121.2	120.4	120.9	121.3	117.5	116.4	129.9
New incorporations (1,000)	68.2	68.5	702	663	635	602	566	534
Failures, number (1,000)	57.1	61.2	61.6	57.1	52.0	31.3	24.9	11.7
Rate per 10,000 concerns	98	102	120	115	107	110	88	42

1. Preliminary. *Sources:* U.S. Bureau of Economic Analysis and Dun & Bradstreet Corporation. NOTE: Data are most recent available.

50 Leading Stocks in Market Value

Stock	Market value (millions)	Listed shares (millions)	Stock	Market value (millions)	Listed shares (millions)
Exxon Corp.	$93,808	1,812.7	Pacific Telesis	$19,585	432.8
International Business Machines	64,591	571.6	American Home Products	18,695	355.2
General Electric	53,272	926.5	Schlumberger Ltd.	17,610	304.3
Morris (Philip)	48,403	935.3	American International Group	17,284	224.8
Merck & Co.	40,940	455.5	Waste Management	16,990	482.0
Coca-Cola Co.	38,947	839.8	Southwestern Bell	16,850	300.9
Bristol-Myers Squibb	35,769	531.9	Texaco Inc.	16,595	274.3
Wal-Mart Stores	34,578	1,143.1	Boeing Co.	15,935	349.3
American Telephone & Telegraph	32,815	1,089.3	US WEST	15,649	402.6
Procter & Gamble	31,444	363.0	Eastman Kodak	15,552	373.6
Johnson & Johnson	27,529	383.7	Dow Chemical	15,538	327.1
BellSouth Corporation	26,703	486.6	Royal Dutch Petroleum	15,283	194.1
Amoco Corp.	26,468	505.3	NYNEX Corp.	14,678	206.4
Mobil Corporation	25,401	438.0	Anheuser-Busch	14,460	335.3
Chevron Corp.	24,846	342.1	Disney (Walt)	13,894	136.7
du Pont de Nemours	24,750	673.5	Pfizer Inc.	13,401	165.4
PepsiCo., Inc.	22,643	862.6	McDonald's Corp.	12,164	417.7
General Motors	21,740	630.2	Ford Motor	11,893	444.6
Bell Atlantic	21,423	399.5	Ralston Purina	11,749	114.6
Eli Lilly	20,721	282.9	Kellogg Co.	11,719	154.5
Atlantic Richfield	20,705	167.7	Schering-Plough Corporation	11,598	261.4
GTE Corp.	20,600	704.3	Warner-Lambert Company	10,822	160.3
Minnesota Mining & Manufacturing	20,238	236.0	Westinghouse Electric	10,544	370.0
Abbott Laboratories	19,692	437.6	Pacific Gas & Electric	10,537	419.4
American Information Technologies (Ameritech)	19,612	293.8	BCE Inc.	10,386	304.4
			Total	**$1,177,048**	**23,023.9**

NOTE: As of Dec. 31, 1990. *Source:* New York Stock Exchange.

Top 50 Banks in the World

Bank	Country	Assets (U.S. dollars)	Bank	Country	Assets (U.S. dollars)
Dai-Ichi Kangyo Bank Ltd., Tokyo	Japan	$428,167,138,042[1]	Hongkong and Shanghai Banking Corp., Hong Kong	Hong Kong	$148,488,419,200[1]
Sumitomo Bank Ltd., Osaka	Japan	409,160,813,636[1]	Commerzbank, Frankfurt	Germany	144,165,990,896[1]
Mitsu Taiyo Kobe Bank Ltd., Tokyo	Japan	408,754,426,386[1]	Toyo Trust & Banking Co., Ltd., Tokyo	Japan	141,744,450,966[2]
Sanwa Bank Ltd., Osaka	Japan	402,698,761,938[1]	Bayerische Vereinsbank, Munich	Germany	137,747,100,000[1]
Fuji Bank, Ltd., Tokyo	Japan	399,545,460,096[1]	Banca Nazionale del Lavoro, Rome	Italy	137,713,846,000[1]
Mitsubishi Bank Ltd., Tokyo	Japan	391,528,117,262[1]	Deutsche Genossenschaftsbank, Frankfurt	Germany	136,453,080,611[1]
Credit Agricole Mutuel, Paris	France	305,205,855,320[1]	Westdeutsche Landesbank Girozentrale, Dusseldorf	Germany	135,824,394,000[1]
Banque Nationale de Paris	France	291,872,593,200[1]	Istituto Bancario San Paola di Torino, Turin	Italy	133,486,857,257[1]
Industrial Bank of Japan, Ltd., Tokyo	Japan	290,067,480,950[1]	Nippon Credit Bank, Ltd., Tokyo	Japan	128,321,129,734[1]
Credit Lyonnais, Paris	France	287,330,254,000[1]	Algemene Bank Nederland, Amsterdam[3]	Netherlands	122,042,365,000[1]
Deutsche Bank, AG, Frankfurt	Germany	266,286,358,959[1]	Rabobank Nederland, Utrecht	Netherlands	119,728,479,000[1]
Barclays Bank Plc., London	United Kingdom	258,983,040,000[1]	Credit Suisse, Zurich	Switzerland	117,345,984,000[1]
Tokai Bank Ltd., Nagoya	Japan	249,751,219,342[1]	Bayerische Hypotheken-und Wechsel-Bank, Munich	Germany	116,410,504,469[1]
Norinchukin Bank, Tokyo	Japan	249,666,548,514	Midland Bank Plc, London	United Kingdom	114,501,120,000[1]
Mitsubishi Trust & Banking Corp., Tokyo	Japan	237,695,564,610[2]	Amsterdam-Rotterdam Bank, Amsterdam	Netherlands	112,460,671,000[1]
National Westminster Bank Plc, London	United Kingdom	232,512,000,000[1]	Banque Paribas, Paris[4]	France	111,555,200,000[1]
Bank of Tokyo, Ltd.	Japan	223,184,576,804[1]	Kyowa Bank, Ltd., Tokyo[5]	Japan	111,546,886,854[1]
Societe Generale, Paris	France	219,983,122,800[1]	Lloyds Bank Plc, London	United Kingdom	105,987,840,000[1]
Sumitomo Trust & Banking Co., Ltd., Osaka	Japan	218,916,041,638[2]	Saitama Bank Ltd., Urawa[5]	Japan	105,634,996,346
Mitsui Trust & Banking Co., Ltd. Tokyo	Japan	210,934,667,188[2]	Bayerische Landesbank Girozentrale, Munich	Germany	103,722,030,945[1]
Long-Term Credit Bank of Japan, Ltd., Tokyo	Japan	200,678,534,326[2]	NMB Postbank Group, N.V., Amsterdam	Netherlands	102,894,395,000[1]
Dresdner Bank, Frankfurt	Germany	186,935,643,693[1]	Shoko Chukin Bank, Tokyo	Japan	102,672,847,684
Union Bank of Switzerland, Zurich	Switzerland	83,442,672,000[1]	Cassa di Risparmio delle Provincie Lombarde, Milan	Italy	99,946,273,000[1]
Yasuda Trust & Banking Co., Ltd., Tokyo	Japan	175,552,377,192[2]			
Daiwa Bank, Ltd., Osaka	Japan	171,238,796,178[2]			
Citibank NA, New York	United States	155,394,000,000			
Swiss Bank Corp., Basel	Switzerland	151,260,090,576[1]			

NOTE: As of Dec. 31, 1990. 1. Consolidated data. 2. Data are not consolidated for affiliates more than 50% owned. 3. A subsidiary of the $231.4 billion-asset ABN Amro Holding N.V., Amsterdam, Netherlands, the 17th largest banking company in the world. 4. A subsidiary of the $185.6-billion-asset Compagnie Financiere de Paribas, Paris, the 25th largest banking company in the world. 5. On April 1, 1991, Kyowa Bank and Saitama Bank merged to form Kyowa Saitama Bank Ltd. *Source: American Banker, July 26, 1991.* Reprinted by permission of American Banker/Bond Buyer.

National Labor Organizations With Membership Over 100,000

Members[1]	Union
921,926	Automobile, Aerospace and Agricultural Implement Workers of America, International Union, United
145,000	Bakery, Confectionery, and Tobacco Workers International Union
106,174	Bricklayers and Allied Craftsmen, International Union of
140,000	Bridge, Structural and Ornamental Iron Workers, International Association of
609,000	Carpenters and Joiners of America, United Brotherhood of
250,000	Clothing and Textile Workers Union, Amalgamated
650,000	Communications Workers of America
2,000,000	Education Association, National (Ind.)
845,000	Electrical Workers, International Brotherhood of
180,000	Electronic, Electrical, Salaried, Machine and Furniture Workers, International Union of
180,000	Fire Fighters, International Association of
1,235,000	Food and Commercial Workers International Union, United
210,000	Government Employees, American Federation of
185,585	Graphic Communications International Union
301,300	Hotel Employees and Restaurant Employees International Union
570,000	Laborers' International Union of North America
150,000	Ladies' Garment Workers' Union, International
315,000	Letter Carriers, National Association of
767,000	Machinists and Aerospace Workers, International Association of
171,000	Mine Workers of America, United (Ind.)
198,000	Nurses Association, American (Ind.)
125,000	Office and Professional Employees International Union
100,000	Oil, Chemical and Atomic Workers International Union
365,000	Operating Engineers, International Union of
155,000	Painters and Allied Trades of the United States and Canada, International Brotherhood of
250,000	Paper Workers International Union, United
325,000	Plumbing and Pipe Fitting Industry of the United States and Canada, United Association of Journeymen and Apprentices of the
330,000	Postal Workers Union, American
130,000	Retail, Wholesale, and Department Store Union
100,000	Rubber, Cork, Linoleum, and Plastic Workers of America, United
950,000	Service Employees International Union
147,000	Sheet Metal Workers' International Association
1,250,000	State, County and Municipal Employees, American Federation of
650,000	Steelworkers of America, United
750,000	Teachers, American Federation of
1,700,000	Teamsters, Chauffeurs, Warehousemen and Helpers of America, International Brotherhood of
165,000	Transit Union, Amalgamated
150,000	Transportation • Communications International Union
100,000	Transportation Union, United

1. Data are for 1991.

Persons in the Labor Force

Year	Labor force[1] Number (thousands)	% Working-age population	Percent in labor force in[2] Farm occupation	Nonfarm occupation	Year	Labor force[1] Number (thousands)	% Working-age population	Percent in labor force in[2] Farm occupation	Nonfarm occupation
1830	3,932	45.5	70.5	29.5	1910	37,371	52.2	31.0	69.0
1840	5,420	46.6	68.6	31.4	1920	42,434	51.3	27.0	73.0
1850	7,697	46.8	63.7	36.3	1930	48,830	49.5	21.4	78.6
1860	10,533	47.0	58.9	41.1	1940	52,789	52.2	17.4	82.6
1870	12,925	45.8	53.0	47.0	1950	60,054	53.5	11.6	88.4
1880	17,392	47.3	49.4	50.6	1960	69,877	55.3	6.0	94.0
1890	23,318	49.2	42.6	57.4	1970	82,049	58.2	3.1	96.9
1900	29,073	50.2	37.5	62.5	1980	106,085	62.0	2.2	97.8

1. For 1830 to 1930, the data relate to the population and gainful workers at ages 10 and over. For 1940 to 1960, the data relate to the population and labor force at ages 14 and over; for 1970 and 1980, the data relate to the population and labor force at age 16 and over. For 1940 to 1980, the data include the Armed Forces. 2. The farm and nonfarm percentages relate only to the experienced civilian labor force. *Source:* Department of Commerce, Bureau of the Census. NOTE: Data are most recent available.

Corporate Profits[1]

(in billions of dollars)

Item	1991[2]	1990	1989	1988	1985	1980	1975	1970
Domestic industries	221.4	236.4	253.5	285.0	190.8	161.9	107.6	62.4
Financial	22.5	18.7	27.3	35.7	21.0	26.9	11.8	12.1
Nonfinancial	198.9	217.7	226.2	249.3	169.7	134.9	95.8	50.2
Manufacturing	67.1	88.8	86.9	98.4	73.0	72.9	52.6	26.6
Wholesale and retail trade	46.2	41.5	39.1	40.1	49.7	23.6	21.3	9.5
Other	43.7	45.9	36.0	36.0	14.0	38.4	21.9	14.1
Rest of world	68.2	56.9	47.8	43.7	31.8	29.9	13.0	6.5
Total	**289.7**	**293.3**	**301.3**	**328.6**	**222.6**	**191.7**	**120.6**	**68.9**

1. Corporate profits with inventory valuation adjustment. 2. Preliminary. *Source:* U.S. Bureau of Economic Analysis, *Survey of Current Business.*

National Income by Type

(in billions of dollars)

Type of share	1990	1989	1985	1980	1975	1970	1965	1960	1950
National income	$4,418.4	$4,223.3	$3,222.3	$2,121.4	$1,215.0	$800.5	$564.3	$414.5	$241.1
Compensation of employees	3,244.2	3,079.0	2,368.2	1,596.5	931.1	603.9	393.8	294.2	154.6
Wages and salaries	2,705.3	2,573.2	1,965.8	1,343.6	805.9	542.0	358.9	270.8	146.8
Supplements to wages and salaries	538.9	505.8	402.4	252.9	125.2	61.9	35.0	23.4	7.8
Proprietors' income[1][2]	402.5	379.3	254.4	130.6	87.0	66.9	57.3	46.2	37.5
Business and professional	352.6	330.7	225.2	107.2	63.5	50.0	42.4	34.2	24.0
Farm	49.9	48.6	29.2	23.4	23.5	16.9	14.8	12.0	13.5
Rental income of persons	6.9[1]	8.2[1]	7.6[1]	31.8	22.4	23.9	19.0	15.8	9.4
Corporate profits[1][2]	298.3	311.6	280.7	182.7	95.9	69.4	76.1	49.9	37.7
Net interest	466.7	445.1	311.4	179.8	78.6	36.4	18.2	8.4	2.0

1. Includes capital consumption adjustment. 2. Includes inventory valuation adjustment. *Source:* Department of Commerce, Bureau of Economic Analysis.

Per Capita Personal Income by States

State	1990[1]	1989	1988	1980	State	1990[1]	1989	1988	1980
Alabama	$14,826	$13,668	$12,845	$7,465	Montana	$15,110	$14,142	$12,896	$8,342
Alaska	21,761	21,365	19,042	13,007	Nebraska	17,221	15,685	14,783	8,895
Arizona	16,297	15,846	15,000	8,854	Nevada	19,416	18,985	17,521	10,848
Arkansas	14,218	12,995	12,212	7,113	New Hampshire	20,789	20,308	19,230	9,150
California	20,795	19,834	18,757	11,021	New Jersey	24,968	23,736	22,146	10,966
Colorado	18,794	17,510	16,465	10,143	New Mexico	14,228	13,196	12,469	7,940
Connecticut	25,358	24,085	23,039	11,532	New York	21,975	20,818	19,261	10,179
Delaware	20,039	18,742	17,693	10,059	North Carolina	16,203	15,283	14,293	7,780
D.C.	24,181	23,131	21,471	12,251	North Dakota	15,255	13,690	12,764	8,642
Florida	18,586	17,710	16,603	9,246	Ohio	17,473	16,446	15,530	9,399
Georgia	16,944	16,057	15,273	8,021	Oklahoma	15,444	14,147	13,355	9,018
Hawaii	20,254	18,413	16,775	10,129	Oregon	17,156	16,003	14,876	9,309
Idaho	15,160	13,761	12,596	8,105	Pennsylvania	18,672	17,392	16,224	9,353
Illinois	20,303	18,873	17,588	10,454	Rhode Island	18,841	18,101	16,846	9,227
Indiana	16,864	15,824	14,856	8,914	South Carolina	15,099	13,641	12,934	7,392
Iowa	17,249	15,864	14,680	9,226	South Dakota	15,872	13,838	12,741	7,800
Kansas	17,986	16,521	15,736	9,880	Tennessee	15,798	14,728	13,859	7,711
Kentucky	14,929	13,823	12,830	7,679	Texas	16,759	15,515	14,592	9,439
Louisiana	14,391	12,926	12,298	8,412	Utah	14,083	14,142	12,180	7,671
Maine	17,200	16,417	15,088	7,760	Vermont	17,436	16,496	15,303	7,957
Maryland	21,864	20,912	19,565	10,394	Virginia	19,746	18,985	17,671	9,413
Massachusetts	22,642	22,234	20,834	10,103	Washington	18,858	17,679	16,452	10,256
Michigan	18,346	17,535	16,544	9,801	West Virginia	13,747	12,439	11,696	7,764
Minnesota	18,731	17,643	16,649	9,673	Wisconsin	17,503	16,532	15,625	9,364
Mississippi	12,735	11,804	11,123	6,573	Wyoming	16,398	14,547	13,634	11,018
Missouri	17,497	16,449	15,458	8,812	**United States**	**18,685**	**17,594**	**16,491**	**9,494**

1. Preliminary. *Source:* U.S. Department of Commerce, Bureau of Economic Analysis, *Survey of Current Business.*

The Federal Budget—Receipts and Outlays

(in billions of dollars)

Description	1992[1]	1991	1990	Description	1992[1]	1991	1990
RECEIPTS BY SOURCE				Commerce & housing credit	92.8	119.5	67.1
Individual income taxes	529.5	492.6	466.9	Transportation	32.7	31.5	29.5
Corporate income taxes	93.5	95.9	93.5	Community development	6.5	7.7	8.5
Social insurance taxes				Education	45.5	42.8	38.5
and contributions	429.4	402.0	380.0	Health	81.3	71.2	57.7
Excise taxes	47.8	44.8	35.3	Medicare	113.7	104.4	98.1
Estate and gift taxes	13.3	12.2	11.5	Income security	184.8	173.2	147.3
Customs duties	19.3	17.7	16.7	Social security	288.6	269.0	248.6
Miscellaneous receipts	23.9	26.2	27.3	Veterans benefits	33.0	31.5	29.1
Total budget receipts	**1,165.0**	**1,091.4**	**1,031.3**	Administration of justice	14.5	12.6	10.0
OUTLAYS BY FUNCTION				General government	13.2	11.2	10.7
National Defense	295.2	298.9	299.3	Net interest	206.3	197.0	184.2
International affairs	17.8	17.0	13.8	Allowances	4.7	8.2	—
Gen. science	17.5	15.8	14.4	Undistributed receipts	−40.8	−39.1	−36.6
Energy	3.7	2.6	2.4	**Total outlays**	**1,445.9**	**1,409.6**	**1,251.7**
Natural resources	19.5	18.8	17.1	**Total deficit**	**−280.9**	**−318.2**	**−220.4**
Agriculture	15.3	15.9	12.0				

1. Estimated. NOTE: The fiscal year is from Oct. 1 to Sept. 30. *Source:* Executive Office of the President, Office of Management and Budget.

Foreign Assistance

(in millions of dollars)

	Non-military programs			Military proframs		
Calendar years	Net new grants	Net new credits	Net other assistance	Net grants	Net credits	Total net assistance[1]
1945–1950[2]	$18,413	$8,086	—	$ 1,525	—	$28,023
1951–60	18,750	2,012	2,767	26,555	49	50,123
1961–70	18,192	14,776	12	21,591	176	54,747
1971–80	27,216	16,399	−1,011	22,602	9,003	74,209
1981–85	29,025	7,071	−2	9,295	10,836	56,226
1986	7,898	298	5	4,125	1,212	13,538
1987	7,419	−2,666	−27	3,131	334	8,191
1988	7,231	202	−36	3,576	−4,205	6,768
1989	7,662	−431	−2	3,728	−1,924	9,033
1990	10,144	372	−34	6,085	−4,644	11,924
Total postwar period	**151,950**	**46,119**	**1,672**	**102,213**	**10,838**	**312,793**

1. Excludes investment in international nonmonetary financial institutions of $20,922 million. 2. Includes transactions after V-J Day (Sept. 2, 1945). NOTE: Detail may not add to total due to rounding. *Source:* Department of Commerce, Bureau of Economic Analysis.

Women in the Civilian Labor Force

(16 years of age and over; in thousands)

Labor force status	1990	1989	1988	1987	1986	1985
In the labor force:	56,554	56,030	54,742	53,658	52,413	51,050
16 to 19 years of age	3,544	3,818	3,872	3,875	3,824	3,767
20 years and over	53,010	52,212	50,870	49,783	48,589	47,283
Employed	53,479	53,027	51,696	50,334	48,706	47,259
16 to 19 years of age	3,024	3,282	3,313	3,260	3,149	3,105
20 years and over	50,455	49,745	48,383	47,075	45,557	44,154
Unemployed	3,075	3,003	3,046	3,324	3,707	3,791
16 to 19 years of age	519	536	558	616	675	661
20 years and over	2,555	2,467	2,487	2,709	3,032	3,129
Not in the labor force:	41,845	41,601	42,014	42,195	42,376	42,686
Women as percent of labor force	45.3	45.2	45.0	44.8	44.5	44.2
Total civilian noninstitutional population	98,399	97,630	96,756	95,853	94,789	93,736

Source: Department of Labor, Bureau of Labor Statistics, annual averages.

Employed Persons 16 Years and Over, by Race and Major Occupational Groups

(number in thousands)

	1990		1989	
Race and occupational group	Number	Percent distri-bution	Number	Percent distri-bution
WHITE				
Managerial and professional specialty	27,638	27.1	27,459	27.0
Executive, administrative, & managerial	13,539	13.3	13,555	13.3
Professional specialty	14,099	13.8	13,903	13.7
Technical, sales, & administrative support	32,135	31.5	31,619	31.1
Technicians & related support	3,308	3.2	3,125	3.1
Sales occupations	12,857	12.6	12,741	12.5
Administrative support, including clerical	15,970	15.6	15,752	15.5
Service occupations	12,413	12.2	12,237	12.0
Precision production, craft, and repair	12,221	12.0	12,369	12.2
Operators, fabricators, and laborers	14,553	14.3	14,752	14.5
Farming, forestry, fishing	3,127	3.1	3,149	3.1
Total	**102,087**	**100.0**	**101,584**	**100.0**
BLACK				
Managerial and professional specialty	1,913	16.0	1,862	15.6
Executive, administrative, & managerial	853	7.1	840	7.0
Professional specialty	1,060	8.9	1,022	8.5
Technical, sales, & administrative support	3,377	28.2	3,346	28.0
Technicians & related support	349	2.9	347	2.9
Sales occupations	912	7.6	906	7.6
Administrative support, including clerical	2,117	17.7	2,094	17.5
Service occupations	2,728	22.8	2,731	22.9
Precision production, craft, and repair	1,065	8.9	1,089	9.1
Operators, fabricators, and laborers	2,675	22.4	2,714	22.7
Farming, forestry, and fishing	208	1.7	210	1.8
Total	**11,966**	**100.0**	**11,953**	**100.0**

Source: Department of Labor, Bureau of Labor Statistics.

Mothers Participating in Labor Force

(figures in percentage)

	Mother with children		
Year	Under 18 years	6 to 17 years	Under 6 years[1]
1955	27.0	38.4	18.2
1965	35.0	45.7	25.3
1975	47.4	54.8	38.9
1980	56.6	64.4	46.6
1981	58.1	65.5	48.9
1982	58.5	65.8	49.9
1983	58.9	66.3	50.5
1984	60.5	68.2	52.1
1985	62.1	69.9	53.5
1986	62.8	70.4	54.4
1987	64.7	72.0	56.7
1988	65.0	73.3	56.1
1989	n.a.	n.a.	n.a.
1990	66.7	74.7	58.2

1. May also have older children. NOTE: For 1955 data are for April; for 1965 and 1975–90, data are for March. *Source:* Department of Labor, Bureau of Labor Statistics. NOTE: Data are most recent available.

Women in the Labor Force

Year	Number[1] (thousands)	% Female population aged 16 and over[1]	% of Labor force population aged 16 and over[1]
1900	5,319	18.8	18.3
1910	7,445	21.5	19.9
1920	8,637	21.4	20.4
1930	10,752	22.0	22.0
1940	12,845	25.4	24.3
1950	18,408	33.9	29.0
1960[2]	23,268	37.8	32.5
1970	31,580	43.4	37.2
1980	45,611	51.6	42.0
1988	54,904	56.6	44.5
1989	56,198	57.5	44.8
1990	56,554	57.5	45.3

1. For 1900–1930, data relate to population and labor force aged 10 and over; for 1940, to population and labor force aged 14 and over; beginning 1950, to population and labor force aged 16 and over. 2. Beginning in 1960, figures include Alaska and Hawaii. *Sources:* Department of Commerce, Bureau of the Census, and Department of Labor, Bureau of Labor Statistics.

Persons Below the Poverty Level, 1970–1989

(in thousands)

Year	All persons	White	Black	Hispanic origin[1]	Year	All persons	White	Black	Hispanic origin[1]
1970	25,420	17,484	7,548	—	1980	29,272	19,699	8,579	3,491
1971	25,559	17,780	7,396	—	1981	31,822	21,553	9,173	3,713
1972	24,460	16,203	7,710	—	1982	34,398	23,517	9,697	4,301
1973	22,973	15,142	7,388	2,366	1983	35,303	23,984	9,882	4,633
1974	23,370	15,736	7,182	2,575	1984	33,700	22,955	9,490	4,806
1975	25,877	17,770	7,545	2,991	1985	33,064	22,860	8,926	5,236
1976	24,975	16,713	7,595	2,783	1986	32,370	22,183	8,983	5,117
1977	24,720	16,416	7,726	2,700	1987[2]	32,221	21,195	9,520	5,422
1978	24,497	16,259	7,625	2,607	1988[2]	31,745	20,715	9,356	5,357
1979	26,072	17,214	8,050	2,921	1989	31,534	20,788	9,305	5,430

1. Persons of Hispanic origin may be of any race. 2. Revised. Source: U.S. Department of Commerce, Bureau of the Census.

Manufacturing Industries—Gross Average Weekly Earnings and Hours Worked

	1990		1989		1985		1980		1975		1970	
Industry	Earnings	Hours worked	Earnings	Hours worked	Earnings	Hours worked	Earnings	Hours worked	Earnings	Hours worked	Earnings	Hours worked
All manufacturing	$442.27	40.8	$429.27	41.0	$385.56	40.5	$288.62	39.7	$189.51	39.4	$133.73	39.8
Durable goods	468.76	41.3	457.60	41.6	415.71	41.2	310.78	40.1	205.09	39.9	143.07	40.3
Primary metal industries	550.83	42.7	531.48	43.0	484.72	41.5	391.78	40.1	246.80	40.0	159.17	40.5
Iron and steel foundries	484.99	42.1	474.99	42.6	429.62	40.8	328.00	40.0	220.99	40.4	151.03	40.6
Nonferrous foundries	413.48	40.3	406.70	41.5	388.74	41.8	291.27	39.9	190.03	39.1	138.16	39.7
Fabricated metal products	447.28	41.3	438.05	41.6	398.96	41.3	300.98	40.4	201.60	40.0	143.67	40.7
Hardware, cutlery, hand tools	440.08	40.9	429.08	41.1	396.42	40.7	275.89	39.3	187.07	39.3	132.33	40.1
Other hardware	448.63	40.6	440.37	40.7	385.40	41.3	195.42	39.4	133.46	40.2		
Structural metal products	416.56	41.0	408.70	41.2	369.00	41.0	291.85	40.2	202.61	40.2	142.61	40.4
Electric and electronic equipment	420.65	40.8	423.50	40.8	384.48	40.6	276.21	39.8	180.91	39.5	130.54	39.8
Machinery, except electrical	494.34	42.0	480.82	42.4	427.04	41.5	328.00	41.0	219.22	40.9	154.95	41.1
Transportation equipment	592.20	42.0	580.88	42.4	542.72	42.7	379.61	40.6	242.61	40.3	163.22	40.3
Motor vehicles and equipment	619.46	42.4	615.47	43.1	584.64	43.5	394.00	40.0	262.68	40.6	170.07	40.3
Lumber and wood products	365.82	40.2	355.29	40.1	326.36	39.8	252.18	38.5	167.35	39.1	117.51	39.7
Furniture and fixtures	333.52	39.1	325.88	39.5	283.29	39.4	209.17	38.1	142.13	37.9	108.58	39.2
Nondurable goods	405.60	40.0	391.55	40.2	342.86	39.5	255.45	39.0	168.78	38.8	120.43	39.1
Textile mill products	320.40	40.0	314.88	41.0	266.39	39.7	203.31	40.1	133.28	39.2	97.76	39.9
Apparel and other textile products	239.88	36.4	234.95	37.0	208.00	36.3	161.42	35.4	111.97	35.1	84.37	35.3
Leather and leather products	258.43	37.4	249.38	37.9	217.09	37.3	169.09	36.7	120.80	37.4	92.63	37.2
Food and kindred products	392.90	40.8	379.73	40.7	341.60	40.0	271.95	39.7	184.17	40.3	127.98	40.5
Tobacco manufactures	645.23	39.2	593.28	38.6	448.26	37.2	294.89	38.1	171.38	38.0	110.00	37.8
Paper and allied products	532.59	43.3	516.57	43.3	466.34	43.1	330.85	42.2	207.58	41.6	144.14	41.9
Printing and publishing	426.38	37.9	410.89	37.8	365.31	37.7	279.36	37.1	198.32	37.0	147.78	37.7
Chemicals and allied products	576.80	42.6	553.74	42.4	484.78	41.9	344.45	41.5	219.63	40.9	153.50	41.6
Petroleum and allied products	723.86	44.6	683.99	44.3	603.72	43.0	422.18	41.8	267.07	41.6	182.76	42.7

Source: Department of Labor, Bureau of Labor Statistics.

Nonmanufacturing Industries—Gross Average Weekly Earnings and Hours Worked

Industry	1990 Earnings	1990 Hours worked	1989 Earnings	1989 Hours worked	1985 Earnings	1985 Hours worked	1975 Earnings	1975 Hours worked	1970 Earnings	1970 Hours worked
Bituminous coal and lignite mining	$740.52	44.0	$696.78	43.0	$630.77	41.4	$284.53	39.2	$186.41	40.8
Metal mining	602.07	42.7	585.08	42.8	547.24	40.9	250.72	42.3	165.68	42.7
Nonmetallic minerals	524.12	45.3	513.91	45.6	451.68	44.5	213.09	43.4	155.11	44.7
Telephone communications	578.74	40.9	561.15	40.9	512.52	41.1	221.18	38.4	131.60	39.4
Radio and TV broadcasting	438.61	34.7	424.86	35.2	381.39	37.1	214.50	39.0	147.45	38.2
Electric, gas, and sanitary services	636.76	41.7	619.28	41.9	534.59	41.7	246.79	41.2	172.64	41.5
Local and suburban transportation	376.65	38.2	369.02	38.4	309.85	38.3	196.89	40.1	142.30	42.1
Wholesale trade	411.48	38.1	395.48	38.1	358.36	38.7	188.75	38.6	137.60	40.0
Retail trade	195.26	28.8	189.01	28.9	177.31	29.7	108.22	32.4	82.47	33.8
Hotels, tourist courts, motels	214.68	30.8	206.82	31.1	176.90	30.5	89.64	31.9	68.16	34.6
Laundries and dry cleaning plants	232.22	34.0	225.04	34.2	198.70	34.2	106.05	35.0	77.47	35.7
General building contracting	487.08	37.7	471.24	37.4	414.78	37.1	254.88	36.0	184.40	36.3

Source: Department of Labor, Bureau of Labor Statistics.

Median Income Comparisons of Year-Round Workers by Educational Attainment 1989
(persons 25 years and over)

Years of school completed	Median income Women	Median income Men	Income gap in dollars	Women's income as a percent of men's	Percent men's income exceeded women's
Elementary school:					
8 years or less	$11,712	$17,204	$5,492	68	47
High School:					
1 to 3 years	13,222	20,623	7,401	64	56
4 years	16,865	25,859	8,994	65	53
College:					
1 to 3 years	20,764	30,406	9,642	68	46
4 years	25,908	36,845	10,937	70	42

Source: Department of Commerce, Bureau of the Census. NOTE: Data are latest available. n.a. = not available.

Money Income of Households with Female Householder, 1989
(No husband present)

Income bracket	Number of Households All	White	Black	Hispanic[1]
Less than $5,000	1,540,000	796,000	708,000	223,000
$5,000 to $9,999	1,921,000	1,113,000	734,000	271,000
$10,000 to $14,999	1,587,000	1,033,000	504,000	161,000
$15,000 to $19,999	1,289,000	883,000	376,000	122,000
$20,000 to $24,999	1,035,000	800,000	226,000	87,000
$25,000 to $29,999	863,000	637,000	197,000	74,000
$30,000 to $34,999	678,000	497,000	167,000	40,000
$35,000 to $39,999	528,000	411,000	99,000	26,000
$40,000 to $44,999	391,000	312,000	78,000	38,000
$45,000 to $49,999	233,000	181,000	43,000	17,000
$50,000 to $54,999	207,000	167,000	33,000	17,000
$55,000 to $59,999	139,000	97,000	36,000	11,000
$60,000 to $64,999	129,000	106,000	18,000	6,000
$65,000 to $69,999	66,000	43,000	17,000	1,000
$70,000 to $74,999	58,000	44,000	12,000	5,000
$75,000 to $79,999	49,000	41,000	6,000	—
$80,000 to $84,999	36,000	29,000	5,000	6,000
$85,000 to $89,999	22,000	21,000	—	4,000
$90,000 to $94,999	18,000	15,000	2,000	—
$95,000 to $99,999	19,000	11,000	6,000	4,000
$100,000 and over	82,000	69,000	10,000	2,000
Median income	$16,442	$18,946	$11,630	$11,745
Mean income	$21,730	$23,866	$16,844	$17,235

1. Persons of Hispanic origin may be of any race. *Source:* Department of Commerce, Bureau of the Census, *Current Population Reports, Consumer Income, Series P-60, No. 172.*

Unemployment by Marital Status, Sex, and Race[1]

Marital status and race	Men Number	Men Unemployment rate	Women Number	Women Unemployment rate
White, 16 years and over	2,866,000	4.8	2,225,000	4.6
Married, spouse present	1,172,000	3.1	984,000	3.6
Widowed, divorced, or separated	382,000	6.2	471,000	5.2
Single (never married)	1,312,000	8.5	770,000	6.8
Black, 16 years and over	793,000	11.8	734,000	10.8
Married, spouse present	197,000	6.2	135,000	5.6
Widowed, divorced, or separated	104,000	10.5	178,000	9.1
Single (never married)	492,000	19.5	421,000	17.3
Total, 16 years and over	3,799,000	5.6	3,075,000	5.4
Married, spouse present	1,429,000	3.4	1,176,000	3.8
Widowed, divorced, or separated	503,000	6.8	671,000	5.9
Single (never married)	1,866,000	10.0	1,228,000	8.6

1. 1990 Annual Averages. *Source: Employment and Earnings,* January 1991, U.S. Department of Labor, Bureau of Labor Statistics.

Earnings Distribution of Year-Round, Full-Time Workers, by Sex, 1989

(persons 15 years old and over as of March 1990)

Earnings group	Number Women	Number Men	Distribution (percent) Women	Distribution (percent) Men	Likelihood of a woman in each earnings group (percent)[1]
$2,499 or less	427,000	548,000	1.4	1.1	1.3
$2,500 to $4,999	440,000	358,000	1.4	0.7	2.0
$5,000 to $7,499	1,274,000	889,000	4.1	1.8	2.3
$7,500 to $9,999	1,982,000	1,454,000	6.3	2.9	2.2
$10,000 to $14,999	6,291,000	5,081,000	20.1	10.2	2.0
$15,000 to $19,999	6,555,000	6,386,000	20.9	12.9	1.6
$20,000 to $24,999	5,169,000	6,648,000	16.5	13.4	1.2
$25,000 to $49,999	8,255,000	20,984,000	26.3	42.1	0.6
$50,000 and over	947,000	7,377,000	3.0	14.9	0.2
Total	**31,340,000**	**49,678,000**	**100.0**	**100.0**	—

Figures obtained by dividing percentages for women by percentages for men. Figures may not add to totals because of rounding. *Source:* Department of Commerce, Bureau of the Census.

Comparison of Median Earnings of Year-Round, Full-Time Workers 15 Years and Over, by Sex, 1960 to 1989

Year	Median earnings Women	Median earnings Men	Earnings gap in current dollars	Women's earnings as a percent of men's	Percent men's earnings exceeded women's	Earnings gap in constant 1989 dollars
1960	$3,257	$5,368	$2,111	60.7	64.8	8,843
1970	5,323	8,966	3,643	59.4	68.4	11,643
1975	7,504	12,758	5,254	58.8	70.0	12,110
1980	11,197	18,612	7,415	60.2	66.2	11,158
1981	12,001	20,260	8,259	59.2	68.8	11,266
1982	13,014	21,077	8,063	61.7	62.0	10,361
1983	13,915	21,881	7,966	63.6	57.2	9,918
1984	14,780	23,218	8,438	63.7	57.1	10,070
1985	15,624	24,195	8,571	64.7	54.9	9,877
1986	16,232	25,256	9,024	64.3	55.6	10,210
1987	16,911	25,946	9,035	65.2	53.4	9,862
1988	17,606	26,656	9,050	66.0	51.4	9,486
1989	18,778	27,430	8,652	68.0	46.1	8,652

Source: Department of Commerce, Bureau of the Census.

Occupations of Employed Women

(16 years of age and over. Figures are percentage)

Occupations	1990	1989[1]	1988[1]	1987[1]	1986[1]	1985[1]	1984[1]
Managerial and professional	26.2	25.9	25.2	24.4	23.7	23.4	22.5
Technical, sales, administrative support	44.4	44.2	44.6	45.1	45.6	45.5	45.6
Service occupations	17.7	17.7	17.9	18.1	18.3	18.5	18.7
Precision production, craft and repair	2.2	2.2	2.3	2.3	2.4	2.4	2.4
Operators, fabricators, laborers	8.5	8.9	8.9	9.0	8.9	9.1	9.6
Farming, forestry, fishing	1.0	1.1	1.1	1.1	1.1	1.2	1.23

1. Annual averages. NOTE: Details may not add up to totals because of rounding. *Source:* Department of Labor.

Employed and Unemployed Workers by Full- and Part-Time Status, Sex, and Age: 1970 to 1990

(In thousands)

	1990	1989	1988	1987	1985	1980	1975	1970
Total 16 yr and over								
Employed	117,914	117,342	114,968	112,440	107,150	99,303	85,846	78,678
Full time	97,994	97,369	95,214	92,957	88,535	82,564	71,585	66,752
Part time	19,920	19,973	19,754	19,483	18,615	16,742	14,260	11,924
Unemployed	6,874	6,528	6,701	7,425	8,312	7,637	7,929	4,093
Full time	5,541	5,211	5,357	5,979	6,793	6,269	6,523	3,206
Part time	1,332	1,317	1,343	1,446	1,519	1,369	1,408	889
Men, 20 yr and over								
Employed	61,198	60,837	59,781	58,726	56,562	53,101	48,018	45,581
Full time	56,640	56,386	55,353	54,381	52,425	49,699	45,051	43,138
Part time	4,558	4,451	4,427	4,345	4,137	3,403	2,966	2,444
Unemployed	3,170	2,867	2,987	3,369	3,715	3,353	3,476	1,638
Full time	2,936	2,651	2,778	3,147	3,479	3,167	3,255	1,502
Part time	234	215	209	222	236	186	223	137
Women, 20 yr. and over								
Employed	50,455	49,745	48,383	47,074	44,154	38,492	30,726	26,952
Full time	39,036	38,408	37,299	36,121	33,604	29,391	23,242	20,654
Part time	11,419	11,337	11,084	10,953	10,550	9,102	7,484	6,297
Unemployed	2,555	2,467	2,487	2,709	3,129	2,615	2,684	1,349
Full time	2,044	1,963	1,987	2,178	2,536	2,135	2,210	1,077
Part time	511	504	500	530	593	480	474	271
Both sexes 16–19 yr.								
Employed	6,261	6,759	6,805	6,640	6,434	7,710	7,104	6,144
Full time	2,318	2,574	2,562	2,454	2,507	3,474	3,292	2,960
Part time	3,943	4,185	4,243	4,185	3,927	4,237	3,810	3,183
Unemployed	1,149	1,194	1,226	1,347	1,468	1,669	1,767	1,106
Full time	561	596	592	653	777	966	1,057	626
Part time	587	598	634	694	690	701	709	480

Source: U.S. Dept. of Labor, Bureau of Labor Statistics.

Work Stoppages Involving 1,000 Workers or More[1]

Year	Work stoppages	Workers involved (thousands)	Man-days idle (thousands)	Year	Work stoppages	Workers involved (thousands)	Man-days idle (thousands)
1950	424	1,698	30,390	1982	96	656	9,061
1955	363	2,055	21,180	1983	81	909	17,461
1960	222	896	13,260	1984	68	391	8,499
1965	268	999	15,140	1985	61	584	7,079
1970	381	2,468	52,761	1986	72	900	11,861
1975	235	965	17,563	1987	46	174	4,456
1979	235	1,021	20,409	1988	40	118	4,381
1980	187	795	20,844	1989	51	452	16,996
1981	145	729	16,908	1990	44	185	5,926

1. The number of stoppages and workers relate to stoppages that began in the year. Days of idleness include all stoppages in effect. Workers are counted more than once if they were involved in more than one stoppage during the year. *Source:* U.S. Department of Labor. Bureau of Labor Statistics, *Monthly Labor Review. July 1991.*

Livestock on Farms (in thousands)

Type	1991	1990	1989	1985	1980	1975	1970	1965	1960	1950
Cattle[1]	99,436	98,162	98,065	109,582	111,242	132,028	112,369	109,000	96,236	77,963
Dairy cows[1]	10,159	10,153	10,212	10,311	10,758	11,220	13,303	16,981	19,527	23,853
Sheep[1]	11,200	11,363	10,858	10,716	12,699	14,515	20,423	25,127	33,170	29,826
Swine[2]	52,360	51,150	52,965	54,073	67,318	54,693	57,046	56,106	59,026	58,937
Chickens[3]	1,088,152	3,236,993	3,229,801	4,689,973	4,201,706	3,173,820	3,220,085	2,535,141	1,976,737	535,266
Turkeys[4]	105,800	304,863	242,421	185,427	165,243	124,165	116,139	105,914	84,458	44,134

1. As of Jan. 1. 2. As of Jan. 1 of the previous year for 1950–60; Dec. 1 of the previous year for 1965–85; As of March 1 for 1989–91. 3. As of Jan. 1 of the previous year for 1950–60; Dec. of the previous year for 1965–85; 1989, 1990 totals for calendar year, and 1991 as of April. 4. 1975–89 as of Dec. of previous year, 1990 total for calendar year, 1991 as of April. *Source:* Department of Agriculture, Statistical Reporting Service, Economic Research Service.

Agricultural Output by States, 1990 Crops

State	Corn (1,000 bu)	Wheat (1,000 bu)	Cotton (1,000 ba[1])	Potatoes (1,000 cwt)	Tobacco (1,000 lb)	Cattle[2] (1,000 head)	Swine[3] (1,000 head)
Alabama	13,920	6,650	400.0	1,943	—	1,750	—
Alaska	—	—	—	—	—	8.2	—
Arizona	1,120	9,266	1,015.0	1,794	—	830	—
Arkansas	6,935	49,000	1,100.0	—	—	1,700	—
California	25,600	47,906	2,805.8	17,783	—	4,800	—
Colorado	128,650	86,950	—	24,032	—	2,900	—
Connecticut	—	—	—	—	3,000	76	—
Delaware	19,780	3,060	—	2,009	—	31	—
Florida	5,325	1,815	45.0	9,792	19,040	1,925	—
Georgia	37,400	20,650	410.0	—	103,200	1,400	1,100
Hawaii	—	—	—	—	—	205	—
Idaho	3,900	99,600	—	112,340	—	1,660	—
Illinois	1,320,800	91,200	—	837	—	1,950	5,700
Indiana	703,050	50,440	—	858	13,440	1,250	4,300
Iowa	1,562,400	3,375	—	160	—	4,500	13,800
Kansas	188,500	472,000	1.1	—	—	5,700	1,500
Kentucky	120,000	20,000	—	—	437,153	2,420	920
Louisiana	21,576	12,870	1,180.0	—	—	1,050	—
Maine	—	—	—	20,520	—	116	—
Maryland	53,100	9,880	—	324	9,443	315	—
Massachusetts	—	—	—	650	776	71	—
Michigan	238,050	41,250	—	12,115	—	1,225	1,250
Minnesota	762,600	138,620	—	16,110	—	2,600	4,500
Mississippi	11,200	15,600	1,851.1	—	—	1,370	—
Missouri	205,800	76,000	305.0	957	5,625	4,400	2,800
Montana	855	145,865	—	2,492	—	2,300	4,300
Nebraska	934,400	85,500	—	3,539	—	5,800	—
Nevada	—	980	—	2,345	—	570	—
New Hampshire	—	—	—	—	—	46	—
New Jersey	8,850	1,247	—	1,012	—	70	—
New Mexico	7,975	8,125	126.0	3,400	—	1,360	—
New York	60,760	7,105	—	7,890	—	1,540	—
North Carolina	72,760	22,550	271.0	3,380	639,620	900	2,800
North Dakota	36,800	385,220	—	16,675	—	1,700	—
Ohio	417,450	79,650	—	1,911	20,500	1,650	2,000
Oklahoma	10,032	201,600	380.0	—	—	5,250	—
Oregon	2,700	57,616	—	23,014	—	1,400	—
Pennsylvania	109,610	10,500	—	5,400	19,780	1,860	920
Rhode Island	—	—	—	294	—	7.0	—
South Carolina	14,400	14,440	145.0	—	109,905	590	—
South Dakota	234,000	128,004	—	1,980	—	3,380	1,770
Tennessee	43,860	17,640	490.0	—	99,416	2,300	620
Texas	130,500	130,200	5,085.0	3,072	—	13,200	—
Utah	2,660	7,170	—	1,643	—	780	—
Vermont	—	—	—	—	—	297	—
Virginia	36,500	12,220	6.6	1,980	109,498	1,700	—
Washington	14,000	150,080	—	67,980	—	1,330	—
West Virginia	5,250	552	—	—	2,880	490	—
Wisconsin	354,000	10,085	—	23,075	13,575	4,170	1,200
Wyoming	6,000	6,113	—	561	—	1,220	—
U.S. Total	7,933,068	2,738,594	15,616.6	393,867	1,606,851	98,162	54,362[4]

1. 480-lb net-weight bales. 2. Number on farms as of Jan. 1, 1991. 3. Number on farms as of Dec. 1, 1990. 4. Includes states not listed as individual states as data are not available. The 16 listed states account for approximately 91% of the total. *Source:* Department of Agriculture, Statistical Reporting Service.

Farm Income

(in millions of dollars)

Year	Crops	Livestock, livestock products	Government payments	Total cash income[1]
		Cash receipts from marketings		
1925	5,545	5,476	—	11,021
1930	3,868	5,187	—	9,055
1935	2,977	4,143	$573	7,693
1940	3,469	4,913	723	9,105
1945	9,655	12,008	742	22,405
1950	12,356	16,105	283	28,764
1955	13,523	15,967	229	29,842
1960	15,023	18,989	703	34,958
1965	17,479	21,886	2,463	42,215
1970	20,977	29,532	3,717	54,768
1975	45,813	43,089	807	90,707
1980	71,746	67,991	1,285	143,295
1984	69,471	72,968	8,431	155,253
1985	74,290	69,845	7,705	156,882
1986	64,005	71,534	11,814	152,473
1987	63,751	75,717	16,747	162,023
1988	72,569	78,862	14,480	171,579
1989	75,449	83,724	10,886	170,060

1. Includes items not listed. *Source:* Department of Agriculture, Economic Research Service. NOTE: Figures are latest available.

Per Capita Consumption of Principal Foods[1]

Food	1990	1989	1988
Red meat[2]	112.3	115.9	119.5
Poultry[2]	63.8	60.8	57.4
Fish and shellfish[2]	15.4	15.6	15.2
Eggs	29.6	29.9	31.2
Fluid milk and cream[3]	233.2	236.4	234.6
Ice cream	15.7	16.1	17.3
Cheese (excluding cottage)	24.7	23.9	23.7
Butter (actual weight)	4.4	4.4	4.5
Margarine (actual weight)	10.9	10.2	10.3
Total fats and oils	62.7	61.1	63.0
Selected fresh fruits (farm weight)	92.2	99.7	99.1
Peanuts (shelled)	6.2	7.0	6.9
Selected fresh vegetable	95.2	101.0	98.7
White potatoes[4]	126.8	126.2	123.2
Sugar (refined)	64.2	62.5	62.1
Corn sweeteners (dry weight)	71.9	70.3	69.7
Flour and cereal products	184.8	175.0	172.9
Soft drinks (gal)	n.a.	32.0	31.9
Coffee bean equivalent	10.2	10.3	9.8
Cocoa (chocolate liquor equivalent)	4.2	3.9	3.8

1. As of August 1991. Except where noted, consumption is from commercial sources and is in pounds retail weight. 2. Boneless, trimmed equivalent. 3. Includes milk and cream produced and consumed on farms. 4. Farm-weight equivalent of fresh and processed use. n.a. = not available.

Government Employment and Payrolls

Year and function	Total	Federal[1]	State	Local	Total	Federal[1]	State	Local
	Employees (in thousands)				**October payrolls (in millions)**			
1940	4,474	1,128	3,346		$566	$177	$389	
1945	6,556	3,375	3,181		1,110	642	468	
1950	6,402	2,117	1,057	3,228	1,528	613	218	696
1955	7,432	2,378	1,199	3,855	2,265	846	326	1,093
1960	8,808	2,421	1,527	4,860	3,333	1,118	524	1,691
1965	10,589	2,588	2,028	5,973	4,884	1,484	849	2,551
1970	13,028	2,881	2,755	7,392	8,334	2,428	1,612	4,294
1975	14,973	2,890	3,271	8,813	13,224	3,584	2,653	6,987
1980	16,213	2,898	3,753	9,562	19,935	5,205	4,285	10,445
1981	15,968	2,865	3,726	9,377	21,193	5,239	4,668	11,287
1982	15,841	2,848	3,744	9,249	23,173	5,959	5,022	12,192
1983	16,034	2,875	3,816	9,344	24,525	6,302	5,346	12,878
1984	16,436	2,942	3,898	9,595	26,904	7,137	5,815	13,952
1985	16,690	3,021	3,984	9,685	28,945	7,580	6,329	15,036
1986	16,933	3,019	4,068	9,846	30,670	7,561	6,810	16,298
1987	17,212	3,091	4,116	10,005	32,669	7,924	7,263	17,482
1988	17,588	3,112	4,236	10,240	34,203	7,976	7,842	18,385
1990, total	18,369	3,105	4,503	10,760	39,228	8,999	9,083	21,146
National defense and international relations	1,038	1,038	(2)	(2)	2,998	2,998	(2)	(2)
Postal service	816	816	(2)	(2)	2,321	2,321	(2)	(2)
Education	7,971	13	1,984	5,974	15,116	37	3,426	11,652
Instructional employees	4,545	n.a.	614	3,931	10,637	n.a.	1,576	9,061
Highways	573	4	261	308	1,199	14	596	588
Health and Hospitals	1,793	291	730	772	3,820	826	1,522	1,472
Police protection	832	79	89	664	2,134	275	257	1,603
Fire protection	327	(2)	(2)	327	739	(2)	(2)	739
Sewerage & solid waste management	238	(2)	2	236	489	(2)	4	484
Parks & recreation	336	24	45	266	464	58	70	336
Natural resources	427	225	164	38	1,074	673	335	66
Financial administration	488	140	147	202	1,045	357	326	362
All other	3,530	475	1,081	1,973	7,829	1,440	2,547	3,844

1. Civilians only. 2. Not applicable. NOTE: n.a. = not available. Detail may not add to totals because of rounding. *Source:* Department of Commerce, Bureau of the Census.

Receipts and Outlays of the Federal Government

(in millions of dollars)

From 1789 to 1842, the federal fiscal year ended Dec. 31; from 1844 to 1976, on June 30; and beginning 1977, on Sept. 30.

		Receipts				
		Internal revenue		**Miscel-**		
Year	**Customs (including tonnage tax)[1]**	**Income and profits tax**	**Other**	**laneous taxes and receipts**	**Total receipts**	**Net receipts[2]**
1789–1791	$ 4	—	—	—	$ 4	$ 4
1800	9	—	$ −1	$ 1	11	11
1810	9	—	—	1	9	9
1820	15	—	—	3	18	18
1830	22	—	—	3	25	25
1840	14	—	—	6	20	20
1850	40	—	—	4	44	44
1860	53	—	—	3	56	56
1870	195	—	185	32	411	411
1880	187	—	124	23	334	334
1890	230	—	143	31	403	403
1900	233	—	295	39	567	567
1910	334	—	290	52	675	675
1915	210	$ 80	335	72	698	683
1929	602	2,331	607	493	4,033	3,862
1933	251	746	858	225	2,080	1,997
1939	319	2,189	2,972	188	5,668	4,979
1943	324	16,094	6,050	934	23,402	21,947
1944	431	34,655	7,030	3,325	45,441	43,563
1945	355	35,173	8,729	3,494	47,750	44,362
1950	423	28,263	11,186	1,439	41,311	36,422
1956[4]	705	56,639	20,564	389	78,297	74,547
1960	1,123	67,151	28,266	1,190	97,730	92,492
1965	1,478	79,792	39,996	1,598	122,863	116,833
1970	2,494	138,689	65,276	3,424	209,883	193,743
1975	3,782	202,146	108,371	6,711	321,010	280,997
1980	7,482	359,927	192,436	12,797	572,641	520,050
1985	12,079	474,074	311,092	18,576	815,821	733,996
1986	13,323	412,102	323,779	19,887	(5)	769,091
1987	15,085	476,483	343,268	19,307	(5)	854,143
1988	16,198	495,376	377,469	19,909	(5)	908,953
1989	16,334	549,273	402,200	22,800	(5)	990,691
1990	16,707	560,391	426,893	27,470	(5)	1,031,462

			Outlays			
Year	**Department of Defense (Army, 1789–1950)**	**Department of the Navy**	**Interest on public debt**	**All other**	**Net outlays[3]**	**Surplus (+) or deficit (−)**
1789–1791	$ 1	—	$ 2	$ 1	$ 4	—
1800	3	$ 3	3	1	11	—
1810	2	2	3	1	8	$ +1
1820	3	4	5	6	18	—
1830	5	3	2	5	15	+10
1840	7	6	—	11	24	−4
1850	9	8	4	18	40	+4
1860	16	12	3	32	63	−7
1870	58	22	129	101	310	+101
1880	38	14	96	120	268	+66
1890	45	22	36	215	318	+85
1900	135	56	40	290	521	+46
1910	190	123	21	359	694	−19
1915	202	142	23	379	746	−63
1929	426	365	678	1,658	3,127	+734
1933	435	349	689	3,125	4,598	−2,602
1939	695	673	941	6,533	8,841	−3,862

			Outlays			
Year	Department of Defense (Army, 1789–1950)	Department of the Navy	Interest on public debt	All other	Net outlays[3]	Surplus (+) or deficit (–)
1943	42,526	20,888	1,808	14,146	79,368	–57,420
1944	49,438	26,538	2,609	16,401	94,986	–51,423
1945	50,490	30,047	3,617	14,149	98,303	–53,941
1950	5,789	4,130	5,750	23,875	39,544	–3,122
1956[4]	35,693	—	6,787	27,981	70,460	+4,087
1960	43,969	—	9,180	39,075	92,223	+269
1965	47,179	—	11,346	59,904	118,430	–1,596
1970	78,360	—	19,304	98,924	196,588	–2,845
1975	87,471	—	32,665	205,969	326,105	–45,108
1980	136,138	—	74,860	368,013	579,011	–58,961
1985	244,054	—	178,945	513,810	936,809	–202,813
1986	273,369	—	135,284	581,136	989,789	–220,698
1987	282,016	—	138,519	581,612	1,002,147	–148,004
1988	290,349	—	151,711	621,995	1,064,055	–155,102
1989	303,600	—	169,100	649,943	1,142,643	–123,785
1990	299,355	—	183,790	768,725	1,251,850	–220,388

1. Beginning 1933, tonnage tax is included in "Other receipts." 2. Net receipts equal total receipts less (a) appropriations to federal old-age and survivors' insurance trust fund beginning fiscal year 1939 and (b) refunds of receipts beginning fiscal year 1933. 3. Includes Air Force 1950–65 (in millions): 1950—$3,521; 1956—$16,750; 1960—$19,065; 1965—$18,471. 4. Beginning 1956, computed on unified budget concepts; not strictly comparable with preceding figures. 5. Net receipts are now the total receipts. Public Law 99–177 moved two social security trust funds off-budget. *Source:* Department of the Treasury, Financial Management Service, and *Budget of the United States Government Fiscal Year 1991.* NOTE: Totals figures may not add to totals because of rounding of some items.

Contributions to International Organizations

(for fiscal year 1990 in millions of dollars)

Organization	Amount[1]	Organization	Amount[1]
United Nations and Specialized Agencies		Customs Cooperation Council	2.39
United Nations	$206.92	General Agreement on Tariffs and Trade	6.65
Food and Agriculture Organization	21.80	International Agency for Research on Cancer	1.25
International Atomic Energy Agency	37.79	International Criminal Police Organization	1.11
International Civil Aviation Organization	7.91	Others (34 Programs, less than $1 million)	6.17
Joint Financing Program	2.46	Special Voluntary Programs	
International Labor Organization	53.16	Consultative Group on International	
International Telecommunication Union	5.32	Agricultural Research	40.00
United Nations Industrial Development		International Atomic Energy Agency	
Organization	19.11	Technical Assistance Fund	21.55[2]
World Health Organization	71.07	International Fund for Agricultural	
World Meteorological Organization	6.68	Development	34.40
Others (5 Programs, less than $1 million)	2.38	International Organization for Migration	16.21
Peacekeeping Forces		OAS Special Development Assistance Fund	3.93
United Nations Disengagement Observer		OAS Special Multilateral Fund (Education	
Force (UNDOF) and UNIFIL	40.75	and Science)	4.68
United Nations Force in Cyprus	8.84	OAS Special Projects fund (Mar del Plata)	1.00
United Nations Iran-Iraq Military Observer		OAS Special Program	2.25
Group (UNIMOG)	12.49	PAHO Special Health Promotion Funds	11.00
United Nations Observer Group in Central		United Nations Children's Fund	63.95
America (ONUCA)	17.73	United Nations Development Program	105.00
Multinational Force and Observers	23.73	United Nations Environment Program	11.80
Inter-American Organizations		U.N. Afghanistan Emergency Trust Fund	
Organization of American States	46.33	(UNOCA)	13.28
Inter-American Institute for Cooperation		U.N. Capital Development Fund	1.48
on Agriculture	14.24	U.N./FAO World Food Program	163.00[3]
Inter-American Tropical Tuna Commission	2.84	U.N. Fund for Drug Abuse Control	4.00
Pan American Health Organization	39.20	U.N. High Commissioner for Refugees Program:	
Others (4 Programs, less than $1 million)	.58	Regular Programs (5)	74.32
Regional Organizations		Special Programs (7)	52.67
North Atlantic Assembly	1.03	United Nations Relief and Works Agency:	
NATO Civilian Headquarters	23.30	Regular Program	57.00
Organization for Economic Cooperation		WHO Special Programs	40.00
and Development	36.08	WMO Voluntary Cooperation Program	1.97
Others (2 Programs, less than $1 million)	.89	Others (10 Programs, less than $1 million)	4.32
Other International Organizations		**Total U.S. Contributions**	**$1,448.01**

1. Estimated. 2. Includes cash, commodities and services, and $7.32 million for the Safeguards Program and other non-proliferation activities. 3. Includes cash, commodities and services, and $22.1 million for the International Emergency Food Reserve, and $55.9 million for WFP protracted refugee operations.

Social Welfare Expenditures Under Public Programs

(in millions of dollars)

Year and source of funds	Social insurance	Public aid	Health and medical programs[1]	Veterans' programs	Education	Housing	Other social welfare	All health and medical care[2]	Total social welfare	Total social welfare as: Percent of gross national product	Percent of total gov't outlays
FEDERAL											
1960	14,307	2,117	1,737	5,367	868	144	417	2,918	24,957	5.0	28.1
1970	45,246	9,649	4,775	8,952	5,876	582	2,259	16,600	77,337	8.1	40.1
1980	191,162	48,666	12,886	21,254	13,452	6,608	8,786	68,989	303,276	11.5	53.2
1981	224,574	55,946	13,596	23,229	13,372	6,045	7,304	80,505	344,066	11.6	54.0
1982	250,551	52,485	14,598	24,463	11,917	7,176	6,500	90,776	367,691	12.0	52.5
1983	274,212	55,895	15,594	25,561	12,397	8,087	7,046	100,274	398,792	12.0	51.9
1984	288,743	58,480	16,622	25,970	13,010	10,226	7,349	103,927	420,399	11.3	50.2
1985	313,108	61,985	18,630	26,704	13,796	11,088	7,548	118,955	452,860	11.5	47.8
1986	326,588	65,615	19,926	27,072	15,022	10,164	7,977	125,730	472,364	11.3	47.6
1987	345,082	69,233	22,219	27,641	16,054	11,110	8,504	143,020	499,844	11.0	50.4
1988	358,412	74,137	22,681	28,845	16,952	14,006	8,112	149,102	523,144	10.9	49.1
STATE AND LOCAL											
1960	4,999	1,984	2,727	112	16,758	33	723	3,478	27,337	5.5	60.1
1970	9,446	6,839	5,132	127	44,970	120	1,886	8,791	68,519	7.1	64.0
1980	38,592	23,133	14,771	212	107,597	601	4,813	31,309	189,720	7.2	66.5
1981	42,821	26,477	17,124	212	114,773	688	4,679	36,327	206,774	7.0	63.1
1982	52,481	28,367	19,195	245	121,957	778	5,154	40,738	228,178	7.4	62.6
1983	56,846	29,935	20,382	265	129,416	1,003	5,438	42,854	243,285	7.3	60.1
1984	52,378	32,206	20,383	301	139,046	1,306	5,946	44,540	251,569	6.8	58.9
1985	59,420	34,792	22,430	338	152,622	1,540	6,398	48,587	277,540	7.0	59.0
1986	63,816	37,464	24,408	373	163,495	1,872	6,728	53,884	298,158	7.1	58.2
1987	69,941	41,462	25,400	410	188,486	2,129	6,773	60,566	344,601	7.4	59.6
1988	73,783	46,237	29,859	409	202,416	2,550	7,368	70,511	362,622	7.6	60.1
TOTAL											
1960	19,307	4,101	4,464	5,479	17,626	177	1,139	6,395	52,293	10.5	38.4
1970	54,691	16,488	9,907	9,078	50,846	701	4,145	25,391	145,856	15.2	48.2
1980	229,754	71,799	27,657	21,466	121,050	7,210	13,599	100,298	492,534	18.7	57.4
1981	267,395	82,424	30,720	23,441	128,145	6,734	11,983	116,832	550,841	18.6	56.9
1982	303,033	80,852	33,793	24,708	133,874	7,954	11,654	131,514	595,869	19.4	55.7
1983	331,058	85,830	35,976	25,826	141,813	9,090	12,484	143,128	642,077	19.3	54.5
1984	341,120	90,685	37,006	26,275	152,056	11,532	13,295	148,467	671,969	18.2	52.8
1985	372,529	96,777	41,060	27,042	166,418	12,627	13,946	167,542	730,399	18.5	51.2
1986	390,404	103,079	44,334	27,445	178,518	12,036	14,705	179,614	770,522	18.4	47.9
1987	415,023	110,695	47,619	28,051	204,540	13,240	15,278	203,586	834,446	18.4	53.5
1988	432,195	120,375	52,540	29,254	219,368	16,556	15,480	219,613	885,766	18.5	52.8
PERCENT OF TOTAL, BY TYPE											
1960	36.9	7.8	8.5	10.5	33.7	0.3	2.2	12.2	100.0	(3)	(3)
1970	37.5	11.3	6.7	6.2	34.9	0.5	3.0	17.2	100.0	(3)	(3)
1980	46.6	14.6	5.6	4.4	24.6	1.5	2.8	20.4	100.0	(3)	(3)
1984	50.9	13.4	5.6	3.9	22.6	1.5	2.0	23.1	100.0	(3)	(3)
1985	51.0	13.2	5.6	3.7	22.8	1.7	1.9	22.9	100.0	(3)	(3)
1986	50.7	13.4	5.8	3.6	23.2	1.6	1.9	23.3	100.0	(3)	(3)
1987	49.7	13.3	5.7	3.4	24.5	1.6	1.8	24.4	100.0	(3)	(3)
1988	48.8	13.6	5.9	3.3	24.8	1.9	1.7	24.8	100.0	(3)	(3)
FEDERAL PERCENT OF TOTAL											
1960	74.1	51.6	38.9	98.0	4.9	81.2	36.6	45.6	47.7	(3)	(3)
1970	82.7	58.5	48.2	98.6	11.6	82.9	54.5	65.4	53.0	(3)	(3)
1980	83.2	67.8	46.6	99.0	11.1	91.7	64.6	68.8	61.6	(3)	(3)
1984	84.7	64.2	43.6	99.0	8.5	87.4	54.7	70.0	62.4	(3)	(3)
1985	84.0	64.0	45.4	98.8	8.3	87.8	54.1	71.0	62.0	(3)	(3)
1986	83.6	63.7	44.9	98.6	8.4	84.4	54.2	70.0	61.3	(3)	(3)
1987	83.1	62.5	46.7	98.5	7.8	83.9	55.7	70.3	59.9	(3)	(3)
1988	82.9	61.6	43.2	98.6	7.7	84.6	52.4	67.9	59.1	(3)	(3)

1. Excludes program parts of social insurance, public aid, veterans, and other social welfare. 2. Combines health and medical programs with medical services provided in connection with social insurance, public aid, veterans, and other social welfare programs. 3. Not applicable. NOTE: Figures are latest available. *Source:* Department of Health and Human Services. *Social Security Bulletin,* May 1991.

Domestic Freight Traffic by Major Carriers

(in millions of ton-miles)[1]

	Railroads		Inland waterways[2]		Motor trucks		Oil pipelines		Air carriers	
Year	Ton-miles	% of total	Ton-miles	% of total	Ton-miles	% of total	Ton-miles	% of total	Ton-miles	% of total
1940	379,201	61.3	118,057	19.1	62,043	10.0	59,277	9.6	14	—
1945	690,809	67.3	142,737	13.9	66,948	6.5	126,530	12.3	91	—
1950	596,940	56.2	163,344	15.4	172,860	16.3	129,175	12.1	318	—
1955	631,385	49.5	216,508	17.0	223,254	17.5	203,244	16.0	481	—
1960	579,130	44.1	220,253	16.8	285,483	21.7	228,626	17.4	778	—
1965	708,700	43.3	262,421	16.0	359,218	21.9	306,393	18.7	1,910	0.1
1970	771,168	39.8	318,560	16.4	412,000	21.3	431,000	22.3	3,274	0.2
1975	759,000	36.7	342,210	16.5	454,000	22.0	507,300	24.6	3,732	0.2
1980	932,000	37.2	420,000	16.9	567,000	22.6	588,000	23.1	4,528	0.2
1983	841,000	36.0	359,000	15.4	575,000	24.6	556,000	23.8	5,870	0.3
1985	895,000	36.4	382,000	15.6	610,000	24.9	564,000	22.9	6,080	0.2
1986	889,000	35.5	393,000	15.7	634,000	25.4	578,000	23.1	7,100	0.3
1987	972,000	36.8	411,000	15.6	661,000	25.1	587,000	22.2	8,670	0.3
1988	1,028,000	37.0	438,000	15.8	699,000	25.1	605,000	21.8	9,300	0.3
1989	1,048,000	37.3	448,000	15.9	716,000	25.4	591,000	21.0	10,210	0.36
1990[3]	1,080,000	37.6	461,000	16.0	735,000	25.6	585,000	20.4	10,480	0.37

1. Mail and express included, except railroads for 1970. 2. Rivers, canals, and domestic traffic on Great Lakes. 3. Preliminary. *Source:* For 1987 on, *Transportation in America, 9th Edition,* Eno Foundation for Transportation.

Tonnage Handled by Principal U.S. Ports

(Over 10 million tons annually; in thousands of tons)

Port	1989	1988	Port	1989	1988
New Orleans	177,523	175,501	Chicago	23,446	22,894
New York	148,590	155,062	Tacoma Harbor, Wash.	22,451	20,668
Houston	125,583	124,887	Newport News, Va.	21,852	21,391
Valdez Harbor, Alaska	95,436	107,145	Seattle	21,763	18,646
Baton Rouge, La.	82,400	78,857	Paulsboro, N.J.	21,446	22,004
Corpus Christi, Texas	60,479	57,932	Detroit	20,701	15,331
Long Beach, Calif.	54,808	46,560	Boston, Port of	18,989	20,641
Norfolk Harbor, Va.	52,055	46,872	Huntington, W.V.	15,707	17,701
Tampa Harbor, Fla.	49,281	50,252	Freeport, Texas	15,176	15,138
Los Angeles	47,272	45,214	Indiana Harbor, Ind.	15,055	16,643
Baltimore Harbor, Md.	44,884	41,926	Jacksonville, Fla.	15,002	15,806
Texas City, Texas	41,272	42,747	Toledo Harbor, Ohio	14,806	14,742
Lake Charles, La.	40,813	37,312	Cleveland	14,688	14,551
Duluth-Superior, Minn.	40,803	40,002	Port Everglades, Fla.	14,685	14,207
Mobile, Ala.	39,980	36,476	Lorain Harbor, Ohio	14,568	17,476
Philadelphia	36,060	37,827	San Juan, P.R.	13,874	13,503
Pittsburgh	33,416	34,373	Anacortes, Wash.	13,169	13,638
Beaumont, Texas	31,668	31,947	Savannah, Ga.	12,830	13,981
Pascagoula, Miss.	31,546	28,528	Presque Isle, Mich.	12,156	11,433
Port Arthur, Texas	31,128	23,801	Memphis, Tenn.	11,844	10,200
Portland, Ore.	30,030	31,971	Galveston, Texas	11,838	12,355
Marcus Hook, Pa.	29,904	29,815	Cincinnati, Ohio	11,557	11,243
St. Louis (Metropolitan)	26,037	29,011	Honolulu, Hawaii	10,360	10,655
Ricmond, Calif.	25,103	18,913	Ashtabula, Ohio	10,322	10,335

Source: Department of the Army, Corps of Engineers.

Annual Railroad Carloadings

Year	Total	Year	Total	Year	Total	Year	Total
1930	30,173,000	1960	27,886,950[1]	1981	21,342,987[1]	1986	19,588,666[1]
1940	36,358,000	1965	28,344,381[1]	1982	18,584,760[1]	1987	20,602,204[1]
1945	41,918,000	1970	27,015,020[1]	1983	19,013,250[1]	1988	22,599,993[1]
1950	38,903,000	1975	22,929,843[1]	1984	20,945,536[1]	1989	21,226,015[1]
1955	32,761,707[1]	1980	22,223,000[1]	1985	19,501,242[1]	1990	21,884,649[1]

1. Only Class 1 railroads. *Source:* Association of American Railroads.

Estimated Motor Vehicle Registration, 1990

(in thousands; including publicly owned vehicles)

State	Autos[1]	Trucks and buses	Motor-cycles	Total	State	Autos[1]	Trucks and buses	Motor-cycles	Total
Alabama	2,720	963	44	3,683	Montana	452	306	27	758
Alaska	233	135	8	368	Nebraska	913	474	22	1,387
Arizona	2,014	837	80	2,851	Nevada	591	256	17	847
Arkansas	929	519	14	1,448	New Hampshire	754	201	36	955
California	17,103	5,073	627	22,176	New Jersey	5,130	463	84	5,593
Colorado	2,355	889	113	3,244	New Mexico	820	499	34	1,319
Connecticut	2,514	158	50	2,672	New York	8,807	1,350	196	10,157
Delaware	408	123	8	531	North Carolina	3,712	1,514	54	5,226
Dist. of Col.	238	16	3	254	North Dakota	370	259	20	629
Florida	9,239	2,293	206	11,532	Ohio	7,567	1,824	248	9,391
Georgia	3,767	1,611	67	5,378	Oklahoma	1,679	913	57	2,592
Hawaii	661	99	19	760	Oregon	1,831	609	64	2,440
Idaho	631	403	42	1,034	Pennsylvania	6,418	1,609	168	8,027
Illinois	6,487	1,636	223	8,123	Rhode Island	554	115	29	669
Indiana	3,222	1,192	93	4,414	South Carolina	1,895	660	30	2,555
Iowa	1,866	733	174	2,599	South Dakota	425	297	29	722
Kansas	1,401	601	70	2,002	Tennessee	3,533	876	83	4,409
Kentucky	1,902	988	32	2,890	Texas	8,649	4,059	175	12,708
Louisiana	2,002	1,011	30	3,013	Utah	806	385	26	1,191
Maine	732	214	39	946	Vermont	348	122	18	470
Maryland	2,942	638	55	3,580	Virginia	3,807	1,175	57	4,982
Massachusetts	3,286	501	53	3,787	Washington	3,002	1,289	126	4,291
Michigan	5,628	1,582	175	7,210	West Virginia	823	399	17	1,222
Minnesota	2,617	724	112	3,341	Wisconsin	2,774	823	216	3,567
Mississippi	1,452	450	27	1,902	Wyoming	290	203	18	493
Missouri	2,741	1,149	59	3,890	**Total**	**145,010**	**45,218**	**4,274**	**190,228**

1. Includes taxicabs. NOTE: Figures are latest available. *Source:* Department of Transportation, Federal Highway Administration.

Passenger Car Production by Make

Companies and models	1990	1989	1985	1980	1975	1970
American Motors Corporation	—	—	109,919	164,725	323,704	276,127
Chrysler Corporation						
Plymouth	212,354	258,847	369,487	293,342	443,550	699,031
Dodge	361,769	453,428	482,388	263,169	354,482	405,699
Chrysler	136,339	203,624	414,193	82,463	102,940	158,614
Imperial	16,280	—	—	—	1,930	10,111
Total	726,742	915,899	1,266,068	638,974	902,902	1,273,455
Ford Motor Company						
Ford	933,466	1,165,886	1,098,627	929,627	1,301,414	1,647,918
Mercury	221,436	297,678	374,446	324,528	405,104	310,463
Lincoln	222,449	213,517	163,077	52,793	101,520	58,771
Total	1,377,351	1,677,081	1,636,150	1,306,948	1,808,038	2,017,152
General Motors Corporation						
Chevrolet	1,025,379	1,196,953	1,691,254	1,737,336	1,687,091	1,504,614
Pontiac	649,255	732,177	702,617	556,429	523,469	422,212
Oldsmobile	418,742	520,981	1,168,982	783,225	654,342	439,632
Buick	405,123	470,052	1,001,461	783,575	535,820	459,931
Cadillac	252,540	293,589	322,765	203,991	278,404	152,859
Saturn	4,245	—	—	—	—	—
Total	2,755,284	3,213,752	4,887,079	4,064,556	3,679,126	2,979,248
Checker Motors Corporation	—	—	—	—	3,197	4,146
Volkswagen of America	—	—	96,458	197,106	3,181	—
Honda	435,437	362,274	238,159	145,337	—	—
Mazda	184,428	216,501	—	—	—	—
Nissan	95,844	115,584	43,810	—	—	—
Toyota	321,523	231,279	—	—	—	—
Diamond Star	148,379	—	—	—	—	—
Subaru Legacy	32,461	—	—	—	—	—
Industry total	6,077,449	6,823,097	8,184,821	6,375,506	6,716,951	6,550,128

Source: Motor Vehicle Manufacturers Association of the United States.

Motor Vehicle Data

	1989	1988	1980	1970	1960
U.S. passenger cars and taxis registered (thousands)	143,081	141,252	121,724	89,280	61,671
Total mileage of U.S. passenger cars (millions)	1,485,474	1,429,579	1,111,596	916,700	588,083
Total fuel consumption of U.S. passenger cars (millions of gallons)	72,333	71,949	71,883	67,820	41,169
World registration of cars, trucks, and buses (thousands)	556,931	539,790	411,113	246,368	126,955
U.S. registration of cars, trucks, and buses (thousands)	187,261	184,397	155,796	108,418	73,858
U.S. share of world registration of cars, trucks, and buses	33.6%	34.2%	37.9%	44.0%	58.2%

Source: Motor Vehicle Manufacturers Association of the U.S.

Domestic Motor Vehicles Sales

(in thousands)

Type of Vehicle	1988	1987	1986	1985	1984	1983	1980	1975
Passenger Cars								
Passenger car factory sales	7,105	7,085	7,516	8,002	7,621	6,739	6,400	6,713
Passenger car (new) retail sales[1]	10,626	10,278	11,460	11,042	10,390	9,182	8,979	8,640
Domestic[2]	7,526	7,081	8,215	8,205	7,952	6,795	6,581	7,050
Subcompact[3]	1,019	1,101	1,325	1,297	2,322	1,776	1,604	700
Compact[3]	2,781	2,388	2,461	2,563	1,336	1,110	1,659	2,336
Standard[3]	1,722	1,565	1,888	1,882	1,817	1,825	1,358	1,956
Intermediate[3]	2,017	2,026	2,540	2,464	2,484	2,071	1,957	2,058
Imports[4]	3,100	3,197	3,245	2,838	2,439	2,387	2,398	1,587
Trucks								
Truck and bus factory sales	4,121	3,821	3,393	3,357	3,075	2,414	1,667	2,272
Truck and bus retail sales[5]	4,608	4,174	4,031	3,984	3,538	2,709	2,232	2,351
Light duty (up to 14,000 GVW)[6]	4,273	3,885	3,766	3,700	3,261	2,521	1,964	2,076
Med. duty (14,000–26,000 GVW)[6]	83	55	51	53	61	48	92	169
Heavy duty (over 26,000 GVW)[6]	251	234	214	231	216	141	176	106
Motorcycles								
Motorcycles (new) retail sales[7]	710	935	1,045	1,260	1,305	1,185	1,070	940
All-terrain vehicles	290	395	465	550	550	425	n.a.	n.a.
All-terrain vehicle imports	209	320	498	683	635	430	n.a.	n.a.
Motorcycle imports total[8]	287	318	550	733	441	540	1,120	948

1. Based on data from U.S. Dept. of Commerce. 2. Includes domestic models produced in Canada and Mexico. 3. Beginning 1980, cars produced in U.S. by foreign manufacturers are included. 4. Excludes domestic models produced in Canada. 5. Excludes motorcoaches and light-duty imports from foreign manufacturers. Includes imports sold by franchised dealers of U.S. manufacturers. Starting in 1986 includes sales of trucks over 10,000 lbs. GVW by foreign manufacturers. 6. Gross vehicle weight (fully loaded vehicles). 7. Estimates by Motorcycle Industry Council Inc., Costa Mesa, Calif. Includes all-terrain vehicles and scooters. Excludes mopeds/motorized bicycles. 8. *Source:* Motorcycle Industry Council Inc. Data from U.S. Dept. of Commerce. Excludes mopeds/motorized bicycles and all-terrain vehicles. NOTE: n.a. = not available. *Source: Statistical Abstract of the United States 1990.* NOTE: Data are most recent available.

Domestic and Export Factory Sales of Motor Vehicles

(in thousands)

		From plants in United States							
	Passenger cars			Motor trucks and buses			Total motor vehicles		
Year	Total	Domestic	Exports	Total	Domestic	Exports	Total	Domestic	Exports
1970	6,547	6,187	360	1,692	1,566	126	8,239	7,753	486
1975	6,713	6,073	640	2,272	2,003	269	8,985	8,076	909
1980	6,400	5,840	560	1,667	1,464	203	8,067	7,304	763
1985	8,002	7,337	665	3,357	3,126	231	11,359	10,463	896
1986	7,516	6,869	647	3,393	3,130	263	10,909	9,999	910
1987	7,085	6,487	598	3,821	3,509	312	10,906	9,996	910
1988	7,105	6,437	668	4,120	3,795	325	11,225	10,232	993
1989	6,807	6,181	626	4,062	3,752	310	10,869	9,933	936
1990	6,050	5,502	548	3,719	3,448	271	9,769	8,950	819

Source: Motor Vehicle Manufacturers Association of the U.S.

U.S. Direct Investment in EEC Countries, 1990

(in millions of dollars)

Countries	All industries	Petroleum	Manufacturing	Wholesale	Banking	Finance & insurance	Services	Other industries
Belgium	$9,462	$327	$4,331	$2,177	(¹)	$2,059	$352	(¹)
Denmark	1,633	(¹)	286	566	(¹)	295	98	−2
France	17,134	(¹)	11,051	3,025	174	960	375	(¹)
Germany, Federal Republic of	27,715	3,136	17,489	1,505	1,694	2,863	−41	1,069
Greece	300	37	84	71	81	(¹)	(¹)	(¹)
Ireland	6,776	−41	4,885	(¹)	4	1,549	352	(¹)
Italy	12,971	605	8,535	1,677	361	1,005	298	490
Luxembourg	1,119	22	539	(¹)	301	238	0	(¹)
Netherlands	22,778	1,636	8,144	2,490	169	8,642	1,439	258
Portugal	590	(¹)	285	110	(¹)	(¹)	(¹)	(¹)
Spain	7,480	116	4,998	1,011	879	3	312	160
United Kingdom	64,983	11,331	20,636	2,746	3,575	23,071	2,249	1,375
Total	$172,940	$18,761	$81,264	$15,420	$7,504	$40,718	$5,501	$3,772

1. Suppressed to avoid disclosure of data of individual companies. *Source: Survey of Current Business,* June 1991.

Balance of International Payments

(in billions of dollars)

Item	1990	1989	1988	1985	1980	1975	1970	1965	1960
Exports of goods, services, and income	$652.9	$603.2	$533.4	$366.0	$343.2	$157.9	$68.4	$42.7	$30.5
Merchandise, adjusted, excluding military	389.5	360.5	319.2	214.4	224.0	107.1	42.5	26.5	19.7
Transfers under U.S. military agency sales contracts	9.8	8.3	10.0	9.0	8.2	3.9	1.5	0.8	0.3
Receipts of income on U.S. investments abroad	130.0	127.5	107.8	90.0	75.9	25.4	11.8	7.4	4.6
Other services	123.3	106.9	92.7	45.0	36.5	19.3	9.9	6.4	4.3
Imports of goods and services	−722.7	−689.5	−641.7	−461.2	−333.9	−132.6	−60.0	−32.8	−23.7
Merchandise, adjusted, excluding military	−497.6	−475.3	−446.5	−339.0	−249.3	−98.0	−39.9	−21.5	−14.8
Direct defense expenditures	−17.1	−14.6	−14.6	−12.0	−10.7	−4.8	4.9	−3.0	−3.1
Payments of income on foreign assets in U.S.	−118.1	−128.4	−105.5	−65.0	−43.2	−12.6	−5.5	−2.1	−1.2
Other services	−89.8	−80.0	−75.0	−46.0	−30.7	−17.2	−9.8	−6.2	−4.6
Unilateral transfers, excluding military grants, net	−22.3	−14.7	−14.6	−15.0	−7.0	−4.6	−3.3	−2.9	−2.3
U.S. Government assets abroad, net	2.9	1.2	−3.0	−2.8	−5.2	−3.5	−1.6	−1.6	−1.1
U.S. private assets abroad, net	−58.5	−102.9	−81.5	−26.0	−71.5	−35.4	−10.2	−5.3	−5.1
U.S. assets abroad, net	−57.7	−127.0	−84.2	−27.7	−86.1	−39.7	−9.3	−5.7	−4.1
Foreign assets in U.S., net	86.3	214.6	219.3	127.1	50.3	15.6	6.4	0.7	2.3
Statistical discrepancy	63.5	22.4	−10.6	23.0	29.6	5.5	−0.2	−0.5	−1.0
Balance on goods, services, and income	−69.7	−95.3	−113.8	−106.8	9.5	25.2	8.5	10.0	6.9
Balance on current account	−92.1	−110.0	−126.5	−118.0	3.7	18.4	2.4	5.4	2.8

NOTE: — denotes debits. *Source:* Department of Commerce, Bureau of Economic Analysis.

Foreign Investors in U.S. Business Enterprises

	Number				Investment outlays (millions of dollars)			
	1990¹	1989	1988	1987	1990¹	1989	1988	1987
Investments, total	1,565	1,580	1,424	978	$64,423	$71,163	$72,692	$40,310
Acquisitions	796	837	869	543	56,773	59,708	64,855	33,933
Establishments	769	743	555	435	7,651	11,455	7,837	6,377
Investors, total	1,682	1,742	1,542	1,051	64,423	71,163	72,692	40,310
Foreign direct investors	628	727	566	480	12,498	22,538	18,569	11,773
U.S. affilates	1,054	1,015	976	571	51,925	48,625	54,123	28,536

1. Figures are preliminary. *Source:* U.S. Department of Commerce, *Survey of Current Business,* May 1991.

Imports of Leading Commodities
(value in millions of dollars)

Commodity	1990	1989
Food and agricultural commodities	**$17,209.9**	**$16,539.6**
Animal feeds	282.7	279.0
Cocoa	784.3	732.0
Coffee	1,768.8	2,273.5
Corn	23.2	55.1
Cotton, raw	0.5	3.3
Dairy products, eggs	502.2	440.9
Fish	2,011.7	2,132.2
Furskins, undressed	78.2	115.8
Hides and skins, undressed	94.8	97.9
Live animals	1,183.2	869.6
Meat and preparations	2,956.2	2,560.0
Oils and fats, animal	0.5	(z)
Oils and fat, vegetable	717.5	655.5
Rice	71.6	61.9
Soybeans	15.4	23.9
Sugar	852.7	605.3
Tobacco, unmanufactured	696.6	667.6
Vegetables and fruits	5,800.8	4,908.6
Wheat	80.0	57.5
Machinery and transport equipment	**134,849.5**	**132,492.2**
Airplanes	2,836.0	2,947.8
Airplane parts	3,337.8	2,929.1
Cars and trucks	53,556.6	52.960.6
Parts	15,235.1	15,248.3
Spacecraft and parts	204.1	80.0
General industrial machinery	14,483.6	14,486.9
Metalworking machinery	3,687.9	3,867.9
Office machinery	26,917.3	25,714.5
Power generating machinery	14,591.1	14,257.1
Manufactured goods	**118,163.3**	**113,695.4**
Artwork and antiques	2,341.0	2,172.2
Chemicals—fertilizers	955.2	1,003.2
Chemicals—medicinal, pharmaceutical	2,500.2	2,087.6
Chemicals—organic and inorganic	10,625.4	10,248.3
Clothing and footwear	35,108.5	32,931.2
Gem diamonds	3,977.8	4,347.3
Glass	759.5	788.8
Iron and steel mill products	8,810.6	9,392.7
Metal manufactures	6,445.7	6,371.6
Paper, paperboard and articles	8,510.5	8,491.8
Photographic apparatus and supplies	3,359.2	3,435.6
Plastic articles	3,142.3	2,998.6
Pottery	1,222.1	1,243.9
Printed matter	1,670.2	1,617.8
Rubber articles	1,020.8	912.5
Scientific instruments and parts	6,207.6	5,848.9
Textile yarns, fabrics, and articles	6,397.6	6,087.1
Tires and tubes, automotive	2,220.1	2,383.8
Toys, games, sporting goods	9,086.6	8,396.1
Watches, clocks and parts	1,762.2	907.7
Wood manufactures	2,040.2	2,028.7
Mineral fuels and related products	**63,592.2**	**51,638.2**
Coal	86.3	84.1
Natural gas	2,149.4	1,849.7
Petroleum and petroleum products	61,356.5	49,704.4
Crude materials excluding agricultural products	**9,965.3**	**10,416.2**
Cork, wood and lumber	3,126.3	3,499.4
Pulp and waste paper	2,867.0	3,050.4
Metal ores, scrap	3,972.3	3,866.4
Tobacco excluding agricultural, beverages	**1,781.4**	**1,637.0**
Cigarettes	53.6	49.3
Distilled alcoholic beverages	1,727.8	1,587.7
All others	**148,769.4**	**146,792.2**
Total	**495,042.0**	**473,210.8**

Exports of Leading Commodities
(value in millions of dollars)

Commodity	1990	1989
Food and agricultural commodities	**$34,922.3**	**$36,773.9**
Animal feeds	2,855.0	3,081.1
Cocoa	38.2	22.0
Coffee	11.9	12.7
Corn	6,205.2	6,734.2
Cotton, raw	2,782.7	2,244.1
Dairy products, eggs	373.2	446.5
Fish	1,757.4	1,436.8
Furskins, undressed	144.3	173.3
Hides and skins, undressed	1,613.1	1,576.6
Live animals	513.8	531.7
Meat and preparations	3,187.9	2,963.8
Oils and fats, animal	30.6	37.9
Oils and fats, vegetable	664.5	739.6
Rice	801.4	981.4
Soybeans	3,595.2	4,011.5
Sugar	8.2	3.3
Tobacco, unmanufactured	1,441.1	1,339.9
Vegetables and fruits	5,011.6	4,530.4
Wheat	3,887.0	5,907.1
Machinery and transport equipment	**115,244.3**	**106,384.5**
Airplanes	19,615.5	14,432.6
Airplane parts	9,554.1	8,791.6
Cars and trucks	11,901.9	12,267.6
Parts	14,547.7	13,224.8
Spacecraft and parts	894.0	554.0
General industrial machinery	15,688.5	15,034.5
Metalworking machinery	2,747.5	2,738.5
Office machinery	24,725.5	23,992.2
Power generating machinery	15,569.6	15,348.7
Manufactured goods	**70,320.0**	**67,469.7**
Artwork and antiques	2,266.7	1,653.0
Chemicals—fertilizers	2,574.6	2,707.8
Chemicals—medicinal, pharmaceutical	4,103.2	3,692.5
Chemicals—organic and inorganic	14,215.5	14,710.4
Clothing and footwear	2,957.5	2,530.5
Gem diamonds	320.1	1,097.6
Glass	1,058.9	979.0
Iron and steel mill products	3,423.1	3,559.1
Metal manufactures	4,722.7	4,494.4
Paper paperboard and articles	4,991.8	4,585.5
Photographic apparatus and supplies	2,773.4	2,535.0
Plastic articles	1,939.4	1,700.0
Pottery	71.3	69.6
Printed matter	3,158.5	3,002.2
Rubber articles	728.4	670.5
Scientific instruments and parts	12,108.0	11,488.6
Textile yarns, fabrics, and articles	4,922.0	4,301.7
Tires and tubes, automotive	913.6	819.1
Toys, games and sporting goods	1,820.2	1,630.9
Watches, clocks and parts	209.3	177.3
Wood manufactures	1,221.8	1,064.9
Mineral fuels and related products	**11,375.5**	**9,323.7**
Coal	4,464.5	4,087.1
Natural gas	198.7	215.5
Petroleum and petroleum products	6,712.3	5,021.1
Crude material excluding agricultural products	**14,207.4**	**15,118.9**
Cork, wood, lumber	5,224.5	5,203.5
Pulp and waste paper	4,040.2	4,394.5
Metal ores, scrap	4,942.7	5,520.9
Tobacco excluding agricultural, beverages	**5,015.0**	**3,584.8**
Cigarettes	4,761.0	3,362.4
Distilled alcoholic beverages	254.0	222.4
All other	**142,960.4**	**125,156.0**
Total	**394,044.9**	**363,811.5**

Source: Department of Commerce, Bureau of the Census, Foreign Trade Division. NOTE: (z) less than one half unit of measurement shown.

RESOURCE GUIDE

Social Security

The original Social Security Act was passed in 1935 and amended in 1939, 1946, 1950, 1952, 1954, 1956, 1958, 1960, 1961, 1965, 1967, 1969, 1972, 1974, 1977, 1980-1984, 1986, and 1988-1989.

The act is administered by the Social Security Administration and the Health Care Financing Administration, and other agencies within the Department of Health and Human Services.

For purposes of clarity, the explanations given below will describe the provisions of the act as amended.

Old Age, Disability, and Survivors Insurance

Practically everyone who works fairly regularly is covered by social security. Most state and local government employees are covered under voluntary agreements between states and the Secretary of Health and Human Services. Workers not covered include most federal civilian employees hired prior to January 1984, career railroad workers, and a few other exceptions.

Cash tips count for Social Security if they amount to $20 or more in a month from employment with a single employer.

To qualify for benefits or make payments possible for your survivors, you must be in work covered by the law for a certain number of "quarters of coverage." Before 1978, a quarter of coverage was earned if a worker was paid $50 or more wages in a 3-month calendar quarter. A self-employed person got 4 "quarters of coverage" for a year in which his net earnings were $400 or more.

In 1978, a worker, whether employed or self-employed, received one quarter of coverage for each $250 of covered annual earnings up to a maximum of four for a year. The quarter of coverage measure was increased to $260 in 1979 and $290 in 1980, $310 in 1981, $340 in 1982, $370 in 1983, $390 in 1984, $410 in 1985, $440 in 1986, $460 in 1987, $470 in 1988, $500 in 1989, $520 in 1990, $540 in 1991, and will increase automatically in future years to keep pace with increases in average wages. The number of quarters needed differs for different persons and depends on the date of your birth; in general, it is related to the number of years after 1950, or after the year you reach 21, if later, and up to the year you reach 62, become disabled, or die. One "quarter of coverage" is required for each such year in order for you or your family to get benefits. No one will need more than 40 quarters. Your local Social Security office can tell you how long you need to work.

Who Pays for the Insurance?

Both workers and their employers pay for the workers' insurance. Self-employed persons pay their own social security contributions annually along with their income tax. The rates include the cost of Medicare hospital insurance. The contribution and benefit base is $53,400 for 1991 for retirement, survivor and disability coverage, and $125,000 for Medicare coverage, and will increase automatically in future years

as earnings levels rise. The contribution rate schedules under present law are shown in a table in this section.

Social Security Contribution and Rate Schedule
(percent of covered earnings)

Year	Retirement survivors, and disability insurance	Hospital insurance	Year
EMPLOYERS AND EMPLOYEES			
1978	4.95 %	1.10 %	6.05 %
1979-80	5.08	1.05	6.13
1981	5.35	1.30	6.65
1982-83	5.40	1.30	6.70
1984	5.70	1.30	7.00
1985	5.70	1.35	7.05
1986-87	5.70	1.45	7.15
1988-89	6.06	1.45	7.51
1990 & later	6.20	1.45	7.65
SELF-EMPLOYED			
1978	7.00 %	1.10 %	8.10 %
1979-80	7.05	1.05	8.10
1981	8.00	1.30	9.30
1982	8.05	1.30	9.35
1983	8.05	1.30	9.35
1984	11.40	2.60	*14.00
1985	11.40	2.70	*14.10
1986-87	11.40	2.90	*14.30
1988-89	12.12	2.90	*15.02
1990 & later	12.40	2.90	*15.30

*The law provides credit against self-employment tax liability in the following manner: 2.7% in 1984; 2.3% in 1985; 2.09% 1986-1989 and, beginning with the 1990 taxable year, the credit is replaced.

The separate payroll contribution to finance hospital insurance is placed in a separate trust fund in the U.S. Treasury. In addition, the medical insurance premiums, currently $29.90 a month in 1991, and the government's shares go into another separate trust fund.

How to Apply for Benefits

You apply for benefits by filing a claim either in person, by mail, or by telephone at any social security office. You can get the address either from the post office or from the phone book under the listing, United States Government—Department of Health and Human Services—Social Security Administration. You will need certain kinds of proof, depending upon the type of benefit you are claiming. If it is a retirement benefit, you should provide a birth certificate, or religious record. If you are unable to get these documents, other old documents showing your age or date of birth—such as census records, school

Delayed Retirement Credit Rates

Age 62	Monthly percentage	Yearly percentage
Prior to 1979	1/12 of 1%	1%
1979-1986	1/4 of 1%	3%
1987-1988	7/24 of 1%	3.5%
1989-1990	1/3 of 1%	4%
1991-1992	3/8 of 1%	4.5%
1993-1994	5/12 of 1%	5%
1995-1996	11/24 of 1%	5.5%
1997-1998	1/2 of 1%	6%
1999-2000	13/24 of 1%	6.5%
2001-2002	7/12 of 1%	7%
2003-2004	5/8 of 1%	7.5%
2005 or later	2/3 of 1%	8%

records, early naturalization certificate, etc.—may be acceptable. A widow, or widower, 60 or older who is claiming widow's benefits based on his or her spouse's earnings should have both proof of age and a copy of the marriage certificate. A child claiming child's benefits should provide a birth certificate. If formal proof is not available, the Social Security office will tell you what kinds of information will be acceptable.

What Does Social Security Offer?

The Social Security contribution you pay gives you four different kinds of protection: (1) retirement benefits, (2) survivors' benefits, (3) disability benefits, and (4) Medicare hospital insurance benefits.

Retirement benefits. Currently, a worker becomes eligible for the full amount of his retirement benefits at age 65, if he has retired under the definition in the law. A worker may retire at 62 and get 80% of his full benefit. The closer he is to age 65 when he starts collecting his benefit, the larger is the fraction of his full benefit that he will get.

The amount of the retirement benefit you are entitled to at 65 is the key to all other benefits under the program. The retirement benefit is based on covered earnings, generally those after 1950. Your covered earnings will be updated (indexed) to the second year before you reach age 62, become disabled, or die, and will reflect the increases in average wages that have occurred since the earnings were paid.

A worker who delays his retirement past age 65, or who does not receive a benefit for some months after age 65 because of high earnings will get a special credit that can mean a larger benefit. The credit adds to a worker's benefits 1% (3% for workers age 62 after 1978) for each year (1/12 of 1% for each month) from age 65 to age 70 for which he did not get benefits. (*See* table.)

The law provides a special minimum benefit at retirement for people who worked under Social Security for many years. The provision will help people who had low incomes, but above a specific level, in their working years. The amount of the special minimum depends on the number of years of coverage. For a worker retiring at 65 in Jan. 1991 with 30 or more years of coverage, the special minimum benefit would be $461.20 (effective December 1984). These benefits are reduced if a worker is under 65 and are increased automatically for increases in the cost of living.

If you retired at age 65 in Jan. 1991 with average earnings, you would get a benefit of $750.50.

If your spouse is also 65, then he or she will get a spouse's benefit that is equal to half your benefit. So if your benefit is $750.50, your spouse gets $375.20.

If your spouse is between ages 62 and 65, he or she can draw a reduced benefit; the amount depends on the number of months before 65 that he or she starts getting checks. If he or she draws his or her benefit when he or she is 62, he or she will get about 3/8 of your basic benefit, or $281.40. (He or she will get this amount for the rest of his or her life, unless you should die first; then he or she can start getting widow's or widower's benefits, described below.)

If the spouse is entitled to a worker's retirement benefit on his or her own earnings, he or she can draw whichever amount is larger. If the spouse is entitled to a retirement benefit which is less than the spouse's benefit, he or she will receive his or her own retirement benefit plus the difference between the retirement benefit and the spouse's benefit.

If you have children under 18 or a child under age 19 in full-time attendance at an elementary or secondary school or a son or daughter who became totally disabled prior to reaching age 22, when you retire they will get a benefit equal to half your full retirement benefits (subject to maximum payments that can be made to a family). If your spouse is caring for a child who is under 16 or who became disabled before 22 (and getting benefits too), he or she is eligible for benefits, even if he or she is under 62.

In general, the highest retirement check that can be paid to a worker who retired at 65 in Jan. 1991 is about $1022.90 a month. Maximum payment to the family of this retired worker is about $1,790.60 in Jan. 1991. When your children reach age 18, their benefits will stop except for children under age 19 attending an elementary or secondary school and except for a benefit that is going to a son or daughter who became totally disabled before attaining age 22. Such a person can continue to get his benefits as long as his disability meets the definition in the law.

If you are divorced, you can get Social Security benefits (the same as a spouse or widow, or widower), based on your ex-spouse's earnings record if you were married at least 10 years and if your ex-spouse has retired, become disabled, or died. If a divorced spouse has been divorced for at least 2 years, the spouse may be eligible for benefits even if the worker is not receiving benefits. However, both the worker and spouse must be age 62 or over and the worker must be fully insured.

Survivor benefits. This feature of the social security program gives your family valuable life insurance protection—in some cases benefits to a family could amount to $100,000 or more over a period of years. The amount of protection is again geared to what the worker would be entitled to if he had been age 65 when he died. Your survivors could get:

1. A one-time cash payment. [NOTE: There is no restriction on the use of the lump-sum death payment.] This "lump-sum death payment" is $255.

2. A benefit for each child until he reaches 18, or 19 if the child is in full-time attendance at an elementary or secondary school or at any age if disabled before 22. Each eligible child receives 75% of the basic benefit (subject to reduction for the family maximum). (A disabled child can continue to collect benefits after age 22.) If certain conditions are met, dependent grandchildren of insured workers can receive survivor or dependent benefits.

3. A benefit for your widow(er) at any age, if she/he has children under 16 or disabled in care. Her/his

benefit is also 75% of the basic benefit. She/he can collect this as long as she/he has a child under 16 or disabled now "in care." Payments stop then (they will start again upon application when she/he is 60 at a slightly lower amount).

Total family survivor benefits are estimated to be as high as $2,183.20 a month if the worker dies in 1991.

4. If there are no children either under 16 or disabled, your spouse can get a widow's, or widower's benefit starting at age 60. This would come to 71 1/2% of the basic amount at age 60. A widow, or widower, who first becomes entitled at 65 or later may get 100% of his or her deceased spouse's basic amount (provided neither he nor she ever drew reduced benefits).

5. Dependent parents can sometimes collect survivors' benefits. They are usually eligible if: (a) they were getting at least half their support from the deceased worker at (1) the time of the worker's death if the worker did not qualify for disability benefits before death, or (2) if the worker had been entitled to disability benefits which had not been terminated before death either at the beginning of the period of disability or at the time of death; (b) they have reached 62; and (c) they are not eligible for a greater retirement benefit based on their own earnings. A single surviving parent can then get 82 1/2% of the basic benefit. If two parents are eligible, each would get 75%.

Here is an example of survivors' benefits in one family situation: John Jones died at age 29 in June 1990 leaving a wife and two children aged one and three. He had average covered earnings under Social Security. Family survivors' benefits would include: (1) a cash lump-sum death payment of $255, and (2) a total monthly benefit of $1,317 for the family. When the children reach 18, their benefits stop unless they are attending an elementary or secondary school full time, in which case payments continue up to age 19. When the older child no longer collects benefits, the widow and younger child continue to get benefits until that child is 16. He will still get a benefit until age 18 (or age 19, if he continues in elementary or secondary school), but Mrs. Jones' checks will stop. When Mrs. Jones becomes 60 (assuming she has not remarried), she will be able to get a reduced widow's benefit if she so chooses, or she can wait until age 65 to get a full benefit.

If in addition to your Social Security benefit as a wife, husband, widow, or widower you receive a pension based on your work in employment not covered by Social Security, your benefit as a spouse or survivor will be reduced by 2/3rds of the amount of that pension. Under an exception in the law, your government pension will not affect your spouse's or survivor's benefit if you became eligible for that pension before December 1982 and if, at the time you apply or become entitled to your social security benefit as a spouse or survivor, you could have qualified for that benefit if the law in effect in January 1977 had remained in effect (i.e., at that time, men had to prove they were dependent upon their wives for support to be eligible for benefits as a spouse or survivor.) There are also several other exceptions in the law. Your government pension, however, currently will not affect any Social Security benefit based on your own work covered by social security.

Disability Benefits. Disability benefits can be paid to several groups of people:

Disabled workers under 65 and their families.

Work Credit for Disabilty Benefits

Born after 1929, become disabled at age	Born before 1930, become disabled before 62 in	Years of work credit you need
42 or younger	1971	5
44	1973	5 1/2
46	1975	6
48	1977	6 1/2
50	1979	7
51	1980	7 1/4
52	1981	7 1/2
54	1983	8
56	1985	8 1/2
58	1987	9
60	1989	9 1/2
62 or older	1991 or later	10

NOTE: Five years of this credit must have been earned in the 10 years ending when you became disabled; years need not be continuous or in units of full years.

Persons disabled before 22 who continue to be disabled. These benefits are payable as early as 18 when a parent (or grandparent under certain circumstances) receives social security retirement or disability benefits or when an insured parent dies.

Disabled widows and widowers and (under certain conditions) disabled surviving divorced spouses of workers who were insured at death. These benefits are payable as early as 50.

A disabled person is eligible for Medicare after being entitled to disability payments for 24 months.

If you are a worker and become severely disabled, you will be eligible for monthly benefits if you have worked under Social Security long enough and recently enough. The amount of work you will need depends on your age when you become disabled:

Before 24: You need credit for 1 1/2 years of work in the 3-year period ending when your disability begins.

24 through 30: You need credit for having worked half the time between 21 and the time you become disabled.

31 or older: All workers disabled at 31 or older—except the blind—need the amount of credit shown in the chart.

To be considered disabled under the social security law you must be: (1) unable to engage in any substantial activity because of any medically determinable physical or mental impairment which can be expected to result in death or has lasted for 12 continuous months, or (2) blind. A person whose vision is no better than 20/200 even with glasses, or who has a limited visual field of 20 degrees or less, is considered "blind" under the social security law.

If you meet these conditions, you may be able to get payments even if your recovery from the disability is expected.

The medical evidence from your physician or other sources will show the severity of your condition and the extent to which it prevents you from doing substantial gainful work. Your age, education, training, and work experience also may be considered in deciding whether you are able to work. If you can't do your regular work but can do other substantial gainful work, you will not be considered disabled.

While you are receiving benefits as a disabled worker, payments can also be made to certain members of your family. These family members include:

Your unmarried children under 18.

Your children under 19 if they are unmarried and attending an elementary or secondary school full time.

Your unmarried children 18 or older who were disabled before reaching 22 and continue to be disabled.

Your spouse at any age if she/he has in-care a child who is under 16 or disabled and who is getting benefits based on your social security record.

Your spouse 62 or older even if there are no children entitled to benefits.

A child may be eligible on a grandparent's social security record only if the child's parents are disabled or deceased and the child was living with and receiving 1/2 support from the grandparent at the time the grandparent qualified for benefits.

Benefits begin after a waiting period of 5 full calendar months. No benefits can be paid for these first 5 months of disability; therefore, the first payment is for the 6th full month. If you are disabled more than 6 full months before you apply, back benefits may be payable, but not before the 6th full month of disability. It is important to apply soon after the disability starts because back payments are limited to the 12 months preceding the month you apply.

Certain disabled people under 65 are eligible for Medicare. They include disabled workers at any age, persons who became disabled before age 22, and disabled widows and widowers age 50 or over who have been entitled to disability checks for 2 years or more.

Medicare protection generally ends when monthly disability benefits end, and can continue an additional 3 years after benefits stop because an individual returns to gainful work. (Under certain circumstances, former disability beneficiaries may purchase continued Medicare coverage. *See* "Do You Qualify for Hospital Insurance?" in this section.)

If a person becomes entitled to disability benefits again, Medicare coverage starts at the same time if a worker becomes disabled again within 5 years after benefits end (or within 7 years for a disabled widow, widower, or person disabled after age 22).

Benefits to workers disabled after 1978 and their dependents are based, in part, on earnings that have been adjusted to take account of increases in average wages since they were earned. The adjusted earnings are averaged together and a formula is applied to the adjusted average to figure the benefit rate.

Monthly benefits in Jan. 1991 or later can be as high as $1,214.20 for a worker and as high as $1,821.30 for a worker with a family. Once a person starts receiving benefits, the amount will increase automatically in future years to keep pace with the rising cost of living.

If you receive benefits as a disabled worker, an adult disabled since childhood, or a disabled widow or widower, you are not subject to the general rule under which some benefits are withheld if you have substantial earnings. There are special rules, which include medical considerations, for determining how any work you do might affect your disability payments.

If one of your dependents who is under 65 and who is not disabled works and earns more than $7,080 in 1991, some of the dependent's benefits may be withheld. In general, $1 in benefits is withheld for each $2 over $7,080. Different rules apply to your dependents who are 65 or over. A person 65 or over can earn $9,720 in 1991 without having benefits withheld. For persons 65 or over, $1 in benefits is withheld for $3 in earnings over $9,720.

The amount a person can earn without having any

benefits withheld will increase in future years as the level of average wages rises.

If you are receiving disability benefits, you are required by law to let the Social Security Administration know if your condition improves or if you return to work no matter how little you earn.

If at any time medical evidence shows that you no longer meet the requirements for entitlement to disability benefits, you will still receive benefits for a 3-month period of adjustment. Benefits will then be stopped.

Whether or not you report a return to work or that your condition has improved, Social Security will review your claim periodically to see if you continue to meet the requirements for benefits.

If you are a disabled worker or a person disabled in childhood and you return to work in spite of a severe condition, your benefits may continue to be paid during a trial work period of up to 9 months—not necessarily consecutive months. This will give you a chance to test your ability to work. If after 9 service months it is decided that you are able to do substantial gainful work, your benefits will be paid for an adjustment period of 3 additional months.

Thus, if you go to work in spite of your disability, you may continue to receive disability benefits for up to 12 months, even though the work is substantial gainful work. If it is decided that the work you are able to do is not substantial and gainful, you may continue to receive benefits. Of course, should you no longer meet the requirements for entitlement to disability, your benefits would be stopped after a 3-month adjustment period even though your trial work period might not be over.

Disabled widows and widowers also can have a trial work period. If your benefits are stopped because you return to work and you become unable to continue working within the next 33 months, your benefits can be restarted automatically. You do not have to file a new disability application.

You Can Earn Income Without Losing Benefits

If you are 70 or over you can earn any amount and still get all your benefits. If you are under 70, you can receive all benefits if your earnings do not exceed the annual exempt amount. The annual amount for 1991 is $9,720 for people 65 or over and $7,080 for people under 65.

If your earnings go over the annual amount, $1 in benefits is withheld for each $2 ($3 if age 65-69) of earnings above the limit.

The monthly measure used for 1977 and earlier years to determine whether benefits could be paid for any month during which they earned 1/12 or less of the annual exempt amount and did not substantial work in their business has been eliminated. A person can now use the monthly test only in the first year that he or she has a month in which earnings do not exceed 1/12 of the annual exempt amount or does not perform substantial services in self-employment. If such a month occurs in 1991, a benefit can be paid for any month in which you earn $810 or less (if 65 or older) or $590 (if under 65) and don't perform substantial services in self-employment even though your total yearly earnings exceed the annual amount.

The annual exempt amount will increase automatically as the level of average wages rises.

If a worker's earnings exceed the exempt amount, social security benefits to his dependents may be reduced. However, a dependent's benefits will not be reduced if another dependent has excess earnings.

Anyone earning over the annual exempt amount a year while receiving benefits (and under age 70) must report these earnings to the Social Security Administration. If you continue to work after you have applied for social security, your additional earnings may increase the amount of your monthly payment. This will be done automatically by the Social Security Administration. You need not ask for it.

Medicare

The Medicare program is administered by the Health Care Financing Administration.

Most people 65 and over and many under 65 who have been entitled to disability checks for at least 2 years have Medicare protection. So do insured people and their dependents who need a kidney transplant or dialysis treatment because of permanent kidney failure.

The hospital insurance part of Medicare helps pay the cost of inpatient hospital care and certain kinds of follow-up care. The medical insurance part helps pay for the cost of doctors' services, outpatient hospital services, and for certain other medical items and services.

A person who is eligible for monthly benefits at 65 gets hospital insurance automatically and does not have to pay a premium. He does pay a monthly premium for medical insurance.

Supplemental Security Income

The supplemental security income (SSI) program is a federally funded program administered by the Social Security Administration. Its basic purpose is to assure a minimum level of income to people who are elderly (65 or over), blind or disabled, and who have limited income and resources.

In 1991, the maximum Federal SSI payment was $407 a month for an individual and $610 a month for a couple. But in many States, SSI payments are much higher because the State adds to the Federal payment.

Countable resources must be valued at $2,000 or less for an individual or $3,000 or less for a couple. But not all the things people own count for SSI. For instance, the house a person lives in and the land around it, and usually, one car does not count.

Generally, depending on the State, people who get SSI can also get Medicaid to pay for their health care costs as well as food stamps and other social services. And in many States an application for SSI is an application for Medicaid, so people do not have to make separate applications. Certain people can also apply for food stamps at the same Social Security office where they apply for SSI.

Social Security representatives will need information about the income and resources and the citizenship or alien status of people applying for benefits. If the person is living with a spouse, or the application is for a disabled child living with parents, the same information is needed about the spouse/parents.

People who are age 65 or over will need proof of their age such as a birth certificate, or religious record. And if a person who is filing is disabled or blind, Social Security will need information about the impairment and its treatment history.

It helps if people have this information and evidence with them when they talk to their Social Security representative. But they do not need to have **any** of these things to **start** their application. All they need to do is to call Social Security to find out if they are eligible for SSI payments and the other benefits that come with it. Benefits are not retroactive, so delay can cost money.

The Social Security representative will explain just what information/evidence is needed for the SSI claim, and will provide help in getting it if help is needed. Most Social Security offices will make an appointment for an office visit or for a telephone interview if that is more convenient. Or people can just walk in, and wait until someone is free to help them.

Over 4.8 million people receive SSI benefits now. Many receive both SSI and Social Security. Do not wait. Call 1-800-234-5SSA, and find out more about SSI. Even the call is free!

How to Protect Your Social Security Record

Always show your Social Security card when you start a new job. In that way you will be sure that your earnings will be credited to *your* Social Security record and not someone else's. If you lose your Social Security card, contact Social Security to find out how to apply for a new one. When a woman marries, she should apply for a new card showing her married name (and the same number).

Public Assistance

The Federal government makes grants to the states to help them provide financial assistance, medical care, and social services to certain persons in need, including children dependent because of the death, absence from home, incapacity, or (in some states) unemployment of a parent. In addition, some help is provided from only state and/or local funds to some other needy persons.

Federal sharing in state cash assistance expenditures made in accordance with the Social Security Act is based on formulas which are set forth in the Act. The Social Security Act gives the states the option of using one of two formulas, whichever is to its benefit. One formula limits the amount of assistance payment in which there is federal sharing. The other formula permits federal sharing without a limit on the amount of assistance payment. Administrative costs in all the programs are shared equally by the federal and state governments.

Within these and other general patterns set by the requirements of the Social Security Act and their administrative interpretations, each state initiates and administers its own public assistance programs, including the determination of who is eligible to receive assistance, and how much can be granted and under what conditions. Assistance is in the form of cash payments made to recipients, except that direct payments are used for medical care, and restricted payments may be used in cases of mismanagement. Other social services are provided, in some instances, to help assistance recipients increase their capacity for self-care and self-support or to strengthen family life.

In the medical assistance Medicaid program, federal funds pay 50% to 83% of the costs for medical care. If it is to a state's benefit, it may use the Medicaid formula for federal sharing for its money payment programs, ignoring the maximum on dollar amounts per recipient.

Medicare Program

The Medicare program is a federal health-insurance program for persons 65 and over, disabled people under 65 who have been entitled to social security disability benefits at least 24 months, or have worked long enough in Federal employment to be insured for Medicare, and insured workers and their dependents at any age who need dialysis treatment or a kidney transplant because of permanent kidney failure.

Enacted under the Social Security Amendments of 1965, Medicare's official name is Title XVIII of the Social Security Act. These amendments also carried Title XIX, providing federal assistance to state medical-aid programs, which has come to be known as Medicaid.

Medicare

It will be helpful to your understanding of the Medicare program if you keep the following points in mind:

- The federal health-insurance program does not of itself offer medical services. It helps pay hospital, doctor, and other medical bills. You choose your own doctor, who prescribes your treatment and place of treatment. But, you should always make sure that health care facilities or persons who provide you with treatment or services are participating in Medicare. Usually, Medicare cannot pay for care from non-participating health care organizations.
- There are two parts of the program: (1) The hospital insurance part for the payment of most of the cost of covered care provided by participating hospitals, skilled nursing facilities, and home health agencies. (2) The medical insurance part which helps pay doctors' bills and certain other expenses.
- Another important point to remember: While Medicare pays the major share of the costs of many illnesses requiring hospitalization, it does not offer adequate protection for long-term illness or mental illness.
- Therefore, it may be advisable not to cancel any private health insurance you now carry. You may wish to cancel a policy whose benefits are duplicated by the federal program, and consider a new policy that will provide for the payment of costs not covered by the federal program. Private insurance companies offer policies supplementing the protection offered by the federal program.
- If you want help in deciding whether to buy private supplemental insurance, ask at any social security office for the pamphlet, *Guide to Health Insurance for People with Medicare.* This free pamphlet describes the various types of supplemental insurance available.

Do You Qualify for Hospital Insurance?

If you're entitled to monthly social security or railroad retirement checks (as a worker, dependent, or survivor), you have hospital insurance protection automatically when you're 65. Disabled people under 65 will have hospital insurance automatically after they have been entitled to social security disability benefits for 24 months. Effective July 1, 1990, for-

mer disability beneficiaries will be able to purchase hospital insurance after their premium-free coverage stops due to work activity. Federal employees who are disabled before 65 may be eligible on the basis of Federal employment. (Disabled people who get railroad annuities must meet special requirements.) People 65 or older who are not entitled to monthly benefits must have worked long enough under Social Security or the railroad retirement system or in covered Federal employment to get hospital insurance without paying a monthly premium. If they do not have enough work, they can buy hospital insurance. The premium is $177 a month in 1991. People are eligible at any age if they need maintenance dialysis or a kidney transplant for permanent kidney failure and are getting monthly Social Security or railroad retirement benefits or have worked long enough.

To be sure your protection will start the month you reach 65, apply for Medicare insurance 3 months before reaching 65, even if you don't plan to retire.

Do You Qualify for Voluntary Medical Insurance?

The voluntary medical insurance plan is a vital supplement to the hospital plan. It helps pay for doctors' and other medical services. Many people have not been able to obtain such insurance from private companies because they could not afford it or because of their medical histories.

One difference between the hospital insurance plan and the medical insurance plan is that you do not have to be under the social security or railroad retirement systems to enroll in the medical plan. Almost anyone who is 65 or older or who is eligible for hospital insurance can enroll in medical insurance.

People who get social security benefits or retirement benefits under the railroad retirement system will be enrolled automatically for medical insurance—unless they say they don't want it—when they become entitled to hospital insurance. Automatic enrollment does not apply to people who plan to continue working past 65, who are disabled widows or widowers between 50 and 65 who aren't getting disability checks, who are 65 but have not worked long enough to be eligible for hospital insurance, who have permanent kidney failure, who are eligible for Medicare on the basis of Federal employment, or who live in Puerto Rico or foreign countries. These people have to apply for medical insurance if they want it. People who have medical insurance pay a monthly premium covering part of the cost of this protection. The other part is paid from general federal revenues. The basic premium for enrollees is $29.90 a month in 1991.

Is Other Insurance Necessary?

As already indicated, Medicare provides only partial reimbursement. Therefore, you should know how much medical cost you can bear and perhaps arrange for other insurance.

In 1991, for the first 60 days of inpatient hospital care in each benefit period, hospital insurance pays for all covered services except for the first $628. For the 61st through 90th day of a covered inpatient hospital stay, hospital insurance pays for all covered services except for $157 a day. People who need to be in a hospital for more than 90 days in a benefit period can use some or all of their 60 lifetime reserve days. Hospital insurance pays for all covered services except for $314 a day for each reserve day used. Hospital insurance also does not pay the full cost of an inpatient stay in a skilled nursing facility.

Under medical insurance, the patient must meet an annual deductible. In 1991, the annual deductible is $100. After the patient has met the deductible, each year, medical insurance generally pays 80% of the approved amounts for any additional covered services the patient receives during the rest of the year.

How You Obtain Coverage

If you are receiving Social Security or railroad retirement monthly benefits, you will receive from the government information concerning Medicare about 3 months before you become entitled to hospital insurance.

All other eligible people have to file an application for Medicare. They should contact a social security office to apply for Medicare.

New in 1991

Breast Cancer Screening (Mammography): Medicare medical insurance now helps pay for X-ray screenings to detect breast cancer. Women 65 or older can use the benefit ever other year. Younger disabled women covered by Medicare can use it more frequently. Medicare will pay 80 percent of up to $55 for each screening.

Physician Payment Reforms: In 1991, physicians who do not accept assignment may not charge you for office and hospital visits more than 140 percent of the Medicare prevailing charge for non-participating physicians. For most other services (surgery, for example) the limit is 125 percent. Physicians who knowingly charge more than these amounts are subject to sanctions.

You no longer have to file claims to Medicare for covered medical insurance services received after September 1, 1990. Doctors, suppliers, and other providers of services must submit the claims to Medicare within one year of providing the service to you or be subject to certain penalties.

Copyrights

Source: Library of Congress, Copyright Office.

U.S. is a Member of the Berne Union

On March 1, 1989, the United States joined the Berne Union by entering into an international treaty called the Berne Convention, whose full title is the Berne Convention for the Protection of Literary and Artistic Works. Also on that date, amendments to the U.S. copyright law that satisfy U.S. treaty obligations under the Convention took effect and some of them are listed herein. Contact the U.S. Copyright Office for details of Berne Convention obligations.

The U.S. Law continues to govern the protection and registration of works in the United States.

Beginning March 1, 1989, copyright in the works of U.S. authors is protected automatically in all member nations of the Berne Union and the works of foreign authors who are nationals of a Berne Union country, and works first published in a Berne Union country are automatically protected in the United States.

In order to fulfill its Berne Convention obligations, the United States made certain changes in its copyright law by passing the Berne Convention Implementation Act of 1988. These changes are not retroactive and are effective only on and after March 1, 1989.

The copyright law (Title 17 of the United States Code) was amended by the enactment of a statute for its general revision, Public Law 94–553 (90 Stat. 2541), which was signed by the President on October 19, 1976. The new law superseded the copyright act of 1909, as amended, which remained effective until the new enactment took effect on January 1, 1978.

Under the new law, all copyrightable works, whether published or unpublished, are subject to a single system of statutory protection which gives a copyright owner the exclusive right to reproduce the copyrighted work in copies or phonorecords and distribute them to the public by sale, rental, lease, or lending. Among the other rights given to the owner of a copyright are the exclusive rights to prepare derivative works based upon the copyrighted work, to perform the work publicly if it be literary, musical, dramatic, choreographic, a pantomime, motion picture, or other audiovisual work, and in the case of literary, musical, dramatic, and choreographic works, pantomimes, and pictorial, graphic, or sculptural works, including the individual images of a motion picture or other audiovisual work, to display the copyrighted work publicly. All of these rights are subject to certain exceptions, including the principle of "fair use" which the new statute specifically recognizes.

Special provisions are included which permit compulsory licensing for the recording of musical compositions, noncommercial transmissions by public broadcasters of published musical and graphic works, performances of copyrighted music by jukeboxes, and the secondary transmission of copyrighted works on cable television systems.

Copyright protection under the new law extends to original works of authorship fixed in a tangible medium of expression, from which they can be perceived, reproduced, or otherwise communicated, either directly or with the aid of a machine or device.

Works of authorship include books, periodicals and other literary works, musical compositions with accompanying lyrics, dramas and dramatico-musical compositions, pantomimes and choreographic works, motion pictures and other audiovisual works, sound recordings, and works of the visual arts.

As a mandatory condition of copyright protection under the law in effect before 1978, all published copies of a work were required to bear a copyright notice. The 1976 Act provides for a notice on published copies, but omission or errors will not immediately result in forfeiture of the copyright, and can be corrected within certain time limits. Innocent infringers misled by the omission or error may be shielded from liability.

In accordance with the Berne agreement, mandatory notice of copyright has been abolished for works published for the first time on or after March 1, 1989. Failure to place a notice of copyright on copies or phonorecords of such works can no longer result in the loss of copyright.

Voluntary use of notice is encouraged. Placing a notice of copyright on published works is still strongly recommended. One of the benefits is that an infringer will not be able to claim that he or she "innocently infringed" a work. (A successful innocent infringement claim may result in a reduction in damages for infringement that the copyright owner would otherwise receive.)

A sample notice of copyright is: © 1991 John Brown.

The notice requirement for works incorporating a predominant portion of U.S. government work has been eliminated as of March 1, 1989. For these works to receive the evidentiary benefit of voluntary notice, in addition to the notice, a statement is required on the copies identifying what is copyrighted.

A sample is: © 1991 Jane Brown. Copyright claimed in Chapters 7–10, exclusive of U.S. government maps.

Notice Unchanged for Works Published Before March 1, 1989

The Berne Convention Implementation Act is not retroactive. Thus, the notice requirements that were in place before March 1, 1989, govern all works first published during that period (regardless of national origin).

• Works first published between January 1, 1978, and February 28, 1989: If a work was first published without notice during this period, it is still necessary to register the work before or within five years after publication and add the notice to copies distributed in the United States after discovery of the omission.

• Works first published before January 1, 1978: If a work was first published without the required notice before 1978, copyright was lost immediately (with the possible exception of works seeking "ad interim" protection). Once copyright is lost, it can never be restored in the United States, except by special legislation.

Registration in the Copyright Office is not a condition of copyright protection but will be a prerequisite to bringing an action in a court of law for infringement. With certain exceptions, the remedies of statutory damages and attorney's fees will not be available for infringements occurring before registration. Most copies or phonorecords published in the United States with notice of copyright are required to be deposited for the collections of the Library of Congress, not as a condition of copyright protection, but under provisions of the law subjecting the copyright owner to certain penalties for failure to deposit after a demand by the Register of Copyrights. Registration is permissive, but may be made either at the time the depository requirements are satisfied or at any other time during the subsistence of the copyright.

For works already under statutory protection, the new law retains the present term of copyright of 28 years from first publication (or from registration in some cases), renewable by certain persons for a second period of protection, but it increases the length of the second period to 47 years. Copyrights in their first term on January 1, 1978, must still be renewed during the last (28th) year of the original copyright term to receive the maximum statutory term of 75 years (a first term of 28 years plus a renewal term of 47 years).

Copyrights in their second term on January 1, 1978, are automatically extended up to a maximum of 75 years. Unpublished works that are already in existence on January 1, 1978, but are not protected by statutory copyright and have not yet gone into the public domain, will generally obtain automatic Federal copyright protection for the author's life, plus an additional 50 years after the author's death, but in any event, for a minimal term of 25 years (that is, until December 31, 2002), and if the work is published before that date, then for an additional term of 25 years, through the end of 2027.

For works created on or after January 1, 1978, the new law provides a term lasting for the author's life, plus an additional 50 years after the author's death. For works made for hire, and for anonymous and pseudonymous works (unless the author's identity is revealed in Copyright Office records), the new term will be 75 years from publication or 100 years from creation, whichever is shorter. The new law provides that all terms of copyright will run through the end of the calendar year in which they would otherwise expire. This will not only affect the duration of copyrights, but also the time-limits for renewal registrations.

Works already in the public domain cannot be protected under the new law. The 1976 Act provides no procedure for restoring protection to works in which copyright has been lost for any reason. In general, works published before January 1, 1916, are not under copyright protection in the United States, at least insofar as any version published before that date is concerned.

The new law requires that all visually perceptible copies published in the United States or elsewhere bear a notice of copyright affixed in such manner and location as to give reasonable notice of the claim of copyright. (Abolished in or after March 1, 1989, according to the Berne agreement) The notice consists of the symbol © (the letter C in a circle), the word "Copyright," or the abbreviation "Copr.," and the year of first publication of the work, and the name of the owner of copyright in the work. EXAMPLE: © *1991 John Doe.*

The notice of copyright prescribed for sound recordings consists of the symbol ℗ (the letter P in a circle), the year of first publication of the sound recording, and the name of the owner of copyright in the sound recording, placed on the surface of the phonorecord, or on the phonorecord label or container, in such manner and location as to give reasonable notice of the claim of copyright. EXAMPLE: ℗ *1991 Doe Records, Inc.*

According to the Berne Agreement, copyright owners must deposit in the Copyright Office two complete copies or phonorecords of the best edition of all works subject to copyright that are publicly distributed in the United States, whether or not the work contains a notice of copyright. In general, this deposit requirement may be satisfied by registration. For more information about mandatory deposit, request Circular 7d.

Renewal Is Still Required

Works first federally copyrighted before 1978 must still be renewed in the 28th year in order to receive the second term of 47 years. If such a work is not timely renewed, it will fall into the public domain in the United States at the end of the 28th year.

Recordation

Recordation as a Prerequisite to an Infringement Suit. The copyright owner no longer has to record a transfer before bringing a copyright lawsuit in that owner's name.

Benefits of recordation. The benefits of recordation in the Copyright Office are unchanged:

- Under certain conditions, recordation establishes priorities between conflicting transfers and nonexclusive licenses;
- Under certain conditions, recordation establishes priority between conflicting transfers; and,
- Recordation establishes a public record of the contents of the transfer or document.

Jukebox Licenses

Section 116 of the 1976 Copyright Act provides for a compulsory license to publicly perform nondramatic musical works by means of coin-operated phonorecord players (jukeboxes). The Berne Convention Implementation Act amends the law to provide for negotiated licenses between the user (the jukebox operator) and the copyright owner. If necessary, the parties are encouraged to submit to arbitration to facilitate negotiated licenses. Such licenses take precedence over the compulsory license.

For detailed information about the admendments to U.S. copyright law under the Berne Convention agreement, request circulars 93, "Highlights of U.S. Adherence to the Berne Convention," and 93a, "The United States Joins The Berne Union" from the Copyright Office.

For publications, call the Forms and Publications Hotline, 202-707-9100, or write:

Copyright Office
Publications Section, LM-455
Library of Congress
Washington, D.C. 20559

To speak with an information specialist or to request further information, call 202-479-0700, or write:

Copyright Office
Information Section, LM-401
Library of Congress
Washington, D.C. 20559

Counterfeit Products

Source: U.S. Office of Consumer Affairs.

Counterfeit products include any product bearing an unauthorized representation of a manufacturer's trademark or trade name. Examples of products which have been counterfeited include prescription and over-the-counter drugs, clothing, credit cards, watches, pacemakers, and machine and automobile replacement parts. Because counterfeit products are often of sub-standard quality, there are potential safety risks which may cause personal injury as well as economic loss.

Avoiding counterfeit products takes practice. The following are usually associated with counterfeit products:

- incorrect, smeared or blurred product packaging
- incorrect spelling of brand name
- no warranty or guarantee available
- "unbelievably" low prices

Unemployment Insurance

Unemployment insurance is managed jointly by the states and the federal government. Most states began paying benefits in 1938 and 1939.

Under What Conditions Can the Worker Collect?

The laws vary from state to state. In general, a waiting period of one week is required after a claim is filed before collecting unemployment insurance; the worker must be able to work, must not have quit without good cause or have been discharged for misconduct; he must not be involved in a labor dispute; above all, he must be ready and willing to work. He may be disqualified if he refuses, without good cause, to accept a job which is suitable for him in terms of his qualifications and experience, unless the wages, hours and working conditions offered are substantially less favorable than those prevailing for similar jobs in the community.

The unemployed worker must go to the local state employment security office and register for work. If that office has a suitable opening available, he must accept it or lose his unemployment payments, unless he has good cause for the refusal. If a worker moves out of his own state, he can still collect at his new residence; the state in which he is now located will act as agent for the other state, which will pay his benefits.

Benefits are paid only to unemployed workers who have had at least a certain amount of recent past employment or earnings in a job covered by the state law. The amount of employment or earnings, and the period used to measure them, vary from state to state, but the intent of the various laws is to limit benefits to workers whose recent records indicate that they are members of the labor force. The amount of benefits an unemployed worker may receive for any week is also determined by application to his past wages of a formula specified in the law. The general objective is to provide a weekly benefit which is about half the worker's customary weekly wages, up to a maximum set by the law (see table). In a majority of states, the total benefits a worker may receive in a 12-month period is limited to a fraction of his total wages in a prior 12-month period, as well as to a stated number of weeks. Thus, not all workers in a state are entitled to benefits for the number of weeks shown in the table.

Who Pays for the Insurance?

The total cost is borne by the employer in all but a few states. Each state has a sliding scale of rates. The standard rate is set at 6.2% of taxable payroll in most states. But employers with records of less unemployment (that is, with fewer unemployment benefits paid to their former workers) are rewarded with rates lower than the standard state rate.

During periods of high unemployment in a state, federal-state extended benefits are available to workers who have exhausted their regular benefits. An unemployed worker may receive benefits equal to the weekly benefit he received under the state program for one half the weeks of his basic entitlement to benefits up to a maximum (including regular benefits) of 39 weeks.

Federal Programs

Amendments to the Social Security Act provided unemployment insurance for Federal civilian employees (1954) and for ex-servicemen (1958). Benefits under these programs are paid by state employment security agencies as agents of the federal government under agreements with the Secretary of Labor. For federal civilian employees, eligibility for benefits and the amount of benefits paid are determined according to the terms and conditions of the applicable state unemployment insurance law. Ex-servicemen are subject to specific eligibility and benefit payment provisions: benefits are not payable before the fifth week subsequent to the week of release or discharge from service and such benefits are limited to 13 weeks of duration.

State Unemployment Compensation Maximums, 1991

State	Weekly benefit[1]	Maximum duration, weeks	State	Weekly benefit[1]	Maximum duration, weeks
Alabama	150	26	Nebraska	144	26
Alaska	212–284	26	Nevada	202	26
Arizona	165	26	New Hampshire	168	26
Arkansas	220	26	New Jersey	291	26
California	210	26	New Mexico	177	26
Colorado	229	26	New York	260	26
Connecticut	270–320	26	North Carolina	245	26
Delaware	225	26	North Dakota	198	26
D.C.	293	26	Ohio	196–291	26
Florida	225	26	Oklahoma	197	26
Georgia	185	26	Oregon	247	26
Hawaii	275	26	Pennsylvania	291–299	26
Idaho	206	26	Puerto Rico	120	20
Illinois	206–270	26	Rhode Island	269–336	26
Indiana	96–161	26	South Carolina	175	26
Iowa	186–228	26	South Dakota	154	26
Kansas	222	26	Tennessee	165	26
Kentucky	199	26	Texas	224	26
Louisiana	181	26	Utah	221	26
Maine	188–282	26	Vermont	182	26
Maryland	215	26	Virgin Islands	191	26
Massachusetts	282–423	30	Virginia	198	26
Michigan	276	26	Washington	246	30
Minnesota	260	26	West Virginia	251	26
Mississippi	145	26	Wisconsin	225	26
Missouri	170	26	Wyoming	200	26
Montana	193	26			

1. Maximum amounts. When two amounts are shown, higher includes dependents' allowances. *Source:* Department of Labor, Employment and Training Administration.

Employment and Unemployment
(in millions of persons)

Category	1991[2]	1990	1989	1985	1980	1975	1970	1950	1945	1932	1929
EMPLOYMENT STATUS[1]											
Civilian noninstitutional population	189.4	188.0	186.4	178.2	167.7	153.2	137.1	105.0	94.1	—	—
Civilian labor force	125.7	124.8	123.9	115.5	106.9	93.8	82.8	62.2	53.9	—	—
Civilian labor force participation rate	66.4	66.4	66.5	64.8	63.8	61.2	60.4	59.2	57.2	—	—
Employed	117.4	117.9	117.3	107.2	99.3	85.8	78.7	58.9	52.8	38.9	47.6
Employment-population ratio	62.0	62.7	63.0	60.1	59.2	56.1	57.4	56.1	56.1	—	—
Agriculture	3.2	3.2	3.2	3.2	3.4	3.4	3.5	7.2	8.6	10.2	10.5
Nonagricultural industries	114.2	114.7	14.1	104.0	95.9	82.4	75.2	51.8	44.2	28.8	37.2
Unemployed	8.3	6.9	6.5	8.3	7.6	7.9	4.1	3.3	1.0	12.1	1.6
Unemployment rate	6.6	5.5	5.3	7.2	7.1	8.5	4.9	5.3	1.9	23.6	3.2
Not in labor force	63.7	63.3	62.5	62.7	60.8	59.4	54.3	42.8	40.2	—	—
INDUSTRY											
Total nonagricultural employment	108.7	110.0	108.3	97.5	90.4	76.9	70.9	45.2	40.4	23.6	31.3
Goods-producing industries	23.8	25.0	25.3	24.9	25.7	22.6	23.6	18.5	17.5	8.6	13.3
Mining	0.7	0.7	0.7	0.9	1.0	0.8	0.6	0.9	0.8	0.7	1.1
Construction	4.7	5.1	5.2	4.7	4.3	3.5	3.6	2.4	1.1	1.0	1.5
Manufacturing: Durable goods	10.6	11.1	11.4	11.5	12.2	10.7	11.2	8.1	9.1	—	—
Nondurable goods	7.8	8.0	8.0	7.8	8.1	7.7	8.2	7.2	6.4	—	—
Services-producing industries	84.9	85.0	83.0	72.7	64.7	54.3	47.3	26.7	22.9	15.0	18.0
Transportation and public utilities	5.8	5.8	5.6	5.2	5.1	4.5	4.5	4.0	3.9	2.8	3.9
Trade, Wholesale	6.1	6.2	6.2	5.7	5.3	4.4	4.0	2.6	1.9	—	—
Retail	19.3	19.7	19.5	17.3	15.0	12.6	11.0	6.7	5.4	—	—
Finance, insurance, and real estate	6.7	6.7	6.7	6.0	5.2	4.2	3.6	1.9	1.5	1.3	1.5
Services	28.6	28.2	27.1	22.0	17.9	13.9	11.5	5.4	4.2	2.9	3.4
Federal government	3.0	3.1	3.0	2.9	2.9	2.7	2.7	1.9	2.8	0.6	0.5
State and local government	15.5	15.2	14.8	13.5	13.4	11.9	9.8	4.1	3.1	2.7	2.5

1. For 1929–45, figures on employment status relate to persons 14 years and over; beginning in 1950, 16 years and over.
2. As of April; seasonally adjusted. *Source:* Bureau of Labor Statistics.

Trademarks

Source: Department of Commerce, Patent and Trademark Office.

A trademark may be defined as a word, letter, device, or symbol, as well as some combination of these, which is used in connection with merchandise and which points distinctly to the origin of the goods.

Certificates of registration of trademarks are issued under the seal of the Patent and Trademark Office and may be registered by the owner if he is engaged in interstate or foreign commerce which may lawfully be regulated by Congress since any Federal jurisdiction over trademarks arises under the commerce clause of the Constitution. Effective November 16, 1989, applications to register may also be based on a "bona fide intention to use the mark in commerce." Trademarks may be registered by foreign owners who comply with our law, as well as by citizens of foreign countries with which the U.S. has treaties relating to trademarks. American citizens may register trademarks in foreign countries by complying with the laws of those countries. The right to registration and protection of trademarks in many foreign countries is guaranteed by treaties.

General jurisdiction in trademark cases involving Federal Registrations is given to Federal courts. Adverse decisions of examiners on applications for registration are appealable to the Trademark Trial and Appeal Board, whose affirmances, and decisions in *inter partes* proceedings, are subject to court review. Before adopting a trademark, a person should make a search of prior marks to avoid infringing unwittingly upon them.

The duration of a trademark registration is 10 years, but it may be renewed indefinitely for 10-year periods, provided the trademark is still in use at the time of expiration.

The application fee is $175.

Patents

Source: Department of Commerce, Patent and Trademark Office.

A patent, in the most general sense, is a document issued by a government, conferring some special right or privilege. The term is now restricted mainly to patents for inventions; occasionally, land patents.

The grant of a patent for an invention gives the inventor the privilege, for a limited period of time, of excluding others from making, using, or selling a certain article. However, it does not give him the right to make, use, or sell his own invention if it is an improvement on some unexpired patent whose claims are infringed thereby.

In the U.S., the law provides that a patent may be granted, for a term of 17 years, to any person who has invented or discovered any new and useful art, machine, manufacture, or composition of matter, as well as any new and useful improvements thereof. A patent may also be granted to a person who has invented or discovered and asexually reproduced a new and distinct variety of plant (other than a tuber-propagated one) or has invented a new, original and ornamental design for an article of manufacture.

A patent is granted only upon a regularly filed application, complete in all respects; upon payment of the fees; and upon determination that the disclosure is complete and that the invention is new, useful, and, in view of the prior art, unobvious to one skilled in the art. The disclosure must be of such nature as to enable others to reproduce the invention.

A complete application, which must be addressed to the Commissioner of Patents and Trademarks, Washington, D.C. 20231, consists of a specification with one or more claims; oath or declaration; drawing (whenever the nature of the case admits of it); and a basic filing fee of $315.[1] The filing fee is not returned to the applicant if the patent is refused. If the patent is allowed, another fee of $525[1] is required before the patent is issued. The fee for design patent application is $125; the issue fee is $185[1]. Maintenance fees are required on utility patents at stipulated intervals.

Applications are ordinarily considered in the order in which they are received. Patents are not granted for printed matter, for methods of doing business, or for devices for which claims contrary to natural laws are made. Applications for a perpetual-motion machine have been made from time to time, but until a working model is presented that actually fulfills the claim, no patent will be issued.

1. Fees quoted are for small entities. Fees are double for corporations.

Beware of Illegal Patent Services

It is illegal under patent law (35 USC 33) for anyone to hold himself out as qualified to prepare and prosecute patent applications unless he is registered with the Patent Office. Also, Patent Office regulations forbid registered practitioners advertising for patent business. Some inventors, unaware of this, enter into binding contracts with persons and firms which advertise their assistance in making patent searches, preparing drawings, specifications, and patent applications, only to discover much later that their applications require the services of fully qualified agents or attorneys.

State Consumer Protection Offices

Source: U.S. Office of Consumer Affairs.

State consumer protection offices resolve individual consumer complaints, conduct informational and educational programs, and enforce consumer protection and fraud laws. Most of these offices require complaints in writing. Call to find out the correct procedure for filing a complaint and what sales documents are needed. Phone numbers are subject to change.

Alabama
Montgomery (205) 261-7334
1 (800) 392-5658 (Alabama only)

Alaska
Anchorage (907) 279-0428
Fairbanks (907) 456-8588

Arizona
Phoenix (602) 542-3702 (fraud only)
1 (800) 352-8431 (Arizona only)

Arkansas
Little Rock (501) 682-2007
1 (800) 482-8982 (Arkansas only)

California
Sacramento-Consumer Affairs
(916) 445-0660 (complaint assistance)
(916) 445-1254 (consumer information)
(916) 322-3360 (Attorney General)
1 (800) 952-5225 (California only)
(916) 366-5100 (auto repairs)
1 (800) 952-5210 (California only—auto repairs)
Los Angeles (213) 974-1452

Colorado
Denver (303) 866-5167
(303) 866-3561 (agriculture)

Connecticut
Hartford (203) 566-4999
1 (800) 842-2649 (Connecticut only)

Delaware
Wilmington (302) 571-3250
(302) 571-3849 (economic crime)

District of Columbia
Washington, DC (202) 727-7000

Florida
Tallahassee (904) 488-2226
1 (800) 327-3382 (education)
Miami (305) 377-5619

Georgia
Atlanta (404) 656-7000
1 (800) 282-5808 (Georgia only)

Hawaii
Honolulu (808) 548-2560 (legal—Hawaii only)
(808) 548-2540 (complaints—Hawaii only)
Hilo (808) 961-7433
Lihue (808) 245-4365
Wailuku (808) 244-4387

Illinois
Springfield (217) 782-0244
1 (800) 642-3112 (Illinois only)
Chicago (312) 917-3580
(312) 917-3289 (citizens' rights)

Indiana
Indianapolis (317) 232-6330
1 (800) 382-5516 (Indiana only)

Iowa
Des Moines (515) 281-3592
1 (800) 358-5510 (Iowa only)
(515) 281-5926 (consumer protection)

Kansas
Topeka (913) 296-3751
1 (800) 432-2310 (Kansas only)

Kentucky
Frankfort (502) 564-2200
1 (800) 432-9257 (Kentucky only)

Louisiana
Baton Rouge (504) 342-7013
New Orleans (504) 568-5472

Maine
Augusta (207) 582-8718
(207) 289-3716 (9 a.m.-1 p.m.)
Portland (207) 797-8978 (1 p.m.-4 p.m.)

Maryland
Baltimore (301) 528-8662 (9 a.m.-2 p.m.)
Hagerstown (301) 791-4780
Glen Burnie (301) 768-7420
Salisbury (301) 543-6620

Massachusetts
Boston (617) 727-8400 (information & referral only)
(617) 727-7780 (information & referral only)
Springfield (413) 784-1240

Michigan
Lansing (517) 373-1140
(517) 373-0947 (Consumers Council)
(517) 373-7858 (automotive regulation)
1 (800) 292-4204 (Michigan only)

Minnesota
Duluth (218) 723-4891
St. Paul (612) 296-2331

Mississippi
Jackson (601) 354-6018
(601) 354-7063 (agriculture and commerce)
Biloxi (601) 436-6000

Missouri
Jefferson City (314) 751-4962
(314) 751-2616 (trade offenses)
1 (800) 392-8222 (Missouri only)

Montana
Helena (406) 444-4312

Nebraska
Lincoln (402) 471-4723

Nevada
Carson City (702) 885-4340
Las Vegas (702) 486-4150

New Hampshire
Concord (603) 271-3641

New Jersey
Newark (201) 648-4010 (consumer affairs)
(201) 648-4730 (Attorney General)
Trenton (609) 292-7087
1 (800) 792-8600 (New Jersey only)

New Mexico
Santa Fe (505) 872-6910
1 (800) 432-2070 (New Mexico only)

New York
Albany (518) 474-8583
(518) 474-5481
New York (212) 587-4908
(212) 341-2300

North Carolina
Raleigh (919) 733-7741

North Dakota
Bismarck (701) 224-2210
(701) 224-3404 (Consumer Fraud)
1 (800) 472-2600 (North Dakota only)

Ohio
Columbus (614) 466-4986
1 (800) 282-0515 (Ohio only)
(614) 466-9605 (Consumers' Counsel)
1 (800) 282-9448 (Ohio only)

Oklahoma
Oklahoma City (405) 521-3921
(405) 521-3653

Oregon
Salem (503) 378-4320

Pennsylvania
Allentown (215) 821-6690
Erie (814) 871-4371
Harrisburg (717) 787-9707
1 (800) 441-2555 (Pennsylvania only)
(717) 783-5048 (utilities only)
(717) 787-7109 (consumer protection)
Scranton (717) 963-4913
Philadelphia (215) 560-2414
Pittsburgh (412) 565-5135

Puerto Rico
Old San Juan (809) 721-2900
Santurce (809) 722-7555

Rhode Island
Providence (401) 277-2104
(401) 277-2764

South Carolina
Columbia (803) 734-3970 (fraud)
(803) 734-9452 (Consumer affairs)
1 (800) 922-1594 (South Carolina only)
(803) 734-0457 (State Ombudsman)

South Dakota
Pierre (605) 773-4400

Tennessee
Nashville (615) 741-2672 (consumer protection)

(615) 741-4737 (consumer affairs)
1 (800) 342-8385 (Tennessee only)

Texas
Austin (512) 463-2070
Dallas (214) 742-8944
El Paso (915) 772-9476
Houston (713) 223-5886
Lubbock (806) 747-5238
McAllen (512) 682-4547
San Antonio (512) 225-4191

Utah
Salt Lake City (801) 530-6601
(801) 538-1331 (consumer affairs)

Vermont
Montpelier (802) 828-3171
(802) 828-2436 (agriculture)

Virgin Islands
St. Thomas (809) 774-3130

Virginia
Richmond (804) 786-2116
(804) 786-2042 (agriculture)
1 (800) 552-9963 (Virginia only)

Washington
Olympia (206) 753-6210
Seattle (206) 464-7744
1 (800) 551-4636 (Washington only)
Spokane (509) 456-3123
Tacoma (206) 593-2904

West Virginia
Charleston (304) 348-8986
1 (800) 368-8808 (West Virginia only)

(304) 348-7890

Wisconsin
Altoona (715) 839-3848
Green Bay (414) 436-4087 (agriculture)
Milwaukee (414) 257-8956 (agriculture)
(414) 227-4948
Madison (608) 266-1852 (Consumer protection)
1 (800) 362-8189 (Wisconsin only)
(608) 266-9836 (agriculture)
1 (800) 362-3020 (Wisconsin only)

Wyoming
Cheyenne (307) 777-7841, 6286

How to Write a Complaint Letter

Source: United States Office of Consumer Affairs.

• Include your name, address, and home and work phone numbers.
• Type your letter if possible. If it is handwritten, make sure it is neat and easy to read.
• Make your letter brief and to the point. Include all important facts about your purchase, including the date and place where you made the purchase and any information you can give about the product or service such as serial or model numbers or specific type of service.

• State exactly what you want done about the problem and how long you are willing to wait to get it resolved. Be reasonable.
• Include all documents regarding your problem. Be sure to send COPIES, not originals.
• Avoid writing an angry, sarcastic, or threatening letter. The person reading your letter probably was not responsible for your problem, but may be very helpful in resolving it.
• Keep a copy of the letter for your records.

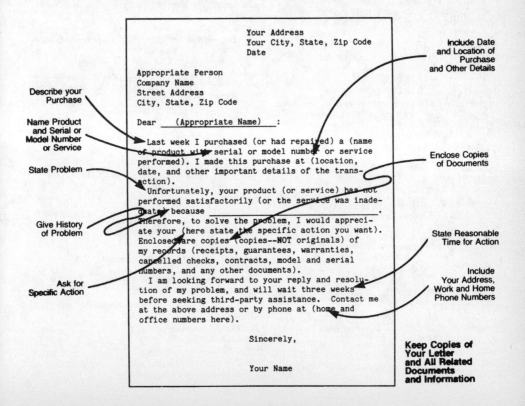

Toll-Free Numbers

Please note that the numbers and services listed are subject to change.

AIDS
National AIDS Hotline
U.S. Public Health Service
1-800-342-2437
Hours: 24 hours, 7 days
SIDA (Spanish line) 1-800-344-7432
8 a.m.–2 a.m. EST
TTY (hearing impaired) 1-800-243-7889
10 a.m.–10 p.m. EST

Provides the latest information to the public about Acquired Immune Deficiency Syndrome (AIDS).

AIDS Drugs Hotline
National Institute of Allergies and Infectious Diseases
1-800-874-2572
Hours: 9 a.m.–7 p.m., Mon.-Fri.

Callers learn the status of research and how to get into a government-sponsored clinical trial.

AUTOMOBILE
Auto Safety Hotline
National Highway Traffic Safety Administration
202-366-0123 (Washington, D.C.)
1-800-424-9393 (Elsewhere)
Hours: 8:00–4:00, EST Mon.–Fri.
Answering service after hours

Handles complaints on safety-related defects, and receives reports of vehicle safety problems. Provides information and in some cases literature on:
•motor vehicle safety recalls •car seats •automobile equipment •tires •motor homes •drunk driving •gas mileage

BANKING
Federal Deposit Insurance Corporation
202-898-3536 (Washington, D.C.)
1-800-424-5488 (Elsewhere)
Hours: 9:00–4:00, EST Mon.–Fri.

Provides general banking information on consumer banking laws. Will refer consumer to proper regulatory agency that supervises institution complaint is being filed against.

BOATING SAFETY HOTLINE
U.S. Coast Guard
1-800-368-5647
1-202-267-0973, 0780 (Washington, D.C.)
Hours: 8:00–4:00 EST Mon.-Fri.

Provides information on boats, safe boating, and associated equipment involved in safety defect (recall) campaigns for past five model years. Takes complaints about possible safety defects. Cannot resolve non-safety problems between consumer and manufacturer and cannot recommend or endorse specific boats or products.

BLIND
National Federation of the Blind
1-800-638-7518, 8-5 EST, Mon.-Fri.
1-301-659-9314 (Maryland)

Provides job information. Concerned about the rights of the blind. Free package of information about blindness.

CHEMICALS
Chemical Referral Center

1-800-262-8200
1-202-887-1315 (Washington, D.C.)
Hours: 9:00-6:00, EST, Mon.-Fri.

Refers callers to health and safety contacts at chemical manufacturers.

CHILD ABUSE
Parents Anonymous
1-800-352-0386 (California)—machine on 24 hours—can leave message
1-800-421-0353 (Elsewhere) provides referrals for all states
Hours: 8:30–5:00 Mon.–Fri., PST

CIVICS
National Civic League
1-800-223-6004
303-571-4343 in Colorado
Hours: 8 A.M.—5 P.M. MST, Mon.-Fri.

Nonprofit organization that seeks to improve state and local governments.

CIVIL RIGHTS
Civil Rights Complaint Hotline
1-800-368-1019
Answering machine

Accepts complaints regarding discrimination on the basis of race, color, national origin, handicap, or age occurring in Health and Human Services programs, i.e. in admission to hospitals, nursing homes, day care centers, or federally funded state health care assistance.

EDUCATION
U.S. Department of Education's Inspector General's Office
1-800-MIS-USED

This number is to report suspected fraud, waste, or abuse involving Federal student aid funds. Callers may remain anonymous.

1-800-433-3243

For complaints on procedure a school is using to distribute financial aid.

DEPARTMENT OF DEFENSE
1-800-424-9098 (Washington, D.C.)
223-5080 (Autovon Line)
693-5080 (FTS)
Hours: 8:00–4:30, EST

Operated for citizens to report suspected cases of fraud and waste involving the Department of Defense. The anonymity of callers will be respected.

DRUG ABUSE
National Institute on Drug Abuse
1-800-662-HELP
Hours: 9:00–3:00 (Monday to Friday), 12:00-3:00 (Saturday & Sunday).

Provides information on drug abuse, and treatment referrals.

National Cocaine Hotline
1-800-COCAINE
Hours: 24 hours—7days

Provides information on cocaine and drug-related problems for cocaine abusers.

ALCOHOLISM
National Council on Alcoholism and Drug Dependence Helpline
1-800-622-2255
Hours: 24 hours—7 days

The National Council on Alcoholism, Inc. (NCA), is a national nonprofit organization that combats alcoholism, other drug addictions, and related problems. The council provides an automated referral service for affiliate offices and will mail information. All names and addresses are kept confidential.

Mothers Against Drunk Driving (MADD)
1-800-438-6233
Hours: 24-hours (Business hours: 8 A.M.—5 P.M. Central Time, Mon.-Fri.)
In New York state, call 1-800-245-6233 8:30—5 P.M.

Provides counseling, victim hotline, and nearest chapter referrals. Sends free literature.

"Just Say No Clubs" Hotline (Drug Abuse)
"Just Say No" International
1-800-258-2766
Hours: 8:00 A.M.—5:00 P.M., PCT, Mon.-Fri.

These nationwide clubs provide support and positive peer reinforcement to youngsters through workshops, seminars, newsletters, walk-a-thons, and a variety of other activities. Clubs are organized by schools, communities, and parent groups.

ELECTIONS
Federal Election Commission
Clearinghouse on Election Administration
1-800-424-9530
202-376-3120 (Wash. D.C., Alaska, and Hawaii)
Hours: 8:30—5:30, EST Mon.-Fri.

Provides information on campaign financing.

ENERGY
Conservation and Renewable Energy Inquiry and Referral Service
1-800-523-2929
Hours: 9:00–5:00, EST Mon.–Fri.

Provides non-technical information on solar, wind, and other energy heating and cooling technologies, energy conservation, and alcohol fuels.

ENVIRONMENT
Hazardous Waste
RCRA Superfund Hotline
Environmental Protection Agency
202-382-3000 (Washington, D.C.)
1-800-424-9346 (Elsewhere)
Hours: 8:30–7:30, EST Mon.–Fri.

Provides information and interpretation of federal hazardous waste regulations. Will provide referrals regarding other hazardous waste matters.

Pesticide Hotline
National Pesticide Telecommunications Network
1-800-858-7378
Hours: 24 hours—7 days

Provides information on health hazards, cleanup and disposal of pesticides. Will refer callers to human and animal poison control centers in their states if necessary.

FOOD
The Meat and Poultry Hotline
U.S. Department of Agriculture
1-800-535-4555
202-447-3333 in Washington, D.C.

Hours: 10 A.M.—4 P.M. EST, Mon.-Fri.

Provides information on proper handling, preparation, storing, and cooking of meat, poultry, and eggs. Answers questions about the safe cooking of poultry and meat in microwave ovens.

HEALTH CARE
ALZHEIMER'S DISEASE
Alzheimer's Disease and Related Disorders Association, Inc.
1-800-621-0379
1-800-572-6037 (Illinois)
Hours: 8 a.m.–5:30 p.m., M–F CST

Information and referral service. Provides support for patients and their families, aids research efforts, etc.

Cancer Information Service
National Cancer Institute
National Institutes of Health
Department of Health & Human Services
1-800-638-6694 (National)
1-800-4-Cancer (State)
Hours: 9:00 A.M.–10:00 P.M., EST Mon.–Fri.

Provides information on cancer, prevention, treatment and ongoing research; fills requests for pamphlets and other literature on cancer.

National Health Information Center
Department of Health & Human Services
301-565-4167 (Maryland)
1-800-336-4797 (Elsewhere)
Hours: 9:00–5:00 EST Mon.–Fri.

Provides referrals to sources of information on health-related issues.

Sexually Transmitted Diseases (STDs)
National STD Hotline
Operated by The American Social Health Association
1-800-227-8922
Hours: 8 A.M.—11 P.M. EST Mon.-Fri.

Provides latest information about STDs (sometimes called VD) and where to get confidential, free treatment in your area.

HOUSING
Fair Housing Discrimination Hotline
Fair Housing and Equal Opportunity
Department of Housing and Urban Development
202-708-3500 (Washington, D.C.)
1-800-669-9777 (Elsewhere)
Hours: 8:45—5:15, EST Mon.—Fri.

Receives housing discrimination complaints due to race, color, religion, sex, familial status, handicap, or national origin.

INSURANCE
Federal Crime Insurance
Federal Emergency Management Administration
1-800-638-8780 (National Number)
Hours: 8:30–5:00, EST Mon.–Fri.
Answering service after hours.

Provides information on federal crime insurance for both homes and businesses which have been robbed or burglarized.

National Insurance Consumer Helpline
Sponsored by insurance industry trade associations
1-800-942-4242
Hours: 8:00–8:00 EST Mon.–Fri.

Trained personnel provide answers on a wide range of questions about various insurance matters, are able to refer consumer complaints to appropriate sources, and send consumer brochures upon reqeust.

National Flood Insurance
1-800-492-6605 (Maryland)
1-800-638-6831 (Alaska, Hawaii, Puerto Rico, Virgin Islands, Guam)
1-800-638-6620 (Elsewhere)
Hours: 8:00–8:00, EST Mon.–Fri.

Provides information on community participation in the flood program (emergency or regular). If the community does not have a program, it is not eligible for government-subsidized insurance relief. Complaints are referred to the proper office within the agency.

PREGNANCY
Pro-Choice
Abortion Hotline
National Abortion Federation
1-800-772-9100
Hours: 9:30 A.M.—5:30 P.M. EST, Mon.-Fri.

Provides facts about abortion, counseling, and referrals to member clinics.

Right-To-Life
Birthright, Inc. (U.S.A.)
1-800-848-LOVE
1-800-328-LOVE in Canada
Hours: 8 A.M.—3 A.M., EST 7-days

Birthright, Inc. provides alternative advice to abortion. Operates crisis centers, and provides help such as pregnancy testing, housing, medical care, and adoption referral.

PRODUCT SAFETY
Consumer Product Safety Commission
1-800-638-2772
Hours: 10:30–4:00, EST Mon.–Fri.

Provides recorded information on the safety of consumer products. Receives reports of product-related deaths, illnesses, and injuries. Products are not rated or recommended.

RUNAWAYS
Runaway Hotline
1-800-231-6946 (U.S.A. except Texas)
1-800-392-3352 (Texas)
Hours: 24 hours, 7 days

Helps runaways by referring them to shelters, clinics, local hotlines. Will relay messages from the runaway to the parent.

SOCIAL SECURITY AND MEDICARE FRAUD
Inspector General's Hotline
Department of Health and Human Services
1-800-368-5779
Hours: 10:00–4:00, EST Mon.-Fri.

Takes calls on fraud in Social Security payments or abuse, Medicaid and Medicare fraud and other HHS programs. Recording machine after hours.

1-800-234-5772
Hours: 9:00–4:30, EST Mon–Fri.

Provides Social Security information.

VIETNAM VETERANS
Vietnam Veterans of America
1-800-424-7275 (answering machine)
202-332-2700 (Washington, D.C.)
Hours: 9:00–5:30, EST Mon.-Fri.

Answering machine takes messages for information and help. Provides information on Agent Orange, post-traumatic stress disorder, and other matters. Will answer questions on direct line.

Veterans of the Vietnam War, Inc.
1-800-VIETNAM
1-800-NAM-9090 (Pennsylvania)
Hours: 8 a.m.–6 p.m., Mon.-Fri., service after hours.

Provides information on filing claims against the Agent Orange Settlement, filing claims for veterans benefits with the VA, how to take the VA to court, and information on MIAs and POWs. Veterans newsletter is available, also provides Veterans location services.

Tips For Shopping by Mail, Telephone, or Television

Source: Consumer's Resource Handbook, United States Office of Consumer Affairs.

Be suspicious of exaggerated product claims or very low prices, and read product descriptions carefully—sometimes pictures of products are misleading. If you have any doubt about the company, check with the U.S. Postal Service, your state or local consumer protection agency, or Better Business Bureau before ordering.

Ask about the firm's return policy. If it is not stated, ask before you order. For example, does the company pay charges for shipping and return? Is a warranty or guarantee available? Does the company sometimes substitute comparable goods for the product you want to order?

Keep a record of your order, including the company's name, address, and telephone number, the price of the items ordered, any handling or other charges, the date you mailed (or telephoned) in the order, and your method of payment. Keep copies of canceled checks and/or statements.

If you order by mail, your order should be shipped within 30 days after the company receives your complete order, unless another period is agreed upon when placing the order or is stated in an advertisement. If your order is delayed, a notice of delay should be sent to you within the promised shipping period along with an option to cancel the order.

If you buy a product through a television shopping program, check the cost of the same item sold by other sources, including local stores, catalogs, etc.

If you want to buy a product based on a telephone call from the company, ask for the name, address, and phone number where you can reach the caller after considering the offer. Never give your credit card or social security number over the telephone as proof of your identity.

Postal regulations allow you to write a check payable to the sender, rather than the delivery company, for cash on delivery (C.O.D.) orders. If, after examining the merchandise, you feel there has been a misrepresentation or fraud, you can stop payment on the check and file a complaint with the U.S. Postal Inspector's Office.

You can have a charge removed from your bill if you did not receive the goods or services or if your order was obtained through misrepresentation or fraud. You must notify the credit card company in writing, at the billing/inquiries/disputes address, within 60 days after the charge first appeared on your bill. □

U.S. Societies & Associations

Source: Questionnaires to organizations. Names are listed alphabetically according to key word in title; figure in parentheses is year of founding; other figure is membership. An asterisk (*) before a name indicates that up-to-date information has not been provided.

The following is a partial list selected for general readership interest. A comprehensive listing of approximately 20,000 national and international organizations can be found in the **"Encyclopedia of Associations,"** 20th Ed., 1986, Vol. I, Parts 1-3 (Katherine Gruber, Editor; Iris Cloyd, Research Editor), published by Gale Research Company, Book Tower, Detroit, Mich. 48226, available in most public libraries.

Abortion Federation, National (1977): 1436 U St. N.W., Suite 103, Washington, D.C., 20009. Phone: (202) 667-5881.

Abortion Rights Action League, National (1969): 1101 14th St. N.W., Washington, D.C. 20005. 400,000. Phone: (202) 408-4600.

Accountants, American Institute of Certified Public (1887): 1211 Avenue of the Americas, New York, N.Y. 10036. 304,000. Phone: (212) 575-6200.

Accountants, National Association of (1919): 10 Paragon Dr., Montvale, N.J., 07645-1760. Phone: (201) 573-9000.

Acoustical Society of America (1929): 500 Sunnyside Blvd., Woodbury, N.Y. 11797. 6,700. Phone: (516) 349-7800.

ACSM: American Congress on Surveying and Mapping (1941): 5410 Grosvenor Lane, Bethesda, Md. 20814. 10,000. Phone: (301) 493-0200.

Actors' Equity Association (1913): 165 W. 46th St., New York, N.Y. 10036. Phone: (212) 869-8530.

Actuaries, Society of (1949): 475 N. Martingale Rd., Suite 800, Schaumburg, Ill. 60173-2226. 13,000. Phone: (708) 706-3500.

Adirondack Mountain Club (1922): RD 3, Box 3055, Luzerne Rd., Lake George, N.Y. 12845. 17,000. Phone: (518) 668-4447.

Aeronautic Association, National (1905): 1815 N. Fort Myer Dr., Arlington, Va. 22209. 300,000. Phone: (703) 527-0226.

Aeronautics and Astronautics, American Institute of (1932): The Aerospace Center, 370 L'Enfant Promenade S.W., Washington, D.C. 20024. 40,000+. Phone: (202) 646-7400.

Aerospace Industries Association of America (1919): 1250 Eye St. N.W., Washington, D.C. 20005. 55 companies. Phone: (202) 371-8400.

Aerospace Medical Association (1929): 320 S. Henry St., Alexandria, Va. 22314-3524. 4,350. Phone: (703) 739-2240.

African-American Institute, The (1953): 833 United Nations Plaza, New York, N.Y. 10017. Phone: (212) 949-5666.

AFS Intercultural Programs (American Field Service) (1947): 313 E. 43rd St., New York, N.Y. 10017. 100,000. Phone: (212) 949-4242 or (800) AFS-INFO.

Aging Association, American (1970): 600 S. 42nd St., Omaha, Neb. 68198-4635. 500. Phone: (402) 559-4416.

Agricultural Engineers, American Society of (1907): 2950 Niles Rd., St. Joseph, Mich. 49085. 12,000. Phone: (616) 429-0300.

Agricultural History Society (1919): 1301 New York Ave. N.W., Washington, D.C. 20005-4788. 1,400. Phone: (202) 219-0787.

Agronomy, American Society of (1907): 677 S. Segoe Rd., Madison, Wis. 53711-1086. 13,000. Phone: (608) 273-8080.

Air & Waste Management Association (1907): P.O. Box 2861, Pittsburgh, Pa. 15230. 11,000. Phone: (412) 232-3444.

Aircraft Association, Experimental (1953): 3000 Poberezny Rd., Oshkosh, Wis. 54903-3086. 125,000. Phone: (414) 426-4800.

Aircraft Owners and Pilots Association (1939): 421 Aviation Way, Frederick, Md. 21701-4798. 300,000. Phone: (301) 695-2000.

Air Force Association (1946): 1501 Lee Highway, Arlington, Va., 22209-1198. 194,000. Phone: (703) 247-5800.

Air Line Pilots Association (1931): 1625 Massachusetts Ave. N.W., Washington, D.C. 20036 and 535 Herndon Pkwy., Herndon, Va. 22070. 43,000. Phone: (703) 689-2270.

Air Transport Association of America (1936): 1709 New York Ave. N.W., Washington, D.C. 20006. 21 airlines. Phone: (202) 626-4000.

Al-Anon Family Group Headquarters, Inc. For families and friends of alcoholics. (1951): P.O. Box 862, Midtown Station, New York, N.Y. 10018-0862. 31,000 groups worldwide. Phone: (800) 356-9996.

Alateen. For children of alcoholics: P.O. Box 862, Midtown Station, New York, N.Y. 10018-0862. 3,500 groups worldwide. Phone: 1 (800) 356-9996.

Alcoholics Anonymous (1935): P.O. Box 459, Grand Central Station, New York, N.Y. 10163. 1,800,000. Address communications to General Service Office. Phone: (212) 686-1100.

Alcoholism, and Drug Dependence, National Council on (1944): 12 W. 21st St., New York, N.Y. 10010. 200 affiliates. Phone: (212) 206-6770.

Alcohol Problems, American Council on (1895): 3426 Bridgeland Dr., Bridgeton, Mo. 63044. 3,500. Phone: (314) 739-5944.

Alexander Graham Bell Association for the Deaf (1890): 3417 Volta Place N.W., Washington, D.C. 20007. 6,000. Phone: (202) 337-5220.

Allergy and Immunology, American Academy of (1943): 611 E. Wells St., Milwaukee, Wis. 53202. 4,200. Phone: (414) 272-6071.

Alzheimer's Disease and Related Disorders Association, Inc. (1980): 70 E. Lake St., Suite 600, Chicago, Ill. 60601-5997. More than 200 Chapters and Affiliates, over 1,600 Family Support Groups. Toll-free information: (800) 621-0379; in Illinois: (800) 572-6037.

American Federation of Labor and Congress of Industrial Organizations (AFL-CIO) (1955): 815 16th St. N.W., Washington, D.C. 20006. 14,100,000. Phone: (202) 637-5010.

American Film and Video Association (formerly Educational Film Library Assn.) (1943): 920 Barnsdale Rd., Suite 152, La Grange Park, Ill. 60525. 1,400. Phone: (708) 482-4000.

American Foundrymen's Society, Inc. (1896): 505 State St., Des Plaines, Ill. 60016-8399. 14,000. Phone: (708) 824-0181.

American Friends Service Committee (1917): 1501 Cherry St., Philadelphia, Pa. 19102-1479. Phone: (215) 241-7000.

American Historical Association (1884): 400 A St. S.E., Washington, D.C. 20003. 19,000. Phone: (202) 544-2422.

American Indian Affairs, Association on (1923): 245 Fifth Ave., New York, N.Y. 10016. 35,000. Phone: (212) 689-8720.

American Legion, The (1919): P.O. Box 1055, Indianapolis, Ind. 46206. 2,900,000. Phone: (317) 635-8411.

American Legion Auxiliary (1919): 777 N. Meridian St., Indianapolis, Ind. 46204. 963,483. Phone: (317) 635-6291.

American Mensa, Ltd. (1960): 2626 E. 14th St., Brooklyn, N.Y. 11235-3992. 55,000. Phone: (718) 934-3700.

American Montessori Society (1960): 150 Fifth Ave., New York, N.Y. 10011. 12,000. Phone: (212) 924-3209.

American Philosophical Society (1743): 104 S. 5th St., Philadelphia, Pa. 19106-3387. 682. Phone: (215) 440-3400.

American Planning Association (1909): 1776 Massachusetts Ave. N.W., Washington, D.C. 20036 (headquarters). 26,000. Phone: (202) 872-0611. Membership office: 1313 E. 60th St., Chicago, Ill. 60637. Phone: (312) 955-9100.

Americans for Democratic Action, Inc. (1947): 1511 K St. N.W., Suite 941, Washington, D.C. 20005. 40,000. Phone: (202) 638-6447.

American Society for Public Administration (ASPA) (1939): 1120 G St. N.W., Suite 500, Washington, D.C. 20005. 16,000. Phone: (202) 393-7878.

American Society of CLU & ChFC (1928): 270 Bryn Mawr Ave., Bryn Mawr, Pa. 19010-2195. Phone: (215) 526-2500.

American Universities, Association of (1900): One Dupont Circle N.W., Suite 730, Washington, D.C. 20036. Phone: (202) 466-5030.

AMIDEAST (America-Mideast Educational and Training Services) (1951): 1100 17th St. N.W., Washington, D.C. 20036-4601. 217 institutional members. Phone: (202) 785-0022.

Amnesty International/USA (1961): 322 Eighth Ave., New York, N.Y. 10001-4808. 385,000. Phone: (212) 807-8400.

AMVETS (American Veterans of World War II, Korea, and Vietnam) (1944): 4647 Forbes Blvd., Lanham, Md. 20706. 200,000. Phone: (301) 459-9600.

Animal Protection Institute of America (1968): 2831 Fruitridge Rd., P.O. Box 22505, Sacramento, Calif. 95822. Phone: (916) 731-5521.

Animals, Fund For (1967): 200 W. 57th St., New York, N.Y. 10019. 175,000. Phone: (212) 246-2096.

Animals, The American Society for the Prevention of Cruelty to (ASPCA) (1866): 441 E. 92nd St., New York, N.Y. 10128. 400,000+. Phone: (212) 876-7700..

Animal Welfare Institute (1951): P.O. Box 3650, Washington, D.C. 20007. 8,600. Phone: (202) 337-2332.

Anthropological Association, American (1902): 1703 New Hampshire Ave. N.W., Washington, D.C. 20009. 11,500. Phone: (202) 232-8800.

Anti-Defamation League of B'nai B'rith (1913): 823 United Nations Plaza, New York, N.Y. 10017-3560. Phone: (212) 490-2525.

Antiquarian Society, American (1812): 185 Salisbury St., Worcester, Mass. 01609. 543. Phone: (508) 755-5221.

Anti-Vivisection Society, The American (1883): Suite 204, Noble Plaza, 801 Old York Rd., Jenkintown, Pa. 19046-1685. 15,000. Phone: (215) 887-0816.

Appraisers, American Society of (1936): P.O. Box 17265, Washington, D.C. 20041. 6,000. Phone: (703) 478-2228.

Arbitration Association, American (1926): 140 W. 51st St., New York, N.Y. 10020-1203. 5,500. Phone: (212) 484-4000.

Arboriculture, International Society of (1924): 303 W. University, Urbana, Ill. 61801-1746. 6,000. Phone: (217) 328-2032.

Archaeological Institute of America (1879): 675 Commonwealth Ave., Boston, Mass. 02215. 10,000. Phone: (617) 353-9361.

Architects, The American Institute of (1857): 1735 New York Ave. N.W., Washington, D.C. 20006. 56,000. Phone: (202) 626-7300.

Architectural Historians, Society of (1940): 1232 Pine St., Philadelphia, Pa. 19107-5944. 4,000. Phone: (215) 735-0224.

Army, Association of the United States (1950): 2425 Wilson Blvd., Arlington, Va. 22210-0860. 150,000. Phone: (703) 841-4300.

Arthritis Foundation (1948): 1314 Spring St. N.W., Atlanta, Ga. 30309. 70 local chapters. Phone: (404) 872-7100.

Arts, National Endowment for the (1965): 1100 Pennsylvania Ave. N.W., Washington, D.C. 20506. Phone: (202) 682-5400.

Arts, The American Federation of (1909): 41 E. 65th St., New York, N.Y. 10021. 1,400. Phone: (212) 988-7700.

Arts and Letters, American Academy and Institute of (1898): 633 W. 155th St., New York, N.Y. 10032. 250. Phone: (212) 368-5900.

ASM International® (1913): Materials Park, Ohio 44073. 54,000. Phone: (216) 338-5151.

Association for Investment Management and Research (1947): 1633 Broadway, 16th Floor, New York, N.Y. 10019. 17,500. Phone: (212) 957–2860.

Astronomical Society, American (1899): Astronomy Program, University of Maryland, College Park, Md. 20742. 5,700. Phone: (301) 405–1818.

Atheists, American (1963): P.O. Box 140195, Austin, Tex. 78714-0195. 40,000 Families. Phone: (512) 458-1244.

Auctioneers Association, National (1949): 8880 Ballentine, Overland Park, Kan. 66214-1985. 6,000. Phone: (913) 541-8084.

Audubon Society, National (1905): 950 Third Ave., New York, N.Y. 10022. 546,000. Phone: (212) 832-3200.

Authors League of America (1912): 330 W. 42nd St., 29th Floor, New York, N.Y. 10036-6902. 14,000. Phone: (212) 564–8350.

Autism Society of America (1965): 8601 Georgia Ave., Suite 503, Silver Spring, Md. 20910. 10,000. Phone: (301) 565–0433.

Automobile Association, American (1902): 1000 AAA Dr., Heathrow, Fla., 32746-5063. Phone: (407) 444-7000.

Automobile Club, National (1924): Bayside Plaza, 188 The Embarcadero, #300, San Francisco, Calif. 94105. 300,000. Phone: (415) 777-4000.

Automotive Hall of Fame (1939): P.O. Box 1727, Midland, Mich. 48641-1727. Phone: (517) 631-5760.

Bar Association, American (1878): 750 N. Lake Shore Dr., Chicago, Ill. 60611-4497. 371,000. Phone: (312) 988-5000.

Barber Shop Quartet Singing in America, Society for the Preservation and Encouragement of (1938): 6315 Third Ave., Kenosha, Wis., 53143-5199. 38,000. Phone: (414) 656-8440.

*Better Business Bureaus, Council of (1970): 4200 Wilson Blvd., Suite 800, Arlington, Va. 22203. Phone: (703) 276-0100.

Bible Society, American (1816): 1865 Broadway, New York, N.Y. 10023-9980. 320,000. Phone: (212) 408-1200.

Biblical Literature, Society of (1880): 1549 Clairmont Rd., Suite 204, Decatur, Ga. 30033-4635. 7,000. Phone: (404) 636-4744.

Bibliographical Society of America (1904): P.O. Box 397, Grand Central Station, New York, N.Y. 10163. 1,300. Phone: (212) 995-9151.

Bide-A-Wee Home Association, Inc. (1903): 410 E. 38th St., New York, N.Y. 10016. Phone: Adoptions (pets) (212) 532-4455; Clinic and Hospital (212) 532-5884.

Big Brothers/Big Sisters of America (1977): 230 N. 13th St., Philadelphia, Pa. 19107. Phone: (215) 567-7000.

Biochemistry and Molecular Biology, American Society for (1906): 9650 Rockville Pike, Bethesda, Md. 20814. 8,200. Phone: (301) 530-7145.

Biological Sciences, American Institute of (1947): 730 11th St. N.W., Washington, D.C. 20001-4521. 14,000. Phone: (202) 628-1500.

Blind, American Council of the (1961): 1155 15th St. N.W., Suite 720, Washington, D.C. 20005. 20,000. Phone: (202) 467–5081.

Blind, National Federation of the (1940): 1800 Johnson St., Baltimore, Md. 21230. 50,000. Phone: (301) 659-9314.

Blindness, National Society to Prevent (1908): 500 E. Remington Rd., Schaumburg, Ill. 60173-4557. 26 affiliates. Phone: (708) 843-2020.

Blindness, Research to Prevent (1960): 598 Madison Ave., New York, N.Y. 10022. 3,300. Phone: (212) 752-4333.

Blue Cross and Blue Shield Association (1948 and 1946): 676 N. St. Clair St., Chicago, Ill. 60611. 74 Plans. Phone: (312) 440-6000.

B'nai B'rith International (1843): 1640 Rhode Island Ave. N.W., Washington, D.C. 20036-3278. 500,000. Phone: (202) 857-6500.

Booksellers Association, American (1900): 137 W. 25th St., New York, N.Y. 10001. 8,298. Phone: (212) 463-8450.

Botanical Gardens & Arboreta, American Association of (1940): 786 Church Rd., Wayne, Pa. 19087. 2,000. Phone: (215) 688-1120.

Boys & Girls Clubs of America (1906): 771 First Ave., New York, N.Y. 10017. 1,410,995. Phone: (212) 351-5900.

Boy Scouts of America (1910): 1325 W. Walnut Hill Lane, P.O. Box 152079, Irving, Tex. 75015-2079. 5,448,197. Phone: (214) 580-2000.

Bridge, Tunnel, and Turnpike Association, International (1932): 2120 L St. N.W., Suite 305, Washington, D.C. 20037-1527. 215 agencies. Phone: (202) 659-4620.

Broadcasters, National Association of (1922): 1771 N St. N.W., Washington, D.C. 20036. 6,000. Phone: (202) 429-5300.

Brookings Institution, The (1916): 1775 Massachusetts Ave. N.W., Washington, D.C. 20036-2188. Phone: (202) 797-6000.

Brooks Bird Club, Inc., The (1932): 707 Warwood Ave., Wheeling, W. Va. 26003. 1,000. Phone: (304) 547-5253.

Business Clubs, National Association of American (1922): 3315 No. Main St., High Point, N.C. 27265. 7,000. Phone: (919) 869-2166.

Business Education Association, National (1946): 1914 Association Dr., Reston, Va. 22091-1596. 16,000. Phone: (703) 860-8300.

Business Women's Association, American (1949): 9100 Ward Parkway, P.O. Box 8728, Kansas City, Mo. 64114-0728. More than 100,000. Phone: (816) 361-6621.

Campers & Hikers Association, National (1949): 4804 Transit Rd., Bldg. 2, Depew, N.Y. 14043-4906. 24,000 families. Phone: (716) 668-6242.

Camp Fire Boys and Girls (1910): 4601 Madison Ave., Kansas City, Mo. 64112-1278. 600,000. Phone: (816) 756-1950.

Camping Association, The American (1910): 5000 State Rd. 67 N., Martinsville, Ind. 46151-7902. 5,500. Phone: (317) 342-8456.

Cancer Society, American (1913): 1599 Clifton Rd., N.E.. Atlanta Ga. 30329. 2,646,070 volunteers. Phone: (800) ACS-2345 or check local listings.

CARE, Inc. (1945): 660 First Ave., New York, N.Y. 10016. 19 agencies plus 22 public members. Phone: (212) 686-3110.

Carnegie Endowment for International Peace (1910): 2400 N St. N.W., Washington, D.C. 20037. Phone: (202) 862-7900.

Cartoonists Society, National (1946): 157 W. 57th St., Suite 904, New York, N.Y. 10019. Phone: (212) 333-7606.

Catholic Charities USA (1910): 1731 King St., Alexandria, Va. 22314. 4,000 individuals, 735 agencies and institutions. Phone: (703) 549-1390.

Catholic Daughters of the Americas (1903): 10 W. 71st St., New York, N.Y. 10023. 150,000. Phone: (212) 877-3041.

Catholic Historical Society, American (1884): 263 S. Fourth St., Philadelphia, Pa. 19106. 950. Phone: (215) 925-5752.

Catholic War Veterans of the U.S.A. Inc. (1935): 419 N. Lee St., Alexandria, Va. 22314. 30,000. Phone: (703) 549-3622.

Ceramic Society, Inc., The American (1899): 757 Brooksedge Plaza Dr., Westerville, Ohio 43081-6136. Phone: (614) 890-4700.

Cerebral Palsy Associations, Inc., United (1949): 7 Penn Plaza, Suite 804, New York, N.Y. 10001. 163 affiliates. Phone: (800) USA IUCP.

Chamber of Commerce of the U.S. (1912): 1615 H St. N.W., Washington, D.C. 20062. 180,000. Phone: (202) 659-6000.

Chemical Engineers, American Institute of (1908): 345 E. 47th St., New York, N.Y. 10017. 52,000. Phone: (212) 705-7338.

Chemical Manufacturers Association, Inc. (1872): 2501 M St. N.W., Washington, D.C. 20037. 185 companies. Phone: (202) 887-1100.

Chemical Society, American (1876): 1155 16th St. N.W., Washington, D.C. 20036. 140,089. Phone: (202) 872-4600.

Chemists, American Institute of (1923): 7315 Wisconsin Ave., Bethesda, Md. 20814. 5,000. Phone: (301) 652-2447.

Chess Federation, United States (1939): 186 Rt. 9W, New Windsor, N.Y. 12553. 60,000. Phone: (914) 562-8350/(800) 388–KING.

Child Labor Committee, National (1904): 1501 Broadway, Rm. 1111, New York, N.Y. 10036. Phone: (212) 840-1801.

Children, American Association for Protecting (a Div. of the American Humane Association) (1877): 63 Inverness Dr. East, Englewood, Colo. 80112. Phone: (303) 792-9900.

Children's Aid Society, The (1853): 105 E. 22nd St., New York, N.Y. 10010. Child welfare services, community centers, camps and health services. Phone: (212) 949-4800.

Children's Book Council (1945): 568 Broadway, Suite 404, New York, N.Y. 10012. 61 publishing houses. Phone: (212) 966-1990.

Child Welfare League of America (1920): 440 First St. N.W., Suite 310, Washington, D.C. 20001-2085. Phone: (202) 638-2952.

Chiropractic Association, American (1963): 1701 Clarendon Blvd., Arlington, Va. 22209. 21,300. Phone: (703) 276-8800.

Christians and Jews, National Conference of (1927): 71 Fifth Ave., New York, N.Y. 10003. 200,000. Phone: (212) 206-0006.

Churches of Christ in the USA, National Council of the (1950): 475 Riverside Drive, New York, N.Y. 10115. 32 Protestant and Orthodox communions. Phone: (212) 870-2511.

Cities, National League of (1924): 1301 Pennsylvania Ave. N.W., Washington, D.C. 20004. 16,000 cities and towns. Phone: (202) 626-3000.

Civil Air Patrol (1941): Maxwell AFB, Ala. 36112-5572. 61,720. Phone: (205) 953-5463.

Civil Engineers, American Society of (1852): 345 E. 47th St., New York, N.Y. 10017. 110,000. Phone: (212) 705-7496.

Civil Liberties Union, American (1920): 132 W. 43rd St., New York, N.Y. 10036. 290,000. Phone: (212) 944-9800.

Clinical Chemistry, Inc., American Association for (1948): 2029 K St. N.W., 7th Floor, Washington, D.C. 20006. 9,000. Phone (202) 857-0717.

Clinical Pathologists, American Society of (1922): 2100 W. Harrison St., Chicago, Ill. 60612. 50,000. Phone: (312) 738-1336.

Collectors Association, American (1939): Box 39106, Minneapolis, Minn. 55439-0106. Over 3,600 debt collection agencies. Phone: (612) 926-6547.

College Board, The (1900): 45 Columbus Ave., New York, N.Y. 10023-6992. 2,800 institutions. Phone: (212) 713-8000.

College Placement Council (1956): 62 E. Highland Ave., Bethlehem, Pa. 18017. 3,100. Phone: (215) 868-1421.

Common Cause (1970): 2030 M St. N.W., Washington, D.C. 20036. 270,000. Phone: (202) 833-1200.

Community and Junior Colleges, American Association of (1920): One Dupont Circle N.W., Suite 410, Washington, D.C. 20036-1176. 1,124 institutions. Phone: (202) 728-0200.

Community Cultural Center Association, American (1978): 19 Foothills Dr., Pompton Plains, N.J. 07444. Phone: (201) 835-2661.

Composers, Authors, and Publishers, American Society of (ASCAP) (1914): One Lincoln Plaza, New York, N.Y. 10023. 48,000. Phone: (212) 621-6000.

Composers/USA, National Association of (1932): P.O. Box 49652, Barrington Station, Los Angeles, Calif. 90049. 550. Phone: (213) 541-8213.

*Congress of Racial Equality (CORE) (1942): 1457 Flatbush Ave., Brooklyn, N.Y. 11210. Nationwide network of chapters. Phone: (718) 434-3580.

Conscientious Objectors, Central Committee for (1948): 2208 South St., Philadelphia, Pa. 19146. Phone: (215) 545-4626.

Conservation Engineers, Association of (1961): Alabama Dept. of Cons. & Natural Resources, Engineering Section, 64 N. Union St., Montgomery, Ala. 36130. Phone: (205) 242-3476.

Consulting Chemists & Chemical Engineers, Inc., Association of (1928): 295 Madison Ave., 27th Floor, New York, N.Y. 10017. 130. Phone: (212) 983-3160.

Consulting Organizations, Council of (1989): 230 Park Ave., Suite 544, New York, N.Y. 10169. 2,100 individual members in DMC Division, 50 firms in ACME Division. Phone: (212) 697-9693.

Consumer Federation of America (1968): 1424 16th St. N.W., Suit 604, Washington, D.C. 20036. 240 member organizations. Phone: (202) 387-6121.

Consumer Interests, American Council on (1953): 240 Stanley Hall, Univ. of Missouri, Columbia, Mo. 65211. 1,800. Phone: (314) 882-3817.

Consumers League, National (1899): 815 15th St. N.W., Suite 928-N, Washington, D.C. 20005. Phone: (202) 639-8140.

Consumers Union (1936): 101 Truman Ave., Yonkers, N.Y. 10703-1057. 4,900,000 subscribers to *Consumer Reports*. Phone: (914) 378-2000.

Contract Bridge League, American (1927): 2990 Airways Blvd., Memphis, Tenn. 38116-3847. Phone: (901) 332-5586.

Cooperative Business Association, National (formerly Cooperative League of the U.S.A) (1916): 1401 New York Ave. N.W., Suite 1100, Washington, D.C. 20005. Phone: (202) 638-6222.

Counselors and Family Therapists, National Academy of (1972): 55 Morris Ave., Springfield, N.J. 07081-1422. Phone: (201) 379-7496.

Country Music Association (1958): One Music Circle South, Nashville, Tenn. 37203. 6,000. Phone: (615) 244-2840.

Credit Association, International (1912): P.O. Box 27357, St. Louis, Mo. 63141-1757. 11,500 members, 125 local associations. Phone: (314) 991-3030.

Credit Management, National Association of (1896): 8815 Centre Park Dr., Suite 200, Columbia, Md. 21045. Phone: (301) 740-5560.

Credit Union National Association (1934): P.O. Box 431, Madison, Wis. 53701. 52 state leagues representing 14,500 credit unions. Phone: (608) 231-4000.

*Crime and Delinquency, National Council on (1907): 685 Market St., #620, San Francisco, Calif. 94105. Nationwide membership. Phone: (415) 896-6223.

CSA/USA, Celiac Sprue Association/United States of America: P.O. Box 31700, Omaha, Neb. 68131-0700. 6 regions in U.S., 36 chapters, 60 active resource units. Phone: (402) 558-0600.

Dairy Council, National (1915): 6300 N. River Rd., Rosement, Ill. 60018. Phone: (708) 696-1020.

Daughters of the American Revolution, National Society (1890): 1776 D St. N.W., Washington, D.C. 20006. 200,000. Phone: (202) 628-1776.

Daughters of the Confederacy, United (1894): 328

N. Boulevard, Richmond, Va. 23220-4057. 27,000. Phone: (804) 355-1636.

Deaf, National Association of the (1880): 814 Thayer Ave., Silver Spring, Md. 20910. Phone: (301) 587-1788; (301) 587-1789 TDD.

Defenders of Wildlife (1947): 1244 19th St. N.W., Washington, D.C. 20036. 84,000 members and supporters. Phone: (202) 659-9510.

Defense Preparedness Association, American (1919): Two Colonial Place, Suite 400, 2101 Wilson Blvd., Arlington, Va. 22201-3061. 45,000 individual, 1,000 corporate. Phone: (703) 522-1820.

Dental Association, American (1859): 211 E. Chicago Ave., Chicago, Ill. 60611. 150,000. Phone: (312) 440-2500.

Diabetes Association, American (1940): 1660 Duke St., Alexandria, Va. 22314. Phone: (703) 549-1500.

Dignity (1969): 1500 Massachusetts Ave. N.W., Suite 11, Washington, D.C. 20005. 5,000. Phone: (202) 861-0017.

Disabled American Veterans (1920): 807 Maine Ave. S.W., Washington, D.C. 20024. Phone: (202) 554-3501.

Dowsers, Inc., The American Society of (1961): P.O. Box 24, Danville, Vt. 05828-0024. 3,500. Phone: (802) 684-3417.

Drug, Chemical, & Allied Trades Association, Inc., The (1890): 2 Roosevelt Ave., Syosset, N.Y. 11791. 575. Phone (516) 496-3317.

Ducks Unlimited, Inc. (1937): One Waterfowl Way, Long Grove, Ill. 60047. 550,000. Phone: (708) 438-4300.

Earthwatch (1971): 680 Mt. Auburn St., Box 403N, Watertown, Mass. 02272. 75,000. Phone: (617) 926-8200.

Eastern Star, Order of, General Grand Chapter (1876): 1618 New Hampshire Ave. N.W., Washington, D.C. 20009. 2,087,063. Phone: (202) 667-4737.

Easter Seal Society, The National (1921): 70 E. Lake St., Chicago, Ill. 60601. 58 affiliated state societies and Puerto Rico. Phone: (312) 726-6200 and (312) 726-4258 TDD.

Economic Association, American (1885): 2014 Broadway, Suite 305, Nashville, Tenn. 37203. 21,000. 6,000 inst. subscribers. Phone: (615) 322-2595.

Economic Development, Committee for (1942): 477 Madison Ave., New York, N.Y. 10022. 250 trustees. Phone: (212) 688-2063.

Edison Electric Institute (1933): 701 Pennsylvania Ave. N.W., Washington, D.C. 20004-2696.

Education, American Council on (1918): One Dupont Circle N.W., Washington, D.C. 20036. 1,750 institutional members. Phone: (202) 939-9300.

Education, Council for Advancement and Support of (CASE) (1974): 11 Dupont Circle N.W., Suite 400, Washington, D.C. 20036-1207. 14,000. Phone: (202) 328-5900.

Educational Exchange, International, Council on (1947): 205 E. 42nd St., New York, N.Y. 10017. 203. Phone: (212) 661-1414.

Educational Research Association, American (1916): 1230 17th St. N.W., Washington, D.C. 20036. 17,000. Phone: (202) 223-9485.

Education Association, National (1857): 1201 16th St. N.W., Washington, D.C. 20036-3290. 2 million. Phone: (202) 833-4000.

Electrochemical Society, The (1902): 10 S. Main St., Pennington, N.J. 08534-2896. 6,274. Phone: (609) 737-1902.

Electronic Industries Association (1924): 2001 Pennsylvania Ave. N.W., Washington, D.C. 20006-1813. 1,000 member companies. Phone: (202) 457-4900.

Electroplaters and Surface Finishers Society, American (1909): 12644 Research Pkwy., Orlando, Fla. 32826. 10,000. Phone: (407) 281-6441.

Elks of the U.S.A., Benevolent and Protective Order of the (1868): 2750 Lake View Ave., Chicago, Ill. 60614. 1,400,000. Phone: (312) 477-2750.

Energy Engineers, Association of (1977): 4025 Pleasantdale Rd., Suite 420, Atlanta, Ga. 30340. 7,500. Phone: (404) 447-5083.

English-Speaking Union of the United States (1920): 16 E. 69th St., New York, N.Y. 10021. 25,000. Phone: (212) 879-6800.

Entomological Society of America (1889): 9301 Annapolis Rd., Lanham, Md. 20706-3115. 9,000. Phone: (301) 731-4535.

Esperanto League for North America, The (1952): P.O. Box 1129, El Cerrito, Calif. 94530. Over 1,000. Phone: (415) 653-0998.

Exceptional Children, The Council for (1922): 1920 Association Dr., Reston, Va. 22091. 54,000. Phone: (703) 620-3660.

Experimental Test Pilots, The Society of (1956): 44814 Elm St., Lancaster, Calif. 93534. 1,800. Phone: (805) 942-9574.

Exploration Geophysicists, Society of (1930): P.O. Box 702740, Tulsa, Okla. 74170-2740. 15,000. Phone: (918) 493-3516.

Family Physicians, American Academy of (1947): 8880 Ward Pkwy., Kansas City, Mo. 64114-2797. 70,000. Phone: (816) 333-9700.

Family Relations, National Council on (1938): 3989 Central Ave. N.E., #550, Minneapolis, Minn. 55421-3921. 3,800. Phone: (612) 781-9331.

Family Service America (1911): 11700 W. Lake Park Dr., Park Place, Milwaukee, Wis. 53224. Approximately 300 member agencies. Phone: (414) 359-1040.

Farm Bureau Federation, American (1919): 225 Touhy Ave., Park Ridge, Ill. 60068. 3.8 million member families. Phone: (312) 399-5700.

Farmer Cooperatives, National Council of (1929): 50 F St. N.W., Washington, D.C. 20001. 135. Phone: (202) 626-8700.

Federal Bar Association (1920): 1815 H St. N.W., Suite 408, Washington, D.C. 20006-3697. 15,000. Phone: (202) 638-0252.

Federal Employees, National Federation of (1917): 1016 16th St. N.W., Washington, D.C. 20036. Rep. 150,000. Phone: (202) 862-4400.

Feline and Canine Friends, Inc. (1973): 505 N. Bush St., Anaheim, Calif. 92805. 1,000. Phone: (714) 635-7975.

Fellowship of Reconciliation (1915): Box 271, Nyack, N.Y. 10960. 36,000. Phone: (914) 358-4601.

Female Executives, National Association for (1972): 127 W. 24th St., New York, N.Y. 10011. 250,000. Phone: (212) 645-0770.

FFA Organization, National (1928): 5632 Mt. Vernon Memorial Hwy., P.O. Box 15160, Alexandria, Va. 22309-0160. 387,042. Phone: (703) 360-3600.

Fire Protection Association, National (1896): One Batterymarch Park, P.O. Box 9101, Quincy, Mass. 02269-9101. 56,000. Phone: (617) 770-3999.

Flag Foundation, National (1968): Flag Plaza, Pittsburgh, Pa. 15219-3630. 3,000+. Phone: (412) 261-1776.

Fleet Reserve Association (1924): 125 N. West St., Alexandria, Va. 22314-2754. 153,000. Phone:

(703) 683-1400.

Flight Test Engineers, Society of (1968): P.O. Box 4047, Lancaster, Calif. 93539. 1,100. Phone: (805) 948-3067.

Foreign Policy Association (1918): 729 Seventh Ave., New York, N.Y. 10019. Phone: (212) 764-4050.

Foreign Relations, Council on (1921): 58 E. 68th St., New York, N.Y. 10021. 2,600. Phone: (212) 734-0400.

Foreign Study, American Institute for (1965): 102 Greenwich Ave., Greenwich, Conn. 06830. Phone: (203) 869-9090/(800) 727-AIFS.

Foreign Trade Council, Inc., National (1914): 100 E. 42nd St., New York, N.Y. 10017. Over 550 companies. Phone: (212) 867-5630. Also, 1625 K St. N.W., Washington, D.C. 20006. Phone: (202) 887-0278.

Forensic Sciences, American Academy of (1948): 218 E. Cache La Poudre/80903, P.O. Box 669, Colorado Springs, Colo. 80901-0669. 3,500. Phone: (719) 636-1100.

Forest Council, American (1932): 1250 Connecticut Ave. N.W., Suite 320, Washington, D.C. 20036. 100. Phone: (202) 463 -2455.

Foresters, Society of American (1900): 5400 Grosvenor Lane, Bethesda, Md. 20814-2198. 19,000. Phone: (301) 897-8720.

Forestry Association, American (1875): 1516 P St. N.W., Washington, D.C. 20005. 35,000. Phone: (202) 667-3300.

Fortean Organization, International (1965): P.O. Box 367, Arlington, Va. 22210-0367. 900. Phone: (703) 522-9232.

Foster Parents Plan International (1937). Box 804, East Greenwich, R.I. 02818. Phone: (401) 826-2500.

4-H Program (early 1900s): Room 3860-S, U.S. Department of Agriculture, Washington, D.C. 20250. 5,492,120. Phone: (202) 447-5853.

Freedom of Information Center (1958): 20 Walter Williams Hall, Univ. of Missouri, Columbia, Mo. 65211. Phone: (314) 882-4856.

French-American Chamber of Commerce in the U.S. Inc. (1896): 509 Madison Ave., Suite 1900, New York, N.Y. 10022. 605. Membership Association. Phone: (212) 371-4466.

French Institute/Alliance Française (1911): 22 E. 60th St., New York, N.Y. 10022-1077. 9,000. Phone: (212) 355-6100.

Friendship and Good Will, International Society of (Esperanto) (1978): 211 W. Fourth Ave., P.O. Box 2637, Gastonia, N.C. 28053-2637. 3,922 in 166 countries. Phone: (704) 864-7906.

Friends of Animals Inc. (1957): P.O. Box 1244, Norwalk, Conn. 06856. 104,000. Phone: (203) 866-5223. For low-cost spay/neuter info. call: (800) 321-PETS.

Friends of the Earth (1969): 218 D St. S.E., Washington, D.C. 20003. Phone: (202) 544-2600.

Future Homemakers of America, Inc. (1945): 1910 Association Dr., Reston, Va. 22091. 280,000. Phone: (703) 476-4900.

Gamblers Anonymous: Box 17173, Los Angeles, Calif. 90017. Phone: (213) 386-8789.

Genealogical Society, National (1903): 4527 17th St. N., Arlington, Va. 22207-2399. 10,000. Phone: (703) 525-0050.

Genetic Association, American (1903): P.O. Box 39, Buckeystown, Md. 21717. 1,600. Phone: (301) 695-9292.

Geographers, Association of American (1904): 1710 16th St. N.W., Washington, D.C. 20009-3198. 6,300. Phone: (202) 234-1450.

Geographical Society, The American (1851): 156 Fifth Ave., Suite 600, New York, N.Y. 10010-7002. 1,500. Phone: (212) 242-0214.

Geographic Education, National Council for (1915): Indiana University of Pennsylvania, Indiana, Pa. 15705. 3,700. Phone: (412) 357-6290.

Geographic Society, National (1888): 17th and M Sts. N.W., Washington, D.C. 20036. 10,000,000. Phone: (202) 857-7000.

Geological Institute, American (1948): 4220 King St., Alexandria, Va. 22302-1507. 20 member societies representing 70,000 geoscientists. Phone: (703) 379-2480.

Geological Society of America, Inc. (1888): 3300 Penrose Pl., P.O. Box 9140, Boulder, Colo. 80301. 17,000. Phone: (303) 447-2020.

Geriatrics Society, American (1942): 770 Lexington Ave., Suite 300, New York, N.Y. 10021. 6,200. Phone: (212) 308-1414.

German American National Congress, The (Deutsch-Amerikanischer National Congress— D.A.N.K.) (1958): 4740 N. Western Ave., Chicago, Ill. 60625. 30,000, plus Associates. Phone: (312) 275-1100.

Gideons International, The (1889): 2900 Lebanon Rd., Nashville, Tenn. 37214-0800. 105,000. Phone: (615) 883-8533.

Gifted, The Association for the (1958): The Council for Exceptional Children, 1920 Association Dr., Reston, Va. 22091. 2,200. Phone: (703) 620-3660.

Girls Incorporated (1945): 30 E. 33rd St., New York, N.Y. 10016. 250,000. Phone: (212) 689-3700.

Girl Scouts of the U.S.A. (1912): 830 Third Ave., New York, N.Y. 10022-7522. 3,268,630. Phone: (212) 940-7500.

Graphic Artists, Society of American (1916): 32 Union Square, Rm. 1214, New York, N.Y. 10003. Phone: (212) 260-5706.

Graphoanalysis Society, International (1929): 111 N. Canal St., Chicago, Ill. 60606. 10,000. Phone: (312) 930-9446.

Gray Panthers Project Fund (1970): 1424 16th St. N.W., Suite 602, Washington, D.C. 20036. Over 80 chapters (networks). Phone: (202) 387-3111.

Greenpeace U.S.A. (1979): 1436 U St. N.W., Washington, D.C. 20009. 800,000. Phone: (202) 462-1177.

Group Psychotherapy Association, American (1942): 25 E. 21st St., 6th Floor, New York, N.Y. 10010. 3,500 Phone: (212) 477-2677.

Guide Dog Foundation for the Blind, Inc. (1946): 371 E. Jericho Turnpike, Smithtown, N.Y. 11787-2976. 15,000. Phone: (516) 265-2121; outside N.Y. city call (800) 548-4337.

Hadassah, The Women's Zionist Organization of America (1912): 50 W. 58th St., New York, N.Y. 10019. 385,000. Phone: (212) 355-7900.

Handgun Control, Inc. (1974): 1225 Eye St. N.W., Washington, D.C. 20005. 250,000. Phone: (202) 898-0792.

Health, Physical Education, Recreation, and Dance, American Alliance for (1885): 1900 Association Dr., Reston, Va. 22091. 35,000. Phone: (703) 476-3400.

Heart Association, American (1924): 7320 Greenville Ave., Dallas, Tex. 75231-4599. 3,200,000 volunteers. Phone: (214) 373-6300.

Heating, Refrigerating, and Air-Conditioning Engineers, Inc., American Society of (1894): 1791 Tullie Circle N.E., Atlanta, Ga. 30329. 50,000.

Phone: (404) 636-8400.

Helicopter Association International (1948): 1619 Duke St., Alexandria, Va. 22314-3439. Phone: (703) 683-4646.

Hemispheric Affairs, Council on (1975): 724 9th St. N.W., Rm. 401, Washington, D.C. 20001. Phone: (202) 393-3322.

Historians, The Organization of American (1907): Indiana Univ., 112 N. Bryan St., Bloomington, Ind. 47408. 9,000. Phone: (812) 855-7311.

Historic Preservation, National Trust for (1949): 1785 Massachusetts Ave. N.W., Washington, D.C. 20036. 230,000. Phone: (202) 673-4000.

Home Economics Association, American (1909): 1555 King St., Alexandria, Va. 22314. 23,000. Phone: (800) 424-8080.

Horse Council, Inc., American (1969): 1700 K St. N.W., #300, Washington, D.C. 20006. More than 180 organizations and 2,400 individuals. Phone: (202) 296-4031.

Horse Shows Association, Inc., American (1917): 220 E. 42nd St., New York, N.Y. 10017-5806. 55,000. Phone: (212) 972-2472.

Horticultural Association, National Junior (1935): 441 E. Pine, Freemont, Mich. 49412. 12,500. Phone: (616) 924-5237.

Horticultural Society, American (1922): Box 0105, Mt. Vernon, Va. 22121. 20,000. Phone: (703) 768-5700 or (800) 777-7931.

Hospital Association, American (1898): 840 N. Lake Shore Dr., Chicago, Ill. 60611. 5,500 institutions. Phone: (312) 280-6000.

Housing Science, International Association for (1972): P.O. Box 340254, Coral Gables/Miami, Fla. 33114. 500 professionals. Phone: (305) 448-3532.

Humane Association, American (1877): P.O. Box 1266, Denver, Colo. 80201-1266. Phone: (303) 792-9900.

Humane Society of the United States (1954): 2100 L St. N.W., Washington, D.C. 20037. 1,000,000. Phone: (202) 452-1100.

Humanities, National Endowment for the (1965): 1100 Pennsylvania Ave. N.W., Washington, D.C. 20506. Phone: (202) 786-0443.

Hydrogen Energy, International Association for (1975): P.O. Box 248266, Coral Gables, Fla. 33124. 2,500. Phone: (305) 284-4666.

Illustrators, Society of (1901): 128 E. 63rd St., New York, N.Y. 10021. 975. Phone: (212) 838-2560 .

Industrial Engineers, Institute of (1948): 25 Technology Park/Atlanta, Norcross, Ga. 30092. 40,000. Phone: (404) 449-0460.

Interfraternity Conference, National (1909): 3901 W. 86th St., Suite 390, Indianapolis, Ind. 46268. 59. Phone: (317) 872-1112.

Iron and Steel Institute, American (1908): 1133 15th St. N.W., Suite 300, Washington, D.C. 20005-2701. 1,200. Phone: (202) 452-7100.

Izaak Walton League of America (1922): 1401 Wilson Blvd., Level B, Arlington, Va. 22209. 53,000. Phone: (703) 528-1818.

Jaycees, The United States (The U.S. Junior Chamber of Commerce) (1920): P.O. Box 7, Tulsa, Okla. 74121. 234,000. Phone: (918) 584-2481.

Jewish Community Centers, World Confederation of (1946): 12 Hess St., Jerusalem, Israel 94185. Phone: (02) 231 371/221 265.

Jewish Community Centers Association of North America (1917): 15 E. 26th St., New York, N.Y. 10010-1579. 275 affiliated Jewish Community Centers, YM-YWHAs, and camps. Phone: (212)

532-4949.

Jewish Congress, American (1918): 15 E. 84th St., New York, N.Y. 10028. 50,000. Phone: (212) 879-4500.

Jewish Historical Society, American (1892): 2 Thornton Rd., Waltham, Mass. 02154. 3,500. Phone: (617) 891-8110.

Jewish War Veterans of the U.S.A. (1896): 1811 R St. N.W., Washington, D.C. 20009-1659. Phone: (202) 265-6280.

Jewish Women, National Council of (1893): 53 W. 23rd St., New York, N.Y. 10010. 100,000. Phone: (212) 645-4048.

John Birch Society (1958): P.O. Box 8040, Appleton, Wis. 54913. Under 100,000. Phone: (414) 749-3780.

Journalists, Society of Professional (1909): 16 S. Jackson, Greencastle, Ind. 46135-0077. 20,000. Phone: (317) 653-3333.

Journalists and Authors, American Society of (1948): 1501 Broadway, Suite 302, New York, N.Y. 10036. 800. Phone: (212) 997-0947.

Judaism, American Council for (1943): P.O. Box 9009, Alexandria, Va. 22304. 10,000. Phone: (703) 836-2546.

Junior Achievement Inc. (1919): 45 East Clubhouse Dr., Colorado Springs, Colo. 80906. 1.5 million. Phone: (719) 540-8000.

Junior Leagues International, Inc., Association of (1921): 660 First Ave., New York, N.Y. 10016-3241. 276 Leagues, 188,000 members. Phone: (212) 683-1515.

Junior Statesmen of America (1934): 650 Bair Island Rd., Suite 201, Redwood City, Calif. 94063. 10,000. Phone: (415) 366-2700.

Kennel Club, American (1884): 51 Madison Ave., New York, N.Y. 10010. 473 member clubs. Phone: (212) 696-8200.

Kiwanis International (1915): 3636 Woodview Trace, Indianapolis, Ind. 46268-3196. 323,000. Phone: (317) 875-8755.

Knights of Columbus (1882): One Columbus Plaza, New Haven, Conn. 06507-0901. 1,509,641. Phone: (203) 772-2130.

Knights of Pythias, Supreme Lodge (1864): 2785 E. Desert Inn Rd. #150, Las Vegas, Nev. 89121. 89,000. Phone: (702) 735-3302.

Knights Templar, Grand Encampment of (1816): 14 E. Jackson Blvd., Suite 1700, Chicago, Ill. 60604. 340,000. Phone: (312) 427-5670.

La Leche League International (1956): 9616 Minneapolis Ave., Franklin Park, Ill. 60131-8209. 40,000. Phone: (708) 455-7730.

Law, American Society of International (1906): 2223 Massachusetts Ave. N.W., Washington, D.C. 20008. 4,500. Phone: (202) 265-4313.

League of Women Voters of the U.S. (1920): 1730 M St. N.W., Washington, D.C. 20036. 114,000. Phone: (202) 429-1965.

Legal Aid and Defender Association, National (1911): 1625 K St. N.W., Suite 800, Washington, D.C. 20006. 5,000. Phone: (202) 452-0620.

Legal Secretaries, National Association of (1950): 2250 E. 73rd St., Suite 550, Tulsa, Okla. 74136-6864. 18,000. Phone: (918) 493-3540.

Leukemia Society of America (1949): 733 Third Ave., New York, N.Y. 10017. Phone: (212) 573-8484.

Library Association, American (1876): 50 E. Huron St., Chicago, Ill. 60611. 51,500. Phone: (312) 944-6780.

Life Insurance, American Council of (1976): 1001

Pennsylvania Ave. N.W., Washington, D.C. 20004-2599. 617. Phone: (202) 624-2000.

Life Underwriters, National Association of (1890): 1922 F St. N.W., Washington, D.C. 20006-4387. Phone: (202) 331-6000.

Lions Clubs International (1917): 300 22nd St., Oak Brook, Ill. 60521-8842. 1,376,470. Phone: (708) 571-5466.

Longwave Club of America (1974): 45 Wildflower Rd., Levittown, Pa. 19057. 530. Phone: (215) 945-0543.

Lung Association, American (1904): 1740 Broadway, New York, N.Y. 10019-4374. 132 constituent and affiliate associations. Phone: (212) 315-8700.

Magazine Editors, American Society of (1963): 575 Lexington Ave., New York, N.Y. 10022. 700. Phone: (212) 752-0055.

Magazine Publishers of America (1919): 575 Lexington Ave., New York, N.Y. 10022. 197 companies, 725 publications. Phone: (212) 752-0055.

Management Association, American (1923): 135 W. 50th St., New York, N.Y. 10020-1201. 75,000. Phone: (212) 586-8100.

Manufacturers, National Association of (1895): 1331 Pennsylvania Ave. N.W., Suite 1500-North Lobby, Washington, D.C. 20004-1703. 13,500. Phone: (202) 637-3065.

Manufacturers' Agents National Association (MANA) (1947): 23016 Mill Creek Rd., P.O. Box 3467, Laguna Hills, Calif. 92654. 9,000. Phone: (714) 859-4040.

March of Dimes Birth Defects Foundation (1938): 1275 Mamaroneck Ave., White Plains, N.Y. 10605. 133 chapters. Phone: (914) 428-7100.

Marine Conservation, Center for (1972): 1725 De Sales St. N.W., Suite 500, Washington, D.C. 20036. 110,000. Phone: (202) 429-5609.

Marine Corps Association (1913): Bldg. #715, Marine Corps Base, Quantico, Va. 22134. 104,419. Phone: (800) 336-0291.

Marine Corps League (1923): 8626 Lee Hwy., Fairfax, Va. Correspondence address: P.O. Box 3070, Merrifield, Va. 22116. 30,000. Phone: (703) 207-9588 or (703) 207-9589.

Marine Technology Society (1963): 1825 K St. N.W., Suite 218, Washington, D.C. 20006. 2,700. Phone: (202) 775-5966.

Masons, Ancient and Accepted Scottish Rite, Northern Masonic Jurisdiction, Supreme Council (1813): 33 Marrett Rd., Lexington, Mass. 02173. 412,612. Phone: (617) 862-4410.

Masons, Ancient and Accepted Scottish Rite, Southern Jurisdiction, Supreme Council (1801): 1733 16th St. N.W., Washington, D.C. 20009. 575,746. Phone: (202) 232-3579.

Masons, Royal Arch, General Grand Chapter International (1797): P.O. Box 489, 111 S. Fourth St., Danville, Ky. 40422. 277,340. Phone: (606) 236-0757.

Massachusetts Audubon Society (1896): South Great Rd., Lincoln, Mass. 01773. 49,000 member households. Phone: (508) 259-9500.

Mathematical Association of America (1915): 1529 18th St. N.W., Washington, D.C. 20036. 33,000. Phone: (202) 387-5200.

Mathematical Society, American (1888): P.O. Box 6248, Providence, R.I. 02940-6248. 28,710. Phone: (401) 455-4000.

Mathematical Statistics, Institute of (1935): 3401 Investment Blvd. #7, Hayward, Calif. 94545. 3,800. Phone: (415) 783-8141.

Mayflower Descendants, General Society of (1897): 4 Winslow St., P.O. Box 3297, Plymouth, Mass. 02361. 25,000. Phone: (508) 746-3188.

Mayors, U.S. Conference of (1932): 1620 Eye St. N.W., Washington, D.C. 20006. 8 standing committees. Phone: (202) 293-7330.

Mechanical Engineers, American Society of (1880): 345 E. 47th St., New York, N.Y. 10017. 118,000. Phone: (212) 705-7722.

Mechanics, American Academy of (1969): 4205 EBUI, AMES, 0411, University of CA, San Diego, 9500 Gilman Dr., La Jolla, Calif. 92093-0411. 1,600. Phone: (619) 534-2036.

Medical Association, American (1847): 515 N. State St., Chicago, Ill. 60610-4377. Phone: (312) 464-5000.

Medical Library Association (1898): Six N. Michigan Ave., Suite 300, Chicago, Ill. 60602. 5,000. Phone: (312) 419-9094.

Mental Health Association, National (1909): 1021 Prince St., Alexandria, Va., 22314-2971. 1,000,000. Phone: (703) 684-7722.

Meteorological Society, American (1919): 45 Beacon St., Boston, Mass. 02108-3693. 10,000. Phone: (617) 227-2425.

Military Chaplains Association of the U.S.A. (1925): P.O. Box 42660, Washington, D.C. 20015-0660. 1,500. Phone: (202) 574-2423.

Mining, Metallurgy and Exploration, Society for; The Minerals, Metals & Materials Society (1871): 345 E. 47th St., New York, N.Y. 10017. 4 Member Societies: Society of Mining Engineers, The Minerals, Metals and Materials Society, Iron & Steel Society, Society of Petroleum Engineers. Phone: (212) 705-7695.

Mining and Metallurgical Society of America (1910): 9 Escalle Lane, Larkspur, Calif. 94939. 300. Phone: (415) 924-7441.

Model Aeronautics, Academy of (1936): 1810 Samuel Morse Dr., Reston, Va. 22090. 150,000. Phone: (703) 435-0750.

Modern Language Association of America (1883): 10 Astor Place, New York, N.Y. 10003. 33,285. Phone: (212) 475-9500.

Modern Woodmen of America (1883): 1701 1st Ave., Rock Island, Ill. 61201. 649,000. Phone: (309) 786-6481.

Moose, Loyal Order of (1888): Mooseheart, Ill. 60539. 1,804,198. Phone: (708) 859-2000.

Mothers Against Drunk Driving (MADD) (1980): P.O. Box 541688, Dallas, Tex. 75354-1688. 2.95 million. Phone: (214) 744-6233.

Motion Picture & Television Engineers, Society of (1916): 595 W. Hartsdale Ave., White Plains, N.Y. 10607. 9,500. Phone: (914) 761-1100.

Motion Picture Arts & Sciences, Academy of (1927): 8949 Wilshire Blvd., Beverly Hills, Calif. 90211-1972. Phone: (213) 247-3000.

Multiple Sclerosis Society, National (1946): 205 E. 42nd St., New York, N.Y. 10017-5706. 400,000. Phone: (212) 986-3240.

Muscular Dystrophy Association (1950): 3561 East Sunrise Dr., Tucson, Ariz. 85718. 2,300,000 volunteers. Phone: (602) 529-2000.

Museum of Natural History, American (1869): Central Park West at 79th St., New York, N.Y. 10024-5192. 520,000. Phone: (212) 769-5100.

Museums, American Association of (1906): 1225 Eye St. N.W., Suite 200, Washington, D.C. 20005. 11,500. Phone: (202) 289-1818.

Music Council, National (1940): P.O. Box 5551, Englewood, N.J. 07631-5551. 50 National Music Organizations. Phone: (201) 871-9088.

Musicians, American Federation of (1896): 1501 Broadway, Suite 600 Paramount Bldg., New York, N.Y. 10036. Phone: (212) 869-1330.

Music Publishers Association, Inc., National (1917): 205 E. 42nd St., New York, N.Y. 10017. Trade Organization/Harry Fox Agency-Licensing Organization. Phone: (212) 370-5330.

Muzzle Loading Rifle Association, National (1933): P.O. Box 67, Friendship, Ind. 47021. 30,000. Phone: (812) 667-5131.

NAFSA: Association of International Educators (1948): 1875 Connecticut Ave. N.W., Suite 1000, Washington, D.C. 20009-5728. 6,500. Phone: (202) 462-4811.

Narcolepsy and Cataplexy Foundation of America (1975): 445 E. 68th St., Suite 12L, New York, N.Y. 10021. 3,991. Phone: (212) 628-6315.

National Association for the Advancement of Colored People (1909): 4805 Mt. Hope Dr., Baltimore, Md. 21215. 500,000+. Phone: (301) 358-8900.

National Grange, The (1867): 1616 H St. N.W., Washington, D.C. 20006. 330,000. Phone: (202) 628-3507.

National PTA (National Congress of Parents and Teachers) (1897): 700 N. Rush St., Chicago, Ill. 60611. 7.0 million. Phone: (312) 787-0977.

National Rifle Association of America (1871): 1600 Rhode Island Ave. N.W., Washington, D.C. 20036. 3,000,000. Phone: (202) 828-6000.

Natural Science for Youth Foundation (1961): 130 Azalea Dr., Roswell, Ga. 30075. 350. Phone: (404) 594-9367.

Nature Conservancy, The (1951): 1815 N. Lynn St., Arlington, Va. 22209. 680,000. Phone: (703) 841-5300.

Naval Architects and Marine Engineers, The Society of (1893): 601 Pavonia Ave., Jersey City, N.J. 07306. 12,200. Phone: (201) 798-4800.

Naval Engineers, American Society of (1888): 1452 Duke St., Alexandria, Va. 22314. 7,500. Phone: (703) 836-6727.

Naval Institute, United States (1873): Annapolis, Md. 21402. 100,000. Phone: (301) 268-6110.

Navigation, The Institute of (1945): 1026 16th St. N.W., Suite 104, Washington, D.C. 20036. 3,200. Phone: (202) 783-4121.

Navy League of the United States (1902): 2300 Wilson Blvd., Arlington, Va. 22311. 70,500; Dudley L. Carlson, Vice Admiral, USN (Ret.), Executive Director.

Neurofibromatosis Foundation, The National (1978): 141 Fifth Ave., Suite 7-S, New York, N.Y. 10010. 27,000. Phone: (212) 460-8980; toll-free (800) 323-7938.

Newspaper Editors, American Society of (1922): P.O. Box 17004, Washington, D.C. 20041. 1,000. Phone: (703) 648-1144.

Newspaper Publishers Association, American (1887): The Newspaper Center, P.O. Box 17407, Dulles International Airport, Washington, D.C. 20041. 1,400. Phone: (703) 648-1000.

Ninety-Second Street Young Men's and Young Women's Hebrew Association (1874): 1395 Lexington Ave., New York, N.Y. 10128. Phone: (212) 427-6000.

Nondestructive Testing, Inc., The American Society for (1941): 1711 Arlingate Lane, P.O. Box 28518, Columbus, Ohio 43228-0518. 10,841. Phone: Natl. (800) 222-ASNT; Ohio (800) NDT-OHIO.

North American Shortwave Assn. (1964): 45 Wildflower Rd., Levittown, Pa. 19057. 1,800.

Phone: (215) 945-0543.

NOT SAFE (National Organization Taunting Safety and Fairness Everywhere) (1980): P.O. Box 5743, Montecito, Calif. 93108. 975. Phone: (805) 969-6217.

Nuclear Society, American (1954): 555 N. Kensington Ave., La Grange Park, Ill. 60525. 16,000. Phone: (708) 352-6611.

Numismatic Association, American (1891): 818 N. Cascade Ave., Colorado Springs, Colo. 80903-3279. 34,000. Phone: (719) 632-2646.

Nurses Association, American (1896): 2420 Pershing Rd., Kansas City, Mo. 64108. 200,000. Phone: (816) 474-5720.

Nutrition, American Institute of (1928): 9650 Rockville Pike, Bethesda, Md. 20814. 2,950. Phone: (301) 530-7050.

Odd Fellows, Sovereign Grand Lodge, Independent Order of (1819): 422 Trade St., Winston-Salem, N.C. 27101-2830. 500,000. Phone: (919) 725-5955.

Olympic Committee, United States (1921): 1750 East Boulder St., Colorado Springs, Colo. 80909-5760. Phone: (719) 632-5551.

Optical Society of America (1916): 2010 Massachusetts Ave. N.W., Washington, D.C. 20036. 11,000. Phone: (202) 223-8130.

Optimist International (1919): 4494 Lindell Blvd., St. Louis, Mo. 63108. 170,000. Phone: (314) 371-6000.

Optometric Association, American (1898): 243 N. Lindbergh Blvd., St. Louis, Mo. 63141. 28,000. Phone: (314) 991-4100.

*Organization of American States, General Secretariat (1890): 1889 F St. N.W., Washington, D.C. 20006. 32 member nations. Phone: (202) 458-3000.

Ornithologists' Union, American (1883): c/o National Museum of Natural History, Smithsonian Institution, Washington, D.C. 20560. 5,000. Phone: (202) 357-1970.

ORT Federation, American (1922): 817 Broadway, 10th Floor, New York, N.Y. 10003. 160,000. Phone: (212) 677-4400.

Overeaters Anonymous (1960): P.O. Box 92870, Los Angeles, Calif. 90009. 150,000. Phone: (213) 542-8363.

Parents Without Partners (1957): 8807 Colesville Rd., Silver Spring, Md. 20910. 115,000. Phone: (301) 588-9354 or (800) 637-7974.

Parks & Conservation Association, National (1919): 1015 31st St. N.W., Washington, D.C. 20007. 289,000. Phone: (202) 944-8530.

Pathologists, American Association of (1976): 9650 Rockville Pike, Bethesda, Md. 20814-3993. 2,300. Phone: (301) 530-7130.

People for the American Way (1980): 2000 M St. N.W., Suite 400, Washington, D.C. 20036. 280,000. Phone: (202) 467-4999.

Petroleum Geologists, American Association of (1917): P.O. Box 979, Tulsa, Okla. 74101-0979. 34,700. Phone: (918) 584-2555.

Pharmaceutical Association, American (1852): 2215 Constitution Ave. N.W., Washington, D.C. 20037. 40,000. Phone: (202) 628-4410.

Philatelic Society, American (1886): P.O. Box 8000, State College, Pa. 16803. 57,000. Phone: (814) 237-3803.

Photogrammetry and Remote Sensing, American Society for (1934): 5410 Grosvenor Lane, Suite 210, Bethesda, Md. 20814-2160. Phone: (301) 493-0290.

Photographic Society of America (1934): 3000 United Founders Blvd., Suite 103, Oklahoma

City, Okla. 73112. Phone: (405) 843-1437.

Photography, International Center of (1974): 1130 Fifth Ave., New York, N.Y. 10128. Midtown branch: 1133 Avenue of the Americas, New York, N.Y. 10036. Phone: (212) 860-1777.

Physical Society, American (1899): 335 E. 45th St., New York, N.Y. 10017-3483. 39,000. Phone: (212) 682-7341.

Physical Therapy Association, American (APTA) (1921): 1111 N. Fairfax St., Alexandria, Va. 22314. 50,000. Phone: (703) 684-2782.

Physics, American Institute of (1931): 335 E. 45th St., New York, N.Y. 10017. 102,500. Phone: (212) 661-9404.

Pilot Club International (1921): Pilot International World Headquarters, 244 College St., P.O. Box 4844, Macon, Ga. 31213-0599. 21,000. Phone: (912) 743-7403.

Planetary Society, The (1979): 65 N. Catalina Ave., Pasadena, Calif. 91106. 120,000. Phone: (818) 793-5100.

Planned Parenthood® Federation of America, Inc., (1916): 810 Seventh Ave., New York, N.Y. 10019. 171 affiliates. Phone: (212) 541-7800.

Plastics Engineers, Society of (1942): 14 Fairfield Dr., Brookfield, Conn. 06804-0403. 35,000. Phone: (203) 775-0471.

Police, American Federation of (1966): Records Center, 3801 Biscayne Blvd., Miami, Fla. 33137. 55,000. Phone: (305) 573-0070.

Police, International Association of Chiefs of (1893): 1110 N. Glebe Rd., Suite 200, Arlington, Va. 22201. 13,000. Phone (703) 243-6500.

Police Hall of Fame, American (1960): 3801 Biscayne Blvd., Miami, Fla. 33137. 55,000. Phone: (305) 573-0070.

Political and Social Science, American Academy of (1889): 3937 Chestnut St., Philadelphia, Pa. 19104. Phone: (215) 386-4594.

Political Science, Academy of (1880): 475 Riverside Dr., Suite 1274, New York, N.Y. 10115-0012. 9,000. Phone: (212) 870-2500.

Powder Metallurgy Institute, American (1958): 105 College Rd. East, Princeton, N.J. 08540. 2,800. Phone: (609) 452-7700.

Practical Nurse Education and Service, National Association for (1941): 1400 Spring St., Suite 310, Silver Spring, Md. 20910. Phone: (301) 588-2491.

Press Club, National (1908): National Press Bldg., 529 14th St. N.W., Washington, D.C. 20045. 4,800. Phone: (202) 662-7500.

Professional Engineers, National Society of (1934): 1420 King St., Alexandria, Va. 22314. 75,000. Phone: (703) 684-2800.

Professional Photographers of America, Inc. (1880): 1090 Executive Way, Des Plaines, Ill. 60018. 17,000. Phone: (708) 299-8161.

Psychiatric Association, American (1844): 1400 K St. N.W., Washington, D.C. 20005. 36,900. Phone: (202) 682-6000.

Psychoanalytic Association, The American (1911): 309 E. 49th St., New York, N.Y. 10017. 3,000 psychoanalysts. Phone: (212) 752-0450.

Psychological Association, American (1892): 1200 17th St. N.W., Washington, D.C. 20036. 108,000. Phone: (202) 955-7600.

Public Health Association, American (1872): 1015 15th St. N.W., Washington, D.C. 20005. 50,000+. Phone: (202) 789-5600.

Puppeteers of America (1937): 5 Cricklewood Path, Pasadena, Calif. 91107-1002. Phone: (818) 797-5748.

Quality Control, The American Society for (1946): 310 W. Wisconsin Ave., Milwaukee, Wis. 53203. 80,184. Phone: (414) 272-8575.

Railroads, Association of American (1934): 50 F St. N.W., Washington, D.C. 20001-1564. Phone: (202) 639-2100.

Recording Arts and Sciences, Inc., National Academy of (1958): 303 N. Glenoaks Blvd., Suite 140, Burbank, Calif. 91502-1178. 8,200. Phone: (213) 849-1313.

Red Cross, American (1881): 17th and D Sts. N.W., Washington, D.C. 20006. Over 2,800 chapters. Phone: (202) 737-8300.

Rehabilitation Association, National (1925): 633 S. Washington St., Alexandria, Va. 22314-4193. 18,000. Phone: (703) 836-0850.

Research and Enlightenment, Association for (1931): 67th St. & Atlantic Ave. (P.O. Box 595), Virginia Beach, Va. 23451. 75,000. Phone: (804) 428-3588.

Reserve Officers Association of the United States (1922): 1 Constitution Ave. N.E., Washington, D.C. 20002. 125,000. Phone: (202) 479-2200.

Retarded Citizens of the United States, Association for (1950): P.O. Box 1047, Arlington, Tex. 76004. 1,200 chapters. Phone: (817) 261-6003.

Retired Federal Employees, National Association of (1921): 1533 New Hampshire Ave. N.W., Washington, D.C. 20036-1279. 500,000. Phone: (202) 234-0832.

*Retired Persons, American Association of (1958): 1909 K St. N.W., Washington, D.C. 20049. 29,000,000. Phone: (202) 872-4700.

Reye's Syndrome Foundation, National (1974): 426 N. Lewis St., Bryan, Ohio 43506. Phone: (800) 233-7393. In Ohio: (800) 231-7393.

RID-USA (Remove Intoxicated Drivers) (1978): Box 520, Schenectady, N.Y. 12301. Over 155/42 state chapters. Phone: (518) 372-0034.

Right to Life, National Committee (1973): 419 7th St. N.W., Washington, D.C. 20004. Phone: (202) 626-8800.

Rotary International (1905): One Rotary Center, 1560 Sherman Ave., Evanston, Ill. 60201. 1,116,000 in 172 countries. Phone: (708) 866-3000.

SAE International (1905): 400 Commonweatlh Dr., Warrendale, Pa. 15096-0001. 60,000. Phone: (412) 776-4841.

Safety Council, National (1913): 444 N. Michigan Ave., Chicago, Ill. 60611. Phone: (312) 527-4800.

Salvation Army, The (1865): National Headquarters, 615 Slaters Lane, Alexandria, Va. 22314. 445,566. Phone: (703) 979-3380.

SANE/FREEZE: Campaign for Global Security (a merger of SANE and the Nuclear Weapons Freeze Campaign) (1957): 1819 H St. N.W., Suite 640, Washington, D.C. 20006-3603. 170,000. Phone: (202) 862-9740.

Save-the-Redwoods League (1918): 114 Sansome St., Suite 605, San Francisco, Calif. 94104. 45,000. Phone: (415) 362-2352.

Savings Institutions, National Council of (1920): 1101 15th St. N.W., Suite 400, Washington, D.C. 20005-5070. Phone: (202) 857-3100.

Science, American Association for the Advancement of (1848): 1333 H St. N.W., Washington, D.C. 20005. 133,000. Phone: (202) 326-6400.

Science and Health, American Council on (1978): 1995 Broadway, 16th Floor, New York, N.Y. 10023-5860. Phone: (212) 362-7044.

Science Fiction Society, World (1939): c/o Southern California Institute for Fan Interests, P.O. Box 8442, Van Nuys, Calif. 91409. 6,000. Phone:

(818) 366-3827.

Science Writers, Inc., National Association of (1934): P.O. Box 294, Greenlawn, N.Y. 11740. 1,650. Phone: (516) 757-5664.

Scientists, Federation of American (FAS) (1945): 307 Massachusetts Ave. N.E., Washington, D.C. 20002. 4,000. Phone: (202) 546-3300.

SCRABBLE® Association, National (1972): P.O. Box 700, Front Street Garden, Greenport, N.Y. 11944. 15,000. Phone: (516) 477-0033.

Screen Actors Guild (1933): 7065 Hollywood Blvd., Hollywood, Calif. 90028-6065. 76,000. Phone: (213) 465-4600.

Sculpture Society, National (1893): 15 E. 26th St., New York, N.Y. 10010. 350. Phone: (212) 889-6960.

Seeing Eye Inc., The (1929): P.O. Box 375. Morristown, N.J. 07963-0375. Phone: (201) 539-4425.

Senior Citizens, National Alliance of (1974): 2525 Wilson Blvd., Arlington, Va. 22201. 65,000. Phone: (703) 528-4380.

Separationists, Society of (1963): P.O. Box 140195, Austin, Tex. 78714-0195. 37,216 families. Phone: (512) 458-1244.

Shriners of North America and Shriners Hospitals for Crippled Children, The (1872): Box 31356, Tampa, Fla. 33631-3356. 750,000. Phone: (813) 281-0300.

Sierra Club (1892): 730 Polk St., San Francisco, Calif. 94109. 650,000. Phone: (415) 776-2211.

SIETAR INTERNATIONAL (1974) 733 15th St. N.W., Suite 900, Washington, D.C. 20005. 1,500. Phone: (202) 737-5000.

Simon Wiesenthal Center (1978): 9760 W. Pico Blvd., Los Angeles, Calif. 90035. 375,000. Phone: (213) 553-9036.

Small Business United, National (1937): 1155 15th St. N.W., #710, Washington, D.C. 20005. 50,000. Phone: (202) 293-8830.

Social Work Education, Council on (1919): 1600 Duke St., Alexandria, Va. 22314-3421. Phone: (703) 683-8080.

Social Workers, National Association of (1955): 7981 Eastern Ave., Silver Spring, Md. 20910. Phone: (301) 565-0333.

Sociological Association, American (1905): 1722 N St. N.W., Washington, D.C. 20036-2981. 13,000. Phone: (202) 833-3410.

Soil and Water Conservation Society (1945): 7515 N.E. Ankeny Rd., Ankeny, Iowa 50021. 13,000. Phone: (515) 289-2331.

Songwriters Guild of America, The (1931): 276 Fifth Ave., Suite 306, New York, N.Y. 10001. 4,200. Phone: (212) 686-6820.

Sons of Italy in America, Order (1905): 219 E St. N.E., Washington, D.C. 20002. 175,000. Phone: (202) 547-2900.

Sons of the American Revolution, National Society of the (1889): 1000 S. 4th St., Louisville, Ky. 40203. 26,000. Phone: (502) 589-1776.

Soroptimist International of the Americas (1921): 1616 Walnut St., Philadelphia, Pa. 19103. 50,000. Phone: (215) 732-0512.

Southern Association on Children Under Six (1948): Box 5403, Brady Station, Little Rock, Ark. 72215. 16,000. Phone: (501) 663-0353.

Space Education Association, U.S. (1973): 746 Turnpike Rd., Elizabethtown, Pa. 17022-1161. 1,000. Phone: (717) 367-3265.

Space Society, National (1974): 922 Pennsylvania Ave. S.E., Washington, D.C. 20003. 30,000. Phone: (202) 543-1900.

Special Olympics International (1968): 1350 New York Ave. N.W., Suite 500, Washington, D.C., 20005. 1,000,000. Phone: (202) 628-3630.

Speech-Language-Hearing Association, American (1925): 10801 Rockville Pike, Rockville, Md. 20852. 62,000. Phone: (301) 897-5700.

Sports Car Club of America Inc. (1944): 9033 E. Easter Place, Englewood, Colo. 80112-2105. 54,000. Phone: (303) 694-7222.

State Garden Clubs, Inc., National Council of (1929): 4401 Magnolia Ave., St. Louis, Mo. 63110. 280,992. Phone: (314) 776-7574.

State Governments, The Council of (1933): P.O. Box 11910, Iron Works Pike, Lexington, Ky. 40578-1910. All state officials, all 50 states. Phone: (606) 231-1939.

Statistical Association, American (1839): 1429 Duke St., Alexandria, Va. 22314. 15,103.

Student Association, United States (1947): 1012 14th St. N.W., #207, Washington, D.C. 20005. Phone: (202) 347-8772.

Surgeons, American College of (1913): 55 E. Erie, St., Chicago, Ill. 60611-2797. 50,000+. Phone: (312) 664-4050.

Symphony Orchestra League, American (1942): 777 Fourteenth St. N.W., Suite 500, Washington, D.C. 20005. 4,713. Phone: (202) 628-0099.

TASH: The Association for Persons with Severe Handicaps (1973): 7010 Roosevelt Way N.E., Seattle, Wash. 98115. 9,000. Phone: (206) 523-8446.

Tax Foundation, Inc. (1937): 470 L'Enfant Plaza S.W., Suite 7112, Washington, D.C. 20024. Phone: (202) 863-5454.

Teachers, American Federation of (1916): 555 New Jersey Ave. N.W., Washington, D.C., 20001. 660,000. Phone: (202) 879-4400.

Television Arts and Sciences, National Academy of (1948): 111 W. 57th St., New York, N.Y., 10019. 15,000. Phone: (212) 586-8424.

Testing & Materials, American Society for (1898): 1916 Race St., Philadelphia, Pa. 19103. 32,000. Phone: (215) 299-5400.

Theatre Guild (1919): 226 W. 47th St., New York, N.Y. 10036. 105,000. Phone: (212) 869-5470.

Theosophical Society in America, The (1875): P.O. Box 270, Wheaton, Ill. 60189-0270. 5,600. Phone: (708) 668-1571.

Tin Can Sailors, Inc. (1976): Battleship Cove, Fall River, Mass. 02721. 14,000. Phone: (617) 678-1905.

Toastmasters International (1924): P.O. Box 9052, Mission Viejo, Calif. 92690-7052, and 23182 Arroyo Vista, Rancho Santa Margarita, Calif. 92688. 160,000. Phone: (714) 542-6793 and (714) 858-8255.

TOUGHLOVE International (1977): P.O. Box 1069, Doylestown, Pa. 18901. 750 registered groups. Phone: (215) 348-7090.

TransAfrica Forum (1982): 545 Eighth St. S.E., Suite 200, Washington, D.C. 20003. Phone: (202) 547-2550.

Travel Agents, American Society of (ASTA) (1931): P.O. Box 23992, Washington, D.C. 20026-3992. 20,000. Phone: (703) 739-2782.

Travelers Aid Services (1905/1982): 2 Lafayette St., New York, N.Y. 10007. Lucy N. Friedman, Executive Director. (Result of merger of Travelers Aid Society of New York and Victim Services Agency in 1982). Phone: (212) 577-7700. **Client Services:** Times Square Office, 158-160 W. 42nd St., Manhattan (212) 944-0013; JFK Airport Office, International Arrivals Bldg., Jamaica, Queens (718) 656-4870; 24-hour Crime Victims

Hotline (212) 577-7777; Immigration Hotline (718) 899-4000.

Tuberous Sclerosis Association, Inc., National (1975): 8000 Corporate Dr., Suite 120, Landover, Md. 20785. 5,000. Phone: (301) 459-9888 or (800) 225-6872.

UFOs, National Investigations Committee on (1967): 14617 Victory Blvd., Suite 4, Van Nuys, Calif. 91411. Phone: (818) 989-5942.

UNICEF, U.S. Committee for (1947): 333 E. 38th St., New York, N.Y. 10016. 20,000 volunteers. Phone: (212) 686-5522.

Union of Concerned Scientists (1969): 26 Church St., Cambridge, Mass. 02238. 90,000. Phone: (617) 547-5552.

United Jewish Appeal (1939): 99 Park Ave., New York, N.Y. 10016. Phone: (212) 818-9100.

United Negro College Fund Inc. (1944): 500 E. 62nd St., New York, N.Y. 10021. Phone: (212) 326-1100.

United Way of America (1918): 701 N. Fairfax St., Alexandria, Va. 22314-2045. 2,300 local United Ways. Phone: (703) 836-7100.

University Foundation, International (1973): 1301 S. Noland Rd., Independence, Mo. 64055. 35,000. Phone: (816) 461-3633.

University Women, American Association of (1881): 1111 16th St. N.W., Washington, D.C. 20036. 140,000. Phone: (202) 785-7700.

Urban League, National (1910): 500 E. 62nd St., New York, N.Y. 10021. 116. Phone: (212) 310-9000.

USO (United Service Organizations) (1941): World Headquarters, 601 Indiana Ave. N.W., Washington, D.C. 20004. Phone: (202) 783-8121.

Variety Clubs International (1927): 1560 Broadway, Suite 1209, New York, N.Y. 10036. 15,000. Phone: (212) 704-9872.

Veterans Committee, American (AVC) (1944): 6309 Bannockburn Dr., Bethesda, Md. 20817. 15,000. Phone: (301) 320-6490.

Veterans of Foreign Wars of the U.S. (1899): V.F.W. Bldg., 34th and Broadway, Kansas City, Mo. 64111. V.F.W. and Auxiliary, 2,850,000. Phone: (816) 756-3390.

Veterinary Medical Association, American (1863): 930 N. Meacham Rd., Schaumburg, Ill. 60196-1074. 50,000. Phone: (708) 605-8070.

Visually Handicapped, Division for the (1948): The Council for Exceptional Children, 1920 Association Dr., Reston, Va. 22091. 1,000. Phone: (703) 620-3660.

Volunteers of America (1896): 3813 N. Causeway Blvd., Metairie, La. 70002. Provides human services in over 200 communities. Phone: (504) 837-2652.

War Resisters League (1923): 339 Lafayette St., New York, N.Y. 10012. 18,000. Phone: (212) 228-0450.

Washington Legal Foundation (1976): 1705 N St. N.W., Washington, D.C. 20036. 200,000. Phone: (202) 857-0240.

Water Quality Association (1974): 4151 Naperville Rd., Lisle, Ill. 60532. Phone: (708) 505-0160.

Water Resources Association, American (1964): 5410 Grosvenor Lane, Suite 220, Bethesda, Md. 20814. 4,000. Phone: (301) 493-8600.

Welding Society, American (1919): 550 N.W. Le-

Jeune Rd., Miami, Fla. 33126. 38,000. Phone: (305) 443-9353; toll free (800) 443-9353.

Wildlife Federation, National (1936): 1400 16th St. N.W., Washington, D.C. 20036-2266. 5,600,000. Phone: (202) 797-6800.

Wildlife Fund, World (1961): 1250 24th St. N.W., Washington, D.C. 20037. 1.1 million. Phone: (202) 293-4800.

Woman's Christian Temperance Union, National (1874): 1730 Chicago Ave., Evanston, Ill. 60201. Under 50,000. Phone: (708) 864-1396.

Women, National Organization for (NOW) (1966): 1000 16th St. N.W., Suite 700, Washington, D.C. 20036-5705. 270,000. Phone: (202) 331-0066.

Women's American ORT (1927): 315 Park Ave. South, New York, N.Y. 10010. Over 1,000 Chapters. Phone: (212) 505-7700.

Women's Clubs, General Federation of (1890): 1734 N St., N.W., Washington, D.C. 20036-2990. 400,000. Phone: (202) 347-3168.

Women's Educational and Industrial Union (1877): 356 Boylston St., Boston, Mass. 02116. 2,200. Phone: (617) 536-5651.

Women's International League for Peace and Freedom (1915): 1213 Race St., Philadelphia, Pa. 19107-1691. 50,000. Phone: (215) 563-7110.

World Future Society (1966): 4916 Saint Elmo Ave., Bethesda, Md. 20814. 30,000. Phone: (301) 656-8274.

World Health, American Association for (1951): 2001 S St. N.W., Suite 530, Washington, D.C. 20009. 800. Phone: (202) 265-0286.

World Peace, International Association of Educators for (1969): P.O. Box 3282, Mastin Lake Station, Huntsville, Ala. 35810. 20,000. Phone: (205) 534-5501.

World Peace Foundation (1910): 22 Batterymarch St., Boston, Mass. 02109. Phone: (617) 482-3875.

Worldwatch Institute (1974): 1776 Massachusetts Ave. N.W., Washington, D.C. 20036. Research organization. Phone: (202) 452-1999.

Writers Union, National (1983): 13 Astor Pl., 7th Fl., New York, NY 10003. 3,000. Phone: (212) 254-0279.

YMCA of the USA (1844): 101 N. Wacker Dr., Chicago, Ill. 60606. 12,800,000. Phone: (312) 977-0031.

*Young Women's Christian Association of the U.S.A. (1858 in U.S.A., 1855 in England): 726 Broadway, New York, N.Y. 10003. 2,030,922. Phone: (212) 614-2846.

Youth Hostels, Inc., American (1934): P.O. Box 37613, Washington, D.C. 20013-7613. 100,000. Phone: (202) 783-6161.

Zero Population Growth (1968): 1400 Sixteenth St. N.W., Suite 320, Washington, D.C. 20036. 33,000. Phone: (202) 332-2200.

Zionist Organization of America (1897): ZOA House, 4 E. 34th St., New York, N.Y. 10016. 135,000. Phone: (212) 481-1500.

Zoological Parks and Aquariums, American Association of (1924): Oglebay Park, Wheeling, W. Va. 26003. 6,000. Phone: (304) 242-2160.

Zoologists, American Society of (1890): 104 Sirius Circle, Thousand Oaks, Calif. 91360. 4,000. Phone: (805) 492-3585.

EDUCATION

School Enrollment, October 1990
(in thousands)

Age	White Enrolled	White Percent	Black Enrolled	Black Percent	Hispanic origin[1] Enrolled	Hispanic origin[1] Percent	All races Enrolled	All races Percent
3 and 4 years	2,700	44.9	452	41.6	249	29.8	3,292	44.4
5 and 6 years	5,750	96.5	1,129	96.3	835	94.8	7,207	96.5
7 to 9 years	8,848	99.7	1,628	99.9	1,296	99.6	10,976	99.7
10 to 13 years	11,228	99.6	2,204	99.9	1,498	99.2	14,040	99.6
14 to 15 years	5,265	99.1	1,023	99.2	739	99.0	6,555	99.0
16 and 17 years	4,858	92.5	962	91.7	592	85.4	6,098	92.5
18 and 19 years	3,271	57.1	596	55.2	329	44.1	4,044	57.3
20 and 21 years	2,402	41.0	305	28.4	213	27.2	2,852	39.7
22 to 24 years	1,781	20.2	274	20.0	121	9.9	2,231	21.0
25 to 29 years	1,706	9.9	162	6.1	130	6.3	2,013	9.7
30 to 34 years	1,090	5.9	119	4.4	72	3.6	1,281	5.8
Total	**48,899**	**49.5**	**8,854**	**51.9**	**6,073**	**47.4**	**60,588**	**50.2**

1. Persons of Hispanic origin may be of any race. NOTE: Figures include persons enrolled in nursery school, kindergarten, elementary school, high school, and college. *Source:* Department of Commerce, Bureau of the Census.

Persons Not Enrolled in School, October 1990
(in thousands)

Age	Population	Total not enrolled Number	Total not enrolled Percent	High school graduate Number	High school graduate Percent	Not high school graduate (dropouts)[1] Number	Not high school graduate (dropouts)[1] Percent
14 and 15 years	6,620	64	1.0	12	0.2	57	0.9
16 and 17 years	6,591	493	7.5	248	3.8	418	6.3
18 and 19 years	7,064	3,020	42.8	5,037	71.3	1,003	14.2
20 and 21 years	7,183	4,331	60.3	6,180	86.0	918	12.8
22 to 24 years	10,605	8,374	79.0	9,094	85.8	1,458	13.8

1. Persons who are not enrolled in school and who are not high school graduates are considered dropouts. *Source:* Department of Commerce, Bureau of the Census.

School Enrollment by Grade, Control, and Race
(in thousands)

Grade level and type of control	White Oct. 1990[3]	White Oct. 1980[4]	White Oct. 1970	Black Oct. 1990[3]	Black Oct. 1980[4]	Black Oct. 1970	All races[1] Oct. 1990[3]	All races[1] Oct. 1980[4]	All races[1] Oct. 1970
Nursery school: Public	896	432	198	283	180	129	1,212	633	333
Private	1,961	1,205	695	148	115	49	2,188	1,354	763
Kindergarten: Public	2,609	2,172	2,233	574	440	374	3,332	2,690	2,674
Private	472	423	473	62	50	53	567	486	536
Grades 1–8: Public	20,997	19,743	24,923	4,431	4,058	4,668	26,615	24,398	30,001
Private	2,359	2,768	3,715	199	202	200	2,676	3,051	3,949
Grades 9–12: Public	9,429	12,056[2]	11,599	1,937	2,200[2]	1,794	11,911	14,556[2]	13,545
Private	810	—	1,124	65	—	41	906	—	1,170
College: Public	9,049	8,875[2]	5,168	1,120	1,007[2]	422	10,754	10,180[2]	5,699
Private	2,439	—	1,591	274	—	100	2,869	—	1,714
Total: Public	42,954	—	44,121	8,344	—	7,387	53,823	—	52,225
Private	8,041	—	7,598	748	—	443	9,204	—	8,132
Grand Total	**50,995**	**47,673**	**51,719**	**9,092**	**8,251**	**7,830**	**63,027**	**57,348**	**60,357**

1. Includes persons of Spanish origin. 2. Total public and private. Breakdown not available. 3. Estimates controlled to 1980 census base. 4. Estimates controlled to 1970 census base. *Source:* Department of Commerce, Bureau of the Census.

State Compulsory School Attendance Laws, November 1989

State	Enactment[1]	Age limits	State	Enactment[1]	Age limits
Alabama	1915	7–16	Montana[4]	1883	7–16
Alaska[2]	1929	7–16	Nebraska	1887	7–16
Arizona	1899	8–16	Nevada	1873	7–17
Arkansas	1909	5–17	New Hampshire	1871	6–16
California	1874	6–16	New Jersey	1875	6–16
Colorado	1889	7–16	New Mexico	1891	6–18
Connecticut	1872	7–16	New York[5]	1874	6–16
Delaware	1907	5–16	North Carolina	1907	7–16
D. C.	1864	7–17	North Dakota	1883	7–16
Florida	1915	6–16	Ohio	1877	6–18
Georgia	1916	7–16	Oklahoma	1907	7–18
Hawaii	1896	6–18	Oregon	1889	7–18
Idaho	1887	7–16	Pennsylvania	1895	8–17
Illinois	1883	7–16	Rhode Island	1883	6–16
Indiana	1897	7–16	South Carolina[6]	1915	5–17
Iowa	1902	7–16	South Dakota[4]	1883	7–16
Kansas	1874	7–16	Tennessee	1905	7–17
Kentucky[3]	1896	6–16	Texas[7]	1915	7–17
Louisiana	1910	7–17	Utah	1890	6–18
Maine	1875	7–17	Vermont	1867	7–16
Maryland	1902	6–16	Virginia	1908	5–17
Massachusetts	1852	6–16	Washington	1871	8–18
Michigan	1871	6–16	West Virginia	1897	6–16
Minnesota	1885	7–16	Wisconsin	1879	6–18
Mississippi	1918	6–14	Wyoming	1876	7–16
Missouri	1905	7–16			

1. Date of enactment of first compulsory attendance law. 2. Ages 7 to 16 or high school graduation. 3. Must have parental signature for leaving school between ages of 16 and 18. 4. May leave after completion of eighth grade. 5. The ages are 6 to 17 for New York City and Buffalo. 6. Permits parental waiver of kindergarten at age 5. 7. Must complete academic year in which 16th birthday occurs. *Source:* Department of Education, National Center for Educational Statistics.

High School and College Graduates

School Year	High School			College[1]		
	Men	Women	Total	Men	Women	Total
1900	38,075	56,808	94,883	22,173	5,237	27,410
1910	63,676	92,753	156,429	28,762	8,437	37,199
1920	123,684	187,582	311,266	31,980	16,642	48,622
1929–30	300,376	366,528	666,904	73,615	48,869	122,484
1939–40	578,718	642,757	1,221,475	109,546	76,954	186,500
1949–50	570,700	629,000	1,199,700	328,841	103,217	432,058
1959–60	898,000	966,000	1,864,000	254,063	138,377	392,440
1964–65	1,314,000	1,351,000	2,665,000	316,286	213,717	530,003
1969–70	1,433,000	1,463,000	2,896,000	484,174	343,060	827,234
1970–71	1,456,000	1,487,000	2,943,000	511,138	366,538	877,676
1971–72	1,490,000	1,518,000	3,008,000	541,313	389,371	930,684
1972–73	1,501,000	1,536,000	3,037,000	564,680	407,700	972,380
1973–74	1,515,000	1,565,000	3,080,000	575,843	423,749	999,592
1974–75	1,541,000	1,599,000	3,140,000	533,797	425,052	978,849
1975–76	1,554,000	1,601,000	3,155,000	557,817	430,578	988,395
1976–77	1,548,000	1,606,000	3,154,000	547,919	435,989	983,908
1977–78	1,535,000	1,599,000	3,134,000	487,000	434,000	921,000
1978–79	1,531,800	1,602,400	3,134,200	529,996	460,242	990,238
1979–80	1,500,000	1,558,000	3,058,000	526,327	473,221	999,548
1980–81	1,483,000	1,537,000	3,020,000	470,000	465,000	935,000
1981–82	1,474,000	1,527,000	3,001,000	473,000	480,000	953,000
1982–83	1,437,000	1,451,000	2,888,000	479,140	490,370	969,510
1983–84	n.a.	n.a.	2,767,000	482,319	491,990	974,309
1984–85	n.a.	n.a.	2,677,000	482,528	496,949	979,477
1985–86	n.a.	n.a.	2,643,000	485,923	501,900	987,823
1986–87	n.a.	n.a.	2,694,000	480,854	510,485	991,339
1987–88	n.a.	n.a.	2,801,000	476,842[2]	516,520[2]	993,362[2]
1988–89	n.a.	n.a.	2,787,000[3]	483,613[3]	533,115[3]	1,016,728[3]

1. Includes bachelor's and first-professional degrees for years 1900–1960. 2. Preliminary data. 3. Estimated. n.a. = not available. NOTE: Includes graduates from public and private schools. Beginning in 1959–60, figures include Alaska and Hawaii. Because of rounding, details may not add to totals. Most recent data available. *Source:* Department of Education, Center for Education Statistics.

Federal Funds for Some Major Programs for Education, Fiscal Year 1992[1]

Program	Amount in thousands	Program	Amount in thousands
Elementary-secondary		College housing loans	53,072
Educationally disadvantaged	$6,424,344	**Vocational and adult education**	1,261,667
School improvement programs	1,500,528	**Education for the handicapped**	
Bilingual education	200,789	Special education	2,729,853
School assistance in federally		Rehabilitation services and	
affected areas	620,130	disability research	2,003,380
Higher education		All other	114,208
Student financial assistance	6,713,681	**Indian education**	77,400
Guaranteed student loans	3,025,952	**Education research and improvement**	295,751
Higher education facliities loans	9,023	**Total**	**$25,029,778**

1. Estimated outlay for fiscal year 1992. *Source: Budget of the United States Government,* Fiscal Year 1992.

Funding for Public Elementary and Secondary Education, 1981–82 to 1987–88

(In thousands except percent)

School year	Total	Federal	State	Local[1]	% Federal	& State	% Local[1]
1981–82	110,191,257	8,186,466	52,436,435	49,568,356	7.4	47.6	45.0
1982–83	117,497,502	8,339,990	56,282,157	52,875,354	7.1	47.9	45.0
1983–84	126,055,419	8,576,547	60,232,981	57,245,892	6.8	47.8	45.4
1984–85	137,294,678	9,105,569	67,168,684	61,020,425	6.6	48.9	44.4
1985–86	149,127,779	9,975,622	73,619,575	65,532,582	6.7	49.4	43.9
1986–87	158,523,693	10,146,013	78,830,437	69,547,243	6.4	49.7	43.9
1987–88	169,650,907	10,719,821	84,042,408	74,888,679	6.3	49.5	44.1

1. Includes a relatively small amount from nongovernmental sources (gifts and tuition and transportation fees from patrons). *Source:* U.S. Department of Education, National Center for Education Statistics.

Major U.S. College and University Libraries

(Top 50 based on number of volumes in library)

Institution	Volumes	Microforms[1]	Institution	Volumes	Microforms[1]
Harvard	11,874,148	5,557,388	Iowa	3,104,621	3,381,454
Yale	8,862,768	3,393,479	Pennsylvania State	3,095,863	3,125,463
U of Illinois–Urbana	7,748,736	3,502,629	New York	3,092,620	2,039,077
U of California–Berkeley	7,540,234	4,455,669	U of Florida	2,892,301	2,704,717
U of Michigan	6,369,490	4,063,879	U of Georgia	2,889,108	4,518,130
U of Texas	6,265,236	4,413,304	U of Pittsburgh	2,878,713	2,525,370
U of California–Los Angeles	6,156,761	5,618,652	U of Kansas	2,868,223	2,218,777
Columbia	6,032,545	4,094,213	Johns Hopkins	2,835,664	1,548,084
Stanford	5,871,063	3,709,144	Rochester	2,686,996	1,214,830
Cornell	5,216,501	5,036,410	U of Southern California	2,626,271	2,987,801
U of Chicago	5,191,998	1,535,955	Arizona State	2,599,701	3,371,362
U of Wisconsin	5,036,144	3,413,874	SUNY–Buffalo	2,591,006	3,761,902
U of Washington	4,908,988	5,337,134	U of Missouri	2,486,014	4,777,547
U of Minnesota	4,651,111	3,141,452	Louisiana State	2,460,219	2,144,615
Ohio State	4,430,132	3,248,867	South Carolina	2,431,129	3,467,747
Princeton	4,276,086	2,395,378	U of Massachusetts	2,409,946	1,781,928
Indiana	4,133,331	1,754,286	U of Hawaii	2,385,601	3,640,718
Duke	3,846,295	1,481,804	U of California–Davis	2,376,157	2,828,257
North Carolina	3,751,660	3,159,522	Wayne State	2,374,831	2,099,908
U of Pennsylvania	3,665,786	2,427,600	Syracuse	2,332,676	3,654,447
U of Arizona	3,549,281	4,020,838	U of Oklahoma	2,297,087	2,903,183
Northwestern	3,474,423	2,215,175	U of Colorado	2,286,736	1,290,062
Michigan State	3,417,388	3,526,349	Washington U–St. Louis	2,277,203	1,849,845
Rutgers	3,219,823	3,705,472	U of Connecticut	2,271,849	2,842,144
U of Virginia	3,193,260	4,302,386	Brown	2,227,301	1,116,626

1. Includes reels of microfilm and number of microcards, microprint sheets, and microfiches. *Source:* Association of Research Libraries.

College and University Endowments, 1989–90
(top 75 in millions of dollars)

Institution	Endowment (market value)	Voluntary support[1]	Expenditures[2]	Institution	Endowment (market value)	Voluntary support[1]	Expenditures[2]
Harvard U	$4,683.2	$213.5	$1,025.7	Ohio State U	321.9	63.3	771.2
Yale U	2,585.3	130.0	617.3	Wake Forest U	318.0	21.7	230.9
Princeton U	2,475.1	75.2	276.4	U of Cincinnati	314.5	27.4	366.1
Stanford U	2,053.1	202.2	864.0	Texas Christian U	314.4	11.7	74.8
Columbia U	1,515.8	123.2	789.7	U of California–Los Angeles	304.3	96.5	0.0
Texas A&M	1,485.9	50.8	307.8	Carnegie–Mellon U	299.2	36.1	250.7
Massachusetts Inst. of Tech.	1,404.6	117.6	606.3	George Washington U	296.7	15.5	247.2
Washington U	1,386.9	49.6	542.2	Pomona C	296.0	21.4	36.8
Northwestern U	1,202.6	68.1	427.3	Grinnell C	286.8	6.5	28.5
Emory U	1,106.0	38.8	322.8	Indiana U	285.9	79.1	815.0
U of Chicago	1,074.5	67.1	556.7	Trinity U	285.6	10.3	44.8
Rice U	1,068.5	25.8	118.2	U of Richmond	283.0	13.6	49.1
Cornell U	926.9	161.3	789.6	Loyola U of Chicago	278.4	36.3	150.5
U of Pennsylvania	808.4	140.0	685.3	U of Pittsburgh	278.1	36.6	504.4
Dartmouth C	653.8	51.1	197.2	Boston C	277.1	20.0	159.3
U of Notre Dame	605.6	53.8	124.0	Berea C	271.1	14.6	18.8
Vanderbilt U	604.0	43.3	329.5	Wesleyan U	271.0	12.3	71.3
U of Rochester	589.0	34.8	349.2	Amherst C	269.4	10.9	45.0
Johns Hopkins U	560.5	111.8	684.8	Lehigh U	260.4	21.7	113.2
New York U	546.7	74.7	696.2	Baylor U	250.5	23.0	99.4
Rockefeller U	544.9	24.9	92.2	Oberlin C	244.6	10.4	63.0
Duke U	505.0	108.0	428.5	Vassar C	242.5	13.4	53.2
U of Michigan	495.9	83.6	929.4	Georgetown U	242.3	28.6	283.5
U of Southern California	495.6	126.1	689.3	Tulane U	233.4	22.8	219.9
U of Virginia	487.5	51.3	364.9	Rensselaer Poly. Inst.	230.2	23.6	147.9
California Inst. of Tech.	467.0	37.2	184.8	Lafayette C	228.9	13.9	44.1
U of Minnesota	466.3	105.3	965.7	Middlebury C	227.8	9.7	53.3
Brown U	440.7	42.0	200.7	U of Kansas	226.0	23.7	220.0
Case Western Reserve U	420.0	40.8	242.6	Boston U	218.0	28.9	494.8
Princeton Theol. Sem.	379.0	4.3	21.8	U of Wisconsin–Madison	217.5	124.4	802.5
Wellesley C	374.1	29.2	64.4	U of Tennessee System	210.0	33.5	587.6
U of Texas–Austin	355.6	56.7	544.2	Georgia Inst. of Tech.	200.4	28.5	282.0
Southern Methodist U	352.3	22.0	131.5	U of North Carolina at Chapel Hill	200.2	54.2	496.5
Purdue U	350.4	27.5	539.9	U of Illinois	190.5	86.6	1,153.9
Smith C	341.9	35.3	88.8	Saint Louis U	188.1	29.5	174.8
Swarthmore C	336.0	13.3	40.6	Pennsylvania State U	186.3	62.4	825.5
Williams C	333.1	20.0	55.5	U of Florida	185.1	54.8	712.3
Macalester C	326.3	5.5	29.7				

1. Gifts from business, alumni, religious denominations, and others. 2. Figure represents about 80% of typical operating budget. Does not include auxiliary enterprises and capital outlays. NOTE: C = College; U = University. Source: Council for Aid to Education.

Institutions of Higher Education—Average Salaries and Fringe Benefits for Faculty Members, 1970–1989[1]
(in thousands of dollars)

Control and Acadmic Rank	1989	1988	1987	1986	1985	1984	1983	1982	1980	1975	1970
Average Salaries											
Public: All ranks	39.6	37.2	35.8	33.4	31.2	29.4	28.6	26.2	22.1	16.6	13.1
Professor	50.1	47.2	45.3	42.3	39.6	37.1	36.0	33.7	28.8	21.7	17.3
Associate professor	37.9	35.6	34.2	32.2	30.2	28.4	27.5	25.7	21.9	16.7	13.2
Assistant professor	31.7	29.6	28.5	26.7	25.0	23.5	22.6	21.2	18.0	13.7	10.9
Instructor	23.9	22.2	21.8	20.9	19.5	19.1	17.7	16.7	14.8	11.2	9.1
Private:[2] All ranks	42.4	39.7	37.8	35.4	33.0	31.1	29.2	26.8	22.1	16.6	13.1
Professor	55.9	52.2	50.3	47.0	44.1	41.5	38.8	35.8	30.1	22.4	17.8
Associate professor	38.8	36.6	34.9	32.9	30.9	29.4	27.5	25.4	21.0	16.0	12.6
Assistant professor	31.9	28.3	26.8	25.0	23.7	22.1	20.4	17.0	13.0	10.3	
Instructor	24.1	22.7	20.4	19.8	19.0	18.4	17.6	15.9	13.3	10.9	8.6
Average Fringe Benefits—All Ranks Combined											
Public	9.0	8.2	7.8	7.3	7.0	6.0	5.4	5.1	3.9	2.5	1.9
Private[2]	10.0	9.2	8.6	8.0	7.2	6.4	5.7	5.4	4.1	2.8	2.2

1. Figures are for 9 months teaching for full-time faculty members in four-year colleges and universities. 2. Excludes church-related colleges and universities. Source: U.S. Bureau of the Census, Statistical Abstract of the United States: 1990. NOTE: Data are latest available.

Accredited U.S. Senior Colleges and Universities

Source: The Guidance Information System™, a product of The Riverside Publishing Company, a Houghton Mifflin Company.

Schools listed are four-year institutions that offer at least a Bachelor's degree and are fully accredited by one of the institutional and professional accrediting associations. Included are accredited colleges outside the U.S.

Tuition, room, and board listed are average annual figures (including fees) subject to fluctuation, usually covering two semesters, two out of three trimesters, or three out of four quarters, depending on the school calendar.

For further informmation, write to the Registrar of the school concerned.

NOTE: n.a. = information not available. — = does not apply. Enrollment figures are approximate. (C) = Coeducational, (M) = primarily for men, (W) = primarily for women.

Abbreviations used for controls:

P   Private   Pub   Public

Institution and location	Enrollment	Control	Tuition ($) Res.	Nonres.	Rm/Bd ($)
Abilene Christian University; Abilene, Tex. 79699	3,529 (C)	P	6,944	6,944	3,200
Academy of Art College; San Francisco, Calif. 94108	2,156 (C)	P	4,800	4,800	5,400
Academy of the New Church College; Bryn Athyn, Pa. 19009	139 (C)	P	3,483	3,483	3,039
Adams State College; Alamosa, Colo. 81102	2,161 (C)	Pub	1,445	3,792	2,632
Adelphi University; Garden City, N.Y. 11530	4,813 (C)	P	9,450	9,450	4,520
Adrian College; Adrian, Mich. 49221	1,180 (C)	P	9,340	9,340	3,175
Aeronautics, College of; Flushing, N.Y. 11371	1,333 (C)	P	5,600	5,600	n.a.
Aero-Space Institute; Chicago, Ill. 60605-10717	103 (C)	P	6,000	6,000	n.a.
Agnes Scott College; Decatur, Ga. 30030	591 (W)	P	10,575	10,575	4,180
Akron, University of; Akron, Ohio 44325	24,665 (C)	Pub	2,431	5,971	3,200
Alabama, University of; Tuscaloosa, Ala. 35487-0132	15,910 (C)	Pub	1,936	4,800	3,288
Alabama, University of–Birmingham; Birmingham, Ala. 35294	10,616 (C)	Pub	1,920	3,660	2,545
Alabama, University of–Huntsville; Huntsville, Ala. 35899	10,616 (C)	Pub	2,019	4,038	2,705
Alabama A&M University; Normal, Ala. 35762	3,710 (C)	Pub	1,248	2,236	2,036
Alabama State University; Montgomery, Ala. 36101-0271	4,024 (C)	Pub	1,268	2,428	2,110
Alaska, University of-Anchorage; Anchorage, Alas. 99508	12,860 (C)	Pub	1,300	3,900	3,600
Alaska, University of-Fairbanks; Fairbanks, Alas. 99701	6,989 (C)	Pub	1,490	4,090	2,880
Alaska Southeast, University of-Juneau; Juneau, Alas. 99801	2,158 (C)	Pub	1,300	3,900	3,850
Alaska Bible College; Glennallen, Alas. 99588	111 (C)	P	2,100	2,100	3,200
Alaska Pacific University; Anchorage, Alas. 99508	1,267 (C)	P	6,330	6,330	4,050
Albany College of Pharmacy; Albany, N.Y. 12208	651 (C)	P	7,375	7,375	4,000
Albany State College; Albany, Ga. 31705	2,355 (C)	Pub	1,680	4,260	2,484
Albertus Magnus College; New Haven, Conn. 06511	540 (C)	P	10,120	10,120	4,930
Albion College; Albion, Mich. 49224	1,616 (C)	P	11,134	11,134	4,064
Albright College; Reading, Pa. 19603	1,306 (C)	P	13,560	13,560	4,015
Alcorn State University; Lorman, Miss. 39096	2,853 (C)	Pub	3,700	4,882	1,900
Alderson-Broaddus College; Philippi, W. Va. 26416	760 (C)	P	8,666	8,666	2,860
Alfred University; Alfred, N.Y. 14802	2,086 (C)	P	13,960	13,960	4,470
Alice Lloyd College; Pippa Passes, Ky. 41844	534 (C)	P	3,240	3,240	2,664
Allegheny College; Meadville, Pa. 16335	1,810 (C)	P	14,850	14,850	4,120
Allentown College of St. Francis De Sales; Center Valley, Pa. 18034	873 (C)	P	7,200	7,200	4,150
Alma College; Alma, Mich. 48801	1,227 (C)	P	10,635	10,635	3,878
Alvernia College; Reading, Pa. 19607	1,113 (C)	P	6,932	6,932	3,600
Alverno College; Milwaukee, Wis. 53215	2,414 (W)	P	6,792	6,792	3,030
Ambassador College; Big Sandy, Tex. 75755	635 (C)	P	1,925	1,925	2,450
Amber University; Garland, Tex. 75041	722 (C)	P	3,938	3,938	n.a.
American Baptist College; Nashville, Tenn. 37207	163 (C)	P	2,012	2,012	784
American University of Paris; 75007 Paris, France	1,024 (C)	P	13,526	13,526	n.a.
American College of Switzerland; Switzerland	320 (C)	P	18,600	18,600	3,900
American Conservatory of Music; Chicago, Ill. 60602	124 (C)	P	6,800	6,800	n.a.
American International College; Springfield, Mass. 01109	1,384 (C)	P	8,079	8,079	3,762
American University; Washington, D.C. 20016	5,373 (C)	P	13,506	13,506	6,014
American University in Cairo; New York, N.Y. 10017	2,872 (C)	P	6,860	6,860	3,220
American University of Beirut; Beirut, Lebanon	4,500 (C)	P	3,200	3,200	2,925
American Universtity of Puerto Rico; Bayamon, PR 00621	4,208 (C)	P	2,100	2,100	n.a.
Amherst College; Amherst, Mass. 01002	1,570 (C)	P	15,515	15,515	4,400
Anderson College; Anderson, SC 29621	1,038 (C)	P	5,500	5,500	3,530
Anderson University; Anderson, Ind. 46012	2,015 (C)	P	8,060	8,060	2,870
Andrews University; Berrien Springs, Mich. 49104	2,009 (C)	P	9,105	9,105	3,675
Angelo State University; San Angelo, Tex. 76909	6,003 (C)	Pub	975	4,095	3,280
Anna Maria College for Men and Women; Paxton, Mass. 01612	633 (C)	P	9,480	9,480	4,380
Antillian College; Mayaguez, P.R. 00709	775 (C)	P	2,620	2,620	2,300
Antioch College; Yellow Springs, Ohio 45387	557 (C)	P	14,430	14,430	2,880

Institution and location	Enrollment	Control	Tuition ($) Res.	Tuition ($) Nonres.	Rm/Bd ($)
Antioch Los Angeles; Marina Del Rey, Calif. 90292	157 (C)	P	7,500	7,500	n.a.
Antioch Santa Barbara; Santa Barbara, Calif. 93101	66 (C)	P	6,750	6,750	n.a.
Antioch School for Adult & Experiential Learning; Yellow Springs, Ohio 45387	222 (C)	P	5,580	5,580	n.a.
Antioch Seattle; Seattle, Wash. 98121	115 (C)	P	7,575	7,575	n.a.
Appalachian Bible College; Bradley, W. Va. 25818	186 (C)	P	1,820	1,820	1,300
Appalachian State University; Boone, N.C. 28608	9,785 (C)	Pub	1,465	6,351	2,550
Aquinas College; Grand Rapids, Mich. 49506	2,218 (C)	P	8,960	8,960	3,950
Arizona, University of; Tucson, Ariz. 85721	27,932 (C)	Pub	1,540	6,546	3,192
Arizona College of the Bible; Phoenix, Ariz. 85021	177 (C)	P	4,370	4,370	3,020
Arizona State University; Tempe, Ariz. 85287-0112	32,027 (C)	Pub	1,590	6,996	4,100
Arkansas, Univ. of; Fayetteville, Ark. 72701	11,513 (C)	Pub	1,598	3,950	2,750
Arkansas, Univ. of-Little Rock; Little Rock, Ark. 72204	9,405 (C)	Pub	1,550	3,850	n.a.
Arkansas, Univ. of-Monticello; Monticello, Ark. 71655	1,854 (C)	Pub	1,410	3,230	1,880
Arkansas, Univ. of-Pine Bluff; Pine Bluff, Ark. 71601	3,333 (C)	Pub	1,320	3,140	1,300
Arkansas Baptist College; Little Rock, Ark. 72202	233 (C)	P	4,670	4,670	2,200
Arkansas College; Batesville, Ark. 72501	855 (C)	P	7,040	7,040	3,140
Arkansas State University; State University, Ark. 72467	8,429 (C)	Pub	1,400	2,650	2,010
Arkansas Tech. University; Russellville, Ark. 72801	3,453 (C)	Pub	1,200	2,400	3,280
Arlington Baptist College; Arlington, Tex. 76012	179 (C)	P	2,250	2,250	2,350
Armstrong College; Berkeley, Calif. 94704	100 (C)	P	4,500	4,500	n.a.
Armstrong State College; Savannah, Ga. 31419	4,170 (C)	Pub	1,467	4,047	2,850
Arnold & Marie Schwartz College of Pharmacy & Health Sciences. See Long Island University Center, Brooklyn Center					
Art Academy of Cincinnati; Cincinnati, Ohio 45202	247 (C)	P	7,200	7,200	n.a.
Art Center College of Design; Pasadena, Calif. 91103	1,268 (C)	P	11,780	11,780	n.a.
Art Institute of Chicago, School of the; Chicago, Ill. 60603	2,066 (C)	P	11,500	11,500	n.a.
Art Institute of Southern California; Laguna Beach, Calif. 92651	130 (C)	P	7,700	7,700	n.a.
Arts, The University of the; Philadelphia, Pa. 19102	1,245 (C)	P	10,775	10,775	3,570
Asbury College; Wilmore, Ky. 40390	1,053 (C)	P	7,350	7,350	2,476
Ashland University; Ashland, Ohio 44805	1,651 (C)	P	9,965	9,965	4,120
Assumption College; Worcester, Mass. 01615-0005	1,787 (C)	P	9,835	9,835	5,370
Athens State College; Athens, Ala. 35611	2,770 (C)	Pub	1,700	3,400	2,800
Atlanta Christian College; East Point, Ga. 30344	169 (C)	P	3,620	3,620	2,600
Atlanta College of Art; Atlanta, Ga. 30309	368 (C)	P	7,500	7,500	2,720
Atlantic, College of the; Bar Harbor, Maine 04609	226 (C)	P	11,625	11,625	3,295
Atlantic Christian College; Wilson, N.C. 27893	1,434 (C)	P	6,173	6,173	2,814
Atlantic Union College; South Lancaster, Mass. 01561	782 (C)	P	9,800	9,800	3,300
Auburn University; Auburn University, Ala. 36849	18,645 (C)	Pub	1,596	4,788	3,000
Auburn University-Montgomery; Montgomery, Ala. 36193	5,286 (C)	Pub	1,428	4,284	6,660
Augsburg College; Minneapolis, Minn. 55454	2,872 (C)	P	10,233	10,233	3,832
Augusta College; Augusta, Ga. 30910	5,205 (C)	Pub	1,431	3,909	3,175
Augustana College; Rock Island, Ill. 61201	2,235 (C)	P	11,118	11,118	3,666
Augustana College; Sioux Falls, S.D. 57197	1,952 (C)	P	9,330	9,330	3,100
Aurora University; Aurora, Ill. 60506	1,602 (C)	P	8,730	8,730	3,405
Austin College; Sherman, Tex. 75090	1,203 (C)	P	9,465	9,465	3,745
Austin Peay State University; Clarksville, Tenn. 37040	4,784 (C)	Pub	1,353	3,241	2,450
Averett College; Danville, Va. 24541-3692	1,042 (C)	P	8,750	8,750	4,200
Avila College; Kansas City, Mo. 64145	1,397 (C)	P	7,300	7,300	3,200
Azusa Pacific University; Azusa, Calif. 91702	1,720 (C)	P	8,900	8,900	3,590
Babson College; Wellesley, Mass. 02157	1,584 (C)	P	14,838	14,838	6,498
Baker University; Baldwin City, Kan. 66006	870 (C)	P	6,850	6,850	4,450
Baldwin-Wallace College; Berea, Ohio 44017	4,138 (C)	P	9,945	9,945	3,900
Ball State University; Muncie, Ind. 47306	18,993 (C)	Pub	2,110	4,870	2,790
Baltimore, University of; Baltimore, Md. 21201	3,216 (C)	Pub	2,047	3,635	n.a.
Baltimore Hebrew University; Baltimore, Md. 21215	612 (C)	P	1,920	1,920	n.a.
Baptist Bible College; Springfield, Mo. 65803	793 (C)	P	1,600	1,600	2,190
Baptist Bible College of Pennsylvania; Clarks Summit, Pa. 18411	494 (C)	P	8,590	8,590	5,510
Baptist Christian College; Shreveport, La. 71108	350 (C)	P	2,100	2,100	n.a.
Barat College; Lake Forest, Ill. 60045	685 (C)	P	8,640	8,640	3,300
Barber-Scotia College; Concord, N.C. 28025	370 (C)	P	4,000	4,000	2,487
Bard College; Annandale-on-Hudson, N.Y. 12504	1,023 (C)	P	16,790	16,790	5,565
Barnard College of Columbia University; New York, N.Y. 10027	2,200 (W)	P	16,468	16,468	6,892
Barry University; Miami Shores, Fla. 33161	4,442 (C)	P	8,490	8,490	3,340
Bartlesville Wesleyan College; Bartlesville, Okla. 74003	489 (C)	P	5,650	5,650	2,900
Bassist College; Portland, Ore. 97201	157 (C)	P	7,900	7,900	4,100
Bates College; Lewiston, Maine 04240	1,500 (C)	P	21,400	21,400	—
Baylor University; Waco, Tex. 76798-7032	10,389 (C)	P	6,060	6,060	3,658
Beaver College; Glenside, Pa. 19038	1,215 (C)	P	10,820	10,820	4,750
Behrend College. See Pennsylvania State University					
Beirut University College; Beirut, Lebanon	2,438 (C)	P	1,300	1,300	500
Belhaven College; Jackson, Miss. 39202	693 (C)	P	5,880	5,880	2,310
Bellarmine College; Louisville, Ky. 40205	1,853 (C)	P	6,615	6,615	2,450
Bellevue College; Bellevue, Neb. 68005	1,956 (C)	P	2,916	2,916	n.a.

Institution and location	Enrollment	Control	Tuition ($) Res.	Tuition ($) Nonres.	Rm/Bd ($)
Bellin College of Nursing; Green Bay, Wis. 54305-3400	180 (C)	P	5,222	5,222	n.a.
Belmont Abbey College; Belmont, N.C. 28012	1,023 (C)	P	6,870	7,870	3,804
Belmont College; Nashville, Tenn. 37203	2,508 (C)	P	6,100	6,100	3,150
Beloit College; Beloit, Wis. 53511	1,152 (C)	P	13,050	13,050	3,300
Bemidji State University; Bemidji, Minn. 56601	4,642 (C)	Pub	1,944	2,976	2,259
Benedict College; Columbia, S.C. 29204	1,448 (C)	P	5,084	5,084	2,292
Benedictine College; Atchison, Kan. 66002	788 (C)	P	7,150	7,150	3,060
Bennett College; Greensboro, N.C. 27401	572 (W)	P	4,850	4,850	2,600
Bennington College; Bennington, Vt. 05201	570 (C)	P	19,400	19,400	3,800
Bentley College; Waltham, Mass. 02254	5,503 (C)	P	11,390	11,390	4,768
Berea College; Berea, Ky. 40404	1,535 (C)	P	177	177	2,457
Berklee College of Music; Boston, Mass. 02215	2,734 (C)	P	9,085	9,085	6,190
Bernard M. Baruch Coll. *See* New York, City Univ. of					
Berry College; Mount Berry, Ga. 30149	1,714 (C)	P	6,990	6,990	3,360
Bethany Bible College; Santa Cruz, Calif. 95066	533 (C)	P	5,850	5,850	3,000
Bethany College; Bethany, W. Va. 36032	844 (C)	P	11,170	11,170	4,000
Bethany College; Lindsborg, Kan. 67456	653 (C)	P	7,028	7,028	3,241
Bethel College; McKenzie, Tenn. 38201	469 (C)	P	4,100	4,100	2,350
Bethel College; Mishawaka, Ind. 46545	679 (C)	P	7,200	7,200	2,750
Bethel College; North Newton, Kan. 67117	605 (C)	P	6,990	6,990	2,800
Bethel College; St. Paul, Minn. 55112	1,832 (C)	P	9,950	9,950	3,590
Bethune-Cookman College; Daytona Beach, Fla. 32015	2,351 (C)	P	4,944	4,944	2,787
Biola University; La Mirada, Calif. 90639	1,834 (C)	P	9,902	9,902	4,060
Birmingham-Southern College; Birmingham, Ala. 35254	1,846 (C)	P	8,900	8,900	4,135
Blackburn College; Carlinville, Ill. 62626	508 (C)	P	7,070	7,070	3,400
Black Hills State University; Spearfish, S.D. 57783	2,545 (C)	Pub	1,949	3,402	2,355
Bloomfield College; Bloomfield, N.J. 07003	1,701 (C)	P	7,300	7,300	3,700
Bloomsburg State Coll. *See* Bloomsburg Univ. of Pennsylvania					
Bloomsburg University of Pennsylvania; Bloomsburg, Pa. 17815	6,808 (C)	Pub	2,278	4,312	2,466
Bluefield College; Bluefield, Va. 24605	435 (C)	P	5,400	5,400	3,620
Bluefield State College; Bluefield, W. Va. 24701	2,706 (C)	Pub	1,454	3,424	n.a.
Blue Mountain College; Blue Mountain, Miss. 38610	364 (W)	P	3,434	3,434	2,040
Bluffton College; Bluffton, Ohio 45817	684 (C)	P	8,100	8,100	3,324
Bob Jones University; Greenville, S.C. 29614	4,003 (C)	P	3,660	3,660	3,360
Boca Raton, College of; Boca Raton, Fla. 33431	1,100 (C)	P	10,900	10,900	4,400
Boise State University; Boise, Idaho 83725	10,725 (C)	Pub	1,378	3,578	2,923
Boricua College; New York, N.Y. 10032	1,100 (C)	P	4,900	4,9900	n.a.
Boston Architecture Center School of Architecture; Boston, Mass. 02115	653 (C)	P	2,280	2,280	n.a.
Boston College; Chestnut Hill, Mass. 02167	8,649 (C)	P	13,925	13,925	6,150
Boston Conservatory; Boston, Mass. 02215	385 (C)	P	9,650	9,650	5,151
Boston University; Boston, Mass. 02215	14,572 (C)	P	16,190	16,190	6,320
Bowdoin College; Brunswick, Maine 04011	1,350 (C)	P	16,380	16,380	5,590
Bowie State University; Bowie, Md. 20715	2,879 (C)	Pub	2,254	4,179	3,418
Bowling Green State University; Bowling Green, Ohio 43403	15,847 (C)	Pub	2,162	2,162	2,514
Bradford College; Bradford, Mass. 01835	456 (C)	P	10,650	10,650	5,450
Bradley University; Peoria, Ill. 61625	5,255 (C)	P	9,060	9,060	3,950
Brandeis University; Waltham, Mass. 02254	2,920 (C)	P	16,535	16,535	6,250
Brenau: The Women's College; Gainesville, Ga. 30501	477 (W)	P	7,242	7,242	5,658
Brescia College; Owensboro, Ky. 42301	756 (C)	P	5,600	5,600	2,700
Brewton-Parker College; Mount Vernon, Ga. 30445	1,350 (C)	P	3,150	3,150	2,130
Briar Cliff College; Sioux City, Iowa 51104	1,131 (C)	P	8,760	8,760	3,147
Bridgeport, University of; Bridgeport, Conn. 06601	2,903 (C)	P	11,465	11,465	5,300
Bridgeport Engineering Institute; Bridgeport, Conn. 06606	830 (C)	P	5,450	5,450	n.a.
Bridgewater College; Bridgewater, Va. 22812	1,007 (C)	P	9,195	9,195	4,295
Bridgewater State College; Bridgewater, Mass. 02325	5,262 (C)	Pub	1,250	4,325	3,675
Brigham Young University; Provo, Utah 84602	25,812 (C)	P	2,850	2,850	3,120
Brigham Young University-Hawaii; Laie, Oahu, Hawaii 96762	2,040 (C)	P	2,280	2,280	2,530
Brooklyn Center. *See* Long Island University Center					
Brooklyn College. *See* New York, City University of					
Bristol University; Bristol, Tenn. 37621	700 (C)	P	4,360	4,360	n.a.
Brooks Institute of Photography; Santa Barbara, Calif. 93108	665 (C)	P	9,900	9,900	n.a.
Brown University; Providence, R.I. 02912	5,804 (C)	P	16,860	16,860	5,220
Bryan College; Dayton, Tenn. 37321	551 (C)	P	6,410	6,410	3,520
Bryant College; Smithfield, R.I. 02917	2,923 (C)	P	10,993	10,993	5,932
Bryn Mawr College; Bryn Mawr, Pa. 19010	1,177 (W)	P	15,750	15,750	5,850
Bucknell University; Lewisburg, Pa. 17837	3,373 (C)	P	15,650	15,650	3,825
Buena Vista College; Storm Lake, Iowa 50588	1,032 (C)	P	10,900	10,900	3,110
Burlington College; Burlington, Vt. 05401	206 (C)	P	6,865	6,864	n.a.
Butler University; Indianapolis, Ind. 46208	2,457 (C)	P	10,500	10,500	3,840
Cabrini College; Radnor, Pa. 19087	832 (C)	P	7,860	7,860	4,700
Caldwell College; Caldwell, N.J. 07006	1,186 (C)	P	7,600	7,600	4,000

Institution and location	Enrollment	Control	Tuition ($) Res.	Tuition ($) Nonres.	Rm/Bd ($)
California, University of; Berkeley, Calif. 94720:					
UC-Berkeley; Berkeley, Calif. 94720	22,262 (C)	Pub	1,640	7,556	5,134
UC-Davis; Davis, Calif. 95616	18,395 (C)	Pub	1,829	8,373	4,655
UC-Irvine; Irvine, Calif. 92717	13,150 (C)	Pub	1,796	7,712	5,350
UC-Los Angeles; Los Angeles, Calif. 90024	24,284 (C)	Pub	2,200	8,050	3,700
UC-Riverside; Riverside, Calif. 92521	6,747 (C)	Pub	1,644	7,560	4,850
UC-San Diego; La Jolla, Calif. 92093	14,105 (C)	Pub	2,284	7,650	5,250
UC-Santa Barbara; Santa Barbara, Calif. 93106	15,975 (C)	Pub	1,638	5,916	5,338
UC-Santa Cruz; Santa Cruz, Calif. 95064	8,883 (C)	Pub	1,813	7,729	4,787
California Baptist College; Riverside, Calif. 92504	617 (C)	P	5,076	5,076	4,198
California College of Arts and Crafts; Oakland, Calif. 94618	1,039 (C)	P	9,760	9,760	3,700
California Institute of Technology; Pasadena, Calif. 91125	810 (C)	P	13,300	13,300	5,422
California Institute of the Arts; Valencia, Calif. 91355	640 (C)	P	12,200	12,200	3,725
California Lutheran University; Thousand Oaks, Calif. 91360	1,636 (C)	P	9,450	9,450	4,200
California Maritime Academy; Vallejo, Calif. 94590	431 (C)	Pub	1,391	1,391	4,002
California Polytechnic State University; San Luis Obispo, Calif. 93407	16,530 (C)	Pub	948	5,604	3,960
California State Coll. (Pa.). See California Univ. of Pennsylvania					
California State Polytechnic University-Pomona; Pomona, Calif. 91768	17,933 (C)	Pub	820	5,670	4,116
California State University-Bakersfield; Bakersfield, Calif. 93311-1099	3,679 (C)	Pub	878	5,548	3,475
California State University-Chico; Chico, Calif. 95929	14,491 (C)	Pub	914	6,654	3,720
California St. Univ.-Dominguez Hills; Carson, Calif. 90747	6,158 (C)	Pub	876	5,796	4,480
California State Univ.-Fresno; Fresno, Calif. 93740	15,854 (C)	Pub	906	6,123	3,633
California State Univ.-Fullerton; Fullerton, Calif. 92634	21,210 (C)	Pub	916	6,586	4,056
California State Univ.-Hayward; Hayward, Calif. 94542	9,405 (C)	Pub	894	5,826	4,605
California State Univ.-Long Beach; Long Beach, Calif. 90840	27,131 (C)	Pub	862	6,526	4,400
California State Univ.-Los Angeles; Los Angeles, Calif. 90032	16,094 (C)	Pub	961	5,345	4,602
California State Univ.-Northridge; Northridge, Calif. 91330	24,664 (C)	Pub	972	5,892	5,500
California State Univ.-Sacramento; Sacramento, Calif. 95819	20,846 (C)	Pub	1,050	8,430	3,944
California State Univ.-San Bernardino; San Bernardino, Calif. 92407	7,914 (C)	Pub	845	5,670	4,043
California State Univ.-Stanislaus; Turlock, Calif. 95380	4,268 (C)	Pub	870	5,406	3,845
California Univ. of Pennsylvania; California, Pa. 15419	5,995 (C)	Pub	2,648	4,682	2,940
Calumet College of St. Joseph; Whiting, Ind. 46394	976 (C)	P	3,600	3,600	n.a.
Calvary Bible College; Kansas City, Mo. 64147	305 (C)	P	3,400	3,400	2,570
Calvin College; Grand Rapids, Mich. 49506	4,097 (C)	P	8,150	8,150	3,350
Cameron University; Lawton, Okla. 73505	4,894 (C)	Pub	1,209	2,965	1,862
Campbellsville College; Campbellsville, Ky. 42718	760 (C)	P	4,500	4,500	2,760
Campbell University; Buies Creek, N.C. 27506	3,941 (C)	P	7,296	7,296	2,690
Canisius College; Buffalo, N.Y. 14208	3,753 (C)	P	8,800	8,800	4,650
Capital University; Columbus, Ohio 43209	2,015 (C)	P	11,085	11,085	3,700
Capitol College; Laurel, Md. 20708	737 (C)	P	6,588	6,588	4,230
Cardinal Stritch College; Milwaukee, Wis. 53217	2,125 (C)	P	6,960	6,960	3,150
Carleton College; Northfield, Minn. 55057	1,850 (C)	P	16,290	16,290	3,330
Carlow College; Pittsburgh, Pa. 15213	1,125 (W)	P	8,336	8,336	4,000
Carnegie-Mellon University; Pittsburgh, Pa. 15213	4,327 (C)	P	15,350	15,350	5,110
Carroll College; Helena, Mont. 59625	1,234 (C)	P	6,570	6,570	3,230
Carroll College; Waukesha, Wis. 53186	1,495 (C)	P	11,068	11,068	3,560
Carson-Newman College; Jefferson City, Tenn. 37760	2,031 (C)	P	6,670	6,670	2,790
Carthage College; Kenosha, Wis. 53140	1,116 (C)	P	10,640	10,640	3,350
Case Western Reserve University; Cleveland, Ohio 44106	3,067 (C)	P	13,600	13,600	4,930
Castleton State College; Castleton, Vt. 05735	1,461 (C)	Pub	3,300	6,850	4,300
Catawba College; Salisbury, N.C. 28144	1,000 (C)	P	7,700	7,700	3,700
Catholic University of America; Washington, D.C. 20064	2,950 (C)	P	10,850	10,850	5,400
Catholic University of Puerto Rico; Ponce, P.R. 00732	11,598 (C)	P	2,457	2,457	2,265
Cayey University College. See Puerto Rico, University of					
Cazenovia College; Cazenovia, N.Y. 13035	1,070 (C)	P	7,654	7,654	3,832
Cedar Crest College; Allentown, Pa. 18104-6196	497 (W)	P	12,210	12,210	4,911
Cedarville College; Cedarville, Ohio 45314	1,923 (C)	P	5,710	5,710	3,390
Centenary College; Hackettstown, N.J. 07840	388 (C)	P	10,390	10,390	4,890
Centenary College of Louisiana; Shreveport, La. 71104	849 (C)	P	6,500	6,500	2,910
Center for Creative Studies, College of Art and Design; Detroit, Mich. 48202	953 (C)	P	8,900	8,900	4,950
Central Arkansas, University of; Conway, Ark. 72032	6,670 (C)	Pub	1,260	2,520	2,156
Central Baptist College; Conway, Ark. 72032	201 (C)	P	2,190	2,190	1,785
Central Bible College; Springfield, Mo. 65803	1,042 (C)	P	3,120	3,120	2,600
Central Christian College of the Bible; Moberly, Mo. 65270	79 (C)	P	2,815	2,815	2,200
Central College; Pella, Iowa 50219	1,695 (C)	P	9,198	9,198	3,417
Central Connecticut State University; New Britain, Conn. 06050	11,250 (C)	Pub	2,414	6,144	3,830
Central Florida, University of; Orlando, Fla. 32816	16,548 (C)	Pub	1,471	4,782	3,360
Central Methodist College; Fayette, Mo. 65248	824 (C)	P	6,710	6,710	3,270
Central Michigan University; Mt. Pleasant, Mich. 48859	15,628 (C)	Pub	2,065	5,110	3,350
Central Missouri State University; Warrensburg, Mo. 64093	9,755 (C)	Pub	1,870	3,580	2,982
Central Oklahoma, University of; Edmond, Okla. 73034-0419	11,165 (C)	Pub	1,065	2,811	1,992

Institution and location	Enrollment	Control	Tuition ($) Res.	Tuition ($) Nonres.	Rm/Bd ($)
Central State University; Wilberforce, Ohio 45384	2,550 (C)	Pub	2,247	4,788	3,753
Central Texas, University of; Killeen, Tex. 76540	336 (C)	P	3,660	3,660	2,484
Central Washington University; Ellensburg, Wash. 98926	7,298 (C)	Pub	1,674	5,712	2,993
Central Wesleyan College; Central, S.C. 29630	934 (C)	P	7,090	7,090	2,980
Centre College; Danville, Ky. 40422	859 (C)	P	10,110	10,110	3,930
Chadron State College; Chadron, Neb. 69337	2,062 (C)	Pub	1,457	2,273	2,614
Chaminade University of Honolulu; Honolulu, Hawaii 96816	2,704 (C)	P	5,930	6,680	3,715
Chapman College; Orange, Calif. 92666	1,489 (C)	P	11,910	11,910	4,640
Charleston, College of; Charleston, S.C. 29424	6,663 (C)	Pub	2,400	4,650	3,000
Charleston Southern University; Charleston, S.C. 29411	2,036 (C)	P	6,522	6,522	2,990
Charleston, University of; Charleston, W. Va. 25304	1,510 (C)	P	7,840	7,840	3,500
Charter Oak College; Farmington, Conn. 06032-1909	884 (C)	Pub	615	855	n.a.
Chatham College; Pittsburgh, Pa. 15232	686 (W)	P	11,065	11,065	4,745
Chestnut Hill College; Philadelphia, Pa. 19118-2695	850 (W)	P	8,250	8,250	4,800
Cheyney University of Pennsylvania; Cheyney, Pa. 19319	1,314 (C)	Pub	2,588	4,622	2,956
Chicago, University of—The College; Chicago, Ill. 60637	3,478 (C)	P	15,945	15,945	5,685
Chicago State University; Chicago, Ill. 60628	5,129 (C)	Pub	1,772	4,916	n.a.
Christ College-Irvine; Irvine, Calif. 92715	574 (C)	P	8,800	8,800	4,170
Christian Brothers College; Memphis, Tenn. 38104	1,678 (C)	P	7,640	7,640	2,960
Christian Heritage College; El Cajon, Calif. 92019	328 (C)	P	6,877	6,877	3,522
Christian Life College; Stockton, Calif. 95210	173 (C)	P	2,140	2,140	2,400
Christopher Newport College; Newport News, Va. 23606—2998	4,861 (C)	Pub	2,010	4,460	n.a.
Church College of Hawaii. *See* Brigham Young University— Hawaii Campus					
Cincinnati, University of; Cincinnati, Ohio 45221	13,885 (C)	Pub	3,008	7,180	4,185
Cincinnati Bible College; Cincinnati, Ohio 45204	633 (C)	P	3,762	3,762	2,966
Cincinnati College of Mortuary Science Cohen Center; Cincinnati, Ohio 45212	120 (C)	P	6,080	6,080	4,200
Circleville Bible College; Circleville, Ohio 43113	162 (C)	P	3,514	3,514	2,580
Citadel-The Military College of South Carolina; Charleston, S.C. 29409	1,960 (M)	Pub	8,607	11,945	—
City College (NYC). *See* New York, City University of					
City University; Bellevue, Wash. 98008	2,222 (C)	P	6,030	6,030	n.a.
Claflin College; Orangeburg, S.C. 29115	756 (C)	P	6,413	6,413	2,140
Claremont Colleges:					
Claremont McKenna College; Claremont, Calif. 91711	847 (C)	P	13,850	13,850	4,840
Claremont Men's College. *See* Claremont McKenna College					
Harvey Mudd College; Claremont, Calif. 91711-5990	568 (C)	P	14,490	14,490	5,990
Pitzer College; Claremont, Calif. 91711	750 (C)	P	15,428	15,428	5,742
Pomona College; Claremont, Calif. 91711	1,375 (C)	P	14,030	14,030	5,700
Scripps College; Claremont, Calif. 91711	607 (W)	P	13,920	13,920	6,000
Clarion State College. *See* Clarion University of Pennsylvania					
Clarion University of Pennsylvania; Clarion, Pa. 16214	5,789 (C)	Pub	2,278	4,438	2,558
Clark Atlanta University; Atlanta, Ga. 30314	2,339 (C)	P	6,600	6,600	3,500
Clarke College; Dubuque, Iowa 52001	820 (C)	P	8,780	8,780	3,000
Clarkson College of Technology. *See* Clarkson University					
Clarkson University; Potsdam, N.Y. 13676	3,035 (C)	P	13,675	13,675	4,732
Clark University; Worcester, Mass. 01610	2,200 (C)	P	15,200	15,200	4,500
Clearwater Christian College; Clearwater, Fla. 33519	295 (C)	P	4,575	4,575	3,220
Cleary College; Ypsilanti, Mich. 48197	940 (C)	P	5,790	5,790	n.a.
Clemson University; Clemson, S.C. 29634	13,010 (C)	Pub	2.623	7,001	3,153
Cleveland College of Jewish Studies; Deachwood, Ohio 44122	350 (C)	P	3,015	3,015	n.a.
Cleveland Institute of Art; Cleveland, Ohio 44106	495 (C)	P	10,800	10,800	4,310
Cleveland Institute of Music; Cleveland, Ohio 44106	173 (C)	P	11,800	11,800	4,875
Cleveland State University; Cleveland, Ohio 44115	13,408 (C)	Pub	2,538	5,076	3,069
Clinch Valley College. *See* Virginia, University of					
Coe College; Cedar Rapids, Iowa 52402	1,217 (C)	P	10,280	10,280	3,940
Cogswell College; Cupertino, Calif. 95014	275 (C)	P	6,240	6,240	n.a.
Coker College; Hartsville, S.C. 29550	778 (C)	P	8,339	8,339	3,818
Colby College; Waterville, Me. 04901	1,695 (C)	P	16,460	16,460	5,350
Colby-Sawyer College; New London, N.H. 03257	550 (C)	P	12,185	12,185	4,715
Coleman College; La Mesa, Calif. 92041	1,080 (C)	P	7,990	7,990	n.a.
Colgate University; Hamilton, N.Y. 13346	2,680 (C)	P	16,102	16,102	5,070
College for Human Services; New York, N.Y. 10014. *See* Human Services, College for					
College Misericordia; Dallas, Pa. 18612	900 (C)	P	8,650	8,650	4,446
College of Great Falls; Great Falls, Mont. 59405. *See* Great Falls, College of					
Colorado, University of; Boulder, Colo. 80309:					
U. of Colorado-Boulder; Boulder, Colo. 80309	18,927 (C)	Pub	2,346	4,875	3,340
U. of Colorado-Colorado Springs; Colorado Springs, Colo. 80933	4,216 (C)	Pub	1,942	5,856	n.a.
U. of Colorado-Denver; Denver, Colo. 80202	5,843 (C)	Pub	1,891	6,991	n.a.
Colorado Christian University; Lakewood, Colo. 80226	658 (C)	P	5,030	5,030	2,990
Colorado College; Colorado Springs, Colo. 80903	1,880 (C)	P	12,710	12,710	3,410

Institution and location	Enrollment	Control	Tuition ($) Res.	Tuition ($) Nonres.	Rm/Bd ($)
Colorado School of Mines; Golden, Colo. 80401	1,623 (C)	Pub	3,540	9,812	3,400
Colorado State University; Fort Collins, Colo. 80523	16,911 (C)	Pub	2,223	6,589	3,915
Colorado Technical College; Colorado Springs, Colo. 80907	1,200 (C)	P	5,670	5,670	n.a.
Colorado Women's College. *See* Denver, Univ. of					
Columbia Bible College and Seminary; Columbia, S.C. 29230	518 (C)	P	5,025	5,025	2,913
Columbia Christian College; Portland, Ore. 97216	250 (C)	P	5,952	5,952	2,872
Columbia College; Chicago, Ill. 60605	6,535 (C)	P	5,828	5.828	n.a.
Columbia College; Columbia, Mo. 65216	714 (C)	P	6,844	6,844	3,082
Columbia College; Columbia, S.C. 29203	1,147 (W)	P	8,725	8,725	3,255
Columbia College-Hollywood; Los Angeles, Calif. 90038	233 (C)	P	6,350	6,350	n.a.
Columbia Union College; Takoma Park, Md. 20912	1,356 (C)	P	8,200	8,200	2,900
Columbia University-Columbia College; New York, N.Y. 10027	3,200 (C)	P	14,793	14,793	5,735
Columbus College; Columbus, Ga. 31993	3,661 (C)	Pub	1,413	3,891	n.a.
Columbus College of Art and Design; Columbus, Ohio 43215	1,631 (C)	P	8,550	8,550	4,500
Conception Seminary College; Conception, Mo. 64433	76 (M)	P	4,254	4,254	2,736
Concord College; Athens, W. Va. 24712	2,651 (C)	Pub	1,622	3,642	2,894
Concordia College; Ann Arbor, Mich. 48105	416 (C)	P	7,812	7,812	3,580
Concordia College; Bronxville, N.Y. 10708	560 (C)	P	8,370	8,370	4,200
Concordia College; Moorhead, Minn. 56560	2,948 (C)	P	8,690	8,690	2,710
Concordia College; Portland, Ore. 97211	555 (C)	P	8,707	8,707	2,550
Concordia College; St. Paul, Minn. 55104	1,235 (C)	P	8,268	8,268	2,910
Concordia College; Seward, Neb. 68434	818 (C)	P	6,600	6,600	2,790
Concordia Lutheran College; Austin, Tex. 78705	603 (C)	P	6,090	6,090	3,200
Concordia University; River Forest, Ill. 60305	952 (C)	P	7,328	7,328	3,603
Concordia University Wisconsin; Mequon, Wis. 53092	1,606 (C)	P	7,400	7,400	3,100
Connecticut, University of; Storrs, Conn. 06269	13,715 (C)	Pub	3,463	9,173	4,522
Connecticut College; New London, Conn. 06320	1,650 (C)	P	16,270	16,270	5,370
Conservatory of Music of Puerto Rico; Hato Rey, P.R. 00918	264 (C)	Pub	210	210	n.a.
Converse College; Spartanburg, S.C. 29301	860 (W)	P	10,368	10,368	3,240
Cooper Union; New York, N.Y. 10003	973 (C)	P	300	300	5,250
Coppin State College; Baltimore, Md. 21216	2,325 (C)	Pub	2,281	4,045	n.a.
Corcoran School of Art; Washington, D.C. 20006	302 (C)	P	9,500	9,500	4,955
Cornell College; Mt. Vernon, Iowa 52314	1,155 (C)	P	12,360	12,360	3,960
Cornell University; Ithaca, N.Y. 14853	7,600 (C)	P	16,192	16,192	5,414
Cornish College of the Arts; Seattle, Wash. 98102	598 (C)	P	8,010	8,010	n.a.
Corpus Christi State Univ.; Corpus Christi, Tex. 78412	2,070 (C)	Pub	958	4,286	3,500
Covenant College; Lookout Mountain, Ga. 30750	606 (C)	P	8,130	8,130	3,480
Creighton University; Omaha, Neb. 68178	3,576 (C)	P	8,996	8,996	3,798
Crichton College; Memphis, Tenn. 38175-7830	358 (C)	P	3,899	3,899	3,050
Culver-Stockton College; Canton, Mo. 63435	1,129 (C)	P	6,650	6,650	2,600
Cumberland College; Williamsburg, Ky. 40769	1,712 (C)	P	5,280	5,280	3,076
Cumberland University of Tennessee; Lebanon, Tenn. 37087	707 (C)	P	4,700	4,700	2,830
Curry College; Milton, Mass. 02186	1,001 (C)	P	11,125	11,125	5,810
Curtis Institute of Music; Philadelphia, Pa. 19103	119 (C)	P	450	450	n.a.
C. W. Post Center. *See* Long Island Univ. Center					
D'Youville College; Buffalo, N.Y. 14201	1,166 (C)	P	7,750	7,750	3,730
Daemen College; Amherst, N.Y. 14226	1,962 (C)	P	7,920	7,920	3,950
Dakota State University; Madison, S.D. 57042	1,311 (C)	Pub	7,822	7,822	2,176
Dakota Wesleyan University; Mitchell, S.D. 57301	706 (C)	P	6,250	6,250	2,530
Dallas, University of; Irving, Tex. 75062	1,101 (C)	P	8,600	8,600	4,000
Dallas Baptist University; Dallas, Tex. 75211	2,333 (C)	P	5,100	5,100	2,928
Dallas Christian College; Dallas, Tex. 75234	114 (C)	P	2,040	2,040	2,500
Dana College; Blair, Neb. 68008	507 (C)	P	7,370	7,370	2,770
Daniel Webster College; Nashua, N.H. 03063	550 (C)	P	9,710	9,710	4,140
Dartmouth College; Hanover, N.H. 03755	3,752 (C)	P	16,335	16,335	5,160
David Lipscomb University; Nashville, Tenn. 37203	2,284 (C)	P	6,165	6,165	3,020
Davidson College; Davidson, N.C. 28036	1,406 (C)	P	13,280	13,280	4,160
Davis and Elkins College; Elkins, W. Va. 26241	890 (C)	P	7,820	7,820	3,930
Dayton, University of; Dayton, Ohio 45469	6,737 (C)	P	9,410	9,410	3,760
Defiance College; Defiance, Ohio 43512	1,006 (C)	P	8,690	8,690	3,290
Delaware, University of; Newark, Del. 19716	14,615 (C)	P	2,890	7,680	3,571
Delaware State College; Dover, Del. 19901	2,510 (C)	Pub	1,295	3,170	4,182
Delaware Valley College of Science and Agriculture; Doylestown, Pa. 18901	1,050 (C)	P	8,500	8,500	3,900
Delta State University; Cleveland, Miss. 38732	3,330 (C)	Pub	1,706	2,888	1,690
Denison University; Granville, Ohio 43023	2,024 (C)	P	14,700	14,700	3,980
Denver, University of; Denver, Colo. 80208	2,765 (C)	P	12,990	12,990	4,206
CWC Campus Weekend College-Women's Program; Denver, Colo. 80220	419 (W)	P	6,300	6,300	n.a
DePaul University; Chicago, Ill. 60604	9,416 (C)	P	9,342	9,342	5,843
DePauw University; Greencastle, Ind. 46135	2,347 (C)	P	12,288	12,288	4,420
Deree College-Division of the American College of Greece; Athens, Greece GR-153 42	4,081 (C)	P	2,400	2,400	n.a.
Design Institute of San Diego; San Diego, Calif. 92121	190 (C)	P	5,700	5,700	n.a.

Institution and location	Enrollment	Control	Tuition ($) Res.	Tuition ($) Nonres.	Rm/Bd ($)
Detroit Bible College. *See* William Tyndale College					
Detroit College of Business; Dearborn, Mich. 48126	4,528 (C)	P	4,248	4,248	n.a.
Detroit Mercy, University of; Detroit, Mich. 48221	3,206 (C)	P	8,850	8,850	3,300
DeVry Institute of Technology; Chicago, Ill. 60618-5994	3,261 (C)	P	5,015	5,015	n.a.
DeVry Institute of Technology; City of Industry, Calif. 91744-3495	1,886 (C)	P	5,012	5,012	n.a.
DeVry Institute of Technology; Columbus, Ohio 43209-2764	2,715 (C)	P	5,015	5,015	n.a.
DeVry Institute of Technology; Decatur, Ga. 30030-2198	3,121 (C)	P	5,015	5,015	n.a.
DeVry Institute of Technology; Irving, Tex. 75038-4299	2,292 (C)	P	5,015	5,015	n.a.
DeVry Institute of Technology; Kansas City, Mo. 64131-3626	1,748 (C)	P	5,015	5,015	n.a.
DeVry Institute of Technology; Lombard, Ill. 60148-4299	2,453 (C)	P	5,012	5,012	n.a.
DeVry Institute of Technology; Phoenix, Ariz. 85021	2,647 (C)	P	5,012	5,012	n.a.
Dickinson College; Carlisle, Pa. 17013	2,003 (C)	P	15,565	15,565	4,530
Dickinson State University; Dickinson, N.D. 58601	1,429 (C)	Pub	1,659	4,731	1,750
Dillard University; New Orleans, La. 70122	1,200 (C)	P	5,500	5,500	3,250
District of Columbia, Univ. of the; Washington, D.C. 20008	11,280 (C)	Pub	664	2,464	n.a.
Divine Word College; Epworth, Iowa 52045	62 (M)	P	5,200	5,200	1,200
Doane College; Crete, Neb. 68333	651 (C)	P	8,320	8,320	2,600
Dr. Martin Luther College; New Ulm, Minn. 56073	443 (C)	P	3,132	3,132	1,770
Dominican College of Blauvelt; Orangeburg, N.Y. 10962	1,480 (C)	P	6,890	6,890	5,150
Dominican College of San Rafael; San Rafael, Calif. 94901	430 (C)	P	10,390	10,390	5,150
Dominican School of Philosophy and Theology; Berkeley, Calif. 94709	8 (C)	P	4,500	4,500	n.a.
Dordt College; Sioux Center, Iowa 51250	1,038 (C)	P	7,900	7,900	2,250
Dowling College; Oakdale, N.Y. 11769	3,242 (C)	P	7,130	7,130	2,500
Drake University; Des Moines, Iowa 50311	4,352 (C)	P	11,040	11,040	4,215
Drew University-College of Liberal Arts; Madison, N.J. 07940	1,485 (C)	P	16,502	16,502	4,840
Drexel University; Philadelphia, Pa. 19104	7,100 (C)	P	10,859	10,859	5,400
Drury College; Springfield, Mo. 65802	1,130 (C)	P	7,510	7,510	3,184
Dubuque, University of; Dubuque, Iowa 52001	836 (C)	P	9,105	9,105	3,100
Duke University; Durham, N.C. 27706	5,950 (C)	P	15,101	15,101	5,050
Duquesne University; Pittsburgh, Pa. 15282	4,200 (C)	P	8,850	8,850	4,317
Dyke College; Cleveland, Ohio 44115	1,261 (C)	P	4,900	4,900	n.a.
Earlham College; Richmond, Ind. 47374	1,200 (C)	P	13,479	13,479	3,726
East Carolina University; Greenville, N.C. 27834	12,982 (C)	Pub	1,140	5,512	2,720
East Central University; Ada, Okla. 74820-6899	3,459 (C)	Pub	1,215	3,210	1,988
Eastern College; St. Davids, Pa. 19087	1,115 (C)	P	9,500	9,500	3,786
Eastern Connecticut State Univ.; Willimantic, Conn. 06226	4,190 (C)	Pub	2,406	6,136	3,434
Eastern Illinois University; Charleston, Ill. 61920	9,352 (C)	Pub	2,114	5,258	2,574
Eastern Kentucky University; Richmond, Ky. 40475	15,371 (C)	Pub	1,440	4,040	3,046
Eastern Mennonite College; Harrisonburg, Va. 22801	969 (C)	P	7,900	7,900	3,300
Eastern Michigan University; Ypsilanti, Mich. 48197	19,700 (C)	Pub	2,116	5,189	3,951
Eastern Montana College; Billings, Mont. 59101	3,533 (C)	Pub	1,308	2,991	2,839
Eastern Nazarene College; Quincy, Mass. 02170	746 (C)	P	7,020	7,020	3,100
Eastern New Mexico University; Portales, N.M. 88130	3,187 (C)	Pub	1,233	4,251	2,594
Eastern Oregon State College; La Grande, Ore. 97850	1,767 (C)	Pub	1,755	1,755	2,840
Eastern Washington University; Cheney, Wash. 99004	7,465 (C)	Pub	1,611	5,649	2,971
Eastman School of Music; Rochester, N.Y. 14604	411 (C)	P	14,039	14,039	5,996
East Stroudsburg University of Pennsylvania; East Stroudsburg, Pa. 18301	4,735 (C)	Pub	2,278	4,676	3,065
East Tennessee State University; Johnson City, Tenn. 37614	9,761 (C)	Pub	1,390	4,594	2,400
East Texas Baptist University; Marshall, Tex. 75670	924 (C)	P	4,050	4,050	2,750
East Texas State University; Commerce, Tex. 75428	4,881 (C)	Pub	1,022	4,082	3,082
East-West University; Chicago, Ill. 60605	238 (C)	P	5,360	5,360	n.a.
Eckerd College; St. Petersburg, Fla. 33711	1,350 (C)	P	13,040	13,040	3,210
Edgewood College; Madison, Wis. 53711	1,067 (C)	P	6,950	6,950	3,330
Edinboro University of Pennsylvania; Edinboro, Pa. 16444	6,750 (C)	Pub	2,590	4,624	2,904
Edward Waters College; Jacksonville, Fla. 32209	686 (C)	P	3,476	3,476	3,400
Electronic Data Processing College of Puerto Rico; Hato Rey, P.R. 00918	1,176 (C)	P	2,334	2,334	n.a.
Elizabeth City State University; Elizabeth City, N.C. 27909	1,694 (C)	Pub	1,273	5,261	2,549
Elizabethtown College; Elizabethtown, Pa. 17022	1,451 (C)	P	11,650	11,650	3,950
Elmhurst College; Elmhurst, Ill. 60126-3296	1,758 (C)	P	7,532	7,532	3,442
Elmira College; Elmira, N.Y. 14901	1,002 (C)	P	11,380	11,380	3,900
Elms College; Chicopee, Mass. 01013-2839	600 (W)	P	9,650	9,650	4,400
Elon College; Elon College, N.C. 27244	3,205 (C)	P	7,320	7,320	3,550
Embry-Riddle Aeronautical Univ.-Daytona Beach Campus; Daytona Beach, Fla. 32114	4,975 (C)	P	6,400	6,400	3,550
Prescott Campus; Prescott, Ariz. 86301	1,676 (C)	P	6,390	6,390	3,550
Emerson College; Boston, Mass. 02116	2,065 (C)	P	12,096	12,096	6,832
Emmanuel College; Boston, Mass. 02115	902 (W)	P	10,345	10,345	5,420
Emmanuel College School of Christian Ministries; Franklin Springs, Ga. 30639	51 (C)	P	3,501	3,501	2,610
Emory and Henry College; Emory, Va. 24327	853 (C)	P	7,270	7,270	3,956
Emory University; Atlanta, Ga. 30322	4,747 (C)	P	14,700	14,700	4,532

Institution and location	Enrollment	Control	Tuition ($) Res.	Tuition ($) Nonres.	Rm/Bd ($)
Emporia State University; Emporia, Kan. 66801	4,472 (C)	Pub	1,490	4,005	2,695
Endicott College; Beverly, Mass. 01915	755 (W)	P	9,640	9,640	5,310
Erskine College; Due West, S.C. 29639	514 (C)	P	9,650	9,650	3,340
Esther Boyer College of Music, Temple University; Philadelphia, Pa. 19122	350 (C)	Pub	4,294	7,892	4,400
ETI Technical College; Cleveland, Ohio 44114	900 (C)	P	4,080	4,080	2,995
Eugene Bible College; Eugene, Ore. 97405	145 (C)	P	3,192	3,192	2,250
Eureka College; Eureka, Ill. 61530	478 (C)	P	9,425	9,425	3,160
Evangel College; Springfield, Mo. 65802	1,540 (C)	P	6,064	6,064	2,880
Evansville, University of; Evansville, Ind. 47722	3,006 (C)	P	9,710	9,710	3,750
Evergreen State College; Olympia, Wash. 98505	3,250 (C)	Pub	1,611	5,649	3,600
Fairfield University; Fairfield, Conn. 06430	2,928 (C)	P	12,650	12,650	5,350
Fairhaven College-Western Washington University; Bellingham, Wash. 98225	282 (C)	Pub	1,611	5,649	3,550
Fairleigh Dickinson Univ.-Madison; Madison, N.J. 07940	2,501 (C)	P	10,178	10,178	6,104
Fairleigh Dickinson Univ.-Rutherford; Rutherford, N.J. 07070	1,505 (C)	P	10,184	10,184	4,596
Fairleigh Dickinson Univ.-Teaneck; Teaneck, N.J. 07666	4,402 (C)	P	10,184	10,184	5,273
Fairmont State College; Fairmont, W. Va. 26554	6,306 (C)	Pub	1,424	3,454	2,720
Faith Baptist Bible College and Theological Seminary; Ankeny, Iowa 50021	263 (C)	P	4,206	4,206	2,622
Faulkner University; Montgomery, Ala. 36193	1,690 (C)	P	4,150	4,150	2,700
Fayetteville State University; Fayetteville, N.C. 28301	2,307 (C)	Pub	1,354	5,670	2,147
Felician College; Lodi, N.J. 07644	750 (C)	P	6,950	6,950	n.a.
Ferris State University; Big Rapids, Mich. 49307	11,813 (C)	Pub	2,412	4,896	3,018
Ferrum College; Ferrum, Va. 24088	1,238 (C)	P	7,725	7,725	3,075
Findlay, University of; Findlay, Ohio 45840	2,215 (C)	P	9,005	9,005	3,895
Finlay Engineering College; Kansas City, Mo. 64114	100 (C)	P	3,500	3,500	n.a.
Fisk University; Nashville, Tenn. 37203	520 (C)	P	5,050	5,050	3,050
Fitchburg State College; Fitchburg, Mass. 01420	6,030 (C)	Pub	2,530	5,605	3,104
Flagler College; St. Augustine, Fla. 32085	1,187 (C)	P	4,550	4,550	2,840
Flaming Rainbow University; Stilwell, Okla. 74960	129 (C)	P	3,400	3,400	n.a.
Florida, University of; Gainesville, Fla. 32611	26,435 (C)	Pub	1,320	4,640	3,330
Florida A&M University; Tallahassee, Fla. 32307	8,082 (C)	Pub	1,295	4,606	2,482
Florida Atlantic University; Boca Raton, Fla. 33431-0991	8,498 (C)	Pub	1,300	4,040	3,345
Florida Baptist Theological College; Graceville, Fla. 32440	386 (C)	P	1,463	1,463	2,725
Florida Christian College; Kissimmee, Fla. 34744	123 (C)	P	3,296	3,296	3,076
Florida Institute of Technology; Melbourne, Fla. 32901	3,865 (C)	P	11,526	11,526	3,465
Florida International University; Miami, Fla. 33199	14,814 (C)	Pub	1,324	4,627	5,422
Florida Memorial College; Miami, Fla. 33054	1,750 (C)	P	4,450	4,450	2,800
Florida Southern College; Lakeland, Fla. 33801	1,770 (C)	P	6,600	6,600	4,200
Florida State University; Tallahassee, Fla. 32306	21,341 (C)	Pub	1,307	4,619	3,419
Fontbonne College; St. Louis, Mo. 63105	821 (C)	P	7,470	7,470	3,500
Fordham Univ.-Rose Hill Campus; New York, N.Y. 10458	7,020 (C)	P	11,254	11,254	6,525
Forsyth School for Dental Hygienists; Boston, Mass. 02115	117 (C)	P	10,130	10,130	6,249
Fort Hays State University; Hays, Kan. 67601	3,792 (C)	Pub	1,470	3,600	2,502
Fort Lauderdale College; Fort Lauderdale, Fla. 33301	1,300 (C)	P	4,500	4,500	4,600
Fort Lewis College; Durango, Colo. 81301	3,842 (C)	Pub	1,420	5,048	2,520
Fort Valley State College; Fort Valley, Ga. 31030	1,748 (C)	Pub	1,650	4,230	2,310
Framingham State College; Framingham, Mass. 01701	3,248 (C)	Pub	2,329	5,404	3,160
Franciscan University of Steubenville; Steubenville, Ohio 43952	1,419 (C)	P	7,190	7,190	3,925
Francis Marion College; Florence, S.C. 29501	3,687 (C)	Pub	2,140	4,280	3,078
Franklin and Marshall College; Lancaster, Pa. 17604-3003	1,876 (C)	P	16,905	16,905	3,980
Franklin College; Franklin, Ind. 46131	811 (C)	P	8,250	8,250	3,110
Franklin College; Switzerland	225 (C)	P	15,150	15,150	3,450
Franklin Pierce College; Rindge, N.H. 03461	1,300 (C)	P	11,325	11,325	4,160
Franklin University; Columbus, Ohio 43215-5399	4,005 (C)	P	4,371	4,371	n.a.
Freed-Hardeman University; Henderson, Tenn. 38340	1,150 (C)	P	5,040	5,040	2,810
Free Will Baptist Bible College; Nashville, Tenn. 37205	269 (C)	P	3,074	3,074	2,970
Fresno Pacific College; Fresno, Calif. 93702	488 (C)	P	8,200	8,200	3,300
Friends Bible College; Haviland, Kan. 67059	106 (C)	P	5,400	5,400	2,500
Friends University; Wichita, Kan. 67213	1,135 (C)	P	7,260	7,260	2,520
Friends World College; Huntington, N.Y. 11743	300 (C)	P	9,000	9,000	4,750
Frostburg State University; Frostburg, Md. 21532	4,127 (C)	Pub	2,016	3,666	3,690
Furman University; Greenville, S.C. 29613	2,522 (C)	P	10,922	10,922	3,728
Gallaudet University, Washington, D.C. 20002	1,558 (C)	P	3,334	3,334	4,160
Gannon University; Erie, Pa. 16541	3,975 (C)	P	8,744	8,744	3,800
Gannon University–Willa Marie Campus; Erie, Pa. 16505	699 (W)	P	8,830	8,830	3,500
Gardner-Webb College; Boiling Springs, N.C. 28017	824 (C)	P	6,720	6,720	3,580
General Motors Institute. See GMI Engineering and Management Institute					
Geneva College; Beaver Falls, Pa. 15010	1.264 (C)	P	7,565	7,565	3,680
George Fox College; Newberg, Ore. 97132	820 (C)	P	8,950	8,950	3,440
George Mason University; Fairfax, Va. 22030	13,371 (C)	Pub	2,988	7,464	4,910
Georgetown College; Georgetown, Ky. 40324	1,188 (C)	P	6,250	6,250	3,286

Institution and location	Enrollment	Control	Tuition ($) Res.	Tuition ($) Nonres.	Rm/Bd ($)
Georgetown University; Washington, D.C. 20057	5,906 (C)	P	15,510	15,510	6,550
George Washington University; Washington, D.C. 20052	6,532 (C)	P	14,902	14,902	6,356
Georgia, University of; Athens, Ga. 30602	21,494 (C)	Pub	2,076	5,520	3,438
Georgia College; Milledgeville, Ga. 31061	4,703 (C)	Pub	1,461	2,448	2,205
Georgia Institute of Technology; Atlanta, Ga. 30332	9,270 (C)	Pub	2,913	7,074	3,855
Georgia Southern University; Statesboro, Ga. 30458	12,250 (C)	Pub	1,563	4,041	2,730
Georgia Southwestern College; Americus, Ga. 31709	1,873 (C)	Pub	1,527	4,005	2,220
Georgian Court College; Lakewood, N.J. 08701	1,672 (W)	P	7,180	7,180	3,750
Georgia State University; Atlanta, Ga. 30303	16,470 (C)	Pub	1,812	5,780	n.a.
Gettysburg College; Gettysburg, Pa. 17325	1,900 (C)	P	16,500	16,500	3,470
Glassboro State College; Glassboro, N.J. 08208	5,427 (C)	Pub	2,302	3,200	4,105
Glenville State College; Glenville, W. Va. 26351	2,238 (C)	Pub	1,280	3,150	2,590
GMI Engineering & Management Institute; Flint, Mich. 48504	2,505 (C)	P	9,490	9,490	2,840
Goddard College; Plainfield, Vt. 05667	225 (C)	P	15,344	15,344	—
Golden Gate University; San Francisco, Calif. 94105	2,049 (C)	P	4,500	4,500	n.a.
God's Bible School and College; Cincinnati, Ohio 45201	203 (C)	P	2,670	2,670	2,140
Goldey Beacom College; Wilmington, Del. 19808	1,920 (C)	P	5,600	5,600	4,189
Gonzaga University; Spokane, Wash. 99258	2,567 (C)	P	10,300	10,300	3,650
Gordon College, Wenham, Mass 01984	1,146 (C)	P	11,400	11,400	3,630
Goshen College; Goshen, Ind. 46526	1,107 (C)	P	7,720	7,720	3,275
Goucher College; Baltimore, Md. 21204	909 (C)	P	11,750	11,750	5,380
Governors State University; University Park, Ill. 60466	2,770 (C)	Pub	1,646	4,838	n.a.
Grace Bible College; Grand Rapids, Mich. 49509	127 (C)	P	3,600	3,600	2,750
Grace College; Winona Lake, Ind. 46590	665 (C)	P	7,011	7,011	3,328
Grace College of the Bible; Omaha, Neb. 68108	256 (C)	P	3,780	3,780	2,400
Graceland College; Lamoni, Iowa 50140	935 (C)	P	7,850	7,850	2,650
Grambling State University; Grambling, La. 71245	5,896 (C)	Pub	1,812	3,362	2,612
Grand Canyon University; Phoenix, Ariz. 85017	1,835 (C)	P	6,730	6,730	2,800
Grand Rapids Baptist College; Grand Rapids, Mich. 49505	752 (C)	P	5,852	5,852	3,630
Grand Valley State University; Allendale, Mich. 49401-9401	9,529 (C)	Pub	2,132	4,910	3,300
Grand View College; Des Moines, Iowa 50316	1,349 (C)	P	7,750	7,750	2,900
Gratz College; Melrose Park , Pa. 19126	92 (C)	P	3,500	3,500	n.a.
Great Falls, College of; Great Falls, Mont. 59405	1,127 (C)	P	3,790	3,790	n.a.
Great Lakes Bible College; Lansing, Mich. 48901	150 (C)	P	5,600	5,600	3,675
Green Mountain College; Poultney, Vt. 05764	600 (C)	P	7,495	7,495	4,690
Greensboro College; Greensboro, N.C. 27401	1,116 (C)	P	6,830	6,830	3,280
Greenville College; Greenville, Ill. 62246	753 (C)	P	8,960	8,960	3,730
Griffin College; Seattle, Wash. 98121	1,700 (C)	P	5,200	5,200	n.a.
Grinnell College; Grinnell, Iowa 50112	1,251 (C)	P	13,724	13,724	3,868
Grove City College; Grove City, Pa. 16127	2,139 (C)	P	4,630	4,630	2,670
Guam, University of; Mangilao, Guam 96913	2,057 (C)	Pub	1,408	2,016	3,805
Guilford College; Greensboro, N.C. 27410	1,154 (C)	P	10,510	10,510	4,514
Gustavus Adolphus College; St. Peter, Minn. 56082	2,371 (C)	P	11,900	11,900	2,900
Gwynedd-Mercy College; Gwynedd Valley, Pa. 19437	1,861 (C)	P	8,600	8,600	4,500
Hahnemann University School of Health Sciences and Humanities; Philadelphia, Pa. 19102	793 (C)	P	7,150	7,150	5,164
Hamilton College; Clinton, N.Y. 13323	1,673 (C)	P	16,650	16,650	4,550
Hamline University; St. Paul, Minn. 55104	1,507 (C)	P	11,725	11,725	3,631
Hampden-Sydney College; Hampden-Sydney, Va. 23943	950 (M)	P	11,685	11,685	3,797
Hampshire College; Amherst, Mass. 01002	1,253 (C)	P	16,000	16,000	4,240
Hampton University, Hampton, Va. 23668	4,490 (C)	P	6,550	6,550	3,000
Hannibal-LeGrange College; Hannibal, Mo. 63401	830 (C)	P	4,980	4,980	2,110
Hanover College; Hanover, Ind. 47243	1,060 (C)	P	6,450	6,450	2,885
Harding University; Searcy, Ark. 72143	3,311 (C)	P	4,500	4,500	2,850
Hardin-Simmons University; Abilene, Tex. 79698	1,636 (C)	P	4,950	4,950	2,436
Harrington Institute of Interior Design; Chicago, Ill. 60605	404 (C)	P	7,565	7,565	n.a.
Harris-Stowe State College; St. Louis, Mo. 63103	1,480 (C)	Pub	1,407	2,800	n.a.
Hartford, University of; West Hartford, Conn. 06117	5,858 (C)	P	12,990	12,990	6,018
Hartwick College; Oneonta, N.Y. 13820	1,498 (C)	P	13,450	13,450	4,350
Harvard and Radcliffe Colleges; Cambridge, Mass. 02138	6,601 (C)	P	16,560	16,560	5,520
Harvey Mudd College. *See* Claremont Colleges					
Hastings College; Hastings, Neb. 68901	925 (C)	P	8,090	8,090	2,910
Haverford College; Haverford, Pa. 19041	1,147 (C)	P	16,275	16,275	5,400
Hawaii, Univ. of-Hilo Colleges of Arts and Sciences and Agriculture; Hilo, Hawaii 96720-4091	1,408 (C)	Pub	450	2,510	3,254
Hawaii, University of-Manoa; Honolulu, Hawaii 96822	12,763 (C)	Pub	1,230	3,680	3,276
Hawaii, University of-West Oahu; Pearl City, Hawaii 96782	652 (C)	Pub	850	2,590	n.a.
Hawaii Loa College; Kaneohe, Hawaii 96744	597 (C)	P	7,800	7,800	4,200
Hawaii Pacific University; Honolulu, Hawaii 96813	5,025 (C)	P	4,950	4,950	n.a.
Health Sciences, University of-School of Related Health Sciences; North Chicago, Ill. 60064	65 (C)	P	10,280	10,280	n.a.
Hebrew Theological College; Skokie, Ill. 60077	266 (C)	P	4,795	4,795	3,790
Heidelberg College; Tiffin, Ohio 44883	1,200 (C)	P	11,680	11,680	3,730
Hellenic College; Brookline, Mass. 02146	41 (C)	P	7,260	7,260	3,800

Institution and location	Enrollment	Control	Tuition ($) Res.	Tuition ($) Nonres.	Rm/Bd ($)
Henderson State University; Arkadelphia, Ark. 71923	3,223 (C)	Pub	1,200	2,400	2,092
Hendrix College; Conway, Ark. 72032	1,029 (C)	P	6,653	6,653	2,595
Herbert H. Lehman College. *See* New York, City University of					
Heritage College; Toppenish, Wash. 98948	383 (C)	P	4,923	4,923	n.a.
High Point College; High Point, N.C. 27261	2,023 (C)	P	6,085	6,085	2,985
Hillsdale College; Hillsdale, Mich. 49242	1,080 (C)	P	9,400	9,400	3,900
Hillsdale Free Will Baptist College; Moore, Okla. 73153	170 (C)	P	2,738	2,738	2,740
Hiram College; Hiram, Ohio 44234	900 (C)	P	11,800	11,800	3,780
Hobart and William Smith Colleges; Geneva, N.Y. 14456	1,838 (C)	P	16,477	16,477	5,166
Hofstra University; Hempstead, N.Y. 11550	8,541 (C)	P	8,507	8,507	5,992
Hollins College; Roanoke, Va. 24020	919 (W)	P	10,810	10,810	4,350
Holy Apostles College and Seminary; Cromwell, Conn. 06416	54 (C)	P	3,400	3,400	4,320
Holy Cross, College of the; Worcester, Mass. 01610	2,684 (C)	P	15,530	15,530	5,700
Holy Family College; Philadelphia, Pa. 19914	986 (C)	P	7,000	7,000	n.a.
Holy Names College; Oakland, Calif. 94619	596 (C)	P	9,256	9,256	4,422
Hong Kong Baptist College; Kowloon, Hong Kong	3,028 (C)	Pub	1,100	1,100	n.a.
Hood College; Frederick, Md 21701	1,161 (W)	P	12,208	12,208	5,675
Hope College; Holland, Mich. 49423	2,813 (C)	P	10,086	10,086	3,826
Houghton College, Houghton, N.Y. 14744	1,164 (C)	P	8,676	8,676	3,134
Houghton College-Buffalo Suburban Campus; West Seneca, N.Y. 14225	86 (C)	P	7,056	7,056	3,020
Houston, Univ. of; Houston, Tex. 77284-2161	25,052 (C)	Pub	990	3,438	3,770
Houston, Univ. of-Clear Lake; Houston, Tex. 77058	3,957 (C)	Pub	914	4,154	n.a.
Houston, Univ. of-Downtown; Houston, Tex .77002	8,056 (C)	Pub	1,010	4,310	3,034
Houston, Univ. of-Victoria; Victoria, Tex. 77901	480 (C)	Pub	648	4,392	n.a.
Houston Baptist University; Houston, Tex. 77074	1,868 (C)	P	4,695	4,695	2,590
Howard Payne University; Brownwood, Tex. 76801	1,247 (C)	P	4,160	4,160	2,710
Howard University; Washington, D.C. 20059	8,820 (C)	P	6,446	6,446	3,540
Human Services, College for; New York, N.Y. 10014	911 (C)	P	8,400	8,400	n.a.
Humboldt State University; Arcata, Calif. 95521	6,245 (C)	Pub	904	5,440	3,945
Humphreys College; Stackton, Calif. 95207	414 (C)	P	3,730	3,730	3,730
Hunter College. *See* New York, City University of					
Huntingdon College; Montgomery, Ala. 36194	866 (C)	P	6,500	6,500	3,200
Huntington College; Huntington, Ind. 46750	545 (C)	P	7,770	7,770	3,100
Huron University; Huron, S.D. 57350	602 (C)	P	6,150	6,150	2,816
Husson College; Bangor, Me. 04401	1,846 (C)	P	7,320	7,320	3,770
Huston-Tillotson College; Austin, Tex. 78702	502 (C)	P	4,230	4,230	3,679
Idaho, College of; Caldwell, Idaho 83605	581 (C)	P	10,152	10,152	2,710
Idaho, University of; Moscow, Idaho 83843	7,210 (C)	Pub	1,236	3,746	2,808
Idaho State University; Pocatello, Idaho 83209	6,047 (C)	Pub	1,086	2,986	2,667
Illinois, Univ. of, at Chicago; Chicago, Ill. 60680	16,465 (C)	Pub	2,730	6,270	4,100
Illinois, Univ. of, at Urbana-Champaign; Urbana, Ill. 61801	26,445 (C)	Pub	2,846	6,385	3,658
Illinois Benedictine College; Lisle, Ill. 60532	1,623 (C)	P	8,850	8,850	3,605
Illinois College; Jacksonville, Ill. 62650	813 (C)	P	6,600	6,600	3,250
Illinois Institute of Technology; Chicago, Ill. 60616	2,612 (C)	P	12,690	12,690	4,350
Illinois State University; Normal, Ill. 61761	19,651 (C)	Pub	2,306	5,734	2,560
Illinois Wesleyan University; Bloomington, Ill. 61702	1,744 (C)	P	11,015	11,015	3,695
Immaculata College; Immaculata, Pa. 19345	2,100 (W)	P	8,500	8,500	4,400
Incarnate Word College; San Antonio, Tex. 78209	2,141 (C)	P	7,200	7,200	3,500
Indiana Institute of Technology; Fort Wayne, Ind. 46803	936 (C)	P	5,850	5,850	3,030
Indianapolis, University of; Indianapolis, Ind. 46227	2,788 (C)	P	9,020	9,020	3,470
Indiana Institute of Technology; Fort Wayne, Ind. 46803	936 (C)	P	7,200	7,200	3,500
Indiana State University; Terre Haute, Ind. 47809	10,308 (C)	Pub	2,104	5,056	3,332
Indiana University of Pennsylvania; Indiana, Pa. 15705	13,000 (C)	Pub	2,524	4,380	2,350
Indiana University-Bloomington; Bloomington, Ind. 47405	26,685 (C)	Pub	2,368	6,900	3,370
Indiana University-East; Richmond, Ind. 47374	1,860 (C)	Pub	1,490	3,668	n.a.
Indiana University-Kokomo; Kokomo, Ind. 46902	2,857 (C)	Pub	1,790	4,512	n.a.
Indiana University-Northwest; Gary, Ind. 46408	4,325 (C)	Pub	1,836	4,177	n.a.
Indiana University-Purdue University at Fort Wayne; Fort Wayne, Ind. 46805	10,961 (C)	Pub	2,216	3,934	n.a.
Indiana University-Purdue University at Indianapolis; Indianapolis, Ind. 46202-5143	20,087 (C)	Pub	1,971	5,777	n.a.
Indiana University-South Bend; South Bend, Ind. 46634	5,799 (C)	Pub	1,895	4,617	n.a.
Indiana University-Southeast; New Albany, Ind. 47150	5,182 (C)	Pub	1,790	4,512	n.a.
Indiana Wesleyan University; Marion, Ind. 46953	1,656 (C)	P	7,590	7,590	3,392
Industrial Engineering College of Chicago; Chicago, Ill. 60601	120 (C)	P	4,420	4,420	n.a.
Insurance, College of; New York, N.Y. 10007	650 (C)	P	8,790	8,790	6,280
Inter-American University-Arecibo Regional College; Arecibo, P.R. 00612	3,715 (C)	P	2,445	2,445	n.a.
International Bible College; Florence, Ala. 35630	119 (C)	P	2,920	2,920	2,500
International Institute of A.C.E.; Lewisville, Tex. 75067	75 (C)	P	2,000	2,000	2,800
International Institute of the Americas of World University; Carolina, P.R. 00628	4,600 (C)	P	2,280	2,280	n.a.
International Training, School for; Brattleboro, Vt. 05301	60 (C)	P	9,820	9,820	3,578

Institution and location	Enrollment	Control	Tuition ($) Res.	Nonres.	Rm/Bd ($)
Iona College; New Rochelle, N.Y. 10801	3,420 (C)	P	9,090	9,090	5,900
Iowa, University of; Iowa City, Iowa 52242	20,160 (C)	Pub	1,952	6,470	2,920
Iowa State University; Ames, Iowa 50011	21,188 (C)	Pub	1,952	6,406	2,870
Iowa Wesleyan College; Mount Pleasant, Iowa 52641	914 (C)	P	7,800	7,800	3,000
Ithaca College; Ithaca, N.Y. 14850	6,267 (C)	p	12,040	12,040	5,100
ITT Technical Institute; West Covina, Calif. 91790-2767	700 (C)	P	6,490	6,490	n.a.
Jackson College for Women. *See* Tufts University					
Jackson State Universityi; Jackson, Miss. 39217	6,051 (C)	Pub	1,786	2,968	2,424
Jacksonville State University; Jacksonville, Ala. 36265	7,272 (C)	Pub	1,420	2,130	2,354
Jacksonville University; Jacksonville, Fla. 32211	2,099 (C)	P	8,245	8,245	3,840
James Madison University; Harrisonburg, Va. 22807	9,860 (C)	Pub	3,298	6,650	4,102
Jamestown College; Jamestown, N.D. 58401	841 (C)	P	6,670	6,670	2,980
Jarvis Christian College; Hawkins, Tex. 75765	560 (C)	P	4,015	4,015	2,999
Jersey City State College; Jersey City, N.J. 07305	5,728 (C)	Pub	2,212	2,902	4,450
Jewish Theological Seminary of America; New York, N.Y. 10027	134 (C)	P	5,910	5,910	5,720
John Brown University; Siloam Springs, Ark. 72761	912 (C)	P	5,390	5,390	3,060
John Carroll University; University Heights, Ohio 44118	3,400 (C)	P	9,253	9,253	5,050
John F. Kennedy University-Evenings; Orinda, Calif. 94563	327 (C)	P	5,160	5,160	n.a.
John Jay Coll. of Criminal Justice. *See* New York, City Univ. of					
Johns Hopkins Universtiy; Baltimore, Md. 21218	2,898 (C)	P	16,400	16,400	6,120
Johnson and Wales University; Providence, R.I. 02903	7,019 (C)	P	8,235	8,235	4,000
Johnson Bible College; Knoxville, Tenn. 37998	409 (C)	P	3,350	3,350	2,645
Johnson C. Smith University; Charlotte, N.C. 28216	1,197 (C)	P	5,876	5,876	2,158
Johnson State College; Johnson, Vt. 05656	1,200 (C)	Pub	2,870	6,152	4,086
Johnston College, Calif. *See* Redlands, University of					
John Wesley College; High Point, N.C. 27260	67 (C)	P	3,639	3,639	4,400
Jones College—Jacksonville; Jacksonville, Fla. 32211	1,700 (C)	P	3,240	3,240	n.a.
Jordan College; Cedar Springs, Mich. 49319	2,322 (C)	P	4,340	4,340	n.a.
Judson College; Elgin, Ill. 60120	498 (C)	P	8,090	8,090	4,090
Judson College; Marion, Ala. 36756	411 (W)	P	4,750	4,750	3,090
Juilliard School; New York, N.Y. 10023	485 (C)	P	10,350	10,350	5,830
Juniata College; Huntingdon, Pa. 16652	1,134 (C)	P	12,470	12,470	3,690
Kalamazoo College; Kalamazoo, Mich. 49007	1,265 (C)	P	12.719	12,719	4,053
Kansas, University of; Lawrence, Kan. 66045	19,261 (C)	Pub	1,546	4,670	2,500
Kansas, University of, Medical Center; Kansas City, Kan. 66103	597 (C)	Pub	1,358	4,482	n.a.
Kansas City Art Institute; Kansas City, Mo. 64111	533 (C)	P	11,260	11,260	3,500
Kansas City College and Bible School; Overland Park, Kan. 66204	49 (C)	P	2,275	2,275	2,450
Kansas Newman College; Wichita, Kan. 67213	756 (C)	P	6,523	6,523	3,168
Kansas State University; Manhattan, Kan. 66506	20,110 (C)	Pub	1,699	5,377	2,680
Kansas Wesleyan University; Salina, Kan. 67401	550 (C)	P	6,220	6,220	2,900
Kean College of New Jersey; Union, N.J. 07083	10,907 (C)	Pub	1,950	2,640	2,920
Keene State College; Keene, N.H. 03431	3,512 (C)	Pub	2,544	6,394	3,430
Kendall College; Evanston, Ill. 60201	371 (C)	P	7,005	7,005	4,473
Kendall College of Art and Design; Grand Rapids, Mich. 49503	742 (C)	P	8,124	8,124	n.a.
Kennesaw College, Marietta, Ga. 30061	8,404 (C)	Pub	1,461	4,041	n.a.
Kent State University; Kent, Ohio 44242	19,636 (C)	Pub	3,006	6,006	3,008
Kentucky, University of; Lexington, Ky. 40506	17,300 (C)	Pub	1,844	5,084	3,534
Kentucky Christian College; Grayson, Ky. 41143	479 (C)	P	3,250	3,250	2,950
Kentucky State University; Frankfort, Ky. 40601	2,425 (C)	Pub	1,452	4,051	2,468
Kentucky Wesleyan College; Owensboro, Ky. 42301	711 (C)	P	6,690	6,690	3,760
Kenyon College; Gambier, Ohio 43022	1,530 (C)	P	16,050	16,050	3,375
Keuka College; Keuka Park, N.Y. 14478	651 (C)	P	7,660	7,660	3,580
King College; Bristol, Tenn. 37620	535 (C)	P	6,650	6,650	3,050
Kings College; Briarcliff Manor, N.Y. 10510	508 (C)	P	8,310	8,310	3,820
King's College; Wilkes-Barre, Pa 18711	2,257 (C)	P	8,500	8,500	4,120
Knox College; Galesburg, Ill. 61401	1,000 (C)	P	12,765	12,765	3,675
Knoxville College; Knoxville, Tenn. 37921	1,225 (C)	P	5,100	5,100	3,600
Kutztown University; Kutztown, Pa. 19530	6,883 (C)	Pub	2,552	4,586	2,548
Laboratory Institute of Merchandising; New York, N.Y. 10022	258 (C)	P	8,300	8,300	n.a.
Lafayette College; Easton, Pa. 18042	2,323 (C)	P	15,475	15,475	4,900
LaGrange College; LaGrange, Ga. 30240	961 (C)	P	5,127	5,127	3,000
Lake Erie College; Painesville, Ohio 44077	613 (C)	P	8,480	8,480	4,000
Lake Forest College; Lake Forest, Ill. 60045	1,121 (C)	P	13,885	13,885	3,155
Lakeland College; Sheboygan, Wis. 53082	1,967 (C)	P	8,050	8,050	3,250
Lake Superior State University; Sault Ste. Marie, Mich. 49783	3,078 (C)	Pub	1,998	4,119	3,454
Lamar University; Beaumont, Tex. 77710	11,174 (C)	Pub	890	3,400	2,800
Lambuth College; Jackson, Tenn. 38301	804 (C)	P	4,600	4,600	3,000
Lancaster Bible College; Lancaster, Pa. 17601	395 (C)	P	6,560	6,560	2,940
Lander College; Greenwood S.C. 29649	2,309 (C)	Pub	3,180	3,180	2,430
Lane College; Jackson, Tenn. 38301	525 (C)	P	4,357	4,357	2,473
Langston University; Langston, Okla. 73050	2,103 (C)	Pub	1,103	3,041	2,192
Laredo State University; Laredo, Tex. 78040-9960	541 (C)	Pub	1,338	4,398	n.a.
La Roche College; Pittsburgh, Pa. 15237	1,868 (C)	P	7,138	7,138	3,878
La Salle University; Philadelphia, Pa. 19141	3,396 (C)	P	10,250	10,250	4,800

Institution and location	Enrollment	Control	Tuition ($) Res.	Tuition ($) Nonres.	Rm/Bd ($)
Lasell College; Newton, Mass. 02166	444 (W)	P	8,575	8,575	5,175
La Verne, University of; La Verne, Calif 91750	1,485 (C)	P	10,060	10,060	3,646
Lawrence Technological University; Southfield, Mich. 48075	5,182 (C)	P	5,826	5,826	4,246
Lawrence University; Appleton, Wis. 54912	1,176 (C)	P	14,685	14,685	3,363
Lebanon Valley College; Annville, Pa. 17003	1,211 (C)	P	11,750	11,750	4,325
Lee College; Cleveland, Tenn. 37311	1,738 (C)	P	4,379	4,379	2,774
Lee College of the University of Judaism; Los Angeles, Calif. 90077	70 (C)	P	7,200	7,200	5,140
Lehigh University; Bethlehem, Pa. 18015	4,493 (C)	P	15,650	15,650	4,940
Le Moyne College; Syracuse, N.Y. 13214-1399	2,354 (C)	P	9,270	9,270	4,220
Le Moyne-Owen College; Memphis, Tenn. 38126	955 (C)	P	3,650	3,650	n.a.
Lenoir-Rhyne College; Hickory, N.C. 28603	1,544 (C)	P	8,584	8,584	3,326
Lesley College; Cambridge, Mass. 02138-2790	571 (W)	P	10,140	10,140	4,770
LeTourneau University; Longview, Tex. 75607	773 (C)	P	7,250	7,250	3,640
Lewis and Clark College; Portland, Ore. 97219	1,896 (C)	P	13,470	13,470	4,653
Lewis-Clark State College; Lewiston, Idaho 83501	2,275 (C)	Pub	1,118	2,206	2,700
Lewis University; Romeoville, Ill. 60441	3,091 (C)	P	7,850	7,850	3,965
Liberty University; Lynchburg, Va. 24506	8,367 (C)	P	6,045	6,045	3,970
L.I.F.E. Bible College; Los Angeles, Calif. 90086-2529	370 (C)	P	4,090	4,090	2,800
L.I.F.E. Bible College East; Christiansburg, V.A. 24073	112 (C)	P	2,160	2,160	2,240
Limestone College; Gaffney, S.C. 29340	295 (C)	P	6,464	6,464	3,122
Lincoln Christian College; Lincoln, Ill. 62656	327 (C)	P	3,965	3,965	2,470
Lincoln Memorial University; Harrogate, Tenn. 37752	1,609 (C)	P	4,780	4,780	2,430
Lincoln University; San Francisco, Calif. 94118	159 (C)	P	1,000	1,000	n.a.
Lincoln University; Jefferson City, Mo. 65101	3,242 (C)	Pub	1,930	3,840	2,728
Lincoln University; Lincoln University, Pa. 19352	1,180 (C)	Pub	2,510	3,730	2,700
Lindenwood College; St. Charles, Mo. 63301	1,412 (C)	P	8,180	8,180	4,400
Lindsey Wilson College; Columbia, Ky. 42728	1,060 (C)	P	5,168	5,168	3,280
Linfield College; McMinnville, Ore. 97128	1,590 (C)	P	11,050	11,050	3,500
Livingstone College; Salisbury, N.C. 28144	580 (C)	P	5,028	5,028	3,140
Livingstone University; Livingston, Ala. 35470	1,641 (C)	Pub	1,524	1,524	2,055
Lock Haven University of Pennsylvania; Lock Haven, Pa. 17745	3,521 (C)	Pub	2,318	4,214	2,274
Lockyear College; Evansville, Ind. 47706	721 (C)	P	2,850	2,850	n.a.
Loma Linda University; Loma Linda, Calif. 92350	2,322 (C)	P	9,360	9,360	3,246
Loma Linda University-La Sierra; Riverside, Calif. 92515	1,800 (C)	P	9,360	9,360	3,246
Long Island University; Greenvale, N.Y. 11548:					
Brooklyn Campus; Brooklyn, N.Y. 11201	3,441 (C)	P	8,100	8,100	6,000
C.W. Post Campus; Greenvale, N.Y. 11548	4,906 (C)	P	8,700	8,700	4,580
Southampton Campus; Southampton, N.Y. 11968	1,162 (C)	P	9,100	9,100	4,500
Longwood College; Farmville, Va. 23901	2,947 (C)	Pub	3,190	6,790	3,554
Loras College; Dubuque, Iowa 52001	1,807 (C)	P	9,115	9,115	3,200
Louisiana College; Pineville, La. 71359	1,017 (C)	P	3,300	3,300	2,808
Louisiana State Univ. and A&M Coll.; Baton Rouge, La. 70803	20,792 (C)	Pub	2,043	5,243	2,710
LSU-Shreveport; Shreveport, La. 71115	3,594 (C)	Pub	1,910	4,830	n.a.
Louisiana Tech University; Ruston, La. 71272	9,078 (C)	Pub	1,841	2,996	2,115
Louisville, University of; Louisville, Ky, 40292	17,835 (C)	Pub	1,740	4,980	3,040
Lourdes College; Sylvania, Ohio 43560	886 (C)	P	4,680	4,680	n.a.
Lowell, University of; Lowell, Mass. 01854	11,328 (C)	Pub	3,168	6,685	3,990
Loyola College; Baltimore, Md. 21210	3,134 (C)	P	9,640	9,640	5,080
Loyola Marymount University; Los Angeles, Calif. 90045	4,076 (C)	P	11,367	11,367	5,671
Loyola University; New Orleans, La. 70118	3,642 (C)	P	9,370	9,370	4,848
Loyola University of Chicago; Chicago, Ill. 60611	6,037 (C)	P	9,270	9,270	4,908
Lubbock Christian University; Lubbock, Tex. 79407	1,035 (C)	P	5,630	5,630	2,330
Lutheran Bible Institute of Seattle; Issaquah, Wash. 98027	148 (C)	P	2,455	2,455	3,240
Luther College; Decorah, Iowa 52101	2,265 (C)	P	10,600	10,600	3,300
Lycoming College; Williamsport, Pa. 17701	1,271 (C)	P	11,000	11,000	3,975
Lynchburg College; Lynchburg, Va. 24501	1,958 (C)	P	10,330	10,330	5,050
Lyndon State College; Lyndonville, Vt. 05851	1,067 (C)	Pub	4,801	7,033	4,290
Macalester College; St. Paul, Minn. 55105	1,744 (C)	P	13,331	13,331	3,970
MacMurray College; Jacksonville, Ill. 62650	569 (C)	P	8,150	8,150	3,350
Madonna University; Livonia, Mich. 48150	4,055 (C)	P	4,050	4,050	3,200
Maharishi International University; Fairfield, Iowa 52556	360 (C)	P	7,250	7,250	2,532
Maine, Univ. of, at Augusta; Augusta, Me. 04330	4,773 (C)	Pub	1,920	4,650	n.a.
Maine, Univ. of, at Farmington; Farmington, Me. 04938	2,438 (C)	Pub	2,410	5,470	3,586
Maine, Univ. of, at Fort Kent; Fort Kent, Me. 04743-1292	576 (C)	Pub	1,920	4,650	3,395
Maine, Univ. of, at Machias; Machias, Me. 04654	1,008 (C)	Pub	1,920	4,650	3,090
Maine, Univ. of, at Orono; Orono, Me. 04469	11,262 (C)	Pub	2,679	6,843	4,241
Maine, Univ. of, at Presque Isle; Presque Isle, Me. 04769	1,394 (C)	Pub	1,920	4,650	3,090
Maine Maritime Academy—College of Engineering, Transportation, and Management; Castine, Me. 04420	555 (C)	Pub	3,320	3,320	4,000
Malone College; Canton, Ohio 44709	1,515 (C)	P	7,860	7,860	3,000
Manchester College; North Manchester, Ind. 46962	1,113 (C)	P	8,270	8,270	3,246
Manhattan Christian College; Manhattan, Kan. 66502	206 (C)	P	3,180	3,180	2,434
Manhattan College; Riverdale, N.Y. 10471	3,146 (C)	P	11,100	11,100	5,800

Institution and location	Enrollment	Control	Tuition ($) Res.	Tuition ($) Nonres.	Rm/Bd ($)
Manhattan School of Music; New York, N.Y. 10027	398 (C)	P	10,250	10,250	n.a.
Manhattanville College; Purchase, N.Y. 10577	1,004 (C)	P	12,690	12,690	5,600
Mankato State University; Mankato, Minn. 56001	13,141 (C)	Pub	1,976	3,224	2,388
Mannes College of Music; New York, N.Y. 10024	14 (C)	P	10,030	10,030	6,200
Mansfield University of Pennsylvania; Mansfield, Pa. 16933	2,661 (C)	Pub	2,908	4,764	2,316
Marian College; Indianapolis, Ind. 46222	1,233 (C)	P	7,584	7,584	3,104
Marian College of Fond du Lac; Fond du Lac, Wis. 54935	1,168 (C)	P	7,400	7,400	3,300
Marietta College; Marietta, Ohio 45750	1,285 (C)	P	16,817	16,817	5,155
Marist College; Poughkeepsie, N.Y. 12601	2,941 (C)	P	9,195	9,195	5,100
Marlboro College; Marlboro, Vt. 05344	275 (C)	P	15,000	15,000	5,150
Marquette University; Milwaukee, Wis. 53233	9,053 (C)	P	8,284	8,284	3,450
Mars Hill College; Mars Hill, N.C. 28754	1,097 (C)	P	6,650	6,650	3,300
Marshall University; Huntington, W. Va. 25705	10,581 (C)	Pub	2,712	4,042	3,630
Martin University; Indianapolis, Ind. 46218	475 (C)	P	4,500	4,500	n.a.
Mary, University of; Bismarck, N.D. 58504	1,190 (C)	P	5,568	5,568	2,448
Mary Baldwin College; Staunton, Va. 24401	677 (W)	P	9,165	9,165	6,175
Marygrove College; Detroit, Mich. 48221	1,099 (C)	P	6,420	6,420	3,360
Mary Hardin-Baylor, University of; Belton, Tex. 76513	1,812 (C)	P	4,400	4,400	2,680
Maryland, Univ. of-Baltimore County; Baltimore, Md. 21228	8,542 (C)	Pub	2,380	6,330	3,860
Maryland, Univ. of-College Park; College Park, Md. 20742	22,553 (C)	Pub	2,269	6,325	4,712
Maryland, Univ. of-Eastern Shore; Princess Anne, Md. 21853	1,925 (C)	Pub	2,114	5,764	3,534
Maryland, Univ. of, University College; College Park, Md. 20742	11,715 (C)	Pub	3,865	4,015	n.a.
Maryland Institute-College of Art; Baltimore, Md. 21217	850 (C)	P	10,600	10,600	4,125
Marylhurst College; Marylhurst, Ore. 97036	865 (C)	P	7,200	7,200	n.a.
Marymount College; Tarrytown, N.Y. 10591	1,108 (W)	P	10,200	10,200	5,750
Marymount Manhattan College; New York, N.Y. 10021	1,484 (W)	P	9,258	9,258	4,200
Marymount Univ.; Arlington, Va. 22207	1,878 (C)	P	9,707	9,707	4,650
Maryville College; Maryville, Tenn. 37801	855 (C)	P	7,750	7,750	3,550
Maryville College-St. Louis; St. Louis, Mo. 63141	3,143 (C)	P	7,800	7,800	3,850
Mary Washington College; Fredericksburg, Va. 22401	3,395 (C)	Pub	2,618	6,076	4,250
Marywood College; Scranton, Pa. 18509	2,052 (C)	P	8,250	8,250	3,800
Massachusetts, Univ. of-Amherst; Amherst, Mass. 01003	17,961 (C)	Pub	3,200	8,222	3,640
Massachusetts, Univ. of-Boston; Boston, Mass. 02125	10,336 (C)	Pub	2,200	6,400	n.a.
Massachusetts College of Art; Boston, Mass. 02115	1,109 (C)	Pub	3,311	7,101	5,142
Massachusetts College of Pharmacy and Allied Health Sciences; Boston, Mass. 02115	785 (C)	P	8,500	8,500	6,115
Massachusetts Institute of Technology; Cambridge, Mass. 02139	4,242 (C)	P	16,900	16,900	4,076
Massachusetts Maritime Academy; Buzzards Bay, Mass. 02532	600 (C)	Pub	2,010	5,980	3,800
Master's College, The; Newhall, Calif. 91322	845 (C)	P	7,180	7,180	3,810
Mayville State University; Mayville, N.D. 58257	764 (C)	Pub	1,482	3,954	2,054
McKendree College; Lebanon, Ill. 62258	1,100 (C)	P	6,626	6,626	3,420
McMurry College; Abilene, Tex. 79697	1,711 (C)	P	6,255	6,255	3,371
McNeese State University; Lake Charles, La. 70609	6,662 (C)	Pub	1,626	3,176	2,160
McPherson College; McPherson, Kan. 67460	462 (C)	P	6,660	6,660	3,110
Medaille College; Buffalo, N.Y. 14214	1,105 (C)	P	3,590	3,590	n.a.
Medical College of Georgia; Augusta, Ga. 30912	780 (C)	Pub	1,962	5,406	2,590
Medical University of South Carolina; Charleston, S.C. 29425	964 (C)	Pub	1,750	3,500	3,300
Memphis College of Art; Memphis, Tenn. 38112	251 (C)	P	8,140	8,140	4,000
Memphis State University; Memphis, Tenn. 38152	16,207 (C)	Pub	1,472	4,675	2,740
Menlo College; Atherton, Calif. 94027-4185	490 (C)	P	12,100	12,100	6,320
Mercer University; Macon, Ga. 31207	2,596 (C)	P	9,450	9,450	3,780
Mercer University-Atlanta; Atlanta, Ga. 30341	1,405 (C)	P	5,600	5,600	n.a.
Mercy College; Dobbs Ferry, N.Y. 10522	5,283 (C)	P	6,990	6,990	n.a.
Mercyhurst College; Erie, Pa. 16546	2,086 (C)	P	8,754	8,754	3,345
Meredith College; Raleigh, N.C. 27607	2,038 (W)	P	5,720	5,720	2,820
Merrimack College; North Andover, Mass. 01845	2,240 (C)	P	10,350	10,350	5,700
Mesa State College; Grand Junction, Colo. 81502	3,242 (C)	Pub	1,546	4,094	3,144
Messiah College; Grantham, Pa. 17027	2,252 (C)	P	8,700	8,700	4,380
Methodist College; Fayettesville, N.C. 28311-1499	1,190 (C)	P	7,700	7,700	3,100
Metropolitan State College; Denver, Colo. 80204	16,262 (C)	Pub	1,710	4,435	n.a.
Metropolitan State University; St. Paul, Minn. 55101	5,535 (C)	Pub	1,740	1,740	n.a.
Miami, University of; Coral Gables, Fla. 33124	8,714 (C)	P	14,095	14,095	5,575
Miami Christian College; Miami, Fla. 33167	173 (C)	P	5,170	5,170	2,760
Miami University; Oxford, Ohio 45056	14,467 (C)	Pub	6,880	6,880	3,460
Michigan, Univ. of-Ann Arbor; Ann Arbor, Mich. 48109	21,811 (C)	Pub	3,366	11,874	3,853
Michigan, Univ. of-Dearborn; Dearborn, Mich. 48128	6,737 (C)	Pub	3,744	11,988	n.a.
Michigan, Univ. of-Flint; Flint, Mich. 48502	6,174 (C)	Pub	2,104	6,860	n.a.
Michigan Christian College; Rochester Hills, Mich. 48307	282 (C)	P	4,200	4,200	3,030
Michigan State University; East Lansing, Mich. 48824	34,829 (C)	Pub	3,302	8,143	3,168
Michigan Technological University; Houghton, Mich. 49931	6,107 (C)	Pub	2,436	5,907	3,186
Mid-America Bible College; Oklahoma City, Okla. 73170	236 (C)	P	3,640	3,640	2,936
Mid-America Nazarene College; Olathe, Kan. 66061	1,189 (C)	P	5,090	5,090	2,990
Middlebury College; Middlebury, Vt. 05753	1,950 (C)	P	20,460	20,460	—

Institution and location	Enrollment	Control	Tuition ($) Res.	Tuition ($) Nonres.	Rm/Bd ($)
Middle Tennessee State University; Murfreesboro, Tenn. 37132	12,744 (C)	Pub	1,346	4,550	1,914
Midland Lutheran College; Fremont, Neb. 68025	960 (C)	P	8,100	8,100	2,550
Midway College; Midway, Ky. 40347	335 (W)	P	5,840	5,840	3,550
Midwestern State University; Wichita Falls, Tex. 76308	4,805 (C)	Pub	1,190	4,430	2,830
Miles College; Birmingham, Ala. 35208	566 (C)	P	3,760	3,760	2,300
Millersville University of Pennsylvania; Millersville, Pa. 17551	6,996 (C)	Pub	2,536	4,392	2,810
Milligan College; Milligan College, Tenn. 37682	600 (C)	P	6,214	6,214	2,736
Millikin University; Decatur, Ill. 62522	1,805 (C)	P	10,081	10,081	3,784
Millsaps College; Jackson, Miss. 39210	1,325 (C)	P	9,720	9,720	4,620
Mills College; Oakland, Calif. 94613	789 (W)	P	13,005	13,005	5,400
Milwaukee Institute of Art and Design; Milwaukee, Wis. 53202	408 (C)	P	7,600	7,600	n.a.
Milwaukee School of Engineering; Milwaukee, Wis. 53201-0644	1,808 (C)	P	9,150	9,150	3,225
Minneapolis Coll. of Art and Design; Minneapolis, Minn. 55404	629 (C)	P	10,300	10,300	3,610
Minnesota, Univ. of-Duluth; Duluth, Minn. 55812	7,800 (C)	Pub	2,614	5,000	3,066
Minnesota, Univ. of-Morris; Morris, Minn. 56267	2,021 (C)	Pub	2,585	6,089	2,835
Minnesota, Univ. of-Twin Cities; Minneapolis, Minn. 55455	29,082 (C)	Pub	2,337	5,341	2,900
Minnesota Bible College; Rochester, Minn. 55902	96 (C)	P	3,940	3,940	2,770
Minot State University; Minot, N.D. 58701	3,236 (C)	Pub	1,703	4,249	1,746
Mississippi, University of; University, Miss. 38677	7,589 (C)	Pub	2,059	3,240	2,934
Mississippi, Univ. of, Medical Center; Jackson, Miss. 39216	472 (C)	Pub	1,595	2,777	2,600
Mississippi College; Clinton, Miss. 39058	2,078 (C)	P	5,403	5,403	2,550
Mississippi State University; Mississippi State, Miss. 39762	11,123 (C)	Pub	2,223	3,685	2,800
Mississippi University for Women; Columbus, Miss. 39701	2,407 (C)	Pub	2,043	3,503	2,092
Mississippi Valley State University; Itta Bena, Miss. 38941	1,848 (C)	Pub	1,750	2,932	1,924
Missouri, Univ. of-Columbia; Columbia, Mo. 65211	18,763 (C)	Pub	2,230	6,253	3,004
Missouri, Univ. of-Kansas City; Kansas City, Mo. 64110	6,703 (C)	Pub	2,217	6,240	3,270
Missouri, Univ. of-Rolla; Rolla, Mo. 65401	4,126 (C)	Pub	2,340	6,138	3,100
Missouri, Univ. of-St. Louis; St. Louis, Mo. 63121	10,737 (C)	Pub	2,310	6,333	n.a.
Missouri Baptist College; St. Louis, Mo. 63141	951 (C)	P	5,820	5,820	2,650
Missouri Southern State College; Joplin, Mo. 64801	6,012 (C)	Pub	1,784	3,056	2,340
Missouri Valley College; Marshall, Mo. 65340	1,130 (C)	P	8,178	8,178	4,656
Missouri Western State College; St. Joseph, Mo. 64507	4,338 (C)	Pub	1,648	3,112	2,154
Mobile College; Mobile, Ala. 36613	1,032 (C)	P	4,650	4,650	2,900
Molloy College; Rockville Centre, N.Y. 11570	1,476 (C)	P	8,164	8,164	n.a.
Monmouth College; Monmouth, Ill. 61462	655 (C)	P	12,450	12,450	3,350
Monmouth College; West Long Branch, N.J. 07764	3,078 (C)	P	10,470	10,470	5,000
Montana, University of; Missoula, Mont. 59812	8,135 (C)	Pub	1,447	3,520	3,029
Montana College of Mineral Science and Technology; Butte, Mont. 59701	1,690 (C)	Pub	1,309	3,382	3,000
Montana State University; Bozeman, Mont. 59717	10,024 (C)	Pub	1,764	3,837	3,000
Montclair State College; Upper Montclair, N.J. 07043	10,200 (C)	Pub	2,400	3,392	4,132
Monterey Institute of Intl. Studies; Monterey, Calif. 93940	108 (C)	P	11,345	11,345	n.a.
Montevallo, University of; Montevallo, Ala. 35115	2,648 (C)	Pub	1,954	3,784	2,820
Montreat-Anderson College; Montreat, N.C. 28757	386 (C)	P	5,250	5,250	3,000
Moody Bible Institute; Chicago, Ill. 60610	1,434 (C)	P	900	900	3,750
Moore College of Art and Design; Philadelphia, Pa. 19103	590 (W)	P	10,700	10,700	4,600
Moorhead State University; Moorhead, Minn. 56560	8,709 (C)	Pub	1,758	3,062	2,256
Moravian College; Bethlehem, Pa. 18018	1,215 (C)	P	12,698	12,698	4,044
Morehead State University; Morehead, Ky. 40351	7,083 (C)	Pub	1,420	4,020	2,900
Morehouse College; Atlanta, Ga. 30314	2,720 (M)	P	6,210	6,210	4,462
Morgan State University; Baltimore, Md. 21239	3,878 (C)	Pub	2,124	4,048	4,380
Morningside College; Sioux City, Iowa 51106	1,282 (C)	P	9,206	9,206	2,980
Morris Brown College; Atlanta, Ga. 30314	1,500 (C)	P	6,550	6,550	3,800
Morris College; Sumter, S.C. 29150	760 (C)	P	3,939	3,939	2,387
Morrison College/Reno Business College; Reno, Nev. 89503	400 (C)	P	8,235	8,235	n.a.
Mount Angel Seminary; St. Benedict, Ore. 97373	27 (M)	P	3,300	3,300	2,900
Mount Holyoke College; South Hadley, Mass. 01075	1,954 (W)	P	15,050	15,050	4,600
Mount Ida College; Newton Centre, Mass. 02159	1,400 (C)	P	8,300	8,300	5,865
Mount Marty College; Yankton, S.D. 57078	685 (C)	P	6,690	6,690	2,705
Mount Mary College; Milwaukee, Wis. 53222	1,418 (W)	P	6,950	6,950	2,447
Mount Mercy College; Cedar Rapids, Iowa 52402	1,529 (C)	P	7,750	7,750	3,150
Mount Olive College; Mount Olive, N.C. 28365	756 (C)	P	6,600	6,600	2,550
Mount St. Joseph, College of; Mount St. Joseph, Ohio 45051	2,398 (C)	P	8,170	8,170	3,810
Mount Saint Mary College; Newburgh, N.Y. 12550	1,239 (C)	P	7,335	7,335	4,300
Mount Saint Mary's College; Emmitsburg, Md. 21727	1,413 (C)	P	9,875	9,875	5,700
Mount St. Clare College; Clinton, Iowa 52732	325 (C)	P	7,267	7,267	3,230
Mount St. Mary's College; Los Angeles, Calif. 90049	910 (W)	P	9,250	9,250	4,535
Mount St. Vincent, College of; New York, N.Y. 10471	1,043 (C)	P	9,920	9,920	4,900
Mount Senario College; Ladysmith, Wis. 54848	403 (C)	P	6,300	6,300	2,625
Mount Union College; Alliance, Ohio 44601	1,360 (C)	P	11,320	11,320	3,280
Mount Vernon College; Washington, D.C. 20007	528 (W)	P	12,510	12,510	6,090
Mount Vernon Nazarene College; Mount Vernon, Ohio 43050	1,061 (C)	P	5,750	5,750	3,350
Muhlenberg College; Allentown, Pa. 18104	1,615 (C)	P	15,180	15,180	4,260
Multnomah School of the Bible; Portland, Ore. 97220	508 (C)	P	5,090	5,090	3,056

Institution and location	Enrollment	Control	Tuition ($) Res.	Nonres.	Rm/Bd ($)
Mundelein College; Chicago, Ill. 60660	917 (W)	P	9,260	9,260	4,730
Murray State University; Murray, Ky. 42071	6,296 (C)	Pub	1,410	5,000	2,490
Museum of Fine Arts, School of the-Tufts University; Boston, Mass. 02115	690 (C)	P	10,355	10,355	n.a.
Museum Art School, Portland. *See* Pacific Northwest College of Art					
Muskingum College; Concord, Ohio 43762	1,092 (C)	P	11,855	11,855	3,510
NAES College; Chicago, Ill. 60659	119 (C)	P	4,300	4,300	n.a.
Naropa Institute; Boulder, Colo. 80302	135 (C)	P	7,580	7,580	n.a.
Nathaniel Hawthorne College. *See* Hawthorne College					
National College-Albuquerque; Albuquerque, N.M. 87108-7439	134 (C)	P	5,472	5,472	n.a.
National College, Colorado Springs Branch; Colorado Springs, Colo. 80909	207 (C)	P	3,800	3,800	n.a.
National College; Rapid City, S.D. 57709	585 (C)	P	5,460	5,460	2,790
National-Louis University; Evanston, Ill. 60201	2,910 (C)	P	6,975	6,975	4,065
National University; San Diego, Calif. 92108	7,121 (C)	P	5,950	5,950	n.a.
Nazareth College in Kalamazoo; Nazareth, Mich. 49001-1282	564 (C)	P	7,664	7,664	3,076
Nazareth College of Rochester; Rochester, N.Y. 14610	1,370 (C)	P	8,750	8,750	4,480
Nebraska, University of–Kearney; Kearney, Neb. 68849	7,458 (C)	Pub	1,415	2,135	2,030
Nebraska, University of-Lincoln; Lincoln, Neb. 68588-0415	19,791 (C)	Pub	1,284	3,492	3,125
Nebraska, University of-Omaha; Omaha, Neb. 68182	14,057 (C)	Pub	1,358	3,669	n.a.
Nebraska Christian College; Norfolk, Neb. 68701	139 (C)	P	2,600	2,600	2,240
Nebraska Wesleyan University; Lincoln, Neb. 68504	1,682 (C)	P	8,227	8,227	2,950
Neumann College; Aston, Pa. 19014	1,206 (C)	P	7,800	7,800	n.a.
Nevada, University of-Las Vegas; Las Vegas, Nev. 89154	16,320 (C)	Pub	1,426	4,726	4,200
Nevada, University of-Reno; Reno, Nev. 89557	7,507 (C)	Pub	1,593	3,600	3,720
Newberry College; Newberry, S.C. 29108	701 (C)	P	7,400	7,400	3,000
New College of California; San Francisco, Calif. 94110	200 (C)	P	5,850	5,850	n.a.
New College of the University of South Florida; Sarasota, Fla. 34243-2197	525 (C)	Pub	1,419	4,730	3,300
New England, University of; Biddeford, Me. 04005	801 (C)	P	9,750	9,750	4,300
New England College; Henniker, N.H. 03242	1,073 (C)	P	11,290	11,290	4,700
New England College-Arundel Campus; England	220 (C)	P	10,570	10,570	3,420
New England Conservatory of Music; Boston, Mass. 02115	348 (C)	P	12,840	12,840	6,150
New England Institute of Technology; Warwick, R.I. 02886	1,950 (C)	P	7,425	7,425	n.a.
New Hampshire, University of; Durham, N.H. 03824	10,121 (C)	Pub	3,014	8,804	3,276
New Hampshire College; Manchester, N.H. 03104	1,897 (C)	P	10,008	10,008	4,635
New Haven, University of; West Haven, Conn. 06516	3,839 (C)	P	9,640	9,640	5,000
New Jersey Institute of Technology; Newark, N.J. 07102	4,957 (C)	Pub	4,000	4,000	4,632
New Mexico, University of; Albuquerque, N.M. 87131	19,927 (C)	Pub	1,554	5,520	3,123
New Mexico Highlands University; Las Vegas, N.M. 87701	1,889 (C)	Pub	1,248	4,488	2,230
New Mexico Inst. of Mining & Technology; Socorro, N.M. 87801	1,311 (C)	Pub	1,393	4,842	3,026
New Mexico State University; Las Cruces, N.M. 88003-0001	12,312 (C)	Pub	1,488	5,184	2,588
New Orleans, University of; New Orleans, La. 70148	12,609 (C)	Pub	1,924	4,616	2,368
New Rochelle, College of-School of Arts & Sciences and School of Nursing; New Rochelle, N.Y. 10805	766 (W)	P	10,150	10,150	4,420
New School for Social Research Eugene Lang College; New York, N.Y. 10011	400 (C)	P	11,794	11,794	7,346
New York, City University of; New York, N.Y. 10021:					
Bernard M. Baruch College; New York, N.Y. 10010	12,835 (C)	Pub	1,250	4,050	n.a.
Brooklyn College; Brooklyn, N.Y. 11210	12,000 (C)	Pub	1,250	4,050	n.a.
City College; New York, N.Y. 10031	11,206 (C)	Pub	1,450	4,050	n.a.
College of Staten Island; Staten Island, N.Y. 10301	11,000 (C)	Pub	1,450	4,050	n.a.
Hunter College; New York, N.Y. 10021	14,866 (C)	Pub	1,450	4,050	3,200
John Jay College of Criminal Justice; New York, N.Y. 10019	8,090 (C)	Pub	1,316	4,150	n.a.
Lehman College; Bronx, N.Y. 10468	8,298 (C)	Pub	1,250	4,050	n.a.
Medgar Evers College; Brooklyn, N.Y. 11225	2,823 (C)	Pub	1,225	2,025	n.a.
New York City Technical College; Brooklyn, N.Y. 11201	10,323 (C)	Pub	1,274	4,054	n.a.
Queens College; Flushing, N.Y. 11367	17,500 (C)	Pub	1,433	4,233	n.a.
York College; Jamaica, N.Y. 11451	5,455 (C)	Pub	1,532	4,132	n.a.
New York, State University of; Albany, N.Y. 12246:					
SUNY-Albany; Albany, N.Y. 12222	11,870 (C)	Pub	1,350	4,700	3,301
SUNY-Buffalo; Buffalo, N.Y. 14214	18,831 (C)	Pub	1,525	4,875	4,020
SUNY-College at Brockport; Brockport, N.Y. 14420	7,096 (C)	Pub	1,586	4,936	3,690
SUNY-College at Buffalo; Buffalo, N.Y. 14222	10,520 (C)	Pub	1,465	4,815	3,090
SUNY-College at Cortland; Cortland, N.Y. 13045	3,467 (C)	Pub	1,350	4,700	3,610
SUNY-College at Fredonia; Fredonia, N.Y. 14063	4,473 (C)	Pub	1,529	4,879	3,580
SUNY-College at Geneseo; Geneseo, N.Y. 14454-1471	4,968 (C)	Pub	1,500	4,900	3,050
SUNY-College at New Paltz; New Paltz, N.Y. 12561	4,728 (C)	Pub	1,495	4,095	3,360
SUNY-College at Old Westbury; Old Westbury, N.Y. 11568	3,999 (C)	Pub	1,475	4,825	3,898
SUNY-College at Oneonta; Oneonta, N.Y. 13820	5,218 (C)	Pub	1,350	4,700	3,500
SUNY-College at Oswego; Oswego, N.Y. 13126	6,574 (C)	Pub	1,475	4,825	3,236
SUNY-College at Plattsburgh; Plattsburgh, N.Y. 12901	5,754 (C)	Pub	1,475	3,825	3,400
SUNY-College at Potsdam; Potsdam, N.Y. 13676	4,194 (C)	Pub	1,475	4,825	4,225

Institution and location	Enrollment	Control	Tuition ($) Res.	Tuition ($) Nonres.	Rm/Bd ($)
SUNY-College of Agriculture and Life Sciences at Cornell University; Ithaca, N.Y. 14853	2,970 (C)	Pub	6,472	11,972	5,414
SUNY-College of Environmental Science and Forestry; Syracuse, N.Y. 13210	942 (C)	Pub	1,460	4,760	5,210
SUNY-College of Human Ecology at Cornell University; Ithaca, N.Y. 14853	1,225 (C)	Pub	6,472	11,972	5,414
SUNY-College of Technology-Farmingdale; Farmingdale, N.Y. 11735	11,106 (C)	Pub	1,650	5,000	3,850
SUNY-Empire State College; Saratoga Springs, N.Y. 12866	7,072 (C)	Pub	2,081	7,106	n.a.
SUNY-Fashion Institute of Technology; New York, N.Y. 10001-5992	4,443 (C)	Pub	1,570	3,920	4,500
SUNY-Health Science Center at Syracuse; Syracuse, N.Y. 13210	304 (C)	Pub	1,475	4,825	4,102
SUNY-Institute of Technology at Utica/Rome; Utica, N.Y. 13054-3050	2,344 (C)	Pub	1,510	4,860	n.a.
SUNY-Maritime College; Throggs Neck, N.Y. 10465	688 (C)	Pub	1,350	4,700	3,632
SUNY-Purchase; Purchase, N.Y. 10577	4,587 (C)	Pub	1,650	5,000	3,590
SUNY-School of Industrial and Labor Relations at Cornell University; Ithaca, N.Y. 14853	625 (C)	Pub	6,472	11,972	5,414
SUNY-Stony Brook; Stony Brook, N.Y. 11794	11,403 (C)	Pub	1,350	4,700	3,894
SUNY-University Center at Binghamton; Binghamton, N.Y. 13901	9,310 (C)	Pub	1,943	5,293	4,474
New York City Technical Coll. *See* New York, City Univ. of					
New York Institute of Technology; Old Westbury, N.Y. 11568	6,428 (C)	P	6,700	6,700	n.a.
New York Institute of Technology Central Islip Campus; Central Islip, N.Y. 11722	1,616 (C)	P	6,770	6,770	4,400
New York Institute of Technology, Metropolitan Center; New York, N.Y. 10023	2,841 (C)	P	6,700	6,700	n.a.
New York School of Interior Design; New York, N.Y. 10022	643 (C)	P	10,115	10,115	n.a.
New York University; New York, N.Y. 10011	15,801 (C)	P	15,820	15,820	7,064
New York, University of the State of, Regents College Degrees; Albany, N.Y. 12230	13,305 (C)	Pub	425	425	n.a.
Niagara University; Niagara University, N.Y. 14109	2,425 (C)	P	9,030	9,030	2,060
Nicholls State University; Thibodaux, La. 70310	6,639 (C)	Pub	1,590	3,390	2,350
Nichols College; Dudley, Mass. 01570	848 (C)	P	7,130	7,130	4,100
Norfolk State University; Norfolk, Va. 23504	7,241 (C)	Pub	2,330	5,160	3,320
North Adams State College; North Adams, Mass. 01247	2,204 (C)	Pub	2,202	5,277	3,460
North Alabama, University of; Florence, Ala. 35632	5,006 (C)	Pub	1,620	1,914	4,000
North Carolina, Univ. of-Asheville; Asheville, N.C. 28804	3,259 (C)	Pub	1,116	4,958	2,990
North Carolina, Univ. of-Chapel Hill; Chapel Hill, N.C. 27514	15,251 (C)	Pub	1,084	5,584	3,472
North Carolina, Univ. of-Charlotte; Charlotte, N.C. 28223	11,143 (C)	Pub	1,035	5,565	2,456
North Carolina, Univ. of-Greensboro; Greensboro, N.C. 27412	9,191 (C)	Pub	1,364	5,978	3,345
North Carolina, Univ. of-Wilmington; Wilmington, N.C. 28403	6,642 (C)	Pub	1,188	5,719	3,034
North Carolina Agricultural and Technical State University; Greensboro, N.C. 27411	5,716 (C)	Pub	1,040	5,412	2,188
North Carolina Central University; Durham, N.C. 27707	4,070 (C)	Pub	1,121	5,652	2,764
North Carolina School of the Arts; Winston-Salem, N.C. 27127-2189	502 (C)	Pub	1,848	5,918	3,039
North Carolina State University-Raleigh; Raleigh, N.C. 27695	22,121 (C)	Pub	1,044	5,546	2,900
North Carolina Wesleyan College; Rocky Mount, N.C. 27801	724 (C)	P	7,160	7,160	3,540
North Central Bible College; Minneapolis, Minn. 55404	1,182 (C)	P	4,768	4,768	3,110
North Central College; Naperville, Ill. 60566-7063	2,216 (C)	P	9,960	9,960	3,735
North Dakota, University of; Grand Forks, N.D. 58202	10,086 (C)	Pub	2,040	5,058	2,190
North Dakota State University; Fargo, N.D. 58105	8,518 (C)	Pub	1,890	5,046	2,178
Northeastern Illinois University, Chicago, Ill. 60625	7,457 (C)	Pub	1,706	4,870	n.a.
Northeastern State Univ.; Tahlequah, Okla. 74464	6,985 (C)	Pub	1,255	3,268	1,880
Northeastern University; Boston, Mass. 02115	13,788 (C)	P	10,178	10,178	2,410
Northeast Louisiana University; Monroe, La. 71209	9,522 (C)	Pub	1,615	3,199	1,950
Northeast Missouri State University; Kirksville, Mo. 63501	5,610 (C)	Pub	1,800	3,504	2,584
Northern Arizona University; Flagstaff, Ariz. 86011	11,029 (C)	Pub	1,580	6,246	2,714
Northern Colorado, University of; Greeley, Colo. 80639	8,442 (C)	Pub	1,820	5,190	3,211
Northern Illinois University; DeKalb, Ill. 60115	18,220 (C)	Pub	2,650	6,250	2,900
Northern Iowa, University of; Cedar Falls, Iowa 50614	11,495 (C)	Pub	1,991	5,012	2,455
Northern Kentucky University; Highland Heights, Ky. 41076	10,195 (C)	Pub	1,410	4,010	2,920
Northern Michigan University; Marquette, Mich. 49855	7,656 (C)	Pub	1,987	3,907	3,157
Northern Montana College; Havre, Mont. 59501	1,489 (C)	Pub	1,272	2,955	2,910
Northern State University; Aberdeen, S.D. 57401	3,100 (C)	Pub	1,735	3,094	1,798
North Florida, University of; Jacksonville, Fla. 32216	6,497 (C)	Pub	1,200	3,800	2,800
North Georgia College; Dahlonega, Ga. 30579	2,180 (C)	Pub	1,650	4,230	2,295
Northland College; Ashland, Wis. 54806	547 (C)	P	8,380	8,380	3,450
North Park College; Chicago, Ill. 60625	1,083 (C)	P	10,665	10,665	4,035
Northrop University; Los Angeles, Calif. 90045	954 (C)	P	11,706	11,706	4,952
North Texas, University of; Denton, Tex. 76203	19,970 (C)	Pub	1,036	4,156	3,304
Northwest Christian College; Eugene, Ore. 97401	279 (C)	P	5,130	5,130	3,072
Northwest College; Kirkland, Wash. 98083-0579	681 (C)	P	5,277	5,277	2,900
Northwestern College; Orange City, Iowa 51041	1,047 (C)	P	8,000	8,000	2,800
Northwestern College; St. Paul, Minn. 55113	1,115 (C)	P	9,096	9,096	2,640
Northwestern Oklahoma State University; Alva, Okla. 73717	1,642 (C)	Pub	1,277	3,282	1,772
Northwestern State Univ. of Louisiana; Natchitoches, La. 71497	6,594 (C)	Pub	1,767	3,567	2,143
Northwestern University; Evanston, Ill. 60201-3060	7,360 (C)	P	14,370	14,370	4,827
Northwest Missouri State University; Maryville, Mo. 64468	4,997 (C)	Pub	1,590	2,880	2,645

Institution and location	Enrollment	Control	Tuition ($) Res.	Nonres.	Rm/Bd ($)
Northwest Nazarene College; Nampa, Idaho 83651	1,095 (C)	P	5,823	5,823	2,529
Northwood Institute of Florida; West Palm Beach, Fla. 33409	528 (C)	P	7,770	7,770	4,725
Northwood Institute of Michigan; Midland, Mich. 48640	1,850 (C)	P	7,500	7,500	3,555
Northwood Institute of Texas; Cedar Hill, Tex. 75104	290 (C)	P	7,290	7,290	3,891
Norwich University; Northfield, Vt. 05663	1,900 (C)	P	11,800	11,800	4,500
Notre Dame, College of, Belmont, Calif. 94002	667 (C)	P	10,165	10,165	5,100
Notre Dame, University of; Notre Dame, Ind. 46556	7,500 (C)	P	13,500	13,500	3,600
Notre Dame College; Manchester, N.H. 03104	600 (C)	P	8,376	8,376	4,635
Notre Dame of Maryland, College of; Baltimore, Md. 21210	672 (W)	P	9,500	9,500	4,800
Notre Dame College of Ohio; Cleveland, Ohio 44121	849 (W)	P	6,850	6,850	3,460
Nova University; Ft. Lauderdale, Fla. 33314	3,560 (C)	P	7,050	7,050	3,265
Nyack College; Nyack, N.Y. 10960	519 (C)	P	7,430	7,430	2,940
Oakland City College; Oakland City, Ind. 47660	636 (C)	P	6,300	6,300	2,840
Oakland University; Rochester, Mich. 48063	9,472 (C)	Pub	2,200	6,000	3,200
Oakwood College; Huntsville, Ala. 35896	1,223 (C)	P	5,925	5,925	3,486
Oberlin College; Oberlin, Ohio 44074	2,850 (C)	P	15,220	15,220	4,890
Oblate College; Washington, D.C. 20017	8 (C)	P	3,750	3,750	n.a.
Occidental College; Los Angeles, Calif. 90041	1,677 (C)	P	14,640	14,640	5,216
Oglala Lakota College; Kyle, S.D. 57752	800 (C)	Pub	1,720	1,720	n.a.
Oglethorpe University; Atlanta, Ga. 30319	1,092 (C)	P	10,250	10,250	4,000
Ohio Dominican College; Columbus, Ohio 43219	1,365 (C)	P	7,020	7,020	3,740
Ohio Institute of Technology; Columbus. *See* DeVry Institute of Technology, Columbus					
Ohio Northern University; Ada, Ohio 45810	2,225 (C)	P	12,255	12,255	3,390
Ohio State University; Columbus, Ohio 43210	41,161 (C)	Pub	2,343	6,295	3,750
Ohio State University-Lima; Lima, Ohio 45804	1,312 (C)	Pub	2,253	6,852	n.a.
Ohio State University-Mansfield; Mansfield, Ohio 44906	1,236 (C)	Pub	2,106	6,195	n.a.
Ohio State University-Marion; Marion, Ohio 43302	1,021 (C)	Pub	2,253	6,852	n.a.
Ohio State University-Newark; Newark, Ohio 43055	1,499 (C)	Pub	2,253	6,852	n.a.
Ohio University; Athens, Ohio 45701	14,500 (C)	Pub	2,730	5,922	3,549
Ohio University-Lancaster; Lancaster, Ohio 43130	1,500 (C)	Pub	2,070	4,929	n.a.
Ohio University-Zanesville, Zanesville, Ohio 43701	985 (C)	Pub	2,199	5,283	n.a.
Ohio Valley College; Parkersburg, W.Va. 26101	224 (C)	P	4,435	4,435	3,005
Ohio Wesleyan University; Delaware, Ohio 43015	2,055 (C)	P	13,610	13,610	4,884
Oklahoma, University of-Norman; Norman, Okla. 73019	14,709 (C)	Pub	1,513	4,420	3,172
Oklahoma, University of-Health Sciences Center; Oklahoma City, Okla. 73190	1,186 (C)	Pub	1,419	4,581	n.a.
Oklahoma Baptist University; Shawnee, Okla. 74801	2,208 (C)	P	5,390	5,390	2,800
Oklahoma Christian University of Science and Arts; Oklahoma City, Okla. 73136-1100	1,645 (C)	P	4,715	4,715	2,720
Oklahoma City University; Oklahoma City, Okla. 73106	1,882 (C)	P	5,500	5,500	3,520
Oklahoma Panhandle State University; Goodwell, Okla. 73939	1,276 (C)	Pub	1,382	3,320	1,800
Oklahoma State University; Stillwater, Okla. 74078	15,141 (C)	Pub	1,568	4,525	2,876
Old Dominion University; Norfolk, Va. 23529-0050	11,679 (C)	Pub	2,848	6,928	4,134
Olivet College; Olivet, Mich. 49076	766 (C)	P	7,890	7,890	2,860
Olivet Nazarene University; Kankakee, Ill. 60901	1,566 (C)	P	6,476	6,476	3,510
O'More College of Design; Franklin, Tenn. 37604	147 (C)	P	5,900	5,900	n.a.
Oral Roberts University; Tulsa, Okla. 74171	3,250 (C)	P	6,025	6,025	3,495
Oregon, University of; Eugene, Ore. 97403	14,018 (C)	Pub	1,782	5,043	3,389
Oregon Coll. of Education. *See* Western Oregon State Coll.					
Oregon Health Sciences University; Portland, Ore. 97201	400 (C)	Pub	2,061	4,929	2,849
Oregon Institute of Technology; Klamath Falls, Ore. 97601	2,873 (C)	Pub	1,890	5,592	3,180
Oregon State University; Corvallis, Ore. 97331	12,419 (C)	Pub	1,833	5,541	2,810
Orlando College; Orlando, Fla. 32810	810 (C)	P	4,300	4,300	n.a.
Otis Art Institute of Parsons School of Design; Los Angeles, Calif. 90057	735 (C)	P	10,050	10,050	4,600
Ottawa University; Ottawa, Kan. 66067	536 (C)	P	6,450	6,450	2,998
Ottawa University-Phoenix Center; Phoenix, Ariz. 85021	560 (C)	P	3,000	3,000	n.a.
Otterbein College; Westerville, Ohio 43081	2,352 (C)	P	10,800	10,800	3,912
Ouachita Baptist University; Arkadelphia, Ark. 71923	1,284 (C)	P	5,210	5,210	2,300
Our Lady of Angels College. *See* Neumann College					
Our Lady of Holy Cross College; New Orleans, La. 70131-7399	1,033 (C)	P	4,600	4,600	n.a.
Our Lady of the Lake-University of San Antonio; San Antonio, Tex. 78285	2,101 (C)	P	5,992	5,992	4,000
Ozark Christian College; Joplin, Mo. 64801	538 (C)	P	2,866	2,866	2,600
Ozarks, College of the; Point Lookout, Mo. 65726	1,512 (C)	P	—	—	1,700
Ozarks, University of the; Clarksville, Ark. 72830	616 (C)	P	3,520	3,520	2,330
Pace University; New York, N.Y. 10038	6,148 (C)	P	8,754	8,754	4,180
Pace University-College of White Plains; White Plains, N.Y. 10603	1,431 (C)	P	8,754	8,754	4,180
Pace University-Pleasantville-Briarcliff; Pleasantville, N.Y. 10570	3,937 (C)	P	8,754	8,754	4,180
Pacific, University of the; Stockton, Calif. 95211	3,802 (C)	P	14,480	14,480	5,100
Pacific Christian College; Fullerton, Calif. 92631	466 (C)	P	5,000	5,000	4,000
Pacific Lutheran University; Tacoma, Wash. 98447	3,049 (C)	P	11,075	11,075	3,890

Institution and location	Enrollment	Control	Tuition ($) Res.	Tuition ($) Nonres.	Rm/Bd ($)
Pacific Northwest College of Art; Portland, Ore. 97205					
Pacific Oaks College; Pasadena, Calif. 91103	150 (C)	P	9,945	9,945	n.a.
Pacific States University; Los Angeles, Calif. 90006	300 (C)	P	3,600	3,600	n.a.
Pacific Union College; Angwin, Calif. 94508	1,676 (C)	P	9,595	9,595	3,335
Pacific University; Forest Grove, Ore. 97116	899 (C)	P	10,200	10,200	3,175
Paier College of Art, Inc.; Hamden, Conn. 06511	309 (C)	P	8,700	8,700	n.a.
Paine College; Augusta, Ga. 30910	581 (C)	P	5,256	5,256	2,660
Palm Beach Atlantic College; West Palm Beach, Fla. 33401	1,375 (C)	P	5,600	5,600	3,170
Pan American University; Edinburg, Tex. 78539	9,000 (C)	Pub	762	1,629	2,288
Park College; Parkville, Mo. 64152	450 (C)	P	6,820	6,820	3,300
Parks College of St. Louis University; Cahokia, Ill. 62206	1,100 (C)	P	7,000	7,000	3,700
Parsons School of Design; New York, N.Y. 10011	1,760 (C)	P	12,050	12,050	6,200
Patten College; Oakland, Calif. 94601	333 (C)	P	3,490	3,490	3,695
Paul Quinn College; Waco, Tex. 76704	509 (C)	P	3,635	3,635	2,975
Peabody Conservatory of Music; Baltimore, Md. 21202	256 (C)	P	11,480	11,480	4,770
Pembroke State University; Pembroke, N.C. 28372	2,712 (C)	Pub	800	4,642	1,920
Pennsylvania, University of; Philadelphia, Pa. 19104	9,949 (C)	P	15,894	15,894	6,030
Pennsylvania State Erie –The Behrend College; Erie, Pa. 16563	2,648 (C)	Pub	4,048	8,444	3,510
Pennsylvania State Harrisburg–The Capital College; Middletown, Pa. 17057	1,959 (C)	Pub	3,754	7,900	3,610
Pennsylvania State University Park; University Park, Pa. 16802	31,621 (C)	Pub	3,754	7,900	3,570
Pepperdine University School of Business and Management; Culver City, Calif. 90230	520 (C)	P	13,500	13,500	n.a.
Pepperdine University-Seaver College; Malibu, Calif. 90265	2,562 (C)	P	15,230	15,230	6,070
Peru State College; Peru, Neb. 68421	1,724 (C)	Pub	1,489	2,305	2,450
Pfeiffer College; Misenheimer, N.C. 28109	830 (C)	P	7,295	7,295	3,050
Pharmacy, School of (Ga.). *See* Mercer Univ.					
Philadelphia College of Bible; Langhorne, Pa. 19047	647 (C)	P	6,245	6,245	3,580
Philadelphia College of Pharmacy and Science; Philadelphia, Pa. 19104	1,543 (C)	P	9,250	9,250	4,266
Philadelphia College of Textiles and Science; Philadelphia, Pa. 19144	1,711 (C)	P	9,735	9,735	4,500
Philander Smith College; Little Rock, Ark. 72202	572 (C)	P	2,350	2,350	2,300
Phillips University; Enid, Okla. 73702	828 (C)	P	8,530	8,530	2,770
Phoenix, University of; Phoenix, Ariz. 85040	3,023 (C)	P	5,588	5,588	n.a.
Piedmont Bible College; Winston-Salem, N.C. 27101	298 (C)	P	3,190	3,190	2,500
Piedmont College; Demorest, Ga. 30535	495 (C)	P	3,600	3,600	3,050
Pikeville College; Pikeville, Ky. 41501	753 (C)	P	4,200	4,200	2,400
Pillsbury Baptist Bible College; Owatonna, Minn. 55060	367 (C)	P	3,672	3,672	2,700
Pine Manor College; Chestnut Hill, Mass. 02167	525 (W)	P	13,700	13,700	5,700
Pittsburgh, University of; Pittsburgh, Pa. 15260	18,475 (C)	Pub	4,314	8,886	3,514
Pittsburgh, University of-Bradford; Bradford, Pa. 16701-2898	1,204 (C)	Pub	4,298	8,870	3,460
Pittsburgh, University of-Greensburg; Greensburg, Pa. 15601	1,504 (C)	Pub	4,278	8,850	3,120
Pittsburgh, University of-Johnstown; Johnstown, Pa. 15904	3,210 (C)	Pub	4,262	8,834	3,186
Pittsburg State University; Pittsburg, Kan. 66762	4,476 (C)	Pub	1,450	3,964	2,600
Pitzer College. *See* Claremont Colleges.					
Plymouth State College; Plymouth, N.H. 03264	4,000 (C)	Pub	2,574	5,934	3,442
Point Loma Nazarene College; San Diego, Calif. 92106	1,837 (C)	P	8,058	8,058	3,624
Point Park College; Pittsburgh, Pa. 15222	2,881 (C)	P	7,980	7,980	3,940
Polytechnic University; Brooklyn, N.Y. 11201	1,655 (C)	P	12,800	12,800	4,500
Pomona College. *See* Claremont Colleges.					
Pontifical College Josephinum; Columbus, Ohio 43235-1498	58 (M)	P	4,500	4,500	3,000
Portland, University of; Portland, Ore. 97203	2,084 (C)	P	9,250	9,250	3,580
Portland School of Art; Portland, Me. 04101	305 (C)	P	8,300	8,300	5,085
Portland State University; Portland, Ore. 97207	11,504 (C)	Pub	1,917	5,676	3,434
Post College; Waterbury, Conn. 06708	2,082 (C)	P	10,075	10,075	4,180
Potsdam Coll. of Arts & Science. *See* New York, State Univ. of					
Prairie View A&M University; Prairie View, Tex. 77446	5,240 (C)	Pub	931	4,051	2,938
Pratt Institute; Brooklyn, N.Y. 11205	2,687 (C)	P	11,184	11,184	6,130
Presbyterian College; Clinton, S.C. 29325	1,126 (C)	P	10,326	10,326	3,184
Prescott College; Prescott, Ariz. 86301	320 (C)	P	7,200	7,200	n.a.
Presentation College; Anerdeen, S.D. 57401	464 (C)	P	5,146	5,146	2,535
Princeton University; Princeton, N.J. 08544	4,524 (C)	P	16,570	16,570	5,311
Principia College; Elsah, Ill. 62028	622 (C)	P	11,310	11,310	4,590
Providence College; Providence, R.I. 02918	3,805 (C)	P	12,290	12,290	5,300
Puerto Rico, University of-Cayey University College; Cayey, P.R. 00633	3,332 (C)	Pub	662	2,000	n.a.
Puerto Rico, University of-Humacao University College; Humacao, P.R. 00661	3,982 (C)	Pub	707	2,257	n.a.
Puerto Rico, University of-Mayaguez Campus; Mayaguez, P.R. 00708	9,123 (C)	Pub	838	2,838	2,950
Puerto Rico, University of-Medical Science; San Juan, P.R. 00936	1,037 (C)	Pub	([2])	([3])	n.a.

Institution and location	Enrollment	Control	Tuition ($) Res.	Tuition ($) Nonres.	Rm/Bd ($)
Puget Sound, University of; Tacoma, Wash. 98416	3,214 (C)	P	12,690	12,690	3,980
Puget Sound Christian College; Edmonds, Wash. 98020	70 (C)	P	4,485	4,485	3,000
Purdue University; West Lafayette, Ind. 47907	29,537 (C)	Pub	2,152	6,764	3,320
Purdue University-Calumet; Hammond, Ind. 46323	7,710 (C)	Pub	1,789	4,504	n.a.
Purdue University-North Central; Westville, Ind. 46391	3,013 (C)	Pub	1,789	4,504	n.a.
Queens College; Charlotte, N.C. 28274	1,369 (C)	P	9,300	9,300	4,400
Queens College (NYC). *See* New York, City University of					
Quincy College; Quincy, Ill. 62301	1,559 (C)	P	8,604	8,604	3,440
Quinnipiac College; Hamden, Conn. 06518	2,950 (C)	P	10,350	10,350	4,990
Rabbinical College of America; Morristown, N.J. 07960	230 (M)	P	4,100	4,100	3,400
Rabbinical Seminary of America; Forest Hills, N.Y. 11375	200 (M)	P	3,000	3,000	3,000
Radcliffe College. *See* Harvard and Radcliffe Colleges					
Radford University; Radford, Va. 24142	9,175 (C)	Pub	2,436	5,584	3,718
Ramapo College of New Jersey, Mahwah, N.J. 07403	4,525 (C)	Pub	3,644	3,644	4,782
Randolph-Macon College; Ashland, Va. 23005	1,141 (C)	P	10,810	10,810	4,600
Randolph-Macon Woman's College; Lynchburg, Va. 24503	750 (W)	P	11,680	11,680	5,140
Redlands, University of; Redlands, Calif. 92373-0999	1,220 (C)	P	12,960	12,960	5,070
Reed College; Portland, Ore. 97202	1,261 (C)	P	16,700	16,700	4,640
Reformed Bible College; Grand Rapids, Mich. 49506	193 (C)	P	5,166	5,166	3,000
Regis College; Denver, Colo. 80221	1,041 (C)	P	10,340	10,340	6,100
Regis College; Weston, Mass. 02193	1,145 (W)	P	10,650	10,650	5,200
Rensselaer Polytechnic Institute; Troy, N.Y. 12180	4,436 (C)	P	15,625	15,625	5,150
Research College of Nursing; Kansas City, Mo. 64132	133 (C)	P	6,850	6,850	3,200
Rhode Island, University of; Kingston, R.I. 02881	12,646 (C)	Pub	2,437	6,819	4,230
Rhode Island, University of, College of Continuing Education; Providence, R.I. 02908-5090	4,400 (C)	Pub	(4)	(5)	n.a.
Rhode Island College; Providence, R.I. 02908	5,433 (C)	Pub	2,000	5,119	5,200
Rhode Island School of Design; Providence, R.I. 02903	1,809 (C)	P	14,121	14,121	5,892
Rhodes College Memphis; Memphis, Tenn. 38112	1,407 (C)	P	12,958	12,958	4,516
Rice University; Houston, Tex. 77251	2,741 (C)	P	8,125	8,125	4,900
Richmond, University of; Richmond, Va. 23173	2,749 (C)	P	11,695	11,695	2,865
Richmond College; Surrey, TW10 6JP England	1,044 (C)	P	9,550	9,550	4,745
Rider College; Lawrenceville, N.J. 08648	3,080 (C)	P	10,900	10,900	4,650
Ringling School of Art and Design; Sarasota, Fla. 34234	578 (C)	P	8,900	8,900	4,700
Ripon College; Ripon, Wis. 54971	854 (C)	P	12,740	12,740	3,150
Rivier College; Nashua, N.H. 03060	778 (C)	P	9,050	9,050	4,310
Roanoke Bible College; Elizabeth City, N.C. 27909	114 (C)	P	5,280	5,280	2,400
Roanoke College; Salem, Va. 24153	1,668 (C)	P	11,250	11,250	4,000
Robert Morris College; Coraopolis, Pa. 15108	4,945 (C)	P	5,100	5,100	3,800
Roberts Wesleyan College; Rochester, N.Y. 14624	969 (C)	P	8,508	8,508	2,976
Rio Grande, University of; Rio Grande, Ohio 45674	2,000 (C)	P	2,865	4,620	3,000
Rochester, University of; Rochester, N.Y. 14627	4,823 (C)	P	15,651	15,651	5,750
Rochester Institute of Technology; Rochester, N.Y. 14623	10,789 (C)	P	11,952	11,952	5,100
Rockford College; Rockford, Ill. 61108	1,168 (C)	P	9,400	9,400	3,400
Rockhurst College; Kansas City, Mo. 64110	3,085 (C)	P	8,560	8,560	3,750
Rocky Mountain College; Billings, Mont. 59102	769 (C)	P	7,197	7,197	3,328
Roger Williams College; Bristol, R.I. 02809	2,111 (C)	P	10,560	10,560	5,120
Rollins College; Winter Park, Fla. 32789	1,500 (C)	P	12,800	13,900	4,295
Roosevelt University; Chicago, Ill. 60605	4,293 (C)	P	7,470	7,470	4,500
Rosary College; River Forest, Ill. 60305-1099	1,042 (C)	P	9,276	9,276	4,176
Rose-Hulman Institute of Technology; Terre Haute, Ind. 47803	1,300 (M)	P	10,785	10,785	3,600
Rosemont College; Rosemont, Pa. 19010	627 (W)	P	9,445	9,445	5,400
Rush University Colleges of Nursing and Health Sciences; Chicago, Ill. 60612	175 (C)	P	9,800	9,800	5,920
Russell Sage College; Troy, N.Y. 12180	1,000 (W)	P	10,470	10,470	4,240
Rust College; Holly Springs, Miss. 38635	936 (C)	P	4,152	4,152	1,948
Rutgers, The State University of New Jersey–Camden College of Arts and Sciences; Camden, N.J. 08102	2,695 (C)	Pub	3,279	6,237	3,826
Rutgers, The State University of New Jersey–College of Engineering; New Brunswick, N.J. 08903	2,537 (C)	Pub	3,740	7,026	3,826
Rutgers, The State University of New Jersey–College of Nursing-Newark; Newark, N.J. 07102	401 (C)	Pub	3,274	6,232	3,826
Rutgers, The State University of New Jersey–College of Pharmacy; New Brunswick, N.J. 08903	783 (C)	Pub	3,595	6,881	3,826
Rutgers, The State Universit of New Jersey–Cook College; New Brunswick, N.J. 08903	2,874 (C)	Pub	3,766	7,052	3,826
Rutgers, The State University of New Jersey–Douglass College; New Brunswick, N.J. 08903	3,227 (W)	Pub	3,424	6,382	3,826
Rutgers, The State University of New Jersey–Livingston College; New Brunswick, N.J. 08903	3,776 (C)	Pub	3,444	6,402	3,826
Rutgers, The State University of New Jersey–Mason Gross School of the Arts; New Brunswick, N.J. 08903	428 (C)	Pub	3,281	6,239	3,826

Institution and location	Enrollment	Control	Tuition ($) Res.	Tuition ($) Nonres.	Rm/Bd ($)
Rutgers, The State University of New Jersey–Newark College of Arts and Sciences; Newark, N.J. 07102	3,396 (C)	Pub	3,281	6,239	3,826
Rutgers, The State University of New Jersey–Rutgers College; New Brunswick, N.J. 08903	8,377 (C)	Pub	3,432	6,390	3,826
Rutgers, The State University of New Jersey–University College–Camden; Camden, N.J. 08102	872 (C)	Pub	(^{6})	(^{7})	n.a.
Rutgers, The State University of New Jersey–University College–New Brunswick; New Brunswick, N.J. 08903	3,087 (C)	Pub	(^{6})	(^{7})	n.a.
Rutgers, The State University of New Jersey–University College–Newark; Newark, N.J. 07102	1,758 (C)	Pub	(^{6})	(^{7})	n.a.
Sacred Heart, Univ. of the; Santurce, P.R. 00924	7,044 (C)	P	3,130	3,130	3,340
Sacred Heart Seminary; Detroit, Mich. 48206	194 (C)	P	2,900	2,900	2,400
Sacred Heart University; Fairfield, Conn. 06432	3,218 (C)	P	8,970	8,970	5,010
Saginaw Valley State University; University Center, Mich. 48710	5,263 (C)	Pub	2,344	4,672	3,200
Saint Ambrose University; Davenport, Iowa 52803	1,700 (C)	P	8,530	8,530	3,420
Saint Andrews Presbyterian College; Laurinburg, N.C. 28352	794 (C)	P	8,875	8,875	3,920
Saint Anselm College; Manchester, N.H. 03102	1,890 (C)	P	10,160	10,160	5,000
Saint Augustine's College; Raleigh, N.C. 27611	1,716 (C)	P	5,000	5,000	3,200
St. Benedict, College of; St. Joseph, Minn. 56374-2099	1,916 (W)	P	10,135	10,135	3,750
St. Bonaventure University; St. Bonaventure, N.Y. 14778	2,396 (C)	P	9,067	9,067	4,510
St. Catherine, College of; St. Paul, Minn. 55105	2,463 (W)	P	10,140	10,140	3,674
St. Cloud State University; St. Cloud, Minn. 56301	14,454 (C)	Pub	1,977	2,990	2,300
St. Edward's University; Austin, Tex. 78704	2,524 (C)	P	7,764	7,764	3,644
St. Elizabeth, College of; Convent Station, N.J. 07961	1,068 (W)	P	9,600	9,600	4,400
St. Francis, College of; Joliet, Ill. 60435	1,080 (C)	P	7,980	7,980	3,580
St. Francis College; Brooklyn Heights, N.Y. 11201	1,743 (C)	P	5,250	5,250	n.a.
St. Francis College; Fort Wayne, Ind. 46808	751 (C)	P	7,158	7,158	3,450
St. Francis College; Loretto, Pa. 15940	1,001 (C)	P	9,596	9,596	4,490
St. Hyacinth College and Seminary; Granby, Mass. 01033	25 (M)	P	3,600	3,600	4,000
St. John Fisher College; Rochester, N.Y. 14618	1,668 (C)	P	9,320	9,320	5,094
St. John's College; Annapolis, Md. 21404	444 (C)	P	14,262	14,262	4,696
St. John's College; Santa Fe, N.M. 87501	409 (C)	P	13,040	13,040	4,410
St. John's Seminary College; Camarillo, Calif. 93012	86 (M)	P	4,012	4,012	—
St. John's Seminary College of Liberal Arts; Brighton, Mass. 02135	70 (M)	P	3,600	3,600	2,600
St. John's University; Collegeville, Minn. 56321	1,971 (M)	P	10,135	10,135	3,680
St. John's University–Queens–Staten Island; Jamaica, N.Y. 11439	14,154 (C)	P	7,530	7,530	n.a.
St. John Vianney College Seminary; Miami, Fla. 33165	47 (M)	P	5,600	5,600	3,000
St. Joseph College; West Hartford, Conn. 06117	1,215 (W)	P	10,400	10,400	4,264
St. Joseph in Vermont, College of; Rutland, Vt. 05701	377 (C)	P	6,085	6,085	3,550
St. Joseph's College; Brooklyn, N.Y. 11205	827 (C)	P	6,156	6,156	n.a.
St. Joseph's College-Suffolk; Patchogue, N.Y. 11772	1,936 (C)	P	6,356	6,356	n.a.
Saint Joseph's College; Rensselaer, Ind. 47978	1,032 (C)	P	9,410	9,410	3,570
Saint Joseph's College; Windham, Me. 04062-1198	660 (C)	P	8,500	8,500	4,300
St. Joseph Seminary College; St. Benedict, La. 70457	55 (M)	P	5,400	5,400	3,500
Saint Joseph's University; Philadelphia, Pa. 19131	3,884 (C)	P	10,150	10,150	4,962
St. Lawrence University; Canton, N.Y. 13617	1,967 (C)	P	15,951	15,951	5,050
Saint Leo College; Saint Leo, Fla. 33574	6,000 (C)	P	7,230	7,230	3,480
St. Louis Christian College; Florissant, Mo. 63033	142 (C)	P	3,343	3,343	2,360
St. Louis College of Pharmacy; St. Louis, Mo. 63110	701 (C)	P	5,935	5,935	3,750
St. Louis Conservatory of Music; St. Louis, Mo. 63130	70 (C)	P	7,750	7,750	n.a.
St. Louis University; St. Louis, Mo. 63103	7,729 (C)	P	9,160	9,160	4,242
St. Martin's College; Lacey, Wash. 98503	577 (C)	P	9,605	9,605	3,720
St. Mary, College of; Omaha, Neb. 68124	1,133 (W)	P	3,880	3,880	3,160
Saint Mary College; Leavenworth, Kan. 66048	566 (C)	P	6,450	6,450	3,250
St. Mary of the Plains College; Dodge City, Kan. 67801	911 (C)	P	5,800	5,800	3,100
St. Mary-of-the-Woods Coll.; St. Mary-of-the-Woods, Ind. 47876	858 (W)	P	9,110	9,110	3,775
St. Mary's College; Notre Dame, Ind. 46556	1,798 (W)	P	9,390	9,390	4,096
St. Mary's College; Orchard Lake, Mich. 48033	307 (C)	P	3,850	3,850	2,800
St. Mary's College; Winona, Minn. 55987	1,275 (C)	P	9,225	9,225	3,150
St. Mary's College of California; Moraga, Calif. 94575	2,583 (C)	P	10,294	10,294	5,058
St. Mary's College of Maryland; St. Mary's City, Md. 20686	1,568 (C)	Pub	2,860	4,660	4,100
St. Mary's University of San Antonio; San Antonio, Tex. 78284	2,404 (C)	P	7,300	7,300	3,346
Saint Meinrad College; St. Meinrad, Ind. 47577	96 (M)	P	5,413	5,413	4,064
Saint Michael's College; Colchester, Vt. 05439	1,710 (C)	P	11,265	11,265	5,090
St. Norbert College; De Pere, Wis. 54115	1,936 (C)	P	10,225	10,225	3,900
St. Olaf College; Northfield, Minn. 55057	3,097 (C)	P	12,080	12,080	3,345
St. Paul Bible College; Bible College, Minn. 55375	526 (C)	P	6,240	6,240	3,318
Saint Paul's College; Lawrenceville, Va. 23868	736 (C)	P	4,806	4,806	3,180
Saint Peter's College; Jersey City, N.J. 07306	3,152 (C)	P	7,590	7,590	3,100
Saint Rose, The College of; Albany, N.Y. 12203	2,361 (C)	P	8,530	8,530	5,010
St. Scholastica, College of; Duluth, Minn. 55811	1,741 (C)	P	9,921	9,921	3,255
St. Thomas, College of; St. Paul, Minn. 55105	5,129 (C)	P	10,625	10,625	3,543
St. Thomas, University of; Houston, Tex. 77006	1,105 (C)	P	6,090	6,090	3,240

Institution and location	Enrollment	Control	Tuition ($) Res.	Nonres.	Rm/Bd ($)
St. Thomas Aquinas College; Sparkill, N.Y. 10968	1,875 (C)	P	6,750	6,750	4,200
Saint Thomas University; Miami, Fla. 33054	1,383 (C)	P	8,125	8,125	4,100
Saint Vincent College; Latrobe, Pa. 15650	1,238 (C)	P	9,080	9,080	3,520
St. Xavier College; Chicago, Ill. 60655	2,177 (C)	P	8,820	8,820	3,692
Salem College; Winston-Salem, N.C. 27108	694 (W)	P	8,950	8,950	5,600
Salem State College; Salem, Mass. 01970	5,388 (C)	Pub	1,250	3,930	2,841
Salem-Teikyo University; Salem, W.Va. 26426	400 (C)	P	6,380	6,380	4,320
Salisbury State University, Salisbury, Md. 21801	5,183 (C)	Pub	2,444	4,498	4,090
Salve Regina University; Newport, R.I. 02840-4192	1,830 (C)	P	11,700	11,700	5,500
Samford University; Birmingham, Ala. 35229	3,203 (C)	P	6,540	6,540	3,576
Sam Houston State University; Huntsville, Tex. 77341	12,750 (C)	Pub	1,060	4,360	2,490
San Diego, University of; San Diego, Calif. 92110	3,886 (C)	P	11,360	11,360	5,000
San Diego State University; San Diego, Calif. 92182	28,712 (C)	Pub	894	5,430	3,968
Imperial Valley Campus; Calexico, Calif. 92231	253 (C)	Pub	838	5,500	n.a.
San Francisco, University of; San Francisco, Calif. 94117	3,326 (C)	P	10,960	10,960	5,214
San Francisco Art Institute; San Francisco, Calif. 94133	514 (C)	P	11,350	11,350	n.a.
San Francisco Conservatory of Music; San Francisco, Calif. 94122	155 (C)	P	8.550	8,550	n.a.
San Francisco State Univ.; San Francisco, Calif. 94132	22,251 (C)	Pub	864	5,670	3,904
Sangamon State University; Springfield, Ill. 62708	2,342 (C)	Pub	1,644	5,218	2,554
San Jose Christian College; San Jose, Calif. 95108	235 (C)	P	5,361	5,361	3,240
San Jose State University; San Jose, Calif. 95192-0009	24,001 (C)	Pub	1,056	7,356	4,550
Santa Clara University; Santa Clara, Calif. 95053	3,830 (C)	P	11,271	11,271	5,292
Santa Fe, College of; Santa Fe, N.M. 87501	1,652 (C)	P	7,506	7,506	2,580
Sarah Lawrence College; Bronxville, N.Y. 10708	902 (C)	P	15,530	15,530	5,960
Savannah College of Art and Design; Savannah, Ga. 31401	1,835 (C)	P	7,575	7,575	4,800
Savannah State College; Savannah, Ga. 31404	1,754 (C)	Pub	1,635	4,215	2,145
Schiller International University; 6900 Heidelberg, Germany	1,345 (C)	P	9,740	9,740	4,400
Schreiner College; Kerrville, Tex. 78028	658 (C)	P	6,975	6,975	4,800
Science and Arts, University of, of Oklahoma; Chickasha, Okla. 73018	1,551 (C)	Pub	1,317	3,616	1,820
Scranton, University of; Scranton, Pa. 18510	3,849 (C)	P	9,700	9,700	4,500
Scripps College. *See* Claremont Colleges					
Seattle Pacific University; Seattle, Wash. 98119	2,268 (C)	P	10,630	10,630	3,969
Seattle University; Seattle, Wash. 98122	3,406 (C)	P	10,770	10,770	4,251
Seaver College. *See* Pepperdine University					
Selma University; Selma, Ala. 36701	217 (C)	P	2,380	2,380	1,740
Seton Hall University; South Orange, N.J. 07079	5,380 (C)	P	11,110	11,110	5,517
Seton Hill College; Greensburg, Pa. 15601	1,037 (W)	P	9,030	9,030	3,760
Shawnee State University; Portsmouth, Ohio 45662	2,900 (C)	Pub	1,893	2,697	3,400
Shaw University; Raleigh, N.C. 27611	1,500 (C)	P	4,894	4,894	3,282
Sheldon Jackson College; Sitka, Alaska 99835	300 (C)	P	5,960	5,960	4,215
Shenandoah College and Conservatory; Winchester, Va. 22601-9986	818 (C)	P	7,900	7,900	4,100
Shepherd College; Shepherdstown, W. Va. 25443	3,700 (C)	Pub	1,894	4,314	3,690
Shimer College; Waukegan, Ill. 60085	100 (C)	P	8,800	8,800	3,150
Shippensburg University of Pennsylvania; Shippensburg, Pa. 17257	5,324 (C)	Pub	2,396	3,818	2,282
Shorter College; Rome, Ga. 30161	858 (C)	P	5,810	5,810	3,450
Siena College; Loudonville, N.Y. 12211	3,551 (C)	P	8,850	8,850	4,465
Siena Heights College; Adrian, Mich. 49221	1,493 (C)	P	7,170	7,170	3,550
Sierra Nevada College; Incline Village, Nev. 89450	300 (C)	P	6,750	6,750	4,400
Silver Lake College; Manitowoc, Wis. 54220	748 (C)	P	7,480	7,480	n.a.
Simmons Bible College; Louisville, Ky. 40210	103 (C)	P	520	520	n.a.
Simmons College; Boston, Mass. 02115	1,417 (W)	P	13,632	13,632	6,000
Simon's Rock of Bard College; Great Barrington, Mass. 01230	298 (C)	P	14,450	14,450	4,810
Simpson College; Indianola, Iowa 50125	1,735 (C)	P	9,585	9,585	3,375
Simpson College; Redding, Calif. 96003	356 (C)	P	6,388	6,388	3,480
Sinte Gleska College; Rosebud, S.D. 57570	485 (C)	P	1,927	1,927	n.a.
Sioux Falls College; Sioux Falls, S.D. 57105	937 (C)	P	7,496	7,496	2,927
Skidmore College; Saratoga Springs, N.Y. 12866	2,174 (C)	P	16,000	16,000	5,090
Slippery Rock State College. *See* Slippery Rock University of Pennsylvania					
Slippery Rock Univ. of Pennsylvania; Slippery Rock, Pa. 16057	7,084 (C)	Pub	2,668	4,702	2,794
Smith College; Northampton, Mass. 01063	2,662 (W)	P	15,770	15,770	6,100
Sojourner-Douglass College; Baltimore, Md. 21205	298 (C)	P	4,515	4,515	n.a.
Sonoma State University; Rohnert Park, Calif. 94928	4,983 (C)	Pub	882	5,418	4,820
South, University of the; Sewanee, Tenn. 37375	1,096 (C)	P	13,505	13,505	3,510
South Alabama, University of; Mobile, Ala. 36688	9,658 (C)	Pub	1,905	2,505	2,565
Southampton College. *See* Long Island Univ. Center					
South Carolina, University of; Columbia, S.C. 29208	16,017 (C)	Pub	3,328	7,168	2,700
South Carolina, Univ. of-Aiken; Aiken, S.C. 29801	2,967 (C)	Pub	1,800	4,500	2,470
South Carolina, Univ. of-Coastal Carolina; Conway, S.C. 29526	4,080 (C)	Pub	1,920	4,800	4,000
South Carolina, Univ. of-Spartanburg; Spartanburg, S.C. 29303	3,501 (C)	Pub	1,920	4,800	2,540
South Carolina State College; Orangeburg, S.C. 29117	3,531 (C)	Pub	3,470	5,500	1,216
South Dakota, University of; Vermillion, S.D. 57069	5,501 (C)	Pub	2,089	3,802	2,270

Institution and location	Enrollment	Control	Tuition ($) Res.	Tuition ($) Nonres.	Rm/Bd ($)
South Dakota School of Mines and Technology; Rapid City, S.D. 57701	2,015 (C)	Pub	3,555	4,676	2,300
South Dakota State University; Brookings, S.D. 57007	6,816 (C)	Pub	1,936	3,539	1,722
Southeast Missouri State Univ.; Cape Girardeau, Mo. 63701	7,810 (C)	Pub	1,836	3,276	2,825
Southeastern Baptist College; Laurel, Miss. 39440	70 (C)	P	2,200	2,200	1,700
Southeastern Bible College; Birmingham, Ala. 35243	138 (C)	P	3,400	3,400	2,400
Southeastern College; Lakeland, Fla. 33801	1,192 (C)	P	3,168	3,168	2,948
Southeastern Louisiana University; Hammond, La. 70402	9,500 (C)	Pub	1,703	3,503	2,280
Southeastern Massachusetts University; North Dartmouth, Mass. 02747	5,354 (C)	Pub	1,600	5,485	3,822
Southeastern Oklahoma State Univ.; Durant, Okla. 74701	3,546 (C)	Pub	1,200	3,000	2,330
Southeastern University; Washington, D.C. 20024	559 (C)	P	5,190	5,190	n.a.
Southern Arkansas University; Magnolia, Ark. 71753	2,388 (C)	Pub	1,155	1,848	2,310
Southern California, Univ. of; Los Angeles, Calif. 90089	16,113 (C)	P	14,375	14,375	5,650
Southern California College; Costa Mesa, Calif. 92626	828 (C)	P	6,720	6,720	3,300
Southern California Institute of Architecture; Santa Monica, Calif. 90404	310 (C)	P	7,960	7,960	n.a.
Southern College of Seventh-Day Adventists; Collegedale, Tenn. 37315	1,534 (C)	P	7,100	7,100	3,040
Southern College of Technology; Marietta, Ga. 30060	3,829 (C)	Pub	1,431	3,909	3,215
Southern Colorado, University of; Pueblo, Colo. 81001	4,246 (C)	Pub	1,720	5,525	3,370
Southern Connecticut State Univ.; New Haven, Conn. 06515	6,723 (C)	Pub	2,199	5,929	3,986
Southern Illinois Univ.-Carbondale; Carbondale, Ill. 62901	19,888 (C)	Pub	2,332	5,452	3,764
Southern Illinois Univ.-Edwardsville; Edwardsville, Ill. 62026	8,841 (C)	Pub	1,821	4,743	3,619
Southern Indiana, University of; Evansville, Ind. 47714	6,480 (C)	Pub	1,800	7,212	2,860
Southern Maine, University of; Gorham, Me. 04038	8,819 (C)	Pub	2,214	5,994	3,844
Southern Methodist University; Dallas, Tex. 75275	5,749 (C)	P	11,768	11,768	4,832
Southern Missionary College. *See* Southern College of Seventh-Day Adventists					
Southern Mississippi, Univ. of; Hattiesburg, Miss. 39406	10,118 (C)	Pub	3,087	5,460	3,420
Southern Nazarene Univ.; Bethany, Okla. 73008	1,254 (C)	P	5,588	5,588	3,256
Southern Oregon State College; Ashland, Ore. 97520	4,453 (C)	Pub	2,400	5,600	3,300
Southern University-Baton Rouge; Baton Rouge, La. 70813	9,448 (C)	Pub	1,576	5,482	2,350
Southern University-New Orleans; New Orleans, La. 70126	3,200 (C)	Pub	1,452	3,010	n.a.
Southern Utah State College; Cedar City, Utah 84720	3,600 (C)	Pub	1,345	3,596	2,070
Southern Vermont College; Bennington, Vt. 05201	676 (C)	P	7,230	7,230	3,828
South Florida, University of; Tampa, Fla. 33620	21,565 (C)	Pub	1,410	4,750	3,100
Southwest, College of the; Hobbs, N.M. 88240	277 (C)	P	2,700	2,700	2,755
Southwest Baptist University; Bolivar, Mo. 65613	2,920 (C)	P	6,204	6,204	2,340
Southwestern Adventist College; Keene, Tex. 76059	785 (C)	P	6,552	6,552	3,242
Southwestern Assemblies of God College; Waxahachie, Tex. 75165	686 (C)	P	3,540	3,540	2,762
Southwestern College; Winfield, Kan. 67156	653 (C)	P	5,050	5,050	2,810
Southwestern Conservative Baptist Bible College; Phoenix, Ariz. 85032	146 (C)	P	5,160	5,160	2,090
Southwestern Louisiana, University of; Lafayette, La. 70504	14,103 (C)	Pub	1,490	3,140	1,945
Southwestern Oklahoma State Univ.; Weatherford, Okla. 73096	5,401 (C)	Pub	1,172	2,928	1,770
Southwestern University; Georgetown, Tex. 78626	1,219 (C)	P	9,400	9,400	4,081
Southwest Missouri State Univ.; Springfield, Mo. 65804	17,037 (C)	Pub	1,718	1,718	3,024
Southwest State University; Marshall, Minn. 56258	3,035 (C)	Pub	1,800	3,000	2,400
Southwest Texas State Univ.; San Marcos, Tex. 78666	20,511 (C)	Pub	1,042	4,178	2,968
Spalding University; Louisville, Ky. 40203	735 (C)	P	6,696	6,696	2,760
Spelman College; Atlanta, Ga. 30314	1,757 (W)	P	6,707	6,707	4,770
Spring Arbor College; Spring Arbor, Mich. 49283	847 (C)	P	7,556	7,556	3,100
Spring Garden College; Philadelphia, Pa. 19119	1,465 (C)	P	8,800	8,800	3,850
Spring Hill College; Mobile, Ala. 36608	1,160 (C)	P	10,114	10,114	4,060
Stanford University; Stanford, Calif. 94305	6,505 (C)	P	14,280	14,280	5,930
Staten Island, Coll. of (NYC). *See* New York, City Univ. of					
Stephen F. Austin State Univ. Nacogdoches, Tex. 75962	11,471 (C)	Pub	900	3,262	2,950
Stephens College; Columbia, Mo. 65215	1,191 (W)	P	11,475	11,475	4,500
Sterling College; Sterling, Kan. 67579	468 (C)	P	6,785	6,785	3,000
Stetson University; Deland, Fla. 32720	2,113 (C)	P	10,020	10,020	4,070
Stevens Institute of Technology; Hoboken, N.J. 07030	1,600 (C)	P	16,285	16,285	4,595
Stillman College; Tuscaloosa, Ala. 35403	770 (C)	P	4,260	4,260	2,640
Stockton State College; Pomona, N.J. 08240	5,639 (C)	Pub	2,456	3,096	4,332
Stonehill College; North Easton, Mass. 02357	1,964 (C)	P	10,290	10,290	5,366
Strayer College; Washington, D.C. 20036	2,288 (C)	P	4,950	4,950	n.a.
Suffolk University; Boston, Mass. 02108	2,845 (C)	P	8,535	8,535	n.a.
Sul Ross State University; Alpine, Texas 79832	1,580 (C)	Pub	985	4,252	2,730
Sul Ross State University–Uvalde Study Center; Uvalde, Texas 78801	347 (C)	Pub	708	3,204	n.a.
Summit Christian College; Fort Wayne, Ind. 46807	376 (C)	P	6,625	6,625	2,860
Susquehanna University; Selinsgrove, Pa. 17870	1,465 (C)	P	13,950	13,950	4,030
Swarthmore College; Swarthmore, Pa. 19081	1,302 (C)	P	16,640	16,640	5,520
Sweet Briar College; Sweet Briar, Va. 24595	539 (W)	P	12,500	12,500	4,850
Syracuse University; Syracuse, N.Y. 13210	12,577 (C)	P	12,958	12,958	5,570
Tabor College; Hillsboro, Kan. 67063	436 (C)	P	6,160	6,160	2,760
Talladega College; Talladega, Ala. 35160	615 (C)	P	4,449	4,449	2,364

Institution and location	Enrollment	Control	Tuition ($) Res.	Tuition ($) Nonres.	Rm/Bd ($)
Tampa, University of; Tampa, Fla. 33606	2,026 (C)	P	10,100	10,100	3,720
Tampa College; Tampa, Fla. 33614	1,350 (C)	P	4,725	4,725	n.a.
Tarleton State University; Stephensville, Tex. 76402	5,585 (C)	Pub	1,132	3,120	2,592
Taylor University; Upland, Ind. 46989	1,740 (C)	P	9,353	9,353	3,542
Teikyo Westmar University; Le Mars, Iowa 51031	658 (C)	P	8,397	8,397	3,339
Teikyo Marycrest University; Davenport, Iowa 52804	1,309 (C)	P	8,440	8,440	3,100
Temple University, Philadelphia, Pa. 19122	22,336 (C)	Pub	4,294	7,892	4,398
Temple University-Ambler; Ambler, Pa. 19002	4,242 (C)	Pub	3,996	7,258	4,056
Tennessee, Univ. of-Chattanooga; Chattanooga, Tenn. 37402	6,698 (C)	Pub	1,493	4,696	4,748
Tennessee, Univ. of-Knoxville; Knoxville, Tenn. 37996	19,532 (C)	Pub	1,712	4,916	2,964
Tennessee, Univ. of-Martin; Martin, Tenn. 38238	5,056 (C)	Pub	1,546	4,750	2,440
Tennessee, Univ. of-Memphis, The Health Science Center; Memphis, Tenn. 38163	315 (C)	Pub	1,644	4,650	2,892
Tennessee State University; Nashville, Tenn. 37203	7,012 (C)	Pub	1,400	4,604	2,290
Tennessee Technological Univ.; Cookeville, Tenn. 38505	6,954 (C)	Pub	1,462	4,666	1,300
Tennessee Temple University; Chattanooga, Tenn. 37404	1,400 (C)	P	3,700	3,700	3,180
Tennessee Wesleyan College; Athens, Tenn. 37303	605 (C)	P	5,569	5,569	3,144
Texas, University of-Arlington; Arlington, Tex. 76019	20,735 (C)	Pub	1,700	6,692	3,852
Texas, University of-Austin; Austin, Tex. 78712	37,152 (C)	Pub	1,100	4,220	3,400
Texas, University of-Dallas; Richardson, Tex. 75083-0688	4,493 (C)	Pub	950	4,070	n.a.
Texas, University of-El Paso; El Paso, Tex. 79968	14,047 (C)	Pub	990	4,230	3,300
Texas, University of-Health Science Center-San Antonio; San Antonio, Tex. 78284	810 (C)	Pub	733	3,973	n.a.
Texas, University of, Medical Branch-Galveston; Galveston, Tex. 77550	655 (C)	Pub	864	5,760	5,400
Texas, University of-Permian Basin; Odessa, Tex. 79762	1,258 (C)	Pub	960	4,080	3,175
Texas, University of-San Antonio; San Antonio, Tex. 78285	12,459 (C)	Pub	930	4,050	3,345
Texas, University of, Southwestern Medical Center at Dallas; Dallas, Tex. 75235	356 (C)	Pub	990	5,400	n.a.
Texas, University of-Tyler; Tyler, Tex. 75701	2,579 (C)	Pub	900	4,020	n.a.
Texas A&I University-Kingsville; Kingsville, Tex. 78363	4,911 (C)	Pub	910	4,030	2,624
Texas A&M University; College Station, Tex. 77843	32,204 (C)	Pub	1,200	4,362	3,884
Texas A&M University-Galveston; Galveston, Tex. 77553	1,075 (C)	Pub	970	4,395	3,119
Texas Christian University; Fort Worth, Tex. 76129	5,415 (C)	P	8,166	8,166	2,735
Texas College; Tyler, Tex. 75702	450 (C)	P	3,275	3,275	2,430
Texas Lutheran College; Seguin, Tex. 78155	1,014 (C)	P	5,820	5,820	2,820
Texas Southern University; Houston, Tex. 77004	7,179 (C)	Pub	1,098	4,360	3,320
Texas Tech University; Lubbock, Tex. 79409	20,990 (C)	Pub	1,198	4,258	3,348
Texas Wesleyan University; Fort Worth, Tex. 76105	1,300 (C)	P	5,600	5,600	3,230
Texas Woman's University; Denton, Tex. 76204	4,992 (W)	Pub	964	4,084	2,678
Thiel College; Greenville, Pa. 16125	918 (C)	P	9,355	9,355	4,230
Thomas Aquinas College; Santa Paula, Calif. 93060	196 (C)	P	10,350	10,350	4,420
Thomas College; Waterville, Me. 04901	822 (C)	P	8,050	8,050	4,150
Thomas Edison State College, Trenton, N.J. 08608-1176	7,811 (C)	Pub	220	365	n.a.
Thomas Jefferson University, College of Allied Health Sciences; Philadelphia, Pa. 19107	1,333 (C)	P	10,600	10,600	4,650
Thomas More College; Crestview Hills, Ky. 41017	1,297 (C)	P	7,430	7,430	3,400
Tiffin University; Tiffin, Ohio 44883	854 (C)	P	6,100	6,100	3,380
Toccoa Falls College; Toccoa Falls, Ga. 30598	840 (C)	P	4,894	4,894	3,333
Toledo, University of; Toledo, Ohio 43606	21,585 (C)	Pub	2,526	5,781	2,805
Tougaloo College; Tougaloo, Miss. 39174	788 (C)	P	4,190	4,190	1,690
Touro College; New York, N.Y. 10001	4,298 (C)	P	6,730	6,730	6,050
Towson State University; Towson, Md. 21204-7097	13,519 (C)	Pub	2,458	4,380	2,205
Transylvania University; Lexington, Ky. 40508	1,076 (C)	P	9,619	9,619	4,048
Trenton State College; Trenton, N.J. 08650	6,760 (C)	Pub	2,720	3,795	4,400
Trevecca Nazarene College; Nashville, Tenn. 37210	1,051 (C)	P	4,896	4,896	2,660
Tri-State University; Angola, Ind. 46703	1,185 (C)	P	7,272	7,272	3,333
Trinity Bible College; Ellendale, N.D. 58436	394 (C)	P	4,088	4,088	3,098
Trinity Christian College; Palos Heights, Ill. 60463	546 (C)	P	8,250	8,250	3,340
Trinity College; Burlington, Vt. 05401	1,108 (W)	P	8,850	8,850	4,452
Trinity College; Deerfield, Ill. 60015	849 (C)	P	8,610	8,610	3,850
Trinity College; Hartford, Conn. 06106	1,969 (C)	P	16,960	16,960	4,820
Trinity College; Washington, D.C. 20017	884 (W)	P	10,600	10,600	6,280
Trinity University; San Antonio, Tex. 78284	2,383 (C)	P	9,676	9,676	4,340
Troy State University; Troy, Ala. 36802	3,642 (C)	Pub	1,470	2,172	2,632
Troy State University-Dothan; Dothan, Ala. 36303	1,169 (C)	Pub	1,419	1,824	n.a.
Troy State University-Montgomery; Montgomery, Ala. 36195-4419	2,242 (C)	Pub	1,370	2,090	n.a.
Tufts University; Medford, Mass. 02155	4,556 (C)	P	17,179	17,179	5,300
Tulane University; New Orleans, La. 70118	7,369 (C)	P	16,980	16,980	5,505
Tulsa, University of; Tulsa, Okla. 74104	2,980 (C)	P	8,700	8,700	3,600
Tusculum College; Greeneville, Tenn. 37743	720 (C)	P	5,700	5,700	3,100
Tuskegee University; Tuskegee, Ala. 36088	3,096 (C)	P	6,250	6,250	3,000
Union College; Barbourville, Ky. 40906	781 (C)	P	5,590	5,590	2,560
Union College; Lincoln, Neb. 68506	627 (C)	P	8,200	8,200	1,970
Union College; Schenectady, N.Y. 12308	1,957 (C)	P	15,579	15,579	5,395

Institution and location	Enrollment	Control	Tuition ($) Res.	Tuition ($) Nonres.	Rm/Bd ($)
Union Institute, The; Cincinnati, Ohio 45202-2407	300 (C)	P	7,284	7,284	n.a.
Union University; Jackson, Tenn. 38305	1,638 (C)	P	4,550	4,550	2,540
U.S. Air Force Academy; Colorado Springs, Colo. 80840	4,443 (C)	Pub	1,500	1,500	—
U.S. Coast Guard Academy; New London, Conn. 06320	951 (C)	Pub	1,500	1,500	—
U.S. International University; San Diego, Calif. 92131	1,254 (C)	P	8,550	8,550	4,155
U.S. Merchant Marine Academy; Kings Point, N.Y. 11024	844 (C)	Pub	2,980	2,980	—
U.S. Military Academy; West Point, N.Y. 10996	4,322 (C)	Pub	1,000	1,000	—
U.S. Naval Academy; Annapolis, Md. 21402	4,000 (C)	Pub	1,500	1,500	—
Unity College; Unity, Me. 04988	410 (C)	P	7,150	8,300	4,400
Universidad de las Americas—Puebla; Puebla, Mexico 72820	4,488 (C)	P	4,000	4,000	1,000
Universidad Politecnica de Puerto Rico; Hato Rey, San Juan, P.R. 00918	3,116 (C)	P	(8)	(8)	n.a.
Upper Iowa University; Fayette, Iowa 52142	2,215 (C)	P	8,540	8,540	2,860
Upsala College; East Orange, N.J. 07019	1,228 (C)	P	10,079	10,079	4,528
Urbana Univ.; Urbana, Ohio 43078	852 (C)	P	7,130	7,130	3,710
Ursinus College; Collegeville, Pa. 19426	1,128 (C)	P	12,530	12,530	4,500
Ursuline College; Pepper Pike, Ohio 44124	1,460 (C)	P	6,600	6,600	3,380
Utah, University of; Salt Lake City, Utah 84112	21,009 (C)	Pub	2,008	5,695	3,200
Utah State University; Logan, Utah 84322	10,030 (C)	Pub	1,686	4,668	2,790
Utica College of Syracuse University; Utica, N.Y. 13502	1,700 (C)	P	10,490	10,490	4,450
Valdosta State College; Valdosta, Ga. 31698	6,033 (C)	Pub	1,638	4,218	2,760
Valley City State University; Valley City, N.D. 58072	1,085 (C)	Pub	1,638	4,110	1,920
Valley Forge Christian College; Phoenixville, Pa. 19460	511 (C)	P	3,346	3,346	2,700
Valparaiso University; Valparaiso, Ind. 46383	3,243 (C)	P	9,110	9,110	2,700
Vanderbilt University; Nashville, Tenn. 37212	5,097 (C)	P	15,483	15,483	5,420
VanderCook College of Music; Chicago, Ill. 60616	104 (C)	P	7,545	7,545	3,992
Vassar College; Poughkeepsie, N.Y. 12601	2,306 (C)	P	14,950	14,950	4,980
Vennard College; University Park, Iowa 52595	153 (C)	P	4,172	4,172	2,310
Vermont, University of; Burlington, Vt. 05401-3596	8,032 (C)	Pub	4,200	12,800	4,026
Villa Julie College; Stevenson, Md. 21153	1,596 (C)	P	5,770	5,700	n.a.
Villanova University; Villanova, Pa. 19085	6,400 (C)	P	12,050	12,050	5,420
Virginia, University of; Charlottesville, Va. 22906	11,304 (C)	Pub	3,350	9,550	3,450
Virginia, University of—Clinch Valley College; Wise, Va. 24293	1,528 (C)	Pub	2,056	3,716	2,900
Virginia Commonwealth University; Richmond, Va. 23284-2526	15,920 (C)	Pub	2,719	6,698	3,350
Virginia Intermont College; Bristol, Va. 24201	521 (C)	P	6,570	6,570	3,930
Virginia Military Institute; Lexington, Va. 24450	1,300 (M)	Pub	4,325	9,865	3,525
Virginia Polytechnic Institute and State University; Blacksburg, Va. 24061	18,574 (C)	Pub	3,304	8,152	2,754
Virginia State University; Petersburg, Va. 23803	3,308 (C)	Pub	2,908	6,628	3,977
Virginia Union University; Richmond, Va. 23220	1,165 (C)	P	6,131	6,131	3,162
Virginia Wesleyan College; Norfolk-Virginia Beach, Va. 23502	1,390 (C)	P	8,740	8,740	4,425
Virgin Islands, University of the; St. Thomas, V.I. 00802	2,432 (C)	Pub	1,122	3,336	3,600
Visual Arts, School of; New York, N.Y. 10010	2,035 (C)	P	9,950	9,950	5,100
Viterbo College; La Crosse, Wis. 54601	1,122 (C)	P	7,900	7,900	3,100
Voorhees College; Denmark, S.C. 29042	574 (C)	P	6,292	6,292	2,522
Wabash College; Crawfordsville, Ind. 47933	850 (M)	P	10,700	10,700	3,665
Wadhams Hall Seminary—College; Ogdensburg, N.Y. 13669-9308	43 (M)	P	3,550	3,550	3,400
Wagner College; Staten Island, N.Y. 10301	1,290 (C)	P	10,050	10,050	4,850
Wake Forest University; Winston-Salem, N.C. 27109	3,483 (C)	P	10,800	10,800	3,900
Walla Walla College; College Place, Wash. 99324	1,534 (C)	P	9,540	9,540	2,985
Walsh College; Canton, Ohio 44720	1,315 (C)	P	6,528	6,528	3,350
Walsh College of Accountancy and Business Administration; Troy, Mich. 48007	1,734 (C)	P	4,034	4,034	n.a.
Warner Pacific College; Portland, Ore. 97215	496 (C)	P	7,472	7,472	3,298
Warner Southern College; Lake Wales, Fla. 33853	423 (C)	P	5,320	5,320	2,090
Warren Wilson College; Swannanoa, N.C. 28778	502 (C)	P	8,515	8,515	2,852
Wartburg College; Waverly, Iowa 50677	1,440 (C)	P	9,640	9,640	3,080
Warwick, University of; Coventry, CV4 7AL, England	5,626 (C)	Pub	3,071	3,071	2,456
Washburn University; Topeka, Kan. 66621	5,492 (C)	Pub	2,342	3,632	2,734
Washington, University of; Seattle, Wash. 98195	24,566 (C)	Pub	1,941	5,421	3,918
Washington and Jefferson College; Washington, Pa. 15301	1,205 (C)	P	12,850	12,850	3,290
Washington and Lee University; Lexington, Va. 24450	1,624 (C)	P	11,575	11,575	4,068
Washington Bible College; Lanham, Md. 20706	325 (C)	P	5,143	5,143	2,210
Washington College; Chestertown, Md. 21620	899 (C)	P	11,400	11,400	4,600
Washington State University; Pullman, Wash. 99164	13,814 (C)	Pub	1,954	5,434	3,300
Washington University; St. Louis, Mo. 63130	4,916 (C)	P	16,110	16,110	5,127
Wayland Baptist University; Plainview, Tex. 79072	2,052 (C)	P	4,654	4,654	3,073
Waynesburg College; Waynesburg, Pa. 15370	1,196 (C)	P	7,490	7,490	3,050
Wayne State College; Wayne, Neb. 68787	2,714 (C)	Pub	1,421	2,186	2,290
Wayne State University; Detroit, Mich. 48202	21,085 (C)	Pub	2,128	4,702	4,860
Webber College; Babson Park, Fla. 33827	247 (C)	P	5,390	5,390	2,730
Webb Institute of Naval Architecture; Glen Cove, N.Y. 11542	78 (C)	P	—	—	4,200
Weber State College; Ogden, Utah 84408	12,783 (C)	Pub	1,400	3,753	2,535

Institution and location	Enrollment	Control	Tuition ($) Res.	Tuition ($) Nonres.	Rm/Bd ($)
Webster University; St. Louis, Mo. 63119	2,275 (C)	P	7,340	7,340	3,650
Wellesley College; Wellesley, Mass. 02181	2,279 (W)	P	15,966	15,966	5,657
Wells College; Aurora, N.Y. 13026	400 (W)	P	11,690	11,690	4,300
Wentworth Institute of Technology; Boston, Mass. 02115	3,034 (C)	P	7,716	7,716	5,954
Wesleyan College; Macon, Ga. 31297	511 (W)	P	9,845	9,845	3,950
Wesleyan University; Middletown, Conn. 06457	2,671 (C)	P	16,250	16,250	4,990
Wesley College; Dover, Del. 19901	1,295 (C)	P	8,055	8,055	3,800
Wesley College; Florence, Miss. 39073	65 (C)	P	1,740	1,740	1,980
West Chester Univ. of Pennsylvania; West Chester, Pa. 19383	9,770 (C)	Pub	2,279	4,562	3,194
West Coast Christian College; Fresno, Calif. 93710	274 (C)	P	2,880	2,880	2,640
West Coast University; Los Angeles, Calif. 90020-1765	850 (C)	P	8,250	8,250	n.a.
Western Baptist College; Salem, Ore. 97301	358 (C)	P	7,150	7,150	3,350
Western Carolina University; Cullowhee, N.C. 28723	5,106 (C)	Pub	1,213	5,744	2,180
Western Connecticut State University; Danbury, Conn. 06810	5,163 (C)	Pub	2,490	6,202	3,200
Western Illinois University; Macomb, Ill. 61455	11,004 (C)	Pub	2,229	5,541	2,869
Western International University; Phoenix, Ariz. 85021	1,173 (C)	P	4,370	4,370	n.a.
Western Kentucky University; Bowling Green, Ky. 42101	13,130 (C)	Pub	1,440	4,040	2,570
Western Maryland College; Westminster, Md. 21157	1,315 (C)	P	12,505	12,505	4,740
Western Michigan University; Kalamazoo, Mich. 49008	20,598 (C)	Pub	2,270	5,370	3,375
Western Montana College; Dillon, Mont. 59725	905 (C)	Pub	1,364	3,035	3,010
Western New England College; Springfield, Mass. 01119	2,232 (C)	P	7,982	7,982	4,900
Western New Mexico University; Silver City, N.M. 88061	1,546 (C)	Pub	1,122	4,352	2,110
Western Oregon State College; Monmouth, Ore. 97361	3,461 (C)	Pub	1,806	4,566	2,940
Western State College of Colorado; Gunnison, Colo. 81230	2,500 (C)	Pub	1,599	4,693	2,958
Western Washington University; Bellingham, Wash. 98225	8,882 (C)	Pub	1,611	5,649	3,200
Westfield State College; Westfield, Mass. 01085	3,043 (C)	Pub	1,250	4,325	2,160
West Florida, University of; Pensacola, Fla. 32514	6,625 (C)	Pub	1,321	4,632	3,204
West Georgia College; Carrollton, Ga. 30118	5,269 (C)	Pub	1,587	4,065	2,304
West Liberty State College; West Liberty, W. Va. 26074	2,386 (C)	Pub	1,500	3,470	2,650
West Los Angeles, University of, School of Paralegal Studies; Los Angeles, Calif. 90066	319 (C)	P	2,904	2,904	n.a.
Westminster Choir College; Princeton, N.J. 08540	230 (C)	P	11,100	11,100	4,780
Westminster College; Fulton, Mo. 65251	761 (C)	P	8,200	8,200	3,350
Westminster College; New Wilmington, Pa. 16172	1,392 (C)	P	10,580	10,580	3,150
Westminster Coll. of Salt Lake City; Salt Lake City, Utah 84105	1,609 (C)	P	7,254	7,254	3,550
Westmont College; Santa Barbara, Calif. 93108	1,264 (C)	P	10,900	10,900	4,650
West Oahu College. *See* Hawaii, University of					
West Texas State University; Canyon, Tex. 79016	4,813 (C)	Pub	1,060	4,128	2,686
West Virginia Institute of Technology; Montgomery, W. Va. 25136	2,883 (C)	Pub	3,082	3,082	3,010
West Virginia State College; Institute, W. Va. 25112	4,834 (C)	Pub	1,432	3,542	2,800
West Virginia University; Morgantown, W. Va. 26506	14,984 (C)	Pub	1,850	5,000	3,846
West Virginia Wesleyan College; Buckhannon, W. Va. 26201	1,461 (C)	P	11,930	11,930	3,150
Wheaton College; Norton, Mass. 02766	1,264 (C)	P	16,040	16,040	5,300
Wheaton College; Wheaton, Ill. 60187	2,235 (C)	P	9,500	9,500	3,800
Wheeling Jesuit College; Wheeling, W. Va. 26003	1,224 (C)	P	8,550	8,550	3,840
Wheelock College; Boston, Mass. 02215	750 (C)	P	11,212	11,212	5,078
White Plains, Coll. of, of Pace Univ. *See* Pace Univ.					
Whitman College; Walla Walla, Wash. 99362	1,239 (C)	P	13,210	13,210	4,340
Whittier College; Whittier, Calif. 90608	1,029 (C)	P	14,632	14,632	4,966
Whitworth College; Spokane, Wash. 99251	1,237 (C)	P	10,415	10,415	3,850
Wichita State University; Wichita, Kan. 67208	17,419 (C)	Pub	1,608	4,715	3,127
Widener University; Chester, Pa. 19013	2,403 (C)	P	10,500	10,500	4,560
Wilberforce University; Wilberforce, Ohio 45384	779 (C)	P	6,346	6,346	3,686
Wiley College; Marshall, Tex. 75670	505 (C)	P	4,146	4,146	2,544
Wilkes University; Wilkes-Barre, Pa. 18766	1,886 (C)	P	9,275	9,275	4,700
Willamette University; Salem, Ore. 97301	1,535 (C)	P	12,480	12,480	3,950
William and Mary, College of; Williamsburg, Va. 23185	5,286 (C)	Pub	3,730	10,450	3,746
William Carey College; Hattiesburg, Miss. 39401	1,546 (C)	P	4,555	4,555	2,250
William Jewell College; Liberty, Mo. 64068	1,477 (C)	P	7,450	7,450	2,560
William Paterson College; Wayne, N.J. 07470	7,370 (C)	Pub	2,385	3,135	2,085
William Penn College; Oskaloosa, Iowa 52577	737 (C)	P	9,190	9,190	2,720
Williams Baptist College; Walnut Ridge, Ark. 72476	504 (C)	P	3,110	3,110	2,220
Williams College; Williamstown, Mass. 01267	2,060 (C)	P	15,535	15,535	4,975
William Smith College. *See* Hobart and William Smith Colleges					
William Tyndale College; Farmington Hills, Mich. 48108	396 (C)	P	5,060	5,060	3,400
William Woods College; Fulton, Mo. 65251	750 (W)	P	8,208	8,208	3,560
Wilmington College; New Castle, Del. 19720	1,796 (C)	P	4,945	4,945	n.a.
Wilmington College of Ohio; Wilmington, Ohio 45177	890 (C)	P	8,780	8,780	3,250
Wilson College; Chambersburg, Pa. 17201-1285	853 (W)	P	10,582	10,582	4,936
Wingate College; Wingate, N.C. 28174	1,791 (C)	P	5,900	5,900	3,120
Winona State University; Winona, Minn. 55987	7,100 (C)	Pub	2,000	3,200	2,450
Winston-Salem State University; Winston-Salem, N.C. 27110	2,517 (C)	Pub	896	4,268	2,265
Winthrop College; Rock Hill, S.C. 29733	4,173 (C)	Pub	2,568	4,612	2,668
Wisconsin, University of-Eau Claire; Eau Claire, Wis. 54701	10,003 (C)	Pub	1,829	5,476	2,420

Institution and location	Enrollment	Control	Tuition ($) Res.	Tuition ($) Nonres.	Rm/Bd ($)
Wisconsin, University of-Green Bay; Green Bay, Wis. 54302	4,590 (C)	Pub	1,754	5,300	2,350
Wisconsin, University of-La Crosse; La Crosse, Wis. 54601	8,120 (C)	Pub	1,970	5,830	2,130
Wisconsin, University of-Madison; Madison, Wis. 53706	29,248 (C)	Pub	2,107	6,831	3,445
Wisconsin, University of-Milwaukee; Milwaukee, Wis. 53201	20,686 (C)	Pub	2,054	6,881	3,476
Wisconsin, University of-Oshkosh; Oshkosh, Wis. 54901	9,543 (C)	Pub	1,850	5,700	2,110
Wisconsin, University of-Parkside; Kenosha, Wis. 53141	4,896 (C)	Pub	1,781	5,059	2,916
Wisconsin, University of-Platteville; Platteville, Wis. 53818	5,213 (C)	Pub	1,877	5,524	2,260
Wisconsin, University of-River Falls; River Falls, Wis. 54022	4,583 (C)	Pub	1,760	5,120	2,292
Wisconsin, University of-Stevens Point; Stevens Point, Wis. 54481	8,429 (C)	Pub	1,879	5,526	2,614
Wisconsin, University of-Stout; Menomonie, Wis. 54751	6,889 (C)	Pub	1,866	5,513	2,263
Wisconsin, University of-Superior; Superior, Wis. 54880	2,112 (C)	Pub	1,677	5,401	2,200
Wisconsin, University of-Whitewater; Whitewater, Wis. 53190	9,147 (C)	Pub	1,800	5,493	2,100
Wisconsin Lutheran College; Milwaukee, Wis. 53226	283 (C)	P	7,578	7,578	3,200
Wittenberg University; Springfield, Ohio 45501	2,341 (C)	P	13,491	13,491	4,044
Wofford College; Spartanburg, S.C. 29303-3663	1,076 (C)	P	9,790	9,790	4,150
Woodbury University; Burbanks, Calif. 91510-7846	865 (C)	P	9,342	9,342	5,100
Wooster, College of; Wooster, Ohio 44691	1,891 (C)	P	13,410	13,410	4,240
Worcester Polytechnic Institute; Worcester, Mass. 01609	2,820 (C)	P	14,295	14,295	4,590
Worcester State College; Worcester, Mass. 01602	3,600 (C)	Pub	1,812	4,506	3,630
World College West; Petaluma, Calif. 94952	125 (C)	P	8,850	8,850	3,900
Wright State University; Dayton, Ohio 45435	13,783 (C)	Pub	2,469	4,938	3,642
Wyoming, University of; Laramie, Wyo. 82071	9,408 (C)	Pub	1,293	4,097	3,262
Xavier University; Cincinnati, Ohio 45207	3,912 (C)	P	9,000	9,000	3,910
Xavier University of Louisiana; New Orleans, La. 70125	2,563 (C)	P	5,500	5,500	2,900
Yale University; New Haven, Conn. 06520	5,182 (C)	P	16,300	16,300	5,900
Yeshiva University; New York, N.Y. 10033-3299	1,754 (C)	P	10,310	10,310	5,130
York College of Pennsylvania; York, Pa. 17405	2,746 (C)	P	4,448	4,448	2,972
Youngstown State Univ.; Youngstown, Ohio 44555	13,647 (C)	Pub	2,190	3,390	3,405

1. Graduate school only. 2. $15 per credit. 3. $50 per credit. 4. $86 per credit. 5. $273 per credit. 6. $93 per credit. 7. $188 per credit. 8. $65 per credit.

Public Education Expenditures Exceeded $286 Billion in 1989

Source: U.S. Department of Commerce, Bureau of the Census.

Federal, state, and local governments spent more than $286 billion in 1989 to fund higher education institutions and provide elementary-secondary education according to a report issued by the Commerce Department's Census Bureau.

The federal government spent $38.5 billion, or 13 percent of the total public education costs, to fund programs such as school lunch and milk, impact aid, education for the handicapped, and project Head Start. The federal share increased by 9.2 percent over 1988.

State governments contributed nearly $159 billion, or 55 percent of the total, for public education. This included more than $91.5 billion to elementary-secondary school systems and $67 billion to state-operated higher education institutions, special schools, and scholarship/fellowship payments.

Local school systems, the primary recipients of federal and state intergovernmental payments for education, supplied an additional $89 billion, or 31 percent.

The report also shows that:

• State support for elementary-secondary education increased by 7.2 percent from 1988 to 1989, and local tax support by 8.2 percent.

• Local funding for elementary-secondary education ranged from a high of 89 percent in New Hampshire to a low of 13 percent in New Mexico.

• Systems with the greatest percentage of state funding were Hawaii (100 percent), New Mexico (76 percent), and Washington (70 percent).

• The federal government's funding share was highest in Mississippi (16 percent).

• Of the $194 billion spent by public school systems for elementary-secondary education, $106 billion—almost 55 percent—was allocated to instructional programs, while $78 billion was spent on teachers and other instructional salaries. Although instructional salaries increased by 5.2 percent from the $74 billion spent in 1988, its share of total elementary-secondary expenditures shrank from 41.7 to 40.4 percent.

• Spending per pupil for instruction averaged $2,635 in 1989.

Selected Degree Abbreviations

A.B. Bachelor of Arts
AeEng. Aeronautical Engineer
A.M.T. Master of Arts in Teaching
B.A. Bachelor of Arts
B.A.E. Bachelor of Arts in Education, or Bachelor of Art Education, Aeronautical Engineering, Agricultural Engineering, or Architectural Engineering
B.Ag. Bachelor of Agriculture
B.A.M. Bachelor of Applied Mathematics
B.Arch. Bachelor of Architecture
B.B.A. Bachelor of Business Administration
B.C.E. Bachelor of Civil Engineering
B.Ch.E. Bachelor of Chemical Engineering
B.C.L. Bachelor of Canon Law
B.D. Bachelor of Divinity
B.E. Bachelor of Education or Bachelor of Engineering
B.E.E. Bachelor of Electrical Engineering
B.F. Bachelor of Forestry
B.F.A. Bachelor of Fine Arts
B.J. Bachelor of Journalism
B.L.S. Bachelor of Liberal Studies or Bachelor of Library Science
B.Lit. Bachelor of Literature
B.M. Bachelor of Medicine or Bachelor of Music
B.M.S. Bachelor of Marine Science
B.N. Bachelor of Nursing
B.Pharm. Bachelor of Pharmacy
B.R.E. Bachelor of Religious Education
B.S. Bachelor of Science
B.S.Ed. Bachelor of Science in Education
C.E. Civil Engineer
Ch.E. Chemical Engineer
D.B.A. Doctor of Business Administration
D.C. Doctor of Chiropractic
D.D. Doctor of Divinity[1]
D.D.S. Doctor of Dental Surgery or Doctor of Dental Science
D.L.S. Doctor of Library Science
D.M.D. Doctor of Dental Medicine
D.O. Doctor of Osteopathy
D.M.S. Doctor of Medical Science
D.P.A. Doctor of Public Administration[2]
D.P.H. Doctor of Public Health
D.R.E. Doctor of Religious Education
D.S.W. Doctor of Social Welfare or Doctor of Social Work
D.Sc. Doctor of Science[3]
D.V.M. Doctor of Veterinary Medicine
Ed.D. Doctor of Education[2]
Ed.S. Education Specialist
E.E. Electrical Engineer

E.M. Engineer of Mines
E.Met. Engineer of Metallurgy
I.E. Industrial Engineer or Industrial Engineering
J.D. Doctor of Laws[2]
J.S.D. Doctor of Juristic Science
L.H.D. Doctor of Humane Letters[3]
Litt.B. Bachelor of Letters
Litt.M. Master of Letters[4]
LL.B. Bachelor of Laws
LL.D. Doctor of Laws[3]
LL.M. Master of Laws
M.A. Master of Arts
M.Aero.E. Master of Aeronautical Engineering
M.B.A. Master of Business Administration
M.C.E. Master of Christian Education or Master of Civil Engineering
M.C.S. Master of Computer Science
M.D. Doctor of Medicine
M.Div. Master of Divinity
M.E. Master of Engineering
M.Ed. Master of Education
M.Eng. Master of Engineering
M.F.A. Master of Fine Arts
M.H.A. Master of Hospital Administration
M.L.S. Master of Library Science
M.M. Master of Music
M.M.E. Master of Mechanical Engineering or Master of Music Education
M.Mus. Master of Music
M.N. Master of Nursing
M.R.E. Master of Religious Education
M.S. Master of Science
M.S.W. Master of Social Work
M.Th. Master of Theology
Nuc.E. Nuclear Engineer
O.D. Doctor of Optometry
Pharm.D. Doctor of Pharmacy[2]
Ph.B. Bachelor of Philosophy
Ph.D. Doctor of Philosophy
S.B. Bachelor of Science
Sc.D. Doctor of Science[3]
S.J.D. Doctor of Juridical Science or Doctor of the Science of Law
S.Sc.D. Doctor of Social Science
S.T.B. Bachelor of Sacred Theology
S.T.D. Doctor of Sacred Theology
S.T.M. Master of Sacred Theology
Th.B. Bachelor of Theology
Th.D. Doctor of Theology
Th.M. Master of Theology

1. Honorary. 2. Earned and honorary. 3. Usually honorary. 4. Sometimes honorary.

Academic Costume: Colors Associated With Fields

Field	Color	Field	Color
Agriculture	Maize	Medicine	Green
Arts, Letters, Humanities	White	Music	Pink
Commerce, Accountancy,		Nursing	Apricot
Business	Drab	Oratory (Speech)	Silver gray
Dentistry	Lilac	Pharmacy	Olive green
Economics	Copper	Philosophy	Dark blue
Education	Light blue	Physical Education	Sage green
Engineering	Orange	Public Admin. including Foreign Service	Peacock blue
Fine Arts, Architecture	Brown	Public Health	Salmon pink
Forestry	Russet	Science	Golden yellow
Journalism	Crimson	Social Work	Citron
Law	Purple	Theology	Scarlet
Library Science	Lemon	Veterinary Science	Gray

WRITER'S GUIDE

A Concise Guide to Style

From *Webster's II New Riverside University Dictionary.* © 1984 by Houghton Mifflin Company.

This section discusses and illustrates the basic conventions of American capitalization, punctuation, and italicization.

Capitalization

Capitalize the following: **1.** the first word of a sentence: Some spiders are poisonous; others are not. Are you my new neighbor?
2. the first word of a direct quotation, except when the quotation is split: Joyce asked, "Do you think that the lecture was interesting?" "No," I responded, "it was very boring." Tom Paine said, "The sublime and the ridiculous are often so nearly related that it is difficult to class them separately."
3. the first word of each line in a poem in traditional verse: Half a league, half a league,/Half a league onward,/All in the valley of Death/Rode the six hundred.—Alfred, Lord Tennyson
4. the names of people, of organizations and their members, of councils and congresses, and of historical periods and events: Marie Curie, Benevolent and Protective Order of Elks, an Elk, Protestant Episcopal Church, an Episcopalian, the Democratic Party, a Democrat, the Nuclear Regulatory Commission, the U.S. Senate, the Middle Ages, World War I, the Battle of Britain.
5. the names of places and geographic divisions, districts, regions, and locales: Richmond, Vermont, Argentina, Seventh Avenue, London Bridge, Arctic Circle, Eastern Hemisphere, Continental Divide, Middle East, Far North, Gulf States, East Coast, the North, the South Shore.
Do not capitalize words indicating compass points unless a specific region is referred to: Turn north onto Interstate 91.
6. the names of rivers, lakes, mountains, and oceans: Ohio River, Lake Como, Rocky Mountains, Atlantic Ocean.
7. the names of ships, aircraft, satellites, and space vehicles: U.S.S. *Arizona, Spirit of St. Louis,* the spy satellite Ferret-D, Voyager II, the space shuttle Challenger.
8. the names of nationalities, races, tribes, and languages: Spanish, Maori, Bantu, Russian.
9. words derived from proper names, except in their extended senses: the Byzantine Empire. *But:* byzantine office politics.
10. words indicating family relationships when used with a person's name as a title: Aunt Toni and Uncle Jack. *But:* my aunt and uncle, Toni and Jack Walker.
11. a title (i.e., civil, judicial, military, royal and noble, religious, and honorary) when preceding a name: Justice Marshall, General Jackson, Mayor Daley, Queen Victoria, Lord Mountbatten, Pope John Paul II, Professor Jacobson, Senator Byrd.
12. all references to the President and Vice President of the United States: The President has entered the hall. The Vice President presides over the Senate.

13. all key words in titles of literary, dramatic, artistic, and musical works: the novel *The Old Man and the Sea,* the short story "Notes from Underground," an article entitled "On Passive Verbs," James Dickey's poem "In the Tree House at Night," the play *Cat on a Hot Tin Roof,* Van Gogh's *Wheat Field and Cypress Trees,* Beethoven's *Emperor Concerto.*
14. *the* in the title of a newspaper if it is a part of the title: *The Wall Street Journal. But:* the New York *Daily News.*
15. the first word in the salutation and in the complimentary close of a letter: My dear Carol, Yours sincerely.
16. epithets and substitutes for the names of people and places: Old Hickory, Old Blood and Guts, The Oval Office, the Windy City.
17. words used in personifications: When is not Death at watch/Within those secret waters?/What wants he but to catch/Earth's heedless sons and daughters?—Edmund Blunden
18. the pronoun *I*: I told them that I had heard the news.
19. names for the Deity and sacred works: God, the Almighty, Jesus, Allah, the Supreme Being, the Bible, the Koran, the Talmud.
20. days of the week, months of the year, holidays, and holy days: Tuesday, May, Independence Day, Passover, Ramadan, Christmas.
21. the names of specific courts: The Supreme Court of the United States, the Massachusetts Appeals Court, the United States Court of Appeals for the First Circuit.
22. the names of treaties, accords, pacts, laws, and specific amendments: Panama Canal Treaty, Treaty of Paris, Geneva Accords, Warsaw Pact countries, Sherman Antitrust Law, Labor Management Relations Act, took the Fifth Amendment.
23. registered trademarks and service marks: Day-Glo, Comsat.
24. the names of geologic eras, periods, epochs, and strata and the names of prehistoric divisions: Paleozoic Era, Precambrian, Pleistocene, Age of Reptiles, Bronze Age, Stone Age.
25. the names of constellations, planets, and stars: Milky Way, Southern Crown, Saturn, Jupiter, Uranus, Polaris.
26. genus but not species names in binomial nomenclature: *Rana pipiens.*
27. New Latin names of classes, families, and all groups higher than genera in botanical and zoological nomenclature: Nematoda.
But do not capitalize derivatives from such names: nematodes.
28. many abbreviations and acronyms: Dec., Tues., Lt. Gen., M.F.A., UNESCO, MIRV.

Italicization

Use italics to:
1. indicate titles of books, plays, and epic poems:

412

War and Peace, The Importance of Being Earnest, Paradise Lost.

2. indicate titles of magazines and newspapers: *New York* magazine, *The Wall Street Journal,* the New York *Daily News.*

3. set off the titles of motion pictures and radio and television programs: *Star Wars, All Things Considered, Masterpiece Theater.*

4. indicate titles of major musical compositions: Handel's *Messiah,* Adam's *Giselle.*

5. set off the names of paintings and sculpture: *Mona Lisa, Pietà.*

6. indicate words, letters, or numbers that are referred to: The word *hiss* is onomatopoeic. *Can't* means *won't* in your lexicon. You form your *n*'s like *u*'s. A *6* looks like an inverted *9.*

7. indicate foreign words and phrases not yet assimilated into English: *C'est la vie* was the response to my complaint.

8. indicate the names of plaintiff and defendant in legal citations: *Roe* v. *Doe.*

9. emphasize a word or phrase: When you appear on the national news, you are *somebody.*
Use this device sparingly.

10. distinguish New Latin names of genera, species, subspecies, and varieties in botanical and zoological nomenclature: *Homo sapiens.*

11. set off the names of ships and aircraft but not space vehicles: U.S.S. *Arizona, Spirit of St. Louis,* Voyager II, the space shuttle Challenger, the spy satellite Ferret-D.

Punctuation

Apostrophe. 1. indicates the possessive case of singular and plural nouns, indefinite pronouns, and surnames combined with designations such as *Jr., Sr.,* and *II:* my sister's husband, my three sisters' husbands, anyone's guess, They answer each other's phones, John Smith, Jr.'s car.

2. indicates joint possession when used with the last of two or more nouns in a series: Doe and Roe's report.

3. indicates individual possession or authorship when used with each of two or more nouns in a series: Smith's, Roe's, and Doe's reports.

4. indicates the plurals of words, letters, and figures used as such: 60's and 70's; *x*'s, *y*'s, and *z*'s.

5. indicates omission of letters in contractions: aren't, that's, o'clock.

6. indicates omission of figures in dates: the class of '63.

Brackets.

1. enclose words or passages in quoted matter to indicate insertion of material written by someone other than the author: A tough but nervous, tenacious but restless race [the Yankees]; materially ambitious, yet prone to introspection. . . .—Samuel Eliot Morison

2. enclose material inserted within matter already in parentheses: (Vancouver [B.C.] January 1, 19—).

Colon.

1. introduces words, phrases, or clauses that explain, amplify, or summarize what has gone before: Suddenly I realized where we were: Rome.
"There are two cardinal sins from which all the others spring: impatience and laziness."—Franz Kafka

2. introduces a long quotation: In his original draft of the *Declaration of Independence,* Jefferson wrote: "We hold these truths to be sacred and undeniable; that all men are created equal and independent, that

from that equal creation they derive rights inherent and inalienable. . . ."

3. introduces a list: We need the following items: pens, paper, pencils, blotters, and erasers.

4. separates chapter and verse numbers in Biblical references: James 1:4.

5. separates city from publisher in footnotes and bibliographies: Chicago: Riverside Press, 1983.

6. separates hour and minute(s) in time designations: 9:30 a.m., a 9:30 meeting.

7. follows the salutation in a business letter: Gentlemen:

Comma.1. separates the clauses of a compound sentence connected by a coordinating conjunction: A difference exists between the musical works of Handel and Haydn, and it is a difference worth noting.
The comma may be omitted in short compound sentences: I heard what you said and I am furious. I got out of the car and I walked and walked.

2. separates *and* or *or* from the final item in a series of three or more: Red, yellow, and blue may be mixed to produce all colors.

3. separates two or more adjectives modifying the same noun if *and* could be used between them without altering the meaning: a solid, heavy gait. *But:* a polished mahogany dresser.

4. sets off nonrestrictive clauses or phrases (i.e., those that if eliminated would not affect the meaning of the sentences): The burglar, who had entered through the patio, went straight to the silver chest.
The comma should not be used when a clause is restrictive (i.e., essential to the meaning of the sentence): The burglar who had entered through the patio went straight to the silver chest; the other burglar searched for the wall safe.

5. sets off words or phrases in apposition to a noun or noun phrase: Plato, the famous Greek philosopher, was a student of Socrates.
The comma should not be used if such words or phrases precede the noun: The Greek philosopher Plato was a student of Socrates.

6. sets off transitional words and short expressions that require a pause in reading or speaking: Unfortunately, my friend was not well traveled. Did you, after all, find what you were looking for? I live with my family, of course.

7. sets off words used to introduce a sentence: No, I haven't been to Paris. Well, what do you think we should do now?

8. sets off a subordinate clause or a long phrase that precedes a principal clause: By the time we found the restaurant, we were starved. Of all the illustrations in the book, the most striking are those of the tapestries.

9. sets off short quotations and sayings: The candidate said, "Actions speak louder than words." "Talking of axes," said the Duchess, "chop off her head"—Lewis Carroll

10. indicates omission of a word or words: To err is human; to forgive, divine.

11. sets off the year from the month in full dates: Nicholas II of Russia was shot on July 16, 1918.
But note that when only the month and the year are used, no comma appears: Nicholas II of Russia was shot in July 1918.

12. sets off city and state in geographic names: Atlanta, Georgia, is the transportation center of the South. 34 Beach Drive, Bedford, VA 24523.

13. separates series of four or more figures into thousands, millions, etc.: 67,000; 200,000.

14. sets off words used in direct address: "I tell you, folks, all politics is applesauce."—Will Rogers Thank you for your expert assistance, Dolores.

15. Separates a tag question from the rest of a sentence: You forgot your keys again, didn't you?

16. sets off sentence elements that could be misunderstood if the comma were not used: Some time after, the actual date for the project was set.

17. follows the salutation in a personal letter and the complimentary close in a business or personal letter: Dear Jessica, Sincerely yours.

18. sets off titles and degrees from surnames and from the rest of a sentence: Walter T. Prescott, Jr.; Gregory A. Rossi, S.J.; Susan P. Green, M.D., presented the case.

Dash.

1. indicates a sudden break or abrupt change in continuity: "If—if you'll just let me explain—" the student stammered. And the problem—if there really is one—can then be solved.

2. sets apart an explanatory, a defining, or an emphatic phrase: Foods rich in protein—meat, fish, and eggs—should be eaten on a daily basis.

More important than winning the election, is governing the nation. That is the test of a political party—the acid, final test.—Adlai E. Stevenson

3. sets apart parenthetical matter: Wolsey, for all his faults—and he had many—was a great statesman, a man of natural dignity with a generous temperament. . . .—Jasper Ridley

4. marks an unfinished sentence: "But if my bus is late—" he began.

5. sets off a summarizing phrase or clause: The vital measure of a newspaper is not its size but its spirit—that is its responsibility to report the news fully, accurately, and fairly.—Arthur H. Sulzberger

6. sets off the name of an author or source, as at the end of a quotation: A poet can survive everything but a misprint.—Oscar Wilde

Ellipses.

1. indicate, by three spaced points, omission of words or sentences within quoted matter: Equipped by education to rule in the nineteenth century, . . . he lived and reigned in Russia in the twentieth century.—Robert K. Massie

2. indicate, by four spaced points, omission of words at the end of a sentence: The timidity of bureaucrats when it comes to dealing with . . . abuses is easy to explain. . . .—*New York*

3. indicate, when extended the length of a line, omission of one or more lines of poetry:

Roll   on,   thou   deep   and   dark   blue ocean—roll!
. . . .
Man marks the earth with ruin—his control
Stops with the shore.—Lord Byron

4. are sometimes used as a device, as for example, in advertising copy:

To help you Move and Grow
    with the Rigors of
Business in the 1980's . . .
    and Beyond.—*Journal of Business Strategy*

Exclamation Point.

1. terminates an emphatic or exclamatory sentence: Go home at once! You've got to be kidding!

2. terminates an emphatic interjection: Encore!

Hyphen. 1. indicates that part of a word of more than one syllable has been carried over from one line to the next:

During the revolution, the nation was
beset with problems—looting, fighting, and famine.

2. joins the elements of some compounds: great-grandparent, attorney-at-law, ne'er-do-well.

3. joins the elements of compound modifiers preceding nouns: high-school students, a fire-and-brim-

stone lecture, a two-hour meeting.

4. indicates that two or more compounds share a single base: four- and six-volume sets, eight- and nine-year olds.

5. separates the prefix and root in some combinations; check the Dictionary when in doubt about the spelling: anti-Nazi, re-elect, co-author, re-form/reform, re-cover/recover, re-creation/-recreation.

6. substitutes for the word *to* between typewritten inclusive words or figures: pp. 145–155, the Boston-New York air shuttle.

7. punctuates written-out compound numbers from 21 through 99: forty-six years of age, a person who is forty-six, two hundred fifty-nine dollars.

Parentheses. 1. enclose material that is not essential to a sentence and that if not included would not alter its meaning: After a few minutes (some say less) the blaze was extinguished.

2. often enclose letters or figures to indicate subdivisions of a series: A movement in sonata form consists of the following elements: (1) the exposition, (2) the development, and (3) the recapitulation.

3. enclose figures following and confirming written-out numbers, especially in legal and business documents: The fee for my services will be two thousand dollars ($2,000.00).

4. enclose an abbreviation for a term following the written-out term, when used for the first time in a text: The patient is suffering from acquired immune deficiency syndrome (AIDS).

Period. 1. terminates a complete declarative or mild imperative sentence: There could be no turning back as war's dark shadow settled irrevocably across the continent of Europe.—W. Bruce Lincoln. Return all the books when you can. Would you kindly affix your signature here.

2. terminates sentence fragments: Gray clouds—and what looks like a veil of rain falling behind the East German headland. A pair of ducks. A tired or dying swan, head buried in its back feathers, sits on the sand a few feet from the water's edge.—Anthony Bailey

3. follows some abbreviations: Dec., Rev., St., Blvd., pp., Co.

Question Mark. 1. punctuates a direct question: Have you seen the new play yet? Who goes there? *But:* I wonder who said "Nothing is easy in war." I asked if they planned to leave.

2. indicates uncertainty: Ferdinand Magellan (1480?–1521), Plato (427?–347 B.C.).

Quotation Marks. 1. Double quotation marks enclose direct quotations: "What was Paris like in the Twenties?" our daughter asked. "Ladies and Gentlemen," the Chief Usher said, "the President of the United States." Robert Louis Stevenson said that "it is better to be a fool than to be dead." When advised not to become a lawyer because the profession was already overcrowded, Daniel Webster replied, "There is always room at the top."

2. Double quotation marks enclose words or phrases to clarify their meaning or use or to indicate that they are being used in a special way: This was the border of what we often call "the West" or "the Free World." "The Windy City" is a name for Chicago.

3. Double quotation marks set off the translation of a foreign word or phrase: *die Grenze,* "the border."

4. Double quotation marks set off the titles of series of books, of articles or chapters in publications, of essays, of short stories and poems, of individual radio and television programs, and of songs and short musical pieces: "The Horizon Concise History" series; an article entitled "On Reflexive Verbs in

English"; Chapter Nine, "The Prince and the Peasant"; Pushkin's "The Queen of Spades"; Tennyson's "Ode on the Death of the Duke of Wellington"; "The Bob Hope Special"; Schubert's "Death and the Maiden."

5. Single quotation marks enclose quotations within quotations: The blurb for the piece proclaimed, "Two years ago at Geneva, South Vietnam was virtually sold down the river to the Communists. Today the spunky little . . . country is back on its own feet, thanks to "a mandarin in a sharkskin suit who's upsetting the Red timetable.' "—Frances FitzGerald

Put commas and periods inside quotation marks; put semicolons and colons outside. Other punctuation, such as exclamation points and question marks, should be put inside the closing quotation marks only if part of the matter quoted.

Semicolon. 1. separates the clauses of a compound sentence having no coordinating conjunction: Do not let us speak of darker days; let us rather speak of sterner days.—Winston Churchill

2. separates the clauses of a compound sentence in which the clauses contain internal punctuation, even when the clauses are joined by conjunctions: Skis in hand, we trudged to the lodge, stowed our lunches, and donned our boots; and the rest of our party waited for us at the lifts.

3. separates elements of a series in which items already contain commas: Among those at the diplomatic reception were the Secretary of State; the daughter of the Ambassador to the Court of St. James's, formerly of London; and two United Nations delegates.

4. separates clauses of a compound sentence joined by a conjunctive adverb, such as *however, nonetheless,* or *hence:* We insisted upon a hearing; however, the Grievance Committee refused.

5. may be used instead of a comma to signal longer pauses for dramatic effect: But I want you to know that when I cross the river my last conscious thought will be of the Corps; and the Corps; and the Corps.—General Douglas MacArthur

Virgule. 1. separates successive divisions in an extended date: fiscal year 1983/84.

2. represents *per:* 35 km/hr, 1,800 ft/sec.

3. means *or* between the words *and* and *or:* Take water skis and/or fishing equipment when you visit the beach this summer.

4. separates two or more lines of poetry that are quoted and run in on successive lines of a text: The student actress had a memory lapse when she came to the lines "Double, double, toil and trouble/Fire burn and cauldron bubble/Eye of newt and toe of frog/Wool of bat and tongue of dog" and had to leave the stage in embarrassment.

Forms of Address[1]

Source: Webster's II New Riverside University Dictionary. Copyright © 1984 by Houghton Mifflin Company.

Academics

Dean, college or university. *Address:* Dean _____. *Salutation:* Dear Dean _____

President. *Address:* President _____ _____. *Salutation:* Dear President _____.

Professor, college or university. *Address:* Professor _____ _____. *Salutation:* Dear Professor _____.

Clerical and Religious Orders

Abbot. *Address:* The Right Reverend _____ _____ O.S.B. Abbot of _____. *Salutation:* Right Reverend Abbot or Dear Father Abbot.

Archbishop, Eastern Orthodox. *Address:* The Most Reverend Joseph, Archbishop of _____. *Salutation:* Your Eminence.

Archbishop, Roman Catholic. The Most Reverend _____ _____, Archbishop of _____. *Salutation:* Your Excellency.

Archdeacon, Episcopal. *Address:* The Venerable _____ _____, Archdeacon of _____. *Salutation:* Venerable Sir or Dear Archdeacon _____.

Bishop, Episcopal. *Address:* The Right Reverend _____ _____, Bishop of _____. *Salutation:* Right Reverend Sir or Dear Bishop _____.

Bishop, other Protestant. *Address:* The Reverend _____ _____. *Salutation:* Dear Bishop _____.

Bishop, Roman Catholic. *Address:* The Most Reverend _____ _____, Bishop of _____. *Salutation:* Your Excellency or Dear Bishop _____.

Brotherhood, Roman Catholic. *Address:* Brother _____ _____, C.F.C. *Salutation:* Dear Brother or Dear Brother Joseph.

Brotherhood, superior of. *Address:* Brother Joseph C.F.C. Superior. *Salutation:* Dear Brother Joseph.

Cardinal. *Address:* His Eminence Joseph Cardinal Stone. *Salutation:* Your Eminence.

Clergyman/woman, Protestant. *Address:* The Reverend _____ _____ or The Reverend _____ _____, D.D. *Salutation:* Dear Mr./Ms. _____ or Dear Dr. _____.

Dean of a cathedral, Episcopal. *Address:* The Very Reverend _____ _____, Dean of _____. *Salutation:* Dear Dean _____.

Monsignor. *Address:* The Right Reverend Monsignor _____ _____. *Salutation:* Dear Monsignor.

Patriarch, Greek Orthodox. *Address:* His All Holiness Patriarch Joseph. *Salutation:* Your All Holiness.

Patriarch, Russian Orthodox. *Address:* His Holiness the Patriarch of _____. *Salutation:* Your Holiness.

Pope. *Address:* His Holiness The Pope. *Salutation:* Your Holiness or Most Holy Father.

Priest, Roman Catholic. *Address:* The Reverend _____ _____, S.J. *Salutation:* Dear Reverend Father or Dear Father.

Rabbi, man or woman. *Address:* Rabbi _____ _____ or _____ _____ D.D.. *Salutation:* Dear Rabbi _____ or Dear Dr. _____.

Sisterhood, Roman Catholic. *Address:* Sister _____ _____, C.S.J. *Salutation:* Dear Sister or Dear Sister _____.

Sisterhood, superior of. *Address:* The Reverend Mother Superior, S.C. *Salutation:* Reverend Mother.

Diplomats

Ambassador, U.S. *Address:* The Honorable _____ _____ The Ambassador of the United States. *Salutation:* Sir/Madam or Dear Mr./Madam Ambassador.

Ambassador to the U.S. *Address:* His/Her Excellency _____ _____, The Ambassador of _____. *Salutation:* Excellency or Dear Mr./Madam Ambassador.

Chargé d'Affaires, U.S. *Address:* The Honorable _____ _____, United States Chargé d'Affaires. *Salutation:* Dear Mr./Ms. _____ .

Consul, U.S. *Address:* _____ _____, Esq., United States Consul. *Salutation:* Dear Mr./Ms. _____ .

Minister, U.S. or to U.S. *Address:* The Honorable _____ _____, The Minister of _____ . *Salutation:* Sir/Madam or Dear Mr./Madame Minister.

Secretary General, United Nations. *Address:* His/Her Excellency _____ _____, Secretary General of the United Nations. *Salutation:* Dear Mr./Madam/Madame Secretary General.

United Nations Representative (Foreign). *Address:* His/Her Excellency _____ Representative of _____ to the United Nations. *Salutation:* Excellency or My dear Mr./Madame _____

United Nations Representative (U.S.) *Address:* The Honorable _____ _____, United States Representative to the United Nations. *Salutation:* Sir/Madam or Dear Mr./Ms. _____ .

Government Officials

Assemblyman. *Address:* The Honorable _____ . *Salutation:* Dear Mr./Ms. _____ .

Associate Justice, U.S. Supreme Court. *Address:* Mr./Madam Justice _____ . *Salutation:* Dear Mr./Madam Justice or Sir/Madam.

Attorney General, U.S. *Address:* The Honorable _____ _____, Attorney General of the United States. *Salutation:* Dear Mr./Madam or Attorney General.

Cabinet member: *Address:* The Honorable _____ _____, Secretary of _____ . *Salutation:* Sir/Madam or Dear Mr./Madam Secretary.

Chief Justice, U.S. Supreme Court. *Address:* The Chief Justice of the United States. *Salutation:* Dear Mr. Chief Justice.

Commissioner (federal, state, local). *Address:* The Honorable _____ . *Salutation:* Dear Mr./Ms. _____ .

Governor. *Address:* The Honorable _____ _____, Governor of _____ . *Salutation:* Dear Governor _____ .

Judge, Federal: *Address:* The Honorable _____ _____, Judge of the United States District Court for the _____, District of _____ .

Salutation: Sir/Madam or Dear Judge _____ .

Judge, state or local. *Address:* The Honorable _____ _____, Judge of the Court of _____ . *Salutation:* Dear Judge _____ .

Lieutenant Governor. *Address:* The Honorable _____ _____, Lieutenant Governor of _____ . *Salutation:* Dear Mr./Ms. _____ .

Mayor. *Address:* The Honorable _____ _____, Mayor of _____ . *Salutation:* Dear Mayor _____ .

President, U.S. *Address:* The President. *Salutation:* Dear Mr. President.

President, U.S., former. *Address:* The Honorable _____ _____ . *Salutation:* Dear Mr. _____ .

Representative, state. *Address:* The Honorable _____ _____ . *Salutation:* Dear Mr./Ms. _____ .

Representative, U.S. *Address:* The Honorable _____ _____, United States House of Representatives. *Salutation:* Dear Mr./Ms. _____ .

Senator, state. *Address:* The Honorable _____ _____, The State Senate, State Capitol. *Salutation:* Dear Senator _____ .

Senator, U.S. *Address:* The Honorable _____ _____, United States Senate. *Salutation:* Dear Senator _____ .

Speaker, U.S. House of Representatives. *Address:* The Honorable _____ _____, Speaker of the House of Representatives. *Salutation:* Dear Mr./Madam Speaker.

Vice President, U.S. *Address:* The Vice President of the United States. *Salutation:* Sir or Dear Mr. Vice President.

Military and Naval Officers

Rank. *Address:* Full rank, USN (or USCG, USAF, USA, USMC). *Salutation:* Dear (full rank) _____ .

Professions

Attorney. *Address:* Mr./Ms. _____ _____, Attorney at law or _____ _____, Esq. *Salutation:* Dear Mr./Ms. _____ .

Dentist. *Address:* _____ _____, D.D.S. *Salutation:* Dear Dr. _____ .

Physician. *Address:* _____ _____, M.D. *Salutation:* Dear Dr. _____ .

Veterinarian. *Address:* _____ _____, D.V.M. *Salutation:* Dear Dr. _____ .

1. Forms of address do not always follow set guidelines; the type of salutation is often determined by the relationship between correspondents or by the purpose and content of the letter. However, a general style applies to most occasions. In highly formal salutations, when the addressee is a woman, "Madam" should be substituted for "Sir." When the salutation is informal, "Ms.," "Miss," or "Mrs." should be substituted for "Mr." If a woman addressee has previously indicated a preference for a particular form of address, that form should be used.

Reference Books and Other Sources

This cannot be a record of all the thousands of available sources of information. Nevertheless, these selected references will enable the reader to locate additional facts about many subjects. The editors have chosen sources that they believe will be helpful to the general reader.

General References

Encyclopedias are a unique category, since they attempt to cover most subjects quite thoroughly. The most valuable multivolume encyclopedias are the **Encyclopaedia Britannica** and the **Encyclopedia Americana.** Useful one-volume encyclopedias are the **New Columbia Encyclopedia** and the **Random House Encyclopedia.**

Dictionaries and similar "word books" are also unique: **The American Heritage Dictionary, Second College Edition,** containing 200,000 definitions and specialized usage guidance; **The American Heritage Illustrated Encyclopedic Dictionary,** containing 180,000 entries, 275 boxed encyclopedic features, and 175 colored maps of the world; **Webster's Third New International Dictionary, Unabridged; Webster's II New Riverside University Dictionary,** containing 200,000 definitions plus hundreds of word history paragraphs; and the multivolume **Oxford English Dictionary,** providing definitions in historical order. **Roget's II The New Thesaurus,** containing thousands of synonyms grouped according to meaning, assists writers in choosing just the right word. The quick reference set—**The Word Book III** (over 40,000 words spelled and divided), **The Right Word III** (a concise thesaurus), and **The Written Word III** (a concise guide to writing, style, and usage)—are based on **The American Heritage Dictionary** and are intended for the busy reader needing information fast. Two excellent books of quotations are **Bartlett's Familiar Quotations** and **The Oxford Dictionary of Quotations.**

There are a number of useful atlases: the **New York Times Atlas of the World,** a number of historical atlases (Penguin Books), **Oxford Economic Atlas of the World, Rand McNally Cosmopolitan World Atlas: New Census Edition,** and **Atlas of the Historical Geography of the United States** (Greenwood). Many contemporary road atlases of the United States and foreign countries are also available.

A source of information on virtually all subjects is the United States Government Printing Office (GPO). For information, write: Superintendent of Documents, Washington, D.C. 20402.

For help on any subject, consult: **Subject Guide to Books in Print, The New York Times Index,** and the **Reader's Guide to Periodical Literature** in your library.

Specific References

AIDS Answer Book (Network Publishers)
America Votes (Congressional Quarterly, Inc.)
American Indian, Reference Encyclopedia of the (Todd Publications)
American Recipe Collection (Fell)
American Revolution, The (Houghton Mifflin)
Anatomy, Gray's (Churchill)
Antiques and Collectibles Price List, the Kovels' (Crown)
Architectural & Building Technology, Dictionary of (Elsevier)

Architecture, Encyclopedia of World (Orient Book Distributors)
Art, History of (Prentice-Hall)
Art, Oxford Companion to (Oxford University Press)
Art, Who's Who in American (R.R. Bowker)
Art Directory, American (R.R. Bowker)
Associations, Encyclopedia of (Gale Research Co.)
Astronomy, Peterson First Guide (Houghton Mifflin)
Authors, 1000–1900, European (H.W. Wilson)
Authors, Twentieth Century (H.W. Wilson)
Automobile Facts and Figures (Kallman)
Automotive Yearbook (Wards Communication)
Ballet & Modern Dance: A Concise History (Princeton Book Co.)
Banking and Finance, Encyclopedia of (Bankers Publishing Co.)
Baseball Encyclopedia (Macmillan)
Biographical Dictionary, Cambridge (Cambridge University Press)
Biography Yearbook, Current (H.W. Wilson)
Birds, Field Guide to the, Peterson Field Guide Series (Houghton Mifflin)
Black Americans, Who's Who Among (Gale)
Book Review Digest, 1905– (H.W. Wilson)
Catholic Encyclopedia, New (Publishers Guild)
Chemistry, Encyclopedia of (Van Nostrand Rinehold)
Chemistry, Lange's Handbook of, 13th Edition (McGraw Hill)
Christian Church, Oxford Dictionary of the (Oxford University Press)
Citizens Band Radio Rules and Regulations (AMECO)
College Cost Book, 1986–87, The (The College Board)
Composers, Great 1300–1900 (H.W. Wilson)
Composers Since 1900 (H .W. Wilson)
Computer Science and Technology, Encyclopedia of (Dekker)
Computer Software (W.H. Freeman)
Computer Terms, Dictionary of (Barron)
Condo and Co-op Information Book, Complete (Houghton Mifflin)
Congressional Quarterly Almanac (Congressional Quarterly, Inc.)
Consumer Reports (Consumers Union)
Costume, The Dictionary of (Macmillan)
Drama As You Like It (DOK Publications)
Cultural Literacy, The Dictionary of (Houghton Mifflin)
Drama, 20th Century, England, Ireland, the United States (McGraw Hill)
Ecology (Wiley)
Energy: Facts and Future (CRC Printing)
Environmental Politics and Policy, 2nd Edition (Congressional Quarterly)
Environmental Science (Prentice-Hall)
Europa World Year Book (Taylor & Francis)
Fact Books, The Rand McNally (Macmillan)
Facts, Famous First (H.W. Wilson)
Facts on File (Facts on File, Inc.)
Film: A Reference Guide (Greenwood)
(Film) Guide to Movies on Video-cassette (Consumers Reports)
(Finance) Touche Ross Guide to Personal Financial Management (Prentice-Hall)
Football Made Easy (Jonathan David)
Games, Book of (Jazz Press)

Gardening, Encyclopedia of (Revisionist Press)
Gardening, Taylor's Pocket Guides (Houghton Mifflin)
Geography, Dictionary of (Penguin Books)
Government Manual, U.S. (U.S. Office of the Federal Register, Government Printing Office)
History, Album of American (Macmillan)
History, Dictionary of American (Littlefield)
History, Documents of American (Prentice-Hall)
History, Encyclopedia of Latin-American (Greenwood)
History, Encyclopedia of World (Houghton Mifflin)
Hockey, the Illustrated History: An Official Publication of the National Hockey League (Doubleday)
How the World Works, A Guide to Science's Greatest Discoveries (Quill/William Morrow)
Infomania, The Guide to Essential Electronic Services (Houghton Mifflin Company)
Islam, Dictionary of (Orient Book Distributors)
Jazz in the Seventies, Encyclopedia of (Da Capo)
Jewish Concepts, Encyclopedia of (Hebrew Publishers)
Legal Word Book, The (Houghton Mifflin)
Libraries, World Guide to (K. G. Saur)
Library Directory, American (R.R. Bowker)
Literary Market Place (R. R. Bowker)
Literature, Oxford Companion to American (Oxford University Press)
Literature, Oxford Companion to Classical (Oxford University Press)
Literature, Oxford Companion to English (Oxford University Press)
(Literature) Reader's Adviser: A Layman's Guide to Literature (R.R. Bowker)
Medical Encyclopedia, Home (Been Porter)
Medical & Health Sciences Word Book (Houghton Mifflin)
Museums of the World (K.G. Saur)
Music and Musicians, Handbook of American (Da Capo)
Music, Concise Oxford Dictionary of (Oxford University Press)
Music, Harvard Dictionary of (Harvard University Press)
Musical Terms, Dictionary of (Gordon Press)
Mystery Writers, Twentieth Century Crime and (St. Martin's Press)
Mythology (Little, Brown and Co.)
National Park Guide (Prentice-Hall)
New Nations: A Student Handbook (Shoe String)
Numismatist's Fireside Companion, Vol. 2 (Bowers & Merena)
Occupational Outlook Handbook (U.S. Bureau of Labor Statistics, Government Printing Office)
Operas, New Milton Cross Complete Stories of the Great (Doubleday)
Performing Arts Information (Kansas State University)
Physics (Wiley)
Pocket Data Book, U.S.A. (U.S. Department of Commerce, Bureau of the Census, Government Printing Office)
Poetry, Granger's Index to (Columbia University Press)
Politics, Almanac of American (Barone & Co.)
Politics, Who's Who in American (R.R. Bowker)

Popular Music, America, Vol. 2 The Age of Rock (Bowling Green University)
Prescription & Non-Prescription Drugs, Complete Guide to (Price Stern)
Private Schools of the United States (Council for American Private Education (CAPE) Schools)
Radon, A Citizen's Guide to (Government Printing Office)
Religions, The Facts on File Dictionary of (Facts on File)
Robert's Rules of Order Revised (Morrow & Co.)
Science, American Men and Women of (R.R. Bowker)
Science and Technology, Asimov's Biographical Encyclopedia of (Doubleday)
Scientific Encyclopedia, VanNostrand's (VanNostrand Reinhold)
Secretary's Handbook, The Professional (Houghton Mifflin)
Senior Citizens Information Resources, Encyclopedia of (Gale Research Co.)
Shakespeare, The Riverside (Houghton Mifflin)
Ships, Boats, & Vessels, Illustrated Encyclopedia of (Overlook Press)
Social Security Handbook (USGPO)
Stamp Collecting for Beginners (Wilshire)
Stars and Planets, Field Guide to the (Houghton Mifflin)
States, Book of the (Council of State Governments)
Statesman's Year-Book (St. Martin's)
Theater, Oxford Companion to the (Oxford University Press)
United Nations, Demographic Yearbook (Unipub)
United Nations, Statistical Yearbook of the (Unipub)
United States, Historical Statistics of the Colonial Times to 1970 (Revisionist Press)
United States, Statistical Abstract of the (U.S. Department of Commerce, Bureau of the Census, Government Printing Office)
Vitamin Book: A No-Nonsense Consumer Guide (Bantam)
Washington Information Directory (Congressional Quarterly, Inc.)
The Way Things Work (Houghton Mifflin)
Who's Who in America (Marquis)
Wines, Dictionary of American (Morrow)
Women, Notable American (Harvard University Press)
World War I (Houghton Mifflin)
World War II (Houghton Mifflin)
Writer's Market (Writers Digest)
Zip Code and Post Office Directory, National (U.S. Postal Service, Government Printing Office)

See the full range of publications of Dun & Bradstreet and Standard & Poor's for corporate financial and stockholder information.

For detailed information on American colleges and universities, see the many publications of the **American Council on Education.**

Also see many other specialized **Who's Who** volumes not listed here for biographies of famous people in many fields.

WEATHER & CLIMATE

Climate of 100 Selected U.S. Cities

| City | Average Monthly Temperature (°F)[1] | | | | Precipitation | | Snowfall | |
	Jan.	April	July	Oct	Average (in.)[1]	annual (days)[2]	Average annual (in.)[2]	Years[2]
Albany, N.Y.	21.1	46.6	71.4	50.5	35.74	134	65.5	38
Albuquerque, N.M.	34.8	55.1	78.8	57.4	8.12	59	10.6	45
Anchorage, Alaska	13.0	35.4	58.1	34.6	15.20	115	69.2	41[3]
Asheville, N.C.	36.8	55.7	73.2	56.0	47.71	124	17.5	20
Atlanta, Ga.	41.9	61.8	78.6	62.2	48.61	115	1.9	50
Atlantic City, N.J.	31.8	51.0	74.4	55.5	41.93	112	16.4	40[3]
Austin, Texas	49.1	68.7	84.7	69.8	31.50	83	0.9	43
Baltimore, Md.	32.7	54.0	76.8	56.9	41.84	113	21.8	34
Baton Rouge, La.	50.8	68.4	82.1	68.2	55.77	108	0.1	34[3]
Billings, Mont.	20.9	44.6	72.3	49.3	15.09	96	57.2	50
Birmingham, Ala.	42.9	62.8	80.1	62.6	54.52	117	1.3	41
Bismark, N.D.	6.7	42.5	70.4	46.1	15.36	96	40.3	45
Boise, Idaho	29.9	48.6	74.6	51.9	11.71	92	21.4	45
Boston, Mass.	29.6	48.7	73.5	54.8	43.81	127	41.8	49[3]
Bridgeport, Conn.	29.5	48.6	74.0	56.0	41.56	117	26.0	36
Buffalo, N.Y.	23.5	45.4	70.7	51.5	37.52	169	92.2	41
Burlington, Vt.	16.6	42.7	69.6	47.9	33.69	153	78.2	41
Caribou, Maine	10.7	37.3	65.1	43.1	36.59	160	113.3	45
Casper, Wyom.	22.2	42.1	70.9	47.1	11.43	95	80.5	34
Charleston, S.C.	47.9	64.3	80.5	65.8	51.59	113	0.6	42
Charleston, W.Va.	32.9	55.3	74.5	55.9	42.43	151	31.5	37
Charlotte, N.C.	40.5	60.3	78.5	60.7	43.16	111	6.1	45
Cheyenne, Wyom.	26.1	41.8	68.9	47.5	13.31	98	54.1	49
Chicago, Ill.	21.4	48.8	73.0	53.5	33.34	127	40.3	26
Cleveland, Ohio	25.5	48.1	71.6	53.2	35.40	156	53.6	43
Columbia, S.C.	44.7	63.8	81.0	63.4	49.12	109	1.9	37
Columbus, Ohio	27.1	51.4	73.8	53.9	36.97	137	28.3	37[3]
Concord, N.H.	19.9	44.1	69.5	48.3	36.53	125	64.5	43
Dallas–Ft. Worth, Texas	44.0	65.9	86.3	67.9	29.46	78	3.1	31
Denver, Colo.	29.5	47.4	73.4	51.9	15.31	88	59.8	50
Des Moines, Iowa	18.6	50.5	76.3	54.2	30.83	107	34.7	45
Detroit, Mich.	23.4	47.3	71.9	51.9	30.97	133	40.4	26
Dodge City, Kan.	29.5	54.3	80.0	57.7	20.66	78	19.5	42
Duluth, Minn.	6.3	38.3	65.4	44.2	29.68	135	77.4	41[3]
El Paso, Texas	44.2	63.6	82.5	63.6	7.82	47	5.2	45
Fairbanks, Alaska	−12.7	30.2	61.5	25.1	10.37	106	67.5	33
Fargo, N.D.	4.3	42.1	70.6	46.3	19.59	100	35.9	42
Grand Junction, Colo.	25.5	51.7	78.9	54.9	8.00	72	26.1	38
Grand Rapids, Mich.	22.0	46.3	71.4	50.9	34.35	143	72.4	21
Hartford, Conn.	25.2	48.8	73.4	52.4	44.39	127	50.0	30
Helena, Mont.	18.1	42.3	67.9	45.1	11.37	96	47.9	44
Honolulu, Hawaii	72.6	75.7	80.1	79.5	23.47	100	0.0	38[3]
Houston, Texas	51.4	68.7	83.1	69.7	44.76	105	0.4	50
Indianapolis, Ind.	26.0	52.4	75.1	54.8	39.12	125	23.1	53[3]
Jackson, Miss.	45.7	65.1	81.9	65.0	52.82	109	1.2	21
Jacksonville, Fla.	53.2	67.7	81.3	69.5	52.76	116	T	43
Juneau, Alaska	21.8	39.1	55.7	41.8	53.15	220	102.8	41
Kansas City, Mo.	28.4	56.9	80.9	59.6	29.27	98	20.0	43
Knoxville, Tenn .	38.2	59.6	77.6	59.5	47.29	127	12.3	42
Las Vegas, Nev.	44.5	63.5	90.2	67.5	4.19	26	1.4	36
Lexington, Ky.	31.5	55.1	75.9	56.8	45.68	131	16.3	40
Little Rock, Ark.	39.9	62.4	82.1	63.1	49.20	104	5.4	42
Long Beach, Calif.	55.2	60.9	72.8	67.5	11.54	32	T	41[3]
Los Angeles, Calif.	56.0	59.5	69.0	66.3	12.08	36	T	49
Louisville, Ky.	32.5	56.6	77.6	57.7	43.56	125	17.5	37
Madison, Wisc.	15.6	45.8	70.6	49.5	30.84	118	40.8	36
Memphis, Tenn.	39.6	62.6	82.1	62.9	51.57	107	5.5	34
Miami, Fla.	67.1	75.3	82.5	77.9	57.55	129	0.0	42
Milwaukee, Wisc.	18.7	44.6	70.5	50.9	30.94	125	47.0	44

419

City	Average Monthly Temperature (°F)[1]				Precipitation		Snowfall	
	Jan.	April	July	Oct	Average (in.)[1]	annual (days)[2]	Average annual (in.)[2]	Years[2]
Minneapolis–St. Paul, Minn.	11.2	46.0	73.1	49.6	26.36	115	48.9	46
Mobile, Ala.	50.8	68.0	82.2	68.5	64.64	123	0.3	43
Montgomery, Ala.	46.7	65.2	81.7	65.3	49.16	108	0.3	40
Mt. Washington, N.H.	5.1	22.4	48.7	30.5	89.92	209	246.8	52
Nashville, Tenn.	37.1	59.7	79.4	60.2	48.49	119	11.1	43
Newark, N.J.	31.2	52.1	76.8	57.2	42.34	122	28.2	43
New Orleans, La.	52.4	68.7	82.1	69.2	59.74	114	0.2	38[3]
New York, N.Y.	31.8	51.9	76.4	57.5	42.82	119	26.1	40[3]
Norfolk, Va.	39.9	58.2	78.4	61.3	45.22	115	7.9	36
Oklahoma City, Okla.	35.9	60.2	82.1	62.3	30.89	82	9.0	45
Olympia, Wash.	37.2	47.3	63.0	50.1	50.96	164	18.0	43
Omaha, Neb.	20.2	52.2	77.7	54.5	30.34	98	31.1	49[3]
Philadelphia, Pa.	31.2	52.9	76.5	56.5	41.42	117	21.9	42[3]
Phoenix, Ariz.	52.3	68.1	92.3	73.4	7.11	36	T	47[3]
Pittsburgh, Pa.	26.7	50.1	72.0	52.5	36.30	154	44.6	32
Portland, Maine	21.5	42.8	68.1	48.5	43.52	128	72.4	44
Portland, Ore.	38.9	50.4	67.7	54.3	37.39	154	6.8	44
Providence, R.I.	28.2	47.9	72.5	53.2	45.32	124	37.1	31
Raleigh, N.C.	39.6	59.4	77.7	59.7	41.76	112	7.7	40
Reno, Nev.	32.2	46.4	69.5	50.3	7.49	51	25.3	42
Richmond, Va.	36.6	57.9	77.8	58.6	44.07	113	14.6	47
Roswell, N.M.	41.4	61.9	81.4	61.7	9.70	52	11.4	37[3]
Sacramento, Calif.	45.3	58.2	75.6	63.9	17.10	58	0.1	36[3]
Salt Lake City, Utah	28.6	49.2	77.5	53.0	15.31	90	59.1	56
San Antonio, Texas	50.4	69.6	84.6	70.2	29.13	81	0.4	42
San Diego, Calif.	56.8	61.2	70.3	67.5	9.32	43	T	44
San Francisco, Calif.	48.5	54.8	62.2	60.6	19.71	63	T	57
Savannah, Ga.	49.1	66.0	81.2	66.9	49.70	111	0.3	34
Seattle–Tacoma, Wash.	39.1	48.7	64.8	52.4	38.60	158	12.8	40
Sioux Falls, S.D.	12.4	46.4	74.0	49.4	24.12	96	39.9	39
Spokane, Wash.	25.7	45.8	69.7	47.5	16.71	114	51.5	37
Springfield, Ill.	24.6	53.3	76.5	56.0	33.78	114	24.5	37
St. Louis, Mo.	28.8	56.1	78.9	57.9	33.91	111	19.8	48[3]
Tampa, Fla.	59.8	71.5	82.1	74.4	46.73	107	T	38
Toledo, Ohio	23.1	47.8	71.8	51.7	31.78	137	38.3	29
Tucson, Ariz.	51.1	64.9	86.2	70.4	11.14	52	1.2	44
Tulsa, Okla.	35.2	61.0	83.2	62.6	38.77	89	9.0	46
Vero Beach, Fla.	61.9	71.7	81.1	75.2	51.41	n.a.	n.a.	0
Washington, D.C.	35.2	56.7	78.9	59.3	39.00	112	17.0	41[3]
Wilmington, Del.	31.2	52.4	76.0	56.3	41.38	117	20.9	37
Wichita, Kan.	29.6	56.3	81.4	59.1	28.61	85	16.4	31

1. Based on 30 year period 1951–80. Data latest available. 2. Data through 1984 based on number of years as indicated in Years column. 3. For snowfall data where number of years differ from that for precipitation data. T = trace. n.a. = not available. *Source:* National Oceanic and Atmospheric Administration.

Wind Chill Factors

Wind speed (mph)	Thermometer reading (degrees Fahrenheit)																
	35	30	25	20	15	10	5	0	–5	–10	–15	–20	–25	–30	–35	–40	–45
5	33	27	21	19	12	7	0	–5	–10	–15	–21	–26	–31	–36	–42	–47	–52
10	22	16	10	3	–3	–9	–15	–22	–27	–34	–40	–46	–52	–58	–64	–71	–77
15	16	9	2	–5	–11	–18	–25	–31	–38	–45	–51	–58	–65	–72	–78	–85	–92
20	12	4	–3	–10	–17	–24	–31	–39	–46	–53	–60	–67	–74	–81	–88	–95	–103
25	8	1	–7	–15	–22	–29	–36	–44	–51	–59	–66	–74	–81	–88	–96	–103	–110
30	6	–2	–10	–18	–25	–33	–41	–49	–56	–64	–71	–79	–86	–93	–101	–109	–116
35	4	–4	–12	–20	–27	–35	–43	–52	–58	–67	–74	–82	–89	–97	–105	–113	–120
40	3	–5	–13	–21	–29	–37	–45	–53	–60	–69	–76	–84	–92	–100	–107	–115	–123
45	2	–6	–14	–22	–30	–38	–46	–54	–62	–70	–78	–85	–93	–102	–109	–117	–125

NOTES: This chart gives equivalent temperatures for combinations of wind speed and temperatures. For example, the combination of a temperature of 10° Fahrenheit and a wind blowing at 10 mph has a cooling power equal to –9° F. Wind speeds of higher than 45 mph have little additional cooling effect.

World and U.S. Extremes of Climate

Highest recorded temperature

	Place	Date	Degree Fahrenheit	Degree Centigrade
World (Africa)	El Azizia, Libya	Sept. 13, 1922	136	58
North America (U.S.)	Death Valley, Calif.	July 10, 1913	134	57
Asia	Tirat Tsvi, Israel	June 21, 1942	129	54
Australia	Cloncurry, Queensland	Jan. 16, 1889	128	53
Europe	Seville, Spain	Aug. 4, 1881	122	50
South America	Rivadavia, Argentina	Dec. 11, 1905	120	49
Canada	Midale and Yellow Grass, Saskatchewan	July 5, 1937	113	45
Persian Gulf (sea–surface)		August 5, 1924	96	36
South Pole		Dec. 27, 1978	7.5	−14
Antarctica	Vanda Station	Jan. 5, 1974	59	15

Lowest recorded temperature

	Place	Date	Degree Fahrenheit	Degree Centigrade
World (Antarctica)	Vostok	July 21, 1983	−129	−89
Asia	Verkhoyansk/Oimekon	Feb. 6, 1933	−90	−68
Greenland	Northice	Jan. 9, 1954	−87	−66
North America (excl. Greenland)	Snag, Yukon, Canada	Feb. 3, 1947	−81	−63
Alaska	Prospect Creek, Endicott Mts.	Jan. 23, 1971	−80	−62
U.S., excluding Alaska	Rogers Pass, Mont.	Jan. 20, 1954	−70	−56.5
Europe	Ust 'Shchugor, U.S.S.R.	n.a.	−67	−55
South America	Sarmiento, Argentina	Jan. 1, 1907	−27	−33
Africa	Ifrane, Morocco	Feb. 11, 1935	−11	−24
Australia	Charlotte Pass, N.S.W.	July 22, 1947	−8	−22
United States	Prospect Creek, Alaska	Jan. 23, 1971	−80	−62

Greatest rainfalls

	Place	Date	Inches	Centimeters
1 minute (World)	Unionville, Md.	July 4, 1956	1.23	3.1
20 minutes (World)	Curtea–de–Arges, Romania	July 7, 1889	8.1	20.5
42 minutes (World)	Holt, Mo.	June 22, 1947	12	30.5
12 hours (World)	Foc–Foc, La Réunion	Jan. 7–8, 1966	45	114
24 hours (World)	Foc–Foc, La Réeunion	Jan. 7–8, 1966	72	182.5
24 hours (N. Hemisphere)	Paishih, Taiwan	Sept. 10–11, 1963	49	125
24 hours (Australia)	Bellenden Ker, Queensland	Jan. 4, 1979	44	114
24 hours (U.S.)	Alvin, Texas	July 25–26, 1979	43	109
24 hours (Canada)	Ucluelet Brynnor Mines, British Columbia	Oct. 6, 1967	19	49
5 days (World)	Commerson, La Réunion	Jan. 23–28, 1980	156	395
1 month (World)	Cherrapunji, India	July 1861	366	930
12 months (World)	Cherrapunji, India	Aug. 1860–Aug. 1861	1,042	2,647
12 months (U.S.)	Kukui, Maui, Hawaii	Dec. 1981–Dec. 1982	739	1878

Greatest snowfalls

	Place	Date	Inches	Centimeters
1 month (U.S.)	Tamarack, Calif.	Jan. 1911	390	991
24 hours (N. America)	Silver Lake, Colo.	April 14–15, 1921	76	192.5
24 hours (Alaska)	Thompson Pass	Dec. 29, 1955	62	157.5
19 hours (France)	Bessans	April 5–6, 1969	68	173
1 storm (N. America)	Mt. Shasta Ski Bowl, Calif.	Feb. 13–19, 1959	189	480
1 storm (Alaska)	Thompson Pass	Dec. 26–31, 1955	175	445.5
1 season (N. America)	Paradise Ranger Sta., Wash.	1971–1972	1,122	2,850
1 season (Alaska)	Thompson Pass	1952–1953	974.5	2,475
1 season (Canada)	Revelstoke Mt. Copeland, British Columbia	1971–1972	964	2,446.5

Source: U.S. Army Corps of Engineers, Engineer Topographic Laboratories.

Tropical Storms and Hurricanes, 1886–1990

	Jan.–April	May	June	July	Aug.	Sept.	Oct.	Nov.	Dec.	Total
Number of tropical storms (incl. hurricanes)	3	14	56	68	215	299	186	42	6	889
Number of tropical storms that reached hurricane intensity	1	3	23	36	149	188	95	21	3	519

Other Recorded Extremes

Highest average annual mean temperature (World): Dallol, Ethiopia (Oct. 1960–Dec. 1966), 94° F (35° C). **(U.S.):** Key West, Fla. (30–year normal), 78.2° F (25.7° C).

Lowest average annual mean temperature (Antarctica): Plateau Station –70° F (–57° C). **(U.S.):** Barrow, Alaska (30–year normal), 9.3° F (–13° C).

Greatest average yearly rainfall (U.S.): Mt. Waialeale, Kauai, Hawaii (32–year avg), 460 in. (1,168 cm). **(India):** Cherrapunji (74–year avg), 450 in. (1,143 cm).

Minimum average yearly rainfall (Chile): Arica (59–year avg), 0.03 in. (0.08 cm) (no rainfall for 14 consecutive years). **(U.S.):** Death Valley, Calif. (42–year avg), 1.63 in. (4.14 cm). Bagdad, Calif., holds the U.S. record for the longest period with no measurable rain, 767 days, from Oct. 3, 1912 to Nov. 8, 1914).

Hottest summer avg in Western Hemisphere (U.S.): Death Valley, Calif., 98° F (36.7° C).

Longest hot spell (W. Australia): Marble Bar, 100° F (38° C) (or above) for 162 consecutive days, Oct. 30, 1923–Apr. 7, 1924.

Largest hailstone (U.S.): Coffeyville, KS, 17.5 in. (44.5 cm), Sept. 3, 1979.

Weather Glossary

blizzard: storm characterized by strong winds, low temperatures, and large amounts of snow.

blowing snow: snow lifted from ground surface by wind; restricts visibility.

cold wave warning: indicates that a change to abnormally cold weather is expected; greater than normal protective measures will be required.

cyclone: circulation of winds rotating counterclockwise in the northern hemisphere and clockwise in the southern hemisphere. Hurricanes and tornadoes are both examples of cyclones.

drifting snow: strong winds will blow loose or falling snow into significant drifts.

drizzle: uniform close precipitation of tiny drops with diameter of less than .02 inch.

flash flood: dangerous rapid rise of water levels in streams, rivers, or over land area.

freezing rain or drizzle: rain or drizzle that freezes on contact with the ground or other objects forming a coating of ice on exposed surfaces.

gale warning: winds in the 33–48 knot (38–55 mph) range forecast.

hail: small balls of ice falling separately or in lumps; usually associated with thunderstorms and temperatures that may be well above freezing.

hazardous driving warnings: indicates that drizzle, freezing rain, snow, sleet, or strong winds make driving conditions difficult.

heavy snow warnings: issued when 4 inches or more of snow are expected to fall in a 12–hour period or when 6 inches or more are anticipated in a 24–hour period.

hurricane: devastating cyclonic storm; winds over 74 mph near storm center; usually tropical in origin; called cyclone in Indian Ocean, typhoon in the Pacific.

hurricane warning: winds in excess of 64 knots (74 mph) in connection with hurricane.

rain: precipitation of liquid particles with diameters larger than .02 inch.

sleet: translucent or transparent ice pellets; frozen rain; generally a winter phenomenon.

small craft warning: indicates winds as high as 33 knots (38 mph) and sea conditions dangerous to small boats.

snow flurries: snow falling for a short time at intermittent periods; accumulations are usually small.

snow squall: brief, intense falls of snow, usually accompanied by gusty winds.

storm warnings: winds greater than 48 knots (55 mph) are forecast.

temperature–humidity index (THI): measure of personal discomfort based on the combined effects of temperature and humidity. Most people are uncomfortable when the THI is 75. A THI of 80 produces acute discomfort for almost everyone.

tidal waves: series of ocean waves caused by earthquakes; can reach speeds of 600 mph; they grow in height as they reach shore and can crest as high as 100 feet.

thunder: the sound produced by the rapid expansion of air heated by lightning.

tornado: dangerous whirlwind associated with the cumulonimbus clouds of severe thunderstorms; winds up to 300 mph.

tornado warning: tornado has actually been detected by radar or sighted in designated area.

tornado watch: potential exists in the watch area for storms that could contain tornadoes.

travelers' warning: *see* hazardous driving warning.

tsunami: *see* tidal waves.

wind–chill factor: combined effect of temperature and wind speed as compared to equivalent temperature in calm air.

During a Hurricane

Source: Federal Emergency Management Agency and NOAA.

Remain indoors during a hurricane. Blowing debris can injure and kill. Travel is extremely dangerous. Be especially wary of the "eye" of the hurricane. If the storm center passes directly overhead, there will be a lull in the wind lasting from a few minutes to half-an-hour or more. At the other side of the "eye" the winds will increase rapidly to hurricane force, and will come from the opposite direction.

Record Highest Temperatures by State

State	Temp. °F	Temp °C	Date	Station	Elevation, feet
Alabama	112	44	Sept. 5, 1925	Centerville	345
Alaska	100	38	June 27, 1915	Fort Yukon	est. 420
Arizona	127	53	July 7, 1905*	Parker	345
Arkansas	120	49	Aug. 10, 1936	Ozark	396
California	134	57	July 10, 1913	Greenland Ranch	−178
Colorado	118	48	July 11, 1888	Bennett	5,484
Connecticut	105	41	July 22, 1926	Waterbury	400
Delaware	110	43	July 21, 1930	Millsboro	20
D.C.	106	41	July 20, 1930	Washington	410
Florida	109	43	June 29, 1931	Monticello	207
Georgia	113	45	May 27, 1978	Greenville	860
Hawaii	100	38	Apr. 27, 1931	Pahala	850
Idaho	118	48	July 28, 1934	Orofino	1,027
Illinois	117	47	July 14, 1954	E. St. Louis	410
Indiana	116	47	July 14, 1936	Collegeville	672
Iowa	118	48	July 20, 1934	Keokuk	614
Kansas	121	49	July 24, 1936*	Alton (near)	1,651
Kentucky	114	46	July 28, 1930	Greensburg	581
Louisiana	114	46	Aug. 10, 1936	Plain Dealing	268
Maine	105	41	July 10, 1911*	North Bridgton	450
Maryland	109	43	July 10, 1936*	Cumberland & Frederick	623;325
Massachusetts	107	42	Aug. 2, 1975	New Bedford & Chester	120;640
Michigan	112	44	July 13, 1936	Mio	963
Minnesota	114	46	July 6, 1936*	Moorhead	904
Mississippi	115	46	July 29, 1930	Holly Springs	600
Missouri	118	48	July 14, 1954*	Warsaw & Union	687;560
Montana	117	47	July 5, 1937	Medicine Lake	1,950
Nebraska	118	48	July 24, 1936*	Minden	2,169
Nevada	122	50	June 23, 1954*	Overton	1,240
New Hampshire	106	41	July 4, 1911	Nashua	125
New Jersey	110	43	July 10, 1936	Runyon	18
New Mexico	116	47	July 14, 1934*	Orogrande	4,171
New York	108	42	July 22, 1926	Troy	35
North Carolina	110	43	Aug. 21, 1983	Fayetteville	81
North Dakota	121	49	July 6, 1936	Steele	1,857
Ohio	113	45	July 21, 1934*	Gallipolis (near)	673
Oklahoma	120	49	July 26, 1943*	Tishomingo	670
Oregon	119	48	Aug. 10, 1898	Pendleton	1,074
Pennsylvania	111	44	July 10, 1936*	Phoenixville	100
Rhode Island	104	40	Aug. 2, 1975	Providence	51
South Carolina	111	44	June 28, 1954*	Camden	170
South Dakota	120	49	July 5, 1936	Gannvalley	1,750
Tennessee	113	45	Aug. 9, 1930*	Perryville	377
Texas	120	49	Aug. 12, 1936	Seymour	1,291
Utah	117	47	July 5, 1895	Saint George	2,880
Vermont	105	41	July 4, 1911	Vernon	310
Virginia	110	43	July 15, 1954	Balcony Falls	725
Washington	118	48	Aug. 5, 1961*	Ice Harbor Dam	475
West Virginia	112	44	July 10, 1936*	Martinsburg	435
Wisconsin	114	46	July 13, 1936	Wisconsin Dells	900
Wyoming	114	46	July 12, 1900	Basin	3,500

*Also on earlier dates at the same or other places. *Source:* National Climatic Data Center, Atlanta, and Storm Phillips, STORMFAX, INC.

Record Lowest Temperatures by State

State	Temp. °F	Temp °C	Date	Station	Elevation, feet
Alabama	−27	−33	Jan. 30, 1966	New Market	760
Alaska	−80	−62	Jan. 23, 1971	Prospect Creek	1,100
Arizona	−40	−40	Jan. 7, 1971	Hawley Lake	8,180
Arkansas	−29	−34	Feb. 13, 1905	Pond	1,250
California	−45	−43	Jan. 20, 1937	Boca	5,532
Colorado	−60	−51	Jan. 1, 1979*	Maybell	5,920
Connecticut	−32	−36	Feb. 16, 1943	Falls Village	585
Delaware	−17	−27	Jan. 17, 1893	Millsboro	20
D.C.	−15	−26	Feb. 11, 1899	Washington	410
Florida	−2	−19	Feb. 13, 1899	Tallahassee	193
Georgia	−17	−27	Jan. 27, 1940	CCC Camp F–16	est. 1,000
Hawaii	14	−11	Jan. 2, 1961	Haleakala, Maui Is	9,750
Idaho	−60	−51	Jan. 18, 1943	Island Park Dam	6,285
Illinois	−35	−37	Jan. 22, 1930	Mount Carroll	817
Indiana	−35	−37	Feb. 2, 1951	Greensburg	954
Iowa	−47	−44	Jan. 12, 1912	Washta	1,157
Kansas	−40	−40	Feb. 13, 1905	Lebanon	1,812
Kentucky	−34	−37	Jan. 28, 1963	Cynthiana	684
Louisiana	−16	−27	Feb. 13, 1899	Minden	194
Maine	−48	−44	Jan. 19, 1925	Van Buren	510
Maryland	−40	−40	Jan. 13, 1912	Oakland	2,461
Massachusetts	−34	−37	Jan. 18, 1957	Birch Hill Dam	840
Michigan	−51	−46	Feb. 9, 1934	Vanderbilt	785
Minnesota	−59	−51	Feb. 16, 1903*	Pokegama Dam	1,280
Mississippi	−19	−28	Jan. 30, 1966	Corinth	420
Missouri	−40	−40	Feb. 13, 1905	Warsaw	700
Montana	−70	−57	Jan. 20, 1954	Rogers Pass	5,470
Nebraska	−47	−44	Feb. 12, 1899	Camp Clarke	3,700
Nevada	−50	−46	Jan. 8, 1937	San Jacinto	5,200
New Hampshire	−46	−43	Jan. 28, 1925	Pittsburg	1,575
New Jersey	−34	−37	Jan. 5, 1904	River Vale	70
New Mexico	−50	−46	Feb. 1, 1951	Gavilan	7,350
New York	−52	−47	Feb. 18, 1979*	Old Forge	1,720
North Carolina	−29	−37	Jan. 30, 1966	Mt. Mitchell	6,525
North Dakota	−60	−51	Feb. 15, 1936	Parshall	1,929
Ohio	−39	−39	Feb. 10, 1899	Milligan	800
Oklahoma	−27	−33	Jan. 18, 1930	Watts	958
Oregon	−54	−48	Feb. 10, 1933*	Seneca	4,700
Pennsylvania	−42	−41	Jan. 5, 1904	Smethport	est. 1,500
Rhode Island	−23	−31	Jan. 11, 1942	Kingston	100
South Carolina	−20	−28	Jan. 18, 1977	Caesars Head	3,100
South Dakota	−58	−50	Feb. 17, 1936	McIntosh	2,277
Tennessee	−32	−36	Dec. 30, 1917	Mountain City	2,471
Texas	−23	−31	Feb. 8, 1933*	Seminole	3,275
Utah	−50	−51	Jan. 5, 1913*	Strawberry Tunnel	7,650
Vermont	−50	−46	Dec. 30, 1933	Bloomfield	915
Virginia	−29	−34	Feb. 10, 1899	Monterey	—
Washington	−48	−44	Dec. 30, 1968	Mazama & Winthrop	2,120;1,765
West Virginia	−37	−38	Dec. 30, 1917	Lewisburg	2,200
Wisconsin	−54	−48	Jan. 24, 1922	Danbury	908
Wyoming	−63	−53	Feb. 9, 1933	Moran	6,770

*Also on earlier dates at the same or other places. *Source:* National Climatic Data Center, Atlanta, and Storm Phillips, STORMFAX, INC.

Record High and Low Temperature in U.S. for Each Month

Source: National Climatic Data Center, Atlanta, and Storm Phillips, STORMFAX, Inc.

January

The highest temperature ever recorded for the month of January occurred on January 17, 1936, again in 1954, in Laredo, Tex. (elevation 421 ft) where the temperature reached 98° F.

The lowest temperature ever recorded for the month of January occurred on January 20, 1954, in Rogers Pass, Mont. (elevation 5,470 ft) where the temperature fell to –70° F.

February

The highest temperature ever recorded for the month of February occurred on February 3, 1963, in Montezuma, Ariz. (elevation 735 ft) where the temperature reached 105° F.

The lowest temperature ever recorded for the month of February occurred on February 9, 1933, at the Riverside Ranger Station in Montana (elevation 6,700 ft) where the temperature fell to –66° F.

March

The highest temperature ever recorded for the month of March occurred on March 31, 1954, in Rio Grande City, Tex. (elevation 168 ft) where the temperature reached 108° F.

The lowest temperature ever recorded for the month of March occurred on March 17, 1906, in Snake River, Wyo. (elevation 6,862 ft) where the temperature dropped to –50° F.

April

The highest temperature ever recorded for the month of April occurred on April 25, 1898, at Volcano Springs, Calif. (elevation –220 ft) where the temperature reached 118° F.

The lowest temperature ever recorded for the month of April occurred on April 5, 1945, in Eagle Nest, N. Mex. (elevation 8,250 ft) where the temperature dropped to –36° F.

May

The highest temperature ever recorded for the month of May occurred on May 27, 1896, in Salton, Calif. (elevation –263 ft) where the temperature reached 124° F.

The lowest temperature ever recorded for the month of May occurred on May 7, 1964, in White Mountain 2, Calif. (elevation 12,470 ft) where the temperature dropped to –15° F.

June

The highest temperature ever recorded for the month of June occurred on June 15, 1896, at Fort Mohave, Ariz. (elevation 555 ft) where the temperature reached 127° F.

The lowest temperature ever recorded for the month of June occurred on June 13, 1907, in Tamarack, Calif. (elevation 8,000 ft) where the temperature dropped to 2° F.

July

The highest temperature ever recorded for the month of July occurred on July 10, 1913, at Greenland Ranch, Calif. (elevation –178 ft) where the temperature reached 134° F.

The lowest temperature ever recorded for the month of July occurred on July 21, 1911, at Painter, Wyo. (elevation 6,800 ft) where the temperature fell to 10° F.

August

The highest temperature ever recorded for the month of August occurred on August 17, 1885, at Amos, Calif. (elevation –172 ft) where the temperature reached 130° F.

The lowest temperature ever recorded for the month of August occurred on August 25, 1910, in Bowen, Mont. (elevation 6,080 ft) where the temperature fell to 10° F.

September

The highest temperature ever recorded for the month of September occurred on September 2, 1950, in Mecca, Calif. (elevation –175 ft) where the temperature reached 126° F.

The lowest temperature ever recorded for the month of September occurred on September 24, 1926, at Riverside Ranger Station, Mont. (elevation 6,700 ft) where the temperature fell to –9 F.

October

The highest temperature ever recorded for the month of October occurred on October 5, 1917, in Sentinel, Ariz. (elevation 685 ft) where the temperature reached 116° F.

The lowest temperature ever recorded for the month of October occurred on October 29, 1917, in Soda Butte, Wyo. (elevation 6,600 ft) where the temperature fell to –33° F.

November

The highest temperature ever recorded for the month of November occurred on November 12, 1906, in Craftonville, Calif. (elevation 1,759 ft) where the temperature reached 105° F.

The lowest temperature ever recorded for the month of November occurred on November 16, 1959, at Lincoln, Mont. (elevation 5,130 ft) where the temperature fell to –53° F.

December

The highest temperature ever recorded for the month of December occurred on December 8, 1938, in La Mesa, Calif. (elevation 539 ft) where the temperature reached 100° F.

The lowest temperature ever recorded for the month of December occurred on December 19, 1924, at Riverside Ranger Station, Mont. (elevation 6,700 ft) where the temperature fell to –59° F.

Temperature Extremes in The United States

Source: National Oceanic and Atmospheric Administration, Environmental Data and Information Service, and National Center Climatic Center

The Highest Temperature Extremes

Greenland Ranch, California, with 134° F (56.67° C) on July 10, 1913, holds the record for the highest temperature ever officially observed in the United States. This station was located in barren Death Valley, 178 feet below sea level. Death Valley is about 140 miles long, four to six miles wide, and oriented north to south in southwestern California. Much of the valley is below sea level and is flanked by towering mountain ranges with Mt. Whitney, the highest landmark in the 48 conterminous states, rising to 14,495 feet above sea level, less than 100 miles to the west. Death Valley has the hottest summers in the Western Hemisphere, and is the only known place in the United States where nightime temperatures sometimes remain above 100° F (37.78° C).

The highest annual normal (1941–70 mean) temperature in the United States, 78.2° F (25.67° C), and the highest summer (June–August) normal temperature, 92.8° F (33.78° C), are for Death Valley, California. The highest winter (December–February) normal temperature is 72.8° F (22.67° C) for Honolulu, Hawaii.

Amazing temperature rises of 40° to 50° F (4.44 to 10° C) in a few minutes occasionally may be brought about by chinook winds.

Some Outstanding Temperature Rises

In 12 hours: 83° F (46.11° C), Granville, N.D., Feb. 21, 1918, from –33° F to 50° F (–36.11 to 10° C) from early morning to late afternoon.

In 15 minutes: 42° F (23.34° C), Fort Assinniboine, Mont., Jan. 19, 1892, from –5° F to 37° F (–20.56 to 2.78° C).

In seven minutes: 34° F (18.89° C), Kipp, Mont., Dec. 1, 1896. The observer also reported that a total rise of 80° F (44.44° C) occurred in a few hours and that 30 inches of snow disappeared in one–half day.

In two minutes: 49° F (27.22° C), Spearfish, S.D., Jan. 22, 1943 from –4° F (–20° C) at 7:30 a.m. to 45° F (7.22° C) at 7:32 a.m.

The Lowest Temperature Extremes

The lowest temperature on record in the United States, –79.8° F (–62.1° C), was observed at Prospect Creek Camp in the Endicott Mountains of northern Alaska (latitude 66° 48′N, longitude 150° 40′W) on Jan. 23, 1971. The lowest ever recorded in the conterminous 48 states, –69.7° F (–56.5° C), occurred at Rogers Pass, in Lewis and Clark County, Mont., on Jan. 20, 1954. Rogers Pass is in mountainous and heavily forested terrain about one–half mile east of and 140 feet below the summit of the Continental Divide.

The lowest annual normal (1941–70 mean) temperature in the United States is 9.3° F (–12.68° C) for Barrow, Alaska, which lies on the Arctic coast. Barrow also has the coolest summers (June–August) with a normal temperature of 36.4° F (2.44° C). The lowest winter (December–February) normal temperature, is –15.7° F (–26.5° C) for Barter Island on the arctic coast of northeast Alaska.

In the 48 conterminous states, Mt. Washington, N.H. (elevation 6,262 feet) has the lowest annual normal temperature 26.9° F (–2.72° C) and the lowest normal summer temperature, 46.8° F (8.22° C). A few stations in the northeastern United States and in the upper Rocky Mountains have normal annual temperatures in the 30s; summer normal temperatures at these stations are in the low 50s. Winter normal temperatures are lowest in northeastern North Dakota, 5.6° F (–14.23° C) for Langdon Experiment Farm, and in northwestern Minnesota, 5.3° F (–14.83° C) for Hallock.

Some Outstanding Temperature Falls

In 24 hours: 100° F (55.57° C), Browning, Mont., Jan. 23–24, 1916, from 44° to –56° F (6.67° to –48.9° C).

In 12 hours: 84° F (46.67° C), Fairfield, Mont., Dec. 24, 1924, from 63° (17.22° C) at noon to –21° F (–29.45° C) at midnight.

In 2 hours: 62° F (34.45° C), Rapid City, S.D., Jan. 12, 1911, from 49° F (9.45° C) at 6:00 a.m. to –13° F (–25° C) at 8:00 a.m.

In 27 minutes: 58° F (32.22° C), Spearfish, S.D., Jan. 22, 1943, from 54° F (12.22 ° C) at 9:00 a.m. to –4° F (–20° C) at 9:27 a.m.

In 15 minutes: 47° F (26.11° C), Rapid City, S.D., Jan. 10, 1911, from 55° F (12.78° C) at 7:00 a.m. to 8° F (–13.33° C). at 7:15 a.m.

1. A warm, dry wind that descends from the eastern slopes of the Rocky Mountains, causing a rapid rise in temperature.

Winter Indoor Comfort and Relative Humidity

Compared to summer when the moisture content of the air (relative humidity) is an important factor of body discomfort, air moisture has a lesser effect on the human body during outdoor winter activities. But it is a big factor for winter indoor comfort because it has a direct bearing on health and energy consumption.

The colder the outdoor temperature, the more heat must be added indoors for body comfort. However, the heat that is added will cause a drying effect and lower the indoor relative humidity, unless an indoor moisture source is present.

While a room temperature between 71° and 77° F may be comfortable for short periods of time under very dry conditions, prolonged exposure to dry air has varying effects on the human body and usually causes discomfort. The moisture content of the air is important, and by increasing the relative humidity to

Average Indoor Relative Humidity, %, for January

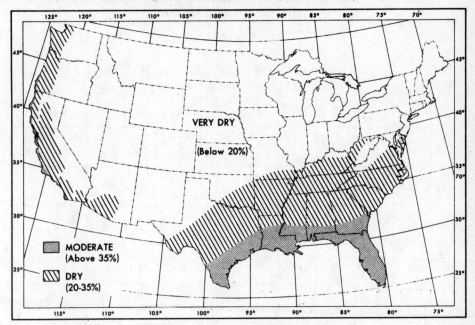

VERY DRY

(Below 20%)

MODERATE
(Above 35%)

DRY
(20-35%)

Source: National Oceanic and Atmospheric Administration, Environmental Data and Information Service, National Climatic Center.

above 50% within the above temperature range, 80% or more of all average dressed persons would feel comfortable.050

Effects of Dry Air on the Body

Studies have shown that dry air has four main effects on the human body:

1. Breathing dry air is a potential health hazard which can cause such respiratory ailments as asthma, bronchitis, sinusitis, and nosebleeds, or general dehydration since body fluids are depleted during respiration.

2. Skin moisture evaporation can cause skin irritations and eye itching.

3. Irritative effects, such as static electricity which causes mild shocks when metal is touched, are common when the air moisture is low.

4. The "apparent temperature" of the air is lower than what the thermometer indicates, and the body "feels" colder.

These problems can be reduced by simply increasing the indoor relative humidity. This can be done through use of humidifiers, vaporizers, steam ge nerators, sources such as large pans, or water containers made of porous ceramics. Even wet towels or water in a bathtub will be of some help. The lower the room temperature the easier the relative humidity can be brought to its desired level. A relative humidity indicator (hygrometer) may be of assistance in determining the humidity in the house.

Referring to item 4, a more detailed discussion is necessary. While the indoor temperature as read from a thermometer may be 75° F, the apparent temperature (what it feels like) may be warmer or colder depending on the moisture content of the air. Apparent temperature can vary as much as 8° F within a relative humidity range of 10 to 80 percent (these limits are generally possible in a closed room). Because of evaporation the human body cools when exposed to dry air, and the sense of coldness increases as the humidity decreases. With a room temperature of 70° F, for example, a person will feel colder in a dry room than in a moist room; this is especially noticeable when entering a dry room after bathing.

The table on the following page gives apparent temperatures for various combinations of room temperature and relative humidity. As an example of how to read the table, a room temperature of 70° F combined with a relative humidity of 10% feels like 64° F, but at 80% it feels like 71° F.

Although degrees of comfort vary with age, health, activity, clothing, and body characteristics, the table can be used as a general guideline when raising the apparent temperature and the level of comfort through an increase in room moisture, rather than by an addition of heat to the room. This method of changing the apparent temperature can give the direct benefit of reducing heating costs because comfort can be maintained with a lower thermostat setting if moisture is added. For example, an apparent comfortable temperature can be maintained with a thermostat setting of 75° F with 20% relative humidity or with a 70° F setting with 80 percent humidity. A relative humidity of 20 percent is common for homes without a humidifier during winter in the northern United States.

Apparent Temperature for Values of Room Temperature and Relative Humidity

RELATIVE HUMIDITY (%)

ROOM TEMPERATURE (F)	0	10	20	30	40	50	60	70	80	90	100
75	68	69	71	72	74	75	76	76	77	78	79
74	66	68	69	71	72	73	74	75	76	77	78
73	65	67	68	70	71	72	73	74	75	76	77
72	64	65	67	68	70	71	72	73	74	75	76
71	63	64	66	67	68	70	71	72	73	74	75
70	63	64	65	66	67	68	69	70	71	72	73
69	62	63	64	65	66	67	68	69	70	71	72
68	61	62	63	64	65	66	67	68	69	70	71
67	60	61	62	63	64	65	66	67	68	68	69
66	59	60	61	62	63	64	65	66	67	67	68
65	59	60	61	61	62	63	64	65	65	66	67
64	58	59	60	60	61	62	63	64	64	65	66
63	57	58	59	59	60	61	62	62	63	64	64
62	56	57	58	58	59	60	61	61	62	63	63
61	56	57	57	58	59	59	60	60	61	61	62
60	55	56	56	57	58	58	59	59	60	60	61

Source: National Oceanic and Atmospheric Administration, Environmental Data and Information Service and National Climatic Center.

WEIGHTS & MEASURES

Measures and Weights

Source: Department of Commerce, National Bureau of Standards.

The International System (Metric)

The International System of Units is a modernized version of the metric system, established by international agreement, that i.e. provides a logical and interconnected framework for all measurements in science, industry, and commerce. The system is built on a foundation of seven basic units, and all other units are derived from them. (Use of metric weights and measures was legalized in the United States in 1866, and our customary units of weights and measures are defined in terms of the meter and kilogram.)

Length. Meter. Up until 1893, the meter was defined as 1,650,764.73 wavelengths in vacuum of the orange-red line of the spectrum of krypton-86. Since then, it is equal to the distance traveled by light in a vacuum in 1/299,792,458 of a second.

Time. Second. The second is defined as the duration of 9,192,631,770 cycles of the radiation associated with a specified transition of the cesium 133 atom.

Mass. Kilogram. The standard for the kilogram is a cylinder of platinum-iridium alloy kept by the International Bureau of Weights and Measures at Paris. A duplicate at the National Bureau of Standards serves as the mass standard for the United States. The kilogram is the only base unit still defined by a physical object.

Temperature. Kelvin. The kelvin is defined as the fraction 1/273.16 of the thermodynamic temperature of the triple point of water; that is, the point at which water forms an interface of solid, liquid and vapor. This is defined as 0.01°C on the Centigrade or Celsius scale and 32.02°F on the Fahrenheit scale. The temperature 0°K is called "absolute zero."

Electric Current. Electric current. The ampere is defined as that current that, if maintained in each of two long parallel wires separted by one meter in free space, would produce a force between the two wires (due to their magnetic fields) of 2×10^{-7} newton for each meter of length. (A newton is the unit of force which when applied to one kilogram mass would experience an acceleration of one meter per second per second.)

Luminous Intensity. Candela. The candela is defined as the luminous intensity of 1/600,000 of a square meter of a cavity at the temperature of freezing platinum (2,042K).

Amount of Substance. Mole. The mole is the amount of substance of a system that contains as many elementary entities as there are atoms in 0.012 kilogram of carbon-12.

Tables of Metric Weights and Measures

LINEAR MEASURE

10 millimeters (mm) = 1 centimeter (cm)
10 centimeters = 1 decimeter (dm) = 100 millimeters
10 decimeters = 1 meter (m) = 1,000 millimeters
10 meters = 1 dekameter (dam)
10 dekameters = 1 hectometer (hm) = 100 meters
10 hectometers = 1 kilometer (km) = 1,000 meters

AREA MEASURE

100 square millimeters (mm^2) = 1 sq centimeter (cm^2)
10,000 square centimeters = 1 sq meter (m^2) = 1,000,000 sq millimeters
100 square meters = 1 are (a)
100 ares = 1 hectare (ha) = 10,000 sq meters
100 hectares = 1 sq kilometer (km^2) = 1,000,000 sq meters

VOLUME MEASURE

10 milliliters (ml) = 1 centiliter (cl)
10 centiliters = 1 deciliter (dl) = 100 milliliters
10 deciliters = 1 liter (l) = 1,000 milliliters
10 liters = 1 dekaliter (dal)
10 dekaliters = 1 hectoliter (hl) = 100 liters
10 hectoliters = 1 kiloliter (kl) = 1,000 liters

CUBIC MEASURE

1,000 cubic millimeters (mm^3) = 1 cu centimeter (cm^3)
1,000 cubic centimeters = 1 cu decimeter (dm^3) = 1,000,000 cu millimeters
1,000 cubic decimeters = 1 cu meter (m^3) = 1 stere = 1,000,000 cu centimeters = 1,000,000,000 cu millimeters

WEIGHT

10 milligrams (mg) = 1 centigram (cg)
10 centigrams = 1 decigram (dg) = 100 milligrams
10 decigrams = 1 gram (g) = 1,000 milligrams
10 grams = 1 dekagram (dag)
10 dekagrams = 1 hectogram (hg) = 100 grams
10 hectograms = 1 kilogram (kg) = 1,000 grams
1,000 kilograms = 1 metric ton (t)

Tables of Customary U.S. Weights and Measures

LINEAR MEASURE

12 inches (in.) =	1 foot (ft)
3 feet =	1 yard (yd)
5 1/2 yards =	1 rod (rd), pole, or perch (16 1/2 ft)
40 rods =	1 furlong (fur) = 220 yds = 660 ft
8 furlongs =	1 statute mile (mi.) = 1,760 yds = 5,280 ft
3 land miles =	1 league
5,280 feet =	1 statute or land mile
6,076.11549 feet =	1 international nautical mile

AREA MEASURE

144 square inches =	1 sq ft
9 square feet =	1 sq yd = 1,296 sq in.
30 1/4 square yards =	1 sq rd = 272 1/4 sq ft
160 square rods =	1 acre = 4,840 sq yds = 43,560 sq ft
640 acres =	1 sq mi.
1 mile square =	1 section (of land)
6 miles square =	1 township = 36 sections = 36 sq mi.

CUBIC MEASURE

1,728 cubic inches =	1 cu ft
27 cubic feet =	1 cu yd

LIQUID MEASURE

When necessary to distinguish the liquid pint or quart from the dry pint or quart, the word "liquid" or the abbreviation "liq" should be used in combination with the name or abbreviation of the liquid unit.

4 gills (gi) =	1 pint (pt) (= 28.875 cu in.)
2 pints =	1 quart (qt) (= 57.75 cu in.)
4 quarts =	1 gallon (gal) (= 231 cu in.) = 8 pts = 32 gills

APOTHECARIES' FLUID MEASURE

60 minims (min.) =	1 fluid dram (fl dr) (= 0.2256 cu in.)
8 fluid drams =	1 fluid ounce (fl oz) (= 1.8047 cu in.)
16 fluid ounces =	1 pt (= 28.875 cu in.) = 128 fl drs
2 pints =	1 qt (= 57.75 cu in.) = 32 fl oz = 256 fl drs
4 quarts =	1 gal (= 231 cu in.) = 128 fl oz = 1,024 fl drs

DRY MEASURE

When necessary to distinguish the dry pint or quart from the liquid pint or quart; the word "dry" should be used in combination with the name or abbreviation of the dry unit.

2 pints =	1 qt (=67.2006 cu in.)
8 quarts =	1 peck (pk) (=537.605 cu in.) = 16 pts
4 pecks =	1 bushel (bu) (= 2,150.42 cu in.) = 32 qts

AVOIRDUPOIS WEIGHT

When necessary to distinguish the avoirdupois dram from the apothecaries dram, or to distinguish the avoirdupois dram or ounce from the fluid dram or ounce, or to distinguish the avoirdupois ounce or pound from the troy or apothecaries, ounce or pound, the word "avoirdupois" or the abbreviation "avdp" should be used in combination with the name or abbreviation of the avoirdupois unit. (The "grain" is the same in avoirdupois, troy, and apothecaries weights.)

27 11/32 grains =	1 dram (dr)
16 drams =	1 oz = 437 1/2 grains
16 ounces =	1 lb = 256 drams = 7,000 grains
100 pounds =	1 hundredweight (cwt)[1]
20 hundredweights =	1 ton (tn) = 2,000 lbs[1]

In "gross" or "long" measure, the following values are recognized:

112 pounds =	1 gross or long cwt[1]
20 gross or long hundredweights =	1 gross or long ton = 2,240 lbs[1]

1. When the terms "hundredweight" and "ton" are used unmodified, they are commonly understood to mean the 100–pound hundredweight and the 2,000–pound ton, respectively; these units may be designated "net" or "short" when necessary to distinguish them from the corresponding units in gross or long measure.

UNITS OF CIRCULAR MEASURE

Second (") =	—
Minute (') =	60 seconds
Degree (°) =	60 minutes
Right angle =	90 degrees
Straight angle =	180 degrees
Circle =	360 degrees

TROY WEIGHT

24 grains =	1 pennyweight (dwt)
20 pennyweights =	1 ounce troy (oz t) = 480 grains
12 ounces troy =	1 pound troy (lb t) = 240 pennyweights = 5,760 grains

APOTHECARIES' WEIGHT

20 grains =	1 scruple (s ap)
3 scruples =	1 dram apothecaries' (dr ap) = 60 grains
8 drams apothecaries =	1 ounce apothecaries' (oz ap) = 24 scruples = 480 grains
12 ounces apothecaries =	1 pound apothecaries' (lb ap) = 96 drams apothecaries' = 288 scruples = 5,760 grains

GUNTER'S OR SURVEYOR'S CHAIN MEASURE

7.92 inches =	1 link (li)
100 links =	1 chain (ch) = 4 rods = 66 ft
80 chains =	1 statute mile = 320 rods = 5,280 ft

Metric and U.S. Equivalents

1 angstrom[1] (light wave measurement)	0.1 millimicron 0.000 1 micron 0.000 000 1 millimeter 0.000 000 004 inch
1 cable's length	120 fathoms 720 feet 219.456 meters
1 centimeter	0.3937 inch
1 chain (Gunter's or surveyor's)	66 feet 20.1168 meters
1 decimeter	3.937 inches
1 dekameter	32.808 feet
1 fathom	6 feet 1.8288 meters
1 foot	0.3048 meter
1 furlong	10 chains (surveyor's) 660 feet 220 yards 1/8 statute mile 201.168 meters

1 inch	2.54 centimeters
1 kilometer	0.621 mile
1 league (land)	3 statute miles 4.828 kilometers
1 link (Gunter's or surveyor's)	7.92 inches 0.201 168 meter
1 meter	39.37 inches 1.094 yards
1 micron	0.001 millimeter 0.000 039 37 inch
1 mil	0.001 inch 0.025 4 millimeter
1 mile (statute or land)	5,280 feet 1.609 kilometers
1 mile (nautical international)	1.852 kilometers 1.151 statute miles 0.999 U.S. nautical miles
1 millimeter	0.03937 inch
1 millimicron (m+GRKm)	0.001 micron 0.000 000 039 37 inch
1 nanometer	0.001 micrometer or 0.000 000 039 37 inch
1 point (typography)	0.013 837 inch 1/72 inch (approximately) 0.351 millimeter
1 rod, pole, or perch	16 1/2 feet 5.0292 meters
1 yard	0.9144 meter

AREAS OR SURFACES

1 acre	43,560 square feet 4,840 square yards 0.405 hectare
1 are	119.599 square yards 0.025 acre
1 hectare	2.471 acres
1 square centimeter	0.155 square inch
1 square decimeter	15.5 square inches
1 square foot	929.030 square centimeters
1 square inch	6.4516 square centimeters
1 square kilometer	0.386 square mile 247.105 acres
1 square meter	1.196 square yards 10.764 square feet
1 square mile	258.999 hectares
1 square millimeter	0.002 square inch
1 square rod, square pole or square perch	25.293 square meters
1 square yard	0.836 square meters

CAPACITIES OR VOLUMES

1 barrel, liquid	31 to 42 gallons[2]
1 barrel, standard for fruits, vegetables, and other dry commodities except cranberries	7,056 cubic inches 105 dry quarts 3.281 bushels, struck measure
1 barrel, standard, cranberry	5.286 cubic inches 86 45/64 dry quarts 2.709 bushels, struck measure
1 bushel (U.S.) struck measure	2,150.42 cubic inches 35.238 liters
1 bushel, heaped (U.S.)	2,747.715 cubic inches 1.278 bushels, struck measure[3]
1 cord (firewood)	128 cubic feet
1 cubic centimeter	0.061 cubic inch
1 cubic decimeter	61.024 cubic inches
1 cubic foot	7.481 gallons 28.316 cubic decimeters
1 cubic inch	0.554 fluid ounce 4.433 fluid drams 16.387 cubic centimeters
1 cubic meter	1.308 cubic yards
1 cubic yard	0.765 cubic meter
1 cup, measuring	8 fluid ounces 1/2 liquid pint
1 dram, fluid or liquid (U.S.)	1/8 fluid ounces 0.226 cubic inch 3.697 milliliters 1.041 British fluid drachms
1 dekaliter	2.642 gallons 1.135 pecks
1 gallon (U.S.)	231 cubic inches 3.785 liters 0.833 British gallon 128 U.S. fluid ounces
1 gallon (British Imperial)	277.42 cubic inches 1.201 U.S. gallons 4.546 liters 160 British fluid ounces
1 gill	7.219 cubic inches 4 fluid ounces 0.118 liter
1 hectoliter	26.418 gallons 2.838 bushels
1 liter	1.057 liquid quarts 0.908 dry quart 61.024 cubic inches
1 milliliter	0.271 fluid dram 16.231 minims 0.061 cubic inch
1 ounce, fluid or liquid (U.S.)	1.805 cubic inch 29.574 milliliters 1.041 British fluid ounces

1 peck	8.810 liters	1 hundredweight, net or short	100 pounds 45.359 kilograms
1 pint, dry	33.600 cubic inches 0.551 liter	1 kilogram	2.205 pounds
1 pint, liquid	28.875 cubic inches 0.473 liter	1 microgram [μg (the Greek letter mu in combination with the letter g)]	0.000 001 gram
1 quart, dry (U.S.)	67.201 cubic inches 1.101 liters 0.969 British quart	1 milligram	0.015 grain
1 quart, liquid (U.S.)	57.75 cubic inches 0.946 liter 0.833 British quart	1 ounce, avoirdupois	437.5 grains 0.911 troy or apothecaries, ounce 28.350 grams
1 quart (British)	69.354 cubic inches 1.032 U.S. dry quarts 1.201 U.S. liquid quarts	1 ounce, troy or apothecaries	480 grains 1.097 avoirdupois ounces 31.103 grams
1 tablespoon, measuring	3 teaspoons 4 fluid drams 1/2 fluid ounce	1 pennyweight	1.555 grams
		1 point	0.01 carat 2 milligrams
1 teaspoon, measuring	1/3 tablespoon 1 1/3 fluid drams	1 pound, avoirdupois	7,000 grains 1.215 troy or apothecaries pounds 453.592 37 grams
1 assay ton[4]	29.167 grams		
1 carat	200 milligrams 3.086 grains	1 pound, troy or apothecaries	5,760 grains 0.823 avoirdupois pound 373.242 grams
1 dram, apothecaries'	60 grains 3.888 grams		
1 dram, avoirdupois	27 11/32 (=27.344) grains 1.772 grams	1 ton, gross or long[5]	2,240 pounds 1.12 net tons 1.016 metric tons
1 grain	64.798 91 milligrams	1 ton, metric	2,204.623 pounds 0 .984 gross ton 1.102 net tons
1 gram	15.432 grains 0.035 ounce, avoirdupois	1 ton, net or short	2,000 pounds 0.893 gross ton 0.907 metric ton
1 hundredweight, gross or long[5]	112 pounds 50.802 kilograms		

1. The angstrom is basically defined as 10^{-10} meter. 2. There is a variety of "barrels" established by law or usage. For example, federal taxes on fermented liquors are based on a barrel of 31 gallons; many state laws fix the "barrel for liquids" at 31 1/2 gallons; one state fixes a 36–gallon barrel for cistern measurement; federal law recognizes a 40–gallon barrel for "proof spirits"; by custom, 42 gallons comprise a barrel of crude oil or petroleum products for statistical purposes, and this equivalent is recognized "for liquids" by four states. 3. Frequently recognized as 1 1/4 bushels, struck measure. 4. Used in assaying. The assay ton bears the same relation to the milligram that a ton of 2,000 pounds avoirdupois bears to the ounce troy; hence the weight in milligrams of precious metal obtained from one assay ton of ore gives directly the number of troy ounces to the net ton. 5. The gross or long ton and hundredweight are used commercially in the United States to only a limited extent, usually in restricted industrial fields. These units are the same as the British "ton" and "hundredweight."

Miscellaneous Units of Measure

Acre: An area of 43,560 square feet. Originally, the area a yoke of oxen could plow in one day.

Agate: Originally a measurement of type size (5 1/2 points). Now equal to 1/14 inch. Used in printing for measuring column length.

Ampere: Unit of electric current. A potential difference of one volt across a resistance of one ohm produces a current of one ampere.

Astronomical Unit (A.U.): 93,000,000 miles, the average distance of the earth from the sun. Used for astronomy.

Bale: A large bundle of goods. In the U.S., the ap-

proximate weight of a bale of cotton is 500 pounds. The weight varies in other countries.

Board Foot (fbm): 144 cubic inches (12 in. × 12 in. × 1 in.). Used for lumber.

Bolt: 40 yards. Used for measuring cloth.

Btu: British thermal unit. Amount of heat needed to increase the temperature of one pound of water by one degree Fahrenheit (252 calories).

Carat (c): 200 milligrams or 3.086 grains troy. Originally the weight of a seed of the carob tree in the Mediterranean region. Used for weighing precious stones. *See also* Karat.

Chain (ch): A chain 66 feet or one–tenth of a furlong in length, divided into 100 parts called links. One mile is equal to 80 chains. Used in surveying and sometimes called Gunter's or surveyor's chain.

Cubit: 18 inches or 45.72 cm. Derived from distance between elbow and tip of middle finger.

Decibel: Unit of relative loudness. One decibel is the smallest amount of change detectable by the human ear.

Ell, English: 1 1/4 yards or 1/32 bolt. Used for measuring cloth.

Freight, Ton (also called Measurement Ton): 40 cubic feet of merchandise. Used for cargo freight.

Great Gross: 12 gross or 1728.

Gross: 12 dozen or 144.

Hand: 4 inches or 10.16 cm. Derived from the width of the hand. Used for measuring the height of horses at withers.

Hertz: Modern unit for measurement of electromagnetic wave frequencies (equivalent to "cycles per second").

Hogshead (hhd): 2 liquid barrels or 14,653 cubic inches.

Horsepower: The power needed to lift 33,000 pounds a distance of one foot in one minute (about 1 1/2 times the power an average horse can exert). Used for measuring power of steam engines, etc.

Karat (kt): A measure of the purity of gold, indicating how many parts out of 24 are pure. For example: 18 karat gold is 3/4 pure. Sometimes spelled *carat*.

Knot: Not a distance, but the rate of speed of one nautical mile per hour. Used for measuring speed of ships.

League: Rather indefinite and varying measure, but usually estimated at 3 miles in English-speaking countries.

Light-Year: 5,880,000,000,000 miles, the distance light travels in a vacuum in a year at the rate of 186,281.7 miles (299,792 kilometers) per second. (If an astronomical unit were represented by one inch, a light-year would be represented by about one mile.) Used for measurements in interstellar space.

Magnum: Two-quart bottle. Used for measuring wine, etc.

Ohm: Unit of electrical resistance. A circuit in which a potential difference of one volt produces a current of one ampere has a resistance of one ohm.

Parsec: Approximately 3.26 light-years of 19.2 million miles. Term is combination of first syllables of *par*allax and *sec*ond, and distance is that of imaginary star when lines drawn from it to both earth and sun form a maximum angle or parallax of one second (1/3600 degree). Used for measuring interstellar distances.

Pi (π): 3.14159265+. The ratio of the circumference of a circle to its diameter. For practical purposes, the value is used to four decimal places: 3.1416.

Pica: 1/6 inch or 12 points. Used in printing for measuring column width, etc.

Pipe: 2 hogsheads. Used for measuring wine and other liquids.

Point: .013837 (approximately 1/72) inch or 1/12 pica. Used in printing for measuring type size.

Quintal: 100,000 grams or 220.46 pounds avoirdupois.

Quire: Used for measuring paper. Sometimes 24 sheets but more often 25. There are 20 quires to a ream.

Ream: Used for measuring paper. Sometimes 480 sheets, but more often 500 sheets.

Roentgen: International Unit of radiation exposure produced by X-rays.

Score: 20 units.

Sound, Speed of: Usually placed at 1,088 ft per second at 32°F at sea level. It varies at other temperatures and in different media.

Span: 9 inches or 22.86 cm. Derived from the distance between the end of the thumb and the end of the little finger when both are outstretched.

Square: 100 square feet. Used in building.

Stone: Legally 14 pounds avoirdupois in Great Britain.

Therm: 100,000 Btu's.

Township: U.S. land measurement of almost 36 square miles. The south border is 6 miles long. The east and west borders, also 6 miles long, follow the meridians, making the north border slightly less than 6 miles long. Used in surveying.

Tun: 252 gallons, but often larger. Used for measuring wine and other liquids.

Watt: Unit of power. The power used by a current of one ampere across a potential difference of one volt equals one watt.

Kelvin Scale

Absolute zero, –273.16° on the Celsius (Centigrade) scale, is 0° Kelvin. Thus, degrees Kelvin are equivalent to degrees Celsuis plus 273.16. The freezing point of water, 0°C. and 32°F., is 273.16°K. The conversion formula is K° = C° + 273.16.

Conversion of Miles to Kilometers and Kilometers to Miles

Miles	Kilometers	Miles	Kilometers	Miles	Kilometers	Kilometers	Miles	Kilometers	Miles	Kilometers	Miles
1	1.6	8	12.8	60	96.5	1	0.6	8	4.9	60	37.2
2	3.2	9	14.4	70	112.6	2	1.2	9	5.5	70	43.4
3	4.8	10	16.0	80	128.7	3	1.8	10	6.2	80	49.7
4	6.4	20	32.1	90	144.8	4	2.4	20	12.4	90	55.9
5	8.0	30	48.2	100	160.9	5	3.1	30	18.6	100	62.1
6	9.6	40	64.3	1,000	1609	6	3.7	40	24.8	1,000	621
7	11.2	50	80.4			7	4.3	50	31.0		

Bolts and Screws: Conversion from Fractions of an Inch to Millimeters

Inch	mm	Inch	mm	Inch	mm	Inch	mm
1/64	0.40	17/64	6.75	33/64	13.10	49/64	19.45
1/32	0.79	9/32	7.14	17/32	13.50	25/32	19.84
3/64	1.19	19/64	7.54	35/64	13.90	51/64	20.24
1/16	1.59	5/16	7.94	9/16	14.29	13/16	20.64
5/64	1.98	21/64	8.33	37/64	14.69	53/64	21.03
3/32	2.38	11/32	8.73	19/32	15.08	27/32	21.43
7/64	2.78	23/64	9.13	39/64	15.48	55/64	21.83
1/8	3.18	3/8	9.53	5/8	15.88	7/8	22.23
9/64	3.57	25/64	9.92	41/64	16.27	57/64	22.62
5/32	3.97	13/32	10.32	21/32	16.67	29/32	23.02
11/64	4.37	27/64	10.72	43/64	17.06	59/64	23.42
3/16	4.76	7/16	11.11	11/64	17.46	15/16	23.81
13/64	5.16	29/64	11.51	45/64	17.86	61/64	24.21
7/32	5.56	15/32	11.91	23/32	18.26	31/32	24.61
15/64	5.95	31/64	12.30	47/64	18.65	63/64	25.00
1/4	6.35	1/2	12.70	3/4	19.05	1	25.40

U.S.—Metric Cooking Conversions

U.S. customary system				Metric			
Capacity		**Weight**		**Capacity**		**Weight**	
1/5 teaspoon	1 milliliter	1 fluid oz	30 milliliters	1 milliliter	1/5 teaspoon	1 gram	.035 ounce
1 teaspoon	5 ml		28 grams	5 ml	1 teaspoon	100 grams	3.5 ounces
1 tablespoon	15 ml	1 pound	454 grams	15 ml	1 tablespoon	500 grams	1.10 pounds
1/5 cup	50 ml			34 ml	1 fluid oz	1 kilogram	2.205 pounds
1 cup	240 ml						35 oz
2 cups (1 pint)	470 ml			100 ml	3.4 fluid oz		
4 cups (1 quart)	.95 liter			240 ml	1 cup		
4 quarts (1 gal.)	3.8 liters			1 liter	34 fluid oz		
					4.2 cups		
					2.1 pints		
					1.06 quarts		
					0.26 gallon		

Cooking Measurement Equivalents

16 tablespoons =	1 cup		2 tablespoons =	1/8 cup
12 tablespoons =	3/4 cup		2 tablespoons + 2 teaspoons =	1/6 cup
10 tablespoons + 2 teaspoons =	2/3 cup		1 tablespoon =	1/16 cup
8 tablespoons =	1/2 cup		2 cups =	1 pint
6 tablespoons =	3/8 cup		2 pints =	1 quart
5 tablespoons + 1 teaspoon =	1/3 cup		3 teaspoons =	1 tablespoon
4 tablespoons =	1/4 cup		48 teaspoons =	1 cup

Prefixes and Multiples

Prefix	Suffix	Equivalent	Multiple/ submultiple	Prefix	Suffix	Equivalent	Multiple/ submultiple
atto	a	quintillionth part	10^{-18}	deci	d	tenth part	10^{-1}
femto	f	quadrillionth part	10^{-15}	deka	da	tenfold	10
pico	p	trillionth part	10^{-12}	hecto	h	hundredfold	10^2
nano	n	billionth part	10^{-9}	kilo	k	thousandfold	10^3
micro	μ	millionth part	10^{-6}	mega	M	millionfold	10^6
milli	m	thousandth part	10^{-3}	giga	G	billionfold	10^9
centi	c	hundredth part	10^{-2}	tera	T	trillionfold	10^{12}

Common Formulas

Circumference

Circle: $C = \pi d$, in which π is 3.1416 and d the diameter.

Area

Triangle: $A = \dfrac{ab}{2}$, in which a is the base and b the height.

Square: $A = a^2$, in which a is one of the sides.

Rectangle: $A = ab$, in which a is the base and b the height.

Trapezoid: $A = \dfrac{h(a+b)}{2}$, in which h is the height, a the longer parallel side, and b the shorter.

Regular pentagon: $A = 1.720a^2$, in which a is one of the sides.

Regular hexagon: $A = 2.598a^2$, in which a is one of the sides.

Regular octagon: $A = 4.828a^2$, in which a is one of the sides.

Circle: $A = \pi r^2$, in which π is 3.1416 and r the radius.

Volume

Cube: $V = a^3$, in which a is one of the edges.

Rectangular prism: $V = abc$, in which a is the length, b is the width, and c the depth.

Pyramid: $V = \dfrac{Ah}{3}$, in which A is the area of the base and h the height.

Cylinder: $V = \pi r^2 h$, in which π is 3.1416, r the radius of the base, and h the height.

Cone: $V = \dfrac{\pi r^2 h}{3}$, in which π is 3.1416, r the radius of the base, and h the height.

Sphere: $V = \dfrac{4 \pi r^3}{3}$, in which π is 3.1416 and r the radius.

Miscellaneous

Distance in feet traveled by falling body: $d = 16t^2$, in which t is the time in seconds.

Speed in sound in feet per second through any given temperature of air:
$$V = \frac{1087 \sqrt{273 + t}}{16.52}$$
in which t is the temperature Centigrade.

Cost in cents of operration of electrical device: $C = \dfrac{Wtc}{1000}$, in which W is the number of watts, t the time in hours, and c the cost in cents per hilowatt-hour.

Conversion of matter into energy (Einstein's Theorem): $E = mc^2$, in which E is the energy in ergs, m the mass of the matter in grams, and c the speed of light in centimeters per second ($c^2 = 3 \times 10^{20}$).

Decimal Equivalents of Common Fractions

1/2	.5000	1/10	.1000	2/7	.2857	3/11	.2727	5/9	.5556	7/11	.6364
1/3	.3333	1/11	.0909	2/9	.2222	4/5	.8000	5/11	.4545	7/12	.5833
1/4	.2500	1/12	.0833	2/11	.1818	4/7	.5714	5/12	.4167	8/9	.8889
1/5	.2000	1/16	.0625	3/4	.7500	4/9	.4444	6/7	.8571	8/11	.7273
1/6	.1667	1/32	.0313	3/5	.6000	4/11	.3636	6/11	.5455	9/10	.9000
1/7	.1429	1/64	.0156	3/7	.4286	5/6	.8333	7/8	.8750	9/11	.8182
1/8	.1250	2/3	.6667	3/8	.3750	5/7	.7143	7/9	.7778	10/11	.9091
1/9	.1111	2/5	.4000	3/10	.3000	5/8	.6250	7/10	.7000	11/12	.9167

Conversion Factors

To change	To	Multiply by
acres	hectares	.4047
acres	square feet	43,560
acres	square miles	.001562
atmospheres	cms. of mercury	76
BTU	horsepower-hour	.0003931
BTU	kilowatt-hour	.0002928
BTU/hour	watts	.2931
bushels	cubic inches	2150.4
bushels (U.S.)	hectoliters	.3524
centimeters	inches	.3937
centimeters	feet	.03281
circumference	radians	6.283
cubic feet	cubic meters	.0283
cubic meters	cubic feet	35.3145
cubic meters	cubic yards	1.3079
cubic yards	cubic meters	.7646
degrees	radians	.01745
dynes	grams	.00102
fathoms	feet	6.0
feet	meters	.3048
feet	miles (nautical)	.0001645
feet	miles (statute)	.0001894
feet/second	miles/hour	.6818
furlongs	feet	660.0
furlongs	miles	.125
gallons (U.S.)	liters	3.7853
grains	grams	.0648
grams	grains	15.4324
grams	ounces avdp	.0353
grams	pounds	.002205
hectares	acres	2.4710
hectoliters	bushels (U.S.)	2.8378
horsepower	watts	745.7
hours	days	.04167
inches	millimeters	25.4000
inches	centimeters	2.5400
kilograms	pounds avdp or t	2.2046
kilometers	miles	.6214
kilowatts	horsepower	1.341
knots	nautical miles/hour	1.0
knots	statute miles/hour	1.151
liters	gallons (U.S.)	.2642
liters	pecks	.1135
liters	pints (dry)	1.8162
liters	pints (liquid)	2.1134
liters	quarts (dry)	.9081
liters	quarts (liquid)	1.0567
meters	feet	3.2808
meters	miles	.0006214
meters	yards	1.0936
metric tons	tons (long)	.9842
metric tons	tons (short)	1.1023
miles	kilometers	1.6093
miles	feet	5280
miles (nautical)	miles (statute)	1.1516
miles (statute)	miles (nautical)	.8684
miles/hour	feet/minute	88
millimeters	inches	.0394
ounces avdp.	grams	28.3495
ounces	pounds	.0625
ounces (troy)	ounces (avdp)	1.09714
pecks	liters	8.8096
pints (dry)	liters	.5506
pints (liquid)	liters	.4732
pounds ap or t	kilograms	.3782
pounds avdp	kilograms	.4536
pounds	ounces	16
quarts (dry)	liters	1.1012
quarts (liquid)	liters	.9463
radians	degrees	57.30
rods	meters	5.029
rods	feet	16.5
square feet	square meters	.0929
square kilometers	square miles	.3861
square meters	square feet	10.7639
square meters	square yards	1.1960
square miles	square kilometers	2.5900
square yards	square meters	.8361
tons (long)	metric tons	1.016
tons (short)	metric tons	.9072
tons (long)	pounds	2240
tons (short)	pounds	2000
watts	Btu/hour	3.4129
watts	horsepower	.001341
yards	meters	.9144
yards	miles	.0005682

Fahrenheit and Celsius (Centigrade) Scales

Zero on the Fahrenheit scale represents the temperature produced by the mixing of equal weights of snow and common salt.

	F	C
Boiling point of water	212°	100°
Freezing point of water	32°	0°
Absolute zero	−459.6°	−273.1°

Absolute zero is theoretically the lowest possible temperature, the point at which all molecular motion would cease.

To convert Fahrenheit to Celsius (Centigrade), subtract 32 and multiply by 5/9.

To convert Celsius (Centigrade) to Fahrenheit, multiply by 9/5 and add 32.

°Centigrade	°Fahrenheit	°Centigrade	°Fahrenheit
−273.1	−459.6	30	86
−250	−418	35	95
−200	−328	40	104
−150	−238	45	113
−100	−148	50	122
−50	−58	55	131
−40	−40	60	140
−30	−22	65	149
−20	−4	70	158
−10	14	75	167
0	32	80	176
5	41	85	185
10	50	90	194
15	59	95	203
20	68	100	212
25	77		

Roman Numerals

Roman numerals are expressed by letters of the alphabet and are rarely used today except for formality or variety.

There are three basic principles for reading Roman numerals:

1. A letter repeated once or twice repeats its value that many times (XXX = 30, CC = 200, etc.).

2. One or more letters placed after another letter of greater value increases the greater value by the amount of the smaller. (VI = 6, LXX = 70, MCC = 1200, etc.).

3. A letter placed before another letter of greater value decreases the greater value by the amount of the smaller. (IV = 4, XC = 90, CM = 900, etc.).

Letter	Value	Letter	Value	Letter	Value	Letter	Value	Letter	Value
I	1	VII	7	XXX	30	LXXX	80	$\overline{V}$	5,000
II	2	VIII	8	XL	40	XC	90	$\overline{X}$	10,000
III	3	IX	9	L	50	C	100	$\overline{L}$	50,000
IV	4	X	10	LX	60	D	500	$\overline{C}$	100,000
V	5	XX	20	LXX	70	M	1,000	$\overline{D}$	500,000
VI	6							$\overline{M}$	1,000,000

Mean and Median

The mean, also called the average, of a series of quantities is obtained by finding the sum of the quantities and dividing it by the number of quantities. In the series 1, 3, 5, 18, 19, 20, 25, the mean or average is 13—i.e., 91 divided by 7.

The median of a series is that point which so divided it that half the quantities are on one side, half on the other. In the above series, the median is 18.

The median often better expresses the common-run, since it is not, as is the mean, affected by an excessively high or low figure. In the series 1, 3, 4, 7, 55, the median of 4 is a truer expression of the common-run than is the mean of 14.

Prime Numbers Between 1 and 1,000

2	3	5	7	11	13	17	19	23
29	31	37	41	43	47	53	59	61	67
71	73	79	83	89	97	101	103	107	109
113	127	131	137	139	149	151	157	163	167
173	179	181	191	193	197	199	211	223	227
229	233	239	241	251	257	263	269	271	277
281	283	293	307	311	313	317	331	337	347
349	353	359	367	373	379	383	389	397	401
409	419	421	431	433	439	443	449	457	461
463	467	479	487	491	499	503	509	521	523
541	547	557	563	569	571	577	587	593	599
601	607	613	617	619	631	641	643	647	653
659	661	673	677	683	691	701	709	719	727
733	739	743	751	757	761	769	773	787	797
809	811	821	823	827	829	839	853	857	859
863	877	881	883	887	907	911	919	929	937
941	947	953	967	971	977	983	991	997	(1009)

Definitions of Gold Terminology

The term "fineness" defines a gold content in parts per thousand. For example, a gold nugget containing 885 parts of pure gold, 100 parts of silver, and 15 parts of copper would be considered 885-fine.

The word "karat" indicates the proportion of solid gold in an alloy based on a total of 24 parts. Thus, 14-karat (14K) gold indicates a composition of 14 parts of gold and 10 parts of other metals.

The term "gold-filled" is used to describe articles of jewelry made of base metal which are covered on one or more surfaces with a layer of gold alloy. No article having a gold alloy portion of less than one twentieth by weight may be marked "gold-filled." Articles may be marked "rolled gold plate" provided the proportional fraction and fineness designations are also shown.

Electroplated jewelry items carrying at least 7 millionths of an inch of gold on significant surfaces may be labeled "electroplate." Plate thicknesses less than this may be marked "gold-flashed" or "gold-washed."

Portraits and Designs of U.S. Paper Currency[1]

Currency	Portrait	Design on back	Currency	Portrait	Design on back
$1	Washington	ONE between obverse and reverse of Great Seal of U.S.	$50	Grant	U.S. Capitol
$2[2]	Jefferson	Monticello	$100	Franklin	Independence Hall
$2[3]	Jefferson	"The Signing of the Declaration of Independence"	$500	McKinley	Ornate FIVE HUNDRED
			$1,000	Cleveland	Ornate ONE THOUSAND
			$5,000	Madison	Ornate FIVE THOUSAND
$5	Lincoln	Lincoln Memorial	$10,000	Chase	Ornate TEN THOUSAND
$10	Hamilton	U.S. Treasury Building	$100,000[4]	Wilson	Ornate ONE HUNDRED THOUSAND
$20	Jackson	White House			

1. Denominations of $500 and higher were discontinued in 1969. 2. Discontinued in 1966. 3. New issue, April 13, 1976.
4. For use only in transactions between Federal Reserve System and Treasury Department.

TRAVEL

U.S. Passport and Customs Information

Source: Department of State, Bureau of Consular Affairs and Department of the Treasury, Customs Service.

Passports

With a few exceptions, a passport is required for all U.S. citizens to depart and enter the United States and to enter most foreign countries. A valid U.S. passport is the best documentation of U.S. citizenship available. Persons who travel to a country where a U.S. passport is not required should be in possession of documentary evidence of their U.S. citizenship and identity to facilitate reentry into the United States. Travelers should check passport and visa requirements with consular officials of the countries to be visited well in advance of their departure date.

Application for a passport may be made at a passport agency; to a clerk of any Federal court or State court of record; or a judge or clerk of any probate court accepting applications; or at a post office selected to accept passport applications. Passport agencies are located in Boston, Chicago, Honolulu, Houston, Los Angeles, Miami, New Orleans, New York, Philadelphia, San Francisco, Seattle, Stamford, Conn., and Washington, D.C.

All persons are required to obtain individual passports in their own names. Neither spouses nor children may be included in each others' passports. Applicants between the ages of 13 and 18 must appear in person before the clerk or agent executing the application. For children under the age of 13, a parent or legal guardian may execute an application for them.

First time passport applicants must apply in person. Applicants must present evidence of citizenship (e.g., a certified copy of birth certificate), personal identification (e.g., a valid driver's license), two identical black and white or color photographs taken within six months (2 × 2 inches, with the image size measured from the bottom of the chin to the top of the head [including hair] not less than 1 inch nor more than 1 3/8 inches on a plain white or off–white background, vending machine photographs not acceptable), plus a completed passport application (DSP–11). If you were born abroad, you may also use as proof of citizenship: a Certificate of Naturalization, a Certificate of Citizenship, a Report of Birth abroad of a Citizen of the United States of America or a Certification of Birth. A fee of $35 plus a $7 execution fee is charged for adults 18 years and older for a passport valid for ten years from the date of issue. The fee for minor children under 18 years of age is $20 for a five–year passport plus $7 for the execution of the application.

You may apply for a passport by mail if you have been the bearer of a passport issued within 12 years prior to the date of a new application, are able to submit your most recent U.S. passport with your new application, and your previous passport was not issued before your 16th birthday. If you are eligible to apply by mail, include your previous passport, a completed, signed, and dated DSP–82 "Application for Passport by Mail," new photographs, and the passport fee of $35. The $7 execution fee is not required when applying by mail. Mail the application and attachments to one of the 13 passport agencies.

Passports may be presented for amendment to show a married name or legal change of name or to correct descriptive data. Any alterations to the passport by the bearer *other than* in the spaces provided for change of address and next of kin data are forbidden.

Loss, theft or destruction of a passport should be reported to Passport Services, 1425 K Street, N.W., Washington, D.C. 20524 immediately, or to the nearest passport agency. If you are overseas, report to the nearest U.S. Embassy or consulate and to local police authorities. Your passport is a valuable citizenship and identity document. It should be carefully safeguarded. Its loss could cause you unnecessary travel complications as well as significant expense. It is advisable to photocopy the data page of your passport and keep it in a place separate from your passport to facilitate the issuance of a replacement passport should one be necessary.

Customs

United States residents must declare all articles acquired abroad and in their possession at the time of their return. In addition, articles acquired in the U.S. Virgin Islands, American Samoa, or Guam and not accompanying you must be declared at the time of your return. The wearing or use of an article acquired abroad does *not* exempt it from duty. Customs declaration forms are distributed on vessels and planes, and should be prepared in advance of arrival for presentation to the customs inspectors.

If you have not exceeded the duty–free exemption allowed, you may make an oral declaration to the customs inspector. A written declaration is necessary when (1) total fair retail value of articles exceeds $1,400 ($400 duty–free exemption plus $1,000 dutiable at a flat 10% rate) (keep your sales slips); (2) over 1 liter of liquor, 200 cigarettes, or 100 cigars are included; (3) items are not intended for your personal or household use, or articles brought home for another person; and (4) when a customs duty or internal revenue tax is collectible on any article in your possession.

An exception to the above are regulations applicable to articles purchased in the U.S. Virgin Islands, American Samoa, or Guam where you may receive a customs exemption of $1,200. Not more than $400 of this exemption may be applied to merchandise obtained elsewhere than in these islands or $600 if acquired in a beneficiary country. Five liters of alcoholic beverages and 1000 cigarettes may be included provided not more than one liter and 200 cigarettes were acquired elsewhere than in these islands. Articles acquired in and sent from these islands to the United States may be claimed under your duty–free personal exemption if properly declared at the time of your return. For information on rules applying to beneficiary countries and a list of them check with your customs office or write for the pamphlet "GSP and the Traveler" from the Department of the Treasury, U.S. Customs Service, Washington, D.C. 20229. Since rules change, it is always wise to check with customs before leaving, to get information pertinent to the areas you will be visiting.

Articles accompanying you, in excess of your personal exemption, up to $1000 will be assessed at a flat rate of duty of 10% based on fair retail value in country of acquisition. (If articles were acquired in the insular possessions, the flat rate of duty is 5% and these goods may accompany you or be shipped home.) These articles must be for your personal use or for use as gifts and not for sale. This provision may be used every 30 days, excluding the day of your last arrival. Any items which have a "free" duty rate will be excluded before duty is calculated.

Other exemptions include in part: automobiles, boats, planes, or other vehicles taken abroad for non-commercial use. Foreign–made personal articles (e.g., watches, cameras, etc.) taken abroad should be registered with Customs before departure. Customs will register anything with a serial number or identifying marks, or documented by sales receipts or insurance documents. Gifts of not more than $50 can be shipped back to the United States tax and duty free ($100 if mailed from the Virgin Islands, American Samoa, or Guam). Household effects and tools of trade which you take out of the United States are duty free at time of return.

Prohibited and restricted articles include in part: ab-sinthe, narcotics and dangerous drugs, obscene articles and publications, seditious and treasonable materials, hazardous articles (e.g., fireworks, dangerous toys, toxic and poisonous substances, and switchblade knives), biological materials of public health or veterinary importance, fruit, vegetables and plants, meats, poultry and products thereof, birds, monkeys, and turtles.

If you understate the value of an article you declare, or if you otherwise misrepresent an article in your declaration, you may have to pay a penalty in addition to payment of duty. Under certain circumstances, the article could be seized and forfeited if the penalty is not paid.

If you fail to declare an article acquired abroad, not only is the article subject to seizure and forfeiture, but you will be liable for a personal penalty in an amount equal to the value of the article in the United States. In addition, you may also be liable to criminal prosecution.

If you carry more than $10,000 into or out of the United States in currency (either United States or foreign money), negotiable instruments in bearer form, or travelers checks in any form, a report must be filed with United States Customs at the time you arrive or depart with such amounts.

Foreign Embassies in the United States

Source: U.S. Department of State

Embassy of the Republic of Afghanistan, 2341 Wyoming Ave., N.W., Washington, D.C. 20008. Phone: (202) 234–3770, 3771.

Embassy of the Democratic & Popular Republic of Algeria, 2118 Kalorama Rd., N.W., Washington, D.C. 20008. Phone: (202) 265–2800.

Embassy of Antigua & Barbuda, 3400 International Dr., N.W., Suite 4M, Washington, D.C. 20008. Phone: (202) 362–5211, 5166, 5122.

Embassy of the Argentine Republic, 1600 New Hampshire Ave., N.W., Washington, D.C. 20009. Phone: (202) 939–6400 to 6403, inclusive.

Embassy of Australia, 1601 Massachusetts Ave., N.W., Washington, D.C. 20036. Phone: (202) 797–3000.

Embassy of Austria, 2343 Massachusetts Ave., N.W., Washington, D.C. 20008. Phone: (202) 483–4474.

Embassy of the Commonwealth of the Bahamas, 2220 Massachusetts Ave., N.W., Washington, D.C. 20008. Phone: (202) 319–2660.

Embassy of the State of Bahrain, 3502 International Dr., N.W., Washington, D.C. 20008. Phone: (202) 342–0741, 0742.

Embassy of the People's Republic of Bangladesh, 2201 Wisconsin Ave., N.W., Washington, D.C. 20007. Phone: (202) 342–8372 to 8376.

Embassy of Barbados, 2144 Wyoming Ave., N.W., Washington, D.C. 20008. Phone: (202) 939–9218, 9219.

Embassy of Belgium, 3330 Garfield St., N.W., Washington, D.C. 20008. Phone: (202) 333–6900.

Embassy of Belize, 3400 International Dr., N.W., Suite 2J, Washington, D.C. 20008. Phone: (202) 363–4505.

Embassy of the People's Republic of Benin, 2737 Cathedral Ave., N.W., Washington, D.C. 20008. Phone: (202) 232–6656.

Embassy of Bolivia, 3014 Massachusetts Ave., N.W., Washington, D.C. 20008. Phone: (202) 483–4410, 4411, 4412.

Embassy of the Republic of Botswana, 3400 International Dr., N.W., Suite 7M, Washington, D.C. 20008. Phone: (202) 244–4990, 4991.

Brazilian Embassy, 3006 Massachusetts Ave., N.W., Washington, D.C. 20008. Phone: (202) 745–2700.

Embassy of the State of Brunei Darussalam, 2600 Virginia Ave., N.W., Suite 300, Washington, D.C. 20037. Phone: (202) 342–0159.

Embassy of the Republic of Bulgaria, 1621 22nd St., N.W., Washington, D.C. 20008. Phone: (202) 387–7969.

Embassy of Burkina Faso, 2340 Massachusetts Ave., N.W., Washington, D.C. 20008. Phone: (202) 332–5577, 6895.

Embassy of the Republic of Burundi, 2233 Wisconsin Ave., N.W., Suite 212, Washington, D.C. 20007. Phone: (202) 342–257 4.

Embassy of the Republic of Cameroon, 2349 Massachusetts Ave., N.W., Washington, D.C. 20008. Phone: (202) 265–8790 to 8794.

Embassy of Canada, 501 Pennsylvania Ave., N.W., Washington, D.C. 20001. Phone: (202) 682–1740.

Embassy of the Republic of Cape Verde, 3415 Massachusetts Ave., N.W., Washington, D.C. 20007. Phone: (202) 965–6820.

Embassy of Central African Republic, 1618 22nd St. N.W., Washington, D.C. 20008. Phone: (202) 483–7800, 7801.

Embassy of the Republic of Chad, 2002 R St., N.W., Washington, D.C. 20009. Phone: (202) 462–4009.

Embassy of Chile, 1732 Massachusetts Ave., N.W., Washington, D.C. 20036. Phone: (202) 785–1746.

Embassy of the People's Republic of China, 2300 Connecticut Ave., N.W., Washington, D.C. 20008. Phone: (202) 328–2500, 2501, 2502.

Embassy of Colombia, 2118 Leroy Pl., N.W., Washington, D.C. 20008. Phone: (202) 387–8338.

Embassy of the Federal and Islamic Republic of Comoros, c/o Permanent Mission of the Federal and Islamic Republic of Comoros to the United

Nations, 336 E. 45th St., 2nd floor, New York, N.Y. 10017. Phone: (212) 972–8010.

Embassy of the People's Republic of the Congo, 4891 Colorado Ave., N.W., Washington, D.C. 20011. Phone: (202) 726–5500, 5501.

Embassy of Costa Rica, 1825 Connecticut Ave., N.W., Suite 211, Washington, D.C. 20009. Phone: (202) 234–2945 to 2947.

Embassy of the Republic of Cote d'Ivoire, 2424 Massachusetts Ave., N.W., Washington, D.C. 20008. Phone: (202) 797–0300.

Embassy of the Republic of Cyprus, 2211 R St. N.W., Washington, D.C. 20008. Phone: (202) 462–5772.

Embassy of the Czech and Slovak Federal Republic, 3900 Linnean Ave., N.W., Washington, D.C. 20008. Phone: (202) 363–6315, 6316.

Cuban Interests Section, 2630 and 2639 16th St., N.W., Washington, D.C. 20009. Phone: (202) 797–8518 to 8520, 8609, 8610.

Royal Danish Embassy, 3200 Whitehaven St., N.W., Washington, D.C. 20008. Phone: (202) 234–4300.

Embassy of the Republic of Djibouti, 1156 15th St., N.W., Suite 515, Washington, D.C. 20005. Phone: (202) 331-0270.

Embassy of the Dominican Republic, 1715 22nd St., N.W., Washington, D.C. 20008. Phone: (202) 332–6280.

Embassy of Ecuador, 2535 15th St., N.W., Washington, D.C. 20009. Phone: (202) 234–7200.

Embassy of the Arab Republic of Egypt, 2310 Decatur Pl., N.W., Washington, D.C. 20008. Phone: (202) 232–5400.

Embassy of El Salvador, 2308 California St., N.W., Washington, D.C. 20008. Phone: (202) 265–9671, 9672.

Embassy of Equatorial Guinea, 801 Second Ave., Suite 1403, New York, N.Y. 10017. Phone: (202) 745–3680.

Legation of Estonia, 9 Rockefeller Plaza, New York, N.Y. 10020. Phone: (212) 247–1450.

Embassy of Ethiopia, 2134 Kalorama Rd., N.W., Washington, D.C. 20008. Phone: (202) 234–2281, 2282.

Embassy of the Republic of Fiji, 2233 Wisconsin Ave., N.W., Suite 240, Washington, D.C. 20007. Phone: (202) 337–8320.

Embassy of Finland, 3216 New Mexico Ave., N.W., Washington, D.C. 20016. Phone: (202) 363–2430.

Embassy of France, 4101 Reservoir Rd., N.W., Washington, D.C. 20007. Phone: (202) 944–6000.

Embassy of the Gabonese Republic, 2034 20th St., N.W., Washington, D.C. 20009. Phone: (202) 797–1000.

Embassy of The Gambia, 1030 15th St., N.W., Suite 720, Washington, D.C. 20005. Phone: (202) 842–1356, 1359.

Embassy of the Federal Republic of Germany, 4645 Reservoir Rd., N.W., Washington, D.C. 20007. Phone: (202) 298–4000.

Embassy of Ghana, 3512 International Dr., N.W., Washington, D.C. 20008 (202) 686–4520.

Embassy of Greece, 2221 Massachusetts Ave., N.W., Washington, D.C. 20008. Phone (202) 939–5800.

Embassy of Grenada, 1701 New Hampshire Ave., N.W., Washington, D.C. 20009. Phone: (202) 265–2561.

Embassy of Guatemala, 2220 R St., N.W., Washington, D.C. 20008. Phone: (202) 745–4952 to 4954.

Embassy of the Republic of Guinea, 2112 Leroy Pl., N.W., Washington, D.C. 20008. Phone: (202) 483–9420.

Embassy of the Republic of Guinea-Bissau, 918 16th St., N.W., Mezzanine Suite, Washington, D.C. 20006. Phone: (202) 872–4222.

Embassy of Guyana, 2490 Tracy Pl., N.W. Washington, D.C. 20008. Phone: (202) 265–6900, 6903.

Embassy of Haiti, 2311 Massachusetts Ave., N.W., Washington, D.C. 20008. Phone: (202) 332–4090 to 4092.

Apostolic Nunciature of the Holy See, 3339 Massachusetts Ave., N.W., Washington, D.C. 20008. Phone: (202) 333–7121.

Embassy of Honduras, 3007 Tilden St., N.W., Washington, D .C. 20008. Phone: (202) 966–7702, 2604, 5008, 4596.

Embassy of the Republic of Hungary, 3910 Shoemaker St., N.W., Washington, D.C. 20008. Phone: (202) 362–6730.

Embassy of Iceland, 2022 Connecticut Ave., N.W., Washington, D.C. 20008. Phone: (202) 265–6653 to 6655.

Embassy of India, 2107 Massachusetts Ave., N.W., Washington, D.C. 20008. Phone: (202) 939–7000.

Embassy of the Republic of Indonesia, 2020 Massachusetts Ave., N.W., Washington, D.C. 20036. Phone: (202) 775–5200.

Embassy of the Republic of Iraq, 1801 P St., N.W., Washington, D.C. 20036. Phone: (202) 483–7500.

Embassy of Ireland, 2234 Massachusetts Ave., N.W., Washington, D.C. 20008. Phone: (202) 462–3939.

Embassy of Israel, 3514 International Dr., N.W., Washington, D.C. 20008. Phone: (202) 364–5500.

Embassy of Italy, 1601 Fuller St., N.W., Washington, D.C. 20009. Phone: (202) 328–5500.

Embassy of Jamaica, 1850 K St., N.W., Suite 355, Washington, D.C. 20006. Phone: (202) 452–0660.

Embassy of Japan, 2520 Massachusetts Ave., N.W., Washington, D.C. 20008. Phone: (202) 939–6700.

Embassy of the Hashemite Kingdom of Jordan, 3504 International Dr., N.W., Washington, D.C. 20008. Phone: (202) 966–2664.

Embassy of Kenya, 2249 R St., N.W., Washington, D.C. 20008. Phone: (202) 387–6101.

Embassy of Korea, 2370 Massachusetts Ave., N.W., Washington, D.C. 20008. Phone: (202) 939–5600.

Embassy of the State of Kuwait, 2940 Tilden St., N.W., Washington, D.C. 20008. Phone: (202) 966–0702.

Embassy of the Lao People's Democratic Republic, 2222 S St., N.W., Washington, D.C. 20008. Phone: (202) 332–6416, 6417.

Legation of Latvia, 4325 17th St., N.W., Washington, D.C. 20011. Phone: (202) 726–8213, 8214.

Embassy of Lebanon, 2560 28th St., N.W., Washington, D.C. 20008. Phone: (202) 939–6300.

Embassy of the Kingdom of Lesotho, 2511 Massachusetts Ave., N.W., Washington, D.C. 20008. Phone: (202) 797–5534 to 5536.

Embassy of the Republic of Liberia, 5201 16th St., N.W., Washington, D.C. 20011. Phone: (202) 291–0761.

Legation of Lithuania, 2622 16th St., N.W., Washington, D.C. 20009. Phone: (202) 234–5860, 2639.

Embassy of Luxembourg, 2200 Massachusetts Ave., N.W., Washington, D.C. 20008. Phone: (202) 265–4171.

Embassy of the Democratic Republic of Madagascar, 2374 Massachusetts Ave., N.W., Washington, D.C. 20008. Phone: (202) 265–5525, 5526.

Malawi Embassy, 2408 Massachusetts Ave., N.W., Washington, D.C. 20008. Phone: (202) 797–1007.

Embassy of Malaysia, 2401 Massachusetts Ave., N.W., Washington, D.C. 20008. Phone: (202) 328–2700.

Embassy of the Republic of Mali, 2130 R St., N.W., Washington, D.C. 20008. Phone: (202) 332–2249; (202) 939–8950.

Embassy of Malta, 2017 Connecticut Ave., N.W., Washington, D.C. 20008. Phone: (202) 462–3611, 3612.

Embassy of the Republic of the Marshall Islands, 2433 Massachusetts Ave., N.W., Washington, D.C. 20008. Phone: (202) 234–5414.

Embassy of the Islamic Republic of Mauritania, 2129 Leroy Pl., N.W., Washington, D.C. 20008. Phone: (202) 232–5700.

Embassy of Mauritius, 4301 Connecticut Ave., N.W., Suite 134, Washington, D.C. 20008. Phone: (202) 244–1491, 1492.

Embassy of Mexico, 1911 Pennsylvania Ave., N.W., 20006, Washington, D.C. Phone: (202) 728–1600.

Embassy of the Federated States of Micronesia, 1725 N St., N.W., Washington, D.C. 20036. Phone: (202) 223–4383.

Embassy of the Mongolian People's Republic, Washington, D.C. Phone: (202) 983–1962.

Embassy of Morocco, 1601 21st St., N.W., Washington, D.C. 20009. Phone: (202) 462–7979 to 7982, inclusive.

Embassy of the People's Republic of Mozambique, 1990 M St., N.W., Suite 570, Washington, D.C. 20036. Phone: (202) 293–7146.

Embassy of the Union of Myanmar, 2300 S St., N.W., Washington, D.C. 20008. Phone: (202) 332–9044, 9045.

Embassy of the Republic of Namibia, 1413 K St., N.W., 7th floor, Washington, D.C. 20005. Phone: (202) 289–3871.

Royal Nepalese Embassy, 2131 Leroy Pl., N.W., Washington, D.C. 20008. Phone: (202) 667–4550.

Embassy of the Netherlands, 4200 Linnean Ave., N.W., Washington, D.C. 20008. Phone: (202) 244–5300; after 6 p.m. (202) 244–5304.

Embassy of New Zealand, 37 Observatory Circle, N.W., Washington, D.C. 20008. Phone: (202) 328–4800.

Embassy of Nicaragua, 1627 New Hampshire Ave., N.W., Washington, D.C. 20009. Phone: (202) 939–6570.

Embassy of the Republic of Niger, 2204 R St., N.W., Washington, D.C. 20008. Phone: (202) 483–4224 to 4227, inclusive.

Embassy of the Federal Republic of Nigeria, 2201 M St., N.W., Washington, D.C. 20037. Phone: (202) 822–1500.

Royal Norwegian Embassy, 2720 34th St., N.W., Washington, D.C. 20008. Phone: (202) 333–6000.

Embassy of the Sultanate of Oman, 2342 Massachusetts Ave., N.W., Washington, D.C. 20008. Phone: (202) 387–1980 to 1982.

Embassy of Pakistan, 2315 Massachusetts Ave., N.W., Washington, D.C. 20008. Phone: (202) 939–6200.

Embassy of Panama, 2862 McGill Terrace, N.W., Washington, D.C. 20008. Phone: (202) 483–1407.

Embassy of Papua New Guinea, 1615 New Hampshire Ave., N.W., 3rd floor, Washington, D.C. 20009. Phone: (202) 745–3680.

Embassy of Paraguay, 2400 Massachusetts Ave., N.W., Washington, D.C. 20008. Phone: (202) 483–6960 to 6962.

Embassy of Peru, 1700 Massachusetts Ave., N.W., Washington, D.C. 20036. Phone: (202) 833–9860 to 9869.

Embassy of the Philippines, 1617 Massachusetts Ave., N.W., Washington, D.C. 20036. Phone: (202) 483–1414.

Embassy of the Republic of Poland, 2640 16th St., N.W., Washington, D.C. 20009. Phone: (202) 234–3800 to 3802.

Embassy of Portugal, 2125 Kalorama Rd., N.W., Washington, D.C. 20008. Phone: (202) 328–8610.

Embassy of the State of Qatar, 600 New Hampshire Ave., N.W., Suite 1180, Washington, D.C. 20037. Phone: (202) 338–0111.

Embassy of Romania, 1607 23rd St., N.W., Washington, D.C. 20008. Phone: (202) 232–4747, 6593, 6634.

Embassy of the Republic of Rwanda, 1714 New Hampshire Ave., N.W., Washington, D.C. 20009. Phone: (202) 232–2882.

Embassy of Saint Kitts and Nevis, 2100 M St., N.W., Suite 608, Washington, D.C. 20037. Phone: (202) 833–3550.

Embassy of Saint Lucia, 2100 M St., N.W., Suite 309, Washington, D.C. 20037. Phone: (202) 463–7378, 7379.

Embassy of Saint Vincent and the Grenadines, 1717 Massachusetts Ave., N.W., Suite 102, Washington, D.C. 20036. Phone: (202) 462–7806, 7846.

Embassy of São Tomé and Príncipe, 801 Second Ave., Suite 603, New York, N.Y. 10017 (temporary address). Phone: (212) 697–4211.

Embassy of Saudi Arabia, 601 New Hampshire Ave., N.W., Washington, D.C. 20037. Phone: (202) 342–3800.

Embassy of the Republic of Senegal, 2112 Wyoming Ave., N.W., Washington, D.C. 20008. Phone: (202) 234–0540, 0541.

Embassy of the Republic of Seychelles, c/o Permanent Mission of Seychelles to the United Nations, 820 Second Ave., Suite 900F, New York, N.Y. 10017. Phone: (212) 687–9766/9767.

Embassy of Sierra Leone, 1701 19th St., N.W., Washington, D.C. 20009. Phone: (202) 939–9261.

Embassy of the Republic of Singapore, 1824 R St., N.W., Washington, D.C. 20009. Phone: (202) 667–7555.

Embassy of the Solomon Islands, c/o Permanent Mission of the Solomon Islands to the United Nations, 820 Second Ave., Suite 800, New York, N.Y. 10017. Phone: (212) 599-6193.

Embassy of the Somali Democratic Republic, 600 New Hampshire Ave., N.W., Suite 710, Washington, D.C. 20037. Phone: (202) 342–1575.

Embassy of South Africa, 3051 Massachusetts Ave., N.W., Washington, D.C. 20008. Phone: (202) 232–4400.

Embassy of Spain, 2700 15th St., N.W., Washington, D.C. 20009. Phone: (202) 265–0190, 0191.

Embassy of the Democratic Socialist Republic of Sri Lanka, 2148 Wyoming Ave., N.W., Washington, D.C. 20008. Phone: (202) 483–4025 to 4028.

Embassy of the Republic of the Sudan, 2210 Massachusetts Ave., N.W., Washington, D.C. 20008. Phone: (202) 338–8565 to 8570.

Embassy of the Republic of Suriname, 4301 Connecticut Ave., N.W., Suite 108, Washington, D.C. 20008. Phone: (202) 244–7488, 7490 to 7492.

Embassy of the Kingdom of Swaziland, 3400 International Drive, N.W., Washington, D.C. 20008. Phone: (202) 362–6683, 6685.

Embassy of Sweden, 600 New Hampshire Ave., N.W., Suites 1200 and 715, Washington, D.C. 20037. Phone: (202) 944–5600.

Embassy of Switzerland, 2900 Cathedral Ave., N.W., Washington, D.C. 20008. Phone: (202) 745–7900.

Embassy of the Syrian Arab Republic, 2215 Wyoming Ave., N.W., Washington, D.C. 20008. Phone: (202) 232–6313.

Embassy of the United Republic of Tanzania, 2139 R St., N.W., Washington, D.C. 20008. Phone: (202) 939–6125.

Embassy of Thailand, 2300 Kalorama Rd., N.W., Washington, D.C. 20008. Phone: (202) 483–7200.

Embassy of the Republic of Togo, 2208 Massachusetts Ave., N.W., Washington, D.C. 20008. Phone: (202) 234–4212, 4213.

Embassy of Trinidad and Tobago, 1708 Massachusetts Ave., N.W., Washington, D.C. 20036. Phone: (202) 467–6490.

Embassy of Tunisia, 1515 Massachusetts Ave., N.W., Washington, D.C. 20005. Phone: (202) 862–1850.

Embassy of the Republic of Turkey, 1714 Massachusetts Ave. N.W., Washington, D.C. 20036. Phone: (202) 659–8200.

Embassy of the Republic of Uganda, 5909 16th St., N.W., Washington, D.C. 20011. Phone: (202) 726–7100 to 7102.

Embassy of the Union of Soviet Socialist Republics, 1125 16th St., N.W., Washington, D.C. 20036. Phone: (202) 628–7551, 8548.

Embassy of the United Arab Emirates, 600 New Hampshire Ave., N.W., Suite 740, Washington, D.C. 20037. Phone: (202) 338–6500.

United Kingdom of Great Britain & Northern Ireland—British Embassy, 3100 Massachusetts Ave., N.W., Washington, D.C. 20008. Phone: (202) 462–1340.

Embassy of Uruguay, 1918 F St., N.W., Washington, D.C. 20006. Phone: (202) 331–1313 to 1316, inclusive.

Embassy of Venezuela, 1099 30th St., N.W., Washington, D.C. 20007. Phone: (202) 342-2214.

Embassy of Western Samoa, 1155 15th St. N.W., # 510, Washington, D.C. 20005. Phone: (202) 833–1743.

Embassy of the Republic of Yemen, 600 New Hampshire Ave., N.W., Suite 840, Washington, D.C. 20037. Phone: (202) 965–4760, 4761.

Embassy of the Socialist Federal Republic of Yugoslavia, 2410 California St., N.W., Washington, D.C. 20008. Phone: (202) 462–6566.

Embassy of the Republic of Zaire, 1800 New Hampshire Ave., N.W., Washington, D.C. 20009. Phone: (202) 234–7690, 7691.

Embassy of the Republic of Zambia, 2419 Massachusetts Ave., N.W., Washington, D.C. 20008. Phone: (202) 265–9717 to 9721.

Embassy of Zimbabwe, 1608 New Hampshire Ave., N.W., Washington, D.C. 20009. Phone: (202) 332–7100.

Diplomatic Personnel To and From the U.S.

Country	U.S. Representative to[1]	Rank	Representative from[2]	Rank
Afghanistan	—	—	Abdul Ghafoor Jawshan	Min.-Consl.
Algeria	Christopher W. S. Ross	Amb.	Abderrahmane Bensid	Amb.
Antigua and Barbuda	(Vacancy)	Amb.	Paul O. Spencer	Min.-Consl.
Argentina	Terance A. Todman	Amb.	Carlos Ortiz de Rosas	Amb.
Australia	Melvin F. Sembler	Amb.	Michael John Cook	Amb.
Austria	Roy Michael Huffington	Amb.	Friedrich Hoess	Amb.
Bahamas	Chic Hecht	Amb.	Margaret E. McDonald	Amb.
Bahrain	Charles W. Hostler	Amb.	Ghazi Mohamed Algosaibi	Amb.
Bangladesh	William B. Milam	Amb.	A.H.S. Ataul Karim	Amb.
Barbados	G. Philip Hughes	Amb.	Sir William Douglas	Amb.
Belgium	Maynard W. Gitman	Amb.	Jean Cassiers	Amb.
Belize	Eugene L. Scassa	Amb.	James V. Hyde	Amb.
Benin	Harriet W. Isom	Amb.	Candide Pierre Ahouansou	Amb.
Bolivia	Robert S. Gelbard	Amb.	Jorge Crespo–Velasco	Amb.
Botswana	David Passage	Amb.	Botsweletse Kingsley Sebele	Amb.
Brazil	Richard H. Melton	Amb.	Marcilio Marques Moreira	Amb.
Brunei	Christopher H. Phillips	Amb.	Dato Haji Mohammad Kassim	Amb.
Bulgaria	H. Kenneth Hill	Amb.	Ognian Raytchev Pishev	Amb.
Burkina Faso	Edward P. Byrnn	Amb.	Paul-Désiré Kabore	Amb.
Burundi	Cynthia S. Perry	Amb.	Julien Kavakure	Amb.
Cameroon	Frances D. Cook	Amb.	Paul Pondi	Amb.
Canada	Edward N. Ney	Amb.	Derek H. Burney	Amb.
Cape Verde	Francis T. McNamara	Amb.	Jorge M. Custodio Dos Santos	Amb.
Central African Republic	Daniel H. Simpson	Amb.	Jean-Pierre Sohahong-Kombet	Amb.
Chad	Richard W. Bogosian	Amb.	Mahamat Ali Adoum	Amb.
Chile	Charles A. Gillespie Jr.	Amb.	Patricio Silva	Amb.
China	James R. Lilley	Amb.	Qizhen Zhu	Amb.
Colombia	Thomas E. McNamara	Amb.	Jaime Garcia-Parra	Amb.
Comoros	Kenneth N. Peltier	Amb.	Amini Ali Moumin	Amb.
Congo, People's Republic of	James D. Phillips	Amb.	Roger Issombo	Amb.

Country	U.S. Representative to[1]	Rank	Representative from[2]	Rank
Costa Rica	(Vacancy)	Amb.	Gonzalo J. Facio	Amb.
Côte d'Ivoire	Kenneth L. Brown	Amb.	Charles Gomis	Amb.
Cyprus	Robert E. Lamb	Amb.	Michael E. Sherifis	Amb.
Czechoslovakia	Shirley Temple Black	Amb.	Rita Klimova	Amb.
Denmark	Keith L. Brown	Amb.	Peter P. Dyvig	Amb.
Djibouti	Robert S. Barrett IV	Amb.	Roble Olhaye	Amb.
Dominica	—	—	Edward I. Watty	Amb.
Dominican Republic	Paul D. Taylor	Amb.	Dr. Dario Suro	Min.
Ecuador	Paul C. Lambert	Amb.	Jaime Moncayo	Amb.
Egypt	Frank G. Wisner	Amb.	El Sayed Abdel Raouf El Reedy	Amb.
El Salvador	William G. Walker	Amb.	Miguel Angel Salaverria	Amb.
Equatorial Guinea	(Vacancy)	Amb.	Damaso Obiang Ndong	Amb.
Ethiopia	Robert G. Houdek	Cd'A.	Girma Amare	Consul.
Fiji	Evelyn I. H. Teegen	Amb.	Ratu Finau Mara	Consul.
Finland	John G. Weinmann	Amb.	Jukka Valtasaari	Amb.
France	Alan P. Larson	Amb.	Jacques Andreani	Amb.
Gabon	Keith L. Wauchope	Amb.	Alexandre Sambat	Amb.
Gambia	Arlene Render	Amb.	Ousman A. Sallah	Amb.
Germany	Vernon A. Walters	Amb.	Juergen Ruhfus	Amb.
Ghana	Raymond C. Ewing	Amb.	Dr. Joseph L.S. Abbey	Amb.
Greece	Michael G. Sotirhos	Amb.	Christo Zacharakis	Amb.
Grenada	(Vacancy)	Cd'A.	Denneth Modeste	Amb.
Guatemala	Thomas F. Stroock	Amb.	Norma J. Vazquez	Min.-Consl.
Guinea	Dane F. Smith, Jr.	Amb.	Camara Ansoumane	Consul.
Guinea-Bissau	William H. Jacobsen, Jr.	Amb.	Alfredo Lopes Cabral	Amb.
Guyana	(Vacancy)	Amb.	Dr. Cedric Hilburn Grant	Amb.
Haiti	Alvin P. Adams, Jr.	Amb.	Louis Harold Joseph	Min.-Consl.
Holy See	Thomas P. Melady	Amb.	Most Rev. Agostino Cacciavillan	Pro-Nuncio
Honduras	Cresencio S. Arcos	Amb.	Jorge Ramon Hernandez-Alcerro	Amb.
Hungary	Charles H. Thomas	Amb.	Eniko Bollobas	Min.-Consl.
Iceland	Charles E. Cobb, Jr.	Amb.	Tomas A. Tomasson	Amb.
India	William Clark, Jr.	Amb.	Abid Hussain	Amb.
Indonesia	John C. Monjo	Amb.	Abdul Rachman Ramly	Amb.
Iraq	Operations have been temporarily suspended			
Ireland	Richard A. Moore	Amb.	Padraic N. MacKernan	Amb.
Israel	William A. Brown	Amb.	Zalman Shoval	Amb.
Italy	Peter F. Secchia	Amb.	Rinaldo Petrignani	Amb.
Jamaica	Glen A. Holden	Amb.	Richard Leighton Bernal	Amb.
Japan	Michael H. Armacost	Amb.	Ryohei Murata	Amb.
Jordan	Roger G. Harrison	Amb.	Hussein A. Hammami	Amb.
Kenya	Smith Hempstone, Jr.	Amb.	Denis D. Afande	Amb.
Korea, South	Donald P. Gregg	Amb.	Hong-Choo Hyun	Amb.
Kuwait	Edward Gnehm	Amb.	Shaikh Saud Nasir Al-Sabah	Amb.
Laos	Charles B. Salmon, Jr.	Cd'A.	Linthong Phetsavan	1st Secy.
Lebanon	Ryan C. Crocker	Amb.	Nassib S. Lahoud	Amb.
Lesotho	Leonard H.O. Spearman, Jr.	Amb.	W. T. Van Tonder	Amb.
Liberia	Peter J. de Vos	Amb.	Eugenia A. Wordsworth-Stevenson	Amb.
Luxembourg	Edward M. Rowell	Amb.	Andre Philippe	Amb.
Madagascar	Howard K. Walker	Amb.	Pierrot J. Rajaonarivelo	Amb.
Malawi	George A. Trail, III	Amb.	Robert B. Mbaya	Amb.
Malaysia	Paul M. Cleveland	Amb.	A.R. Ahmad Fuzi	Min.
Mali	Herbert Donald Gelber	Amb.	Mohamed Alhousseyni Toure	Amb.
Malta	Sally J. Novetzke	Amb.	Salv. J. Stellini	Amb.
Marshall Islands	William Bodde, Jr.	Cd'A.	Wilfred I. Kendall	Amb.
Mauritania	William H. Twaddell	Amb.	Abdellah Ould Daddah	Amb.
Mauritius	Penne Percy Korth	Amb.	Chitmansing Jesseramsing	Amb.
Mexico	John D. Negroponte	Amb.	Gustavo Petricioli	Amb.
Micronesia	Aurelia Brazeal	Amb.	Jesse B. Marehalau	Amb.
Mongolia	Joseph E. Lake	Amb.	Gendengiin Nyamdoo	Amb.
Morocco	E. Michael Ussery	Amb.	Mohamed Belkhayat	Amb.
Mozambique	Townsend B. Friedman, Jr.	Amb.	Hipolito Pereira Zozimo Patricio	Amb.
Myanmar (Burma)	Burton Levin	Amb.	U Hla Myint OO	Consul.
Namibia	Genta Hawkins Holmes	Amb.	Hinyangerwa Pius Asheeke	Min.
Nepal	Julia Chang Bloch	Amb.	Mohan Man Sainju	Amb.
Netherlands	C. Howard Wilkins, Jr.	Amb.	Johan H. Meesman	Amb.
New Zealand	Della M. Newman	Amb.	Denis Bazeley Gordon McLean	Amb.
Nicaragua	Harry W. Shlaudeman	Amb.	Ernesto Palazio	Amb.
Niger	Carl C. Cundiff	Amb.	Moumouni Adamou Djermakoye	Amb.
Nigeria	Lannon Walker	Amb.	Kevin Efiong Efretei	Min.
Norway	Loret Miller Ruppe	Amb.	Kjeld Vibe	Amb.
Oman	Richard W. Boehm	Amb.	Awadh Bader Al-Shanfari	Amb.

Country	U.S. Representative to[1]	Rank	Representative from[2]	Rank
Pakistan	Robert B. Oakley	Amb.	Najmuddin A. Shaikh	Amb.
Panama	Deane R. Hinton	Amb.	Miguel A. Corro	Min.-Consl.
Papua New Guinea	Robert W. Farrand	Amb.	Margaret Taylor	Amb.
Paraguay	Timothy L. Towell	Amb.	Marcos Martinez Mendieta	Amb.
Peru	Anthony C.E. Quainton	Amb.	Roberto MacLean	Amb.
Philippines	Nicholas Platt	Amb.	Emmanuel Pelaez	Amb.
Poland	Thomas W. Simons, Jr.	Amb.	Kazimierz Dziewanowski	Amb.
Portugal	Everett Ellis Briggs	Amb.	Joao Eduardo M. Pereira Bastos	Amb.
Qatar	Mark G. Hambley	Amb.	Dr. Hamad Abdelaziz Al-Kawari	Amb.
Romania	Alan Green, Jr.	Amb.	Virgil Constantinescu	Amb.
Rwanda	Robert A. Flaten	Amb.	Aloys Uwimana	Amb.
Saint Kitts and Nevis	—	—	Erstein M. Edwards	Amb.
Saint Lucia	—	—	Dr. Joseph Edsel Edmunds	Amb.
Saint Vincent and the Grenadines	—	—	Kingsley C.A. Layne	Amb.
São Tomé and Príncipe	—	—	Joaquim Rafael Branco	Amb.
Saudi Arabia	Charles W. Freeman, Jr.	Amb.	Prince Bandar Bin Sultan	Amb.
Senegal	George E. Moose	Amb.	Ibra Deguene Ka	Amb.
Seychelles	James B. Moran	Amb.	Marc R. Marengo	2nd Secy.
Sierra Leone	Johnny Young	Amb.	Dr. George Carew	Amb.
Singapore	Robert D. Orr	Amb.	S.R. Nathan	Amb.
Solomon Islands	Robert W. Farrand	Amb.	Francis Bugotu	Amb.
Somalia	—	—	Embassy ceased operations	—
South Africa	William L. Swing	Amb.	Harry Heinz Schwarz	Amb.
Spain	Joseph Zappala	Amb.	Jaime de Ojeda y Eiseley	Amb.
Sri Lanka	Marion V. Creekmore, Jr.	Amb.	W. Susanta DeAlwis	Amb.
Sudan	James R. Cheek	Amb.	Abdalla Ahmed Abdalla	Amb.
Suriname	John P. Leonard	Amb.	Willem A. Udenhout	Amb.
Swaziland	Stephen H. Rogers	Amb.	Absalom Vusani Mamba	Amb.
Sweden	Charles E. Rednam	Amb.	Anders Ingmar Thunborg	Amb.
Switzerland	Joseph B. Gildenhorn	Amb.	Edouard Brunner	Amb.
Syria	Edward P. Djerejian	Amb.	Walid Al-Moualem	Amb.
Tanzania	Edward DeJarnette	Amb.	Charles Musama Nyirabu	Amb.
Thailand	Daniel A. O'Donohue	Amb.	Krit Garnjana-Goonchorn	Min.
Togo	Harmon E. Kirby	Amb.	Ellom-Kodjo Schuppius	Amb.
Trinidad and Tobago	Charles A. Gargano	Amb.	Angus Albert Khan	Amb.
Tunisia	Robert H. Pelletreau, Jr.	Amb.	Ismail Khelil	Amb.
Turkey	Morton I. Abramowitz	Amb.	Nuzhet Kandemir	Amb.
Uganda	John A. Burroughs, Jr.	Amb.	Stephen Kapimpina Katenta-Apuli	Amb.
U.S.S.R.	Robert S. Strauss	Amb.	Viktor Georgivevich Komplektov	Amb.
United Arab Emirates	Edward S. Walker, Jr.	Amb.	Abdulla bin Zayed Al-Nahayyan	Amb.
United Kingdom	Raymond G.H. Seitz	Amb.	Sir Robin Renwick	Amb.
Uruguay	Richard C. Brown	Amb.	Dr. Eduardo MacGillycuddy	Amb.
Venezuela	Michael M. Skol	Amb.	Simon Alberto Consalvi	Amb.
Western Samoa	Della Newman	Amb.	Tuaopepe Fili Wendt	Amb.
Yemen	Charles F. Dunbar	Amb.	Mohsin A. Alaini	Amb.
Yugoslavia	Warren Zimmerman	Amb.	Dzevad Mujezinovic	Amb.
Zaire	William C. Harrop	Amb.	Tatanene Manata	Amb.
Zambia	Gordon L. Street	Amb.	Dr. Paul J.F. Lusaka	Amb.
Zimbabwe	(Vacancy)	Amb.	Stanislaus Garikai Chigwedere	Amb.

1. As of Jan. 1991. 2. As of May 1991. NOTE: Amb.=Ambassador; Cd'A.=Charge d'Affaires; Secy.=Secretary; Consl.=Counselor; Min.=Minister; P.O.=Principal Officer. *Source:* U.S. Department of State.

Health Hints for the International Traveler

Source: U.S. Department of Health and Human Services, Public Health Service, Centers for Disease Control

Introduction

This article includes practical information on how to avoid potential health problems. Some of these recommendations are common–sense precautions; others have been scientifically documented.

Personal and specific preventive measures against certain diseases may require advance planning and advice from a physician concerning immunization and prophylaxis. If more specific information is needed, travelers should contact their local health department or physician.

Travelers who take prescription medications should carry an adequate supply accompanied by a signed and dated statement from a physician; the statement should indicate the major health problems and dosage of such medications, to provide information for medical authorities in case of emergency. The traveler should take an extra pair of glasses or lens prescription, and a card, tag, or bracelet that identifies any physical condition that may require emergency care.

Medical Care

If medical care is needed abroad, travel agents or the American Embassy or Consulate can usually provide names of hospitals, physicians, or emergency medical service agencies. Prior to departure, travelers should contact their own insurance companies concerning their coverage.

WHO Blood Transfusion Guidelines

There is a growing public awareness of the AIDS epidemic, and a resulting concern about acquiring the AIDS virus through blood transfusion. Systematic screening of blood donations is not yet feasible in all developing countries. Requests have been made by persons planning international travels, to have their own blood, or blood from their home country, available to them in case of urgent need. These requests raise logistic, technical and ethical issues which are not easy to resolve. Ultimately, the safety of blood for such persons will depend upon the quality of blood transfusion services in the host country. The strengthening of these services is of the highest priority. While efforts are being made to achieve this end, other approaches are also needed.

Basic Principles:

1. Unexpected, emergency, blood transfusion is rarely required. It is needed only in situations of massive hemorrhage like severe trauma, gynecological and obstetric emergency, or gastrointestinal bleeding.

2. In many cases, resuscitation can be achieved by use of colloid or crystalloid plasma expanders[1] instead of blood.

3. Blood transfusion is not free of risk, even in the best of conditions. In most developing countries, the risk is increased by limited technical resources for screening blood donors for HIV infection and other diseases transmissible by blood.

4. The international shipment of blood for transfusion is practical only when handled by agreement between two responsible organizations, such as national blood transfusion services. This mechanism is not useful for emergency needs of individual patients and should not be attempted by private individuals or organizations not operating recognized blood programs.

Therefore:

1. There are no medical indications for travelers to take blood with them from their home country.

2. The limited storage period of blood and the need for special equipment negate the feasibility of independent blood banking for individual travelers or small groups.

3. Blood should be transfused only when absolutely indicated. This applies even more forcefully in those countries where screening of blood for transmissible diseases is not yet widely performed.

Proposed Options:

1. When urgent resuscitation is necessary, the use of plasma expanders rather than blood should always be considered.

2. In case of emergency need of blood, use of plasma expanders and urgent evacuation home may be the actions of choice.

3. When blood transfusion cannot be avoided, the attending physician should make every effort to ensure that the blood has been screened for transmissible diseases, including HIV.

4. International travelers should: (a) take active steps to minimize the risk of injury; (b) establish a plan for dealing with medical emergencies; (c) support the development within countries of safe and adequate blood supplies.

This information is taken from the WHO publication "World Health Organization Global Programme on AIDS: Blood transfusion guidelines for international travelers."

Motion Sickness

Travelers with a history of motion sickness or sea sickness can attempt to avoid symptoms by taking anti–motion–sickness pills or antihistaminics before departure.

Pregnant Women

The problems that a pregnant woman might encounter during international travel are basically the same problems that other international travelers have. These have to do with exposure to infectious diseases and availability of good medical care. There is the additional potential problem that air travel late in pregnancy might precipitate labor.

Potential health problems vary from country to country; therefore, if the traveler has specific questions, she should be advised to check with the embassy or local consulate general office of the country in question before traveling.

Disabled Travelers

The Airport Operators Council International, Incorporated, publishes "Access Travel: A Guide to Accessibility of Terminals." The 40–page guide lists design features, facilities, and services for handicapped persons in 472 airport terminals in over 50 countries. Single copies are available at no cost from the Architectural and Transportation Barriers Compliance Board. For a copy, you may write or call, ATBCB, 1111 18th Street, N.W., Suite 50, Washington, D.C. 20036–3894, (202) 653–7834.

Risks From Food and Drink

Contaminated food and drink are common sources for the introduction of infection into the body. Among the more common infections that travelers may acquire from contaminated food and drink are *Escherichia coli* infections, shigellosis or bacillary dysentery, giardiasis, cryptosporidiosis, and hepatitis A. Other less common infectious disease risks for travelers include typhoid fever and other salmonelloses, cholera, infections caused by rotaviruses and Norwalk–like viruses, and a variety of protozoan and helminth parasites (other than those that cause giardiasis and cryptosporidiosis). Many of the infectious diseases transmitted in food and water can also be acquired directly through the fecal–oral route.

Water

Water that has been adequately chlorinated, using minimum recommended water–works standards as practiced in the United States, will afford significant protection against viral and bacterial waterborne diseases. However, chlorine treatment alone, as used in the routine disinfection of water, may not kill some enteric viruses and the parasitic organisms that cause giardiasis and amebiasis. In areas where chlorinated tap water is not available, or where hygiene and sanitation are poor, travelers should be advised that only the following may be safe to drink:

1. Beverages, such as tea and coffee, made with boiled water.

Treatment of Water With Tincture of Iodine

Tincture of iodine (from medicine chest or first aid kit)	Drops* to be added per quart or litre	
	Clear water	Cold or cloudy water+
2%	5	10

*1 drop = 0.05 ml
Let stand for 30 minutes.
Water is safe to use.
+Very turbid or cloudy water may require prolonged contact time; let stand up to several hours prior to use, if possible.

2. Canned or bottled *carbonated* beverages, including *carbonated* bottled water and soft drinks.
3. Beer and wine.

Where water may be contaminated, ice (or containers for drinking) also should be considered contaminated. Thus, in these areas ice should not be used in beverages. If ice has been in contact with containers used for drinking, the containers should be thoroughly cleaned, preferably with soap and hot water, after the ice has been discarded.

It is safer to drink directly from a can or bottle of a beverage than from a questionable container. However, water on the outside of cans or bottles of beverages might be contaminated. Therefore, wet cans or bottles should be dried before being opened, and surfaces which are contacted directly by the mouth in drinking should first be wiped clean. Where water may be contaminated, travelers should avoid brushing their teeth with tap water.

Treatment of Water

Boiling is by far the most reliable method to make water of uncertain purity safe for drinking. Water should be brought to a vigorous boil and allowed to cool to room temperature—do not add ice. At very high altitudes, for an extra margin of safety, boil for several minutes or use chemical disinfection. Adding a pinch of salt to each quart, or pouring the water several times from one container to another will improve the taste.

Chemical disinfection with iodine is an alternative method of water treatment when it is not feasible to boil water. Two well-tested methods for disinfection with iodine are the use of tincture of iodine (*See* table), and the use of tetraglycine hydroperiodide tablets (Globaline, Potable-Agua, Coghlan's,[2] etc.). The tablets are available from pharmacies and sporting goods stores. The manufacturer's instructions should be followed. If water is cloudy, the number of tablets should be doubled; if water is extremely cold, an attempt should be made to warm the water, and the recommended contact time should be increased to achieve reliable disinfection. Cloudy water should be strained through a clean cloth into a container to remove any sediment or floating matter, and then the water should be treated with heat or iodine. Chlorine, in various forms, has also been used for chemical disinfection. However, its germicidal activity varies greatly with pH, temperature, and organic content of the water to be purified, and is less reliable than iodine.

There are a variety of portable filters currently on the market which according to the manufacturers' data will provide safe drinking water. Although the iodide–impregnated resins and the microstrainer type filters will kill and/or remove many micoorganisms, there are very few published reports in the scientific literature dealing both with the methods used and the results of the tests employed to evaluate the efficacy of these filters against water–borne pathogens. Until there is sufficient independent verification of the efficacy of these filters, The Centers for Disease Control makes no recommendation regarding their use.

As a last resort, if no source of safe drinking water is available or can be obtained, tap water that is uncomfortably hot to touch is usually safe. After allowing such hot water to cool to room temperature in a thoroughly cleaned container, it may be used for brushing teeth, as well as for drinking.

Food

To avoid illness, food should be selected with care. All raw food is subject to contamination. Particularly in areas where hygiene and sanitation are inadequate, the traveler should be advised to avoid salads, uncooked vegetables, unpasteurized milk and milk products such as cheese, and to eat only food that has been cooked and is still hot, or fruit that has been peeled by the traveler. Undercooked and raw meat, fish, and shellfish may carry various intestinal pathogens.

The easiest way to guarantee a safe food source for an infant less than 6 months of age is to have the child breast–feed. If the infant has already been weaned from the breast, formula prepared from commercial powder and boiled water is the safest and most practical food.

Some species of fish and shellfish can contain poisonous biotoxins, even when well cooked. The most common type of fish poisoning in travelers is ciguatera fish poisoning. Red snapper, grouper, barracuda, amberjack, sea bass, and a wide range of tropical reef fish contain the toxin at unpredictable times. The potential for ciguatera poisoning exists in all subtropical and tropical insular areas of the West Indies, Pacific and Indian Oceans where the implicated fish species are consumed.

1. See World Health Organization documents LAB/81,5: "Use of plasma volume substitutes and plasma in developing countries," for further details, and WHO/GPA/INF/88.5 "Guidelines for Treatment of Acute Blood Loss."

2. Use of trade names is for identification only and does not imply endorsement by the Public Health Service or the U.S. Department of Health and Human Services.

Travel Tips

The booklet, *Your Trip Abroad,* contains some valuable information on loss and theft of a passport as well as other travel tips. To obtain a copy, write to the Superintendent of Documents, U.S. Government Printing Office, Washington, D.C. 20402 and ask for publication #8969. The single copy price is $1.

State and City Tourism Offices

The following is a selected list of state tourism offices. Where a toll-free 800 number is available, it is given. However, the numbers are subject to change.

ALABAMA
Bureau of Tourism & Travel
401 Adams Ave.
Montgomery, AL
36104-4331
205–242–4169 or
1–800–ALABAMA

ALASKA
Alaska Division of Tourism
P.O. Box E
Juneau, AK 99811
907–465–2010

ARIZONA
Arizona Office of Tourism
1100 West Washington
Phoenix, AZ 85007
602 542–TOUR

ARKANSAS
Arkansas Department of
Parks and Tourism
1 Capitol Mall
Little Rock, AR 72201
501–682–7777 or
1–800–NATURAL
(both in and out of state)

CALIFORNIA
California Office of Tourism
Department of Com-
merce
801 K Street
Suite 1600
Sacramento, CA 95814
Write or phone for free
200-page Guide Infor-
mation Packet: (Outside
Calif.) 800–862–2543

COLORADO
Colorado Tourism Board
1625 Broadway, Suite 1700
Denver, CO 80202
303–592–5410
For a vacation planning kit,
call Toll-free
1–800–433–2656

CONNECTICUT
Tourism Promotion Service
CT Dept. of Economic
Development
865 Brook Street
Rocky Hill, CT 06067-3405
203–258–4355 or 800–CT
BOUND (nationwide)

DELAWARE
Delaware Tourism Office
Delaware Development
Office
99 Kings Highway
P.O. Box 1401, Dept. RB
Dover, DE 19903
302–736–4271 or
1–800–441–8846
(out of state)

DISTRICT OF COLUMBIA
Washington Convention

and Visitors Association
1212 New York Ave., NW
Washington, D.C. 20005
202–789–7000

FLORIDA
Department of Commerce
Visitors Inquiry
126 Van Buren St.
Tallahassee, FL 32399-2000
904–487–1462

GEORGIA
Tourist Division
P.O. Box 1776
Atlanta, GA 30301-1776
404–656–3590
1–800–VISIT GA
(1–800–847–4842)

HAWAII
Hawaii Visitors Bureau
2270 Kalakaua Ave., Suite
801
Honolulu, HI 96815
808–923–1811

IDAHO
Department of Commerce
700 W. State St.
Second Floor
Boise, ID 83720
208–334–2470 or
1–800–635–7820

ILLINOIS
Illinois Department of
Commerce and
Community
Affairs, Bureau of
Tourism
620 East Adams Street
Springfield, IL 62701
217–782–7139

INDIANA
Indiana Dept. of Commerce
Tourism & Film Develop-
ment Division
One North Capitol
Suite 700
Indianapolis, IN
46204-2288
317–232–8860 or
1–800–289–ONIN

IOWA
Iowa Department of
Economic Development
Division of Tourism
200 East Grand Avenue
Des Moines, IA 50309
515–242–4705
1–800–345–IOWA

KANSAS
Travel & Tourism Develop-
ment Division
Department of Commerce
400 W. 8th St., 5th Floor
Topeka, KS 66603

913–296–2009
1–800–2 KANSAS

KENTUCKY
Department of Travel
Development
550 Mero Street
2200 Capital Plaza Tower
Frankfort, KY 40601-1968
502–564–4930 or
1–800–225–TRIP
(Continental United States
and provinces of Ontario
and Quebec, Canada)

LOUISIANA
Office of Tourism
P.O. Box 94291
Baton Rouge, LA
70804-9291
504–342–8119 or
1–800–33GUMBO

MAINE
Maine Publicity Bureau
97 Winthrop St., P.O. Box
2300
Hallowell, ME 04347-2300
207–289–6070

MARYLAND
Office of Tourism
Development
217 E. Redwood St.
Baltimore, MD 21202
1–800–543–1036

MASSACHUSETTS
Office of Travel and
Tourism
100 Cambridge St., 13th
Floor
Boston, MA 02202
617–727–3201

MICHIGAN
Travel Bureau
Department of Commerce
P.O. Box 30226
Lansing, MI 48909
1–800–5432–YES

MINNESOTA
Minnesota Office of
Tourism
375 Jackson St.
250 Skyway Level
Farm Credit Services Bldg.
St. Paul, MN 55101-1848
612–296–5029 or
1–800–657–3700

MISSISSIPPI
Department of Economic
and Community
Development
Tourism Development
P.O. Box 22825
Jackson, MS 39205-2825
601–359–3297 or
1–800–647–2290

Average Daily Temperatures (°F) in Tourist Cities

Location	January High	January Low	April High	April Low	July High	July Low	October High	October Low
U.S. CITIES (See Weather and Climate Section)								
CANADA								
Ottawa	21	3	51	31	81	58	54	37
Quebec	18	2	45	29	76	57	51	37
Toronto	30	16	50	34	79	59	56	40
Vancouver	41	32	58	40	74	54	57	44
MEXICO								
Acapulco	85	70	87	71	89	75	88	74
Mexico City	66	42	78	52	74	54	70	50
OVERSEAS								
Australia (Sydney)	78	65	71	58	60	46	71	56
Austria (Vienna)	34	26	57	41	75	59	55	44
Bahamas (Nassau)	77	65	81	69	88	75	85	73
Bermuda (Hamilton)	68	58	71	59	85	73	79	69
Brazil (Rio de Janeiro)	84	73	80	69	75	63	77	66
Denmark (Copenhagen)	36	29	50	37	72	55	53	42
Egypt (Cairo)	65	47	83	57	96	70	86	65
France (Paris)	42	32	60	41	76	55	59	44
Germany (Berlin)	35	26	55	38	74	55	55	41
Greece (Athens)	54	42	67	52	90	72	74	60
Hong Kong	64	56	75	67	87	78	81	73
India (Calcutta)	80	55	97	76	90	79	89	74
Italy (Rome)	54	39	68	46	88	64	73	53
Israel (Jerusalem)	55	41	73	50	87	63	81	59
Japan (Tokyo)	47	29	63	46	83	70	69	55
Nigeria (Lagos)	88	74	89	77	83	74	85	74
Netherlands (Amsterdam)	40	34	52	43	69	59	56	48
Puerto Rico (San Juan)	81	67	84	69	87	74	87	73
South Africa (Cape Town)	78	60	72	53	63	45	70	52
Spain (Madrid)	47	33	64	44	87	62	66	48
United Kingdom (London)	44	35	56	40	73	55	58	44
United Kingdom (Edinburgh)	43	35	50	39	65	52	53	44
U.S.S.R. (Moscow)	21	9	47	31	76	55	46	34
Venezuela (Caracas)	75	56	81	60	78	61	79	61
Yugoslavia (Belgrade)	37	27	64	45	84	61	65	47

MISSOURI
Missouri Division of
    Tourism
Truman State Office Bldg.
301 W. High St.
P.O. Box 1055
Jefferson City, MO 65102
314–751–4133

MONTANA
Department of Commerce
Travel Montana
1424 9th Avenue
Helena, MT 59620
406–444–2654 or
    1–800–541–1447

NEBRASKA
Dept. of Economic
    Development
Division of Travel and
    Tourism
301 Centennial Mall South
P.O. Box 94666
Lincoln, NE 68509
402–471–3796 or
    1–800–742–7595 (in
    state) or 1–800–228–4307
    (out of state)

NEVADA
Commission on Tourism

Capitol Complex
Carson City, NV 89710
1–800–Nevada–8

NEW HAMPSHIRE
Office of Vacation Travel
P.O. Box 856
Concord, NH 03302
603–271–2666
or for recorded weekly
    events, ski conditions,
    foliage reports
1–800–258–3608
Toll free number is for
    northeast only

NEW JERSEY
Division of Travel and
    Tourism
CN–826
Trenton, NJ 08625
1–800–JERSEY–7

NEW MEXICO
New Mexico Department
    of Tourism
Joseph Montoya Building
Room 1057
1100 St. Francis Dr.
Santa Fe, NM 87503
505–827–0291 or
    1–800–545–2040

NEW YORK
Division of Tourism
1 Commerce Plaza
Albany, NY 12245
Toll free from anywhere in
    the U.S. and its territorial
    possessions
1–800–225–5697. From
    Canada, call (518) 474–4116

NORTH CAROLINA
Travel and Tourism Division
Department of Economic
    and Community
    Development
430 North Salisbury St.
Raleigh, NC 27611
919–733–4171 or
    1–800–VISIT NC

NORTH DAKOTA
North Dakota Tourism
    Promotion
Liberty Memorial Building
Capitol Grounds
604 E. Boulevard
Bismarck, ND 58505
701–224–2525 or
    1–800–437–2077 (out
    of state)
1–800–537–8879 (Canada)

OHIO
Ohio Division of Travel and Tourism
P.O. Box 1001
Columbus, OH 43266-0001
614-466-8844 (Business Office)
1-800-BUCKEYE (National Toll-Free Travel Hotline)

OKLAHOMA
Oklahoma Tourism and Recreation Dept.
Literature Distribution Center
P.O. Box 60000
Oklahoma City, OK 73146
405-521-2409 (In Oklahoma City area) or nationwide at 1-800-652-6552

OREGON
Tourism Division
Oregon Economic Development Dept.
775 Summer St. NE
Salem, OR 97310
503-373-1270 or 1-800-547-7842 (Out of state); 1-800-543-8838 (in state)

PENNSYLVANIA
Bureau of Travel Marketing
453 Forum Building
Harrisburg, PA 17120
717-787-5453 (Business Office)
1-800-VISIT PA, ext. 257 (To order single free copy of PA Travel Guide)

RHODE ISLAND
Rhode Island Tourism Division

7 Jackson Walkway
Providence, RI 02903
401-277-2601 or 1-800-556-2484

SOUTH CAROLINA
South Carolina Division of Tourism
Box 71
Columbia, SC 29202
803-734-0235

SOUTH DAKOTA
Department of Tourism
Capitol Lake Plaza
Pierre, South Dakota 57501
605-773-3301 or 1-800-843-1930

TENNESSEE
Department of Tourist Development
P.O. Box 23170
Nashville, TN 37202
615-741-2158

TEXAS
Travel Information Services
State Highway Department
P.O. Box 5064
Austin, TX 78763-5064
512-483-3705

UTAH
Utah Travel Council
Council Hall, Capitol Hill
Salt Lake City, UT 84114
801-538-1030

VERMONT
Agency of Development and Community Affairs
Travel Division
134 State St.
Montpelier, VT 05602
802-828-3236

VIRGINIA
Virginia Division of Tourism

1021 East Cary St.
Richmond, VA 23219
804-786-4484
1-800-VISIT-VA

WASHINGTON
Washington State Dept. of Trade and Economic Development
101 General Administration Bldg.
AX-13
Olympia, WA 98504-0613
206-753-5630

WASHINGTON, D.C.
See District of Columbia

WEST VIRGINIA
Division of Tourism and Parks
2101 Washington St. E.
Charleston, WV 25305
304-348-2286 or 1-800-CALL-WVA

WISCONSIN
Department of Development
Division of Tourism Development
Box 7606
Madison, WI 53707
Toll free in WI and neighbor states 1-800-372-2737
others: 608-266-2161
Nationally 1-800-432-TRIP

WYOMING
Wyoming Division of Tourism
I-25 at College Drive
Cheyenne, WY 82002-0660
307-777-7777 or 1-800-225-5996

Travel Advisories

Source: U.S. Department of State.

The Department of State tries to alert American travelers to adverse conditions abroad—including violence—through the travel advisory program. In consultation with our embassies and consulates overseas, and various bureaus of the Department of State, the Office of Overseas Citizens Services in the Bureau of Consular Affairs issues travel advisories about conditions in specific countries. Advisories generally do not pertain to isolated international terrorist incidents since these can occur anywhere and at any time. Some mention conditions of political or civil unrest which could pose a threat to personal safety.

There are only a few advisories in effect which advise avoiding all travel to a particular country because of a high incidence of terrorism within the region or because a long–term problem exists. Most of the security–related advisories do not recommend against travel to an entire country but suggest avoiding specific areas within a country where unrest is endemic.

Ask about current travel advisories for specific countries at any of the 13 regional U.S. passport agencies and at U.S. Embassies and consulates abroad. Travel advisories are also widely disseminated to interested organizations, travel associations, and airlines.

Travel advisories may be heard by calling (24 hours a day) the State Department's Citizens Emergency Center at 202-647-5225.

Passport Travel Tips

The American Society of Travel Agents (ASTA) advises those traveling abroad to photocopy important pages in their passports, especially the pages featuring their photos and passport numbers, and dates and places of issue. Also copy those pages containing visas of countries you plan to visit.

In the case of a lost passport, U.S. embassies will usually accept photocopies as proof that you actually possess a passport. Losing a passport abroad can be a time–consuming and expensive process to replace.

Keep a list of your credit cards and other important numbers (driver's license, traveler's checks) in a separate location from your cards in case they are lost.

Road Mileages Between U.S. Cities[1]

Cities	Birming-ham	Boston	Buffalo	Chicago	Cleveland	Dallas	Denver
Birmingham, Ala.	—	1,194	947	657	734	653	1,318
Boston, Mass.	1,194	—	457	983	639	1,815	1,991
Buffalo, N.Y.	947	457	—	536	192	1,387	1,561
Chicago, Ill.	657	983	536	—	344	931	1,050
Cleveland, Ohio	734	639	192	344	—	1,205	1,369
Dallas, Tex.	653	1,815	1,387	931	1,205	—	801
Denver, Colo	1,318	1,991	1,561	1,050	1,369	801	—
Detroit, Mich.	754	702	252	279	175	1,167	1,301
El Paso, Tex.	1,278	2,358	1,928	1,439	1,746	625	652
Houston, Tex.	692	1,886	1,532	1,092	1,358	242	1,032
Indianapolis, Ind.	492	940	510	189	318	877	1,051
Kansas City, Mo.	703	1,427	997	503	815	508	616
Los Angeles, Calif.	2,078	3,036	2,606	2,112	2,424	1,425	1,174
Louisville, Ky.	378	996	571	305	379	865	1,135
Memphis, Tenn.	249	1,345	965	546	773	470	1,069
Miami, Fla.	777	1,539	1,445	1,390	1,325	1,332	2,094
Minneapolis, Minn.	1,067	1,402	955	411	763	969	867
New Orleans, La.	347	1,541	1,294	947	1,102	504	1,305
New York, N.Y.	983	213	436	840	514	1,604	1,780
Omaha, Neb.	907	1,458	1,011	493	819	661	559
Philadelphia, Pa.	894	304	383	758	432	1,515	1,698
Phoenix, Ariz.	1,680	2,664	2,234	1,729	2,052	1,027	836
Pittsburgh, Pa.	792	597	219	457	131	1,237	1,411
St. Louis, Mo.	508	1,179	749	293	567	638	871
Salt Lake City, Utah	1,805	2,425	1,978	1,458	1,786	1,239	512
San Francisco, Calif.	2,385	3,179	2,732	2,212	2,540	1,765	1,266
Seattle, Wash.	2,612	3,043	2,596	2,052	2,404	2,122	1,373
Washington, D.C.	751	440	386	695	369	1,372	1,635

Cities	Detroit	El Paso	Houston	Indian-apolis	Kansas City	Los Angeles	Louisville
Birmingham, Ala.	754	1,278	692	492	703	2,078	378
Boston, Mass.	702	2,358	1,886	940	1,427	3,036	996
Buffalo, N.Y.	252	1,928	1,532	510	997	2,606	571
Chicago, Ill.	279	1,439	1,092	189	503	2,112	305
Cleveland, Ohio	175	1,746	1,358	318	815	2,424	379
Dallas, Tex.	1,167	625	242	877	508	1,425	865
Denver, Colo.	1,310	652	1,032	1,051	616	1,174	1,135
Detroit, Mich.	—	1,696	1,312	290	760	2,369	378
El Paso, Tex.	1,696	—	756	1,418	936	800	1,443
Houston, Tex.	1,312	756	—	1,022	750	1,556	981
Indianapolis, Ind.	290	1,418	1,022	—	487	2,096	114
Kansas City, Mo.	760	936	750	487	—	1,609	519
Los Angeles, Calif.	2,369	800	1,556	2,096	1,609	—	2,128
Louisville, Ky.	378	1,443	981	114	519	2,128	—
Memphis, Tenn.	756	1,095	586	466	454	1,847	396
Miami, Fla.	1,409	1,957	1,237	1,225	1,479	2,757	1,111
Minneapolis, Minn.	698	1,353	1,211	600	466	2,041	716
New Orleans, La.	1,101	1,121	365	839	839	1,921	725
New York, N.Y.	671	2,147	1,675	729	1,216	2,825	785
Omaha, Neb.	754	1,015	903	590	204	1,733	704
Philadelphia, Pa.	589	2,065	1,586	647	1,134	2,743	703
Phoenix, Ariz.	1,986	402	1,158	1,713	1,226	398	1,749
Pittsburgh, Pa.	288	1,778	1,395	360	847	2,456	416
St. Louis, Mo.	529	1,179	799	239	255	1,864	264
Salt Lake City, Utah	1,721	877	1,465	1,545	1,128	728	1,647
San Francisco, Calif.	2,475	1,202	1,958	2,299	1,882	403	2,401
Seattle, Wash.	2,339	1,760	2,348	2,241	1,909	1,150	2,355
Washington, D.C.	526	1,997	1,443	565	1,071	2,680	601

1. These figures represent estimates and are subject to change.

Road Mileages Between U.S. Cities

Cities	Memphis	Miami	Minne–apolis	New Orleans	New York	Omaha	Phila–delphia
Birmingham, Ala.	249	777	1,067	347	983	907	894
Boston, Mass.	1,345	1,539	1,402	1,541	213	1,458	304
Buffalo, N.Y.	965	1,445	955	1,294	436	1,011	383
Chicago, Ill.	546	1,390	411	947	840	493	758
Cleveland, Ohio	773	1,325	763	1,102	514	819	432
Dallas, Tex.	470	1,332	969	504	1,604	661	1,515
Denver, Colo.	1,069	2,094	867	1,305	1,780	559	1,698
Detroit, Mich.	756	1,409	698	1,101	671	754	589
El Paso, Tex.	1,095	1,957	1,353	1,121	2,147	1,015	2,065
Houston, Tex.	586	1,237	1,211	365	1,675	903	1,586
Indianapolis, Ind.	466	1,225	600	839	729	590	647
Kansas City, Mo.	454	1,479	466	839	1,216	204	1,134
Los Angeles, Calif.	1,847	2,757	2,041	1,921	2,825	1,733	2,743
Louisville, Ky.	396	1,111	716	725	785	704	703
Memphis, Tenn.	—	1,025	854	401	1,134	658	1,045
Miami, Fla.	1,025	—	1,801	892	1,328	1,683	1,239
Minneapolis, Minn.	854	1,801	—	1,255	1,259	373	1,177
New Orleans, La.	401	892	1,255	—	1,330	1,043	1,241
New York, N.Y.	1,134	1,328	1,259	1,330	—	1,315	93
Omaha, Neb.	658	1,683	373	1,043	1,315	—	1,233
Philadelphia, Pa.	1,045	1,239	1,177	1,241	93	1,233	—
Phoenix, Ariz.	1,464	2,359	1,644	1,523	2,442	1,305	2,360
Pittsburgh, Pa.	810	1,250	876	1,118	386	932	304
St. Louis, Mo.	295	1,241	559	696	968	459	886
Salt Lake City, Utah	1,556	2,571	1,243	1,743	2,282	967	2,200
San Francisco, Calif.	2,151	3,097	1,997	2,269	3,036	1,721	2,954
Seattle, Wash.	2,363	3,389	1,641	2,606	2,900	1,705	2,818
Washington, D.C.	902	1,101	1,114	1,098	229	1,170	140

Cities	Phoenix	Pitts–burgh	St. Louis	Salt Lake City	San Francisco	Seattle	Wash–ington
Birmingham, Ala.	1,680	792	508	1,805	2,385	2,612	751
Boston, Mass.	2,664	597	1,179	2,425	3,179	3,043	440
Buffalo, N.Y.	2,234	219	749	1,978	2,732	2,596	386
Chicago, Ill.	1,729	457	293	1,458	2,212	2,052	695
Cleveland, Ohio	2,052	131	567	1,786	2,540	2,404	369
Dallas, Tex.	1,027	1,237	638	1,239	1,765	2,122	1,372
Denver, Colo.	836	1,411	871	512	1,266	1,373	1,635
Detroit, Mich.	1,986	288	529	1,721	2,475	2,339	526
El Paso, Tex.	402	1,778	1,179	877	1,202	1,760	1,997
Houston, Tex.	1,158	1,395	799	1,465	1,958	2,348	1,443
Indianapolis, Ind.	1,713	360	239	1,545	2,299	2,241	565
Kansas City, Mo.	1,226	847	255	1,128	1,882	1,909	1,071
Los Angeles, Calif.	398	2,456	1,864	728	403	1,150	2,680
Louisville, Ky.	1,749	416	264	1,647	2,401	2,355	601
Memphis, Tenn.	1,464	810	295	1,556	2,151	2,363	902
Miami, Fla.	2,359	1,250	1,241	2,571	3,097	3,389	1,101
Minneapolis, Minn.	1,644	876	559	1,243	1,997	1,641	1,114
New Orleans, La.	1,523	1,118	696	1,743	2,269	2,626	1,098
New York, N.Y.	2,442	386	968	2,282	3,036	2,900	229
Omaha, Neb.	1,305	932	459	967	1,721	1,705	1,178
Philadelphia, Pa.	2,360	304	886	2,200	2,954	2,818	140
Phoenix, Ariz.	—	2,073	1,485	651	800	1,482	2,278
Pittsburgh, Pa.	2,073	—	599	1,899	2,653	2,517	241
St. Louis, Mo.	1,485	599	—	1,383	2,137	2,164	836
Salt Lake City, Utah	651	1,899	1,383	—	754	883	2,110
San Francisco, Calif.	800	2,653	2,137	754	—	817	2,864
Seattle, Wash.	1,482	2,517	2,164	883	817	—	2,755
Washington, D.C.	2,278	241	836	2,110	2,864	2,755	—

Air Distances Between U.S. Cities in Statute Miles

Cities	Birming-ham	Boston	Buffalo	Chicago	Cleveland	Dallas	Denver
Birmingham, Ala.	—	1,052	776	578	618	581	1,095
Boston, Mass.	1,052	—	400	851	551	1,551	1,769
Buffalo, N.Y.	776	400	—	454	173	1,198	1,370
Chicago, Ill.	578	851	454	—	308	803	920
Cleveland, Ohio	618	551	173	308	—	1,025	1,227
Dallas, Tex.	581	1,551	1,198	803	1,025	—	663
Denver, Colo.	1,095	1,769	1,370	920	1,227	663	—
Detroit, Mich.	641	613	216	238	90	999	1,156
El Paso, Tex.	1,152	2,072	1,692	1,252	1,525	572	557
Houston, Tex.	567	1,605	1,286	940	1,114	225	879
Indianapolis, Ind.	433	807	435	165	263	763	1,000
Kansas City, Mo.	579	1,251	861	414	700	451	558
Los Angeles, Calif.	1,802	2,596	2,198	1,745	2,049	1,240	831
Louisville, Ky.	331	826	483	269	311	726	1,038
Memphis, Tenn.	217	1,137	803	482	630	420	879
Miami, Fla.	665	1,255	1,181	1,188	1,087	1,111	1,726
Minneapolis, Minn.	862	1,123	731	355	630	862	700
New Orleans, La.	312	1,359	1,086	833	924	443	1,082
New York, N.Y.	864	188	292	713	405	1,374	1,631
Omaha, Neb.	732	1,282	883	432	739	586	488
Philadelphia, Pa.	783	271	279	666	360	1,299	1,579
Phoenix, Ariz.	1,456	2,300	1,906	1,453	1,749	887	586
Pittsburgh, Pa.	608	483	178	410	115	1,070	1,320
St. Louis, Mo.	400	1,038	662	262	492	547	796
Salt Lake City, Utah	1,466	2,099	1,699	1,260	1,568	999	371
San Francisco, Calif.	2,013	2,699	2,300	1,858	2,166	1,483	949
Seattle, Wash.	2,082	2,493	2,117	1,737	2,026	1,681	1,021
Washington, D.C.	661	393	292	597	306	1,185	1,494

Cities	Detroit	El Paso	Houston	Indian-apolis	Kansas City	Los Angeles	Louisville
Birmingham, Ala.	641	1,152	567	433	579	1,802	331
Boston, Mass.	613	2,072	1,605	807	1,251	2,596	826
Buffalo, N.Y.	216	1,692	1,286	435	861	2,198	483
Chicago, Ill.	238	1,252	940	165	414	1,745	269
Cleveland, Ohio	90	1,525	1,114	263	700	2,049	311
Dallas, Tex.	999	572	225	763	451	1,240	726
Denver, Colo.	1,156	557	879	1,000	558	831	1,038
Detroit, Mich.	—	1,479	1,105	240	645	1,983	316
El Paso, Tex.	1,479	—	676	1,264	839	701	1,254
Houston, Tex.	1,105	676	—	865	644	1,374	803
Indianapolis, Ind.	240	1,264	865	—	453	1,809	107
Kansas City, Mo.	645	839	644	453	—	1,356	480
Los Angeles, Calif.	1,983	701	1,374	1,809	1,356	—	1,829
Louisville, Ky.	316	1,254	803	107	480	1,829	—
Memphis, Tenn.	623	976	484	384	369	1,603	320
Miami, Fla.	1,152	1,643	968	1,024	1,241	2,339	919
Minneapolis, Minn.	543	1,157	1,056	511	413	1,524	605
New Orleans, La.	939	983	318	712	680	1,673	623
New York, N.Y.	482	1,905	1,420	646	1,097	2,451	652
Omaha, Neb.	669	878	794	525	166	1,315	580
Philadelphia, Pa.	443	1,836	1,341	585	1,038	2,394	582
Phoenix, Ariz.	1,690	346	1,017	1,499	1,049	357	1,508
Pittsburgh, Pa.	205	1,590	1,137	330	781	2,136	344
St. Louis, Mo.	455	1,034	679	231	238	1,589	242
Salt Lake City, Utah	1,492	689	1,200	1,356	925	579	1,402
San Francisco, Calif.	2,091	995	1,645	1,949	1,506	347	1,986
Seattle, Wash.	1,938	1,376	1,891	1,872	1,506	959	1,943
Washington, D.C.	396	1,728	1,220	494	945	2,300	476

Source: National Geodetic Survey.

Air Distances Between U.S. Cities in Statute Miles

Cities	Memphis	Miami	Minne–apolis	New Orleans	New York	Omaha	Phila–delphia
Birmingham, Ala.	217	665	862	312	864	732	783
Boston, Mass.	1,137	1,255	1,123	1,359	188	1,282	271
Buffalo, N. Y.	803	1,181	731	1,086	292	883	279
Chicago, Ill.	482	1,188	355	833	713	432	666
Cleveland, Ohio	630	1,087	630	924	405	739	360
Dallas, Tex.	420	1,111	862	443	1,374	586	1,299
Denver, Colo.	879	1,726	700	1,082	1,631	488	1,579
Detroit, Mich.	623	1,152	543	939	482	669	443
El Paso, Tex.	976	1,643	1,157	983	1,905	878	1,836
Houston, Tex.	484	968	1,056	318	1,420	794	1,341
Indianapolis, Ind.	384	1,024	511	712	646	525	585
Kansas City, Mo.	369	1,241	413	680	1,097	166	1,038
Los Angeles, Calif.	1,603	2,339	1,524	1,673	2,451	1,315	2,394
Louisville, Ky.	320	919	605	623	652	580	582
Memphis, Tenn.	—	872	699	358	957	529	881
Miami, Fla.	872	—	1,511	669	1,092	1,397	1,019
Minneapolis, Minn.	699	1,511	—	1,051	1,018	290	985
New Orleans, La.	358	669	1,051	—	1,171	847	1,089
New York, N. Y.	957	1,092	1,018	1,171	—	1,144	83
Omaha, Neb.	529	1,397	290	847	1,144	—	1,094
Philadelphia, Pa.	881	1,019	985	1,089	83	1,094	—
Phoenix, Ariz.	1,263	1,982	1,280	1,316	2,145	1,036	2,083
Pittsburgh, Pa.	660	1,010	743	919	317	836	259
St. Louis, Mo.	240	1,061	466	598	875	354	811
Salt Lake City, Utah	1,250	2,089	987	1,434	1,972	833	1,925
San Francisco, Calif.	1,802	2,594	1,584	1,926	2,571	1,429	2,523
Seattle, Wash.	1,867	2,734	1,395	2,101	2,408	1,369	2,380
Washington, D.C.	765	923	934	966	205	1,014	123

Cities	Phoenix	Pitts–burgh	St. Louis	Salt Lake City	San Francisco	Seattle	Wash–ington
Birmingham, Ala.	1,456	608	400	1,466	2,013	2,082	661
Boston, Mass.	2,300	483	1,038	2,099	2,699	2,493	393
Buffalo, N. Y.	1,906	17 8	662	1,699	2,300	2,117	292
Chicago, Ill.	1,453	410	262	1,260	1,858	1,737	597
Cleveland, Ohio	1,749	115	492	1,568	2,166	2,026	306
Dallas, Tex.	887	1,070	547	999	1,483	1,681	1,185
Denver, Colo.	586	1,320	796	371	949	1,021	1,494
Detroit, Mich.	1,690	205	455	1,492	2,091	1,938	396
El Paso, Tex.	346	1,590	1,034.	689	995	1,376	1,728
Houston, Tex.	1,017	1,137	679	1,200	1,645	1,891	1,220
Indianapolis, Ind.	1,499	330	231	1,356	1,949	1,872	494
Kansas City, Mo.	1,049	781	238	925	1,506	1,506	945
Los Angeles, Calif.	357	2,136	1,589	579	347	959	2,300
Louisville, Ky.	1,508	344	242	1,402	1,986	1,943	476
Memphis, Tenn.	1,263	660	240	1,250	1,802	1,867	765
Miami, Fla.	1,982	1,010	1,061	2,089	2,594	2,734	923
Minneapolis, Minn.	1,280	743	466	987	1,584	1,395	934
New Orleans, La.	1,316	919	598	1,434	1,926	2,101	966
New York, N. Y.	2,145	317	875	1,972	2,571	2,408	205
Omaha, Neb.	1,036	836	354	833	1,429	1,369	1,014
Philadelphia, Pa.	2,083	259	811	1,925	2,523	2,380	123
Phoenix, Ariz.	—	1,828	1,272	504	653	1,114	1,983
Pittsburgh, Pa.	1,828	—	559	1,668	2,264	2,138	192
St. Louis, Mo.	1,272	559	—	1,162	1,744	1,724	712
Salt Lake City, Utah	504	1,668	1,162	—	600	701	1,848
San Francisco, Calif.	653	2,264	1,744	600	—	678	2,442
Seattle, Wash.	1,114	2,138	1,724	701	678	—	2,329
Washington, D.C.	1,983	192	712	1,848	2,442	2,329	—

Source: National Geodetic Survey.

Air Distances Between World Cities in Statute Miles

Cities	Berlin	Buenos Aires	Cairo	Calcutta	Cape Town	Caracas	Chicago
Berlin	—	7,402	1,795	4,368	5,981	5,247	4,405
Buenos Aires	7,402	—	7,345	10,265	4,269	3,168	5,598
Cairo	1,795	7,345	—	3,539	4,500	6,338	6,129
Calcutta	4,368	10,265	3,539	—	6,024	9,605	7,980
Cape Town, South Africa	5,981	4,269	4,500	6,024	—	6,365	8,494
Caracas, Venezuela	5,247	3,168	6,338	9,605	6,365	—	2,501
Chicago	4,405	5,598	6,129	7,980	8,494	2,501	—
Hong Kong	5,440	11,472	5,061	1,648	7,375	10,167	7,793
Honolulu, Hawaii	7,309	7,561	8,838	7,047	11,534	6,013	4,250
Istanbul	1,078	7,611	768	3,638	5,154	6,048	5,477
Lisbon	1,436	5,956	2,363	5,638	5,325	4,041	3,990
London	579	6,916	2,181	4,947	6,012	4,660	3,950
Los Angeles	5,724	6,170	7,520	8,090	9,992	3,632	1,745
Manila	6,132	11,051	5,704	2,203	7,486	10,620	8,143
Mexico City	6,047	4,592	7,688	9,492	8,517	2,232	1,691
Montreal	3,729	5,615	5,414	7,607	7,931	2,449	744
Moscow	1,004	8,376	1,803	3,321	6,300	6,173	4,974
New York	3,965	5,297	5,602	7,918	7,764	2,132	713
Paris	545	6,870	1,995	4,883	5,807	4,736	4,134
Rio de Janeiro	6,220	1,200	6,146	9,377	3,773	2,810	5,296
Rome	734	6,929	1,320	4,482	5,249	5,196	4,808
San Francisco	5,661	6,467	7,364	7,814	10,247	3,904	1,858
Shanghai, China	5,218	12,201	5,183	2,117	8,061	9,501	7,061
Stockholm	504	7,808	2,111	4,195	6,444	5,420	4,278
Sydney, Australia	10,006	7,330	8,952	5,685	6,843	9,513	9,272
Tokyo	5,540	11,408	5,935	3,194	9,156	8,799	6,299
Warsaw	320	7,662	1,630	4,048	5,958	5,517	4,667
Washington, D.C.	4,169	5,218	5,800	8,084	7,901	2,059	597

Cities	Hong Kong	Honolulu	Istanbul	Lisbon	London	Los Angeles	Manila
Berlin	5,440	7,309	1,078	1,436	579	5,724	6,132
Buenos Aires	11,472	7,561	7,611	5,956	6,916	6,170	11,051
Cairo	5,061	8,838	768	2,363	2,181	7,520	5,704
Calcutta	1,648	7,047	3,638	5,638	4,947	8,090	2,203
Cape Town, South Africa	7,375	11,534	5,154	5,325	6,012	9,992	7,486
Caracas, Venezuela	10,167	6,013	6,048	4,041	4,660	3,632	10,620
Chicago	7,793	4,250	5,477	3,990	3,950	1,745	8,143
Hong Kong	—	5,549	4,984	6,853	5,982	7,195	693
Honolulu, Hawaii	5,549	—	8,109	7,820	7,228	2,574	5,299
Istanbul	4,984	8,109	—	2,012	1,552	6,783	5,664
Lisbon	6,853	7,820	2,012	—	985	5,621	7,546
London	5,982	7,228	1,552	985	—	5,382	6,672
Los Angeles, Calif.	7,195	2,574	6,783	5,621	5,382	—	7,261
Manila	693	5,299	5,664	7,546	6,672	7,261	—
Mexico City	8,782	3,779	7,110	5,390	5,550	1,589	8,835
Montreal	7,729	4,910	4,789	3,246	3,282	2,427	8,186
Moscow	4,439	7,037	1,091	2,427	1,555	6,003	5,131
New York	8,054	4,964	4,975	3,364	3,458	2,451	8,498
Paris	5,985	7,438	1,400	904	213	5,588	6,677
Rio de Janeiro	11,021	8,285	6,389	4,796	5,766	6,331	11,259
Rome	5,768	8,022	843	1,161	887	6,732	6,457
San Francisco	6,897	2,393	6,703	5,666	5,357	347	6,967
Shanghai, China	764	4,941	4,962	6,654	5,715	6,438	1,150
Stockholm	5,113	6,862	1,348	1,856	890	5,454	5,797
Sydney, Australia	4,584	4,943	9,294	11,302	10,564	7,530	3,944
Tokyo	1,794	3,853	5,560	6,915	5,940	5,433	1,866
Warsaw	5,144	7,355	863	1,715	899	5,922	5,837
Washington, D.C.	8,147	4,519	5,215	3,562	3,663	2,300	8,562

Source: Encyclopaedia Britannica.

Air Distances Between World Cities in Statute Miles

Cities	Mexico City	Montreal	Moscow	New York	Paris	Rio de Janeiro	Rome
Berlin	6,047	3,729	1,004	3,965	545	6,220	734
Buenos Aires	4,592	5,615	8,376	5,297	6,870	1,200	6,929
Cairo	7,688	5,414	1,803	5,602	1,995	6,146	1,320
Calcutta	9,492	7,607	3,321	7,918	4,883	9,377	4,482
Cape Town, South Africa	8,517	7,931	6,300	7,764	5,807	3,773	5,249
Caracas, Venezuela	2,232	2,449	6,173	2,132	4,736	2,810	5,196
Chicago	1,691	744	4,974	713	4,134	5,296	4,808
Hong Kong	8,782	7,729	4,439	8,054	5,985	11,021	5,768
Honolulu	3,779	4,910	7,037	4,964	7,438	8,285	8,022
Istanbul	7,110	4,789	1,091	4,975	1,400	6,389	843
Lisbon	5,390	3,246	2,427	3,364	904	4,796	1,161
London	5,550	3,282	1,555	3,458	213	5,766	887
Los Angeles	1,589	2,427	6,003	2,451	5,588	6,331	6,732
Manila	8,835	8,186	5,131	8,498	6,677	11,259	6,457
Mexico City	—	2,318	6,663	2,094	5,716	4,771	6,366
Montreal	2,318	—	4,386	320	3,422	5,097	4,080
Moscow	6,663	4,386	—	4,665	1,544	7,175	1,474
New York	2,094	320	4,665	—	3,624	4,817	4,281
Paris	5,716	3,422	1,544	3,624	—	5,699	697
Rio de Janeiro	4,771	5,097	7,175	4,817	5,699	—	5,684
Rome	6,366	4,080	1,474	4,281	697	5,684	—
San Francisco	1,887	2,539	5,871	2,571	5,558	6,621	6,240
Shanghai, China	8,022	7,053	4,235	7,371	5,754	11,336	5,677
Stockholm	5,959	3,667	762	3,924	958	6,651	1,234
Sydney, Australia	8,052	9,954	9,012	9,933	10,544	8,306	10,136
Tokyo	7,021	6,383	4,647	6,740	6,034	11,533	6,135
Warsaw	6,365	4,009	715	4,344	849	6,467	817
Washington, D.C.	1,887	488	4,858	205	3,829	4,796	4,434

Cities	San Francisco	Shanghai	Stockholm	Sydney	Tokyo	Moscow	Washington
Berlin	5,661	5,218	504	10,006	5,540	320	4,169
Buenos Aires	6,467	12,201	7,808	7,330	11,408	7,662	5,218
Cairo	7,364	5,183	2,111	8,952	5,935	1,630	5,800
Calcutta	7,814	2,117	4,195	5,685	3,194	4,048	8,084
Cape Town, South Africa	10,247	8,061	6,444	6,843	9,156	5,958	7,901
Caracas, Venezuela	3,904	9,501	5,420	9,513	8,799	5,517	2,059
Chicago	1,858	7,061	4,278	9,272	6,299	4,667	597
Hong Kong	6,897	764	5,113	4,584	1,794	5,144	8,147
Honolulu	2,393	4,941	6,862	4,943	3,853	7,355	4,519
Istanbul	6,703	4,962	1,348	9,294	5,560	863	5,215
Lisbon	5,666	6,654	1,856	11,302	6,915	1,715	3,562
London	5,357	5,715	890	10,564	5,940	899	3,663
Los Angeles	347	6,438	5,454	7,530	5,433	5,922	2,300
Manila	6,967	1,150	5,797	3,944	1,866	5,837	8,562
Mexico City	1,887	8,022	5,959	8,052	7,021	6,365	1,887
Montreal	2,539	7,053	3,667	9,954	6,383	4,009	488
Moscow	5,871	4,235	762	9,012	4,647	715	4,858
New York	2,571	7,371	3,924	9,933	6,740	4,344	205
Paris	5,558	5,754	958	10,544	6,034	849	3,829
Rio de Janeiro	6,621	11,336	6,651	8,306	11,533	6,467	4,796
Rome	6,240	5,677	1,234	10,136	6,135	817	4,434
San Francisco	—	6,140	5,361	7,416	5,135	5,841	2,442
Shanghai, China	6,140	—	4,825	4,899	1,097	4,951	7,448
Stockholm	5,361	4,825	—	9,696	5,051	501	4,123
Sydney, Australia	7,416	4,899	9,696	—	4,866	9,696	9,758
Tokyo	5,135	1,097	5,051	4,866	—	5,249	6,772
Warsaw	5,841	4,951	501	9,696	5,249	—	4,457
Washington, D.C.	2,442	7,448	4,123	9,758	6,772	4,457	—

Source: Encyclopaedia Britannica.

World's 25 Busiest Airports in 1990

Airport	Passengers[1]	Cargo		Operations	
1. Chicago, Ill. (O'Hare)	59,936,137	986,673	(5)	810,865	(1)
2. Dallas/Ft. Worth, Texas	48,515,464	556,749	(16)	731,036	(3)
3. Atlanta, Georgia	48,024,566	610,450	(14)	790,502	(2)
4. Los Angeles (International)	45,810,221	1,164,926	(4)	679,861	(4)
5. London (Heathrow)	42,964,200	779,400	(8)	390,485	(18)
6. Tokyo, Japan (Haneda)	40,233,031	614,610	(13)	183,950	(77)
7. San Francisco (International)	31,059,820	566,068	(15)	430,253	(11)
8. New York (Kennedy)	29,786,657	1,322,353	(2)	302,038	(36)
9. Frankfurt, Germany	28,912,145	1,259,398	(3)	324,387	(27)
10. Denver, Colorado	27,432,989	280,136	(32)	484,040	(8)
11. Miami, Fla. (International)	25,837,445	966,443	(6)	480,987	(9)
12. Paris (Orly)	24,329,700	287,895	(30)	193,451	(74)
13. Osaka, Japan	23,511,611	493,947	(19)	130,550	(128)
14. Honolulu, Oahu, Hawaii	23,367,770	374,901	(23)	407,048	(15)
15. Boston, Massachusetts	22,935,844	364,275	(24)	424,568	(12)
16. New York (LaGuardia)	22,753,812	116,844	(62)	354,229	(24)
17. Detroit (Metro Wayne Co.)	22,585,156	191,421	(44)	387,848	(19)
18. Paris (Charles De Gaulle)	22,506,107	647,369	(10)	235,350	(52)
19. Newark, N.J. (International)	22,255,002	504,980	(18)	379,432	(22)
20. Phoenix, Arizona	21,718,068	114,238	(65)	498,752	(6)
21. London (Gatwick)	21,185,400	228,000	(35)	203,200	(69)
22. Minneapolis/St. Paul, Minn.	20,381,314	266,355	(34)	379,785	(21)
23. Toronto, Ont. (Pearson)	20,304,271	322,929	(26)	353,682	(25)
24. St. Louis, Missouri	20,065,737	108,047	(67)	439,002	(10)
25. Tokyo, Japan (Narita)	19,264,650	1,387,552	(1)	125,187	(136)

1. Enplaned, deplaned, and transfer, in millions. NOTE: Figures in ( ) next to cargo and operations totals represent rank for those categories. *Source:* Airport Operators Council International.

A

Abbreviations:
Degrees, Academic, 411
Postal, 148
Abidjan, Côte d'Ivoire, 208
Absolute zero, 433, 435
Abu Dhabi, United Arab Emirates, 307
Academic costume, 411
Acadia, 199
Accidents:
Deaths from, 27
Motor vehicle, 27
Rates, 27
Accra, Ghana, 230
Aconcagua Peak, 170, 186
Acre, 430, 431, 432
ACTION, 112
Addis Ababa, Ethiopia, 219
Address, forms of, 415–16
Adenauer, Konrad, 228
Administration, Office of, 111
Admirals (U.S.), 123
First, 97
Adriatic Sea, 245, 284, 321
Advent (season), 6
Aegean Islands, 231
Aegean Sea, 231, 305
Afars and Issas. See Djibouti
Afghanistan, 183, 292, 293
See also Countries
AFL-CIO, 369
Africa, 167
Explorations and discoveries, 159
Portuguese territory, 281
Southernmost point, 289
See also Continents; Countries
Agate (measure), 432
Age:
Arrests by, 131, 132
At first marriage, 22
Death rates by, 28, 29
Life expectancy by, 29, 153
Of unmarried mothers, 25
Population by, 12–13, 16, 17, 19, 20
School enrollment by, 381
Age limits:
School attendance, 382
Agencies (U.N.), 180–81
Agencies (U.S.), 112–13
Aggtelek Cavern, 177
Aging
See Social Security & Aging
Agnew, Spiro T., 99, 105
Agriculture:
Animals on farms, 343
Economic statistics, 329, 342, 343
Employment, 334, 337, 341
Farm laborers, 334, 337, 341
Income, 343
Production by state, 342
See also Food
Agriculture, U.S. Dept. of, 111
Secretaries of, 108–10
AIDS
Hot line, 366, 367, 368
Air distances, cities, 452–55
Air Force, U.S., 125
See also Armed Forces
Air Force, U.S. Department of:
Secretary of, 111
Air Force Academy, U.S., 125
Airlines:
Freight, 347
Passenger traffic, 456
See also Travel
Airmail, 145, 147
Firsts, 97
International, 147
Priority mail, 145
Stamps for, 146
Airplanes:
Exports and imports, 351
Passenger traffic, 456
Airports, world's busiest, 456
Alabama, 35
See also States of U.S.
Alabama–Coosa River, 33
Alamo, Battle of the, 57
Aland Islands, 220

Alaska, 35–36
Bought, 16, 36
Discovered, 36, 160
Gold Rush, 36
Mountain peaks, 33
Oil, 36
Volcanoes, 36, 161
See also States of U.S.
Albania, 183–84
See also Countries
Alberta, Canada, 199, 200
Albuquerque, New Mexico, 66
See also Cities (U.S.)
Alcohol. See Liquor
Aleutian Islands, 161
Alexander the Great, 159, 216, 241
Alexandria, Egypt, 216
Alfred the Great, 308
Algeria, 184
War of Independence, 222
See also Countries
Aliens, in U.S., 19
Allende, Salvador, 203
All Saints' Day, 5
Alps, 188, 221, 245, 299, 321
Altamaha–Ocmulgee River, 33
Altamira Cave, 177
Altiplano, 193
Altitudes. See Elevations
Amazon River, 194, 206, 160, 173
Amendments to Constitution, 86–90
Civil rights, 86–90
Right to bear arms, 86
Search and seizure, 86
American Academy and Institute of Arts and Letters, 370
American Federation of Labor, 369
American History. See United States History
American Independent Party, 105
American Indians. See Indians
American Red Cross, 378
American Revolution. See Revolutionary War
American Samoa, 63
American's Creed, The, 94
Amman, Jordan, 248
Ampere, 429, 432, 433
Amsterdam, Netherlands, 269
Amu Darya River, 174
Amur River, 204, 292
Amusement. See Recreation
Andaman Islands, 237
Andaman Sea, 171
Andes, 170–71, 186, 203, 206, 277
Andorra, 184–85
Andropov, Yuri V., 294
Angel Falls, 174
Angola, 185, 281
See also Countries
Angstrom, 430, 432
Anguilla, 312
Animals:
Farm, 329, 342, 343
State animals, 35–61
Ankara, Turkey, 305
Annapolis, Md., 44, 45
Naval Academy, 45, 124–25
Anniversaries, wedding, 7
Antananarivo, Madagascar, 258
Antarctica, 160, 165, 167
Australian Antarctic Territory, 167
British Antarctic Territory, 312
Exploration, 160
Falkland Islands, 313
French Antarctica, 225
Ross Dependency, 271
Volcanoes, 165
Antarctic Circle, 4, 160
Anthem, National, 92
Anti-Comintern Treaty, 228, 248
Antigua, 186
Antigua and Barbuda, 185–86
See also Countries
Antiparos Cavern, 177
Antipodes Islands, 270
Antwerp, Belgium, 190
Apalachicola–Chattahoochee River, 33
Apartheid, 290
Apennine Mountains, 245, 284, 299
Aphelion, 8
Apia, Western Samoa, 319
Apothecaries fluid measure, 430

Apothecaries weight, 430
Appendicitis, 27
Appomattox surrender, 59
Aqaba, Gulf of, 216, 244
Aquino, Benigno, 279
Aquino, Corazon C., 278, 279
Arabia, explored, 159
See specific Arab countries for other data
Arabian Desert, 176
Arab-Israeli wars, 216–17, 241, 244–45. 248–49, 254, 285, 300–01, 306
See also Egypt; Israel; Jordan; Lebanon; Saudi Arabia; Syria
Arab League, 241, 252, 285, 306, 307, 320
Aral Lake, 172
Arbor Day, 6
Arctic Area, 160
Exploration, 160
Arctic Circle, 4
Arctic Ocean, 171
Ardennes, 191
Area:
Cities of U.S., 66–78
Continents, 167
Countries, 150–51, 183–324
Deserts, 176
Formulas for, 435
Islands, 175–76
Lakes, 172–73
Measure of, 429–31
Oceans, seas, 171
States of U.S., 35–61
U.S. and territories, 12, 16
U.S. growth, 12, 16
World, 167
Argentina, 186–87
Volcanoes, 164
See also Countries
Arithmetic. See Mathematics
Arizona, 36
See also States of U.S.
Arkansas, 36–37
See also States of U.S.
Arkansas River, 33, 160, 174
Arlington National Cemetery, 95, 99
Armada, Spanish, 295, 309
Armed Forces (U.S.), 123–27, 129
Defense expenditures, 343, 344–45
History, 123–24
Joint Chiefs of Staff, 111
Medal of Honor, 129
Officers, 123
Ranks, 123
Service academies, 124–26
Spending for, 343, 344–45
Veterans' benefits, 128–29
War casualties, 126, 127
See also Defense; Selective Service; Veterans
Armenia, 293
Armistice Day, 6
Arms Control and Disarmament Agency, U.S., 113
Army, U.S. Department of the, 123
Expenditures, 344–45
Secretary of, 111
See also Armed Forces
Arrests, 131–32
See also Law enforcement; Crime
"Arsenal of the Nation," 38
Arson, arrests for, 131–32
Articles of Confederation, 94
Arts and the Humanities, National Foundation on the, 112
Arts and Letters, American Academy and Institute of, 370
Aruba, 270
Asama, Mount, 161
Ascension Day, 5
Ascension Island, 314
Ashmore Islands, 187
Ash Wednesday, 4
Asia, 161, 167
Exploration and discoveries, 159
See also Continents; Countries
Assault, 131, 132, 133, 134
Assistance, public, 346
Associations, 369–80
Assyrian Empire, 241
Astronauts, 97
Astronomical unit, 432
Astronomy

Measures, 432, 433
Seasons, 3–4
Asunción, Paraguay, 277
Aswan Dam, 172, 216
See also High Aswan Dam
Atacama Desert, 176, 203
Athens, Greece, 230
See also Cities (world)
Atlanta, Ga., 39, 40, 66–67
See also Cities (U.S.)
Atlantic Ocean, 171
Islands, 175–76
Volcanoes, 164
Atlas Mountains, 265
Atom bomb, dropped on Japan, 248
Atomic Energy Agency, International, 180
Atonement, Day of, 5
Attlee, Clement, 310
Attorneys General:
State, 35–61
United States, 106–10, 111
Auckland Islands, 270
Austin, Tex., 57, 58, 67
See also Cities (U.S.)
Australasia, *See* Oceania
Australia, 160, 187–88
Explored, 160
Islands of, 176, 187–88
See also Continents; Countries
Australian Antarctic Territory, 188
Australian Desert, 176, 187
Austria, 188
See also Countries
Automobiles:
Accident deaths, 27
Drunken driving arrests, 131, 132
Economic statistics, 348–49
Exports and imports, 349, 351
Industry, hours and wages, 338
Registrations, 348, 349
Sales, 349
Services, 330
Theft statistics: 131–32, 133–34
U.S. production, 348
World production, 156
See also Motor Vehicles
Average, mathematical, 437
Aviation:
Airports, world's busiest, 456
International Civil Aviation Organization, 180
Traffic (passengers, freight), 347, 456
See also Airlines; airplanes
Avoirdupois weight, 430
Axel Heiberg, 176
Ayatollah Khomeini, 240–41
Azerbaijan, 293
Azores, 280
Azov, Sea of, 171
Aztecs, 263
Azuma, 161

B

Babylonian Empire, 241
Baffin Bay, discovered, 160
Baffin Island, 175
Baghdad, Iraq, 241
Bagnell Dam, 48
Bahamas, 188–89
See also Countries
Bahrain, 189
See also Countries
Baikal, Lake, 172
Baker Island, 63
Balance of payments, 350
Balaton, Lake, 235
Balearic Islands, 295
Bale (weight), 432
Balfour Declaration, 243
Balkans, 282, 321
Baltic Sea, 171
Baltimore, Md., 45, 67
See also Cities (U.S.)
Bamako, Mali, 260
Bandar Seri Begawan, Brunei, 195
Bangkok, Thailand, 302
See also Cities (world)
Bangladesh, 189–90, 237, 238, 275
See also Countries
Bangui, Central African Republic, 201
Banjul, Gambia, 226
Bank of North America, 97
Banks and banking:
Firsts, 97
Largest, 332, 333
Banks (island), 176

Barbados, 190
See also Countries
Barbuda. *See* Antigua and Barbuda
Baseball Hall of Fame, 52
Basseterre, St. Kitts–Nevis, 283
Basutoland. *See* Lesotho
Battle of Hastings, 309
Battles. *See* specific battles
Bay of Pigs, 209–10
Bechuanaland. *See* Botswana
Bedloe's Island, 96
Begin, Menachem, 217, 244
Beijing, China, 204
See also Peking
Beirut, Lebanon, 244, 253–54
Belfast, Northern Ireland, 311
Belgian Congo. *See* Zaire
Belgium, 190–91
See also Countries
Belgrade, Yugoslavia, 320
See also Cities (world)
Belize, 191–92
See also Countries
Belmopan, Belize, 191
Benelux, 228, 258
Benin, 192
See also Countries
Bering Sea, 171
Bering Strait, 160
Berlin, Germany, 226, 229, 230
Airlift (1948), 228
East Berlin uprising (1953), 229
Wall (1961) (1990), 229
See also Cities (world)
Berlin, Treaty of (1899), 63
Bermuda, 312
See also Countries
Bern, Switzerland, 299
Bessarabia, 282, 293
Bhutan, 192–93
See also Countries
Biafra, 272–73
Bikini Atoll, 261
Bill of Rights, 86–87
Bills (Congressional):
How a bill becomes a law, 117
Procedure, 82, 117
Bills (money), 437
Bioko (formerly Fernando Po), 218
Birds:
State birds, 35–61
Birmingham, Alabama, 35
Birmingham, England, 308
Birth rates, 24–26
Births (U.S.):
Age of mother, 25
Live, 24–26
To unmarried women, 25
Bismarck, Otto von, 227
Bissau, Guinea–Bissau, 233
Black Death, 309
Black Hills, 56
Black Rock Desert, 176
Black Sea, 171, 253
Blacks in U.S.:
Births, birth rates, 25, 26
Elected officials, 121
Employment, 337, 340
Population statistics, 12–13, 16, 19, 20
School enrollment, 381
See also Civil rights; Nonwhite persons; Racial statistics; Slavery
Blanc, Mont, 221
Blue Grotto, 177
Blue Nile, 219
Board foot (measure), 432
Boers, 289, 290
Boer War, 289, 290, 310
Bogotá, Colombia, 206
Bohemia, 211
Boiling point of water, 436
Bolivia, 193
See also Countries
Bolsheviks, 292
Bolt (measure), 432
Bolts and screws, 434
Bombay, India, 237
See also Cities (world)
Bonaire, 270
Bonaparte, Napoleon, 221, 222
Bonn, Germany, 226, 228, 229
Books, Reference, 417–18
Boone, Daniel, 43
Bophuthatswana, 290
See also Countries
Boquerón (volcano), 164
Borneo (island), 175, 239, 259
Brunei, 175, 195

Boroughs, New York City, 72
Bosnia, 321
Boston, Mass., 45, 46, 67
See also Cities (U.S.)
Boston Tea Party, 45
Botanic garden, first, 97
Botswana, 193–94
See also Countries
Boulder Dam. *See* Hoover Dam
Bounty, H.M.S., 314
Bourbon Kings of France, 222, 223
Boxer Rebellion, 204
Boy Scouts of America, 371
Brahmaputra River, 173. 190, 237
Brandt, Willy, 228, 229
Brazil, 160, 194–95
See also Countries
Brazos River, 33
Brazzaville, Congo, 207
Brest–Litovsk, Treaty of, 292
Brezhnev, Leonid, 293, 294
Bridgetown, Barbados, 190
British Columbia, Canada, 199–200
British Commonwealth. *See* Commonwealth of Nations
British Guiana. *See* Guyana
British Honduras. *See* Belize
British Indian Ocean Territory, 312–13
British New Guinea. *See* Papua New Guinea
British Solomon Islands. *See* Solomon Islands
British thermal unit, 432
British Virgin Islands, 313
Bronx, The, 72
Brooklyn, 72
Brunei Darussalam, 195
See also Countries
Brussels, Belgium, 190
See also Cities (world)
Bryan, William Jennings
Presidential candidate, 104
Secretary of State, 108
Btu, 432, 436
Bucharest, Romania, 282
See also Cities (world)
Budapest, Hungary, 235
See also Cities (world)
Budget, Federal, 336, 343, 344–45, 346
Budget, Office of Management and, 111
Budget. *See* Expenditures; Revenue
Buenos Aires, Argentina, 186
See also Cities (world)
Buffalo, N.Y., 67
See also Cities (U.S.)
Buildings:
New construction (U.S.), 329
Bujumbura, Burundi, 197
Bulganin, Nikolai A., 294
Bulgaria, 195–96
See also Countries
Bull Run, Battle of, 96
Burger, Warren E., 119
Burgesses, House of, 97
Burglary, 131, 132, 133, 134
Burkina Faso, 196
See also Countries
Burma. *See* Myanmar
Burr, Aaron, 98, 102
Burundi, 196–97
See also Countries
Buses, 348. 349
Economic statistics, 348, 349
Bush, George, 98, 99
Business, economy, 325–51
Investments, foreign, in U.S. business, 350
Largest, 331–32
Retail sales, 330
See also Retail trade; Wholesale trade; Industry
Butter:
Economic statistics, 343
Byelorussia, 292, 293

C

Cabinets (U.S.), 106–10
First black member, 97
First woman member, 97
Salaries, 121
Caesar, Julius, 221
Cairo, Egypt, 215, 216
See also Cities (world)
Calcutta, India, 237
See also Cities (world)

Calendar, 1–9
  History, 1, 2
  Names of days and months, 3
  Perpetual, 8–9
Calgary, Alberta, Canada, 201
Calhoun, John C., 102
California, 37
  Gold Rush, 37
  Mountain peaks, 33
  Volcanoes, 163
  See also States of U.S.
Cambodia, 197–98
  See also Countries
Cambrian Mountains, 309
Cameroon, 198
  See also Countries
Camp Fire Boys and Girls, 371
Canada, 199–201
  Economy, 199
  Geography, 199
  Government, 199
  History, 199
  Latitude and longitude, 32
  Population, 199
  Provinces, 199
  Territories, 199
  Time zones, 3
  See also Countries
Canadian River, 33
Canary Islands, 164, 295
Cancer, 27
Cancer, Tropic of, 4
Candela, 429
Canton Island, 63
Cape Horn, 160, 203
Cape of Good Hope, 159, 289
Capetian Dynasty, 221, 223
Cape Town, South Africa, 289
  See also Cities (world)
Cape Verde, 164, 203–04
  See also Countries
Capitalization, rules for, 412
Capital punishment, first state to abolish, 97
  See also Executions
Capitals, foreign, 182–324
Capitals of states, 35–61
Capitals of U.S.:
  Early capitals, 51, 55, 94
  Washington, D.C., 76
Capitol, U.S., 95
Capri, 177
Capricorn, Tropic of, 4
Caracas, Venezuela, 317
  See also Cities (world)
Carat (measure), 432, 433
Cardiovascular disease, 27
Caribbean area:
  Islands, 164, 176
  Volcanoes, 164
  See also specific countries
Caribbean Sea, 171, 176
Carloadings, railroad, 347
Carlsbad Caverns, 177
Carnival season, 4
Caroline Islands, 64
Carolingian Dynasty, 221, 222
Carpathian Mountains, 279, 282
Cartoons, first colored, 97
Casablanca, Morocco, 265
Caspian Sea, 171, 172, 240, 292
Castries, St. Lucia, 283
Castro, Fidel, 209–10
Casualties, war, 126, 127
Catholic Church
  See Roman Catholic Church
Cattle, 342
Caucasus, 161, 292
Caves, caverns, 177
Cayman Islands, 313
CEA, 111
Celebes, 175, 239
Celsius (Centigrade) scale, 429, 433, 436
Cemeteries, National
  Arlington, 95, 99
Census. *See* Population
Centigrade (Celsius) scale, 429, 433, 436
Central African Republic, 201–02
  See also Countries
Central America, 161
  Volcanoes, 164
  See also specific countries
Central Intelligence Agency, 111
Cerebrovascular diseases, 27
Certified mail, 146
Ceylon. *See* Sri Lanka
Chaco, 186, 277
Chad, 202–03

Chad, Lake, 172, 202
Chain (measure), 430, 433
Chamberlain, Neville, 310
Channel Islands, 313
Charlemagne, 221, 222, 227
Charles I of England, 45, 52, 56, 308
Charlotte, N.C., 52, 67–68
  See also Cities (U.S.)
Cheese:
  Economic statistics, 343
Chemicals, 351
Chernenko, Konstantin U., 293, 294
Chernobyl nuclear accident, 294
Chesapeake Bay, 45
Chiang Kai-shek, 204, 301
Chicago, Ill., 41, 68
  Climate, 419
  See also Cities (U.S.)
Chickens:
  Economic statistics, 342, 343
Children:
  Abuse and neglect, 134
  Birth statistics, 24–26
  Births to unmarried women, 25
  Death statistics, 27–29
  Education statistics, 381–84
  Life expectancy, 29
  Number of, 16
  Runaways, 131, 132
Chile, 203
  Volcanoes, 164
  See also Countries
China, 204–06
  Boxer Rebellion, 204
  Great Wall, 204
  History, 204–06
  Japan and, 204, 205, 247–48
  Ming dynasty, 204
  Nuclear weapons testing, 205
  Provinces and regions, 205
  U.S. and, 205–06
  Yuan dynasty, 204
  See also Countries
China (Taiwan). *See* Taiwan
China Sea, 171
"China seat" (U.N.), 205, 301
Chinese in U.S.:
  Births, birth rates, 26
  See also Nonwhite persons
Chinese-Japanese War (1894–95), 204, 247
Chou En-lai. *See* Zhou Enlai
Christian holidays, 4–6
Christianity. *See* Religion; Roman Catholic Church
Christmas, 6
Christmas Island, 188, 288
Churches (buildings):
  In largest cities, 66–78
Churches (organizations). *See* Religion
Churchill, Sir Winston, 310
Church of England, 309
CIA, 111
Cimarron River, 33
Cincinnati, Ohio, 53, 68
  See also Cities (U.S.)
Circular measure, 430, 435, 436
Circumference, formula for, 435
Ciskei, 290–91
Cities (Canadian):
  Latitude and longitude, 32
  Time of day, 32
Cities (U.S.), 66–78
  Chambers of Commerce, 66–78
  Climate, 419–20
  Consumer Price Index, 326
  Crime rates, 134
  Distances between, 450–53
  Latitudes and longitudes, 32
  Mayors, managers, 66–78
  Population figures:
    Largest, 13–15, 66–78
    Largest by state, 35–61
  Ports, 347
  Time of day, 3
  See also specific cities
Cities (world):
  Distances between, 454–55
  Largest, by country, 182–324
  Large (table), 151–52
  Population, 151–52, 182–324
  Latitudes and longitudes, 169
  Southernmost, 203
  Time of day, 169
  See also specific cities
City managers, 66–78
Civilian labor force, 10, 334, 336

Civil rights:
  Bill of rights, 86–87
  Emancipation Proclamation, 92–93
  Fourteenth Amendment, 87
  Other Constitutional provisions, 85, 87, 88, 89, 90
Civil Rights, Commission on, 113
Civil Service Commission, U.S.
  See Office of Personnel Management
Civil time, 3
Civil War, American, 126
  Confederate States, 93
  Gettysburg Address, 93
Civil War, English, 310
Civil War, Russian, 292
Civil War, Spanish, 295
Clark, Charles Joseph, 200, 201
Clay, Henry, 102
Cleopatra, 216
Cleveland, Ohio, 53, 68
  See also Cities (U.S.)
Climate. *See* Weather
Clothing:
  Economic statistics, 328, 338, 351
  Industry, hours and wages, 338
  Price indexes, 328
Cloture rule, 117
Coal, 351
  Economic statistics, 154–55, 339, 351
  Industry, hours and wages, 339
  World production, 154–55
Coast Guard, U.S., 124, 125
Coast Guard Academy, U.S., 125
Coastline of U.S., 30
Cochise, 36
Cocoa, 343, 351
Cocos (Keeling) Islands, 288
C.O.D. mail, 146
Coffee, 343, 351
Coins. *See* Money
Collect-on-delivery mail, 146
Colleges and Universities, 385–410
  Accredited, 385–410
  Endowments, 384
  Enrollments, 381, 385–410
  Firsts, 97
  Faculty salaries, 384
  Graduates, 382
  Libraries, 383
  United States, 385–410
Colombia, 206–07
  Volcanoes, 164
  See also Countries
Colombo, Sri Lanka, 296
  See also Sri Jayewardenapura Kotte
Colonial Williamsburg, 59
Colorado, 37–38
  Mountain peaks, 33
  See also States of U.S.
Colorado Desert, 176
Colorado River (Colorado-Mexico), 33, 159, 174
Colorado River (Texas), 33
  Hoover Dam, 49
Colorado Springs, Colo., 37
  Air Force Academy, U.S., 125
Colors, state, 35–61
Columbia River, 33, 60, 174
  Grand Coulee Dam, 60
Columbus, Christopher, 159, 214, 232, 246, 304
Columbus, Ohio, 53, 68
  See also Cities (U.S.)
Columbus Day, 5
Colville River, 33
Commerce. *See* Foreign trade; Interstate Commerce
Commerce, U.S. Dept. of, 111
  Secretaries of, 108–10
Commodities, Producer Price Index. 328
Common Market. *See* European Economic Community
Commonwealth of Nations, 233, 237, 258, 259, 261, 298, 304, 323
Commonwealth, Puritan, 308, 310
Communicable diseases, 27
Communications:
  FCC, 112
  Industry, hours and wages, 338
  ITU, 181
  See also specific type of communication
Communist Party (U.S.S.R.), 294
Community, European Economic, 296, 311
Como, Lake, 245
Comoros, 207
  Volcanoes, 164

See also Countries
Comstock Lode, 49
Conakry, Guinea, 232
Confederate Memorial Day, 6
Confederate States, 95
  Flag, 96
  Secession, readmission dates, 95
Confucius, 168
Congo, 207–08
  See also Countries
Congo, Democratic Republic of the. See
** Zaire**
Congo River, 159, 173, 207, 322
Congresses, Continental, 79–80, 94
Congress of Vienna, 188, 223
Congress (U.S.), 114–17
  Adjournment, 82
  Assembling time, 82, 89
  Compensation and privileges, 82
  Constitutional provisions, 81–90
  First Black member, 97
  First sessions, 94
  First women members, 97
  Legislative powers, 83, 88–89, 117
  Powers and duties, 81–83
  Salary of members, 82, 122
  See also House of Representatives; Sen-
  ate
Connecticut, 38
  See also States of U.S.
Connecticut River, 33, 38
Constantinople, 231, 305
  See also Istanbul
Constitutions (state):
  Dates adopted, 35–61
  First, 39, 97
Constitution (U.S.), 55, 81–90
  Amendment procedure, 85
  Amendments, 86–90
  Drafting of, 81
  Ratification, 81, 86, 94
  Supremacy of, 85
Consumer Price Index, 326
Consumer Product Safety Commission,
** 112**
Consumers:
  Complaints, 365
  Credit, 327
  Metric conversion tables, 434, 436
  Price indexes, 326
  Toll-free numbers, 366–68
Continental Congresses, 79–80, 94
Continental Divide, 31, 48
Construction industry, 329, 362
Continental Drift, 160
Continents, 160–61
  Area, 167
  Elevations, 167
  Explorations, discoveries, 159–60
  Populations, 167
  See also specific continents
Controllers (of states), 35–61
Conventions, National, 101
Cook Islands, 270
Copenhagen, Denmark, 212
  See also Cities (world)
Coptic Christians, 215, 219
Copyrights, 359–60
Coral Sea Islands, 188
Corn:
  Economic statistics, 155, 156, 342
  Exports and imports, 156
  World production, 155
Corporations:
  Profits, 335
  Taxes, 138, 140
Corruption, public, prosecutions for, 132
Corsica, 221, 245
Cortés, Hernando, 159, 263
Costa Rica, 208
  See also Countries
Côte d'Ivoire, 208–09
  See also Countries
Cotopaxi, 164
Cotton, 342
Council of Economic Advisors, 111
Council of Trent, 1
Council on Environmental Quality, 111
Counterfeiting, 131, 132, 133
Counties (per state), 35–61
Countries of world, 182–324
  Agriculture, 155, 156, 182–324
  Areas, 150–51, 182–324
  Birth rates, 182–324
  Capitals, 182–324
  Cities, large, 151–52, 182–324
  Economic conditions, 182–324

Explorations and discoveries of selected
  areas, 159–60
  Foreign trade, 158, 182–324
  Governments, 182–324
  History, 182–324
  Holidays, 7
  Immigration to U.S., 18
  Industry, 182–324
  Languages, 182–324
  Life expectancy, 153
  Monetary units, 182–324
  Natural features, 182–324
  Petroleum production, 154–55
  Political parties, 182–324
  Population densities, 182–324
  Populations, 182–324
  Population (table) 150–51
  Premiers, prime ministers, 182–324
  Presidents, 182–324
  Rulers, 182–324
  U.N. members, 178
  World Wars I and II, 127
  See also Geography (world); History
  (world)
Couples, unmarried, by sex and age, 21
Court, International, 180
Courts (federal), 84–85, 119–20
  See also Supreme Court
Courts (state), 65–66
Cows:
  Economic statistics, 342
  See also Cattle
CPI, 43
Crater Lake National Park, 161
Cream, economic statistics, 343
Credit, consumer, 327
Creed, The American's, 94
Crete, 161, 231
Crime:
  Corruption, prosecutions for, 132
  Rates, 134
  Recidivism, 130
  Statistics, 10, 130–34
  Trial rights, 85, 86–87
Crimean War, 306, 310
Croatia, 321
Cromwell, Oliver, 308, 310
Cuba, 209–10
  Bay of Pigs invasion, 210
  Island, 293
  Missile crisis, 210, 293
  Refugees, 210
  See also Countries
Cubic measure, 429–30
Cubit (measure), 433
Cultural Revolution, 205
Cumberland River, 33
Curaçao, 270
Curfew law arrests, 131, 132
Currency. See Money
Custer, Gen. George, 48, 53
Custer's Last Stand, 48
Customs, declarations, 438–39
Cyprus, 210–11, 231, 306
  Greek–Turkish crisis, 210, 306
  See also Countries
Czechoslovakia, 211–12
  Warsaw Pact invasion of, 211
  See also Countries

D

Dahomey. See Benin
Dairy products:
  Economic statistics, 343, 351
Dakar, Senegal, 286
Dallas, Tex., 57, 68
  See also Cities (U.S.)
Damascus, Syria, 300
Damavend, Mount, 240
Danube River, 173, 188, 195, 211, 235,
  282, 321
Dardanelles, 305
Dare, Virginia, 52, 97
Dar es Salaam, Tanzania, 302
Darling River, 174
Dasht-e-Kavir Desert, 176
Dasht-e-Lut Desert, 176
Date line, 3
Davis, Jefferson, 6
Days:
  Names of, 3
  Sidereal and solar, 2
Dead Sea, 243
Death penalty, 136

Deaths and death rates:
  Accidental, 27
  Diseases, 27
  Motor vehicle, 27
  War casualties, 126, 127
Death Valley, 30, 31, 176
Debs, Eugene V., 104
Debts, National, 328, 344–45
Decibel, 433
Decimals, fractions, 435
Declaration of Independence, 55, 79–80
Decoration Day. See Memorial Day
Defense, U.S. Dept. of, 111
  Expenditures, 343, 344–45
  Secretaries of, 109–10
  See also Armed Forces (U.S.)
de Gaulle, Charles, 222, 223
Degrees, academic, 411
  First for women, 97
Delaware, 38–39
  See also States of U.S.
Delaware River, 33
Democratic Party:
  Members of Congress, 114–17
  Senate floor leaders, 118
Denali National Park, 36
Deng, Xiaoping, 205, 206
Denmark, 212–13
  See also Countries
Densities of Population:
  United States, 12–17
  World, 167, 182–324
Denver, Colo., 37, 38, 69, 419
  See also Cities (U.S.)
Deserts, 176
Detroit, Mich., 46, 69
  See also Cities (U.S.)
Devil's Hole, 177
Devon Island, 176
Dhaka, Bangladesh, 189
Diabetes mellitus, 27
Diamond mine (Arkansas), 37
Diamonds, 289
Dinaric Alps, 321
Diphtheria, 27
Diplomatic personnel, first Black, 97
Directory, French, 222
Disability benefits, 128
Discoveries, geographical, 159–60
Diseases:
  Cardiovascular, 27
  Communicable, 27
  Deaths from, 27
Distance:
  Between cities, 450–55
Distilled spirits. See Liquor
District of Columbia, 39, 76
  See also Washington, D.C.
"Divorce capitals," 49
Divorce statistics, 20
Djibouti, Republic of, 213–14
  See also Countries
Dnieper River, 174, 292
Doctors (physicians), first woman, 97
Dodecanese Islands, 231
Dominica, 214
  See also Countries
Dominican Republic, 214–15
  U.S. interventions in, 214–15
  See also Countries
Don River, 174, 292
Dram (measure), 430
Drivers:
  Accidents, 27
  Arrests for drunkenness, 131, 132
Dropouts, high school, 381
Drug Control Policy, National Office of,
  111
Drugs & Drug Abuse:
  Economic statistics, 351
  Hotline (toll-free), 366
  See also Narcotics
Drunkenness, arrests for, 131, 132
Dry measure, 430
Duarte, José, Napoleón, 217
Dublin, Ireland, 242
  See also Cities (world)
Durable goods, 328, 362
  See also individual items
Dutch East Indies. See Indonesia
Dutch Guiana. See Suriname

E

Earth (planet). See World

Earthquakes, 168
East China Sea, 171
East Germany. *See* Germany
Easter Island, 203
Easter Rebellion, 242
Easter Sunday, 5
Ebert, Friedrich, 228
Economic Advisers, Council of, 111
Economic and Social Council, U.N.,
179–80
Economic statistics (U.S.), 155–58, 326–51
Economic statistics (world), 154–58, 351
Economy:
   U.S., 326–51
   World, 154–58
Ecuador, 215
   Volcanoes, 164
   See also Countries
Ecumenical Councils, 316
   Vatican Council II, 316
Eden, Anthony, Sir, 310
Edinburgh, Scotland, 308
Education, 10, 381–411
   Attendance laws, 382
   College costs, 385–410
   Employment, payrolls, 343
   Enrollments, 381, 385–410
   Expenditures, college, 383, 384
   Federal aid, 383
   Graduates, 382
   School statistics, 381–411
   Service academies, 124–26
   Teachers, 384
   Veterans' benefits, 128
   See also Colleges & Universities
Education, Department of, 112
   Secretaries, 110
Edward VIII, 308
Eggs:
   Economic statistics, 343
Egypt, Arab Republic of, 215–17
   Israel and, 215–17, 244
   Suez Canal, 216, 217, 244
   See also Arab–Israeli wars; Countries
Eire. *See* Ireland (Republic)
Elbe River, 211, 227
Elbert, Mount, 33
Election Day, 5–6
Elections, presidential, 102–05
   Election results (1789–1988), 102–05
Electoral College, 87, 89, 101
   Voting, 101
Electrical appliances and equipment, 330
Electricity:
   Economic statistics, 326
   Electric current, 429
Electrocution, first, 97
Elementary schools, 381, 383
Elevations:
   Cities of U.S., 66–78
   Continents, 167
   Deserts, 176
   Extremes of U.S., 30
   Mountain peaks, 33, 170–71
   States of U.S., 31
   Volcanoes, 161, 164–65
Elizabeth I, Queen, 308, 309
Elizabeth II, Queen, 307, 308, 309, 311
Elks (BPOE), 373
Ellesmere Island, 175
Ellice Islands. *See* Tuvalu
Ell (measure), 433
El Paso, Tex., 57, 69
   See also Cities (U.S.)
El Salvador, 217–18
   Volcanoes, 164
   See also Countries
Emancipation Proclamation, 92–93
Embezzlement arrests, 131, 132, 133
Empire, Second (French), 221, 222, 223
Employment, 327, 334, 336, 337, 338, 339,
341, 362
   Average weekly earnings, 338, 339
   By race, occupation, 337
   Government, 343
   Labor force, 66–78, 334, 336, 337, 340,
   341
   Taxes, 138
   Unemployment, 66–78, 340, 362
   Unions, 334
   Women, 336, 337, 339, 341
   See also Labor
Enderbury Island, 63
Energy:
   Consumption, 154–55
   World production, 154–55
Energy, U.S. Department of, 112
   Secretaries, 110

Eniwetak (Enewetok) Atoll, 261
England, 307–11
   Area, population, 307
   Rulers, 308
   See also United Kingdom
Enrollment, school. *See* Education
Environmental Protection Agency, 112
Environmental Quality, Council on, 111
EPA, 112
Epiphany, 4
"E pluribus unum," 94
Equal Employment Opportunity Commis-
sion, 112
Equatorial Guinea, 218
   See also Countries
Equinox(es), 1–2, 4
Equipment expenditures, 329
Ericson, Leif, 6, 199
Erie, Lake, 172
   Battle of, 53
   Erie Canal, 51
Eritrea, Ethiopia, 220
Estate & gift taxes, 138, 140
Estonia, 218–19
   See also Countries
Ethiopia, 219–20, 246
   See also Countries
Etna, Mount, 164, 245
Euphrates River, 174, 241
Eurasia, 161
Europe, 161, 167
   Explorations and discoveries, 159
   See also Continents; Countries
European Economic Community, 296,
311, 350
Everest, Mount, 167, 170, 268
Everglades National Park, 39
Executions:
   First electrocution, 97
   Methods by state, 136
   See also Capital punishment
Executive Departments and Agencies,
111–13
Expectation of life, 29, 153
Expenditures:
   Education, 383
   Federal government, 336, 343, 344–45,
   346
   Gross national product, 328
   Plant and equipment, 329
   State governments, 65–66
Explorations, 159–60
Export–Import Bank, 113
Exports:
   United States, 158, 349, 351
   Value by country, 158
Express Mail, 145
Extradition between states, 85

F

Faeroe Islands, 213
Fahrenheit scale, 429, 436
Falkland Islands, 186, 311, 313
Falling bodies:
   Formulas for, 435
   Law of, 435
Families:
   Characteristics, 23–24
   Income, 23–24, 327, 329
   Of U.S. Presidents, 100
   Statistics, 22, 23–24, 327, 329
Farm Credit Administration, 112
Farm Index, 329
Farms. *See* Agriculture
Farragut, David G., Adm., 97
Fascists, 246
Fats and oils, 343, 351
Fat Tuesday. *See* Shrove Tuesday
FBI, 111
FCA, 112
FDIC, 112
Feasts, Jewish, 4–6
FEC, 112
Federal budget, 336, 343, 344–45, 346
   Foreign assistance, 336
   Public debt, 328, 344–45
   Social welfare expenditure, 336, 346
Federal Bureau of Investigation, 111
Federal Communications Commission,
112
Federal Courts, 84–85, 119–20
   See also Supreme Court
Federal Deposit Insurance Corporation,
112
Federal Election Commission, 112

Federal Energy Administration. *See* Ener-
gy, U.S. Dept. of
Federal Government. *See* United States
Government
Federalist Party, 98, 102
Federal Maritime Commission, 112
Federal Mediation and Conciliation Serv-
ice, 112
Federal Power Commission. *See* Enerfy,
U.S. Dept. of
Federal Reserve Board, 112
Federal Reserve System, 112
Federal Trade Commission, 112
Fernando Po, Equatorial Guinea. *See*
Bioko
Fertilizers, 351
Festival of Lights, 6
Fifth Republic (French), 222, 223
Fiji, 220
   See also Countries
Filibusters, 117
Fingal's Cave, 177
Finland, 220–21
   See also Countries
Firearms:
   As murder weapons, 133–34
Fireman, 343
Fires:
   Arson arrests, 131, 132
First Fruits, Feast of, 5
Firsts in America, 97
Fish:
   Economic statistics, 351
Five and ten-cent store, first, 97
Flag (Confederate), 96
Flag Day, 5
Flag (U.S.), 96
   Pledge to, 96
Flights, Orbital, 293
Floor Leaders of Senate, 118
Florence, Italy, 245
Florida, 39
   See also States of U.S.
Flour, economic statistics, 343
Flowers:
   State, 35–61
FMCS, 112
FM radio stations, 66–78
Food:
   Economic statistics, 338, 342, 343, 351
   Industry, hours and wages, 338
   Price indexes, 326
   U.S. consumption, 343
   See also Agriculture
Food and Agriculture Organization, U.N.,
180
Foreign aid (U.S.), 336, 345
Foreign embassies, 439–42
Foreign mail. *See* International mail
Foreign trade (U.S.), 349, 350, 351
Foreign trade (world):
   By country, 158, 182–324
   Exports–imports table, 158
Forests:
   Resources of countries, 182–324
   State forests, 35–61
Forgery, 131, 132, 133
Formosa. *See* Taiwan
Forms of address, 415–16
Formulas, math, physics, 435
Fort Dodge, 42
Fort Sumter, Battle of, 56
Fort Ticonderoga, 52, 58
Fort Worth, Tex., 57, 69
   See also Cities (U.S.)
Fourth of July, 5
Fractions, decimals, 435
France, 221–25
   NATO, 223
   Rulers (table), 222
   See also Countries
Franco, Francisco, 295
Franco-Prussian War, 223
Frankfurt, Germany, 226
Franklin, Benjamin, 79, 94
Fraternity, first, 97
"Freedom March," 35
Freedom of the press, 86
Freedoms, Constitutional, 86–90
Freetown, Sierra Leone, 287
Freezing point of water, 433
Freight ton (measure), 433
Freight traffic, 347
FRELIMO, 266
French and Indian War, 41, 46, 47, 53, 57,
58, 61
French Guiana, 223
French Polynesia, 224–25

French Revolution, 221
French Somaliland. *See* Djibouti
French Southern and Antarctic Lands, 225
French Sudan. *See* Mali
French Territory of the Afars and Issas.
   See Djibouti
Fresno, Calif., 69
   See also Cities (U.S.)
Friendly Islands, 304
FRS, 112
Fruit:
   Economic statistics, 343
FTC, 112
Fuel, 328, 351
   See also specific fuels
Fujiyama, 161, 247
Funafuti, Tuvalu, 306
"Fundamental Orders," 38, 97
Fur, 351
Furniture:
   Economic statistics, 328, 330, 338
   Industry, hours and wages, 338

G

Gabon, 225–26
   See also Countries
Gadsden Purchase, 16, 36, 51
Gagarin, Yuri A., 293
Galápagos Islands, 160, 215
Galilee, Sea of, 243
Gambia, 226
   See also Countries
Gambia River, 159, 226
Gambier Island, 225
Gambling, 49, 50, 131, 132, 264
Gandhi, Indira, 238
Gandhi, Mohandas K., 237–38
Ganges River, 172, 190, 237
"Gang of Four," 205
Gas, natural, manufactured, 351
Gasoline service stations, 330
GATT, 180
Gaza Strip, 216, 244
General Agreement on Tariffs and Trade
   (GATT), 180
General Assembly, U.N., 179
General Services Administration, 112
General Sherman Tree, 37
Generals (U.S.), 123
Geneva, Lake, 299
Geneva, Switzerland, 299
Genghis Khan, 182
Geographic centers:
   Of states, 35–61
   Of United States, 30
Geographic Society, National, 374
Geography:
   Caves and caverns, 177
   Coastline of U.S., 30
   Continental Divide, 31
   Continents, 159–61, 167
   Deserts, 176
   Elevations, 31, 167
   Explorations, discoveries, 159–60
   Islands, 175–76
   Lakes, 172–73
   Mountain peaks, 33, 170–71
   Oceans, seas, 171
   Of countries, 182–324
   Rivers, 33–34, 173–74
   United States, 10, 30–34
   Volcanoes, 161–65
      Map, 162–63
   Waterfalls, 174–75
   World, 159–77
Geometric formulas, 435
Georgetown, Guyana, 233
Georgia, 39–40
   See also States of U.S.
Georgia, Republic of, 293
Germany, 226–30
   History, 227–30
   Nazi regime, 228
   Rulers (table), 228
   World War I, 227
   World War II, 228
   See also Countries
Geronimo, 36, 51
Gettysburg Address, 93
Gettysburg, Battle of, 55, 93
Ghana, 230
   See also Countries
Gibraltar, 313
Gift taxes, federal, 138, 140
Gila River, 33

Gilbert Islands, 250
   See also Kiribati
Girl Scouts of U.S.A., 374
Giscard d'Estaing, Valéry, 222
Glacier National Park, 48
Glasgow, Scotland, 308
   See also Cities (world)
Glass, economic statistics, 351
Glenn, John H., Jr., 115
Glossary:
   Weather, 422
GNP, 328
Gobi Desert, 176, 204
Godwin Austen, Mount (K–2), 170
Golan Heights, 216, 244, 300
Gold:
   Karat (measure of purity), 433, 437
Gold Coast: *See* Ghana
Golden Gate Bridge, 37
Golden Temple (India), 238
Gold Rush:
   Alaska, 36
   California, 37
Good Friday, 5
Gorbachev, Mikhail S., 294, 295
Gotland, Sweden, 298
Government, U.S. *See* United States Gov-
   ernment
Government employment, 343
Government (foreign), 182–324
   Heads of state, 182–324
Governors of states, 35–61
   First Black, 97
   First woman, 61, 97
   Puerto Rico, 62
   Terms and salaries, 65–66
   U.S. Territories, 62–65
Graduates, high school, college, 382
Grain, 351
   See also specific grains
Gram (measure), 429, 432, 434, 436
Grand Coulee Dam, 60
   Hydroelectric plant, 60
Grants for education, 383
Graves, Presidential, 99
Great Arabian Desert, 176
Great Australian Desert, 176
Great Bear Lake, 172
Great Britain (country).*See* United King-
   dom
Great Britain (island) 175
Great gross (measure), 433
Great Lakes, 172
Great Salt Lake, 58
Great Salt Lake Desert, 176
Great Seal of U.S., 94
Great Slave Lake, 172
Great Smoky Mountains National Park,
   52, 57
Great Wall of China, 204
Greece, 230–31
   See also Countries
Greece, ancient, 231
Greenback Party, 103
Greenland, 159, 160, 161, 175
Green Mountain Boys, 58
Green River (Ky.), 33
Green River (Wyoming–Utah), 33
Greenwich time, 3
Gregorian calendar, 1–2
Grenada, 231–32
   U.S. military intervention, 232
   See also Countries
Gromyko, Andrei A., 294
Gross (measure), 433
Gross National Product, 182–324, 328
GSA, 112
Guadalcanal, 288
Guadalupe Mountains National Park, 58
Guadeloupe, 224
Guam, 62, 65
Guatemala, 232
   Volcanoes, 164
   See also Countries
Guernsey, 313
Guevara, Ché, 193, 209
Guiana, British. *See* Guyana
Guiana, Dutch. *See* Suriname
Guiana, French, 223
Guinea, Portuguese. *See* Guinea–Bissau
Guinea, Spanish. *See* Equatorial Guinea
Guinea–Bissau, 233
   See also Countries
Guinea (republic), 232–33
   See also Countries
Gulf of Mexico, 171, 263
Guns. *See* Firearms
Gunter's chain (measure), 430, 433

Guyana, 233–34
   See also Countries

H

Hague, The, The Netherlands, 269
Hailstone, largest, 422
Haile Selassie, 219
Hainan Island, 204
Haiti, 234
   Duvalier, Jean–Claude, 234
   U.S. intervention in, 234
   See also Countries
Hall of Fame, baseball, 52
Halloween, 5
Hamburg, Germany, 226
Hamilton, Alexander, 106
Hammarskjöld, Dag, 180, 322
Hand (measure), 433
Hanging as death penalty, 136
Hanoi, Vietnam, 318
Hanover, House of, 308
Hanukkah, 6
Hapsburg, House of, 188, 235
Harare (formerly Salisbury), Zimbabwe,
   323
Hardware, 330
Harvard University, 97
Harvest, Feast of, 5
Hashemite Kingdom. *See* Jordan
Hastings, Battle of, 309
Havana, Cuba, 209
Hawaii, 40
   Volcanoes, 40, 164, 167
   See also States of U.S.
Hawaii Volcanoes National Park, 40
Health, Education, and Welfare, U.S.
   Dept. of, 112
   Secretaries of, 109–10
   See also Health and Human Services,
   Dept. of; Education, Dept. of
Health and Human Services, Dept. of,
   111–12
   Secretaries of, 110
Heard Island, 188
Heart disease, human, 27
Heath, Edward, 310
Hebrew Pentecost, 5
Hebrides, 309
Hectare, 431
Helsinki, Finland, 220
Hermitage, The (Andrew Jackson's
   home), 57, 99
Hertz (measure), 433
Herzegovina, 321
Hides, 328, 351
High Aswan Dam, 172, 216
Highest points, U.S., 31
High schools, 381, 382, 383
   Graduates, 322
Highways, road mileages, 451–52
Himalayas, 170–71, 237, 238
Hindenburg, Paul von, 228
Hindu Kush range, 182
Hirohito, Emperor, 247
Hiroshima, Japan, 247
   Atomic bombing, 248
Hispanics, Population, 16, 19
Hispaniola, 176, 214, 234
History (U.S.). *See* United States History
History (world), 182–324
   Discoveries, 159–60
   Explorations, 159–60
Hitler, Adolf, 228
Ho Chi Minh, 318
Ho Chi Minh City, Vietnam, 318
Hogshead (measure), 433
Hokkaido, 176, 247
Holidays, 4–7
   National, by country, 7
   Religious, 4–6
Holland. *See* Netherlands
Holy Roman Empire, 227
Homestake Mine, 56
Homicide. *See* Murder
Honduras, 234–35
   See also Countries
Honduras, British. *See* Belize
Hong Kong, 204, 214, 314
Honolulu, Hawaii, 70
   See also Cities (U.S.)
Honshu, Japan, 175, 247
Hood, Mount, 31, 54, 161
Hoover Dam, 36, 50, 172
   Lake Mead, 36, 50
Horn, Cape, 160, 203

Horsepower, 433
Horse racing:
Kentucky Derby, 43
Hostages, American, 240
Hotels, hours and wages, 339
Hot Springs National Park, 37
Households, 21, 22–24, 331, 339
House of Burgesses, 97
House of Representatives (U.S.), 81–82, 115–17
Apportionment, 81, 88
Eligibility, 81
First Black member, 97
First woman member, 97
Speakers, 118
See also Congress (U.S.)
Housing:
Construction, 329
Economic statistics, 326, 329
Housing and Urban Development, U.S. Dept. of, 112
Secretaries of, 109–10
Houston, Tex., 57, 70
See also Cities (U.S.)
Howland Island, 63
Hsi River (Si Kiang). *See* Xi Jiang
Huang Ho, 173, 204
Hudson Bay, 160, 171, 199
Hudson River, 52, 160
Hudson's Bay Company, 199
Humidity, relative, 426–28
Humphrey, Hubert H., 99
Hundred Years' War, 221, 309
Hungary, 235–36
1956 uprisings, 236
See also Countries
Huns. *See* Mongols
Huron, Lake, 46, 172, 199
Hus, Jan, 211
Hurricanes, 422
Hussein, King, 248–49, 320
Hussein, Saddam, 241, 242, 252
Hyde Park, N.Y. (F.D.R.), 52, 99
Hydrogen bomb, 293

I

ICC, 112
Iceland, 159, 161, 236–37
Island, 176
Volcanoes, 164
See also Countries
Idaho, 40–41
See also States of U.S.
Illinois, 41
See also States of U.S.
Illinois River, 33
IMF, 181
Immigration statistics, 18, 19
Impeachment, 81–82, 84
Imperial gallon, 431
Imports:
United States, 158, 351
Value by country, 158
Inca Empire, 193, 203, 215, 278
Income:
By occupation, 327, 338, 339
Family, 327, 329
Farm income, 343
Household, 327, 329
National income, 335
Per capita, 66–78, 326, 335
See also Revenue; Salaries; Wages
Income tax (federal), 137–41, 344
Collections, 138, 344
Established, 88
Independence, Declaration of, 79–80
Independence Day, 5
Independence Hall, 55, 95
India, 190, 237–38, 274, 310
Sikh rebellion, 238
See also Countries
Indiana, 41–42
See also States of U.S.
Indianapolis, Ind., 41, 42, 70
See also Cities (U.S.)
Indian Ocean, 171
Islands, 175, 176
Volcanoes, 164
Indians (American):
Births and birth rates, 26
Population of reservations, 19
Reservations, 19, 36
Indochina. *See* Cambodia; Laos; Vietnam
Indonesia, 238–39
Volcanoes, 164

See also Countries
Indus River, 173, 237, 274
Industry:
Employment, 337, 361
Foreign countries, 154–58
Hours and wages, 338, 339
Plant and equipment costs, 329
Production indexes, 328
See also individual industries
Infant mortality, 27, 28
Influenza, 27
Information Agency, U.S., 113
"Information Please" quiz show, 97
Ingathering, Feast of, 5
Inini, 223
Insurance:
Life insurance, 329
Unemployment, 361–62
Insured mail, 146
Interest on the public debt, 344–45
Interior, U.S. Dept. of, 111
Secretaries of, 107–10
Internal Revenue Service. *See* Taxes
International Atomic Energy Agency, 180
International Bank, 180
International Civil Aviation Organization, 180
International Court, 180
International Date Line, 3
International Development Association, 180
International Development Cooperation Agency, U.S., 113
International Finance Corp., 180–81
International Labor Organization, 181
International mail, 147
International Maritime Organization, 181
International Monetary Fund, 181
International organizations, U.S. contributions to, 345
International System of Units, 429–32
International Telecommunication Union, 181
International Trade Commission, U.S., 113
Interstate commerce, 347
Interstate Commerce Commission, 112
Iolani Palace, 40
Ionian Islands, 231
Iowa, 42
See also States of U.S.
IRA (Irish Republic Army), 242, 311, 312
Iran, 239–41
Hostage crisis, 240
Shah of, 240
War with Iraq, 240, 241
See also Countries
Iraq, 241–42
Israel and, 240
War with Iran, 240
See also Countries
Ireland, Northern, 242, 309, 311–12
See also United Kingdom
Ireland (island), 176
Ireland (republic), 242–43
See also Countries
Irish Republican Army, 242, 311, 312
Iron:
Economic statistics, 338, 351
Irrawaddy River, 174
Irtish River, 173
Islamabad, Pakistan, 274
Islands, 175–76
See also specific islands
Isle of Man, 314
Israel, 243–45
Balfour Declaration, 243
Independence (1948), 244
Invasion of Lebanon, 244, 254
Wars with Arabs, 216–17, 241, 244–45, 248–49, 254, 285, 300–01, 305
See also Countries
Istanbul, Turkey, 305
See also Constantinople
Italy, 245–46
Volcanoes, 164
See also Countries; Roman Empire
Ivory Coast. *See* Côte d'Ivoire
Iwo Jima, 161

J

Jackson, Miss., 47
Jacksonville, Fla., 39, 70
See also Cities (U.S.)
Jakarta, Indonesia, 239

Jamaica, 246–47
See also Countries
James River, 33
Jamestown, Va., 59, 160
Jammu, 238
Japan, 159, 247–48
China and, 204, 205, 247–48
Islands, 175, 176, 247
Russia and, 247
Volcanoes, 161, 247
World War II peace treaty, 248
See also Countries
Japanese in U.S.:
Births and birth rates, 26
See also Nonwhite persons
Japan Sea, 171, 247
Japurá River, 174
Jarvis Island, 63
Java, 175, 239
See also Indonesia
Jefferson, Thomas, 79
Birthday, 6
Jenolan Caves, 177
Jersey (island), 313
Jerusalem, 243
Jewish holidays, 4–6
Jewish New Year, 5
Jobs. *See* Employment
Johnston Atoll, 64
Joint Chiefs of Staff, 111
Jordan (kingdom), 248–49
Israel and, 248–49
See also Countries
Juan Fernández Islands, 203
Judaism:
Holidays, 4–6
Judiciary, U.S.:
Act of 1789, 97
Constitutional provisions, 84–85
See also Supreme Court
Julian Calendar, 1, 2
Jura Mountains, 299
Jury trial, 85, 86, 87
Justice, U.S. Department of, 111
Attorneys General, 106–10
Justices. *See* Supreme Court

K

Kabul, Afghanistan, 183
Kalahari Desert, 176
Kamchatka, 161
Kampala, Uganda, 306
Kampuchea. *See* Cambodia
Kanawha-New River, 33
Kansas, 42–43
See also States of U.S.
Kansas City, Mo., 47, 70, 421
See also Cities (U.S.)
Karafuto. *See* Sakhalin
Kara Kum Desert, 176
Karat (measure), 433, 437
Kariba Lake, 172
Katanga (now Shaba), 322
Kashmir, 237, 274
Katmandu, Nepal, 268
Kazakhstan, 293
Kelvin (scale), 429, 433
Kennedy, Edward M., 114
Kennedy, Jacqueline. *See* Onassis, Jacqueline
Kennedy, Robert F., 109
Kennedy International Airport, 52, 456
Kennedy Space Center, 39
Kent's Cavern, 177
Kentucky, 43
See also States of U.S.
Kentucky Derby, 43
Kenya, 249
See also Countries
Key, Francis Scott, 92
Kharkov, 291
Khartoum, Sudan, 296
Khmer Republic. *See* Cambodia
Khomeini, Ayatollah, 240–41
Khrushchev, Nikita, 294
Kiev, 291, 293
Kigali, Rwanda, 283
Kilauea, 164
Kilogram, 429, 432, 436
Kilometer, 429, 431, 434, 436
Kindergarten, 381
Kingman Reef, 64
Kings:
Of England, 308
Of France, 222

Of Prussia, 228
Of Russia, 294
Kingston, Jamaica, 246
Kingstown, St. Vincent and the Grenadines, 284
Kinshasa, Zaire, 322
Kirghizia, 293
Kiribati, 249–50
    See also Countries
Kissinger, Henry A., 109, 110, 205, 216, 244, 319
Kitty Hawk, N.C., 52
Kiwanis International, 375
Kjólen Mountains, 298
Knights of Columbus, 375
Knights of Pythias, 375
Knot (measure), 433
Know–Nothing Party, 105
Korea, North, 250
    See also Countries; Korean War
Korea, South, 251
    See also Countries; Korean War
Korean War, 251
    Casualties, U.S., 126
    Unknown Soldier of, 95
Kosciusko, Mount, 187
Kosygin, Aleksei N., 293
Koyukuk River, 33
Krakatau, 164
K–2 (Mount Godwin Austen), 170
Kuala Lumpur, Malaysia, 259
Kublai Khan, 204, 265
Kunlun Mountains, 204
Kuomintang, 204, 301
Kurile Islands, 161, 247, 293
Kuskokwim River, 33
Kuwait, 251–52
    See also Countries
Kyushu (island), 176, 247
Kyzyl Kum Desert, 176

L

Labor:
    Civilian labor force, 66–67, 334, 336, 341
    ILO, 181
    NLRB, 112
    Statistics, 337, 340, 341, 343, 362
    Unions, leading, 334
    See also Employment
Labor, U.S. Department of, 111
    Secretaries of, 108–10
Labor Day, 5
Labrador, 159, 199
Laccadive Islands, 237
Lagos, Nigeria, 272
Lakes, 172–73
    See also specific lakes
"Lame Duck" Amendment, 89
Lancaster, House of, 308
Land:
    Area of cities, 66–78
    Area of countries, 150–51, 182–324
    Area of states, 35–61
    World area, 167
Land rushes, 54
Languages:
    Use by country, 182–324
Laos, 252–53
    See also Countries
Lao-tse, 204
La Paz, Bolivia, 193
    See also Cities (world)
Larceny, 131, 132, 134
Largest businesses, 1990, 331–32
Lassen Peak, 37, 161
Lateran Treaty, 316
Latin America. *See* specific countries
Latitudes of cities, 32, 169
Latvia, 253
    See also Countries
Laundries, hours, wages, 339
Lausanne, Switzerland, 299
Law, first unconstitutional, 97
Law enforcement, 130–36
    Corruption, prosecutions for, 132
    Prisoners under death sentence, 136
    See also Crime; Arrests
Laws. *See* Bills (Congressional)
Lawyers:
    First woman, 97
League (measure), 433
League of Nations, 228, 300
Leather:
    Economic statistics, 328, 338
    Industry, hours and wages, 338

Lebanon, 244, 253–54
    Civil War, 254
    Israeli Invasion, 254
    U.S. military action in, 254
    See also Countries
Lee, Robert E., 6
Leeward Islands. *See* British Virgin Islands; Montserrat
Legal holidays, 4–6
Legislatures (state), 65–66
    Only unicameral, 49, 66
Legislatures (world), 182–324
    Oldest, 236
Lena River, 173, 292
Length, units of, 429–31
    Metric System, 429–32, 434, 436
Lenin, Vladimir, 292, 294
Leningrad, 291, 292
    See also St. Petersburg
Lent, 4
Lesbos, 231
Lesotho, 255
    See also Countries
Lesser Antilles, volcanoes, 164
Letters:
    Complaint letters, 365
    Forms of address, 415–16
    Postal regulations, 145–48
Lewis and Clark expedition, 41, 43, 53, 54, 56, 59–60, 160
Lexington-Concord, Battle of, 45
Liberia, 255–56
    See also Countries
Liberty, Statue of, 52, 96
Liberty Bell, 55, 95
Libraries, 383
    College and university, 383
    First circulating, 97
Libreville, Gabon, 225
Libya, 256
    See also Countries
Libyan Desert, 176
Licking River, 33
Lie, Trygve, 179
Liechtenstein, 256–57
    See also Countries
Life expectancy, 29, 153
Life insurance, 329
"Lighthouse of the Mediterranean," 164
Light-year, 433
Lilongwe, Malawi, 258
Lima, Peru, 277
    See also Cities (world)
Lincoln, Abraham, 41
    Emancipation Proclamation, 92–93
    Gettysburg Address, 93
    Home, 41
    See also Presidents (U.S.)
Lincoln's Birthday, 4
Linear measure, 429–32
Lions Clubs, 376
Lipari Islands, 164
Liquid measure, 430, 431, 432, 434, 436
Liquor:
    Economic statistics, 330, 351
    Law violations, 131, 132
    Taxes, 138
    See also Prohibition
Lisbon, Portugal, 280
    See also Cities (world)
Liter, 429, 431, 432, 434, 436
Lithuania, 257, 293
    See also Countries
Little Big Horn, Battle of, 48
Little Missouri River, 33
"Little White House," 40
Livestock, 342, 343
Loans:
    Educational loans, 383
    VA loans, 128
Logan, Mount, 199
Lomé, Togo, 303
London, England, 308
    See also Cities (world)
Long Beach, Calif., 71
    See also Cities (U.S.)
Longitude of cities, 32, 169
Los Angeles, Calif., 37, 71, 419
    See also Cities (U.S.)
Lots, Feast of, 4
Louisiana, 43–44
    See also States of U.S.
Louisiana Purchase, 16, 36, 41, 42, 43, 44, 46, 48, 49, 54, 56, 61
Louis XVI, 222
Louisville, Ky., 43
    See also Cities (U.S.)

Lowest points, U.S., 31
Luanda, Angola, 185
Lumber and wood:
    Economic statistics, 328, 330, 338, 351
    Industry, hours and wages, 338
    See also Forests
Lunation, 1
Luray Cavern, 177
Lusaka, Zambia, 323
Luther, Martin, 227
Luxembourg, 257–58
    See also Countries
Luzon, Philippines, 176, 278

M

Macao, 281
MacArthur, Douglas, 248, 251
MacDonald, Ramsay, 310
Macedonia, 231, 321
Machinery:
    Economic statistics, 328, 330, 351
    Industry, hours and wages, 338
Mackenzie River, 160, 173, 199
Macmillan, Harold, 310
Madagascar, 175, 258
    See also Countries
Madeira, Portugal, 280
Madeira River, 173
Madrid, Spain, 295
    See also Cities (world)
Magellan, Ferdinand, 160, 278
Maggiore, Lake, 245, 299
Magna Carta, 309
Magnum (measure), 433
Mail:
    Air-mail route, first, 97
    Postal regulations, 145–48
Maine, 44
    See also States of U.S.
Maine (battleship), 209
Major, John, 307, 310, 311
Majorca, 295
Malabo, Equatorial Guinea, 218
Malagasy, 258
Malawi, 258–59
    See also Countries
Malaya. *See* Malaysia
Malay Archipelago, 239
Malaysia, 259
    See also Countries
Maldives, 260
    See also Countries
Malé, Maldives, 260
Malenkov, Georgi M., 294
Mali, 260
    See also Countries
Malta, 261
    See also Countries
Mammoth Cave, 43, 177
Man, Isle of, 314
Management and Budget, Office of, 111
Managerial workers, 337
Managua, Nicaragua, 271
Manama, Bahrain, 189
Manchu Dynasty, 204, 248
Manchukuo, 204, 247
Manchuria, 204, 247
Manhattan, 51, 72
Manila, Philippines, 278
    See also Cities (world)
Manitoba, 199, 200
Manslaughter, 131, 132
Manufacturing. *See* Industry
Mao Tse-tung. *See* Mao Zedong
Mao Zedong, 204–05
Maputo, Mozambique, 266
Marco Polo, 159
Mardi Gras, 4
Margarine, 61
Mariana Islands, 64–65
Marine Corps, U.S., 123, 124
    Actions, 127, 217, 271
    Commandant of, 111
    See also Armed Forces
Marquesas Islands, 225
Marriage statistics, 20–22, 23–24
Marshall, John, 119
Marshall Islands, 261
Martinique, 224
Mount Pelée, 164
Martin Luther King Day, 4
Maryland, 44–45
    See also States of U.S.
Maseru, Lesotho, 255

Mason and Dixon's Line, 31
Mass:
 Metric System, 429
Massachusetts, 45–46
 See also States of U.S.
Mass–energy theorem, 435
Massive, Mount, 33
Maternal mortality, 27
Mathematics:
 Averages, 437
 Decimals and fractions, 435
 Formulas, 435
 Mean and median, 437
 Metric and U.S. equivalents, 429–32
 Prefixes and multiples, 435
 Prime numbers, 437
Matter–energy theorem, 435
Mauna Kea, 31, 40, 164
Mauna Loa, 40, 164
Mauritania, 261–62
 See also Countries
Mauritius, 262
 See also Countries
Maximilian, Emperor, 263
Mayflower Compact, 91
Mayflower (ship), 91
Mayors, U.S., 66–78
Mayotte, 225
Mbabane, Swaziland, 298
McDonald Islands, 188
McHenry, Fort, 92
McKinley, Mount, 30, 31, 33, 167
McNary Dam, 54
Mean and median, 437
Measles, 27
Measurement ton, 433
Measures, weights, 429–37
 Capacities and volumes, 429–32
 Conversion factors, 436
 Cooking, 434
Meat:
 Economic statistics, 157, 343, 351
 World production, 157
Mecca, Saudi Arabia, 285
Medal of Honor, 129
Mediation and Conciliation Service, Federal, 112
Mediation Board, National, 112
Medical care, economic statistics, 326
Medina, Saudi Arabia, 285
Mediterranean Sea, 171
 Volcanoes, 164
Mekong River, 173, 318
Melville Island, 176
Memorial Day, 5
Memphis, Tenn., 57, 71
 See also Cities (U.S.)
Merced River, waterfalls, 174–75
Merchant Marine Academy, U.S., 125–26
Mesabi Range, 46
Mesa Verde National Park, 38
Mesopotamia, 241
Metals:
 Economic statistics, 328, 351
 Industry, hours and wages, 338
 Mineral wealth in countries, 182–324
Meter (measure), 429–31, 436
Metric System, 429–32, 434, 436
 Conversion tables, 434, 436
Metropolitan areas, 13–15
Mexican Cession, 16, 263
Mexican War, 36, 37, 49, 51, 58, 61, 126, 263
Mexico, 262–63
 Conquest of, 159, 263
 U.S. military actions in, 127, 263
 Volcanoes, 164
 See also Countries
Mexico, Gulf of, 171
Mexico City, Mexico, 262
 See also Cities (world)
Miami, Fla., 71, 419
 See also Cities (U.S.)
Michigan, 46
 See also States of U.S.
Michigan, Lake, 42, 46, 160, 172
Micronesia, 263
Middle East:
 Arab–Israeli conflicts, 216–17, 243–44, 248–49, 254, 285, 300–01
Midway Islands, 64
Mileage:
 U.S. cities, between, 450–53
 World cities, between, 454–55
Military. *See* National defense; Armed Forces
Military Academy, U.S., 52, 125
Military forces. *See* Armed Forces

Milk:
 Economic statistics, 343
Milk River, 33
Milwaukee, Wis., 60, 71
 See also Cities (U.S.)
Mindanao, Philippines, 176, 278
Mindszenty, Jozsef Cardinal, 236
Minerals. *See* Coal; Metals
Ming Dynasty, 204
Mining:
 Hours and wages, 339
 Union, 334
Minneapolis, Minn., 46, 72
 See also Cities (U.S.)
Minnesota, 46–47
 See also States of U.S.
Minority Presidents, 122
Minsk, Byelorussia, U.S.S.R., 291, 292
Minutemen, 45
Miquelon. *See* St. Pierre
Mississippi, 47
 See also States of U.S.
Mississippi-Missouri-Red Rock River, 34, 173
Mississippi River, 34, 44, 47, 159, 160, 173
Missouri, 47–48
 See also States of U.S.
Missouri Compromise, 48
Missouri-Red Rock River, 34
Missouri River, 34, 173
Mistletoe, 6
Mitterrand, François, 221, 222, 223
Mmabatho, Bophuthatswana, 290
Mobile-Alabama-Coosa River, 34
Mobile homes, 329
Modified Mercalli Intensity Scale, 168
Mogadishu, Somalia, 288
Mohammed, 285
Mojave Desert, 176
Moldavia, 293
Mole (measure), 429
Moluccas islands, 239
Monaco, 264
 See also Countries
Mondale, Walter F., 99
Monetary Fund, International, 181
Money:
 Designs of U.S. bills, 437
 Of countries, 182–324
 Portraits on U.S. bills, 437
Money orders, postal, 146
Mongolia, 159, 264–65
 See also Countries
Mongols, 204, 292
Monroe Doctrine, 91
Monrovia, Liberia, 255
Montana, 48
 See also States of U.S.
Mont Blanc, 221
Monte Carlo, Monaco, 264
Montenegro, 321
Montevideo, Uruguay, 315
 See also Cities (world)
Months, 3
Monticello, Va., 59
Montreal, Quebec, Canada, 199, 200
Montserrat, 314
"Monumental Mountain," 177
Moravia, 211
Mormons, 58
Morocco, 265–66
 See also Countries
Moroni, Comoros, 207
Mortality. *See* Deaths
Moscow, 291, 293
 See also Cities (world)
"Mother of Presidents," 59
Motor vehicles:
 Accident deaths, 27
 Economic statistics, 348–49
 Registration, 348
 Theft, 131, 132, 133, 134
 See also Automobiles; Buses
Mottoes:
 National, 99
 State, 35–61
Mountains:
 United States, 31, 33, 171
 World, 170–71
 See also names of mountains; Volcanoes
Mount McKinley National Park. *See* Denali National Park
Mount Rainier National Park, 60
Mount Vernon, Va., 59, 99
Mozambique, 266, 281
 See also Countries
Mubarak, Hosni, 215, 217

Mulroney, Brian, 199, 200, 201
Munich, Germany, 226
Munich Conference (1938), 211, 228
Murder, 130, 131, 132, 133, 134
Murray River, 174
Muscat, Oman, 274
Museums, first science museum, 97
Mussolini, Benito, 247
Myanmar, 266–67
 See also Countries

N

NAACP, 377
Nagasaki, Japan, 248
Nairobi, Kenya, 249
Names:
 Days, 3
 Months, 3
 States, origins of, 35–61
Namibia, 267–68
 See also Countries
Napoleon Bonaparte. *See* Bonaparte, Napoleon
Napoleonic Wars, 221, 223, 292, 310
Narcotics:
 Violations, arrests for, 131, 132, 133
NASA, 112
Nashville-Davidson, Tenn., 57, 72
 See also Cities (U.S.)
Nassau, Bahamas, 188
Nasser, Gamal Abdel, 216, 244, 285, 320
National Aeronautics and Space Administration, 112
National Anthem, 92
National Cemetery, Arlington, 95, 99
National Conventions, 101
National debt, 328, 344–45
 Interest, 344–45
 Validity, 88
National defense:
 Spending for, 327, 336, 343, 344–45
National Foundation on the Arts and Humanities, 112
National income, 335
National Labor Relations Board, 112
National Mediation Board, 112
National Republican Party, 103
National Science Foundation, 112
National Security Council, 111
National Transportation Safety Board, 112
NATO. *See* North Atlantic Treaty Organization
Natural features (of countries), 182–324
 See also Geography
Naturalization statistics, 19
Natural resources:
 Countries, 182–324
 States of U.S., 35–61
Nauru, 268
 See also Countries
Naval Academy, U.S., 45, 124–25
Navy (U.S.), 123
 Expenditures, 344–45
 First admiral, 97
 Secretaries of, 106–10, 111
 See also Armed Forces
Nazis, 228
N'Djamena, Chad, 202
Nebraska, 48–49
 See also States of U.S.
Negev Desert, 243
Negroes. *See* Blacks
Nehru, Jawaharlal, 238
Nelson River, 174
Neosho River, 34
Nepal, 268
 See also Countries
Netherlands, 268–69
 See also Countries
Netherlands Antilles, 269–70
Nevada, 49
 See also States of U.S.
Nevis, 283
New Amsterdam, 51
New Brunswick, 199, 200
New Caledonia, 225
"New Colossus, The," 96
New Cornelia Tailings, 36
New Delhi, India, 237
Newfoundland, Canada, 176, 199
New Guinea. *See* Papua New Guinea
New Hampshire, 50
 See also States of U.S.
New Hebrides. *See* Vanuatu

New Jersey, 50
 See also States of U.S.
New Mexico, 51
 See also States of U.S.
New Orleans, 43–44, 72, 420
 See also Cities (U.S.)
New Orleans, Battle of, 44
Newspapers:
 First Black, 97
 Firsts, 97
 Oldest still published, 38
 Postal rates, 145
Newsreel, first, 97
Newton (measure), 429
New Year, Jewish, 5
New Year's Day, 4
New York City, 13, 51–52, 72
 Boroughs, 72
 Climate, 420
 Kennedy Airport, 52, 456
 Statue of Liberty, 52, 96
 U.N. Headquarters, 52, 179
 See also Cities (U.S.)
New York (State), 51–52
 See also States of U.S.
New Zealand, 270–71
 First visited, 160
 Volcanoes, 161
 See also Countries
Niagara Falls, 52, 175
Niamey, Niger, 272
Nicaragua, 271
 U.S. military actions in, 271
 Volcanoes, 164
 See also Countries
Nicknames:
 States (U.S.), 35–61
Nicobar Islands, 237
Nicosia, Cyprus, 210
Niger, 272
 See also Countries
Nigeria, 272–73
 See also Countries
Niger River, 173, 272
Nile River, 173, 216, 297
 High Aswan Dam, 216
Niobrara River, 34
Niue (island), 271
NLRB, 112
Noatak River, 34
Nonwhite persons in U.S.:
 Deaths and death rates, 28, 29, 130–31
 Life expectancy, 29, 130–31
 Population statistics, 12–13, 16, 19
 See also Chinese; Indians; Japanese;
 Blacks in U.S.
Norfolk Island, 187
Normandy, House of, 308
North America, 161, 167
 Explorations, discoveries, 159–60
 Population, 167
 See also Continents; Countries
North Atlantic Treaty Organization:
 France and, 223
 Turkey and, 306
North Canadian River, 34
North Carolina, 52
 See also States of U.S.
North Dakota, 52–53
 See also States of U.S.
Northeast Passage, 160
Northern Ireland, 242, 307, 311–12
 See also United Kingdom
Northern Rhodesia. *See* Zambia
North Island (New Zealand), 175, 270
North Platte River, 34
North Pole, 160
 Reached, 160
North Sea, 171, 191, 212, 227, 269, 273
Northwest Passage, 54, 160
Northwest Territories, 199, 200
Norway, 273–74
 See also Countries
Nouakchott, Mauritania, 261
Nova Scotia, 169, 199, 200
NRC, 112
NSF, 112
Nubian Desert, 176
Nuclear Regulatory Commission, 112
Nuku'alofa, Tonga, 304
Numbers:
 Decimals and fractions, 435
 Prime, 437
 Roman, 437
Nyasa, Lake, 172
Nyasaland. *See* Malawi

O

Oakland, Calif., 37, 72–73
 See also Cities (U.S.)
OAS. *See* Organization of American
 States
Oaths:
 Constitutional, 84, 86
 Presidential, 84
Oberlin College, 97
Ob River, 173
Occupational Safety and Health Review
 Commission, 113
Oceania, 161, 167
 Countries, 167
 Elevations, 167
 Explorations and discoveries, 160
 Population, 167
 Entries under Continents *may also apply*
Oceans, 171
Odd Fellows, Independent Order of, 377
Oder-Neisse Line, 228
Office of Personnel Management, 113
Offices, Executive, 111–13
Ohio, 53
 See also States of U.S.
Ohio-Allegheny River, 34, 174
Ohio River, 34
Ohm, 433
Oil (petroleum):
 Crude production, 154–55
 Economic statistics, 154–55, 338, 351
 First well in U.S., 97
 Industry, hours and wages, 338
 World production, 154–55
Oils, fats: 343, 351
O.K. Corral, 36
Okhotsk Sea, 171
Okinawa, 248
Oklahoma, 53–54
 See also States of U.S.
Oklahoma City, Okla., 53, 54, 73
 See also Cities (U.S.)
Öland, 298
Old North Church, 46
Olympic Games:
 1984 Games, 294
Omaha, Neb., 48, 73
 See also Cities (U.S.)
Oman, 274
 See also Countries
Onassis, Jacqueline, 100
Ontario, Canada, 199
Ontario, Lake, 172
OPEC, 286
OPM, 113
Orange River, 174
Oregon, 54
 Volcanoes, 161
 See also States of U.S.
Organization of American States:
 Dominican Republic and, 214
Organization of Petroleum Exporting
 Countries, 286
Organizations, 369–90
Orinoco River, 174, 206
Orkney Islands, 309
Osage River, 34, 48
Oslo, Norway, 273
Ottawa, Ontario, Canada, 199
Ottoman Turks, 300, 305
Ouachita River, 34
Ouagadougou, Burkina Faso, 196
Outer Mongolia. *See* Mongolia
Owen Falls Lake, 172
Ozark Mountains, 48

P

Pacific Islands (U.S.), 65
Pacific Ocean, 171
 Discovery, 159
 Islands, 175–76
 "Ring of Fire," 161–64
 U.S. coastline, 30
 Volcanoes, 161, 164
 See also Oceania
Painted Desert, 176
Pakistan, 237, 274–75
 See also Countries
Palau Islands, 65
Palestine, 243

Palestine Liberation Organization, 244,
 249, 254
Palm Sunday, 4–5
Pamir Mountain Range, 170–71
Panama, 275–76
 See also Countries
Panama Canal, 275–76
 Treaties, 275–76
Panama City, Panama, 275
Pancake Tuesday, 4
Panel quiz radio show, first, 97
Panmunjom, North Korea, 250
Papal States, 316–17
Papeete, French Polynesia, 225
Paper:
 Economic statistics, 328, 338, 351
 Industry, hours and wages, 338
Paper currency, portraits on, 437
Papua New Guinea, 175. 276
 First visited, 160
 See also Countries
Paraguay, 277
 See also Countries
Paraguay River, 174, 194, 277
Paramaribo, Suriname, 297
Paraná River, 173, 194, 277
Parcel post, 145
Paricutín, 164
Paris, France, 221
 World War II, 223
Paris, Treaty of (1947), 236
Parks:
 City–owned, 66–78
 State parks, 35–61
Parliament (Great Britain), 309
Parsec (measure), 433
Parties, political (world), 182–324
Passover, 5
Passports and Customs, 438–39
Patagonia, 186
Patents, 363
Paulo Afonso Falls, 194
Peace Corps, 113
Peace River, 174
Peak Cavern, 177
Pearl Harbor attack, 40, 248
Pearl River, 34
Peary, Robert E., 160
Pee Dee-Yadkin River, 34
Peking, China, 204
 See also Beijing; Cities (world)
Pelée, Mount, 164
Pend Oreille-Clark Fork, 34
Pennsylvania, 54–55
 See also States of U.S.
Pennyweight, 430
Pensions:
 Veterans, 128
Pentagon, 111
Pentecost, 5
Pentecost, Hebrew, 5
People's Party (Populists), 103, 104
Per capita income:
 By states, 335
 Countries, 182–324
Pérez de Cuéllar, Javier, 179
Perihelion, 3–4
Perón, Juan D., 186
Perpetual calendar, 8–9
Persia, modern. *See* Iran
Persian Gulf States. *See* United Arab
 Emirates
Persian Gulf War, 242, 252
Peru, 160, 277–78
 See also Countries
Petition, right of, 86
Petroleum. *See* Oil
Philadelphia, Pa., 55, 73
 Continental Congresses, 94
 Liberty Bell, 55, 95
 See also Cities (U.S.)
Philippines, 278–79
 Marcos, Ferdinand, 279
 Tydings–McDuffie Act, 278
 U.S. Territory, 16
 Volcanoes, 161
 See also Countries
Phnom Penh, Cambodia, 197
Phoenix, Ariz., 36, 73, 420
 See also Cities (U.S.)
Phoenix Islands, 63, 250
Photography equipment, 351
Physical Fitness, President's Council
 on,113
Pi (measure), 433, 435
Pica (measure), 433
Pigs, Bay of, 209–10

Pikes Peak, 33, 37
Pilcomayo River, 174
Pilgrims, 45
Pindus Mountains, 231
Pipe (measure), 433
Pitcairn Island, 314
Pittsburgh, Pa., 55, 73
  See also Cities (U.S.)
Pizarro, Francisco, 160, 215, 278, 295
Plague, 309
Plantagenet, House of, 308, 309
Plastics:
  Economic statistics, 351
Plata River, 194, 315
Plate–tectonics theory, 167
Pledge to flag, 96
PLO, 244, 249, 254
Plymouth Colony, 45
Pneumonia, 27
Pocket veto, 117
Point (measure), 433
Poland, 279–80
  Solidarity Union, 279–80
  Workers strikes, 279–80
  World War II (1939), 228, 280
  See also Countries
Policy Development, White House Office of, 111
Political parties (U.S.) *See* specific parties
Political parties (world), 182–324
Poll–tax, 90
Polo, Marco, 159
Pol Pot, 197, 319
Polynesia, French, 224–25
Pompeii, 164
Pompidou, Georges, 222, 223
Pony Express, 48
Popes:
  John Paul I, 317
  John Paul II, 317
  John XXIII, 316
  Paul VI, 316–17
Popocatépetl, 164
Population (U.S.), 10–20
  Age, by, 12–13, 16, 17, 19, 20, 66–78
  Black, 12–13, 16, 19, 20, 23, 66–78
  Census required by Constitution, 81
  Census years, 12
  Cities:
    Largest, 13–15, 66–78
    Largest of each state, 35–61
  Civilian labor force, 10, 334, 336, 337
  Colonial estimates, 12
  Densities (1790–1990), 12, 17
  Family groups, 22, 23–24
  Female, 12–13, 16
  Foreign–born, 12–13, 16, 18, 19
  Growth, 11, 12–16
  Hispanic origin, 16, 19, 66–78
  Households, 22
  Indians on reservations, 19
  Male, 12–13, 16
  Marital status, 20, 21, 22
  Married couples, 22
  Metropolitan areas, 13–15
  Nativity, 12–13
  Poverty level, persons below, 19
  Projections, 20
  Race, 12–13, 16, 19, 20
  Sex, 12–13, 16
  Shifts, 11, 15
  65 and over, 12–13, 16, 19, 20, 66–78
  States, 1790–1990, 17, 35–61
  Territories, 16, 62–65
  Total, 16
  Urban, 13–15
  Working population, 334, 336, 337, 341
Population (world), 150–52
  Cities, by country, 182–324
  Cities, large (table), 151–52
  Continents, 167
  Countries, 150–51, 182–324
  Countries (table), 150–51
  Densities, 167
Populists. *See* People's party
Porcupine River, 34
Port-au-Français, French Southern and Antarctic Lands, 225
Port-au-Prince, Haiti, 234
Portland, Ore., 74
  See also Cities (U.S.)
Port Louis, Mauritius, 262
Port Moresby, Papua New Guinea, 276
Port-of-Spain, Trinidad and Tobago, 304
Porto–Novo, Benin, 192
Portraits on U.S. currency, 437
Ports, U.S., commerce at, 347

Portsmouth, Treaty of, 50
Portugal, 280–81
  See also Countries
Portuguese Guinea. *See* Guinea–Bissau
Portuguese West Africa. *See* Angola
Port Vila, Vanuatu, 316
Postal regulations, 145–48
Postal Service, U.S., 113, 145–48
  Employment, 343
  Rates, 145–48
Postal Union, Universal, 181
Postcards, 145
Postmasters General, 106–110
Post Office Department. *See* Postal Service
Postojna Grotto, 177
Potatoes, economic statistics, 342, 343
Potomac River, 34, 76
Poultry:
  Economic statistics, 342, 343
Poverty level, persons below, 19
Powder River, 34
Prague, Czechoslovakia, 211
  See also Cities (world)
Praia, Cape Verde, 201
Precipitation, 419–20
Premiers and Prime Ministers:
  Canada, 200
  Countries, 182–324
  Great Britain, 310
  Soviet Union, 294
Presidential candidates, 100–05
  First woman, 97
Presidential elections, 100–05
Presidential oath, 84
"Presidents, Mother of," 59
President's Council on Physical Fitness and Sports, 113
Presidents (foreign), 182–324
  France, 221, 222
  Germany, 228
Presidents (U.S.), 98, 106–10
  Burial places, 99
  Cabinets, 106–10
  Constitutional provisions, 83–84
  Continental Congresses, 94
  Election procedure, 83–84, 87, 100–01
  Elections, 100–05
  Families, 100
  Minority Presidents, 122
  Powers, duties, 83–84
  Mount Rushmore carvings, 56
  Nomination, 100–01
  Oath of Office, 84
  Portraits on currency, 437
  Qualifications, 84
  Religious affiliations, 98
  Salary, 84, 122
  Succession to, 84, 89, 90, 122
  Tabulated data, 98
  Term of office, 83, 89, 98
  Wives and children, 100
  See also entries under Presidential
Press, freedom of, 86
Price Indexes:
  Consumer, 326
  GNP deflator, 328
  Producer, 328
Prime Ministers. *See* Premiers
Prime numbers, 437
Prince Edward Island, 199, 200
Prince of Wales, 309
Principe, 284–85
Printing:
  Economic statistics, 338
  Industry, hours and wages, 338
  Measures, 432, 433
  See also Publishing
Priority mail. *See* Airmail
Private schools, 381, 384, 385–40
Production indexes, U.S. industries, 328
  See also kind of industry or product
Professional personnel, 337
Progressive Party (1912, 1924, 1948), 104
Prohibition, 88, 89
Promontory Summit, 58
Prostitution, arrests for, 131, 132
Protestant Reformation, 227
Prudhoe Bay, Alaska, 36
Prussia, 227
  Kings of, 228
Public assistance, 346
Public schools, 381, 383, 384
Public utilities:
  Hours and wages, 339
  Largest companies, 332
Publishing:

Printed matter, 351
Puerto Rico, 62
  Execution methods, 136
  Holidays, 6
Punctuation rules, 413–15
Punjab, 159, 238, 274
Pupils. *See* Students
Purim, 4
Puritan Commonwealth, 316
Purús River, 173
Pyongyang, North Korea, 250

Qaddafi, Muammar el, 202, 256, 297
Qatar, 281–82
  See also Countries
Quart, 430, 431, 432, 436
Quebec, Canada, 199
Quebec, Que., Canada, 199
  See also Cities (world)
Queens (NYC), 72
Queens of England, 308
Quintal (measure), 433
Quire, 433
Quisling, Maj. Vidkun, 273
Quito, Ecuador, 215
Quiz show, first panel, 97

Racial statistics:
  Births and birth rates, 26
  Crime, 132, 136
  Deaths and death rates, 28
  Employment, 337, 362
  Family characteristics, 22, 23–24
  Population, 12–13, 16, 19, 20
  School enrollment, 381
Radio:
  Stations in U.S. cities, 66–78
Railroad Retirement Board, 113
Railroads:
  Economic statistics, 347
  Firsts, 97
  Freight, 347
Rainfall, greatest, 421
Rainier, Mount, 31, 33, 60, 161
Rangoon, Burma. *See* Yangon, Myanmar
Rape, 130, 131, 132, 134
Ream (measure), 433
Recreation:
  Government employment in, 343
Red Cross, American, 378
Red Desert (An Nafud), 176
Red Guards (1966), 204
Red River (N.M.–La.), 34
Red Rock River, 34, 173
Red Sea, 171
Reference books, 417–18
Reformation, 227
Registered mail, 145–46
Rejoicing of the Law, 5
Religion:
  Churches in U.S. cities, 66–78
  Colleges, affiliation with, 385–410
  Freedom of religion, 86
  Holidays, 4–6
  Practice by country, 182–324
  See also specific religions and churches
Religious affiliations:
  Presidents, 98
  Supreme Court Justices, 119–120
Rent, 326
Representatives. *See* House of Representatives
Republic, oldest, 284
Republican Party:
  Members of Congress, 114–17
  National conventions, 100–01
  Senate floor leaders, 118
Republican River, 34
Reservations, Indian, 19, 36
Residence requirements, for voting, 121
Resources, world, by country, 182–324
Retail Trade:
  Hours and wages, 339
  Sales, 330
Retirement:
  See Social Security & Aging
Réunion, 164, 224
Revenue:
  Bills for raising, 82
  National, 336, 344

Revolutionary War, American:
  Casualties, 126
  Continental Congresses, 79–80, 94
  Declaration of Independence, 79–80
Reykjavik, Iceland, 236
  See also Cities (world)
Rhine River, 221, 227, 269, 299
Rhode Island, 55
  See also States (U.S.)
Rhodes, Cecil, 289, 324
Rhodesia. *See* Zambia; Zimbabwe
Rhodope Mountains, 195
Rhône River, 221, 299
Ribbon Falls, 174
Rice:
  Economic statistics, 155, 156
  World production, 155, 156
Richmond (NYC). *See* Staten Island
Richter Magnitude Scale, 168
Ride, Sally K., 97
Riga, Latvia, 253
"Ring of Fire," 161, 162–63, 164, 167
Rio de Janeiro, Brazil, 194
  See also Cities (world)
Rio de la Plata, 315
Rio Grande, 34, 173
Río Muni, 218
Rivers:
  U.S., 33–34
  World, 173–74
Riyadh, Saudi Arabia, 285
Roads, mileages, 450–51
Roanoke Island, 52
Roanoke River, 34, 52
Robbery, 131, 132, 133, 134
Roentgen (measure), 433
Roman Catholic Church:
  Vatican, 316–17
  Vatican Council II, 316
Roman Empire, 245
Romania, 282
  See also Countries
Roman numerals, 437
Rome, Italy, 247
  See also Cities (world)
Roosevelt, Eleanor, 100
Roosevelt's (FDR) Birthday, 6
Roseau, Dominica, 214
Roses, War of the, 309
Rosh Hashana, 5
Ross, Betsy, 96
Ross Dependency, 271
Rotary International, 378
Rubber:
  Economic statistics, 351
Rulers of countries, 182–324
Rumania. *See* Romania
Rupert's Land, 200
Rushmore, Mount, 56
Russia:
  History, 292–95
  Revolution, 292
  Rulers, 294
  World War I, 292
  World War II, 293
  See also Countries; Soviet Union
Russo–Finnish War, 221, 293
Russo–Japanese War, 247, 292
  Treaty signed in Portsmouth, N.H., 50
Russo–Turkish War, 306
Rwanda, 282–83
  See also Countries
Ryukyu Islands, 248

S

Sabah, Malaysia, 195, 259
Sabine River, 34
Sacramento, Calif., 74
Sacramento River, 34
Sadat, Anwar el-, 216, 244
Sahara, 159, 176, 184, 256, 265, 305
Saigon, Vietnam. *See* Ho Chi Minh City
St. Christopher–Nevis. *See* St. Kitts and Nevis
St. Croix, V.I., 62
St. Francis River, 34
St. George's, Grenada, 231
St. Helena, 314
St. Helens, Mount, 60, 161
St. John, V.I., 62
St. John's, Antigua and Barbuda, 185
St. Kitts and Nevis, 283
  See also Countries
St. Lawrence River, 159, 173, 199
St. Lawrence Seaway, 52

St. Louis, Mo., 47, 74
  See also Cities (U.S.)
St. Lucia, 283–84
  See also Countries
St. Patrick's Day, 4
St. Paul, Minn., 46, 47
  See also Cities (U.S.)
St. Petersburg, 291, 292
  See also Leningrad
St. Pierre and Miquelon, 224
St. Thomas, V.I., 62
St. Valentine's Day, 4
St. Vincent and the Grenadines, 284
  See also Countries
Saipan, 65
Sakhalin, 176
Salaries:
  Federal government, 122
  Industrial wages, 339
  National income and, 335
  State governments, 65–66
Sales, retail and wholesale, 330
Sales taxes, state, 144
Sales workers, 337
Salisbury, Zimbabwe. *See* Harare
Salmon River, 34
SALT. *See* Strategic Arms Limitation Talks
Salvador, El. *See* El Salvador
Salvation Army, 378
Salween River, 174
Samoa, American, 63
Samoa, Western, 319–20
Samoan archipelago, 164
Samos, 231
San'a', Yemen, 320
San Antonio, Tex., 57, 74
  See also Cities (U.S.)
San Diego, Calif., 37, 74
  See also Cities (U.S.)
Sandinista guerrillas, 271
Sandwich Islands, 40
San Francisco, Calif., 37, 74–75
  Climate, 420
  See also Cities (U.S.)
San Jacinto, Battle of, 57
San Joaquin River, 34
San Jose, Calif., 37, 75
  See also Cities (U.S.)
San José, Costa Rica, 208
San Juan River, 34
San Marino, 284
  See also Countries
San Salvador, El Salvador, 217
Santa Claus, 6
Santee–Wateree–Catawba River, 34
Santiago, Chile, 203
Santiago de Cuba, 209
Santo Domingo, Dominican Rep., 214
São Francisco River, 173, 194
São Tomé and Príncipe, 284–85
  See also Countries
Sarawak, Malaysia, 195, 239, 259
Sardinia, 245
Saskatchewan, Canada, 199, 200
Saskatchewan River, 174
Saudi Arabia, 285–86
  See also Countries
Sault Ste. Marie Canal, 46
Savings bank, first in U.S., 97
Saxe-Coburg, House of, 308
Saxon kings, 308
SBA, 113
Scarlet fever, 27
Schmidt, Helmut, 228, 229
Schools:
  First public, 97
  Statistics, 381–84
  See also Colleges and universities; Education
Science:
  Metric System, 429–32, 434, 436
  UNESCO, 181
  Weights and measures, 429–37
  See also Astronomy; Mathematics
Science and Technology, Office of, 111
Science Foundation, National, 112
Score (measure), 433
Scotland, 309
  See also United Kingdom
Seal of U.S., Great, 94
Seas, 171
Seasons, 3–4
Seattle, Wash., 59, 75, 420
  See also Cities (U.S.)
SEC, 113
Secondary schools, 381, 382, 383
Secretaries-General (U.N.), 179

Securities and Exchange Commission, 113
Security Council, National, 111
Security Council, U.N., 179
Seine River, 221
Selassie, Haile. *See* Haile Selassie
Selective Service System, 113
Senate (U.S.), 81–82, 114–15
  Birthdates of members, 114–15
  Eligibility, 81
  First Black member, 97
  First woman member, 97
  Floor leaders, 118
  Impeachment cases, 81–82
  See also Congress (U.S.)
Senegal, 286
  See also Countries
Seoul, South Korea, 251
  See also Cities (world)
Sepoy Mutiny, 237
Sequoia National Park, 37
Serbia, 321
Service academies, 124–26
Service industries, employment, 362
Seven Cities of Gold, 36
Seven Years' War, 200
Seward, William, 6, 38, 107
"Seward's Folly," 36
Sexes, distribution by:
  Arrests, 131
  Colleges, 136
  Death rates, 28
  Degrees received, 382
  Employment, 327, 340, 362
  Graduates, 382
  Life expectancy, 29
  Marriage statistics, 21, 22
  Population in U.S., 16
  Ratio of men to women, 12–13, 26
Sex offenses, arrests for, 131, 132, 133
Seychelles, 286–87
Shaba, Zaire, 322
Shah of Iran, 240
Shanghai, China, 204
  See also Cities (world)
Shannon River, 242
Shasta, Mount, 33, 161
Shatt-al-Arab, 174, 241
Shavuot, 5
Shenandoah National Park, 59
Shetland Islands, 159, 309
Shikoku, 247
Shipping, commerce, 347
Shooting, death rates from, 133
Shoreline of U.S., 30
Shrove Tuesday, 4
Siam. *See* Thailand
Siberia, 247
Sicily, 245, 246
  Volcanoes, 164
Sidereal time, 2
Sierra Leone, 159, 287
  See also Countries
Sihanouk, Norodom, 197
Sikh Rebellion (India), 238
Sikkim, 238
Simhat Torah, 5
Sinai Peninsula, 216, 244
Singapore, 259, 287–88
  See also Countries
Singing Cave, 177
Single persons, 21
Six-day War, 244
  See also Arab–Israeli wars
Skyscrapers, first, 97
Slavery:
  Emancipation Proclamation, 92–93
  First slaves to United States, 59, 97
  First state to forbid, 58
  Prohibited in U.S., 87
Small Business Administration, 113
Smoky Hill River, 34
Snake River, 34
Snowdon, Mount, 309
Snowfall, greatest, 421
Social Security & Aging, 352–58
  Medicare, 356, 357–58
  Social Security Act, 352–55
Socialist parties (U.S.), 104
Societies and associations, 369–80
Society Islands, 225
Sofia, Bulgaria, 195
Solar time, 2
Solomon Islands, 288
Somalia, 288–89
  See also Countries
Somaliland, French. *See* Djibouti
Somoza Debayle, Gen. Anastasio, 271

Songs, state, 35–61
"Sooners," 54
Sorority, first, 97
Sound:
　Speed of, 433, 435
Sources, reference, 417–18
South Africa, Rep. of,289–91
　See also Countries
South America, 161, 167
　Explorations, discoveries, 160
　Southernmost point, 203
　See also Continents; Countries
South Carolina, 56
　See also States of U.S.
South China Sea, 171
South Dakota, 56
　See also States of U.S.
Southeast Asia War. *See* Vietnam War
Southern Alps, 270
Southern and Antarctic Lands, 225
Southern Cameroons. *See* Nigeria
Southern Rhodesia. *See* Zimbabwe
South Georgia Island, 313
South Island (New Zealand), 175, 270
South Manchurian Railway, 204
South Orkney Islands, 313
South Platte River, 34
South Pole:
　Reached, 160
South Shetland Islands, 313
South-West Africa. *See* Namibia
Soviet Union, 291–95
　Afghanistan invasion, 183, 293
　Area, elevations, and population densi-
　ty, 167
　Constitution, 292
　Germany, nonaggression pact with
　(1939), 293
　Government, 292
　Hydrogen bomb, 293
　Moscow Summer Olympics, 293
　Rulers, 294
　World War II, 293
　See also Countries; Russia
Spain, 295–96
　See also Countries
Span (measure), 433
Spanish-American War, 126, 209
Spanish Armada, 295, 309
Spanish Civil War, 295
Spanish origin, persons of. *See* Hispanics
Speakers of the House, 118
Special-delivery mail, 146
Speech, freedom of, 86
Speed:
　Of sound, 433, 435
Spitsbergen, 160, 273
Sputnik I (satellite), 293
Square (measure), 433
Sri Jayewardenepura Kotte, Sri Lanka,
　296
Sri Lanka, 176, 296
　See also Countries
Stalin, Joseph, 293, 294
Stamps, postage, 97, 146
　United Nations, 148
Standard time, 3
"Star-Spangled Banner," 92
START. *See* Strategic Arms Reduction
　Talks
State, Secretaries of (states), 35–61
State, U.S. Department of, 111
　Secretaries of, 106–10
Staten Island, 72
　See also New York City
States, Confederate, 93
States of U.S., 35–66
　Agricultural production, 342
　Areas, 35–61
　Births and birth rates, 26
　Coastlines, 30
　Congress members, 114–17
　Constitutional provisions, 83, 85
　Deaths and death rates, 27, 28
　Education, 382
　Execution methods, 136
　Firsts, 97
　General Sales and Use Taxes, 143
　Government employment, 343
　Government statistics, 65–66
　Governors, 35–61
　Highest court members, term and
　salary, 65–66
　Holidays, 6
　Motor vehicle deaths, 27
　Motor vehicle registrations, 348
　Per capita personal income, 335
　Population, 17, 35–61

Procedure for admitting new states, 85
Representatives, 115–17
School attendance laws, 382
Senators, 114–15
Taxes. *See* Taxes
Tax Freedom Day, by 143
Thirteen original, 81
Tourism offices, 447–49
Unemployment benefits, 362
Voting qualifications, 121
States' rights, 83, 85, 87
States' Rights Democratic Party, 104
Statue of Liberty, 52, 96
Steel, 157, 338, 351
　World consumption, 157
　World production, 157
Stockholm, Sweden, 298
　See also Cities (world)
Stock market, 330, 331, 333
　50 leading stocks, 333
　50 most active stocks, 330
　Shareholders, 330, 331
　Stock exchange seat sales, 331
Stone (measure), 433
Stone Mountain, 40
Stores, retail. *See* Retail trade
Strategic Arms Limitation Talks, 293
Strategic Arms Reduction Talks, 293
Strikes (labor), 341
　First strike in U.S., 97
Stromboli, 164
Stuart, House of, 308
Students:
　College and professional, 381, 384, 410
　Elementary and secondary school, 381
Subways, first in U.S., 97
Sucre, Bolivia, 193
Sudan, 159, 296–97
　See also Countries
Suez Canal, 216, 244
　Egypt seizes (1956), 216
Suffrage. *See* Voting
Sugar:
　Economic statistics, 343, 351
Sukarno, 239
Sukkot, 5
Sumatra, 175, 239
　Volcanoes, 164
Sun:
　Seasons, 3–4
　Time based on, 2–3
Sungari River, 174
Sun Yat-sen, 204
Superior, Lake, 46, 172, 199
Supreme Court (U.S.):
　Constitutional provisions, 84, 85
　First Black member, 97
　First law declared unconstitutional, 97
　First woman member, 97
　Justices, 119–20
　Salaries, 122
Supreme Courts, state, 65–66
Suribachi, Mount, 161
Suriname, 297–98
　See also Countries
Surveying measures, 430
Susquehanna River, 34
Sutter's Mill, 37
Suva, Fiji, 220
Svendrup Islands, 200
Swains Islands, 63
Swaziland, 298
　See also Countries
Sweden, 298–99
　See also Countries
Switzerland, 299–300
　See also Countries
Sydney, Australia, 187
　See also Cities (world)
Syphilis, 27
Syria, 241, 244, 300–01
　Israel and, 244, 254, 300
　See also Countries

T

Tabernacles, Feast of, 4
Tabloid newspaper, first, 97
Tadzhikistan, 293
Taft, William Howard, 119
　See also Presidents (U.S.)
Tahiti, 225
Taipei, Taiwan, 301
Taiwan (Republic of China), 301
Takla Makan Desert, 176
Tallinn, Estonia, 218

Tamerlane, 183
Tananarive, Madagascar. *See* Antananari-
vo
Tanana River, 34
Tanganyika. *See* Tanzania
Tanganyika, Lake, 159, 172
T'ang Dynasty, 204
Tanzania, 302
　See also Countries
Tarawa, 249
Tasmania, 160, 176, 187
Taxes, 137–44
　Constitutional provisions for, 81, 83, 88,
　90
　Corporation taxes, federal, 138, 140
　Corporation taxes, state, 140, 144
　Estate taxes, federal, 138, 140–41
　Excise, 138
　Franchise taxes, state, 140
　Gift taxes, federal, 138, 140–41
　Income tax, federal, 137–40
　Income tax, history, 137
　Individual returns, 140
　Internal Revenue Service, 137–38
　Sales and use taxes, state, 143
Teachers, 384
Tegucigalpa, Honduras, 234
Teheran, Iran, 239
　See also Cities (world)
Tel Aviv, Israel, 243
Telephones:
　Economic statistics, 339
　Toll-free numbers, 266–68
Television:
　Stations in cities, 66–78
Temperatures:
　International, 448
　In U.S. cities, 419–20
　Scales, 429, 433, 436
　U.S. extremes, 421, 422, 423–24
　World extremes, 421, 422
Tenerife, Canary Islands, 164
Tennessee, 57
　See also States of U.S.
Tennessee River, 34
Tennessee Valley Authority, 57, 113
Territorial expansion of U.S., 16
Territories of U.S., 62–65
　Areas, 16, 62–65
　Execution methods, 136
　Population, 16, 62–65
Terrorism, 244, 254, 256, 312, 317
Teutonic Knights, 279
Texas, 57–58
　War of Independence, 57
　See also States of U.S.
Textiles, economic statistics, 328, 338,
351
Thailand, 302–03
　See also Countries
Thames River, 309
Thanksgiving Day, 6
Thant, U, 179, 322
Thar Desert, 176
Thatcher, Margaret, 310, 311
Theater:
　First vaudeville, 97
Theft, 130, 131, 132, 133, 134
Therm (measure), 433
Thermometer:
　Scales, 433, 436
Thimphu, Bhutan, 192
Thieu, Nguyen Van, 319
"Third World," 321
Thirty Years' War, 227, 299
Thohoyandou, Venda, 291
Tibet, 169, 204, 205
Tidal shoreline of U.S., 30
Tien-Pamir Mountains, 292
Tien Shan Mountains, 204
Tierra del Fuego, 176, 203
Tigris River, 174
Time:
　Kinds of, 2–3
　Universal and civil, 2–3
　Time of day, cities, 32, 169
Time zones, 2–3
Timor, 239, 281
Tinian (island), 65
Tippecanoe, 42
Tirana, Albania, 183
Titicaca, Lake, 172, 193
Tito, Marshal, 321
Tobacco:
　Economic statistics, 338, 342, 351
　In Connecticut, 38
　Taxes, 138
Tobago. *See* Trinidad and Tobago

Tocantins River, 174
Togo, 303–04
  See also Countries
Tokelau Island, 270
Tokyo, Japan, 247
  See also Cities (world)
Toledo, Ohio, 53, 75
  See also Cities (U.S.)
Tomb of the Unknown Soldier, 95
Tombigbee River, 34
Ton:
  Gross or long, 432, 436
  Metric, 429, 432, 436
  Net or short, 432, 436
Tonga, 304
  See also Countries
Torah, 5
Tornadoes, 422
Toronto, Ont., Canada, 199
Toulouse, France, 221
Tourist information. *See* Travel
Township (measure), 433
Toys and games, 351
Trade. *See* Foreign trade; Interstate Commerce
Trade Commission, Federal, 112
Trade Commission, U.S. International, 113
Trademarks, 363
Trade Negotiations, Office of U.S. Trade Representative, 111
Trade unions. *See* Unions, labor
Trains. *See* Railroads
Trans-Alaska Pipeline, 36
Transkei, 291
  See also Countries
Transportation:
  Accident death rates, 27
  Economic statistics, 347–48
  Employment, 362
  Freight traffic, 347
  Industry, hours and wages, 339
  See also kinds of transportation
Transportation, U.S. Department of, 112
  Secretaries of, 109–110
Transportation equipment, 328, 351
Travel, 438–56
  Air distances between cities, 452–55
  Foreign embassies, 439–42
  Health hints abroad, 444–46
  Information sources, 447–49
  Mileages between cities, 450–55
  Passports and Customs, 438–39
  Traveler warnings, 449
Treason defined, 85
Treasurers (of states), 35–61
Treasury, U.S. Dept. of, 111
  Secretaries, 106–110
Trees, State, 35–61
Trieste, 246, 321
Trinidad and Tobago, 304
  See also Countries
Trinity River, 34
Tripoli, Libya, 256
Tristan da Cunha, 314
Tropical storms, 422
Tropic of Cancer, 4
Tropic of Capricorn, 4
Trotsky, Leon, 292
Troy weight, 430
Trucks and trucking, 347, 348, 349
Trucial States. *See* United Arab Emirates
Trudeau, Pierre E., 200
Trusteeship Council, U.N., 180
Trusteeships, U.N., 180
Trust Territory of Pacific Islands, 16, 65
Tuberculosis, 27
Tucson, Ariz., 75
  See also Cities (U.S.)
Tudor, House of, 308
Tugela Falls, 174
Tulsa, Okla., 75–76, 161
  See also Cities (U.S.)
Tunis, Tunisia, 304
Tunisia, 304–05
  See also Countries
Tun (measure), 433
Turkey, 305–06
  See also Countries
Turkish-Russian War, 306
Turkmenistan, 293
Turks and Caicos Islands, 315
Turner, John, 200, 201
Tuskegee Institute, 35
Tuvalu, 306
  See also Countries
TVA, 57, 113

Twelfth Night, 4
Tydings-McDuffie Act (1934), 278
Typhoid fever, 27

U

Uganda, 306–07
  See also Countries
Ukraine, 293
  See also Soviet Union
Ulan Bator, Mongolia, 264
Ulbricht, Walter, 228
Ulster, Northern Ireland, 311
Umtala, Transkei, 291
Unemployment, 340, 341, 362
  Insurance, 361–62
UNESCO, 181
Union Islands. *See* Tokelau Island
Union Labor Party, 103
Union of Soviet Socialist Republics. *See* Soviet Union
Unions, labor, 334
United Arab Emirates, 307
  See also Countries
United Automobile Workers, 334
United Kingdom, 307–15
  Prime Ministers, 310
  Rulers, 308
  See also Countries
United Nations:
  Agencies, 180–81
  Charter, 179
  Economic and Social Council, 179–80
  General Assembly, 179
  International Court, 180
  Member nations, 178
  Persian Gulf War, 242
  Principal organs, 179–81
  Secretariat, 179
  Security Council, 179
  Stamps, 148
  Trusteeship Council, 180
  Trust territories, 65, 180, 276
  U.S. contributions to, 345
United Nations Educational, Scientific, and Cultural Organization, 181
United States, 315
  Aliens admitted, 18, 19
  Area, 16
  Armed forces, 123–29
  Balance of payments, 350
  Birth statistics, 24–26
  Businesses, foreign investments in, 350
  Climate extremes, 421, 422
  Coastline, 30
  Colleges, 384–410
  Crime statistics, 130–34
  Death statistics, 27–28
  District Courts, 133
  Divorce statistics, 20
  Economic statistics, 326–51
  Education statistics, 381–84
  Exports, 158, 349, 351
  Family statistics, 22, 23–24, 327, 329
  Flag, 96
  Geography, 10, 30–34
  Growth, 12–16
  Highest points, 31
  Holidays, 4–6
  Immigration, 18, 19
  Imports, 158, 351
  Labor force, 66–78, 334, 336, 337
  Largest cities, 66–78
  Latitudes and longitudes, 32
  Life expectancy in, 29
  Lowest points, 31
  Marriage statistics, 20–22, 23–24
  Mileages between cities, 450–55
  National Anthem, 92
  Naturalization statistics, 19
  Passports and customs, 438–39
  Population, 10–20
    For detailed listing, *see* Population (U.S.)
  Postal regulations, 145–48
  Societies and associations, 369–80
  State tourism offices, 447–49
  Territories, 16, 62–65
  Travel information, 447–49
  Universities, 384–410
  Weather and climate, 419–28
  See also Cities (U.S.); Countries of the World; Foreign trade; Interstate commerce; States (U.S.); U.S. Govern-

ment; U.S. History
United States Government:
  Armed forces, 123–29
  Cabinet, 106–10
  Congress. *See* Congress (U.S.)
  Constitution, 81–90
  Employment, 343
  Executive Departments, 111–13
  Expenditures and receipts, 336, 343, 344–45
  Federal budget, 336, 344
  Foreign aid, 336, 345
  Great Seal, 94
  Independent agencies, 112–13
  Judicial powers, 84–85
  Presidents, 98
  Salaries of officials, 121
  Supreme Court, 84–85, 119–20
  Unemployment insurance, 361–62
  Veterans' benefits, 128–29
  Voting qualifications, 88, 89, 90, 121
  See also individual entries elsewhere in index for more extensive listing
United States History:
  Armed services, 123–24
  Articles of Confederation, 94
  Cabinets, 106–10
  Constitution, 81–90
  Continental Congresses, 94
  Declaration of Independence, 79–80
  Discoveries and explorations, 159–60
  Elections, presidential, 100–05
  Emancipation Proclamation, 92–93
  Firsts, 97
  Flag, 96
  Gettysburg Address, 93
  Mason and Dixon's Line, 31
  Mayflower Compact, 91
  Minority Presidents, 122
  Monroe Doctrine, 91
  Presidents, 98
  Speakers of the House, 118
  "Star-Spangled Banner," 92
  Statue of Liberty, 96
  Territorial expansion, 16
  Unknown soldiers, 95
  War casualties, 126, 127
  See also names of wars
  White House, 90
Universal Postal Union, 181
Universities, United States, 384–410
  See also Colleges
Unknown Soldier, Tomb of the, 95
Unleavened Bread, Feast of, 5
Upper Volta. *See* Burkina Faso
Ural Mountains, 292
Ural River, 174
Uruguay, 315–16
  See also Countries
Uruguay River, 315
Utah, 58
  See also States of U.S.
Uzbekistan, 293

V

VA, 112
Vaduz, Liechtenstein, 256
Valentine's Day, 4
Valetta, Malta, 261
Valley Forge, Pa., 55
Valois, House of, 222
Vancouver, B.C., Canada, 199
Vandalism arrests, 131, 132
Vanuatu, 316
  See also Countries
Vatican City State, 316–17
  See also Countries; Roman Catholic Church
Vatican Council II, 316
Vaudeville theater, first, 97
Vegetables:
  Economic statistics, 343, 351
Venda, 291
Venezuela, 317–18
  See also Countries
Vermont, 58–59
  See also States of U.S.
Vernal Equinox, 1–2
Versailles, Treaty of, 228
Vesuvius, Mount, 164
Veterans:
  Benefits, 128–29
  Education, 128–29
Veterans Affairs, Department of, 112

Veterans' Day, 6
Veto power, 82
Vice-Presidential Candidates:
First woman, 97
Vice Presidents (U.S.):
As Acting President, 90
Election procedure, 83–84, 87
List of, 98–99
Nomination, 101
Powers and duties, 81
Salary, 122
Succession to Presidency, 84, 89, 90, 91
Term of office, 89, 98
Much of what applies to Presidents (U.S.) also applies to Vice Presidents
Vichy, France, 222, 223, 318
Victoria, Lake, 172, 302, 307
Victoria, Queen, 308, 310
Victoria, Seychelles, 286
Victoria Falls, 159, 175
Victoria (island), 175
Vienna, Austria, 188
Vienna, Congress of, 188, 223
Vientiane, Laos, 252
Viet Cong, 318–19
Vietnam, 252, 318–19
See also Countries
Vietnam War, 318–19
Casualties, U.S., 126
Unknown Serviceman of, 95
See also Cambodia; Laos, Thailand
Vikings, 212, 273
Vilnius, Lithuania, 257
Vinson Massif, 167
Virginia, 59
See also States of U.S.
Virginia Beach, Va., 59, 76
Virgin Islands, British, 313
Virgin Islands, U.S., 62–63
Volcanoes, 161–65, 167
Islands, 164
Principal types, 165
"Ring of Fire," 161–64
Volga River, 172, 173, 292
Volume:
Formulas for, 435
Measure of, 429, 430, 431–32, 433, 434
Voting:
18–year–olds, 90
Presidential elections, 100–05
Qualification by state, 121
Rights, 89, 90
Unusual voting results, 122
Women's suffrage, 89, 97

W

Wabash River, 34
Wages, hours:
Industrial, 338
National income and, 335
See also Income
Wake Island, 64
Waldheim, Kurt, 179, 188
Wales, 309
See also United Kingdom
Wales, Prince of, 309
Walesa, Lech, 279, 280
Wallis and Futuna Islands, 225
Wall of China, 204
War, U.S. Department of, Secretaries of, 106–09
War casualties, 126, 127
War of 1812, 126
Warren, Earl, 119
Wars. *See* individual wars
Warsaw, Poland, 279
See also Cities (world)
Warsaw Treaty Organization, 236, 280, 282, 294
Wars of the Roses, 309
Washington, D.C., 76
Climate, 420
Twenty–third Amendment, 89–90
White House, 90
See also Cities (U.S.); much information under States also applies to Washington, D.C.
Washington, Mount, 31
Washington Monument, 95
Washington's Birthday, 4
Washington (state), 59–60
Mountains and volcanoes, 33
See also States of U.S.
Washita River, 34
Water, boiling and freezing points, 436

Waterfalls, 174–75
Waterloo, Battle of, 227, 310
Waterways, traffic on, 347
Watt (measure), 433
Watusi, 197
Weapons, 131, 132, 133, 134
Weather and climate, 419–28
Glossary, 422
Hail, hailstones, 422
Humidity, relative, 426–28
Hurricanes, 422
Of U.S. cities, 419–28
Tornadoes, 422
Tropical storms, 422
World extremes, 421
Wedding anniversaries, 7
Weights, measures, 429–37
Capacities, volumes, 429–34
Conversion factors, 434, 436
Weimar Republic, 227–28
Welfare. *See* Public Assistance
Wellington, New Zealand, 270
Western Samoa, 319–20
See also Countries
West Indies:
Discovery, 159
Volcanoes, 164
See also specific islands
West Irian, 239
West Point (U.S. Military Academy), 52, 124
West Virginia, 60
See also States of U.S.
Wheat, 154, 155, 342
World production, 155
Wheat flour. *See* Flour
Where to find out more, 417–18
Whig Party (U.S.), 103
White House, 90
White River, 34
Whitney, Mount, 31, 33, 37
Whitsunday, 5
WHO, 181
Wholesale trade:
Employment, 362
Hours and wages, 339
Price indexes, 328
Sales, 330
Whooping cough, 27
Wilhelm, 167
Williamsburg, Va., 59
William the Conqueror, 308, 309
William II, Kaiser, 228
Wilson, Harold, 310
Wind chill factor, 420
Windhoek, Namibia, 267
Windsor, House of, 308
Windward Islands. *See* St. Lucia; St. Vincent and the Grenadines
Winnipeg, Lake, 172
WIPO, 181
Wisconsin, 60–61
See also States of U.S.
Wisconsin River, 34
Wives of Presidents, 100
WMO, 181
Wollaston Islands, 203
Women:
Arrests, 131
Death rates, 28
Earnings, 327, 329, 339, 340
Education, 339, 382
Employment, 336, 337, 339, 340, 341
Families maintained by, 339
Firsts, 97
Heads of families, 22, 339
In labor force, 336, 337, 339, 341
Life expectancy, 29, 153
Marriage statistics, 21–22
Mothers, 25
Mothers employed, 337
Number, 16
Political firsts, 97
Presidents' wives, 100
Ratio of men to women, 12–13
Suffrage, 89, 97
Wood pulp, 328, 351
Wood. *See* Lumber and wood
Working population, 334, 336, 337, 339, 340, 341
World:
Air distances, 453–54
Area, 167
Caves, caverns, 177
Climate extremes, 421, 422
Consumer Price Indexes, 326
Countries of, 182–324
Deserts, 176

Economy, 325–29
Education, expenditure, 383
Elevations, 167
Explorations, discoveries, 159–60
Geography. *See* Geography (world)
Highest mountain peaks, 170–71
History. *See* History (world)
Islands, 175–76
Lakes, 172–73
Population. *See* Population (world)
Rivers, 173–74
Statistics, 150–58
Unemployment, 340, 362
Volcanoes, 161–65
Waterfalls, 174–75
See also Cities (world); Countries; Governments (foreign)
World Bank (IBRD), 180
World Court, International Court of Justice, 180
World Health Organization, 181
World History, 182–324
World Intellectual Property Organization (WIPO), 181
World Meteorological Organization, 181
World Time Zones, 3
World War I:
Casualties, 126, 127
Unknown Soldier of, 95
World War II:
Casualties, 126, 127
Unknown Soldier of, 95
See also involved countries
Wrangell, Mount, 33, 161
Writer's Guide, 412–16
Capitalization, 412
Punctuation, 413–15
Wyandotte Cave, 42, 177
Wyoming, 61
See also States of U.S.

X

Xavier, St. Francis, 159
Xhosa, 291

Y

Yangon, Myanmar, 266
See also Cities (World)
Yangtze Kiang, 173, 204
Yaoundé, Cameroon, 198
Year, defined, 1–2
Yellow River, 173, 204
Yellowstone National Park, 48, 61
Yellowstone River, 34
Yemen, Republic of, 320
See also Countries
Yenisei River, 173, 292
Yom Kippur, 5
York, House of, 308
Yorktown, Battle of, 59
Yosemite National Park, 37
Yosemite, waterfalls, 37
Young Men's Christian Association, 380
Young Women's Christian Association, 380
Yugoslavia, 320–21
See also Countries
Yukon River, 34, 173
Yukon Territory, 199, 200

Z

Zaire, 321–22
U.N. action, 322
See also Countries
Zaire River, 159, 173, 207, 322
Zambezi River, 159, 174, 323
Kariba Dam, 172, 323
Zambia, 323
See also Countries
Zanzibar. *See* Tanzania
Zhou Enlai, 205
Zhujiang River, 204
Zimbabwe, 323–24
Kariba Dam, 172, 323
See also Countries
Zionism, 243–44
Zugspitze (peak), 227
Zwelitsha, Ciskei, 290

Ticks and tick paralysis 256
Tom Sawyer's Cave, Mo. 1
Tonto Natural Bridge, Ariz. 67
Touring cavers 292–296
Tourniquets 240–241
Townsend, Charles 226
Trash removal 141, 251
Traverses 288. *See also* Tyrolean
    traverses
Travertine caves 67–68, 76–78, 311
Tree casts 54, 311
Trenches, lava 51
Tropical caves and karst 9; floods in
    81; hazards of 90, 256–257; sur-
    vival in 93, 124; water exploration
    in 82. *See also* specific countries,
    specific caves and topics
Trousers 132–133
Trypanosomiasis 257
Tuberculosis 257
Tubes, solution 7, 11; inner. *See*
    inner tubes; lava; lava tube caves
Tubes-in-tube 50, 312
Tularemia 256
Two-knot ascent system. *See* ascents
    and ascending, systems of
Typhoid fever 250, 251
Tyrolean traverses 232, 288, 312

Unconsciousness 172, 217, 237, 239,
    241–242. *See also* drugs
Underground Empire 315
Underwear 122, 132, 134
Urbani, Franco 270
Urchins, sea 67
Urine, clue to dehydration 143;
    disposal of 252

Vadose features 6ff, 35, 81, 312. *See
    also* speleogenesis
Valley fever. *See* coccidioidomycosis
Values of caves. *See* specific values;
    conservation
Vampire bats 255; guano 76. *See also*
    bats
Vancouver Island Cave Exploration
    Group 322, 328
Vandalism *xiv*, 6, 44, 50, 74, 296, 312;
    chains 296. *See also* conservation;
    dams; Engineers, U.S. Army
    Corps of

Varnedoe, William 107, 115, 119, 317,
    327, 329
Venereal diseases 257
Venezuelan Speleological Society.
    See Sociedad Venezolana de
    Espeleologia
Vertical caving 156ff, 179ff, 203ff, 318;
    father of *v*. *See also* specific topics
Vineyard, Jerry 329
Vining, Mark 327
Virginia Polytechnic Institute Grotto of
    the National Speleological Society
    102, 329
Vision, problems of 105, 147. *See also*
    steam
Visiting cavers. *See* touring cavers
Vitamins. *See* drugs
Vugs 16, 312
Vulcanospeleology. *See* lava tube
    caves

Wading and its hazards 82–83, 137. *See
    also* chill; hypothermia; immersion,
    foot
Waist belts 281
Wakulla Spring, Fla. 5, 87, 314
Wall walking 221–224, 226, 283–284
Warm River Cave, Va. 78, 124
Warm springs in caves 78. *See also*
    geothermal caves
Washington, Caves of 55, 314
Wasps 247
Water 81ff; burn treatment with 244;
    discovery 296; drinking 143, 144,
    153; purification for 143–144;
    hazards of 72–73, 81ff, 203;
    headlamp 96ff, 144; illusions from
    258; pollution (*see* animals,
    dead; pollution, water; and
    sewage diseases); retention by
    fabrics 131; in rescues 273, 280;
    tracing 297. *See also* chill;
    hypothermia; siphons;
    speleogenesis; other specific
    topics
Waterchill. *See* chill
Waterfalls 72, 89–90, 95, 202, 203, 205,
    236
Watts, Troy 265
Webbing 163–166, 217. *See also* slings
Wedged cavers 289–291
Wefer, Fred L. 179, 318

Weil's disease 256
Welts 20, 312
Western Speleological Survey 315
West Indies 5, 86, 322. *See also*
    Blue Holes
West Virginia, Caves of 314
Wet-cell units. *See* batteries and
    battery units
Wet suits 86, 122, 127, 130, 205, 242,
    312
Whaletails. *See* rappels and rappelling,
    devices for
Wheat lamps 116
White, William B. 16, 313–314, 327,
    329
Wicking of clothing 131, 150, 312
Wildcats 255
Wilderness values of caves 296. *See
    also* conservation

Winches 202
Windbreaks 151
Wind Cave, S.D. 2, 7, 71, 74, 316
Wind Cave, Wyo. 236
Windchill. *See* chill; hypothermia
Winding Stair, Cave of the, Calif. 206
Winds, Cave of the, Colo. 2, 27
Wolf's Den Cave, Conn. 156
Wolves 156, 247
Woodford, Richard 139
Wookey Hole, England 86
Worms, parasitic 250
Wrist loops 228
Wyandotte Cave, Ind. 2

Yellowstone National Park, Wyo. 46,
    63, 67, 77–78
Yucatan 2. *See also* Blue Holes

74 75 76 77 10 9 8 7 6 5 4 3 2 1